Thomas Bros. Maps®

CALIFORNIA
ROAD ATLAS
THE COMPLETE DRIVER'S GUIDE FROM STATE ROADS TO CITY STREETS

FOLLOW THE EASY-TO-USE
1-2-3 TABLE OF CONTENTS

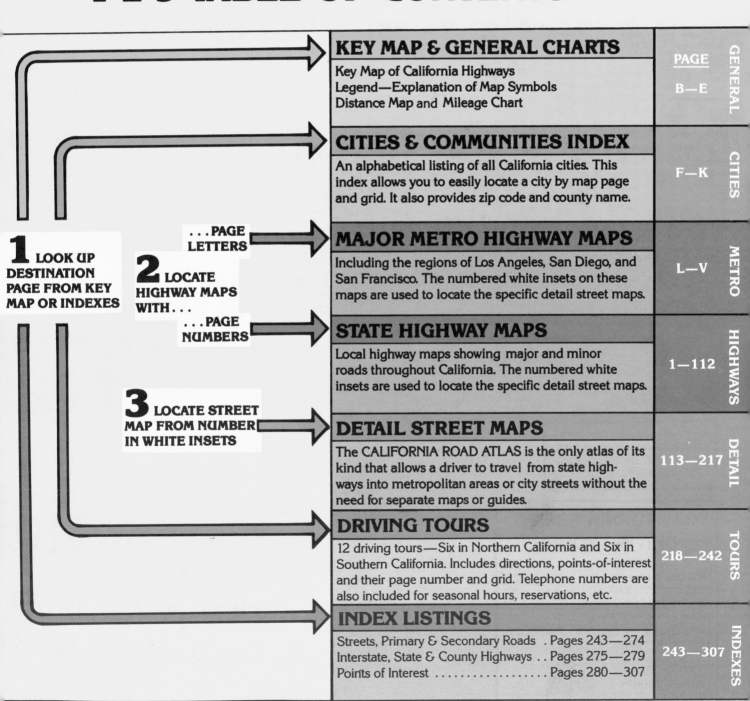

1 LOOK UP DESTINATION PAGE FROM KEY MAP OR INDEXES

2 LOCATE HIGHWAY MAPS WITH...
...PAGE LETTERS
...PAGE NUMBERS

3 LOCATE STREET MAP FROM NUMBER IN WHITE INSETS

17731 Cowan, Irvine, CA 92714 (714) 863-1984
550 Jackson St., San Francisco, CA 94133 (415) 981-7520
603 West 7th St., Los Angeles, CA 90017 (213) 627-4018

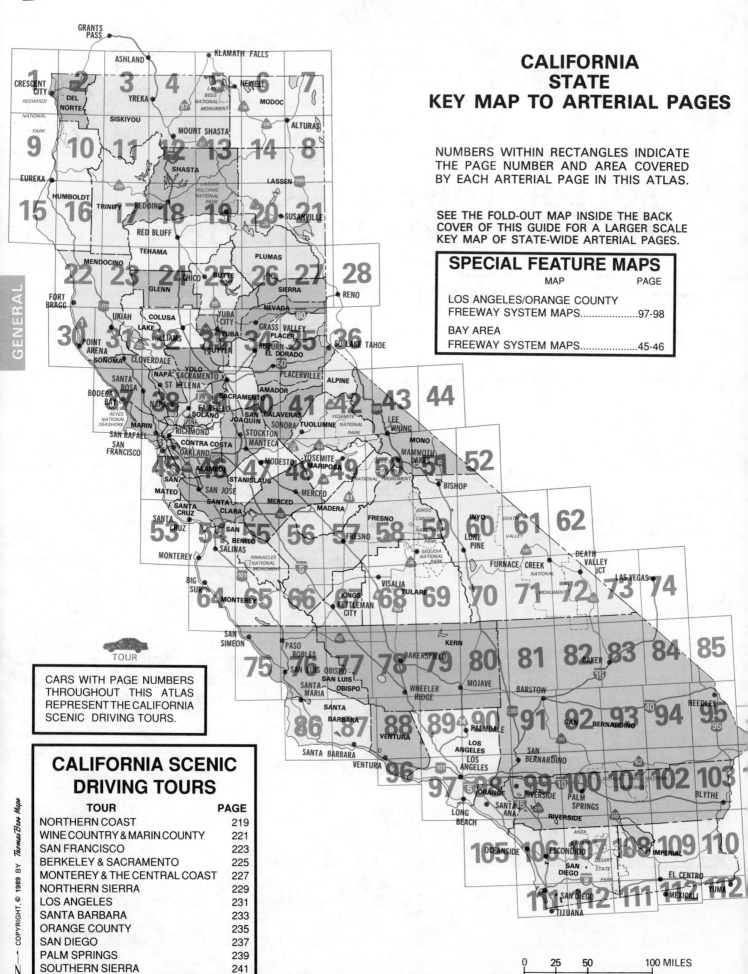

B

CALIFORNIA STATE KEY MAP TO ARTERIAL PAGES

NUMBERS WITHIN RECTANGLES INDICATE THE PAGE NUMBER AND AREA COVERED BY EACH ARTERIAL PAGE IN THIS ATLAS.

SEE THE FOLD-OUT MAP INSIDE THE BACK COVER OF THIS GUIDE FOR A LARGER SCALE KEY MAP OF STATE-WIDE ARTERIAL PAGES.

SPECIAL FEATURE MAPS

MAP	PAGE
LOS ANGELES/ORANGE COUNTY FREEWAY SYSTEM MAPS	97-98
BAY AREA FREEWAY SYSTEM MAPS	45-46

TOUR

CARS WITH PAGE NUMBERS THROUGHOUT THIS ATLAS REPRESENT THE CALIFORNIA SCENIC DRIVING TOURS.

CALIFORNIA SCENIC DRIVING TOURS

TOUR	PAGE
NORTHERN COAST	219
WINE COUNTRY & MARIN COUNTY	221
SAN FRANCISCO	223
BERKELEY & SACRAMENTO	225
MONTEREY & THE CENTRAL COAST	227
NORTHERN SIERRA	229
LOS ANGELES	231
SANTA BARBARA	233
ORANGE COUNTY	235
SAN DIEGO	237
PALM SPRINGS	239
SOUTHERN SIERRA	241

GENERAL

0	25	50	100 MILES

SCALE

DETAIL PAGES

EXPLANATION OF MAP SYMBOLS

ARTERIAL PAGES

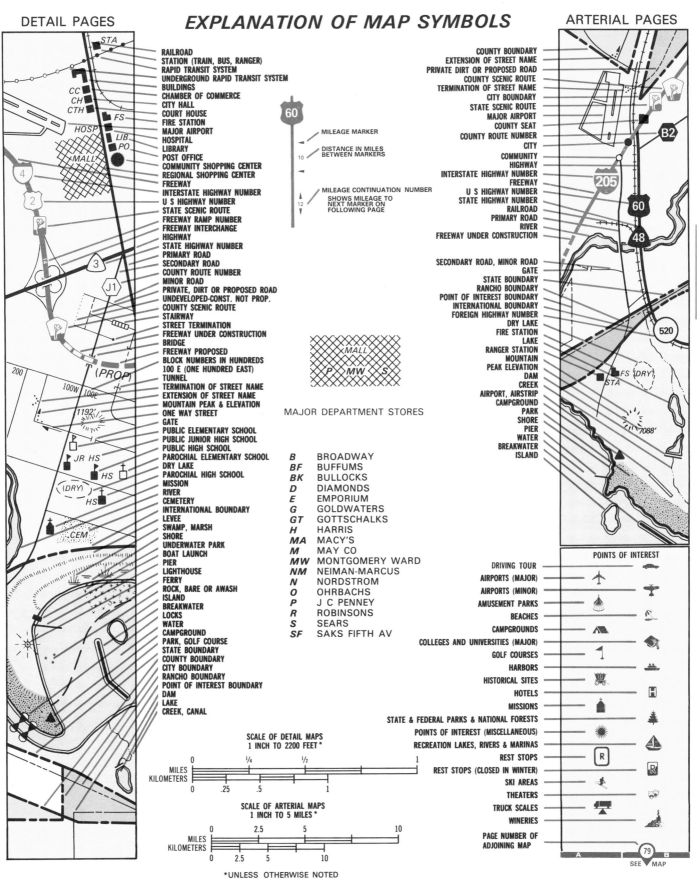

RAILROAD
STATION (TRAIN, BUS, RANGER)
RAPID TRANSIT SYSTEM
UNDERGROUND RAPID TRANSIT SYSTEM
BUILDINGS
CHAMBER OF COMMERCE
CITY HALL
COURT HOUSE
FIRE STATION
MAJOR AIRPORT
HOSPITAL
LIBRARY
POST OFFICE
COMMUNITY SHOPPING CENTER
REGIONAL SHOPPING CENTER
FREEWAY
INTERSTATE HIGHWAY NUMBER
U S HIGHWAY NUMBER
STATE SCENIC ROUTE
FREEWAY RAMP NUMBER
FREEWAY INTERCHANGE
HIGHWAY
STATE HIGHWAY NUMBER
PRIMARY ROAD
SECONDARY ROAD
COUNTY ROUTE NUMBER
MINOR ROAD
PRIVATE, DIRT OR PROPOSED ROAD
UNDEVELOPED-CONST. NOT PROP.
COUNTY SCENIC ROUTE
STAIRWAY
STREET TERMINATION
FREEWAY UNDER CONSTRUCTION
BRIDGE
FREEWAY PROPOSED
BLOCK NUMBERS IN HUNDREDS
100 E (ONE HUNDRED EAST)
TUNNEL
TERMINATION OF STREET NAME
EXTENSION OF STREET NAME
MOUNTAIN PEAK & ELEVATION
ONE WAY STREET
GATE
PUBLIC ELEMENTARY SCHOOL
PUBLIC JUNIOR HIGH SCHOOL
PUBLIC HIGH SCHOOL
PAROCHIAL ELEMENTARY SCHOOL
DRY LAKE
PAROCHIAL HIGH SCHOOL
MISSION
RIVER
CEMETERY
INTERNATIONAL BOUNDARY
LEVEE
SWAMP, MARSH
SHORE
UNDERWATER PARK
BOAT LAUNCH
PIER
LIGHTHOUSE
FERRY
ROCK, BARE OR AWASH
ISLAND
BREAKWATER
LOCKS
WATER
CAMPGROUND
PARK, GOLF COURSE
STATE BOUNDARY
COUNTY BOUNDARY
CITY BOUNDARY
RANCHO BOUNDARY
POINT OF INTEREST BOUNDARY
DAM
LAKE
CREEK, CANAL

60

MILEAGE MARKER

10   DISTANCE IN MILES
      BETWEEN MARKERS

MILEAGE CONTINUATION NUMBER
12   SHOWS MILEAGE TO
      NEXT MARKER ON
      FOLLOWING PAGE

MALL
P   MW   S

MAJOR DEPARTMENT STORES

B	BROADWAY
BF	BUFFUMS
BK	BULLOCKS
D	DIAMONDS
E	EMPORIUM
G	GOLDWATERS
GT	GOTTSCHALKS
H	HARRIS
MA	MACY'S
M	MAY CO
MW	MONTGOMERY WARD
NM	NEIMAN-MARCUS
N	NORDSTROM
O	OHRBACHS
P	J C PENNEY
R	ROBINSONS
S	SEARS
SF	SAKS FIFTH AV

COUNTY BOUNDARY
EXTENSION OF STREET NAME
PRIVATE DIRT OR PROPOSED ROAD
COUNTY SCENIC ROUTE
TERMINATION OF STREET NAME
CITY BOUNDARY
STATE SCENIC ROUTE
MAJOR AIRPORT
COUNTY SEAT
COUNTY ROUTE NUMBER
CITY
COMMUNITY
HIGHWAY
INTERSTATE HIGHWAY NUMBER
FREEWAY
U S HIGHWAY NUMBER
STATE HIGHWAY NUMBER
RAILROAD
PRIMARY ROAD
RIVER
FREEWAY UNDER CONSTRUCTION

SECONDARY ROAD, MINOR ROAD
GATE
STATE BOUNDARY
RANCHO BOUNDARY
POINT OF INTEREST BOUNDARY
INTERNATIONAL BOUNDARY
FOREIGN HIGHWAY NUMBER
DRY LAKE
FIRE STATION
LAKE
RANGER STATION
MOUNTAIN
PEAK ELEVATION
DAM
CREEK
AIRPORT, AIRSTRIP
CAMPGROUND
PARK
SHORE
PIER
WATER
BREAKWATER
ISLAND

POINTS OF INTEREST

DRIVING TOUR
AIRPORTS (MAJOR)
AIRPORTS (MINOR)
AMUSEMENT PARKS
BEACHES
CAMPGROUNDS
COLLEGES AND UNIVERSITIES (MAJOR)
GOLF COURSES
HARBORS
HISTORICAL SITES
HOTELS
MISSIONS
STATE & FEDERAL PARKS & NATIONAL FORESTS
POINTS OF INTEREST (MISCELLANEOUS)
RECREATION LAKES, RIVERS & MARINAS
REST STOPS
REST STOPS (CLOSED IN WINTER)
SKI AREAS
THEATERS
TRUCK SCALES
WINERIES
PAGE NUMBER OF
ADJOINING MAP

79
SEE MAP
A   B

SCALE OF DETAIL MAPS
1 INCH TO 2200 FEET *

MILES   0   ¼   ½   1
KILOMETERS   0   .25   .5   1

SCALE OF ARTERIAL MAPS
1 INCH TO 5 MILES *

MILES   0   2.5   5   10
KILOMETERS   0   2.5   5   10

*UNLESS OTHERWISE NOTED

GENERAL

N

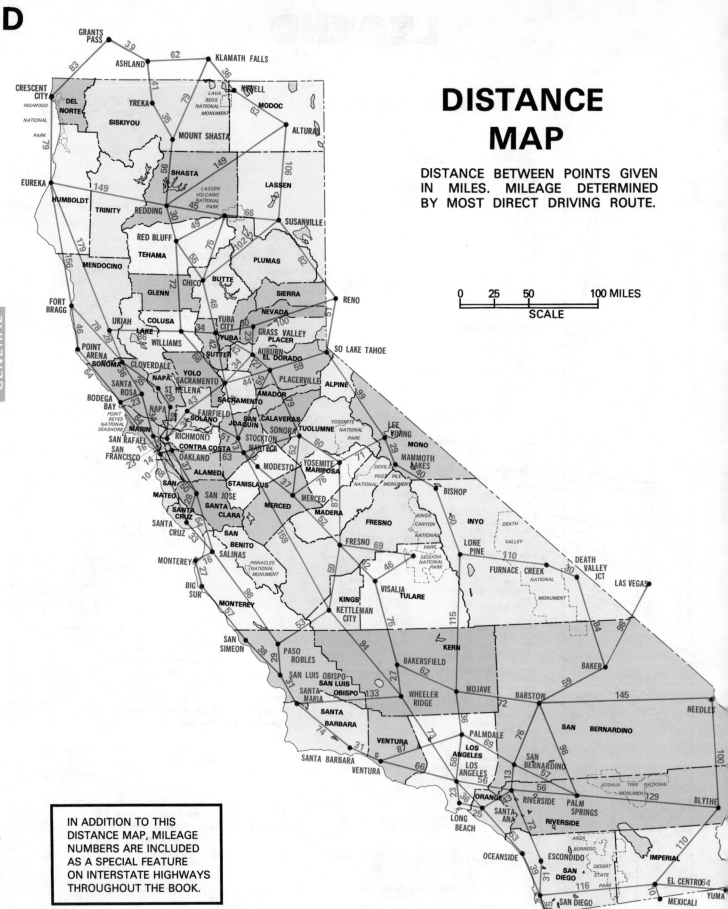

DISTANCE MAP

DISTANCE BETWEEN POINTS GIVEN IN MILES. MILEAGE DETERMINED BY MOST DIRECT DRIVING ROUTE.

0 25 50 100 MILES
SCALE

IN ADDITION TO THIS DISTANCE MAP, MILEAGE NUMBERS ARE INCLUDED AS A SPECIAL FEATURE ON INTERSTATE HIGHWAYS THROUGHOUT THE BOOK.

MILEAGE CHART

MILEAGE DETERMINED BY MOST DIRECT DRIVING ROUTE

	BAKERSFIELD	CHICO	EUREKA	FRESNO	LAS VEGAS	LONG BEACH	LOS ANGELES	MERCED	MODESTO	OAKLAND	PALM SPRINGS	REDDING	RIVERSIDE	SACRAMENTO	SALINAS	SAN DIEGO	SAN FRANCISCO	SAN JOSE	SAN LUIS OBISPO	SANTA ANA	SANTA BARBARA	SANTA ROSA	SOUTH LAKE TAHOE	STOCKTON	VENTURA
ALTURAS	577	207	292	470	624	705	650	415	374	379	720	142	645	297	471	741	360	392	577	683	737	367	241	342	692
ANAHEIM	138	505	718	245	274	24	30	302	341	443	100	577	42	415	346	86	449	403	235	4	128	485	490	370	102
AUBURN	306	90	321	199	601	441	420	143	106	115	518	175	473	34	207	539	121	151	339	452	444	131	86	70	421
BAKERSFIELD		362	555	109	284	132	113	163	200	285	209	433	177	272	206	232	283	241	114	143	146	340	360	227	115
BARSTOW	129	491	684	236	155	123	131	292	330	414	123	559	78	401	335	180	412	385	264	116	205	469	395	356	174
BENECIA	292	144	287	177	578	429	396	123	84	37	510	187	466	58	106	513	43	49	236	456	341	61	164	74	374
BISHOP	222	360	553	235	284	308	277	223	252	314	308	396	242	265	347	360	335	321	357	301	327	382	176	240	296
BLYTHE	339	705	918	446	208	228	230	501	521	622	129	775	171	616	530	222	619	575	433	202	314	676	686	568	287
BODEGA BAY	404	189	266	249	632	491	451	194	156	74	568	246	527	141	165	594	64	109	294	516	400	23	256	152	431
BURBANK	104	465	659	210	294	31	9	266	304	383	111	536	67	376	304	127	377	334	200	45	93	421	446	330	64
CHICO	362		218	254	620	498	475	198	160	172	575	73	543	89	264	638	180	212	389	509	490	166	170	134	477
CLAREMONT	135	497	691	308	246	47	26	298	336	415	79	568	23	408	336	107	409	366	226	23	118	453	469	360	88
DAVIS	287	83	282	180	582	422	399	134	87	66	499	155	454	15	158	520	74	102	320	433	425	83	127	60	402
DEATH VALLEY	238	530	703	395	213	229	206	393	422	484	306	566	262	435	475	407	505	491	352	324	366	552	346	410	336
EL CENTRO	322	706	872	427	303	219	213	482	520	615	110	775	154	618	536	110	601	561	413	201	308	660	596	554	279
EUREKA	555	218		446	797	683	669	390	353	288	788	149	743	287	381	776	269	323	508	722	614	219	388	332	643
FAIRFIELD	278	132	276	171	561	412	391	118	79	45	489	173	457	43	132	554	55	78	260	423	362	57	150	51	389
FORT BRAGG	460	199	156	353	730	597	551	292	255	180	674	288	629	217	280	669	176	216	401	608	507	119	319	233	534
FRESNO	109	254	446		284	239	220	56	93	178	316	325	272	165	134	339	185	151	140	250	245	233	251	120	222
GRASS VALLEY	329	78	320	222	624	464	443	166	129	138	541	163	496	57	230	562	144	174	362	475	467	154	115	93	444
LAGUNA BEACH	162	528	741	269	288	34	55	324	363	465	115	598	62	437	368	75	471	425	257	19	150	507	511	391	123
LA JOLLA	219	625	763	326	319	90	103	382	419	507	122	667	79	492	428	13	517	449	309	79	203	536	529	450	172
LASSEN NATIONAL PARK	437	102	202	329	695	573	550	273	235	247	650	45	618	164	339	713	255	287	459	584	562	241	199	209	552
LAS VEGAS	284	620	797	284		276	286	446	484	567	276	640	231	567	488	332	568	524	414	269	354	610	466	510	323
LONE PINE	159	420	593	285	224	232	209	283	312	374	277	456	233	325	365	337	395	381	273	245	285	442	236	300	254
LONG BEACH	132	498	683	239	276		24	294	333	417	118	568	60	407	338	103	427	383	218	25	120	477	479	361	93
LOS ANGELES	113	475	669	220	286	24		276	314	393	103	546	56	386	314	119	387	344	204	35	96	431	456	340	66
MAMMOTH LAKES	262	320	513	195	324	348	317	283	212	274	348	356	217	225	307	400	295	281	397	341	367	342	130	200	336
MANTECA	215	147	345	108	499	348	329	54	15	63	425	219	380	44	99	447	73	65	248	382	354	123	144	13	330
MARTINEZ	288	146	290	172	571	424	391	118	79	28	507	191	460	61	101	509	38	47	233	453	338	64	168	70	369
MERCED	163	198	390	56	446	294	276		37	123	368	269	326	109	105	395	130	115	195	305	300	172	194	64	278
MODESTO	200	160	353	93	484	333	314	37		84	410	232	365	72	104	432	92	77	233	344	339	135	156	27	315
MOJAVE	62	424	617	169	229	117	94	225	262	347	162	495	118	334	268	213	345	303	190	130	116	402	351	289	87
MONTEREY	216	278	399	149	504	356	334	115	138	111	433	350	388	190	18	442	122	75	145	367	250	170	272	141	273
NAPA	331	150	255	224	613	463	439	169	130	46	540	191	495	61	145	566	56	88	270	492	363	36	168	69	390
NEEDLES	281	638	821	383	108	269	279	439	476	560	190	729	224	548	481	311	561	517	416	262	352	603	552	508	316
NEVADA CITY	334	83	325	227	629	469	448	171	134	143	546	168	501	62	235	567	149	179	367	480	472	159	110	98	449
NEWPORT BEACH	155	519	735	262	279	21	43	317	366	458	108	592	55	430	361	81	465	418	230	12	141	498	502	382	114
OAKLAND	285	172	288	178	567	417	393	123	84		494	218	449	81	99	520	10	42	224	446	317	60	195	73	344
ONTARIO	141	493	696	247	222	44	37	303	341	420	77	573	21	413	341	125	414	371	232	33	123	458	483	367	103
OXNARD	122	485	650	229	316	85	59	271	322	351	165	555	117	395	252	178	379	329	142	97	38	421	478	349	7
PALMDALE	98	460	653	205	244	81	58	261	298	383	126	531	82	370	304	182	381	339	221	94	116	438	387	325	87
PALM SPRINGS	209	575	788	316	276	118	103	368	410	494		658	56	484	415	135	504	460	306	96	199	554	435	438	172
PALO ALTO	261	213	302	171	544	403	364	135	97	43	480	251	433	120	74	482	33	20	205	426	311	89	223	92	342
PASADENA	109	475	688	216	259	31	7	271	310	394	104	554	52	384	315	134	404	360	210	42	95	454	463	338	68
PLACERVILLE	282	133	331	175	525	416	395	122	83	125	493	205	461	44	177	548	131	127	309	427	429	141	59	55	397
REDDING	433	73	149	325	640	568	546	269	232	218	658		600	161	334	680	218	246	431	579	537	223	249	206	548
RENO	432	104	342	297	444	510	504	241	209	216	510	196	465	132	308	561	223	249	434	503	507	229	61	177	496
RICHMOND	299	163	276	192	581	431	407	137	98	14	508	204	462	74	113	534	24	56	238	460	331	50	181	82	358
RIVERSIDE	177	543	743	272	231	60	56	326	365	449	56	600		439	367	92	463	413	259	43	147	509	379	406	125
SACRAMENTO	272	89	287	165	567	407	386	109	72	81	484	161	439		173	505	87	117	305	418	410	97	107	45	387
SALINAS	206	264	381	134	488	338	314	105	104	99	415	334	367	173		441	101	57	125	349	218	160	251	122	245
SAN BERNARDINO	167	534	714	269	228	63	59	325	362	439	57	595	13	436	360	104	444	401	260	48	154	486	436	389	123
SAN DIEGO	232	638	776	339	332	103	119	395	432	520	135	680	92	505	441		530	462	322	84	216	549	542	493	185
SAN FRANCISCO	283	180	269	185	568	427	387	130	92	10	504	218	463	87	101	530		45	230	452	336	56	192	88	367
SAN JOSE	241	212	323	151	524	383	344	115	77	42	460	246	413	117	57	462	45		185	406	291	96	197	72	322
SAN JUAN CAPISTRANO	163	529	742	270	289	40	55	325	364	466	116	599	63	438	369	66	472	426	258	20	151	508	512	114	124
SAN LUIS OBISPO	114	384	508	140	414	218	204	195	233	224	306	431	259	305	125	322	230	185		238	106	281	382	254	137
SAN MATEO	313	199	288	181	554	413	374	125	86	29	490	237	443	106	84	492	19	30	215	436	321	75	209	78	352
SAN PEDRO	134	496	690	242	285	9	22	298	336	415	126	568	68	408	336	118	409	366	213	37	108	454	478	362	75
SAN RAFAEL	306	167	260	199	588	438	414	144	105	21	515	243	470	83	121	559	18	64	246	470	339	39	181	94	366
SANTA ANA	143	509	722	250	269	25	35	305	344	446	96	579	43	418	349	84	452	406	238		131	488	492	372	104
SANTA BARBARA	146	490	614	245	354	120	96	300	339	317	199	537	147	410	218	216	336	291	106	131		387	490	374	31
SANTA CRUZ	239	230	354	150	524	379	344	116	109	75	456	275	411	146	33	462	74	29	162	390	268	129	229	101	300
SANTA MARIA	145	415	539	171	428	194	170	226	264	255	273	462	221	336	156	290	261	216	31	205	74	312	413	285	103
SANTA ROSA	340	166	219	233	610	477	431	172	135	60	554	223	509	97	160	549	56	96	281	488	387		199	113	414
SAUSALITO	298	183	276	200	583	442	402	145	107	25	519	259	478	99	116	545	15	60	245	467	351	55	207	103	382
SEQUOIA NATIONAL PK	129	343	556	84	408	258	234	139	178	335	235	385	303	252	209	361	272	228	178	269	276	329	335	206	262
SONOMA	331	163	239	224	613	468	439	170	130	46	540	204	495	75	146	584	43	89	271	495	364	20	181	82	391
SONORA	215	189	387	108	498	380	366	52	42	105	420	261	391	86	157	447	115	107	247	357	352	165	139	55	330
SOUTH LAKE TAHOE	360	170	388	251	466	479	456	194	156	195	435	249	379	107	251	542	192	197	382	492	490	199		131	471
STOCKTON	227	134	332	120	510	361	340	64	27	73	438	206	406	45	122	493	88	72	254	372	374	113	131		342
SUSANVILLE	465	105	257	356	599	600	577	299	262	275	677	110	645	191	369	714	252	280	465	613	571	257	133	240	582
UKIAH	402	147	179	295	672	539	493	234	197	135	616	184	571	159	222	611	118	158	343	550	449	62	253	175	476
VALLEJO	310	147	265	203	592	442	418	131	92	25	519	186	474	57	124	545	35	67	249	471	342	46	266	65	370
VENTURA	115	477	643	222	323	93	66	278	315	344	172	548	125	387	245	185	367	322	137	104	31	414	471	342	
YOSEMITE NATIONAL PK	199	263	476	92	435	331	307	83	122	174	408	333	364	172	188	434	184	178	236	342	329	234	133	129	330
YREKA	531	171	205	427	698	657	638	372	335	307	747	98	689	263	423	756	317	346	534	668	630	325	315	297	645
YUBA CITY	313	48	290	206	608	448	427	150	113	122	525	133	480	41	214	546	128	158	346	459	451	201	145	86	428
YUMA	379	742	922	491	299	278	271	545	584	674	169	816	221	655	595	173	655	614	473	260	368	702	646	603	337

CITIES AND COMMUNITIES INDEX

COMMUNITY NAME	CO.	ZIP CODE	PAGE	GRID
A				
ACADEMY	FRCO	93612	57	E2
ACAMPO	SJCO	95226	40	A4
ACTIS	KER	93501	80	A5
ACTON	LACO	93510	89	E4
ADAMS	LAK	95496	31	E4
ADELAIDA	SLO	93446	75	E1
• ADELANTO	SBD	92301	91	A3
ADIN	MOD	96006	14	D3
AERIAL ACRES	KER	93523	80	D5
AETNA SPRINGS	NAPA	94567	32	B5
AFTON	GLE	95920	25	A5
AGATE BAY	PLA	95711	35	E1
AGOURA	LACO	91301	97	A1
• AGOURA HILLS	LACO	91301	96	E1
AGUA CALIENTE	SDCO	92086	107	C2
AGUA CALIENTE	SON	95476	38	B3
AGUA CALIENTE HOT SPGS	SDCO	92036	107	E4
AGUA DULCE	LACO	91350	89	D4
AGUANGA	RCO	92302	107	A1
AGUEREBERRY POINT	INY	92328	71	D1
AHWAHNEE	MAD	93601	49	C4
AINSWORTH CORNER	SIS		5	C2
• ALAMEDA	ALA	94501	L	D5
ALAMO	CC	94507	M	A4
ALAMORIO	IMP	92227	109	B4
• ALBANY	ALA	94706	L	D4
ALBERHILL	RCO	92303	99	A4
ALBION	MEN	95410	30	B1
ALDERPOINT	HUM	95411	16	D5
ALDER SPRINGS	FRCO	93602	58	A1
ALDER SPRINGS	GLE	95939	23	E3
ALGODONES	BAJA		112	C5
• ALHAMBRA	LACO	91801	R	C3
ALISO VIEJO	ORA	92656	98	D5
ALLEGHANY	SIE	95910	26	D4
ALLENSWORTH	TUL	93219	68	A4
ALMANOR	PLU	95911	20	B4
ALPAUGH	TUL	93201	67	E4
ALPINE	SDCO	92001	107	B5
ALPINE HEIGHTS	SDCO	92001	107	B5
ALPINE HIGHLANDS	SDCO	92001	107	B5
ALPINE HILLS	SDCO	92001	107	B5
ALPINE HILLS	SMCO	94025	N	D3
ALPINE MEADOWS	PLA	95730	35	D2
ALPINE PEAKS	PLA	95730	35	D2
ALTA	PLA	95701	34	E1
ALTADENA	LACO	91001	R	C2
ALTA LOMA	SBD	91701	U	D2
ALTAMONT	ALA	94550	M	D5
ALTAMONT	KLAM		5	C1
ALTA SIERRA	KER	93285	69	C5
ALTAVILLE	CAL	95221	41	B4
ALTA VISTA	INY	93514	51	C3
ALTON	HUM	95540	15	D2
• ALTURAS	MOD	96101	8	A1
ALUM ROCK	SCL	95127	P	C3
ALVISO	SCL	95002	P	B2
• AMADOR CITY	AMA	95601	40	D2
AMARGOSA VALLEY	NYE		62	E4
AMBLER	TUL	93277	68	B1
AMBOY	SBD	92304	93	E3
AMERICAN HOUSE	PLU	95981	26	C3
• ANAHEIM	ORA	92801	T	D2
ANAHEIM HILLS	ORA	92807	T	E2
• ANDERSON	SHA	96007	18	C3
ANDERSON SPRINGS	LAK	95461	31	E4
ANDRADE	IMP	92283	112	C5
• ANGELS CAMP	CAL	95222	41	B4
ANGELUS OAKS	SBD	92305	99	E1
ANGWIN	NAPA	94508	38	C1
ANNAPOLIS	SON	95412	30	E5
ANTELOPE	SAC	95842	34	A5
ANTELOPE ACRES	LACO	93534	89	D2
• ANTIOCH	CC	94509	M	C3
ANZA	RCO	92306	100	C5
APPLEGATE	PLA	95703	34	D3
APPLE VALLEY	SBD	92307	91	C4
APTOS	SCR	95003	54	B2
ARABIA	RCO	92274	101	B5
ARBUCKLE	COL	95912	32	E3
• ARCADIA	LACO	91006	R	C3
• ARCATA	HUM	95521	9	E5
ARDEN	CLK		74	D3
ARDEN	SAC	95864	40	A1
ARGUS	SBD	93562	71	B5
ARLINGTON	RCO	92503	99	A3
ARMONA	KIN	93202	67	D1
ARNOLD	CAL	95223	41	C3
ARNOLD HEIGHTS	RCO	92508	99	B3
AROMAS	MON	95004	54	C2
ARROWBEAR LAKE	SBD	92308	99	D1
ARROWHEAD SPRINGS	SBD	92404	99	C1
• ARROYO GRANDE	SLO	93420	76	B4
• ARTESIA	LACO	90701	T	A1
ARTOIS	GLE	95913	24	D4
• ARVIN	KER	93203	78	E4
ASHFORD JUNCTION	INY	92328	72	C4
• ASHLAND	JKSN		3	E1
ASPENDELL	INY	93514	51	B5
ASTI	SON	95413	31	C5
• ATASCADERO	SLO	93422	76	A2
• ATHERTON	SMCO	94025	N	D2
ATOLIA	SBD	93558	80	E3
• ATWATER	MCO	95301	48	B4
ATWOOD	ORA	92670	T	E1
• AUBURN	PLA	95603	34	C3
• AVALON	LACO	90704	97	E5
AVENAL	KIN	93204	66	E3
AVERY	CAL	95224	41	C3
AVILA BEACH	SLO	93424	76	A4
AVON	CC	94553	38	E4
• AZUSA	LACO	91702	U	A1
B				
BABBITT	MIN		44	B1
BADGER	TUL	93603	58	D4
BADWATER	INY	92328	72	A2
BAKER	SBD	92309	83	B3
• BAKERSFIELD	KER	93301	78	D3
BALBOA	ORA	92661	T	C4
BALBOA ISLAND	ORA	92662	T	C4
BALCH CAMP	FRCO	93657	58	C2
• BALDWIN PARK	LACO	91706	R	D3
BALLARAT	INY	93562	71	C3
BALLARD	SB	93463	86	E3
BALLENA	SDCO	92065	107	B4
BALLICO	MCO	95303	48	A3
BANGOR	BUT	95914	25	E5
BANKHEAD SPRINGS	SDCO	92034	111	A4
BANNER	SDCO	92036	107	D4
• BANNING	RCO	92220	100	A3
BARD	IMP	92222	112	D5
BARDSDALE	VEN	93015	88	D4
BARRETT JUNCTION	SDCO	92017	112	B2
BARSTOW	FRCO	93702	57	B3
• BARSTOW	SBD	92311	91	E1
BARTLETT	INY	93545	60	B5
BARTLETT SPRINGS	LAK	95443	32	A2
BARTON	AMA	92309	41	B2
BASSETT	LACO	91746	R	D4
BASSETTS	SIE	96125	27	A4
BASS LAKE	MAD	93604	49	E4
BAXTER	PLA	95704	34	E1
BAYSHORE	SMCO	94005	L	C5
BAYSIDE	HUM	95524	9	E5
BAYWOOD PARK	SLO	93401	75	E3
BEAR HARBOR	MEN	95489	22	B2
BEAR VALLEY	ALP	95223	41	E2
BEAR VALLEY	MPA	95338	48	E3
BEAR VALLEY	SDCO	92082	106	E3
BEAR VALLEY SPRINGS	KER	93561	79	B4
BEATTY	NYE		62	B2
BEATTY JUNCTION	INYO	92328	61	E4
• BEAUMONT	RCO	92223	99	E3
BECKWOURTH	PLU	96129	27	C2
BEE ROCK	SLO	93928	65	D5
BEL AIRE	MAR	94920	L	B4
BEL AIR ESTATES	LACO	90077	Q	B4
BELDEN	PLU	95915	26	A1
• BELL	LACO	90201	R	B5
BELLA VISTA	KER	93283	79	E1
BELLA VISTA	SHA	96008	18	D2
• BELLFLOWER	LACO	90706	S	E1
• BELL GARDENS	LACO	90201	R	B5
BELLOTA	SJCO	95236	40	C4
BELL SPRINGS	MEN	95440	22	D1
BEL MARIN KEYS	MAR	94947	L	B2
• BELMONT	SMCO	94002	N	C2
• BELVEDERE	MAR	94920	L	B4
BELVEDERE GARDENS	MAR	94920	L	B4
BENBOW	HUM	95440	22	C1
BEND	TEH	96008	18	D4
• BENICIA	SOL	94510	L	E2
BEN LOMOND	SCR	95005	N	E5
BENTON	MNO	93512	51	C1
BERENDA	MAD	93637	56	E1
• BERKELEY	ALA	94701	L	D4
BERMUDA DUNES	RCO	92201	101	A4
BERRY CREEK	BUT	95916	25	E3
BERRYESSA HIGHLANDS	NAPA	94558	38	D1
BERRYESSA PINES	NAPA	94567	38	C1
BERTELEDA	DN	95531	2	A4
BERTSCH TERRACE	DN	95531	1	E4
BETHANY	SJCO	95376	M	E5
BETHEL ISLAND	CC	94511	M	D3
BETTERAVIA	SB	93455	86	B1
• BEVERLY HILLS	LACO	90210	Q	C3
BIEBER	LAS	96009	14	B3
BIG BAR	AMA	95704	41	A2
• BIG BEAR CITY	SBD	92314	92	A5
• BIG BEAR LAKE	SBD	92315	92	A5
BIG BEND	SHA	96011	13	A4
BIG BEND	SON	95476	38	B3
BIG CREEK	FRCO	93605	50	B5
• BIGGS	BUT	95917	25	B5
BIG MEADOW	CAL	95223	41	E2
BIG OAK FLAT	TUO	95305	48	D1
BIG PINE	INY	93513	51	E5
BIG RIVER	SBD	92242	104	A1
BIG SPRINGS	SIS		4	C5
BIG SUR	MON	93920	64	B2
BINGHAMTON	SOL	95625	39	B2
BIOLA	FRCO	93606	57	B3
BIRCH HILL	SDCO	92060	107	A2
BIRCHVILLE	NEV		34	C1
BIRDS LANDING	SOL	94512	39	B4
• BISHOP	INY	93514	51	D4
BITTERWATER	SBT	93930	65	C1
BLACKHAWK	CC	94526	M	B4
BLACK POINT	MAR	94947	L	B2
BLACKWELLS CORNER	KER	93249	77	C1
BLAIRSDEN	PLU	96103	27	A2
BLOCKSBURG	HUM	95414	16	D4
BLOOMINGTON	SBD	92316	99	A2
BLOSSOM	TEH	96080	18	B5
BLOSSOM VALLEY	SDCO	92021	107	A5
BLUE DIAMOND	CLK		74	B3
BLUE JAY	SBD	92317	91	C5
• BLUE LAKE	HUM	95525	10	A5
BLUE LAKES	LAK	95493	31	C2
• BLYTHE	RCO	92225	103	D5
BOCA	NEV	95737	27	E5
BODEGA	SON	94922	37	C3
BODEGA BAY	SON	94923	37	C3
BODFISH	KER	93205	79	C1
BODIE	MNO	93517	43	D3
BOLINAS	MAR	94924	37	E5
BOLSA KNOLLS	MON	93906	54	C3
BOMBAY BEACH	IMP	92257	108	E2
• BONANZA	KLAM		5	E1
BONDS CORNER	IMP	92250	112	C4
BONITA	SDCO	92002	V	D4
BONNEFOY	AMA	95642	41	A2
BONSALL	SDCO	92003	106	C2
BOONVILLE	MEN	95415	30	E3
BOOTJACK	MPA	95338	49	B3
BORON	KER	93516	80	E5
BORREGO	SDCO	92004	107	E3
BORREGO SPRINGS	SDCO	92004	107	E2
BOSTONIA	SDCO	92021	V	E2
BOULDER CREEK	SCR	95006	N	E5
BOULDER OAKS	SDCO	92062	112	D1
BOULEVARD	SDCO	92005	111	A4
BOUSE	LPAZ	92363	104	D3
BOWLES	FRCO	93725	57	C4
BOWMAN	PLA	95707	34	C3
BOYES HOT SPRINGS	SON	95476	38	B3
BOYLE HEIGHTS	LACO	90033	R	A4
• BRADBURY	LACO	91010	R	E3
BRADLEY	MON	93426	65	E4
BRANSCOMB	MEN	95417	22	D3
• BRAWLEY	IMP	92227	109	A4
• BREA	ORA	92621	T	D1
BRENDA	LPAZ		104	D4
• BRENTWOOD	CC	94513	M	D3
BRENTWOOD	LACO	90049	Q	B4
BRICEBURG	MPA	95345	49	B2
BRICELAND	HUM	95440	16	B5
BRIDGE HAVEN	SON	95450	37	C2
BRIDGE HOUSE	SAC	95683	40	C2
BRIDGEPORT	MPA	95306	49	A4
BRIDGEPORT	MNO	93517	43	B3
BRIDGEPORT	NEV	95975	34	B1
BRIDGEVIEW	JOS		2	D1
BRIDGEVILLE	HUM	95526	16	C3
• BRISBANE	SMCO	94005	L	C5
BRITE VALLEY	KER	93561	79	C4
BRODERICK	YOL	95605	39	D1
BROOKDALE	SCR	95007	N	E5
BROOKINGS	CUR		1	D2
BROOKS	YOL	95606	32	D5
BROWNS VALLEY	YUB	95918	33	E1
BROWNSVILLE	YUB	95919	26	A4
BRUCEVILLE	SAC	95683	39	E3
BRUSH CREEK	BUT	95916	25	E3
BRYN MAWR	SBD	92318	99	C2
BRYTE	YOL	95605	39	D1
BUCKEYE	ED	95634	34	E3
BUCKEYE	SHA	96003	18	B2
BUCKHORN	AMA	95666	41	B2
BUCKHORN SPRINGS	JKSN		4	B2
BUCKMAN SPRINGS	SDCO	92062	112	D1
BUCK MEADOWS	MPA	95321	49	A1
BUCKS BAR	ED	95684	35	A5
BUCKS LAKE	PLU	95971	26	B2
BUELLTON	SB	93427	86	D3
BUENA	SDCO	92083	106	C3
• BUENA PARK	ORA	90620	T	B1
BUENA VISTA	AMA	95640	40	D3
BUHACH	MCO	95340	48	B4
BULLHEAD CITY	MOH		85	D4
BUMMERVILLE	CAL	95257	41	B2
BUNTINGVILLE	LAS	96114	21	B4
• BURBANK	LACO	91501	Q	E2
BURDELL	MAR	94947	L	A1
• BURLINGAME	SMCO	94010	N	C1
BURNEY	SHA	96013	13	C5
BURNT RANCH	TRI	95527	10	D5
BURREL	FRCO	93607	57	B5
BURSON	CAL	95225	40	D4
BUTTE CITY	GLE	95920	25	A5
BUTTE MEADOWS	BUT	95921	25	D1
BUTTONWILLOW	KER	93206	78	A3
BYRON	CC	94514	M	D4
C				
CABAZON	RCO	92230	100	B3
CABBAGE PATCH	CAL	95223	41	E2
CADENASSO	YOL	95607	32	E5
CADIZ	SBD	92319	94	B4
CADWELL	SON		37	E2
CAIRNS CORNER	TUL	93247	68	C2
CAJON JUNCTION	SBD	92358	91	A5
CAJON PASS	SBD	92397	91	A5
CALABASAS	LACO	91302	97	B1
CALAVERITAS	CAL	95249	41	A3
• CALEXICO	IMP	92231	112	B4
CALICO GHOST TOWN	SBD	92398	82	A5
CALIENTE	KER	93518	79	B3
• CALIFORNIA CITY	KER	93505	80	B4
CALIFORNIA HOT SPRINGS	TUL	93207	69	B4
CALIFORNIA VALLEY	SLO	93453	77	B3
CALIMESA	RCO	92320	99	D2
• CALIPATRIA	IMP	92233	109	B3
• CALISTOGA	NAPA	94515	38	A1
CALLAHAN	SIS	96014	11	D2
CALNEVA	LAS	96113	21	E5
CALPELLA	MEN	95418	31	B1
CALPINE	SIE	96124	27	B3
CALWA	FRCO	93725	57	C3
• CAMARILLO	VEN	93010	96	C1
CAMBRIA	SLO	93428	75	C2
CAMDEN	FRCO	93656	57	C5
CAMERON CORNERS	SDCO	92006	112	D2
CAMERON PARK	ED	95682	34	C5
CAMINO	ED	95709	35	A4
• CAMPBELL	SCL	95008	P	B4
CAMP CONIFER	TUL	93271	59	A5
CAMP CONNELL	CAL	95223	41	D3
CAMP KLAMATH	DN	95548	2	A5
CAMP MEEKER	SON	95419	37	D2
CAMPO	SDCO	92006	112	D2
CAMPO SECO	CAL	95226	40	E3
CAMP SIERRA	FRCO	93634	50	B5
CAMPTONVILLE	YUB	95922	26	B5
CANBY	MOD	96015	14	D1
CANE BRAKE	KER	93255	70	B5
CANOGA PARK	LACO	91303	Q	A2
CANTIL	KER	93519	80	C3
CANTUA CREEK	FRCO	93608	56	D5
CANYON CITY	SDCO	92006	112	D2
CANYON COUNTRY	LACO	91351	89	C4
CANYON CREST HEIGHTS	RCO	92507	99	B2
CANYON DAM	PLU	95923	20	C5
CANYON LAKE	RCO	92380	99	C4
CAPAY	YOL	95607	32	E5
CAPETOWN	HUM	95536	15	C3
CAPISTRANO BEACH	ORA	92624	105	D1
• CAPITOLA	SCR	95010	54	A2
CARBONDALE	AMA	95640	40	C2
CARDIFF-BY-THE-SEA	SDCO	92007	106	B4
CARL INN	TUO	95321	49	C1
CARLOTTA	HUM	95528	16	A2
• CARLSBAD	SDCO	92008	106	B3
• CARMEL	MON	93921	54	A5
CARMEL HIGHLANDS	MON	93921	54	A5
CARMEL VALLEY VILLAGE	MON	93924	54	C5
CARMET	SON	94923	37	C2
CARMICHAEL	SAC	95608	34	A5
CARNELIAN BAY	PLA	95711	36	A1
CARPENTERVILLE	CUR		1	C1
• CARPINTERIA	SB	93013	87	E4
CARQUINEZ HEIGHTS	SOL	94590	38	C4
• CARSON	LACO	90745	S	C2
• CARSON CITY	CRSN		36	C2
CARSON HILL	CAL	95222	41	B4
CARTAGO	INY	93549	70	B1
CARUTHERS	FRCO	93609	57	C5
CASA BLANCA	RCO	92504	99	B3
CASA DE ORO	SDCO	92077	V	E3
CASITAS SPRINGS	VEN	93001	88	A4
CASMALIA	SB	93429	86	B1
CASPER	MEN	95420	22	B5
CASSEL	SHA	96016	13	D5
CASTAIC	LACO	91310	89	B4
CASTELLA	SHA	96017	12	C3
CASTELLAMMARE	LACO	90290	Q	A4
CASTLE CRAG	SHA	96013	12	C3
CASTLE PARK	SDCO	92011	V	D5
CASTRO VALLEY	ALA	94546	L	E5
CASTROVILLE	MON	95012	54	B3
• CATHEDRAL CITY	RCO	92234	100	D4
CATHEYS VALLEY	MPA	95306	49	A3
CAVE JUNCTION	JOS		2	D1
CAYTON	SHA	96013	13	C4
CAYUCOS	SLO	93430	75	D2
CAZADERO	SON	95421	37	C1
CECILVILLE	SIS	96018	11	B3
CEDAR BROOK	FRCO	93641	58	D3
CEDAR CREST	FRCO	93605	50	C5
CEDAR FLAT	PLA	95711	35	E1
CEDAR GLEN	SBD	92321	91	D5
CEDAR GROVE	ED	95709	35	A4
CEDAR GROVE	FRCO	93641	59	B3
CEDARPINES PARK	SBD	92322	91	B5
CEDAR RIDGE	NEV	95924	34	C2
CEDAR VALLEY	MAD	93644	49	D4
CEDARVILLE	MOD	96104	7	D5
CENTERVILLE	ALA	94536	P	A2
CENTERVILLE	DGL		36	C3
CENTERVILLE	FRCO	93654	57	E3
CENTERVILLE	SHA	96001	18	B2
CENTRAL VALLEY	SHA	96019	18	C1
CENTURY CITY	LACO	90067	Q	D4
• CERES	STA	95307	47	D3
• CERRITOS	LACO	90701	T	B1
CHALFANT	MNO	93514	51	D3
CHALLENGE	YUB	95925	26	B4
CHAMBERS LODGE	PLA	95718	35	E2
CHARLESTON PARK	CLK		74	A2
CHATSWORTH	LACO	91311	Q	A1
CHAWANAKEE	FRCO	93602	50	A5
CHEMEKETA PARK	SCL	95030	P	A4
CHEROKEE	BUT	95965	25	D3
CHEROKEE	NEV	93602	26	C5
CHERRY VALLEY	RCO	92223	99	E2
CHESTER	PLU	96020	20	A4
CHICAGO PARK	NEV	95712	34	C2
• CHICO	BUT	95926	25	B3
CHILCOOT	PLU	96105	27	D2
CHINATOWN	SFCO	94108	142	D2
CHINESE CAMP	TUO	95309	41	B5
• CHINO	SBD	91710	U	D3
CHINQUAPIN	MPA	95389	49	D2

*INDICATES INCORPORATED CITY

CITIES AND COMMUNITIES INDEX

COMMUNITY NAME	CO.	ZIP CODE	PAGE	GRID
CHIQUITA LAKE	ED	95634	35	A3
CHLORIDE CITY	INY	92328	62	A4
CHOCTAW VALLEY	KER	93306	78	E2
CHOLAME	SLO	93431	66	D5
* CHOWCHILLA	MAD	93610	48	D5
CHROME	GLE	95963	24	A3
CHUALAR	MON	93925	54	D4
* CHULA VISTA	SDCO	92010	V	D4
CIBOLA	LPAZ		110	D2
CIENEGA SPRINGS	LPAZ		104	C1
CIMA	SBD	92323	84	B4
CIRCLE OAKS	NAPA	94599	38	D2
CISCO	PLA	95728	35	B1
CITRUS HEIGHTS	SAC	95610	34	A5
CLAIREMONT	SDCO	92117	V	B2
CLARAVILLE	KER	93283	79	D2
* CLAREMONT	LACO	91711	U	C2
CLARK	STOR		28	E4
CLARKSBURG	YOL	95612	39	D2
CLARKSVILLE	ED	95682	34	C5
CLAY	SAC	95638	40	B3
* CLAYTON	CC	94517	M	B3
CLEAR CREEK	SIS	96039	2	E4
* CLEARLAKE	LAK	95422	32	A3
CLEARLAKE KEYS	LAK	95423	32	A3
CLEARLAKE OAKS	LAK	95423	32	A3
CLEMENTS	SJCO	95227	40	C3
CLEONE	MEN	95437	22	C4
CLIFF HOUSE	TUO	95321	49	B1
CLINTON	AMA	95232	41	A2
CLIPPER GAP	PLA	95703	34	C3
CLIPPER MILLS	BUT	95930	26	A4
CLOVERDALE	SHA	96007	18	B3
* CLOVERDALE	SON	95425	31	C4
* CLOVIS	FRCO	93612	57	D3
CLYDE	CC	94520	M	A3
* COACHELLA	RCO	92236	101	B4
* COALINGA	FRCO	93210	66	D3
COALINGA MINERAL SPGS	FRCO	93210	66	B2
COARSEGOLD	MAD	93614	49	C4
COBB	LAK	95426	31	E4
COCKATOO GROVE	SDCO	92010	V	E4
CODORA	GLE	95970	25	A5
COFFEE CREEK	TRI	96091	11	E3
COHASSET	BUT	95926	25	C1
COLD SPRINGS	TUO	95370	42	A3
COLES STATION	ED	95684	35	B5
COLEVILLE	MNO	96107	42	D1
* COLFAX	PLA	95713	34	D2
COLLEGE CITY	COL	95931	33	A3
COLLEGEVILLE	SJCO	95206	40	B5
COLLIERVILLE	SJCO	95220	40	B3
COLLINSVILLE	SOL	94585	39	B4
* COLMA	SMCO	94015	L	B5
COLOMA	ED	95613	34	D4
COLONIA	VEN	93030	176	C3
* COLTON	SBD	92324	99	B2
COLUMBIA	TUO	95310	41	C4
* COLUSA	COL	95932	32	E2
* COMMERCE	LACO	90040	R	B4
COMPTCHE	MEN	95427	30	C1
* COMPTON	LACO	90220	S	C1
* CONCORD	CC	94520	M	A3
CONFIDENCE	TUO	95370	41	D4
CONSTANTIA	LAS	96019	27	E1
COOKS STATION	AMA	95666	41	C1
COOLIDGE SPRING	IMP		108	C1
COPCO	SIS	96044	4	C2
COPPEROPOLIS	CAL	95228	41	A5
* CORCORAN	KIN	93212	67	E3
CORDELIA	SOL	93063	L	E1
* CORNING	TEH	96021	24	D2
* CORONA	RCO	91720	U	E4
CORONA DEL MAR	ORA	92625	T	C5
* CORONADO	SDCO	92118	V	B4
* CORTE MADERA	MAR	94925	L	A3
COSO JUNCTION	INY	93542	70	C3
* COSTA MESA	ORA	92626	T	C4
COSUMNES	SAC	95683	40	B2
* COTATI	SON	94928	37	E3
COTO DE CAZA	ORA	92678	98	E4
COTTAGE SPRINGS	CAL	95223	41	D2
COTTON CENTER	TUL	93257	68	C3
COTTONWOOD	SHA	96022	18	C3
COULTERVILLE	MPA	95311	48	D2
COURTLAND	SAC	95615	39	D3
COVELO	MEN	95428	23	A3
* COVINA	LACO	91722	U	A2
COVINGTON MILL	TRI	96052	11	E5
COWAN HEIGHTS	ORA	92705	98	C4
COW HOLLOW	SFCO	94123	142	A2
COYOTE	SCL	95013	P	D4
COYOTE WELLS	IMP	92259	111	C3
COZZENS CORNERS	SON	95441	31	D5
CRAFTON	SBD	92373	99	D2
CRANMORE	SUT	95645	33	B3
CRANNELL	HUM	95530	9	E4
* CRESCENT CITY	DN	95531	1	D4
CRESCENT MILLS	PLU	95934	20	C5
CRESSEY	MCO	95312	48	A4
CREST	SDCO	92021	112	A1
CRESTLINE	SBD	92325	91	C5
CRESTMORE	SBD	92316	99	B2
CRESTON	SLO	93432	76	B2
CRESTVIEW	MNO	93514	50	D1
CROCKETT	CC	94525	L	D3
CROMBERG	PLU	96103	27	A2
CROWN POINT	SDCO	92109	V	A3
CROWS LANDING	SIS	95313	47	C4
* CRYSTAL BAY	DGL		36	A1
* CUDAHY	LACO	90201	R	B5
CUESTA BY THE SEA	SLO	93402	75	D3
* CULVER CITY	LACO	90230	Q	D4
CUMMINGS	MEN	95477	22	D2
CUMMINGS VALLEY	KER	93561	79	B4
CUNNINGHAM	SON	95472	37	E2
* CUPERTINO	SCL	95014	P	A3
CURRY VILLAGE	MPA	95389	49	D2
CUTLER	TUL	93615	58	B5
CUTTEN	HUM	95534	15	E1
CUYAMA	SB	93214	87	D1
CUYAMACA	SDCO	92036	107	C4
* CYPRESS	ORA	90630	T	B2
D				
DAGGETT	SBD	92327	92	A1
DAIRY	KLAM		5	D1
DAIRYVILLE	TEH	96080	18	D5
DALES	TEH	96080	18	E4
* DALY CITY	SMCO	94014	L	B5
DANA	SHA	96036	13	D3
* DANA POINT	ORA	92629	105	D1
* DANVILLE	CC	94526	M	A4
DARDANELLE	TUO	95314	42	B2
DARLINGTONIA	DN	95543	2	A3
DARRAH	MPA	95338	49	C3
DARWIN	INY	93522	70	E2
DATE CITY	IMP	92250	112	C3
DAULTON	MAD	93653	57	B1
DAVENPORT	SCR		53	D2
* DAVIS	YOL	95616	39	C1
DAVIS CREEK	MOD	96108	7	C4
DAVIS DAM	MOH		85	D4
DAY	MOD	96056	13	E3
DAYTON	BUT	95926	25	B3
DAYTON	LYON		36	D1
DE BON	SIS	96034	12	C1
DEER PARK	NAPA	94576	38	B1
DEHESA	SDCO	92021	112	A1
* DELANO	KER	93215	68	B5
DEL CERRO	SDCO	92120	V	D3
DEL DIOS	SDCO	92025	106	D3
DELEVAN	COL	95988	24	D5
DELFT COLONY	TUL	93619	58	A5
DELHI	MCO	95315	47	E4
DEL LOMA	TRI	96010	17	A1
* DEL MAR	SDCO	92014	V	A1
DEL PASO HEIGHTS	SAC	95838	33	E5
DEL REY	FRCO	93616	57	E4
* DEL REY OAKS	MON	93940	54	B4
DEL RIO WOODS	SON	95448	37	E1
DEL ROSA	SBD	92404	99	C1
DELTA	SHA	96051	12	B4
DE LUZ	SDCO	92055	106	B1
DEMOCRAT HOT SPRINGS	KER	93301	79	B2
DENAIR	STA	95316	47	E3
DENNY	TRI	95538	10	E5
DENVERTON	SOL	94585	39	A3
DERBY ACRES	KER	93268	77	E3
DE SABLA	BUT	95978	25	C2
DESCANSO	SDCO	92016	107	C5
DESCANSO JUNCTION	SDCO	92016	107	C5
DESERT BEACH	RCO	92254	101	D5
DESERT CENTER	RCO	92239	102	C4
DESERT HAVEN	RCO	92240	100	D3
* DESERT HOT SPRINGS	RCO	92240	100	D2
DESERT LAKE	KER	93516	80	D5
DESERT SHORES	IMP	92274	108	C1
DEVILS DEN	KER	93204	67	B5
DEVORE	SBD	92405	99	B1
DIABLO	CC	94528	M	B4
DIABLO CASA HOT SPGS	MNO	93546	50	E2
DIAMOND BAR	LACO	91765	U	B3
DIAMOND SPRINGS	ED	95619	34	E5
DI GIORGIO	KER	93217	79	A3
DILLON BEACH	MAR	94929	37	D3
DINKEY CREEK	FRCO	93617	58	C1
* DINUBA	TUL	93618	58	A5
DISCOVERY BAY	CC	94514	39	D5
DIXIELAND	IMP	92251	108	D5
* DIXON	SOL	95620	39	B2
DOBBINS	YUB	95935	26	B5
DOG TOWN	CAL	95249	41	B4
DOGTOWN	MPA	95311	48	E2
DOGTOWN	SJCO	95220	40	C3
DORRINGTON	CAL	95223	41	D3
* DORRIS	SIS	96023	5	A2
* DOS PALOS	MCO	93620	56	B2
DOS PALOS Y	MCO	93620	56	A1
DOS RIOS	MEN	95429	23	A3
DOUGLAS CITY	TRI	96024	17	D2
* DOWNEY	LACO	90241	R	B5
DOWNIEVILLE	SIE	95936	26	D4
DOYLE	LAS	96019	27	E1
DOYLES CORNER	SHA	96040	13	D5
DOZIER	SOL	94535	39	B3
DRYTOWN	AMA	95699	40	E2
* DUARTE	LACO	91010	R	D3
* DUBLIN	ALA	94566	M	B5
DUCOR	TUL	93218	68	D4
DULZURA	SDCO	92017	112	B2
DUNCANS MILLS	SON	95430	37	C2
DUNLAP	FRCO	93621	58	C3
DUNLAP	MEN	95490	30	D1
DUNMOVIN	INY	93542	70	C3
DUNNIGAN	YOL	95937	33	A4
* DUNSMUIR	SIS	96025	12	D3
DURHAM	BUT	95938	25	B3
DUSTIN ACRES	KER	93268	78	A4
DUTCH FLAT	PLA	95714	34	D1
DYER	ESM		52	B2
E				
EAGLE LAKE RESORT	LAS	96130	20	D2
EAGLE MOUNTAIN	RCO	92241	102	B3
EAGLE ROCK	LACO	90041	R	A3
EAGLES NEST	SDCO	92086	107	C2
EAGLEVILLE	MOD	96110	8	D2
EARLIMART	TUL	93219	68	B4
EARP	SBD	92242	104	B1
EAST BAKERSFIELD	KER	93307	78	D3
EAST HIGHLANDS	SBD	92346	99	C1
EAST IRVINE	ORA	92720	T	E4
EAST LAKE	ORA	92686	T	E1
EAST NICOLAUS	SUT	95622	33	D3
EASTON	FRCO	93706	57	C4
EAST OROSI	TUL	93647	58	B5
* EAST PALO ALTO	SMCO	94303	N	E2
EAST QUINCY	PLU	95971	26	D1
EAST SAN DIEGO	SDCO	92105	V	C3
EASTSIDE ACRES	MAD	93622	56	C3
EASTSIDE RANCH	MAD	93622	56	C3
ECHO DELL	SDCO	92016	107	C5
ECHO LAKE	ED	95721	35	E4
EDEN GARDENS	SDCO	92075	106	B4
EDEN HOT SPRINGS	RCO	92353	99	D3
EDGEWOOD	SIS	96094	12	C1
EDISON	KER	93220	78	E3
EDNA	SLO	93401	76	B4
EDWARDS AIR FORCE BASE	KER	93523	90	C1
EEL ROCK	HUM	95554	16	C4
EHRENBERG	YUMA		103	E5
EL BONITA	SON	95446	37	C1
* EL CAJON	SDCO	92020	V	E3
* EL CENTRO	IMP	92243	109	A5
* EL CERRITO	CC	94530	L	C3
ELDERS CORNERS	PLA	95603	34	C3
ELDERWOOD	TUL	93286	58	C5
EL DORADO	ED	95623	34	D5
EL DORADO HILLS	ED	95630	34	C5
ELDRIDGE	SON	95431	38	B3
ELECTRA	AMA	95642	41	A2
EL GRANADA	SMCO	94018	N	B2
ELIZABETH LAKE	LACO	93550	89	D3
ELK	MEN	95432	30	C2
ELK CREEK	GLE	95939	24	A4
ELK GROVE	SAC	95624	39	E2
ELK VALLEY	DN	95543	2	C2
ELLWOOD	SB	93117	87	B4
ELMIRA	SOL	95625	39	B2
EL MODENA	ORA	92669	T	E2
* EL MONTE	LACO	91731	R	D3
ELMORE	IMP	92227	108	D3
ELM VIEW	FRCO	93725	57	C4
EL NIDO	MCO	95317	56	C1
* EL PASO DE ROBLES	SLO	93446	76	A1
EL PORTAL	MPA	95318	49	C2
EL PORVENIR	FRE	93608	56	C5
EL RIO	VEN	93030	176	D1
* EL SEGUNDO	LACO	90245	Q	C5
EL SERENO	LACO	90031	R	A3
EL SOBRANTE	CC	94803	L	D3
EL TORO	ORA	92630	98	D4
EL TORO MARINE BASE	ORA	92709	98	D4
EL VERANO	SON	95433	L	B1
ELVERTA	SAC	95626	33	E5
EMERALD BAY	ED	95733	35	E3
EMERALD BAY	ORA	92651	T	D5
* EMERYVILLE	ALA	94608	L	C4
EMIGRANT GAP	PLA	95715	35	A1
EMMATON	SAC		M	D2
EMPIRE	STA	95319	47	D2
ENCANTO	SDCO	92114	V	D4
* ENCINITAS	SDCO	92024	106	B4
ENCINO	LACO	91316	Q	B3
ENGINEER SPRINGS	SDCO	92017	112	B2
ENTERPRISE	SHA	96001	18	C2
* ESCALON	SJCO	95320	47	C1
* ESCONDIDO	SDCO	92025	106	D3
ESPARTO	YOL	95627	33	A5
ESSEX	SBD	92332	94	D2
ESTRELLA	SLO	93415	76	B1
ETHEDA SPRINGS	FRCO	93633	58	D4
* ETNA	SIS	96027	11	D1
ETTERSBURG	HUM	95440	16	A5
EUCALYPTUS HILLS	SDCO	92040	V	E2
* EUREKA	HUM	95501	15	E1
EUREKA VALLEY	SFCO	94114	45	B2
EVELYN	INY	92384	72	E2
* EXETER	TUL	93221	68	C1
F				
* FAIRFAX	MAR	94930	L	A3
* FAIRFIELD	SOL	94533	M	A1
FAIRHAVEN	HUM	95564	15	D1
FAIRMEAD	MAD	93610	56	D1
FAIRMONT	LACO	93534	89	C2
FAIR OAKS	SAC	95628	34	A5
FAIR PLAY	ED	95684	41	A1
FAIRVIEW	TUL	93238	69	C4
FALES HOT SPRINGS	MNO	93517	43	A2
FALLBROOK	SDCO	92028	106	C2
FALLEN LEAF	ED	95716	35	E4
FALLON	MAR	94932	37	D3
FALL RIVER MILLS	SHA	96028	13	E4
FAMOSO	KER	93250	78	C1
* FARMERSVILLE	TUL	93223	68	C1
FAWNSKIN	SBD	92333	91	E5
FEATHER FALLS	BUT	95940	26	A4
FELICITY	IMP		112	C5
FELLOWS	KER	93224	77	E4
FELIX	CAL	95228	41	A4
FELTON	SCR	95018	N	E5
FENNER	SBD	92332	94	E2
FERN	SHA	96096	19	A1
FERNBROOK	SDCO	92065	107	A4
* FERNDALE	HUM	95536	15	D2
FETTERS HOT SPRINGS	SON	95476	38	B3
FIDDLETOWN	AMA	95629	40	E1
FIELDBROOK	HUM	95521	10	A4
FIELDS LANDING	HUM	95537	15	E1
* FILLMORE	VEN	93015	88	D4
FINE GOLD	MAD	93643	49	D5
FINLEY	LAK	95435	31	D3
* FIREBAUGH	FRCO	93622	56	C3
FISH CAMP	MPA	93623	49	D3
FISH ROCK	MEN	95445	30	D4
FISH SPRINGS	INY	93513	59	E1
FIVE CORNERS	LAKE		7	B1
FIVE CORNERS	SJCO	95336	47	C1
FIVE POINTS	FRCO	93624	57	A5
FIVE POINTS	LACO	91732	R	D4
FLEETRIDGE	SDCO	92106	V	A3
FLETCHER HILLS	SDCO	92020	V	D2
FLINN SPRINGS	SDCO	92021	107	A5
FLORIN	SAC	95828	39	E2
FLOURNOY	TEH	96029	24	B2
FLOWING WELLS	RCO	92254	101	C5
* FOLSOM	SAC	95630	34	B5
* FONTANA	SBD	92335	99	B1
FOOTHILL FARMS	SAC	95841	34	A5
FORBESTOWN	BUT	95963	26	A4
FORD CITY	KER	93268	78	A4
FOREST	SIE	95910	26	D4
FORESTA	MPA	95389	49	C2
FOREST FALLS	SBD	92339	100	A2
FOREST GLEN	TRI	96030	17	A3
FORESTHILL	PLA	95631	34	D3
FOREST HOME	AMA	95640	40	C2
FOREST KNOLLS	MAR	94933	38	A5
FOREST LAKE	LAK	95461	32	A4
FOREST RANCH	BUT	95942	25	C2
FOREST SPRINGS	NEV	95945	34	C2
FORESTVILLE	SON	95436	37	D2
FORKS OF SALMON	SIS	96031	11	A2
FORREST PARK	LACO	91350	89	C4
FORT BIDWELL	MOD	96112	7	D3
* FORT BRAGG	MEN	95437	22	C5
FORT DICK	DN	95538	1	D3
FORT IRWIN	SBD	92311	82	B3
* FORT JONES	SIS	96032	3	D5
FORT ORD VILLAGE	MON	93941	54	B4
FORT ROSS	SON	95450	37	B1
FORT SEWARD	HUM	95438	16	D5
* FORTUNA	HUM	95540	15	E2
FOSTER	SDCO	92040	V	E1
* FOSTER CITY	SMCO	94404	N	D1
FOSTER PARK	VEN	93001	88	A5
FOUNTAIN SPRINGS	TUL	93257	68	E4
* FOUNTAIN VALLEY	ORA	92708	T	C3
FOUR CORNERS	SHA	96016	13	C4
FOUTS SPRINGS	COL	95979	24	A5
* FOWLER	FRCO	93625	57	D4
FRANKLIN	SAC	95639	39	E2
FRAZIER PARK	KER	93225	88	D1
FREDALBA	SBD	92382	99	D1
FREDERICKSBURG	ALP	96120	36	B4
FREDS PLACE	ED	95720	35	D4
FREEDOM	SCR	95019	54	B2
FREEMAN	KER	93527	80	C1
FREEPORT	SAC	95832	39	E2
FREESTONE	SON	95472	37	D2
* FREMONT	ALA	94536	P	A2
FREMONT VALLEY	KER	93519	80	B4
FRENCH CAMP	SJCO	95231	40	B5
FRENCH CORRAL	NEV	95975	34	B1
FRENCH GULCH	SHA	96033	18	A1
FRESH POND	ED	95725	35	B4
FRESHWATER	HUM	95504	16	A1
* FRESNO	FRCO	93706	57	C3
FRIANT	FRCO	93626	57	D2
FROGTOWN	CAL	95222	41	B4
FRUITVALE	KER	93308	78	C3
FRUTO	GLE	95988	24	B4
FULLER ACRES	KER	93307	78	E3
* FULLERTON	ORA	92631	T	C1
FULTON	SON	95439	37	E1
FURNACE CREEK RANCH	INY	92328	62	A5
G				
GALLINAS	MAR	94903	L	B3
* GALT	SAC	95632	40	A3
GANNS	CAL	95223	41	D2
GARBERVILLE	HUM	95440	16	C5
* GARDENA	LACO	90247	S	C1
GARDEN FARMS	SLO	93422	76	B2
* GARDEN GROVE	ORA	92640	T	C2
GARDEN PARK	ED	95633	34	D4
GARDEN VALLEY	ED	95633	34	D4
GARDNERVILLE	DGL		36	C3
GAREY	SB	93454	86	C1
GARFIELD	KER	93240	79	C1
GARLOCK	KER	93519	80	D2
GARNET	RCO	92258	100	C3
GASQUET	DN	95543	2	A3
GAVIOTA	SB	93117	86	D4

*INDICATES INCORPORATED CITY

CITIES

CITIES AND COMMUNITIES INDEX

*INDICATES INCORPORATED CITY

CITIES AND COMMUNITIES INDEX

*INDICATES INCORPORATED CITY

CITIES AND COMMUNITIES INDEX

COMMUNITY NAME	CO.	ZIP CODE	PAGE	GRID
• PALM DESERT	RCO	92260	100	D4
PALMS	LACO	90034	Q	C4
• PALM SPRINGS	RCO	92262	100	D3
• PALO ALTO	SCL	94301	N	E2
PALO CEDRO	SHA	96073	18	D2
PALOMA	CAL	95252	40	E3
PALOMAR MOUNTAIN	SDCO	92060	107	A2
• PALOS VERDES ESTATES	LACO	90274	S	A2
PALO VERDE	IMP	92266	110	C1
PALO VERDE	SDCO	92001	107	B5
PANAMA	KER	93309	78	D3
PANAMINT SPRINGS	INY	93545	71	A1
PANOCHE	SBT	95043	55	D4
PANORAMA CITY	LACO	91402	Q	C2
• PARADISE	BUT	95969	25	C3
PARADISE CAY	MAR	94920	38	B5
PARADISE VALLEY	SCL	95037	P	D5
PARAISO SPRINGS	MON	93960	64	E1
• PARAMOUNT	LACO	90723	S	E1
PARKFIELD	MON	93451	66	C4
PARKER	LPAZ		104	B1
PARK VILLAGE	INY	92328	62	A5
• PARLIER	FRCO	93648	57	E4
• PASADENA	LACO	91101	R	B3
PASKENTA	TEH	96074	24	B2
PASO PICACHO	SDCO	92036	107	C4
• PASO ROBLES	SLO	93446	76	A1
PATRICK CREEK	DN	95543	2	B3
• PATTERSON	STA	95363	47	B3
PATTON VILLAGE	LAS	96113	21	D5
PAUMA VALLEY	SDCO	92061	106	E2
PAYNES CREEK	TEH	96075	19	B4
PAYNESVILLE	ALP	96120	36	B4
PEANUT	TRI	96041	17	B3
PEARBLOSSOM	LACO	93553	90	C4
PEARDALE	NEV	95945	34	C1
PEARLAND	LACO	93550	90	B3
PEARSONVILLE	INY	93542	70	C5
PEBBLE BEACH	MON	93953	54	A4
PECWAN	HUM	95546	10	B2
PEDLEY	RCO	92509	99	A2
PELICAN CITY	KLAM		5	B1
PENNGROVE	SON	94951	38	A3
PENNINGTON	SUT	95953	33	C1
PENTZ	BUT	95965	25	D3
PEPPERWOOD	HUM	95565	16	A3
PERKINS	SAC	95826	39	E1
• PERRIS	RCO	92370	99	C4
PESCADERO	SMCO	94060	N	C4
• PETALUMA	SON	94952	L	A1
PETER PAM	TUO	95335	41	E4
PETERS	SJCO	95236	40	C5
PETROLIA	HUM	95558	15	D4
PHILLIPS	ED	95735	35	E4
PHILLIPSVILLE	HUM	95558	16	B5
PHILO	MEN	95466	30	E3
PICACHO	IMP	92222	110	D4
• PICO RIVERA	LACO	90660	R	C4
• PIEDMONT	ALA	94611	L	D4
PIERCY	MEN	95467	22	C1
PIERPONT BAY	VEN	93003	175	D4
PIKE	SIE	95922	26	C5
PILOT HILL	ED	95664	34	C4
PINE COVE	RCO	92349	100	B4
PINECREST	TUO	95364	42	A3
PINEDALE	FRCO	93650	57	C3
PINE FLAT	TUL	93207	69	B4
PINE GROVE	AMA	95665	41	A2
PINE GROVE	LAK	95426	31	E4
PINE GROVE	MEN	95460	30	B1
PINE GROVE	SHA	96003	18	C2
PINE HILLS	SDCO	92036	107	C4
PINEHURST	FRCO	93641	58	D3
PINEHURST	JKSN		4	C1
PINELAND	PLA	95718	35	E2
PINE MEADOW	RCO	92361	100	C5
PINE MOUNTAIN CLUB	KER	93225	88	B1
PINE RIDGE	FRCO	93602	58	B1
PINE VALLEY	SDCO	92062	107	D5
PINO GRANDE	ED	95634	35	A4
• PINOLE	CC	94564	L	C3
PINOLE ESTATES	CC	94564	L	D3
PINON PINES	KER	93225	88	C1
PINYON PINES	RCO	92361	100	D5
PIONEER STATION	AMA	95666	41	B2
PIONEERTOWN	SBD	92268	100	D1
PIRU	VEN	93040	88	E4
• PISMO BEACH	SLO	93449	76	B4
• PITTSBURG	CC	94565	M	B3
PITTVILLE	SHA	96056	13	E4
PIXLEY	TUL	93256	68	B4
• PLACENTIA	ORA	92670	T	D1
• PLACERVILLE	ED	95667	34	E5
PLAINSBURG	MCO	95333	48	D5
PLAINVIEW	TUL	93267	68	C2
PLANADA	MCO	95365	48	D4
PLASSE	AMA	95666	35	E5
PLASTER CITY	IMP	92269	108	D5
PLATINA	SHA	96076	17	D3
PLAYA DEL REY	LACO	90291	97	C2
PLEASANT GROVE	SUT	95668	33	D4
• PLEASANT HILL	CC	94523	L	E3
• PLEASANTON	ALA	94566	M	C5
PLEASANT VALLEY	ED	95709	35	A5
• PLYMOUTH	AMA	95669	40	D2
• POINT ARENA	MEN	95468	30	C4
POINT LOMA	SDCO	92106	V	A3
POINT PLEASANT	SAC	95624	39	D3
POINT REYES STATION	MAR	94956	37	D4
POLLARD FLAT	SHA	96017	12	C4
POLLOCK PINES	ED	95726	35	A4
POMINS	ED	95733	35	E2
POMO	MEN	95469	31	C1
• POMONA	LACO	91766	U	C2
POND	KER	93280	68	B5
PONDEROSA	TUL	93208	69	C3
PONDEROSA BASIN	MPA	95338	49	C3
PONDEROSA SKY RANCH	TEH		19	B4
PONDOSA	SIS	96077	13	C3
POPE VALLEY	NAPA	94567	32	C5
POPLAR	TUL	93257	68	C3
POPPET FLATS	RCO		100	A3
PORT COSTA	CC	94569	L	D3
PORTER RANCH	LACO	91311	Q	A1
• PORTERVILLE	TUL	93257	68	D3
• PORT HUENEME	VEN	93041	96	B1
• PORTOLA	PLU	96122	27	B2
• PORTOLA VALLEY	SMCO	94025	N	D3
POSEY	TUL	93260	69	B5
POSTON	LPAZ		104	A2
POSTON 2	LPAZ		104	A3
POTRERO	SDCO	92063	112	C2
POTTER VALLEY	MEN	95469	31	B1
• POWAY	SDCO	92064	V	D1
POZO	SLO	93453	76	D3
PRATHER	FRCO	93651	57	E1
PRATTVILLE	PLU	95923	20	B4
PRESIDIO	SFCO	94118	141	D2
PRESIDIO OF SAN FRAN	SFCO	94129	141	D2
PRESTON	SON	95425	31	C4
PRIEST	TUO	95305	48	D1
PRINCETON	COL	95970	25	A5
PRINCETON BY THE SEA	SMCO	94018	N	B2
PROBERTA	TEH	96078	24	D1
PROGRESO	BAJA		112	A4
PROJECT CITY	SHA	96079	18	C1
PRUNEDALE	MON	93901	54	C3
PUERTA LA CRUZ	SDCO	92086	107	C2
PULGA	BUT	95965	25	D2
PUMPKIN CENTER	KER	93309	78	D3
Q				
QUAIL VALLEY	RCO	92380	99	C4
QUAKING ASPEN	TUL	93208	69	C3
QUARTZ HILL	LACO	93536	89	E3
QUARTZSITE	LPAZ		104	B4
QUINCY	PLU	95971	26	C1
QUINCY JUNCTION	PLU	95971	26	D1
R				
RACKERBY	YUB	95972	25	E5
RAFAEL VILLAGE	MAR	94947	L	A2
RAILROAD FLAT	CAL	95248	41	B2
RAINBOW	SDCO	92028	106	D1
RAISIN CITY	FRCO	93652	57	B4
RAMONA	SDCO	92065	107	A4
RAMSEY	LPAZ		104	D4
RANCHITA	SDCO	92066	107	D3
RANCHO BERNARDO	SDCO	92128	106	D4
RANCHO CALIFORNIA	RCO	92390	106	D1
RANCHO CORDOVA	SAC	95670	40	B1
• RANCHO CUCAMONGA	SBD	91730	U	D2
• RANCHO MIRAGE	RCO	92270	100	D4
RANCHO MURIETA	SAC	95683	40	C1
• RANCHO PALOS VERDES	LACO	90274	S	B3
RANCHO PENASQUITOS	SDCO	92129	106	D4
RANCHO SAN DIEGO	SDCO	92077	V	E3
RANCHO SANTA FE	SDCO	92067	106	C4
RANCHO SANTA MARGARITA	ORA	92688	98	E4
RANCHO TEHAMA	TEH	96021	24	C1
RANDOLF	SIE	96126	27	C4
RANDSBURG	KER	93554	80	D3
RAVENDALE	LAS	96123	8	C5
RAYMOND	MAD	93653	49	B5
RED APPLE	CAL	95224	41	C3
REDBANK	TEH	96080	18	B5
• RED BLUFF	TEH	96080	18	C5
REDCREST	HUM	95569	16	A3
• REDDING	SHA	96001	18	C2
RED HILL	ORA	92705	T	E3
• REDLANDS	SBD	92373	99	C2
RED MOUNTAIN	SBD	93558	80	E3
• REDONDO BEACH	LACO	90277	S	A2
REDWAY	HUM	95560	16	B5
• REDWOOD CITY	SMCO	94061	N	D2
REDWOOD ESTATES	SCL	95044	P	B4
REDWOOD PARK	SMCO	94062	N	C2
REDWOOD SHORES	SMCO	94065	N	D2
REDWOOD VALLEY	MEN	95470	31	B1
• REEDLEY	FRCO	93654	58	A4
RENO	WSH		28	B4
RENO-STEAD	WSH		28	B3
REPRESA	SAC	95671	34	B5
REQUA	DN	95561	1	E5
RESCUE	ED	95672	34	D5
RESEDA	LACO	91335	Q	B2
REWARD	INY	93526	60	B3
RHEEM VALLEY	CC	94570	45	E1
• RIALTO	SBD	92376	99	B1
RICARDO	KER	93519	80	B3
RICE	SBD	92280	103	B2
RICHARDSON SPRINGS	BUT	95978	25	B2
RICH BAR	PLU	95915	26	B1
RICHFIELD	TEH	96083	24	D1
RICHGROVE	TUL	93261	68	C5
• RICHMOND	CC	94801	L	C3
RICHMOND	SFCO	94121	141	B4
RICHVALE	BUT	95974	25	C4
• RIDGECREST	KER	93555	80	D1
RIMFOREST	SBD	92378	99	C1
RIMROCK	SBD	92268	100	D1
RINCON	SDCO	92082	106	E2
RIO BRAVO	KER	93306	78	E2
• RIO DELL	HUM	95562	15	E3
RIO DELL	SON	95486	37	D2
RIO LINDA	SAC	95673	33	E5
RIO NIDO	SON	95471	37	D1
RIO OSO	SUT	95674	33	D3
• RIO VISTA	SOL	94571	M	D2
RIPLEY	RCO	92272	103	D5
• RIPON	SJCO	95366	47	C2
• RIVERBANK	STA	95367	47	D2
RIVERDALE	FRCO	93656	57	B5
RIVER KERN	KER	93238	69	D5
RIVER PINES	AMA	95675	40	E1
• RIVERSIDE	RCO	92501	99	B2
RIVERTON	ED	95725	35	B4
RIVIERA	MOH		85	D4
RIVIERA HEIGHTS	LAK	95443	31	D3
RIVIERA WEST	LAK	95422	31	E3
ROADS END	TUL	93236	69	C4
ROBBINS	SUT	95676	33	C4
ROBINSONS CORNER	BUT	95948	25	C5
ROBLA	SAC	95673	33	E5
ROCKAWAY BEACH	SMCO	94044	N	B1
ROCK HAVEN	SDCO	92065	106	E4
• ROCKLIN	PLA	95677	34	B4
ROCKPORT	MEN	95488	22	B3
ROCKVILLE	SOL	94585	38	E3
RODEO	CC	94572	L	D3
ROGERS LANDING	MOH		85	D4
• ROHNERT PARK	SON	94928	38	A2
ROHNERVILLE	HUM	95540	15	E2
ROLINDA	FRCO	93705	57	B3
• ROLLING HILLS	LACO	90274	S	B3
• ROLLING HILLS ESTATES	LACO	90274	S	B2
ROMOLAND	RCO	92380	99	D4
ROSAMOND	KER	93560	90	A1
ROSEDALE	KER	93308	78	C3
• ROSEMEAD	LACO	91770	R	C3
ROSEMONT	SDCO	92065	106	E4
• ROSEVILLE	PLA	95678	34	A4
ROSEVILLE	SDCO	92106	V	A3
ROSEWOOD	TEH	96022	18	B4
• ROSS	MAR	94957	L	A3
ROSSMOOR	ORA	90720	T	A2
ROUGH AND READY	NEV	95975	34	B1
ROUND MOUNTAIN	SHA	96084	13	A5
ROVANA	INY	93514	51	B3
ROWLAND HEIGHTS	LACO	91745	U	A3
RUBIDOUX	RCO	92509	99	A2
RUCH	JKSN		3	C1
RUCKER	SCL	95020	P	D5
RUMSEY	YOL	95679	32	D4
RUNNING SPRINGS	SBD	92382	99	D1
RUSSIAN HILL	SFCO	94133	142	C2
RUTH	TRI	95526	17	A4
RUTHERFORD	NAPA	94573	38	B2
RYDE	SAC	95680	M	E1
S				
SABRE CITY	PLA	95660	34	A5
• SACRAMENTO	SAC	95813	39	E1
• SAINT HELENA	NAPA	94574	38	B1
SALIDA	STA	95368	47	C2
• SALINAS	MON	93901	54	C4
SALMON CREEK	SON	94923	37	C2
SALT CREEK LODGE	SHA	96051	12	C5
SALTDALE	KER	93519	80	C3
SALTON	RCO	92257	108	D1
SALTON CITY	IMP	92274	108	C2
SALTON SEA BEACH	IMP	92274	108	C1
SALVADOR	NAPA	94558	38	C3
SALYER	TRI	95563	10	D5
SAMOA	HUM	95560	9	D5
SAN ANDREAS	CAL	95249	41	A3
• SAN ANSELMO	MAR	94960	L	A3
SAN ANTONIO HEIGHTS	SBD	91786	U	D1
SAN ARDO	MON	93450	65	D3
SAN BENITO	SBT	95023	55	C5
• SAN BERNARDINO	SBD	92402	99	C1
SANBORN	KER	93501	80	A5
• SAN BRUNO	SMCO	94066	N	C1
SAN CARLOS	SDCO	92119	V	D2
• SAN CARLOS	SMCO	94070	N	D2
• SAN CLEMENTE	ORA	92672	105	D1
SANDBERG	LACO	93532	89	A2
• SAND CITY	MON	93955	54	A4
• SAN DIEGO	SDCO	92101	V	B3
SAN DIEGO COUNTRY EST	SDCO	92065	107	B4
• SAN DIMAS	LACO	91773	U	B2
SANDY	CLK		74	A5
SAN FELIPE	SDCO	92086	107	C3
• SAN FERNANDO	LACO	91341	Q	C1
• SAN FRANCISCO	SFCO	94101	L	B4
• SAN GABRIEL	LACO	91776	R	C3
• SANGER	FRCO	93657	57	E3
SAN GERONIMO	MAR	94963	38	A5
SAN GORGONIO	RCO	92282	100	B3
SAN GREGORIO	SMCO	94074	N	C3
• SAN JACINTO	RCO	92383	99	E3
• SAN JOAQUIN	FRCO	93660	56	E4
• SAN JOSE	SCL	95103	P	B3
• SAN JUAN BAUTISTA	SBT	95045	54	D3
• SAN JUAN CAPISTRANO	ORA	92675	98	D5
SAN JUAN HOT SPRINGS	ORA	92675	98	E5
• SAN LEANDRO	ALA	94577	L	E5
SAN LORENZO	ALA	94580	L	E5
SAN LUCAS	MON	93954	65	D3
• SAN LUIS OBISPO	SLO	93401	76	B3
SAN LUIS REY	SDCO	92068	106	B2
SAN LUIS REY HEIGHTS	SDCO	92028	106	C2
• SAN MARCOS	SDCO	92069	106	D3
SAN MARIN	MAR	94947	L	A2
• SAN MARINO	LACO	91108	R	C3
SAN MARTIN	SCL	95046	P	D5
• SAN MATEO	SMCO	94401	N	C1
SAN MIGUEL	SLO	93451	66	A5
SAN ONOFRE	SDCO	92672	105	E1
• SAN PABLO	CC	94806	L	C3
SAN PASQUAL	SDCO	92025	106	E3
SAN PEDRO	LACO	90731	S	C3
SAN QUENTIN	MAR	94964	L	B3
• SAN RAFAEL	MAR	94901	L	B3
• SAN RAMON	CC	94583	M	B4
SAN SIMEON	SLO	93452	75	B1
• SANTA ANA	ORA	92701	T	D3
SANTA ANA GARDENS	ORA	92704	T	D3
• SANTA BARBARA	SB	93101	87	C4
• SANTA CLARA	SCL	95050	P	B3
• SANTA CLARITA	LACO	91321	89	C4
• SANTA CRUZ	SCR	95060	53	E2
• SANTA FE SPRINGS	LACO	90670	R	C5
SANTA MARGARITA	SLO	93453	76	B3
• SANTA MARIA	SB	93454	86	B1
• SANTA MONICA	LACO	90402	Q	B4
• SANTA PAULA	VEN	93060	88	C5
SANTA RITA	ALA	94566	M	C5
SANTA RITA	MON	93901	54	C3
SANTA RITA PARK	MER	93660	56	B1
• SANTA ROSA	SON	95401	37	E2
SANTA SUSANA	VEN	93063	89	A5
SANTA VENETIA	MAR	94903	L	B3
SANTA YNEZ	SB	93460	86	E3
SANTA YSABEL	SDCO	92070	107	C3
• SANTEE	SDCO	92071	V	D2
SAN YSIDRO	SDCO	92073	V	D5
• SARATOGA	SCL	95070	P	A4
SATICOY	VEN	93004	88	C5
SATTLEY	SIE	96124	27	C3
SAUGUS	LACO	91350	89	B4
• SAUSALITO	MAR	94965	L	B4
SAWYERS BAR	SIS	96027	11	B2
SCALES	SIE	95981	26	C4
SCHELLVILLE	SON	95476	L	B1
SCISSORS CROSSING	SDCO	92036	107	D3
SCOTIA	HUM	95565	16	A3
SCOTT BAR	SIS	96085	3	C4
SCOTT DAM	LAK	95469	23	C5
SCOTTS CORNER	ALA	94586	P	B1
• SCOTTS VALLEY	SCR	95060	P	A5
SCOTTYS CASTLE	INY	92328	61	B1
SCRIPPS MIRAMAR RANCH	SDCO	92131	V	C1
SEACLIFF	SFCO	94121	141	C2
SEACLIFF	VEN	93001	87	E5
• SEAL BEACH	ORA	90740	T	A3
SEA RANCH	SON	95412	30	E5
SEARCHLIGHT	CLK		85	A2
SEARCHLIGHT JUNCTION	SBD	92332	95	B1
SEARS POINT	SON	94952	L	B2
• SEASIDE	MON	93955	54	B4
• SEBASTOPOL	SON	95472	37	E2
SEDCO HILLS	RCO	92330	99	C4
SEELEY	IMP	92273	108	E5
SEIAD VALLEY	SIS	96086	3	B3
SEIGLER SPRINGS	LAK	95426	31	E4
• SELMA	FRCO	93662	57	E4
SENECA	PLU	95923	20	C5
SEPULVEDA	LACO	91335	Q	B2
SERENE LAKES	PLA	95728	35	C1
SERENO DEL MAR	SON	94923	37	C2
SERRA MESA	SDCO	92123	V	C3
SEVEN PINES	INY	93526	59	E3
SHADOW HILLS	LAK	95461	32	A4
SHADY DELL	SDCO	92065	V	E1
SHADY GLEN	PLA	95713	34	D2
• SHAFTER	KER	93263	78	B2
SHANDON	SLO	93461	76	D1
SHASTA	SHA	96087	18	B2
SHAVER LAKE HEIGHTS	FRCO	93664	58	B1
SHAVER LAKE POINT	FRCO	93664	50	B5
SHEEP RANCH	CAL	95250	41	B3
SHELL BEACH	SLO	93449	76	B4
SHELL TRACT	SON		39	A5
SHELTER VALLEY RANCHOS	SDCO	92036	107	D4
SHERIDAN	SON	95462	37	C2
SHERMAN OAKS	LACO	91403	Q	C3
SHINGLE MILL	SON	95480	31	A5
SHINGLE SPRINGS	ED	95682	34	D5
SHINGLETOWN	SHA	96088	19	A3
SHIVELY	HUM	95565	16	B3
SHORE ACRES	CC	94565	39	A4
SHOSHONE	INY	92384	73	A4
SHUMWAY	LAS		21	B1
SIERRA BROOKS	SIE	96135	27	D3
SIERRA CITY	SIE	96125	27	A4
• SIERRA MADRE	LACO	91024	R	D2
SIERRAVILLE	SIE	96126	27	C4
• SIGNAL HILL	LACO	90806	S	D2
SILVERADO CANYON	ORA	92676	98	E4
SILVER CITY	LYON		36	C1
SILVER CITY	TUL	93271	59	B5
SILVER FORK	ED	95728	35	C4
SILVER LAKE	LACO	90039	Q	E3
SILVERPEAK	ESM		52	D1
SILVER STRAND	VEN	93030	96	B1

***INDICATES INCORPORATED CITY**

CITIES

CITIES AND COMMUNITIES INDEX

COMMUNITY NAME	CO.	ZIP CODE	PAGE	GRID
• SIMI VALLEY	VEN	93065	89	A5
SIMMLER	SLO	93453	77	B3
SISQUOC	SB	93454	86	C1
SITES	COL	95979	32	C1
SKAGGS SPRINGS	SON	95448	31	C5
SKIDOO	INY	92328	61	D5
SKYFOREST	SBD	92385	99	C1
SKY LONDA	SMCO	94062	N	D3
SKY VALLEY	RCO	92240	100	E3
SLEEPY HOLLOW	MAR	94960	L	A3
SLEEPY VALLEY	LACO	91350	89	D4
SLIDE INN	TUO	95335	41	E4
SLOAN	CLK		74	D4
SLOAT	PLU	96127	26	E2
SLOUGHHOUSE	SAC	95683	40	B1
SMARTVILLE	YUB	95977	34	A2
SMITHFLAT	ED	95727	34	E5
SMITH RIVER	DN	95567	1	E3
SMITH STATION	TUO	95321	49	A1
SNELLING	MCO	95369	48	C3
SOBOBA HOT SPRINGS	RCO	92383	99	E3
SODA BAY	LAK	95443	31	D3
SODA SPRINGS	NEV	95728	27	C5
SODA SPRINGS	SON	95728	31	A5
• SOLANA BEACH	SDCO	92075	106	B4
• SOLEDAD	MON	93960	55	A5
• SOLVANG	SB	93463	86	E3
SOMERSET	ED	95684	35	A5
SOMES BAR	SIS	95568	10	E2
SOMIS	VEN	93066	88	D5
• SONOMA	SON	95476	L	B1
• SONORA	TUO	95370	41	C5
SONORA JUNCTION	MNO	93517	42	E2
SOQUEL	SCR	95073	54	A2
SORRENTO VALLEY	SDCO	92121	V	B1
SOULSBYVILLE	TUO	95372	41	D5
SOUTH BELRIDGE	KER	93251	77	D2
SOUTH DOS PALOS	MCO	93665	56	A2
• SOUTH EL MONTE	LACO	91733	R	C4
SOUTH FORK	MAD		49	E5
SOUTH FORK	MPA	95318	49	B2
• SOUTH GATE	LACO	90280	R	A5
SOUTH LAGUNA	ORA	92677	T	E5
SOUTH LAKE	KER	93283	79	D1
• SOUTH LAKE TAHOE	ED	95705	36	A3
SOUTH OF MARKET	SFCO	94103	143	C4
SOUTH OROVILLE	BUT	95965	25	D4
SOUTH PARK	SON	95404	38	A2
• SOUTH PASADENA	LACO	91030	R	B3
SOUTHPORT	YOL	95691	39	D1
• SOUTH SAN FRANCISCO	SMCO	94080	N	C1
SOUTH SAN GABRIEL	LACO	91770	R	B4
SOUTH TAFT	KER	93268	78	A4
SPANISH CREEK	PLU	95971	26	D1
SPANISH FLAT WOODLANDS	NAPA	94558	38	D1
SPANISH RANCH	PLU	95956	26	C1
SPARKS	WSH		28	C4
SPAULDING	LAS	96130	20	D1
SPENCEVILLE	NEV	95945	34	B2
SPRECKELS	MON	93962	54	D4
SPRING GARDEN	PLU	95971	26	E2
SPRING TOWN	ALA	94550	M	C5
SPRING VALLEY	SDCO	92077	V	D3
SPRINGVILLE	TUL	93265	68	E2
SQUAW VALLEY	FRCO	93646	58	B3
SQUIRREL MTN VALLEY	KER	93240	79	D1
STAFFORD	HUM	95565	16	A3
STAGECOACH	LYON		28	E5
STANDARD	TUO	95373	41	D5
STANDISH	LAS	96128	21	B3
STANFIELD HILL	YUB	95918	34	A1
STANFORD	SCL	94305	N	D2
STANISLAUS	TUO	95247	41	C4
• STANTON	ORA	90680	T	B2
• STATELINE	WSH		36	B3
STAUFFER	VEN	93225	88	C2
STENT	TUO	95347	41	C5
STEVINSON	MCO	95374	47	E4
STEWART	CRSN		36	C2
STEWART-LENNOX	KLAM		5	B1
STEWARTS POINT	SON	95480	30	E5
STINSON BEACH	MAR	94970	L	A4
STIRLING CITY	BUT	95978	25	D2
• STOCKTON	SJCO	95201	40	B5
STONYFORD	COL	95979	24	B5
STOVEPIPE WELLS	INY	92328	61	D4
STRATFORD	KIN	93266	67	C2
STRATHMORE	TUL	93267	68	D2
STRAWBERRY	ED	95735	35	D4
STRAWBERRY	TUO	95375	42	A3
STRAWBERRY VALLEY	YUB	95981	26	B4
STRONGHOLD	MOD	96431	5	E3
STUDIO CITY	LACO	91604	Q	C3
SUGAR LOAF	SBD	92386	92	A5
SUGARLOAF VILLAGE	TUL	93260	69	B4
SUGAR PINE	MAD	95389	49	D3
SUGARPINE	TUO	95346	41	D4
• SUISUN CITY	SOL	94585	M	A1
SULTANA	TUL	93666	58	B5
SUMMERHOME PARK	SON	95436	37	D2
SUMMERLAND	SB	93067	87	D4
SUMMIT	SBD	92322	91	A5
SUMMIT	VEN	93023	88	C4
SUMMIT CITY	SHA	96089	18	B1
SUN CITY	RCO	92381	99	C4
SUNLAND	LACO	91040	Q	D1
SUNNYBROOK	AMA	95640	40	D2
SUNNYSIDE	SDCO	92002	V	D4
SUNNYSLOPE	RCO	93656	99	A2
• SUNNYVALE	SCL	94086	P	A3
SUNNY VISTA	SDCO	92010	V	D4
SUNOL	ALA	94586	P	B1
SUNSET	SFCO	94122	141	B5
SUNSET BEACH	ORA	90742	T	A3
SUNSET ESTATES	PLA	95678	33	E4
SUN VALLEY	LACO	91352	Q	D2
SUN VALLEY	WSH		28	B4
SURF	SB	93436	86	A3
SURFSIDE	ORA	90743	T	A3
• SUSANVILLE	LAS	96130	20	E3
SUTCLIFFE	WSH		28	C1
SUTTER	SUT	95982	33	C2
• SUTTER CREEK	AMA	95685	40	E2
SWANSBORO COUNTRY	ED	95727	35	A4
SWANSEA	INY	93545	60	C5
SWEETBRIER	SHA	96017	12	C3
SWEETLAND	NEV	95959	26	B5
SWEETWATER	LYON		43	C1
SYCAMORE	COL	95957	33	A2
SYLMAR	LACO	91342	Q	B1
SYLMAR SQUARE	LACO	91342	Q	C1
SYLVIA PARK	LACO	90290	Q	A3
T				
• TAFT	KER	93268	78	A4
TAFT HEIGHTS	KER	93268	77	E4
TAHOE CITY	PLA	95730	35	E2
TAHOE PINES	PLA	95718	35	D2
TAHOE VILLAGE	DGL	25	36	B3
TAHOE VISTA	PLA	95732	36	A1
TAHOMA	PLA	95733	35	E2
TAKILMA	JOS		2	D2
TALENT	JKSN		3	E1
TALMAGE	MEN	95481	31	B2
TAMALPAIS VALLEY	MAR	94941	L	A4
TAMARACK	CAL	95223	41	E2
TANCRED	YOL	95606	32	D5
TARZANA	LACO	91356	Q	A3
TASSAJARA	CC	94526	46	B1
TASSAJARA HOT SPRGS	MON	93924	64	D2
TAYLORSVILLE	PLU	95983	20	D5
TECATE	BAJA		112	C2
TECATE	SDCO	92080	112	C2
TECOPA	INY	92389	73	A4
TECOPA HOT SPRINGS	INY	92389	73	A4
• TEHACHAPI	KER	93561	79	D4
TEHACHAPI EAST	KER	93561	79	D4
• TEHAMA	TEH	96090	24	D1
TELEGRAPH CITY	CAL	95228	40	E5
TELEGRAPH HILL	SFCO	94133	142	D1
TEMECULA	RCO	92390	106	C1
• TEMPLE CITY	LACO	91780	R	C3
TEMPLETON	SLO	93465	76	A2
TENNANT	SIS	96012	5	B5
TERMINOUS	SJCO	95240	39	E4
TERMO	LAS	96132	8	B5
TERRA BELLA	TUL	93270	68	D3
TERRA LINDA	MAR	94903	L	A3
THE HIGHLANDS	SMCO	94402	N	C2
THE NARROWS	SDCO	92004	108	A3
THERMAL	RCO	92274	101	B5
THERMALANDS	PLA	95648	34	B3
THE WILLOWS	SDCO	92001	107	B5
THISBE	WSH		28	E4
THORNE	MIN		44	B1
THORNTON	SJCO	95686	39	E3
• THOUSAND OAKS	VEN	91360	96	E1
THOUSAND PALMS	RCO	92276	100	E3
THREE ARCH BAY	ORA	92677	98	D5
THREE RIVERS	TUL	93271	58	D5
• TIBURON	MAR	94920	L	B4
TIERRA BUENA	SUT	95991	33	C2
TIERRA DEL SOL	SDCO	92005	112	E2
TIERRASANTA	SDCO	92124	V	C2
TIJUANA	BAJA		111	D2
TIMBER LODGE	MPA	95345	49	B3
TIPTON	TUL	93272	68	B3
TISDALE	SUT	95957	33	B3
TOBIN	PLU	95965	26	A1
TOLLHOUSE	FRCO	93667	58	A2
TOMALES	MAR	94971	37	D3
TOMS PLACE	MNO	93546	51	B3
TOPANGA	LACO	90290	Q	A3
TOPANGA PARK	LACO	90290	97	B1
TOPAZ	MNO	96133	36	D5
TOPOCK	MOH		95	E2
• TORRANCE	LACO	90505	S	B2
TOWER HOUSE	SHA	96095	18	A2
TOYON	SHA	96019	18	C1
TRABUCO CANYON	ORA	92678	98	E4
• TRACY	SJCO	95376	46	E2
TRAIL PARK	ED	95651	34	E4
TRANQUILLITY	FRCO	93668	56	D4
TRAVER	TUL	93673	57	E5
TRAVIS AIR FORCE BASE	SOL	94535	39	A3
TRES PINOS	SBT	95075	55	A3
• TRINIDAD	HUM	95570	9	E4
TRINITY CENTER	TRI	96091	11	E4
TRONA	SBD	93562	71	B5
TROPICO	KER	93560	89	E1
TROWBRIDGE	SUT	95659	33	D3
TROY	PLA	95728	35	B1
TRUCKEE	NEV	95734	27	D5
TUDOR	SUT	95991	33	C3
TUJUNGA	LACO	91042	Q	E1
• TULARE	TUL	93274	68	A2
• TULELAKE	SIS	96134	5	D2
TUOLUMNE	TUO	95379	41	D5
TUOLUMNE MEADOWS	TUO	95379	43	A5
TUPMAN	KER	93276	78	B3
• TURLOCK	STA	95380	47	E3
TURTLE ROCK	ORA	92715	98	C4
• TUSTIN	ORA	92680	T	E3
TUTTLE	MCO	95340	48	D5
TWAIN	PLU	95984	26	B1
TWAIN HARTE	TUO	95383	41	D4
TWAIN HARTE VALLEY	TUO	95383	41	D4
• TWENTYNINE PALMS	SBD	92277	101	B1
TWIN BRIDGES	ED	95735	35	E4
TWIN CITIES	SAC	95632	40	A3
TWIN OAKS	SDCO	92083	106	C3
TWIN PEAKS	SBD	92391	91	C5
TWIN PINES	RCO		100	B3
TYNDALL LANDING	YOL	95698	33	B4
U				
• UKIAH	MEN	95482	31	B2
ULTRA	TUL	93256	68	D3
• UNION CITY	ALA	94587	P	A1
UNIVERSAL CITY	LACO	91608	Q	D3
UNIVERSITY CITY	SDCO	92122	V	A2
• UPLAND	SBD	91786	U	D2
UPPER LAKE	LAK	95485	31	D2
V				
VACATION BEACH	SON	95446	37	C2
• VACAVILLE	SOL	95688	39	A2
VALENCIA	LACO	91355	89	B4
VALERIE	RCO	92274	101	A5
VALINDA	LACO	91744	R	E4
VALLECITO	CAL	95251	41	C4
VALLECITO	SDCO	92036	107	E4
• VALLEJO	SOL	94590	L	D2
VALLEJO HEIGHTS	SOL	94590	38	D4
VALLE VISTA	RCO	92343	99	E4
VALLEY ACRES	KER	93268	78	A4
VALLEY CENTER	SDCO	92082	106	E2
VALLEY FORD	SON	94972	37	D3
VALLEY HOME	STA	95384	47	D1
VALLEY OF ENCHANTMENT	SBD	92322	91	B5
VALLEY SPRINGS	CAL	95252	40	D3
VALLEY WELLS	INY	92366	71	C4
VAL VERDE	LACO	91350	89	A4
VAN NUYS	LACO	91408	Q	C2
• VENICE	LACO	90291	Q	B5
VENTUCOPA	SB	93252	87	E1
VEN-TU PARK	VEN	91320	96	D1
• VENTURA	VEN	93001	88	B5
VERDEMONT	SBD	92407	99	B1
VERDI	WSH		28	A4
VERDI SIERRA PINES	SIE	95737	27	E4
VERDUGO CITY	LACO	91046	Q	E2
• VERNON	LACO	90058	R	A4
VERONA	SUT	95659	33	D4
VICHY SPRINGS	MEN	95482	31	B2
VICTOR	SJCO	95253	40	B4
VICTORIA	SDCO	92001	107	B5
• VICTORVILLE	SBD	92392	91	C3
VIDAL	SBD	92280	103	E1
VIDAL JUNCTION	SBD	92280	103	D1
VILLA GRANDE	SON	95486	37	C2
• VILLA PARK	ORA	92667	T	E2
VINA	TEH	96092	24	E2
VINEBURG	SON	95487	L	C1
VINTON	PLU	96135	27	D2
VIOLA	SHA	96088	19	C2
VIRGILIA	PLU	95984	26	B1
• VIRGINIA CITY	STOR		36	D1
• VISALIA	TUL	93277	68	B1
• VISTA	SDCO	92083	106	C3
VISTA VERDE	SMCO	94025	N	D3
VOLCANO	AMA	95689	41	A2
VOLCANOVILLE	ED	95634	34	E3
VOLLMERS	SHA	96051	12	B4
VOLTA	MER	93635	55	D1
VORDEN	SAC	95690	M	E1
W				
WAHTOKE PARK	FRCO	93654	58	A4
WALKER	MNO	96107	42	E1
WALLACE	ED	95254	40	D3
WALMORT	SAC	95683	40	A2
• WALNUT	LACO	91789	U	A3
• WALNUT CREEK	CC	94595	M	A4
WALNUT GROVE	SAC	95690	M	E1
WALSH LANDING	SON	95450	37	A1
WARM SPRINGS	ALA	94538	P	B2
WARNER SPRINGS	SDCO	92086	107	C2
• WASCO	KER	93280	78	B1
WASHINGTON	NEV	95986	26	E5
WASHOE	SON	94952	37	E3
WASHOE CITY	WSH		28	B5
• WATERFORD	STA	95386	48	A2
WATERLOO	SJCO	95201	40	B4
• WATSONVILLE	SCR	95076	54	C2
WATTS	LACO	90002	Q	E5
WAWONA	MPA	95389	49	D3
WEAVERVILLE	TRI	96093	17	D1
• WEED	SIS	96094	12	C1
WEED PATCH	KER	93307	78	E4
WEIMAR	PLA	95736	34	D3
WEITCHPEC	HUM	95546	10	C3
WELDON	KER	93283	79	D1
WELLSONA	SLO	93446	76	A1
WENDEL	LAS	96136	21	D3
WENTWORTH SPRINGS	ED	95725	35	C3
WEOTT	HUM	95571	16	B4
WEST BRANCH	BUT	95941	25	C1
WEST BUTTE	SUT	95953	33	B2
• WEST COVINA	LACO	91790	U	A2
WESTERN ADDITION	SFCO	94115	143	A4
WEST HAVEN	FRCO	93234	67	B2
• WEST HOLLYWOOD	LACO	90069	Q	D3
• WESTLAKE VILLAGE	LACO	91361	96	E1
WESTLEY	STA	95387	47	B3
WEST LOS ANGELES	LACO	90025	Q	C4
• WESTMINSTER	ORA	92683	T	B3
• WESTMORELAND	IMP	92281	109	A4
WEST OF TWIN PEAKS	SFCO	94122	141	D5
WEST PITTSBURG	CC	94565	M	B3
WEST POINT	CAL	95255	41	B2
WESTPORT	MEN	95488	22	C4
• WEST SACRAMENTO	YOL	95691	39	D1
WEST SIDE	LAKE		7	B1
WESTVILLE	PLA	95631	35	A2
WESTWOOD	LAS	96137	20	C4
WESTWOOD	LACO	90024	97	C4
• WHEATLAND	YUB	95692	33	E3
WHEATON SPRINGS	SBD	92364	84	B2
WHEATVILLE	FRCO	93656	57	A5
WHEELER RIDGE	KER	93284	78	D5
WHEELER SPRINGS	VEN	93023	88	A4
WHISKEYTOWN	SHA	96095	18	A2
WHISPERING PINES	LAK	95461	32	A4
WHITE HALL	ED	95725	35	C4
WHITE HORSE	MOD	96054	13	E2
WHITE PINES	CAL	95223	41	C3
WHITE RIVER	TUL	93257	68	E4
WHITETHORN	HUM	95489	22	B1
WHITEWATER	RCO	92282	100	C3
WHITE WOLF	TUO	95389	42	D5
WHITLEY GARDENS	SLO	93436	76	C1
WHITLOW	HUM	95554	16	C4
WHITMORE	SHA	96096	19	A2
• WHITTIER	LACO	90605	R	D5
WILBUR SPRINGS	COL	95987	32	C3
WILDOMAR	RCO	92395	99	C5
WILDROSE	INY	93562	71	C2
• WILLIAMS	COL	95987	32	D2
WILLIAMS	JOS		3	A1
• WILLITS	MEN	95490	23	A5
WILLOW CREEK	HUM	95573	10	D5
WILLOW RANCH	MOD	96138	7	C3
• WILLOWS	GLE	95988	24	D4
WILLOW SPRINGS	KER	93550	89	D1
WILMINGTON	LACO	90744	S	C2
WILSEYVILLE	CAL	95257	41	B2
WILSONIA	TUL	93633	58	E3
WILTON	SAC	95693	40	B2
WINCHESTER	RCO	92396	99	D4
WINCHUCK	CUR		1	D2
WINDSOR	SON	95492	37	E1
WINTER GARDENS	SDCO	92040	V	E2
WINTERHAVEN	IMP	92283	112	C5
• WINTERS	YOL	95694	39	A1
WINTERWARM	SDCO	92028	106	C2
WISHON	MAD	93669	49	E4
WITCH CREEK	SDCO	92065	107	B3
WITTER SPRINGS	LAK	95493	31	D2
WOFFORD HEIGHTS	KER	93285	69	C5
WOLF	NEV	95945	34	B2
WONDER VALLEY	FRCO	93657	58	B3
WOODACRE	MAR	94973	L	A3
WOODBRIDGE	ORA	92714	T	E4
WOODCREST	RCO	92504	99	B3
WOODFORD	KER	96120	79	B4
WOODFORDS	ALP	96120	36	B4
• WOODLAKE	TUL	93286	58	D5
• WOODLAND	YOL	95695	33	B5
WOODLAND HILLS	LACO	91364	Q	A3
• WOODSIDE	SMCO	94062	N	D2
WOODSIDE VILLAGE	LACO	91792	R	E4
WOODVILLE	TUL	93257	68	C3
WOODY	KER	93287	69	A5
WORDEN	KLAM		5	B2
WRIGHTS LAKE	ED	95720	35	D4
WRIGHTWOOD	SBD	92397	90	E5
WYANDOTTE	BUT	95965	25	D5
WYNOLA	SDCO	92036	107	C3
Y				
YANKEE HILL	BUT	95969	25	D3
YANKEE JIMS	PLA	95631	34	D3
YERMO	SBD	92398	92	A1
YETTEM	TUL	93670	58	B5
YOLO	YOL	95697	33	B5
• YORBA LINDA	ORA	92686	T	D1
YORKVILLE	MEN	95494	31	B4
YOSEMITE FORKS	MAD	93644	49	D4
YOSEMITE VILLAGE	MPA	95389	49	D1
YOUNGSTOWN	SJCO	95220	40	B4
• YOUNTVILLE	NAPA	94599	38	C2
• YREKA	SIS	96097	4	A4
• YUBA CITY	SUT	95991	33	C2
YUCAIPA	SBD	92399	99	D2
YUCCA VALLEY	SBD	92284	100	E1
• YUMA	YUMA		112	D5
Z				
ZAMORA	YOL	95698	33	B4
ZENIA	TRI	95495	16	E4
ZEPHYR COVE	DGL		36	A3

***INDICATES INCORPORATED CITY**

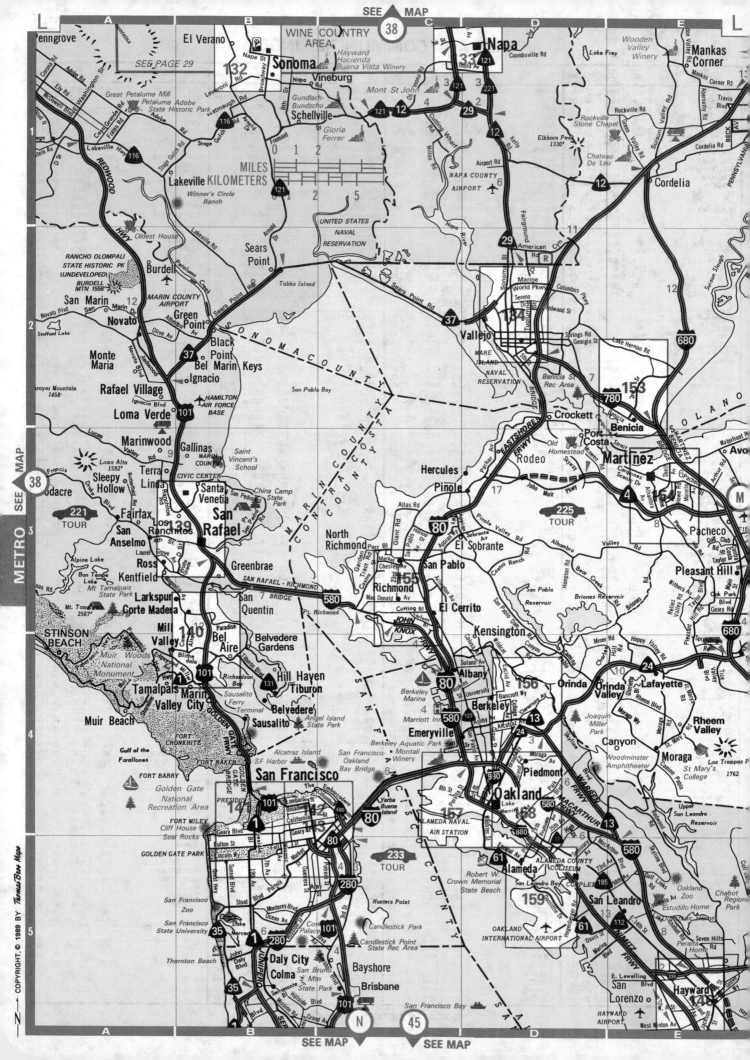

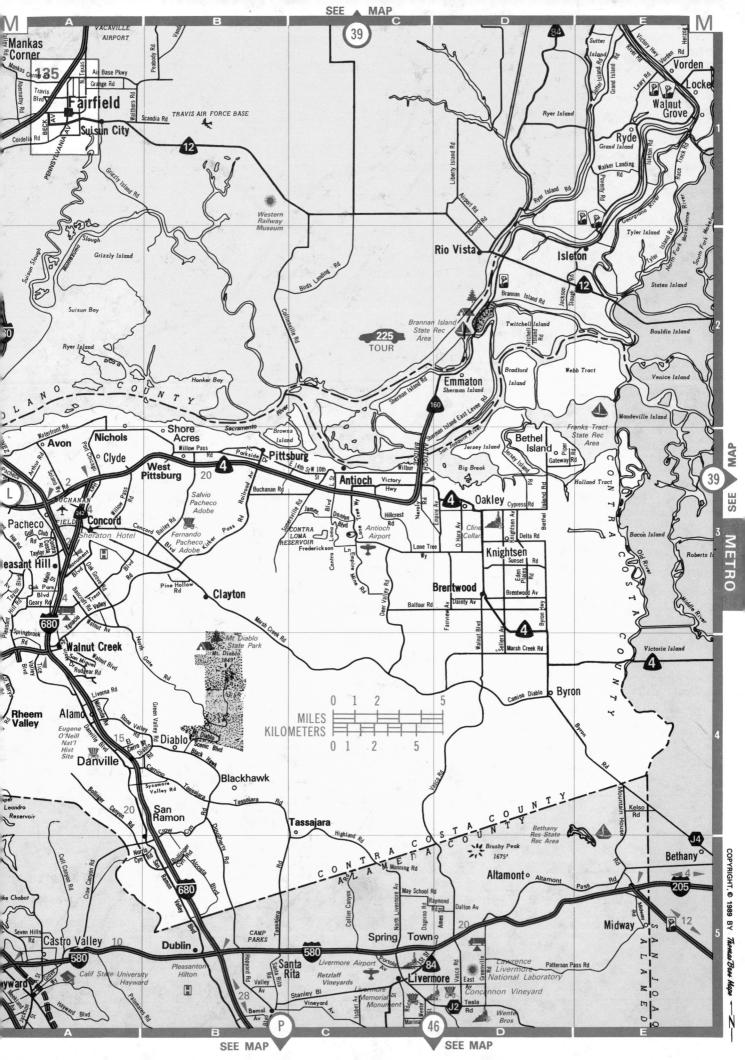

PACIFIC

Pacifica State Beach

35
1
Serramonte Bl Hillside
Mission Rd
Chestnut
Grand Av
101
South San Francisco

Pacifica

4
82 SERRA FRWY
380

Airport Blvd

San Francisco International Airport

San Francisco Airport Marriott

Hyatt

San Francisco Bay

SAN MATEO

ALAMEDA COUNTY

HAYWARD AIRPORT
West Winton Av
W. A St

SHARP PARK BEACH

Rockaway Beach

San Pedro Point

35
San Bruno
144
San Andreas Lake

Millbrae

Linda Mar

DEVILS SLIDE

SAN FRANCISCO
San Francisco State Fish and Game Refuge

Burlingame
Hillsdale Cr
Ralston
San Mateo

Sheraton Inn

SAN MATEO BRIDGE

YOUNGER FRWY

92

13

225 TOUR

Graywhale Cove State Beach

Montara Mountain

Pilarcitos Lake

Hillsborough
16
Black

Foster City

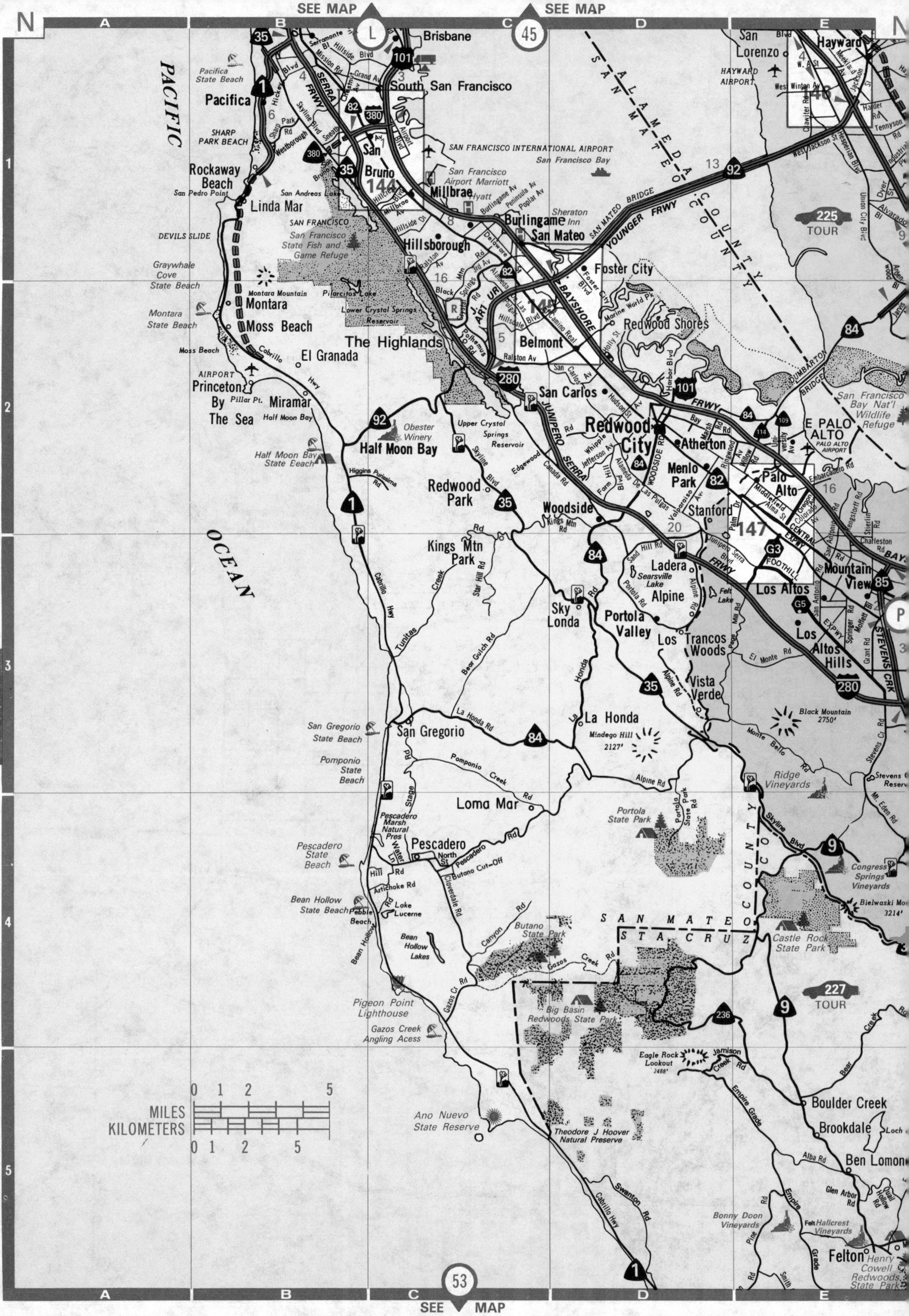

BAYSHORE

84

Montara

Lower Crystal Springs Reservoir

Belmont

Redwood Shores

Montara State Beach

Moss Beach

The Highlands

El Granada

San Carlos Av

280

San Carlos

101 FRWY

84

DUMBARTON BRIDGE

San Francisco Bay Nat'l Wildlife Refuge

Moss Beach

Cobrillo

AIRPORT

Princeton By The Sea

Pillar Pt. Miramar
Half Moon Bay

92

Obester Winery

Upper Crystal Springs Reservoir

JUNIPERO SERRA FRWY

Redwood City
Atherton

E PALO ALTO

PALO ALTO AIRPORT

109
114

Half Moon Bay State Beach

Half Moon Bay

Higgins Purisima Rd

Skyline Blvd

Edgewood Rd

Whipple Av
Jefferson Av

Menlo Park
82

Palo Alto
147

84

1

Redwood Park

35

Woodside
Kings Mtn Rd

Sand Hill Rd

Stanford
20

FOOTHILL

Mountain View

85

Kings Mtn Park

84

Ladera
Searsville Lake
Alpine

G3
G5

Los Altos

OCEAN

Creek

Star Hill Rd

Sky Londa

Portola Valley

Los Trancos Woods

El Monte Rd

Los Altos Hills

280

Bear Gulch Rd

35

Vista Verde

Black Mountain 2750'

STEVENS CRK

La Honda Rd

La Honda

84

Mindego Hill 2127'

Alpine Rd

Monte Bello

Ridge Vineyards

Stevens Cr Reserve

Mt Eden Rd

San Gregorio State Beach

Pomponio State Beach

San Gregorio

Pomponio Creek

Loma Mar

Portola State Park

SAN MATEO COUNTY

9

Congress Springs Vineyards

Bielwaski Mon 3214'

Pescadero Marsh Natural Pres

Pescadero

North St
Butano Cut-Off

Cloverdale Rd

STA CRUZ

Castle Rock State Park

Pescadero State Beach

Hill Rd
Stage Rd

Artichoke Rd

Lake Lucerne

Butano State Park

227 TOUR

Bean Hollow State Beach
Pebble Beach

Bean Hollow Lakes

Canyon

Gazos Creek Rd

Big Basin Redwoods State Park

236
9

Pigeon Point Lighthouse

Gazos Cr Rd

Eagle Rock Lookout 2488'

Jamison Creek Rd

Empire Grade

Gazos Creek Angling Acess

Boulder Creek

Brookdale

MILES
0 1 2 5

KILOMETERS
0 1 2 5

Ano Nuevo State Reserve

Theodore J Hoover Natural Preserve

Cabrillo Hwy

Swanton Rd

Bonny Doon Vineyards

Hallcrest Vineyards

Ben Lomon

Glen Arbor Rd

Alba Rd

1
Felton
Henry Cowell Redwoods State Park

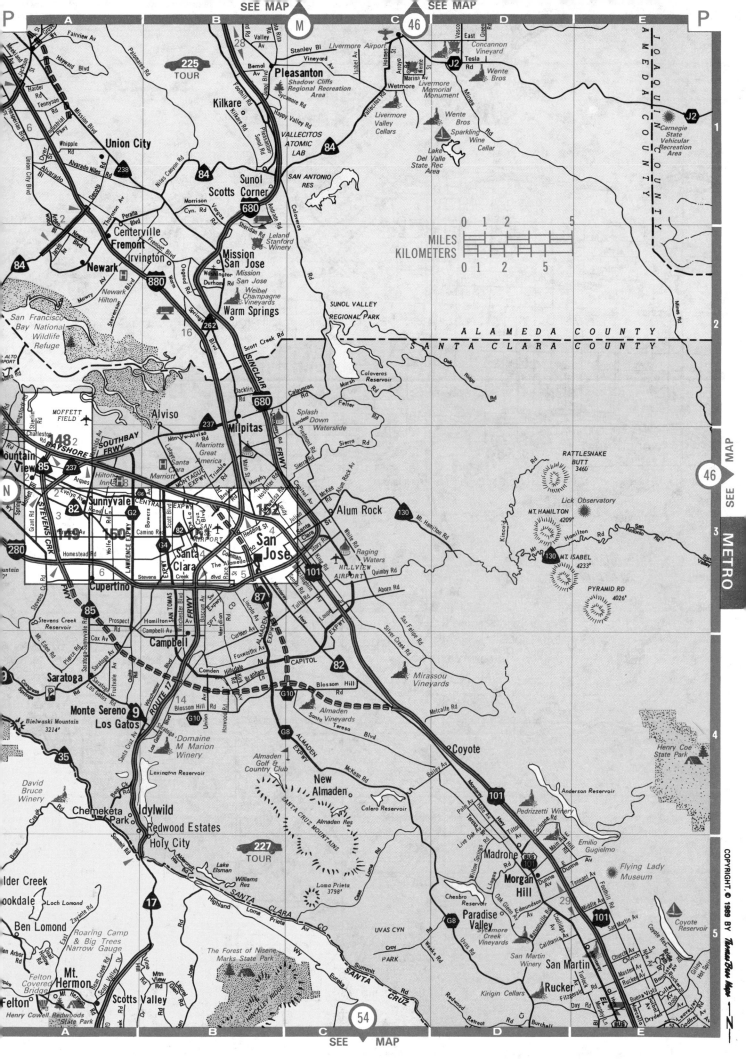

SANTA FE SPRINGS
NORWALK
LA MIRADA
N8
LA HABRA
BREA
OLINDA
98
39
57
TONNER CYN. RD
142
CARBON
90
YORBA LINDA
EAST OLAKE
ARTESIA
CERRITOS
LA PALMA
HAWAIIAN GARDENS
CYPRESS
STANTON
LOS ALAMITOS
ROSSMOOR
BUENA PARK
FULLERTON
PLACENTIA
ATWOOD
ANAHEIM H
35
91
605
22
405
91
5
57
55
OLIVE
ORANGE
VILLA PARK
EL MODENA
COWAN HTS
SEAL BEACH
SURFSIDE
SUNSET BEACH
LEISURE WORLD
WESTMINSTER
MIDWAY CITY
GARDEN GROVE
SANTA ANA
TUSTIN
RED HILL
LEMON HTS
NORTH WOOD
S
98
METRO
FOUNTAIN VALLEY
STA ANA GARDENS
IRVINE
WOODBRIDGE
E IRVINE
TURTLEROCK
HUNTINGTON BEACH
COSTA MESA
NEWPORT BEACH
LIDO ISLE
BALBOA
BALBOA ISLAND
CORONA DEL MAR
NEWPORT CENTER
J WAYNE AIRPORT OR CO
73
133
235 TOUR
Corona Del Mar State Beach
Crystal Cove State Park
EMERALD BAY
LAGUNA BEACH
SOUTH LAGUNA
201

MILES 0 1 2 5
KILOMETERS 0 1 2 5

Bolsa Chica State Beach
Huntington State Beach
Long Beach Marina & Marine Stadium
Huntington Harbour
Movieland Wax Museum
Knotts Berry Farm
Holiday Inn
Embassy Suites

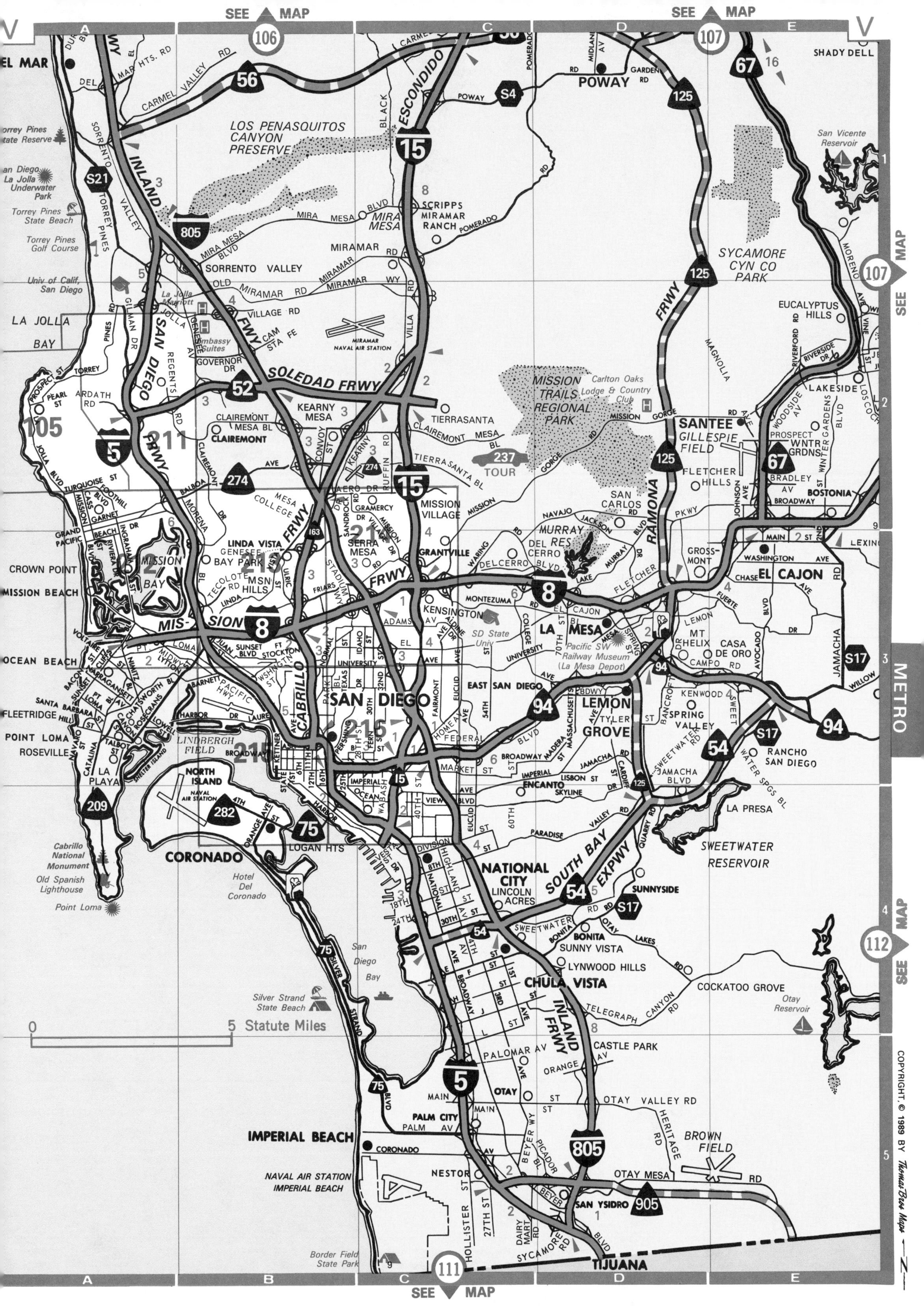

EL MAR

POWAY

LOS PEÑASQUITOS CANYON PRESERVE

SHADY DELL

San Vicente Reservoir

Torrey Pines State Reserve

San Diego La Jolla Underwater Park

Torrey Pines State Beach

Torrey Pines Golf Course

Univ of Calif, San Diego

SORRENTO VALLEY

SCRIPPS MIRAMAR RANCH

MIRA MESA

MIRAMAR

SYCAMORE CYN CO PARK

EUCALYPTUS HILLS

LA JOLLA BAY

LA JOLLA

MIRAMAR NAVAL AIR STATION

SOLEDAD FRWY

KEARNY MESA

CLAIREMONT

TIERRASANTA

MISSION TRAILS REGIONAL PARK

Carlton Oaks Lodge & Country Club

SANTEE

Gillespie Field

LAKESIDE

WNTR GRDNS

BOSTONIA

105

LINDA VISTA

SERRA MESA

MISSION VILLAGE

GRANTVILLE

SAN CARLOS

MURRAY DEL RES CERRO

FLETCHER HILLS

GROSSMONT

EL CAJON

CROWN POINT

MISSION BEACH

MISSION BAY

Bay Park

MSN HILLS

TIERRASANTA

MISSION VALLEY

KENSINGTON

SD State Univ

LA MESA

Pacific SW Railway Museum (La Mesa Depot)

MT HELIX

CASA DE ORO

OCEAN BEACH

MIS-SION

SAN DIEGO

EAST SAN DIEGO

UNIVERSITY

LEMON GROVE

SPRING VALLEY

RANCHO SAN DIEGO

POINT LOMA

ROSEVILLE

LINDBERGH FIELD

NORTH ISLAND NAVAL AIR STATION

LA PLAYA

Cabrillo National Monument

Old Spanish Lighthouse

Point Loma

CORONADO

Hotel Del Coronado

LOGAN HTS

NATIONAL CITY

LINCOLN ACRES

SOUTH BAY

SWEETWATER RESERVOIR

LA PRESA

SUNNYSIDE

COCKATOO GROVE

Otay Reservoir

Silver Strand State Beach

San Diego Bay

BONITA

SUNNY VISTA

LYNWOOD HILLS

CHULA VISTA

INLAND FRWY

CASTLE PARK

0   5 Statute Miles

IMPERIAL BEACH

CORONADO

NAVAL AIR STATION IMPERIAL BEACH

PALM CITY

NESTOR

OTAY

OTAY VALLEY RD

OTAY MESA

BROWN FIELD

SAN YSIDRO 905

Border Field State Park

METRO

HIGHWAYS

CARPENTERVILLE

O R E G O N

THOMAS CK.

101

BOWMAN CK.

CURRY CO.

N. FORK

CHETCO RD.

CHETCO

RIVER

Siskiyou National Forest

NORTH BANK CHETCO RD.

SOUTH BANK

BENHAM LN

BROOKINGS
HARBOR

OCEANVIEW DR

6

101

WINCHUCK

ELK MTN
1688'

S. FORK WINCHUCK RIVER

FOURTH OF JULY CK

COON CK.

HOSSE CK.

E. FORK WINCHUCK RIVER

Pelican
State Beach

D5

S. FORK

CURRY CO
DEL

OREGON
NORTE CO

101

OCEAN VIEW DR

WINCHUCK RIVER

HUNTER ROCK

PRINCE ISLAND

7

WESTBROOK

SMITH
RIVER

SNAVELY

ROWDY

CK.

RD.

LOW DIVIDE

2

1ST ST

SANTA RD.

PALA RD

LOWER LAKE RD.

FRED D HAIGHT

D4

REDWOOD HWY

D E L

N O R T E

C O.

KETTELL BLVD

KELLOGG RD

DISTLERATH
CLOUTIER
ST

MIDDLETON DR

SHUTT ST

MOSELEY RD

FORT
DICK

MOREHEAD

BAILEY RD

S. BANK

OCEAN

STUKEY ST

13

D3

KINGS VLY RD

197

HANDSOMEBLE CK

SIGNAL PK
2055'

199

Lake Earl
State Park

PELICAN
BAY

OLD MILL RD

LOWER

EARL

WONDER STUMP RD

MILL CREEK

D3

LAKE

ELK

VALLEY RD

J. Smith
Redwoods
State Park

SOUTH
FORK

BERTELEDA

PT ST GEORGE

D1

WASHINGTON BL

PACIFIC

BLK

WELL LN

RAILROAD

PARKWAY

LAKE EARL DR

HOWL VALLEY

D2

Redwood Nat'l Park

John McNamara Field

CRESCENT
CITY

HOWLAND HILL RD

BERTSCH
TERRACE

HAMILTON RD

CHILDS HILL
2330'

Undersea World

WHALER
ISLAND

Del Norte County
Historical Society
Museum

Battery
Point
Lighthouse

HUMBOLDT RD

Del Norte Coast
Redwoods
State Park

MILL CK

101

ST PK

CREEK

219
TOUR

SISTER ROCKS

20

WILSON

MATTIE WILSON

HUNTER

FOOTSTEPS ROCK

FALSE KLAMATH
COVE

FALSE KLAMATH
ROCK

REDWOOD HWY

Trees
of
Mystery

MYNOT CK

REQUA

CAMP
KLAMATH

KLAMATH

FLINT ROCK HEAD

WHITE ROCKS

9

169

MCBETH AIRPORT

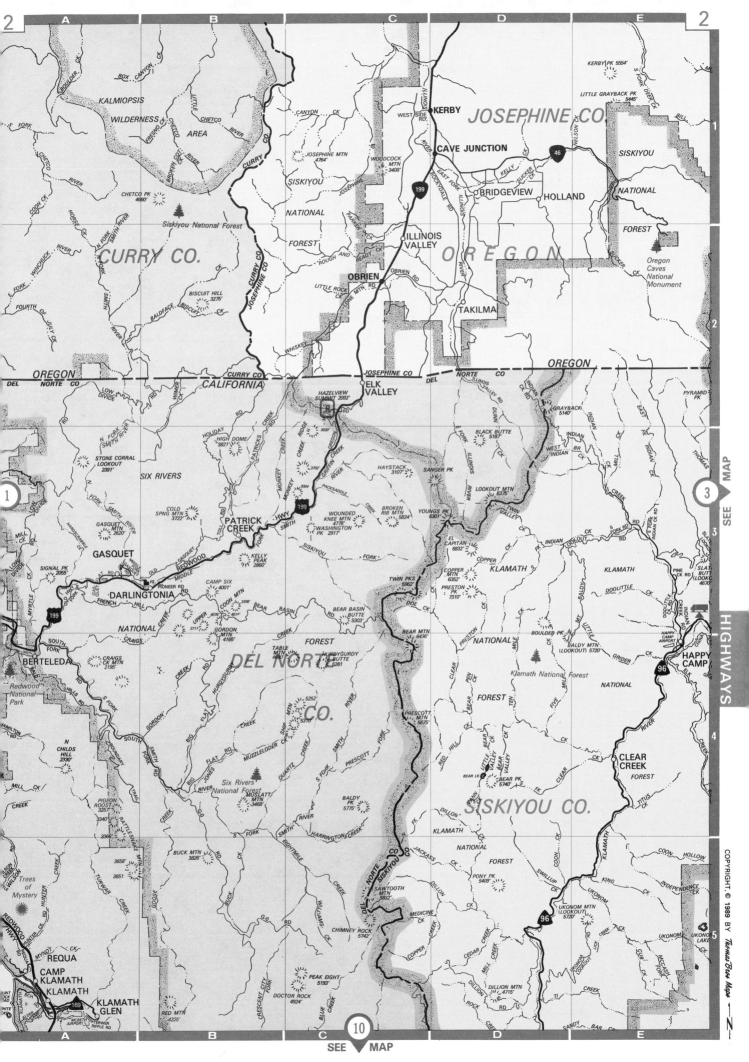

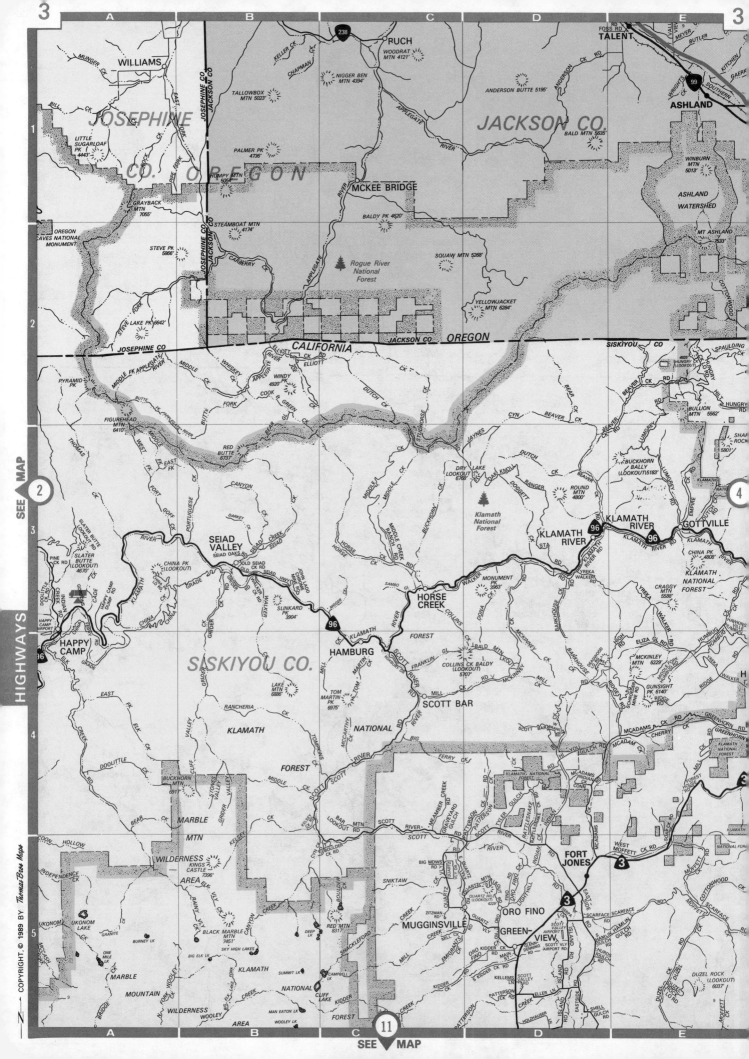

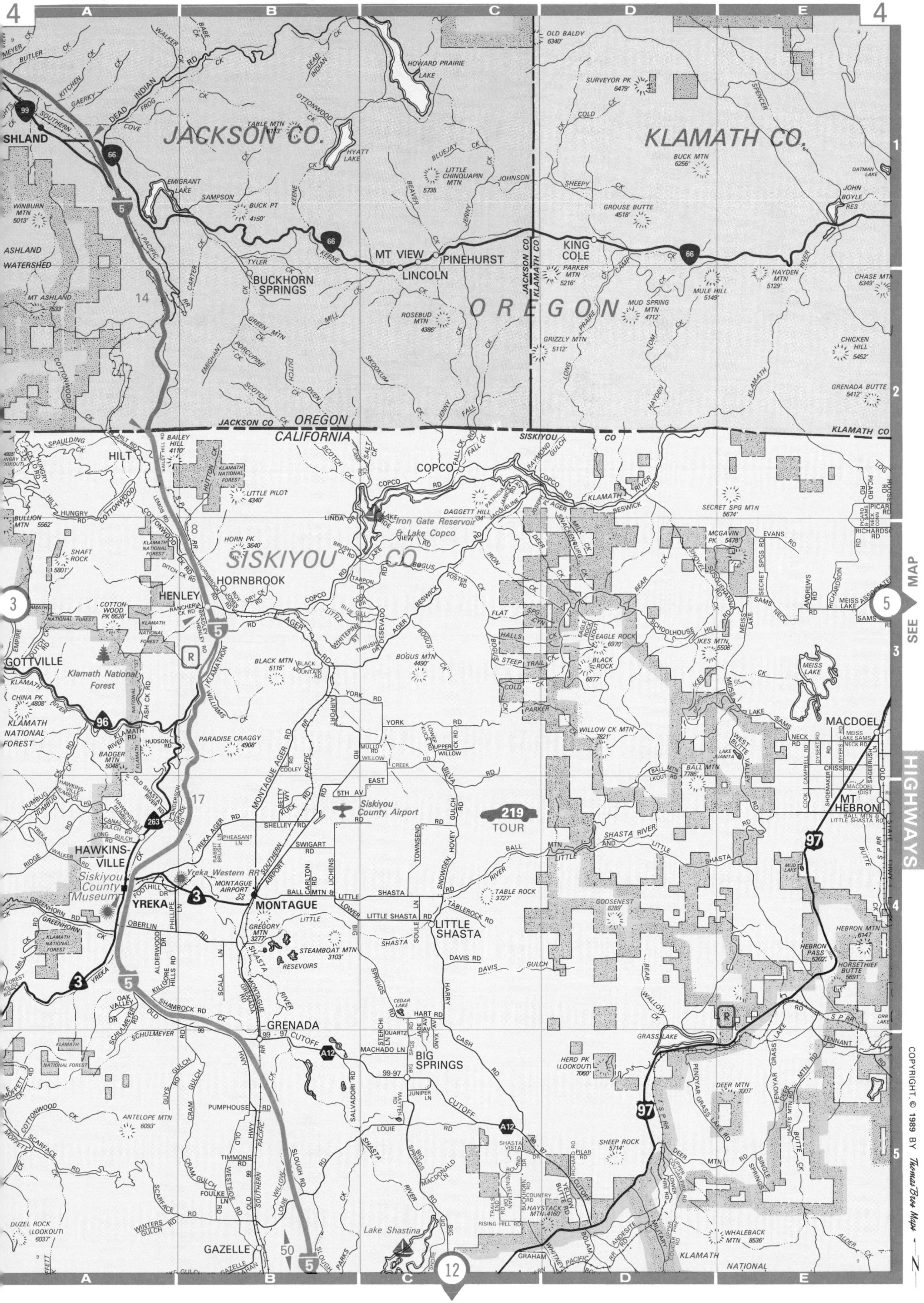

A B C D E
1 2 3 4 5
JACKSON CO.
KLAMATH CO.
OREGON
CALIFORNIA
SISKIYOU CO
JACKSON CO
SISKIYOU CO
KLAMATH CO
ASHLAND
HOWARD PRAIRIE LAKE
HYATT LAKE
EMIGRANT LAKE
OLD BALDY 6340'
SURVEYOR PK 6479'
BUCK MTN 6256'
TABLE MTN 5113'
LITTLE CHINQUAPIN MTN 5735
BUCK PT 4150'
GROUSE BUTTE 4518'
JOHN BOYLE RES
OATMAN LAKE
WINBURN MTN 5013'
ASHLAND WATERSHED
MT ASHLAND 7533'
BUCKHORN SPRINGS
MT VIEW
LINCOLN
PINEHURST
KING COLE
PARKER MTN 5216'
HAYDEN MTN 5129'
MULE HILL 5149'
CHASE MTN 6349'
MUD SPRING MTN 4712'
ROSEBUD MTN 4386'
GRIZZLY MTN 5112'
CHICKEN HILL 5452'
GRENADA BUTTE 5412'
HILT
BAILEY HILL 4110'
COPCO
LITTLE PILOT 4340'
BULLION MTN 5562'
SECRET SPG MTN 5674'
Iron Gate Reservoir & Lake Copco
DAGGETT HILL
HORN PK 3640'
SHAFT ROCK 5801'
MCGAVIN PK 5478'
HORNBROOK
HENLEY
COTTONWOOD PK 6628'
EAGLE ROCK 6970'
BLACK ROCK 6877'
IKES MTN 5506'
MEISS LAKE
BLACK MTN 5115'
BOGUS MTN 4490'
GOTTVILLE
Klamath National Forest
CHINA PK 4808'
KLAMATH NATIONAL FOREST
WILLOW CK MTN 7821'
MACDOEL
PARADISE CRAGGY 4908'
BADGER MTN 5048'
BALL MTN 7786'
MT HEBRON
Siskiyou County Airport
219 TOUR
HAWKINSVILLE
Yreka Western RR
MONTAGUE AIRPORT
Siskiyou County Museum
YREKA
MONTAGUE
TABLE ROCK 3727'
GOOSENEST 8289'
LITTLE SHASTA
GREGORY MTN 3277'
STEAMBOAT MTN 3103'
RESEVOIRS
HEBRON MTN 6147
HEBRON PASS 5202'
HORSETHIEF BUTTE 5691'
OAK VALLEY
GRENADA
GRASS LAKE
CEDAR LAKE
BIG SPRINGS
HERD PK (LOOKOUT) 7060'
DEER MTN 7007'
ANTELOPE MTN 6093'
SHEEP ROCK 5714'
HAYSTACK MTN 4160'
DUZEL ROCK (LOOKOUT) 6037'
WHALEBACK MTN 8536'
GAZELLE
Lake Shastina
KLAMATH NATIONAL
3 5 12
SEE MAP
HIGHWAYS

COPYRIGHT, © 1989 BY Thomas Bros Maps

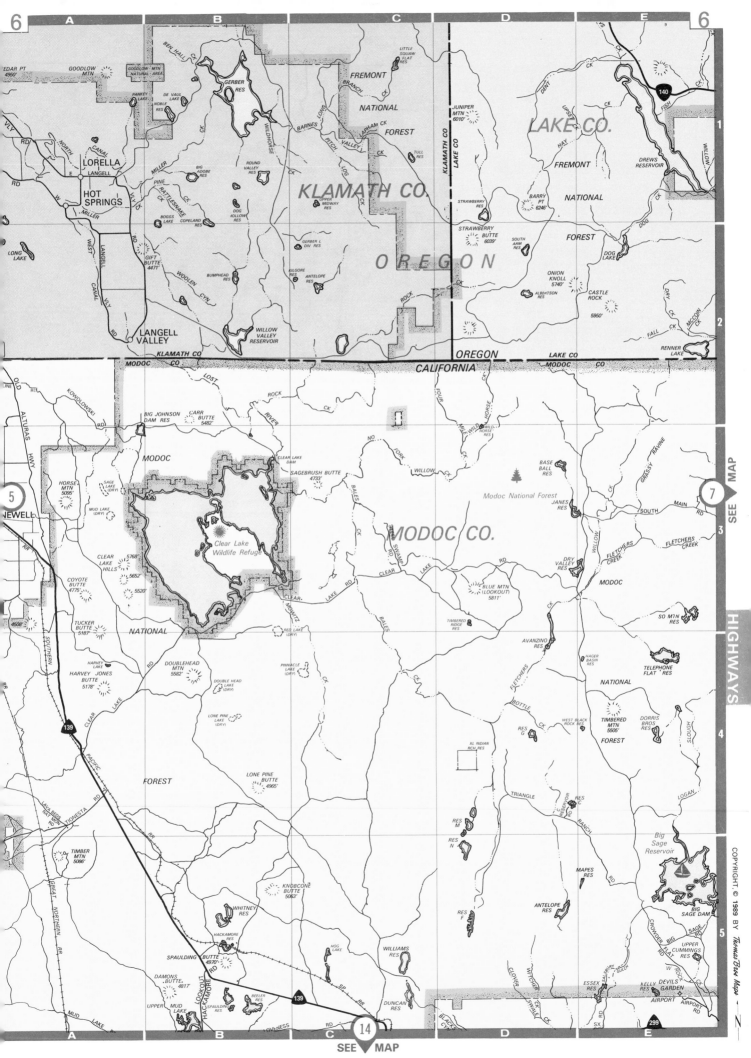

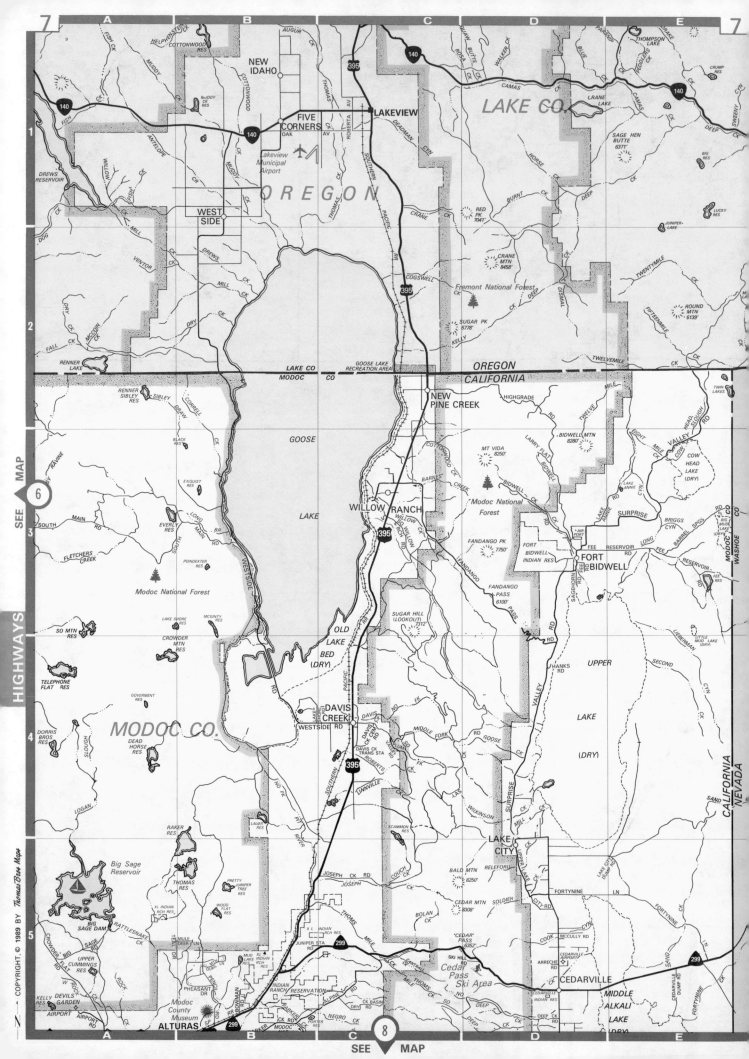

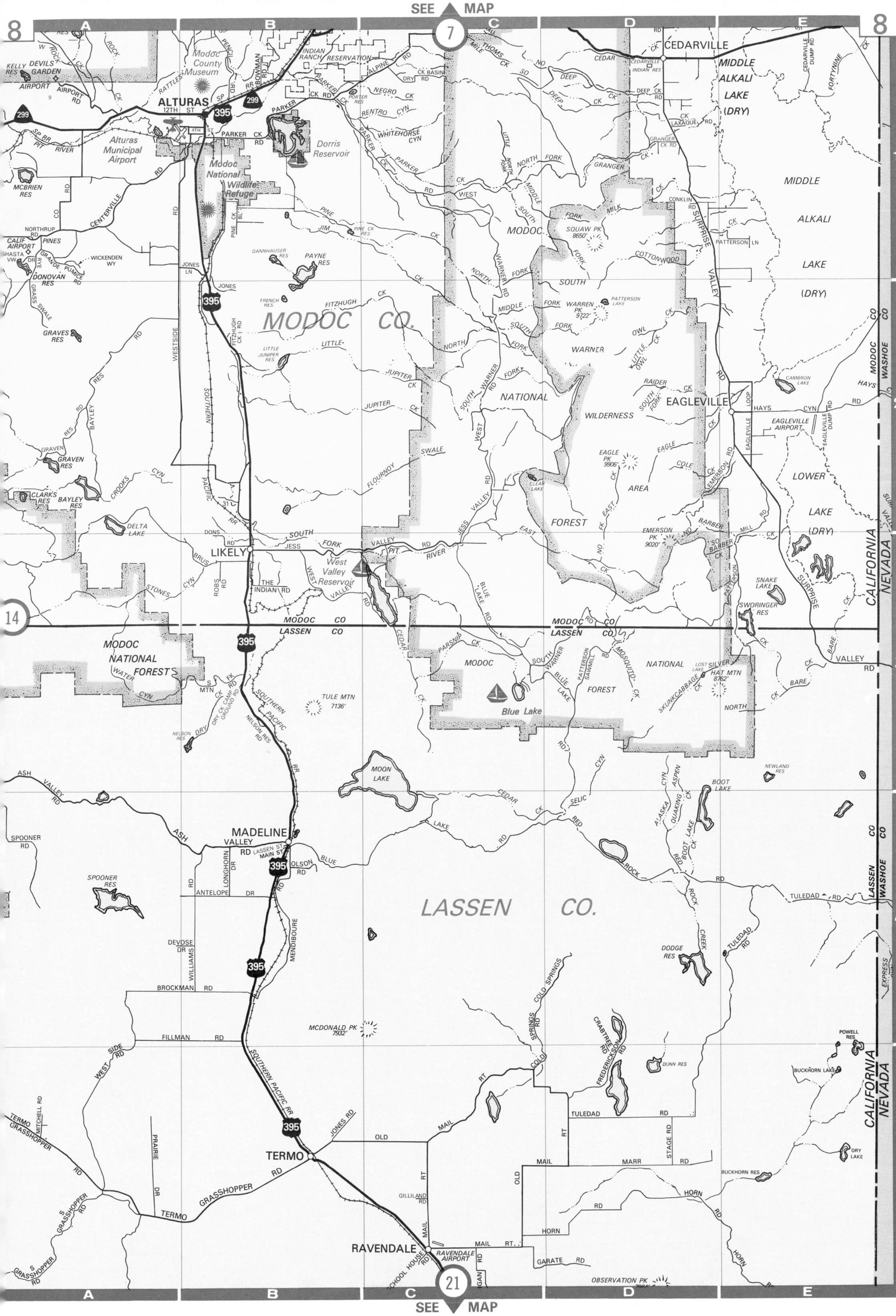

8 | A | B | C | D | E | 8

MODOC COUNTY MUSEUM

ALTURAS
12th ST
299
395

Alturas Municipal Airport

Modoc National Wildlife Refuge

Dorris Reservoir

Indian Ranch Reservation

CEDARVILLE

MIDDLE ALKALI LAKE (DRY)

MODOC CO.

MODOC NATIONAL

SQUAW PK 8650'

SURPRISE VALLEY

MIDDLE ALKALI LAKE (DRY)

WARREN PK 9722'

PATTERSON LAKE

NATIONAL

WARNER

WILDERNESS

EAGLEVILLE

Eagleville Airport

LOWER LAKE (DRY)

EAGLE PK 9906'

AREA

FOREST

CLEAR LAKE

EMERSON PK 9020'

SNAKE LAKE

SWORINGER RES

14

LIKELY

West Valley Reservoir

MODOC CO
LASSEN CO.

MODOC CO.
LASSEN CO.

CALIFORNIA
NEVADA

395

MODOC NATIONAL FOREST

TULE MTN 7136'

Blue Lake

MODOC NATIONAL FOREST

LOST SILVER MTN 8762'

HAT MTN

MOON LAKE

BOOT LAKE

NEWLAND RES

MADELINE
Valley
395

LASSEN CO.

DODGE RES

395

McDONALD PK 7932'

POWELL RES

BUCKHORN LAKE

CALIFORNIA
NEVADA

395

TERMO

DRY LAKE

BUCKHORN RES

RAVENDALE

Ravendale Airport

OBSERVATION PK

A | B | C | D | E

HIGHWAYS

SEE MAP
1

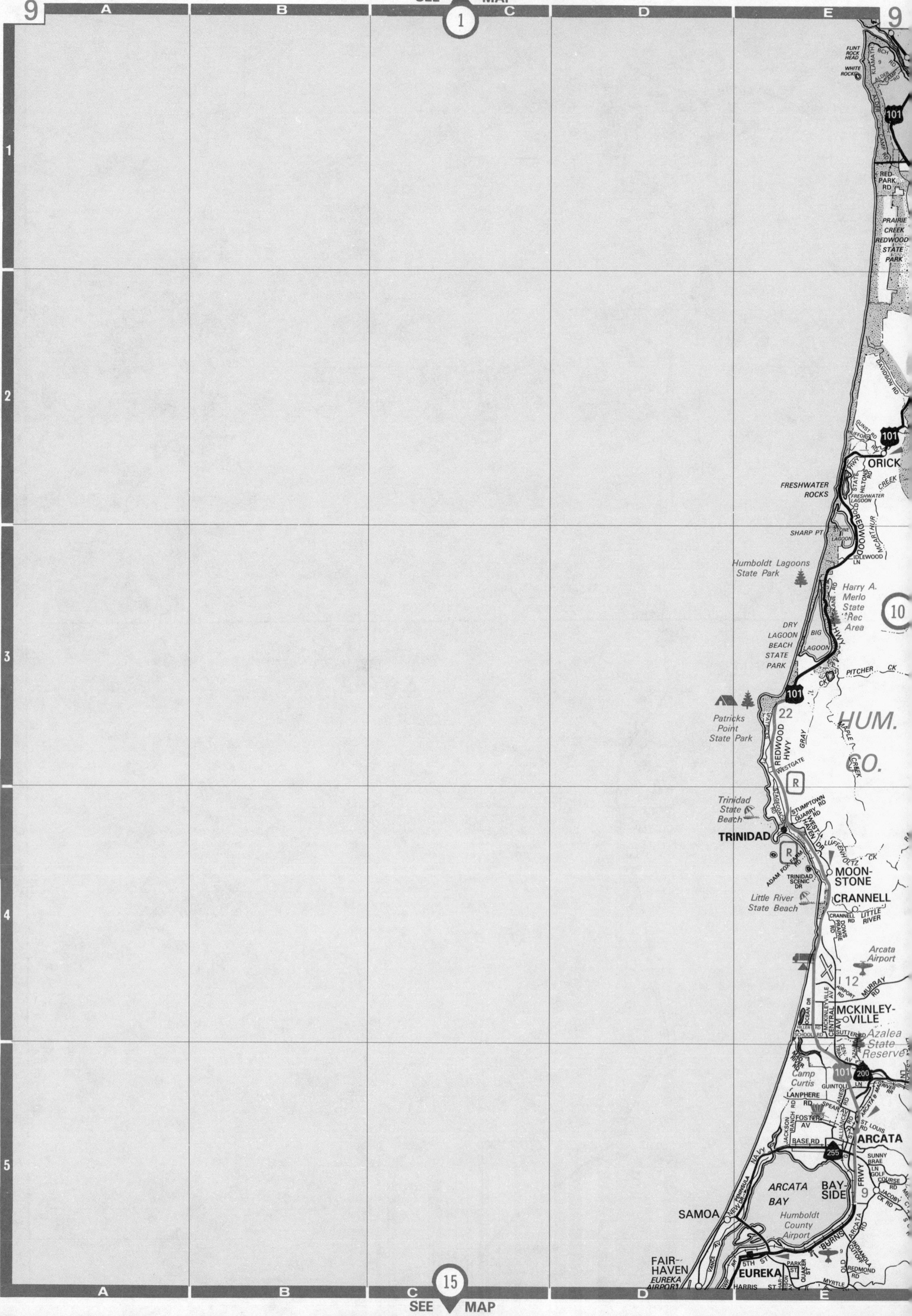

1

FLINT ROCK HEAD
KLAMATH BCH
ALDER CAMP RD
WHITE ROCK
101

RED PARK RD

PRAIRIE CREEK REDWOOD STATE PARK

DAVIDSON RD

2

ORICK
101

FRESHWATER ROCKS

HUFFORD RD
QUIST RD

FRESHWATER LAGOON

SHARP PT
STONE LAGOON
IDLEWOOD LN

Humboldt Lagoons State Park

Harry A. Merlo State Rec Area
KANE RD
10

DRY LAGOON BEACH STATE PARK
BIG LAGOON

3

PITCHER CK

101
22
Patricks Point State Park
REDWOOD HWY
GRAY
WESTGATE

R

Trinidad State Beach
STUMPTOWN RD
QUARRY RD
WEST END RD

TRINIDAD
R

ADAM FOX RD
TRINIDAD SCENIC DR
SCHOLTZ
CK

MOON-STONE
CRANNELL

Little River State Beach

CRANNELL RD
DOW'S PRAIRIE RD
LITTLE RIVER

Arcata Airport

4

12
MURRAY RD

MCKINLEY-VILLE
CENTRAL AV

Azalea State Reserve

Camp Curtis
101 200
GUINTOLI
LANPHERE RD
SPEAR AV

FOSTER AV
ST LOUIS RD

ARCATA
BASE RD
255

5

SUNNY BRAE
GOLF COURSE RD
JACOBY CK RD

ARCATA BAY
BAY-SIDE
9

SAMOA
Humboldt County Airport

FAIR-HAVEN
EUREKA AIRPORT
EUREKA
5TH ST
PARKER
REDMOND RD
HARRIS ST
MYRTLE

HUM. CO.

MAD CREEK

SEE MAP
15

HIGHWAYS

N

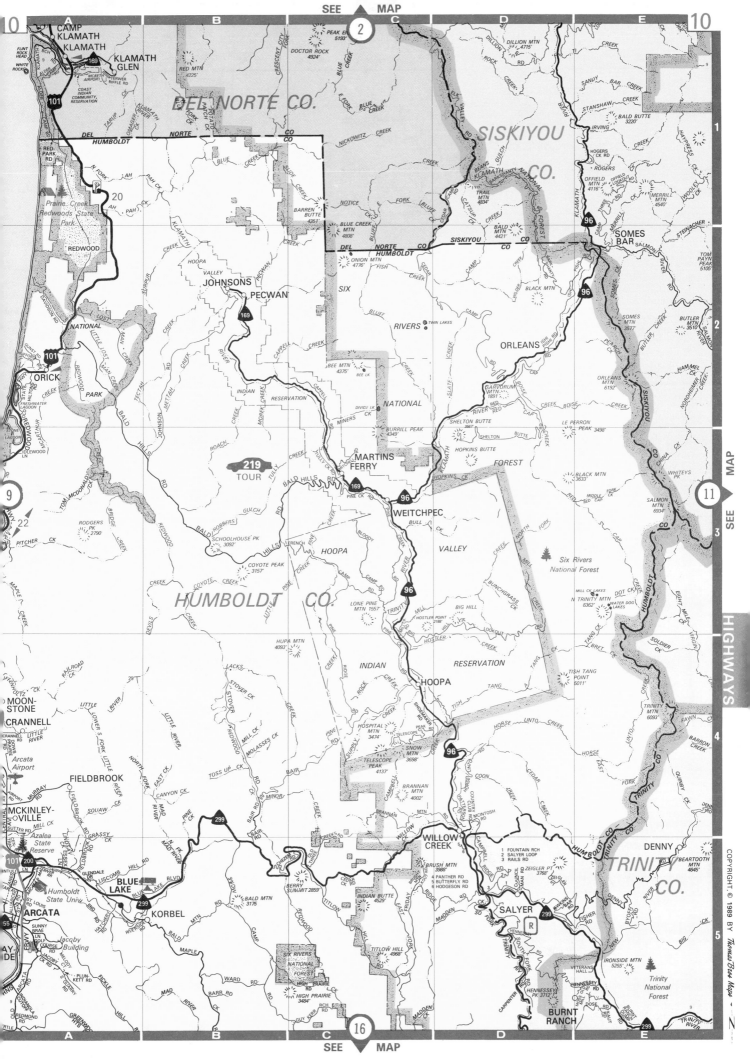

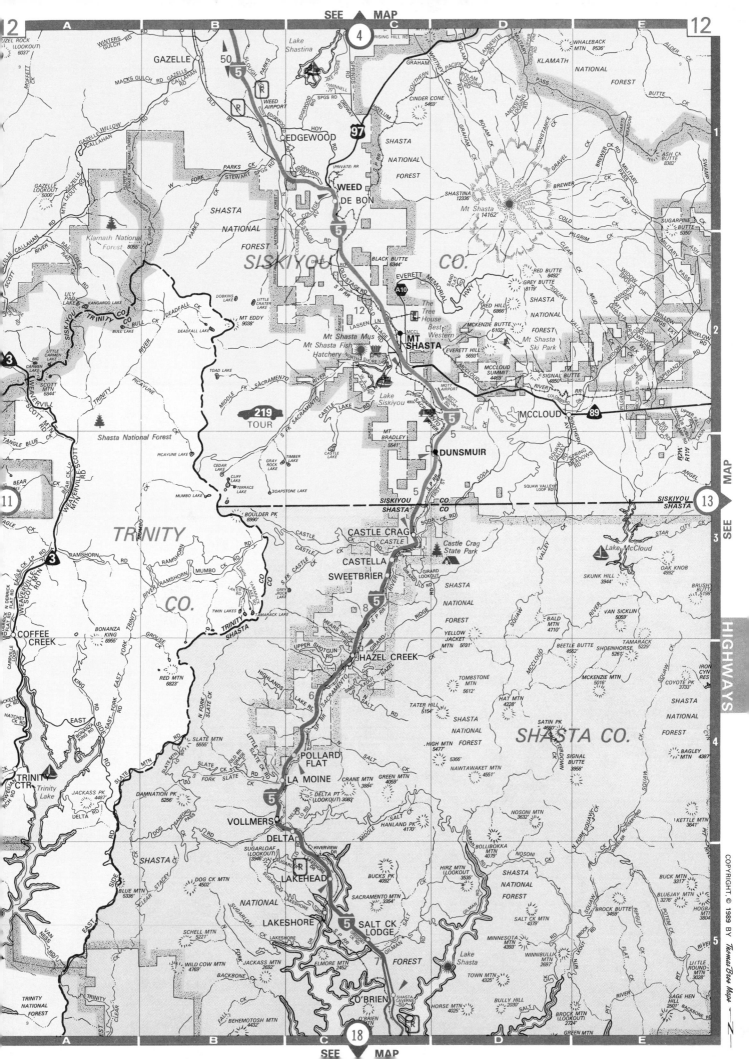

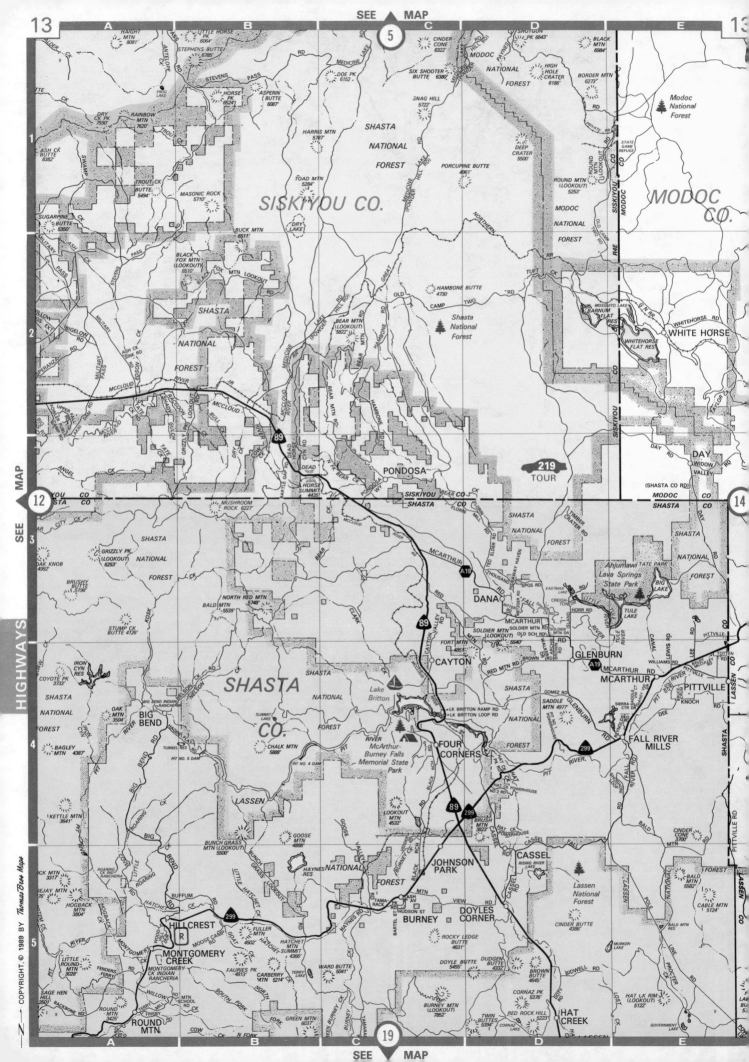

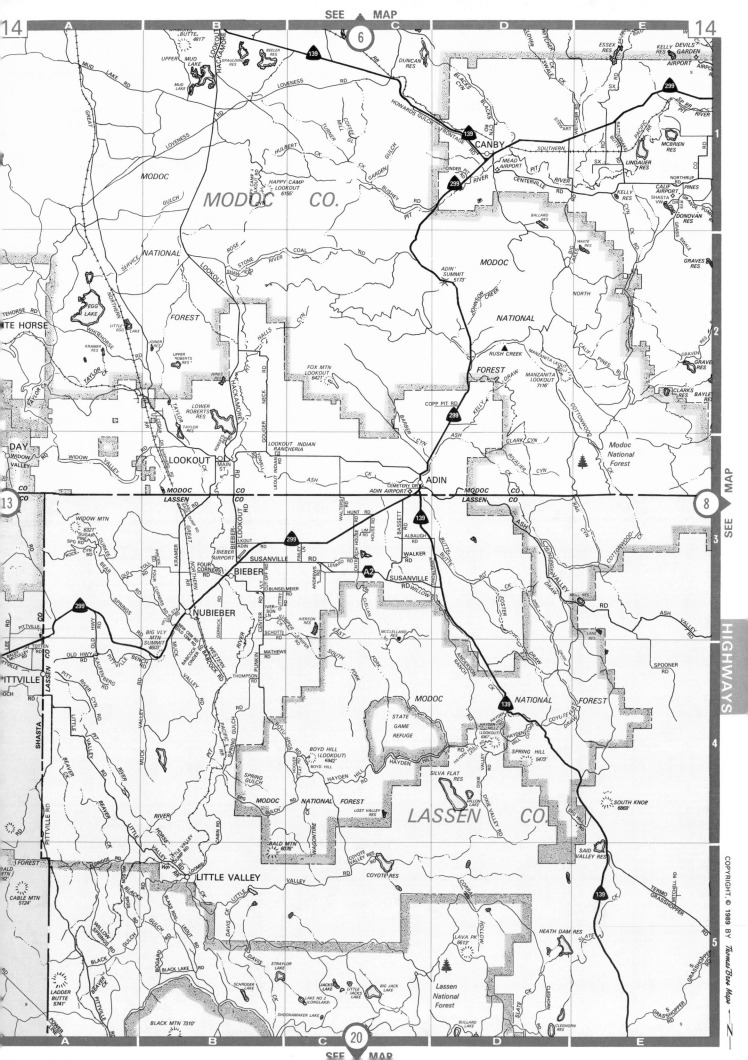

HIGHWAYS

PACIFIC

OCEAN

SAMOA

FAIR-HAVEN
Eureka Airport

HUMBOLDT CO. AIRPORT

EUREKA

CUT-TEN

HUMBOLDT BAY

S JETTY RD

FIELDS LANDING

TABLE BLUFF
TABLE BLUFF RD

INDIANOLA RESERVATION

CANNIBAL

LOLETA

101

EEL RIVER
SALT RIVER

GOBLE LN

211

FERNDALE

PALMER CK RD

FORTUNA

219
TOUR

ROHNER-VILLE

36

ALTON

HYDES-VILLE

FALSE CAPE

RIO DELL

16

101
REDWOOD HWY

CAPE MENDOCINO
SUGAR LOAF ISLAND

CAPETOWN

211
BEAR RIVER

UPPER BEAR RIVER

HUMBOLDT CO.

HUMBOLDT BASE LINE

MT PIERCE 3188'

TAYLOR PK 3390'

MATTOLE RIVER
N FK MATTOLE RIVER

211

PETROLIA

MOORE HILL 1245'

CHAMBERS RD
CONKLIN CK RD

BIG HILL 3040'

CATHEYS PK 3070'

LITTLE CHAPARRAL MTN 2650'

COOSKIE MTN 2951'

HONEYDEW

211

KING RANGE NATIONAL CONSERVATION AREA

OAT HILL 2350'

NORTH SLIDE PK 3512'

HADLEY PK 3020'

KINGS PK 4087'

211

King Range National Conservation Area

SHUBRICK PK 2797'

SADDLE MTN 3290'

HORSE MTN 1929'

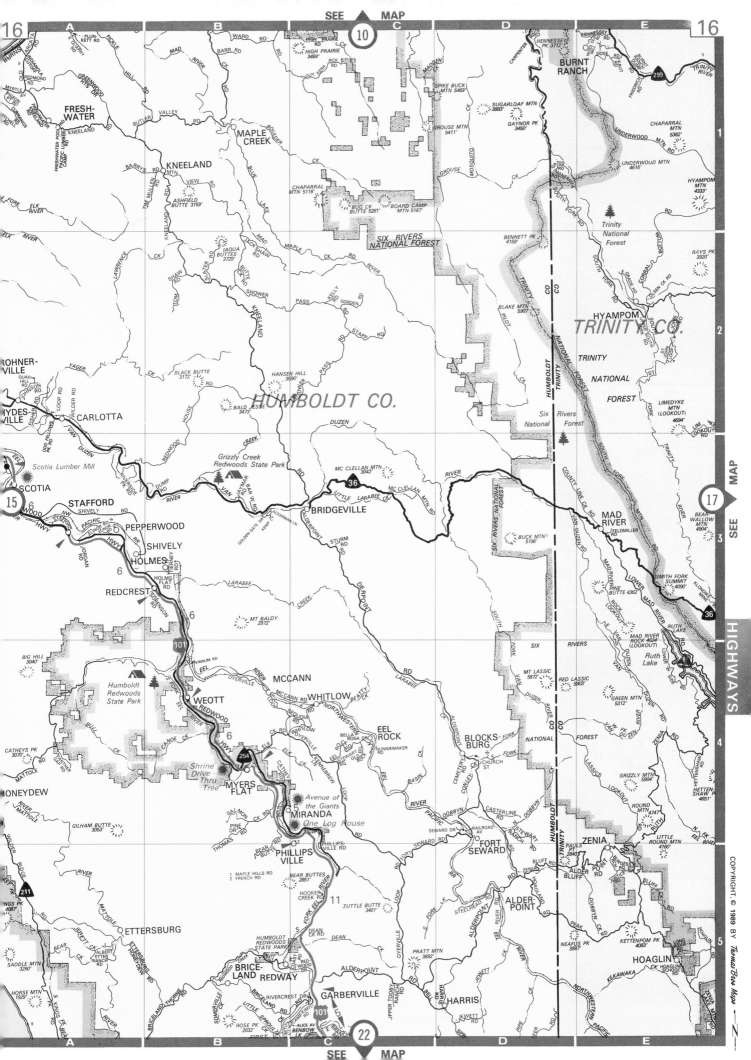

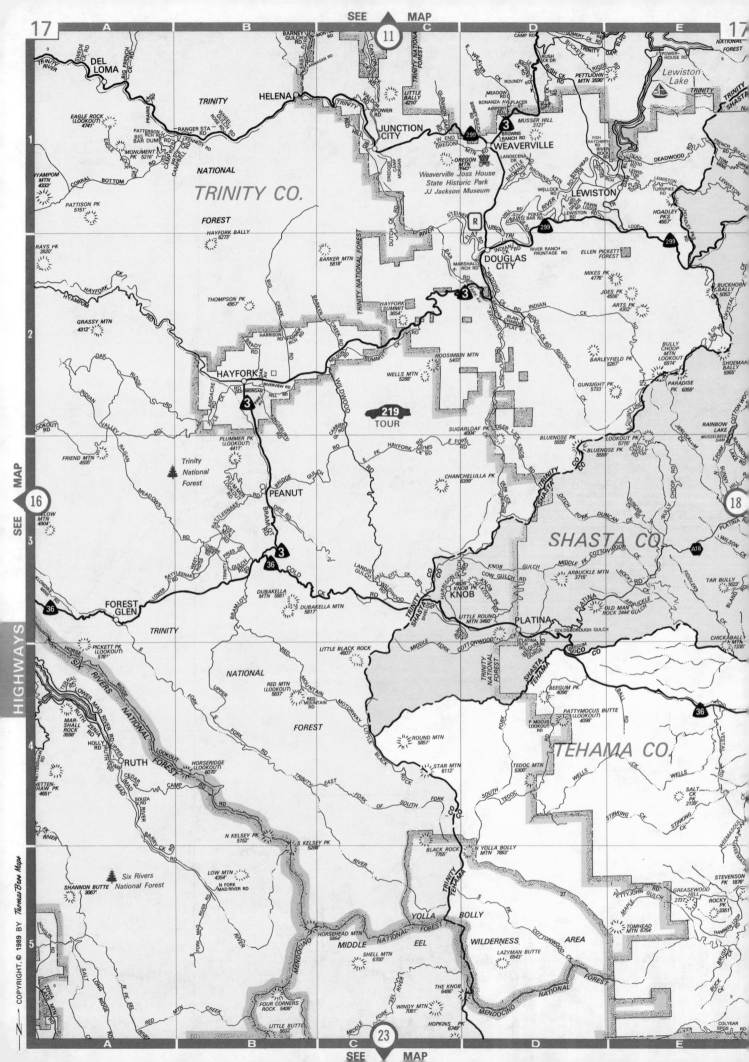

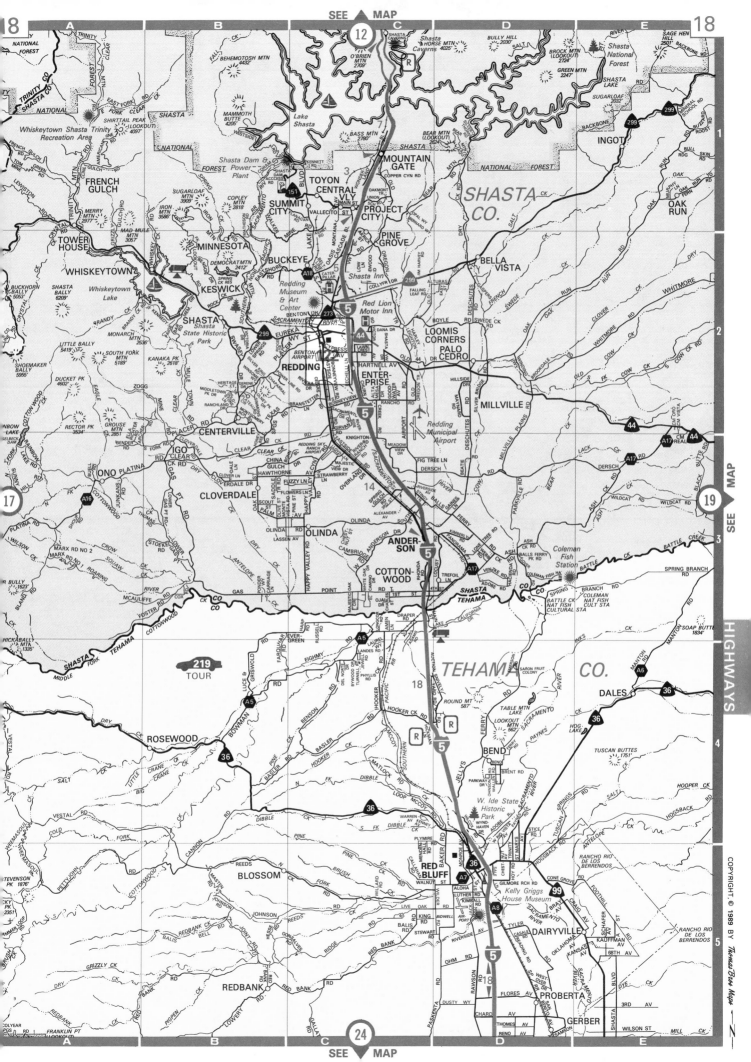

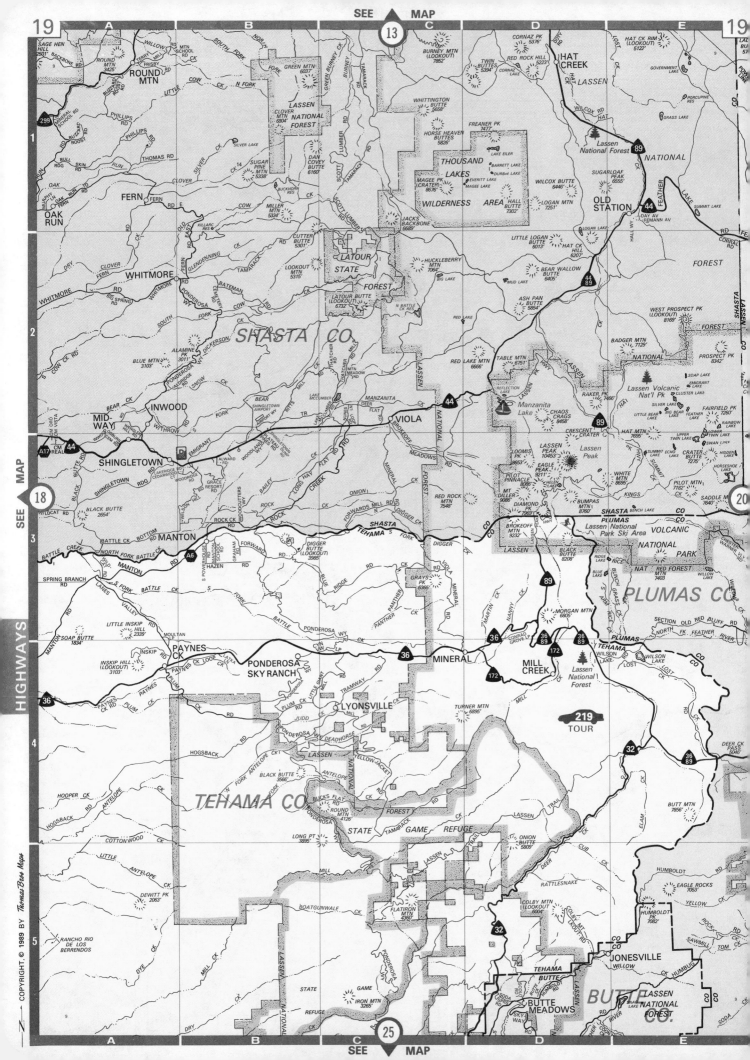

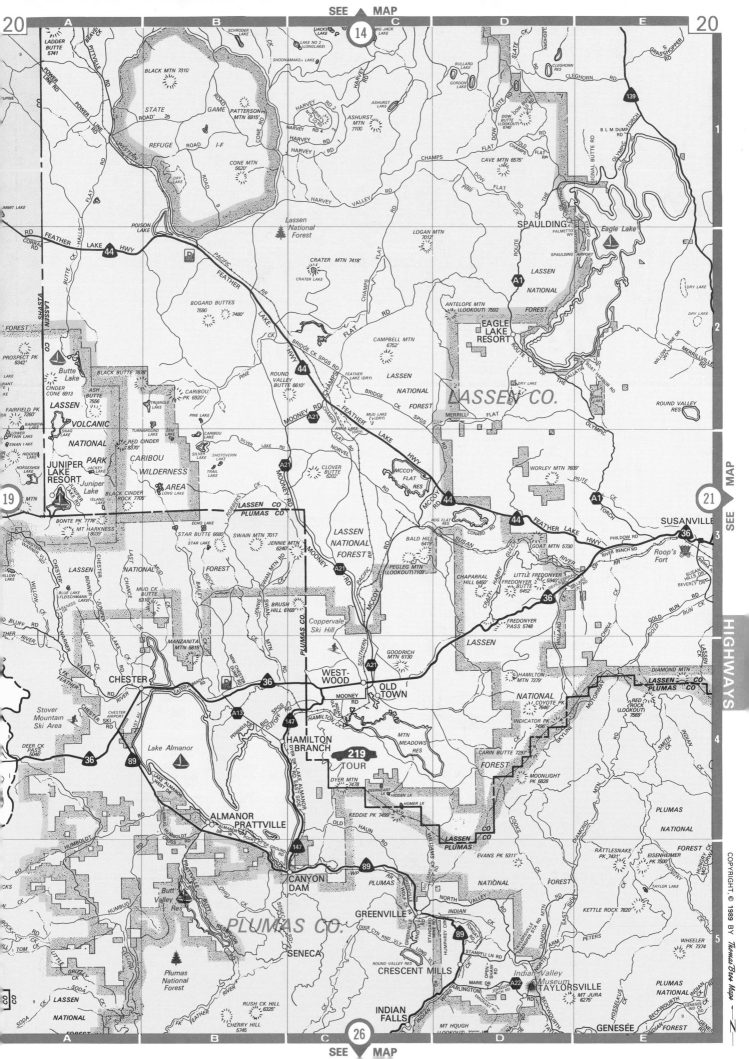

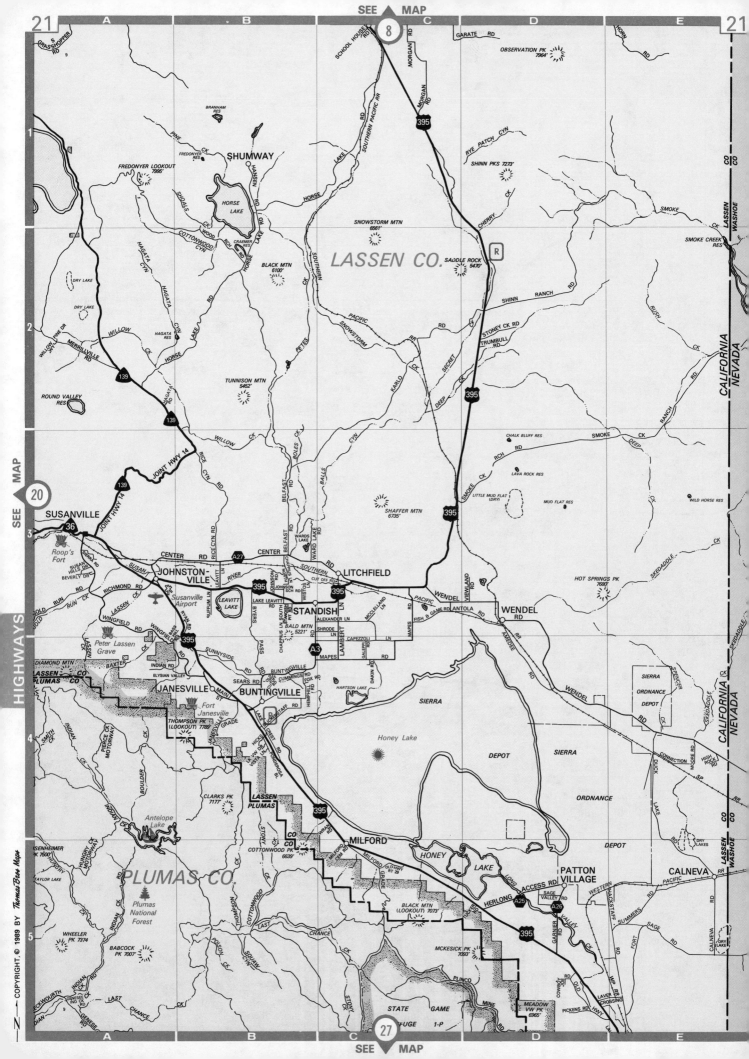

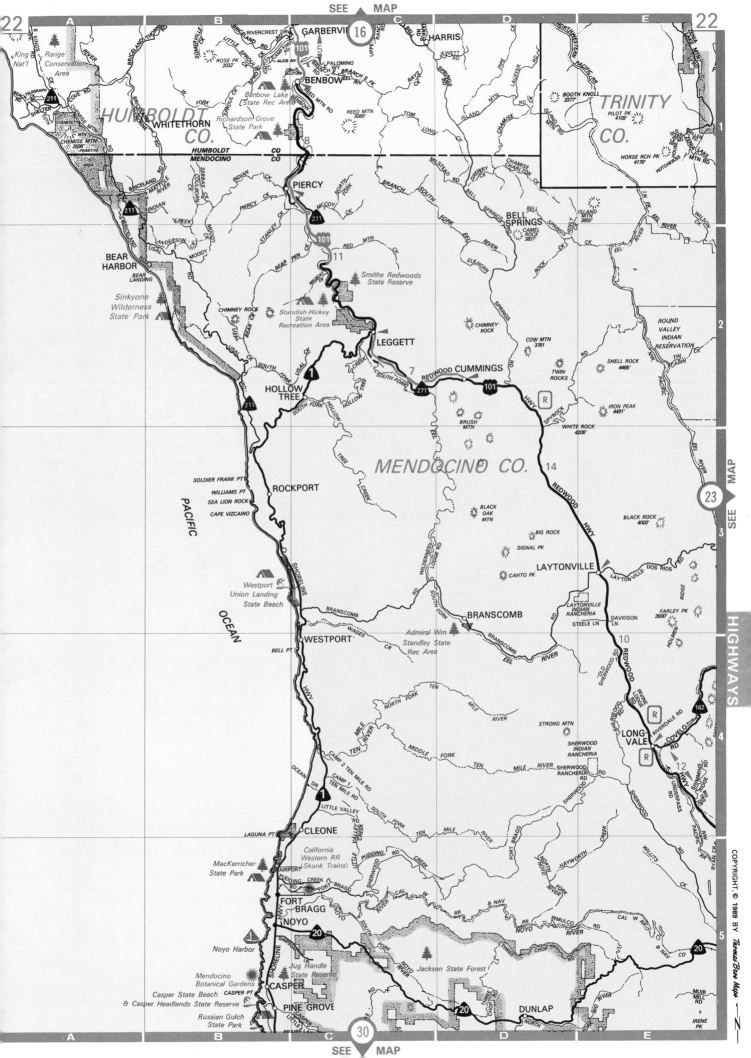

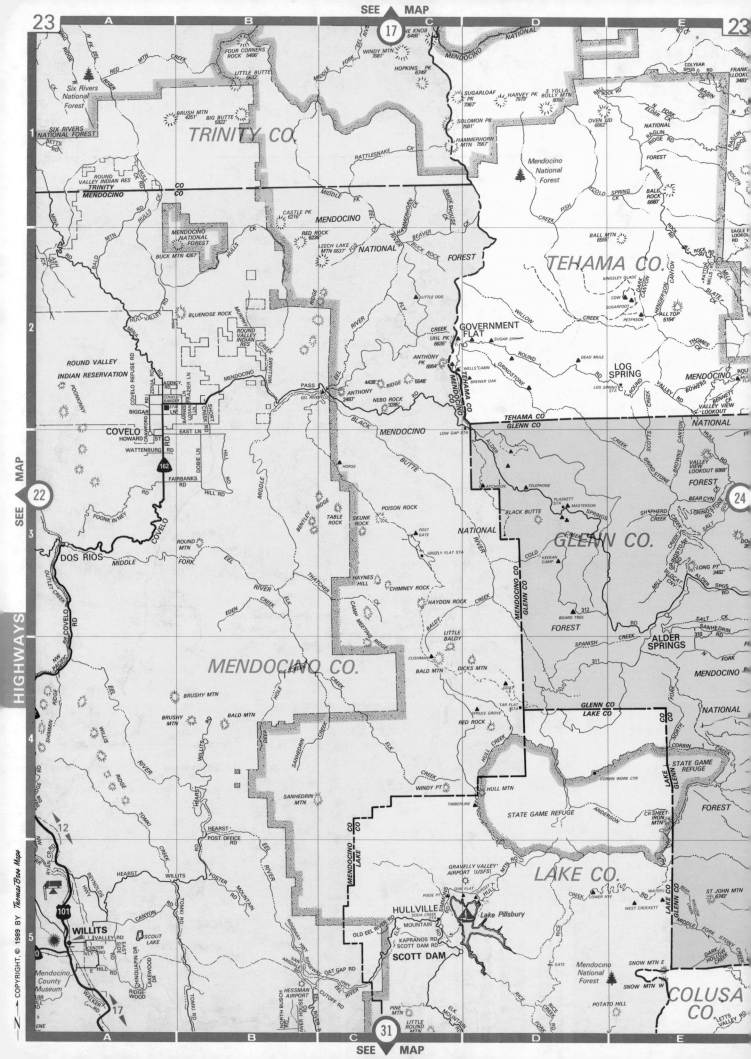

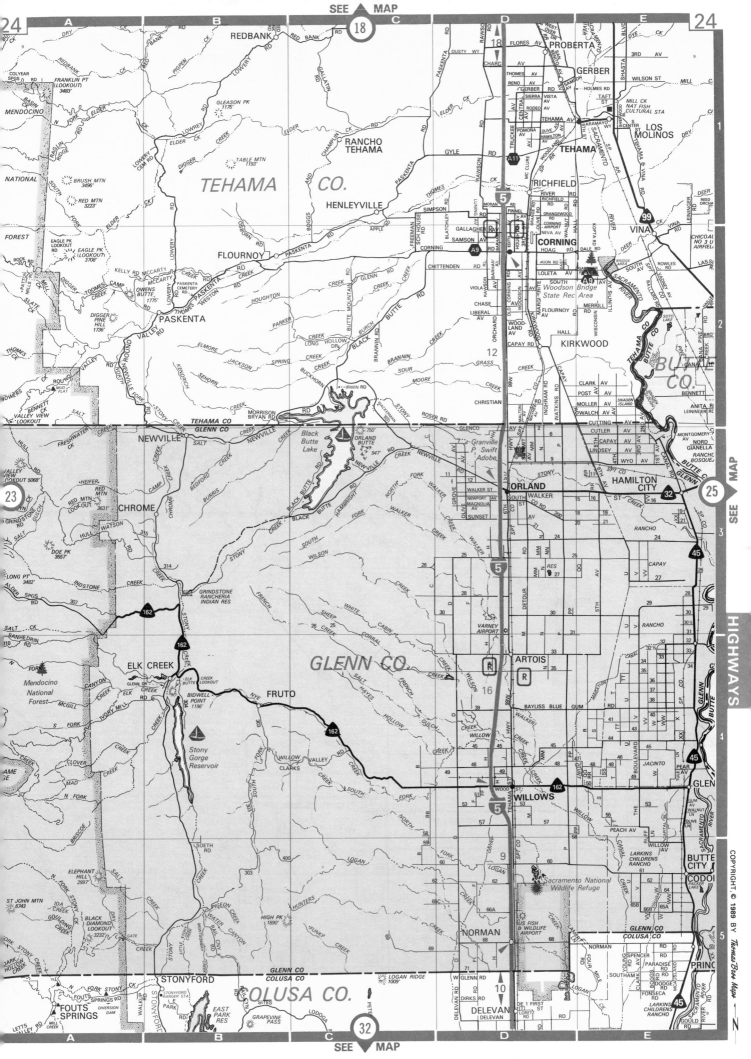

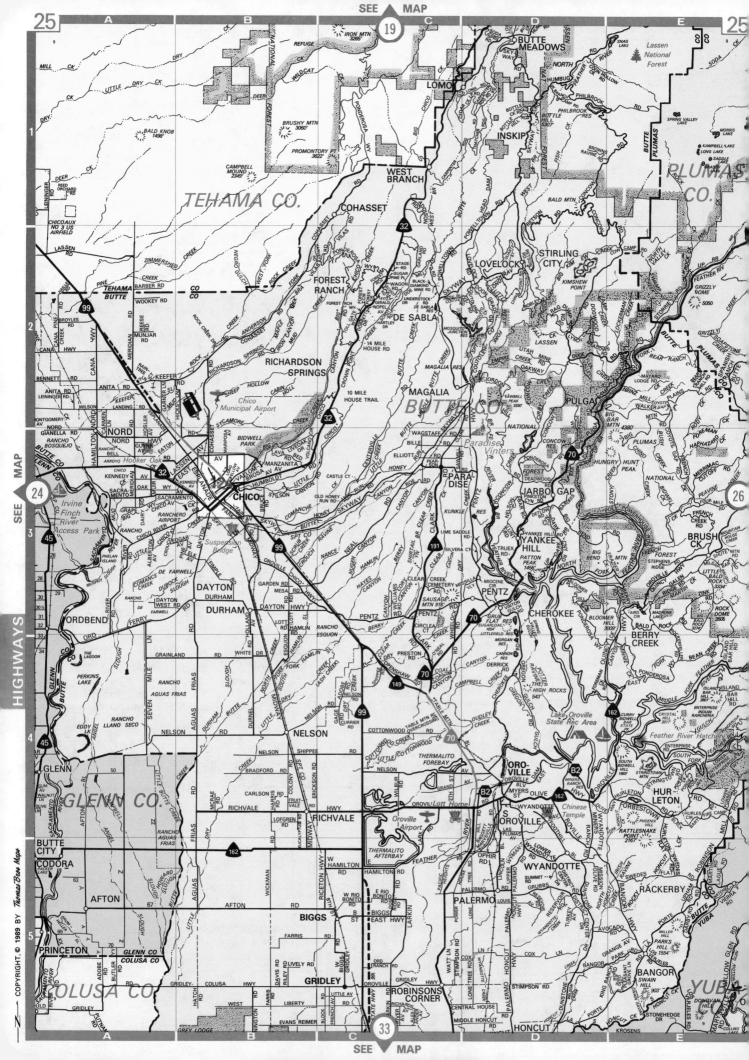

LASSEN NATIONAL FOREST

INDIAN FALLS

TAYLORSVILLE
MT JURA 6275'

GENESEE
PLUMAS NATIONAL FOREST

RICH BAR
TWAIN
VIRGILIA
KEDDIE
BELDEN
BEN LOMAND 6450'

SPANISH CREEK

GRIZZLY PK 7704'
TOWER ROCK 7779'

PLUMAS NATIONAL FOREST

TOBIN

SPANISH RANCH

QUINCY JUNCTION
E QUINCY
QUINCY

SPRING GARDEN

MEADOW VALLEY
SPANISH PK (LOOKOUT) 7010'

Bucks Lake

Plumas National Forest
Plumas Co Mus

SLOAT
CROMBER
MT JACKSON 6565'

BUCKS LAKE

PLUMAS CO.

CLAREMONT 6994'

CRESCENT HILL 6544'
LITTLE VOLCANO 5801'

WHITE CAP 6458'
BIG HILL 5686'

LAVA PK 5882'

Wild and Scenic Feather River

FINGER BOARD 6874'

PILOT PK 7457'

Plumas-Eureka Ski Bowl
Plumas Eureka State Park

Eureka Lake

JOHNSVILLE
Museum of Mining

TABLE MTN 6095'

FLOWER PK 6065'

BALD MTN 6255'
Little Grass Valley Reservoir
GOAT MTN 5696'

GIBSONVILLE
MT FILMORE 7715'

MT ETNA 7163'

BEARTRAP MTN 7232'
GIBRALTAR 7343'

PLUMAS NATIONAL FOREST

PLUMAS CO / BUTTE CO

CAMEL PK 5723'
CASCADE

LA PORTE BALD MTN

LA PORTE

HOWLAND FLAT

CHIMNEY ROCK
RATTLESNAKE PK 7219'

DEADWOOD PK 6477'

BUNKER HILL 6967'
MT ALMA 6477'

Tahoe National Forest

BUTTE CO.

ROCK DOME 3509'

FEATHER FALLS

PLUMAS CO / BUTTE CO

AMERICAN HOUSE

POVERTY HILL 5518'

SCALES

SIERRA CO.

DOWNIEVILLE

SIERRA BUTTES 8587'

COUNTRY (49) HWY

STRAWBERRY VALLEY

GOODYEARS BAR

GOLD

FORBESTOWN
CLIPPER MILLS

BROWNSVILLE
CHALLENGE

KEYSTONE MTN 6908'
GRANITE MTN 6481'

(49) GOLD
229 TOUR

ALLEGHANY

TAHOE

PYRAMID PK 5973'

CAMPTONVILLE
PIKE

GRANITEVILLE
NEVADA

YUBA CO.

DOBBINS

NORTH SAN JUAN
CHEROKEE

N COLUMBIA
NORTH BLOOMFIELD

Malakoff Diggins State Hist Park

NATIONAL FOREST

OREGON HOUSE

SWEET LAND
BIRCHVILLE

LK CITY

WASHINGTON

NEVADA CO.

HIGHWAYS

COPYRIGHT © 1989 BY Thomas Bros Maps

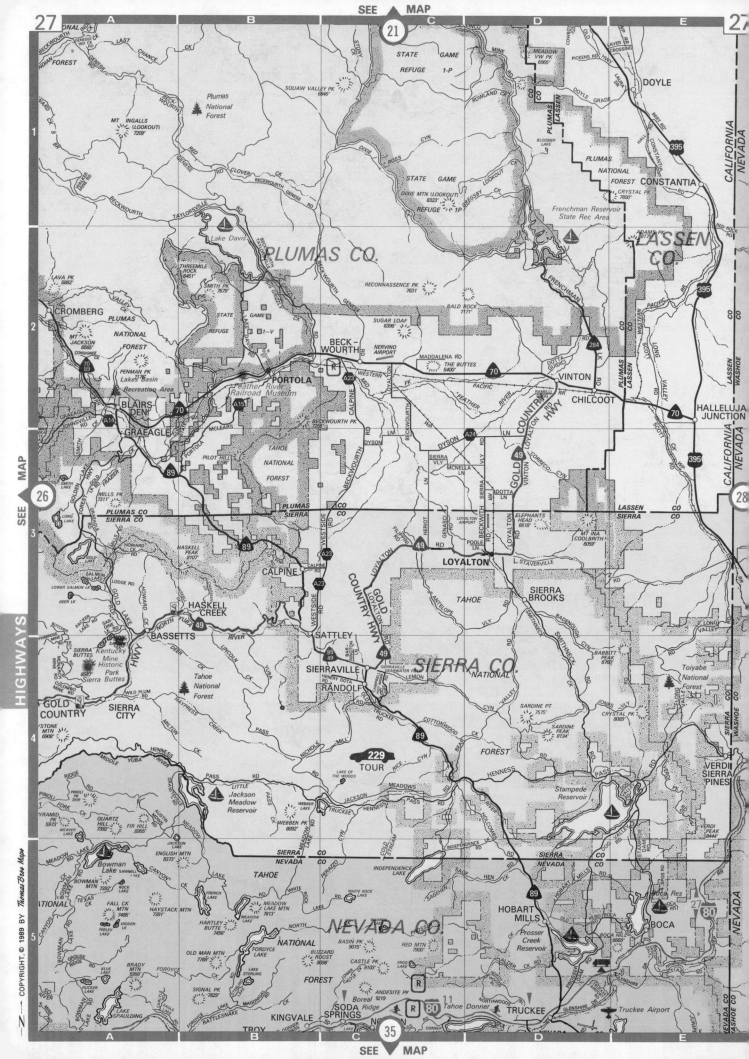

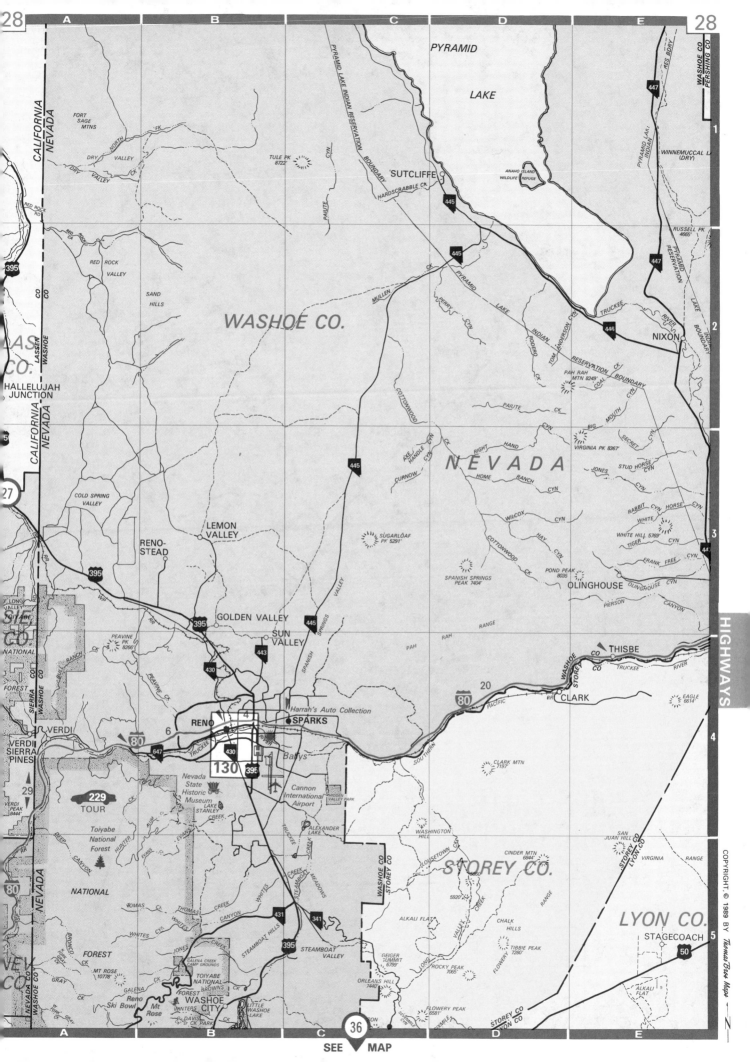

PYRAMID

LAKE

WASHOE CO
PERSHING CO

447

RES BDRY

1

CALIFORNIA
NEVADA

FORT
SAGE
MTNS

DRY
VALLEY

NORTH
FK

DRY
VALLEY

CK

TULE PK
8722'

PAIUTE

CYN

SUTCLIFFE

WINNEMUCCAL L.
(DRY)

ANAHO ISLAND
WILDLIFE REFUGE

RUSSELL PK
4665'

PYRAMID LAKE INDIAN RESERVATION BOUNDARY

HARDSCRABBLE CK

445

RED ROCK
RD

395

RED
CA

RED ROCK
VALLEY

SAND
HILLS

WASHOE CO.

MULLEN

CK

445

PERRY

CYN

PYRAMID

RODEO

LAKE

INDIAN

TOM ANDERSON CYN

TRUCKEE

RIVER

446

NIXON

447

PYRAMID
RESERVATION

INDIAN
LAKE
BOUNDARY

2

LASSEN CO.

HALLELUJAH
JUNCTION

LASSEN
WASHOE

CO
WASHOE

CALIFORNIA
NEVADA

COTTONWOOD

AXE
HANDLE
CYN

CK

CURNOW

RIGHT

HAND

CYN

HOME

NEVADA

RESERVATION BOUNDARY

COAL

CYN

PAH RAH
MTN 8249'

PAIUTE

CK

BIG

MOUTH

CYN

SECRET
CYN

VIRGINIA PK 8367'

RANCH

CYN

STUD HORSE
CYN

JONES

CYN

27

COLD SPRING
VALLEY

LEMON
VALLEY

RENO-
STEAD

445

SUGARLOAF
PK 5291'

WILCOX

CYN

COTTONWOOD

HAY

CK

CYN

RABBIT

CYN

HORSE

CYN

WHITE

WHITE HILL 5769'

TIGER

FRANK

FREE

CYN

CYN

447

3

395

TOIYABE

CO.

NATIONAL

LONG

FOREST

SIERRA CO
WASHOE CO

PEAVINE
PK
8266'

CK

RENO
SKI BOWL

PEAVINE CK

GOLDEN VALLEY

395

SUN
VALLEY

443

430

445

SPANISH

SPRINGS

VALLEY

SPANISH SPRINGS
PEAK 7404'

PAH

RANGE

RAH

COTTONWOOD

POND PEAK
8035'

OLINGHOUSE

PIERSON

OLINGHOUSE CYN

CANYON

WASHOE CO
STOREY CO

THISBE

TRUCKEE

RIVER

EAGLE
6614'

BULL RANCH

VERDI

VERDI
SIERRA
PINES

80

547

430

RENO

6

TRUCKEE

4

SPARKS

Harrah's Auto Collection

80

20

PACIFIC

RR

CLARK

SOUTHERN

CLARK MTN
7197'

4

29

VERDI
PEAK
8444'

229

TOUR

Toiyabe

National

Forest

HUNTER

PAGE

CK

RUM

EVANS

Nevada
State
Historic
Museum

LAKE
STANLEY

CREEK

130

430

395

H

Baffys

Cannon
International
Airport

HIDDEN VALLEY PARK

ALEXANDER
LAKE

WASHINGTON
HILL

CLOUSETOWN CK

CINDER MTN
6844'

SAN
JUAN HILL
6581'

VIRGINIA

RANGE

STOREY CO
LYON CO

80

NEV
CO

NEVADA CO
WASHOE CO

NEVADA

DEEP

CANYON

RR

NATIONAL

FOREST

BRONCO

CK

THOMAS

CA

THOMAS

CREEK

WHITES

CANYON

WHITES

431

STEAMBOAT HILLS

CREEK

341

CREEK

MEADOWS

STEAMBOAT

395

STEAMBOAT
VALLEY

WASHOE CO
STOREY CO

ALKALI FLAT

5920'

LONG

VALLEY

CK

CHALK
HILLS

STOREY CO.

WASHINGTON
HILL

RANGE

FLOWERY

TIBBIE PEAK
7280'

STOREY CO
LYON CO

LYON CO.

STAGECOACH

50

5

MT ROSE
10778'

GALENA

GRAY

CK

JONES

GALENA CREEK
CAMP GROUNDS

TOIYABE
NATIONAL
FOREST

BROWNS

WINTERS

WASHOE
CITY

Mt
Rose

DAVIS CK PARK

LITTLE
WASHOE
LAKE

GEIGER
SUMMIT
6789'

ORLEANS HILL
7440'

ROCKY PEAK
7065'

FLOWERY PEAK
6581'

SIXMILE

CYN

STOREY CO
LYON CO

ALKALI
FLAT

9

36

SEE ▽ MAP

HIGHWAYS

COPYRIGHT © 1989 BY Thomas Bros Maps

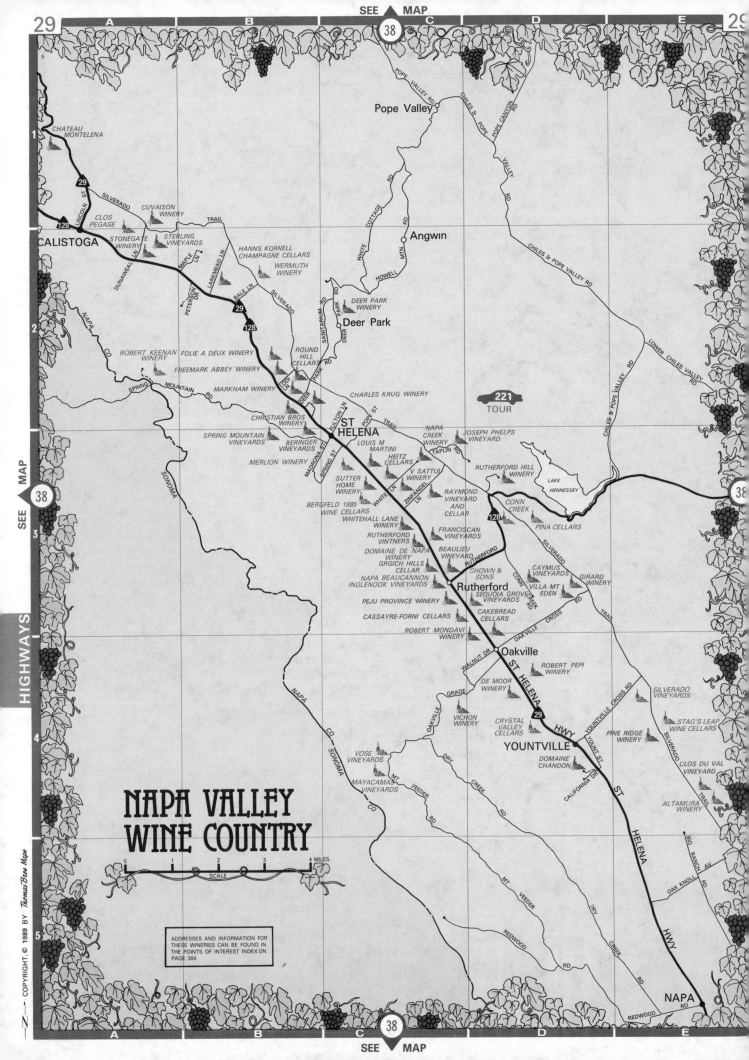

NAPA VALLEY WINE COUNTRY

SCALE 0 1 2 3 4 MILES

ADDRESSES AND INFORMATION FOR THESE WINERIES CAN BE FOUND IN THE POINTS OF INTEREST INDEX ON PAGE 304

HIGHWAYS

SEE ★ MAP
(22) 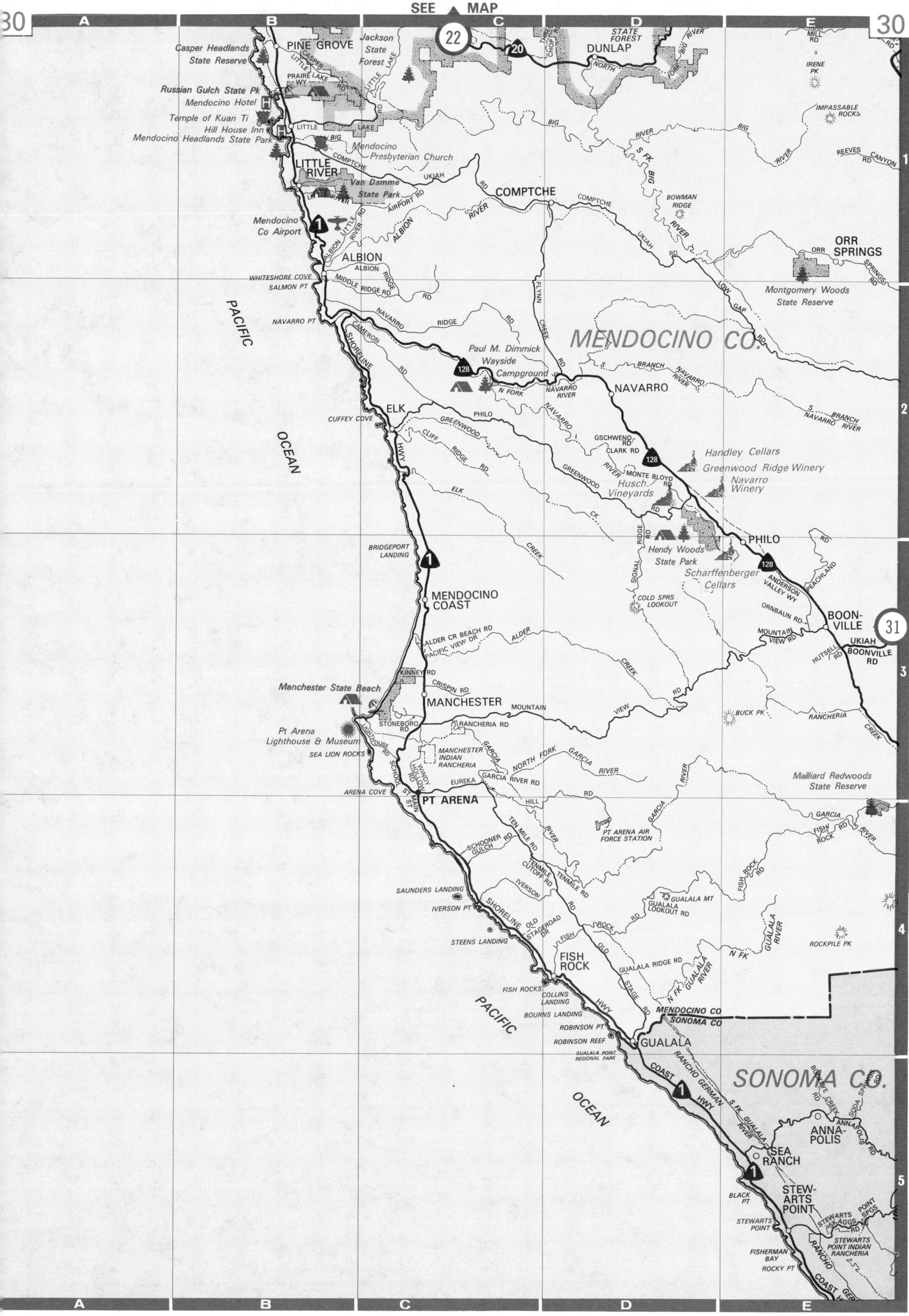
(20)

Casper Headlands State Reserve
PINE GROVE
Jackson State Forest
STATE FOREST
DUNLAP
MILL RD
IRENE PK
PRAIRE LAKE
LITTLE LAKE
Russian Gulch State Pk
Mendocino Hotel
Temple of Kuan Ti
Hill House Inn
Mendocino Headlands State Park
Mendocino Presbyterian Church
LITTLE RIVER
IMPASSABLE ROCKS
REEVES CANYON RD
Van Damme State Park
COMPTCHE
UKIAH
S FK BIG RIVER
Mendocino Co Airport
ORR SPRINGS
ALBION
COMPTCHE
FLYNN CREEK
UKIAH RD
WHITESHORE COVE
SALMON PT
MIDDLE RIDGE RD
Montgomery Woods State Reserve
NAVARRO PT
MENDOCINO CO.
SHORELINE
CAMERON RD
NAVARRO
RIDGE RD
NAVARRO RIVER
Paul M. Dimmick Wayside Campground
(128)
N FORK
BRANCH NAVARRO RIVER
NAVARRO
S BRANCH NAVARRO RIVER
CUFFEY COVE
ELK
HWY
GREENWOOD
CLIFF RIDGE RD
PHILO
GSCHWEND RD
CLARK RD
Handley Cellars
Greenwood Ridge Winery
Navarro Winery
MONTE BLOYD RD
Husch Vineyards
ELK CK
GREENWOOD RIDGE RD
SIGNAL RIDGE RD
Hendy Woods State Park
PHILO
PEACHLAND RD
BRIDGEPORT LANDING
(1)
MENDOCINO COAST
Scharffenberger Cellars
ANDERSON VALLEY WY
(128)
BOONVILLE
ORNBAUN RD
SEE ▶ MAP (31)
ALDER CR BEACH RD
PACIFIC VIEW DR
ALDER
MOUNTAIN VIEW RD
UKIAH BOONVILLE RD
HUTSELL RD
KINNEY RD
CRISPIN RD
Manchester State Beach
MANCHESTER
STONEBORO RD
MOUNTAIN
BUCK PK
RANCHERIA
Pt Arena Lighthouse & Museum
RANCHERIA RD
VIEW RD
Mailliard Redwoods State Reserve
SEA LION ROCKS
MANCHESTER INDIAN RANCHERIA
GARCIA RD
NORTH FORK GARCIA RIVER
GARCIA RIVER
ARENA COVE
LIGHTHOUSE RD
SCHOOL ST
WINDY WILLOW RD
Eureka
GARCIA RIVER RD
HILL
GARCIA RIVER
FISH ROCK RD
PT ARENA
TEN MILE RD
PT ARENA AIR FORCE STATION
GARCIA
SCHOONER GULCH RD
TENMILE CUTOFF RD
TENMILE RD
IVERSON
FISH
SAUNDERS LANDING
SHORELINE
OLD STAGEROAD DR
GUALALA MT
GUALALA LOOKOUT RD
IVERSON PT
ROCK RD
ROCKPILE PK
STEENS LANDING
FISH ROCK
OLD STAGE RD
N FK GUALALA RIVER
FISH ROCKS
COLLINS LANDING
BOURNS LANDING
GUALALA RIDGE RD
N FK GUALALA RIVER
MENDOCINO CO
SONOMA CO
ROBINSON PT
ROBINSON REEF
GUALALA
GUALALA POINT REGIONAL PARK
COAST HWY
RANCHO GERMAN
S FK GUALALA RIVER
SONOMA CO.
(1)
ANNA-POLIS
BLAKES SPRINGS RD
ANNA-POLIS RD
BUCKEYE CREEK RD
SODA SPRINGS RD
SEA RANCH
BLACK PT
(1)
STEWARTS POINT
STEWARTS POINT
STEWARTS POINT INDIAN RANCHERIA
FISHERMAN BAY
ROCKY PT
RANCHO COAST GERMAN

PACIFIC OCEAN

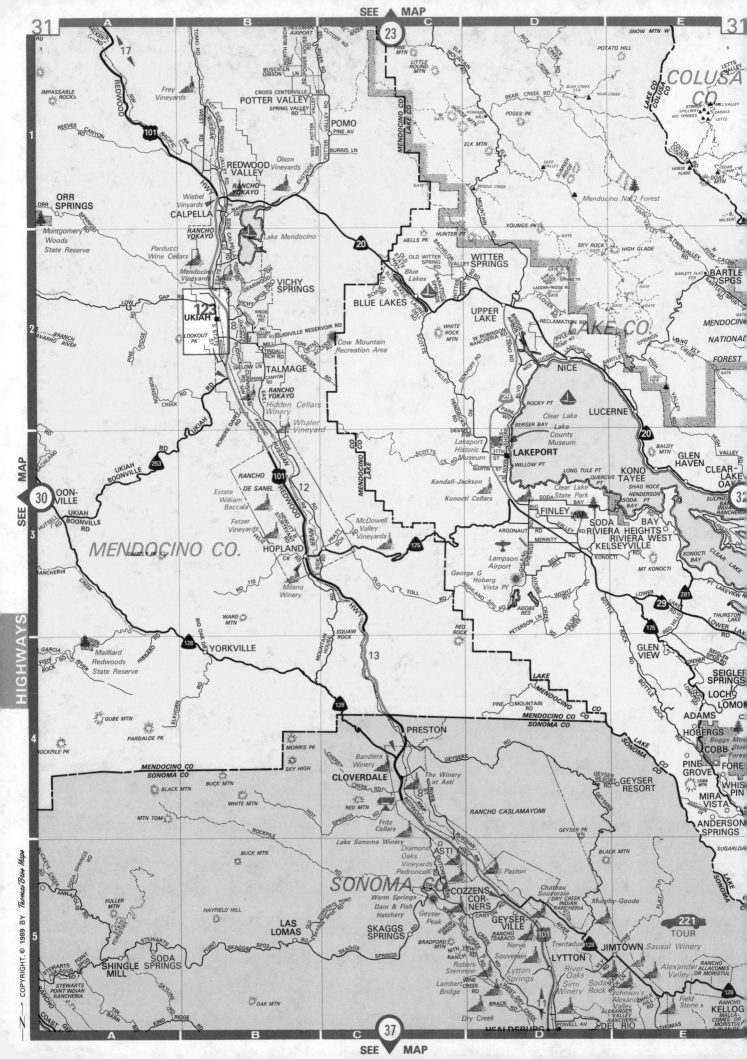

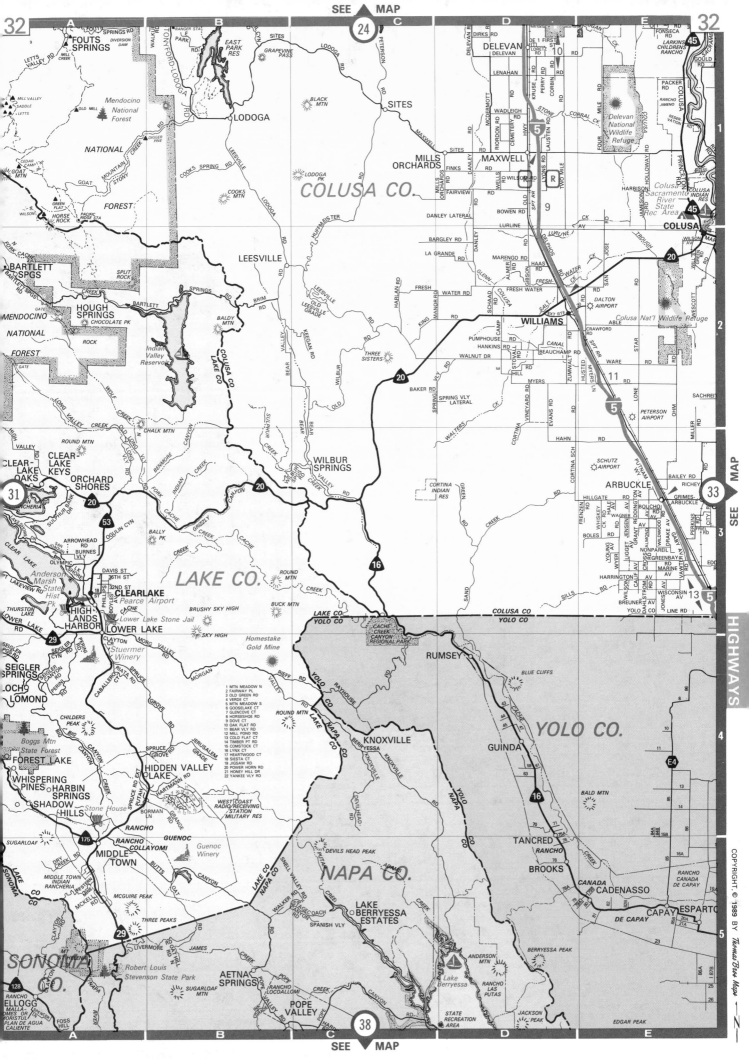

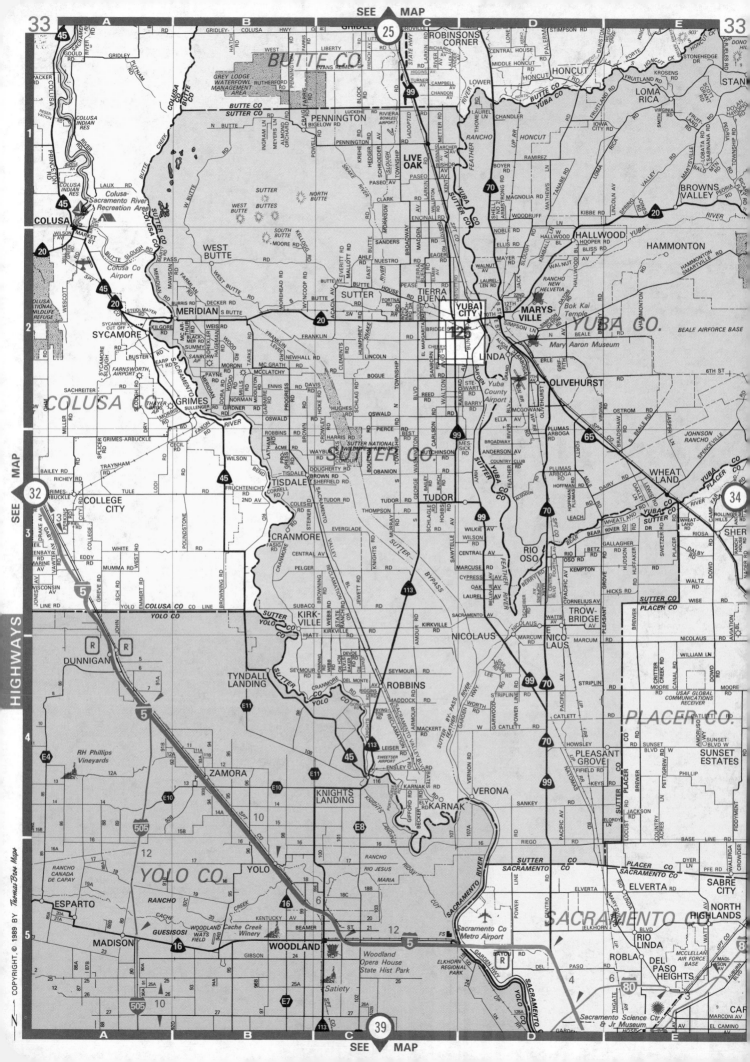

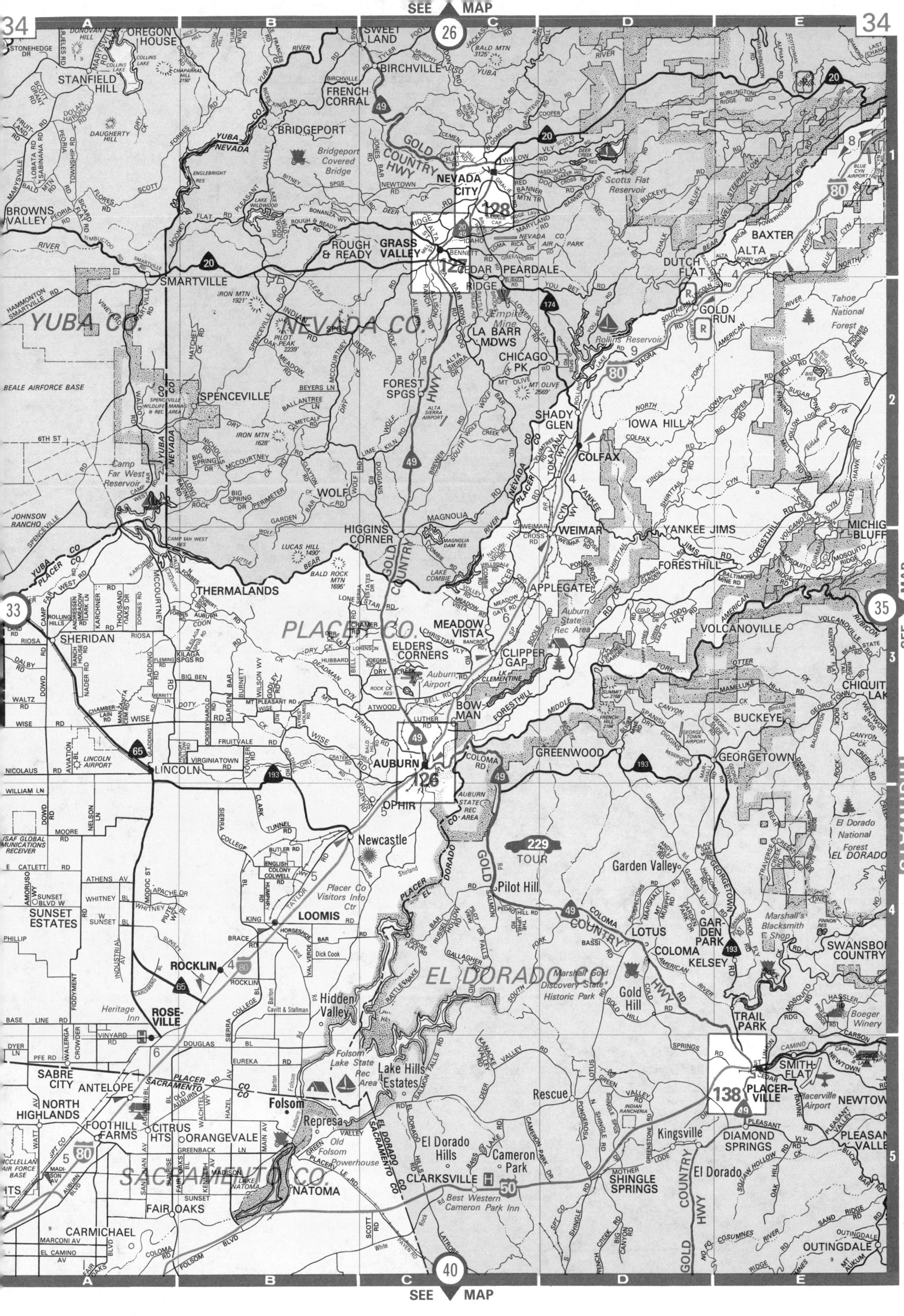

SEE MAP 26

OREGON HOUSE
STANFIELD HILL
BROWNS VALLEY
SMARTVILLE

SWEET LAND
BIRCHVILLE
FRENCH CORRAL
BRIDGEPORT
Bridgeport Covered Bridge

GOLD COUNTRY HWY

NEVADA CITY 128
ROUGH & READY
GRASS VALLEY
CEDAR RIDGE
PEARDALE

BAXTER
ALTA
DUTCH FLAT
GOLD RUN

YUBA CO.
NEVADA CO.
Tahoe National Forest

SPENCEVILLE
FOREST SPGS
LA BARR MDWS
CHICAGO PK
SHADY GLEN
IOWA HILL

Camp Far West Reservoir

WOLF
HIGGINS CORNER

COLFAX
WEIMAR
YANKEE JIMS
FORESTHILL
MICHIGAN BLUFF

THERMALANDS

33

PLACER CO.
MEADOW VISTA
ELDERS CORNERS
APPLEGATE
CLIPPER GAP
VOLCANOVILLE

35

SHERIDAN

BOWMAN
GREENWOOD
GEORGETOWN
BUCKEYE
CHIQUITA LAKE

65
LINCOLN
LOOMIS

AUBURN 126
OPHIR
COLOMA RD

229 TOUR
Garden Valley
EL DORADO National Forest

Newcastle
Placer Co Visitors Info Ctr

PILOT HILL
GOLD COUNTRY
LOTUS
GARDEN PARK
SWANSBORO COUNTRY

ROCKLIN
ROSEVILLE

EL DORADO CO.
Hidden Valley

COLOMA
KELSEY
Marshall's Blacksmith Shop
Gold Hill
TRAIL PARK
Boeger Winery

SUNSET ESTATES

Heritage Inn

Folsom Lake State Rec Area
Lake Hills Estates

Marshall Gold Discovery State Historic Park

SMITH FLAT
PLACERVILLE 138
Placerville Airport

SABRE CITY
ANTELOPE
NORTH HIGHLANDS
FOOTHILL FARMS
CITRUS HTS
ORANGEVALE

Folsom
Represa
Old Folsom Powerhouse

EL DORADO HILLS
CLARKSVILLE
Cameron Park
Best Western Cameron Park Inn

Rescue
SHINGLE SPRINGS
EL DORADO
DIAMOND SPRINGS
Kingsville
PLEASANT VALLEY

80
SACRAMENTO CO.
CARMICHAEL
FAIR OAKS
NATOMA

SHINGLE SPRINGS

OUTINGDALE

HIGHWAYS

COPYRIGHT © 1989 BY Thomas Bros. Maps

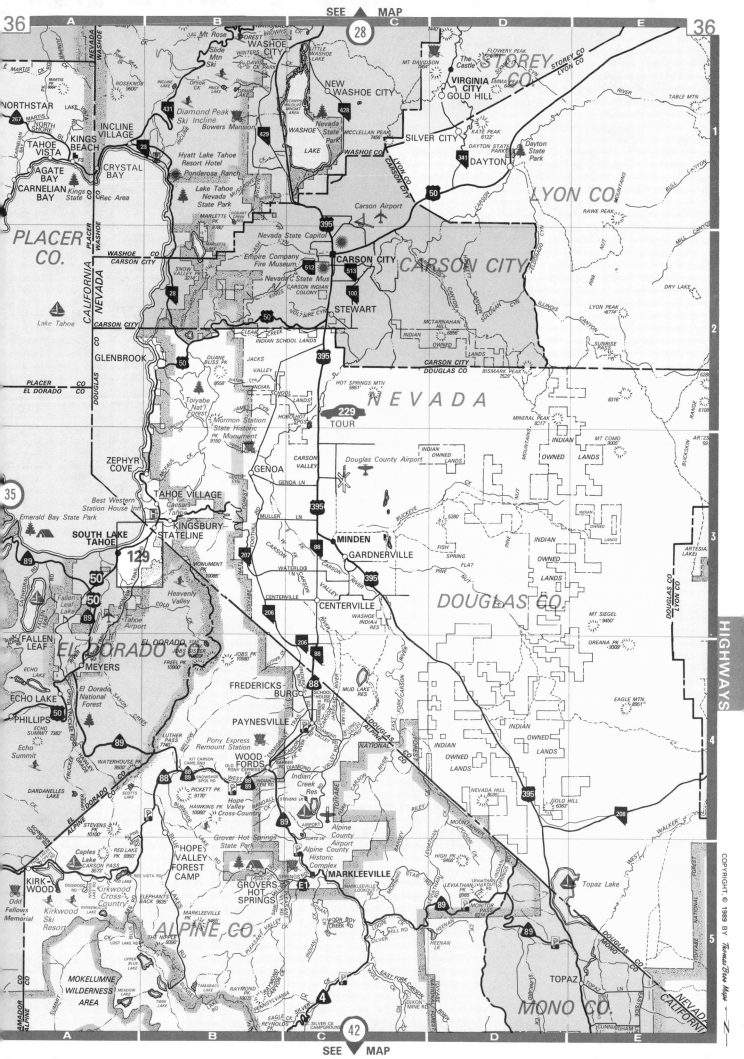

128

SONOMA CO.

HIGHWAYS

COPYRIGHT, © 1989 BY Thomas Bros Maps

OAK MTN

CREEK RD

WEST DRY CREEK RD

Healdsburg Municipal Airport

RANCHO Simi Winery

SOTOYOME RANCHO VALLEY RANCHERIA

EXANDER VALLEY RANCHERIA

CHALK HILL RD

Field Stone

KELLOGG

RANCHO MALLA COMES OR MORISTUL Y PLAN DE LA CALIENTE

FISK MILL COVE

CHO COAST HWY

GERMAN

Kruse Rhododendron State Reserve

SKYLINE RD

KING RIDGE RD

TIN BARN RD

TABLE MTN

KING RD

Salt Point State Park

MILL CREEK RD

HEALDSBURG

POWELL AV

FITCH MTN

Mill Creek Vineyards

BRACK RD

WALLACE CREEK RD

Alderbrook Foppiano Windsor

Piper Sonoma Cellars

William Wheeler Winery

Healdsburg Beach Memorial Regional Park

Clos Du Bois

Brooks White Oak Vineyards

J.W. Morris Winery

Stephen Zellerbach

FRANZ VALLEY RD

MARK WEST SPRINGS

SALT PT GERSTLE COVE

WALSH LANDING

KRUSE RANCH RD

SEAVIEW RD

GUALALA RIVER

HAUSER BR

Sea Ridge Winery

BIG OAT MTN

FOX MTN

ROCKY MT

Austin Creek State Rec Area

Armstrong Redwoods State Reserve

Korbel Champagne Cellars

MT JACKSON

SWEETWATER SPRINGS

Sonoma Cellars Belvedere Winery

Rodney Strong

Landmark Vineyards

ARATA LN

PLEASANT AV

PINER RD

MARK WEST STATION RD

Windsor Water-Works

WINDSOR

RIEBLI RD

WALLACE RD

OCEAN COVE Stillwater Cove

TIMBER COVE WINDERMERE PT

FT ROSS RD

BOHAN DILLON RD

SEAVIEW RD

NIESTRADA RD

MEYERS GRADE RD

Ft Ross State Historic Park

FORT ROSS

BLACK MTN

POLE MTN

CAZADERO

CAZADERO HWY

EL BONITA

RIO NIDO

HACIENDA

GUERNEWOOD PARK

MAYS CYN RD

GUERNE-VILLE

RIVER RD

RIO DELL

Hop Kiln

J. Rochioli Vineyards

HILOH RD

W STATION RD

Sonoma Co Airport RD

AIRPORT BLVD

FULTON

MARK WEST SPRINGS RD

PORTER CREEK RD

Sheraton Round Barn Inn

BADGER RD

FORT ROSS COVE

JENNER-BY-THE-SEA

RANCHO MUNIZ

COAST HWY

116

GOAT ROCK

VILLA GRANDE

AUSTIN CREEK RD

NORTH WOOD

MONTE RIO

VACATION BEACH

MAIN ST

SUMMER HOME PARK

VILLE

116 HWY

FORESTVILLE

Martini & Prati Winery Dehlinger

GREEN VALLEY RD

RANCHO SAN MIGUEL

Piner RD

PINER RD

OLIVET RD

GUERNEVILLE RD

De Loach Vineyards GUERNEVILLE RD

W STATION RD

101

SANTA ROSA

COLLEGE AV

131

SOUTH PARK

BRIDGE HAVEN

RED HILL

Rancho Bodega

COLEMAN VALLEY RD

CAMP MEEKER

BOHEMIAN HWY

VALLEY FORD RD

HALL RD

OCCIDENTAL RD

SR RR

GRATON

HIREEN RD

Sebastopol Indian Rancheria

Ragle Ranch Regional Park

GRATON

HEALDSBURG AV

12

8

OCEAN VIEW

SERENO DEL MAR

DUNCAN POINT

CARMET

IRISH HILL

OCCIDENTAL

JOY RD

GRATON RANCHO CANADA DE JONIVE

PET & SR RR

SEBASTOPOL

TODD RD

RANCHO LLANO DE SANTA ROSA

STONY PT RD

SANTA ROSA AV

RANCHO COTATE

Sonoma Coast State Beach

SALMON CREEK

RANCHO BODEGA

RANCHO ESTERO AMERICANO

PLEASANT HILL RD

FREESTONE

BLOOM FIELD RD

KNOWLES CORNER

CUN-NINGHAM

CADWELL

116

ROHNER PARK

COTATI

38

MUSSEL PT

BODEGA BAY

Doran Regional Park

SAINT TERESA'S CHURCH

BODEGA

BODEGA HWY

VALLEY FORD

VALLEY FORD RD

HESSEL

116

WASHOE

10

STONY PT RD

BODEGA HEAD

Bodega Harbor

BODEGA BAY

FRANKLIN MARSH

BLOOMFIELD RD

ROBLAR RD

RANCHO ROBLAR DE LA MISERIA

WALKER RD

PEPPER RD

PETALUMA

BODEGA

FORD WHITAKER RD

MIDDLE TWO ROCK RD

BLUFF RD

FALLON

FALLON RD

SONOMA CO MARIN CO

TWO ROCK RD

TWO ROCK

PEPPER RD

RANCHO ROBLAR DE LA MISERIA

SPRING HILL RD

BODEGA AV

MIDDLE TWO ROCK RD

DILLON BEACH

DILLON BEACH RD

TOMALES RD

221 TOUR

SPRING HILL RD

CHILENO VALLEY RD

TOMALES BLUFF

BIRD ROCK

TOMALES

TOMALES RD

RANCHO SAN ANTONIO

TOMS PT

MCCLURES BEACH

RANCHO NICASIO

MARIN CO.

MARSHALL-PETALUMA RD

PIERCE POINT RD

TOMALES BAY

SHORELINE HWY

RANCHO NICASIO

REYES HILL RD

PETALUMA PT

PACIFIC OCEAN

POINT REYES BEACH

Tomales Bay State Park

PT REYES

DRAKE BLVD

INVERNESS

1

PT REYES STATION

PT REYES PETALUMA RD

MATEO RD

NICASIO VALLEY RD

NICASIO

NICA SIO RES

SIR FRANCIS DRAKE BLVD

SIR FRANCIS DRAKE BLVD

OLEMA

S.P. Taylor State Park

Golden Gate Nat'l Rec Area

FOREST KNOLL

LAGUNITAS

DRAKES BAY

Point Reyes

National Seashore

PT RESISTANCE

MILLERS PT

KENT LAKE

RANCHO TOMALES

PT REYES

SEA LION COVE

CHIMNEY ROCK

SHORELINE HWY

DOUBLE PT

ABALONE PT

MESA RD

BOLINAS

N

A   B   C   D   E

YOLO CO.

NAPA CO.

SONOMA CO.

MARIN CO.

SOLANO CO.

CONTRA COSTA CO.

KELLOGG
RANCHO MALLA COMES OR MORISTUL Y PLAN DE AGUA CALIENTE
Old Faithful Geyser of California
Mud Baths
Stevenson Mem State Park
Sugarloaf Mtn
AETNA SPRINGS
POPE VALLEY
Lake Berryessa
Rancho Las Putas
JACKSON PEAK
EDGAR PEAK

CALISTOGA
Napa Co Hist Mus
Napa Valley Railroad Depot
ANGWIN
BERRYESSA PINES
Petrified Forest
Bothe-Napa Valley State Park
DEER PARK
Las Posadas State Forest
SPANISH FLAT WOODLANDS

SANTA ROSA
College Av
Annadel State Park
ST HELENA
Bale Grist Mill St Historic Park
Silverado Museum
Hurd Candle Factory
LAKE HENNESSEY
RANCHO CATACULA
BERRY ESSA HIGHLANDS
SOLANO CO

For Detail Page Locations **SEE PAGE 29**

SOUTH PARK
Rancho Los Guilicos
RUTHERFORD
Sugarloaf Ridge St Pk
Chateau St Jean
OAKVILLE
NAPA CO.
CIRCLE OAKS
RANCHO CHIMILES
MT VACA
LAKE CURRY
RANCHO CHIMILES
PUTNAM PEAK
ENGLISH

KENWOOD
Smothers Brothers Wines
St Francis Winery
Las Montanas Winery
Jack London St Hist Pk
YOUNTVILLE
Napa Valley Lodge Best Western
Veterans Peak
CASTLE PEAK
Silverado Country Club Resort

ROHNERT PARK
GLEN ELLEN
Grand Cru
Glen Ellen Winery
Vly of the Moon
SALVADOR
HAGEN RD
MANKAS CORNER
GREEN VALLEY ESTATES
FAIRFIELD

COTATI
PENNGROVE
Eagle Ridge Winery
ELDRIDGE
AGUA CALIENTE
FETTERS HOT SPRINGS
BOYES HOT SPRINGS
MISSION HIGHLANDS
EL VERANO
SONOMA
221 TOUR
NAPA
SKYLINE COUNTY PARK
ROCKVILLE
ELKHORN PEAK
CORDELIA
SUISUN CITY

37
PETALUMA
VINEBURG
BIG BEND
SCHELLVILLE
HUICHICA
Carneros Creek
BAY VIEW AV
LAS AMIGAS RD

LAKEVILLE
WILDCAT MTN
RANCHO PETALUMA
FLY BAY
AIRPORT RD
AMERICAN CANYON RD

SEARS POINT
LITTLE ISLAND
RUSS ISLAND
NAPA CO
SOLANO CO
MARINE WORLD PKWY
SOLANO CO.

SAN MARIN
NOVATO
GREEN POINT
BLACK POINT
SONOMA CO
SOLANO CO SONOMA CO
KNIGHT ISLAND
VALLEJO HTS
VALLEJO

225 TOUR
IGNACIO
MARINWOOD
Hamilton Air Force Base
MAINE NAVAL RES
MARE ISLAND NAVAL RES
BENICIA

For Detail Page Locations **SEE PAGE L**

CARQUINEZ HTS
MORROW COVE
CROCKETT
PORT COSTA
AVON
CLYDE

FOREST KNOLLS
WOODACRE
SLEEPY HOLLOW
SANTA VENETIA
SAN RAFAEL
NORTH RICHMOND
RODEO
HERCULES
PINOLE
MARTINEZ
PACHECO
PLEASANT HILL

LAGUNITAS
SAN GERONIMO
FAIRFAX
SAN ANSELMO
ROSS
SAN RAFAEL BAY
EL SOBRANTE
SAN PABLO
CONTRA COSTA CO.
BRIONES REGIONAL PARK
LAFAYETTE

LARKSPUR
CORTE MADERA
MILL VALLEY
PARADISE CAY
TIBURON
RICHMOND
EL CERRITO
KENSINGTON
ORINDA
WALNUT CREEK

STINSON

HIGHWAYS

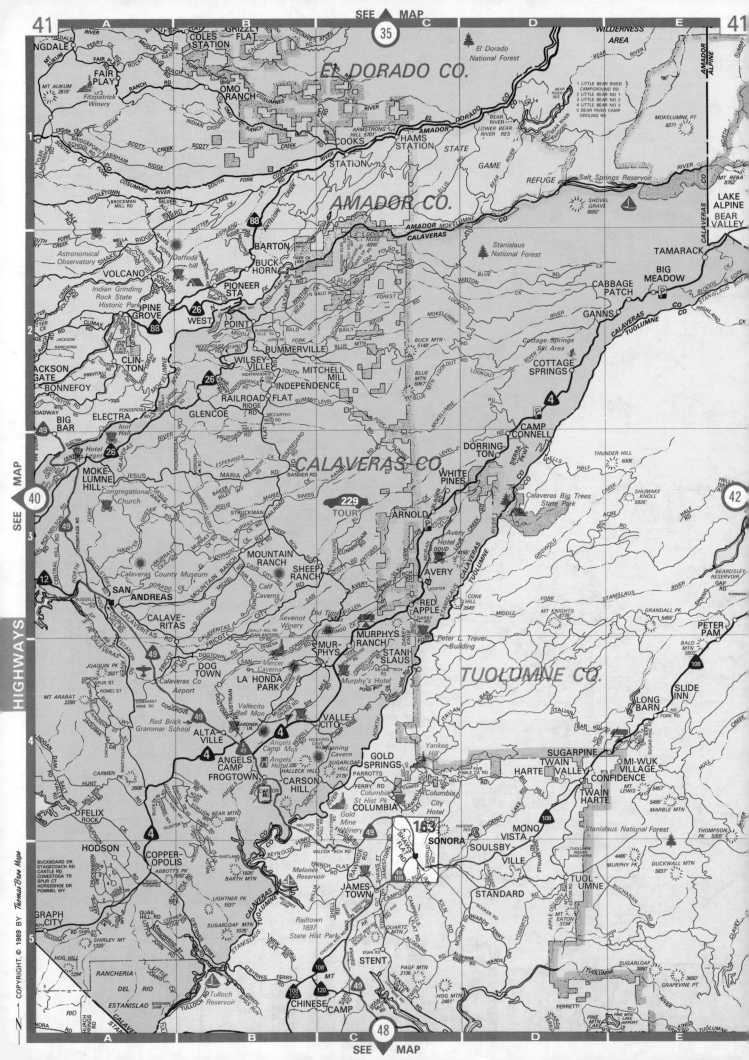

A   B   C   D   E

NEVADA
CALIFORNIA

MOKELUMNE WILDERNESS AREA

MEADOW LAKE
TAMARACK LAKE
TWIN LAKE
RAYMOND PK 10075'
SUNSET LK
PENNSYLVANIA
EAGLE CK
REYNOLDS PK 9800'
UPPER KINNEY RES
LOWER KINNEY RES
SILVER CK CAMPGROUND RD
4
SILVER CK
DIXON MINE RD
CARSON RIVER
TOPAZ LN
CHARLEBOIS LN
CUNNINGHAM LN
OFFAL RD
ANTELOPE RD
PATRICIA LN
EASTSIDE RD

COLEVILLE

HERMIT VALLEY
PACIFIC GRADE SUMMIT 8050'
EBBETTS PASS 8730'
NOBEL CK
STANISLAUS
HIGHLAND LAKE
DIXON
WOLF CK
BRYANT
HIGHLAND PK 10955'

ALPINE CO.

MT REBA
Mt Reba
SILVER TIP CP GRD RD
BEE GULCH RD
ALPINE RD
4
FOLGER PK 9700'
HIGHLAND LAKE
HENRY PK 9309'
ARNOT PK 10036'
BOULDER PK 9359'
TAMARACK LK
ANTELOPE PK 10241'
POISON CK
KINGS CK

MONO

WEST GATE RD
LITTLE LOST CK
SHOSR RD
PINE CR
UTTLE LOST CK
NATIONAL FOREST
395
DEEP CK
COTTONWOOD

WALKER

LAKE ALPINE
BEAR VALLEY
Alpine Lake
Bear Valley Cross-Country
UTICA RES
UNION RES
SAPPS HILL 7187'
BLOODS N FORK STANISLAUS RIVER
WIESER
HIGHLAND
ICEBERG PK 9751'
DISASTER PK 10022'
NATIONAL
DISASTER
FOREST
WHITECLIFF PK 10800'
Toiyabe National Forest
FISH VALLEY PK 10571'
WELLS PK 10833'
WHITE MTN 11398'
LOST CANYON PK 11099'
SILVER
MILL CANYON RD
BURCHAM

DARDANELLES CONE 9502'
SPICER MEADOW RESERVOIR
CLARKS FORK
RED PK 9951'
STANISLAUS PK 11202'
SONORA PK 11429'
CLOUDBURST
BROWNIE
SONORA PASS
108
WALKER TULE LK
CARMEN LK
JUNCTION RES
BUSH MTN 8848'
SONORA JCT
FALES HOT SPGS
POORE LK

DONNELLS RES
108
MIDDLE FORK
108
DARDANELLE
DEADMAN
DOUGLAS
MCKAY
LEAVITT
POORE
BUSH MTN

MONO CO.

Stanislaus National Forest
EAGLE PK 9378'
RELIEF RES
EAST FLANGE ROCK 9909'
KENNEDY
LEAVITT PK 11375'
LEAVITT LK
MT EMMA 10525'
HOOVER
WALKER MTN 11572'
EAGLE PK 11825'

41
HELLS HALF ACRE RD
BULL RUN ROCK 7200'
HERRING CREEK RES
COOPER PK 9581'
CASTLE ROCK 9620'
EMIGRANT
PRIMITIVE
ICELAND LK
GRANITE DOME 10300'
AREA
BLACK HAWK MTN 10327'
RELIEF PK 10788'
KENNEDY PK 10677'
FREMONT LK
ANNA LK
BLUE LK
BONNIE
HANNA MTN 11029'
HUNEWILL PK 11754'
WILDERNESS
AREA
43

STRAW-BERRY
BEARDSLEY RESERVOIR
SPRING GAP
PINE CREST LAKE
DODGE RDG LOOP RD
Dodge Ridge
BEAR LAKE
MEADOW DAM
BURST ROCK 9200'
SUMMIT LK
LONG LK
EMIGRANT LK
SHALLOW LK
SACHSE MTN 9241'
BIGELOW
FORSYTH PK 11180'
DOROTHY LK
Lake Helen
TOWER PK 11704'
CRAIG PK 11041'
EHRNBECK PK 11194'
WELLS PK 11071'
GHOUSE MTN 10784'
CENTER MTN 11220'
CIRQUE MTN 10739'
BARNEY LK
ROBINSON CK

PINECREST
COLD SPRINGS
PETER PAM
BELL
WOOD LK
DEER LK
BUCK LAKES
MAXWELL LK
BLACK
KENDRICK PK 10346'
KEYES PK CREST 11051'
SAURIAN PK 11065'
SNOW PK 10933'
PEELER LK
GLACIER LK
CROWN PT 11358'
SLIDE MTN 11092'
STANISLAUS

TUOLUMNE CO.
PINGREE LK
LAIGHTON LK
BIG LK
HUCKLEBERRY
COW MEADOW
LEKTORA LK
MICHIE PK 10339'
TWIN LK
HAYSTACK PK 9966'
TILDEN LK
ACKER PK 10918'
PRICE PK 10603'
KERRICK
FINGER PKS 11491'
WHORL MTN 12050'

EMIGRANT
GILLETT PK 8300'
WHEELER PK 8877'
SCHOFIELD PK 9913'
RICHARDSON PK 9845'
WILMA LK
CHITTENDEN PK 10133'
ROCK ISLAND LK
BATH MTN 10560'

PRIMITIVE
MERCUR PK 8072'
BARTLETT PK 9264'
NANCE PK 8436'
EDITH LK
FLORA LK
MAHAN PK 9134'
BEARUP LK
ANDREW PK 8508'
TILTILL MTN 8961'
BRANIGAN
PIUTE MTN 10489'
CAMP CK
QUARRY PK 11162'

STANISLAUS
AREA
KIBBIE LK
FROG
FLORA LK
LAKE VERNON
SMEDBERG LK
SISTER LK
BENSON LK
VOLUNTEER PK 10503'
RODGERS LK
PETTIT PK 10775'
MILLER LK

NATIONAL
REYNOLDS
Cherry Lake
LAUREL LK
MT GIBSON 8400'
SADDLE HORSE LK
TABLE LK
WEST PK 10510'
VIRGINIA
COLD MTN 10200'

THOMPSON PK 5305'
MIGUEL CK
SWAMP LK
LAKE ELEANOR
TILTILL
RANCHERIA
LE CONTE PT 6500'
RANCHERIA MTN 9045'
HOOPER PK 9562'
MATTIE LK

FOREST
HETCH HETCHY RES
SMITH PK 7835'
Grand Canyon of The Tuolumne
Grand Canyon of the Tuolumne
HARDEN LK
COLBY MTN 9700'
CATHEDRAL
MT BASE
FAIRVIEW DOME 9737'

MATHER
COTTONWOOD
MORRISON CK
WHITE WOLF
LUKENS
TUOLUMNE
TUOLUMNE PK 10875'

Yosemite National Park

BALD MTN 7338'

HIGHWAYS

N

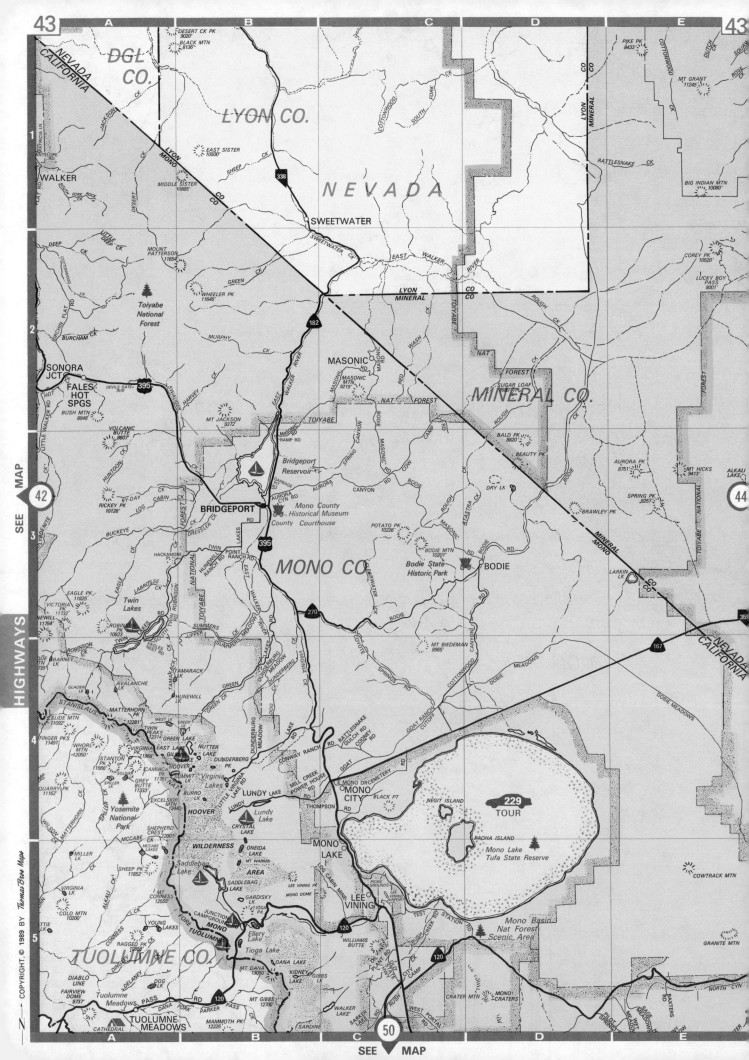

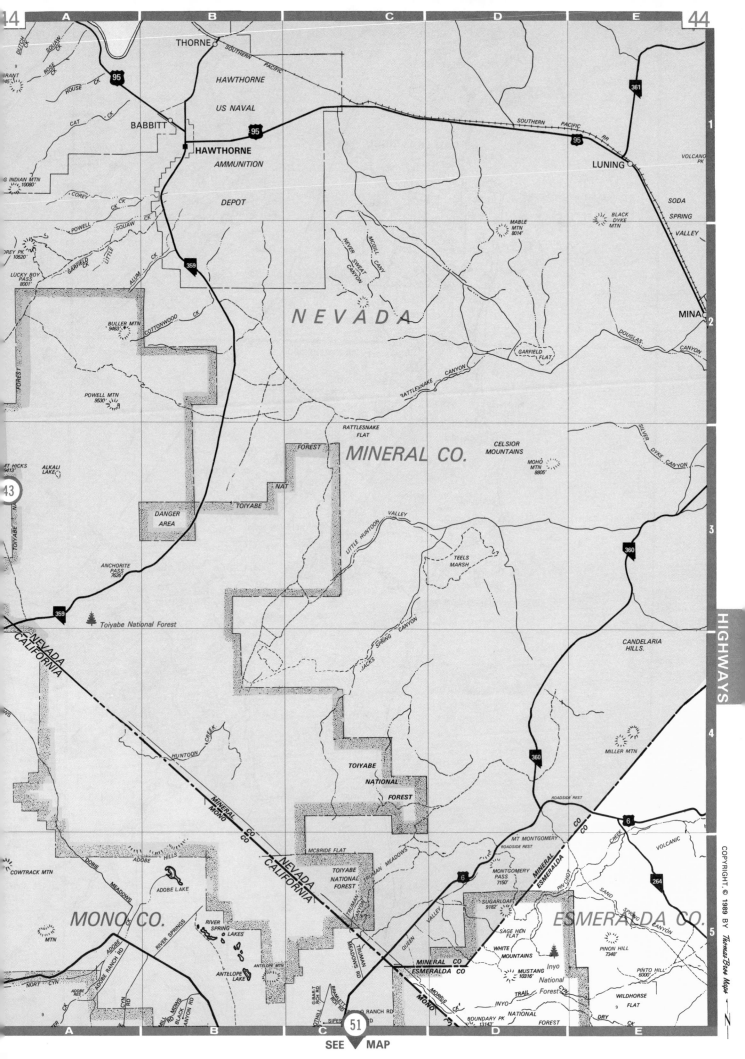

HIGHWAYS

STINSON BEACH
MUIR BEACH
MUIR WOODS NATL MONT
MARIN CITY
MARIN CO.
SAUSALITO
TIBURON
BELVEDERE
CAY PT
CHAUNCEY
BLITHEDALE AV
EDGEWOOD AV
131

GOLDEN GATE BRIDGE

SAN FRANCISCO
101
LOMBARD ST
CALIFORNIA ST
GEARY BL
FULTON ST
LINCOLN
GREAT HWY
SUNSET BL
19TH AV
FELL ST
VAN NESS
MARKET ST
PORTOLA DR
MONTEREY BL
OCEAN AV
GENEVA AV
SLOAT BL
JOHN DALY BL
280
1
35

SAN FRANCISCO CO.

For Detail Page Locations
SEE PAGE L

DALY CITY
COLMA
BRISBANE
BAYSHORE BL
HILLSIDE BL
MISSION RD
GRAND AV
PACIFICA
SOUTH SAN FRANCISCO
SAN BRUNO
MILLBRAE
BURLINGAME
82
380
101
SERRA
ALAMEDA CO
SAN MATEO CO
FRANCISCO CO
SAN MATEO CO

SAN FRANCISCO INTERNATIONAL AIRPORT

ROCKAWAY BEACH
LINDA MAR
SAN ANDREAS LAKE
SAN BRUNO
SKYLINE BL
SHARP PK RD
SNEATH LN
HILLCREST
MILLBRAE
HILLSBOROUGH
SAN MATEO
FOSTER CITY
92
SAN MATEO TOLL BRIDGE
YOUNGER FRWY

MONTARA
MOSS BEACH
PRINCETON BY THE SEA
EL GRANADA
MIRAMAR
HALF MOON BAY
CABRILLO HWY
MOON BAY
92
LOWER CRYSTAL SPRINGS RES
The Highlands
BELMONT
RALSTON AV
SAN CARLOS
REDWOOD CITY
ATHERTON
82
101
84
EAST PALO ALTO
MENLO PARK
114
109
DUMBARTON BRIDGE
35
CANADA RD
UPPER CRYSTAL SPRINGS RES
REDWOOD PARK
WOODSIDE
KINGS MTN RD
SERRA
84
SAND HILL RD
PALO ALTO
Stanford
Ladera
PORTOLA VALLEY
G6
G3
MOUNTAIN VIEW
LOS ALTOS
LOS ALTOS HILLS
G5
280
237

For Detail Page Locations
SEE PAGE N

SAN MATEO CO.

HIGGINS PURISIMA
PURISIMA CK RD
CABRILLO HWY
TUNITAS CK RD
Sky Londa
84
35
SKYLINE BL
ALPINE RD
1
San Gregorio
LA HONDA RD
La Honda
84
CUPERTINO
85
82
FREMONT AV
HOMESTEAD
SANTA CLARA CO.

STAGE RD
Loma Mar
PORTOLA STATE PK RD
Pescadero
ARTICHOKE RD
BUTANO CUT-OFF
BEAN HOLLOW RD
PESCADERO RD
CLOVERDALE RD
CANYON RD
GATOS CK RD
9
85
CONGRESS SPRINGS RD
MONTE SERENO
35
236
9
Redwood

SAN MATEO CO
SANTA CRUZ CO

SANTA CRUZ CO.

OAKLAND
ALAMEDA CO
ALBANY
BERKELEY
EMERYVILLE
ORINDA
ORINDA VILLAGE
MORAGA
PIEDMONT
CANYON
MORAGA
CONTRA COSTA CO
CONTRA COSTA CO.
WALNUT CREEK
24
580
980
13
77
ALAMEDA
61
185
225 TOUR
OAKLAND INTERNATIONAL AIRPORT
SAN LEANDRO
580
112
880
238
ALAMEDA CO.
San Lorenzo
HAYWARD
238
UNION CITY
84
NEWARK
46
237
85

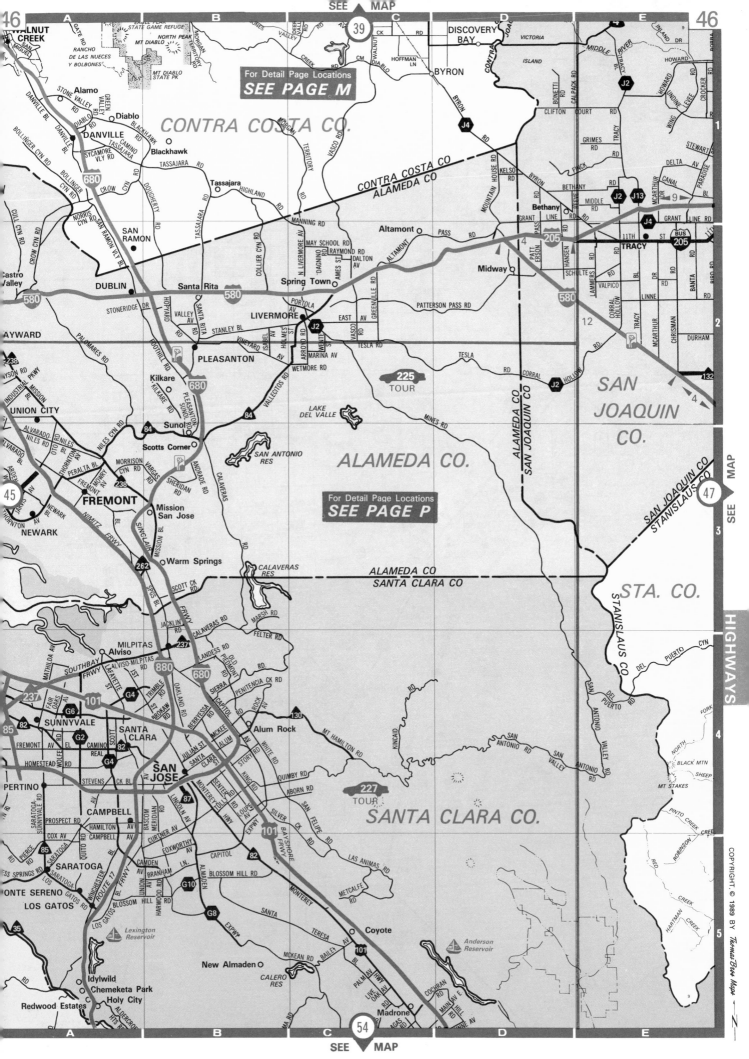

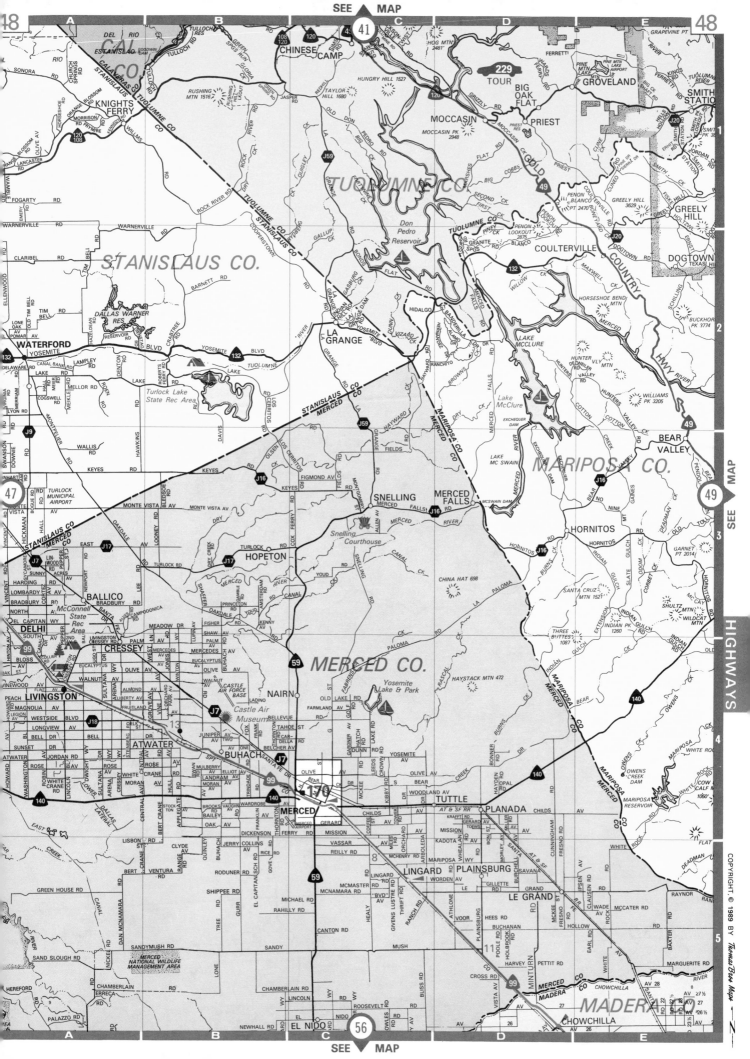

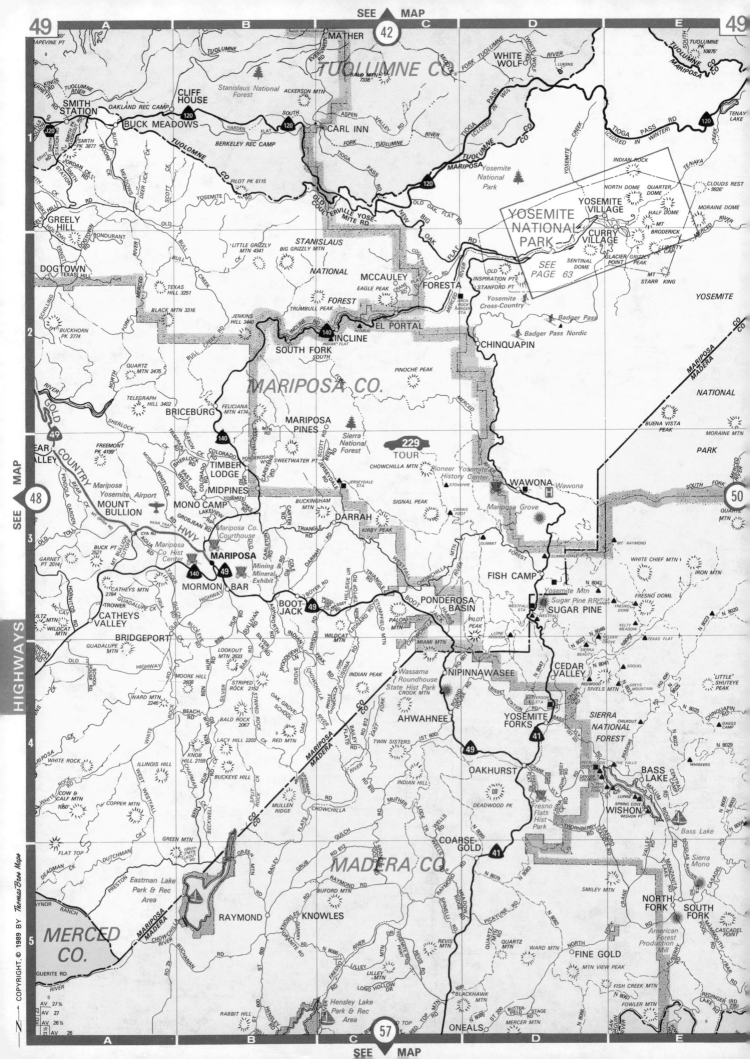

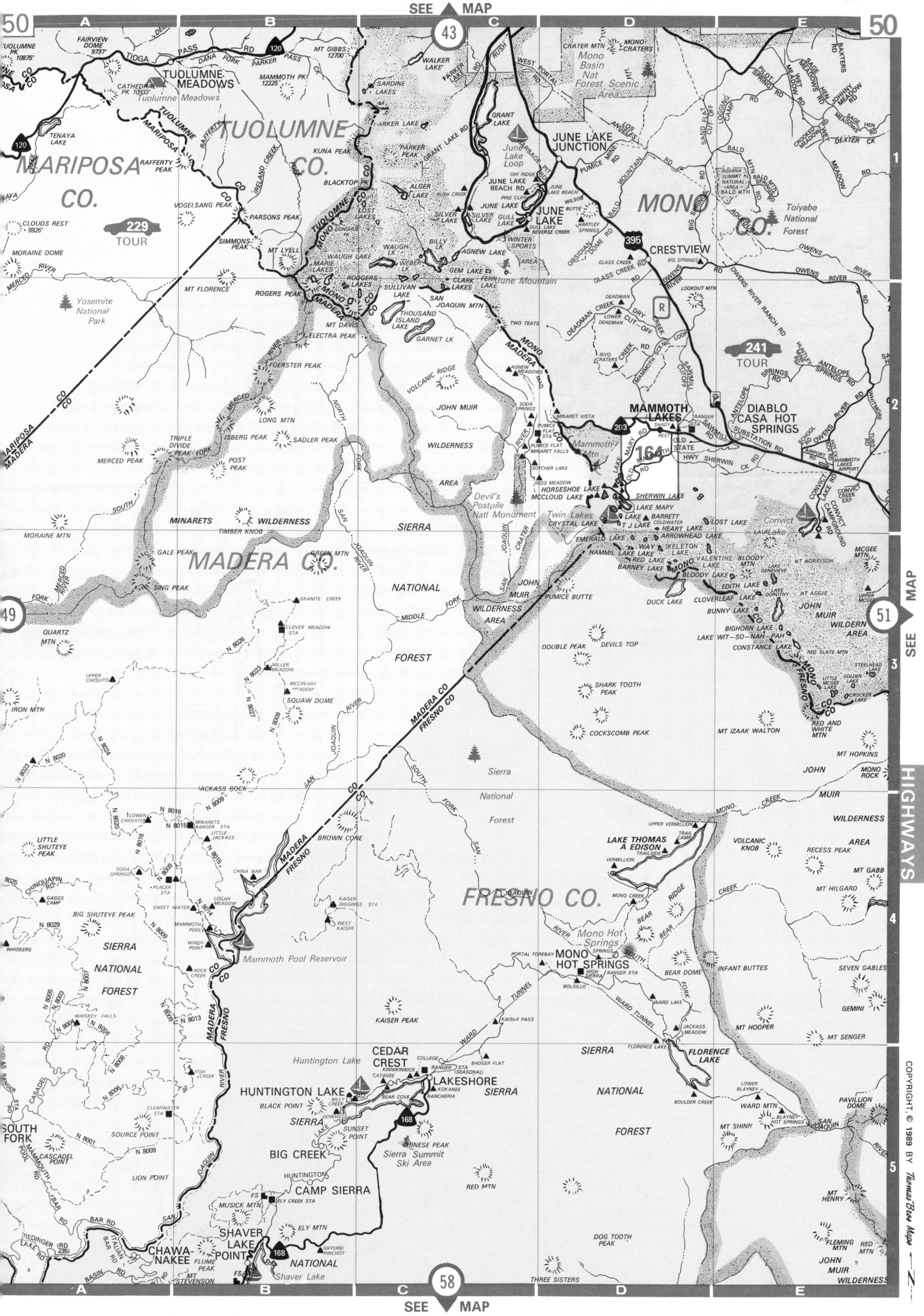

MARIPOSA CO.

TUOLUMNE CO.

MONO CO.

MADERA CO.

FRESNO CO.

SIERRA NATIONAL FOREST

JOHN MUIR WILDERNESS AREA

MINARETS WILDERNESS

Yosemite National Park

Toiyabe National Forest

FAIRVIEW DOME 9737'
TUOLUMNE PK 10875'
CATHEDRAL PK 10933'
TUOLUMNE MEADOWS
Tuolumne Meadows
TIOGA PASS
DANA FORK
BARKER PASS
MT GIBBS 12700
MAMMOTH PK 12225
TENAYA LAKE
CLOUDS REST 9926'
MORAINE DOME
RAFFERTY PEAK
VOGELSANG PEAK
PARSONS PEAK
KUNA PEAK
BLACKTOP PK
MT LYELL
MARIE LAKES
RODGERS LAKES
MT FLORENCE
ROGERS PEAK
MT DAVIS
ELECTRA PEAK
FOERSTER PEAK
LONG MTN
ISBERG PEAK
SADLER PEAK
POST PEAK
MERCED PEAK
TRIPLE DIVIDE PEAK
MORAINE MTN
GALE PEAK
SING PEAK
GREEN MTN
TIMBER KNOB
229 TOUR
241 TOUR

WALKER LAKE
SARDINE LAKES
PARKER LAKE
GRANT LAKE
JUNE LAKE LOOP
JUNE LAKE BEACH RD
SILVER LAKE
GULL LAKE
JUNE LAKE
JUNE LAKE JUNCTION
REVERSE CREEK
WINTER SPORTS AREA
June Mountain
AGNEW LAKE
GEM LAKE
CLARK LAKES
SULLIVAN LAKE
SAN JOAQUIN MTN
THOUSAND ISLAND LAKE
GARNET LK
VOLCANIC RIDGE
AGNEW MEADOWS
SODA SPRINGS
MINARET VISTA
PUMICE FLAT
MINARET FALLS
Mammoth Mtn
SOTCHER LAKE
REDS MEADOW
HORSESHOE LAKE
MCCLOUD LAKE
Devil's Postpile Natl Monument
TWIN LAKES
CRYSTAL LAKE
LAKE MARY
EMERALD LAKE
HAMMIL LAKE
BARNEY LAKE
PUMICE BUTTE
DOUBLE PEAK
DEVILS TOP
SHARK TOOTH PEAK
COCKSCOMB PEAK
MT IZAAK WALTON

CRESTVIEW
395
MAMMOTH LAKES
203
164
OLD STATE HWY
SHERWIN
DIABLO CASA HOT SPRINGS
MAMMOTH LAKES AIRPORT
OWENS RIVER RANCH RD
LOOKOUT MTN
DRY CREEK
DEADMAN CREEK
GLASS CREEK
OBSIDIAN DOME
TWO TEATS
MONO CRATERS
CRATER MTN
Mono Basin Nat Forest Scenic Area
WEST PORTAL
PUMICE MTN

CONVICT LAKE
LOST LAKE
LAVA LAKE
MT MORRISON
VALENTINE LAKE
BLOODY MTN
BLOODY LAKE
CLOVERLEAF LAKE
EDITH LAKE
DUCK LAKE
BUNNY LAKE
BIGHORN LAKE
LAKE WIT-SO-NAH-PAH
CONSTANCE LAKE
MT AGGIE
LAKE GENEVIEVE
LAKE DOROTHY
UPPER MCGEE
MCGEE MTN
LITTLE MCGEE LAKE
CROCKER LAKE
RED SLATE MTN
STEELHEAD LAKE
GOLDEN LAKE
RED AND WHITE MTN
MT HOPKINS
MT HENRY
MONO ROCK

49

51

SEE MAP HIGHWAYS

LAKE THOMAS A EDISON
VERMILION
UPPER VERMILION
TRAIL CAMP
MONO CREEK
BEAR RIDGE
VOLCANIC KNOB
RECESS PEAK
MT GABB
MT HILGARD
MONO HOT SPRINGS
Mono Hot Springs
MONO
PORTAL FOREBAY
BOLSILLO
HIGH SIERRA RANGER STA
BEAR DOME
INFANT BUTTES
SEVEN GABLES
GEMINI
WARD LAKE
MT HOOPER
MT SENGER
JACKASS MEADOW
FLORENCE LAKE
FLORENCE
WARD MTN
BLAYNEY HOT SPRINGS
LOWER BLAYNEY
BOULDER CREEK
PAVILION DOME
SAN JOAQUIN RIVER
MT SHINN

N 8026
N 8023
N 8021
N 8009
N 8024
N 8020
CLOVER MEADOW STA
MILLER MEADOW
MCCREARY MEADOW
SQUAW DOME
GRANITE CREEK
JACKASS ROCK
CHINA BAR
BROWN CONE
MINARETS RANGER STA
LITTLE JACKASS
LOGAN MEADOW
SWEET WATER
MAMMOTH POOL
WINDY POINT
ROCK CREEK
Mammoth Pool Reservoir
KAISER DIGGINGS STA
WEST KAISER
KAISER PEAK
KAISER PASS
WARD TUNNEL

LOWER CHIQUITO
UPPER CHIQUITO
LITTLE SHUTEYE PEAK
BIG SHUTEYE PEAK
SODA SPRINGS
PLACER STA
GAGGS CAMP
CHIQUAPIN RD
WHISKERS
N 8029
N 8025
N 8007
N 8006
N 8005
N 8003
N 8001

HUNTINGTON LAKE
Huntington Lake
CEDAR CREST
LAKESHORE
KINNIKINNICK
CATAVEE
BILLY CREEK
COLLEGE
RANGER STA (SEASONAL)
BADGER FLAT
KOKANEE
RANCHERIA
BEAR COVE
BLACK POINT
DEER CREEK
SUNSET POINT
BIG CREEK
CAMP SIERRA
CHINESE PEAK
Sierra Summit Ski Area
RED MTN
168
MUSICK MTN
ELY CREEK STA
ELY MTN
GIFFORD PINCHOT
SHAVER LAKE POINT
CHAWANAKEE
FLUME PEAK
Shaver Lake
NATIONAL
MT STEVENSON
DOG TOOTH PEAK
THREE SISTERS
FLEMING MTN
RED MTN

SOUTH FORK
REDINGER LAKE
BAR RD
ITALIAN BAR RD
LION POINT
CLEARWATER STA
SOURCE POINT
FISH CREEK
CASCADEL POINT

COPYRIGHT © 1989 BY Thomas Bros Maps

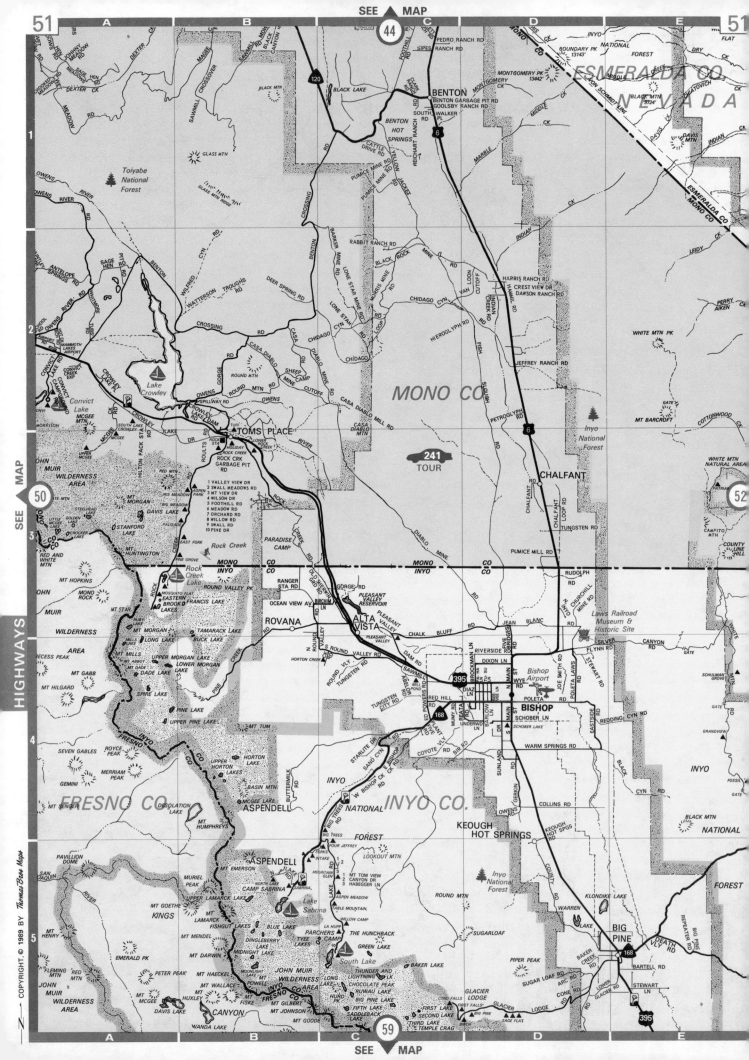

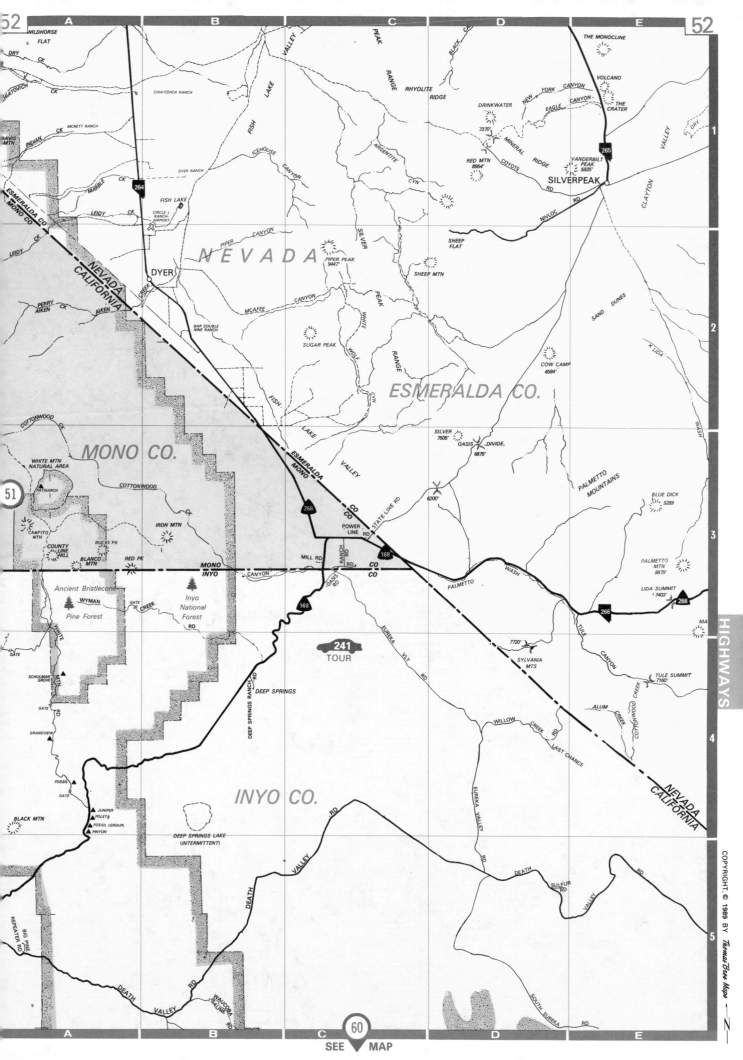

SEE MAP
45

SEE MAP
167

SEE MAP
168

For Detail Page Locations
SEE PAGE N

SANTA CRUZ CO.
227 TOUR

Redwood Estates
Boulder Creek
Brookdale
Ben Lomond
GLEN ARBOR
Santa Cruz Big Trees & Pacific Railway
Felton
MT HERMON
SCOTT

Davenport

SANTA CRUZ
Wilder Ranch State Park
HIGH ST
WATER ST
169

Natural Bridges State Beach

17 MILE DRIVE

SPANISH BAY
Point Joe
Spanish Bay Resort
Clubhouse
Treasure
SEAL
MONTEREY PENINSULA COUNTRY CLUB
Paradise Park

Pacific Grove (Toll)
Pacific Grove Gate (Toll)
Higgins Park
Forest Lodge Country Club Gate CTR

PRESIDIO OF MONTEREY
Veterans Memorial Park

MONTEREY

FRANKLIN ST
JEFFERSON ST
54

MARTIN ST

227 TOUR

MONTEREY CO.

BIRD ROCK
SEAL ROCK
Indian Village
FOREST LAKE
Spyglass Hill Golf Club

Lopez
17 Mile Dr
Poppy Hills Golf Course

Peninsula Community Hosp

CYPRESS POINT
CLUB HOUSE
Cypress Point Country Club

Pebble Beach

Pebble Beach Stables
Collins Polo Field
Peter Hay Golf Course

Highway 1 Gate (Toll)

AGUAJITO

CABRILLO

SUNSET POINT
LONE CYPRESS TREE
MIDWAY POINT

The Lodge At Pebble Beach
Tennis Club

PEBBLE BEACH
STILLWATER COVE
PESCADERO ROCKS
ARROWHEAD POINT
Pebble Beach Golf Links

Forest Hill Park

CARMEL

CARMEL HS
168

PESCADERO POINT

MILES
FEET
0   1000   2000   3000   4000   5000

PACIFIC

CARMEL BAY

OCEAN

HIGHWAYS

N

SEE MAP

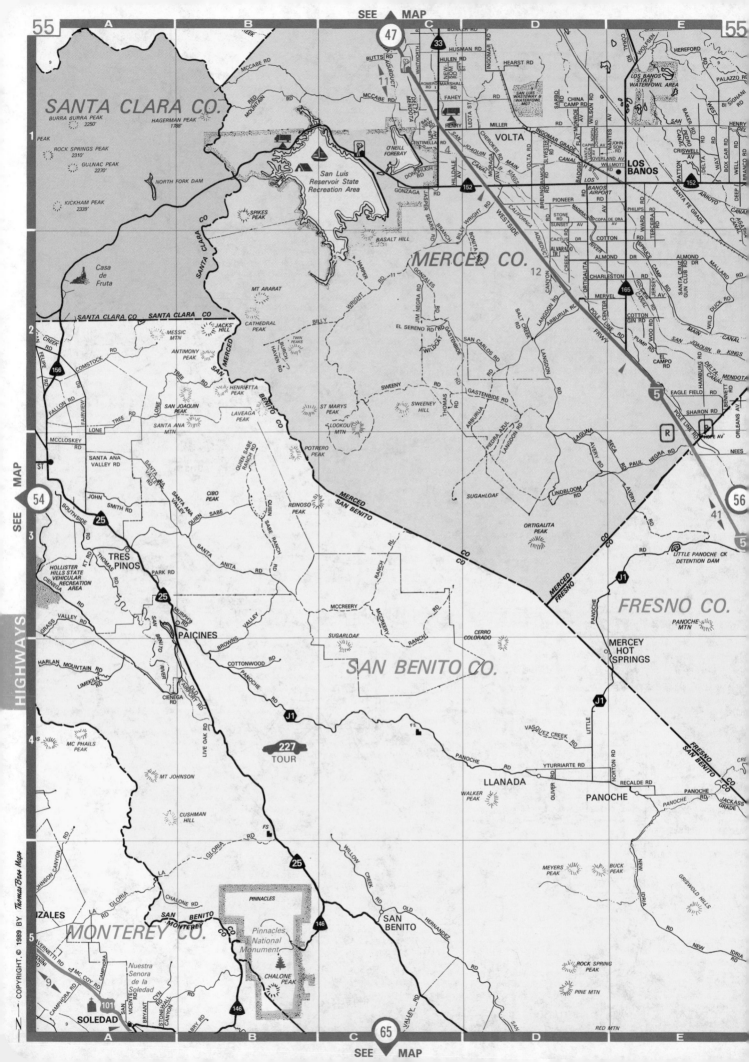

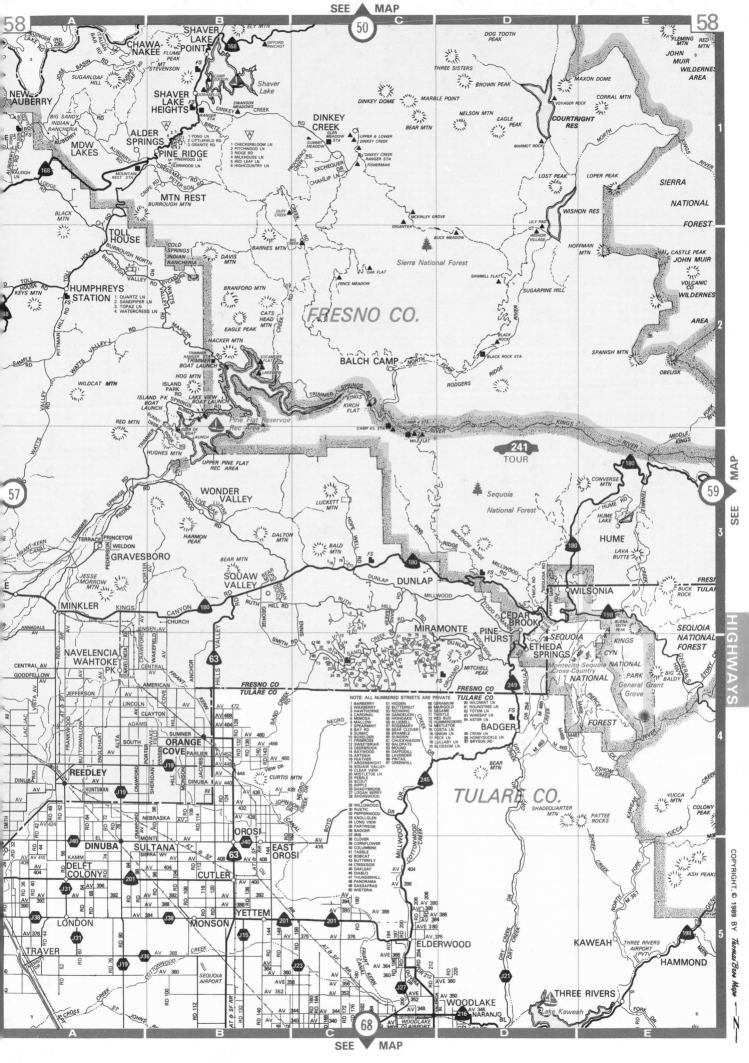

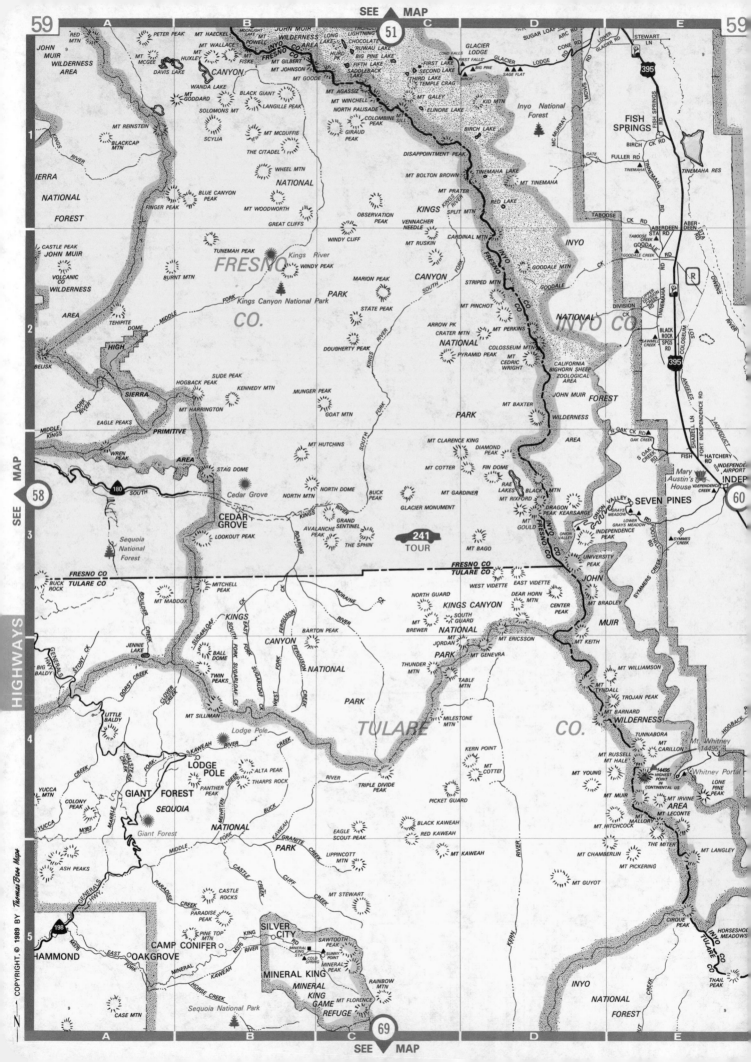

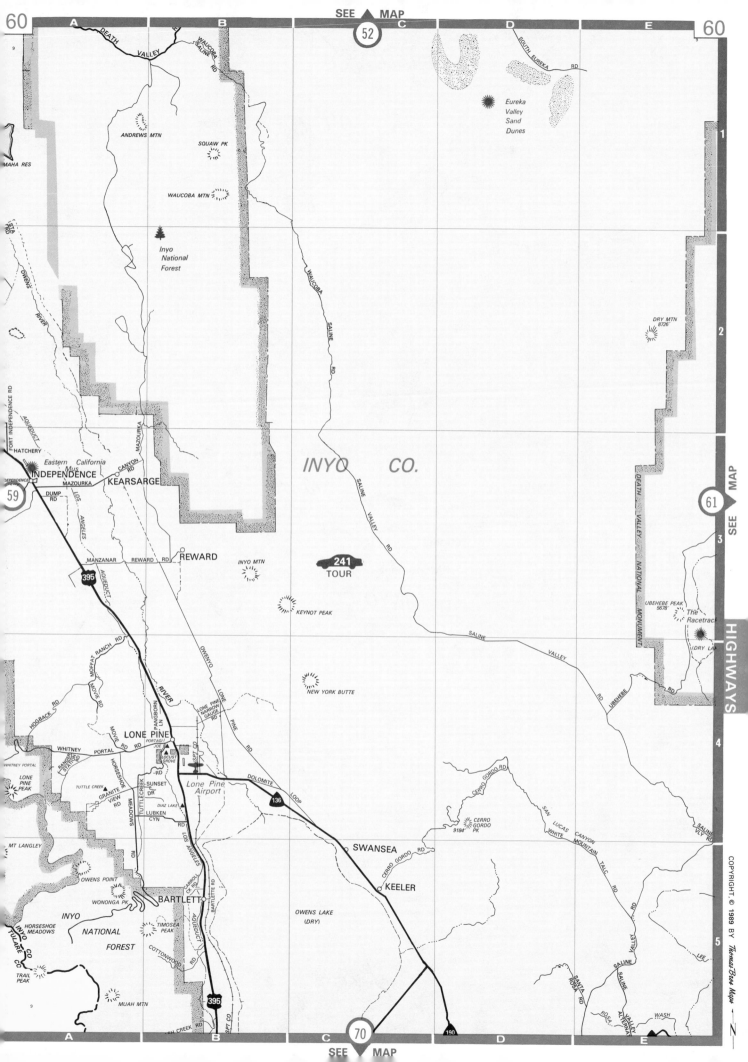

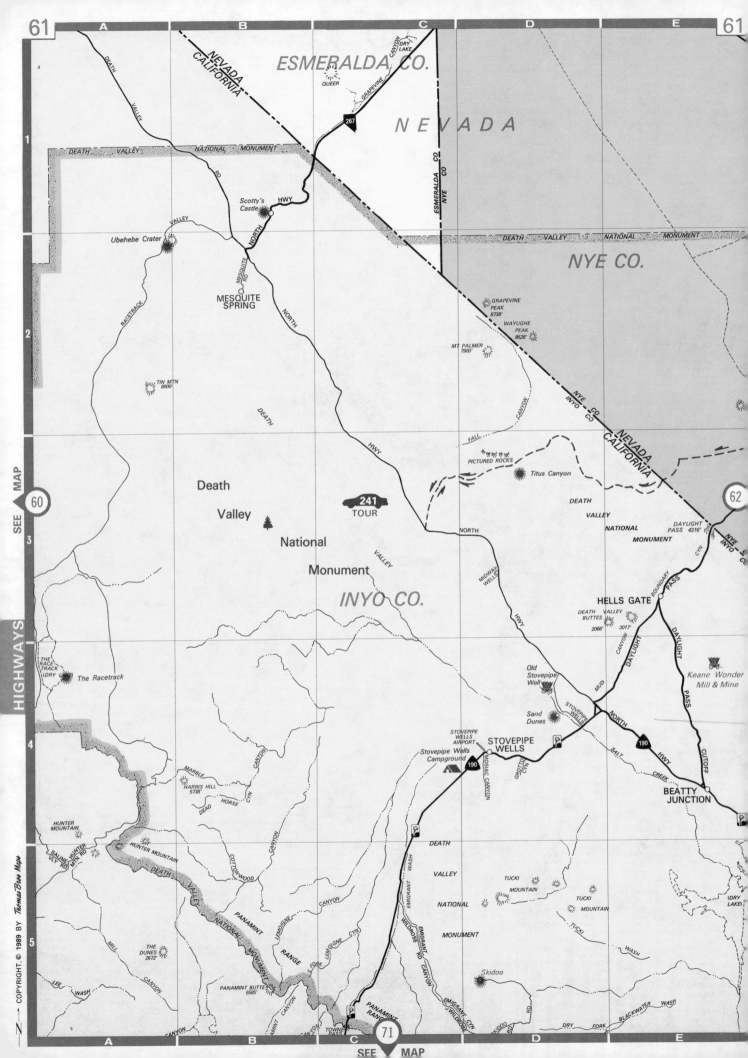

ESMERALDA CO.

DRY LAKE

QUEER

GRAPEVINE CANYON

267

N E V A D A

NEVADA
CALIFORNIA

DEATH VALLEY

DEATH VALLEY NATIONAL MONUMENT

ESMERALDA CO
NYE CO

NYE CO.

DEATH VALLEY NATIONAL MONUMENT

Scotty's Castle

HWY

VALLEY

NORTH

Ubehebe Crater

MESQUITE RD

MESQUITE SPRING

NORTH

RACETRACK

TIN MTN 8900'

DEATH

GRAPEVINE PEAK 8738'

WAYUGHE PEAK 8628'

MT PALMER 7900'

FALL CANYON

NYE CO
INYO CO

NEVADA
CALIFORNIA

Death

Valley

National

Monument

HWY

PICTURED ROCKS

Titus Canyon

241 TOUR

NORTH

MIDWAY WELLS

DEATH

VALLEY

NATIONAL

MONUMENT

DAYLIGHT PASS 4316'

NYE CO
INYO CO

62

INYO CO.

HELLS GATE

BOUNDARY PASS

DAYLIGHT

DAYLIGHT PASS

CYN

DEATH VALLEY BUTTES 2066'

VALLEY 3017'

Keane Wonder Mill & Mine

THE RACE TRACK (DRY LAKE)

The Racetrack

HWY

Old Stovepipe Well

MUD CANYON

NORTH

Sand Dunes

STOVEPIPE WELLS

STOVEPIPE WELLS

190

SALT CREEK

BEATTY JUNCTION

MARBLE CYN

HARRIS HILL 5738'

DEAD HORSE CYN

STOVEPIPE WELLS AIRPORT

Stovepipe Wells Campground

190

MOSAIC CANYON

GROTTO CYN

HUNTER MOUNTAIN

COTTONWOOD

CANYON

DEATH

CUTOFF

(DRY LAKE)

SALINE VLY RD

HUNTER MTN RD

HUNTER MOUNTAIN

VALLEY

CANYON

DEATH VALLEY NATIONAL MONUMENT

LEMOIGNE CANYON

EMIGRANT WASH

VALLEY

TUCKI MOUNTAIN

NATIONAL

TUCKI MOUNTAIN

MILL

CANYON

THE DUNES 2672'

PANAMINT BUTTE 6585'

PANAMINT RANGE

S FORK

LEMOIGNE CYN

WILDROSE CANYON

MONUMENT

Skidoo

TUCKI WASH

LEE WASH

PANAMINT CANYON

CANYON

TOWNE PASS

PANAMINT RANGE

EMIGRANT CYN WILDROSE

SKIDOO RD

DRY FORK

BLACKWATER WASH

SEE MAP 60

SEE MAP 62

71 SEE MAP

HIGHWAYS

N

9

1

2

3

4

5

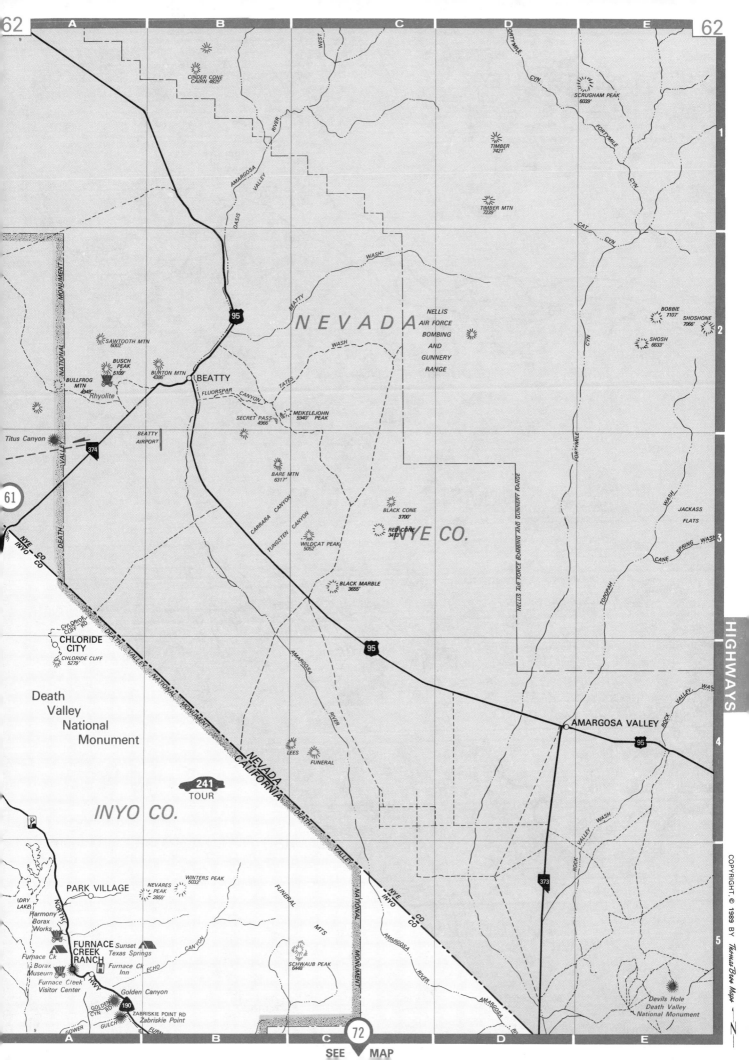

A	B	C	D	E

N E V A D A

NELLIS
AIR FORCE
BOMBING
AND
GUNNERY
RANGE

CINDER CONE
CAIRN 4829'

SCRUGHAM PEAK
6039'

TIMBER
7421'

TIMBER MTN
7239'

BOBBIE
7107'

SHOSHONE
7066'

SHOSH
6633'

1

AMARGOSA

VALLEY

OASIS

WEST

RIVER

BEATTY

WASH

95

SAWTOOTH MTN
6002'

BUSCH
PEAK
5109'

BURTON MTN
4386'

BEATTY

BULLFROG
MTN
4949'

Rhyolite

Titus Canyon

374

FLUORSPAR   CANYON

SECRET PASS
4966'

MEIKELEJOHN
5940' PEAK

TATES

WASH

FORTYMILE

CYN

CAT   CYN

2

BEATTY
AIRPORT

BARE MTN
6317'

CARRARA CANYON

TUNGSTEN CANYON

WILDCAT PEAK
5052'

BLACK CONE
3700'

RED CONE
3413'

N Y E   CO.

JACKASS
FLATS

FORTYMILE

CANE   SPRING   WASH

WASH

3

61

NYE CO.
INYO CO.

DEATH

VALLEY

BLACK MARBLE
3655'

NELLIS AIR FORCE BOMBING AND GUNNERY RANGE

TOPOPAH

CHLORIDE   CLIFF   RD

CHLORIDE
CITY

CHLORIDE CLIFF
5279'

AMARGOSA

RIVER

95

AMARGOSA VALLEY

ROCK   VALLEY   WASH

95

4

Death
Valley
National
Monument

DEATH   VALLEY   NATIONAL   MONUMENT

NEVADA
CALIFORNIA

241
TOUR

INYO CO.

LEES

FUNERAL

NYE
INYO
CO
CO

ROCK   VALLEY   WASH

373

5

PARK VILLAGE

(DRY
LAKE)

Harmony
Borax
Works

FURNACE
CREEK
RANCH

Furnace Ck
Borax
Museum

Furnace Creek
Visitor Center

HWY

HILTON

NEVARES
PEAK
2859'

WINTERS PEAK
5033'

Sunset
Texas Springs

Furnace Ck
Inn

CANYON

ECHO

Golden Canyon

GOLDEN   190
CYN   RD

GOWER   GULCH

FUNERAL

MTS

SCHWAUB PEAK
6448'

NATIONAL   MONUMENT

AMARGOSA

RIVER

AMARGOSA

Devils Hole
Death Valley
National Monument

ZABRISKIE POINT RD
Zabriskie Point

FURN

A	B	C	D	E

SEE   MAP

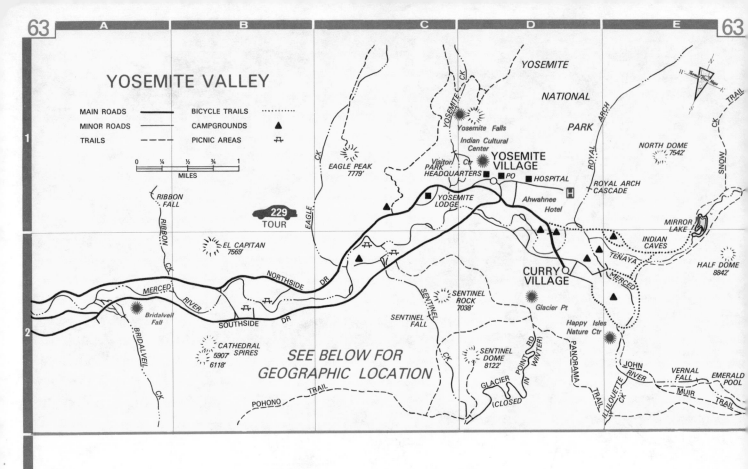

YOSEMITE VALLEY

MAIN ROADS ——
MINOR ROADS —
TRAILS – – –

BICYCLE TRAILS ·······
CAMPGROUNDS ▲
PICNIC AREAS ⛺

0 ¼ ½ ¾ 1
MILES

229 TOUR

SEE BELOW FOR GEOGRAPHIC LOCATION

YOSEMITE NATIONAL PARK

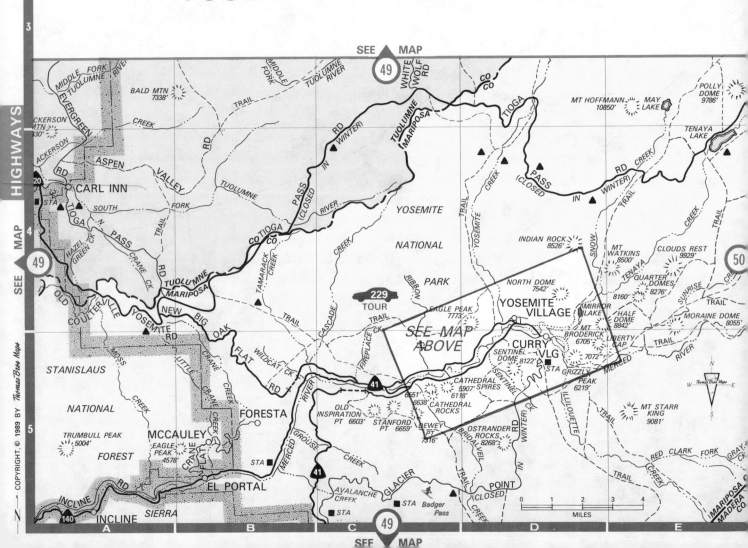

HIGHWAYS

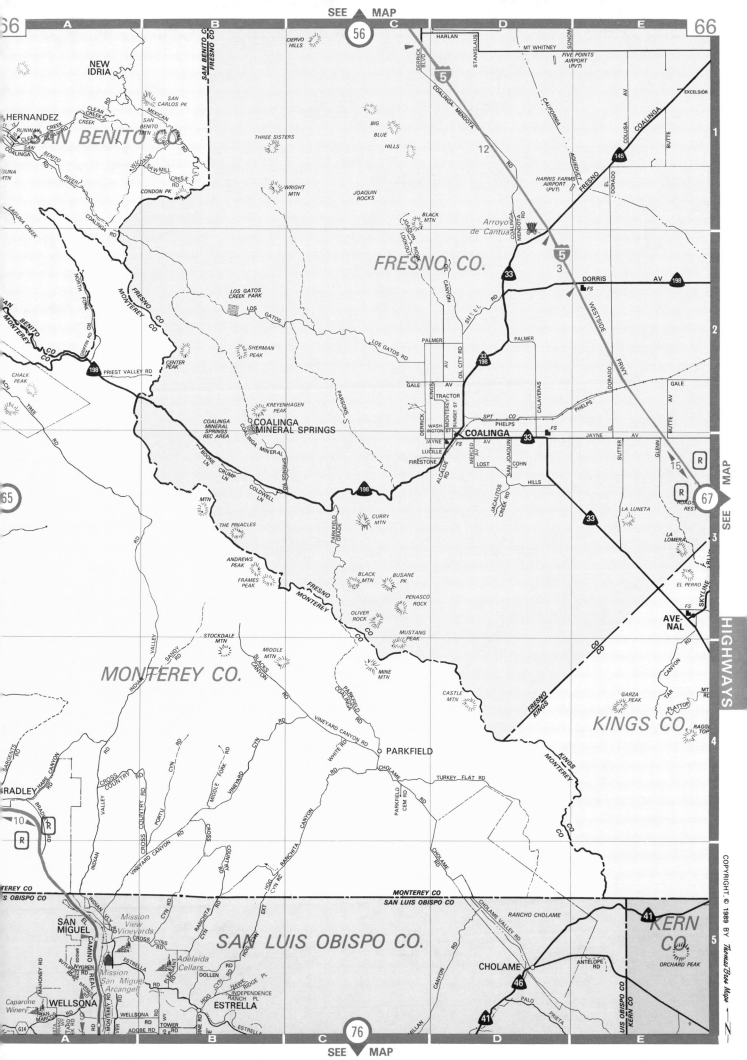

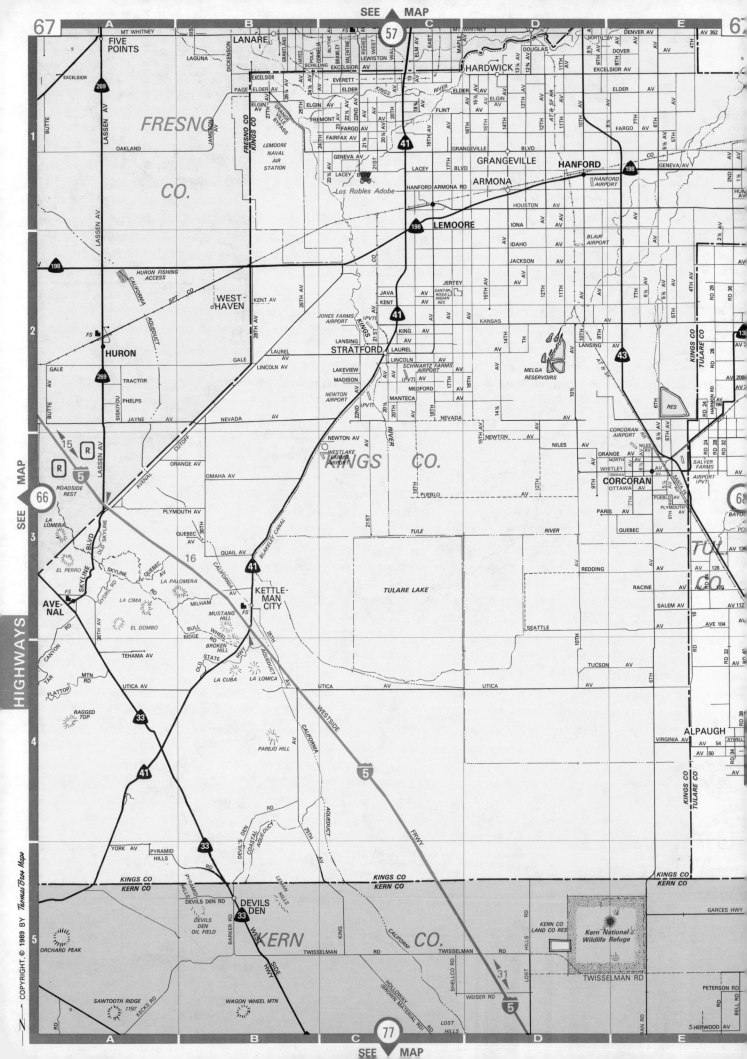

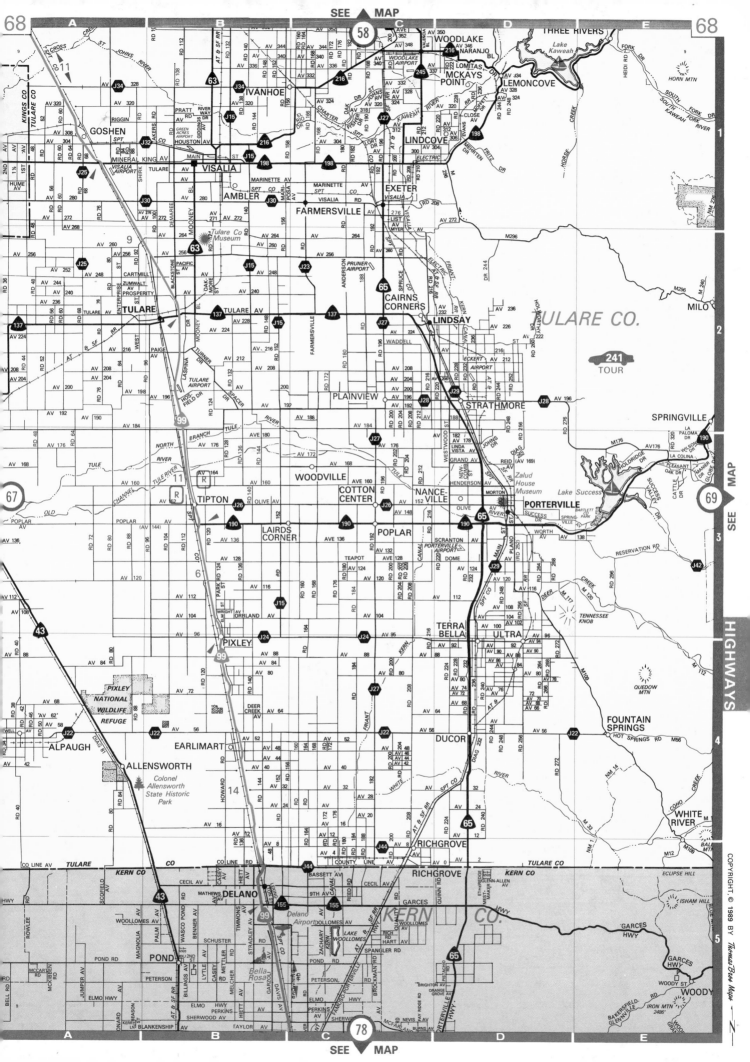

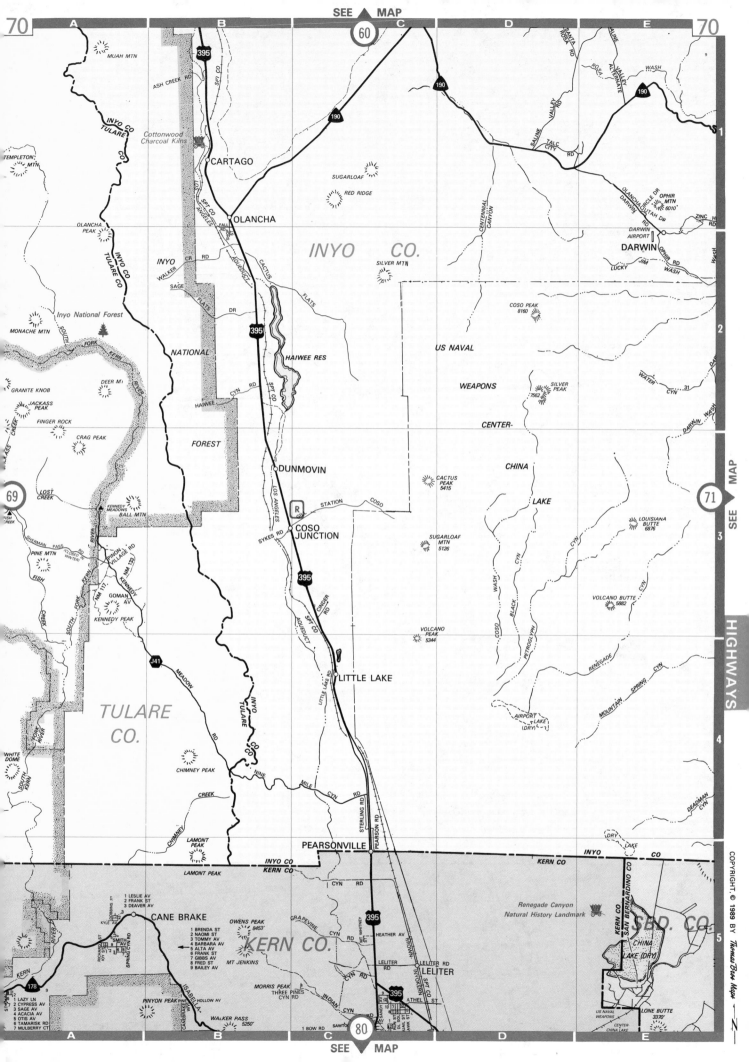

HIGHWAYS

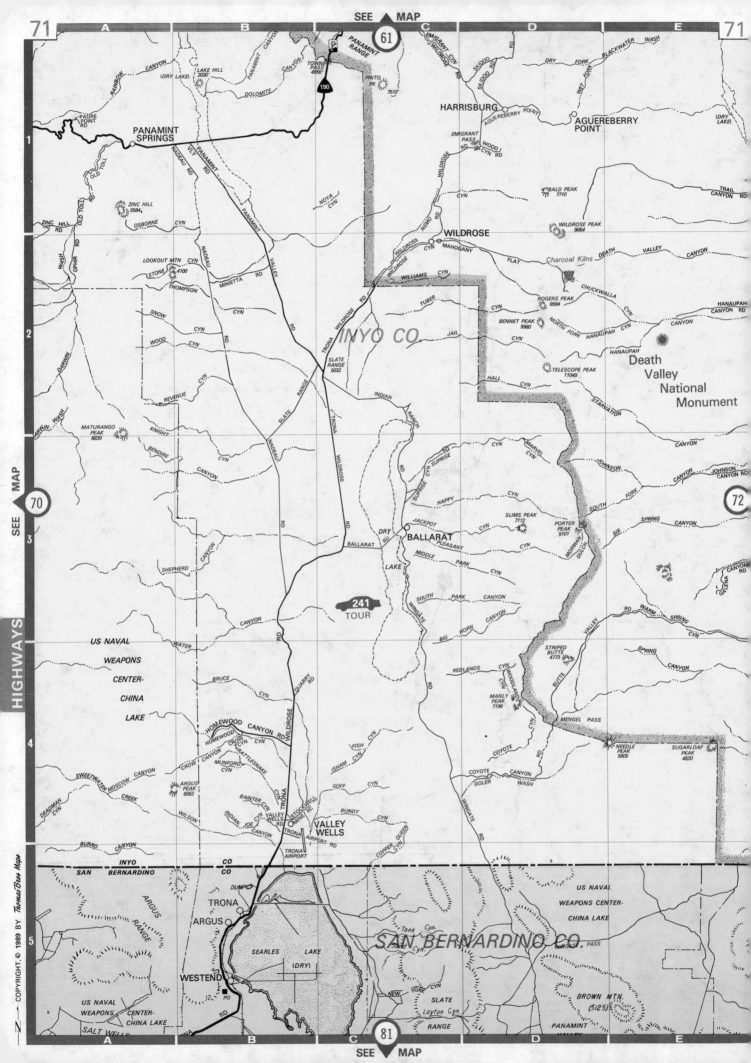

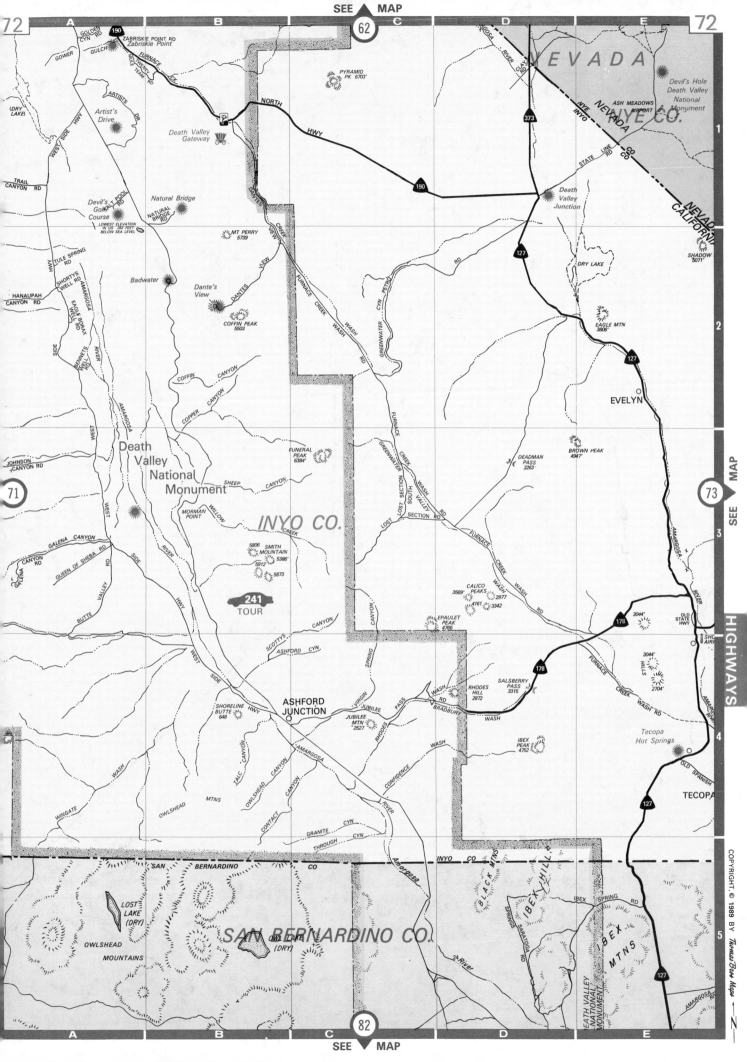

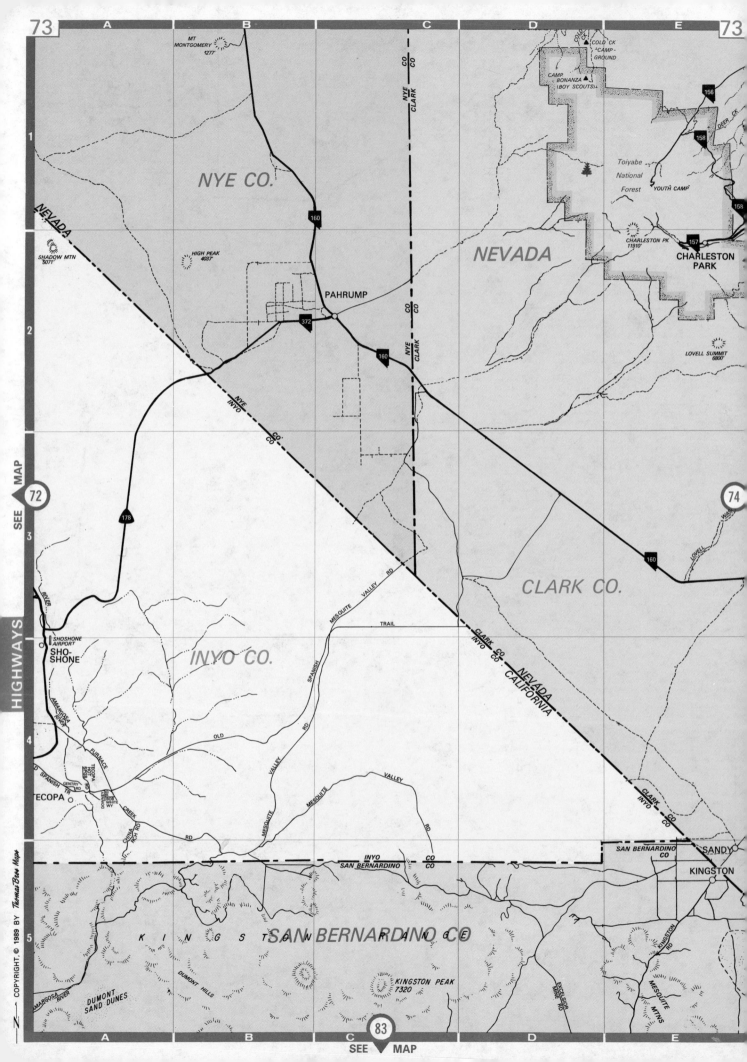

A   B   C   D   E

1

MT
MONTGOMERY
1277'

NYE CO.

COLD CK
COLD CK
"CAMP-
GROUND

CAMP
BONANZA
(BOY SCOUTS)

156

Toiyabe
National
Forest

YOUTH CAMP

158

160

NEVADA

HIGH PEAK
4037'

CHARLESTON PK
11910'

157

CHARLESTON
PARK

158

SHADOW MTN
5071'

NEVADA

PAHRUMP

2

372

160

NYE
CLARK
CO
CO

LOVELL SUMMIT
6800'

NYE
INYO
CO
CO

SEE   MAP
72

178

MESQUITE   VALLEY   RD

TRAIL

CLARK CO.

160

SEE   MAP
74

LOVELL
WASH

3

RIVER

SHOSHONE
AIRPORT

SHO-
SHONE

INYO CO.

CLARK
INYO
CO
CO

NEVADA
CALIFORNIA

SPANISH

AMARGOSA
RIVER

OLD

VALLEY
RD

VALLEY

4

FURNACE

TECOPA
HOT
SPGS

GENTRY
RD

OLD SPANISH
TR

KINGSE
WHITE
HWY

TECOPA

CHINA
RANCH RD

CREEK

MESQUITE

VALLEY

RD

CLARK
INYO
CO

SAN BERNARDINO
CO

SANDY

KINGSTON

RD

INYO
SAN BERNARDINO

CO
CO

KINGSTON
RD

MESQUITE
MTNS

5

K I N G S T O N   SAN BERNARDINO CO

KINGSTON PEAK
7320'

EXCELSIOR
MINE RD

DUMONT
SAND DUNES

DUMONT HILLS

AMARGOSA
RIVER

N

83
SEE   MAP

A   B   C   D   E

GASS PK
6940'

DESERT NATIONAL
WILDLIFE RANGE

NELLIS
SMALL ARMS
RANGE

156

158

TOIYABE

NATIONAL

FOREST

158

157

157

ANGEL
PK
8847'

157

CHARLESTON
PARK

N E V A D A

15

93

RR

RANCHO

North Las Vegas
Air Terminal

PACIFIC

UNION

95

604

Nellis
AIR FORCE
BASE

OWENS

BLVD

LAS
VEGAS

NORTH
LAS VEGAS

BONANZA   RD

LOVELL SUMMIT
6800'

E15

FREMONT

RED
ROCK
SUMMIT
6300'

CHARLESTON

BOULEVARD

LAMB

W

SAHARA   AV

SAHARA   AV

209

73

LOVELL

WASH

PICNIC AREA

BLUE DIAMOND

R
ROADSIDE REST

MOUNTAIN
SPRINGS

160

160

BLVD

PARADISE

10

210

LAS VEGAS

93

95

TROPICANA   AV

McCARRAN
INT'L AIRPORT

HENDERSON

SUNSET

UNION

PACIFIC

RR

LAKE   MEAD
DR

160

ARDEN

15

604

146

POTOSI MTN
8504'

C L A R K   C O.

SLOAN

RR

PACIFIC

22

UNION

SHENANDOAH PK
CAIRN 5866'

GOODSPRINGS

161

JEAN
4

JEAN
LAKE

604

SANDY

KINGSTON

BONANZA

SINGER

WASH

WASH

N E V A D A

C A L I F O R N I A

S.B.D. CO.

LITTLE DEVIL PK
5570'

MESQUITE
LAKE
(DRY)

MESQUITE
MTNS

DEVIL PK
5580'

22

15

R
ROADSIDE
REST

ROACH   LAKE

BEER BOTTLE PASS
3500'

SEE MAP
65

PT SIERRA NEVADA

GARRITY PEAK

RANCHO PIEDRA BLANCA

Hearst San Simeon State Historic Monument

PINE MTN

BLACK OAK MTN
ROCKY BUTTE

CABRILLO

PT PIEDRAS BLANCAS

SAN SIMEON PT

SAN SIMEON

SAN SIMEON BAY

Best Western Cavalier Inn

RED MTN

SAN SIMEON CK. RD.

GORDON RD

RANCHO SAN SIMEON

SAN SIMEON CK

KLAU

ADELAIDA

G14

CHIMNEY ROCK

CYPRESS MTN

L'YPRESS MTN

LIME MTN

ANGEL

RUNNING DEER RD

CHIMNEY

FARM

ROCK

CYPRESS

MTN DR

KLAU MINE RD

GATEWAY DR

NACIMIENTO LAKE

SAN MARC

ADELAIDA

KILER

WILLOW RD

NIDEVER

PEACHY

JENSEN RD

VINEYARD DR

DOVER CYN

OAKDALE

SAN LUIS OBISPO CO.

Wm. Randolph Hearst State Beach

San Simeon State Beach

SIMEON

CAMBRIA

SCOTT ROCK

SANTA ROSA CREEK

NORTHERLY BRANCH GREEN VLY RD

BLACK MTN RD

DOVER

SHADOW CYN RD

YORK MTN RD

JACK CREEK RD

PASO DE

RANCHO

Pesenti

Moonstone Inn Motel
Mariners Inn

MAIN ST

RANCHO

GREEN

VALLEY

233
TOUR

46

York Mountain

CAMBRIA AIR FORCE STA

SANTA ROSA

HARMONY VLY

RANCHO SAN

PICACHO

THUNDER CYN RD

COTTONTAIL CK RD

SANTA

RITA

RANCHO ASUNCION

SAN G

TORO CREEK

PACIFIC

HARMONY

VILLA CREEK RD

GERONIMO

RD

WHALE ROCK RES

OLD CREEK

PARK RANGE PEAK

OCEAN

CAYUCOS

Cayucos State Beach

Morro Strand State Beach

MONTECITO RD

RANCHO MORO Y CAYUCOS

Breakers Motel

Atascadero State Beach

ESTERO

MORRO BAY

SAN BERNARDO CK RD

76

Morro Rock

CABRILLO HWY

MORRO BAY STATE PARK

HOLLISTER PEAK

SAN CK

CABRI

1

Morro Bay Aquarium

MORRO BAY

SANTA YSABEL RD

BAYWOOD PARK

RANCHO CANADA DE LOS Y PECHO Y

Morro Bay Museum Of Natural History

Morro Bay State Park

9TH ST

LOS OSOS

LOS OSOS VALLEY RD

CUESTA BY-THE-SEA

Los Osos Oaks State Reserve

Montana De Oro State Park

LOS OSOS VALLEY RD

PREFUMO CYN RD

SEE CYN

RANCHO

CANADA DE

SADDLE PEAK

LOS OSOS

GREEN PEAK

PG&E NUCLEAR POWER PLANT

Y PECHO Y ISLAY

BAE

RANCH

SAN LUIS HILL

PT SAN LU

PACIFIC

OCEAN

N

WELLSONA

ESTRELLA

Caparone Winery

Arciero Winery

Estrella River Winery

WHITLEY GARDENS

46

SHANDON

41

LUCY BROWN RD

KERN CO.

PASO ROBLES

Martin Bros Winery

Eberle

Paso Robles Muni Airport

Mastantuono Winery

El Paso Santa Ysabel De Robles Winery

TEMPLETON

ATASCADERO

41

CRESTON

SAN LUIS OBISPO CO.

41

RED HILLS

229

233 TOUR

58

Creston Manor

58

BLACK MTN

Los Padres

GARDEN FARMS

58

SANTA MARGARITA

Rancho Santa Margarita

CAMP SAN LUIS OBISPO MILITARY RES

Santa Margarita Lake

LOS PADRES NATIONAL FOREST

LA PANZA

NATIONAL FOREST

PINE MTN

SEE MAP 77

SAN LUIS OBISPO

WOOD PARK

OSOS

BLACK BUTTE

Los Padres National Forest

Lopez Mtn

POZO

GARCIA MTN

MACHESNA MTN

172

227

Edna Valley Vineyard

EDNA

Lopez Lake

LOS PADRES NATIONAL FOREST

BIG BALDY

LOS PADRES NATIONAL FOREST

AVILA BEACH

San Luis Bay Inn

Shore Cliff Lodge

PISMO BEACH

227

BIDDLE REGIONAL PARK

Corbett Canyon

Avila State Beach

PT SAN LUIS

SHELL BEACH

GROVER CITY

Maison Deutz Winery

ARROYO GRANDE

HUASNA

OCEANO

Pismo State Beach

101

NIPOMO

Pismo Dunes State Vehicular Rec Area

Callender Black Lake

Ross-Keller

101 FWY

SHELL PEAK

TWITCHELL RESERVOIR

LOS COCHES MT

SANTA BARBARA CO.

PACIFIC

GUADALUPE

166

SANTA MARIA

166

San Luis Obispo Guadalupe Dunes County Park

SAN LUIS OBISPO CO. / SANTA BARBARA CO.

HIGHWAYS

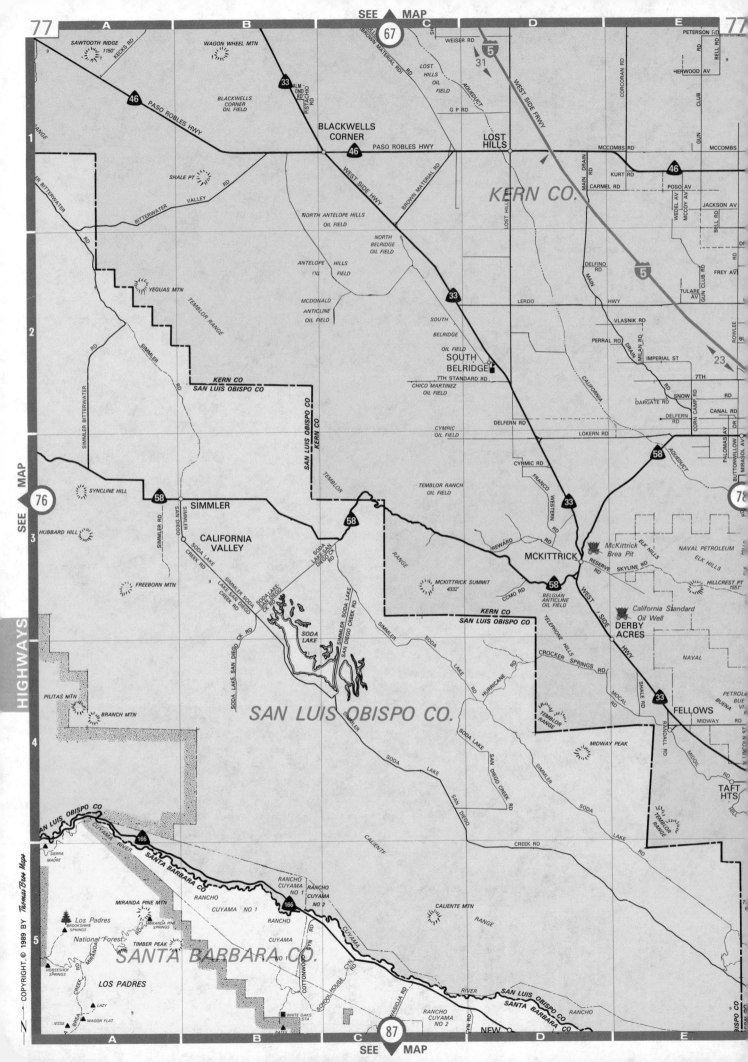

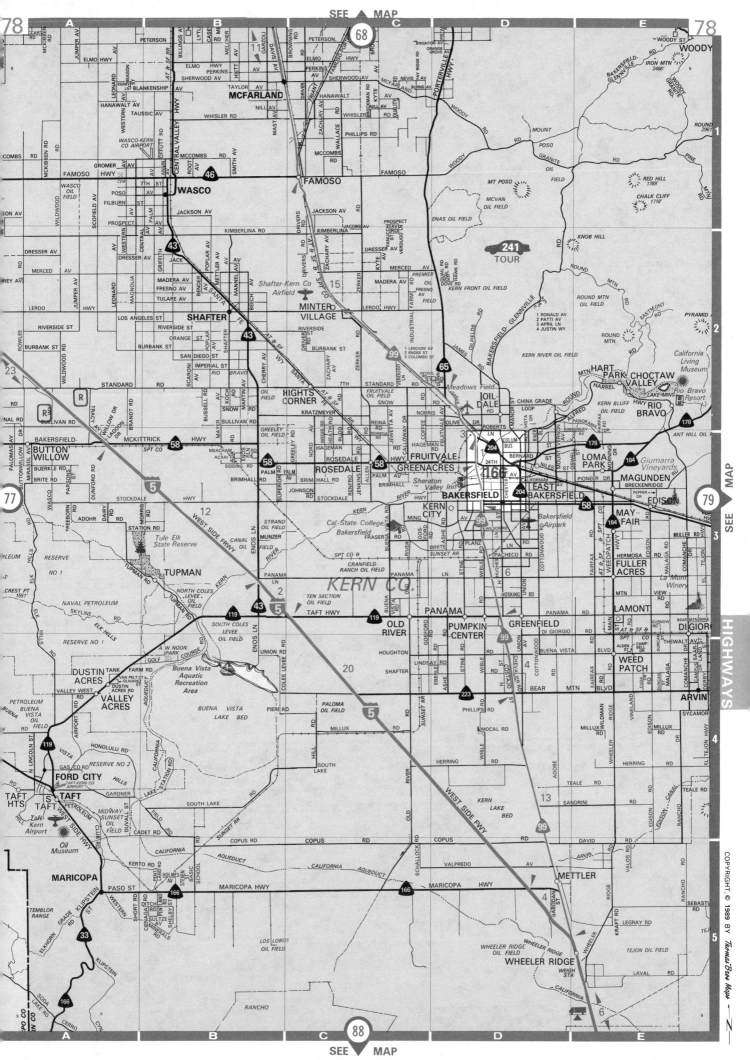

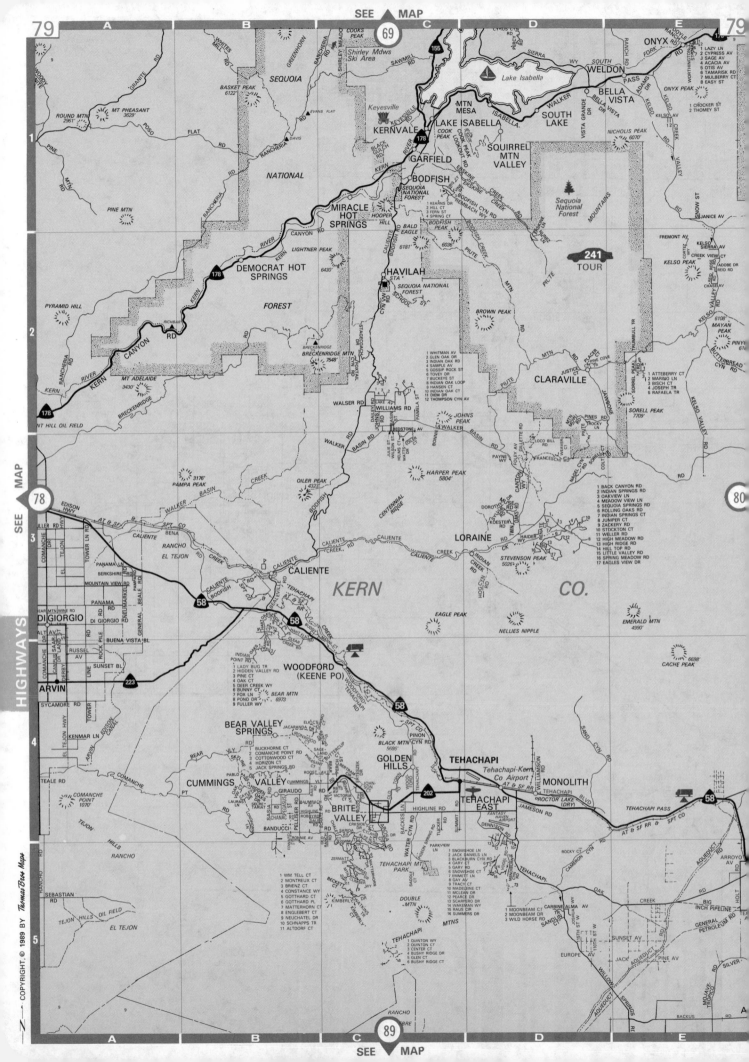

US NAVAL WEAPONS CENTER-CHINA LAKE

SALT WELLS VALLEY

TRONA

178

SALT WELLS CANYON

SPANGLER HILLS

Trona Pinnacles

SLATE

Layton Cyn.

RANGE

BROWN MTN. (5125)

PANAMINT VALLEY

US NAVAL WEAPONS CENTER-

CHINA LAKE

PILOT KNOB VALLEY

US NAVAL

WEAPONS

CENTER-

CHINA LAKE

RANDSBURG RD

RESERVATION

SAN MILITARY

Christmas Cyn.

RANDSBURG RD

DOME MTN 4985

LINKER MTN 5670

BLACK HILLS

ROBBERS MTN. 4530

PILOT KNOB 5428

EAGLE CRAGS

GRANIT

WELLS RD

CUDDEBACK LAKE

AF GUNNERY RANGE

SAN BERNARDINO CO.

GRASS VALLEY

SLOCUM MTN. 5124

SLOCUM MTN RD

SUPERIOR VALLEY

SEE MAP 80

82

CUDDEBACK LAKE (DRY)

HOFFMAN

US NAVAL WEAPONS CENTER CHINA LAKE

OLD

US NAVAL WEAPONS CENTER - CHINA LAKE

COPPER CITY RD

SUPERIOR LAKE (DRY)

GOLDSTONE

FREMONT PK 4584

GRAVEL HILLS

FREMONT PEAK RD

BLACK CANYON

COPPER CITY RD

BLACK CANYON RD

COPPER CITY RD

INDIAN

PARADISE SPRINGS

DOBSON RD

LANE MTN. 4522

LOCKHART

OPAL MOUNTAIN

OPAL MTN. 3950

BLACK MTN. 3939

COOLGARDIE RD

COOLGARDIE RD

WILLIAMS WELL RD

STARBRIGHT MINE

PALMETTO ST

HOFFMAN RD

GEORGIA RD

LUCINDA RD

BLACK

Rainbow Basin Owl Canyon

RAINBOW BASIN

COPPER CITY RD

LOCKHART RD

HOFFMAN RD

HARPER LAKE (DRY)

FOSSIL BED RD

LOCKHART

HALSTEAD

HOLSTEAD

HINKLEY RD

FOSSIL BED RD

BURNT TREE RD

MOUNTAIN VIEW RD

THOMPSON RD

DUMP

BISHOP RD

LARK HAVEN RD

WEBSTER RD

FORT IRWIN

YERMO CUTOFF

SANTA FE AV

AT & SF RR

A | B | SEE MAP 72 | C | D | E |

QUAIL
MOUNTAINS

GRANITE

MOUNTAINS

MCLEAN
LAKE
(DRY)

NELSON LAKE
(DRY)

GOLDSTONE
LAKE
(DRY)

81

FORT IRWIN
MILITARY RESERVATION

FORT
IRWIN

PARADISE
RANGE

STARBRIGHT
MINE
RD

JACKHAMMER
GAP

CALICO
MTNS

PICKHANDLE PASS

CALICO
GHOST
TOWN

DORAN
SCENIC DR

PHILLIPS
DR

MULE CANYON RD

YERMO
CUTOFF

LEACH LAKE
(DRY)

OWL
HOLE
SPRING

FORT   IRWIN

AVAWATZ
MOUNTAINS

DEATH VALLEY NATIONAL MONUMENT

DEATH VAL
NATIONAL
MONUMENT

SARATOGA
SPRINGS
(IRWIN)

AMARGOSA

SALT   CK

SHEEP
SPRING
CREEK
RD

RD)

MILITARY   RESERVATION

AVAWATZ

DRINKWATER LAKE
(DRY)

MOUNTAINS

GRANITE

MOUNTAINS

AVAWATZ
MOUNTAINS

SAN BERNARDINO CO.

MILITARY   RESERVATION

FORT   IRWIN

BICYCLE
LAKE (DRY)

TIEFORT

MOUNTAINS

RED PASS LAKE
(DRY)

LANGFORD WELL
LAKE (DRY)

FORT

IRWIN   MILITARY   RES

ALVORD MTN
3456

COYOTE
LAKE
(DRY)

COYOTE LAKE RD

ALVORD MTN RD

PARADISE SPRINGS

PARADISE SPRINGS RD

PARADISE
SPRINGS
RD

FORT
IRWIN

CALICO
MTNS
ARCHAEOLOGICAL
PROJECT

WEST CRONESE
LAKE (DRY)

CRONESE MTNS

EAST
LAKE

ARROWHEAD
LAKE

CAVE
MOUNTAIN

BASIN

UNION

15   26

AFTON

CANYON

AFTON CANYON
RECREATION
AREA

CLYDE V KANE
ROADSIDE
REST

R

RR

18

15

YERMO RD   UNION

1 LA PEER RD
2 PICASSO RD
3 FLAX ST

CARDIFF ST

DESERT VIEW RD

COYOTE LAKE RD

HARVARD

CHEROKEE
RD

River

SEE MAP 92

83

SEE MAP

HIGHWAYS

N

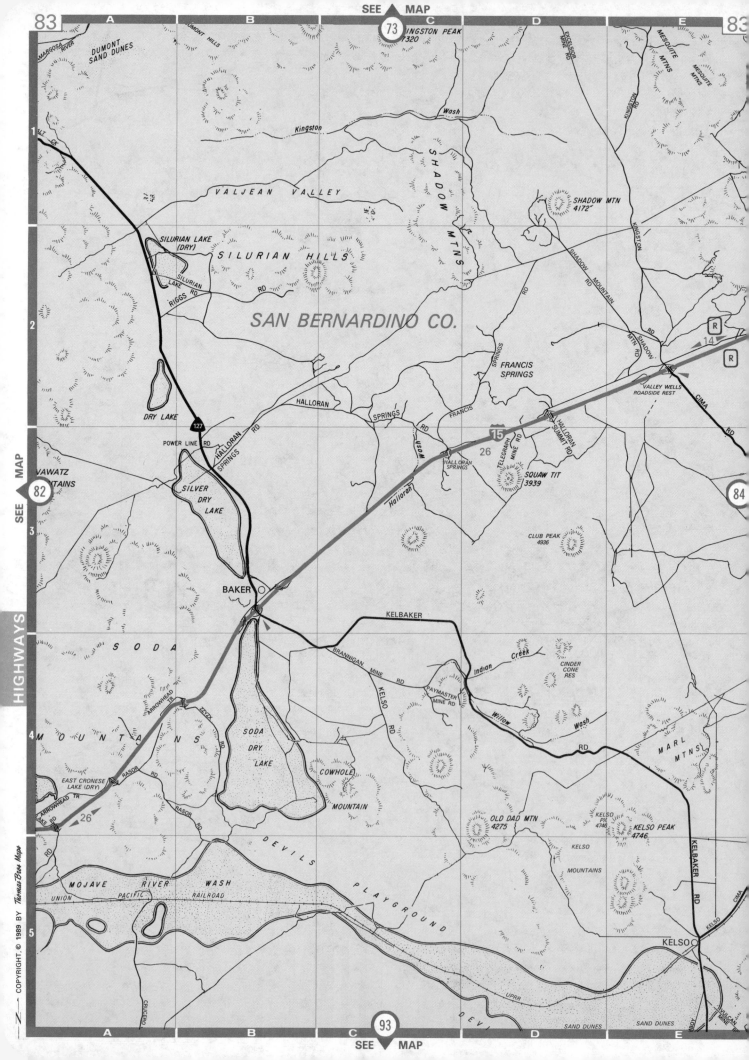

A   B   SEE MAP   C   74   D   E

MESQUITE
LAKE
(DRY)

DEVIL PK
5580'

15

22

ROADSIDE
REST

ROACH LAKE

BEER BOTTLE PASS
3500'

CLARK

MOUNTAIN

RANGE

CLARK
MTN 7903'

MOHAWK
HILL
5948'

MOUNTAIN
PASS

15

Wheaton

R

14

MESCAL
RANGE

KOKOWEEF
PK 6038'

1

McCULLOUGH MTN
6996'

N E V A D A

164

164

IVANPAH
LAKE

(DRY)

YATES
WELL RD

15

Wash

WHEATON SPRINGS

NIPTON

2

NIPTON   RD

CLARK   CO.

CLARK CO.

83

ZINC MINE RD

ZINC MINE

DEEP SPRINGS RD

KESSLER PEAK
6163

MORNING STAR CUTOFF RD

MORNING STAR MINE

IVANPAH-
CIMA RD

TEUTONIA
PK
5710

DEEP SPRING RD

MORNING STAR MINE RD

CIMA

CIMA RD

CIMA

CIMA   RD

CIMA

IVANPAH

BRANT

IVANPAH

UNION

BRANT

CIMA

SADDLE
HORN
RD

IVANPAH   VALLEY

CASTLE PEAKS
5829

IVANPAH

LEASTALK RD
SAN PEDRO
AV

QUARTZ

RD

NEW   YORK   MOUNTAINS

BARNWELL
TOWN SITE

HART
MINE RD

HART MINE RD

85

CASTLE
MTNS

NEVADA
CALIFORNIA

PIUTE

VALLEY

3

MID HILLS

JOSHUA
FOREST

NEW YORK
MOUNTAINS

THEODORIC RD
HUN RD

HOLMES RD

HANCOCK RD

ATTLA RD

FRANKLIN RD

MOUNTAIN

SAN

NEW

NEW   YORK

LANFAIR   RD

BERNARDINO

LANFAIR

NEW YORK   RD

LANDING STRIP

VALLEY

CO.

PIUTE   RANGE

HIGHWAYS

PINTO
MTN

ROUND
VALLEY

CANYON RD

PROVIDENCE RANCH RD

CEDAR

CANYON   RD

CEDAR   RD

GROTTO HILLS

BOBCAT
HILLS

BELSHAW
RD

CHUKKER
TR
PIGEON PASS

VONTRIGGER HILLS

LANFAIR   RD

4

COLUMBIA MTN
5673

TABLE MTN
6176

GOLD   VALLEY

BLACK CANYON RD

FS
(SEASONAL)

WOODS   MOUNTAINS

HACKBERRY MTN
4531

HACKBERRY   MTN

LANFAIR   RD

BILLIE
MTN
3296

SIGNAL HILL
3500

5

UPRR
GLOBE

MINE   RD

CIMA   RD

KELSO

KELSO

PROVIDENCE   MOUNTAINS

COLTON
HILLS

BLACK   CANYON RD

PROVIDENCE MTNS
STATE
REC AREA

FOUNTAIN
PEAK 5996'

F E N N E R

A   B   C   94   D   E

SEE MAP

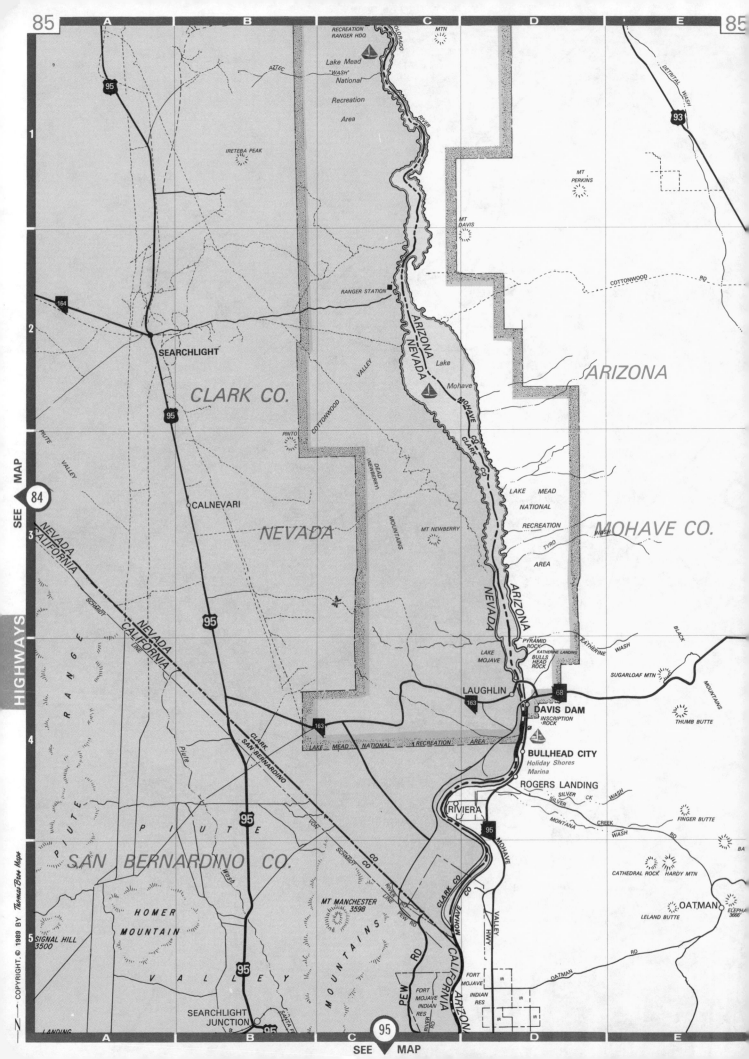

A B C D E

1

2

3

4

5

A B C D E

HIGHWAYS

RECREATION RANGER HDQ
Lake Mead
"WASH" National
Recreation
Area

AZTEC

COLORADO
MTN

DETRITAL WASH

95

93

MT
PERKINS

IRETEBA PEAK

MT
DAVIS

COTTONWOOD   RD

164

SEARCHLIGHT

RANGER STATION

ARIZONA
NEVADA

Lake
Mohave

ARIZONA

95

CLARK CO.

COTTONWOOD

VALLEY

MOHAVE   CO.

SEE MAP 84

PIUTE

VALLEY

NEVADA
CALIFORNIA

CALNEVARI

PINTO

DEAD
(NEWBERRY)

MOUNTAINS

MT NEWBERRY

LAKE   MEAD

NATIONAL

RECREATION

TYRO

AREA

MOHAVE CO.

NEVADA

NEVADA
CALIFORNIA LINE

SCHMIDT

R A N G E

95

CLARK
SAN BERNARDINO

163

PIUTE

PYRAMID
ROCK
KATHERINE LANDING
BULLS
HEAD
ROCK

LAKE
MOJAVE

KATHERINE   WASH

BLACK

SUGARLOAF MTN

LAUGHLIN

163

68

DAVIS DAM
INSCRIPTION
ROCK

MOUNTAINS

THUMB BUTTE

LAKE   MEAD   NATIONAL   RECREATION   AREA

BULLHEAD CITY
Holiday Shores
Marina

ROGERS LANDING

SILVER   CK   WASH

SILVER

P I U T E

PIUTE

WASH

95

SAN   BERNARDINO   CO.

VON
SCHMIDT
RIVER RD

CLARK CO.

RIVIERA

95

MONTANA   CREEK

WASH   RD

FINGER BUTTE

BA

MOJAVE   CO.

HOMER

MOUNTAIN

SIGNAL HILL
3500

MT MANCHESTER
3598

MOUNTAINS

SANTA FE

PEW RD

PEW RD

MOHAVE

VALLEY

HWY

CALIFORNIA
ARIZONA

CATHEDRAL ROCK   HARDY MTN

OATMAN

LELAND BUTTE

ELEPHA
3666'

SEARCHLIGHT
JUNCTION

95

FORT
MOJAVE
INDIAN
RES

FORT
MOJAVE
INDIAN
RES

IR

OATMAN   RD

IR

IR

IR

RD

LANDING

95

95

SEE MAP

N

86 | A B C D E | 86

SANTA BARBARA CO.

Cities & Towns:
GUADALUPE
SANTA MARIA
BETTERAVIA
ORCUTT
CASMALIA
GAREY
SISQUOC
LOS ALAMOS
LOMPOC
SURF
LOS OLIVOS
BALLARD
BUELLTON
SANTA YNEZ
Solvang
LAS CRUCES
GAVIOTA

Parks & Landmarks:
RANCHO GUADALUPE DUNES COUNTY PARK
MUSSEL ROCK
Point Sal State Beach
PT SAL
RANCHO GUADALUPE
RANCHO CASMALIA
CASMALIA HILLS MT LOSPE
VANDENBERG AIR FORCE BASE
RANCHO JESUS MARIA
Santa Maria Airport
RANCHO PUNTA DE LA LAGUNA
RANCHO TODOS SANTOS Y SAN ANTONIO
Mission La Purisima Concepcion
La Purisma Mission State Historic Park
Space Shuttle Launch Complex
VANDENBERG AIR FORCE BASE
RANCHO LOMPO
TRANQUILLON MTN
PT PEDERNALES
PT ARGUELLO
RANCHO PUNTA DE LA CONCEPCION
RANCHO SAN JULIAN
RANCHO CANADA DE SALSIPUEDES
RANCHO SANTA RITA
RANCHO SANTA ROSA
Sanford Winery
Vega Vineyards
Santa Rosa Co Park
RANCHO LAS CRUCES
PALO ALTO HILL
JALAMA PK
RANCHO PUNTA DE LA CONCEPCION
PT CONCEPCION
GOVERNMENT PT
COJO BAY
RANCHO NUESTRA SENORA DEL REFUGIO
Nojoqui Falls County Park
Gaviota State Park
Refugio State Beach
REFUGIO STA
Mission Santa Ines
The Gainey Santa Ynez Valley Winery
J. Carey Vineyard
Best Western Danish Inn
Ramada Inn
Best Western Flagwaver Motor Hotel
Ballard Cyn Winery
Austin Cellars
Brander Vineyard
Ross-Keller Winery
Byron Winery
Rancho Sisquoc Winery
Zaca Mesa Winery
Firestone Winery
RANCHO LA LAGUNA
RANCHO LA ZACA
RANCHO CORRAL DE QUATI
RANCHO SAN CARLOS JONATA
RANCHO NOJOQUI
LOS PADRES
Los Padres National Forest
TEPUSQUET PEAK
BONE MTN
MANZANITA MTN
LOOKOUT MTN
LAZY WAGON FLAT
LA BREA
JESSE
COLSON STA
RANCHO SUEY
RANCHO LOS ALAMOS
SOLOMON HILLS
RANCHO LOS ALAMOS
TINAQUAIC

Highways:
1, 20, 76, 87, 135, 166, 173, 101, 233 TOUR, 246, 26, 9, 6
EL CAMINO REAL
RTE 101 FRWY
FWY 20

Water:
OCEAN
PACIFIC OCEAN
SANTA BARBARA CHANNEL
COJO BAY
SANTA MARIA RIVER
SANTA YNEZ RIVER
JALAMA CREEK
EL JARO CREEK
SANTA ROSA

SEE MAP 87

HIGHWAYS

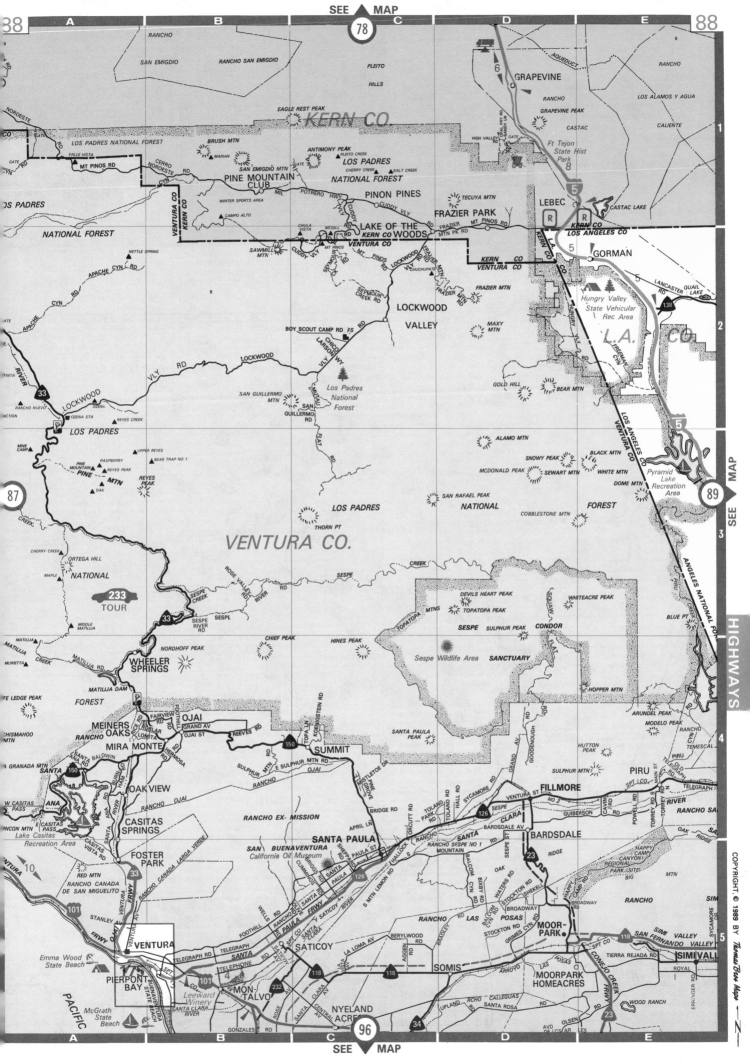

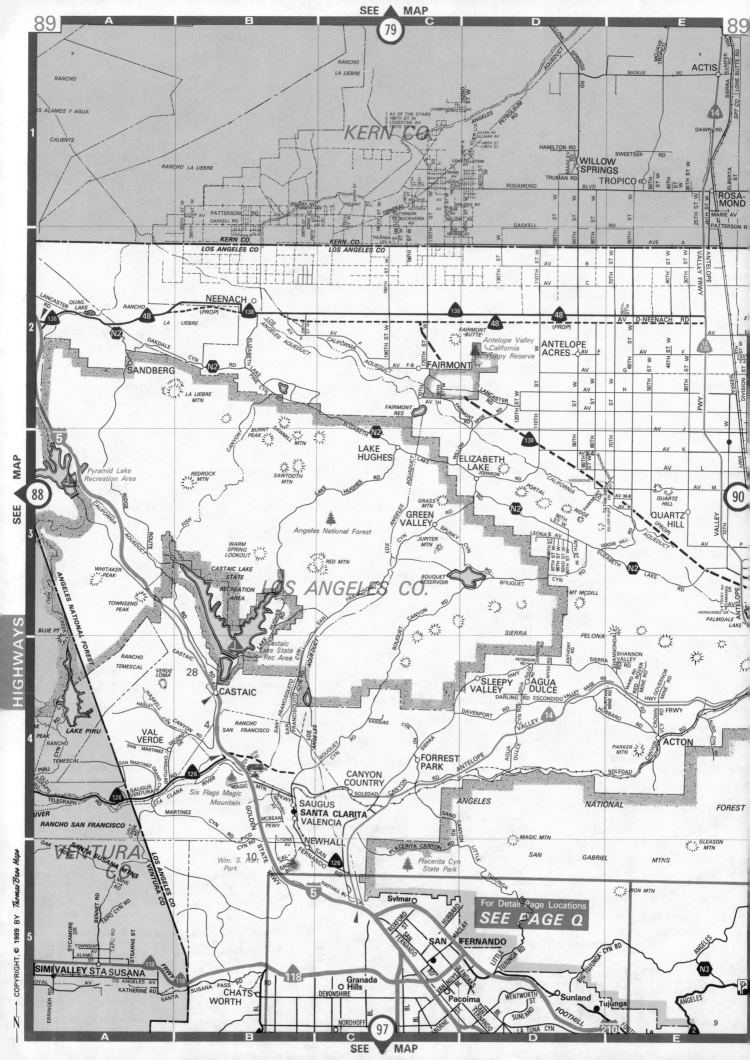

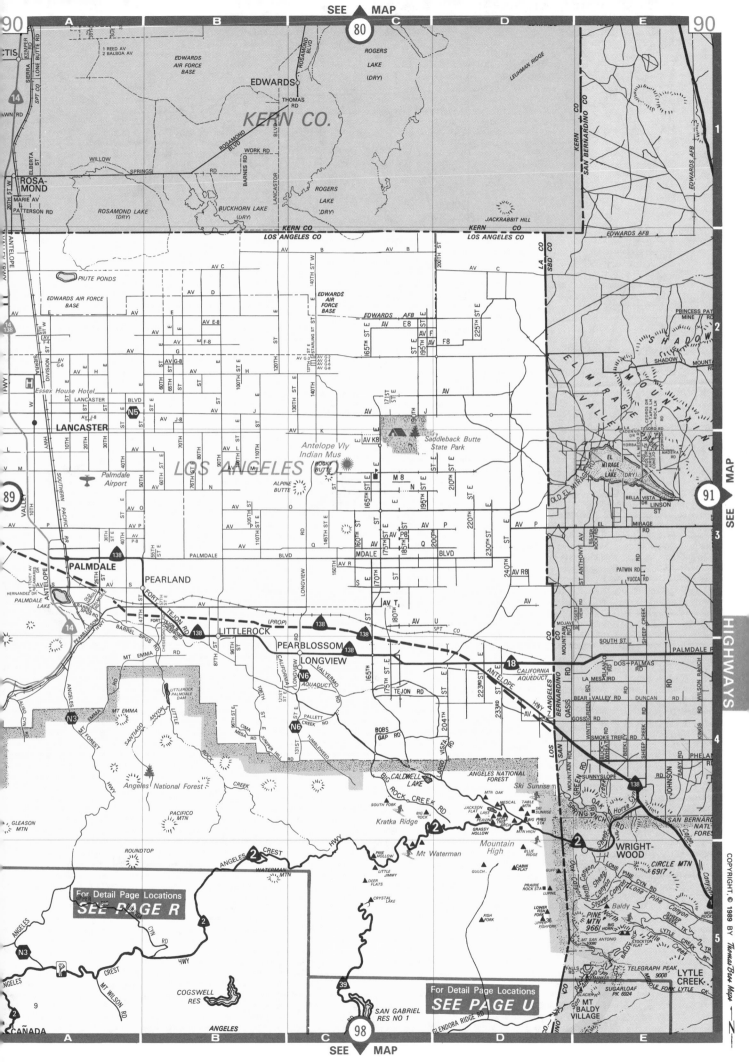

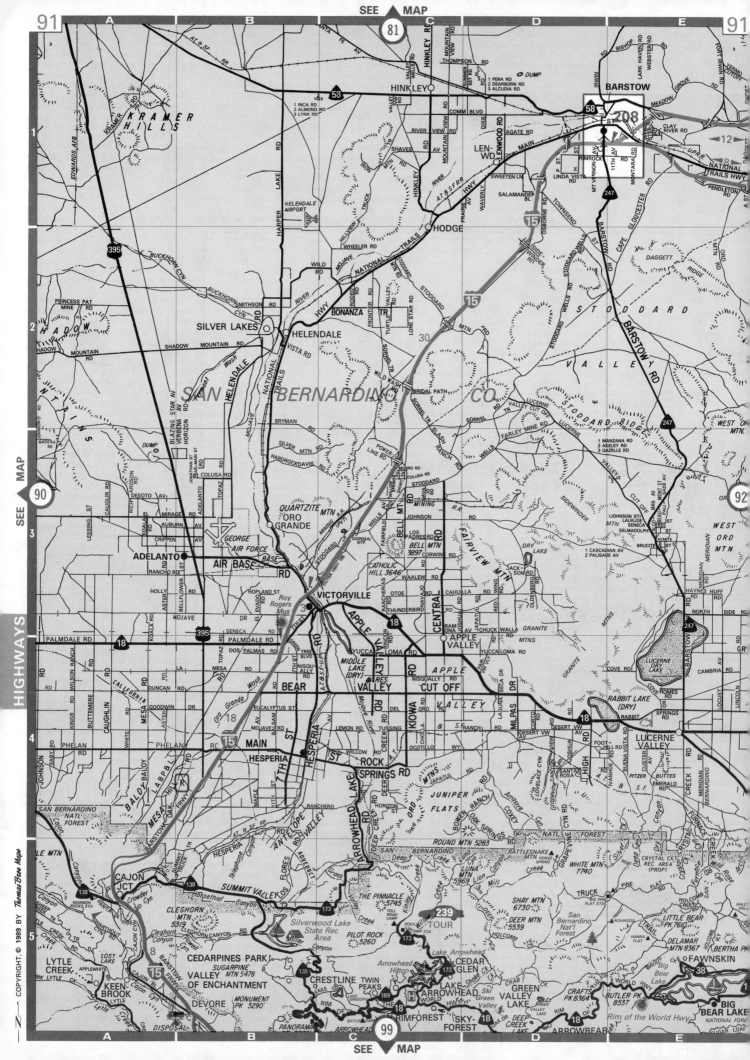

A B C D E

1

DEVILS

SAND DUNES

KELSO

PLAYGROUND

DUNES

GRANITE
MOUNTAINS

BROADWELL LAKE
(DRY)

UPRR

KELSO AMBO

32

2

OLD DAD

40

MOUNTAINS

56

KELBAKER

NATIONAL TRAILS HWY

KELBAKER RD

LUDLOW RD
ELLIOT ST
MAIN ST

AT & SF RR

LAVIC RD

LUDLOW

NATIONAL

TRAILS

HWY

BAGDAD CHASE RD

KLONDIKE RD

SIBERIA ROADSIDE REST

LAVA HILLS

BRISTOL
MOUNTAINS

94

3

USMC TRAINING CTR

NATIONAL

TRAILS

AT AND SF RR

HWY

LANDING STRIP

AMBOY

MOUNTAINS

NATIONAL TRAILS HWY

SAN BERNARDINO CO.

WAY

BAGDAD

DRY
LAKE

LAVA

USMC TRAINING CTR

AMBOY
CUT-OFF
AMBOY
CRATER

CRATER RD

AMBOY RD

SALTUS

NOBLE PASS

BULLION

MTNS

LEAD MTN
2891

SALT
EVAPORATOR

HIDALGO MTN

RAINBOW CYN

WOOD
CANYON

BULLION
MTNS

LAVA

BAGDAD HWY

BAGDAD

HWY

BRISTOL

(DRY)

4

RAINBOW
BULLION
Wash

GYPSUM
RIDGE

CENTER

AMBOY RD

BULLION MOUNTAINS

TRAINING

DEADMAN
LAKE
(DRY)

CLEGHORN PASS

SURPRISE SPRINGS RD

AIRSTRIP

CANYON RD

USMC

TRAINING CTR

USMC

CLEGHORN
LAKES (DRY)

HOT springs RD

RECHE RD

AV

CLEGHORN
LAKES
(DRY)

BULLION
MOUNTAINS

5

SURPRISE
SPRINGS RD

GIANT
RD

VALLEY RD

SHOSHONE VALLEY RD

MESQUITE
SPRINGS
CANYON RD

AV
RD
POLELINE
COYOTE
RD
CASCADE
ROCK RD

MESQUITE
LAKE (DRY)

101

VALLEY MTN

A B C D E

N

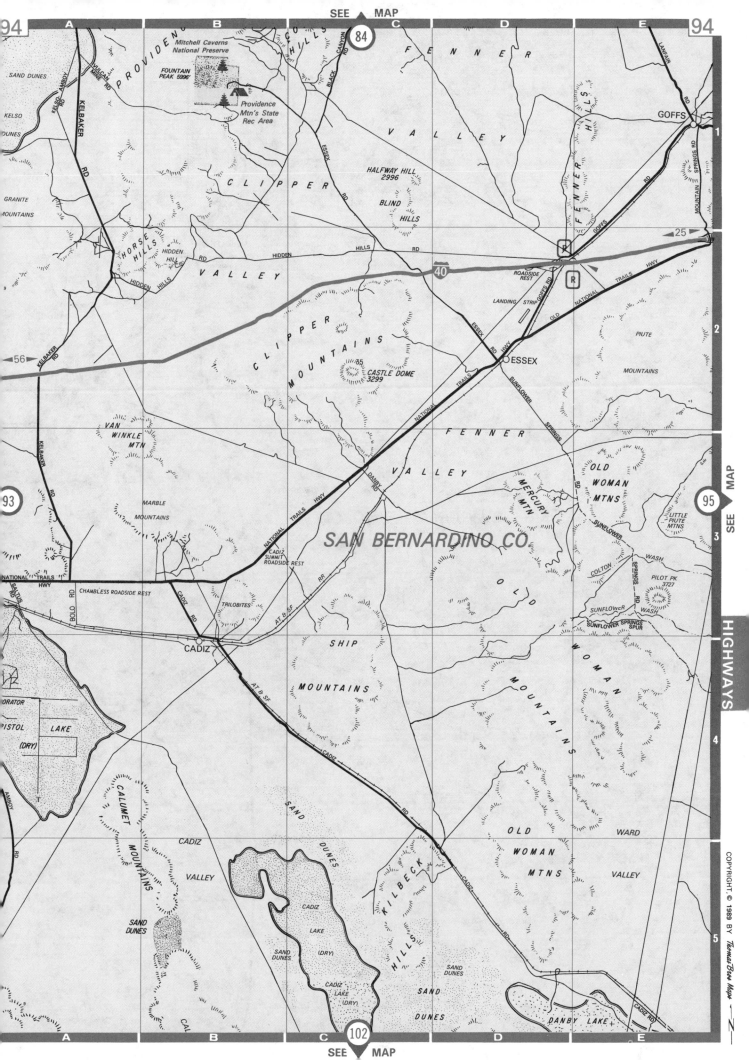

SEE MAP
84

A | B | CO. | C | D | E

PROVIDENCE

Mitchell Caverns
National Preserve

FOUNTAIN
PEAK 5996'

Providence Mtn's
State Rec Area

HILLS

BLACK CANYON RD

FENNER

VALLEY

FENNER HILLS

LANFAIR RD

GOFFS

1

SAND DUNES

VULCAN MINE RD

KELBAKER RD

KELSO AMBOY RD

ESSEX RD

CLIPPER

HALFWAY HILL
2996

BLIND
HILLS

MOUNTAIN SPRINGS RD

GOFFS RD

R

25

KELSO
DUNES

HORSE HILLS

HIDDEN HILL RD

HIDDEN HILLS RD

VALLEY

HIDDEN HILLS RD

40

ROADSIDE REST

R

LANDING STRIP

GOFFS RD

NATIONAL TRAILS HWY

PIUTE

MOUNTAINS

2

GRANITE MOUNTAINS

9

56

KELBAKER RD

CLIPPER

MOUNTAINS

85

CASTLE DOME
3299

ESSEX RD

ESSEX

FENNER

SUNFLOWER SPRINGS

3

93

KELBAKER RD

VAN WINKLE MTN

MARBLE MOUNTAINS

NATIONAL TRAILS HWY

VALLEY

DANBY RD

SAN BERNARDINO CO

MERCURY MTN

OLD WOMAN MTNS

RD

SUNFLOWER

LITTLE PIUTE MTNS

95

SEE MAP

NATIONAL TRAILS HWY

CADIZ SUMMIT ROADSIDE REST

RR

COLTON RD

WASH

PILOT PK
3727

SALTUS RD

BOLO RD

CHAMBLESS ROADSIDE REST

CADIZ RD

TRILOBITES

AT & SF

OLD

SUNFLOWER WASH

SUNFLOWER SPRINGS RD

SUNFLOWER SPRINGS SPUR

WOMAN

4

PISTOL LAKE (DRY)

EVAPORATOR

CADIZ

SHIP

MOUNTAINS

AT & SF

MOUNTAINS

HIGHWAYS

AMBOY

CALUMET

MOUNTAINS

CADIZ RD

CADIZ VALLEY

SAND

DUNES

CADIZ LAKE (DRY)

CADIZ RD

KILBECK HILLS

OLD

WOMAN

MTNS

WARD

VALLEY

5

SAND DUNES

SAND DUNES

CADIZ LAKE (DRY)

SAND DUNES

DANBY LAKE

CADIZ RD

CAL

A | B | C | D | E

102

SEE MAP

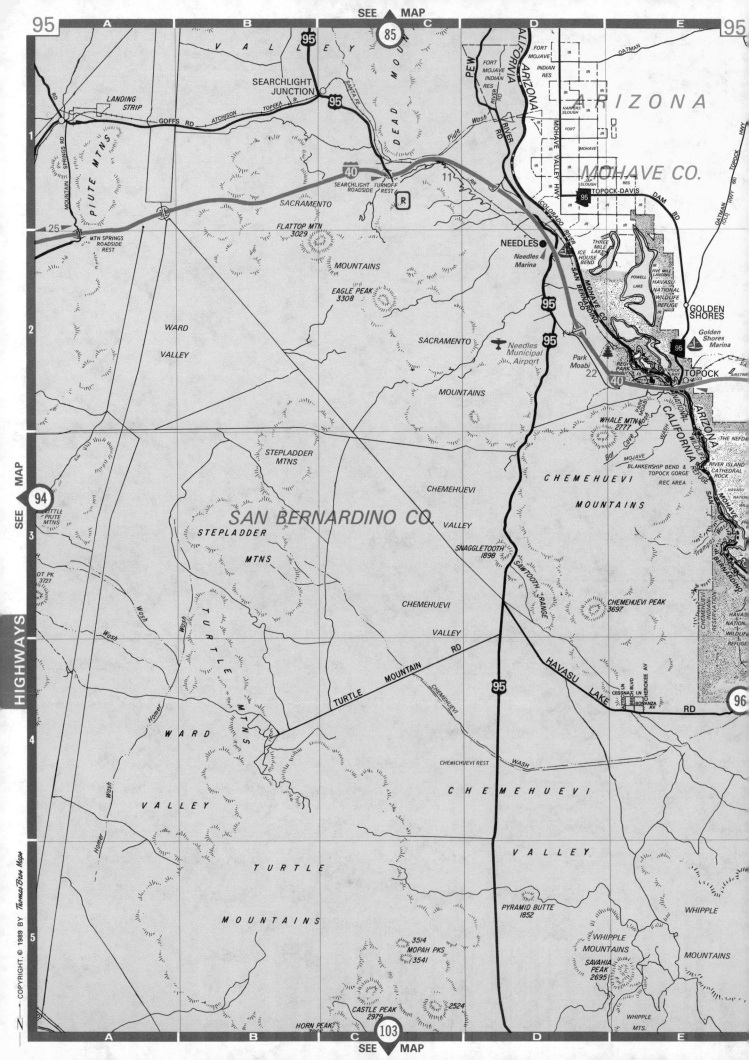

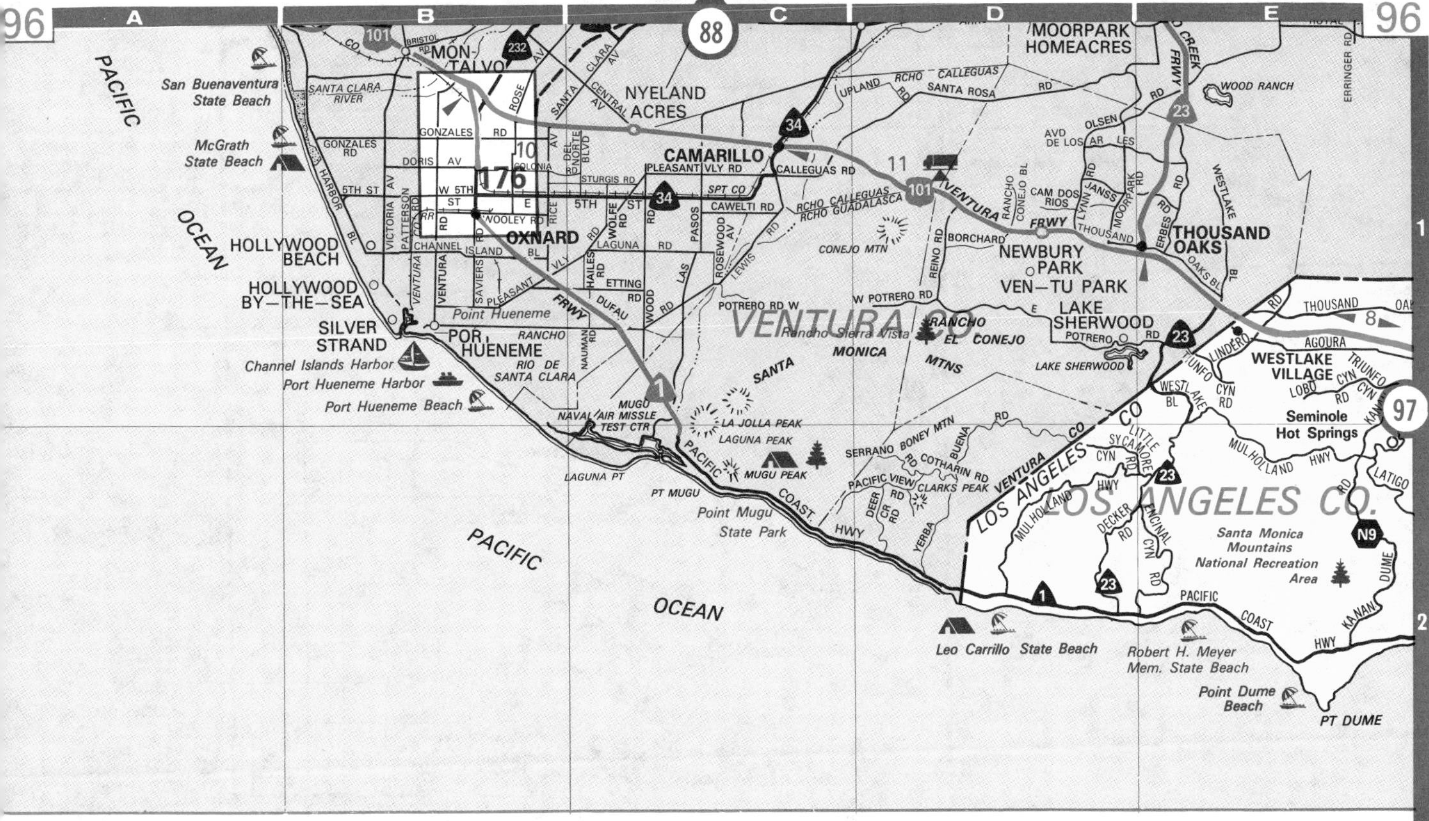

88

A B C D E

PACIFIC OCEAN

San Buenaventura State Beach

McGrath State Beach

MON-TALVO

101
BRISTOL
ROSE

SANTA CLARA RIVER
CENTRAL AV
SANTA CLARA AV

232

NYELAND ACRES

MOORPARK HOMEACRES

WOOD CREEK FRWY

23

WOOD RANCH

EHRINGER

GONZALES RD
DORIS AV
5TH ST
HARBOR BL
VICTORIA AV
PATTERSON
VENTURA RD
VENTURA BL
CHANNEL ISLAND
W 5TH ST
WOOLEY RD

10
176
OXNARD

DEL NORTE BLVD
WOLFE
LAGUNA
5TH ST
LAS POSAS
ROSEWOOD AV
LEWIS
SPT CO
STURGIS RD

34
CAMARILLO
PLEASANT VLY RD
CALLEGUAS RD

UPLAND
RCHO CALLEGUAS
SANTA ROSA RD

34
CAWELTI RD
RCHO CALLEGUAS
RCHO GUADALASCA

11
101
VENTURA

AVD DE LOS ARCES
OLSEN RD
CAM DOS RIOS
JANSS RD
MOORPARK RD

23

WESTLAKE BL

THOUSAND OAKS

HOLLYWOOD BEACH

HOLLYWOOD BY-THE-SEA

SILVER STRAND

Channel Islands Harbor

POR. HUENEME

Port Hueneme Harbor
Port Hueneme Beach

Point Hueneme

SAVIERS RD
PLEASANT VLY
NAUMAN RD
HUENEME RD

RANCHO RIO DE SANTA CLARA

MUGU LAGOON

1

NAVAL AIR MISSLE TEST CTR

POTRERO RD W

W POTRERO RD

BORCHARD

NEWBURY PARK

VEN-TU PARK

REINO RD

LAKE SHERWOOD

Lake Sherwood

23

THOUSAND OAKS BL

8

AGOURA RD

WESTLAKE VILLAGE

Seminole Hot Springs

97

SANTA MONICA MTNS

Rancho Sierra Vista

RANCHO EL CONEJO

Conejo Mtn

POTRERO

SERRANO RD
BONEY MTN
COTHARIN RD
CLARKS PEAK
DEER CR RD
PACIFIC VIEW RD
YERBA

BUENA RD

VENTURA CO
LOS ANGELES CO

MULHOLLAND HWY

LITTLE SYCAMORE CYN

LOBO CYN RD

TRIUNFO CYN RD

LINDERO

TRUNFO CYN

23

LATIGO

La Jolla Peak
LAGUNA PEAK

Mugu Peak

LAGUNA PT

PT MUGU

Point Mugu State Park

PACIFIC COAST HWY

LOS ANGELES CO.

DECKER RD
ENCINAL CYN RD
KANAN DUME RD

Santa Monica Mountains National Recreation Area

N9

23

PACIFIC OCEAN

Leo Carrillo State Beach

1

Robert H. Meyer Mem. State Beach

PACIFIC COAST HWY

2

Point Dume Beach

PT DUME

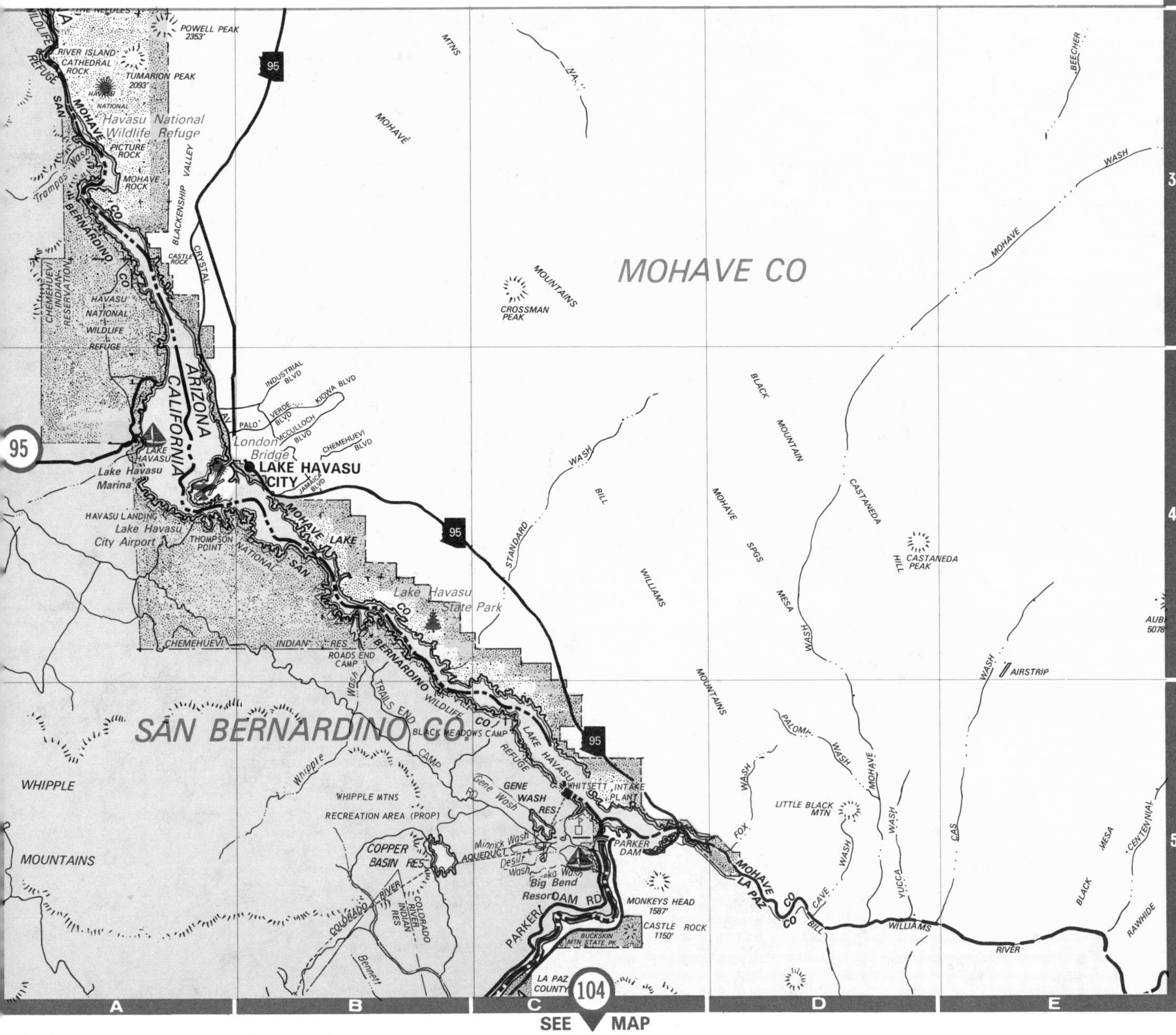

95

THE NEEDLES

POWELL PEAK 2353'

RIVER ISLAND
CATHEDRAL ROCK
TUMARION PEAK 2093'

HAVASU NATIONAL WILDLIFE REFUGE

Havasu National Wildlife Refuge

PICTURE ROCK

MOHAVE ROCK

Trampas Wash

CASTLE ROCK

BLACKENSHIP VALLEY

CRYSTAL

MTNS

MOHAVÉ

MOHAVE WASH

BEECHER

MOHAVE CO

MOUNTAINS
CROSSMAN PEAK

3

SAN BERNARDINO CO

CHEMEHUEVI RESERVATION

HAVASU NATIONAL WILDLIFE REFUGE

ARIZONA
CALIFORNIA

INDUSTRIAL BLVD
KIOWA BLVD
VERDE BLVD
PALO VERDE BLVD
McCULLOCH BLVD
CHEMEHUEVI BLVD

London Bridge
LAKE HAVASU
LAKE HAVASU CITY

BLACK MOUNTAIN

CASTANEDA

CASTANEDA HILL
CASTANEDA PEAK

4

95

Lake Havasu Marina

Havasu Landing
Lake Havasu City Airport
THOMPSON POINT

CHEMEHUEVI INDIAN RES

ROADS END CAMP

MOHAVE
NATIONAL
SAN BERNARDINO WILDLIFE CO REFUGE

LAKE HAVASU

Lake Havasu State Park

95

BILL WILLIAMS WASH

MOHAVE SPGS MESA WASH

STANDARD WASH

MOUNTAINS

AIRSTRIP

AUBREY 5076'

WHIPPLE

MOUNTAINS

SAN BERNARDINO CO

TRAILS END CAMP
BLACK MEADOWS CAMP

Whipple Wash

WHIPPLE MTNS RECREATION AREA (PROP)

COPPER BASIN RES

COLORADO RIVER AQUEDUCT

GENE WASH RES

Minnick Wash

Big Bend Resort

PARKER DAM RD
Eeka Wash
MONKEYS HEAD 1587'

CASTLE ROCK 1150'
BUCKSKIN MTN STATE PK

WHITSETT INTAKE PLANT

PARKER DAM

MOHAVE LA PAZ CO

PALOMA WASH
LITTLE BLACK MTN
FOX WASH
MOHAVE WASH
YUCCA WASH

BLACK
CENTENNIAL
CAS

RAHIDE

RIVER

BLACK MESA

MOHAVE LA PAZ CO BILL
CAVE WASH
WILLIAMS

5

LA PAZ CO

104

A B C D E

HIGHWAYS

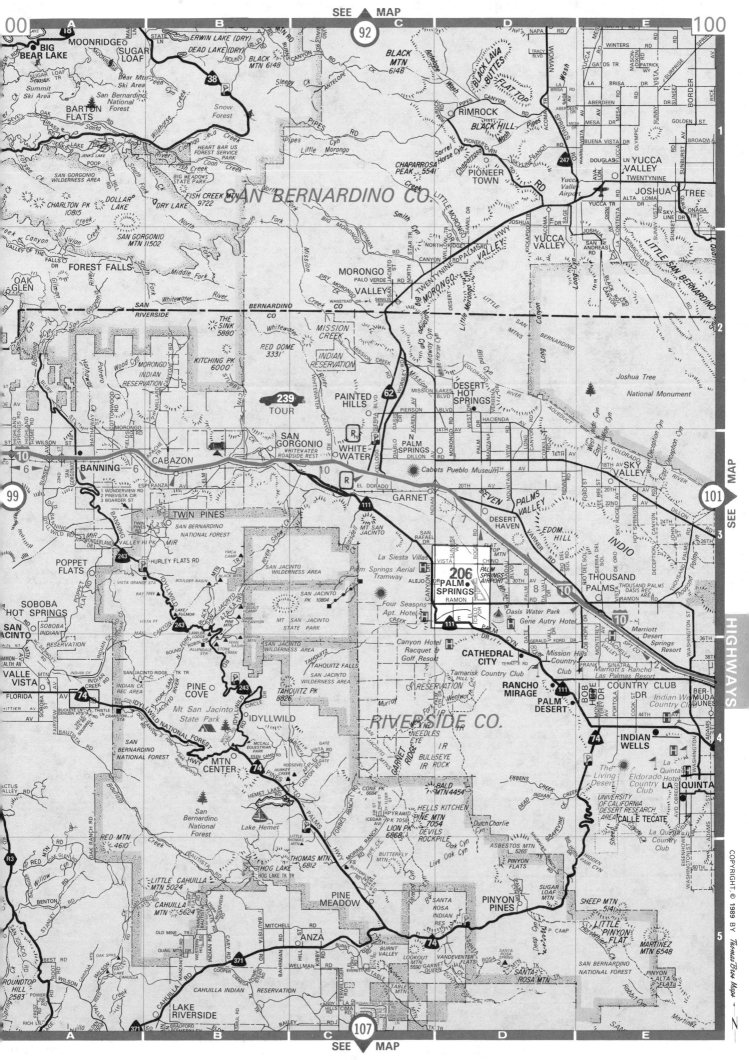

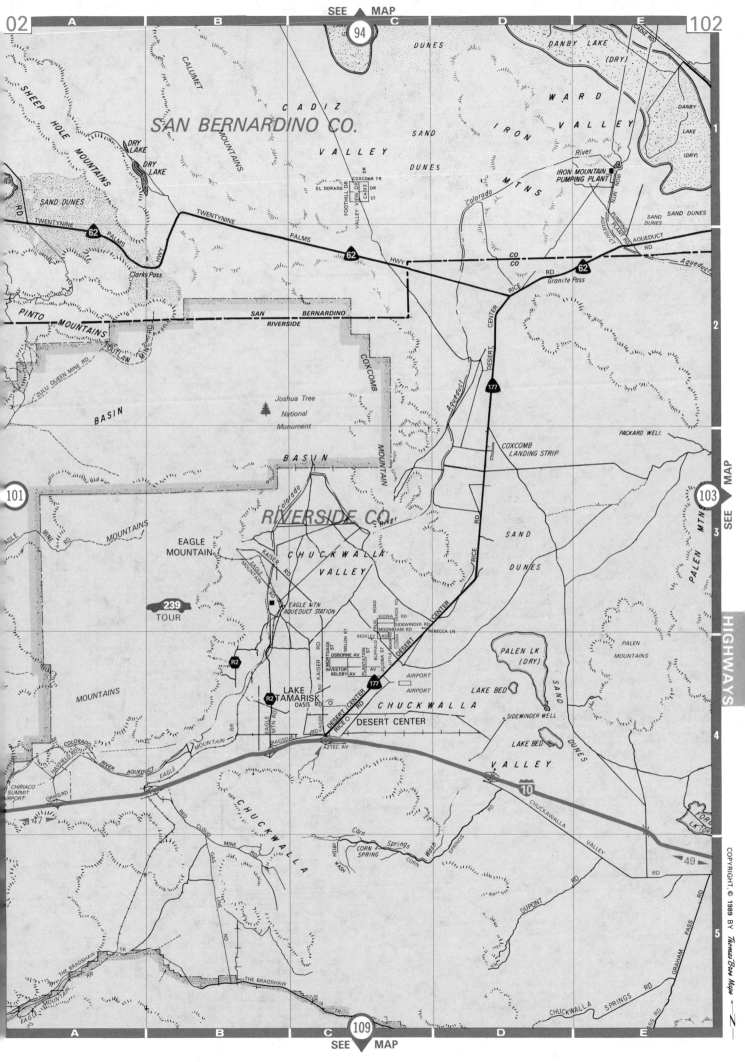

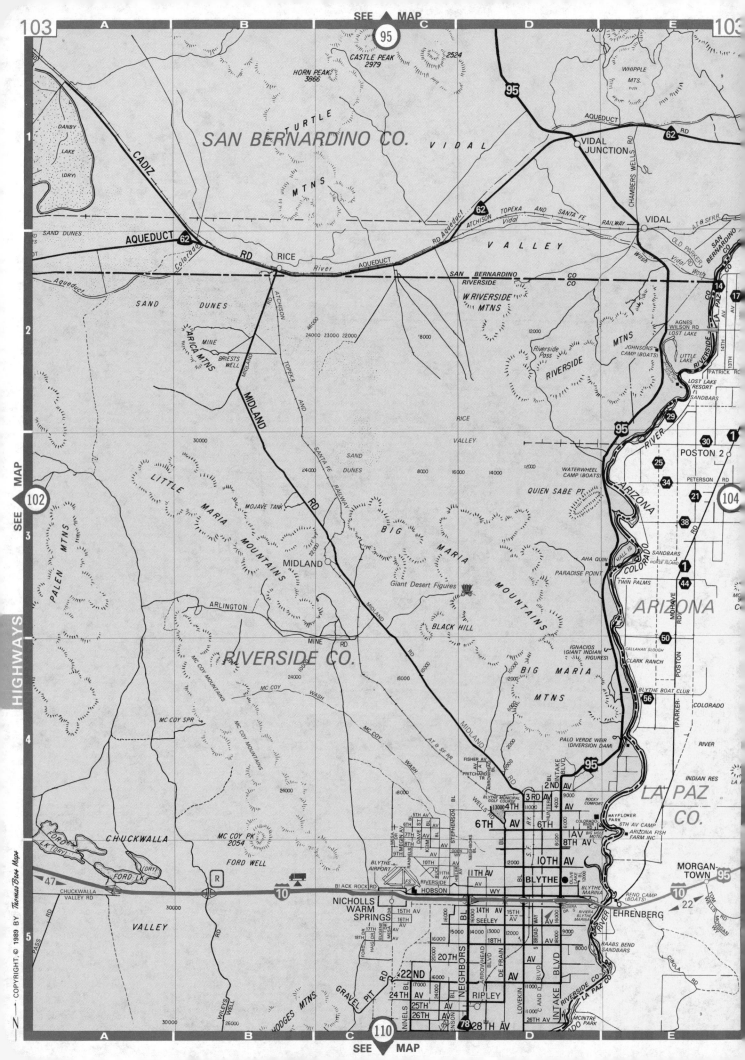

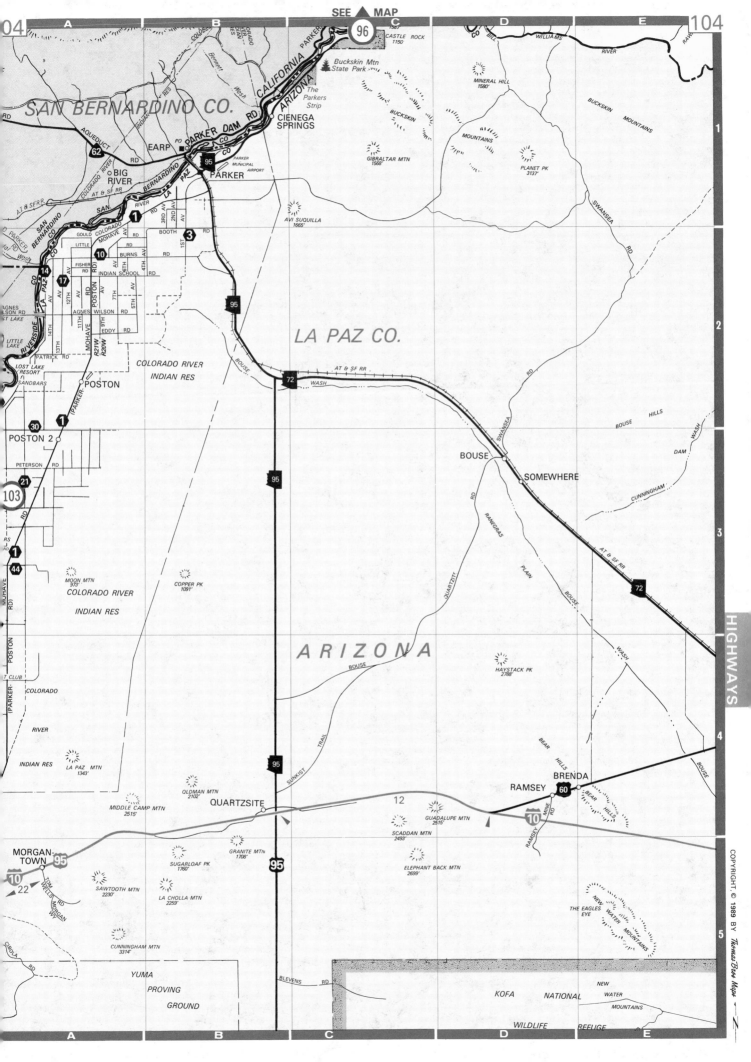

A　B　C　D　E

South Laguna
Three Arch Bay
Ritz Carlton Hotel
DANA POINT

SAN JUAN CAPISTRANO 202
ORANGE CO.
74

Capistrano Beach 7

SAN CLEMENTE

San Clemente State Beach
San Onofre Visitor's Ctr

SAN DIEGO CO.
106
SAN ONOFRE
San Onofre State Park

1

SEE MAP V

La Jolla Shores Beach
ECOLOGICAL RESERVE

SAN DIEGO – LA JOLLA UNDERWATER PARK

LA JOLLA AREA
LA JOLLA BAY

PT LA JOLLA
ELLEN SCRIPPS PARK
Boomer Beach
La Jolla Caves
Spindrift Golf Course

2

CHILDREN'S POOL
SHELL BEACH
Colonial Inn

Wipeout Beach

Hotel La Jolla
COAST BLVD PK

Casa Beach
NICHOLSON'S PT.

PROSPECT RD

La Jolla

237 TOUR

3

OCEAN

Marine Street Beach

VISTA DE LA PLAYA

Windansea Beach

NAUTILUS

SR H.S. LA JOLLA

La Jolla County Club

MUIRLANDS DR

NAUTILUS ST

SAN DIEGO

LA JOLLA SCENIC

211

SOLEDAD MTN

4

PACIFIC

Playa
PLAYA DEL SUR
KOLMAR ST
ROSEMONT
LA JOLLA STRAND PARK
WINAMAR
HERMOSA TERRACE PK
BIG ROCK REEF

CORTEZ PL

Mira Monte

BELLEVUE

SOLEDAD MTN

KATE O SESSIONS MEMORIAL PARK

5

Sun Gold Pt
LA JOLLA HERMOSA PARK

Bird Rock

CHELSEA

CALUMET PK

TURQUOISE

FOOTHILL BL

BERYL

212

A　B　C　D　E

HIGHWAYS

COPYRIGHT © 1989 BY Thomas Bros Maps

N

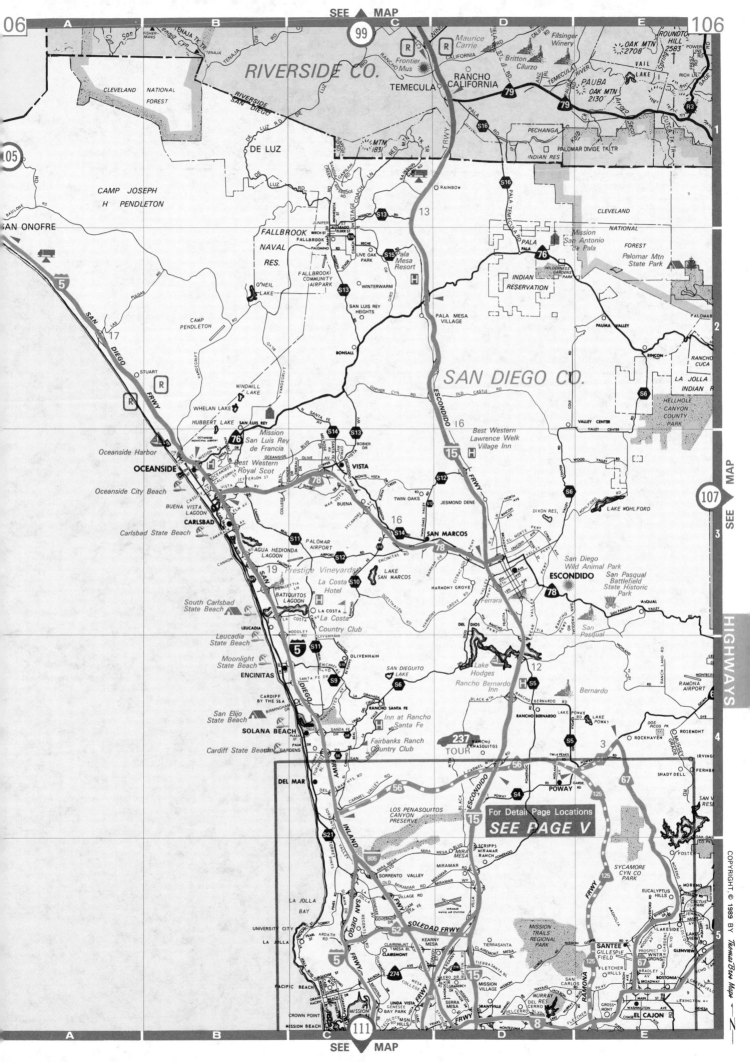

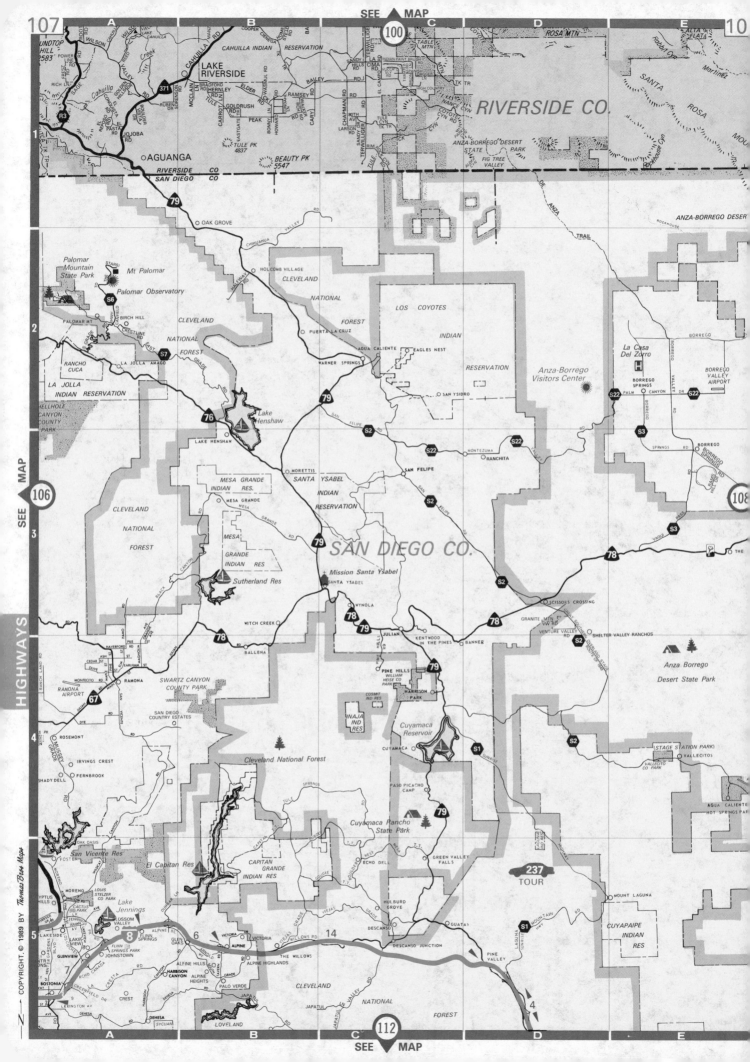

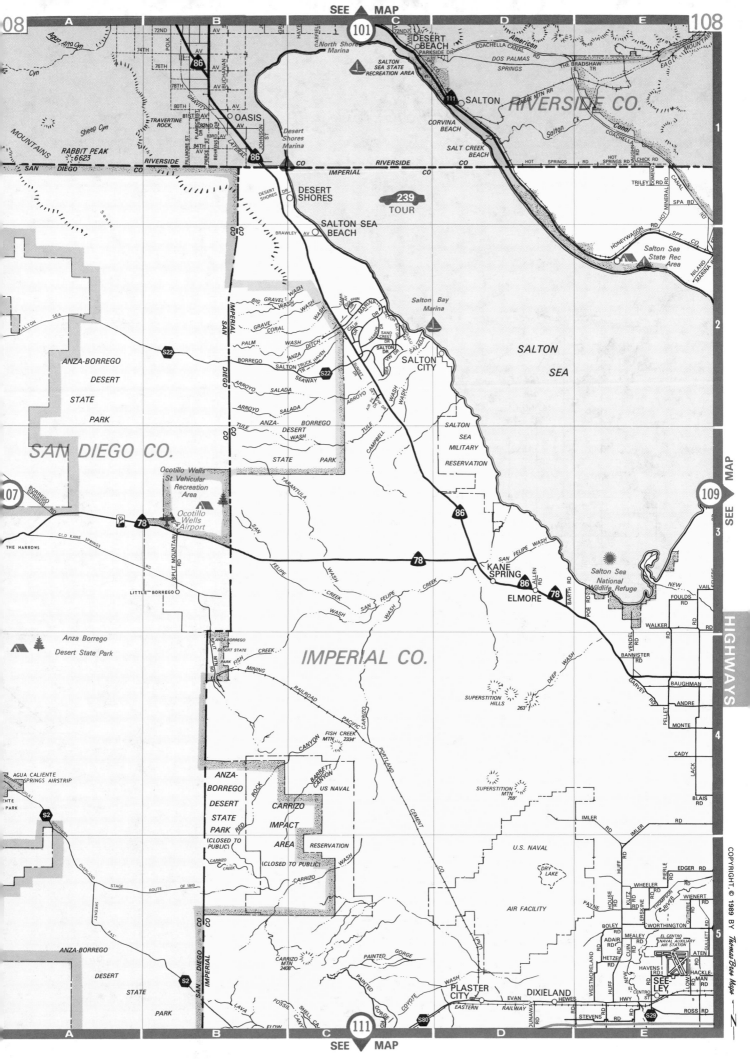

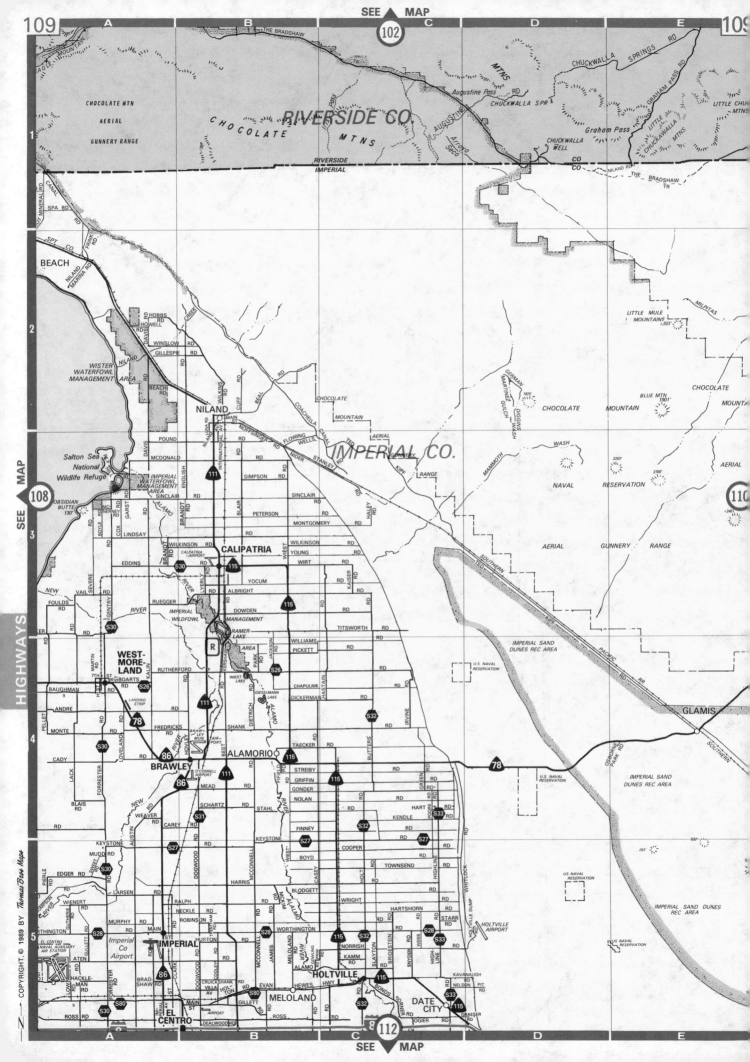

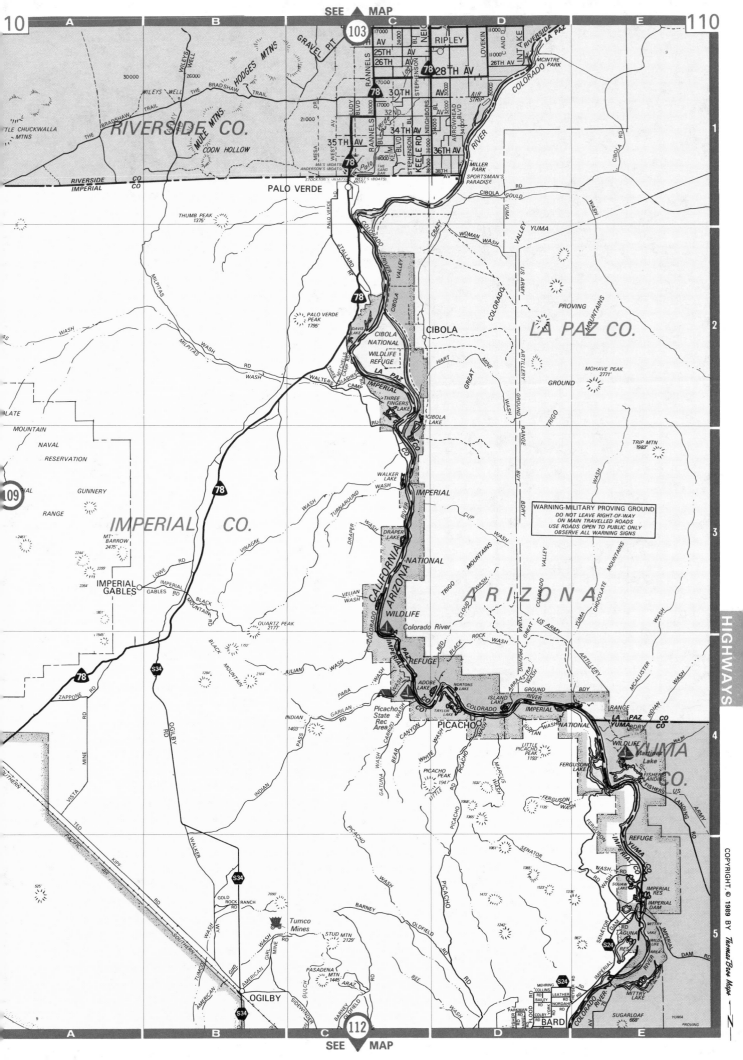

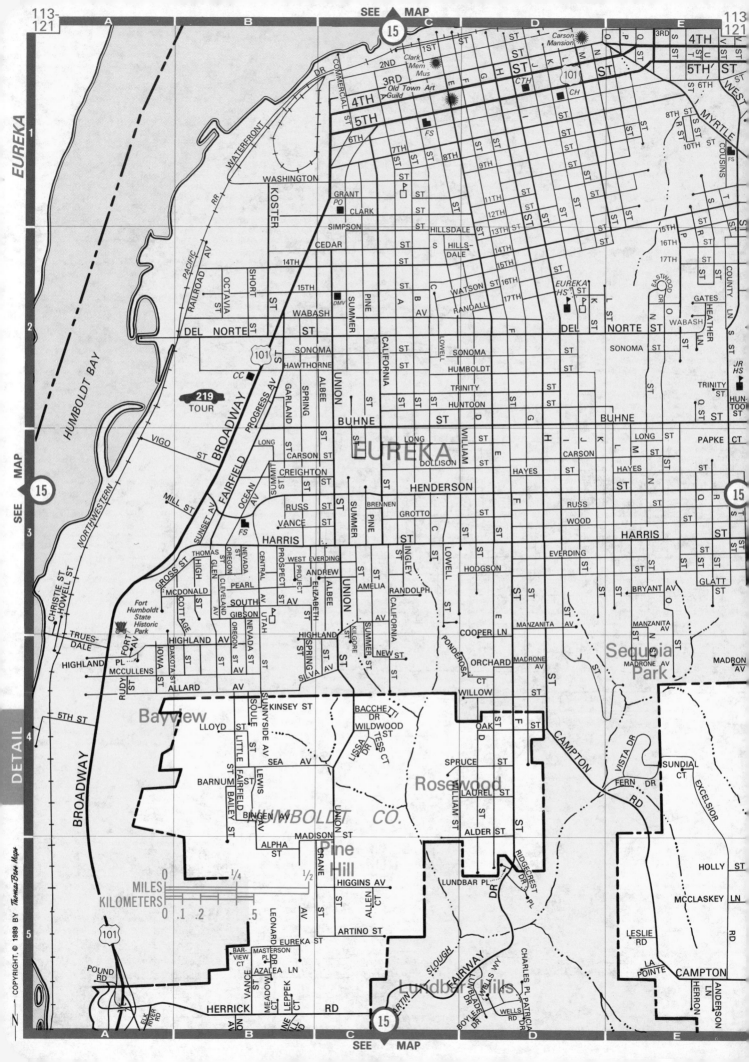

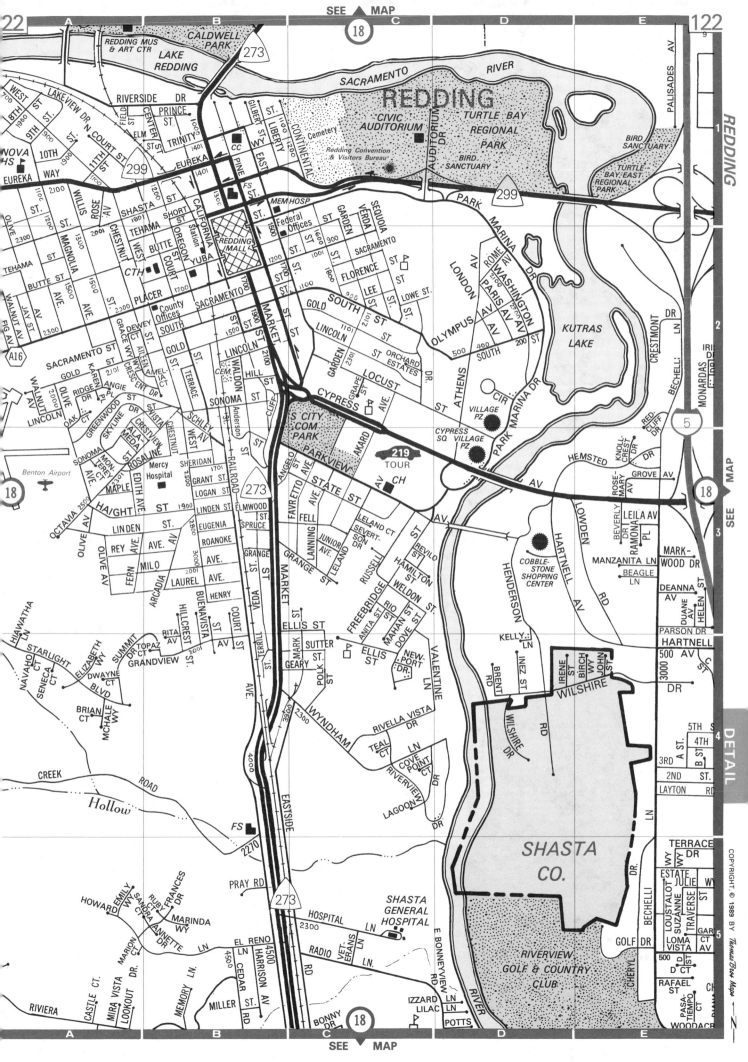

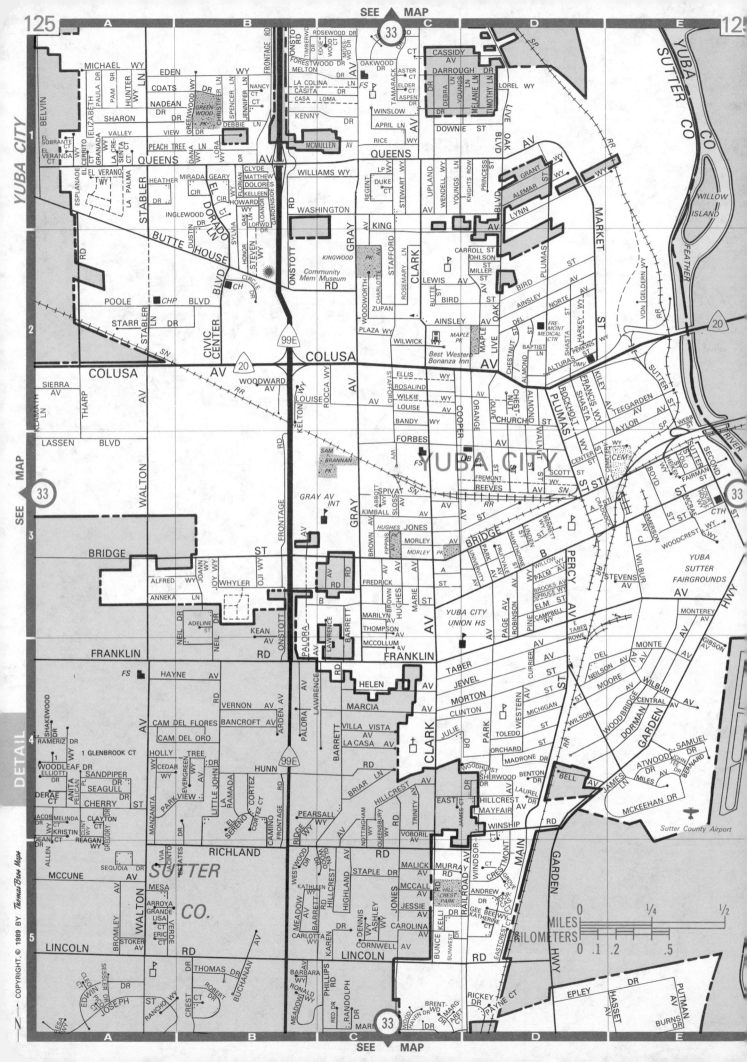

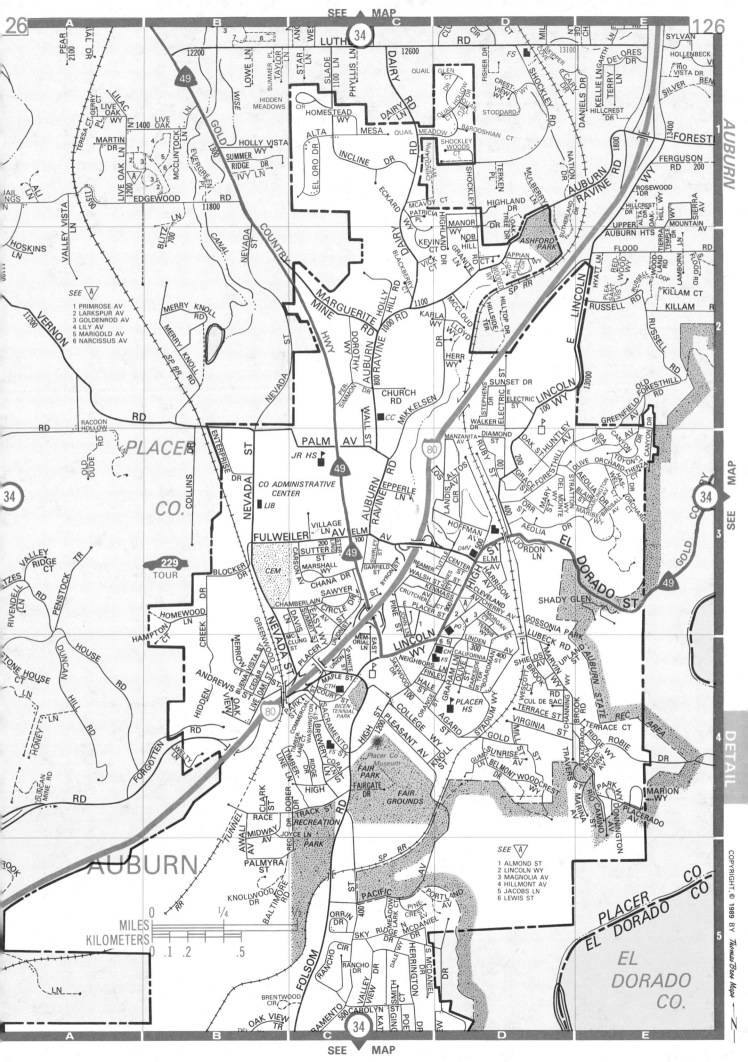

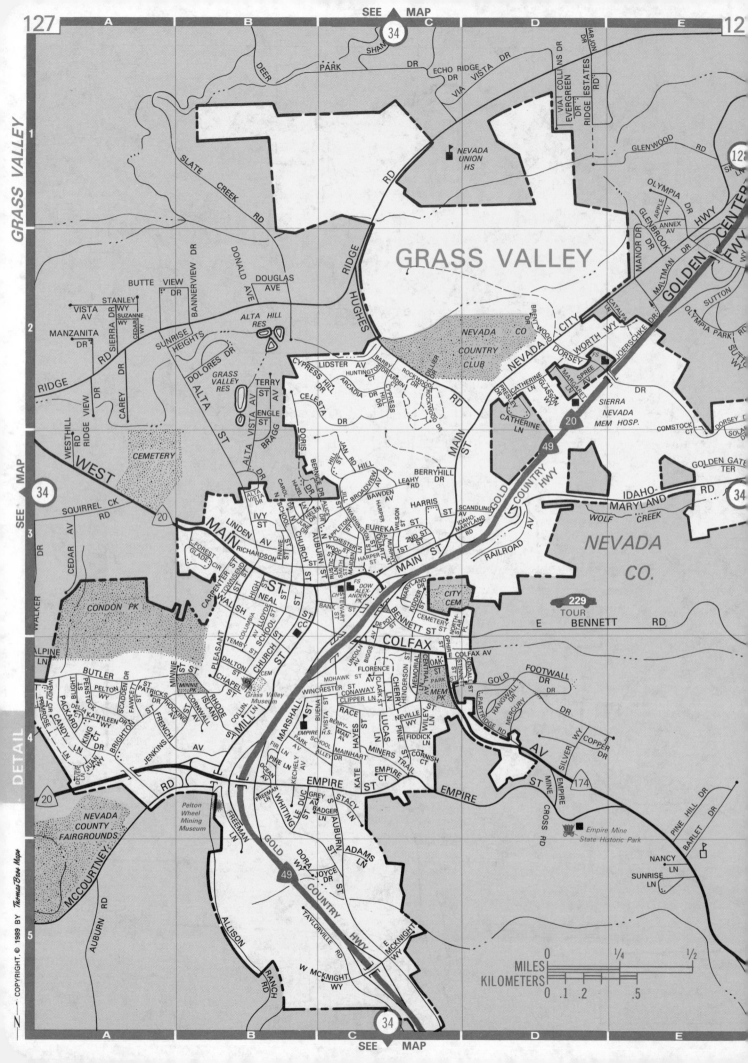

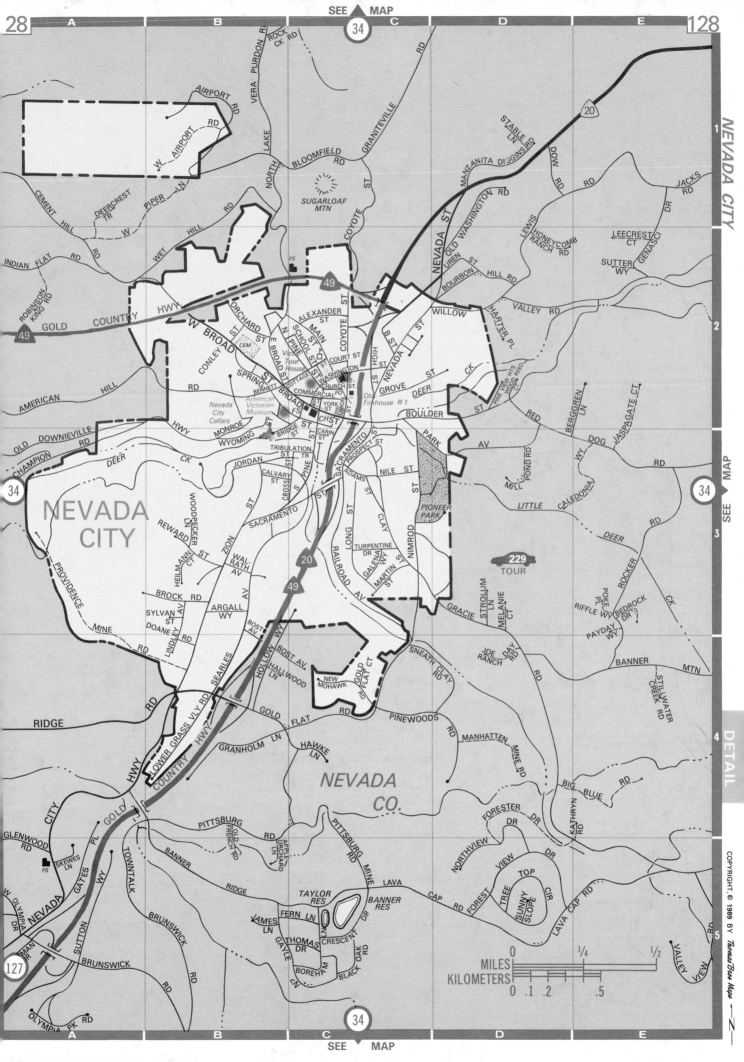

NEVADA CITY

NEVADA CITY

NEVADA
CO.

229
TOUR

DETAIL

SEE MAP

MILES
KILOMETERS

0   1/4   1/2

0 .1 .2   .5

127

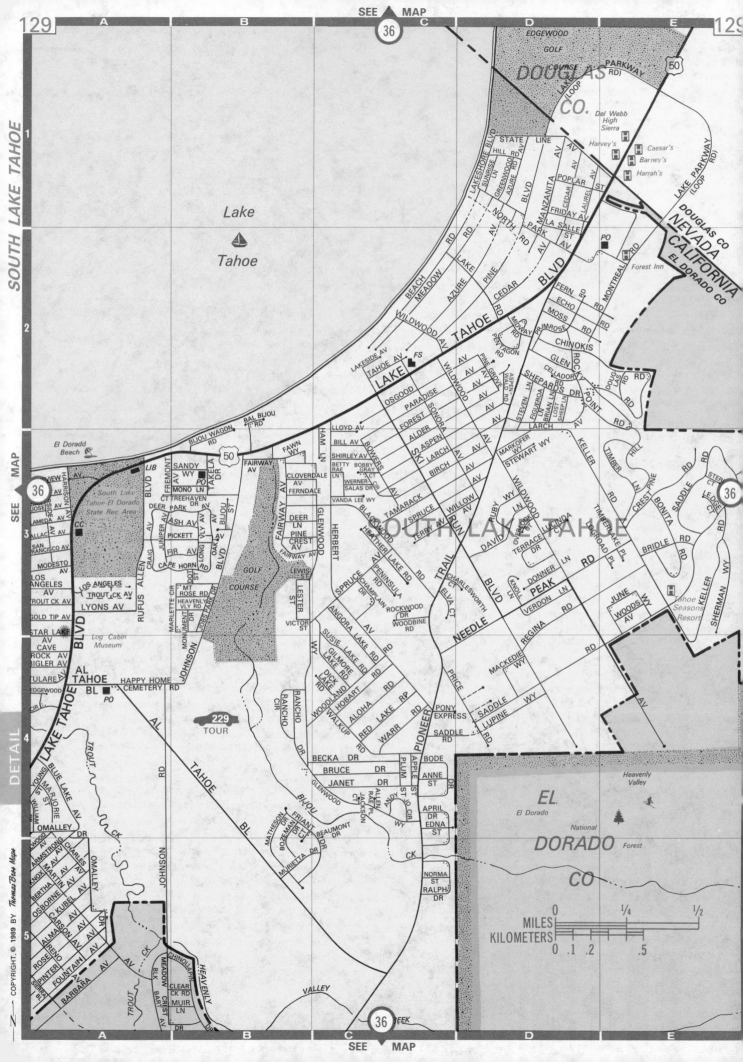

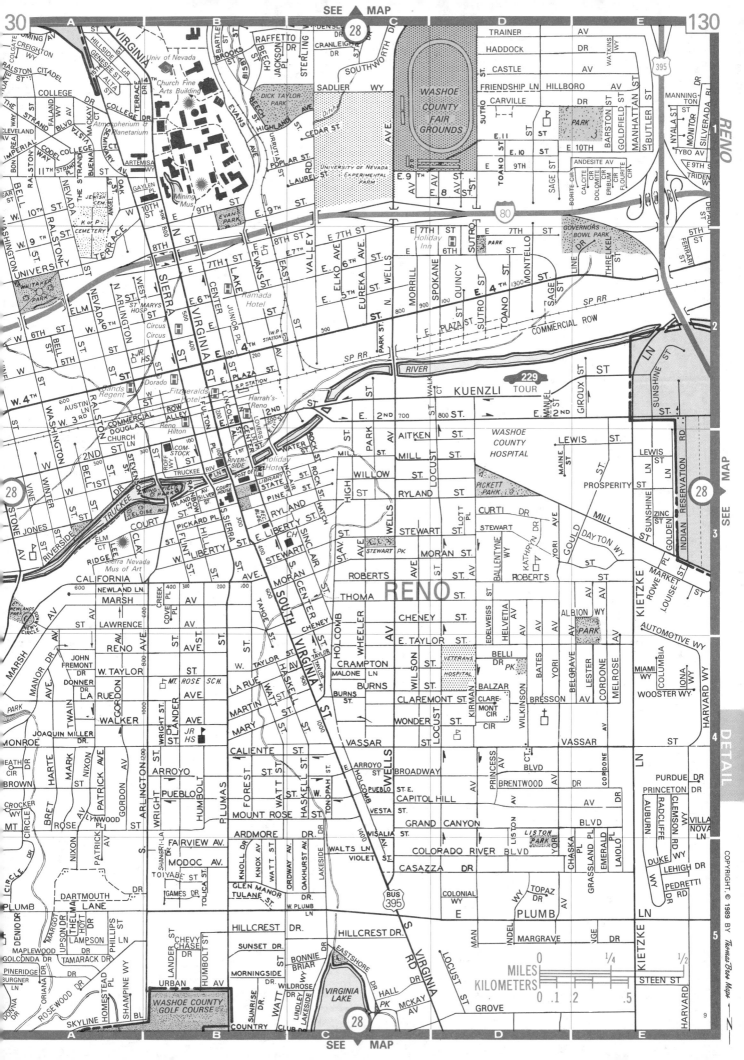

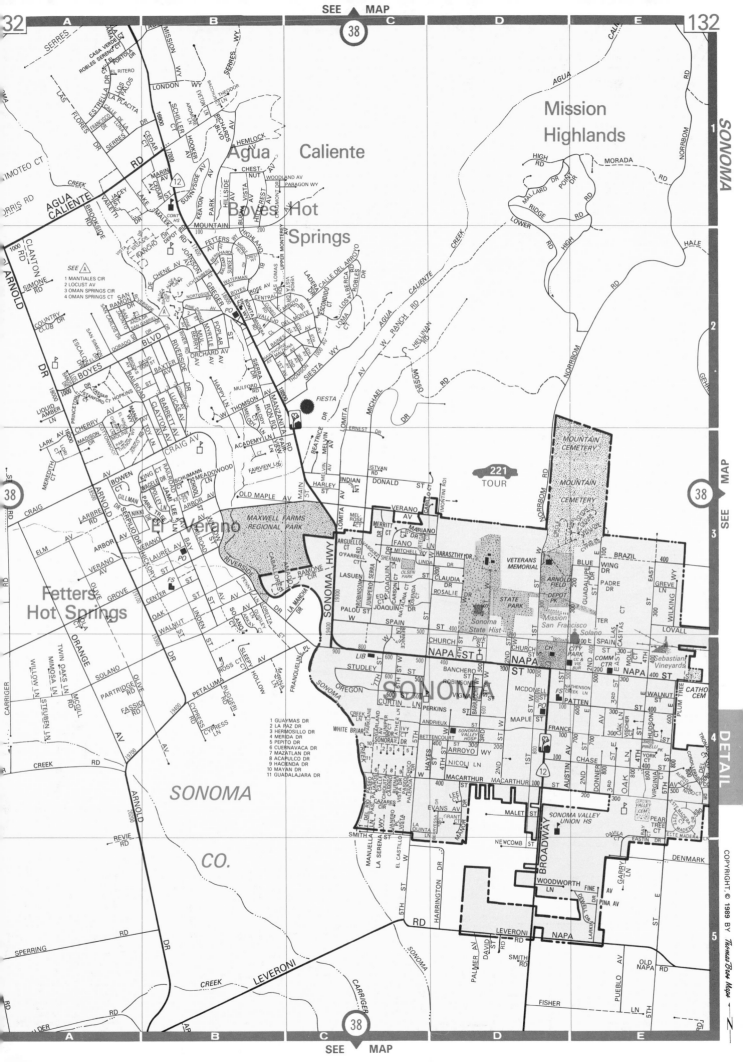

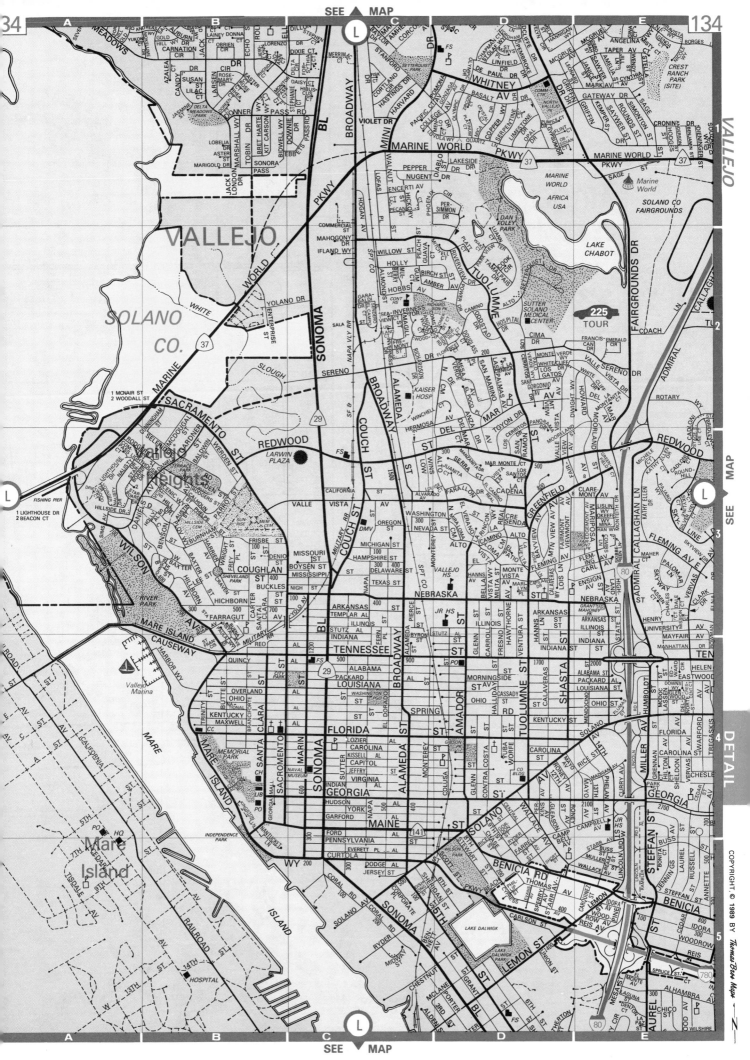

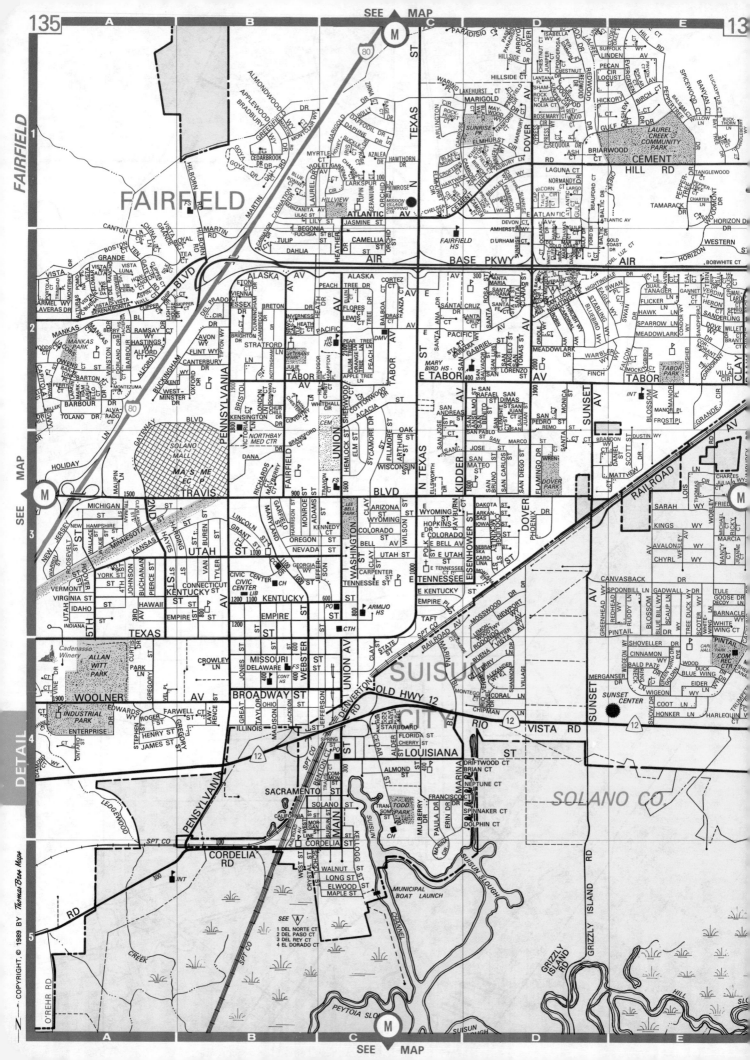

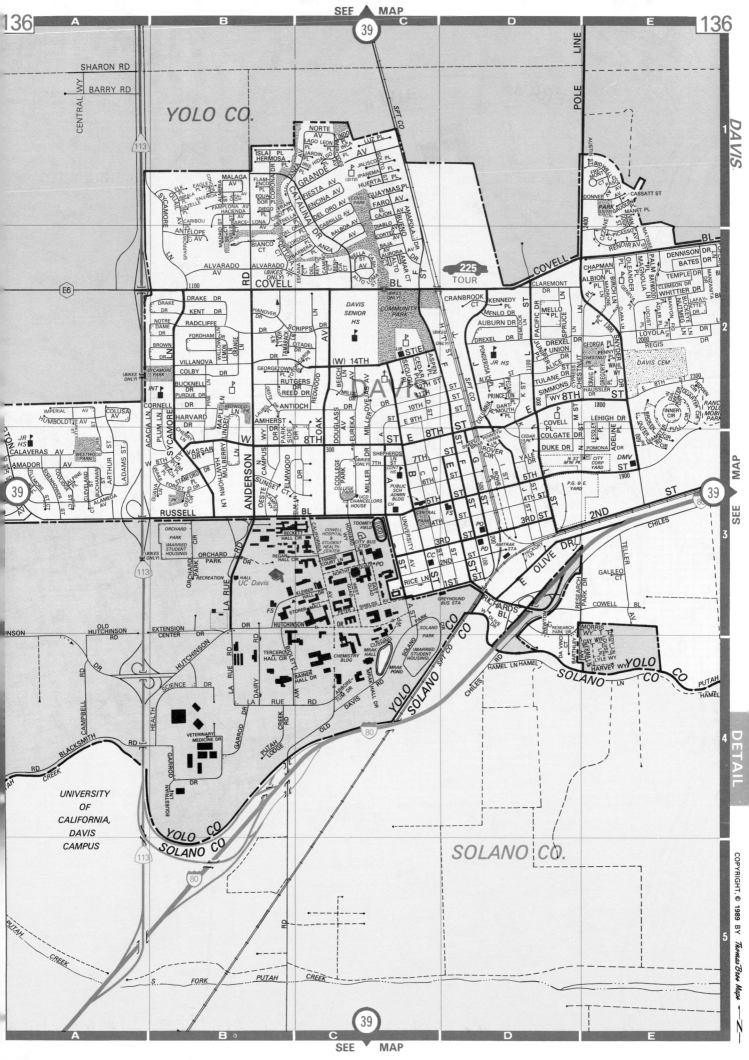

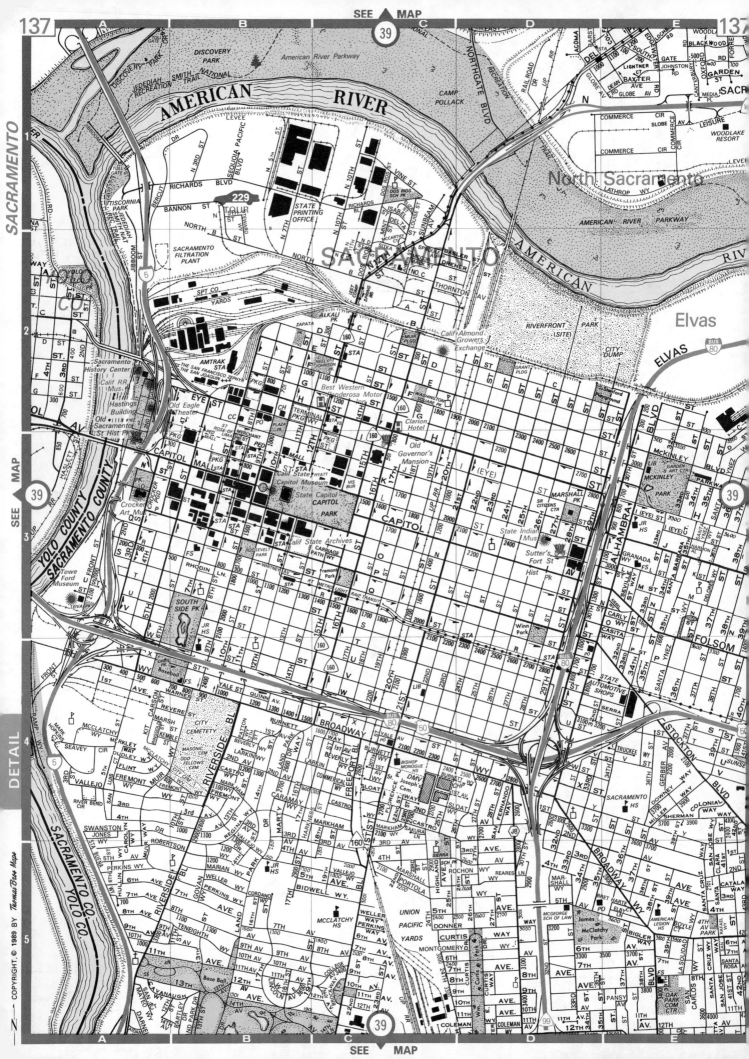

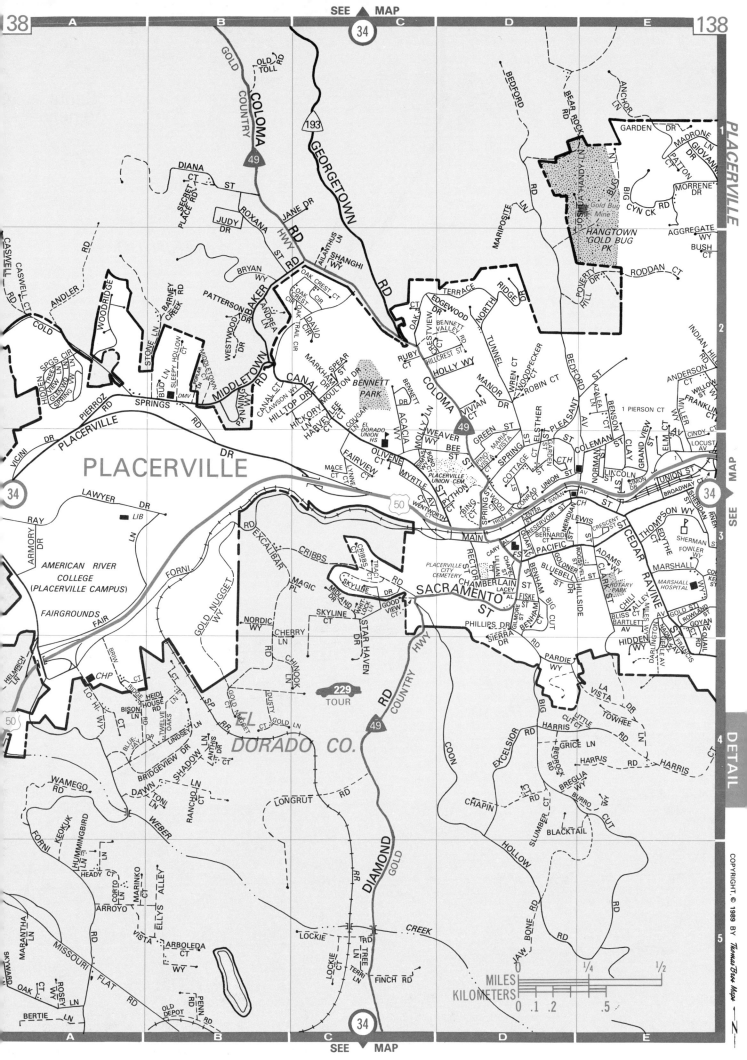

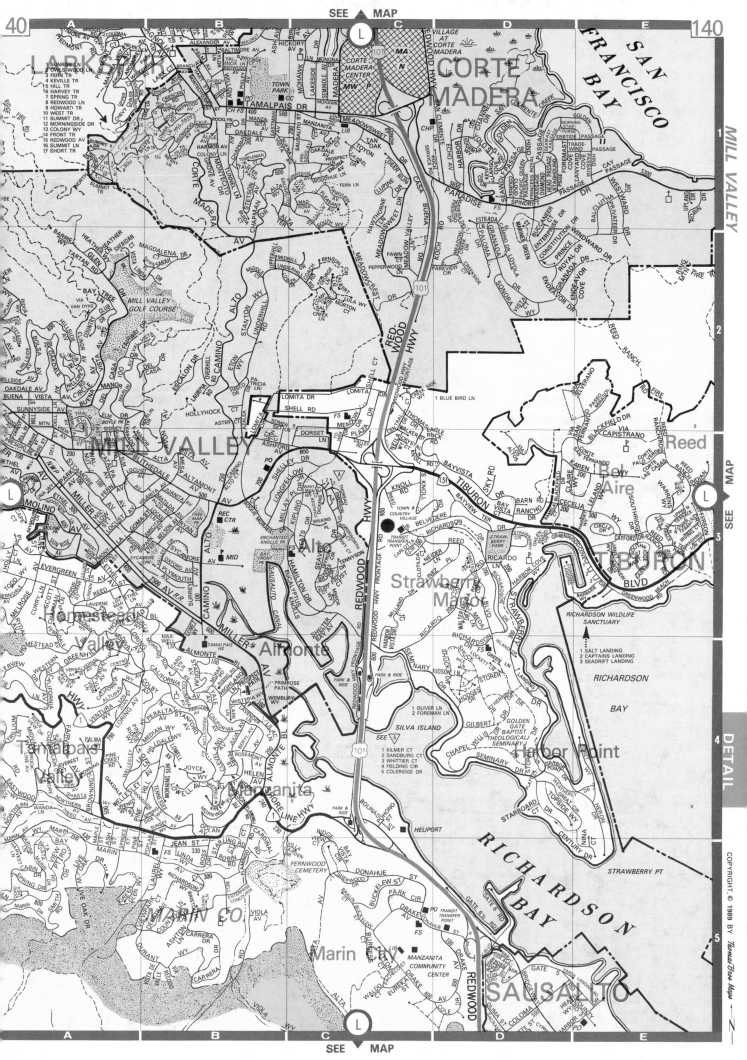

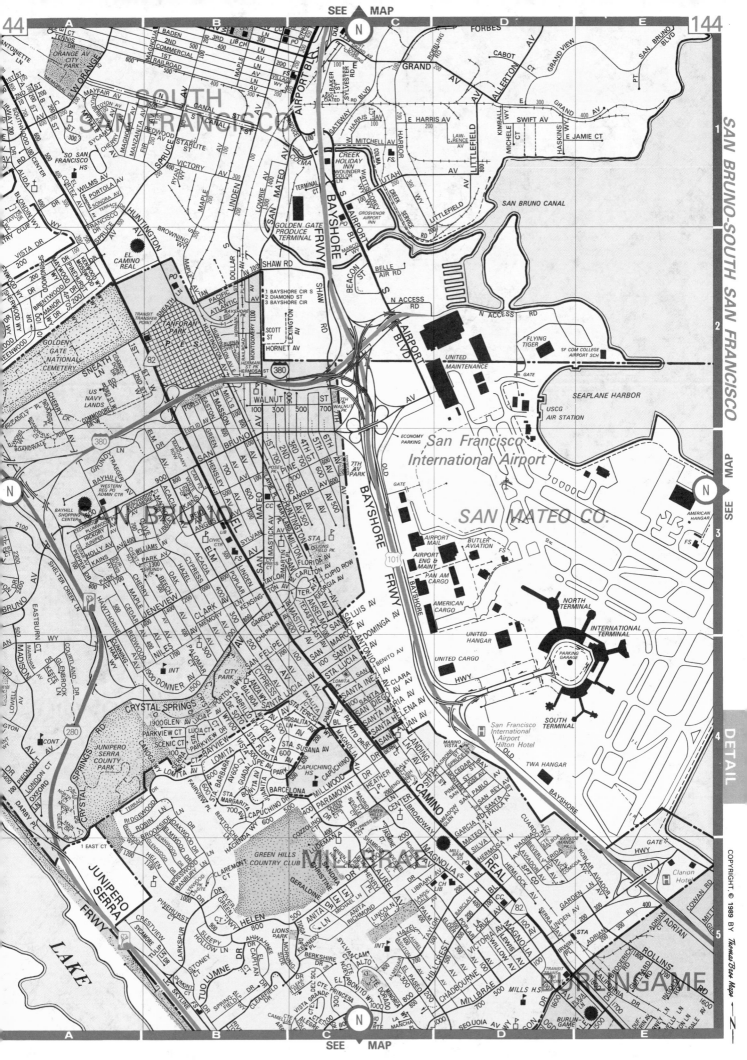

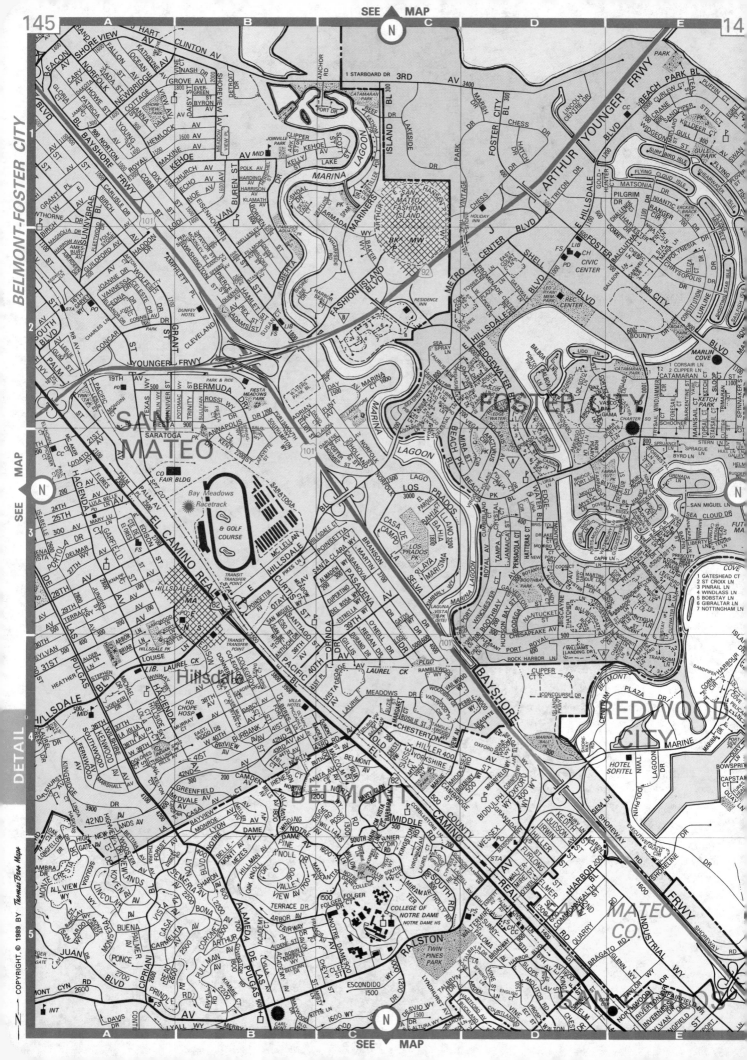

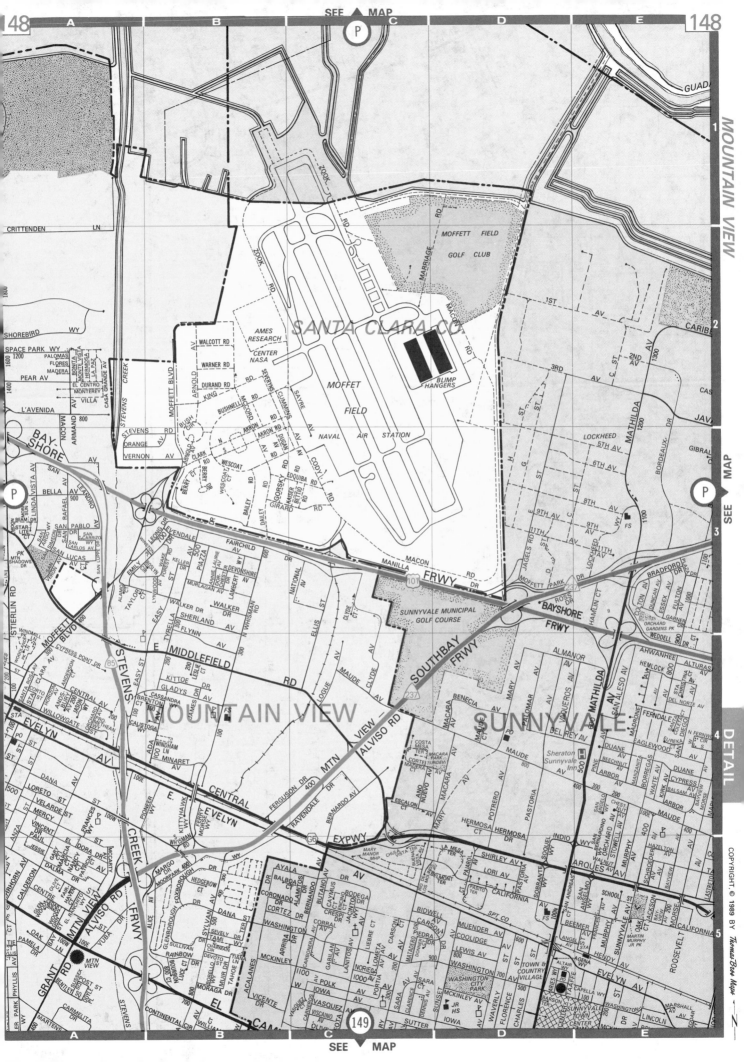

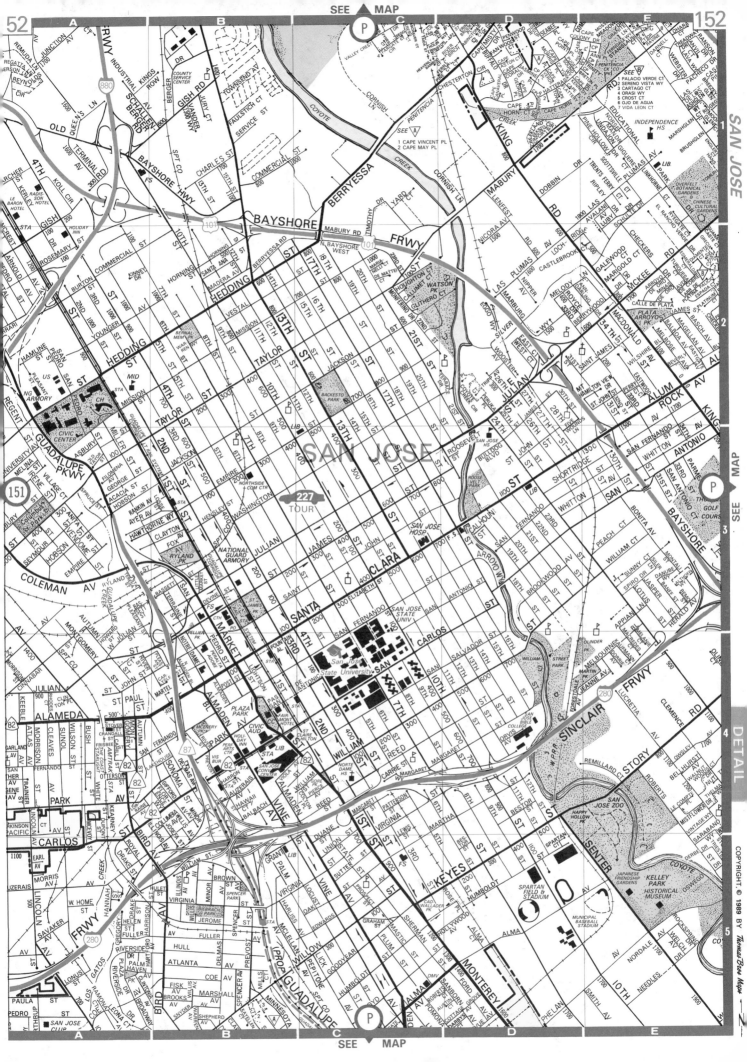

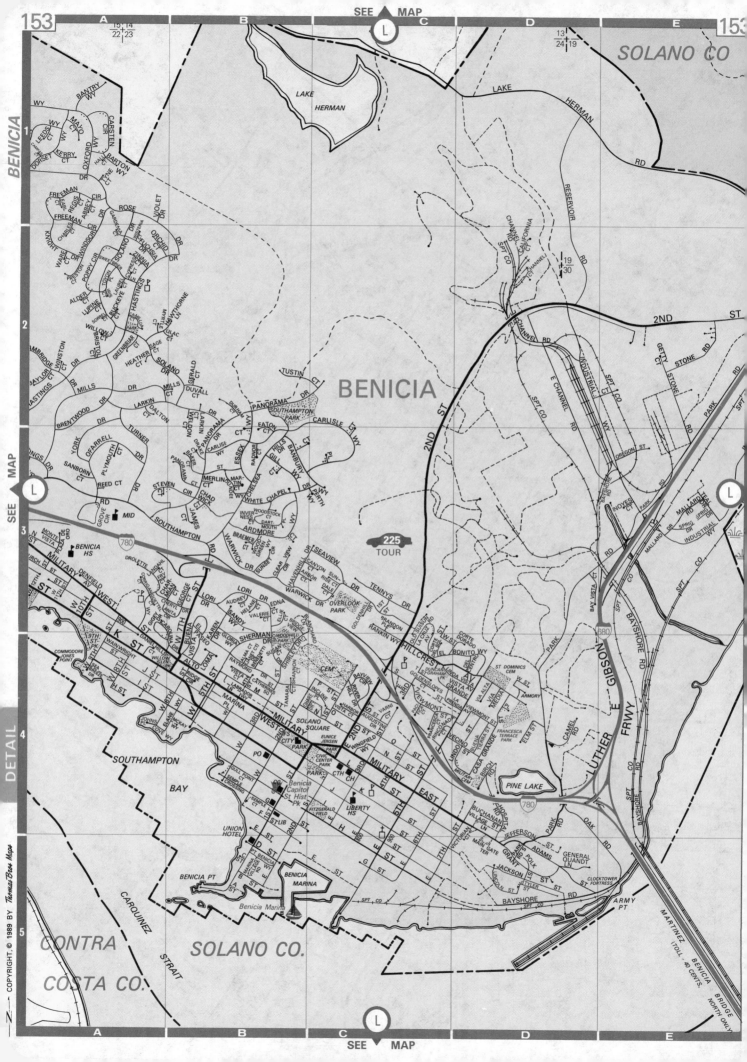

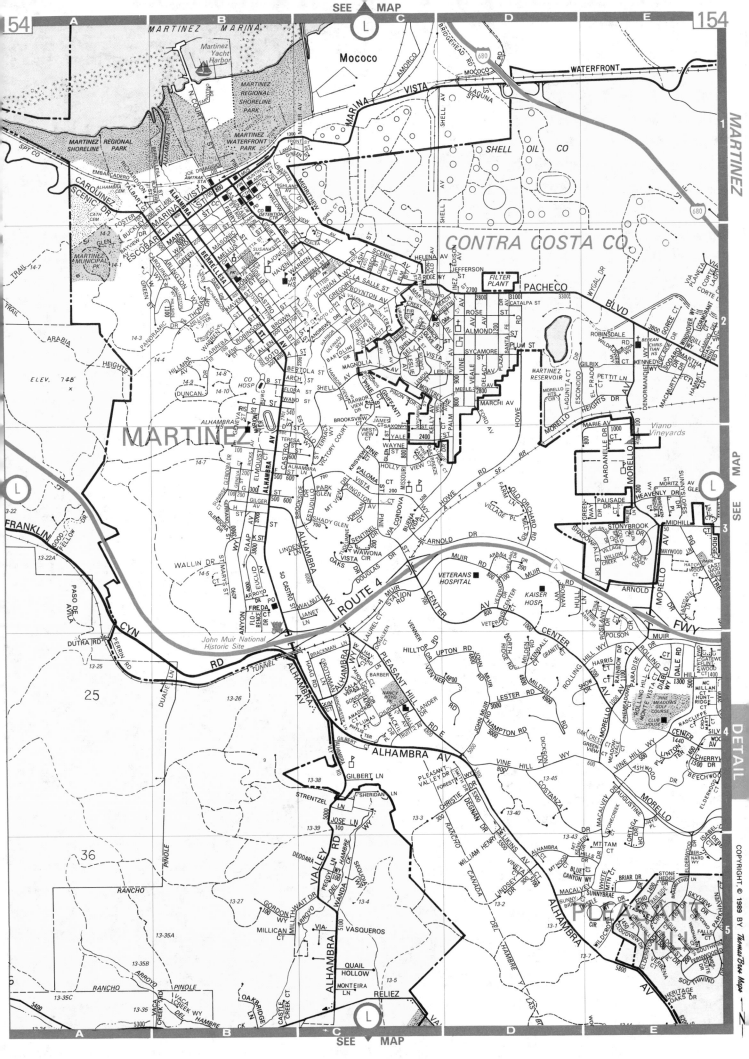

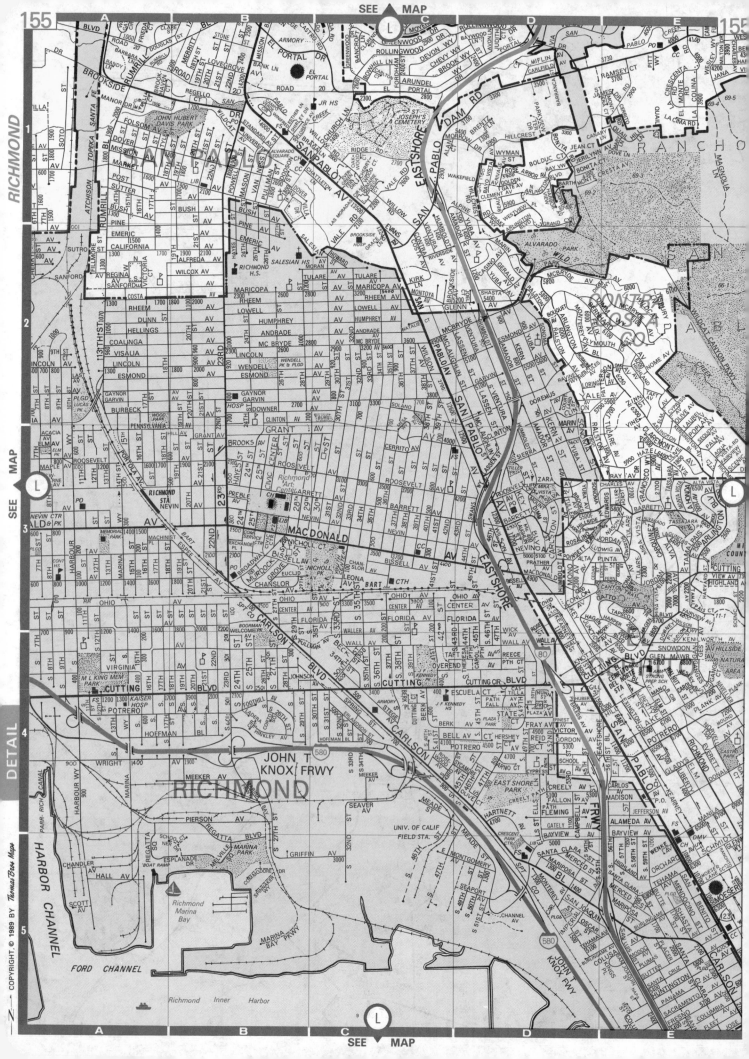

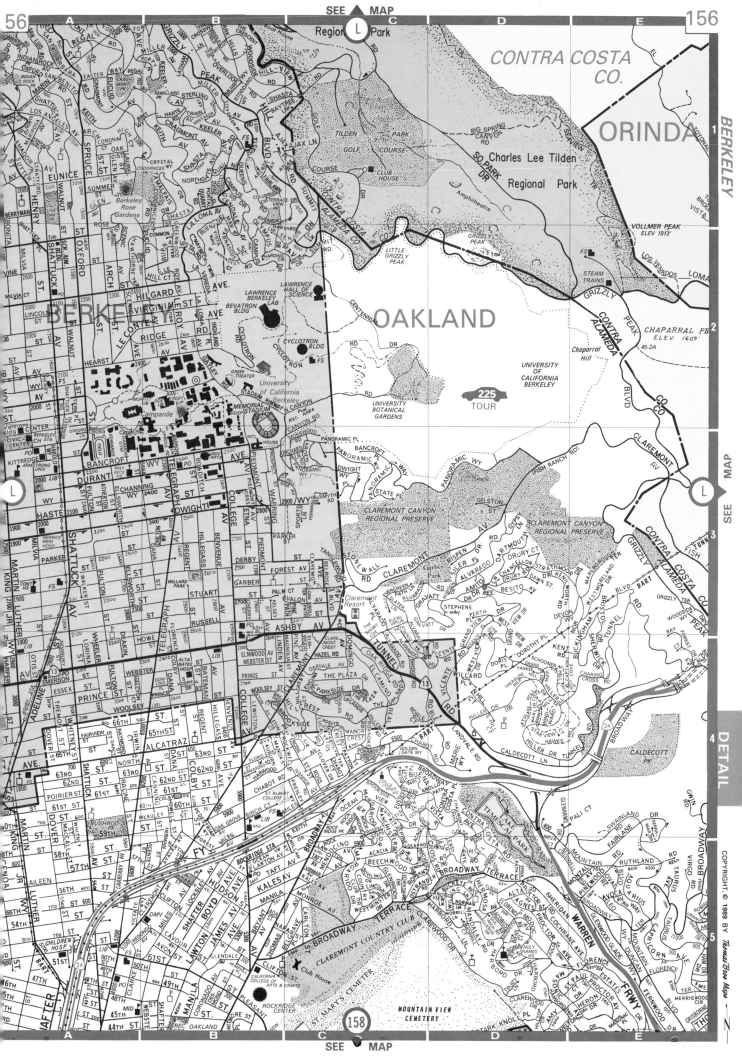

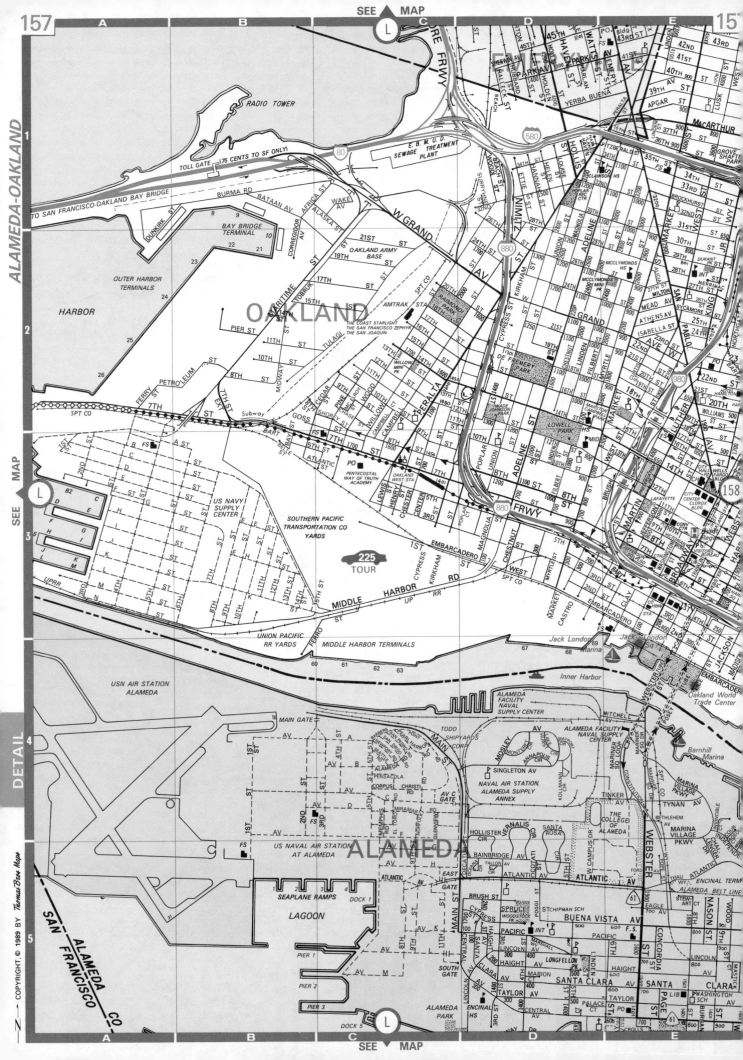

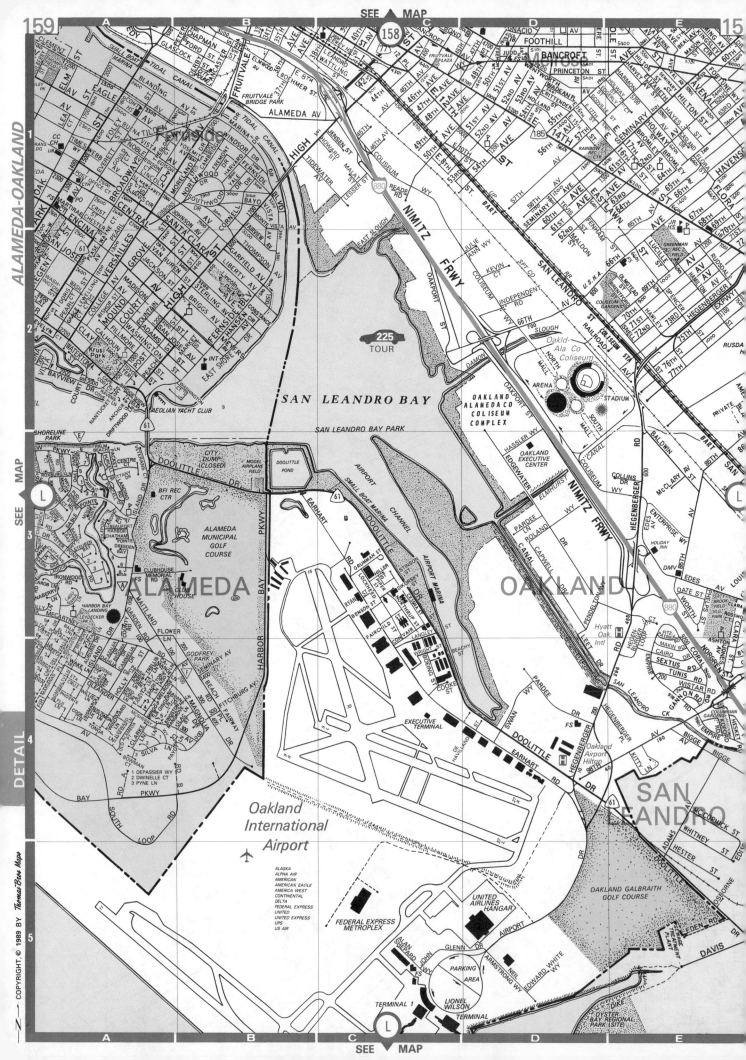

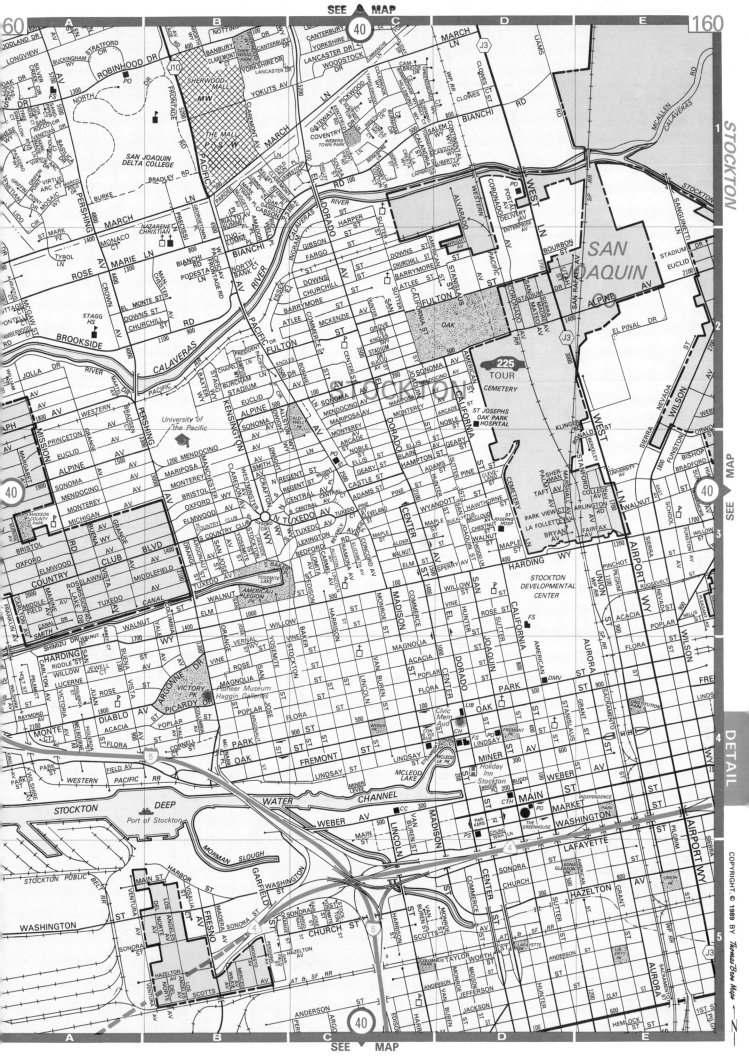

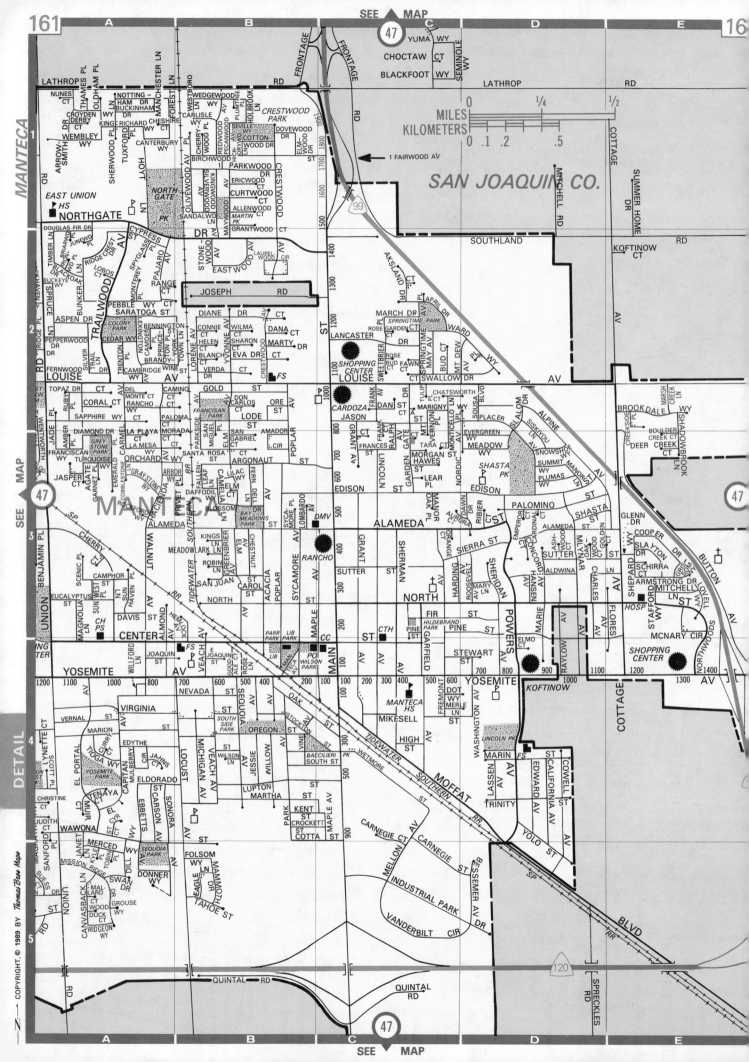

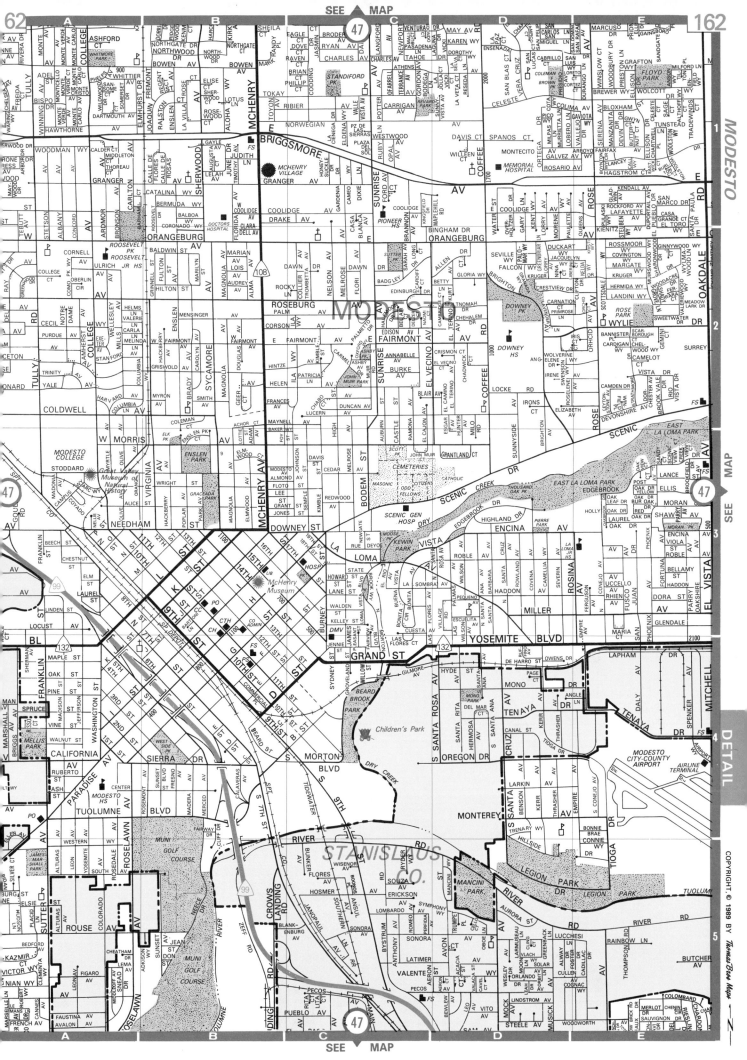

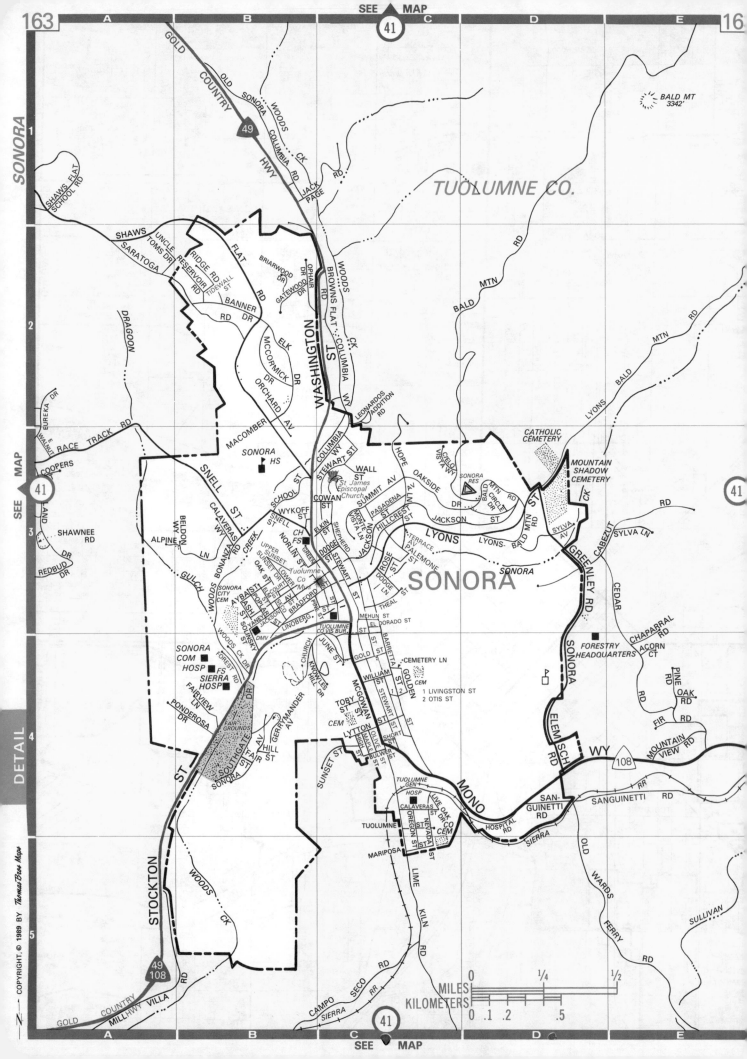

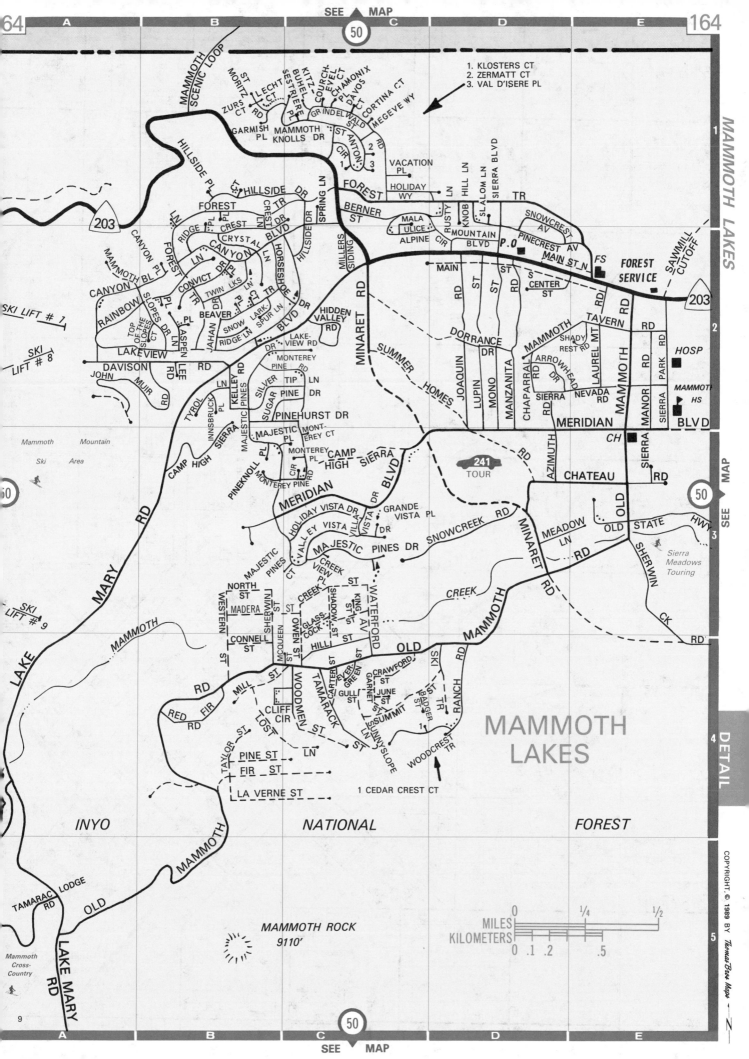

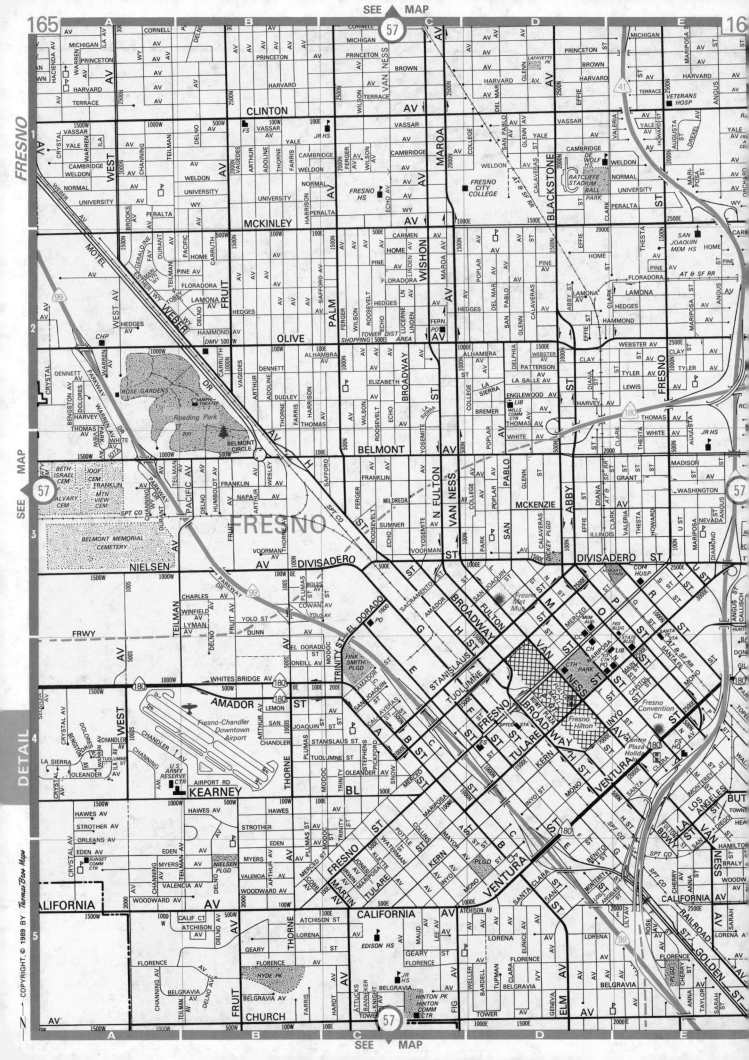

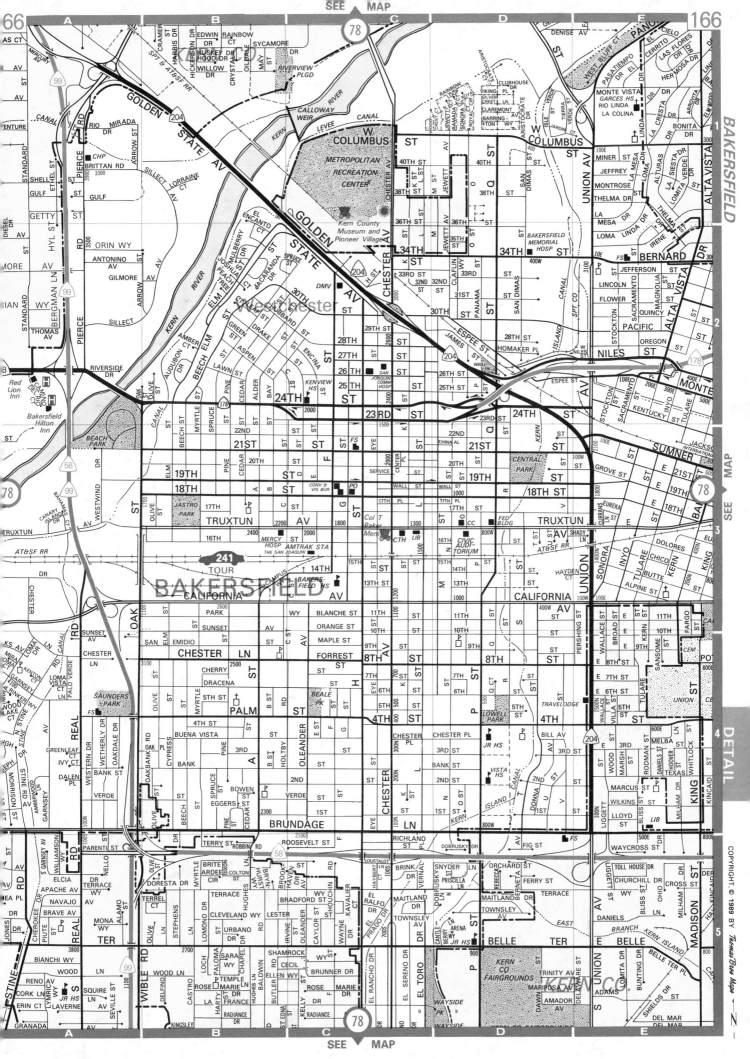

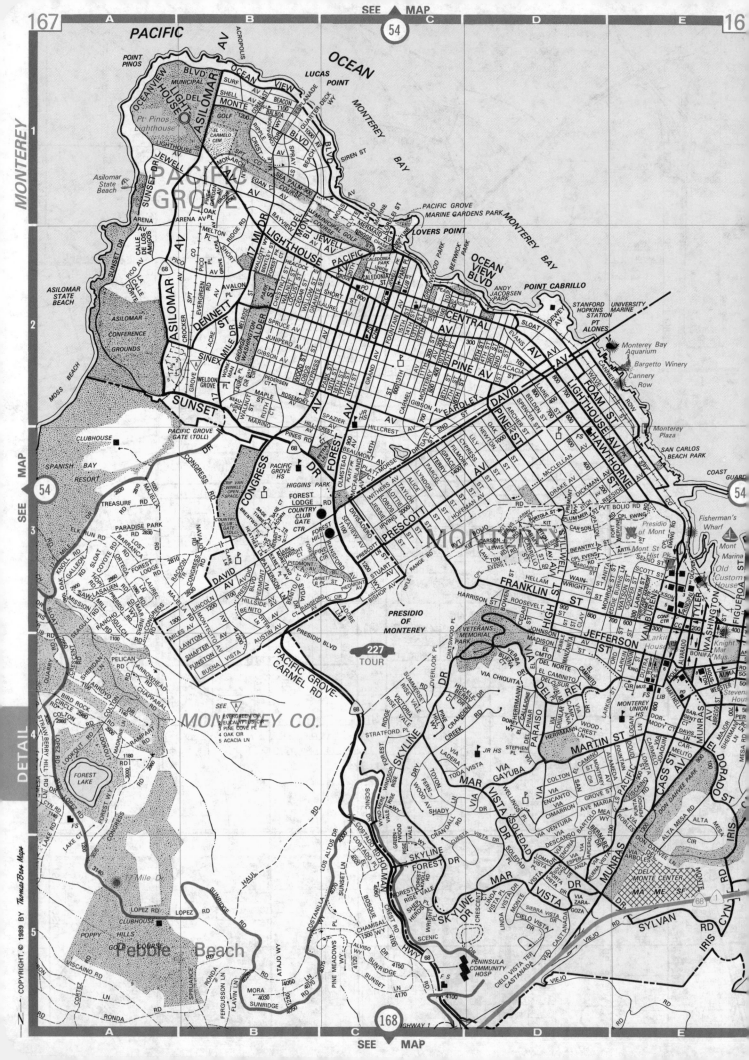

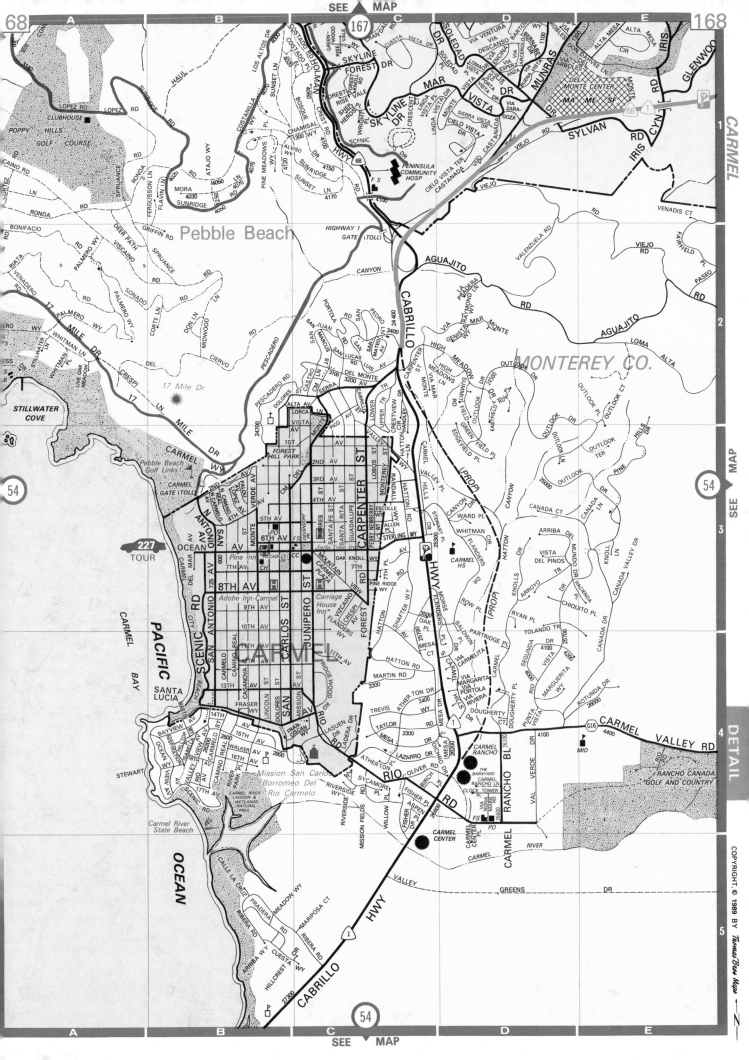

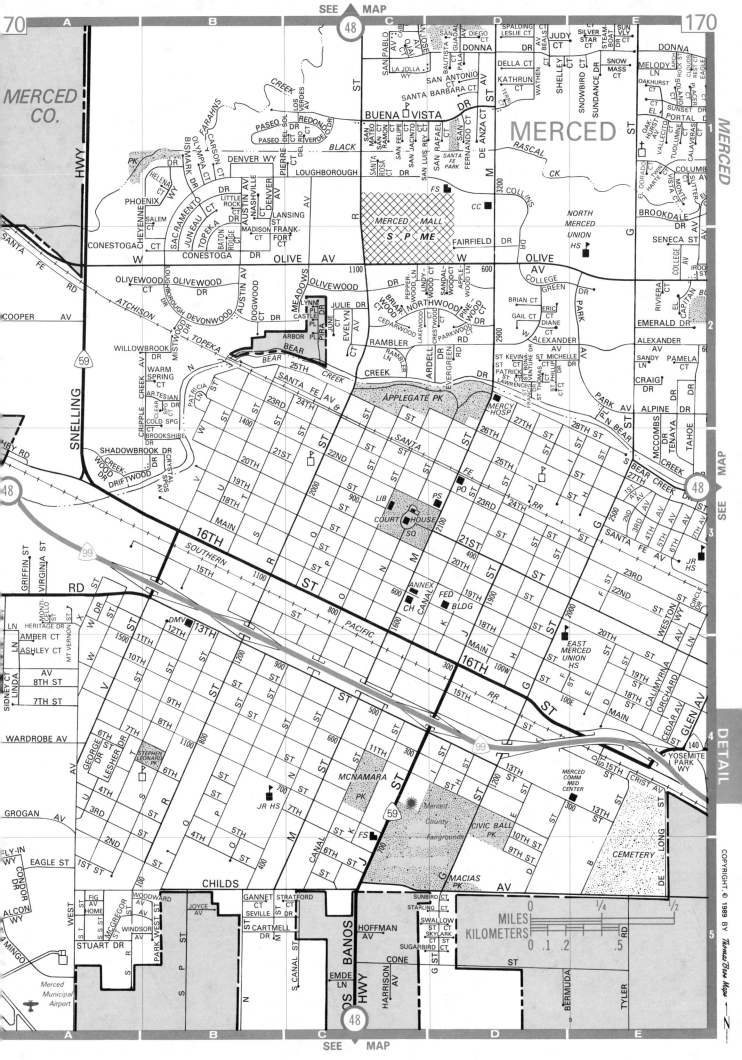

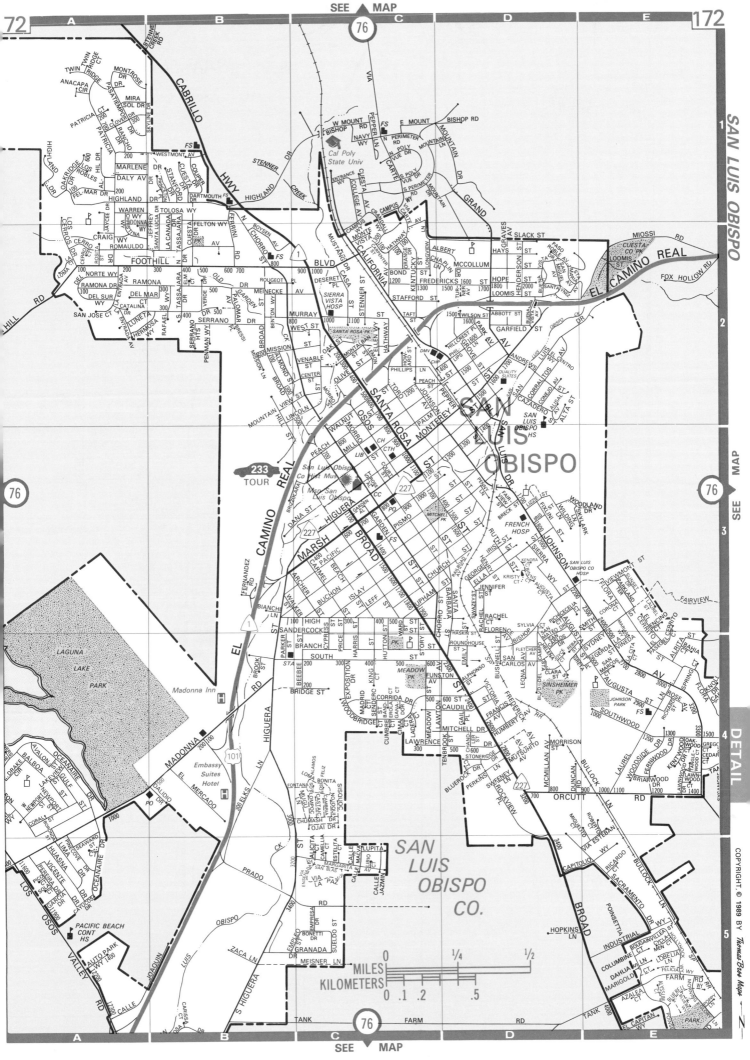

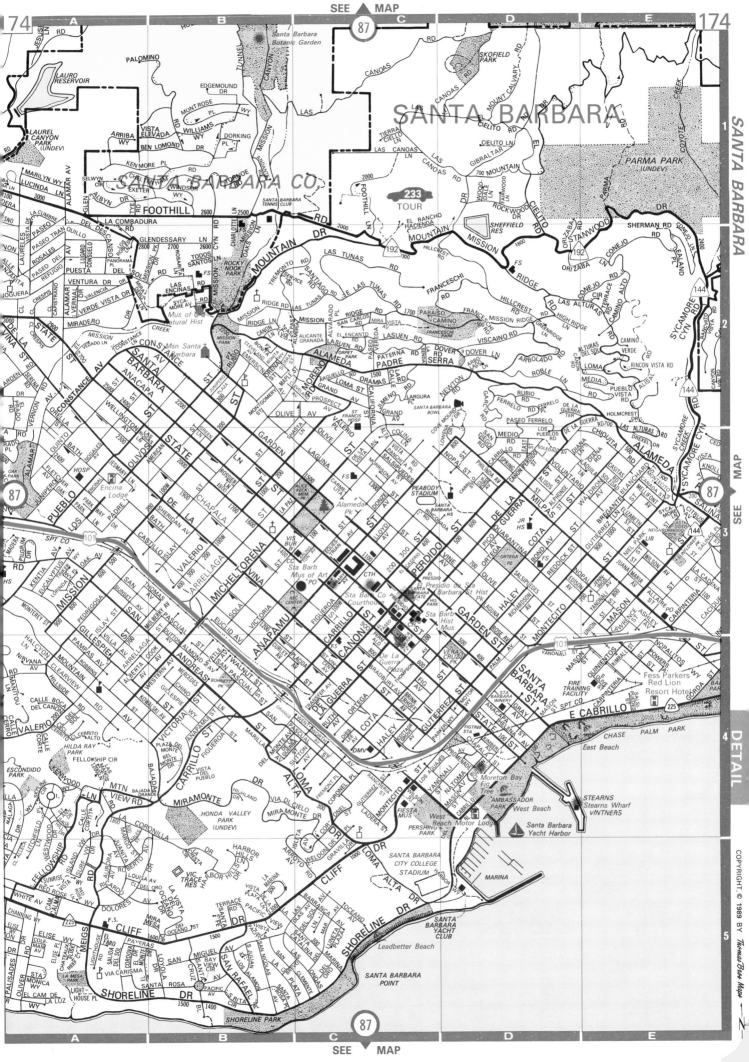

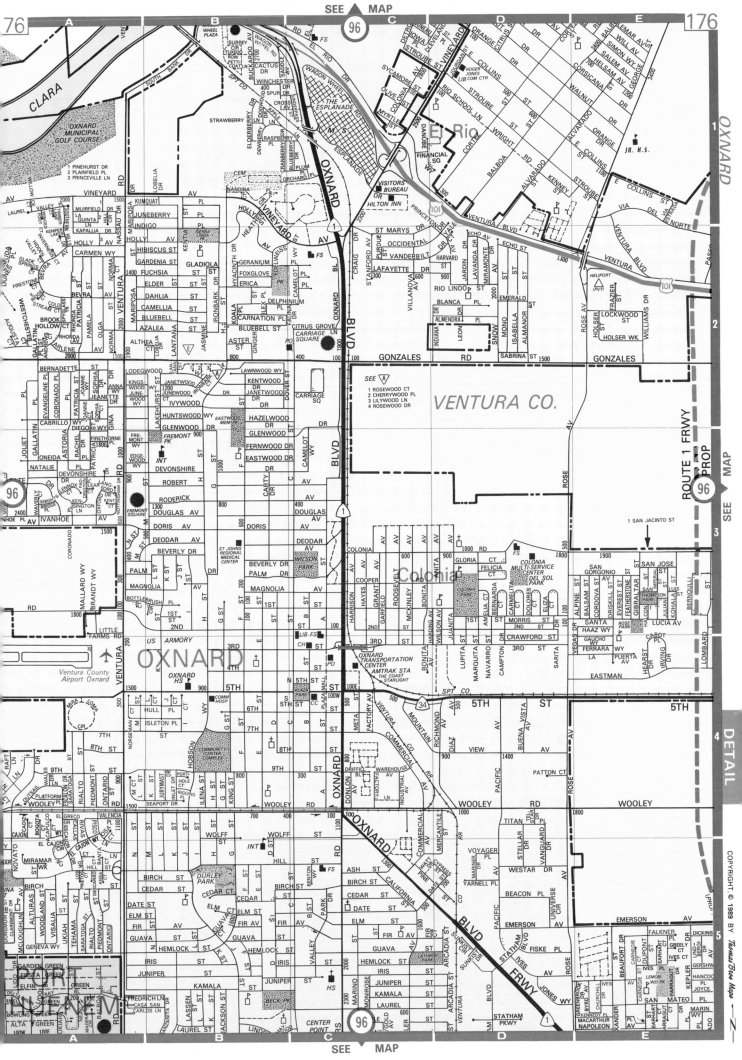

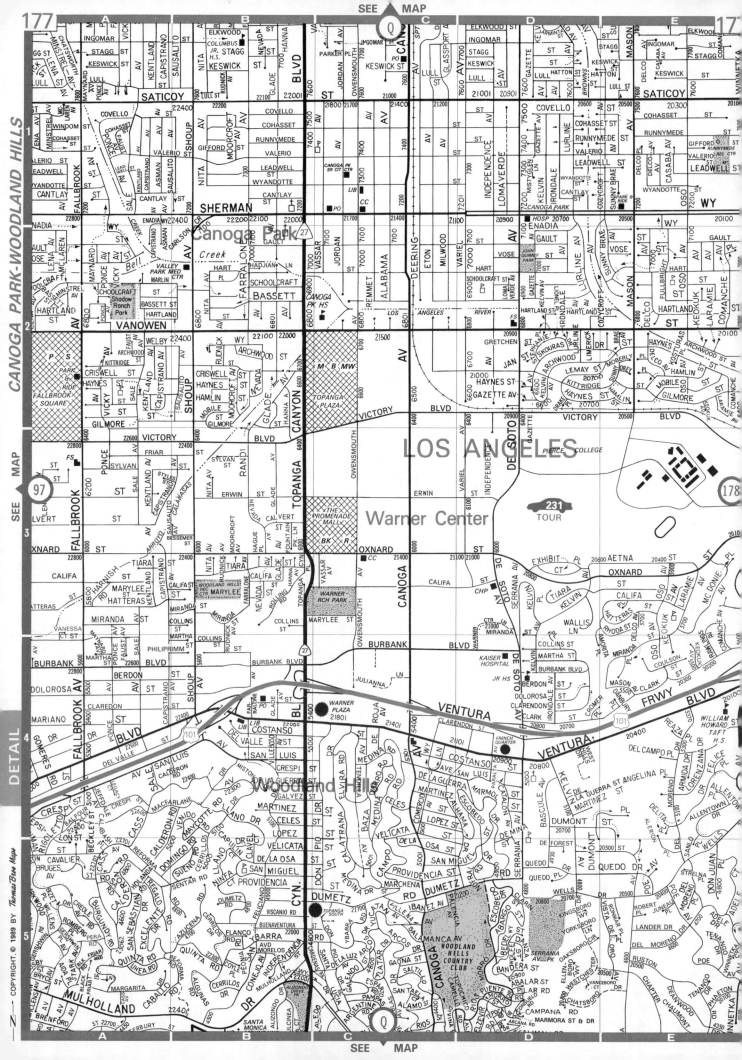

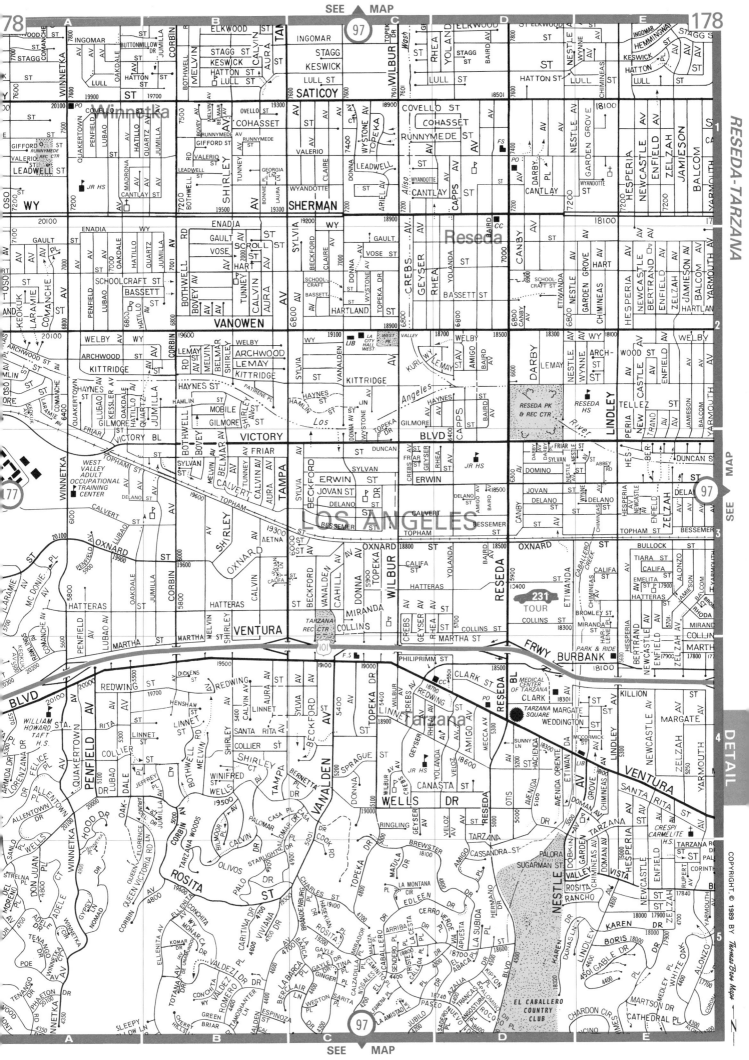

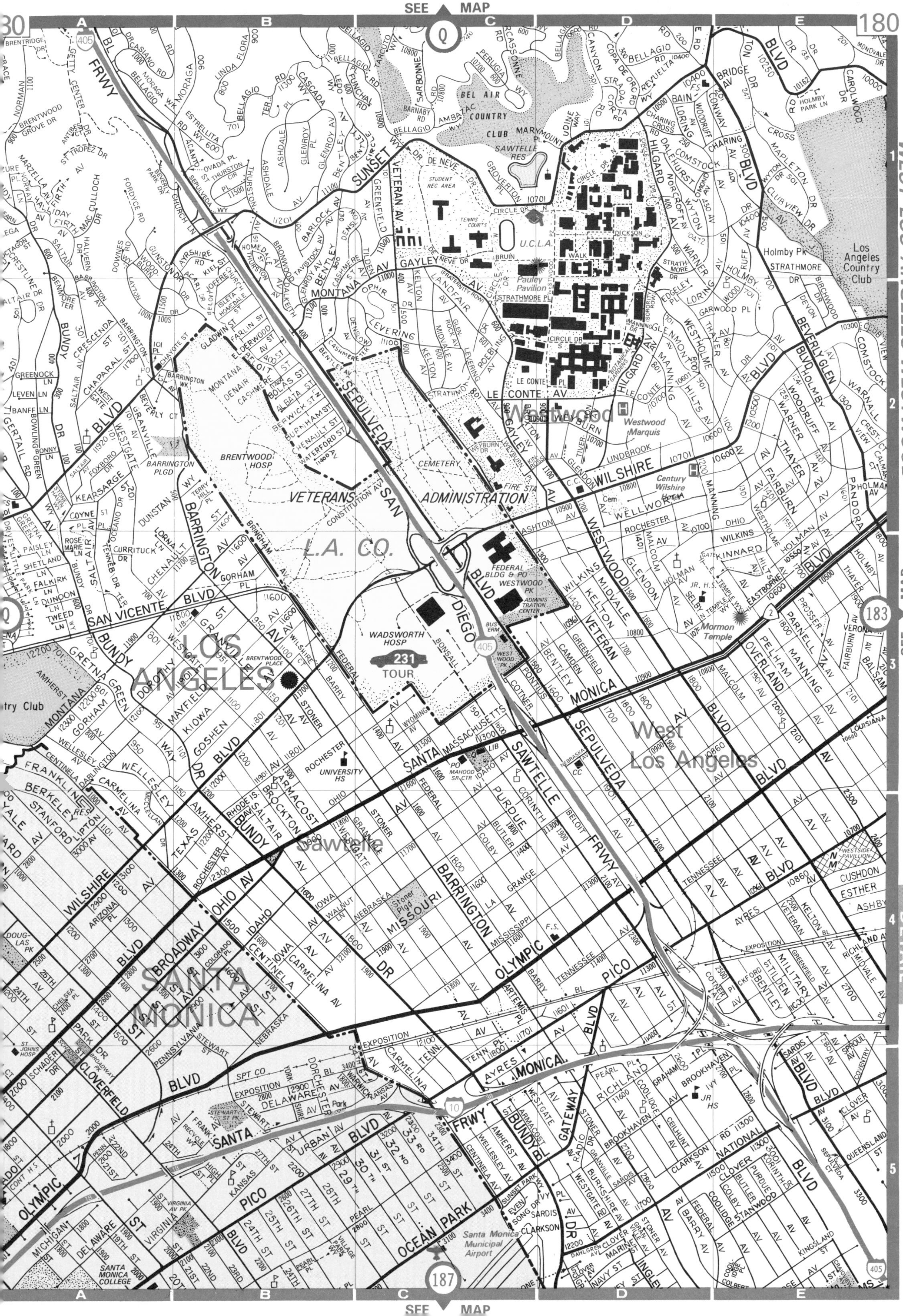

SEE MAP Q

WEST LOS ANGELES-WESTWOOD

405 FRWY

BEL AIR COUNTRY CLUB

MARYMOUNT

SAWTELLE RES

STUDENT REC AREA

U.C.L.A.

Bruin

Pauley Pavilion

DICKSON

WALK

Holmby Pk

STRATHMORE

Los Angeles Country Club

SUNSET BLVD

VETERAN AV

GAYLEY AV

MONTANA AV

LEVERING

LE CONTE AV

Westwood

Westwood Marquis

BEVERLY GLEN BLVD

SEPULVEDA BLVD

BRENTWOOD HOSP

CEMETERY

FIRE STA

WILSHIRE

Century Wilshire Hotel

WELLWORTH

VETERANS ADMINISTRATION

L.A. CO.

SAN DIEGO FRWY

FEDERAL BLDG & PO WESTWOOD PK

ADMINISTRATION CENTER

BUS TERM

Mormon Temple

BARRINGTON

SAN VICENTE BLVD

BUNDY DR

LOS ANGELES

WADSWORTH HOSP

231 TOUR

BRENTWOOD PLACE

405

WEST WOOD PK

SEPULVEDA

MONICA

West Los Angeles

SANTA

Sawtelle

UNIVERSITY HS

SAWTELLE

PURDUE AV

BARRINGTON AV

OLYMPIC

F.S.

WILSHIRE BLVD

OHIO AV

IDAHO AV

MISSOURI AV

STONER

MONICA

PICO

SANTA MONICA

BROADWAY

CENTINELA AV

NEBRASKA AV

ST JOHNS HOSP

PARK DR

CLOVERFIELD

EXPOSITION

SPT CO

10 FRWY

BUNDY BL

GATEWAY

NATIONAL BLVD

MICHIGAN

DELAWARE

PICO

OCEAN PARK

SANTA MONICA COLLEGE

Santa Monica Municipal Airport

405

187 SEE MAP

183 SEE MAP

DETAIL

COPYRIGHT © 1989 BY Thomas Bros. Maps

N

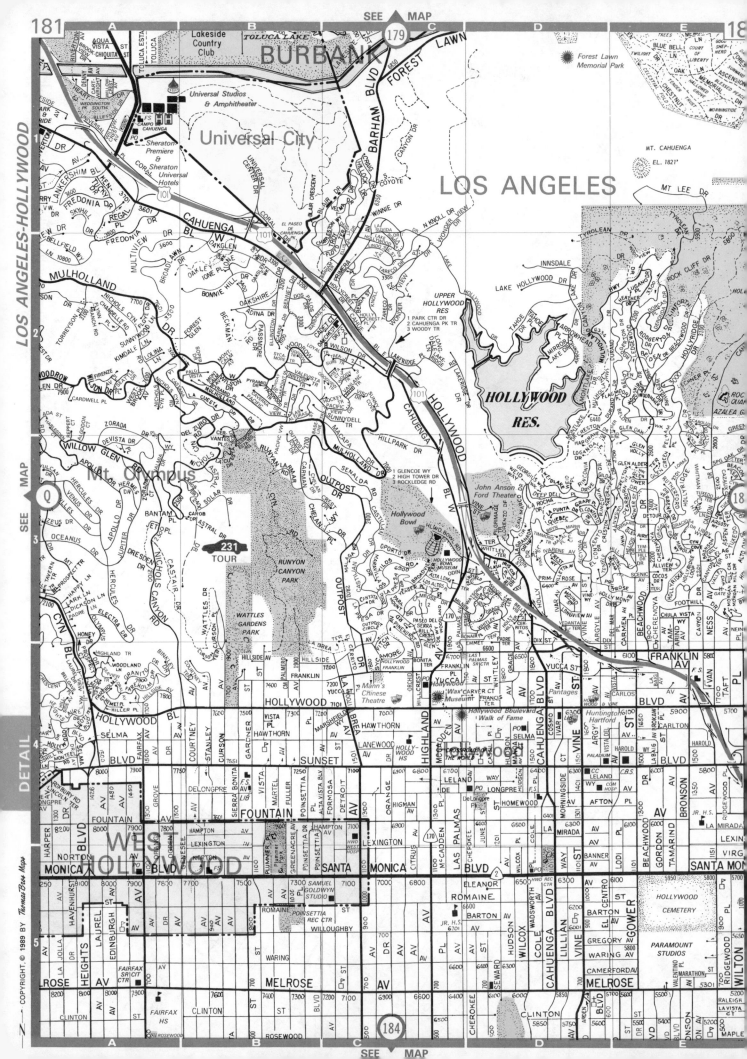

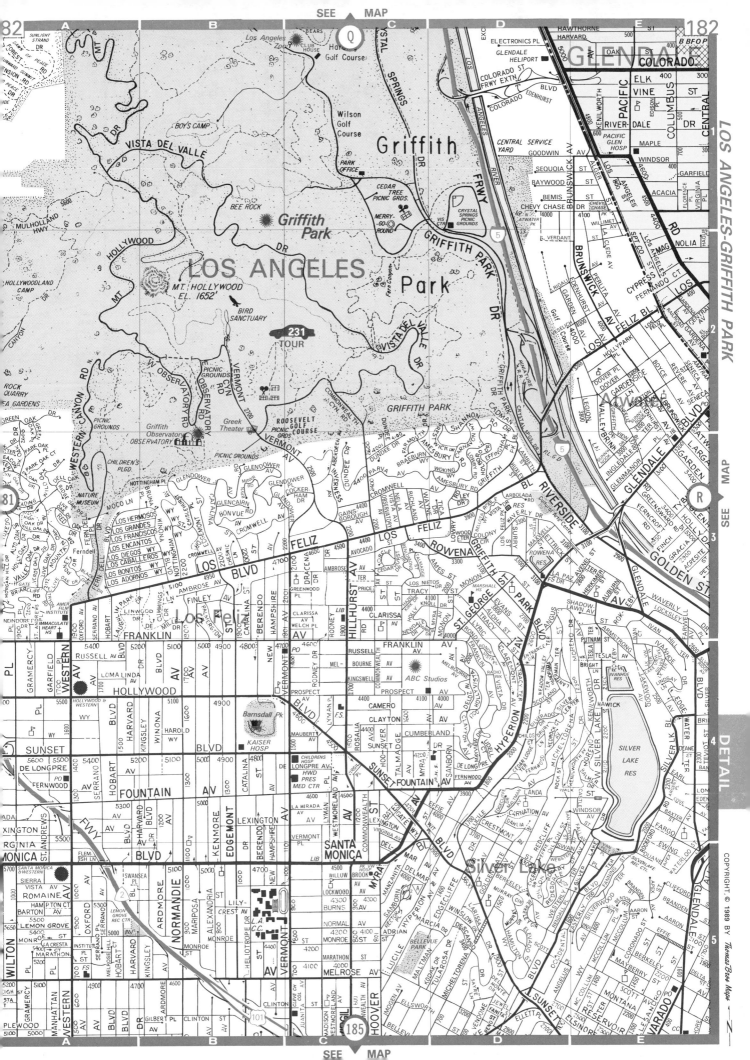

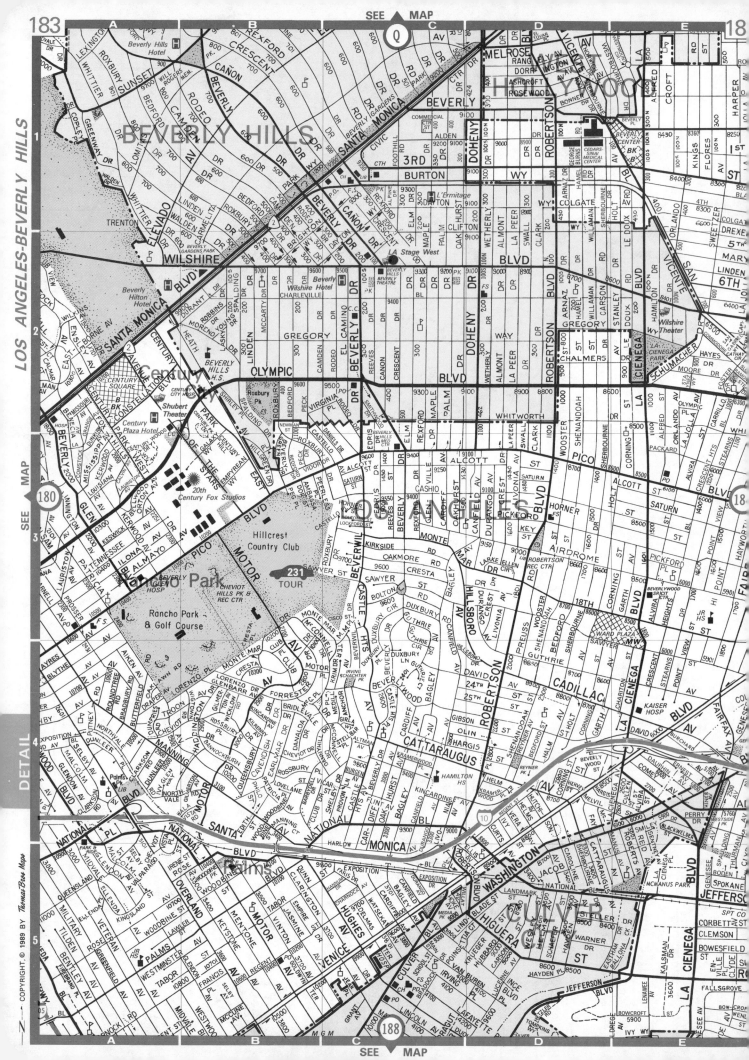

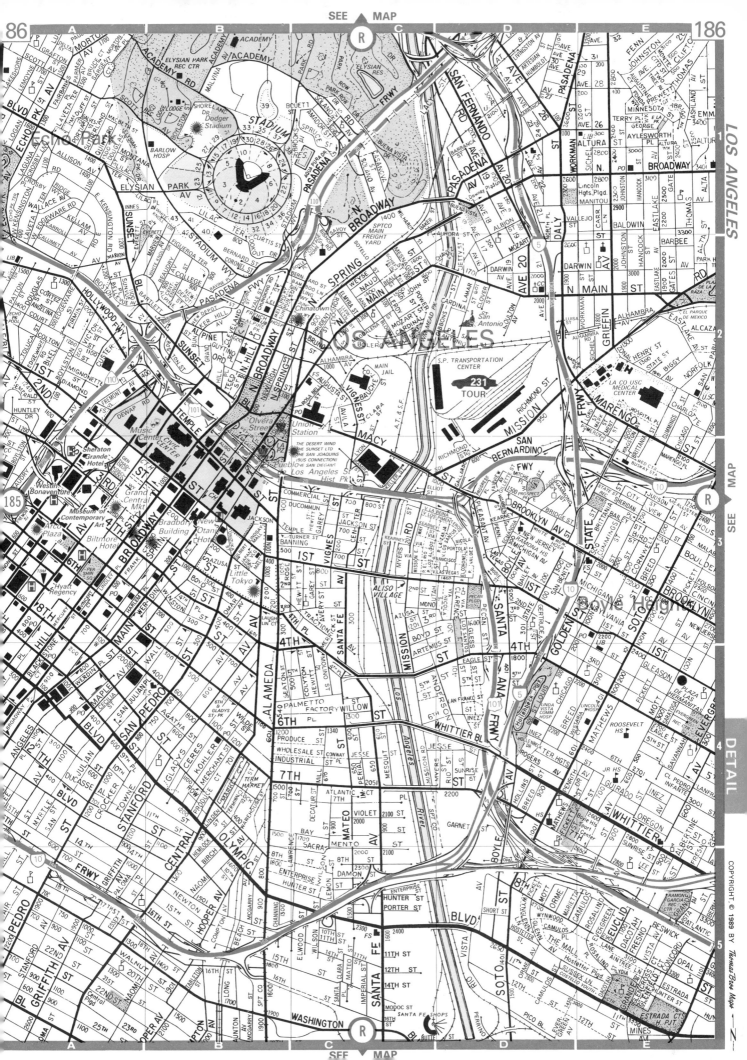

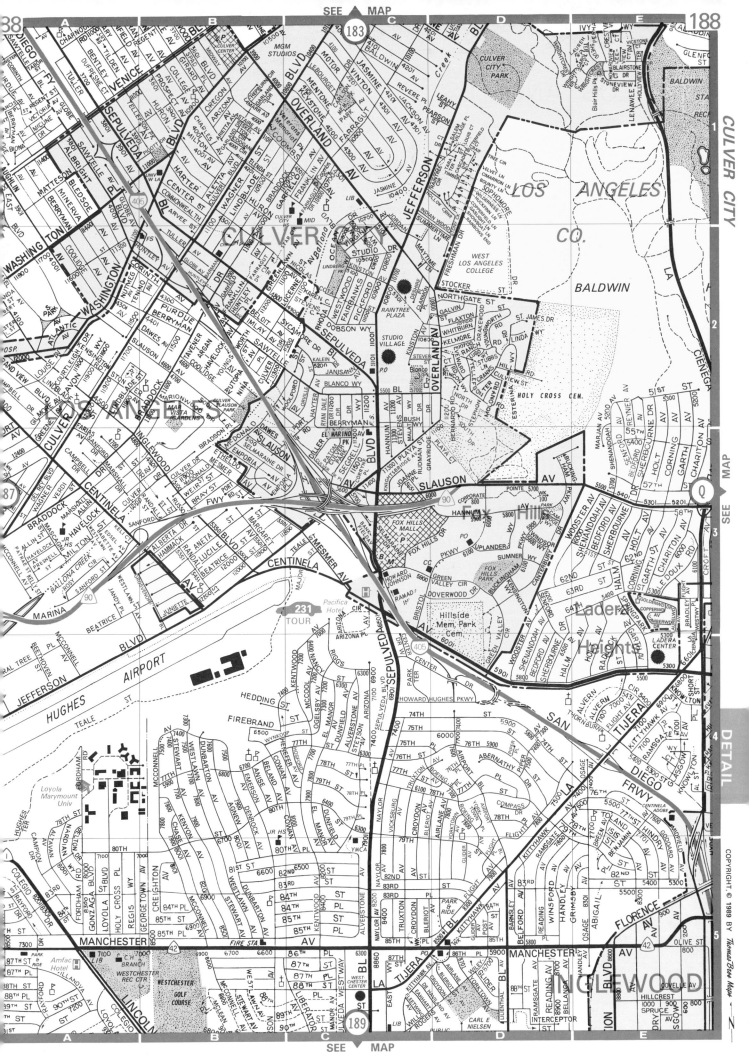

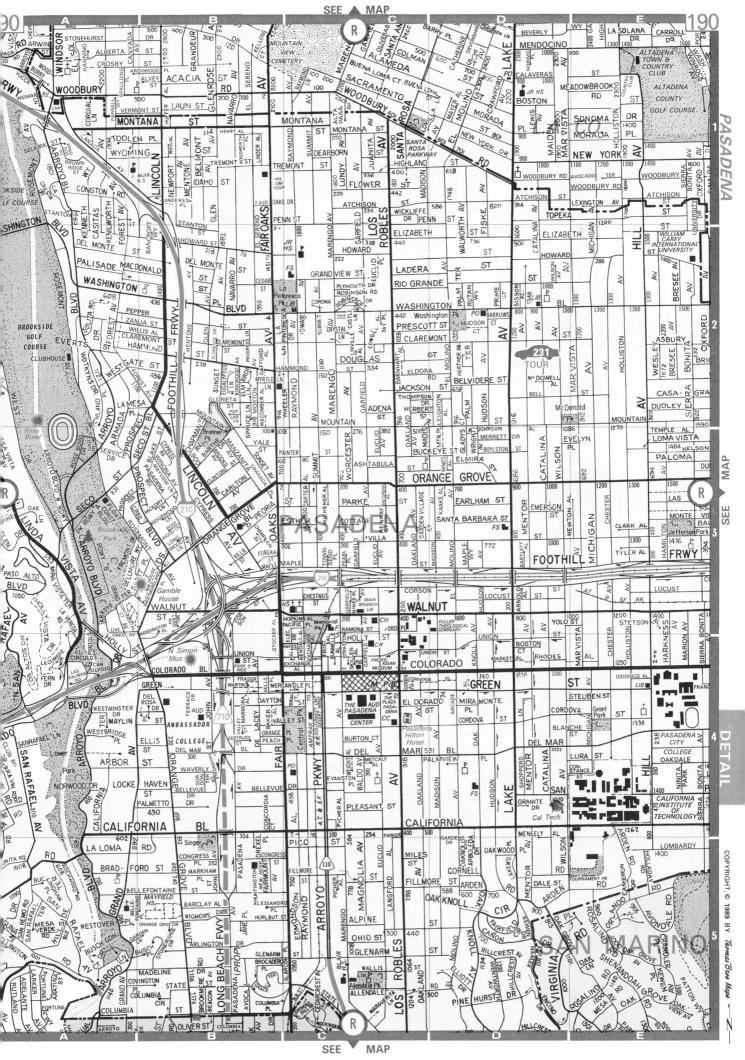

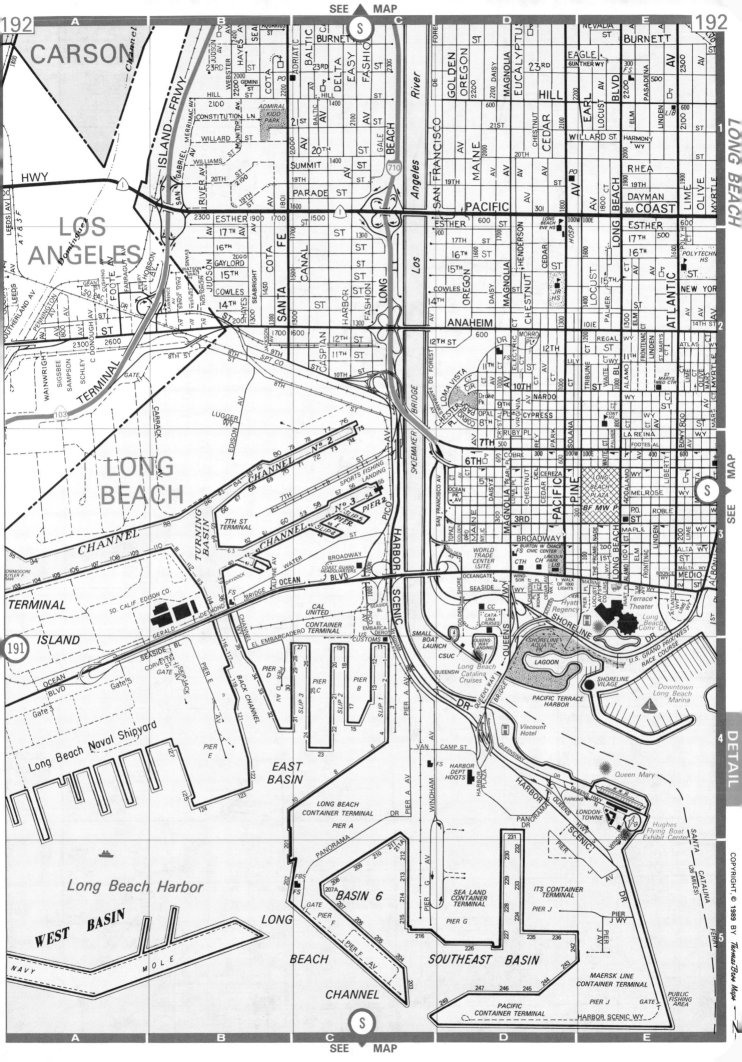

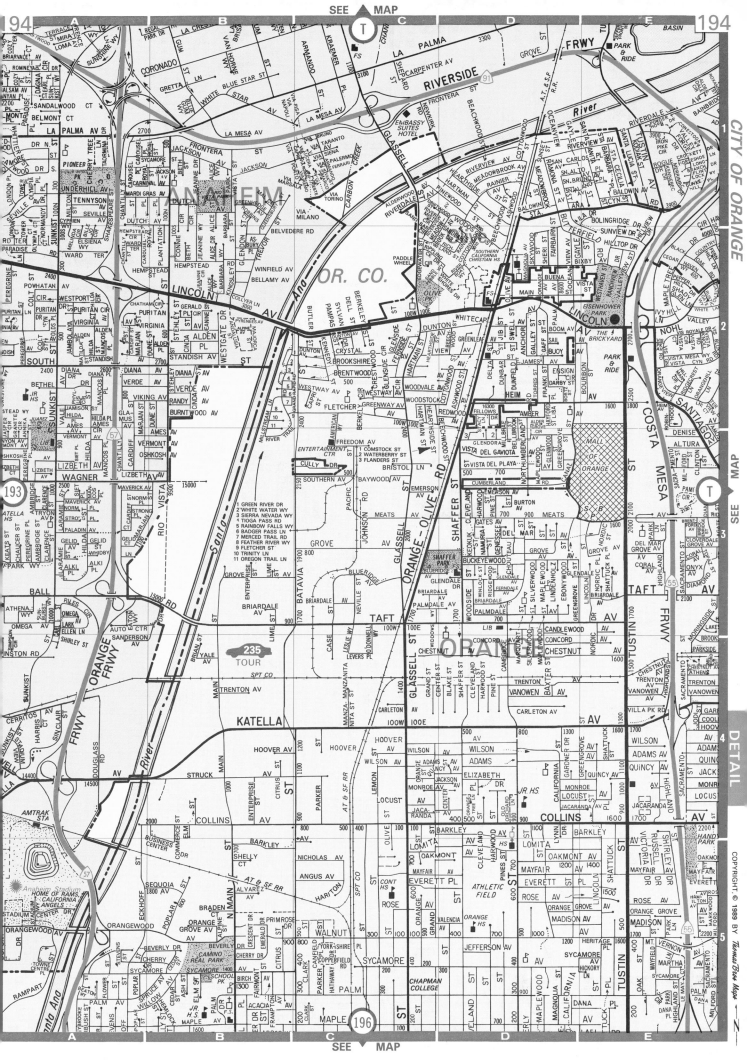

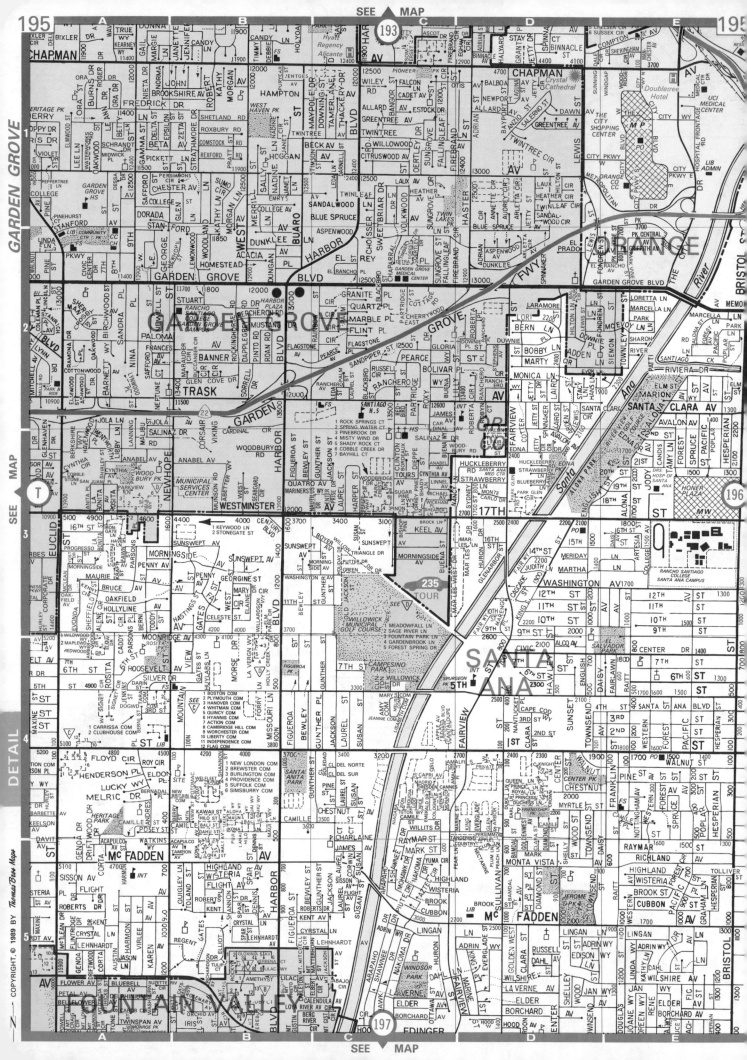

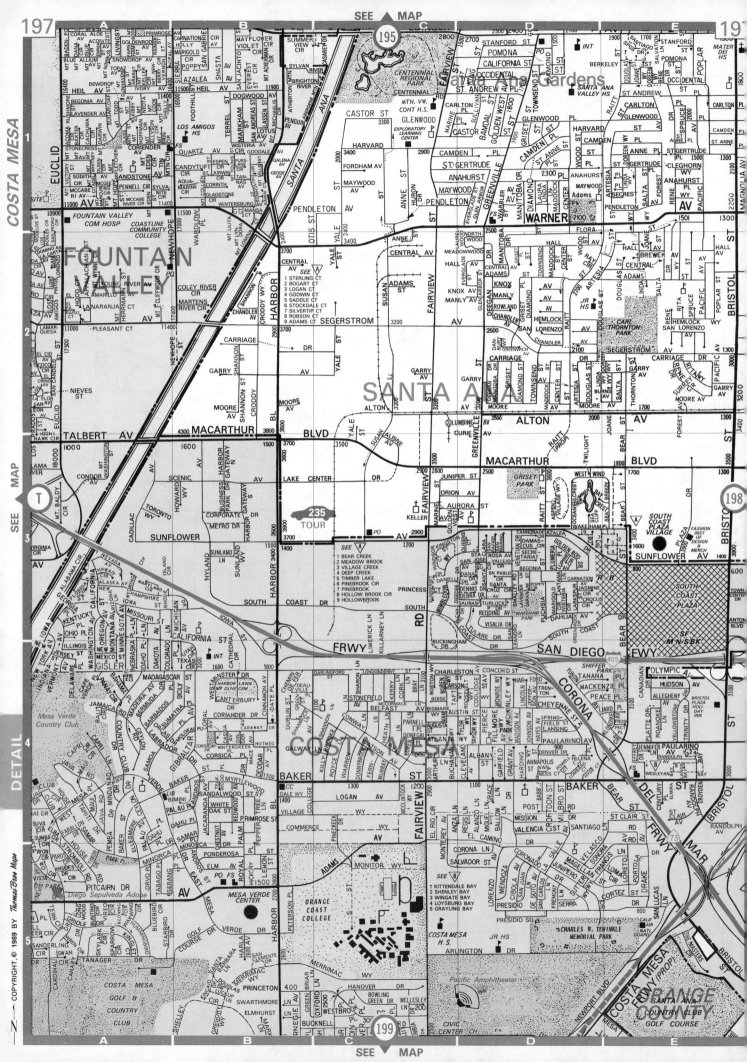

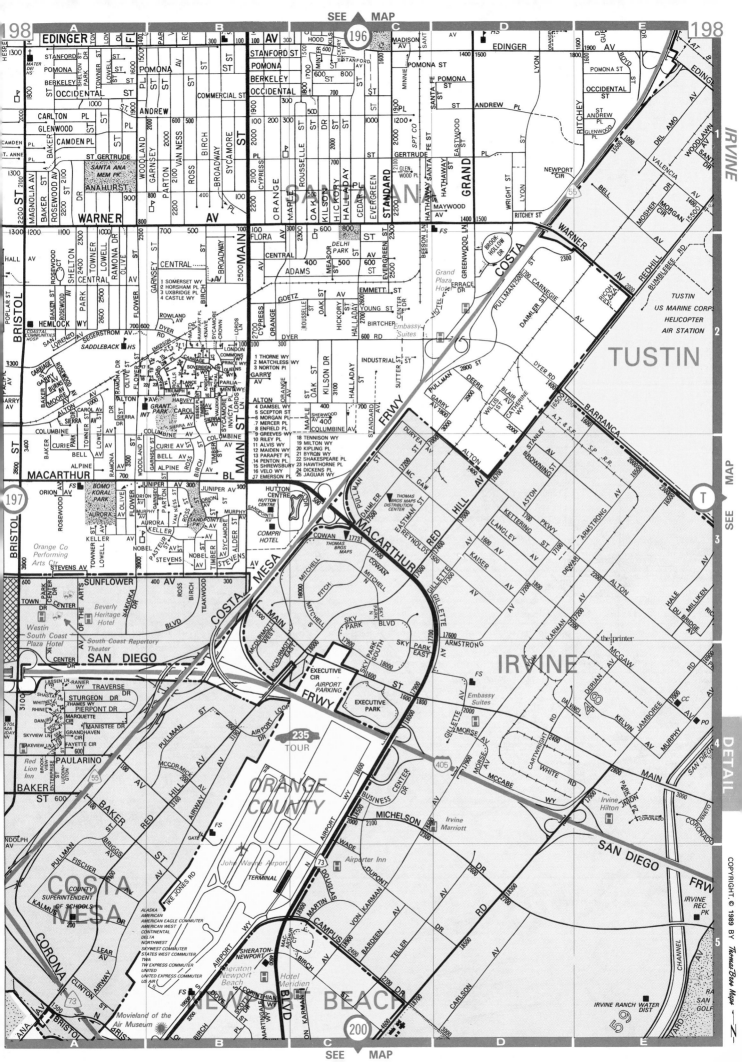

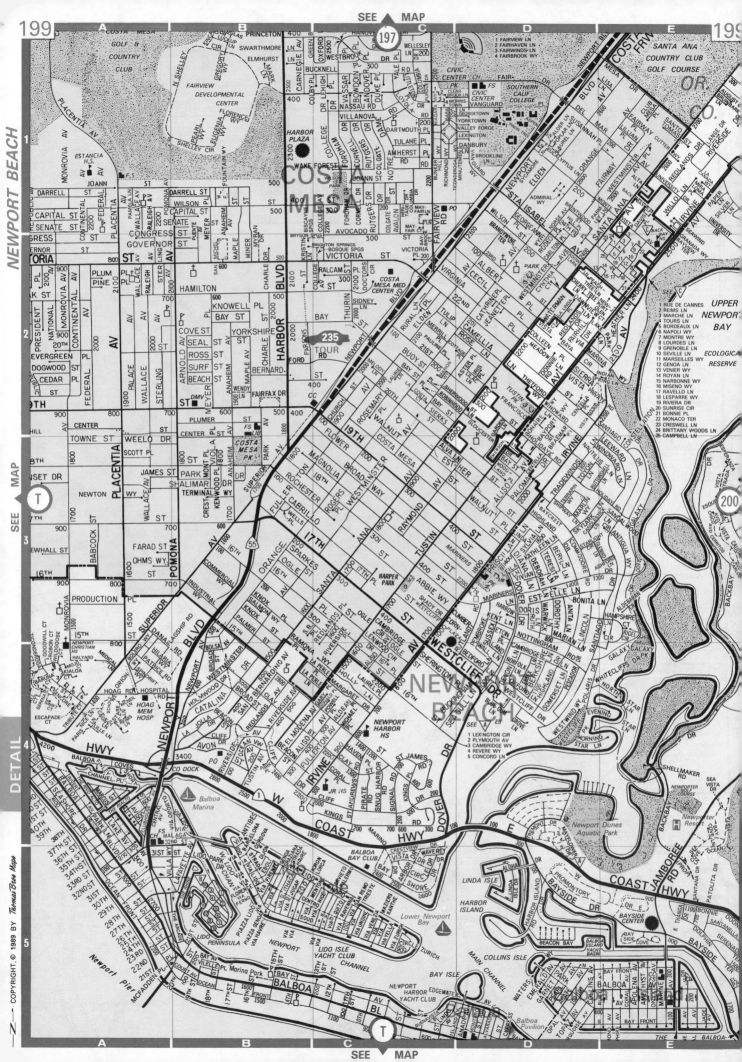

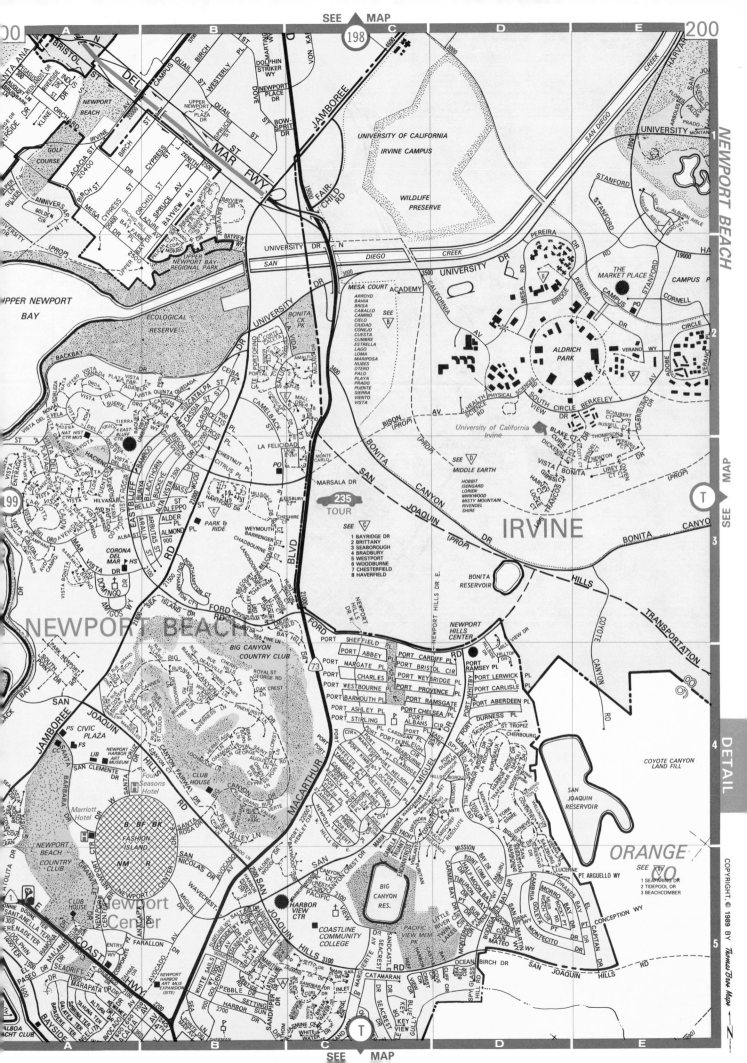

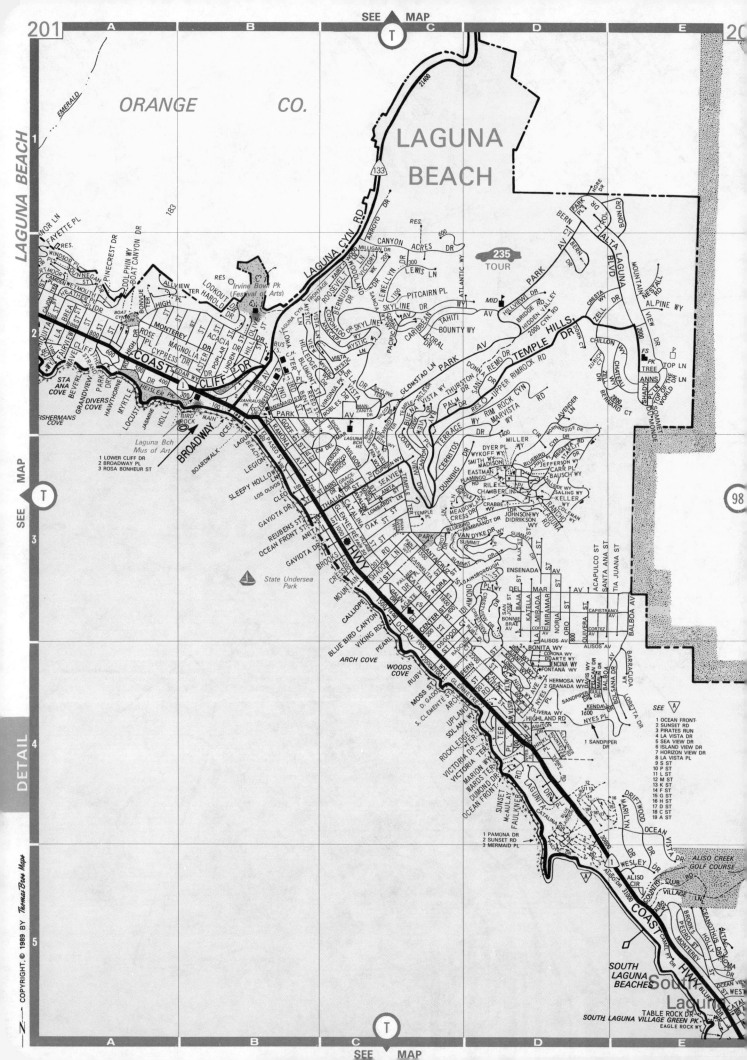

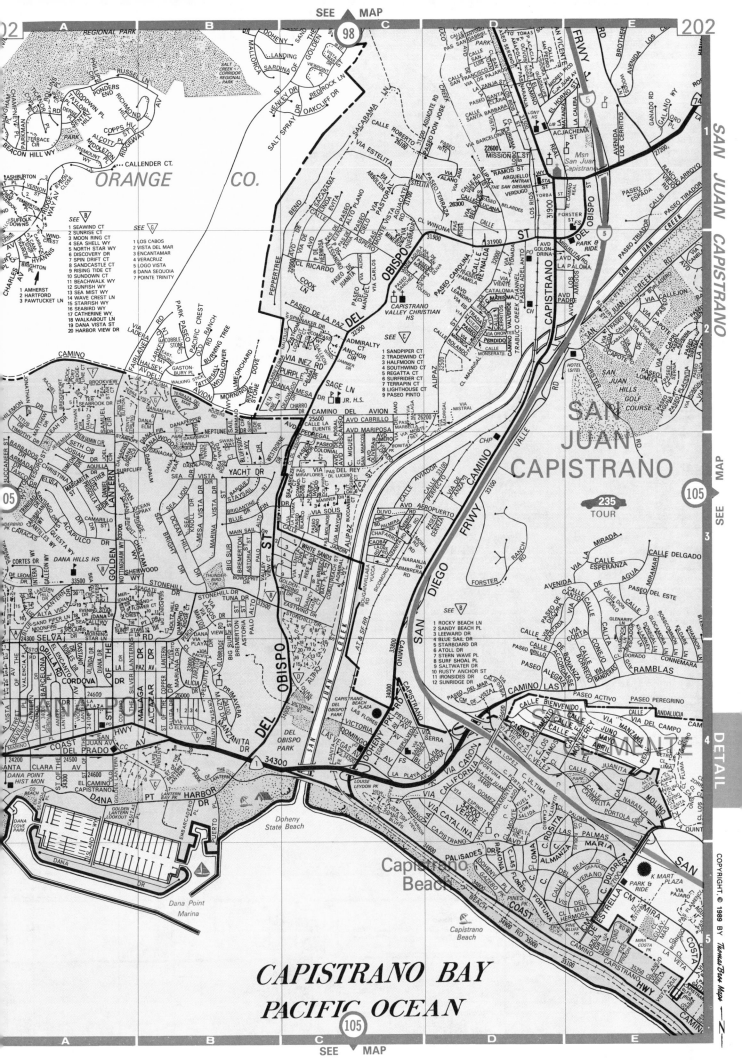

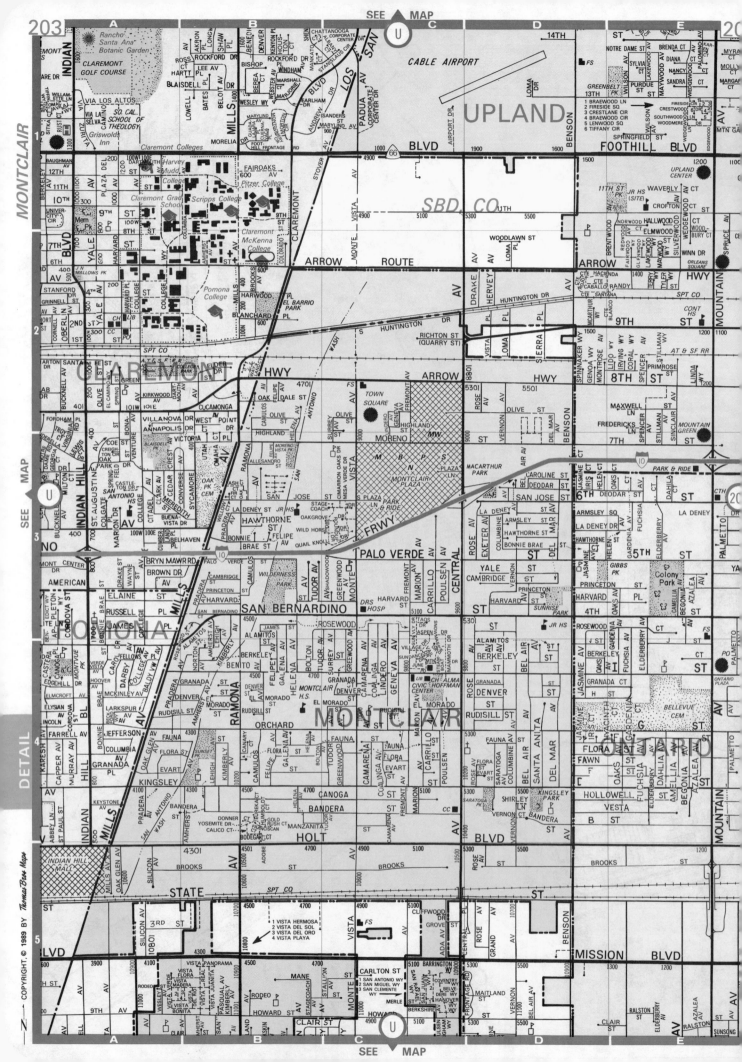

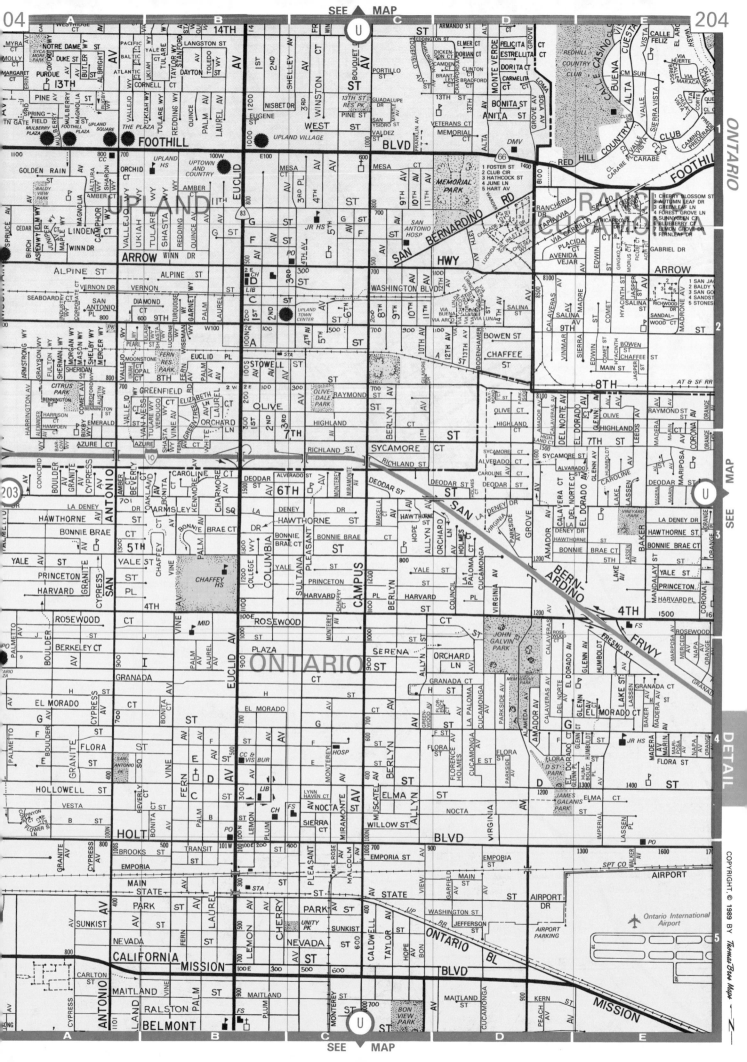

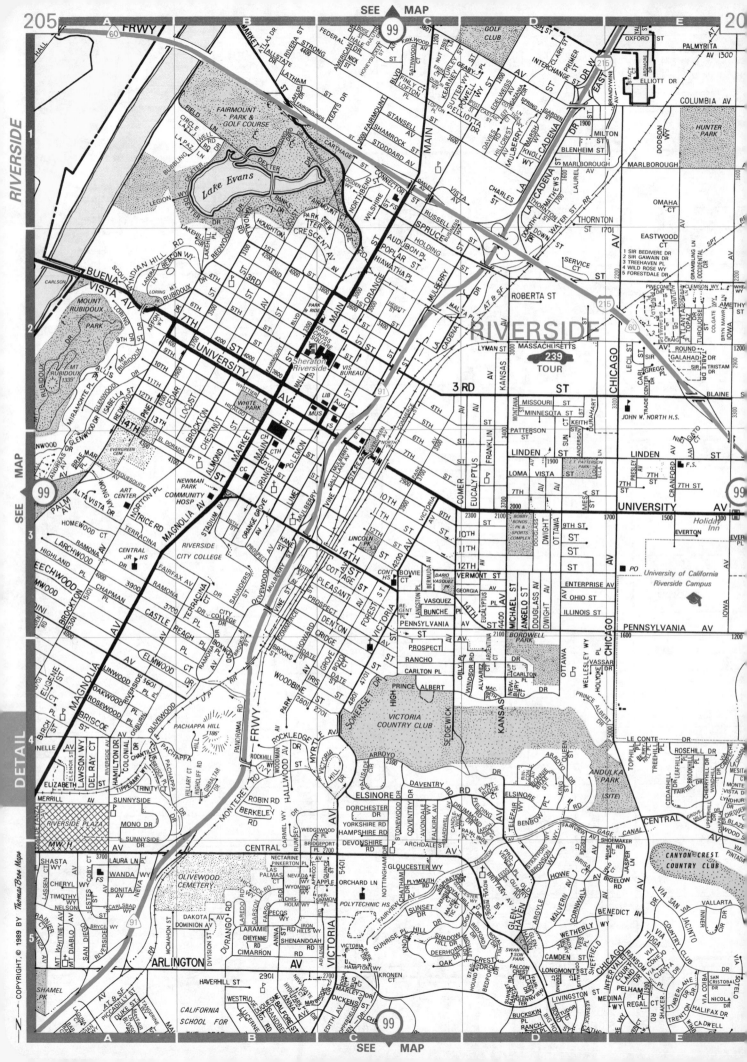

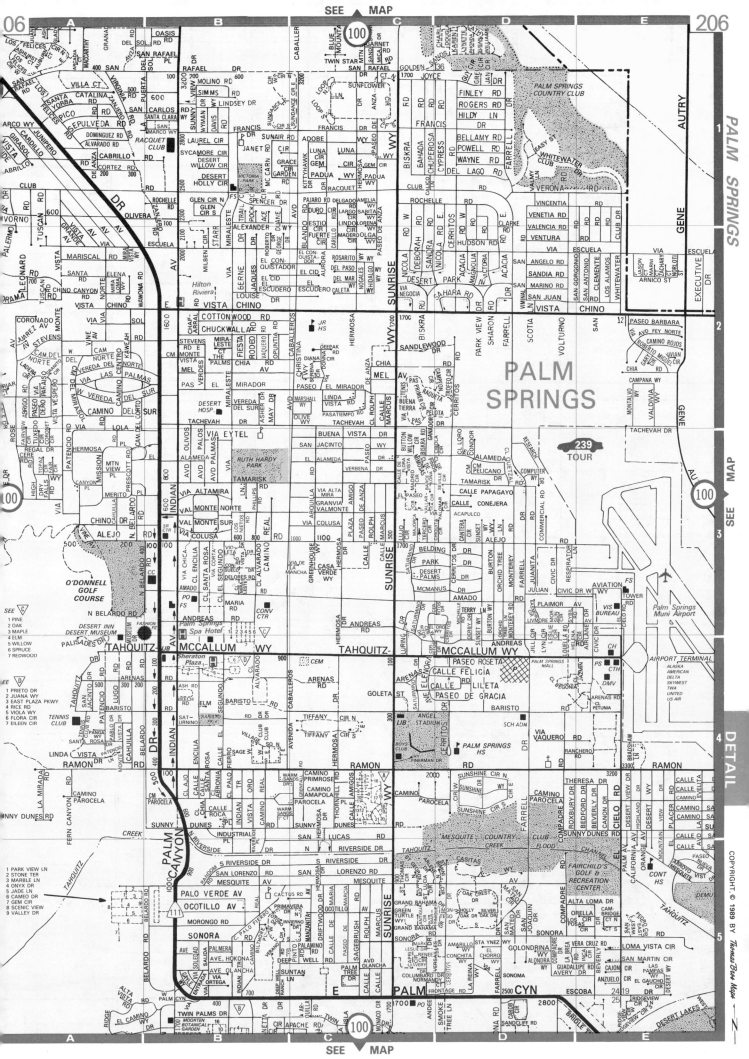

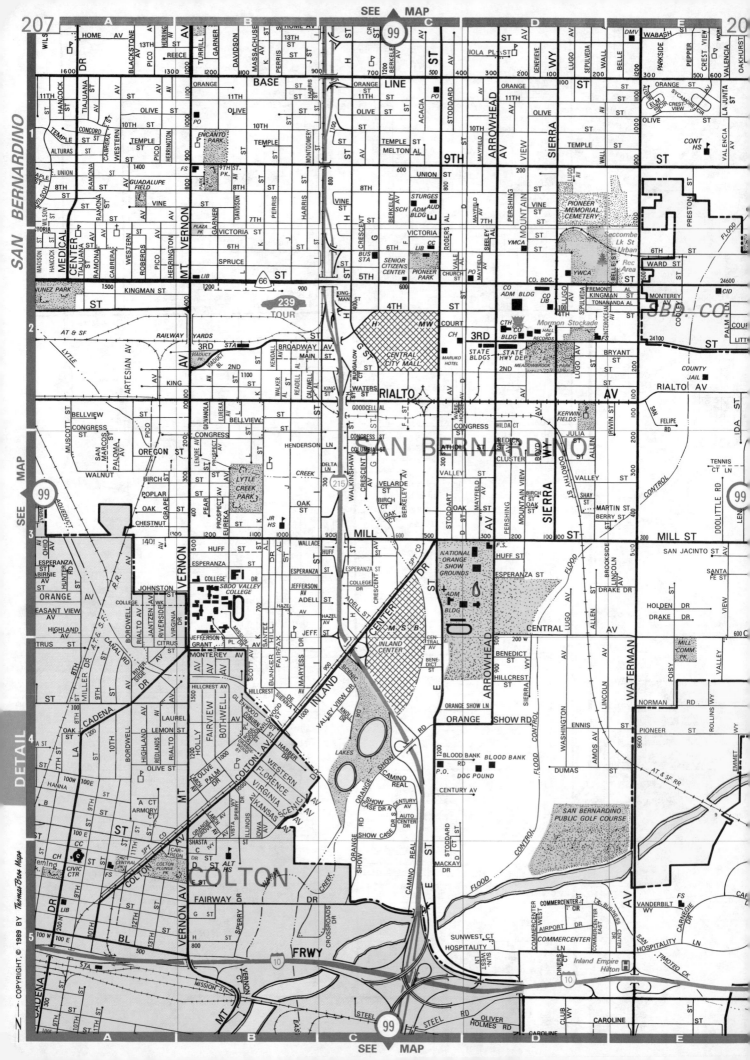

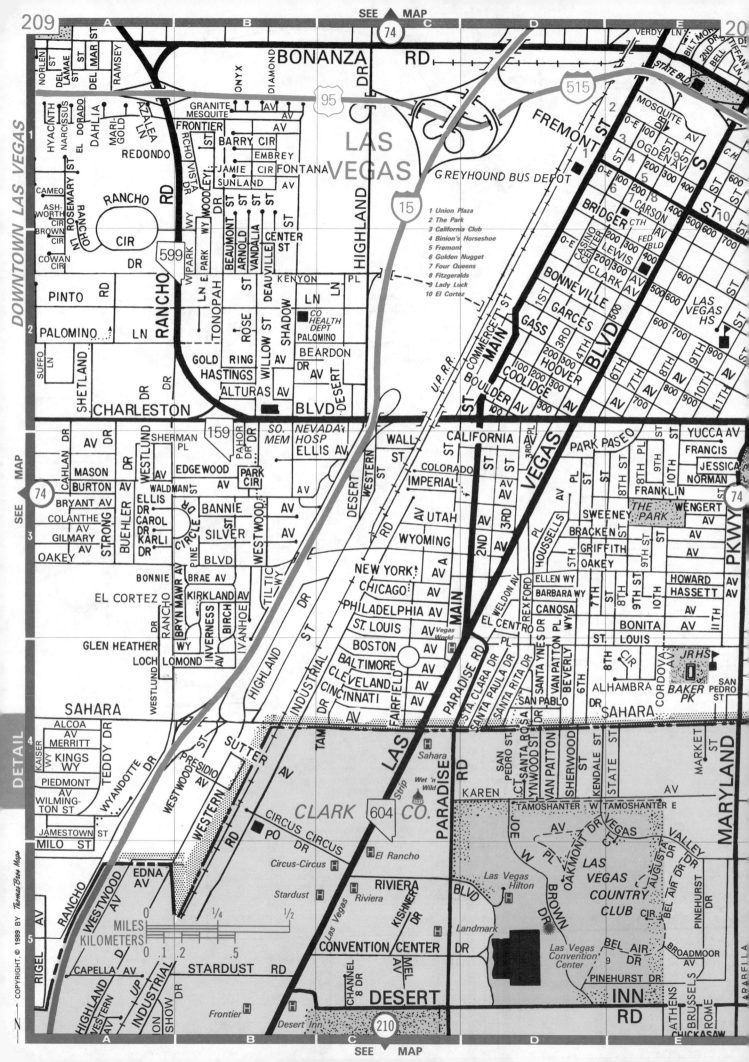

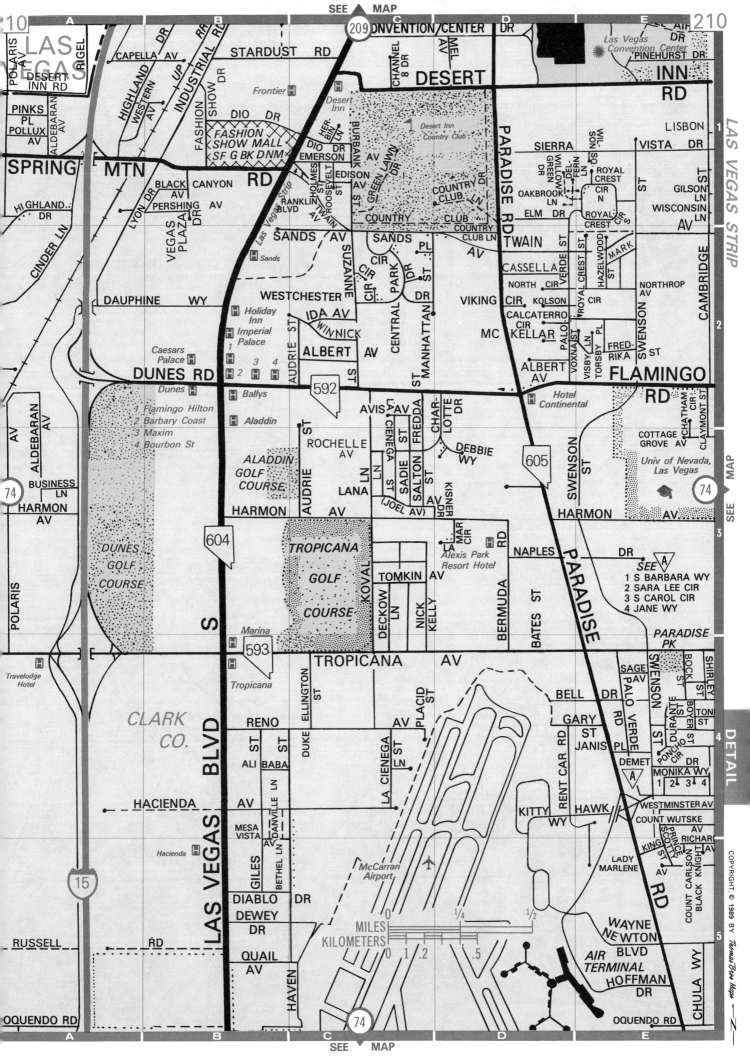

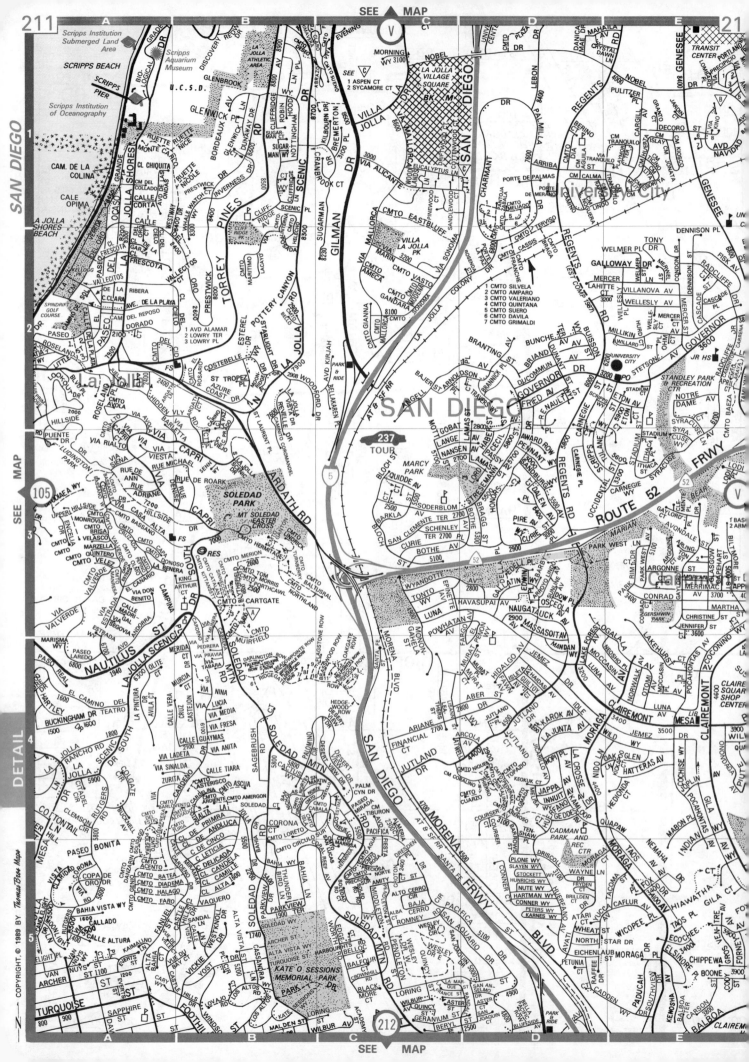

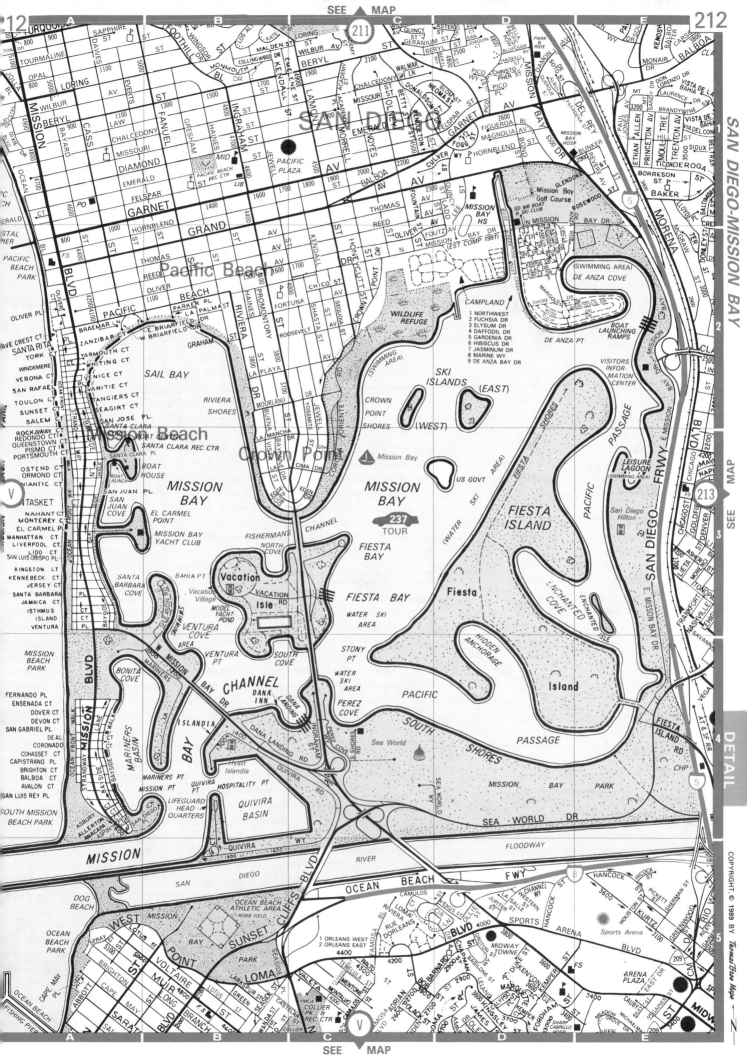

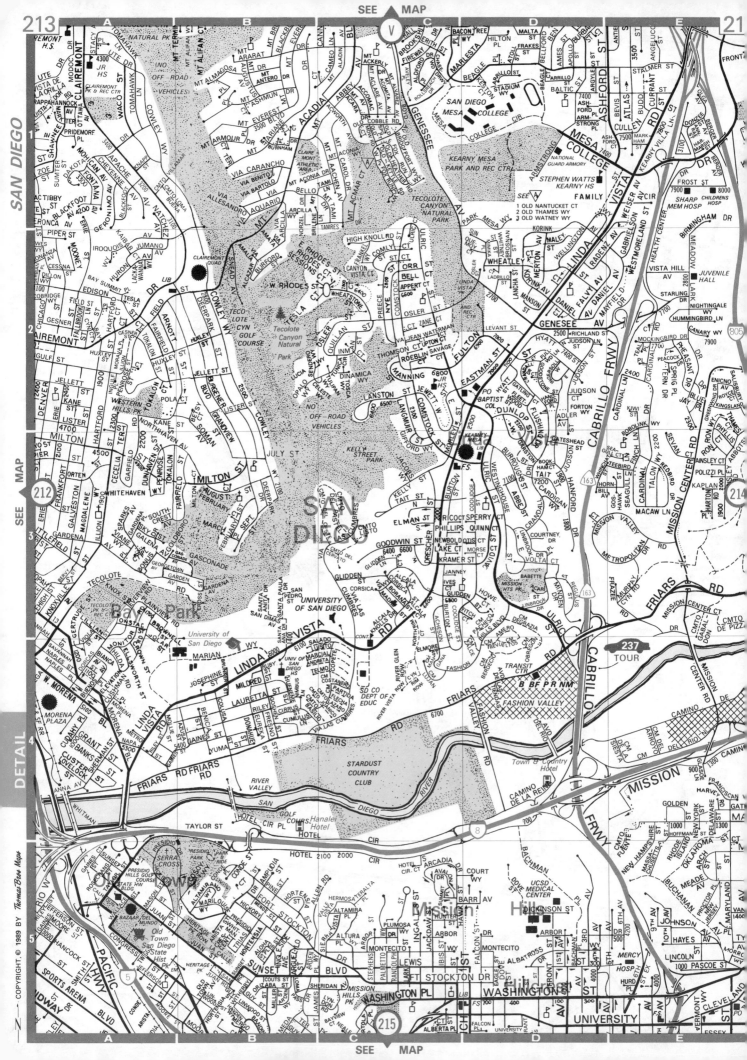

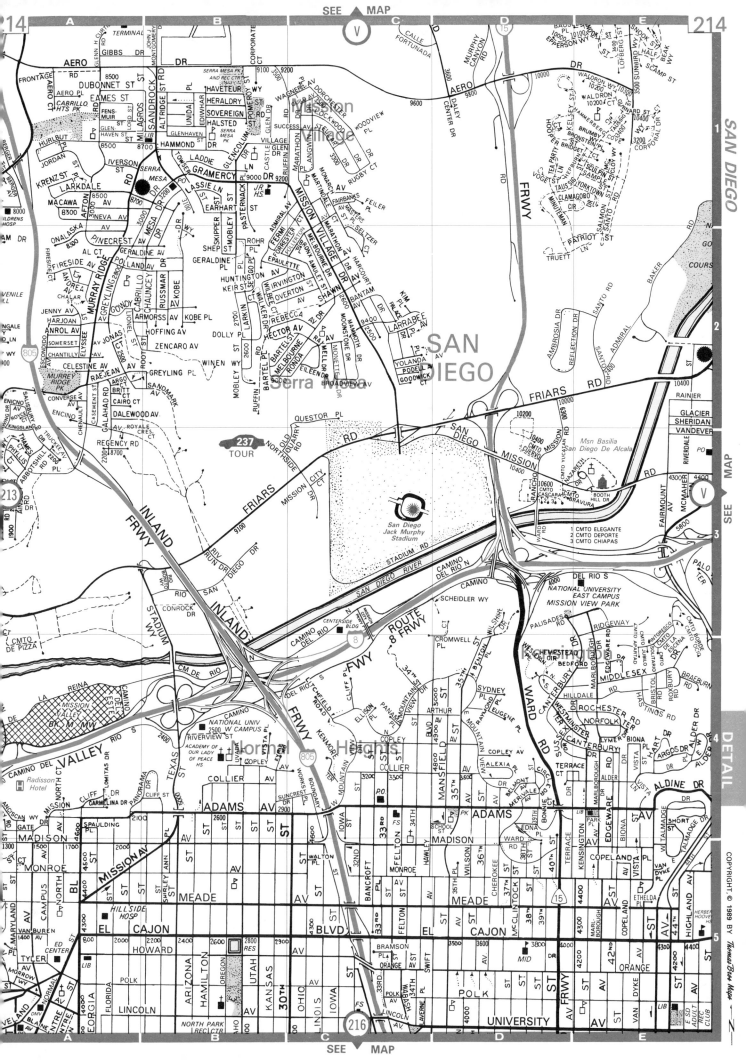

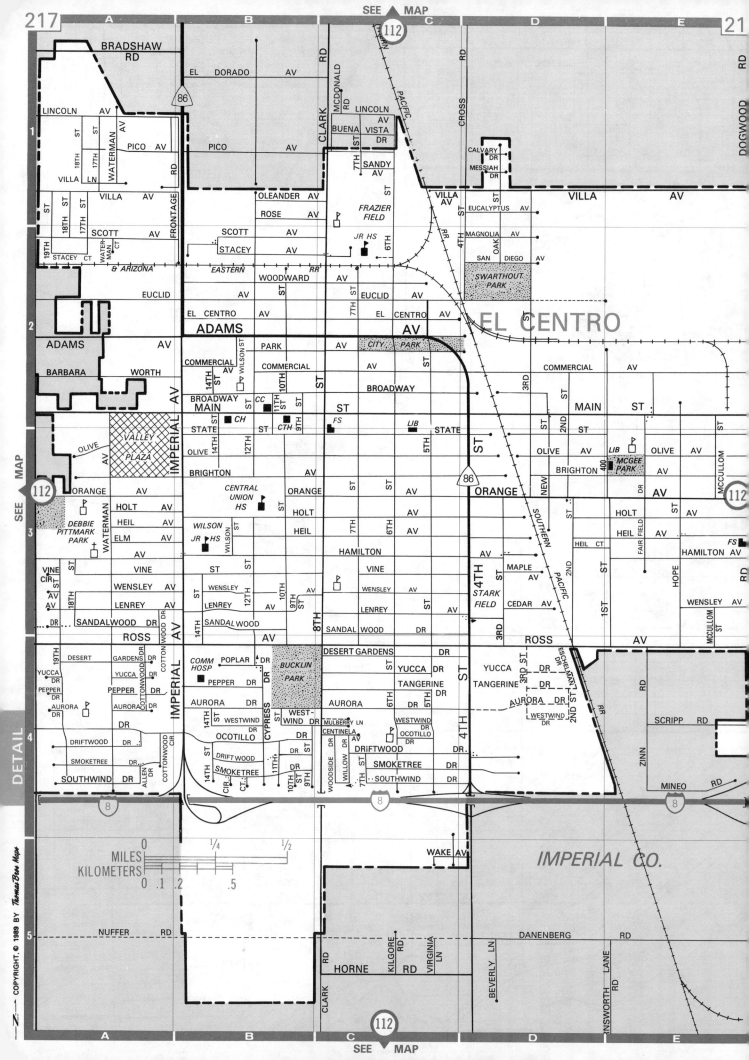

DISCOVER CALIFORNIA

Diverse cultures, natural wonders, historical landmarks and entertainment attractions galore await exploration! Whether you are a visitor, a new arrival or a long-time resident, California has something to spark your curiosity.

From the Danish village of Solvang to Chinatown in San Francisco, every culture in the world is represented in some way. California also boasts the highest mountain in the contiguous U.S.; the lowest elevation; the tallest, the oldest and the largest living things on earth. One location registers the hottest temperature in the Western Hemisphere.

Thirteen hundred miles of coastline and over 250 State maintained parks provide an incredible playground for anyone who loves to investigate the great outdoors.

For the history buff, California's is rich and well-preserved. The dinosaurs, Indian tribes, Spanish explorers and missionaries, gold-seekers and homesteaders all left trails that can be retraced today.

Technology and imagination have made this State an entertainment extravaganza. Disneyland, Hollywood and the Golden Gate Bridge are all internationally recognized symbols of California.

Whether you are a first-time visitor or a native Californian, we encourage you to discover this State along its network of scenic highways and backroads. We hope that you will enjoy your adventure and travel with confidence using the California Road Atlas as your guide.

Table of Contents

We invite your comments and recommendations. Please write to:

Thomas Bros. Maps
17731 Cowan
Irvine, CA 92714
c/o CRA Driving Tours

Thomas Bros. Maps updates this Atlas annually based on field research and available sources, but changes can and do occur. We hope that you will not be inconvenienced by any information that becomes obsolete or inaccurate.

Instructions

We have created twelve Driving Tours which highlight different regions of California. Each tour designates a scenic route and briefly describes some of the points of interest along the way.

An accompanying map outlines the tour with large green numbers indicating the page in this Atlas to refer to for a more detailed map. Also, the extensive indexes and the foldout map in the back of the Atlas will provide additional information. We hope that you have the opportunity to take all of the tours or at least integrate parts of them into your own travel plans.

For road conditions and possible road closures, call the California Department of Transportation (CALTRANS) at (916) 445-7623 or (213) 626-7231.

For general information about California, call the California Office of Tourism at (800) TO-CALIF, Ext. 99.

TOURS

NORTH COAST & MOUNT SHASTA

Northern California is a huge region of unspoiled wilderness, preserved by several state and national park boundaries. The area is dominated by lush forests, clear lakes and streams, wide valleys, mountain ranges and blue skies. It is a paradise for outdoor enthusiasts. There are fascinating natural wonders to explore linked by lonesome roads which meander through miles of spectacular scenery.

REDDING - *(Page 18, C2)* the gateway city to northern California and vital crossroads for travelers and commerce. At this junction, the roads lead north to Mt. Shasta, east to Mt. Lassen, northeast to the Lava Beds, west to the Redwoods, the coast or the wilderness of Klamath River.

Shasta-Cascade Wonderland Association, 1250 Parkview Ave., *(Page 122, C3)* Redding, provides maps, brochures and detailed information of the area. (916) 225-4100.

LASSEN VOLCANIC NATIONAL PARK - *(Page 19, E2)* An eerie wonderland created by a series of volcanic eruptions that occurred between 1914 and 1917. Mt. Lassen is still an active volcano and the area contains such evidence

as boiling lakes, bubbling mud pots, steaming springs and cinder cones. The 106,000 acres are considered safe as long as visitors stay on the designated trails. Maps and brochures are available at the park headquarters. (916) 595-4444.

LAVA BEDS NATIONAL MONUMENT - *(Page 5, D4)* a very remote expanse of dormant volcanoes, lava flows, mud holes and caves. Amateur spelunkers may explore several of the 200 caves, some featuring permanent ice and Indian pictographs. A Visitor's Center provides information and history about the monument. (916) 667-2282.

Tule Lake and Lower Klamath Wildlife Refuges - *(Page 5, D3 & C3)* two lake areas north of Lava Beds Monument which sustain a massive concentration of waterfowl. As many as 500 bald eagles annually migrate to the Klamath Refuge. Self-guided auto trails and canoe routes are available. (916) 667-2231.

MOUNT SHASTA - *(Page 12, D1, D2)* the snow clad 14,162 foot peak is visible for 100 miles in every direction. The now dormant volcano is the majestic central figure of

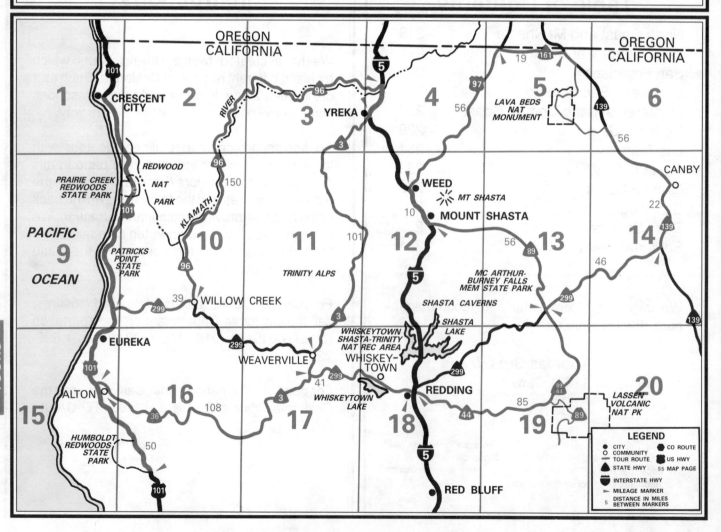

TOURS

LEGEND

	CITY		CO ROUTE
	COMMUNITY		
	TOUR ROUTE		US HWY
	STATE HWY	55	MAP PAGE
	INTERSTATE HWY		
	MILEAGE MARKER		
5	DISTANCE IN MILES BETWEEN MARKERS		

this northern wonderland. The area is popular with hikers, campers, rock climbers, snow skiers, photographers, river rafters, bird watchers, fishermen, geologists, naturalists, and awe-struck tourists. The small town of Mount Shasta sits at the base of the mountain.

McARTHUR-BURNEY FALLS MEMORIAL STATE PARK - *(Page 13, C4)* the 875-acre park is a forest of evergreen trees, wildflowers and streams. The central attractions are twin waterfalls which cascade over 129-foot cliffs into an emerald green pool of water surrounded by lush ferns and mist-shrouded rocks. Throughout the park, visitors are permitted to camp, fish, picnic or canoe. (916) 335-2777.

Highway 299 is an alternate route heading west. It is a scenic road in excellent condition.

WHISKEYTOWN LAKE - *(Page 18, A2)* a man-made alpine lake popular with water sports enthusiasts. Camping is available.

Shasta State Historic Park - located between Redding and Whiskeytown Lake. The small area was a major transportation depot in the gold rush days. A restored Courthouse and museum are open to the public. (916) 243-8194.

SHASTA CAVERNS - *(Page 12, C5)* located 20 miles north of Redding. Take the O'Brien exit 2 miles to the Caverns headquarters. From the headquarters, a shuttle bus takes visitors to Lake Shasta for a 15 minute ride across the lake on a 65' catamaran. A short hike leads to the caverns where guides conduct tours. The caverns have a variety of crystal formations and the view of the lake from the 850' elevation is quite spectacular. There is a gift shop and picnic area. The entire round-trip excursion lasts about 2 hours. (916) 238-2341.

YREKA - *(Page 4, A4)* founded during the gold rush days, it flourished as a mining town. Today, it is a small but important trade center in north central California.

Siskiyou County Museum - an impressive collection of exhibits and displays describing the history of the area. The outdoor museum consists of restored buildings with furnishings and equipment of the gold rush era. (916) 842-3836.

The primitive northwestern area of California along Highway 96 is a fisherman's paradise. The road follows the beautiful Klamath River which is regularly stocked with trout.The challenge of salmon fishing attracts sportsmen from around the world. Rafting, canoeing and kayaking are also popular for the robust sportsmen who brave the icy, white waters.

EUREKA - *(Pages 15, E1 and 121)* a working town which offers a variety of attractions. Visitors view historic and modern lumber mills and fishing fleet operations.

Fort Humboldt State Historic Park -*(Page 121, A3)* includes museums and a logging display. General U.S. Grant was stationed here in 1853. A picnic area and excellent view of Humboldt Bay are additional features. (707) 445-6567.

HUMBOLDT REDWOODS STATE PARK - *(Page 16, A4)* forests of the world's tallest living things - magnificent Redwood Trees, some over 200 feet tall and 2,000 years old. The 33-mile Avenue of the Giants Parkway is a slow-paced, scenic drive with several turnouts. Camping and picnicking are permitted. Call the park for information. (707) 946-2311.

PATRICK'S POINT STATE RESERVE - *(Page 9, E3)* located 30 miles north of Eureka along the rugged coastline. This 630-acre, gorgeous park has 12 trails which allow visitors to walk out near the edge of steep bluffs or onto the sandy beach. There are three state-operated campgrounds. (707) 677-3570.

PRAIRIE CREEK REDWOODS STATE PARK - *(Page 10, A1)* a large meadowland of tall grasses bordered by dense redwoods and fern canyons. Several hiking trails thread through the solemn forest along mountain-fed streams. Elk may be seen in the open areas. The Visitor's Center has displays & information. (707) 488-2171.

TREES OF MYSTERY - *(Page 1, E5)* just north of Prairie Creek Park lies an area of spruce and redwood trees which have grown in unusual, twisted shapes. A walking tour, gift shop and museum are open year-round. (707) 482-5613.

CRESCENT CITY - *(Page 1, D4)* located in the far northwest corner of the State. It is surrounded by rugged coastline and lush forests. Chamber of Commerce has information. (707) 464-3174.

Battery Point Lighthouse - houses a museum with memorabilia and shipwreck artifacts. Tours conducted, tide permitting. (707) 464-3089.

Miller Redwood Company - located 4 miles south on Hwy 101. Tours are conducted of a working sawmill.

Rellim (Miller spelled backwards) **Demonstration Forest** - located near the Miller Redwood Company. A lodge with exhibits of the lumber industry. An area of seedlings which display various trees and reforestation techniques. (707) 464-3144.

WINE COUNTRY & MARIN COUNTY

California is recognized as a world class wine producing region. The climate and soil in the Napa Valley are in perfect balance to produce excellent vintages. This area is also quite beautiful and accessible to tourists. Driving through the countryside and visiting the wineries can be a relaxing respite from the hectic pace of the city. Most of the large wineries offer tours as well as wine tasting.

In conjunction with this tour we have mapped out the wine country from Napa to Calistoga. *(See page 29 for a more detailed map showing specific wineries).*

NAPA - *(Page 38, D3)* synonymous with "The Wine Country", this busy city is actually the southern gateway to the Napa Valley region.
   Hot Air Balloon Rides - an alternative way to see the wine country. Several companies operate out of Napa. Flights last about an hour and often include champagne afterwards.

YOUNTVILLE - *(Page 38, C2)* a quiet, farming community in the heart of Napa Valley.

Vintage 1870 - a converted historic winery, now a major tourist attraction, filled with 42 shops and restaurants. (707) 944-2451.

ST. HELENA - *(Page 38, B2)* has a quaint Victorian flavor in addition to a major concentration of wineries.

   Silverado Museum - displays over 8,000 items of author Robert Louis Stevenson memorabilia. (707) 963-3757.

   Hurd Candle Factory - at the Freemark Abbey Winery, produces handcrafted candles. (707) 963-7211.

CALISTOGA - *(Page 38, A1)* famed health resort with natural hot-water geysers, mineral springs and mud baths. Situated at the foot of Mount St. Helena.

   Petrified Forest - on scenic Petrified Forest Road, 5 miles west of the city. An area of well-preserved examples of ancient redwoods, some 126 feet long. Museum and picnic facilities. (707) 942-6667.

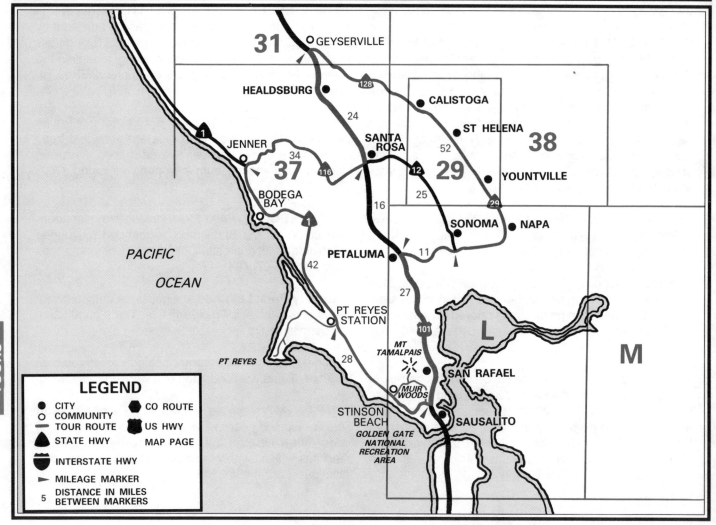

TOURS

LEGEND
- ● CITY
- ○ COMMUNITY
- ▬ TOUR ROUTE
- ◤ STATE HWY
- ⬣ INTERSTATE HWY
- ► MILEAGE MARKER
- 5 DISTANCE IN MILES BETWEEN MARKERS
- ⬡ CO ROUTE
- 🛡 US HWY
- MAP PAGE

Old Faithful Geyser of California - one of the few regularly erupting geysers in the world, spewing steam and vapor 60 feet into the air for 3 minutes at 45 minute intervals. Open year-round. (707) 942-6463.

The area from Geyserville to Healdsburg *(Page 31, D5)* is another massive concentration of wineries.

SANTA ROSA - *(Page 37, E2)* from here west to Sebastopol is known as "apple country". In the spring, thousands of acres of orchards are in full bloom for a spectacular and fragrant display. Roadside stands offer fresh fruit and cider.

The drive along the Russian River, named for the fur traders who flourished here in the 19th century, is dotted with small towns, wineries and peaceful orchards. The road winds through forests of redwoods, occasionally veering sharply around an individual tree, which has been preserved rather than destroyed for the sake of the pavement.

SONOMA COAST STATE BEACH - *(Page 37, C2)* broad shining beaches and secluded coves, rocky coastline and tide pools are protected and maintained by the State. Open to the public at several access points with fire rings on the sand and numerous developed campsites. (707) 875-3483.

BODEGA BAY - *(Page 37, C3)* an active fishing port village and popular recreational area. It is the location for Alfred Hitchcock's famous movie, "The Birds".

POINT REYES STATION - *(Page 37, D4)* small town where you will turn west to reach the Point Reyes National Seashore. The Visitor's Center, with information on facilities, nature trails and exhibits, is located just south of town. Watch for signs. (415) 663-1092.

Point Reyes - mostly undeveloped. The majority of the land is occupied by the Tomales Bay State Park and the Point Reyes National Seashore. The area is a nature refuge with more than 300 species of birds and 72 species of mammals inhabiting the grassy dunes, rolling hills, meadows, swamps and forested inner margin. Tidepools team with life and some 300 varieties of wildflowers bloom in the spring. On a clear day, take the road to the historic Pt. Reyes lighthouse, a remote and scenic picnic spot.

Tomales Bay and Highway 1 south from **Point Reyes Station** (Page 37, D4 & E5) lie directly on the San Andreas Rift Zone. This is one of the rare locations where you can actually drive along the San Andreas Fault and see this geological phenomenon.

STINSON BEACH - *(Page L, A4)* a small town and a popular park now a part of the Golden Gate National Recreation Area. The sandy beaches and good surf attract over one million visitors each year. (415) 868-0942.

Audubon Canyon Ranch - wildlife sanctuary and educational center. Open to the public from March through July. (415) 868-9244.

MUIRWOOD NATIONAL MONUMENT - located 2 miles off the Panoramic Highway. A network of trails thread the 553 acres of redwood forests. There is no camping, picnicking or fishing permitted. (415) 388-2595.

MT. TAMALPAIS STATE PARK - a beautiful area of redwoods laced with roads and trails. The view from "Mt Tam" encompasses the Pacific Ocean and Farallon Islands, San Francisco Bay, and potentially as far as the great Central Valley. Hiking and camping are available, and a natural ampitheatre seats 3,750 people. (415) 388-2070.

SAUSALITO - *(Page L, B4)* an historic artist's colony of 7,500 year-round residents. Its picturesque marina is filled with over 350 houseboats; some elegant, some derelict, while the hillsides are filled with unusual homes, perched precariously above the bay. Sausalito is a popular retreat offering numerous restaurants with spectacular day and evening views of the bay. (415) 332-0505.

Village Fair - forty shops and restaurants in a 3-story complex that was once a gambling hall and haven for crooked politicians.

SAN RAFAEL - *(Page L, B3)* visit the **Mission San Rafael Arcangel**, a replica built in 1949 on the approximate site of the original 1817 mission. (415) 456-3016.

Marin County Civic Center - designed by Frank Lloyd Wright. The 140 acre complex is a combination of futuristic structures and landscapes. (415) 499-7407.

PETALUMA - *(Page L, A1)* a quiet, dairy community.

Petaluma Adobe State Historical Park - one of the largest adobes still standing in California, restored and furnished with period artifacts and historical exhibits. (707) 762-4871.

SONOMA - *(Page L, B1)* site of the first raising of the Bear Flag, June 14, 1846, proclaiming California a republic. A month later, on July 9th, it was replaced by the Stars and Stripes.

Sonoma State Historic Park includes the **Mission San Francisco Solano**, last of the Franciscan Missions established in California, and other historical buildings from the 19th century. (707) 938-1519.

SAN FRANCISCO

Truly a fascinating city, San Francisco is a potpourri of cultures, sights, sounds and excitement. It is a compact urban world center with a rich history and a contemporary flair; ultramodern office buildings share the skyline with refurbished warehouses and fine Victorian homes.

The following 49 Mile Scenic Drive is a planned, counter-clockwise route within San Francisco designed to introduce the first-time visitor to this enchanting "city by the bay". A few tips to remember: 1) the tour is marked by blue, white and orange road signs, featuring a seagull posted every few blocks; 2) the tour involves many of the heavily congested areas and should be driven in off-peak traffic hours, if possible; 3) pedestrians and cable cars ALWAYS have

the right-of-way! The following are some of the many points of interest on the tour. We have started at the Civic Center, but you many begin the scenic drive anywhere along the way.

CIVIC CENTER - *(Page 143, B4)* includes an impressive group of federal, state and city buildings: City Hall, Civic Auditorium, Performing Arts Center, War Memorial, Opera House, Main Public Library and San Francisco Museum of Modern Art.

JAPANTOWN - *(Page 143, A3)* features a 3 square block, Japan Center complex as the focal point of this neighborhood. Traditional shops, restaurants, a theatre, teahouses,

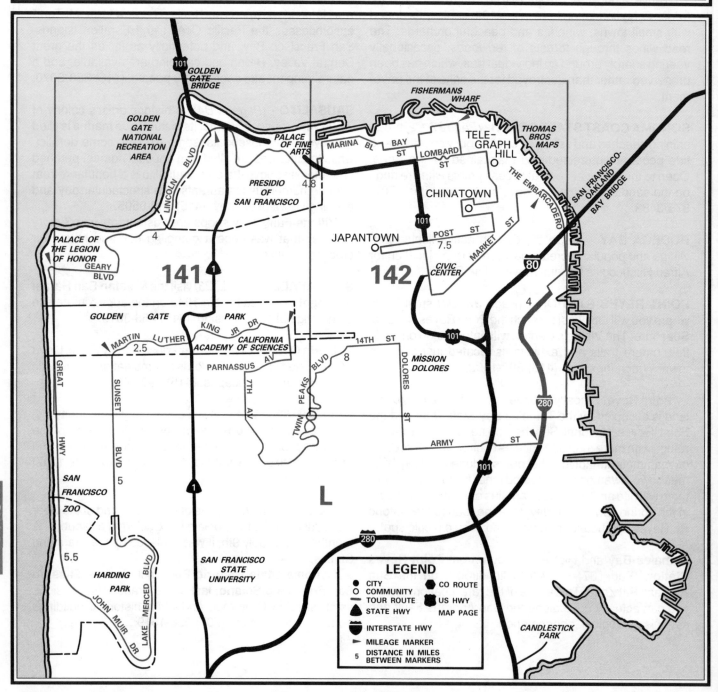

sushi bars, Japanese baths and a five-tiered, 35-foot Peace Pagoda reflect the spirit of the 12,000 San Francisco residents of Japanese descent.

UNION SQUARE - *(Page 143, C3)* the heart of downtown shopping located between Japantown and Chinatown. This attractive square is used for many civic events, fashion shows, rallies and concerts. Around the square and spreading southward are many of San Francisco's fine shops and department stores.

CHINATOWN - *(Page 143, C2)* a 24 block area of bustling activity, pagoda-style architecture, curio shops, street markets, restaurants and temples, home to the largest Chinese community outside the Orient. The main plaza, called Portsmouth Square, is the center of activity.

TELEGRAPH HILL - *(Page 143, C2)* includes **Coit Tower**, a 210 foot monument built in 1934 as a memorial to the city's volunteer firemen. An elevator takes visitors to the top for a panoramic view of San Francisco, the East Bay, the waterfront, the bay bridges and Alcatraz Island.

LOMBARD STREET - *(Page 143, B2)* called "the crookedest street in the world". The steep, one-way, brick street, trimmed in flowers is open to all vehicles except motorhomes and trailers.

FISHERMAN'S WHARF - *(Page 143, A1)* the famous waterfront area of seafood restaurants, harbor cruises, excellent shopping, galleries and entertainment. The refurbished brick buildings of Ghirardelli Square, The Cannery and Pier 39 are especially popular restaurant-shopping meccas.

FORT MASON CENTER - *(Page 143, A1)* a former Army base converted into a cultural center. This artisan's showplace includes 45 studios, 3 theatres and 5 museums. (415) 441-5705.

PALACE OF FINE ARTS - *(Page 142, A1)* built for the 1915 Panama-Pacific International Exposition. It has been beautifully restored and now houses the Exploratorium, a science museum, (415) 561-0362, and the 1,000 seat Palace of Fine Arts Theatre.

PRESIDIO OF SAN FRANCISCO - *(Page 141, C2)* U.S. Sixth Army headquarters. The 1,500 acres of park-like hills and beaches are open to the public. The Presidio Army Museum chronicles over 100 years of San Francisco military history, (415) 561-4115.

PALACE OF THE LEGION OF HONOR - *(Page 141, A3)* modeled after the Palais de la Legion d'Honneur in Paris.

It houses an impressive collection of European art. (415) 750-3614.

SAN FRANCISCO ZOO - ranks among the top six city zoos in the U.S. The collections boasts over 1,000 animals and birds. (415) 661-4844.

GOLDEN GATE PARK - *(Page 141)* formerly 1,000 acres of sand dunes. This park has been transformed into one of the most beautiful metropolitan parks in the world featuring miles of pleasant drives, green lawns, playfields, bridle paths, bicycle routes, lakes and gardens, a stadium and a golf course.
    California Academy of Sciences - includes the Steinhardt Aquarium, Morrison Planetarium, and a large Natural History Museum. (415) 750-7145.
    Conservatory of Flowers - a replica of the Kew Gardens Conservatory in England. It houses many fascinating collections of exotic plants.
    Japanese Tea Garden - an authentic oriental garden built in 1894 which includes a tea house, moon bridge, pagoda, ponds, and bonsai. Each spring the cherry blossoms and oriental landscaping create a delightful wonderland.
    Strybing Arboretum - boasts more than 5,000 species and varieties of plants from around the world.
    M.H. De Young Memorial Museum - houses European and American art and decorative art, with special collections of African and Asian art. (415) 730-3614.

TWIN PEAKS - *(Page 142, A5)* a 360 degree panorama of the city is possible from the overlook at the 910 foot summit.

MISSION SAN FRANCISCO DE ASIS (Mission Dolores) - *(Page 142, C4)* established in 1776 as the sixth in the chain of 21 Franciscan missions. It is the oldest building in San Francisco. (415) 621-8203.
    Some additional points of interest not included on this 49 Mile Scenic Drive which are equally interesting are:
    Alcatraz Island - *(Page L, B4)* formerly a maximum security Federal Penitentiary, now a part of the Golden Gate National Recreation Area. The Island is partially open to the public while extensive restoration is underway. Call for Ferry information at 1-800-445-8880.
    Candlestick Park - *(Page L, C5)* Home of the SF Giants & the SF '49ers.
    Golden Gate Bridge - *(Page L, B4)* completed in 1937. It spans the Bay 4,200 feet from San Francisco to Marin County.

For more information or brochures, contact the **San Francisco Visitor's Center** by calling (415) 974-6900 or **Thomas Bros. Maps,** 550 Jackson Street at (415) 981-7520.

BERKELEY - SACRAMENTO

Across the 8.5 mile bridge from San Francisco lies the center of industrial, shipping and political activity for the seven-county Bay area. *(See pages L & M).*

BERKELEY - *(Page L, D4)* notoriously described as "radical", "revolutionary" and "avant garde". It is regarded as one of the nation's leading educational centers with the **University of California** and its academic populace having shaped the city through the decades. The college campus includes over 1,200 acres of green lawns, classrooms and research buildings, an art museum, a botanical garden and one of the largest computer facilities in the nation. The top of the 307 foot Campanile affords a view of the campus, the East Bay area and San Francisco. The Lawrence Hall of Science, an especially popular attraction, houses numerous displays and hands-on science exhibits for adults and children. Guided walking tours of the campus are conducted from the visitor's center. (415) 642-5215.

OAKLAND - *(Page L, D4)* named for the extensive groves of live oak trees that once flourished here. The city has grown into a major urban center with one of the largest commercial ports in the world. It is also a residential district for thousands of bay area commuters. Call the Visitor's Center at (415) 839-9000.

Lake Merritt - *(Page 158, B3)* a 155-acre body of salt water in the center of the city surrounded by Lakeside Park. It is a favorite recreation spot with a garden center, Children's Fairyland, Gamebird Refuge, Natural Science Center, sailboats for rent, and 122 acres of green lawns. At night, the entire lake is adorned with a string of white lights called the "necklace of lights" which gives an enchanting radiance to the park.

Oakland Museum - *(Page 158, A3)* covering 4 square blocks, the three-tiered complex is really 3 different museums in one: history, natural science and art, with exhibits as intriguing as the building's architecture. (415) 834-2413.

Jack London Square - *(Page 157, E4)* a 10 block area of waterfront considered the historical center of Oakland. Fine restaurants and shops line the wharf where the famous adventure writer spent much of his time.

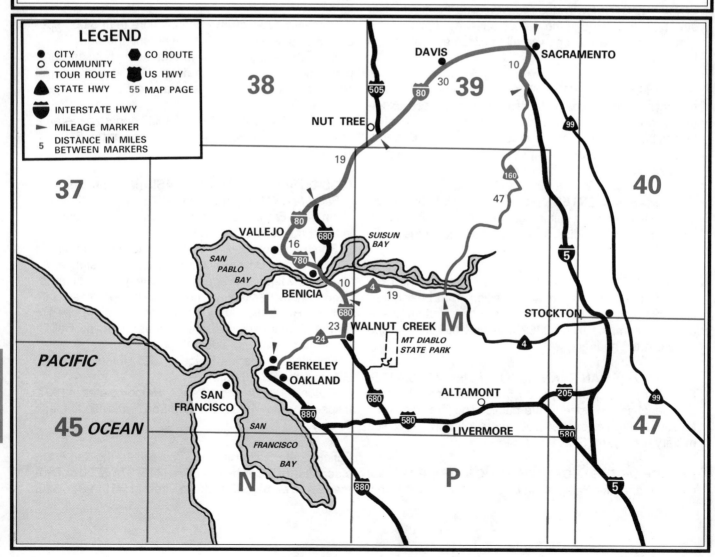

TOURS

Paramount Theatre - *(Page 158, A2)* a sublime example of Art Deco form. The 3,000 seat theatre, built in 1931, has been restored and is an active facility. Tours are available by calling (415) 465-6400.

MT. DIABLO STATE PARK - *(Page M, B4)* located 17 miles southeast of Walnut Creek. On a clear day, the pleasant drive to the 3,849 foot peak provides a view of portions of 35 counties, the Farallon Islands, and the Pacific Ocean, Mt. St. Helena, Mt. Lassen, and the Sierras. Camping and hiking trails. (415) 837-2525.

DELTA - Highway 4 passes through the sprawling flatlands of the richest farmland in the nation. The Antioch Bridge allows large cargo freighters to pass beneath en route to the deep water ports of Sacramento and Stockton. *(Page M, C3)*. On the north side of the bridge, the road becomes a two lane route into the "Mouth of the Delta". Once a swamp, the area is now an intricate network of meandering waterways, hundreds of islands planted in fruit trees, vegetables, grains and vineyards. Several historic communities line the banks of the Sacramento River and thousands of waterfowl make their home in this peaceful refuge. For general information, call (916) 442-5542.

BRANNAN ISLAND STATE RECREATION AREA - *(Page M, C2)* offers year-round camping, picnicking, boating, fishing and swimming. A Visitor's Center provides information and displays. (916) 777-6671.

SACRAMENTO - *(Page 39, E1)* the State Capitol since 1854. The city has a colorful history, well-preserved amid a modern and dynamic environment of current political activity.

State Capitol - *(Page 137, B3)* constructed between 1861 and 1874. The main building is a formidable structure with a 210-foot gold dome, marble floors and radiant, crystal chandeliers. It is the dominant landmark among the state buildings in the area, and is surrounded by a 40-acre park of trees and plants from around the world. Tours of the main building, its chambers and some executive offices are available, as well as historical exhibits, murals and a film. (916) 324-0333.

Old Governor's Mansion - *(Page 137, C3)* located near the State Capitol. It is an elaborate Victorian-Gothic structure built in 1877. It has been the residence of 13 California governors and is now a state historic landmark open to the public. (916) 445-4209.

Old Sacramento State Historic Park - *(Page 137, A2)* a 10-block district along the Sacramento River which recreates the flavor of the gold rush days. Museums, saloons and shops line the western-style streets. The California State Railroad Museum features dozens of historic exhibits and 21 lavishly restored locomotives and cars.

Old Sacramento Visitor's Center - *(Page 137, A2)* located in the Old Sacramento State Historical Park, provides information and walking tours of the city. (916) 443-7815.

Sutters Fort - *(Page 137, D3)* site of the first settlement founded by Captain John Sutter in 1839. The Fort has been restored and houses exhibits and memorabilia of the gold rush days. (916) 445-4209.

Crocker Art Museum - *(Page 137, A3)* a large, converted Victorian mansion built in 1873. The ornate structure has extensive collections of fine art. (916) 449-5423.

DAVIS - *(Page 39, C1)* Highway 80 between Sacramento and Berkeley is the main commuter route. It is a divided, 6-lane expressway slicing through farmlands, pastures of grazing dairy cattle and livestock, and rural communities. Situated along Highway 80 is the thriving city of Davis (pop. 43,200), home of the **University of California at Davis** (student pop. 20,000). The campus covers 3,600 acres, two-thirds of which are devoted to agricultural research. *(Page 136, B3)*. Tours of the main campus, museum, galleries, and special exhibits are available through the Visitor's Center. (916) 752-0539.

NUT TREE - *(Page 39, A2)* of curious origin, the Nut Tree Ranch was settled in 1855 by the Allison family. What started as a single fruit stand beneath a solitary walnut tree in 1921 has grown through family generations into an established visitor attraction. In addition to a bakeshop and candy factory, the Nut Tree complex offers an airport, a railroad, a toy shop, a restaurant of tasty delicacies, and a huge souvenir shop of unique gifts and an impressive selection of aviation books, photographs and related items. In 1962, the United States Postal Service designated the area Nut Tree, California.

VALLEJO - *(Page 38, D4)* founded in 1850 as the state's first capitol. Vallejo is also known for **Marine World Africa USA,** *(Page 134, E1)* a 160-acre oceanarium and wildlife park featuring killer whales, dolphins, sea lions, tigers, elephants, chimps, and exotic birds in exciting and innovative habitats. Call (707) 643-ORCA.

BENICIA - *(Page 38, D4)* Self-proclaimed "Antique Center of the West", Benicia also boasts California's oldest standing capitol building and oldest Masonic temple in the state. *(Page 153, B4)* For a self-guided tour map contact the Chamber of Commerce. (707) 745-2120.

MONTEREY & THE CENTRAL COAST

This area of California offers breathtaking scenery and an impressive range of activities, sites and adventures for every visitor. Unfortunately, the highlights are not laid out in a convenient loop - more of a figure eight. All of the points of interest are special and whatever "backtracking" is necessary simply affords a "second look".

SOLEDAD MISSION - *(Page 65, A1)* exit 3 miles south of Soledad on Hwy 101 to Arroyo Seco Road and the **Mission Nuestra Senora de la Soledad**, "Our Lady of Solitude". Founded in 1791 as the thirteenth in a chain of twenty-one California Missions, it has been partially restored and offers a museum and chapel. (408) 678-2586.

Follow Hwy 17 southwest to Hwy 16, a winding, country drive through the scenic backroads of Carmel Valley to the city of Carmel. At this junction, the road heads west to Carmel, south to Big Sur, or north to Monterey. *(Page 54, A5)*.

POINT LOBOS - just south of Carmel, this 1,500 acre state reserve protects some of the most spectacular shoreline of the California coast. Driving within the reserve is limited, but a short walk leads to the sparkling jade-green water and cliffside gardens. Numerous well-maintained trails provide views of sea lions and sea otters resting among the kelp, gnarled Monterey cypress, tidepools of marine creatures, colonies of birds, and perhaps, depending on the season, migrating whales. The reserve is strictly a day-use area and the number of visitors is limited. (408) 624-4909.

The drive along Hwy 1 is one of the most celebrated stretches of road in California. The two-lane road winds along the craggy, volcanic coastline hugging the Santa Lucia Mountains while providing magnificent vistas of land and sea. The road then turns slightly inland through a wooded canyon.

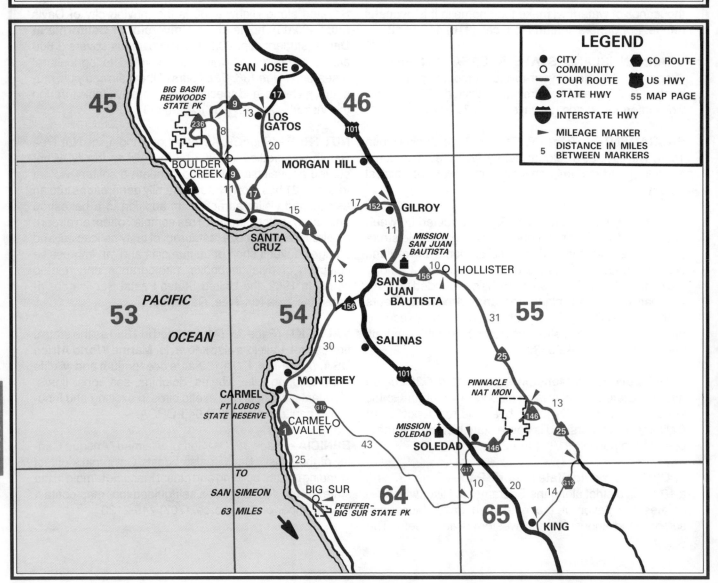

TOURS

PFEIFFER BIG SUR STATE PARK - *(Page 64, B2)* pine trees, chaparral and redwoods create a peaceful refuge from the "city life". Though the park is not large, 807 acres, it provides access to the Los Padres National Forest and the Ventana Wilderness. Combined, there are over 300,000 acres for hiking, camping and fishing along Big Sur River. (408) 667-2315.

Continuing south, Highway 1 returns to the coastline curving its way 63 miles along some of the most photographed spots in America to San Simeon. One popular restaurant, Nepenthe's, has an espcially interesting history and unique design. It is located 3 miles south of Big Sur State Park. Backtracking the 26 miles up the coast to Carmel, motorists will be treated to "seconds" of spectacular shoreline with a "new perspective".

CARMEL - *(Page 54, A5)* the village flavor of Carmel reflects the creativeness and individuality of its many artists and writers. Hilly streets, many without curbs or sidewalks, whimsical architecture, and natural landscaping combine to create a storybook aura. Galleries, unique shops and restaurants abound along the shady main streets.

Mission San Carlos Borromeo - *(Page 168, B4)* founded in 1770 as the second in the eventual chain of 21 missions. Father Serra, the "Father of the Missions", has his final resting place located here. It has been restored and is a fine example of the typical mission architecture. (408) 624-3600.

17 Mile Drive - *(Page 53)* beginning at the north end of Carmel, it winds through scenic, wooded areas of the Del Monte Forest and fabulous shoreline, past the famous Pebble Beach Golf Course and on to Monterey.

MONTEREY - *(Page 54, A4)* a favorite year-round resort that offers an array of activities and attractions. The Chamber of Commerce, (408) 649-3200, can provide detailed information and walking-tour maps. Cannery Row and Fisherman's Wharf are popular areas for restaurants and shopping. The scenic peninsula along Ocean View Boulevard to the Pt. Pinos Lighthouse is lined with Victorian homes and quaint restaurants.

The **Monterey Bay Aquarium** *(Page 167, E2)*, opened in 1984, is particularly exciting. This "hands on" aquarium is one of the largest in the world with special exhibits and habitats for over 5,000 creatures. (408) 375-3333.

The route from Monterey to Santa Cruz *(Page 54)* bends along the coast past miles of pastures, orchards and farmlands. Roadside vendors offer locally grown artichokes, Brussels sprouts and other produce in season.

SANTA CRUZ - *(Page 53, E2)* from the architecture to the festivals, an intriguing mixture of styles created by the evolving social influences throughout its history: the early Indian and Spanish settlers, the turn-of-the-century investors and the influx of a youthful populace when the University opened its campus in the 1960's. Chamber of Commerce Visitor's Center on Cooper Street, (408) 423-1111, distributes free copies of a multi-page publication, *Where to Go & What to Do.* The revitalized Pacific Garden Mall downtown and the Beach Boardwalk with its Giant Dipper roller coaster and famous Coconut Grove, are especially noteworthy attractions. *(Page 169, E4)*.

BIG BASIN REDWOODS STATE PARK - Highway 9 from Santa Cruz weaves through dark, solemn redwoods and passes several mountain communities. At Boulder Creek, take the turnoff to Big Basin, Highway 236. *(Page 53, E1)* Towering redwoods, some over 330 feet tall and 18 feet in diameter, create a lush canopy over the road; rich, green mosses thrive on the stone bridges, wooden fences and tree trunks. Car's headlights are necessary even in mid-afternoon due to the density of the forest. At the park headquarters, where campers and hikers must check in, the road narrows to less than two lanes for the next 8 miles, and is slow going. The road is not suitable for trailers or large RV's, but the scenery is enchanting. (408) 338-6132.

Outside the park, Highway 9 widens slightly but continues to twist along the mountainside to the historic towns of Saratoga and Los Gatos. At this junction Highway 17 leads south to Santa Cruz or north to San Jose. *(Page 46, A5)*.

SAN JOSE - *(Page 46, B4)* located in a region known equally for fine wines and high-technology industries.

Winchester Mystery House - *(Page 151, B5)* created by the heiress of the Winchester Rifle fortune. The 160-room mansion and 6 acres of gardens were designed according to the bizarre superstitious obsessions of its eccentric owner. Tours of the house and gardens are conducted and a museum, gift shop and cafe are open year-round. (408) 247-2101.

The area from Morgan Hill to Gilroy and west to Hecker Pass is noted for several wineries. *(Page 54, C-D1, D2)*

MISSION SAN JUAN BAUTISTA - *(Page 54, D3)* the 15th Franciscan mission. It is well-preserved and still an active Catholic church. (408) 623-4528.

PINNACLES NATIONAL MONUMENT - *(Page 55, B5)* this area is a geological phenomenon, created from an ancient volcano that erupted along the San Andreas Rift Zone, just east of what is today the park. Hiking, rock climbing, cave exploring, picnicking and camping are permitted. Since crags and spires create a ridge through the center of the park, there is not a drivable road connecting both entrances. (408) 389-4485.

TOURS

NORTHERN SIERRA

The Northern half of the Sierra Nevadas is characterized by a rugged backcountry of forests and granite rocks laced with miles of mountain streams. The western slope was the destination for thousands of pioneers who found their fortunes or lost their dreams in a search for gold during the nineteenth century. The eastern slope includes the natural treasures of Yosemite National Park, Mono Lake and Lake Tahoe.

Gold Country Highway (Hwy 49) snakes 300 miles through the historic Mother Lode along the northwestern slope of the Sierras. The area is dotted with rustic gold mining towns, some still thriving mountain communities and others all but ghost towns; each in its own way, capturing the spirit of the Old West.

DOWNIEVILLE - *(Page 26, D4)* a picturesque and well preserved town with a small history museum. (916) 289-3261.

NEVADA CITY - *(Page 34, C1)* a charming town with several historic buildings, Victorian houses, museums and a winery.

GRASS VALLEY - *(Page 34, C1)* once the center of mining activity, it continues to thrive by tourism, lumbering and agriculture.

Empire Mine State Historic Park - the oldest and richest gold mine in California. The park contains displays, exhibits, lectures, and films, with tours conducted daily from the Visitor's Center. (916) 273-8522.

AUBURN - *(Page 34, C3)* one of the first mining camps in California, and a trading center for the region. Devastated several times by fire, it has been rebuilt and restored each time by its residents with the same pioneering spirit that founded it in 1848.

PLACERVILLE - *(Page 34, E5)* also known as "Hangtown" because of its numerous lynchings in 1849. It was a bustling crossroads during the gold rush days.

Gold Bug Mine - visitors can try their luck panning for the still unfound golden treasures of Little Big Creek.

FIDDLETOWN - *(Page 40, E1)* all but a ghost town. The surrounding area has several wineries.

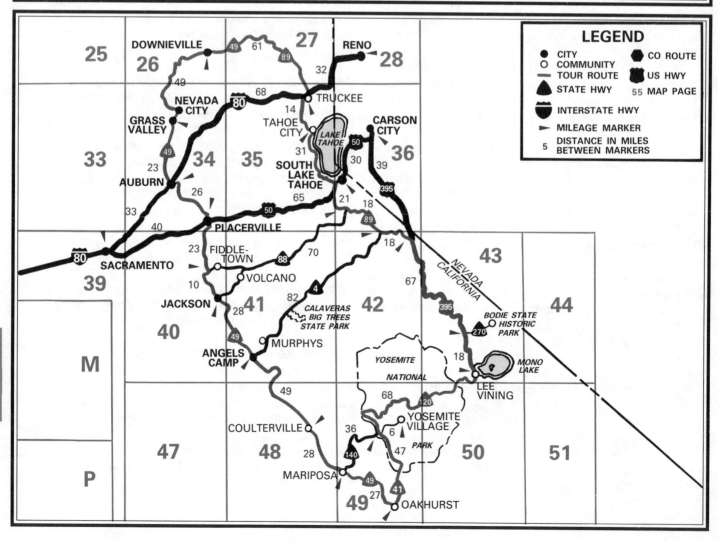

VOLCANO - *(Page 41, A2)* so named because it sits in a deep valley. Volcano offers a pleasant side trip in the Mother Lode with many remnants of the early town.

Daffodil Hill - 3 miles north of town, the private ranch whose owners during the 1850's planted thousands of daffodils in the hills surrounding their home. In the spring, the display is spectacular.

Indian Grinding Rocks State Historic Park - just south of town, the 40 acre park has a very unique story. The area is covered with 363 petroglyphs, or rock carvings, and 1,185 chaw'ses, or mortar cups. The cups were used by the Miwok Indians to grind acorns. Then, through a fascinating assembly line process, the Indians produced acorn meal. Village and Museum Cultural Center are open to visitors. (209) 296-7488.

JACKSON - *(Page 40, E2)* contains several buildings and fine relics of mining activity preserved in a picturesque county park.

ANGELS CAMP - *(Page 41, B4)* made famous twice, first as an important Gold Rush center and again by Mark Twain's short story "The Celebrated Jumping Frog of Calaveras County". Each May the town hosts its Jumping Frog Jubilee and frog-jumping contest.

Angels Camp Museum - scale models of mines and stamp mills, equipment, minerals and artifacts. (209) 736-2963.

MURPHYS - *(Page 41, C4)* charming Victorian homes and beautiful brick buildings line the streets. Murphy's Hotel is restored to its 1800's charm.

Mercer Caverns - *(Page 41, B4)* 1.5 miles north. Open since 1885, the caves invite explorers into 10 rooms of crystal formations. (209) 728-2101.

Calaveras Big Trees State Park - *(Page 41, D3)* two groves of giant redwoods and pines. The sequoias were the first of their kind to receive world-wide attention. Scientists and journalists flocked to the forests in the 1850's to examine and report on these natural phenomenon. (209) 795-2334.

COULTERVILLE - *(Page 48, D2)* a Valley Center for the ranchers and homesteaders who cashed in on the Gold Rush frenzy.

MARIPOSA - *(Page 49, B3)* location of the oldest county courthouse, in use since 1854. Today, the restored town is a visitor's gateway to Yosemite Valley.

YOSEMITE VALLEY - (Page 49, D1) known world-wide for its massive cliffs, cascading waterfalls, pristine high country, glacier-carved valleys, meadows and majestic canyon walls. Summer (June-Sept.) is the busiest time, but early autumn with its colorful and serene valleys act as a wonderful transition into winter. The roads are often closed in the winter. In Spring, the winter thaw creates thousands of splashing waterfalls and wildflowers bloom. Check with park service for road and trail information as well as accomodations, campsite reservations and activities. Park headquarters *(Page 63, D1)* in Yosemite Valley provides guides, maps and information.

MONO LAKE - Tufa State Reserve *(Page 43, D5)* a surrealistic landscape of limestone formations rise from the lake. The area has scant vegetation, and the water is three times saltier than the ocean. The salt water sustains a unique ecosystem of algae, brine shrimp and brine flies which in turn attract 80 species of waterfowl. Some of the tufa has been exposed by the declining water level and walking trails allow a close-up view. (619) 647-6331.

BODIE STATE HISTORIC PARK - *(Page 43, C3)* a "genuine" gold-mining ghost town. What remains of the original town has been left to natural decay. Several buildings and a cemetery present an authentic, unrestored glimpse of the once booming Old West town. The road to Bodie is only partially paved, so call for road conditions. (619) 647-6445.

LAKE TAHOE - *(Pages 35 & 36)* 22 miles long, 12 miles wide, and 1,600 feet deep in places. It is a premiere resort offering a vast array of activities from winter snowskiing to summer water sports to year round casinos. The 71 mile shoreline drive around the lake provides spectacular views and is dotted with mountain inns, motels and campgrounds.

SOUTH LAKE TAHOE - *(Page 36, A3)* the more populated end of the lake with luxury hotels, restaurants and shops. The Nevada side allows gambling casinos.

Emerald Bay/D.L. Bliss State Park - *(Page 35, E3)* includes 6 miles of shoreline and provides the most magnificent panorama of Lake Tahoe, Fannette Island and the Nevada shore. (916) 525-7277.

Vikingsholm - built in 1929 as a private estate, it is a supreme example of Scandinavian architecture. Tours are conducted during the summer months.

TAHOE CITY - *(Page 35, E2)* the north shore of Lake Tahoe includes many popular ski resorts. Pine forests and mountain lodges dominate, making it a quieter, more rustic experience.

TRUCKEE - *(Page 35, D1)* an important crossroads town of 2,500 residents.

Donner Memorial State Park - a popular summer vacation spot. The museum tells the tragic story of the Donner Party that perished in 1846-47. (916) 587-3841.

LOS ANGELES

Reputed for its glamorous celebrities, sunshine and wealth, this "City of the Angels" is composed of a vast array of elements linked together by the most extensive freeway system in the world. *(See pages Q and R).*

The following tour cuts a swath across the center of Los Angeles, giving the first-time visitor a sampling of the cultural, historical and natural diversity of the second largest city in the nation. To visit all the points of interest noted here plus the hundreds which we did not mention would take even the most ambitious explorer many outings.

DOWNTOWN LOS ANGELES - *(Page 185, E3)* revitalized, renovated and massively developed even within the last decade. The first stop should be the Los Angeles Visitor's Information Center, (213) 689-8822, 695 S. Figueroa St. between Wilshire Blvd. and 7th St. (L.A. Hilton) which is within walking distance of THOMAS BROS. MAPS, 603 W. 7th St. (213) 627-4018.

CIVIC CENTER - *(Page 186, B3)* the "heart of Los Angeles", also the second largest governmental center in the U.S. after Washington, D.C.

Music Center - adjacent to the Civic Center, this performing arts complex includes three major theatres. (213) 972-7211.

Olvera Street and El Pueblo de Los Angeles State Historic Park - the founding site of the City of Los Angeles. (213) 628-1274.

EXPOSITION PARK - *(Page 185, C5)* south of the downtown area on Highway110, take the Exposition Blvd. exit.

Natural History Museum - more than 14,000,000 specimens, artifacts and 300 million years of earth history on display in the nation's fourth largest natural history museum. (213) 744-3414.

Also in this area: **California State Museum of Science and Industry, Aerospace Building, Los Angeles Memorial Coliseum, Sports Arena** and **Exposition Park Rose Gardens.** (213) 485-5529.

Nearby is the **University of Southern California campus** and the **Shrine Civic Auditorium.**

DODGER STADIUM - *(Page 186, B1)* home of the 1988 World Champion Los Angeles Dodgers baseball team.

PASADENA - *(Page 190, A3)* home of the Rose Bowl, Cal Tech and host of the New Year's Day Tournament of Roses Parade.

Huntington Library, Art Galleries, and Botanical Gardens (San Marino) - *(Page R, C3)* the 200-acre former estate of Henry E. Huntington houses 18th-century art and one of the world's most extensive manuscript and rare book collections. The sculptured gardens reflect a variety of world climates and cultures. It is open to the public. (818) 405-2100.

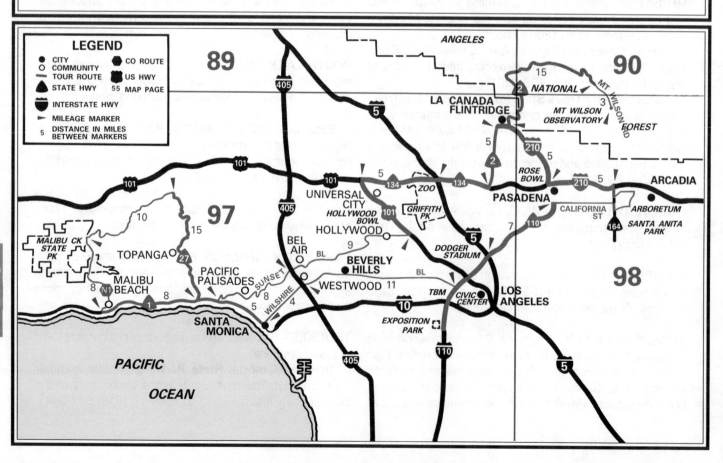

ARCADIA - *(Page R, C3)* follow California Blvd. to Rosemead Blvd., turn right to Baldwin Ave., and turn right. Follow the signs to:

Los Angeles State & County Arboretum - 127 acres of trees, plants and buildings reflecting different time periods and regions of the world. The area has been used by film companies for countless movies. (818) 446-8251.

Santa Anita Park - is one of the most famous thoroughbred horse-racing tracks in the U.S. The park is open January through April. (818) 574-7223.

Go north on Baldwin Avenue to Highway 210, westbound toward Pasadena.

LA CANADA FLINTRIDGE - *(Page R, B2)* scenic Highway 2, also called the Angeles Crest Highway, winds through the rugged San Gabriel Mountains. Turnouts provide a vista of the San Gabriel Valley & Pacific Ocean.

Mount Wilson Observatory - *(Page R, C2)* 3 miles on Mt Wilson Red Box Road, the observatory includes a museum. (818) 577-1122.

Follow Highway 2 south to Highway 134 westbound. Take the Zoo Drive exit *(Page Q, E3)* at the junction of Hwy 134 and Hwy 5.

GRIFFITH PARK - *(Page 182)* the 4,000-acre park includes a zoo, observatory and planetarium, travel museum, Greek Theatre, golf course, the famous "Hollywood" sign, and miles of horse and hiking trails and recreational facilities. (213) 665-5188.

UNIVERSAL CITY - *(Page 181, A1)* the Universal Studios tour takes visitors by tram through the backlots and stages of a movie-land park. (818) 508-9600.

HOLLYWOOD BOWL - *(Page 181, C3)* magnificent outdoor amphitheatre and park. Museum and gift shop. (213) 850-2000.

SUNSET BOULEVARD - *(Page 181, B4)* captures the essence of Los Angeles as it slices 27 miles from downtown LA through the Hollywood glitter, the Beverly Hills glamour and exclusive Pacific Palisades to the Pacific Ocean.

WILL ROGERS STATE HISTORIC PARK - *(Page Q, B4)* home to the late "Cowboy Philosopher", this 31-room house and 186-acre ranch with miles of hiking trails is open to the public. (213) 454-8212.

J. PAUL GETTY MUSEUM - *(Page Q, A4)* the museum and surrounding gardens are a re-creation of an ancient Roman country villa. The museum houses a permanent collection of Greek and Roman antiquities and pre-twentieth century Western European art. Reservations are necessary. (213) 458-2003.

Continue driving west on Pacific Coast Hwy; turn right at (N1) Malibu Canyon Rd. *(Page 97, B2)*.

MALIBU CREEK STATE PARK - *(Page 97, A2)* 4,000 acres of oaks, chaparral and volcanic rock. The area has often been used as the location for Hollywood films.

Turn right on Mulholland Highway, a narrow, winding country road, snaking across the crest of the Santa Monica Mountains with views of the Los Angeles Basin and San Fernando Valley. Mulholland Highway dead-ends at Mulholland Drive. Turn right for a short distance and turn right again onto Topanga Canyon Boulevard. *(Page 97, B1)*.

TOPANGA - *(Page 97, B2)* this rustic mountain town and canyon became a popular mecca for the "counterculture" in the 1960's. The **Topanga State Park** is the nation's second largest urban park and the world's largest wildland situated within the boundaries of a major city. To reach the park, turn east onto Entrada Road from Topanga Canyon Boulevard. (213) 455-2465.

SANTA MONICA - *(Page 97, C2)* a popular seaside resort with numerous shops and restaurants.

Santa Monica Pier - built in 1908, is a popular California landmark. Souvenir shops, restaurants, an arcade and historic carousel share this unique setting. Another Hollywood film location. (213) 458-8900.

Pacific Coast Highway (1) becomes Palisades Beach Road. Take the Pacific Coast Highway ramp to Ocean Avenue. Turn left onto Ocean and right on Wilshire Blvd. *(Page Q, B4)*.

WESTWOOD - *(Page 180)* the village area is an extension of the UCLA campus where trendy restaurants and shops abound. The 400-acre **University of California** campus is beautifully landscaped. Tours are available. (213) 825-4338.

BEVERLY HILLS - *(Page 183)* is one of the more glamourous celebrity residential communities in Southern California with some of the world's most famous shopping streets including Rodeo Drive.

Along **Wilshire Boulevard** are several landmarks and visitor attractions:

Los Angeles County Museum of Art - *(Page 184, A2)* has one of the most comprehensive art collections in the world. (213) 857-6000.

George C. Page Museum of La Brea Discoveries - *(Page 184, B2)* showcases the research and outstanding fossils recovered from the adjacent Rancho La Brea Tar Pits. (213) 857-6309.

TOURS

COPYRIGHT. © 1989 BY *Thomas Bros Maps*

SANTA BARBARA

Nestled against the foothills of the Santa Ynez mountains, Santa Barbara stretches along unspoiled, white beaches. *(Page 87, C4)*. A charming city of adobe buildings, red tile roofs and palm trees, it offers a mixture of rich Spanish history and modern luxury. Among the galleries, restaurants and fine shops in the downtown area, there are many plaques and markers identifying early buildings. *(Page 174)*. The Visitor's Center, 1 Santa Barbara Street, (805) 965-3021, provides copies of a Red Tile Walking Tour which will guide you to over two dozen points of interest in a 12 block area. A 24-mile Scenic Drive highlighting 15 points of interest in and around the area offers further exploration of Santa Barbara.

Leading out of the city north on Hwy 154, *(Page 87)* the road climbs into the Los Padres National Forest. Several turnouts provide a dramatic panorama of mountains, city, coastline and even the Channel Islands.

LAKE CACHUMA RECREATION AREA - *(Page 87, A3)* a large, full-service campground, it is the only point of access to this man-made lake. In addition to 600 campsites, there are hiking trails, a boating and fishing marina, horseback riding, bicycle rentals, a general store, weekend Fireside Theatre and special 2 hour cruises on the lake to view migrating eagles. (805) 688-8780.

SOLVANG - *(Page 86, D3)* a Danish village established in 1911 with old-country architecture, windmills, cobblestone sidewalks, and good luck storks. This enchanting town celebrates its Hans Christian Andersen heritage with authentic shops, bakeries, and many fine restaurants. Of the 3,700 residents, 2,700 claim to be of Danish descent.

City Maps are available at the Visitor's Information Center at 1660 Copenhagen Drive. (805) 688-1981.

TOURS

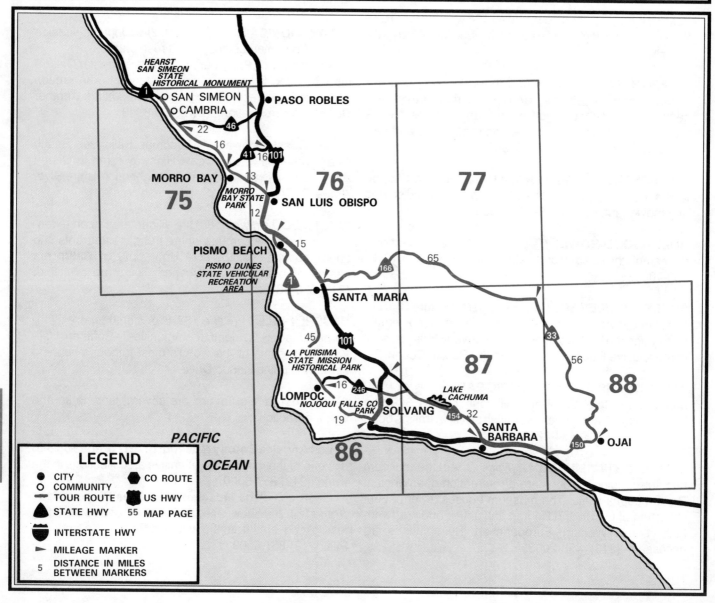

LEGEND

- ● CITY
- ○ COMMUNITY
- ▬ TOUR ROUTE
- ▲ STATE HWY
- ▬ INTERSTATE HWY
- ► MILEAGE MARKER
- 5 DISTANCE IN MILES BETWEEN MARKERS
- ⬡ CO ROUTE
- 🛡 US HWY
- 55 MAP PAGE

Old Mission Santa Ines - located a short distance from the heart of downtown Solvang, is one of the best preserved of the 21 Franciscan missions in California. (805) 688-4815.

NOJOQUI FALLS COUNTY PARK - *(Page 86, E3)* a 164-foot waterfall, 7 miles south of Solvang. This unique local "natural wonder" is a popular picnic and hiking spot.

There are over 22 wineries in the rural Santa Barbara valleys and mountains. A special WINE TOURING MAP is available from the Santa Barbara Vintner's Association. (805) 688-0881.

LOMPOC - *(Page 86, B3)* returning to Hwy 154, continue along the rolling hills turning south on Hwy 101 for a short distance to Hwy 1 toward Lompoc. The road curves through hills and pastures of cattle, offering a very scenic route. Lompoc valley is known as the "Flower Seed Capitol of the World". Experts agree that 50 to 75% of all flower seeds in the world come from this tiny area. A map outlining a 19 mile self-guided tour called the Valley Flower Drive is available from the Lompoc Chamber of Commerce. (805) 736-4567.

La Purisima Mission - *(Page 86, B2)* "Place in Time". Another of the 21 Francisian missions in California, well known as the most fully restored mission. Located in the most original setting, it has 9 buildings with 900 acres of park and 12 miles of foot trails. (805) 733-3713

PISMO BEACH - *(Page 76, B4)* follow the curving highway along country roads and farmland until it changes to groves of tall eucalyptus trees. Planted at the turn of the century, they were meant to be lumbered for railroad ties. When it was discovered that they were not hard enough, they were left to grow and flourish. Today they are a haven for migrating Monarch butterflies that travel from as far away as Canada each Fall to seek protection until the Spring. Pismo is a Chumash Indian word for "blobs of tar", known today as Pismo clams. At one time, as many as 45,000 clams could be commercially harvested in a single day. Now they are scarce and you must have a license to dig for them.

Pismo Dunes State Vehicular Recreation Area - provides access to 12 miles of beach where you may drive your car. Camping, hiking, surf fishing and clam digging are permitted on the dunes. (805) 549-3433.

SAN LUIS OBISPO - *(Page 76, B3)* the County Seat and bustling town of 35,000 residents. The California Polytechnic State University is located here and has an enrollment of approximately 16,000 students. For county-wide visitor's information, call (805) 541-8000.

Mission San Luis Obispo de Tolosa - *(Page 172, C3)* named for a 13 century French Saint. The mission is 5th in the chain of 21 missions and still serves as a parish church. (805) 543-6850.

MORRO BAY - *(Page 75, E3)* exit on Morro Bay Blvd. from Hwy 1, continuing through the heart of the city to the bay. The huge dome shaped rock, for which Morro Bay is named, is actually a centuries-old 576 foot volcanic dome. The Chamber of Commerce on Napa Street, (805) 772-4467, provides a map of the city and lots of helpful information. Morro Bay is an active fishing village as well as a popular resort area. Walk along the Embarcadero to watch the fishermen work, or browse through the interesting shops and enjoy fresh seafood in any of the many restaurants.

Also visit the **Morro Bay Aquarium**, (805) 772-7647, and the nearby **Morro Bay State Park** featuring a natural history museum overlooking the bay, an 18 hole golf course, and camping among the gorgeous Monterey Pines. (805) 772-2560.

CAMBRIA - *(Page 75, C2)* this quaint town tucked away among the pines was a former lumbering, shipping, mining and whaling station. Today the restored town is a popular artist colony, filled with galleries, antique shops and unique gift stores.

HEARST SAN SIMEON STATE HISTORICAL MONUMENT - *(Page 75, B1)* popularly known as Hearst's Castle. The gargantuan estate of the late William Randolph Hearst with its lavish architecture, furnishings, and landscaping was donated to the state and is open to the public. Tours are conducted and reservations are necessary. 1(800) 444-7275.

Continuing up Highway 1 toward Big Sur and Monterey, the road winds along the rugged coast with spectacular views of the ocean and hillsides. The 100 mile drive to Carmel takes approximately 3 hours and is well worth the time.

If you choose to return south, Highway 1 connects to Highway 101 toward Santa Barbara. Or, you may take Highway 166 just before Santa Maria *(Page 76, C5)* and follow it along the western edge of the Sierra Madre Mountains, with miles of picturesque country. Take Highway 33 *(Page 87, E1)* south to Ojai.

OJAI - *(Page 88, B4)* a rural retreat whose Indian name means "the nest". Located at the edge of Los Padres National Forest, the city is filled with art galleries, interesting restaurants, and unique shops. (805) 646-8126.

TOURS

ORANGE COUNTY

ORANGE COUNTY - just may epitomize the Southern California image. The vision of broad, clean beaches, surfers, sunny Mediterranean climate, and casual but affluent lifestyles describes many people's perception of the area. And it's fairly accurate. Orange County has the highest residential real estate prices in the nation and it's not uncommon to see traffic jams of outrageously expensive cars along the congested freeways.

Lying conveniently between the ocean and the mountains, and adjacent to the metropolis of Los Angeles, Orange County enjoys an ideal geographic location. Add to that the sunshine and wealth and you have one of the most attractive tourist destinations in the State. The beautiful beaches and numerous amusement parks welcome millions of visitors each year from around the world.

BUENA PARK - *(Page T, B1 & B2)* gateway to Orange County.

Knotts Berry Farm - a popular family amusement park with six theme areas, shows and over 150 rides. In addition, the Market Place has restaurants and specialty shops, featuring the original Mrs. Knott's jams and preserves. Located at 8039 Beach Blvd. (714) 220-5200.

Movieland Wax Museum - displays over 200 celebrity wax figures in realistic sets and authentic costumes. Located at 7711 Beach Boulevard, Buena Park. (714) 522-1154.

ANAHEIM - *(Page T, C2)*.
Disneyland - *(Page 193, B4)* "The Magic Kingdom" known throughout the world as the spectacular showcase for Mickey Mouse and all the Disney characters. The $200 million amusement park is divided into several theme "lands". A full day is needed to enjoy all of the attractions. (714) 999-4565.

Anaheim Stadium - *(Page 194, A5)* home of the California Angels baseball and Los Angeles Rams football teams. Guided tours are conducted daily. (714) 999-8990.

GARDEN GROVE - *(Page 195, D1)*.
Crystal Cathedral - an enormous steel and glass structure with 10,000 mirrored windows. The cathedral seats 2,862 people and the church services, "Hour Of Power", are televised in the U.S. and in 21 European nations. Tours are available. (714) 971-4000.

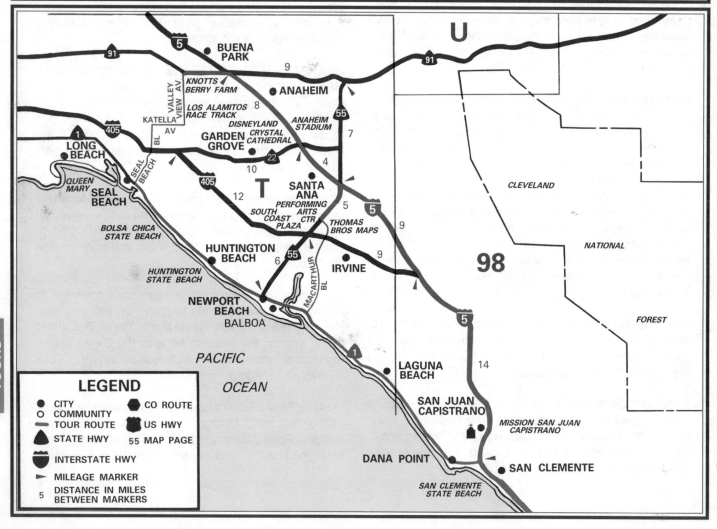

At the junction of Hwys 5 and 55, *(Page 196, E4)* you may take a short-cut southwest to the beach with several points-of-interest along the way.

Thomas Bros. Maps - *(Page 198, C3)* corporate headquarters and retail showroom. Please stop by and say hello. 17731 Cowan, Irvine. (714) 863-1984, 1-800-432-8430.

Orange County Performing Arts Center - *(Page 198, A3)* a 3,000 seat facility for concerts and theatre. For free tour information, call (714) 556-2787. Nearby is the intriguing 1.6 acre sculpture garden "California Scenario" created by the late artist, Isamu Noguchi.

South Coast Plaza - *(Page 197, E3)* a mammoth shopping center, one of the largest in the U.S., with over 270 stores in the main mall and adjoining Crystal Court. Retailers range from Sears to Saks Fifth Avenue. Valet parking available. (714) 241-1700.

BALBOA ISLAND - *(Page 199, E5)* a cute little Island jammed literally wall-to-wall with cozy beach houses, the average of which sells for $600,000. The main street is lined with boutiques and restaurants offering everything from frozen bananas to haute cuisine. Access to the Island is either via a bridge or an auto ferry. The auto ferry takes cars and pedestrians across the bay to the town of Balboa. The peninsula has an amusement area called the "Fun Zone" which includes a ferris wheel and carousel, arcades and shops.

Balboa Pavilion - *(Page 199, D5)* the 1905 landmark contains a restaurant and a gift shop. Also, it is one location where visitors can purchase tickets for harbor cruises, whale-watching expeditions and trips to Catalina Island. (714) 673-5245.

Highway 1 - South of Balboa Island

CRYSTAL COVE STATE PARK - *(Page T, D5)* stretches 3.5 miles along the coast between Corona del Mar and Laguna Beach. Four main parking areas provide access to footpaths and bicycle trails that lead down to the shoreline. The underwater park and marine life refuge is open to swimmers and divers. Park Headquarters is located at **Moro Canyon** where 17 miles of backcountry trails and roads are open to hikers and bicyclers. Camping is now permitted in scenic Moro Canyon. Reservations are encouraged at 1-800-444-7275. For Park information, call (714) 494-3539.

LAGUNA BEACH - *(Page T, E5)* a captivating town with an emphasis on art. The attractive streets are lined with galleries, shops and cafes. The annual **"Festival of the Arts/Pageant of the Masters"** and the **Sawdust Festival** attract thousands of visitors each summer. (714) 494-1145.

DANA POINT - *(Page 105, D1)* a coastal city with a marina that can accommodate over 2,000 boats. Luxury hotels, specialty shops, restaurants and grassy parks line the waterfront. *(Page 202 for detail)*.

SAN CLEMENTE STATE BEACH - *(Page 105, E1)* popular day-use beach and overnight camping spot. Visitors may swim, fish, surf and hike. (714) 492-3156.

SAN JUAN CAPISTRANO - *(Page 105, D1)*.
Mission San Juan Capistrano - *(Page 202, E1)* founded in 1776. The restored structure contains a museum and a self-guided tour explaining the Mission's history. The famous Mission is the place where thousands of swallows return each year on St. Joseph's Day, March 19th. (714) 493-1111.

Highway 1- North of Balboa Island.

UPPER NEWPORT BAY - *(Page 199, E2)* an ecological reserve for waterfowl. Birdwatchers, naturalists and bicyclists will enjoy the quiet walkways that wind along the bay. Entrance is on Backbay Drive off Jamboree Blvd.

HUNTINGTON BEACH - *(Page T, B4)*
Huntington State Beach and Bolsa Chica State Beach - seven miles of clean, sandy beaches maintained by the State. Parking, showers, food concessions, lifeguards and overnight parking for RVs. These beaches are equipped with 1,100 firerings on the sand allowing daytime BBQs and crackling fireside evenings.

SEAL BEACH - *(Page T, A3)* a revitalized beach community with a picturesque Main Street and Pier. Visitors will enjoy a leisurely stroll along the shaded streets lined with shops and pub-style restaurants.

LONG BEACH - *(Page S, D3)* is actually in Los Angeles County but too close and too interesting to miss. **LA Harbor** is here and the **Catalina Island Cruises,** too.

Queen Mary and Spruce Goose - *(Page 192, E4)* the Queen Mary is one of the largest passenger ships ever built. In 1964 she was permanently docked and became a tourist attraction and hotel. Portions of the luxury liner are open to the public as a guided tour and Sunday brunch is still served in the dining room. The Spruce Goose is the largest wooden airplane ever built. Howard Hughes masterminded the giant aircraft's construction in 1942 as a troop carrier, but it has flown only once. (213) 435-3511.

LOS ALAMITOS - *(Page T, A2)*
Los Alamitos Race Track - year-round, alternating thoroughbred, harness and quarter horse racing. Located at 4961 E. Katella Ave. (714) 995-1234.

TOURS

SAN DIEGO

Well endowed with a sunny climate, warm beaches, forested mountains and remote deserts, San Diego County extends a natural year-round vacation invitation. There is something here to please virtually everyone. Its historical sites, recreational parks, natural wonders and luxury accomodations entice thousands of visitors from around the world annually. *(See page V for an overview).*

Downtown - *(Page 215, D3)* the International Visitor's Information Center (619) 236-1212 is located at Horton Plaza Center, a multi-tiered shopping complex with 160 stores, restaurants and seven cinemas. The **Maritime Museum** features three restored ships, one of which is the Star of India, the oldest merchant vessel afloat. (619) 234-9153. The **Embarcadero** is the busy waterfront area where visitors can watch the fleets come in, tour a Navy ship or take an hour cruise around the harbor.

Balboa Park - *(Page 216)* located in the heart of the city. Over 1,000 acres of museums, theatres, gardens, shops and restaurants. The famous **San Diego Zoo** has one of the world's rarest collections of animals. It should not be missed! (619) 234-3153.

Old Town San Diego State Historic Park - *(Page 213, A5)* the location of the first permanent settlement in what is now California. The small cluster of adobe buildings have been restored and the area revitalized into a charming complex of museums, galleries, shops and restaurants. (619) 237-6770.

Cabrillo National Monument - *(Page V, A4)* named for the Portuguese explorer who led an expedition along the Pacific Coast in the 16th Century. The point provides a view of the city and the bay as well as a vantage spot to

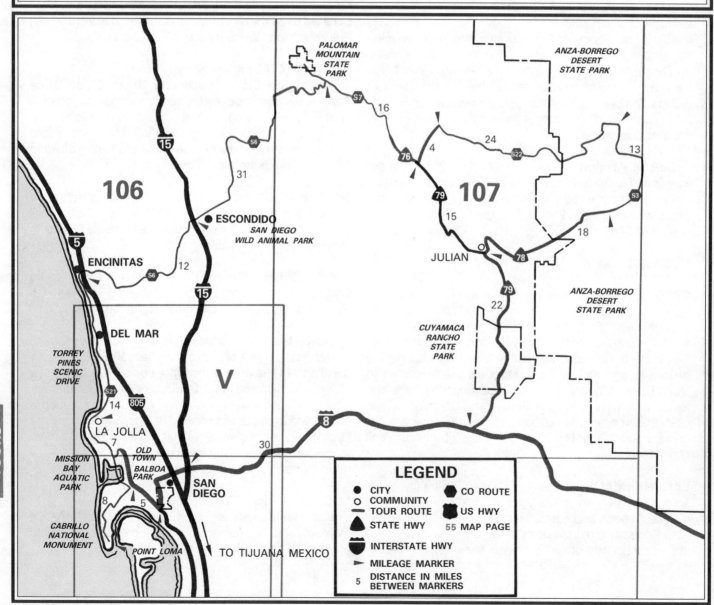

TOURS

watch migratory whales at certain times of the year. A lighthouse, museum and hiking trails are maintained. (619) 557-5450.

Mission Bay - *(Page 212)* an aquatic playground for water sports enthusiasts. Twenty-seven miles of shoreline are open for public swimming, fishing and picnicking. Several boat launches are located around the bay. Motorboating, water skiing and sailing are popular. **Sea World** is one of California's most popular theme parks, featuring 135 acres of fascinating marine exhibits and performances. This is an all-day excursion in itself. (619) 226-3901.

LA JOLLA - the "jewel" of San Diego. Reminiscent of the French Riviera, this gorgeous residential community has a village area along Prospect Street *(Page 105, B2)* of chic restaurants, boutiques and galleries.

La Jolla Museum of Contemporary Art - located at 700 Prospect Street. The Museum and its setting are works of art in themselves; the lovely structure sits on a landscaped bluff overlooking the ocean. Under innovative direction, the museum features fine collections of contemporary art in a broad range of medium including photography, video and musical performances. The gift shop offers unique jewelry and other interesting items. (619) 454-3541.

La Jolla Caves - wave eroded sandstone cliffs have formed several impressive caves which can be reached by an 80-foot staircase through a curio shop. (619) 454-6080.

Scripps Aquarium/Museum - *(Page 211, A1)* world famous center for Marine research. Several displays emphasize those fish and animals found in the Southern California waters. (619) 534-6933.

TORREY PINES SCENIC DRIVE - *(Page V, A1)* curves north of La Jolla to Torrey Pines State Reserve. The park protects over 7,000 gnarled Torrey Pines that grow naturally only one other place in the world, on Santa Rosa Island. (619) 755-2063.

DEL MAR - *(Page V, A1)* where "the turf meets the surf", the oceanside Del Mar Racetrack was founded in 1937 by a group of Hollywood celebrities. Each year, July through September, the pink and green art deco Grandstand is open to the public for championship thoroughbred racing. Other events are held throughout the year. (619) 755-1141.

ENCINITAS - *(Page 106, B4)* a quiet, residential community.

Quail Botanical Gardens - a peaceful setting of foot trails that meander through 30 acres of rare and exotic plants, trees and flowers. Nationally recognized for its diverse and botanically important plant collections. Gift shop and plant sales. (619) 436-3036.

SAN DIEGO WILD ANIMAL PARK - *(Page 106, D3)* located 6 miles south of Escondido. The 1,800 acre wildlife sanctuary exists in conjunction with the San Diego Zoo; animals are often relocated from one park to the other. Within the compound, many of the 2,100 animals are allowed to roam freely in natural settings. A special monorail takes visitors on a one hour safari-like adventure. (619) 234-6541.

PALOMAR MOUNTAIN STATE PARK - *(Page 107, A2)* thick fir and cedar forests resemble the Sierra Nevadas. Fishing and camp sites are available.

Palomar Observatory - has a 200 inch Hale telescope, one of the largest in the world. There is a visitor s gallery, photographs, a film and a small gift shop. (619) 742-2119.

ANZA-BORREGO DESERT STATE PARK - *(Page 107, D2),* 600,000 acre expanse of wilderness, most of which is accessible only by 4-wheel drive vehicles. Even though the area may appear desolate, it is actually a complex and fragile ecosystem; steep canyon walls and feathery palms protect numerous bird and wildlife species. In the spring, the desert is a carpet of colorful wildflowers. Camping is permitted; the visitor's center provides trail maps and information. (619) 767-5311.

JULIAN - *(Page107, C3)* a turn-of-the-century mining town. Old west storefronts harbor quaint shops and home-style restaurants. There are several historic buildings, a museum and a nearby winery. Locally grown apples are a popular dessert ingredient. The Chamber of Commerce provides information, local maps and a calender of events. (619) 765-1857.

Eagle Gold Mine Tour - visitors travel 1,000 feet into an authentic gold mine. Museum and displays of tools, machinery and antique engines. (619) 765-9921.

CUYAMACA RANCHO STATE PARK - *(Page 107,C4)* a tranquil area of oak and pine trees, meadows and streams. There are hundreds of miles of riding & hiking trails within the park. A 3-1/2 mile trail leads to a 6,512 foot summit where the view encompasses the Pacific Ocean to the west and the desert to the east. Camping is permitted. (619) 765-0755.

PALM SPRINGS

Nicknamed "The Springs", "The Village", and "The Golf Capitol of the World", Palm Springs is truly an oasis for the city-weary and the sun worshiper. This playground for all ages lies along the Coachella Valley, snug against the San Jacinto Mountains, less than two hours from Los Angeles. *(Page 100)* There are exclusive shops, fine restaurants and luxury hotels galore along with revitalizing mineral springs and spas, numerous golf courses, and fascinating natural wonders. For visitor information, call (619) 327-8411.

Desert Museum - *(Page 206, A4)* a unique structure that houses an odd combination of contemporary and American fine art collections, natural history and science exhibits, regular concerts and dance performances. (619) 325-7186.

Palm Canyon - 7 miles south of Palm Springs on Palm Canyon Drive. Over 3,000 Washingtonian palms, some 2,000 years old, line the 15 mile long canyon. Follow the signs to Indian canyons. Hiking and horseback riding are permitted. (619) 325-5673.

Moorten Botanical Garden - a 4-acre garden filled with 2,000 varieties of desert plants representing several regions of the world. (619) 327-6555.

Aerial Tramway - *(Page 100, C3)* called the "Eighth Engineering Wonder of the World", it is the longest single-lift passenger tramway in the world. Two 80-passenger trams rise from the desert floor to 8,500 feet for a breathtaking view of Palm Springs, the Coachella Valley and the Salton Sea. At the top is a restaurant, gift shop and picnic area. A 6-mile hike leads to the top of Mt. San Jacinto (10,804') where on a clear day the view extends to the mountain ranges of Las Vegas. (619) 325-1391.

DESERT HOT SPRINGS - *(Page 100, D2)* another popular resort, just northeast of Palm Springs, across Highway 10. It is known for natural hot mineral waters which reach temperatures of 200 degrees F. 1-800-FIND DHS.

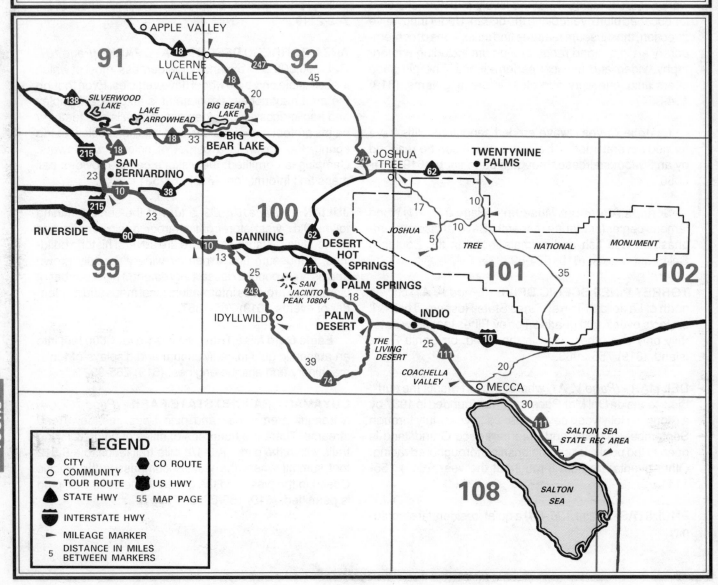

Cabot's Old Indian Pueblo Museum - *(Page 100, C3)* 35-room Hopi-style pueblo filled with odd memorabilia, Indian artifacts, arts and crafts. (619) 329-7610.

LIVING DESERT - *(Page 100, E4)* a 1,200-acre park representing the plants and animals of the high-desert region. Fascinating exhibits and six miles of trails introduce visitors to desert life beyond the civilized world. (619) 346-5694.

PALMS TO PINES HIGHWAY - the 64-mile scenic drive along Highway 74, connecting to Highway 243 to Banning. The road is a two-lane highway and winds through the San Bernardino National Forest.

Idyllwild - *(Page 100, B4)* a small mountain town, site of the Idyllwild School of Music and the Arts.

Mt. San Jacinto State Park - *(Page 100, B4)* combines granite peaks and sub-alpine forests of mostly primitive wilderness. The San Jacinto Peak, at 10,804 feet, is the second highest in California. Camping and extensive hiking trails are available. (714) 659-2607.

San Bernardino County Museum - *(Page 99, C2)* located in Redlands. An especially exciting place for children with "hands-on" exhibits of small animals and reptiles. The museum also boasts a collection of 100,000 bird eggs. (714) 792-1334.

RIM OF THE WORLD HIGHWAY - a 40-mile scenic drive along Highway 18 north of San Bernardino *(Page 99, C1)*. The route threads along the 5,000 to 7,000 foot crest of the San Bernardino Mountains, through several rustic communities and resort areas.

Silverwood State Recreational Area - *(Page 91, B5)* on Highway 138. The park consists of forests of Ponderosa pine, cedar, oak and fir. The area provides excellent camping and picnicking while the manmade lake offers fishing, swimming, waterskiing and boating. (619) 389-2303.

Lake Arrowhead - *(Page 91, C5)* a beautiful manmade lake, in an Alpine setting. A year-round resort for nature lovers and sports enthusiasts. In addition to restaurants, quaint and luxurious lodges, shops and theatres complete the vacation package.

Big Bear Lake - *(Page 91,E5)* for crisp air and spectacular scenery, a wide range of accomodations, restaurants, and activities. In the summer, the 7-mile lake is a playground for water sports; in the winter, the surrounding mountains offer several snow-skiing areas and cozy cabin retreats.

Highway 18 east from Big Bear snakes out of the mountains and onto the desert floor, a dramatic contrast in scenery and climate. The town of Lucerne offers full services before venturing into the vast desert *(Page 91, E4)*. Turn east on Highway 247 and follow it to the junction with Hwy 62 *(Page 100, D1)*. Turn east toward Joshua Tree.

JOSHUA TREE NATIONAL MONUMENT - *(Page 101, A2)*. Brochures and trail maps are available at the West Entrance Information Station. The park is really two deserts:

The Upper Portion is the "high" Mojave Desert where the Joshua Tree grows to 40 feet tall. A giant member of the lily family, it was supposedly named by the Mormons for its upstretched "praying" arms. The Keys View provides a panoramic view of the Coachella Valley and San Jacinto Mountains. There are no services within the park, but the well-maintained roads provide picnic tables and turnouts with information plaques. The unusual rock formations have been used as protection by Indians and hideouts by cattle rustlers in the past and more recently were the backdrop to a private ranch.

The Lower Portion is representative of the "low" Colorado Desert, arid and rocky, with the distinctive Ocotillo Cacti and numerous other plants and wildlife unique to the region.

There are two visitor centers in the park: the **Oasis Visitor Center** at the Twentynine Palms entrance *(Page 101, C1)* has a museum and short self-guided nature walk. The **Cottonwood Visitor Center** is at the south entrance. *(Page 101, D4)* (619) 367-7511.

SALTON SEA STATE RECREATION AREA - *(Page 108)* this 35 mile long inland sea was created in 1905 when the Colorado River flooded. Gradual leaching of minerals from the land has made the water several times saltier than the ocean; fish originally introduced in the 1950's by the Department of Fish and Game have adapted and survived. Seventy-five species of birds make this their permanent home while as many as 300 other species have migrated here at one time or another. The 17,868-acre Salton Sea area is undeveloped but is a popular area for boaters and fishermen. Primitive campsites are available. (619) 393-3052.

INDIO - *(Page 101, A4)* "The Date Capitol of the World", where 200,000 date palms yield 40 million pounds of various varieties of dates. Stop at one of the several roadside stands for a date milkshake.

SOUTHERN SIERRAS

Within this region lie some of nature's remarkable extremes; the world's oldest living things, the world's largest living things, the highest peak in the contiguous U.S., and the lowest spot in the U.S. Perhaps here, more than anywhere else, can we begin to appreciate the kaleidoscope of wonders that California has to offer. These contrasting features not only provide breathtaking scenery but also produce conditions for some of the best outdoor recreation in the state.

The Sierra Nevadas were sculptured eons ago when earth movement pushed the granite rocks upward at sheer angles. The result is a mountain range that rises gradually from the Central Valley on the west and plunges sharply to the desert floor on the east. This characteristic is visually intriguing but also makes the mountains virtually impassable by auto. Only at the far south and north ends can traffic pass through. For this reason, and because both sides of the Sierra Nevadas are equally spectacular, we have divided this tour into two sections: 1) the western slope and 2) the eastern slope.

WESTERN SLOPE - the western portion of the Sierras is dominated by Kings Canyon and Sequoia National Parks, joined end to end along the mountain range. Both park's main entrances, located at Ash Mountain, can be reached by main road Highway180 east from Fresno *(Page 58, D3);* but if time allows you, we recommend taking the zigzag route that threads through the Sequoia National Forest from Lake Isabella.

From Bakersfield *(Page 78, D3)* take scenic Highway 178 east. At Kernvale *(Page 79, C1)* turn north on Highway 155 around the western edge of Lake Isabella, a

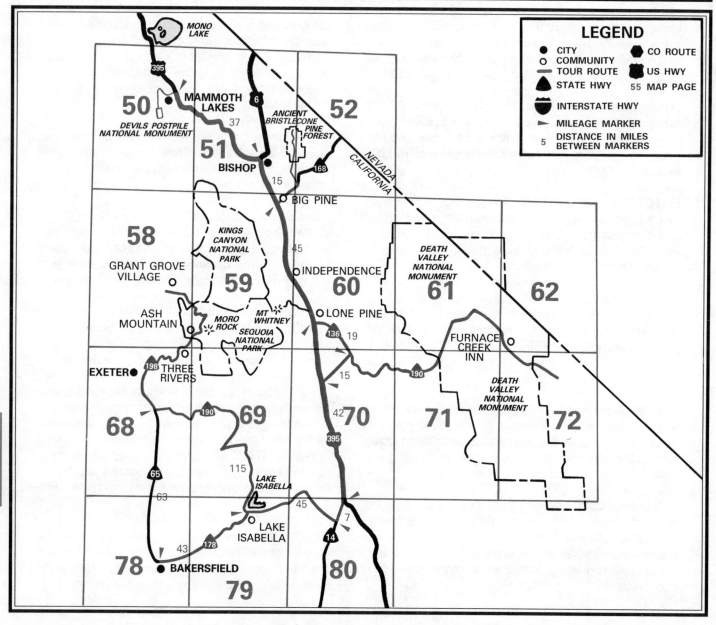

popular man-made recreation area. From here the road north through the Sequoia National Forest *(Page 69)* is two-lane and extremely winding, making the drive slow and tedious, but the scenery is particularly beautiful. Plan to drive it leisurely. Forests of tall trees, craggy granite rocks, waterfalls and numerous campgrounds line the way. The county-maintained road is closed during the winter. Call CALTRANS for road conditions. (916) 445-7623.

KINGS CANYON/SEQUOIA NATIONAL PARKS - from Highway 190, just before Springville, turn north on J37 *(Page 69, A2)* and connect to Highway 198 east of Exeter *(Page 68, D1)*. The headquarters for both parks is located 7 miles north of Three Rivers on Highway 198 *(Page 58, E5)* at the small community of Ash Mountain. The visitors center provides information, maps and brochures of the park. (209) 565-3341.

Along the 46-mile Generals Highway which links the two parks, there are numerous points of interest. The main attractions, of course, are the incredible Sequoias, the largest living things on earth. They have survived the last ice age and are found only along the western slope of the Sierra Nevada range. Unbelievably, these 2,000 year old giants were in danger of being destroyed by greedy loggers. Evidence of this careless harvest is on display at Big Stump Basin and should be a reminder to us of our responsibility to protect these and all natural wonders.

At Moro Rock, climbers can get a 360 degree view of the Sierras. At Giant Forest, the 2,500 year old General Sherman Tree stands 272 feet high with a base large enough for two buses to pass through, side by side. The Congress Trail is a two mile hike through several stands of sequoias. A park ranger leads groups of visitors and explains the history of the trees. Grant Grove is the location of 4 or 5 of the largest sequoias in the world.

There are several full-service campgrounds within the two parks. Hiking and fishing are popular and horses may be rented for trips into the backcountry. The parks are open all year through, although some roads are closed in winter.

EASTERN SLOPE - the eastern portion is a contrasting view of the grand Sierra Nevada range. The route runs straight, slicing through the Owens Valley along the dramatic granite escarpment on the west and the vast Mojave Desert on the east.

From Lake Isabella, continue on scenic Highway 178 east *(Page 79, C1)* to Highway 14 *(Page 80, C1)* at Freeman. Turn north on Highway 14 toward Highway 395.

DEATH VALLEY NATIONAL MONUMENT - at Olancha, Highway 190 angles northeast. *(Page 70, B1)* This scenic drive crosses a series of barren peaks and isolated valleys. At each peak the view is of multicolored desert vistas and unspoiled wilderness. There is a distinct drop in elevation as the road descends to the lowest spot in the continental U.S. (282 feet below sea level). A few communities survive in the harsh desert where summer temperatures may reach 130 degrees F and average less than 2" of rainfall each year.

Stovepipe Wells - *(Page 61, D4)* a small town with a motel and store. Nearby is a great location to play on the huge sand dunes.

Furnace Creek - *(Page 62, A5)* a virtual oasis located in the center of the oblong monument. The Visitors Center provides information, brochures and exhibits concerning the 2 million acres of monument territory. (619) 786-2331, ext. 244.

LONE PINE - on Highway 395 *(Page 60, B4)*, provides an excellent view of Mt. Whitney, the highest point in the contiguous U.S.

Visitor's Center - located 1-1/2 miles south of Lone Pine on Hwy 395 with information on Owen's Valley, Inyo National Forest and Death Valley. (619) 876-4252.

Alabama Hills - a rocky area northwest of town that has been used in countless movie westerns.

Whitney Portal - *(Page 59, E4)* a point 13 miles west of town which is the trail head for hikers attempting to ascend Mt. Whitney.

ANCIENT BRISTLECONE PINE FOREST - *(Page 52, A3)* a 28,000 acre area of the White Mountains that contains the oldest living things on earth. These gnarled pine trees are over 4,000 years old. (619) 873-4207.

The view southwest is the most spectacular panorama of the Sierra Nevadas and Mount Whitney.

MAMMOTH LAKES - *(Page 50, D2)* one of California's most popular resort areas offers excellent year-round accommodations from condominiums to cabins to campgrounds.

Activities range from winter snow-skiing to summer river-rafting. Trout fishing and backpacking are also favorites.

DEVIL'S POSTPILE NATIONAL MONUMENT - *(Page 50, C2)* the monument consists of a sheer wall of symmetrical basaltic columns more than 60 feet high. The unusual formation was created by the crystalization of volcanic matter eons ago. A trail leads to the top where the surface resembles mosaic tiles. (619) 934-2289.

TOURS

COPYRIGHT. © 1989 BY Thomas Bros. Maps

LIST OF ABBREVIATIONS

AL..........ALLEY	CR..........CRESCENT	KPN.....KEY PENINSULA NORTH	RDG..........RIDGE
AR..........ARROYO	CRES..........CRESCENT	KPS.....KEY PENINSULA SOUTH	RES..........RESERVOIR
ARR..........ARROYO	CSWY..........CAUSEWAY	L..........LA	RIV..........RIVER
AV..........AVENUE	CT..........COURT	LN..........LANE	RV..........RIVER
AVD..........AVENIDA	CTE..........CORTE	LP..........LOOP	RO..........RANCHO
AVD D LS......AVENIDA DE LOS	CTO..........CUT OFF	LS..........LAS, LOS	S..........SOUTH
BCH..........BEACH	CTR..........CENTER	MDW..........MEADOW	SN..........SAN
BL..........BOULEVARD	CV..........COVE	MHP..........MOBILE HOME PARK	SPG..........SPRING
BLVD..........BOULEVARD	CY..........CANYON	MNR..........MANOR	SPGS..........SPRINGS
CEM..........CEMETERY	CYN..........CANYON	MT..........MOUNT	SQ..........SQUARE
CIR..........CIRCLE	D..........DE	MTN..........MOUNTAIN	SRA..........SIERRA
CK..........CREEK	DL..........DEL	MTWY..........MOTORWAY	ST..........SAINT
CL..........CALLE	DR..........DRIVE	MTY..........MOTORWAY	ST..........STREET
CL DL..........CALLE DEL	DS..........DOS	N..........NORTH	STA..........SANTA
CL D LS..........CALLE DE LAS	E..........EAST	PAS..........PASEO	STA..........STATION
..........CALLE DE LOS	EST..........ESTATE	PAS DE..........PASEO DE	TER..........TERRACE
CL EL..........CALLE EL	EXPWY..........EXPRESSWAY	PAS DL..........PASEO DEL	THTR..........THEATER
CLJ..........CALLEJON	EXT..........EXTENSION	PAS D LS..........PASEO DE LAS	TK TR..........TRUCK TRAIL
CL LA..........CALLE LA	FRWY..........FREEWAY	..........PASEO DE LOS	TR..........TRAIL
CL LS..........CALLE LAS	FRW..........FREEWAY	PGD..........PLAYGROUND	VIA D..........VIA DE
..........CALLE LOS	FY..........FREEWAY	PK..........PARK	VIA D LS..........VIA DE LAS
CM..........CAMINO	GN..........GLEN	PK..........PEAK	..........VIA DE LOS
CM D..........CAMINO DE	GRDS..........GROUNDS	PKWY..........PARKWAY	VIA DL..........VIA DEL
CM D LA...CAMINO DE LA	GRN..........GREEN	PL..........PLACE	VIS..........VISTA
CM D LS..........CAMINO DE LAS	GRV..........GROVE	PT..........POINT	VLG..........VILLAGE
..........CAMINO DE LOS	HTS..........HEIGHTS	PY..........PARKWAY	VLY..........VALLEY
CMTO..........CAMINITO	HWY..........HIGHWAY	PZ..........PLAZA	VW..........VIEW
CN..........CANAL	HY..........HIGHWAY	RCH..........RANCH	W..........WEST
COM..........COMMON	JCT..........JUNCTION	RCHO..........RANCHO	WK..........WALK
		RD..........ROAD	WY..........WAY

INDEXES

244
A ST
STREET INDEX
AR GRNDE HUASNA

A

STREET	CO.	PAGE	GRID
A ST	ALA	L	E5
A ST	ALA	45	E2
A ST	DVS	136	C3
A ST	DN	1	D4
A ST	H	146	E2
A ST	SBD	92	A1
A ST	SD	215	D3
A ST	TEH	18	E5
A ST W	ALA	L	E5
A ST W	ALA	N	E1
A ST W	H	146	B3
ABBOTT DR	KER	80	B3
ABBOTT RD	LACO	R	A5
ABBOTT ST	MON	54	D4
ABBOTT ST	SAL	171	D4
ABBY ST	FRE	165	D3
ABELIA ST	SBD	92	B3
ABELOR RD	INY	51	C4
ABERDEEN DR	SBD	100	E1
ABERDEEN STA RD	INY	59	E1
ABERNATHY RD	SOL	L	E1
ABERNATHY RD	SOL	M	A1
ABERNATHY RD	SOL	38	E3
ABERNATHY RD	YUB	26	A4
ABLE RD	COL	32	E2
ABORN RD	SCL	P	C3
ABORN RD	SCL	46	C4
ABRAM DR	RCO	100	A5
ACACIA AV	ANA	193	D1
ACACIA AV	STA	47	C3
ACACIA AV	SUT	33	C2
ACACIA ST	SAL	171	A4
ACADEMY AV	FRCO	57	E4
ACAMPO RD	SJCO	40	B4
ACARI RD	KER	78	B3
ACKERMAN LN	HUM	16	B3
ACME RD	SUT	33	B3
ACMITE ST	KER	91	E3
ACOMA TR	SBD	100	D1
ADA RD	KER	78	B3
ADAIR RD	IMP	108	E5
ADAIR RD	STA	47	C2
ADAM FOX FRM RD	HUM	9	E4
ADAMS AV	CM	197	C5
ADAMS AV	EC	217	B2
ADAMS AV	FRCO	56	D4
ADAMS AV	FRCO	57	C4
ADAMS AV	FRCO	58	A4
ADAMS AV	ORA	T	C4
ADAMS AV	SD	214	B4
ADAMS AV	SDCO	V	C3
ADAMS AV	SDCO	111	D1
ADAMS BLVD	LA	184	A4
ADAMS BLVD	LA	185	C4
ADAMS BLVD	LACO	Q	D4
ADAMS DR	KER	79	E1
ADAMS RD	TEH	18	C4
ADAMS ST	IMP	109	A5
ADAMS ST	RCO	99	A2
ADAMS ST	RCO	101	A4
ADDISON RD	BUT	25	C1
ADELAIDA RD	SLO	75	E1
ADELAIDA RD	SLO	76	A1
ADELINE ST	B	156	A4
ADELINE ST	O	157	D2
ADELANTO RD	SBD	91	B3
ADML CALLAHN LN	VAL	134	E3
ADOBE DR	KER	79	E2
ADOBE DR	KER	80	A2
ADOBE PL	MON	65	C4
ADOBE RD	BUT	25	C4
ADOBE RD	COL	25	A5
ADOBE RD	KER	78	D4
ADOBE RD	SBD	101	B1
ADOBE RD	SLO	76	A1
ADOBE RD	SHA	18	D3
ADOBE RD	SON	L	A1
ADOBE RD	SON	38	A3
ADOBE RD	TEH	18	D4
ADOBE CREEK RD	LAK	31	D3
ADOBE RANCH RD	MNO	44	A5
ADOHR RD	KER	78	A3
ADOLFO LOPEZ BL	BAJA	112	B4
AERO DR	SD	214	A1
AERO DR	SDCO	V	B2
AERO DR	SDCO	111	D1
AEROPUERTO HWY	BAJA	111	E2
AFTON BLVD	GLE	25	A4
AFTON RD	BUT	25	B5
AFTON CANYON RD	SBD	82	D5
AGATE RD	SBD	91	D1
AGER RD	SIS	4	B3
AGER RD	SIS	5	D2
AGER BESWICK RD	SIS	4	C3
AGGEN RD	VEN	88	C5
AGNES WILSON RD	LPAZ	104	A2
AGNES WILSON RD	RCO	103	E2
AGOURA RD	LACO	96	E1
AGUA CALIENT BL	BAJA	111	E3
AGUA CALIENT RD	SB	87	D4
AGUA CALIENT RD	SON	132	A1
AGUA DULCE CYN	LACO	89	D4
AGUA FRIA RD	MPA	49	A3
AGUAJITO RD	MON	53	E4
AGUAJITO RD	MON	168	D2
AGUA MANSA RD	RCO	99	B2
AGUAS FRIAS RD	BUT	25	B4
AGUEREBERRY PT	INY	71	D1
AHERN RD	SJCO	47	A2
AHLF RD	SUT	33	C2
AINSWORTH PL	RCO	107	A1

STREET	CO.	PAGE	GRID
AIR BASE PKWY	FRFD	135	C2
AIR BASE PKWY	SOL	M	A1
AIR BASE PKWY	SOL	38	E3
AIR BASE PKWY	SOL	39	A3
AIR BASE RD	SBD	91	B3
AIRD CIR	BUT	25	E3
AIROLA	CAL	41	B4
AIROSA DR	SBD	90	E3
AIROX RD	SB	86	B1
AIR PARK DR	IMP	108	C2
AIRPORT	SJCO	40	B5
AIRPORT BLVD	KER	80	A5
AIRPORT BLVD	LA	188	D5
AIRPORT BLVD	LA	189	D1
AIRPORT BLVD	LACO	Q	D5
AIRPORT BLVD	RCO	101	A4
AIRPORT BLVD	SAL	171	E5
AIRPORT BLVD	SMCO	N	C1
AIRPORT BLVD	SF	144	C1
AIRPORT BLVD	SJ	151	E2
AIRPORT BLVD	SCR	54	B2
AIRPORT BLVD	SON	37	E1
AIRPORT BLVD S	SSF	144	C2
AIRPORT DR	O	159	D5
AIRPORT RD	ALP	36	C4
AIRPORT RD	HUM	9	E4
AIRPORT RD	KER	78	A4
AIRPORT RD	MEN	22	C5
AIRPORT RD	MEN	30	C1
AIRPORT RD	MOD	8	A1
AIRPORT RD	MOD	14	E1
AIRPORT RD	MNO	50	E2
AIRPORT RD	NAPA	L	D1
AIRPORT RD	NAPA	38	C3
AIRPORT RD	O	159	D4
AIRPORT RD	SLO	76	B1
AIRPORT RD	SHA	18	C3
AIRPORT RD	SIS	4	B3
AIRPORT RD	SOL	M	D1
AIRPORT RD	SOL	39	C3
AIRPORT RD	TRI	17	D1
AIRPORT WY	SJCO	40	B5
AIRPORT WY	SJCO	47	B2
AIRWAY DR	KLAM	5	C1
AKER AV	STA	47	D1
AKERS RD	TUL	68	B1
AKINS RD	SIS	5	D2
AKRICH ST	SHA	18	C2
ALABAMA ST	SBD	99	C2
ALAMEDA AV	BUR	179	C5
ALAMEDA AV	LACO	Q	D3
ALAMEDA AV	O	159	B1
ALAMEDA AV	SAL	171	C5
ALAMEDA AV	YOL	39	D2
ALAMEDA ST	LA	186	B4
ALAMEDA ST	LACO	97	E2
ALAMEDA ST	LACO	S	D2
ALAMEDA ST	MAN	161	C3
ALAMEDA ST	VAL	134	C4
ALAMEDA, THE	SJ	151	C2
ALAMEDA, THE	SJ	152	A4
ALAMEDA, THE	SCLR	151	C2
ALAM D LS PULGS	BLMT	145	A4
ALAM D LS PULGS	SMCO	N	C1
ALAM D LS PULGS	SMCO	N	D2
ALAM D LS PULGS	SM	145	A4
ALAM D LS PULGS	SMCO	45	D4
ALAMEDA PAD SER	STB	174	C2
ALAMITOS AV	LACO	S	D3
ALAMO DR	MPA	48	D2
ALAMO RD	IMP	109	B5
ALAMO ST	LACO	88	E5
ALAMO ST	SIS	5	A2
ALAMO ST	VEN	88	E5
ALAMO ST	VEN	89	A5
ALAMO CREEK RD	SLO	76	D5
ALAMO PINTADO	SB	86	E3
ALBA RD	SCR	N	E5
ALBA RD	SCR	53	E1
ALBAUGH RD	LAS	14	C3
ALBERS RD	STA	47	E2
ALBRT ETTER RCH	HUM	16	A5
ALBERTON AV	BUT	25	A3
ALBION LTL RIV	MEN	30	B1
ALBION RIDGE RD	MEN	30	C1
ALBRIGHT RD	IMP	109	B3
ALCALDE RD	FRCO	66	D3
ALCATRAZ AV	ALA	L	D4
ALCATRAZ AV	O	156	B4
ALCOSTA BLVD	CC	M	B5
ALDEN ST	KER	78	E4
ALDER AV	SBD	80	E1
ALDER AV	SBD	99	B1
ALDER ST	PAC	167	B2
ALDER CAMP RD	DN	1	E5
ALDER CAMP RD	DN	9	E1
ALDER CAMP RD	DN	10	A1
ALDER CREEK RD	NEV	27	D5
ALDER CK BCH RD	MEN	30	C3
ALDRCRFT HTS RD	SCL	P	B5
ALDRCRFT HTS RD	SCL	54	A1
ALDERPOINT RD	HUM	16	C3
ALDER PT BLUFF	TRI	16	D5
ALDER SPGS RD	GLE	23	D3
ALDER SPGS RD	GLE	24	A3
ALDERPOINT RD	HUM	16	C3
ALDERWOOD DR	SIS	4	A4
ALDINE DR	SD	214	E4
ALDINE DR	SDCO	V	C3
ALDINE DR	SDCO	111	D1
ALDRIDGE RD	SHA	19	A2
ALEJO DR	RCO	100	C3
ALESSANDRO BLVD	RCO	99	B3
ALEXANDER AV	BUT	33	C1

STREET	CO.	PAGE	GRID
ALEXANDER AV	SHA	18	C3
ALEXANDER LN	LAS	21	C3
ALEXANDR VLY RD	SON	31	D5
ALFALFA AV	STA	47	C4
ALFRD HARRL HWY	KER	78	D2
ALGERINE RD	TUO	41	C5
ALGODON RD	YUB	33	D3
ALGRN WRDS FRRY	TUO	41	C5
ALGOMAN AV	SBD	91	E3
ALHAMBRA	CC	38	E5
ALHAMBRA AV	CC	L	E3
ALHAMBRA AV	M	154	B1
ALHAMBRA BLVD	SCTO	137	E3
ALHAMBRA RD	LACO	R	B3
ALHAMBRA WY	M	154	C3
ALHAMBRA VLY RD	CC	L	D3
ALHAMBRA VLY RD	CC	38	D5
ALHAMBRA VLY RD	CC	154	C5
ALHAMBRA VLY RD	M	154	C4
ALICE AV	HUM	16	C5
ALICIA AV	YUB	33	D2
ALICIA PKWY	ORA	98	D5
ALISAL RD	MON	54	D4
ALISAL RD	SB	86	E3
ALISAL ST E	SAL	171	D4
ALISAL ST W	SAL	171	B4
ALISO CANYON RD	LACO	89	E4
ALISO CANYON RD	SB	87	C1
ALISO CANYON RD	VEN	88	B5
ALISO PARK RD	SB	87	C1
ALISOS AV	SB	87	A3
ALISOS CYN RD	SB	86	D2
ALLAN RD	AMA	41	A1
ALLEGHANY RD	YUB	26	C5
ALLEN AV	LACO	R	C2
ALLEN AV	MCO	48	C3
ALLEN RD	IMP	108	D3
ALLEN RD	KER	78	C3
ALLEN RD	SJCO	47	C1
ALLENDALE RD	SOL	39	A2
ALLERTON AV	SSF	144	D1
ALLIANCE RD	HUM	9	E5
ALLIANCE RD	HUM	10	A5
ALLISON RCH RD	NEV	34	C2
ALLUVIAL AV	FRCO	57	C3
ALMA AV	KER	79	D5
ALMA ST	PA	147	A2
ALMA ST	SJ	152	C5
ALMA ST	SCL	N	E2
ALMA ST	SCL	45	D4
ALMADEN AV	SJ	152	B4
ALMADEN BLVD	SJ	152	B4
ALMADEN EXPWY	SCL	P	B4
ALMADEN EXPWY	SCL	46	B5
ALMANOR DR W	PLU	20	B4
ALMER RD	COL	32	D2
ALMOND AV	CLO	32	E3
ALMOND AV	MCO	48	A4
ALMOND AV	STA	47	C3
ALMOND DR	MCO	55	D2
ALMOND DR	MCO	56	A2
ALMOND DR	SLO	76	B2
ALMOND RD	KER	77	B1
ALMND ORCHRD RD	SUT	33	B1
ALMONDWOOD DR	SJCO	47	B2
ALMONTE BLVD	MAR	140	B4
ALOHA ST	TEH	18	D5
ALONA ST	KER	80	A4
ALONDRA	LACO	97	E3
ALONDRA BLVD	LACO	98	A3
ALOSTA AV	LACO	98	C1
ALOSTA AV	LACO	U	A2
ALPHA RD	NEV	26	E5
ALPINE AV	FRCO	56	D4
ALPINE AV	SJCO	40	A5
ALPINE AV	S	160	A3
ALPINE BLVD	SDCO	107	A5
ALPINE RD	MOD	7	C5
ALPINE RD	MOD	8	C1
ALPINE RD	SJCO	40	B4
ALPINE RD	SMCO	N	D3
ALPINE RD	SMCO	45	D4
ALPINE MINE RD	ALP	36	A5
ALPS DR	KER	79	C5
ALT CT	RCO	107	C1
ALTA	FRCO	58	A4
ALTA ST	MON	54	E5
ALTA ST	NEV	34	C1
ALTA BONNY NOOK	PLA	34	D1
ALTADENA DR	LACO	98	A1
ALTADENA DR	LACO	R	B2
ALTAMONT PS RD	ALA	M	D5
ALTA SIERRA DR	NEV	34	C2
AL TAHOE BLVD	SLT	129	A4
ALTAIR AV	SDCO	106	D5
ALTA LOMA DR	SBD	100	E1
ALTA MESA DR	SHA	18	C2
ALTA MESA RD	SAC	40	B2
ALTAMONT PSS RD	ALA	46	C2
ALTA VISTA	AVLN	105	A4
ALTA VISTA	BKD	166	E2
ALTA VISTA DR	KER	78	D3
ALTHEA AV	FRCO	56	A2
ALTON AV	SA	197	D3
ALTUS AV	KER	80	B5
ALUM ROCK AV	SCL	P	C3
ALUM ROCK AV	SCL	46	B4
ALVARADO BLVD	ALA	N	E1
ALVARADO BLVD	ALA	P	A1
ALVARADO BLVD	ALA	45	E3
ALVARADO RD	MON	65	D4
ALVARADO RD	STA	47	E2
ALVARADO ST	LA	185	C3
ALVARADO ST	LACO	Q	E4

STREET	CO.	PAGE	GRID
ALVARADO ST	SDCO	106	C2
ALVARADO TR	MCO	55	D2
ALVARADO-NILES	ALA	45	E3
ALVARADO NLS RD	ALA	P	A1
ALVES RD	MCO	48	A3
ALVIN AV	SMA	173	B2
ALVIN DR E	SAL	171	D1
ALVIN DR W	SAL	171	C1
ALVISO-MLPTS RD	SCL	46	A4
ALVORD MTN RD	SBD	82	C5
ALWARD RD	SHA	19	B3
AMADOR AV	FRCO	56	D5
AMADOR ST	FRE	165	B4
AMADOR ST	VAL	134	D4
AMADOR CREEK RD	AMA	40	E2
AMAR RD	LACO	98	B2
AMAR RD	LACO	R	E4
AMARGOSA RD	SBD	91	B3
AMARGOSA ST	SBD	92	C2
AMBOY RD	SBD	93	D4
AMBOY RD	SBD	101	C1
AMBOY RD	SBD	101	E1
AMBROSE DR	SAL	171	A4
AMBOY CUTOFF	SBD	93	E3
AMEDEE RD	LAS	21	D4
AMELIA AV	LACO	U	B1
AMEN LN	TEH	18	C3
AMERICAN AV	FRCO	57	A4
AMERICAN AV	FRCO	58	B4
AMERICAN AV	MCO	47	D4
AMERICAN AV	STA	47	C2
AMERICAN CYN RD	NAPA	L	D2
AMERICAN CYN RD	NAPA	38	D4
AMERICN FLAT RD	AMA	40	E2
AMRICAN FLT SDE	AMA	40	E1
AMERICN GIRL MN	IMP	110	B5
AMERICN MINE RD	SHA	18	A1
AMERIGO	SJCO	40	C5
AMES ST	ALA	M	D5
AMES ST	ALA	46	C2
AMESTI RD	SCR	54	B2
AMOROSE ST	RCO	99	B4
AMOUR RD	SUT	33	C4
AMSTERDAM RD	MCO	48	B3
ANAHEIM BLVD	ANA	193	C1
ANAHEIM BLVD	ORA	98	C3
ANAHEIM BLVD	ORA	T	C2
ANAHEIM ST	LB	192	D2
ANAHEIM ST	LA	191	A1
ANAHEIM ST	LA	192	D2
ANAHEIM ST	LACO	97	D4
ANAHEIM ST	LACO	S	C2
ANAPAMU ST	STB	174	C3
ANCHO ERIE MINE	NEV	26	E5
ANCHO MINE RD	NEV	26	E5
ANCHOR	FRCO	58	B4
ANDERHOLT RD	IMP	112	B4
ANDERSON DR W	SHA	18	C3
ANDERSON LN	HUM	15	E2
ANDERSON RD	DVS	136	B3
ANDERSON RD	SLO	76	A1
ANDERSON RD	SOL	39	C4
ANDERSON RD	STA	47	C4
ANDERSON RD	TUL	68	C2
ANDERSON ST	SBD	99	C2
ANDERSON CK RD	JKSN	3	D1
ANDERSON GRADE	SIS	4	A4
ANDERSON RCH RD	LAS	14	D4
ANDERSON VLY WY	MEN	30	E3
ANDESITE RD	SIS	4	D5
ANDESITE RD	SIS	12	D1
ANDESITE LOG RD	SIS	12	D1
ANDRADE RD	ALA	P	B1
ANDRADE RD	ALA	46	B3
ANDRE RD	IMP	109	A4
ANDRESSEN RD	PLA	33	E3
ANDREW AV	SB	86	C1
ANDREWS RD	LAS	14	C3
ANDREWS RD	SIS	4	E3
ANGELES CRST HY	LACO	R	B1
ANGELES FRST HY	LACO	90	A4
ANGELES FRST HY	LACO	R	B1
ANITA RD	BUT	25	A2
ANNADALE AV	FRCO	57	B4
ANNADALE AV	FRCO	58	A3
ANNAPOLIS RD	SON	30	E5
ANNAPOLIS RD	SON	31	A5
ANNETTE RD	KER	76	E1
ANNIN AV	KER	78	B1
ANTELOPE DR	LAS	8	B4
ANTELOPE HWY	LACO	90	D4
ANTELOPE RD	MNO	42	E1
ANTELOPE RD	MNO	43	A1
ANTELOPE RD	RCO	99	C4
ANTELOPE RD	SAC	34	A5
ANTELOPE RD	SLO	66	E5
ANTELOPE SPGS	MNO	50	E2
ANTELOPE VLY FY	LACO	89	E2
ANTELOPE VLY RD	SIE	27	C3
ANTONIO RD	SCL	N	E2
ANTHONY RD	LACO	89	D4
ANTOLA RD	LAS	21	C3
ANZA RD	IMP	112	A4
ANZA RD	RCO	106	D1
ANZAR RD	SBT	54	D2
ANZA TRAIL RD	IMP	111	C4
APACHE TR	RCO	100	B3
APACHE CYN RD	VEN	88	A2
APPALOOSA RD	CAL	41	A4
APPIAN WY	CC	L	C3
APPIAN WY	CC	38	C5
APPLE AV	STA	47	C3
APPLE RD	TEH	24	C2
APPLE CANYON RD	RCO	100	C4

STREET	CO.	PAGE	GRID
APPLE COLONY RD	TUO	41	D5
APPLEGATE RD	MCO	48	B4
APPLE RANCH RD	TUO	41	E4
APPLE SEED LN	RCO	100	A5
APPLE VALLEY RD	SBD	91	C3
APPLEWHITE	SBD	91	A5
APRICOT AV	STA	47	C3
APRIL LN	VEN	88	C4
AQUEDUCT RD	KER	79	E5
AQUEDUCT RD	KER	80	A5
AQUEDUCT RD	SBD	103	A2
AQUEDUCT RD	SBD	104	A1
ARAMAYO WY	TEH	24	E1
ARASTRADERO RD	PA	147	E5
ARATA LN	SON	37	E1
ARBINI RD	STA	47	E1
ARBOGA RD	YUB	33	D2
ARBOLEDA DR	MCO	48	C5
ARBOR AV	BLMT	145	B5
ARBOR RD	SLO	76	A1
ARBOR WY	MCO	56	C1
ARBORETUM RD	PA	147	A3
ARBOR VITAE ST	ING	189	D1
ARBOR VITAE ST	LA	189	D1
ARBOR VITAE ST	LACO	Q	D5
ARBURUA RD	MCO	55	D2
ARC RD	INY	51	D5
ARCH RD	SJCO	40	B5
ARCH AIRPORT RD	SJCO	40	B5
ARCHER AV	SUT	33	C1
ARCHER RD	SHA	18	B3
ARCHERDALE RD	SJCO	40	C5
ARCHIBALD AV	RCO	98	E3
ARCHIBALD AV	SBD	U	E4
ARCHIE BROWN RD	SHA	13	D4
ARDATH RD	SD	211	B3
ARDATH RD	SDCO	V	A2
ARDATH RD	SDCO	106	C5
ARDEN DR	LACO	R	C3
ARDEN WY	SAC	40	A1
ARDENWOOD BLVD	ALA	N	E1
ARDENWOOD BLVD	ALA	P	A1
ARENA WY	MCO	48	A4
ARGO ST	KER	80	D1
ARGONAUT RD	LAK	31	D3
ARGONNE DR	S	160	B4
ARGUELLO BL	SF	141	D2
ARGYLE RD	MON	65	B3
ARLINGTON AV	CC	L	C3
ARLINGTON AV	LA	184	E5
ARLINGTON AV	LACO	Q	D4
ARLINGTON AV	LACO	S	C2
ARLINGTON AV	RIV	205	A5
ARLINGTON AV	RCO	99	A2
ARLINGTON AV S	RENO	130	A5
ARLINGTON RD	PLU	20	D5
ARLINGTON MN RD	RCO	103	B3
ARMORY RD	BARS	208	B3
ARMOUR RD	SUT	33	C4
ARMOUR RANCH RD	SB	86	E3
ARMOUR RANCH RD	SB	87	A3
ARMSTRONG	SJCO	40	A4
ARMSTRONG AV	FRCO	57	D2
ARMSTRONG AV	FRCO	57	D3
ARMSTRONG RD	CAL	41	C3
ARMSTRONG RD	LAS	14	D3
ARMSTRONG RD	RCO	99	A2
ARMSTRONG RD	STA	47	C4
ARMSTRONG RD	YUB	33	D1
ARMSTRNG WDS RD	SON	37	C1
ARMY RD	RCO	110	B1
ARNOLD DR	SON	132	A3
ARMY ST	SFCO	L	B5
ARNOLD RD	IMP	112	C5
ARMY ST	SFCO	45	C2
ARNO RD	SAC	40	A3
ARNOLD DR	SON	L	B2
ARNOLD DR	SON	38	B3
ARNOLD WY	SDCO	107	B5
AROSA RD	KER	79	C4
ARQUES AV	SVL	148	E5
ARQUES RD	SCL	P	A3
ARRECHE RD	MOD	7	D5
ARRELLAGA ST	STB	174	B3
ARROW HWY	CLA	203	C2
ARROW HWY	LACO	98	B1
ARROW HWY	LACO	U	B2
ARROW HWY	MTCL	203	C2
ARROW HWY	ROC	204	A2
ARROW HWY	SBD	U	D2
ARROW HWY	SBD	98	E1
ARROW HWY	UPL	204	A2
ARROW ROUTE	SBD	203	B2
ARROWHEAD AV	SBDO	207	D4
ARROWHEAD BLVD	RCO	103	D5
ARROWHEAD BLVD	RCO	110	D1
ARROWHEAD RD	LAK	32	A3
ARROWHEAD ST	CAL	41	A5
ARROWHEAD TR	SBD	82	E4
ARROWHEAD TR	SBD	83	A4
ARROWHEAD LK RD	SBD	91	C5
ARROYA AV	MCO	56	A1
ARROYO AV	KER	79	E5
ARROYO AV	KER	80	A5
ARROYO BLVD	LACO	R	B2
ARROYO BLVD	PAS	190	A4
ARROYO PKWY	PAS	190	C5
ARROYO RD	ALA	P	C1
ARROYO RD	ALA	46	C2
ARROYO RD	SBD	92	A4
ARROYO BURRO RD	SB	87	C4
AR GRANDE GUADL	SLO	76	B5
AR GRANDE GUADL	SLO	86	A1
AR GRNDE HUASNA	SLO	76	D4

INDEXES

245

ARROYO SECO RD

STREET INDEX

BALFOUR RD

STREET	CO.	PAGE	GRID
ARROYO SECO RD	MON	64	E2
ARROYO SECO RD	MON	65	A1
ARTESIA AV	SB	86	B3
ARTESIA BLVD	LACO	97	D3
ARTESIA BLVD	LACO	98	A3
ARTESIA BLVD	LACO	S	B1
ARTESIA FRWY	LACO	98	A3
ARTESIA FRWY	LACO	S	D1
ARTESIA FRWY	LACO	T	A1
ARTHUR	SJCO	47	C1
ARTHUR RD	CC	L	E3
ARTHUR RD	CC	M	A3
ARTHUR ST	RCO	101	C5
ARTICHOKE RD	SMCO	N	C4
ARTICHOKE RD	SMCO	45	C5
ARTIC MINE RD	NEV	26	E5
ARTISTS DR	INY	72	A1
ASH AV	SHA	13	C5
ASH AV	STA	47	C3
ASH ST	SD	215	D3
ASH ST	SDCO	107	A4
ASHBY AV	ALA	L	D4
ASHBY AV	B	156	B3
ASHBY RD	SHA	18	C2
ASH CREEK RD	INY	60	B5
ASH CREEK RD	SHA	18	E3
ASH CREEK RD	SIS	4	A3
ASH CK SINK RD	SIS	13	A2
ASHE RD	KER	78	D4
ASHLAN AV	FRCO	56	C3
ASHLAN AV	FRCO	57	A5
ASHLEY LN	SJCO	40	B4
ASH VALLEY RD	LAS	8	A3
ASH VALLEY RD	LAS	14	D3
ASHWORTH RD	MPA	49	B3
ASILOMAR AV	PAC	167	A2
ASPEN VALLEY RD	TUO	49	C1
ASPEN VALLEY RD	TUO	63	A4
ASSOCIATED RD	SB	86	B1
ASSOCIATED RD	SIS	4	E3
ASSOCIATED RD	SIS	5	A3
ASTER RD	SBD	91	A3
ASTORIA AV	KER	89	C1
ATEN RD	IMP	109	A5
ATHEL ST	KER	80	C1
ATHERTON AV	MAR	L	A2
ATHERTON BLVD	MAR	38	B4
ATHERTON ST	LACO	S	E2
ATHERTON ST	LACO	T	A2
ATHLONE RD	MCO	48	D5
ATKINS RD	SJCO	40	C4
ATLANTIC AV	A	157	D5
ATLANTIC AV	FRFD	135	C1
ATLANTIC AV	LB	192	E2
ATLANTIC AV	LACO	97	E3
ATLANTIC AV	LACO	S	D1
ATLANTIC AV E	FRFD	135	D1
ATLANTIC BLVD	LACO	98	A2
ATLANTIC BLVD	LACO	R	B4
ATLANTIC BLVD	LACO	S	D2
ATLAS	CC	38	C5
ATLAS RD	CC	L	C3
ATLAS PEAK RD	NAPA	38	D2
ATTERBERRY CT	KER	79	E2
ATTILA RD	SBD	84	C4
ATWATER	MCO	47	E4
ATWELL AV	TUL	67	E4
ATWELL AV	TUL	68	A4
ATWOOD	PLA	34	C3
AUBERRY RD	FRCO	57	E1
AUBERRY RD	FRCO	58	A1
AUBERRY RD	MAD	49	E5
AUBREY AV	MCO	56	A2
AUBURN BLVD	SAC	34	A5
AUBURN RD	NEV	34	C2
AUBURN RD	PLA	34	B3
AUBURN FRST HLL	PLA	34	D3
AUBURN RAVNE RD	AUB	126	C3
AUBURN RAVNE RD	PLA	126	C3
AUCTION SNIVELY	TEH	18	D4
AUDUBON DR	FRCO	57	C2
AUGUST AV	MCO	47	D4
AUGUST RD	STA	47	D4
AUGUSTINE RD	RCO	109	C1
AUKLET RD	SBD	92	C1
AULD RD	RCO	99	D5
AURORA CYN RD	MNO	43	B3
AUSTIN RD	IMP	109	A5
AUSTIN RD	SJCO	40	B5
AUSTIN RD	SJCO	47	B1
AUSTIN CREEK RD	SON	37	C2
AUSTIN MDWS RD	NEV	27	A4
AUSTRIAN RD	CAL	41	B4
AUTOPSTA TIJ-EN	BAJA	111	D3
AVALON AV	SBD	100	E1
AVALON BLVD	LA	191	C1
AVALON BLVD	LACO	97	E3
AVALON BLVD	LACO	S	C1
AVALON CYN RD	AVLN	105	A5
AVENA	SJCO	47	C1
AVENAL CUTOFF	KIN	67	A3
AVD BERMUDAS	RCO	100	E4
AVD DEL CAPITAN	SB	87	A4
AVD D LS ARBLES	VEN	88	D5
AVD D LS ARBLES	VEN	96	D1
AVD DL PRESIDNT	ORA	105	E1
AVENIDA DEL SOL	KER	80	C1
AVENIDA ENCINO	RCO	100	D5
AVD LA CUMBRE	RCO	100	D5
AVD LOS FELIZ	RCO	100	D5
AVENIDA OBREGON	RCO	100	E4
AVENUE A	KER	89	E1
AVENUE A	YUMA	112	D5
AVENUE B	LACO	89	D2

STREET	CO.	PAGE	GRID
AVENUE B	LACO	90	C2
AVENUE C	LACO	89	D2
AVENUE C	LACO	90	D2
AVENUE C	YUMA	112	C5
AVENUE D	LACO	90	B2
AVENUE E	LACO	89	E2
AVENUE E	LACO	90	A2
AVENUE E	RCO	99	B3
AVENUE E	YUMA	112	C5
AVENUE E-8	LACO	90	B2
AVENUE F	LACO	89	B2
AVENUE F	LACO	89	D2
AVENUE F	LACO	90	C2
AVENUE F	SBD	99	D2
AVENUE F-4	LACO	89	E2
AVENUE F-4	LACO	90	A2
AVENUE F-8	LACO	89	C2
AVENUE F-8	LACO	90	D2
AVENUE G	LACO	89	E2
AVENUE G-2	LACO	90	C2
AVENUE G-3	LACO	90	C2
AVENUE G-4	LACO	90	C2
AVENUE G-6	LACO	90	C2
AVENUE G-8	LACO	90	B2
AVENUE H	LACO	89	E2
AVENUE I	LACO	89	E2
AVENUE J	LACO	89	E3
AVENUE J	LACO	90	C2
AVENUE J-8	LACO	90	A2
AVENUE K	LACO	89	E3
AVENUE K	LACO	90	C3
AVENUE K-8	LACO	89	D3
AVENUE L	LACO	89	E3
AVENUE L	LACO	90	B3
AVENUE L	RCO	99	D2
AVENUE M	LACO	89	E3
AVENUE M	LACO	90	B3
AVENUE M-8	LACO	89	E3
AVENUE N	LACO	89	E3
AVENUE N	LACO	90	C3
AVENUE O	LACO	90	A3
AVENUE ONE	MCO	48	B4
AVENUE P	LACO	89	E3
AVENUE P	LACO	90	A3
AVENUE P	LACO	90	D3
AVENUE P-8	LACO	90	A3
AVENUE P-8	LACO	90	C3
AVENUE Q	LACO	90	C3
AVENUE Q	LACO	90	C3
AVENUE R-8	LACO	90	D3
AVENUE S	LACO	89	E3
AVENUE S	LACO	90	A3
AVENUE SAN LUIS	LA	177	B4
AVENUE STANFORD	LACO	89	B4
AVENUE T	LACO	90	B3
AVENUE T	LACO	90	C3
AVENUE TWO	MCO	48	B4
AVENUE U	LACO	90	C3
AVENUE Z	LACO	90	D4
AVENUE 2	TUL	68	D5
AVENUE 4 1/2	MAD	56	E3
AVENUE 5	MAD	56	E3
AVENUE 5 1/2	MAD	56	E3
AVENUE 5 1/2	MAD	57	A3
AVENUE 6	MAD	56	E3
AVENUE 6	MAD	57	A3
AVENUE 6 1/2	MAD	57	A3
AVENUE 7 1/2	MAD	56	D3
AVENUE 7 1/2	MAD	56	E3
AVENUE 7 1/2	MAD	57	A3
AVENUE 8	MAD	56	E3
AVENUE 8	MAD	57	A2
AVENUE 8	MAD	57	C2
AVENUE 8	TUL	68	B5
AVENUE 8 1/2	MAD	57	A2
AVENUE 9	MAD	56	E2
AVENUE 9	MAD	57	C2
AVENUE 9 1/2	MAD	56	E2
AVENUE 10	MAD	56	E2
AVENUE 10	MAD	57	B2
AVENUE 10 1/2	MAD	56	E2
AVENUE 10 1/2	MAD	57	A2
AVENUE 11	MAD	56	E2
AVENUE 11	MAD	57	A2
AVENUE 11 1/2	MAD	56	E2
AVENUE 11 1/2	MAD	57	A2
AVENUE 12	MAD	56	E2
AVENUE 12	MAD	57	B2
AVENUE 12	TUL	68	B5
AVENUE 12	TUL	68	C5
AVENUE 12 1/2	MAD	57	B2
AVENUE 13	MAD	56	E2
AVENUE 13 1/2	MAD	56	E2
AVENUE 13 1/2	MAD	57	A2
AVENUE 14	MAD	56	D2
AVENUE 14	MAD	57	C2
AVENUE 14 1/2	MAD	56	E2
AVENUE 14 1/2	MAD	57	A2
AVENUE 14 1/2	MAD	57	C2
AVENUE 15	MAD	56	E2
AVENUE 15 1/2	MAD	56	E2
AVENUE 15 1/2	MAD	57	B2
AVENUE 16	MAD	56	E2
AVENUE 16	TUL	68	B4
AVENUE 16	TUL	68	C4
AVENUE 16 1/2	MAD	56	E2
AVENUE 17	MAD	56	D2
AVENUE 17 1/2	MAD	56	E2
AVENUE 18	MAD	56	D2
AVENUE 18 1/2	MAD	56	D2
AVENUE 19	MAD	56	D1
AVENUE 19 1/2	MAD	56	D1
AVENUE 20	LA	186	D2
AVENUE 20	MAD	56	D1

STREET	CO.	PAGE	GRID
AVENUE 20 1/2	MAD	56	D1
AVENUE 21	MAD	56	D1
AVENUE 21	MAD	57	A1
AVENUE 21 1/2	MAD	56	D1
AVENUE 22	MAD	56	D1
AVENUE 22 1/2	MAD	56	D1
AVENUE 23 1/2	MAD	56	D1
AVENUE 24	MAD	56	D1
AVENUE 24	TUL	68	B4
AVENUE 24 1/2	MAD	56	E1
AVENUE 25	MAD	56	D1
AVENUE 25 1/2	MAD	56	D1
AVENUE 26	MAD	56	D1
AVENUE 26 1/2	MAD	56	E1
AVENUE 27	MAD	48	D5
AVENUE 27 1/2	MAD	48	E5
AVENUE 28	MAD	48	E5
AVENUE 28	TUL	68	C4
AVENUE 32	TUL	68	B4
AVENUE 40	TUL	68	C4
AVENUE 42	TUL	67	E4
AVENUE 42	TUL	68	C4
AVENUE 42	TUL	68	A4
AVENUE 44	TUL	68	B4
AVENUE 46	TUL	67	E4
AVENUE 46	TUL	68	C4
AVENUE 50	TUL	67	E4
AVENUE 52	TUL	68	B4
AVENUE 52	TUL	68	C4
AVENUE 54	TUL	67	E4
AVENUE 56	TUL	68	B4
AVENUE 58	TUL	68	A4
AVENUE 62	TUL	68	A4
AVENUE 64	TUL	68	D4
AVENUE 66	TUL	68	D4
AVENUE 68	TUL	68	A4
AVENUE 68	TUL	68	D4
AVENUE 70	TUL	68	D4
AVENUE 74	TUL	68	D4
AVENUE 76	TUL	68	D4
AVENUE 78	TUL	68	D4
AVENUE 80	TUL	68	B4
AVENUE 80	TUL	68	C4
AVENUE 84	TUL	68	A4
AVENUE 86	TUL	68	D4
AVENUE 88	TUL	67	E4
AVENUE 88	TUL	68	A4
AVENUE 88	TUL	68	D4
AVENUE 90	TUL	68	D4
AVENUE 92	TUL	68	D4
AVENUE 94	TUL	68	D4
AVENUE 95	TUL	68	C4
AVENUE 96	TUL	68	D4
AVENUE 100	TUL	68	D3
AVENUE 102	TUL	68	D3
AVENUE 104	TUL	67	E3
AVENUE 104	TUL	68	C3
AVENUE 108	TUL	68	A3
AVENUE 108	TUL	68	D3
AVENUE 112	TUL	67	E3
AVENUE 112	TUL	68	D3
AVENUE 116	TUL	68	B3
AVENUE 116	TUL	68	D3
AVENUE 120	TUL	67	E3
AVENUE 120	TUL	68	D3
AVENUE 124	TUL	68	C3
AVENUE 128	TUL	67	E3
AVENUE 128	TUL	68	C3
AVENUE 132	TUL	68	C3
AVENUE 136	TUL	67	E3
AVENUE 136	TUL	68	C3
AVENUE 138	TUL	68	E3
AVENUE 144	TUL	68	A3
AVENUE 152	TUL	68	B3
AVENUE 152	TUL	68	C3
AVENUE 156	TUL	68	D3
AVENUE 160	TUL	68	A3
AVENUE 160	TUL	68	D3
AVENUE 164	TUL	68	B3
AVENUE 168	TUL	68	A3
AVENUE 168	TUL	68	C3
AVENUE 169	TUL	68	D3
AVENUE 172	TUL	68	C3
AVENUE 176	TUL	68	A3
AVENUE 176	TUL	68	C3
AVENUE 178	TUL	68	D3
AVENUE 180	TUL	68	B3
AVENUE 182	TUL	68	D3
AVENUE 184	TUL	68	C2
AVENUE 188	TUL	68	D2
AVENUE 190	TUL	68	A2
AVENUE 192	TUL	68	A2
AVENUE 192	TUL	68	B2
AVENUE 196	TUL	68	B2
AVENUE 196	TUL	68	D2
AVENUE 198	TUL	68	A2
AVENUE 199	TUL	67	E2
AVENUE 200	TUL	68	A2
AVENUE 200	TUL	68	C2
AVENUE 204	TUL	67	E2
AVENUE 204	TUL	68	A2
AVENUE 204	TUL	68	C2
AVENUE 204	TUL	68	C4
AVENUE 206	TUL	68	D2
AVENUE 208	TUL	67	E2
AVENUE 208	TUL	68	A2
AVENUE 208	TUL	68	C2
AVENUE 212	TUL	68	B2
AVENUE 212	TUL	68	D2
AVENUE 216	TUL	68	A2
AVENUE 216	TUL	68	D2
AVENUE 222	TUL	68	D2
AVENUE 224	TUL	68	B2
AVENUE 226	TUL	68	D2

STREET	CO.	PAGE	GRID
AVENUE 228	TUL	68	B2
AVENUE 232	TUL	68	D2
AVENUE 236	TUL	68	A2
AVENUE 236	TUL	68	D2
AVENUE 240	TUL	68	A2
AVENUE 244	TUL	68	D1
AVENUE 248	TUL	68	A2
AVENUE 252	TUL	68	A2
AVENUE 256	TUL	67	E2
AVENUE 260	TUL	68	A2
AVENUE 264	TUL	68	B2
AVENUE 268	TUL	68	A2
AVENUE 271	TUL	68	B1
AVENUE 272	TUL	68	A1
AVENUE 272	TUL	68	D1
AVENUE 276	TUL	68	C1
AVENUE 280	TUL	68	A1
AVENUE 300	TUL	68	C1
AVENUE 304	TUL	68	A1
AVENUE 306	TUL	68	D1
AVENUE 308	TUL	68	A1
AVENUE 312	TUL	68	D1
AVENUE 318	TUL	68	C1
AVENUE 320	TUL	68	A1
AVENUE 320	TUL	68	D1
AVENUE 324	TUL	68	C1
AVENUE 328	TUL	68	A1
AVENUE 328	TUL	68	C1
AVENUE 332	TUL	68	C1
AVENUE 332	TUL	58	C5
AVENUE 334	TUL	58	D5
AVENUE 334	TUL	68	D1
AVENUE 336	TUL	68	B1
AVENUE 336	TUL	58	C5
AVENUE 337	TUL	68	C1
AVENUE 340	TUL	68	B1
AVENUE 340	TUL	58	C5
AVENUE 344	TUL	68	B1
AVENUE 344	TUL	58	C5
AVENUE 346	TUL	68	D1
AVENUE 348	TUL	68	C1
AVENUE 350	TUL	58	D5
AVENUE 352	TUL	57	E5
AVENUE 352	TUL	58	C5
AVENUE 356	TUL	58	B5
AVENUE 356	TUL	58	C5
AVENUE 360	TUL	57	E5
AVENUE 360	TUL	58	C5
AVENUE 364	TUL	58	C5
AVENUE 368	TUL	58	B5
AVENUE 368	TUL	58	C5
AVENUE 376	TUL	57	E5
AVENUE 376	TUL	58	C5
AVENUE 380	TUL	58	C5
AVENUE 384	TUL	58	A5
AVENUE 386	TUL	58	C5
AVENUE 388	TUL	58	C5
AVENUE 390	TUL	57	E5
AVENUE 390	TUL	58	C5
AVENUE 392	TUL	58	A5
AVENUE 394	TUL	58	C5
AVENUE 396	TUL	57	E5
AVENUE 396	TUL	58	A5
AVENUE 398	TUL	58	C5
AVENUE 400	TUL	58	B5
AVENUE 404	TUL	58	B5
AVENUE 404	TUL	58	C5
AVENUE 408	TUL	57	E5
AVENUE 408	TUL	58	B5
AVENUE 410	TUL	57	E5
AVENUE 416	TUL	58	C5
AVENUE 424	TUL	58	A4
AVENUE 428	TUL	58	B4
AVENUE 432	TUL	58	B4
AVENUE 436	TUL	58	B4
AVENUE 438	TUL	58	B4
AVENUE 440	TUL	58	B4
AVENUE 444	TUL	58	B4
AVENUE 448	TUL	58	B4
AVENUE 450	TUL	58	B4
AVENUE 452	TUL	58	B4
AVENUE 456	TUL	58	B4
AVENUE 460	TUL	58	B4
AVENUE 464	TUL	58	B4
AVENUE 468	TUL	58	B4
AVENUE 472	TUL	58	B4
AVERY RD	FRCO	55	E3
AVERY RD	MCO	55	D3
AVERY SHEEP RCH	CAL	41	C3
AVIATION BLVD	ELS	189	E3
AVIATION BLVD	HAW	189	E3
AVIATION BLVD	ING	189	E3
AVIATION BLVD	LA	188	E5
AVIATION BLVD	LA	189	E3
AVIATION BLVD	LACO	97	D3
AVIATION BLVD	LACO	S	B1
AVIATION BLVD	RB	189	E3
AVOCADO BLVD	SDCO	V	E3
AVOCADO BLVD	SDCO	111	E1
AVOCADO RD	BUT	25	E5
AYERS AV	SJCO	47	C1
AYRES HOLMES RD	PLA	34	B3
AZALEA TR	RCO	100	B3
AZEVEDO	MCO	47	D5
AZEVEDO RD	SOL	39	C4
AZEVEDO RD	STA	47	C4
AZTEC AV	RCO	102	C4
AZUSA AV	LACO	98	B2
AZUSA AV	LACO	R	E4
AZUSA CANYON RD	LACO	R	E3
B			
B ST	BUT	25	C5

STREET	CO.	PAGE	GRID
B ST	DVS	136	C3
B ST	FRE	165	C4
B ST	H	146	E2
B ST	IMP	109	A4
B ST	KER	68	B5
B ST	LA	191	B1
B ST	LACO	97	E4
B ST	LACO	98	C2
B ST	LACO	S	C2
B ST	SCTO	137	C2
B ST	SD	215	D3
B ST	SJCO	40	B5
B ST	YUBA	125	D3
B ST	YUB	33	D2
B ST N	SCTO	137	B2
BABCOCK RD	LAS	14	B4
BABCOCK CNDR RD	LAS	14	B4
BABEL SLOUGH RD	YOL	39	D2
BACHELOR VLY RD	LAK	31	C2
BACK BONE RD	NEV	26	D5
BACKBONE RD	SHA	13	A5
BACKBONE RD	SHA	18	E1
BACKES LN	KER	79	C4
BACKUS RD	KER	79	E5
BACON RD	STA	47	B2
BACON ST	SDCO	V	A3
BACON ST	SDCO	111	C1
BACON ISLAND	SJCO	39	E5
BADDAGE RD	RCO	107	B1
BADENOUGH CY RD	SIE	27	D3
BADGER RD	SON	37	E2
BADGER RD	SON	38	A2
BADGER FLAT	MCO	55	D1
BAGDAD HWY	SBD	93	C4
BAGDAD HWY	SBD	101	C1
BAGDAD WY	SBD	93	D4
BAGDAD CHASE RD	SBD	93	B2
BAGGTT MARYSVLL	BUT	25	D5
BAILEY AV	KER	70	A5
BAILEY AV	MCO	48	B4
BAILEY AV	SB	86	B3
BAILEY AV	SCL	P	D4
BAILEY RD	COL	32	E3
BAILEY RD	CC	M	B3
BAILEY RD	CC	39	A5
BAILEY RD	DN	1	E3
BAILEY RD	IMP	110	D5
BAILEY RD	RCO	107	B1
BAILEY RD	SBD	84	A2
BAILEY RD	SCL	46	C5
BAILEY RD	SUT	33	C3
BAILEY FLATS RD	MAD	49	B5
BAILEY HILL RD	SIS	4	A2
BAILY RD	KER	79	B4
BAILY RIDGE RD	CAL	41	C2
BAIN ST	RCO	99	A2
BAIR RD	HUM	10	B4
BAIRD RD	SON	38	A2
BAKER AV	ONT	204	E3
BAKER AV	ORA	T	C3
BAKER AV	ROC	204	E3
BAKER RD	COL	32	C2
BAKER RD	MCO	55	E1
BAKER RD	PLCV	138	B2
BAKER RD	SJCO	40	B4
BAKER RD	STA	47	C3
BAKER RD	TEH	18	D5
BAKER RD	SUT	33	C4
BAKER RD	YUB	26	B5
BAKER ST	CM	197	B4
BAKER ST	CM	198	A4
BAKER CREEK RD	INY	51	D5
BAKER RCH SODA	PLA	34	E2
BAKER RCH SODA	PLA	35	B2
BAKER RILEY WY	CAL	41	B3
BKRSFLD-GLNVLLE	KER	68	E5
BKRSFLD-GLNVLLE	KER	69	A5
BKRSFLD-GLNVLLE	KER	78	D2
BAKRSFLD-MCKITT	KER	78	A3
BALBOA AV	SD	211	E5
BALBOA AV	SD	212	C1
BALBOA AV	SDCO	V	A2
BALBOA AV	SDCO	106	C5
BALBOA BLVD	LACO	97	C1
BALBOA BLVD	NB	199	B5
BALBOA BLVD	ORA	T	C4
BALCH PARK RD	TUL	69	A2
BALCOM CYN RD	VEN	88	D5
BALDERSTON	ED	34	E3
BALD HILL RD	PLA	34	C3
BALD HILLS RD	DN	1	E4
BALD HILLS RD	DN	2	A4
BALD HILLS RD	HUM	10	A2
BALD MTN RD	CAL	41	B2
BALD MTN RD	HUM	10	B5
BALD MTN RD	MEN	23	A2
BALD MTN RD	MNO	50	D1
BALD MTN RD	SHA	13	E4
BALD MTN RD	YUB	33	E1
BALD MTN RD N	CAL	41	C2
BALD MTN LKOUT	SIS	3	D4
BALD MT SPGS RD	MNO	50	E1
BALD ROCK RD	BUT	25	E3
BALDWIN AV	LACO	R	C3
BALDWIN RD	STA	47	D2
BALDWIN RD	STA	47	B3
BALDWIN RD	VEN	88	A4
BALDWIN ST	CAL	40	D4
BALDWIN PARK BL	LACO	R	D4
BALDY RD	SBD	90	E5
BALDY MCCULY RD	SHA	13	E4
BALDY MESA RD	SBD	91	A4
BALE LN	NAPA	29	B2
BALFOUR RD	CC	M	C3

INDEXES

246
BALFOUR RD — STREET INDEX — BLAND RD

STREET	CO.	PAGE	GRID
BALFOUR RD	CC	39	C5
BALIS BELL RD	TEH	18	B5
BALL RD	ANA	193	A3
BALL RD	ANA	194	A3
BALL RD	ORA	98	B3
BALL RD	ORA	T	B2
BALL RD	TEH	17	E4
BALL MT LTL SHA	SIS	4	B4
BALL MT LTL SHA	SIS	5	A4
BALL MTN LKOUT	SIS	4	D3
BALL ROCK RD	TEH	23	E1
BALLANTREE LN	NEV	34	B2
BALLARAT RD	INY	71	C3
BALLARD RD	TEH	24	E2
BALLICO AV	MCO	48	A4
BALLINGER RD	RCO	99	E5
BALLINGR CYN RD	VEN	87	E1
BALLIS RD	TEH	18	C5
BALLS FERRY RD	SHA	18	D3
BALL FERY PK RD	SHA	18	D3
BALSAM RD	SBD	91	B4
BALSAMO RD	SBD	81	A5
BALTIMORE MN RD	PLA	34	E3
BANCROFT AV	O	159	D1
BANCROFT DR	SDCO	V	D3
BANCROFT DR	SDCO	111	E1
BANCROFT RD	CC	M	A3
BANCROFT RD	STA	47	C3
BANCROFT WY	ALA	L	D4
BANCROFT WY	B	156	A3
BANDERILLA DR	MPA	48	D2
BANDINI BLVD	LACO	R	A4
B & R LN	SOL	39	C3
BANDUCCI RD	KER	79	B4
BANGOR AV	KIN	57	E5
BANGOR PARK RD	BUT	25	D5
BANGOR PARK CTO	BUT	25	E5
BANGS AV	STA	47	C2
BANNER RD	CAL	41	B3
BANNER QUAKR HL	NEV	34	D1
BANNER RDG LAVA	NEV	34	C1
BANNING IDYLLWD	RCO	100	A3
BANNISTER AV	SCL	P	E5
BANNISTER RD	IMP	108	E4
BANTA RD	SJCO	47	E2
BAR RD	MAD	49	E5
BAR RD	MAD	50	A5
BARBARA WRTH RD	IMP	112	B4
BARBER	SJCO	39	E3
BARBER LN	RCO	107	B1
BARBER RD	ALP	36	B4
BARBER RD	TEH	25	A2
BARBER MTN RD	SDCO	112	B1
BARD RD	IMP	110	D5
BARDSDALE AV	VEN	88	D4
BARGLEY RD	COL	32	C2
BARHAM AV	TEH	24	D2
BARHAM BLVD	LA	181	C1
BARHAM BLVD	LACO	Q	D3
BAR K RD	TRI	17	C2
BARKER RD	KER	67	B5
BARKER CREEK RD	TRI	17	B2
BARKER MINE RD	MNO	51	C2
BARKHOUSE CK RD	SIS	3	D3
BARKSHANTY RD	SIS	10	D1
BARLOW LN	INY	51	D4
BAR MTN LOOKOUT	SIS	3	C4
BARNES LN	MEN	23	B2
BARNES RD	KER	90	B1
BARNES RD	SBD	92	D4
BARNES RD	SLO	66	A5
BARNES RD	SLO	76	A1
BARNETT AV	SDCO	V	B3
BARNETT RD	STA	48	B2
BARNEY GULCH RD	TRI	11	B5
BARNHART RD	STA	47	C3
BARNY OLDFLD RD	IMP	110	C5
BARR RD	HUM	10	B5
BARRANCA AV	LACO	U	C2
BARRANCA RD	ORA	98	C4
BARRANCA RD	ORA	T	D3
BARRANCA RD	TUS	198	E2
BARREL SPGS RD	LACO	90	A3
BARREL SPGS RD	MOD	7	E3
BARRETT	CC	38	C5
BARRETT AV	FRCO	57	B5
BARRETT AV	FRCO	57	C5
BARRETT LAKE RD	SDCO	112	B2
BARRINGTON AV	LACO	180	B2
BARRINGTON LN	SIE	27	C4
BARRY RD	SUT	33	D2
BARRYS RD	HUM	16	A1
BARSTOW AV	FRCO	57	A3
BARSTOW AV	FRCO	57	C3
BARSTOW AV	KIN	57	E5
BARSTOW FRWY	SBD	91	A5
BARSTOW FRWY	SBD	99	B1
BARSTOW RD	BARS	208	B3
BARSTOW RD	KER	80	D5
BARSTOW RD	SBD	91	E2
BARSTOW RD	SBD	92	A4
BARTEL ST	SHA	13	C5
BARTELL RD	INY	51	E5
BARTH RD	IMP	108	E3
BARTLE GAP RD	SIS	13	B3
BARTLETT RD	SOL	39	C3
BARTLETTE RD	INY	60	B5
BARTLETT SPG RD	LAK	31	E2
BARTLETT SPG RD	LAK	31	E2
BARTOLOMEI	SJCO	40	C5
BARTOLOMEI	SJCO	47	C1
BARTON	PLA	34	B5
BARTON RD	SBD	99	C2
BARTON ST	RCO	99	B3
BARTON HILL RD	YUB	26	B4
BAR W RD	HUM	16	B3
BASCOM AV	SCL	46	B5
BASCOM AV	SJ	151	C4
BASCOM AV	SCL	P	B3
BASE LINE AV	SB	86	E3
BASELINE RD	LACO	98	E1
BASE LINE RD	LACO	U	A2
BASE LINE RD	PLA	33	E5
BASELINE RD	SBD	U	D2
BASELINE RD	SBD	98	E1
BASELINE RD	SBD	101	C1
BASELINE ST	SBDO	207	B1
BASELINE ST	SBD	102	C1
BASIC SCHOOL RD	KER	78	B5
BASILONE RD	SDCO	105	E1
BASIN RD	SBD	82	E5
BASIN ST	KER	79	C2
BASLER RD	TEH	18	B4
BASS	FRCO	56	C3
BASSET RD	LAS	14	C3
BASSETT AV	KER	68	C5
BASS HILL RD	LAS	21	A4
BASS LAKE RD	ED	34	C5
BASS VALLEY RD	MAD	49	D4
BASTANCHURY RD	ORA	T	E1
BATAVIA RD	SOL	39	B2
BATCHELDER RD	SB	86	C2
BATEMAN RD	SHA	19	B2
BATES	SUT	33	C4
BATTL CK BTM RD	SHA	19	A3
BAUGHMAN RD	IMP	108	E4
BAUMBACH AV	KER	79	B4
BAUTISTA RD	RCO	100	A4
BAXTER AV	NAP	133	B2
BAXTER RD	MCO	48	E5
BAXTER RD	RCO	99	C5
BAXTERS RD	MNO	43	E5
BAXTERS RD	MNO	50	E1
BAY DR	SC	169	A3
BAY HWY	SON	37	C3
BAY RD	SMCO	N	D2
BAY RD	SMCO	45	D3
BAY ST	SF	142	B1
BAY ST	SF	143	A2
BAY ST	SC	169	B4
BAYLEY RES RD	MOD	8	A2
BAYLIS BLUE GUM	GLE	24	D4
BAYOU RD	SAC	33	D5
BAYSHORE BLVD	SMCO	L	C5
BAYSHORE BLVD	SMCO	45	C2
BAYSHORE FRWY	BLMT	145	B3
BAYSHORE FRWY	BURL	144	C3
BAYSHORE FRWY	MLBR	144	C3
BAYSHORE FRWY	MVW	148	A3
BAYSHORE FRWY	SJ	151	D1
BAYSHORE FRWY	SJ	152	B1
BAYSHORE FRWY	SM	145	B3
BAYSHORE FRWY	SMCO	45	D3
BAYSHORE FRWY	SMCO	144	C3
BAYSHORE FRWY	SMCO	145	B3
BAYSHORE FRWY	SSF	144	C1
BAYSHORE FRWY	SVL	148	D3
BAYSIDE DR	NB	199	D5
BAYSIDE DR	NB	200	A5
BAY VIEW AV	NAPA	38	C3
BAY VIEW RD	MCO	55	C1
BEACH BLVD	ORA	98	B3
BEACH BLVD	ORA	T	B1
BEACH RD	HUM	22	A1
BEACH RD	IMP	109	A2
BEACH RD	MPA	49	B4
BEACH RD	SCR	54	B3
BEACH ST	SF	143	A2
BEACH PARK BL	FCTY	145	D3
BEACON RD	SLO	76	B1
BEACON ST	AVLN	105	B5
BEAL RD	IMP	109	B2
BEALE RD N	YUB	33	D2
BEALE RD S	YUB	33	E3
BEALE ST	SF	143	D4
BEAL RANCH RD	CAL	40	E3
BEAL RANCH RD	CAL	41	A3
BEALEVILLE RD	KER	79	B3
BEAMER ST	YOL	33	B5
BEAN CLIPPER RD	YUB	26	B4
BEAN CREEK RD	BUT	25	E4
BEAN CREEK RD	SCR	P	A5
BEAN CREEK RD	SCR	54	A1
BEAN HOLLOW RD	SMCO	N	C4
BEAN HOLLOW RD	SMCO	45	C5
BEAR ST	CM	197	E4
BEAR ST	ORA	T	D3
BEAR BASIN RD	DN	2	B3
BEAR BUTTE RD	HUM	16	B5
BEAR CANYON RD	FRCO	66	B2
BEAR CREEK DR N	MCO	48	C4
BEAR CREEK DR S	MCO	48	C4
BEAR CREEK LOOP	TRI	12	A3
BEAR CREEK RD	CC	L	D3
BEAR CREEK RD	CC	38	D5
BEAR CREEK RD	LAK	31	D1
BEAR CREEK RD	SCL	P	A4
BEAR CREEK RD	SCR	N	E5
BEAR CREEK RD	SCR	P	A5
BEAR CREEK RD	SCR	45	E5
BEARD RD	NAP	133	C2
BEAR GULCH RD	SMCO	N	C3
BEAR MTN BLVD	KER	78	D4
BEAR MTN RD	FRCO	58	B3
BEAR MTN RD	SHA	18	C1
BEAR MTN RD	SIS	13	C2
BEAR MTN LKOUT	SHA	18	C1
BEAR MT WINE RD	KER	78	E3
BEAR MT WINE RD	KER	79	A3
BEAR RANCH HILL	BUT	25	E2
BEAR RIVER	AMA	41	D1
BEAR RIVER S	AMA	41	D1
BEAR RIVER DR	SUT	33	D3
BEAR RIV RDG RD	HUM	15	D3
BEAR SPRINGS RD	LAS	14	A3
BEAR TRAP DR	MPA	49	A3
BEAR TRAP RD	NEV	26	C5
BEAR VALLEY	MPA	48	E3
BEAR VLY PKWY	SDCO	106	D4
BEAR VALLEY RD	COL	32	B2
BEAR VALLEY RD	KER	79	B4
BEAR VALLEY RD	SBD	90	E4
BEAR VALLEY RD	SIE	27	D4
BEAR VLY CUTOFF	SBD	91	B4
BEASON ST	KER	78	A1
BEASORE RD	MAD	49	E4
BEATIE RD	SHA	18	D3
BEAUCHAMP RD	COL	32	D2
BEAUMONT AV	RCO	99	E3
BEAUMONT ST	SBD	91	E3
BEAVER CREEK RD	SIS	3	D3
BECHELLI LN	RED	122	E2
BECHELLI LN	SHA	18	C2
BECK AV	SOL	L	E1
BECK AV	SOL	M	A1
BECKER	SUT	33	C4
BECKER RD	SOL	39	C1
BECKET CT	KER	79	C5
BECKWITH RD	SIE	27	D3
BECKWITH RD	STA	47	B2
BECKWRTH CALPNE	PLU	27	C3
BECKWRTH GENESE	PLU	26	E1
BECKWRTH GENESE	PLU	27	B1
BECKWRTH LOYLTN	PLU	27	C3
BCKWRTH TYLRSVL	PLU	26	D1
BCKWRTH TYLRSVL	PLU	27	B2
BEDFORD DR	SBD	92	B1
BEE CANYON RD	RCO	100	A4
BEECH AV	KER	78	B2
BEECH AV	SBD	99	A2
BEECH ST	BKD	166	B2
BEECH ST	SDCO	106	C2
BEECHER RD	SJCO	40	B5
BEE GULCH RD	ALP	42	A1
BEEGUM RD	SHA	17	D4
BEEGUM GORGE RD	SHA	17	D4
BEEKLEY RD	RCO	102	C4
BEEKLEY RD	SBD	90	E4
BEEROCK RD	SLO	65	D5
BEHYMER	FRCO	56	C2
BEHYMER AV	FRCO	57	D2
BELCHER AV	MCO	48	B4
BELFAST RD	LAS	21	B3
BELL	MCO	48	A4
BELL LN	PLU	26	D1
BELL RD	AMA	40	E1
BELL RD	BUT	25	A3
BELL RD	KER	77	E2
BELL RD	KER	78	A2
BELL RD	PLA	34	B3
BELL RD	SB	87	C1
BELL RD	STA	47	C4
BELL ST	SB	86	D2
BELLA ROSA DR	HUM	16	C4
BELLA VISTA DR	KER	79	D1
BELLE TER	KER	166	D5
BELLE GRAVE AV	RCO	99	A2
BELLEVUE AV	SUT	33	D3
BELLEVUE RD	MCO	48	B4
BELLFLOWER BLVD	LACO	98	A3
BELLFLOWER BLVD	LACO	S	E2
BELLFLOWER BLVD	LACO	T	A2
BELLFLOWER ST	SBD	91	B3
BELL HILL RD	LAK	31	D3
BELL MTN RD	SBD	91	C3
BELL SPRINGS RD	HUM	16	C5
BELL SPRINGS RD	MEN	22	D1
BELLVIEW RD	MAD	57	C1
BELMONT AV	FRE	165	C3
BELMONT AV	FRCO	56	C3
BELMONT AV	FRCO	57	C3
BELOMY ST	SCLR	151	B3
BELSBY AV	RCO	102	C4
BELTINE RD	SHA	18	C2
BELVIN RD	YUBA	125	A1
BENA RD	KER	79	A3
BENBOW DR	HUM	22	C1
BEND	TEH	18	D4
BENDER	SJCO	40	A3
BENDER AV	KER	78	B2
BENDER RD	SHA	18	A3
BENDLER RD	STA	47	E2
BENEDICT CYN DR	LACO	Q	C3
BENHAM LN	CUR	1	D2
BEN HUR RD	MPA	49	B4
BENICIA AV	KIN	57	E5
BENICIA RD	SOL	38	D4
BENICIA RD	VAL	134	D5
BENIT JUAREZ BL	BAJA	112	B4
BENNER AV	KER	68	B5
BENNET RD	LACO	89	A5
BENNET RD	VEN	88	E5
BENNETS WELL RD	INY	72	A2
BENNETT RD	BUT	25	A2
BENNETT RD	MCO	55	E2
BENNETT RD	NEV	34	C1
BENNETT RD	RCO	100	D3
BENNETT VLY RD	SON	38	A2
BENNETT VLY RD	STR	131	D4
BENSON AV	MTCL	203	D3
BENSON AV	ONT	203	D5
BENSON AV	SBD	U	D3
BENSON AV	SBD	98	D2
BENSON AV	SBD	203	D3
BENSON AV	UPL	203	D1
BENSON DR	SHA	18	B2
BENSON RD	TEH	18	C4
BENT RD	STA	47	D2
BENTLEY RD	STA	47	D2
BENTON DR	SHA	18	C2
BENTON RD	RCO	99	D5
BENTON RD E	RCO	99	E5
BENTON ST	SCLR	150	C3
BENTON CROSSING	MNO	51	B2
BENTN GBG PT RD	MNO	51	C1
BERDOO CYN RD	RCO	101	B3
BERKELEY AV	STA	47	E3
BERKSHIRE RD	KER	79	A3
BERMUDA DR	SM	145	B2
BERNAL AV	ALA	M	B5
BERNAL AV	ALA	P	B1
BERNAL DR E	SAL	171	C3
BERNARD ST	KER	78	D3
BERNARD WY	SHA	18	C1
BERRELLESA ST	M	154	B2
BERRY AV	H	146	E4
BERRY RD	SUT	33	D3
BERRY CREEK RD	BUT	25	E3
BERRYESSA RD	SJ	152	C1
BERRYESSA RD	SCL	P	B3
BERRYESSA RD	SCL	46	B4
BERRYSSA KNX RD	NAPA	32	C4
BERT RD	LAS	27	E1
BERTAS RD	HUM	15	E1
BERT CRANE RD	MCO	48	B5
BERTRAM CIR	KER	79	C4
BERYL ST	LACO	97	D3
BERYL ST	LACO	S	B1
BERYL ST	SD	212	A1
BERYLWOOD RD	VEN	88	C5
BESSEMR MINE RD	SBD	92	B4
BEST RD	IMP	109	B4
BEST RD	MPA	49	C3
BEST RD	RCO	99	E5
BEST RD	SUT	33	C3
BETHANY RD	SJCO	46	D1
BETHEL AV	FRCO	57	E4
BETHEL RD	SLO	76	A2
BETHEL ISLND RD	CC	M	D3
BETHEL ISLND RD	CC	39	C5
BETTERAVIA RD	STB	173	C5
BETTERAVIA RD	SB	86	B1
BETTERAVIA RD	SMA	173	C5
BETTS RD	TRI	23	A1
BETTY WY	SIS	4	B4
BETZ RD	SUT	33	D3
BEVERLY	LACO	98	A2
BEVERLY BLVD	BH	183	C1
BEVERLY BLVD	LA	183	C1
BEVERLY BLVD	LA	184	B1
BEVERLY BLVD	LA	185	C1
BEVERLY BLVD	LACO	97	D2
BEVERLY BLVD	LACO	183	C1
BEVERLY BLVD	LACO	Q	D4
BEVERLY DR	BH	183	B1
BEVERLY DR	LAS	20	E3
BEVERLY DR	LA	183	B1
BEVERLY DR	LACO	Q	C3
BEVERLY GLEN BL	LA	180	E2
BEVERLY GLEN BL	LA	183	A3
BEVERLY GLEN BL	LACO	97	C1
BEVERLY GLEN BL	LACO	Q	C3
BEVERWIL DR	BH	183	C3
BEVERWIL DR	LA	183	C3
BEYER BLVD	SDCO	V	D5
BEYER BLVD	SDCO	111	D2
BEYER LN	SJCO	40	B5
BEYER WY	SDCO	V	C5
BEYER WY	SDCO	111	D2
BEYERS LN	NEV	34	C5
BIANCHI RD	S	160	B1
BIDDLE	SLO	76	B4
BIDWELL RD	SHA	13	D5
BIDWELL CK RD	MOD	7	D3
BIEBER LKOUT RD	LAS	14	C3
BIG BAR DUMP RD	TRI	17	A1
BIG BAR MTN RD	BUT	25	E2
BIG BEN	PLA	34	B3
BIG BEND RD	BUT	25	D3
BIG BEND RD	SHA	13	A4
BIG CANYON	LAK	32	A4
BIG CREEK RD	PLU	26	B2
BIG CREEK RD	TRI	17	B2
BIG CK SHAFT RD	TUO	48	E1
BIG DIPPER	PLA	34	D2
BIGELOW RD	SIS	13	A2
BIGELOW RD	SUT	33	B1
BIG FLAT RD	DN	2	B4
BIG FRCH CK RD	TRI	11	A5
BIGGAR LN	MEN	23	A2
BIGGS EAST HWY	BUT	25	C5
BIG HILL RD	TUO	41	D4
BIG HILL LKOUT	HUM	10	C3
BIG HORN DR	RCO	100	D5
BIG INCH PIPELN	KER	79	E5
BIG INCH PIPELN	KER	80	A5
BIG LAKES RD	MOD	14	D2
BIG MEADOWS RD	SIS	3	C5
BIG OAK DR	MEN	31	B3
BIG PN REPTR RD	INY	51	E5
BIG RANCH RD	NAPA	29	C5
BIG RANCH RD	NAPA	38	C2
BIG RANCH RD	NAPA	133	C2
BIG RESRVOIR RD	PLA	34	E2
BIG ROCK CK RD	LACO	90	C4
BIG SAGE RD	MOD	6	E5
BIG SAGE RD	MOD	7	A5
BIG SANDY RD	MON	66	B4
BIG SPRING DR	NEV	34	B2
BIG SPRING RD	SHA	19	A2
BIG SPRINGS RD	MNO	50	D1
BIG SPRINGS RD	SIS	4	C5
BIG SPRINGS RD	SIS	12	C1
BIG SPRINGS RD	SIS	13	A2
BIG SPRINGS CTO	PLU	20	B4
BIG STUMP RD	SIS	5	A2
BIG TRAILS DR	MEN	22	E4
BIG TRAILS DR	MEN	23	A4
BIG TREES RD	INY	51	C4
BIG TUJUNGA BL	LACO	Q	E1
BIG TUJUNGA CYN	LACO	89	E5
BIG VALLEY RD	LAK	31	D3
BILBY RD	SAC	39	E2
BILLE RD	BUT	25	C3
BILLIE ST	KER	78	D4
BILLINGS AV	KER	78	B1
BILLINGS LN	RCO	99	B4
BILLY WRIGHT RD	MCO	55	C2
BINET RD	BUT	26	B4
BINGHAMTON RD	SOL	39	B2
BIOLA AV	FRCO	57	B3
BIR RD	INY	51	C4
BIRCH AV	MON	65	A1
BIRCH ST	ORA	98	C3
BIRCH ST	ORA	T	D1
BIRCH ST	ORA	U	A4
BIRCH CREEK RD	INY	59	E1
BIRCHIM LN	INY	51	C3
BIRCHIN FLAT RD	MNO	42	E2
BIRCHIN FLAT RD	MNO	43	A2
BIRCHVILLE RD	NEV	26	B5
BIRD AV	SJ	152	B5
BIRD RD	SJCO	47	A2
BIRDS LANDNG RD	SOL	39	B4
BIRD SPG CYN RD	KER	80	A1
BIRKHEAD	FRCO	57	C2
BIRMINGHAM DR	SDCO	106	B4
BISCH CT	KER	79	E2
BISHOP AV	FRCO	57	B4
BISHOP AV	FRCO	67	B1
BISHOP AV	SUT	33	C1
BISHOP ST	SNLO	172	D4
BISHOP CK RD E	INY	51	C4
BISHOP CK RD W	INY	51	C4
BISIGNANI RD	MCO	55	E1
BISSET STN RD	MAD	49	D4
BITNEY SPGS RD	NEV	34	B1
BITTERWATER RD	MON	65	C2
BITTRWTR VLY RD	KER	77	A1
BIXBY RD	VEN	88	D5
BIXLER RD	CC	39	D5
BLACK RD	SB	86	B1
BLACK BART RD	BUT	25	E4
BLACK BEAR RD	SIS	11	B2
BLACK BUTTE RD	GLE	24	B3
BLACK BUTTE RD	SHA	19	A3
BLACK BUTTE RD	TEH	24	C2
BLACK CANYON RD	INY	51	E4
BLACK CANYON RD	MNO	44	B5
BLACK CANYON RD	MNO	51	B1
BLACK CANYON RD	SBD	81	C5
BLACK CANYON RD	SBD	84	B5
BLACK CANYON RD	SBD	94	C1
BLACK CANYON RD	SDCO	107	A3
BLACK DIAMND WY	CC	39	B5
BLACK DIAMND MN	BUT	25	C2
BLK EAGLE MN RD	RCO	101	E3
BLACK FOX MTN	SIS	13	B2
BLACK GULCH RD	KER	79	C1
BLACK GULCH RD	LAS	14	A5
BLACK HAWK RD	CC	M	B4
BLACK HAWK RD	CC	46	B1
BLACKHAWK RD	PLU	26	C1
BLACK HILLS RD	RCO	100	D4
BLACKIE RD	MON	54	C3
BLACK LAKE RD	LAS	14	B5
BLACKMER RD	SUT	33	B2
BLACKMORE	SJCO	47	C1
BLACK MTN RD	IMP	110	B3
BLACK MTN RD	SDCO	106	D4
BLACK MTN RD	SMCO	N	C2
BLACK MTN RD	SMCO	45	C3
BLACK MTN RD	SIS	4	B3
BLACK MTN TR	RCO	100	B3
BLACK MTN LO RD	SLO	76	D3
BLACK RANCH RD	SHA	13	C4
BLACK ROCK RD	RCO	103	C5
BLACK ROCK CYN	SBD	100	E2
BLACK RCK MN RD	MNO	51	C2
BLACK ROCK SPGS	INY	59	E2
BLACKS CYN RD	MOD	14	D1
BLACKS RDG LKOT	LAS	14	B5
BLACKSTONE AV	FRE	165	D1
BLACKSTONE ST	TUL	68	B2
BLACKWELL LN	DN	1	D4
BLAGEN RD	CAL	41	C3
BLAINE ST	RCO	99	B2
BLAIR RD	IMP	109	B3
BLAIS RD	IMP	109	A4
BLAKE RD	SAC	40	B2
BLAKE ST	SBD	99	B1
BLAKER RD	STA	47	D3
BLANCHARD FT RD	TRI	17	D2
BLANCO	MON	54	C4
BLANCO RD	MPA	48	D2
BLANCO RD E	MON	171	C5
BLANCO RD E	SAL	171	C5
BLANCO RD W	MON	171	A5
BLANCO RD W	SAL	171	A5
BLAND RD	SHA	17	E3

INDEXES

STREET	CO.	PAGE	GRID
BLANEY AV	CPTO	149	E5
BLANKENSHIP AV	KER	78	A1
BLANKO RD	SBD	90	E4
BLATCHLEY RD	TEH	24	D2
BLAZING STAR AV	SBD	91	A3
BLEDSOE RD	MCO	48	B3
BLEVENS RD	LPAZ	104	C5
BLEWETT RD	STA	47	B2
BLICKENSTAFF RD	LAS	21	B4
BLISS DR	RCO	107	C1
BLISS RD	MCO	48	C5
BLISS RD	YUB	33	D2
BLITHEDALE AV	MAR	L	B4
BLITHEDALE AV	MAR	45	B1
BLITHEDALE AV E	MV	140	A3
B L M DUMP RD	LAS	20	E1
BLOCK RD	BUT	25	C5
BLOCK RD	BUT	33	C1
BLODGETT RD	IMP	109	B5
BLOODY CAMP RD	HUM	10	C3
BLOOMR HLL LKOT	BUT	25	D3
BLOOMFIELD AV	LACO	T	A2
BLOOMFIELD AV	SCL	54	D2
BLOOMFIELD RD	SON	37	D3
BLOOMFLD GRNTVL	NEV	26	D5
BLOOMINGTON RD	SBD	99	B2
BLOSS AV	MCO	47	D4
BLOSSER RD	STB	173	A2
BLOSSER RD	SB	86	B1
BLOSSER RD	SMA	173	A4
BLOSSOM	SJCO	39	E3
BLOSSOM AV	MCO	56	A2
BLOSSOM RD	STA	47	E2
BLOSSOM HILL RD	SCL	P	B4
BLOSSOM HILL RD	SCL	46	A5
BLOWERS DR	RCO	99	A4
BLUE GILL RD	SIS	4	B3
BLUE GULCH RD	SIS	11	B3
BLUE GUM AV	STA	47	C2
BLUE LAKE BLVD	HUM	10	A5
BLUE LAKE RD	LAS	8	D3
BLUE LAKE RD	MOD	8	C3
BLUE LK MPLE CK	HUM	16	B1
BLUE LAKES RD	ALP	36	B5
BLUE LAKES RD	LAK	31	C2
BLUE MTN RD	CAL	41	C2
BLUE MTN RD	KER	69	A5
BLUE MTN LKT RD	CAL	41	C2
BLUE RIDGE RD	SOL	38	E2
BLUE RIDGE RD	TEH	19	B3
BLUE SLIDE RD	HUM	15	E3
BLUFF ST	RCO	100	A2
BLUFF CREEK RD	TRI	16	E5
BLYTHE AV	FRCO	57	C3
BLYTHE AV	FRCO	67	B1
BOARDER ST	RCO	100	A3
BOARTS RD	IMP	109	A4
BOAT HARBOR RD	LAS	20	E2
BOBCAT TR	RCO	100	A5
BOB HOPE DR	RCO	100	E4
BOBS GAP RD	LACO	90	C4
BOB WHITE WY	INY	73	A4
BOCA RD	NEV	27	E5
BOCA SPRINGS RD	NEV	27	E5
BOCA SPGS RD E	NEV	27	E5
BOCKMAN RD	ALA	146	A2
BODEGA AV	SON	38	A3
BODEGA HWY	SON	37	D2
BODEM ST	MDO	162	D2
BODFISH CYN RD	KER	79	D1
BODIE RD	MNO	43	C3
BODIE MASONC RD	MNO	43	C3
BOESSOW RD	SAC	40	B3
BOGARD RD	LAS	14	B5
BOGGS RD	COL	24	E5
BOGGS & CHAMLIN	TEH	24	C2
BOGUE RD	STA	47	E3
BOGUE RD	STA	48	A3
BOGUE RD	SUT	33	C2
BOHAN DILLON RD	SON	37	B1
BOHEMIAN HWY	SON	37	C2
BOHN BLVD	SHA	18	C3
BOLAM RD	SIS	4	D5
BOLAM RD	SIS	12	D1
BOLAM LOGGNG RD	SIS	12	D1
BOLES RD	COL	32	E3
BOLEY RD	IMP	108	E5
BOLLINGER CY RD	CC	M	A4
BOLLINGER CY RD	CC	M	B5
BOLINGER CYN RD	CC	45	E1
BOLINGER CYN RD	CC	46	A1
BOLO RD	SBD	94	A3
BOLSA AV	ORA	98	B4
BOLSA CHICA RD	ORA	98	B4
BOLSA CHICA RD	ORA	T	B3
BON ST	MCO	48	D5
BONANZA AV	TRI	17	D1
BONANZA RD	CLK	74	D2
BONANZA RD	LV	209	B1
BONANZA RD	SBD	101	A1
BONANZA TR	SBD	91	C2
BONANZA WY	NEV	34	B1
BONANZA KING RD	TRI	12	A4
BOND RD	SJCO	40	A2
BOND RD	STA	47	E2
BONDS CORNER RD	IMP	112	C4
BONDS FLAT RD	TUO	48	C2
BONDURANT	MPA	49	A2
BONE STEEL RD	IMP	112	C4
BONETTI RD	SJCO	46	D1
BONITA AV	LACO	98	C1
BONITA AV	LACO	U	B2
BONITA RD	MCO	55	D2
BONITA RD	SDCO	V	D4

STREET	CO.	PAGE	GRID
BONITA RD	SDCO	111	D2
BONITA CYN DR	IRV	200	C3
BONITA CYN DR	ORA	98	C4
BONITA CYN DR	ORA	T	D4
BONITA LATERAL	SB	76	C5
BONITA LATERAL	SB	86	B1
BONITA SCHL RD	SLO	76	C5
BONITA SCHL RD	SB	76	C5
BONITA SCHL RD	SB	86	B1
BONITA VISTA RD	RCO	100	C4
BONNER RD	MCO	48	D4
BONNEYVIEW RD E	SHA	18	C2
BONNIE CT	KER	79	C3
BONNY LN	RCO	107	B1
BONNY DOON RD	SCR	53	D2
BONNYVIEW RD S	SHA	18	C2
BONVIEW AV	SBD	98	D2
BOOKER RD	TUO	41	D5
BOONE LN	FRCO	66	B3
BOONE ST	SMA	173	A3
BOOTH RD	LPAZ	104	B2
BOOT JACK	MPA	49	C3
BORAX RD	KER	80	D5
BORAX MILL RD	INY	62	A5
BORBA	SJCO	40	A5
BORBA	SJCO	47	A1
BORCHARD	VEN	96	D1
BORDEN RD	SAC	40	B3
BORDEN ST	MAD	57	A2
BORDER AV	RCO	U	E5
BORDER AV	RCO	98	E3
BORDER AV	SBD	100	E1
BOREL RD	RCO	99	D5
BORMAN LN	LAK	32	B4
BORNT RD	IMP	112	C4
BORON AV	KER	80	E5
BORRGO SLTN SEA	SDCO	108	A2
BORREGO SPGS RD	SDCO	107	E2
BORREGO VLY RD	SDCO	107	E2
BOSCOVICH RD	IMP	112	D5
BOSTON AV	LACO	Q	E2
BOTTINI	TUO	41	E4
BOTTLE CREEK RD	BUT	25	D1
BOTTLE HILL RD	BUT	25	D1
BOTTLE ROCK RD	LAK	31	E4
BOUCHO RD	COL	32	E3
BOULDER AV	SBD	99	C1
BOULDER HWY	CLK	74	D2
BOULDER CK RD	SDCO	107	C5
BOULDER CK RD	SIS	3	C5
BOULEVARD, THE	GLE	24	E4
BL D L AMERICAS	BAJA	112	B4
BOULTON RD	SUT	33	C3
BOUNDARY ST	SD	216	C1
BOUNDARY TR	DN	2	A4
BOUQUET CYN RD	LACO	89	C4
BOUSE QUARTZITE	LPAZ	104	C4
BOW AV	KER	80	C1
BOWEN RD	COL	32	D1
BOWEN RANCH RD	SBD	91	C4
BOWERS AV	SCL	P	B3
BOWERS AV	SCLR	150	D1
BOWKER RD	IMP	112	B3
BOWKER RD	IMP	112	B4
BOWL PL	SB	86	E3
BOWMAN RD	KER	80	D1
BOWMAN RD	MOD	7	B5
BOWMAN RD	SBDO	81	A1
BOWMAN RD	SJCO	47	A1
BOWMAN RD	TEH	18	B4
BOWMAN LAKE RD	NEV	27	A5
BOWMAN LAKE RD	NEV	35	A1
BOX CANYON RD	RCO	101	C5
BOX CAR RD	MCO	55	E1
BOX ELDER ST	RCO	100	C4
BOX SPRINGS BL	RCO	99	B2
BOX SPRINGS RD	RCO	99	C2
BOYCE RD	SOL	39	A1
BOYD	CC	38	E5
BOYD DR	TUL	58	C4
BOYD RD	IMP	109	B5
BOYD SPRINGS RD	LAS	14	B4
BOYER RD	MPA	49	C3
BOYER RD	YUB	33	D1
BOYES BLVD	SON	132	A2
BOYLE RD	IMP	109	A3
BOYLE RD	SHA	18	D2
BOYLES AV	LAK	32	A3
BOY SCOUT CP RD	VEN	88	B2
BRACE RD	PLA	34	B4
BRACK RD	SON	31	D5
BRACK RD	SON	37	D1
BRADBURY RD	MCO	47	E3
BRADBURY RD	MCO	48	A3
BRADBURY RD	STA	47	C3
BRADFORD AV	ORA	T	D1
BRADFORD RD	BUT	25	B4
BRADFORD RD	RCO	107	B1
BRADLEY AV	SDCO	V	E2
BRADLEY AV	SDCO	106	E5
BRADLEY RD	MON	65	E4
BRADLEY RD	RCO	99	C4
BRADLEY RD	VEN	88	C5
BRADLY HENLY RD	SIS	4	B3
BRADLEY LOCK RD	MON	65	C4
BRADSHAW RD	IMP	109	A5
BRADSHAW RD	SAC	40	A2
BRADSHAW RD	YUB	33	E3
BRADSHW TR, THE	RCO	102	A5
BRADSHW TR, THE	RCO	110	B1
BRADY RD	TRI	17	B2
BRAGG RD	RCO	100	A5
BRAMLETT RCH RD	MNO	44	C5
BRAMLOT RD	TRI	17	B3

STREET	CO.	PAGE	GRID
BRANCH RD	SLO	76	B1
BRANCH RD E	HUM	22	C1
BRANCH RD W	SIS	3	D4
BRANCH CAMP W	BUT	25	D1
BRANCH MILL RD	SLO	76	B4
BRANCIFORTE DR	SCR	54	A2
BRANCO RD	MCO	55	E1
BRAND BLVD	LACO	Q	E2
BRANDON RD	ED	40	D1
BRANDT	IMP	109	A3
BRANDT RD	SJCO	40	C4
BRANDT RD	KER	78	A2
BRANDY CITY RD	SIE	26	C4
BRANDY CREEK RD	SHA	18	A2
BRANFORD ST	LACO	Q	C2
BRANHAM LN	SCL	P	B4
BRANHAM LN	SCL	46	B5
BRANNAN ST	SF	143	D5
BRANNAN ISL RD	SAC	39	C4
BRANNAN ISLD RD	SAC	M	D2
BRANNAN MTN RD	RD	10	C4
BRANNIGAN MN RD	SBD	83	C4
BRANNIN RD	TEH	24	C2
BRANNON AV	FRCO	56	B2
BRANSCOMB RD	MEN	22	D4
BRANSTETTER LN	SHA	18	C2
BRANT RD	SBD	84	C3
BRANT CIMA RD	SBD	84	B3
BRAWLEY	IMP	108	C2
BRAWLEY AV	FRCO	57	C5
BRAY AV	TEH	18	D5
BRAZO RD	MCO	47	C4
BREA BLVD	ORA	98	C3
BREA BLVD	ORA	U	A4
BREA BLVD	ORA	T	C1
BREA CANYON RD	LACO	98	C2
BREA CYN CUTOFF	LACO	U	A3
BREA CYN CUTOFF	LACO	98	C2
BRECKENRIDGE RD	KER	78	E3
BRECKENRIDGE RD	KER	79	A2
BREEDLOVE RD	ED	34	E3
BRENDA ST	KER	70	A5
BRENT RD	TEH	18	D4
BRENTWOOD AV	CC	M	D3
BREUING RD	MCO	55	D1
BRENNAN	SJCO	47	C1
BRENTWOOD AV	CC	39	C5
BRETZ RD	FRCO	58	B1
BREUNER AV	COL	32	E3
BREWER RD	NEV	34	C2
BREWER RD	PLA	33	E4
BREWER CREEK RD	SIS	12	E1
BRICELAND RD	HUM	16	B5
BRICELAND RD	MEN	22	B1
BRICELND THORNE	HUM	16	B5
BRIDESTEIN RD	IMP	109	C5
BRIDGE RD	VEN	88	C4
BRIDGE ST	COL	33	A2
BRIDGE ST	RCO	99	D3
BRIDGE ST	SUT	33	C2
BRIDGE ST	SUT	125	A3
BRIDGE ST	YUBA	125	D3
BRIDGE ARBOR	LAK	31	D2
BRIDGE CK SPGS	LAS	20	C2
BRIDGE GULCH RD	TRI	17	B3
BRDGPORT SCH RD	ED	41	A1
BRIDGEWAY	MAR	140	D5
BRIDLE PATH DR	SCL	P	E5
BRIGGS AV	LACO	R	A2
BRIGGS RD	RCO	99	D4
BRIGGS RD	VEN	88	C5
BRIGGS GRIDLY W	BUT	25	C5
BRIGGSMORE AV	STA	47	C2
BRIGHTON AV	MDO	162	E1
BRIGHTWOOD	MAD	57	B1
BRIM RD	COL	32	B2
BRIMHALL RD	KER	78	B3
BRINKERHOFF AV	SB	86	E3
BRINKERHOFF AV	SB	87	A3
BRIONES VLY RD	CC	39	B5
BRISTOL RD	VEN	88	B5
BRISTOL ST	CM	197	E4
BRISTOL ST	CM	198	A4
BRISTOL ST	ORA	98	C4
BRISTOL ST	ORA	197	E4
BRISTOL ST	ORA	T	D3
BRISTOL ST	SA	195	E5
BRISTOL ST	SA	196	A2
BRISTOL ST	SA	197	E2
BRISTOL ST	SA	198	A2
BRISTOL ST N	NB	200	B1
BRITE RD	KER	78	A3
BRITTO RD	MCO	56	A2
BROAD ST	NEVC	128	B2
BROAD ST	SNLO	172	C3
BROAD ST	SLO	172	C3
BROAD ST W	NEVC	128	B2
BROADWAY	A	157	E3
BROADWAY	ALA	L	D4
BROADWAY	ALA	45	D1
BROADWAY	AMA	40	E2
BROADWAY	ANA	193	B2
BROADWAY	EUR	121	A4
BROADWAY	FRE	165	C3
BROADWAY	LB	192	D3
BROADWAY	LA	185	E5
BROADWAY	LA	186	A3
BROADWAY	LACO	Q	E3
BROADWAY	LACO	S	C1
BROADWAY	LACO	S	E2
BROADWAY	O	156	C5
BROADWAY	O	158	A2
BROADWAY	SCTO	137	A4
BROADWAY	SBD	92	D5

STREET	CO.	PAGE	GRID
BROADWAY	SD	215	E3
BROADWAY	SD	216	A3
BROADWAY	SDCO	V	E2
BROADWAY	SDCO	V	B3
BROADWAY	SDCO	106	D3
BROADWAY	SDCO	106	E5
BROADWAY	SDCO	111	D1
BROADWAY	SDCO	111	D2
BROADWAY	SF	143	A3
BROADWAY	SFCO	L	B4
BROADWAY	SMCO	N	C1
BROADWAY	SB	76	C5
BROADWAY	SC	169	E3
BROADWAY	SMA	173	C3
BROADWAY	SMON	180	A4
BROADWAY	SOL	134	C1
BROADWAY	SNMA	132	D5
BROADWAY	SON	L	B1
BROADWAY	SUT	33	C2
BROADWAY	VAL	134	C2
BROADWAY	YUB	33	D3
BROADWAY N	LA	186	C1
BROADWAY N	LACO	R	A3
BROADWAY RD	LACO	R	C5
BROADWAY RD	VEN	88	D5
BROADWAY ST	FRFD	135	B4
BROADWAY ST	SBD	101	A1
BROADWAY TER	O	156	C5
BROCK RD	IMP	112	A3
BROCKMAN LN	INY	51	D4
BROCKMAN RD	KER	78	C1
BROCKMAN RD	LAS	8	A4
BROCKMAN MLL RD	AMA	41	A1
BROCK MTN LKOUT	SHA	12	E5
BROKAW RD	SJ	151	D1
BROKAW RD	SCL	P	B3
BROKAW RD	SCL	46	B4
BROKEOFF MDWS	SHA	19	C2
BROOKDALE RD	SHA	18	D2
BROOKHILL RD	MAD	57	C2
BROOKHURST ST	ORA	98	B4
BROOKHURST ST	ORA	T	C2
BROOKLYN AV	LA	186	D3
BROOKLYN ST	LACO	R	A4
BROOKS RD	MCO	48	B4
BROOKS RD	NEV	34	C2
BROOKS ST	SB	86	D1
BROOKSIDE	FRCO	58	D4
BROOKSIDE AV	RCO	99	E2
BROOKSIDE AV	SBD	99	C2
BROOKSIDE DR	SP	155	A1
BROOKSIDE RD	CAL	41	C2
BROOKSIDE RD	S	160	A2
BROPHY RD	YUB	33	D2
BROWN RD	KER	70	C5
BROWN RD	KER	80	C1
BROWN RD	SB	86	A1
BROWN RD	SHA	13	D4
BROWN RD	SOL	39	B3
BROWN RD	SUT	33	C3
BROWN ST	NAP	133	C3
BROWN ST	RCO	99	B3
BROWNLL LAVA BD	SIS	5	C3
BROWNING	PLA	33	E5
BROWNING RD	COL	33	B5
BROWNING RD	KER	68	C5
BROWNING RD	SUT	33	C3
BROWN MATERL RD	KER	77	C1
BROWNS CREEK RD	TRI	17	D2
BROWNS MTN RD	TRI	17	D1
BROWNS RANCH RD	TRI	17	D1
BROWNS RAVINE	BUT	25	D1
BROWNS VALLEY	SBT	55	B4
BROWNS VLY RD	NAP	133	A3
BROWN VALLEY RD	SOL	39	A2
BROWN VALLEY RD	SCR	54	B2
BROYLE RD	STA	47	C3
BROYLES RD	BUT	25	A2
BROYLES RD	STA	47	C2
BRUCE RD	BUT	25	B3
BRUCE CRUM	SHA	13	E4
BRUCEVILLE RD	SAC	40	A3
BRUCITE ST	KER	91	E3
BRUELLA RD	SJCO	40	B4
BRUGGA LN	HUM	15	D2
BRUNDAGE LN	BKD	166	C5
BRUNDAGE LN	KER	166	C5
BRUNSWICK AV	LA	182	E2
BRUNSWICK RD	NEV	34	C1
BRUS	MOD	8	B3
BRUSH LN	STA	47	C3
BRUSH CREEK RD	SIS	4	B3
BRUSH CREEK RD	SON	37	E2
BRUSH CREEK RD	SON	38	A2
BRUSHY MTN LKOT	HUM	10	C5
BRYAN AV	FRCO	57	B5
BRYANT	FRCO	56	B2
BRYANT ST	SBD	99	D2
BRYANT ST	SF	142	D4
BRYANT ST	SF	143	D5
BRYANT RAVIN RD	BUT	26	A4
BRYANTS CYN RD	MON	55	A5
BRYANTS CYN RD	MON	65	A1
BUARO ST	GGR	195	B2
BUCHANAN RD	CC	M	B3
BUCHANAN RD	CC	39	B5
BUCHANAN RD	MAD	49	B5
BUCHANAN RD	TUO	41	E5
BUCHANAN ST	RCO	101	B5
BUCHANAN HLW RD	MCO	48	D5
BUCK RD	RCO	99	D5
BUCK RD	SJCO	40	B3
BUCKEYE RD	MPA	49	A3
BUCKEYE RD	NEV	34	D1

STREET	CO.	PAGE	GRID
BUCKEYE ARM RD	TRI	11	D5
BUCKEYE CK RD	SON	31	A5
BUCKEYE CK RD	TRI	11	D5
BUCKEYE CK RD	TRI	12	A4
BUCKEYE CK RD	TRI	17	E1
BUCKEYE RDG RD	TRI	11	D5
BUCKHORN	TEH	24	C2
BUCKHORN AV	KER	89	C1
BUCKHORN RD	SIS	4	C5
BUCKHORN RDG RD	AMA	41	B2
BUCKHORN STA LP	TRI	17	E1
BUCKLEY RD	SLO	76	B4
BUCKMAN FUNCK	SJCO	40	D5
BUCK MEADOWS	MPA	49	A1
BUCKNELL RD	KER	80	D3
BUCKS BAR RD	ED	34	E5
BUCKS FLAT RD	TEH	19	B4
BUCKSKIN RD	CAL	41	A4
BUCKS LAKE RD	PLU	26	C1
BUCKWHEAT RD	SBD	90	E4
BUDDY CT	KER	79	B3
BUELL RD	SHA	18	A3
BUENA CREEK RD	SDCO	106	C3
BUENA VISTA	AMA	40	D3
BUENA VISTA	LACO	97	D1
BUENA VISTA	SCL	54	D1
BUENA VISTA AV	A	157	D5
BUENA VISTA AV	A	158	B5
BUENA VISTA AV	MV	140	A2
BUENA VISTA AV	RIV	205	A2
BUENA VISTA AV	RCO	U	E5
BUENA VISTA AV	SCL	P	E5
BUENA VISTA BL	KER	78	D4
BUENA VISTA BL	KER	79	A4
BUENA VISTA DR	MER	170	C1
BUENA VISTA DR	SBD	100	E1
BUENA VISTA DR	SLO	76	A1
BUENA VISTA DR	SCR	54	B2
BUENA VISTA RD	AMA	40	D3
BUENA VISTA RD	KER	78	C3
BUENA VISTA RD	SBD	91	E4
BUENA VISTA RD	SJCO	40	C3
BUENA VISTA ST	BUR	179	C2
BUENA VISTA ST	LACO	Q	D2
BUENA VISTA ST	LACO	R	D3
BUENA VISTA ST	VEN	88	D5
BUERER LN	SJCO	47	C1
BUERKLE RD	KER	78	A3
BUFFALO RUN RD	RCO	102	C4
BUFFUM LN	LAS	21	B3
BUFFUM RD	SHA	13	B5
BUHACH RD	MCO	48	B5
BUHNE ST	EUR	121	C2
BULKLEY RD	SOL	39	C2
BULLARD AV	FRCO	56	C3
BULLARD AV	FRCO	57	B3
BULL CANYON RD	SLO	76	D5
BULL CREEK RD	MPA	49	B2
BULLION MTN RD	SBD	101	C1
BULLIS RD	LACO	S	D1
BULLRIDGE WHEEL	KIN	67	B4
BULL RUN ST	KER	80	C1
BULL SKIN RIDGE	SHA	19	A1
BULLY CHOOP RD	SHA	17	E3
BULS RD	KER	87	E1
BUMMERVILLE RD	CAL	41	B2
BUNCE RD	SUT	33	D2
BUNCH GRASS LKT	SHA	13	B5
BUNDY DR	LA	180	B4
BUNDY DR	LACO	Q	C4
BUNDY CANYON RD	RCO	99	C5
BUNKER RD	MCO	47	C5
BUNKER RD	MCO	55	C1
BUNKER HILL RD	SIE	26	D3
BUNKER STATN RD	SOL	39	C3
BUNNY LN	RCO	100	C5
BUNSELMEIER RD	LAS	14	B3
BUNTE RD	MON	65	C3
BUNTGVLL CUMMGS	LAS	21	B4
BURBANK BLVD	BUR	179	B3
BURBANK BLVD	LA	179	B3
BURBANK BLVD	LACO	97	C1
BURBANK BLVD	LACO	Q	C2
BURBANK ST	KER	78	A2
BURCH RD	SUT	33	C3
BURCHELL AV	MCO	48	D5
BURCHELL RD	SCL	54	C1
BURCH HAVEN RD	MCO	55	B2
BURGESS RCH RD	TRI	16	E5
BURKE LN	SOL	39	B3
BURLANDO RD	KER	69	D5
BURLINGAME AV	SMCO	N	C1
BURLNGTN RDG RD	NEV	34	E1
BURMA RD	NEV	34	C2
BURNES VALLEY	LAK	32	A3
BURNETT	PLA	34	B3
BURNHAM RD	VEN	88	A4
BURNS AV	KER	78	C1
BURNS FRWY	HUM	9	E5
BURNS FRWY	HUM	10	A5
BURNS RD	LPAZ	104	A2
BURNS CANYON RD	SBD	100	B1
BURNS CUTOFF	SJCO	40	A5
BURNSIDE LK RD	ALP	36	B4
BURNT RCH DUMP	TRI	10	E5
BURNT TREE RD	SBD	81	C5
BURRELL RD	HUM	15	E4
BURRIS LN	MEN	31	C1
BURRIS RD	SUT	33	B2
BURROUGH N RD	FRCO	58	A2
BURROUGH VLY RD	FRCO	58	A2
BURSON RD	CAL	40	D4
BURTON WY	BH	183	C1
BURTON WY	LA	183	C1

INDEXES

STREET	CO.	PAGE	GRID
BURTON MESA BL	SB	86	B2
BURWOOD RD	SJCO	47	D2
BUSCH LN	MEN	23	B5
BUSH ST	AMA	40	D2
BUSH ST	SF	142	A3
BUSH ST	SF	143	C4
BUSHARD ST	ORA	T	C3
BUSHEY RD	MOD	14	C1
BUSSEL RD	KER	78	B2
BUSTER RD	COL	33	A2
BUTANO CUTOFF	SMCO	N	C4
BUTANO CUTOFF	SMCO	45	C5
BUTCHER RCH RD	SIE	26	E3
BUTLER AV	FRCO	57	C3
BUTLER RD	COL	25	A5
BUTLER RD	STA	47	B2
BUTLER VLY RD	HUM	16	A1
BUTTE AV	FRCO	66	E1
BUTTE AV	SUT	33	C2
BUTTE RD	LAS	14	D3
BUTTE RD E	SUT	33	C2
BUTTE RD N	SUT	33	B1
BUTTE RD S	SUT	33	B2
BUTTE RD W	SUT	33	B1
BUTTE CREEK RD	HUM	16	B2
BUTTE HOUSE RD	SUT	33	C2
BUTTE HOUSE RD	YUBA	125	A2
BUTTEMER RD	SBD	90	E4
BUTTE MTN RD	AMA	40	E2
BUTTE MTN RD	AMA	41	A2
BUTTE MTN RD	TEH	24	C2
BUTTERBREAD CYN	KER	79	E2
BUTTERBREAD CYN	KER	80	A2
BUTTERCUP CT	KER	79	C4
BUTTERFIELD RD	MAR	L	A3
BUTTRFLD STG RD	MAD	49	D5
BUTTRFLD STG RD	MAD	57	D1
BUTTRFLD STG RD	RCO	99	D5
BUTTERFLY PK RD	RCO	100	C5
BTRFLY VLY TWAN	PLU	26	C1
BUTTERMILK RD	INY	51	B4
BUTTERS RD	IMP	109	C4
BUTTE SLOUGH RD	COL	33	A2
BUTTE VALLEY RD	INY	72	A3
BUTTE VLY RD E	SIS	5	A3
BUTTE VLY RD W	SIS	4	E3
BUTTE VLY AIRPT	SIS	5	A3
BUTTONHOOK RD	SB	86	D3
BUTTONWILLOW AV	FRCO	58	A4
BUTTONWILLOW DR	KER	77	E3
BUTTONWILLOW DR	KER	78	A3
BUTTS RD	MCO	47	C5
BUTTS RD	MCO	55	C1
BUTTS CANYON RD	LAK	32	B5
BUZZARD ROOST	SHA	19	A1
BVD AV	MCO	48	C5
BYERS PASS RD	LAS	21	B3
BYINGTON RD	SUT	33	C4
BYOFF RD	TRI	10	E5
BYRON HWY	CC	M	D3
BYRON HWY	CC	39	D5
BYRON RD	SJCO	46	D1
BYRON RD	CC	M	E4
BYRON RD	CC	46	D1
BYSTRUM RD	STA	47	D3
BYWOOD DR	TEH	18	C4
C			
C ST	KER	68	B5
C ST	SD	215	D3
C ST	YOL	137	A2
CABALLERO CT	LAK	32	A4
CABIN RD	LAS	14	B4
CABRILLO AV	LACO	S	C2
CABRILLO BLVD	STB	174	E4
CABRILLO DR	AVLN	105	B5
CABRILLO FRWY	SD	213	D3
CABRILLO FRWY	SD	215	E2
CABRILLO FRWY	SDCO	V	B3
CABRILLO HWY	MONT	167	D5
CABRILLO HWY	MONT	168	C2
CABRILLO HWY	MON	53	E5
CABRILLO HWY	MON	54	B4
CABRILLO HWY	MON	168	C2
CABRILLO HWY	SNLO	172	A1
CABRILLO HWY	SLO	75	B1
CABRILLO HWY	SLO	76	B5
CABRILLO HWY	SLO	172	A1
CABRILLO HWY	SMCO	N	B2
CABRILLO HWY	SMCO	45	B3
CABRILLO HWY	SB	86	B1
CABRILLO HWY	SC	169	A4
CABRILLO HWY	SCR	N	D5
CABRILLO HWY	SCR	53	D1
CABRILLO HWY	SCR	54	A2
CACHAGUA RD	MON	54	C5
CACHAGUA RD	MON	64	C1
CACHUMA RD	SB	87	A2
CACTUS AV	RCO	99	C3
CACTUS AV	SBD	99	B1
CACTUS DR	MCO	55	D2
CACTUS FLATS	INY	70	B2
CACTUS VLY RD	RCO	99	E4
CADET RD	KER	78	A4
CADILLAC AV	LA	183	D4
CADIZ DR	SBD	102	C1
CADIZ RD	SBD	94	B3
CADIZ RD	SBD	103	A1
CADY RD	IMP	109	A4
CAHUENGA BLVD	LA	179	A3
CAHUENGA BLVD	LA	181	D5
CAHUENGA BLVD	LACO	Q	D3
CAHUENGA BLVD W	LA	181	B2

STREET	CO.	PAGE	GRID
CAHUILLA RD	RCO	100	B5
CAHUILLA RD	SBD	91	C3
CAHUILLA HTS RD	RCO	100	A5
CAIRO	KIN	57	D5
CAJALCO RD	RCO	99	A3
CAJON BLVD	SBD	91	A5
CAJON ST	SBD	99	C2
CALAVERAS AV	FRCO	56	D4
CALAVERAS AV	FRCO	66	D2
CALAVERAS RD	ALA	P	C1
CALAVERAS RD	ALA	46	B3
CALAVERAS RD	SCL	46	B4
CALAVERITAS RD	CAL	41	A3
CALDOR RD	ED	41	B1
CALICO BLVD	SBD	92	A1
CALICO RD	SBD	92	A1
CALIENT-BODF RD	KER	79	B3
CALIENT-BODF RD	KER	79	C2
CALIENTE CK RD	KER	79	C3
CALIFORNIA AV	BKD	166	B3
CALIFORNIA AV	COL	32	E3
CALIFORNIA AV	FRE	165	A5
CALIFORNIA AV	FRCO	56	C3
CALIFORNIA AV	FRCO	57	C3
CALIFORNIA AV	KER	78	D3
CALIFORNIA AV	LACO	R	A5
CALIFORNIA AV	MDO	162	A4
CALIFORNIA AV	RENO	130	A3
CALIFORNIA AV	RCO	98	E2
CALIFORNIA AV	RCO	99	D4
CALIFORNIA AV	SCL	P	D5
CALIFORNIA AV	SCL	54	C1
CALIFORNIA AV	SC	169	C4
CALIFORNIA AV	STA	47	B2
CALIFORNIA BLVD	LACO	R	B3
CALIFORNIA BLVD	NAP	133	B2
CALIFORNIA BLVD	PAS	190	A4
CALIFORNIA BLVD	SNLO	172	B1
CALIFORNIA BLVD	SLO	172	B1
CALIFORNIA DR	IMP	108	C2
CALIFORNIA DR	NAPA	29	D4
CALIFORNIA ST	BUR	179	C3
CALIFORNIA ST	EUR	121	C2
CALIFORNIA ST	LACO	98	A1
CALIFORNIA ST	ONT	204	A5
CALIFORNIA ST	SBD	99	B1
CALIFORNIA ST	SDCO	106	B3
CALIFORNIA ST	SF	141	C3
CALIFORNIA ST	SF	142	A3
CALIFORNIA ST	SF	143	D4
CALIFORNIA ST	SFCO	L	B4
CALIFORNIA ST	SFCO	45	B1
CALIFORNIA ST	SJCO	40	A5
CALIFORNIA ST	S	160	D2
CALIF CITY BLVD	KER	80	B4
CALIFRNIA FARMS	SJCO	47	C1
CALIF PINES BL	MOD	14	E2
CALISTOGA RD	SON	38	A1
CALKINS RD	FRCO	57	E1
CALLAHAN RD	TEH	18	C5
CALLAHAN RD E	SIS	11	D1
CALLE DEL SOL	AVLN	105	B5
CALLE ECUESTRE	SB	87	A4
CALLEGUAS RD	VEN	96	C1
CALLE H COLEGIO	BAJA	112	B4
CALLE LIPPIZANA	SB	87	A4
CALLENDR BLK LK	SLO	76	B5
CALLE QUEBRADA	SB	87	A4
CALLE REAL	SB	86	E4
CALLE REAL	SB	87	A4
CALLOWAY DR	KER	78	C3
CALNEVA RD	LAS	21	E5
CALPACK RD	SJCO	46	E1
CALPINE RD	SIE	27	B3
CALPINE LO RD	SIE	27	B3
CALVIN CREST RD	MAD	49	D4
CALVINE RD	SAC	39	E2
CALVINE RD	SAC	40	A2
CALZ	BAJA	112	B4
CALZADA AV	SB	86	E3
CAMANCHE PKWY	CAL	40	D3
CAMANCHE PKWY N	AMA	40	C3
CAMANCHE PKWY S	CAL	40	D3
CAMARES DR	LACO	90	A3
CAMARILLO ST	LA	179	B4
CAMARILLO ST	LACO	Q	D3
CAMBRIA AV	FRCO	56	A2
CAMBRIA RD	SBD	91	E4
CAMBRIDGE DR	BUR	179	E2
CAMBRIDGE RD	SHA	18	C3
CAMBRIDGE ST	OR	196	D1
CAMBRIDGE ST	SA	196	D1
CAMDEN AV	SCL	P	B4
CAMDEN AV	SCL	46	B5
CAMERON AV	LACO	98	C2
CAMERON AV	LACO	U	A2
CAMERON RD	MEN	30	C2
CAMERON CYN RD	KER	79	D5
CAMERON PARK DR	ED	34	C5
CAMINO AV	IMP	108	C2
CAMINO ALTO	MAR	L	B4
CAMINO ALTO	MV	140	B3
CM CAPISTRANO	SJC	202	D3
CAMINO CIELO	SB	87	A3
CM DE FLORES	AVLN	105	B4
CAMINO DL MONTE	AVLN	105	A4
CAMINO DL MONTE	CAR	53	D5
CAMINO DL MONTE	CAR	168	C3
CAMINO DL MONTE	MON	168	C3
CAMINO DIABLO	CC	M	D4
CAMINO DIABLO	CC	46	C1
CM DOS RIOS	VEN	96	D1
CM LAS RAMBLAS	SJC	202	D4
CM MIRA COSTA	SCL	202	E5

STREET	CO.	PAGE	GRID
CAMINO ORO	SHA	19	A2
CAMINO PABLO	CC	L	D4
CAMINO PABLO	CC	L	E4
CAMINO REAL	LACO	S	A2
CAMINO REAL	SHA	19	A3
CAMINO SANTA FE	SDCO	106	C5
CM SANTA FE DR	SDCO	V	B2
CM TASSAJARA RD	ALA	M	B5
CM TASSAJARA RD	ALA	46	B2
CM TASSAJARA RD	CC	M	B4
CM TASSAJARA RD	CC	46	A1
CAMINO VISTA	SHA	19	A2
CAMMATTI-SHN RD	SLO	76	D1
CAMP RD	SAC	39	E3
CAMP RD E	COL	32	D2
CAMPBELL	SJCO	47	D1
CAMPBELL AV	BUT	33	C1
CAMPBELL AV	SCL	P	B4
CAMPBELL AV	SCL	46	A5
CAMPBELL DR	KER	78	E4
CAMPBELL RD	IMP	111	E3
CAMPBELL RD	SBD	101	D1
CAMPBELL RD	SB	86	C3
CAMPBELL RD	SOL	39	B1
CAMPBL HOT SPGS	SIE	27	C4
CAMPBELL RDG RD	TRI	10	D4
CAMPBLLS FLT RD	TUO	41	C5
CAMP CREEK RD	BUT	25	E2
CAMP CREEK RD	SIS	4	B2
CAMP FAR WST RD	PLA	34	A3
CAMP FAR WST RD	YUB	34	A2
CAMPHORA RD	MON	54	E5
CAMPHORA RD	MON	55	A5
CAMP KIMTU RD	HUM	16	C5
CAMP NINE RD	CAL	41	C4
CAMPO RD	SDCO	V	D3
CAMPO RD	SDCO	111	E1
CAMPODONICA RD	MCO	48	A3
CAMPOS LN	SOL	39	A2
CAMP ROCK RD	SBD	92	A1
CAMPO SECO RD	CAL	40	D3
CAMPO SECO RD	TUO	41	C5
CAMP THREE RD	SIS	10	E1
CAMPTON RD	EUR	121	D4
CAMPTON RD	HUM	15	E1
CAMPTONVILLE RD	SIE	26	C5
CAMPUS AV	ONT	204	C3
CAMPUS AV	SBD	98	D1
CAMPUS AV	UPL	204	C3
CAMPUS DR	IRV	198	C5
CAMPUS DR	KER	78	E4
CAMPUS DR	ORA	198	C5
CAMPUS DR	SCL	147	A3
CAMP WEOTT RD	HUM	15	D2
CMP 1 TEN MI RD	MEN	22	C4
CMP 2 TEN MI RD	MEN	22	C4
CAMP 8 RD	SLO	76	C2
CAMUESA RD	SB	87	D3
CANA HWY	BUT	25	A2
CANADA BLVD	LACO	97	E1
CANADA BLVD	LACO	R	A2
CANADA RD	SMCO	N	D2
CANADA RD	SMCO	45	C3
CANADA RD	SCL	54	D2
CANAL AV	FRCO	57	E1
CANAL BLVD	SJCO	46	E1
CANAL BLVD	SJCO	47	A1
CANAL DR	MCO	47	E4
CANAL DR	MCO	48	A4
CANAL RD	GLE	24	E3
CANAL RD	KER	77	E2
CANAL RD	KER	78	A2
CANAL ST	PLCV	138	C3
CANAL BANK RD	STA	47	E2
CANAL BANK RD	STA	48	A2
CANAL GULCH RD	SIS	4	A4
CANAL SCHOOL RD	MCO	47	C4
CANA PINE CREEK	BUT	25	A2
C AND D BLVD	RCO	103	D5
CANFIELD RD	SDCO	107	A2
CANFIELD RD	SON	37	E3
CANNIBAL RD	HUM	15	D2
CANNON RD	SDCO	106	B3
CANNON RD	TEH	18	B5
CANNON ST	SDCO	V	A3
CANOGA AV	LA	177	C3
CANON DR	BH	183	B1
CANON RD	SOL	39	A3
CANON ST	SDCO	111	C1
CANON PERDIDO	STB	174	C4
CANRIGHT RD	SOL	39	C3
CANTELOW RD	SOL	38	E2
CANTELOW RD	SOL	39	A2
CANTON RD	MCO	48	C5
CANYON DR	RCO	100	C3
CANYON DR	SBD	82	A5
CANYON RD	INY	52	B3
CANYON RD	MEN	23	A5
CANYON RD	MNO	52	B3
CANYON RD	SBD	93	B5
CANYON RD	SBD	100	C2
CANYON RD	SMCO	N	C4
CANYON RD	SMCO	45	C5
CANYON RD	SR	139	B4
CANYON RD	SHA	18	C3
CANYON RD	SON	31	D5
CANYON WY	PLA	34	D3
CANYON CREEK RD	MOD	14	E1
CANYON CREEK RD	SIS	3	B5
CANYON CREEK RD	TRI	17	C1
CANYON CREST DR	RCO	99	B2
CANYON VW LOOP	TEH	19	B4
CANYON VIEW RD	SBD	91	D4
CAPAY AV	GLE	24	E3

STREET	CO.	PAGE	GRID
CAPAY RD	TEH	24	D2
CAPE GLOUCESTER	SBD	91	E2
CAPEZZOLI LN	LAS	21	C4
CAPITAL BLVD	GLE	24	E4
CAPITAN TK TR	SDCO	107	B5
CAPITOL AV	SCTO	137	C3
CAPITOL AV	SCL	P	C3
CAPITOL AV	SCL	46	B4
CAPITOL AV	YOL	137	A2
CAPITOL AV	YOL	39	D1
CAPITOL EXPWY	SCL	P	C4
CAPITOL EXPWY	SCL	46	B5
CAPITOL ST	SAL	171	B3
CAPITOLA RD	SCR	54	A2
CAPPELL RD	HUM	10	C2
CAPPS CROSSING	ED	35	B5
CAPRI AV	MCO	55	D1
CARBINE TR	KER	79	D5
CARBON CYN RD	ORA	98	C3
CARBON CYN RD	ORA	T	E1
CARBON CYN RD	ORA	U	B4
CARBON CYN RD	SBD	98	C3
CARBON CYN RD	SBD	U	C3
CARBONDALE RD	AMA	40	C2
CARBONDALE RD	SAC	40	C2
CARDELLA RD	MCO	48	B4
CARDIFF ST	SDCO	V	D3
CAREY RD	IMP	109	A4
CARGIL LN	RCO	107	C1
CARIBOU RD	SIS	11	C3
CARLETON RD	MPA	49	B3
CARLIN RD	SJCO	46	E1
CARLSBAD BLVD	SDCO	106	B3
CARLSON	CC	38	C5
CARLSON BLVD	CC	L	C3
CARLSON BLVD	R	155	B3
CARLSON RD	BUT	25	B4
CARLSON RD	SUT	33	C3
CARLTON RD	SCR	54	C2
CARLTON RD	SIS	4	B4
CARLUCCI RD	MCO	56	A1
CARLYLE RD	NEV	27	A5
CARMEL RD	KER	77	D1
CARMELLIA AV	FRCO	56	B2
CARMEL MTN RD	SDCO	106	D4
CARMEL RCHO BL	MON	168	D5
CARMEL VLY RD	MON	54	B5
CARMEL VLY RD	MON	64	C1
CARMEL VLY RD	MON	168	E4
CARMEL VLY RD	SDCO	V	A1
CARMEL VLY RD	SDCO	106	D4
CARMEN LN	BUT	25	A3
CARMENCITA AV	SJCO	40	A2
CARMENITA AV	LACO	T	B1
CARNATION RD	MCO	47	D5
CARNELIAN BAY	PLA	35	E1
CARNEROS AV	NAPA	38	C3
CARPENTER RD	HUM	10	D5
CARPENTER RD	SJCO	40	B5
CARPENTER RD	STA	47	C3
CARPENTER ST	CAR	53	D5
CARPENTER ST	CAR	168	C3
CARPENTER ST	MON	168	C3
CARPENTERIA	MON	54	C3
CARPINTERIA ST	STB	174	E3
CARPENTER RIDGE	BUT	25	D1
CARQUINEZ SC DR	CC	L	E3
CARR AV	SBT	54	C2
CARRIAGE LN	SHA	18	B3
CARRIER GLCH RD	TRI	17	C3
CARRILLO ST	STB	174	B4
CARRIZO GRGE RD	SDCO	111	A4
CARROLL RD	SAC	40	A3
CARROLL CK RD	INY	60	B5
CARROLTON	SJCO	47	C1
CARROT LN	RCO	107	B1
CARRVILLE LOOP	TRI	11	E4
CARRVILLE LOOP	TRI	12	A4
CARSON RD	ED	34	E5
CARSON ST	LACO	97	D3
CARSON ST	LACO	S	B2
CARSTENS RD	MPA	49	B3
CARTER RD	MPA	49	B3
CARTER ST	SBD	99	D2
CARTMILL AV	TUL	68	A2
CARUTHERS AV	FRCO	57	C5
CARVER LN	RCO	99	B4
CASADEL RD	MAD	49	E5
CASADEL RD	MAD	50	A5
CASA DIABLO CTO	MNO	51	B2
CASA DIABLO MN	MNO	51	B2
CASA GRANDE RD	SON	L	A1
CASALE RD	TEH	18	D5
CASA LOMA RD	SCL	P	C5
CASA LOMA RD	SCL	54	B1
CASCADE BLVD	SHA	18	C2
CASCADE RD	SBD	101	A1
CASCADIAN AV	SBD	91	D3
CASE RD	RCO	99	C4
CASEY AV	KER	68	B5
CASEY AV	SB	86	E3
CASEY RD	IMP	109	B5
CASEY RD	SOL	39	B2
CASITAS VIS RD	VEN	88	A5
CASPR LTL LK RD	MEN	22	C5
CASS ST	MONT	167	E4
CASS ST	MON	53	E4
CASS ST	SDCO	V	A2
CASS ST	SDCO	106	C5
CASSEL RD	SHA	13	D5
CASSEL FALL RIV	SHA	13	D4
CASSERLY RD	SCR	54	C2
CASSIDY ST	SDCO	106	B3
CASTAIC RD	LACO	89	B4

STREET	CO.	PAGE	GRID
CASTAIC CYN RD	LACO	89	B3
CASTERLINE RD	HUM	16	D4
CASTLE CT	BUT	25	C3
CASTLE ST	S	160	C3
CASTLE CREEK RD	SHA	12	C3
CASTLE LAKE RD	SIS	12	C2
CASTRO	CC	38	C5
CASTRO RD	CC	38	D5
CASTRO RD	RCO	99	D4
CASTRO RANCH RD	CC	L	D3
CASTRO VLY BL	ALA	146	D1
CASTROVILLE BL	MON	54	C3
CATALINA AV	AVLN	105	B5
CATALINA BLVD	SDCO	V	A3
CATALINA DR	DVS	136	C1
CAT CANYON RD	SB	86	D2
CATERPILLAR RD	SHA	18	C2
CATFISH BCH RD	PLU	20	B4
CATHEDRAL RD	ED	35	E3
CATHEY RD	HUM	16	B4
CATLETT RD W	SUT	33	D4
CATRINA RD	MCO	56	B1
CATTARAUGUS AV	CUL	183	C4
CATTARAUGUS AV	LA	183	C4
CATTLE DR	TUL	68	E3
CATTLE DRIVE RD	MNO	51	C1
CATTLEMEN RD	MON	65	D3
CATWAY RD	SB	87	A2
CAUGHLIN RD	SBD	91	A3
CAVE CITY RD	CAL	41	B3
CAVEDALE RD	SON	38	B2
CAVIN RD	VEN	88	E4
CAVITT & STLLMN	PLA	34	B4
CAWELTI RD	VEN	96	C1
CAWSTON AV	RCO	99	E4
CAYLEY DR	KER	79	B4
CAYTON VLY RD	SHA	13	C4
CAYUCOS CK RD	SLO	75	D2
CAZADERO HWY	SON	37	C1
CCMO RD	KER	77	D3
CEBADA CYN RD	SB	86	C3
CECIL AV	KER	68	B5
CECIL RD	COL	33	B3
CECILVILLE RD	SIS	11	C3
CEDAR AV	FRCO	57	C3
CEDAR AV	FRCO	57	C5
CEDAR AV	RCO	100	C4
CEDAR AV	SBD	99	B2
CEDAR DR	MOD	14	B3
CEDAR ST	SBD	80	E1
CEDAR ST	SDCO	107	A4
CEDAR CAMP RD	HUM	10	C2
CEDAR CAMP RD	SIS	10	C1
CEDAR CAMP RD	TRI	17	A4
CEDAR CANYON RD	SBD	84	B4
CEDAR CREEK RD	ED	40	E1
CEDAR CREEK RD	ED	41	A1
CEDAR CREEK RD	HUM	10	C5
CEDAR CK LP RD	BUT	25	C1
CEDAR GROVE RD	SIS	5	A2
CEDAR RAVINE RD	ED	34	E5
CEDAR RAVINE ST	PLCV	138	E3
CEDARVILLE DUMP	MOD	8	E1
CEDAR WELL	SIS	5	A4
CEDARWOOD CT	SHA	19	A3
CEDROS DR	SBD	90	E2
CEMENT HILL RD	FRFD	135	C1
CEMENT HILL RD	NEV	34	C1
CEMETERY DR	MOD	14	C3
CEMETERY RD	COL	32	D1
CEMETERY RD	HUM	16	D4
CEMETERY RD	MCO	47	D4
CEMETERY RD	MNO	43	C4
CEMETERY RD	SBD	82	A5
CEMETERY RD	SHA	19	B2
CEMETERY RD	SIS	5	A2
CENTENNIAL RD	HUM	15	D3
CENTER AV	MCO	56	B2
CENTER RD	LAS	21	A3
CENTER RD	STA	47	B2
CENTER ST	CAL	41	A3
CENTER ST	MAN	161	A4
CENTER ST	RCO	99	B2
CENTER ST	SBD	99	C2
CENTER ST	SC	169	D3
CENTER ST	S	160	D3
CENTER ST EXT	RCO	99	C2
CENTER ST S	TEH	24	E1
CTR SCH HOUSE	LAS	14	C3
CENTERVILLE LN	DGL	36	B3
CENTERVILLE RD	BUT	25	C3
CENTERVILLE RD	HUM	15	D2
CENTERVILLE RD	MOD	8	A1
CENTERVILLE RD	MOD	14	E1
CENTINELA AV	CUL	187	D1
CENTINELA AV	ING	188	B3
CENTINELA AV	LA	187	D1
CENTINELA AV	LACO	Q	C4
CENTINELLA RD	MCO	55	C1
CENTRAL AV	A	158	A5
CENTRAL AV	A	159	A1
CENTRAL AV	FRCO	56	D4
CENTRAL AV	FRCO	57	B4
CENTRAL AV	HUM	9	E4
CENTRAL AV	HUM	10	A4
CENTRAL AV	KER	78	A2
CENTRAL AV	LA	186	B5
CENTRAL AV	LACO	97	E2
CENTRAL AV	LACO	Q	E2
CENTRAL AV	LACO	S	C1
CENTRAL AV	MCO	47	D4
CENTRAL AV	MON	65	B2
CENTRAL AV	MTCL	203	C3
CENTRAL AV	ORA	T	C1

COPYRIGHT, © 1989 BY Thomas Bros Maps

STREET	CO.	PAGE	GRID
CENTRAL AV	ORA	U	A4
CENTRAL AV	PAC	167	C2
CENTRAL AV	RCO	99	B2
CENTRAL AV	RCO	205	B5
CENTRAL AV	SAL	171	A4
CENTRAL AV	SBD	U	D3
CENTRAL AV	SBD	98	D2
CENTRAL AV	RCO	99	B4
CENTRAL AV	SBD	203	C3
CENTRAL AV	SB	86	B3
CENTRAL AV	STA	47	D3
CENTRAL AV	SUT	33	B3
CENTRAL AV	TEH	24	D1
CENTRAL AV	VEN	88	C5
CENTRAL AV	YOL	39	D2
CENTRAL RD	SBD	91	C3
CENTRAL EXPWY	MVW	148	B4
CENTRAL EXPWY	SCL	N	E2
CENTRAL EXPWY	SCL	P	B3
CENTRAL EXPWY	SVL	148	B4
CENTRAL FRWY	SF	143	A5
CENTRAL SKYWAY	SF	142	C4
CENTRAL ST	RC0	99	C5
CENTRAL CAMP RD	MAD	49	E4
CENTRAL HILL RD	CAL	40	E3
CENTRAL HILL RD	CAL	41	A3
CENTRL HOUSE RD	BUT	25	D5
CENTRALIA ST	LACO	S	E2
CENTRALIA ST	LACO	T	A2
CENTRAL VLY HWY	KER	78	B1
CENTURY BLVD	LA	189	D1
CENTURY BLVD	LACO	97	D2
CENTURY BLVD	LACO	Q	D5
CERINI AV	FRCO	57	B5
CERINI AV	FRCO	57	C5
CERRITOS AV	ANA	193	D4
CERRITOS AV	ORA	T	B2
CERRO GORDO RD	INY	60	C5
CERRO GORDO RD	INY	60	D4
CERRO NOROESTE	KER	78	A5
CERRO NOROESTE	KER	87	E1
CERVANTES BLVD	SF	142	A1
CHABOT RD	VAL	134	D1
CHADBOURNE RD	CC	39	B5
CHADBOURNE RD	SOL	38	E3
CHADWICK RD	SBD	101	E1
CHAHLIP LN	FRCO	58	C1
CHALET DR	KER	79	C4
CHALFANT RD	MNO	51	D3
CHALFANT LP RD	MNO	51	D3
CHALK BLUFF RD	INY	51	C4
CHALK BLUFF RD	NEV	34	D1
CHALK HILL RD	SON	37	E1
CHALLNGE CTO RD	YUB	26	A4
CHALONE RD	SBT	55	A5
CHAMBERLAIN	PLA	34	A3
CHAMBERLAIN RD	MCO	48	B5
CHAMBERS RD	HUM	15	D4
CHAMBERS WLS RD	SBD	103	E1
CHAMPAGNE AV	KER	89	C1
CHAMPS FLAT RD	LAS	20	C2
CHANAC RD	KER	79	B4
CHANDLER	YUB	33	D1
CHANDLER BLVD	BUR	179	C3
CHANDLER BLVD	LA	179	A4
CHANDLER BLVD	LACO	Q	C2
CHANDLER RD	PLU	26	D1
CHANDON AV	BUT	33	C1
CHANNEL ISLD BL	VEN	96	B1
CHAPARAJOS ST	CAL	41	A4
CHAPARRAL DR	SHA	18	B2
CHAPMAN AV	GGR	195	A1
CHAPMAN AV	OR	195	D1
CHAPMAN AV	OR	196	B1
CHAPMAN AV	ORA	98	C3
CHAPMAN AV	ORA	T	B2
CHAPMAN AV	ORA	T	C1
CHAPMAN DR	CRTM	140	B2
CHAPMAN RD	RCO	107	C1
CHAPPIUS LN N	LAS	21	B3
CHAPPIUS LN S	LAS	21	B4
CHAPULNIK RD	IMP	109	B4
CHARD AV	TEH	18	D5
CHARLEBOIS RD	MNO	42	E1
CHARLES ST	KER	80	D1
CHARLES ST	SHA	18	C3
CHARLES HILL RD	CC	L	D4
CHARLESTON BLVD	LV	209	A2
CHARLESTON BL E	CLK	74	D2
CHARLESTON RD	MCO	55	D2
CHARLESTON RD	SCL	N	E3
CHARLESTON RD	SCL	P	A3
CHARLESTON RD	SCL	45	E4
CHARLESTON RD W	PA	147	E5
CHRLSTN VOLCANO	AMA	41	A2
CHAROLAIS RD	SLO	76	A1
CHARTER WY	SJCO	40	B5
CHARTER OAK DR	TUL	68	C1
CHASE AV	KER	79	E2
CHASE AV	KER	80	A2
CHASE AV	SDCO	V	E3
CHASE AV	SDCO	111	E1
CHASE AV	TEH	24	D2
CHASE DR	RCO	98	E3
CHASE SCHOOL RD	RCO	100	E3
CHATEAU DR	SMCO	45	C3
CHATEAU RD	ML	164	D3
CHATEAU FRESNO	FRCO	57	B4
CHATEAU FRESNO	FRCO	57	B5
CHATSWORTH BLVD	SDCO	V	A3
CHATSWORTH BLVD	SDCO	111	C1
CHECKMATE RD	RCO	100	A5
CHELSEY AV	CC	L	C3
CHEMEHUEVI BLVD	MOH	96	B4

STREET	CO.	PAGE	GRID
CHEMISE MTN RD	HUM	22	A1
CHEROKEE LN	SAC	40	B3
CHEROKEE LN	SJCO	40	B3
CHEROKEE RD	BUT	25	D4
CHEROKEE RD	MCO	55	D1
CHEROKEE RD	SBD	82	C5
CHEROKEE RD	SJCO	40	B5
CHERRY AV	FRCO	57	C4
CHERRY AV	FRCO	57	C5
CHERRY AV	KER	78	B2
CHERRY AV	LACO	97	E4
CHERRY AV	LACO	S	E2
CHERRY AV	RCO	99	E3
CHERRY AV	SBD	99	A2
CHERRY AV	STA	47	C4
CHERRY ST	SUT	33	C2
CHERRY CREEK RD	SON	31	C4
CHERRY GLEN RD	SOL	38	E3
CHERRY VLY BLVD	RCO	99	E2
CHERT RD	RCO	107	B1
CHESEBORO RD	LACO	90	B4
CHESTER AV	BKD	166	C4
CHESTER AV	KER	78	D3
CHESTER LN	BKD	166	B4
CHESTR JUNPR LK	PLU	20	A3
CHESTER SKI RD	PLU	20	A4
CHESTR WRNR VLY	PLU	19	E3
CHESTR WRNR VLY	PLU	20	A3
CHESTNUT AV	FRCO	57	C2
CHESTNUT AV	FRCO	57	C5
CHESTNUT AV	SMCO	N	B1
CHESTNUT AV	SA	196	B4
CHESTNUT AV	TEH	18	D5
CHESTNUT ST	SF	143	A3
CHESTNUT ST	SHA	18	C3
CHESTNUT WY	CAL	41	B5
CHEVALIER RD	KER	78	D4
CHEVY CHASE DR	LACO	97	E1
CHEVY CHASE DR	LACO	R	A3
CHEZEM RD	HUM	10	B5
CHICAGO AV	RIV	205	E4
CHICAGO AV	STA	47	C2
CHICK RD	IMP	112	B3
CHICK RD	RCO	108	E1
CHICKEN HAWK RD	PLA	34	E2
CHICKEN RCH RD	TUO	41	C5
CHICO AV	KIN	57	E5
CHICO CANYON RD	BUT	25	C2
CHICORB LN	SOL	39	B2
CHICO RIVER RD	BUT	25	A3
CHIDAGO LOOP	MNO	51	C2
CHIDAGO CYN RD	MNO	51	B2
CHIHUAHUA VLY	SDCO	107	B2
CHILDS AV	MER	170	B5
CHILDS AV	MCO	48	C4
CHILE CAMP RD	CAL	40	D3
CHILENO VLY RD	SON	37	E3
CHILENO VLY RD	SON	38	A3
CHILES RD	YOL	39	C1
CHILES POPE VLY	NAPA	29	D1
CHILES POPE VLY	NAPA	38	C1
CHILI HILL	PLA	34	B3
CHIMNEY ROCK RD	SLO	75	D1
CHINA CAMP RD	MCO	55	D1
CHINA CREEK RD	MAD	49	D4
CHINA GRADE	SIS	3	A4
CHINA GRADE LP	KER	78	D2
CHINA GRADE RD	PLU	26	D1
CHINA GULCH DR	SHA	18	B3
CHINA LAKE BLVD	KER	80	D1
CHINA PK LO RD	SIS	3	A3
CHINA POINT RD	BUT	25	D2
CHINA RANCH RD	INY	73	A5
CHINO AV	SBD	U	C3
CHINO AV	SBD	98	D2
CHINO-CORONA RD	SBD	98	E2
CHINQUAPIN RD	MAD	49	E4
CHINQUAPIN RD	MAD	50	A4
CHINQUAPIN DR	MEN	23	A5
CHIRIACO RD	RCO	101	E4
CHITTENDEN RD	TEH	24	C2
CHLORIDE RD	SBD	92	B1
CHLORIDE CLF RD	INY	62	A3
CHOLAME RD	MON	66	C4
CHOLAME VLY RD	SLO	66	D5
CHOLLA RD	SBD	91	C4
CHOLLA RD	SBD	92	C5
CHORRO ST N	SNLO	172	A1
CHORRO ST S	SNLO	172	B2
CHOWCHILLA	MAD	56	D3
CHOWCHILLA BLVD	MAD	56	D1
CHOWCHILLA MTN	MPA	49	C3
CHRISMAN RD	SJCO	47	A2
CHRISTENSEN RD	SAC	40	A3
CHRISTIAN RD	TEH	24	D2
CHRISTN VLY RD	PLA	34	C3
CHROME MINE RD	TRI	17	B3
CHUALAR RD	MON	54	D4
CHUALAR CYN RD	MON	54	E4
CHUALAR RIV RD	MON	54	D5
CHUCKWAGON DR	CAL	41	A5
CHUCKWALLA RD	SBD	91	D3
CHUCKWL SPGS RD	RCO	102	D5
CHUCKWLA VLY RD	RCO	102	D4
CHUCKWLA VLY RD	RCO	103	A5
CHURCH AV	FRE	165	B5
CHURCH AV	FRCO	57	A3
CHURCH AV	FRCO	57	D3
CHURCH AV	SCL	P	E5
CHURCH AV	SCL	54	D1
CHURCH LN	HUM	15	E2
CHURCH LN	SCL	P	E5
CHURCH RD	SOL	M	D2
CHURCH RD	SOL	39	C4

STREET	CO.	PAGE	GRID
CHURCH ST	HUM	16	D4
CHURCH ST	SBD	99	C2
CHURCH ST	STA	47	D2
CHURCH ST	S	160	C5
CHURCH HILL RD	CAL	41	A3
CHURCHILL MN RD	INY	51	D3
CHURCH SPGS RD	STA	48	A1
CHURN CREEK RD	SHA	18	C2
CIBOLA RD	LPAZ	103	E5
CIBOLA RD	LPAZ	110	D1
CIENAGA RD	KER	78	A5
CIENEGA RD	SBT	54	E3
CIENEGA RD	SBT	55	A4
CIMA RD	SBD	83	E2
CIMA RD	SBD	84	A2
CIMA MESA RD	LACO	90	B4
CINCHA ST	CAL	41	A4
CINDER RD	INY	70	C3
CINDER PIT RD	MOD	14	D1
CIRCLE DR	INY	70	E1
CIRCLE DR	RCO	100	B4
CIRCLEA CT	BUT	25	C3
CIRCLE C LN	SOL	39	B2
CITRACADO PKWY	SDCO	106	D3
CITRON ST	ANA	193	B1
CITRUS AV	LACO	98	C2
CITRUS AV	LACO	U	A2
CITRUS AV	SBD	99	A2
CITRUS AV	SBD	99	D2
CITRUS AV	SDCO	106	C3
CITRUS AV	SDCO	106	D3
CITY DR, THE	OR	195	E2
CITY CAMP	MNO	43	C5
CITY CREEK RD	SBD	99	C1
CIVIC CENTER DR	SR	139	C1
CIVIC CENTER DR	SA	196	A3
CLAIREMONT DR	SD	211	E4
CLAIREMONT DR	SD	213	A1
CLAIREMONT DR	SDCO	V	B2
CLAIREMONT DR	SDCO	106	C5
CLAIREMONT MESA	SD	211	D4
CLAIRMNT MSA BL	SDCO	V	B2
CLAIREMONT MESA	SDCO	106	C5
CLARATINA AV	STA	47	D2
CLAREMONT AV	ALA	L	D4
CLAREMONT AV	B	156	C4
CLAREMONT AV	O	156	B5
CLAREMONT BLVD	CLA	203	B2
CLARIBEL RD	STA	47	D2
CLARISSA AV	AVLN	105	B5
CLARK AV	COL	24	E5
CLARK AV	LACO	S	E2
CLARK AV	SB	86	C1
CLARK AV	TEH	24	E2
CLARK AV	YUBA	125	C4
CLARK RD	BUT	25	C3
CLARK RD	IMP	109	A5
CLARK RD	IMP	112	A4
CLARK RD	MEN	30	D2
CLARK RD	MON	65	A1
CLARK RD	SLO	76	C1
CLARK RD	SOL	39	B2
CLARK RD	STA	47	C2
CLARK RD	SUT	33	C1
CLARK ST	NAP	133	E3
CLARKE RD	HUM	15	D4
CLARK MTN RD	SBD	84	A2
CLARK RANCH RD	MNO	51	C1
CLARKSBURG	YOL	39	D2
CLARKS FORK RD	ALP	42	B2
CLARKSON AV	FRCO	56	D5
CLARKSON AV	FRCO	57	C5
CLARKS VLY RD	GLE	24	B4
CLAUS RD	STA	47	D2
CLAUSEN RD	MCO	48	E5
CLAWITER RD	ALA	N	E1
CLAWITER RD	ALA	45	E2
CLAWITER RD	ALA	146	B4
CLAWITER RD	H	146	B4
CLAY RD	INY	72	D1
CLAY ST	SAL	171	B4
CLAY ST	U	123	B3
CLAY BANK RD	SOL	39	A3
CLAY MINE RD	KER	80	C5
CLAY RIVER RD	SBD	91	E1
CLAY STATION RD	SAC	40	B3
CLAYTON AV	FRCO	56	D4
CLAYTON AV	FRCO	58	A4
CLAYTON RD	CC	39	A5
CLAYTON RD	NEV	34	B2
CLAYTON RD	SON	32	A5
CLAYTON RD	SON	38	A1
CLAYTON RD	STA	47	D3
CLAYTON CREEK	LAK	32	A4
CLEAR CREEK RD	KER	79	B4
CLEAR CREEK RD	SBT	65	E1
CLEAR CREEK RD	SBT	66	A1
CLEAR CREEK RD	SHA	18	B3
CLEARFIELD DR	MLBR	144	B5
CLEAR LAKE RD	MOD	6	C3
CLEGHORN RD	LAS	14	D5
CLEGHORN CYN RD	SBD	91	B5
CLEM	SJCO	40	C4
CLEMENCEAU AV	FRCO	57	D5
CLEMENTE AV	AVLN	105	B5
CLEMENTS RD	SJCO	40	C4
CLEMENTS RD	SUT	33	C2
CLEVELAND AV	MAD	57	A2
CLEVELAND AV	SBD	U	E3
CLEVELAND AV	SBD	98	E2
CLEVELAND AV	SD	213	E5
CLEVELAND AV	STA	47	D1
CLEVELAND RD	MCO	56	C1
CLEVELAND ST	RCO	101	C5

STREET	CO.	PAGE	GRID
CLIFF DR	LAG	201	B2
CLIFF DR	NB	199	C4
CLIFF DR	STB	174	A5
CLIFF DR W	SC	169	D4
CLIFF RIDGE RD	MEN	30	C2
CLIFTON CT RD	SJCO	46	D1
CLINE GULCH RD	SHA	18	A1
CLINTON AV	FRE	165	B1
CLINTON AV	FRCO	56	E3
CLINTON AV	FRCO	57	A3
CLINTON AV	KIN	57	E5
CLINTON AV S	SJCO	47	B1
CLINTON RD	AMA	41	A2
CLINTON RD	ED	41	A2
CLINTON RD	STA	47	D2
CLINTON RD E	AMA	41	A2
CLINTON RD W	AMA	41	A2
CLINTN KEITH RD	RC0	99	C5
CLIO STATE RD	PLU	27	B3
CLOSE AV	TUL	68	D1
CLOUGH RD	HUM	15	D2
CLOUTIER ST	DN	1	D3
CLOVER LN	SB	86	E2
CLOVER LN	SB	87	A2
CLOVER LN	SHA	18	B3
CLOVER CREEK RD	KLAM	5	A1
CLOVERDALE DR	SHA	18	B3
CLOVERDALE RD	RCO	U	E3
CLOVERDALE RD	RCO	98	E2
CLOVERDALE RD	SMCO	N	C4
CLOVERDALE RD	SMCO	45	C5
CLOVERFIELD BL	SMON	180	A5
CLOVERLEAF DR	MAD	57	B2
CLOVER VLY RD	LAK	31	D2
CLOVIS AV	FRCO	57	D5
CLUB DR	DN	1	E3
CLYDE AV	MCO	48	B5
COACHELLA CANAL	RCO	108	D1
COACHLA CNAL RD	IMP	109	B2
COACHLLA CYN RD	RCO	101	D5
COAL RD	RCO	99	B4
COAL CANYON RD	BUT	25	C4
COAL CANYON RD	ORA	U	D5
COAL CANYON RD	ORA	98	D3
COALINGA RD	SBT	65	D1
COAL MINE RD	AMA	40	D3
COALINGA RD	SBT	66	A1
COALNGA MNL SPG	FRCO	66	B3
COAST HWY	LAG	201	A2
COAST HWY	ORA	98	C5
COAST HWY	ORA	201	A2
COAST HWY	ORA	202	D5
COAST HWY	SON	30	D5
COAST HWY E	NB	199	D4
COAST HWY E	NB	200	A5
COAST HWY W	NB	199	C4
COAST RD	MON	64	B1
COAST RIDGE TR	MON	64	E4
COCHRANE RD	SCL	P	D4
COCHRAN RD	SCL	54	C1
COCK RBN ISL RD	HUM	15	D2
COCOPAH RD	IMP	112	D5
COD DR	SIS	4	B3
CODONI AV	STA	47	D2
COFFEE RD	KER	78	C2
COFFEE RD	MDO	162	E2
COFFEE RD	STA	47	D2
COFFEE ST	MCO	48	C5
COFFEE CREEK RD	HUM	15	D2
COFFEE CREEK RD	TRI	11	D3
COGSWELL RD	STA	47	E2
COGSWELL RD	STA	48	A2
COHASSET RD	BUT	25	C2
COHASSET RD	C	124	A2
COHEN RD	SJCO	47	A1
COHN AV	FRCO	66	D3
COLBY RD	IMP	110	D5
COLBY MTN LKOUT	TEH	19	D5
COLDEN AV	LACO	Q	E5
COLD CANYON RD	LACO	97	B2
COLD CREEK RD	TRI	17	B3
COLD SPRINGS RD	ED	34	D4
COLD SPRINGS RD	LAS	8	C4
COLDWATR CYN AV	LACO	97	C1
COLDWATR CYN AV	LACO	Q	C2
COLDWATR CYN DR	LACO	97	D1
COLDWELL AV	MDO	162	A2
COLDWELL LN	FRCO	66	B3
COLE RD	IMP	112	B4
COLE RD	MPA	49	B3
COLE GRADE RD	SDCO	106	D2
COLEMAN AV	MP	147	A1
COLEMAN AV	SMCO	147	A1
COLEMAN AV	SCL	P	B3
COLEMAN AV	SCLR	151	C2
COLEMN FSH HTCH	SHA	18	D3
COLEMAN VLY RD	SON	37	C2
COLES RD	SUT	33	B3
COLES LEVEE RD	KER	78	B4
COLEY RD	IMP	112	D5
COLFAX	PLA	34	D2
COLFAX AV	GV	127	C4
COLFAX AV	LACO	Q	D3
COLFAX AV	NEV	127	C4
COLFAX FRST HLL	PLA	34	D2
COLGATE RD	KER	80	D3
COLIMA RD	LACO	98	B3
COLIMA RD	LACO	R	D5
COLIN RD	SBD	80	E1
COLLEGE AV	ALA	L	D4
COLLEGE AV	B	156	B3
COLLEGE AV	MAR	139	B5
COLLEGE AV	MDO	162	A2
COLLEGE AV	O	156	B5

STREET	CO.	PAGE	GRID
COLLEGE AV	SDCO	V	C3
COLLEGE AV	SDCO	111	D1
COLLEGE AV	SIS	12	C1
COLLEGE AV	SON	37	E2
COLLEGE AV	SON	38	A2
COLLEGE AV	STR	131	C3
COLLEGE AV W	STR	131	B3
COLLEGE BLVD	PLA	34	B4
COLLEGE BLVD	SDCO	106	B3
COLLEGE DR	SAL	171	A4
COLLEGE DR	SMA	173	D4
COLLEGE CITY RD	COL	33	A3
COLLEGE HTS BL	KER	80	E1
COLLIER RD	MCO	47	E4
COLLIER RD	MCO	48	A4
COLLIER RD	SJCO	40	B3
COLLIER CYN RD	ALA	46	B2
COLLINS AV	OR	194	D4
COLLINS AV	ORA	T	D2
COLLINS RD	IMP	110	D5
COLLINS RD	INY	51	D4
COLLINSVILLE RD	SOL	M	B2
COLLINSVILLE RD	SOL	39	B4
COLLYER DR	SHA	18	C2
COLOMA RD	ED	34	D4
COLOMA RD	ED	138	B1
COLOMA RD	SAC	40	A1
COLOMA ST	PLCV	138	C2
COLOMBERO DR	SIS	12	D2
COLOMBO MINE RD	SIE	26	E4
COLOMBO MINE RD	SIE	27	A4
COLOMBUS AV	MCO	47	D4
COLONY RD	BUT	25	B4
COLONY RD	MON	64	E1
COLONY RD	MON	65	A1
COLONY RD	SAC	40	B2
COLORADO AV	RCO	99	A3
COLORADO AV	SCL	N	E2
COLORADO AV	SMON	180	A5
COLORADO BLVD	LACO	97	E1
COLORADO BLVD	LACO	98	A1
COLORADO BLVD	LACO	R	D3
COLORADO BLVD	PAS	190	B4
COLORADO RD	FRCO	57	A5
COLORADO RD	MPA	49	B3
COLORADO ST	GLEN	182	E1
COLORADO ST	LACO	Q	E3
COLORADO ST	LACO	S	E2
COLORADO ST	LACO	T	A2
COLORADO RV RD	RCO	103	D4
COLOSEUM	INY	59	E2
COLSEN CYN RD	SB	86	D1
COLT LN	CAL	41	A5
COLTON AV	CLTN	207	B4
COLTON AV	SBD	99	B2
COLUMBIA AV	RCO	99	B2
COLUMBIA RD N	KER	80	D3
COLUMBIA RD S	KER	80	D4
COLUMBINE RD	SIS	12	C2
COLUMBUS AV	SF	143	B2
COLUMBUS AV	SFCO	45	C1
COLUMBUS PKWY	SOL	L	D2
COLUMBUS PKWY	SOL	38	D4
COLUMBUS ST	KER	78	D3
COLUSA AV	CC	L	D4
COLUSA AV	FRCO	56	E4
COLUSA AV	FRCO	66	E1
COLUSA AV	SUT	125	A2
COLUSA AV	YUBA	125	A2
COLUSA RD	SBD	91	B3
COLUSA CO RD	COL	31	E1
COLUSA-PRNTN RD	COL	32	E1
COLYEAR SPGS RD	TEH	17	E5
COMANCHE DR	KER	78	E4
COMANCHE DR	KER	79	A3
COMANCHE PT RD	KER	79	A4
COMBIE RD	NEV	34	C3
COMBIE RD	PLA	34	C3
COMETA RD	SJCO	47	D1
COMM BLVD	SBD	91	C1
COMMERCE AV	LACO	Q	E1
COMMERCIAL ST	SD	216	A4
COMMONS RD	STA	47	D3
COMMONWEALTH	ORA	98	B3
COMMONWEALTH AV	ORA	T	B1
COMMONWEALTH AV	RCO	99	E4
COMPTCHE UKIAH	MEN	30	B1
COMPTON AV	LACO	Q	E5
COMPTON BLVD	LACO	S	B1
COMSTOCK	WSH	130	B3
COMSTOCK RD	SBT	55	A2
COMSTOCK RD	SJCO	40	C4
CONARD RD	LAS	20	D3
CONCHO ST	CAL	41	A4
CONCORD AV	CC	39	C5
CONCORD BLVD	CC	M	A3
CONCORD BLVD	CC	39	A5
CONCOW RD	BUT	25	D1
CONDIT AV	STA	47	B3
CONDOR RD	SBD	92	B1
CONDOR RD	SBD	101	C1
CONDUIT	SUT	33	C3
CONE RD	INY	51	D5
CONE RD 3	LAS	20	B1
CONE GROVE RD	TEH	18	D5
CONEJO AV	FRCO	57	B5
CONEJO AV	FRCO	57	C5
CONEJO DR	SBD	90	E3
CONE PEAK RD	MON	64	E3
CONFER RD	SJCO	40	B5
CONGRESS AV	MONT	53	D3
CONGRESS AV	PAC	167	B3
CONGRESS ST	SD	213	A5
CONGRSS SPGS RD	SCL	N	E4

250
CONGRSS SPGS RD — STREET INDEX — CUNEO RD

STREET	CO.	PAGE	GRID
CONGRSS SPGS RD	SCL	P	A4
CONGRSS SPGS RD	SCL	45	E5
CONKLIN BLVD	KER	80	C4
CONKLIN RD	MOD	8	D1
CONKLIN CK RD	HUM	15	D4
CONKLING RD	IMP	112	A3
CONN CREEK RD	NAPA	29	D4
CONNECTION	LAS	21	E4
CONNELLY RD	IMP	112	C3
CONRAD GROVE LP	TEH	19	D3
CONSTANCE AV	STB	174	A2
CONSTANTIA RD	LAS	27	E1
CONSTELLATN AV	KER	89	C1
CONSUMNES MINE	ED	35	B5
CONTADAS	CC	38	D5
CONTOUR AV	RCO	99	D3
CONTRA COSTA AV	FRCO	56	D4
CONTRA COSTA BL	CC	L	E3
CONTRA COSTA BL	CC	M	A3
CONTRA LOMA BL	CC	M	C3
CONVENTN CTR DR	CLK	209	C5
CONVICT CPGD RD	MNO	50	E2
CONVICT CPGD RD	MNO	51	A2
CONVICT CK EXP	MNO	51	A2
CONVICT LAKE RD	MNO	50	E2
CONVICT LAKE RD	MNO	51	A2
CONVOY ST	SDCO	V	B2
CONVOY ST	SDCO	106	D5
CONWAY RANCH RD	MNO	43	B4
COOK LN	SOL	39	B3
COOK RD	AMA	40	C3
COOK ST	RCO	100	E4
COOK ST	SMA	173	A3
COOK CAMPBLL RD	SIS	4	E4
COOK PEAK LKOUT	KER	79	D1
COOKS CAMP RD	CAL	41	C2
COOKS SPRING RD	COL	32	B1
COOLEY RD	IMP	109	B5
COOLEY RD	SIS	4	B3
COOLGARDIE RD	SBD	81	D4
COOLIDGE AV	O	158	E4
COOLIDGE AV	SCL	P	D5
COOMBSVILLE RD	NAPA	L	D1
COOMBSVILLE RD	NAPA	38	D3
COON HOLLOW CK	BUT	25	D1
COOPER RD	IMP	109	C5
COOPER RD	MON	54	C4
COOPER RD	NEV	34	C1
COOPR CIENG T T	RCO	100	B5
COOPERSTOWN RD	STA	48	B2
COPA DE ORA AV	MCO	55	D1
COPCO RD	SIS	4	B3
COPENHAGEN	HUM	15	D2
COPP AV	KER	89	B1
COPPER	FRCO	57	D2
COPPER AV	FRCO	56	A2
COPPER CYN RD	SHA	18	C1
COPPER CITY RD	SBD	81	D4
COPPER COVE DR	CAL	41	A5
COPPER HEAD RD	MON	65	C4
COPPER MTN RD	SBD	101	B1
COPPEROPOLIS	SJCO	40	D5
COPPER VISTA WY	SDCO	106	C3
COPP PIT RD	MOD	14	D2
COPUS RD	KER	78	B4
CORAL RD	MCO	47	E5
CORAL RD	MCO	55	E1
CORAN RD	SHA	18	B1
CORBETT CYN RD	SLO	76	B4
CORBIN AV	LA	178	B3
CORBIN RD	COL	32	D1
CORCORAN RD	KER	77	E1
CORD	SJCO	40	C3
CORDA RD	MON	54	E5
CORDELIA RD	SOL	L	E1
CORDELIA RD	SOL	M	A1
CORDELIA RD	SOL	38	E3
CORDELIA RD	SOL	135	B5
CORDELIA RD	SUIS	135	B5
CORE RD	SAC	39	E2
CORKILL RD	RCO	100	D3
CORN CAMP RD	KER	77	E3
CORNELIA AV	FRCO	57	B4
CORNELIUS AV	SUT	33	D3
CORNING RD	TEH	24	C2
CORN SPRINGS RD	RCO	102	C5
CORONA AV	KIN	57	E5
CORONA EXPWY	RCO	98	D3
CORONA EXPWY	SBD	98	D2
CORONA FRWY	RCO	98	E3
CORONA RD	SON	L	A1
CORONA RD	SON	38	A3
CORONA D MAR FY	CM	197	D4
CORONA D MAR FY	ORA	98	C4
CORONADO AV	SDCO	V	C5
CORONADO AV	SDCO	111	D2
CORRAL RD	SHA	19	E2
COPPEROPOLIS RD	TRI	17	B5
CORRL DE TIERRA	MON	54	C5
CORRAL HOLLW RD	SJCO	46	E2
CORRALITOS RD	SCR	54	B2
CORREIA RD	SJCO	39	E4
CORRELL RD	SUT	33	B3
CORTE MADERA AV	CRTM	140	B1
CORTEZ AV	MCO	47	E3
CORTEZ AV	MCO	48	A3
CORTEZ WY	KER	79	E2
CORTINA SCH RD	COL	32	D3
CORTINA VNYD RD	COL	32	D3
CORTO RD	SBD	91	D4
CORWIN RD	SBD	91	C3
CORWIN RANCH RD	RCO	99	B5
CORYDON RD	RCO	99	B5
COSGROVE	CAL	41	B4
COSTA RD	YUB	26	A4
COSTNER RD	STA	47	C2
COTA ST	STB	174	C4
COTHARIN RD	VEN	96	D2
COTTA RD	SJCO	39	E4
COTTAGE AV	MAN	161	E1
COTTAGE AV	SJCO	161	E1
COTTLE RD	STA	47	D1
COTTON RD	MCO	55	E2
COTTON CREEK	MPA	48	D2
COTTON GIN RD	MCO	55	E2
COTTNTAIL CK RD	SLO	75	D2
COTTONWOOD AV	RCO	99	C3
COTTONWOOD AV	RCO	99	D4
COTTONWOOD DR	SBD	92	C1
COTTONWOOD RD	BUT	25	C4
COTTONWOOD RD	INY	60	B5
COTTONWOOD RD	KER	78	D3
COTTONWOOD RD	MCO	47	C5
COTTONWOOD RD	RCO	100	A2
COTTONWOOD RD	SBT	55	B4
COTTONWD CYN RD	MNO	43	C4
COTTONWD CYN RD	RCO	99	C4
COTTONWD CYN RD	SB	77	B5
COTTONWD CK RD	SIS	4	A2
COTTONWD SPG RD	RCO	101	D4
COUCH ST	VAL	134	C3
COUGHLAN ST	VAL	134	B3
COULTERVILLE RD	MPA	49	C2
COUNCIL HILL RD	SIE	26	C4
COUNCILMAN RD	HUM	10	D5
COUNTRY	SJCO	40	C5
COUNTRY RD	SIS	4	C5
COUNTRY CLUB BL	SJCO	40	A5
COUNTRY CLUB BL	SJCO	160	A3
COUNTRY CLUB DR	RCO	100	D4
COUNTRY CLUB RD	AVLN	105	A5
COUNTRY CLUB RD	HUM	10	D4
COUNTRY CLUB RD	YUB	33	D3
COUNTRYMAN DR	PLU	26	B2
COUNTY RD	INY	51	D5
COUNTY RD	MOD	8	A1
COUNTY RD	MOD	14	E1
COUNTY RD B	GLE	24	C4
COUNTY RD BB	GLE	24	C4
COUNTY RD C	GLE	24	C3
COUNTY RD D	GLE	24	D4
COUNTY RD F	GLE	24	D3
COUNTY RD H	GLE	24	D3
COUNTY RD H	GLE	24	D4
COUNTY RD I	GLE	24	D3
COUNTY RD J	GLE	24	D3
COUNTY RD M	GLE	24	D4
COUNTY RD MM	GLE	24	D3
COUNTY RD N	GLE	24	D4
COUNTY RD NN	GLE	24	D3
COUNTY RD P	GLE	24	D4
COUNTY RD PP	GLE	24	D4
COUNTY RD QQ	GLE	24	D3
COUNTY RD R	GLE	24	E4
COUNTY RD RR	GLE	24	E3
COUNTY RD S	GLE	24	E4
COUNTY RD SS	GLE	24	E4
COUNTY RD T	GLE	24	E4
COUNTY RD TT	GLE	24	E4
COUNTY RD U	GLE	24	E3
COUNTY RD V	GLE	24	E3
COUNTY RD V	GLE	24	E4
COUNTY RD VV	GLE	24	E3
COUNTY RD VV	GLE	24	E4
COUNTY RD W	GLE	24	E4
COUNTY RD WW	GLE	24	E4
COUNTY RD XX	GLE	24	E3
COUNTY RD XX	GLE	25	A5
COUNTY RD Y	GLE	25	A5
COUNTY RD YY	GLE	25	A5
COUNTY RD Z	GLE	25	A4
COUNTY RD ZZ	GLE	25	A4
COUNTY RD 5	YOL	33	A4
COUNTY RD 6	YOL	33	A4
COUNTY RD 7	YOL	33	A4
COUNTY RD 8	YOL	32	E4
COUNTY RD 9	GLE	24	D3
COUNTY RD 10	YOL	32	E4
COUNTY RD 11	GLE	24	E3
COUNTY RD 11	YOL	32	E4
COUNTY RD 11	YOL	33	A4
COUNTY RD 11A	YOL	33	B4
COUNTY RD 11B	YOL	33	B4
COUNTY RD 12	YOL	33	B4
COUNTY RD 12A	YOL	33	A4
COUNTY RD 13	YOL	32	E4
COUNTY RD 14	YOL	33	A4
COUNTY RD 14A	YOL	33	B4
COUNTY RD 15	GLE	24	E3
COUNTY RD 15	YOL	33	B4
COUNTY RD 15B	YOL	32	E4
COUNTY RD 15B	YOL	33	A4
COUNTY RD 16	GLE	24	E3
COUNTY RD 16	YOL	33	A5
COUNTY RD 16A	YOL	32	E5
COUNTY RD 17	YOL	33	A5
COUNTY RD 18	GLE	24	E3
COUNTY RD 18	YOL	33	B5
COUNTY RD 18B	YOL	33	C5
COUNTY RD 18C	YOL	33	C5
COUNTY RD 19	GLE	24	E3
COUNTY RD 19	GLE	24	E3
COUNTY RD 19	YOL	33	B5
COUNTY RD 19A	YOL	33	A5
COUNTY RD 20	GLE	24	E3
COUNTY RD 20	YOL	33	C5
COUNTY RD 20A	YOL	32	E5
COUNTY RD 21	GLE	24	E3
COUNTY RD 21	GLE	24	E3
COUNTY RD 21A	YOL	32	E5
COUNTY RD 23	GLE	25	A3
COUNTY RD 23	YOL	33	A5
COUNTY RD 24	GLE	24	D3
COUNTY RD 24	YOL	33	B5
COUNTY RD 25	GLE	24	D3
COUNTY RD 25	YOL	33	A5
COUNTY RD 25A	YOL	33	A5
COUNTY RD 26	GLE	24	C3
COUNTY RD 26	YOL	33	A5
COUNTY RD 26A	YOL	33	C5
COUNTY RD 27	GLE	24	D3
COUNTY RD 27	YOL	33	B5
COUNTY RD 28	GLE	24	D3
COUNTY RD 28	YOL	33	A5
COUNTY RD 28H	YOL	39	C1
COUNTY RD 29	GLE	24	E3
COUNTY RD 29	GLE	25	A3
COUNTY RD 29	YOL	39	A1
COUNTY RD 29A	YOL	39	A1
COUNTY RD 30	GLE	24	D3
COUNTY RD 30	GLE	25	A3
COUNTY RD 30	YOL	39	B1
CO RD 30 1/2	GLE	25	A3
COUNTY RD 31	GLE	24	D4
COUNTY RD 31	GLE	25	A3
COUNTY RD 31	YOL	39	A1
COUNTY RD 32	GLE	24	E4
COUNTY RD 32	GLE	25	A4
COUNTY RD 32	YOL	39	B1
CO RD 32 1/2	GLE	24	E4
COUNTY RD 33	GLE	24	D4
COUNTY RD 33	GLE	25	A4
COUNTY RD 34	GLE	24	E4
COUNTY RD 34	GLE	25	A4
COUNTY RD 35	GLE	24	D4
COUNTY RD 36	GLE	24	E4
COUNTY RD 36	YOL	39	C2
COUNTY RD 37	GLE	24	E4
COUNTY RD 38	GLE	24	E4
COUNTY RD 38	YOL	39	C2
COUNTY RD 38A	YOL	39	C2
COUNTY RD 39	GLE	24	D4
COUNTY RD 40	GLE	24	E4
COUNTY RD 41	GLE	24	E4
COUNTY RD 43	GLE	24	D4
COUNTY RD 43	YOL	32	D4
COUNTY RD 44	GLE	24	E4
COUNTY RD 44	YOL	32	D4
COUNTY RD 45	GLE	24	D4
COUNTY RD 45	YOL	32	D4
COUNTY RD 46	GLE	24	E4
COUNTY RD 47	YOL	32	D4
COUNTY RD 48	GLE	24	D4
COUNTY RD 49	GLE	24	D4
COUNTY RD 50	GLE	24	E4
COUNTY RD 50	GLE	25	A4
COUNTY RD 53	GLE	24	E4
COUNTY RD 57	GLE	24	D4
COUNTY RD 58	GLE	24	C4
COUNTY RD 59	GLE	24	C5
COUNTY RD 59	YOL	32	D4
COUNTY RD 60	GLE	24	D5
COUNTY RD 61	GLE	24	E5
COUNTY RD 61	YOL	32	D4
COUNTY RD 62	GLE	24	C5
COUNTY RD 63	GLE	25	A5
COUNTY RD 63	YOL	32	D4
COUNTY RD 64	GLE	24	E5
COUNTY RD 65A	GLE	24	E5
COUNTY RD 65B	GLE	24	C5
COUNTY RD 65C	GLE	24	C5
COUNTY RD 66A	GLE	24	D5
COUNTY RD 66B	GLE	24	E5
COUNTY RD 67	GLE	25	A5
COUNTY RD 68	GLE	24	D5
COUNTY RD 69	GLE	24	C5
COUNTY RD 69	GLE	25	A5
COUNTY RD 70	GLE	25	A5
COUNTY RD 70	YOL	32	D4
COUNTY RD 71	GLE	24	D5
COUNTY RD 71	YOL	32	D4
COUNTY RD 75A	YOL	32	D4
COUNTY RD 76	YOL	32	D5
COUNTY RD 78	YOL	32	D5
COUNTY RD 78A	YOL	32	D5
COUNTY RD 79	YOL	32	E5
COUNTY RD 79A	YOL	32	E5
COUNTY RD 79B	YOL	32	E5
COUNTY RD 80	YOL	32	E5
COUNTY RD 81	YOL	32	E5
COUNTY RD 82	YOL	32	E5
COUNTY RD 82B	YOL	32	E5
COUNTY RD 84A	YOL	32	E4
COUNTY RD 84B	YOL	32	E4
COUNTY RD 85	YOL	32	E5
COUNTY RD 85B	YOL	32	E5
COUNTY RD 86	YOL	32	E4
COUNTY RD 86A	YOL	33	A5
COUNTY RD 87	YOL	33	A5
COUNTY RD 87B	YOL	33	A5
COUNTY RD 88	YOL	33	A4
COUNTY RD 88A	YOL	33	A5
COUNTY RD 88B	YOL	33	A5
COUNTY RD 89	YOL	33	A4
COUNTY RD 90	YOL	39	A1
COUNTY RD 90A	YOL	33	A5
COUNTY RD 91	YOL	33	A5
COUNTY RD 91A	YOL	39	A1
COUNTY RD 91B	YOL	33	A4
COUNTY RD 92	YOL	33	B4
COUNTY RD 92B	YOL	33	A4
COUNTY RD 92C	YOL	33	B5
COUNTY RD 92D	YOL	33	B5
COUNTY RD 92F	YOL	39	B1
COUNTY RD 93	YOL	33	B5
COUNTY RD 93A	YOL	33	B4
COUNTY RD 93B	YOL	33	B4
COUNTY RD 94	YOL	33	B4
COUNTY RD 94A	YOL	33	B5
COUNTY RD 94B	YOL	33	B5
COUNTY RD 95	YOL	33	B4
COUNTY RD 95A	YOL	39	B1
COUNTY RD 96	YOL	33	B5
COUNTY RD 96B	YOL	33	B5
COUNTY RD 97	YOL	33	B5
COUNTY RD 97D	YOL	39	B1
COUNTY RD 98	YOL	33	B5
COUNTY RD 99	YOL	33	B5
COUNTY RD 99E	YOL	33	C5
COUNTY RD 100	YOL	33	C5
COUNTY RD 101	YOL	33	C5
COUNTY RD 101A	YOL	39	C1
COUNTY RD 102	YOL	33	C5
COUNTY RD 102B	YOL	33	C5
COUNTY RD 103	YOL	33	C5
COUNTY RD 104	YOL	39	C1
COUNTY RD 105	YOL	39	C2
COUNTY RD 106	YOL	39	C2
COUNTY RD 107	YOL	33	C5
COUNTY RD 107A	YOL	33	D4
COUNTY RD 108	YOL	33	B4
COUNTY RD 116	YOL	33	C4
COUNTY RD 119	YOL	33	D5
COUNTY RD 122	YOL	33	D5
COUNTY RD 124	YOL	33	D5
COUNTY RD 152	YOL	39	C2
COUNTY RD 155	YOL	39	C2
COUNTY RD 126	YOL	33	D5
COUNTY RD 128A	YOL	39	D1
COUNTY RD 200	GLE	24	D3
COUNTY RD 303	GLE	24	B4
COUNTY RD 304	GLE	24	B4
COUNTY RD 307	GLE	24	A3
COUNTY RD 310	GLE	23	E4
COUNTY RD 314	GLE	24	B3
COUNTY RD 315	GLE	24	A3
COUNTY RD 400	GLE	24	B5
COUNTY HOSP RD	PLU	26	C1
COUNTY LINE RD	KER	68	B5
CO LINE RD E	TRI	17	E2
CO LINE RD E	TRI	17	E2
CO LINE CK RD	TRI	16	E3
COURCHEVEL RD	PLA	35	D2
COURSE RD	KER	78	B4
COURT ST	RED	122	B2
COURTLAND RD N	YOL	39	D2
COURTLANDT CT	KER	79	C4
COUTOLENC RD	BUT	25	D2
COVE AV	FRCO	58	B4
COVE RD	SBD	91	E4
COVE RD	SHA	13	A5
COVELL BL	DVS	136	B2
COVELO RD	MEN	23	A3
COVELO RD	MEN	22	E4
COVELO REFUS RD	MEN	23	A2
COVERT RD	STA	47	C2
COVINA BLVD	LACO	R	E3
COWBOY CNTRY TR	RCO	107	B1
COWBOY JOE RD	LAS	21	D5
COW CAMP RD	BUT	25	E2
COW CAMP RD	MNO	43	C3
COW CREEK RD S	SHA	18	E2
COW CREEK RD S	SHA	19	A2
COWEL RD	CC	38	E5
COW GULCH RD	SHA	17	D3
COW HAVEN CY RD	KER	80	B1
COW MTN ACCESS	MEN	31	B2
COX AV	SCL	P	A4
COX AV	SCL	45	E5
COX LN	BUT	25	D5
COX RD	IMP	109	A3
COX RD	SJCO	40	C4
COX RD	SHA	18	B3
COX RD	STA	47	B3
COX ST	RCO	99	C4
COXCOMB TR	SBD	102	C1
COXEY	SBD	91	D4
COX FERRY RD	MCO	48	B3
COYOTE RD	MCO	56	B1
COYOTE RD	SBD	101	A2
COYOTE #1 RD	IMP	111	C4
COYOTE #2 RD	IMP	111	C4
COYOTE CYN RD	INY	71	D4
COYOTE CYN RD	RCO	107	C1
COYOTE GAP RD	BUT	25	E2
COYOTE LAKE RD	SBD	82	B5
COYOTE RES RD	SCL	P	E5
COYOTE SPGS RD	MNO	43	C4
COYOTE VLY RD	INY	51	C4
COYOTE VLY RD	SBD	93	A5
COYOTE VLY RES	LAS	14	A5
COZZI AV	MCO	56	A1
CRABTREE RD	LAS	8	D4
CRABTREE RD	STA	48	B2
CRAFTON AV	SBD	99	D2
CRAIG	SJCO	47	C1
CRAIG AV	SON	132	B3
CRAIG AV	TEH	18	E5
CRAIG RD	SUT	33	B1
CRAMER	PLA	34	B3
CRAM GULCH RD	SIS	4	B5
CRANE AV	MCO	47	D4
CRANE RD	STA	47	D2
CRANE CANYON RD	SON	38	A2
CRANE FLAT	MPA	63	B5
CRANE FLAT RD	MPA	49	C2
CRANE VALLEY RD	MAD	49	E5
CRANMORE RD	SUT	33	B3
CRANMORE RD	SUT	33	B4
CRANNELL RD	HUM	9	E4
CRANNELL RD	HUM	10	A4
CRATER RD	SBD	93	E3
CRATER HILL RD	PLA	34	B3
CRAWFORD AV	FRCO	58	A4
CRAWFORD RD	CLO	32	E2
CRAWFORD RD	MEN	23	A2
CRAWFORD RD	STA	47	D2
CRAY CROFT RDG	SIE	26	D4
CRAZY HORSE CYN	MON	54	D3
CREED RD	SOL	39	B3
CREEK RD	MCO	55	D2
CREEK RD	RED	122	A4
CREEK RD	VEN	88	B4
CREEKSIDE CT	KER	79	C4
CREEKSIDE LN	STA	47	E2
CREIGHTON DR	SHA	13	D3
CRENSHAW BLVD	LACO	97	D3
CRENSHAW BLVD	LACO	Q	D5
CRENSHAW BLVD	LACO	S	B2
CREOLE MINE RD	SBD	92	E4
CRESCENT AV	AVLN	105	B5
C RESERVOIR RD	MOD	6	D4
CRESSEY WY	MCO	48	A4
CRESSMAN RD	FRCO	58	B1
CREST DR	RCO	99	B2
CREST RD	LACO	S	B2
CRESTLINE RD	SDCO	107	A2
CRESTON RD	SLO	76	B1
CRESTON EUREKA	SLO	76	B2
CRESTN ODONOVAN	SLO	76	C2
CRESTVIEW DR	MNO	51	D2
CRESTVIEW ST	KER	80	C1
CREWS RD	SCL	54	D2
CRIPE RD	FRCO	58	A1
CRIPPEN AV	SBD	91	A3
CRIPPLE CK RD	SLO	76	B2
CRISPIN RD	MEN	30	C3
CRISS RD	SIS	4	E3
CRISS RD	SIS	5	A3
CRISTIANITOS RD	SDCO	105	E1
CRISWELL AV	MCO	55	E1
CROCKER RD	SJCO	46	E1
CROCKER SPGS RD	KER	77	D4
CRONESE LAKE RD	SBD	82	E4
CRONESE LAKE RD	SBD	83	A4
CROOKED MDW RD	MNO	50	E1
CROSBY RD	HUM	15	D2
CROSBY ST	SD	216	A5
CROSBY HAROLD	PLA	34	B3
CROSS RD	COL	32	E3
CROSS RD	MON	65	C4
CROSS CYNS RD	SLO	66	B5
CROSS CTRVILLE	MEN	31	B1
CROSS CNTRY RD	MON	66	B4
CROUCH AV	BUT	25	A3
CROW RD	STA	47	E2
CROW CANYON RD	ALA	M	A5
CROW CANYON RD	ALA	45	E2
CROWDER	PLA	33	E5
CROWDER FLAT RD	MOD	6	E5
CROWLEY RD	SUT	33	C3
CROWLEY LAKE DR	MNO	51	A3
CROWLEY LAKE PL	MNO	51	A2
CROWLY LK DM RD	MNO	51	B2
CROWN RD	MCO	48	C4
CROWN & PICKLE	SBD	92	D5
CROWN POINT RD	BUT	25	C2
CROWN VLY PKWY	ORA	98	D5
CROWN VALLEY RD	LACO	89	E4
CROWS LANDNG RD	MDO	162	C5
CROWS LANDNG RD	STA	47	C4
CROWS LANDNG RD	STA	162	C5
CROY RD	SCL	P	C5
CROY RD	SCL	54	C1
CRUCERO RD	SBD	83	A5
CRUCERO RD	SBD	93	B1
CRUICKSHANK RD	IMP	112	B3
CRUMP LN	FRCO	66	B3
CRUZON GRADE RD	NEV	26	C5
CRYSTAL AV	MOH	96	A3
CRYSTAL CK RD	SHA	18	A2
CRYSTAL SPGS AV	SBR	144	A4
CRYSTAL SPGS DR	LA	182	C1
CRYSTAL SPGS DR	LACO	Q	E3
CRYSTAL SPGS RD	KLAM	5	C1
CRYSTAL SPGS RD	SMCO	N	C2
CRYSTAL SPGS RD	SMCO	45	C3
CUDA DR	KER	78	E4
CUDDEBACK RD	SBD	80	E3
CUDDEBACK RD	SBD	81	A3
CUDDY VALLEY RD	KER	88	C1
CUDDY VALLEY RD	KER	88	C2
CUFF RD	IMP	109	B2
CUIN RD	IMP	108	E5
CULL CANYON RD	ALA	M	A5
CULL CANYON RD	ALA	45	E2
CULLEN AV	SCL	P	E5
CULVER BLVD	CUL	183	C5
CULVER BLVD	CUL	188	A3
CULVER BLVD	LA	183	C5
CULVER BLVD	LA	188	A3
CULVER BLVD	LACO	97	C5
CULVER BLVD	LACO	187	D5
CULVER DR	ORA	98	C4
CULVER DR	ORA	T	E4
CUMMINGS RD	HUM	15	E1
CUMMINGS RD	VEN	88	B5
CUMMINGS SKYWAY	CC	38	D4
CUMMINGS VLY RD	KER	79	B4
CUNEO RD	MPA	48	E1

INDEXES

251
CUNNINGHAM LN
STREET INDEX
DURHAM RD

STREET	CO.	PAGE	GRID
CUNNINGHAM LN	MNO	42	E1
CUNNINGHAM RD	CAL	41	C3
CUNNINGHAM RD	MCO	48	D5
CUNNINGHAM RD	MEN	31	B2
CURLEW ST	SD	215	D1
CURRAN RD	AMA	40	D3
CURREY RD	SOL	39	B1
CURRIE RD	SOL	39	C4
CURRIER RD	BUT	25	C4
CURRY AV	SJCO	40	B4
CURTIS ST	SM	145	B3
CURTIS ST W	SAL	171	C2
CURTNER AV	SCL	P	B4
CURTNER AV	SCL	46	B5
CUSTER AV	FRCO	56	B2
CUSTER AV	SBD	91	E4
CUTCA TRUCK TR	RCO	106	E1
CUTLER AV	GLE	24	E3
CUT OFF RD	LAS	21	C3
CUTOFF RD	MEN	23	C5
CUTTING	CC	38	C5
CUTTING AV	GLE	24	E3
CUTTING BLVD	CC	L	C3
CUTTING BLVD	R	155	A4
CUTTING WHRF RD	NAPA	L	C1
CUTTNGS WHRF RD	NAPA	38	C3
CUYAMA ST	SB	87	D1
CYA RD	MPA	49	A3
CYPRESS AV	LACO	R	E3
CYPRESS AV	SHA	18	C2
CYPRESS AV	SUT	33	D3
CYPRESS RD	CC	M	D3
CYPRESS RD	CC	39	C5
CYPRESS RD	MCO	56	A1
CYPRESS RD	SBD	80	E1
CYPRESS ST	C	124	C4
CYPRESS ST	LACO	98	B2
CYPRESS MTN DR	SLO	75	D1
CYPRUS AV	U	123	B2
CYRMIC RD	KER	77	D3
CYRUS CANYON RD	KER	79	D1
D			
D ST	MAR	L	B3
D ST	MDO	162	C4
D ST	ONT	203	D4
D ST	SR	139	C4
D ST	SON	L	A1
D ST	SON	38	A3
DAGGETT YERMO	SBD	92	A1
DAGNINO RD	ALA	M	C5
DAGNINO RD	ALA	46	C2
DAHLIN RD	SJCO	47	C1
DAHLSTROM RD	COL	32	E3
DAILEY RD	KER	79	C2
DAINTY AV	CC	M	D3
DAINTY AV	CC	39	C5
DAIRY AV	LACO	S	D1
DAIRY LN	MCO	56	A1
DAIRY RD	BUT	25	A3
DAIRY RD	KER	78	A3
DAIRY RD	STA	47	B2
DAIRY RD	YUB	33	E3
DAIRY MART RD	SDCO	V	C5
DAIRY MART RD	SDCO	111	D2
DAKIN RD	LAS	21	C4
DAKOTA AV	FRCO	57	C5
DAKOTA AV	FRCO	56	E3
DAKOTA AV	STA	47	C2
DALBY	PLA	33	E3
DALE LN	SHA	18	B3
DALE RD	KER	79	B4
DALE RD	STA	47	C2
DALE RD	TEH	24	E2
DALE TR	SBD	101	E1
DALE VISTA RD	SBD	101	E1
DALLY RD	SOL	39	B3
DALTON AV	ALA	M	D5
DALTON AV	ALA	46	C2
DALY ST	LA	186	D1
DAMIEN AV	LACO	98	C1
DANA DR	SHA	18	C2
DANA FOOTHLL RD	SLO	76	C5
DANBY RD	SBD	101	D1
DANENBERG RD	IMP	112	B3
DANIELS AV	VAL	134	A3
DANLEY LATERAL	COL	32	C1
DANLEY RD	COL	32	D1
DAN MCNAMARA RD	MCO	48	A5
DANTES VIEW	INY	72	B1
DANVILLE BLVD	CC	M	A4
DANVILLE BLVD	CC	45	E1
DARBY RD	BUT	25	E5
DARBY RD	CAL	41	C3
DARGATE RD	KER	77	E2
DARK CANYON RD	BUT	25	D3
DARLING RD	LACO	89	D4
DARLING RDG RD	ED	34	E4
DARMS LN	NAPA	38	C2
DARRAH RD	MPA	49	B3
DATE ST	SB	86	C1
DATE PALM DR	RCO	100	D4
DATONI RD	YUB	33	D2
DAUBENBERGER RD	STA	47	E3
DAULTON RD	MAD	56	B1
DAULTON RD	MAD	57	B1
DA VALL DR	RCO	100	D3
DAVENPORT RD	LACO	89	D4
DAVEY GLEN RD	SM	145	C4
DAVID AV	MONT	53	C3
DAVID AV	MONT	167	B3
DAVID AV	PAC	167	B3
DAVID RD	KER	78	E5

STREET	CO.	PAGE	GRID
DAVIDSON	FRCO	56	B2
DAVIDSON RD	HUM	9	E2
DAVIDSON RD	HUM	10	A2
DAVIS AV	FRCO	57	A5
DAVIS AV	FRCO	57	C5
DAVIS AV	KER	78	B1
DAVIS RD	BUT	25	B5
DAVIS RD	IMP	109	A2
DAVIS RD	KER	76	E1
DAVIS RD	MON	54	C4
DAVIS RD	MON	171	A4
DAVIS RD	RCO	99	D3
DAVIS RD	SJCO	40	A4
DAVIS RD	SIS	4	C4
DAVIS RD	SIS	5	B4
DAVIS RD	STA	47	C4
DAVIS RD	STA	48	B3
DAVIS RD	SUT	33	B2
DAVIS ST	ALA	L	D5
DAVIS ST	ALA	45	D2
DAVIS ST	LAK	32	A3
DAVIS CK CEM RD	MOD	7	C4
DVS CK TRNS STA	MOD	7	C4
DAWN RD	KER	89	E1
DAWN RD	KER	90	A1
DAWSON RD	RCO	99	C3
DAWSON RANCH RD	MNO	51	D2
DAY AV	SHA	19	E1
DAY RD	MOD	13	E3
DAY RD	SCL	54	C1
DAY RD	SHA	13	E3
DAY ST	RCO	99	C3
DAY RD	SCL	P	E5
DAYLIGHT PASS	INY	61	E4
DAYLIGHT PS CTO	INY	61	E3
DAYTON RD	BUT	25	B3
DAYTON WEST RD	BUT	25	B3
DEAD HRSE CY RD	SIS	13	B3
DEAD INDIAN RD	JKSN	4	A1
DEADMAN CK RD	MNO	50	D2
DEAD MANS GULCH	MON	65	E4
DEADWOOD RD	BUT	25	D3
DEADWOOD RD	PLA	35	A2
DEADWOOD RD	TRI	17	E1
DEADWOOD LO RD	SIS	3	D4
DEALWOOD RD	IMP	109	B5
DEAN CREEK RD	HUM	16	C5
DE ANGELIS RD	MCO	47	D4
DE ANZA BLVD	CPTO	149	D4
DE ANZA DR	RCO	99	E3
DEARBORN RD	IMP	111	E3
DEARDORFF RD	CAL	41	B2
DEARWOOD DR	MEN	31	B2
DEATH VALLEY RD	INY	52	B5
DEAVER AV	KER	70	A5
DECPTION CYN RD	RCO	100	E3
DECKER AV	SBD	92	E5
DECKER RD	SUT	33	B2
DECORD DR	LACO	89	A4
DECOTO RD	ALA	P	A1
DECOTO RD	ALA	45	E3
DEE KNOCH RD	SHA	13	E4
DEEP CREEK RD	MOD	8	D1
DEEP CREEK RD	SBD	91	C5
DEEP SPRINGS RD	SBD	84	A3
DEEP SPGS RANCH	INY	52	B4
DEEP WELL RD	MCO	55	E1
DEER WY	RCO	100	B5
DEER CREEK AV	TUL	68	B5
DEER CREEK RD	SBD	91	C4
DEER CREEK RD	VEN	96	D2
DEER FLAT RD	SHA	19	C2
DEERHORN VLY RD	SDCO	112	B1
DEER LICK KNOB	TRI	17	D2
DEER LICK SPGS	TRI	17	D3
DEER MTN RD	SIS	4	D5
DEER PARK RD	BUT	26	A3
DEER PARK RD	NAPA	29	B2
DEER PARK RD	NAPA	38	B1
DEER SPRING RD	MNO	51	B2
DEER VALLEY	ED	34	C5
DEER VALLEY RD	CC	M	C3
DEER VALLEY RD	CC	39	C5
DEER VALLEY RD	CC	46	C1
DEETZ RD	SIS	12	C2
DEFENDER GRADE	AMA	41	B2
DEFRAIN BLVD	RCO	103	D5
DE HARVEY ST	KER	78	D4
DEHESA RD	SDCO	107	A5
DE LA CRUZ BL	SCL	P	B3
DE LA CRUZ BL	SCLR	151	C2
DE LA GUERRA ST	STB	174	D3
DEL AMO BLVD	LACO	98	A3
DEL AMO BLVD	LACO	S	D2
DE LA VINA ST	STB	174	B3
DELAWARE AV	SC	169	A5
DELAWARE RD	STA	47	E2
DELAWARE ST	SM	N	C1
DELCERRO BLVD	SDCO	V	C3
DELCERRO BLVD	SDCO	111	D1
DEL DIOS HWY	SDCO	106	D4
DELEVAN RD	COL	32	D1
DELFATTI LN	KLAM	5	B1
DELFERN RD	KER	77	D2
DELFIND RD	KER	77	D2
DELHI RD	SOL	39	C2
DELIMA RD	SJCO	47	A1
DEL MAR AV	LACO	R	C4
DEL MAR AV	VAL	134	D3
DEL MAR BLVD	PAS	190	C4
DEL MAR HTS RD	SDCO	106	C4
DEL MAR HTS RD	SDCO	V	A1
DEL MONTE AV	SUT	33	C4
DEL MONTE BLVD	MONT	167	B1

STREET	CO.	PAGE	GRID
DEL NORTE AV	FRCO	57	A4
DEL NORTE DR	TEH	18	C4
DEL NORTE ST	EUR	121	B2
DEL OBISPO ST	ORA	98	D5
DEL OBISPO ST	ORA	202	B4
DEL OBISPO ST	SJC	202	C2
DEL ORO RD	SBD	91	C4
DEL ORTO RD	CAL	40	E3
DEL ORTO RD	CAL	41	A3
DEL PASO RD	SAC	33	D5
DELPHOS RD	CLO	32	D2
DEL PUERTO AV	STA	47	C3
DEL PUERTO CYN	STA	46	E4
DEL PUERTO CYN	STA	47	A3
DEL REY AV	FRCO	57	E3
DEL REY AV	FRCO	57	E5
DEL ROSA AV	SBD	99	C1
DELTA AV	SJCO	46	E1
DELTA AV	SJCO	47	A1
DELTA RD	CC	M	D3
DELTA RD	CC	39	C5
DELTA RD	MCO	55	E1
DE LUZ RD	SDCO	106	B1
DEMAREE RD	TUL	68	B1
DEMAREST MNE RD	CAL	41	A4
DEMPSEY RD	SCL	P	B2
DENISE AV	KER	80	A5
DENNETT ST	PAC	167	B2
DENNISON RD	KER	79	D4
DENNY RD	TRI	10	E5
DENNY RD	TRI	11	A4
DENTON RD	MCO	56	A1
DENTON RD	STA	48	A2
DENTN & LEAK RD	MCO	56	B1
DENVER AV	FRCO	56	E4
DENVER AV	KIN	57	E5
DENVERTON RD	SOL	39	B3
DE PORTOLA RD	RCO	99	E5
DEPOT AV	SB	86	C1
DEPOT RD	ALA	146	B5
DEPOT RD	H	146	B5
DEPOT ST	SMA	173	B3
DERBY ST	B	156	B3
DERRICK BLVD	FRCO	66	C2
DERRICK RD	BUT	25	D4
DERRICK RD	IMP	111	E3
DERRICK RD	LAS	14	B3
DERRICK FT RD N	TRI	11	E3
DERRICK FT RD N	TRI	12	A3
DERRICK FT RD S	TRI	12	A3
DERSCH RD	SHA	18	C3
DESCANSO AV	AVLN	105	B5
DESCHUTES RD	SHA	18	D2
DESERT RD	IMP	112	D3
DESERT CTR RICE	RCO	102	C4
DESERT INN RD	CLK	209	C5
DESERT INN RD	CLK	210	C1
DESERT SHORS DR	IMP	108	C1
DESERT VIEW AV	SBD	91	D4
DESERT WILLW TR	SBD	100	D2
DESEVADO RD	SIS	4	C3
DE SOTO AV	LA	177	D3
DE SOTO AV	LACO	177	D4
DESSIE DR	LAK	31	C3
DETLOW RD	BUT	25	D3
DETOUR RD	GLE	24	D3
DETWEILER RD	MPA	48	D2
DEVILS CORRL RD	LAS	20	D3
DEVILS DEN RD	KIN	67	B5
DEVOE RD	SUT	33	C4
DEVONSHIRE BLVD	LACO	97	C1
DEVORE FRWY	SBD	99	A1
DEVORE RD	SBD	99	B1
DEVOSE DR	LAS	8	A4
DE VRIES	SJCO	40	A4
DEWITT RD	STA	47	D2
DE WOLF AV	FRCO	57	D2
DE WOLF AV	FRCO	57	D5
DE WOLF AV	SB	86	B3
DE 1 FIRST ST	COL	32	D1
DIABLO RD	CC	M	B4
DIABLO RD	CC	46	A1
DIABLO MINE RD	INY	51	C3
DIABLO MINE RD	MNO	51	C3
DIABLO OASIS DR	RCO	100	C3
DIAGONAL 7	MAD	56	C3
DIAGONAL 11	MAD	56	D1
DIAGONAL 232	TUL	68	D4
DIAGONAL 252	TUL	68	D3
DIAGONAL 254	TUL	68	D3
DIAMOND RD	ED	138	C5
DIAMOND BAR BL	LACO	98	C2
DIAMOND BAR BL	LACO	U	B3
DIAMOND MTN RD	PLU	20	E4
DIAMOND VLY RD	ALP	36	C4
DIAZ LN	INY	51	D4
DIAZ ST	KER	80	A4
DICK COOK	PLA	34	B4
DICKERMAN RD	IMP	109	B4
DICKINSON AV	FRCO	57	B4
DICKINSON AV	FRCO	67	B1
DICKNSN FRRY RD	MCO	48	B5
DIDO AV	SBD	92	A3
DIEHL RD	IMP	111	E3
DIEHL RD	STA	47	C4
DIENSTAG RD	STA	48	A2
DIERSSEN RD	SAC	39	E3
DIETRICH	SJCO	40	C5
DIETRICH RD	IMP	109	B4
DIGGER RAVNE RD	PLU	26	C1
DI GIORGIO RD	KER	78	D3
DI GIORGIO RD	KER	79	A3
DILLARD RD	SAC	40	B2
DILLION RD	SIS	10	D1

STREET	CO.	PAGE	GRID
DILLON RD	HUM	15	D2
DILLON RD	RCO	100	E3
DILLON RD	RCO	100	C3
DILLON BEACH RD	MAR	37	D3
DINKELSPIEL RD	SOL	39	B4
DINKEY CREEK RD	FRCO	58	B1
DINKY AV	KER	89	B1
DINUBA AV	FRCO	56	E4
DINUBA AV	FRCO	57	C4
DINUBA AV	FRCO	58	A4
DIPS RD	TRI	17	B3
DIRKS RD	COL	24	D5
DISCH RD	SJCO	40	C4
DISTELRATH DR	DN	1	D3
DISTRICT CTR DR	BUT	25	D5
DITCH RD	KER	78	A5
DITCH RD	SIE	26	C4
DITCH CREEK RD	SIS	4	A3
DIVISADERO ST	FRE	165	B3
DIVISADERO ST	SF	142	A2
DIVISION ST	LACO	89	E2
DIVISION ST	SDCO	V	C4
DIVISION ST	SDCO	111	D1
DIVISION ST	SLO	76	B5
DIVISION CK RD	INY	59	E2
DIXIE RD	BUT	25	D2
DIXIE RD	SBD	91	D1
DXIE CYN RND VY	PLU	20	C5
DIXIE VALLEY RD	LAS	14	D4
DIXON AV E	SOL	39	B2
DIXON AV W	SOL	39	B2
DIXON LN	INY	51	D4
DIXON HILL RD	YUB	26	A5
DIXON MINE RD	ALP	42	C1
DOBBINS ST	KER	70	A5
DOBIE LN	MEN	23	B3
DOBIE MEADOWS	MNO	43	D4
DOBIE MEADOWS	MNO	43	E4
DOBIE MEADOWS	MNO	44	A4
DOBSON RD	SBD	81	E4
DODDS	SJCO	40	C5
DODDS	SJCO	47	C1
DODDS RD	STA	47	C4
DODGE RD	COL	24	E5
DODGE RDG LP RD	TUO	42	A3
DOE MILL RD	BUT	25	C2
DOERKSEN RD	STA	47	E3
DOG BAR RD	NEV	34	C2
DOG CREEK RD	SHA	12	B4
DOGGIE TR	SBD	101	A2
DOGTOWN RD	CAL	41	B4
DOGTOWN RD	MPA	48	E2
DOGTOWN RD	MPA	49	A2
DOG VALLEY RD	SIE	27	E5
DOGWOOD DR	EC	217	E4
DOGWOOD RD	ALP	36	A5
DOGWOOD RD	IMP	109	A5
DOGWOOD RD	IMP	112	A4
DOHENY DR	BH	183	D2
DOHENY DR	LA	183	D2
DOHENY DR	LACO	Q	D4
DOHENY PARK RD	ORA	202	C4
DOLAN RD	MON	54	B3
DOLAN HARDNG RD	YUB	34	A1
DOLLARHIDE RD	NAPA	38	C1
DOLORES ST	SF	142	C5
DOLPHIN AV	KER	80	C1
DOLPHIN DR	IMP	108	C2
DOME AV	TUL	68	D3
DOME ST	SB	86	D1
DOMINION RD	SB	86	C1
DOMINO CT	KER	79	B4
DON RD	SBD	101	D1
DONAHUE RD	SUT	33	C4
DONKIN RD	STA	47	B3
DONLON,JAMES BL	CC	M	C3
DONNER PASS RD	NEV	27	B5
DONOVAN RD	SMA	173	A2
DON PEDRO RD	STA	47	C3
DONS RD	MOD	8	B2
DOOLITTLE DR	A	159	A3
DOOLITTLE DR	ALA	L	D5
DOOLITTLE DR	ALA	45	D2
DOOLITTLE DR	O	159	C3
DOOLITTLE CK RD	SIS	2	E3
DOON GRADE	BUT	25	D2
DORA RD	SUT	33	B2
DORA ST	U	123	C3
DORAN SCENIC DR	SBD	82	A5
DORFF LN	HUM	15	D2
DORIS AV	VEN	96	B1
DORNES RD	PLA	34	A3
DORRETT DR	BUT	25	C2
DORRIS AV	FRCO	66	E2
DORRIS BROWNELL	SIS	5	B3
DORRIS TEHNER	SIS	5	A3
DORSEY RD	STA	47	D1
DOS CABEZA RD	IMP	111	B3
DOSE RD	TRI	10	E5
DOS PALMAS RD	SBD	90	E4
DOS REIS RD	SJCO	47	A1
DOS RIOS DR	SBD	90	E3
DOS RIOS LN	STA	47	B3
DOS RIOS RD	BUT	25	C5
DOSTER RD	CAL	41	A3
DOTTA LN	PLU	27	D3
DOTTA GUIDCI RD	PLU	27	D2
DOTY RD	SHA	13	D5
DOUBLE SPGS RD	CAL	40	E3
DOUGHERTY RD	CC	M	B4
DOUGHERTY RD	CC	46	B1
DOUGHERTY RD	SUT	33	C3
DOUGLAS	KIN	67	D1
DOUGLAS AV	FRCO	56	C4

STREET	CO.	PAGE	GRID
DOUGLAS AV	SB	86	B3
DOUGLAS LN	SBD	100	E1
DOUGLAS RD	SAC	40	B1
DOUGLAS ST	ELS	189	D3
DOUGLAS RGR STA	MAD	49	E5
DOVE	SJCO	47	D1
DOVER AV	FRFD	135	D3
DOVER AV	KIN	67	E1
DOVER DR	NB	199	C4
DOVER DR	ORA	T	C4
DOVER CANYON RD	SLO	75	E1
DOVE SPG CYN RD	KER	80	A2
DOW BUTTE RD	LAS	20	D1
DOW BUTTE LO RD	LAS	20	D1
DOWD RD	PLA	34	A3
DOWD RD	PLA	33	E4
DOWD CAMP RD	PLA	34	A3
DOWDEN RD	IMP	109	B3
DOWER AV	FRCO	57	B3
DOWER AV	FRCO	57	B5
DOW FLAT RD	LAS	20	D1
DOWNEY AV	LACO	S	E1
DOWNEY RD	INY	73	A4
DOWNEY RD	LACO	R	A4
DOWNEY ST	MDO	162	C3
DOWNIE RD	STA	47	E3
DOWNIE RD	STA	48	A3
DOWS PRAIRIE RD	HUM	9	E4
DOYLE DR	SF	141	D1
DOYLE GRADE	LAS	27	D1
DOYLE RD	MCO	47	C5
DOYLE RANCH RD	KER	69	E5
DOYLE RANCH RD	KER	79	E1
DRAIN 10 RD	SIS	5	E2
DRAIS AV	SJCO	40	C5
DRAKE AV	COL	32	E3
DRAKE RD	HUM	15	E2
DRAPER RD	STA	47	C4
DRAPER RD	TEH	18	C3
DREDGR CP MORGN	TRI	17	C1
DRESSER AV	KER	78	A2
DREW RD	IMP	111	E3
DREXLER	SUT	33	B2
DRIVE 212	TUL	58	C5
DRIVE 244	TUL	68	D2
DRIVE 254	TUL	58	D4
DRIVER AV	LACO	97	A1
DRIVER RD	KER	68	C5
DRIVER RD	KER	78	C1
DRIVER RD	KER	78	C2
DROBISH RD	BUT	25	E5
DROGE	SJCO	47	C1
DRUM CANYON RD	SB	86	D3
DRUMMOND AV	KER	80	C1
DRY CREEK RD	LAK	32	A5
DRY CREEK RD	MCO	48	B3
DRY CREEK RD	MNO	50	D2
DRY CREEK RD	NAPA	29	C4
DRY CREEK RD	NAPA	38	B2
DRY CREEK RD	PLA	34	C3
DRY CREEK RD	SJCO	40	B3
DRY CREEK RD	SLO	76	B1
DRY CREEK RD	SHA	18	D2
DRY CREEK RD	SIS	4	B3
DRY CREEK RD	SON	31	C5
DRY CREEK RD	TUL	58	D5
DRY CREEK RD W	SON	31	D5
DRY CREEK RD W	SON	37	D1
DRY CK BASIN RD	MOD	8	C1
DRY CK CMP GRND	LAS	8	B3
DRY CREEK CTOFF	MNO	50	D2
DRYDEN AV	SCL	P	E5
DRY GENESEO RD	SLO	76	B1
DRY SLOUGH RD	COL	33	A3
DRYTOWN AMADOR- -VIA BUNKERHILL	AMA	40	E2
DU BOIS ST	SR	139	D4
DUBOIS TK TR	SDCO	107	B5
DUCK CREEK RD	AMA	40	C3
DUCK LAKE RD	LAS	21	E4
DUDLEY RD	MON	65	D3
DUFAU	VEN	96	C1
DUGGANS RD	NEV	34	C2
DUMETZ RD	LA	177	C5
DUMP RD	HUM	16	B3
DUMP RD	INY	60	A3
DUMP RD	LAK	31	D2
DUNAWAY RD	IMP	111	D3
DUNAWEAL LN	NAPA	29	A2
DUNBAR LN	SDCO	107	A5
DUNCAN RD	SBD	90	E4
DUNCAN RD	SJCO	40	C5
DUNCAN ST	KER	78	E4
DUNCAN CYN RD	SBD	99	A1
DUNCAN CREEK RD	SHA	17	E3
DUNDERBURG MDW	MNO	43	B4
DUNE RD	SBD	92	B1
DUNES RD	CLK	210	B2
DUNFORD RD	KER	78	A3
DUNLAP DR	RCO	99	C3
DUNLAP RD	FRCO	58	C3
DUNLAP RD	KER	69	B5
DUNN LN	CAL	41	B5
DUNN RD	MCO	48	C4
DUNN RD	STA	47	B2
DUNNE AV	SCL	P	D5
DUNNE AV E	SCL	P	D5
DUNSTONE DR	BUT	25	D5
DUNTON RD	STA	40	E5
DUPONT RD	RCO	102	D5
DURANT AV	B	156	A3
DURFEE AV	LACO	R	C4
DURHAM RD	ALA	P	B2
DURHAM RD	SIS	5	A3

STREET	CO.	PAGE	GRID
DURHAM DAYTN HY	BUT	25	B3
DURHAM FERRY RD	SJCO	47	A2
DURKEE RD	LAS	14	A3
DURNEL RD	BUT	25	B4
DUSTIN RD	SJCO	40	B4
DUSTIN AKERS RD	KER	78	A4
DUSTY LN	STA	47	D2
DUSTY WY	TEH	18	D5
DUSTY MILE RD	SBD	92	D5
DUTCH CREEK RD	SIS	3	E3
DUTCH CREEK RD	TRI	17	C2
DUTCHER CK RD	SON	31	C5
DUTCH MINE RD	TUO	41	C5
DUTTON AV	SON	131	C4
DUTTON AV N	STR	131	B3
DUVALL ST	KER	78	A4
DUZEL CREEK RD	SIS	3	E5
DUZEL CREEK RD	SIS	11	E1
DUZEL RCK LO RD	SIS	3	E5
DUZEL RCK LO RD	SIS	11	E1
DWIGHT WY	MCO	48	A4
DWINNELL WY	SIS	4	C5
DWINNELL WY	SIS	12	C1
DYE RD	SDCO	107	A4
DYER DR	PLU	20	C4
DYER LN	PLA	33	E5
DYER RD	ORA	T	D3
DYER ST	ALA	N	E1
DYER ST	ALA	P	A1
DYER ST	ALA	45	E3
DYERVILLE LOOP	HUM	16	B4
DYERVILLE LP RD	HUM	16	C4
DYSERT RD	SIS	4	E3
DYSON LN	PLU	27	C3
E			
E ST	DVS	136	D3
E ST	EUR	121	C1
E ST	FRE	165	C4
E ST	H	146	E2
E ST	SCTO	137	C2
E ST	SBDO	207	C4
E ST	SBD	99	B2
E ST	SDCO	V	C4
E ST	SDCO	111	D2
E ST	YUB	33	D2
EABY RD	SBD	90	E4
EADY RD	IMP	112	A4
EAGER RD	SUT	33	C2
EAGLE AV	FRCO	56	A2
EAGLE BORAX WLL	INY	72	A2
EAGLE CK LP RD	TRI	11	E3
EAGLE CK LP RD	TRI	12	A3
EAGLE FIELD RD	MCO	55	E2
EAGLE LAKE RD	NEV	27	A5
EAGLE MTN RD	RCO	102	B4
EAGLE PK LKOUT	TEH	24	A2
EAGLE ROCK BLVD	LACO	R	A3
EAGLE ROCK RD	TRI	17	A1
EAGLE RCK LKOUT	SIS	4	D3
EAGLES NEST RD	MNO	43	A4
EAGLES NEST RD	SAC	40	B2
EAGLEVL DUMP RD	MOD	8	E2
EAGLEVILLE LOOP	MOD	8	E2
EARDLEY AV	PAC	167	C2
EARHART RD	O	159	D4
EARLHAM ST	SDCO	107	A4
EARP RD	COL	33	A2
EAST AV	ALA	M	D5
EAST AV	ALA	46	C2
EAST AV	BUT	25	B3
EAST AV	BUT	124	B1
EAST AV	C	124	A1
EAST AV	FRCO	57	C5
EAST AV	MCO	48	A3
EAST AV	TEH	24	D2
EAST LN	MEN	23	B3
EAST RD	LACO	R	E5
EAST ST	ANA	193	D1
EAST ST	AUB	126	C3
EAST ST	ORA	T	D2
EAST ST	RED	122	B1
EASTBLUFF DR	NB	200	A3
EAST END AV	SBD	98	D2
EAST END RD	SBD	92	A4
EASTERN AV	LACO	98	A2
EASTERN AV	LACO	R	B5
EAST FORK RD	SHA	18	A1
EAST FORK RD	TRI	11	B5
EAST FORK RD	TRI	17	C3
EAST FORK RD	TRI	12	A4
EAST GRADE RD	SDCO	107	A2
EAST GRADE RD	TRI	16	E2
E FK HAYFORD RD	TRI	17	C3
E FK INDIAN CK	SHA	2	E3
E FK STUART CPG	TRI	11	E5
EASTIN RD	STA	47	C5
EAST LEVEE RD	SAC	M	D2
EASTMAN RD	STA	40	D5
EASTMAN RD	STA	47	D1
EASTMONT RD	KER	78	E2
EASTSHORE FRWY	ELC	155	D3
EASTSHORE FRWY	R	155	D3
EASTSHORE FRWY	SP	155	D3
EASTSHORE RD	SHA	18	B2
EAST SIDE	PLU	20	D5
EASTSIDE LN	MNO	42	E1
EASTSIDE RD	INY	51	D4
EASTSIDE RD	MEN	23	A5
EAST SIDE RD	MEN	31	B2
EASTSIDE RD	MNO	42	E1
EASTSIDE RD	RED	122	B4
EASTSIDE RD	SHA	18	C2

STREET	CO.	PAGE	GRID
EASTSIDE RD	SHA	18	C3
EASTSIDE RD	SIS	3	D5
EASTSIDE RD	SIS	11	D1
EAST SIDE RD	TRI	12	A4
E SIDE CALPELLA	MEN	31	B2
E SDE PORTR VLY	MEN	31	B1
E SDE REDWD VLY	MEN	31	B1
EAST WEST RD	SIS	5	D2
EASY ST	KER	79	C4
EASY ST	SHA	18	D2
EATON RD	BUT	25	B3
EATON RD	STA	47	E1
EBERLE RD	KER	78	C4
ECHO PARK AV	LA	185	E1
ECHO PARK AV	LA	186	A1
ECHO VALLEY RD	MON	54	C3
EDDINS RD	IMP	109	A3
EDDY RD	COL	33	A3
EDDY RD	LPAZ	104	A2
EDDY ST	SF	143	B5
EDDY GULCH RD	SIS	11	B2
EDDY GLH LKOUT	SIS	11	B3
EDEN PLAINS RD	CC	M	D3
EDGAR AV	BUT	25	B3
EDGEMONT ST	LA	182	B5
EDGER RD	IMP	108	E5
EDGEWATER BLVD	FCTY	145	D2
EDGEWATER RD	SMCO	N	C2
EDGEWOOD AV	MAR	L	A4
EDGEWOOD AV	MAR	45	B1
EDGEWOOD RD	SMCO	45	D3
EDGEWOOD RD	SIS	12	C1
EDGEWD BIG SPGS	SIS	12	C1
EDINGER AV	ORA	98	B4
EDINGER AV	ORA	T	B3
EDINGER AV	SA	196	A5
EDINGER AV	SA	197	C1
EDINGER AV	SA	198	A1
EDINGER ST	FTNV	195	C5
EDINGER ST	SA	195	C5
EDISON AV	SBD	98	D2
EDISON BLVD	BUR	179	B3
EDISON HWY	KER	78	E3
EDISON HWY	KER	79	A3
EDISON AV	SBD	U	D3
EDISON RD	KER	78	E3
EDISON ST	SB	86	E3
EDITH AV	TEH	24	D2
EDMINSTER RD	MCO	47	D4
EDMUNDSON AV	SCL	P	D5
EDMUNDSON AV	SCL	54	C1
EDNA RD	SLO	172	D5
ED POWERS RD	INY	51	C4
ED RAU RD	SAC	39	E2
EDSEL LN	STA	47	C2
EDWARD ST	KER	79	B5
EDWARDS	SJCO	47	D1
EDWARDS ST	ORA	T	B3
EEL RIVER RD	MEN	23	B5
EEL RIVER RD	MEN	31	C1
EEL ROCK RD	HUM	16	C4
EGAN RD	TUO	41	C5
EGGERT RD	SOL	39	C2
EHRLICH RD	STA	47	C3
EICKHOFF RD	LAK	31	D2
EIGHMY RD	TEH	18	C4
EIGHTH ST	C	124	C5
EIGHT MILE RD	SJCO	39	E4
EIGHT MILE RD	SJCO	40	A4
EISENHOWER DR	RCO	100	E5
EISENHOWER ST	FRFD	135	D3
ELBERTA ST	KER	89	E1
EL CAJON BLVD	SD	214	A5
EL CAJON BLVD	SDCO	V	D3
EL CAJON BLVD	SDCO	111	D1
EL CAMINO AV	SAC	40	A1
EL CAMINO DR	SHA	18	C3
EL CAMINO RD	SBD	101	D1
EL CAMINO CIELO	SB	87	C4
EL CAMINO REAL	BLMT	145	C4
EL CAMINO REAL	BURL	144	B3
EL CAMINO REAL	MP	147	A2
EL CAMINO REAL	MLBR	144	C4
EL CAMINO REAL	MON	54	D4
EL CAMINO REAL	MON	65	A1
EL CAMINO REAL	MON	66	A5
EL CAMINO REAL	MON	171	B1
EL CAMINO REAL	MVW	148	B5
EL CAMINO REAL	ORA	105	E1
EL CAMINO REAL	PA	147	B3
EL CAMINO REAL	SAL	171	D3
EL CAMINO REAL	SBT	54	D2
EL CAMINO REAL	SBR	144	B3
EL CAMINO REAL	SDCO	106	B3
EL CAMINO REAL	SNLO	172	A4
EL CAMINO REAL	SLO	66	A5
EL CAMINO REAL	SLO	76	B2
EL CAMINO REAL	SLO	172	E1
EL CAMINO REAL	SM	145	A3
EL CAMINO REAL	SMCO	N	D2
EL CAMINO REAL	SMCO	45	C3
EL CAMINO REAL	STB	173	D5
EL CAMINO REAL	SB	86	C1
EL CAMINO REAL	SCL	P	A3
EL CAMINO REAL	SCLR	150	B2
EL CAMINO REAL	SCLR	151	A2
EL CAMINO REAL	SCL	46	A4
EL CAMINO REAL	SCL	54	D2
EL CAMINO REAL	SMA	173	C1
EL CAMINO REAL	SSF	144	B3
EL CAMINO REAL	SVL	150	B2
EL CAMPO RD	MCO	55	E2
EL CAMPO RD	RCO	100	C5
EL CAMPO RD	SLO	76	B5

STREET	CO.	PAGE	GRID
EL CAPITAN WY	MCO	47	E4
EL CAPITAN WY	MCO	48	A3
EL CAPTN SCH RD	MCO	48	B5
EL CARISO TK TR	RCO	99	B4
EL CENTRO AV	NAPA	38	C3
EL CENTRO BLVD	SUT	33	D3
EL CENTRO RD	SAC	33	D5
EL CENTRO ST	IMP	111	E3
EL CERRITO RD	RCO	98	E3
EL CERRO BLVD	CC	M	A4
EL CIELITO RD	STB	174	D1
EL CIELO DR	RCO	100	D3
EL CIELO RD	PMSP	206	E5
EL CONQUISTA RD	RCO	107	A1
ELDER AV	KIN	67	B1
ELDER CREEK RD	RCO	107	B1
ELDER CREEK RD	SAC	40	A1
EL DIABLO RD	SBD	92	E5
EL DORADO AV	FRCO	56	E4
EL DORADO AV	FRCO	66	E2
EL DORADO AV	S	160	C1
EL DORADO DR	RCO	100	C3
EL DORADO DR	SBD	102	C1
EL DORADO ST	AUB	126	D3
EL DORADO ST	FRE	165	C3
EL DORADO ST	MONT	167	E4
EL DORADO ST	SJCO	40	A5
EL DRDO HLLS RD	ED	34	C5
EL DORADO MN RD	RCO	101	C2
ELDRIDGE RD	LAS	14	A5
ELEANOR AV	STA	47	D2
ELEVADO AV	BH	183	A2
ELEVADO RD	SBD	91	B3
ELDER ST	SDCO	106	C2
ELDER CREEK RD	SAC	39	E1
ELECTRA RD	AMA	41	A3
ELEVATOR RD	SOL	39	D3
ELFERS RD	STA	47	B3
ELGIN	MCO	56	B1
ELGIN AV	KIN	67	B1
ELHOLM RD	MCO	47	C5
ELINOR RD N	HUM	16	A3
ELINOR RD S	HUM	16	A3
ELIZA GULCH RD	SIS	3	E4
ELIZABETH LK RD	LACO	89	C3
ELZBTH LK P CYN	LACO	89	B2
ELK	MCO	48	A4
ELK AV	BUT	25	B3
ELK CT	KER	79	B4
ELK CREEK RD	HUM	16	B4
ELK CREEK RD	SIS	3	A4
ELK GROVE BLVD	SAC	39	E2
ELK GROVE BLVD	SAC	40	A2
ELK GRV FLRN RD	SAC	39	E2
ELK GRV FLRN RD	SAC	40	A2
ELK HILLS RD	KER	77	E3
ELK HILLS RD	KER	78	A3
ELKHORN AV	FRCO	56	D5
ELKHORN AV	FRCO	57	D5
ELKHORN BLVD	SAC	33	D5
ELKHORN RD	MEN	31	A4
ELKHORN RD	MON	54	C3
ELKHORN GRAD RD	KER	78	A5
ELKHORN GRADE	FRCO	57	B5
ELK MOUNTAIN RD	LAK	23	C5
ELK MOUNTAIN RD	LAK	31	C1
ELK RIVER RD	HUM	121	A5
ELK RIVER RD	HUM	15	E1
ELK VALLEY RD	DN	1	D4
ELK VALLEY RD	SIS	10	D1
ELK VLY CRSS RD	DN	1	E4
ELLA AV	YUB	33	D2
ELLA RICHTER RD	SHA	18	A3
ELLENA ST	FRCO	57	B5
ELLEN SPGS DR	LAK	32	A4
ELLENWOOD DR	STA	47	E2
ELLENWOOD RD	STA	48	A2
ELLER LN	SIS	3	D5
ELLER LN	SIS	11	D1
ELLIOT	SJCO	40	B3
ELLIOT AV	MCO	48	B4
ELLIOT ST	SBD	93	B2
ELLIOT RCH RD	PLA	34	E2
ELLIOTT RD	BUT	25	C3
ELLIOTT CK RD	SIS	3	B2
ELLIOTT RCH RD	SAC	39	E2
ELLIS AV	RCO	99	C4
ELLIS RD	AMA	41	C1
ELLIS RD	YUB	33	D2
ELLIS ST	SF	143	B5
ELLSWORTH ST	B	156	A3
ELM AV	FRCO	57	C4
ELM AV	MON	65	B1
ELM AV	SBR	144	B3
ELM AV	SDCO	106	B3
ELM ST	BKD	166	B2
ELM ST	RCO	99	C5
ELM ST	SDCO	107	A4
ELM ST	TUL	68	B3
EL MARGARITA RD	SUT	33	C2
EL MEDIO RD	SBD	90	E3
ELMER AV	SUT	33	C2
ELMER ST	RCO	99	B4
ELMIRA RD	SOL	39	A2
EL MIRAGE RD	SBD	90	E3
EL MIRAGE RD	SBD	91	A3
ELMO HWY	KER	78	A1
EL MONTE AV	LACO	R	D3
EL MONTE AV	TUL	58	A4
EL MONTE RD	SCL	N	E3
EL MONTE RD	SCL	45	E4
ELNA RD	INY	59	E1
EL NIDO RD	MCO	48	C5
EL NORTE PKWY	SDCO	106	D3

STREET	CO.	PAGE	GRID
ELORDY LN	SUT	33	E4
EL PASTA RD	RCO	107	A1
EL POMAR AV	STA	47	E2
EL POMAR DR	SLO	76	A2
EL POMAR RD	SLO	76	B2
EL POMAR RO RD	SLO	76	B2
EL PORTAL	CC	38	C5
EL POZO GRADE	SLO	76	D3
EL RANCHO DR	KER	79	C4
EL REPOSO RD	RCO	107	A1
EL RIO DR	TUL	68	C1
EL ROBLAR	VEN	88	A4
EL ROBLAR ST	SB	87	E1
EL SEGUNDO BLVD	ELS	189	D4
EL SEGUNDO BLVD	LACO	97	D3
EL SEGUNDO BLVD	LACO	Q	D5
EL SEGUNDO BLVD	LACO	S	C1
EL SERENO RD	MCO	55	C2
EL SOBRANTE RD	RCO	99	B3
EL TEJON HWY	KER	78	E4
EL TEJON HWY	KER	79	A4
EL TORO DR	BKD	166	C5
EL TORO RD	ORA	98	D5
ELVAS FRWY	SCTO	137	E2
ELVERTA RD	SAC	33	D5
EL VICINO AV	MDO	162	D2
ELWOOD RD	FRCO	58	B3
ELY RD	SON	L	A1
ELY RD	SUT	33	C4
ELYSIAN VLY RD	LAS	21	A4
EMBARCADRO, THE	SF	143	B2
EMBARCADERO RD	PA	147	C2
EMBARCADERO RD	SCL	N	E2
EMBRCDRO SKYWAY	SF	143	D3
EMERALD AV	RCO	100	E3
EMERALD AV	STA	47	C2
EMERALD DR	SDCO	106	C3
EMERALD RD	SBD	91	E4
EMERSON RD	MOD	8	D2
EMERSON RD	TEH	18	D4
EMERY RD	STA	47	E2
EMERY RD	STA	48	A2
EMIGH RD	SOL	39	C4
EMIGRANT RD	PLU	26	D1
EMIGRANT TR	SHA	19	B3
EMMERT RD	COL	33	A3
EMMIGRANT TR	ALP	36	B4
EMPIRE	CC	39	C5
EMPIRE AV	BUR	179	B2
EMPIRE AV	CC	M	D3
EMPIRE ST	GV	127	B4
EMPIRE ST	NEV	127	C4
EMPIRE CREEK RD	SIS	3	E3
EMPIRE GRADE	SCR	N	E5
EMPIRE GRADE	SCR	53	D1
EMPIRE MINE RD	CC	M	C3
EMPIRE MINE RD	CC	39	B5
ENCHNTD FRST RD	RCO	100	A4
ENCINAL	MON	54	D4
ENCINAL AV	ALA	L	D5
ENCINAL AV	ALA	45	D1
ENCINAL RD	SUT	33	C1
ENCINITAS BLVD	SDCO	106	C4
ENCINITAS RD	SDCO	106	C3
END RD W	HUM	10	A5
ENDERTS BCH RD	DN	1	E4
ENGLEHART AV	FRCO	58	A4
ENGLISH RD	IMP	109	A3
ENGLISH COLONY	PLA	34	B4
ENGLISH HILLS	SOL	39	A2
ENNIS RD	FRCO	58	C3
ENNIS RD	SUT	33	B2
ENOS LN	KER	78	B3
ENSLEY RD	SUT	33	C4
ENTERPRISE	SJCO	47	D1
ENTERPRISE RD	BUT	25	E4
ENTERPRISE ST	TUL	68	A3
ERBES RD	VEN	96	E1
EREISTIN DR	SBD	92	D5
ERHIT RD	TUO	48	E1
ERHIT RD	TUO	49	A1
ERICKSON RD	BUT	25	B4
ERLE RD	MCO	48	E5
ERNST	MPA	48	E2
ERNST	MPA	49	A2
ERRECA RD	MCO	48	A5
ERRINGER RD	VEN	88	E5
ERRINGER RD	VEN	89	A5
ERRINGER RD	VEN	96	E1
ERRINGER RD	VEN	97	A1
ERSKINE RD	IMP	108	E5
ERSKINE CK RD	KER	79	D1
ERTESZEK DR	KER	79	C4
ERWIN ST	LA	178	C3
ESCALON BELLOTA	SJCO	40	C5
ESCALON BELLOTA	SJCO	47	C1
ESCHINGER RD	SAC	39	E2
ESCHINGER RD	SAC	40	A2
ESCOBAR ST	M	154	A2
ESCOLLE RD	MON	54	D5
ESCONDIDO AV	SDCO	106	C3
ESCONDIDO FRWY	RCO	99	C3
ESCONDIDO FRWY	SD	216	D3
ESCONDIDO FRWY	SDCO	106	D2
ESCONDIDO RD	LACO	89	D4
ESMERALDA RD	CAL	41	B4
ESPERANZA AV	RCO	100	B3
ESPERANZA RD	MON	54	D4
ESPERANZA RD	SIS	13	A2
ESPINOSA RD	MON	54	C3
ESPINOSA RD	MON	65	B1
ESPLANADE	BUT	25	A2
ESPLANADE AV	RCO	99	D4
ESPLANADE, THE	C	124	B3

STREET	CO.	PAGE	GRID
ESPOLA RD	SDCO	106	D4
ESQUON RD	BUT	25	B4
ESSEX LN	HUM	10	A5
ESSEX RD	SBD	94	D2
ESTHER AV	MCO	56	B2
ESTRELLA RD	SLO	66	A5
ESTRELLA RD	SLO	76	B1
ESTUDILLO AV	ALA	L	E5
ETHANAC RD	RCO	99	C4
ETHEREDGE ST	KER	68	D5
ETIWANDA AV	SBD	98	E2
ETTERBG HONEYDW	HUM	16	A5
ETTING RD	VEN	96	C1
ETZEL RD	SOL	39	C2
EUCALYPTUS AV	MCO	48	A4
EUCALYPTUS AV	RCO	99	C3
EUCALYPTUS AV	SBD	U	E3
EUCALYPTUS AV	SBD	98	E2
EUCALYPTUS AV	STA	47	B3
EUCALYPTUS RD	BUT	25	B5
EUCALYPTUS RD	MCO	56	A2
EUCALYPTUS ST	AVLN	105	B5
EUCALYPTUS ST	SBD	91	B4
EUCLID AV	ALA	L	D4
EUCLID AV	ONT	204	B4
EUCLID AV	SBD	U	D3
EUCLID AV	SBD	98	D2
EUCLID AV	SDCO	V	C3
EUCLID AV	SDCO	111	D1
EUCLID AV	SF	141	E3
EUCLID AV	STA	47	E3
EUCLID AV	UPL	204	B1
EUCLID ST	FTNV	197	A3
EUCLID ST	GGR	195	A3
EUCLID ST	ORA	98	B3
EUCLID ST	ORA	T	C2
EUCLID ST	SA	195	A5
EUREKA RD	PLA	34	B5
EUREKA RD S	INY	52	D5
EUREKA WY	RED	122	B1
EUREKA WY	SHA	18	C2
EUREKA CYN RD	SCR	P	C5
EUREKA CYN RD	SCR	54	B1
EUREKA HILL RD	MEN	30	C3
EUREKA MINE RD	SIE	26	C4
EUREKA VLY RD	INY	52	C4
EUROPE AV	KER	79	D5
EVAN HEWES HWY	IMP	111	D3
EVAN HEWES HWY	IMP	112	D3
EVANS	TUL	68	D1
EVANS AV	FRCO	56	B2
EVANS RD	COL	32	D2
EVANS RD	RCO	107	C1
EVANS RD	SIS	4	E3
EVANS REIMER RD	BUT	25	B5
EVELYN AV	MVW	148	B4
EVELYN AV	SCL	P	A3
EVELYN AV	SVL	148	E5
EVELYN AV	SVL	150	A1
EVERETT AV	KIN	67	C1
EVERETT ST	KER	80	D1
EVERETT MEM HWY	SIS	12	C2
EVERGLADE	SUT	33	C3
EVERGREEN RD	CAL	40	D4
EVERGREEN RD	TEH	18	C4
EVERGREEN RD	TUO	42	B5
EVERGREEN RD	TUO	63	A3
EVERITT RD	SUT	33	C2
EXCELSIOR AV	FRCO	66	E1
EXCELSIOR AV	FRCO	67	C1
EXCELSIOR AV	KIN	67	D1
EXCELSIOR RD	SAC	40	A2
EXCELSIOR MN RD	SBD	73	D5
EXCELSIOR MN RD	SBD	83	D1
EXCELSIOR PT RD	NEV	34	E1
EXCHEQUER	MPA	48	D3
EXCHEQUER RD	FRCO	58	C1
EXCHEQUER DAM	MPA	48	D3
EXP MINE RD	TUO	41	C4
EXPOSITION BLVD	LA	184	C5
EXPOSITION BLVD	LA	185	C5
EXPOSITION BLVD	LACO	97	D2
EXPOSITION BLVD	LACO	Q	D4
EXPOSITION BLVD	SAC	39	E1
F			
F ST	DVS	136	D2
F ST	EUR	121	D3
F ST	FRE	165	C4
F ST	HUM	15	E1
F ST	SBD	99	B1
F ST	SDCO	V	C4
F ST	SDCO	111	D2
FABRY RD	MON	55	B5
FAHEY RD	MCO	55	C1
FAIR ST	BUT	25	B3
FAIR ST	BUT	124	E5
FAIRBANKS RD	MEN	23	B3
FAIRCHILD LN	SJCO	40	B5
FAIRFAX	FRCO	56	B3
FAIRFAX AV	KIN	67	C1
FAIRFAX AV	LA	181	A4
FAIRFAX AV	LA	184	A3
FAIRFAX AV	LACO	Q	D4
FAIRFAX AV	LACO	181	A4
FAIRFAX RD	KER	78	E3
FAIRFAX BOLINAS	MAR	38	A5
FAIRFIELD AV	FRFD	135	B3
FAIRFIELD AV	SBD	91	C3
FAIRFIELD ST	EUR	121	B3
FAIRGROUND DR	NAPA	L	D1
FAIRGROUNDS DR	VAL	134	E2
FAIRHAVEN AV	OR	196	C2

253
FAIRHAVEN AV STREET INDEX FULTON ST

STREET	CO.	PAGE	GRID
FAIRHAVEN AV	ORA	T	E2
FAIRHAVEN AV	SA	196	C2
FAIRLANE RD	SBD	92	A4
FAIRMEAD BLVD	MAD	56	E1
FAIRMONT AV	SDCO	V	C3
FAIRMONT AV	SDCO	111	D1
FAIRMONT AV E	MDO	162	D1
FAIRMONT RD	LACO	89	C2
FAIRMOUNT AV	SD	214	E5
FAIRMOUNT AV	SD	216	E1
FAIROAKS AV	LACO	R	B2
FAIR OAKS AV	LACO	190	B2
FAIR OAKS AV	PAS	190	B4
FAIR OAKS AV	SCL	45	E4
FAIR OAKS AV	SCL	46	A4
FAIR OAKS AV	SVL	149	E1
FAIR OAKS BLVD	SAC	40	A1
FAIR OAKS BLVD	SAC	34	A5
FAIR PLAY RD	ED	41	A1
FAIRVIEW AV	ALA	P	A1
FAIRVIEW AV	CC	M	D3
FAIRVIEW AV	CC	39	C5
FAIRVIEW AV	RCO	100	A4
FAIRVIEW AV	SB	87	B4
FAIRVIEW RD	COL	32	D1
FAIRVIEW RD	CM	199	C1
FAIRVIEW RD	MON	54	E5
FAIRVIEW RD	ORA	98	C4
FAIRVIEW RD	ORA	T	C4
FAIRVIEW RD	SBT	54	E2
FAIRVIEW RD	SBT	55	A2
FAIRVIEW RD	SBD	92	C1
FAIRVIEW RD	VEN	88	B4
FAIRWAY DR	CLTN	207	B5
FAIRWAY DR	EUR	121	C5
FAIRWAY PL	SB	86	E3
FAITH HOME RD	MCO	47	D4
FAITH HOME RD	STA	47	D3
FALL RD	INY	70	B2
FALLBROOK AV	LA	177	A4
FALL CREEK RD	SIS	4	C2
FALLEN LEAF RD	ED	35	E3
FALLING LEAF RD	SHA	18	C2
FALLON RD	SBT	54	E2
FALLON RD	SBT	55	A2
FALL RIVER RD	SHA	13	E4
FALLS CYN RD	AVLN	105	A5
FAMOSO HWY	KER	78	A1
FAMOSO-PRTVL HY	KER	78	C1
FANDANGO PSS RD	MOD	7	C3
FANNING	SJCO	40	B5
FANOE RD	MON	54	E5
FARGO AV	KIN	67	C1
FARGO CANYON RD	RCO	101	B4
FARINA ST	RCO	100	A5
FARLEY MINE RD	SBD	91	D3
FARMER RANCH RD	TRI	17	B2
FARMERSVILLE RD	TUL	68	C2
FARM HILL BLVD	SMCO	N	D2
FARM HILL BLVD	SMCO	45	D4
FARMLAN RD	SUT	33	B2
FARMLAND AV	MCO	48	C4
FARNHAM RDG RD	ED	41	A1
FARQUHAR RD	TEH	18	B4
FARRIS DR	CAL	40	D4
FARRIS RD	BUT	25	B5
FARRIS RD	BUT	33	B1
FASIG RD	SUT	33	B3
FAUST RD	STA	47	C2
FAWCETT RD	IMP	112	A3
FAWN LODGE RD	TRI	17	D1
FAXON RD	COL	33	B3
FAY LN	SIS	11	D1
FAY RD	MCO	47	D4
FAY RANCH RD	KER	69	E5
FAY RANCH RD	KER	79	E1
FAY RIDGE RD	KER	78	C1
FEATHER LAKE HY	LAS	20	A2
FEATHER LAKE HY	LAS	20	D3
FEATHER LAKE RD	SHA	19	E1
FEATHER RIV BL	YUB	33	D3
FEDERAL BLVD	SDCO	V	C3
FEDERAL BLVD	SDCO	111	D1
FEE RD	MOD	7	D3
FEENSTRA RD	SLO	76	B2
FEE RESRVOIR RD	MOD	7	D3
FELCIANA MTN RD	MPA	49	B3
FELDMILLER RD	TRI	16	E3
FELDSPAR AV	KER	80	D1
FELICITA RD	SDCO	106	D3
FELIZ CREEK RD	MEN	31	B3
FELL ST	SFCO	L	B5
FELL ST	SF	141	E4
FELL ST	SF	142	B4
FELL ST	SFCO	45	B1
FELLOWSHIP RD	STB	174	A5
FELTER RD	SCL	46	B4
FELTN EMPIRE RD	SCR	N	E5
FELTON EMPRE RD	SCR	53	E1
FENDERS FERRY	SHA	13	A5
FENSLER RD	SIS	5	D2
FENTEM RD	MCO	47	C5
FERGUSON RD	IMP	110	E4
FERN RD	SHA	19	A2
FERN RD E	SHA	19	A1
FERN ST	SD	216	B3
FERN ST	SDCO	V	C3
FERN ST	SDCO	111	D1
FERN CANYON DR	MEN	31	B2
FERNDALE DMP RD	HUM	15	D2
FERRELL RD	IMP	112	A4
FERRETTI RD	TUO	41	D5
FERRETTI RD	TUO	48	D1
FERRY RD	TEH	18	D4

STREET	CO.	PAGE	GRID
FERRY RD E	HUM	15	E2
FESLER ST	SMA	173	B2
FICKLE HILL RD	HUM	10	A5
FIDDLETOWN RD	AMA	40	E2
FIDLTWN QTZ MTN	AMA	40	E1
FIDLTWN SHNDOAH	AMA	40	E1
FIDDLTWN SLV LK	AMA	41	A1
FIDDYMENT	PLA	33	E4
FIELD RD	SBD	82	C5
FIELDBROOK RD	HUM	10	A4
FIELDS RD	MCO	48	C3
FIELDS RD	RCO	100	A3
FIELDS RIDGE RD	BUT	26	B4
FIESTA ISLND RD	SD	212	E4
FIFIELD RD	IMP	109	B4
FIFIELD RD	SUT	33	D4
FIFTH AV	C	124	B3
FIFTH ST	C	124	B5
FIG AV	FRE	165	C5
FIG AV	FRCO	57	C4
FIG AV	FRCO	57	C5
FIG AV	STA	47	C3
FIGMOND AV	MCO	48	C3
FIG TREE LN	SHA	18	C3
FIGUEROA ST	LA	185	D5
FIGUEROA ST	LA	191	B1
FIGUEROA ST	LACO	R	A3
FIGUEROA ST	LACO	S	C2
FIGUEROA ST	MONT	167	E3
FIGUEROA MTN RD	SB	87	B2
FILBURN ST	KER	78	A1
FILIPPINI RD	SIE	27	C3
FILLMAN RD	LAS	8	A4
FILLMORE ST	RCO	101	B5
FILLMORE ST	SF	142	B2
FILLY LN	CAL	41	B5
FIMPLE RD	BUT	25	B3
FINCK RD	SJCO	46	E1
FINE AV	SJCO	40	C5
FINE AV	STA	47	D2
FINK RD	STA	47	C4
FINKS RD	COL	32	D1
FINLEY LN	LAS	14	C3
FINNEL AV	TEH	24	D1
FINNEY RD	IMP	109	B5
FINNEY RD	STA	47	C2
FINNING HILL RD	PLA	34	E2
FIR ST	C	124	E4
FIR ST	RCO	100	C4
FIRE CAMP RD	BUT	25	E4
FIRESTONE	FRCO	66	C3
FIRESTONE BLVD	LACO	97	E2
FIRESTONE BLVD	LACO	R	A5
FIRETHORN RD	SBD	92	B3
FIRST AV	C	124	B3
FIRST AV	STA	47	C3
FIRST AV E	C	124	D3
FIRST ST	SIS	12	D3
FISCHER RD	IMP	111	E4
FISH & GAME RD	LAS	21	C3
FISHER AV	KER	89	C1
FISHER DR	TUL	68	C1
FISHER RD	HUM	15	E2
FISHER RD	IMP	110	D5
FISHER RD	LPAZ	104	A2
FISHER RD	MCO	48	B4
FISHER RD	TRI	10	E5
FISHERS LANDING	YUMA	110	E4
FISH HATCHRY RD	INY	59	E3
FISH ROCK RD	MEN	31	A4
FISH ROCK RD	MEN	30	D4
FISH SLOUGH RD	MNO	51	D2
FISH SPRINGS RD	INY	59	E1
FISKE	MPA	48	E1
FISKE	MPA	49	A1
FITCH MTN RD	SON	37	D1
FITZGERALD DR	BUT	25	C2
FITZGERALD RD	SCL	P	E5
FITZGERALD RD	SCL	54	D1
FITZHUGH CK RD	MOD	8	B2
FIVE BRIDGES RD	INY	51	D4
FIVE MILE RD	AMA	40	D2
FIVE MILE CK RD	TUO	41	D4
FIVE MI STA RD	SBD	95	D2
FLAMINGO RD	CLK	210	C2
FLANAGAN RD	SHA	18	C1
FLANNERY RD	SOL	39	B3
FLATTOP MTN RD	KIN	67	A4
FLEA VALLEY RD	BUT	25	D2
FLEMING AV E	VAL	134	E3
FLEMING RD	PLA	34	A3
FLETCHER DR	LACO	Q	E3
FLETCHER PKWY	SDCO	V	D3
FLETCHER PKWY	SDCO	111	E1
FLINT AV	KIN	67	C1
FLINT AV	MCO	47	E4
FLINT AV	MCO	48	A4
FLINT ST	KER	80	C5
FLOOD RD	IMP	110	D5
FLOOD RD	SJCO	40	C5
FLORADALE AV	SB	86	B3
FLORAL AV	C	124	D1
FLORAL AV	FRCO	56	D4
FLORAL AV	FRCO	57	B4
FLORENCE AV	ING	188	E5
FLORENCE AV	LACO	97	D2
FLORENCE AV	LACO	Q	D5
FLORES AV	TEH	18	D5
FLORES RD	YUB	34	A1
FLORIDA AV	RCO	99	D4
FLORIDA DR	SD	216	A2
FLORIDA ST	VAL	134	C4
FLORIN RD	SAC	40	A1
FLORIN MILL RD	SHA	13	D3

STREET	CO.	PAGE	GRID
FLORIN PERKINS	SAC	40	A2
FLOURNOY AV	TEH	24	D2
FLOWER ST	LA	185	E4
FLOWER ST	SA	196	A3
FLOWERS LN	SHA	18	C3
FLOWING WELLS	IMP	109	B3
FLOYD AV	FRCO	57	B3
FLOYD AV	STA	47	D2
FLYNN RD	INY	51	D4
FLYNN CREEK RD	MEN	30	D2
FOAM ST	MONT	167	D2
FOAM ST	MON	53	E2
FOGARTY RD	STA	47	E1
FOGARTY RD	STA	48	A1
FOGG RD	SAC	39	E2
FOLETTA RD	MON	54	D5
FOLEY AV	KER	79	D3
FOLSOM AV	FRCO	56	B2
FOLSOM BLVD	SAC	34	B5
FOLSOM BLVD	SAC	39	E1
FOLSOM BLVD	SAC	40	A1
FOLSOM BLVD	SCTO	137	E4
FONSECA RD	COL	24	E5
FONTANA AV	SBD	99	A2
FOOLISH PLSR RD	RCO	107	A1
FOOTE RD	SIE	26	C5
FOOTHILL AV	O	159	D1
FOOTHILL BLVD	ALA	146	D1
FOOTHILL BLVD	BUT	25	D4
FOOTHILL BLVD	CLA	203	C1
FOOTHILL BLVD	CPTO	149	A5
FOOTHILL BLVD	H	146	E2
FOOTHILL BLVD	LACO	89	C5
FOOTHILL BLVD	LACO	89	E5
FOOTHILL BLVD	LACO	98	B1
FOOTHILL BLVD	LACO	Q	B1
FOOTHILL BLVD	LACO	U	A1
FOOTHILL BLVD	NAP	133	B4
FOOTHILL BLVD	O	158	D3
FOOTHILL BLVD	ORA	T	E3
FOOTHILL BLVD	ROC	204	B1
FOOTHILL BLVD	SBD	99	A1
FOOTHILL BLVD	SD	212	B1
FOOTHILL BLVD	SDCO	V	A2
FOOTHILL BLVD	SDCO	106	C5
FOOTHILL BLVD	SNLO	172	A2
FOOTHILL BLVD	UPL	203	C1
FOOTHILL BLVD	UPL	204	B1
FOOTHILL DR	SBD	102	C1
FOOTHILL DR	SIS	4	A4
FOOTHILL DR	SOL	39	A2
FOOTHILL EXPWY	PA	147	C5
FOOTHILL EXPWY	SCL	N	E3
FOOTHILL EXPWY	SCL	45	E4
FOOTHILL EXPWY	SCCO	149	A4
FOOTHILL FRWY	LACO	97	D1
FOOTHILL FRWY	LACO	98	A1
FOOTHILL FRWY	LACO	R	B2
FOOTHILL FRWY	LACO	R	C3
FOOTHILL FRWY	PAS	190	B2
FOOTHILL RD	ALA	P	B1
FOOTHILL RD	ALA	46	B2
FOOTHILL RD	DGL	36	B3
FOOTHILL RD	INY	59	E3
FOOTHILL RD	MNO	51	C1
FOOTHILL RD	MON	64	E1
FOOTHILL RD	MON	65	A1
FOOTHILL RD	SBD	91	D4
FOOTHILL RD	SBD	92	A4
FOOTHILL RD	SLO	76	A3
FOOTHILL RD	STB	174	B1
FOOTHILL RD	SB	87	D1
FOOTHILL RD	SB	174	B1
FOOTHILL RD	SCL	P	E5
FOOTHILL RD	SCL	54	D1
FOOTHILL RD	TEH	18	E5
FOOTHILL RD	VEN	88	B4
FOOTHILL RD	VEN	88	B5
FOPPIANO LN	SJCO	40	B5
FORBES N	PLA	34	B3
FORBES S	PLA	34	A3
FORBES AV	SR	139	C3
FORBES RANCH RD	RCO	100	C4
FORBESTOWN RD	BUT	25	E4
FORBESTOWN RD	BUT	26	A4
FRBSTOWN RES RD	BUT	26	A4
FORD RD	NB	200	B3
FORD ST	RCO	100	E3
FORD ST	SBD	99	C2
FORDYCE LAKE RD	NEV	27	B5
FOREMAN CIR RD	BUT	25	D4
FOREST	MPA	49	D3
FOREST AV	MONT	53	D2
FOREST AV	PAC	167	C3
FOREST BLVD	KER	80	B4
FOREST CIR	BUT	25	C2
FOREST DR	BUT	25	C2
FOREST RD	CAR	168	C4
FOREST TR	ML	164	B1
FOREST HOME BL	SBD	99	E2
FORST HM CRBNDL	AMA	40	D2
FOREST HOUSE	SIS	3	E4
FOREST LAKE	SJCO	40	A3
FOREST LAWN DR	LA	179	E5
FOREST LAWN DR	LA	181	C1
FOREST LAWN DR	LACO	Q	D3
FOREST RANCH RD	BUT	25	C2
FOREST RANCH WY	BUT	25	C2
FORGAY RD	PLU	20	D5
FORREST ST	BKD	166	C4
FORRESTER RD	IMP	109	A4
FORSYTHE RD	YUB	26	A5
FT BRAGG SHERWD	MEN	22	C5
FT CADY RD	SBD	92	C1

STREET	CO.	PAGE	GRID
FORT INDEPNDNCE	INY	59	E3
FORTNA RD	SUT	33	C2
FORT ROMIE RD	MON	64	E1
FORT ROMIE RD	MON	65	A1
FORT ROSS RD	SON	37	B1
FORT SAGE RD	LAS	21	E5
FORT SEWARD RD	HUM	16	C5
FORT STOCKTN DR	SD	213	B5
FORT STOCKTN DR	SDCO	V	B3
FORT STOCKTN DR	SDCO	111	C1
FORT TEJON RD	LACO	90	B3
FT TEJON CHSBRO	LACO	90	B3
FORTUNA BLVD	HUM	15	E2
FORTY MILE RD	YUB	33	D3
FORTYNINE LN	MOD	7	D5
FORTYNINE PALMS	SBD	101	B1
FORWARD RD	TEH	19	B3
FORWARDS MILL	SHA	19	C3
FOSS RD	JKSN	3	D1
FOSS HILL	SON	32	A5
FOSSIL BED RD	SBD	81	C5
FOSTER	MON	54	C4
FOSTER RD	LACO	R	B5
FOSTER RD	LACO	S	E1
FOSTER RD	LACO	T	A1
FOSTER RD	NAP	133	B5
FOSTER RD	SHA	18	B3
FOSTER RD	SIS	4	C3
FOSTER CITY BL	FCTY	145	D2
FOSTER CITY BL	SMCO	N	D1
FOSTER CITY BL	SMCO	45	D3
FOSTER MTN RD	MEN	23	B5
FOULDS RD	IMP	108	E3
FOULKE LN	SIS	4	B5
FOUNTAIN AV	LA	182	A4
FOUNTN HOUSE RD	YUB	26	B5
FOUR CORNERS RD	LAS	14	B3
FOUR MILE RD	COL	24	E5
FOUR MILE RD	COL	32	E1
FOUR MIL RDG RD	BUT	25	E3
FOURTEENTH ST	EUR	121	B2
FOURTH AV	SUT	33	D3
FOURTH ST	C	124	B5
FOUSSAT RD	SDCO	106	B3
FOUTS SPRGS RD	COL	24	A5
FOWLER AV	FRCO	57	D2
FOWLER AV	FRCO	57	D5
FOWLER RD	PLA	34	B3
FOWLER PBLC CMP	SIS	13	A2
FOX RD	LAS	21	B4
FOX RD	MCO	48	B4
FOX RD	STA	47	D2
FOX RD	SOL	39	B2
FOXEN CANYON RD	SB	86	D1
FOXWORTHY AV	SCL	P	B4
FOXWORTHY AV	SCL	46	B5
FRAGUERO RD	TUO	41	C5
FRANCESCHI RD	KER	79	D3
FRANCISCO ST	SF	143	A3
FRANCISQUITO AV	LACO	R	E4
FRANCISQITO CYN	LACO	89	C3
FRANCIS SPGS RD	SBD	83	C2
FRANCO WSTRN RD	KER	77	D3
FRANK AV	KER	70	A5
FRANK COX RD	STA	47	B3
FRANKENHEIMR RD	STA	47	E1
FRANKLIN AV	LA	181	E4
FRANKLIN AV	LA	182	A4
FRANKLIN AV	LACO	Q	E3
FRANKLIN AV	YUBA	125	C4
FRANKLIN BLVD	SAC	39	E2
FRANKLIN BLVD	SCTO	137	D5
FRANKLIN RD	MCO	48	B4
FRANKLIN RD	SBD	84	C4
FRANKLIN RD	SUT	33	B2
FRANKLIN RD	SUT	125	A4
FRANKLIN ST	MDO	162	B4
FRANKLIN ST	MONT	167	D3
FRANKLIN ST	MON	53	E3
FRANKLIN ST	SF	143	B4
FRANKLIN CYN RD	M	154	A3
FRANKLIN LEVEE	SUT	33	B2
FRANK SNATRA DR	RCO	100	D4
FRANKWOOD AV	FRCO	58	A4
FRANZ VALLEY RD	SON	38	A1
FRANZ VLY SCHL	SON	38	A1
FRASER RD	KER	78	C3
FRATES RD	SON	L	A1
FRATES RD	SON	38	A3
FRAZIER LN	MEN	23	B2
FRAZIER RD	FRCO	57	E1
FRAZIER RD	SJCO	40	C4
FRAZIER MTN RD	VEN	88	C2
FRAZR MTN PK RD	KER	88	C2
FRAZIER PK RD	SCL	54	D2
FRAZINE RD	STA	47	D2
FREDERICK AV	SJCO	47	B2
FREDERICK ST	RCO	99	C3
FREDERICKSBURG	ALP	36	C4
FREDERICKSON LN	CC	M	C3
FREDERICKSON RD	LAS	8	D5
FRED HAIGHT DR	DN	1	E3
FREDRICKS RD	IMP	109	A4
FREEBORN RD	KER	78	A3
FREEDOM BLVD	SCR	54	B2
FREEMAN FLAT RD	MON	65	C2
FREEMN SCH HSE	TEH	24	C2
FREEMONT BLVD	ALA	P	B2
FREEPORT BLVD	SCTO	137	C5
FREITAS PKWY	MAR	38	B5
FREITAS RD	STA	47	C4
FREMONT AV	KER	79	E2
FREMONT AV	KIN	67	B1
FREMONT AV	LSAL	149	B2

STREET	CO.	PAGE	GRID
FREMONT AV	LACO	R	B4
FREMONT AV	SCL	P	A3
FREMONT AV	SCL	45	E4
FREMONT AV	SVL	149	B2
FREMONT BLVD	ALA	46	A3
FREMONT DR	SON	L	B1
FREMONT RD	SBD	92	C1
FREMONT RD	SJCO	40	B5
FREMONT ST	CLK	74	D2
FREMONT ST	LV	209	D1
FREMONT ST	SBD	99	D2
FREMONT ST	SF	143	D4
FREMONT ST	S	160	A4
FREMONT PEAK RD	SBD	81	A4
FRENCH AV	BUT	33	C1
FRENCH RD	HUM	16	B5
FRENCH&SUGAR CK	SIS	11	D2
FRENCH BAR RD	AMA	40	E3
FRENCH CAMP RD	HUM	10	C3
FRENCH CAMP RD	SJCO	40	B5
FRENCH CAMP RD	SJCO	47	B1
FRENCH CREEK RD	BUT	25	E3
FRENCH CREEK RD	ED	40	D1
FRENCH CREEK RD	SIS	11	D2
FRENCH FLAT RD	TUO	41	B5
FRENCH GULCH RD	CAL	41	B4
FRENCH GULCH RD	SHA	18	A1
FRENCH HILL RD	DN	2	A3
FRENCHMAN LK RD	PLU	27	D2
FRENCHTOWN RD	YUB	26	A5
FRENZEN RD	COL	32	E3
FRESH WATER RD	COL	32	C2
FRESHWTR KNEELD	HUM	15	E1
FRESHWTR LGN RD	HUM	9	E3
FRESHWATER POOL	HUM	16	A1
FRESNO AV	KER	78	B2
FRESNO AV	KER	78	C2
FRESNO AV	SJCO	40	A5
FRESNO RD	MCO	48	D5
FRESNO ST	FRE	165	E2
FRESNO ST	FRCO	57	C3
FRESNO-COALINGA	FRCO	66	E1
FRESNO FLAT RD	MAD	49	D4
FRESZ RD	RCO	106	E1
FREWERT RD	SJCO	47	A1
FREY AV	KER	77	E2
FREY AV	KER	78	A2
FREY RANCH RD	BUT	26	B3
FRIANT RD	FRCO	57	C2
FRIANT RD	MAD	57	D2
FRIARS RD	SD	213	A4
FRIARS RD	SD	214	D2
FRIARS RD	SDCO	V	B3
FRIARS RD	SDCO	111	D1
FRIARS RD	SDCO	214	B3
FRICOT CITY RD	CAL	41	B4
FRIDAY RIDGE RD	HUM	10	C5
FRIEDRICH RD	TRI	10	E5
FRIEDRICH RD	TRI	16	E1
FRIEL RD	CLO	33	A3
FRINK RD	IMP	109	A2
FRISBY RD	SHA	19	A1
FRITZ DR	TUL	68	D1
FRONT ST	DN	1	D4
FRONT ST	LA	191	A3
FRONT ST	SAL	171	C4
FRONT ST	SF	143	D3
FRONT ST	SC	169	D3
FRONT ST	SOL	39	C4
FRONTAGE RD	CAL	40	E3
FRONTAGE RD	CAL	41	A3
FRONTIER RD	SBD	91	C2
FRUCHTENICHT RD	COL	33	B3
FRUDDEN RD	MON	65	D4
FRUIT AV	FRE	165	B2
FRUIT AV	FRCO	57	C4
FRUIT AV	FRCO	57	C5
FRUIT AV	STA	47	B3
FRUIT ST	SA	196	D3
FRUITLAND AV	MCO	48	A4
FRUITLAND RD	YUB	33	D1
FRUITRIDGE RD	SAC	39	E1
FRUITRIDGE RD	SAC	40	A1
FRUITVALE AV	ALA	L	D4
FRUITVALE AV	ALA	45	D1
FRUITVALE AV	KER	78	D3
FRUITVALE AV	O	158	E4
FRUITVALE AV	O	159	B1
FRUITVALE AV	SCL	P	A4
FRUITVALE RD	BUT	25	B4
FRUITVALE RD	PLA	34	B3
FRY RD	SOL	39	B3
FRYMIRE RD	STA	48	A1
FUENTE ST	ORA	T	C1
FUERTE DR	SDCO	V	E3
FUERTE DR	SDCO	111	E1
FUGLER RD	SB	86	C1
FULKERTH RD	STA	47	C3
FULLEN RD	CAL	41	C3
FULLER LN	AMA	40	E3
FULLER RD	INY	59	E1
FULLERTON RD	LACO	98	B2
FULLERTON RD	LACO	R	E5
FULMOR RD	HUM	15	D2
FULMOR TOPPEN	HUM	15	D2
FULTON AV	SAC	40	A1
FULTON LN	NAPA	29	C2
FULTON RD	SON	37	E2
FULTON ST	B	156	A3
FULTON ST	SF	141	D4
FULTON ST	SF	142	A3
FULTON ST	SF	143	A5
FULTON ST	SFCO	L	B5
FULTON ST	SFCO	45	B1

INDEXES

STREET	CO.	PAGE	GRID
FULTON ST	S	160	B2
FULTON ST N	FRE	165	C3
FULWEILER AV	AUB	126	B3
FURLONG AV	SCL	54	D2
FURNACE CK RD	SBD	91	E4
FURNC CK WSH RD	INY	72	C2
FURNC CK WSH RD	INY	73	A4
FUZZY LN	SHA	18	C3

G

STREET	CO.	PAGE	GRID
G ST	DVS	136	D3
G ST	FRE	165	C4
G ST	HUM	9	E5
G ST	HUM	10	A5
G ST	MER	170	D4
G ST	MCO	48	C4
G ST	MCO	48	C4
G ST	SCTO	137	C2
GABY AV	COL	32	E3
GADDINI	SOL	39	A1
GAFFERY RD	STA	47	A3
GAFFEY ST	LA	191	A5
GAFFEY ST	LACO	S	C3
GAFFNEY RD	YOL	39	D2
GAGE AV	LACO	Q	E5
GAGE RD	BUT	25	C4
GAINES LN	SHA	18	D3
GALE AV	FRCO	66	C2
GALE RD	SBD	91	E2
GALENA ST	RCO	99	A2
GALENA CYN RD	INY	72	A3
GALEPPI RD	LAS	21	C4
GALLAGHER AV	TEH	24	D2
GALLAGHER RD	SUT	33	E3
GALLATIN RD	LAS	20	E2
GALLATIN RD	TEH	18	C5
GALLAWAY RD	SIE	26	D4
GALLINAS AV	SR	139	B1
GALLOPADE TR	SBD	80	E1
GALVEZ AV	FRCO	56	B2
GAMBLE RD	MCO	48	B3
GAMMEL RD	SBD	101	C1
GANESHA BLVD	LACO	98	C2
GANESHA BLVD	LACO	U	B2
GANGER RD	SIS	5	D2
GANN RD	CAL	40	E4
GAP FOLSOM RD	CAL	41	C2
GARAPATOS RD	MON	64	B1
GARATE RD	LAS	8	C5
GARBAGE DUMP RD	LAS	14	B3
GARBAGE PIT RD	MNO	43	B3
GARBAGE PIT RD	MNO	50	D1
GARBONI RD	RCO	99	D4
GARCES HWY	KER	67	E5
GARCES HWY	KER	68	C5
GARCES HWY	KER	69	A5
GARCIA RIVER RD	MEN	30	C3
GARDEN HWY	SAC	39	D1
GARDEN HWY	SUT	33	D2
GARDEN HWY	SUT	125	D5
GARDEN HWY	YUBA	125	E4
GARDEN RD	SDCO	106	E4
GARDEN ST	STB	174	B3
GARDENA BLVD	LACO	S	C1
GARDEN BAR	PLA	34	B3
GARDEN BAR RD	NEV	34	B3
GARDENDALE ST	LACO	R	B5
GARDENDALE ST	LACO	S	E1
GARDEN GROVE BL	GGR	195	A2
GARDEN GROVE BL	OR	195	D2
GARDEN GROVE BL	ORA	98	B4
GARDEN GROVE BL	ORA	T	C2
GARDEN GROVE FY	GGR	195	B2
GARDEN GROVE FY	OR	195	B2
GARDEN GROVE FY	OR	196	C1
GARDEN GROVE FY	ORA	98	B4
GARDEN GROVE FY	ORA	T	C2
GARDEN VLY RD	ED	34	D4
GARDEN VLY RD	YUB	26	B5
GARDINER FRY RD	TEH	24	E2
GARDNER AV	MCO	48	C4
GARDNER LN	CAL	41	B4
GARDNER ST	LA	184	B1
GARDNER ST	VAL	134	B3
GARDNER FLD RD	KER	78	A4
GAREY AV	LACO	98	D2
GAREY AV	LACO	U	C3
GAREY AV	SB	86	C1
GARFIELD AV	FRCO	57	B3
GARFIELD AV	FRCO	57	B5
GARFIELD AV	LACO	98	A2
GARFIELD AV	LACO	R	B5
GARFIELD AV	LACO	S	D1
GARFIELD AV	ORA	98	B4
GARFIELD AV	ORA	T	B3
GARFIELD AV	SAC	34	A5
GARFIELD ST	RCO	101	C5
GARIN RD	MON	54	C2
GARLAND RD	BUT	25	C2
GARLOCK RD	KER	80	D2
GARMIRE RD	SUT	33	B2
GARNER LN	BUT	25	B2
GARNER PL	CAL	40	D4
GARNER RD	STA	47	D2
GARNET AV	SD	212	A1
GARNET AV	SDCO	V	A2
GARNET AV	SDCO	106	C5
GARNET ST	SBD	99	D2
GARNETT LN	SOL	39	B2
GARNIER RD	LAS	21	D5
GARRARD	CC	38	C5
GARRET	PLA	34	D2
GARRETT DR	RCO	100	A5
GARRISON AV	STA	47	C2
GARST RD	IMP	109	A3
GARST RD	STA	47	D2
GARVEY AV	LACO	98	A2
GARVEY AV	LACO	R	C4
GARVEY RD	IMP	108	E4
GARWOOD RD	SUT	33	D4
GARZOLI AV	KER	78	B1
GAS COMPANY RD	KER	78	A4
GASKELL RD	KER	89	B2
GASKELL RD	KER	89	D1
GAS LINE RD	RCO	102	B5
GASPERS RD	SHA	18	D2
GAS POINT RD	SHA	18	B3
GASQUET FLAT RD	DN	2	A3
GASTENBIDE RD	MCO	55	C2
GASTON RD	NEV	26	E5
GATES RD	STA	47	B2
GATES RD	TRI	16	D1
GATES CANYON RD	SOL	38	E2
GATES CANYON RD	SOL	39	A2
GATEWAY	CC	39	D5
GATEWAY BLVD	LA	180	D5
GATEWAY BLVD	KER	80	E1
GATEWAY RD	CC	M	D3
GATOS TR	SBD	100	E1
GAVILAN DR	RCO	99	B3
GAVIOTA	AVLN	105	A4
GAVIOTA BCH RD	SB	86	D4
GAVIOTA STA RD	SB	86	D4
GAVILAN RD	SDCO	106	C1
GAWNE CARTER RD	SJCO	40	C5
GAWNE CARTER RD	SJCO	47	C1
GAZELLE CALLAHN	SIS	4	B5
GAZELLE CALLAHN	SIS	11	E2
GAZELLE CALLAHN	SIS	12	A1
GAZELLE MTN LKT	SIS	12	A1
GAZOS CREEK RD	SMCO	N	C4
GAZOS CREEK RD	SMCO	45	C5
G-BAR-T RCH RD	MNO	44	C5
G-BAR-T RCH RD	MNO	51	C1
GEARY BLVD	SF	141	A3
GEARY BLVD	SF	142	A3
GEARY BLVD	SFCO	L	B4
GEARY BLVD	SFCO	45	B1
GEARY RD	CC	L	E3
GEARY RD	CC	M	A3
GEARY RD	CC	38	E5
GEARY ST	SF	143	A4
GEER AV	MCO	47	D4
GEER RD	STA	47	E3
GELDING RD	CAL	41	B4
GENASCI RD	SIE	27	C3
GENE AUTRY TR	PMSP	206	E2
GENERL BEALE RD	KER	79	A3
GENRL PETROLEUM	KER	79	E5
GENRL PETROLEUM	KER	80	A5
GENRL PETROLEUM	KER	89	C1
GENERALS HWY	TUL	58	E3
GENERALS HWY	TUL	59	A5
GENESEE AV	SD	211	E1
GENESEE AV	SD	213	C1
GENESEE AV	SDCO	V	B2
GENESEE AV	SDCO	106	C5
GENESEE INDN CK	PLU	26	E1
GENESEO RD	SLO	76	B1
GENEVA AV	KIN	67	C1
GENOA LN	DGL	36	B3
GENTRY RD	IMP	109	A3
GENTRY RD	INY	72	E4
GENTRY RD	INY	73	A4
GEORGE RD	IMP	112	A4
GEORGE SMITH RD	FRCO	58	B3
GEORGETOWN	ED	34	E3
GEORGETOWN RD	ED	34	E4
GEORGETOWN RD	PLCV	138	C1
GEO WSHNTN BL S	SUT	33	C3
GEORGIA LN	STA	47	E2
GEORGIA RD	SBD	81	C5
GEORGIA ST	VAL	134	C4
GEORGIA ST	SOL	L	D2
GEORGIA SLID RD	ED	34	D3
GEPHART RD	KER	80	D5
GERARD AV	MCO	48	C4
GERBER RD	SAC	40	A2
GERBER RD	TEH	18	D5
GERKIN RD	INY	51	D4
GERRIE LN	RCO	107	C1
GETTYSBURG AV	FRCO	56	C3
GETTYSBURG AV	FRCO	57	A3
GEYSERS RD	SON	31	D4
GEYSRS RESRT RD	SON	31	D4
GHOST TOWN RD	SBD	92	A1
GIANT RD	CC	L	C3
GIANT ROCK RD	SBD	92	E5
GIANT ROCK RD	SBD	93	A5
GIBRALTAR RD	SB	87	C3
GIBSON LN	MEN	23	B5
GIBSON RD	COL	32	D2
GIBSON RD	YOL	33	B5
GIBSON CYN RD	SOL	39	A2
GIDDINGS AV	TUL	68	B1
GILEOW LN	MEN	31	B2
GIFFORD RD	SUT	33	C4
GILBERT RD	STA	47	D1
GILLAM RD	CAL	40	E3
GILLESPIE RD	IMP	109	A2
GILLESPIE ST	STB	174	A4
GILLETT RD	IMP	109	B5
GILLETT RD	MON	65	C4
GILLETTE RD	KER	79	D3
GILLETTE RD	MCO	48	D5
GILLILAND RD	LAS	8	C5
GILLIS CYN RD	SLO	76	D1
GILLMAN AV	KER	89	D1
GILL RANCH RD	PLU	26	E2
GILL STA COSO	INY	70	C3
GILMAN DR	SD	211	C2
GILMAN DR	SDCO	V	A2
GILMAN DR	SDCO	106	C5
GILMAN RD	SCL	54	D2
GILMAN RD	SHA	12	D4
GILMAN SPGS RD	RCO	99	D3
GILMORE	SJCO	40	C4
GILMOR RANCH RD	TEH	18	D5
GILROY HT SP RD	SCL	54	D1
GIRARD LO RD	SHA	12	C3
GIRARD LOOKOUT	SHA	12	C3
GIRARD RIDGE RD	SHA	12	C4
GIRAUDO RD	KER	79	B4
GIRD RD	SDCO	106	C2
GIRDNER RD	SUT	33	B2
GIRVAN RD	SHA	18	C2
GISH ST	SJ	152	A2
GIVENS LUSTR RD	MCO	48	C5
GLACIER LODG RD	INY	51	D5
GLACIER PT RD	MPA	63	C5
GLADDING RD	PLA	34	A3
GLADSTONE ST	LACO	U	A2
GLASSCOCK RD	SJCO	39	E4
GLASSELL ST	OR	194	C4
GLASSELL ST	OR	196	C1
GLASSELL ST	ORA	98	C3
GLASSELL ST	ORA	T	D2
GLASS FLOW RD	MNO	50	D1
GLEASON RD	SBD	92	D5
GLEN AV	MER	170	E4
GLEN RD	SB	87	B4
GLEN ALPINE RD	ED	35	E4
GLEN ANNIE RD	SB	87	B4
GLEN ARBOR RD	SCR	N	E5
GLEN ARBOR RD	SCR	P	A5
GLEN ARBOR RD	SCR	53	E1
GLENBURN RD	SHA	13	D4
GLEN CANYON RD	SCR	54	A1
GLENCO AV	GLE	24	D3
GLENDALE AV	LACO	97	E1
GLENDALE AV	LACO	Q	E3
GLENDALE BLVD	LA	182	E3
GLENDALE BLVD	LA	185	E2
GLENDALE BLVD	LACO	Q	E3
GLENDALE DR	HUM	10	A5
GLENDALE FRWY	LACO	R	A3
GLENDORA AV	LACO	98	B2
GLENDORA AV	LACO	U	A2
GLENDORA MTN RD	LACO	98	C1
GLENDORA MTN RD	LACO	U	A1
GLENISON GAP RD	TRI	17	C1
GLENN AV	FRCO	66	E3
GLENN DR	GLE	24	A4
GLENN RD	TEH	24	C2
GLENN RD W	COL	24	D5
GLENN-ALLEN AV	KER	68	D5
GLENN COOLDG DR	SC	169	A2
GLENN COOLDG DR	SCR	169	A2
GLENNDENNING RD	SIS	3	D5
GLENOAKS BLVD	BUR	179	C1
GLENOAKS BLVD	LA	179	C1
GLENOAKS BLVD	LACO	89	D5
GLENOAKS BLVD	LACO	97	D1
GLENOAKS BLVD	LACO	Q	C1
GLENOAKS RD	RCO	99	D5
GLENSHIRE DR	NEV	27	D5
GLENWOOD DR	SCR	54	A1
GLENWOOD LN	FRCO	58	B1
GLOBE DR	TUL	69	A3
GLOBE MINE RD	SBD	84	A5
GLORIA RD	MON	54	E5
GLORIA RD	MON	55	A5
GLORIETTA BLVD	CC	L	E4
GLORIETTA BLVD	CC	45	D1
G-O RD	DN	2	B4
GOAT MTN RD	COL	32	A1
GOBBI ST	U	123	C4
GOBLE LN	HUM	15	D2
GODDELL RD	CAL	40	E3
GODFREY AV	SCL	P	E5
GODFREY RCH RD	SLO	75	E1
GODLEY	PLA	34	B3
GODWIN RD	SBD	101	C1
GOETZ RD	RCO	99	C4
GOFFS RD	SBD	94	D2
GOFFS RD	SBD	95	A1
GOGNA	SJCO	40	B5
GOLD CROWN RD	RCO	101	E2
GOLD CROWN RD	SBD	101	E1
GOLDEN AV	SBD	99	C1
GOLDEN RD	SIS	5	D2
GOLDEN ST	SBD	100	E1
GOLDEN CYN RD	INY	72	A1
GOLDEN CTR FRWY	GV	127	E2
GOLDEN CTR FRWY	NEV	127	E2
GOLDEN EAGLE AV	PLU	26	C1
GOLDEN GATE AV	SF	142	A3
GOLDEN GATE AV	SF	143	A5
GOLDEN GATE DR	HUM	16	B3
GOLDEN GATE RD	MNO	42	D1
GOLDN LK FOREST	PLU	26	E3
GOLDENROD AV	FRCO	57	A4
GOLDEN SPGS DR	LACO	U	B3
GOLDEN STATE AV	BKD	166	C2
GOLDEN STATE BL	FRCO	57	E5
GOLDEN STATE BL	STA	47	D3
GOLDEN STATE DR	MAD	57	A2
GOLDEN STATE FY	BUR	179	C1
GOLDEN STATE FY	LA	179	C1
GOLDEN STATE FY	LA	182	D1
GOLDEN STATE FY	LA	186	D3
GOLDEN STATE FY	LACO	89	B4
GOLDEN STATE FY	LACO	97	D1
GOLDEN STATE FY	LACO	Q	B1
GOLDN TROUT CRS	BUT	26	B4
GOLDENWEST AV	ORA	98	B4
GOLDEN WEST ST	ORA	T	B3
GOLD HILL	ED	34	D4
GOLDHILL RD	PLA	34	B3
GOLD HILL RD	SOL	38	D4
GOLD LAKE RD	PLU	27	A3
GOLD LAKE RD	SIE	27	A3
GOLD PARK	SBD	101	C2
GOLD RCK RCH RD	IMP	110	B5
GOLD RUN RD	LAS	20	E4
GOLDRUSH RD	RCO	107	B1
GOLDSBOROUGH GL	SHA	17	D3
GOLD STONE LN	SHA	18	B2
GOLDSTONE RD	SBD	81	E3
GOLD STRIKE RD	CAL	41	A3
GOLER RD	KER	80	E2
GOLF RD	MCO	48	C4
GOLF CLUB RD	CC	L	E3
GOLF CLUB RD	CC	M	A3
GOLF COURSE RD	HUM	10	A5
GOLF LINK RD	AVLN	105	B5
GOLF LINK RD	MCO	47	E4
GOLF LINKS RD	ALA	L	E5
GOLF LINKS RD	ALA	45	E2
GOMAN AV	TUL	70	A3
GOMER AV	KER	78	A1
GOMEZ RD	SHA	13	D4
GONDER RD	IMP	109	B4
GONSALVES RD	TEH	18	C5
GONZAGA RD	MCO	55	C1
GONZALES RD	MCO	55	C2
GONZALES RD	VEN	88	B5
GONZALES RD	VEN	96	B1
GONZALES RIV RD	MON	54	E5
GOODALE RD	INY	59	E2
GOODE HILL RD	LACO	89	E3
GOODENOUGH RD	VEN	88	D4
GOODFELLOW AV	FRCO	57	E4
GOODWATER AV	SHA	18	C2
GOODWIN DR	SBD	91	A4
GOODWIN RD	STA	47	D2
GOODYEAR RD	SOL	38	E4
GOODYEAR CK RD	SIE	26	D4
GOOLSBY RCH RD	MNO	51	C1
GOOSE CREEK RD	AMA	40	C3
GOOSE HAVEN RD	SOL	39	B3
GOOSE RANCH RD	TRI	17	D1
GOOSE VALLEY RD	SHA	13	C4
GOPHER CYN RD	SDCO	106	C2
GOPHR HLL LNDFL	PLU	26	C1
GORDEN RD	HUM	16	C2
GORDONS FRRY RD	SIS	3	A3
GORDON TRACT RD	CC	L	C3
GORDON VLY RD	NAPA	38	E2
GORDON VLY RD	SOL	L	E1
GORDON VLY RD	SOL	38	E2
GORGE RD	INY	51	C3
GORMAN RANCH	PLA	34	E3
GOSFORD RD	KER	78	C3
GOSS RD	SBD	90	E4
GOUDIE TRUCK TR	SDCO	107	C5
GOUGER NECK RD	MOD	14	B3
GOUGH ST	SF	142	C2
GOUGH ST	SF	143	A4
GOULD AV	LACO	S	B1
GOULD RD	COL	25	A5
GOULD RD	LPAZ	104	A2
GOVE RD	MCO	48	B5
GOVER RD	SHA	18	D3
GOVERNOR DR	SD	211	D2
GOVERNOR DR	SDCO	V	B2
GOVERNOR DR	SDCO	106	C5
GOVERNOR MN RD	LACO	89	E4
GOWER ST	LA	181	E5
GOWLING RD	IMP	109	B5
G P RD	KER	77	C1
GRACE RESORT RD	SHA	19	B3
GRACIE RD	NEV	34	C1
GRACIOSA RD	SB	86	C2
GRAEAGLE RD	SIE	26	E3
GRAEAGLE RD	SIE	27	A3
GRAEAGL JHNSVLL	PLU	26	E2
GRAESER RD	IMP	112	C3
GRAHAM	SIS	12	C1
GRAHAM AV	RCO	99	B4
GRAHAM RD	FRCO	57	A4
GRAHAM RD	IMP	111	E3
GRAHAM RD	SJCO	40	B3
GRAHAM RD	TEH	19	B3
GRAHAM HILL RD	SC	169	D1
GRAHAM HILL RD	SCR	54	A1
GRAHAM HILL RD	SCR	169	D1
GRAHAM PASS RD	RCO	109	E1
GRAINLAND RD	BUT	25	A4
GRAMERCY DR	SD	214	B1
GRAMERCY DR	SDCO	V	C2
GRAMERCY DR	SDCO	111	D1
GRANADA AV	SAL	171	D2
GRAND AV	ALA	L	D4
GRAND AV	BUT	25	C4
GRAND AV	ELS	189	A3
GRAND AV	LA	185	D4
GRAND AV	LACO	97	E2
GRAND AV	LACO	98	C2
GRAND AV	LACO	Q	C5
GRAND AV	LACO	U	A2
GRAND AV	LACO	S	A1
GRAND AV	O	158	C4
GRAND AV	ORA	98	C4
GRAND AV	ORA	T	D3
GRAND AV	PAS	190	A5
GRAND AV	P	158	C1
GRAND AV	RCO	99	D4
GRAND AV	RCO	99	B4
GRAND AV	RCO	99	E4
GRAND AV	SA	196	D4
GRAND AV	SA	198	D1
GRAND AV	SD	212	B2
GRAND AV	SDCO	V	A3
GRAND AV	SNLO	172	C1
GRAND AV	SLO	76	B4
GRAND AV	SMCO	L	B5
GRAND AV	SMCO	N	B1
GRAND AV	SMCO	45	C2
GRAND AV	SR	139	D3
GRAND AV	SB	86	E3
GRAND AV	TUL	68	D3
GRAND AV	VEN	88	D4
GRAND AV	YUB	33	D2
GRAND AV E	SSF	144	C1
GRAND AV W	O	157	D2
GRAND ST	MDO	162	C3
GRAND CIRCLE BL	RCO	U	E5
GRAND CIRCLE BL	RCO	98	E3
GRANDE AV	DVS	136	C1
GRANDE PUMICE	MOD	8	A1
GRANDE PUMICE	MOD	14	E1
GRAND ISLAND RD	SAC	M	D1
GRAND ISLAND RD	SAC	39	D4
GRANDON RD	RCO	107	C1
GRAND VIEW AV	LACO	R	C2
GRANDVILLE RD	MCO	56	B2
GRANGE RD	LAK	32	B4
GRANGE AV	PLA	34	B4
GRANGE RD	SOL	M	A1
GRANGE RD	SON	38	A2
GRANGE RD	TEH	24	D2
GRANGER CK RD	MOD	8	D1
GRANGEVILLE BL	KIN	67	C1
GRANGEVLLE BYPS	KIN	67	B1
GRANITE RD	KER	78	D1
GRANITE RD	KER	79	A1
GRANITE RD	MAD	49	B5
GRANITE RD	SBD	92	A4
GRANITE CK RD	SCR	54	A2
GRNIT MTN VW RD	SDCO	107	D3
GRANITE PARK RD	TRI	11	D5
GRANITE SPGS RD	MPA	48	D2
GRANITE VIEW RD	INY	60	A4
GRANITEVILLE RD	NEV	27	A4
GRANIT WELLS RD	SBD	81	A3
GRANT AV	ALCO	146	A2
GRANT AV	COL	32	E3
GRANT AV	SF	143	C2
GRANT RD	LSAL	149	A3
GRANT RD	MCO	56	C1
GRANT RD	MVW	148	A5
GRANT RD	SCL	N	E3
GRANT RD	SCL	P	A3
GRANT RD	SCL	45	E4
GRANT ST	RCO	101	C5
GRANT ST	SM	145	A2
GRANT ST	SMA	173	B1
GRANT LAKE RD	MNO	50	C1
GRANTLAND AV	FRCO	57	B2
GRANTLAND AV	FRCO	67	B1
GRANT LINE RD	SAC	40	A2
GRANT LINE RD	SJCO	47	A2
GRAPE WY	BUT	25	A3
GRAPEFRUIT BLVD	RCO	101	B4
GRAPEVNE CYN RD	KER	70	C5
GRAPEVNE CYN RD	SBD	91	D5
GRAPEVINE GULCH	AMA	40	D3
GRAPP LN	RCO	107	C1
GRASS RD	SBD	100	A1
GRASSHOPPR RD S	LAS	8	A5
GRASSHOPPR RD S	LAS	14	E5
GRASSHOPPER FLT	TRI	11	C5
GRASS VALLEY RD	SBT	54	E3
GRASS VALLEY RD	SBT	55	A3
GRATON RD	SON	37	D2
GRATTON RD	STA	47	E3
GRAVEL PIT RD	RCO	103	C5
GRAVEN RES RD	MOD	8	A2
GRAVEN RES RD	MOD	14	E2
GRAVES RD	SJCO	47	B1
GRAVEYARD GULCH	SIS	3	C5
GRAY AV	YUBA	125	C2
GRAYSON	CC	38	E5
GRAYSON RD	STA	47	B3
GREAT CIR DR	KER	80	B4
GREAT HWY	SFCO	L	B5
GREAT HWY	SFCO	45	B2
GREAT NORTHERN	MOD	5	E3
GREAT SO OVRLND	SDCO	108	A5
GREELEY RD	KER	78	C3
GREELY HILL RD	MPA	48	E1
GREELY HILL RD	MPA	49	A1
GREEN RD	COL	32	D3
GREEN RD	IMP	109	C4
GREEN RD	SAC	40	B2
GREEN RD	SBD	90	D4
GREENBACK LN	SAC	34	B5
GREENBAY RD	COL	32	E3
GREENFIELD AV	VAL	134	D3
GREENFIELD DR	SDCO	107	A5
GREEN HILL RD	SON	37	D2
GREENHORN RD	NEV	34	C1
GREENHORN RD	SIS	4	A4
GREEN HOUSE RD	MCO	47	E5
GREEN HOUSE RD	MCO	48	A5
GREEN LAKES RD	MNO	43	B4
GREENLEAF AV	LACO	R	D5
GREENLEY RD	TUO	41	C5

INDEXES

255
GREENLEY RD
STREET INDEX
HIGH ST

STREET	CO.	PAGE	GRID
GREENLEY RD	TUO	163	D3
GREEN MTN RD	MAD	49	B5
GREEN MTN LKOUT	MPA	49	B5
GREEN RIVER RD	RCO	U	D5
GREEN RIVER RD	RCO	98	D3
GREENSPOT RD	SBD	99	C1
GREENSPOT RD	SBD	99	D2
GREEN SPRING RD	TUO	48	B1
GREENSTONE	ED	34	D5
GREENTREE BLVD	SBD	91	B4
GREEN VALLEY RD	CC	M	B4
GREEN VALLEY RD	CC	46	A1
GREEN VALLEY RD	ED	34	D5
GREEN VALLEY RD	SCR	54	B2
GREEN VALLEY RD	SOL	L	E1
GREEN VALLEY RD	SOL	38	D3
GREEN VALLEY RD	SON	37	D2
GREENVILLE RD	ALA	46	C2
GREENVILLE ST	ORA	T	C3
GREENVILLE ST	SA	197	D3
GRNVLL RND VLY	PLU	20	C5
GREENVLL WLF CK	PLU	20	C5
GREENWALD AV	RCO	99	B4
GREENWOOD AV	FRCO	57	E4
GREENWOOD AV	LACO	R	B4
GREENWOOD RD	ED	34	D4
GREENWOOD RD	SJCO	47	A2
GREENWD HTS DR	HUM	10	A5
GREEN, W S RD	COL	32	E2
GREGORY AV	YOL	39	D1
GREGORY RD	CAL	40	D4
GREGORY CK RD	SHA	12	C5
GREILICH RD	AMA	40	D2
GRIDER RD	SIS	3	B3
GRIDER CREEK RD	SIS	3	B4
GRIDLEY RD	COL	25	B5
GRIDLEY-COLUSA	BUT	25	B5
GRIEVE RD	COL	33	A3
GRIFFIN AV	LA	186	E2
GRIFFIN RD	IMP	109	B4
GRIFFIN RD	STA	47	C2
GRIFFIN ST	SAL	171	D3
GRIFFITH AV	KER	78	B2
GRIFFITH AV	MCO	47	E4
GRIFFITH AV	YUB	33	D2
GRIFFITH PK BL	LA	182	D3
GRIFFITH PK DR	LA	182	D2
GRIFFITH PK DR	LACO	Q	E3
GRIMES AV	STA	47	C2
GRIMES RD	SJCO	46	E1
GRIMES-ARBKL RD	CLU	33	A3
GRIMES CYN RD	VEN	88	D5
GRIMSEL DR	KER	79	C5
GRINDSTONE RD	GLE	23	E3
GRINDSTONE RD	GLE	24	A3
GRIZZLY RD	PLU	27	B2
GRIZZLY RD	TUO	48	D1
GRIZZLY BLUF RD	HUM	15	D2
GRIZZLY GLCH RD	SHA	18	A2
GRIZLY HLL RD N	NEV	26	C5
GRIZZLY ISLD RD	SOL	M	A1
GRIZZLY ISLD RD	SOL	38	E3
GRIZZLY ISLD RD	SOL	39	A3
GRIZZLY ISLD RD	SOL	135	D5
GRIZZLY PEAK BL	B	156	B1
GRIZZLY PEAK BL	CC	156	E2
GRIZZLY PEAK BL	O	156	B1
GRZZLY PK LKOUT	SIS	13	B3
GROOMS	SJCO	47	D1
GROSJEAN	MPA	49	B3
GROTTO CANYON	INY	61	D4
GROUSE CREEK RD	SIS	11	E2
GROUSE RIDGE RD	NEV	27	A5
GROVE AV	GLE	24	D3
GROVE AV	MCO	48	B4
GROVE AV	ONT	204	D3
GROVE AV	ROC	204	D3
GROVE AV	SBD	U	D3
GROVE AV	SBD	98	E2
GROVE AV	U	123	B3
GROVE RD	SUT	33	D3
GROVE ST	ALA	L	D4
GROVE ST	ALA	M	A5
GROVE ST	SON	132	A3
GROVE WY	ALA	L	E5
GROVE WY	ALA	P	A1
GROVE WY	ALCO	146	D2
GROVE SHFTR FWY	O	156	B5
GROVE SHFTR FWY	O	157	E3
GROVE SHFTR FWY	O	158	A2
GRUB GULCH RD	MAD	49	B5
GRUBBS RD	BUT	25	D5
GSCHWEND RD	MEN	30	D2
GUADALUPE PKWY	SJ	151	D1
GUADALUPE PKWY	SJ	152	A3
GUADALUPE ST	SB	86	A1
GUALALA LOOKOUT	MEN	30	D4
GUALALA RDG RD	MEN	30	D4
GUERNEVILLE HWY	SON	37	C1
GUERNEVILLE RD	STR	131	A2
GUERNEVILLE RD	SON	37	E2
GUERRERO ST	SF	142	C4
GUERRERO ST	SFCO	L	B5
GUERRERO ST	SFCO	45	C2
GUIBAL AV	SCL	P	E5
GUIBERSON RD	VEN	88	D4
GUIDIVILLE RES	MEN	31	B2
GUINTOLI LN	HUM	9	E5
GUINTOLI LN	HUM	10	A5
GULCH RD	TRI	17	B3
GULLETT RD	IMP	109	A5
GULLEY VIEW DR	RCO	107	C1
GULLING ST N	PLU	27	B2
GULLING ST S	PLU	27	B2

STREET	CO.	PAGE	GRID
GUM AV	GLE	25	A4
GUN CLUB RD	KER	77	E2
GUN CLUB RD	MCO	47	D5
GUNN AV	LACO	R	C5
GUNST RD	HUM	9	E2
GUNST RD	HUM	10	A2
GURR RD	MCO	48	B5
GUTHERIE RD	IMP	108	E5
GUTIERREZ ST	STB	174	C4
GUTTRY RD	LAS	14	B3
GUY KERR RCH RD	HUM	10	C5
GUYS GULCH RD	SIS	4	A5
GWIN MINE RD	CAL	40	E3
GYLE RD	TEH	24	D1
GYPSUM CYN RD	ORA	U	C5
GYPSUM CYN RD	ORA	98	D3
H			
H ST	BKD	166	C4
H ST	BEN	153	C5
H ST	EUR	121	D1
H ST	FRE	165	B3
H ST	IMP	109	A4
H ST	KER	78	D3
H ST	MCO	55	D1
H ST	SCTO	137	B2
H ST	SAC	39	E1
H ST	SBD	91	D1
H ST	SDCO	V	C4
H ST	SDCO	106	B4
H ST	SDCO	111	D2
H ST	SR	139	C3
H ST	SB	86	B3
HAAS RD	COL	32	D2
HACIENDA AV	RCO	100	D2
HACIENDA AV	SM	145	A3
HACIENDA BLVD	LACO	98	B2
HACIENDA BLVD	LACO	R	D5
HACIENDA BLVD	KER	80	B4
HACIENDA RD	SHA	18	D3
HACKAMORE PL	MNO	43	A3
HACKETT RD	STA	47	C3
HACKLEMAN RD	IMP	109	A5
HACKMAN RD	SOL	39	C2
HACKNEY DR	MNO	42	E1
HACKSTAFF RD	LAS	21	E5
HAGATA RD	LAS	21	A2
HAGEMAN RD	KER	78	C3
HAGEMAN RD	SUT	33	B2
HAGEN RD	NAPA	38	D3
HAGEN RD	NAPA	133	E2
HAGEN FLAT RD	SHA	13	A4
HAHN RD	COL	32	D3
HAIGHT MTN RD	SIS	5	A5
HAILES RD	VEN	96	C1
HAILLE RD	TEH	25	A2
HALE AV	COL	32	E3
HALE AV	SCL	P	D4
HALE RD	AMA	41	A2
HALEY RD	IMP	109	C3
HALEY RD	MCO	47	C5
HALEY ST	STB	174	C4
HALF MOON BY RD	SMCO	45	C3
HALFWAY RD	SDCO	107	B2
HALL AV	SJCO	47	D1
HALL RD	LAS	27	E1
HALL RD	MON	54	C3
HALL RD	SON	37	E2
HALL RD	STA	47	E3
HALL RD	STA	48	A2
HALL RD	TEH	24	D2
HALL RD	VEN	88	D4
HALL WY	SHA	19	E2
HALL CITY CK RD	TRI	17	C3
HALLEY RD	SOL	39	A2
HALLOCK	VEN	88	C5
HALLORAN SPG RD	SBD	83	B3
HALLORAN SUMMIT	SBD	83	D2
HALLOWELL RD	STA	47	C4
HALLS FLAT RD	LAS	20	A2
HALLS GRADE RD	RCO	100	B3
HALLWOOD BLVD	YUB	33	D2
HALLWOOD BLVD W	YUB	33	D2
HALSTEAD	SBD	81	C5
HAM LN	SJCO	40	A4
HAMBONE RD	SIS	13	C2
HAMBURG RD	MCO	55	E2
HAMES RD	SCR	54	B2
HAMILTON	YOL	39	D2
HAMILTON AV	ORA	T	B4
HAMILTON AV	SCL	P	B3
HAMILTON AV	SCL	46	A5
HAMILTON AV	TEH	24	D1
HAMILTON RD	DN	1	E4
HAMILTON RD	KER	89	D1
HAMILTON RD	STA	47	B3
HAMILTON RD E	BUT	25	C5
HAMILTON RD W	BUT	25	C5
HAMLTN NORD CNA	BUT	25	A3
HAMLTN VICTORIA	ORA	98	B4
HAMLIN RD	BUT	25	C3
HAMLIN GULCH RD	SIS	3	E5
HAMLOW RD	STA	47	E3
HAMMER LN	SJCO	40	A5
HAMMER LOOP RD	TEH	18	A5
HAMMETT RD	STA	47	C2
HAMMIL RD	MNO	51	D2
HAMMONTON RD	YUB	33	E2
HAMMNTN SMRTVLL	YUB	33	E2
HAMNER AV	RCO	U	E4
HAMNER AV	RCO	98	E3
HAMPTON RD	CC	L	D3
HANAUPAH CYN RD	INY	72	A2

STREET	CO.	PAGE	GRID
HANAWALT AV	KER	78	A1
HANCOCK RD	SBD	84	C4
HANEY VIEW DR	SHA	13	E4
HANFORD ARMONA	KIN	67	C1
HANKINS RD	COL	32	D2
HANKS RD	MOD	7	D4
HANSEN	FRCO	58	B4
HANSEN AV	RCO	99	D3
HANSEN RD	LAS	21	B1
HANSEN RD	SJCO	46	D2
HANSEN ST	SAL	171	E5
HAPGOOD RD	SB	86	C3
HAPPY TR	SBD	92	D5
HAPPY CAMP LKOT	MOD	14	B1
HAPPY CAMP RD	VEN	88	D5
HAPPY CAMP DUMP	SIS	3	A3
HAPPY CANYON RD	SB	87	A3
HAPPY GAP RD	TUL	58	D3
HAPPY VALLEY RD	ALA	P	B1
HAPPY VALLEY RD	CC	L	E4
HAPPY VALLEY RD	CC	45	D1
HAPPY VALLEY RD	ED	35	A5
HAPPY VALLEY RD	SHA	18	C3
HARBERS LN	HUM	15	E2
HARBISON RD	COL	32	E1
HARBISON CYN RD	SDCO	107	A5
HARBOR	YOL	39	D1
HARBOR BLVD	ANA	193	B1
HARBOR BLVD	CM	197	B5
HARBOR BLVD	CM	199	B2
HARBOR BLVD	FTNV	195	B5
HARBOR BLVD	FTNV	197	B2
HARBOR BLVD	GGR	195	B3
HARBOR BLVD	LA	191	B3
HARBOR BLVD	LACO	S	C3
HARBOR BLVD	ORA	98	B3
HARBOR BLVD	ORA	T	C2
HARBOR BLVD	SMCO	N	D2
HARBOR BLVD	SA	195	B5
HARBOR BLVD	SA	197	B2
HARBOR BLVD	VENT	175	E4
HARBOR BLVD	VEN	96	B1
HARBOR DR	IMP	108	C2
HARBOR DR	SD	215	D4
HARBOR DR	SD	216	B5
HARBOR DR	SDCO	V	B4
HARBOR DR N	SD	215	B2
HARBOR FRWY	LA	185	D4
HARBOR FRWY	LA	191	A2
HARBOR FRWY	LACO	97	D4
HARBOR FRWY	LACO	S	C2
HARBOR WY	R	155	A3
HARBOR SCNIC DR	LB	192	C3
HARDEN FLAT	TUO	49	B1
HARDER RD	ALA	N	E1
HARDER RD	ALA	P	A1
HARDER RD	ALA	45	E2
HARDER RD W	H	146	D4
HARDIN RD	NAPA	32	C5
HARDIN RD	NAPA	38	C1
HARDING AV	STA	47	D3
HARDING RD	MCO	47	E3
HARDING RD	MCO	48	A3
HARDING WY	SJCO	40	A5
HARDING WY	S	160	A4
HARDMAN AV	NAPA	38	C2
HARDRK DAVIS RD	SBD	91	B3
HARDY RD	IMP	111	E3
HARE CANYON RD	MON	65	E4
HARE CANYON RD	MON	66	A4
HARKINS	MON	54	C4
HARKINS RD	SAL	171	E5
HARKINS SLGH RD	SCR	54	B2
HARKNESS DR	PLU	20	A3
HARKNESS ST	NAP	133	A2
HARLAN AV	FRCO	66	D1
HARLAN AV	FRCO	57	C5
HARLAN RD	COL	32	C2
HARLAN MTN RD	SBT	54	E4
HARLAN MTN RD	SBT	55	A4
HARLEY LEIGHTON	SHA	18	C2
HARMON RD	MCO	56	B1
HARMON RD	TUL	67	E2
HARMONY GRVE RD	SDCO	106	C3
HARMONY VLY RD	SLO	75	C2
HARNEY	SJCO	40	A4
HARP RD	TEH	18	C3
HARPER LN	MCO	55	C2
HARPER LN	SOL	39	B2
HARPER RD	IMP	112	D5
HARPER LAKE RD	SBD	81	B5
HARPOLD RD	KLAM	5	D1
HARRIGAN RD	IMP	111	E3
HARRINGTON AV	COL	32	E3
HARRIS	MPA	49	C3
HARRIS RD	BUT	25	B4
HARRIS RD	HUM	16	D5
HARRIS RD	IMP	109	B5
HARRIS RD	MON	54	C4
HARRIS RD	SUT	33	C3
HARRIS ST	EUR	121	B3
HARRIS ST	HUM	9	E5
HARRIS ST	HUM	15	E1
HARRISON AV	HUM	9	E5
HARRISON AV	HUM	15	E1
HARRISON RD	TRI	17	B2
HARRISON ST	O	158	B2
HARRISON ST	RCO	101	B5
HARRISON ST	SF	143	D5
HARRISN GLCH RD	SHA	17	C3
HARRIS RANCH RD	MNO	51	D2
HARROD RD	SBD	92	A4
HARROLD RD	SJCO	47	D1
HARRY CASH RD	SIS	4	C4

STREET	CO.	PAGE	GRID
HART AV	KER	68	C5
HART RD	IMP	109	C4
HART RD	SIS	4	C4
HART RD	STA	47	C2
HART FLAT RD	KER	79	B3
HARTLEY DR	BUT	25	C2
HARTMANN RD	LAK	32	B4
HART MINE RD	SBD	84	D3
HARTNELL	RED	122	E4
HARTNELL AV	SHA	18	C2
HART OAKS DR	KER	79	B3
HARTSHORN RD	IMP	109	C5
HARTS MEADOW	SIS	12	E1
HARTS MTN RD	SIS	4	E5
HARTVICKSON LN	CAL	40	E4
HARVARD AV	IRV	200	E1
HARVARD AV	ORA	T	E3
HARVARD RD	SBD	92	C1
HARVARD MINE RD	TUO	41	C5
HARVEY RD	BUT	25	C2
HARVEY RD	SAC	40	A3
HARVEY RD	STA	47	C4
HARVEY RD 1	LAS	20	C1
HARVEY RD 2	LAS	20	C1
HARVEY RD 4	LAS	20	C1
HARVY MTN LO RD	LAS	20	C1
HARVY PETTIT RD	MCO	48	D5
HARVEY VLY RD	LAS	20	C1
HARWOOD RD	SCL	P	B4
HARWOOD RD	SCL	46	B5
HASKELL AV	LACO	Q	B2
HASKINS RD	SIS	5	D2
HASKINS VALLEY	BUT	26	A3
HASLEY CYN RD	LACO	89	A4
HASSLER RD	ED	34	E4
HASTAIN RD	IMP	109	B4
HASTE ST	B	156	A3
HASTER ST	ANA	193	D5
HASTER ST	ANA	195	C1
HASTER ST	ORA	T	C2
HATCHET CK RD	TRI	11	E4
HAT CREEK PK RD	SHA	13	D4
HAT CK PWRHOUSE	SHA	13	D4
HAT CK PWRHS #2	SHA	13	D4
HATCH RD	BUT	25	B5
HATCH RD	MCO	48	C4
HATCH RD	STA	47	C2
HATCHET CK RD	NEV	34	B2
HATCHET CK RD	TRI	12	A4
HATHAWAY ST	RCO	100	A3
HAUSER BLVD	LA	184	B3
HAUSER BR RD	SON	37	A1
HAVASU LAKE RD	SBD	95	D4
HAVEN AV	SBD	U	E2
HAVEN AV	SBD	98	E2
HAVEN RD	SBD	80	E5
HAVENS RD	IMP	108	E5
HAVERFORD RD	SDCO	107	A4
HAVLINA ST	SIS	5	D2
HAWEE CANYON RD	INY	70	B2
HAWKEYE AV	STA	47	E3
HAWKINS RD	SOL	39	B2
HAWKINS RD	STA	48	A3
HAWKINS BAR RD	TRI	10	D5
HAWKNSVLLE HMBG	SIS	3	E4
HAWKNSVLLE HMBG	SIS	4	A4
HAWKS HILL RD	HUM	15	D2
HAWLEY GRADE	ED	36	A4
HAWTHORNE AV	C	124	D3
HAWTHORNE AV	SHA	18	B3
HAWTHORNE BLVD	LACO	97	D3
HAWTHORNE BLVD	LACO	S	B2
HAWTHORNE ST	MONT	167	D3
HAWTHORNE ST	RCO	99	C5
HAWVER RD	CAL	41	A3
HAYDEN RD	MCO	48	D4
HAYDEN HILL RD	LAS	14	C4
HAYDN HLL CTOFF	LAS	14	D4
HAYDN HLL LKOUT	LAS	14	D4
HAYES AV	FRCO	57	B3
HAYES AV	FRCO	57	B5
HAYES ST	NAP	133	C3
HAYES ST	RCO	101	C5
HAYNES RD	SBD	91	E3
HAYNES RD	SHA	13	C5
HAYS CANYON RD	MOD	8	E2
HAYWARD BLVD	ALA	M	A5
HAYWARD BLVD	ALA	P	A1
HAYWARD RD	MCO	48	C2
HAZEL AV	SAC	34	B5
HAZELDEAN RD	STA	48	A2
HAZEL DELL RD	SCR	54	C2
HAZEL VALLEY RD	ED	35	B4
HAZELTINE AV	LACO	Q	C2
HAZELTON AV	S	160	E5
HAZEN RD	TEH	19	B3
HEACOCK ST	RCO	99	C2
HEAD DAM RD	BUT	25	D1
HEALDSBURG AV	SON	37	E2
HEALY RD	MCO	48	C5
HEARST RD	MCO	47	D5
HEARST RD	MCO	55	D1
HEARST POST OFC	MEN	23	B4
HEARST WLLTS RD	MEN	23	A5
HEATH RD	KER	78	C3
HEATHER AV	KER	70	C5
HEATHER AV	MAD	57	B1
HEATHER DR	FRFD	135	C2
HEBER RD	IMP	112	B3
HECKER PASS HWY	SCL	54	C2
HECTOR RD	SBD	92	D2
HEDDING ST	SJ	151	C4
HEDDING ST	SJ	152	A3
HEDDING ST	SCL	P	B3

STREET	CO.	PAGE	GRID
HEDGER RD	SUT	33	C1
HEFFERNAN AV	IMP	112	A4
HEGAN LN	BUT	25	B3
HEGENBRGR EXPWY	ALA	45	D2
HEGENBRGR EXPWY	O	159	E2
HEGENBERGER RD	ALA	L	D5
HEGENBERGER RD	ALA	45	D2
HEGENBURGER RD	O	159	E3
HEIDI RD	TUL	68	E1
HEINSEN RD	MON	65	D4
HEINZELMAN DR	SIS	4	C5
HEISKELL DR	MAD	57	B1
HEITT AV	KER	68	B5
HELEN DR	MLBR	144	B5
HELENA AV	STA	47	E2
HELENDALE RD	SBD	91	B2
HELLMAN AV	RCO	U	E4
HELLMAN AV	RCO	98	E2
HELLS HALF ACRE	SIE	26	D4
HELLS HALF ACRE	TUO	41	D3
HELLS HALF ACRE	TUO	42	A3
HELLS HOLLOW RD	TUO	48	E1
HELMS CT	KER	79	C3
HEMET LAKE RD	RCO	100	B4
HEMPHILL RD	LAS	21	B4
HENDERSON AV	TUL	68	D3
HENDERSON RD	FRCO	57	B4
HENDERSON RD	FRCO	57	C4
HENDERSON RD	RED	122	D3
HENDERSON ST	EUR	121	C3
HENDRICKS DR	SBD	101	E1
HENDRICKS RD	LAK	31	C2
HENLEY RD	KLAM	5	C1
HENNESSEY RD	HUM	10	D5
HENNESSEY RD	TRI	10	E5
HENNESS PASS RD	SIE	26	D4
HENNESS PASS RD	SIE	27	A4
HENRY RD	SBD	101	D1
HENRY RD	SJCO	40	D5
HENRY RD	SJCO	47	D1
HENRY ST	B	156	A1
HENRY DOTA RD	SIE	27	C4
HENRY FORD AV	LA	191	E1
HENRY FORD AV	LB	191	E2
HENRY MILLER AV	MCO	56	A1
HENRY MILLER RD	MCO	55	C1
HENSLEY RD	MAD	57	B1
HEREFORD RD	MCO	47	E5
HEREFORD RD	MCO	48	A5
HEREFORD RD	MCO	55	E1
HEREFORD RD	SBD	92	B1
HERIOT LN	PLU	27	C3
HERIOT LN	SIE	27	C3
HERITAGE CT	SHA	18	B2
HERITAGE RD	SDCO	V	D5
HERITAGE RD	SDCO	111	E2
HERLONG ACCESS	LAS	21	D5
HERMOSA AV	LACO	S	A1
HERMOSA RD	KER	78	E3
HERMOSA RD	VEN	88	B4
HERNANDEZ DR	LACO	90	A3
HERNANDEZ DR	MPA	48	C2
HERNDON AV	FRCO	56	B3
HERNDON AV	FRCO	57	C3
HERNLEY RD	RCO	107	B1
HERON AV	SBD	101	A1
HERRICK RD	HUM	121	B5
HERRING RD	KER	78	C4
HERZOG RD	SAC	M	D1
HERZOG RD	SAC	39	D3
HESPELER RD	SOL	38	E2
HESPERIA RD	MON	65	C5
HESPERIA RD	SBD	91	B4
HESPERIAN BLVD	ALA	N	E1
HESPERIAN BLVD	ALA	P	A1
HESPERIAN BLVD	ALA	45	E2
HESPERIAN BLVD	ALCO	146	A2
HESPERIAN BLVD	H	146	A2
HESSE RD	TEH	18	B5
HETTENSHAW RD	TRI	16	E4
HETZEL RD	IMP	108	E5
HEWES AV	ORA	98	C4
HEWES AV	ORA	T	E3
HEWITT	SJCO	40	C5
HEWLTT STURTVNT	MEN	31	B3
HEYSER RD	IMP	110	D5
HIALEAH WY	RCO	100	C5
HIATT RD	SUT	33	B4
HIAWATHA AV	AVLN	105	A4
HIBBARD RD	MEN	31	A4
HIBBARD RD	SJCO	40	B4
HICKEY BLVD	SMCO	N	B1
HICKEY BLVD	SMCO	45	B2
HICKMAN LN	TEH	18	C4
HICKMAN RD	STA	47	E3
HICKMAN RD	STA	48	A3
HICKS	LAS	21	B4
HICKS LN	BUT	25	B2
HICKS RD	SUT	33	E3
HIDALGO ST	MPA	48	C2
HIDDEN HILLS RD	SBD	94	A2
HIDDEN OAKS DR	KER	79	B4
HIDDEN VLY RD	SB	87	B4
HIDEAWAY HAVEN	SHA	13	D3
HIEROGLYPH RD	MNO	51	C2
HIETT AV	KER	78	B1
HIGDON RD	CAL	41	B2
HIGGINS AV	BUT	33	C1
HIGGNS PRSMA RD	SMCO	N	B2
HIGGNS PRSMA RD	SMCO	45	C3
HIGH RD	SBD	91	D4
HIGH RD	SIS	3	E4
HIGH ST	ALA	L	D4
HIGH ST	A	159	A2

INDEXES

HIGH ST

STREET INDEX

INLAND DR

256

STREET	CO.	PAGE	GRID
HIGH ST	AUB	126	D3
HIGH ST	MONT	167	D3
HIGH ST	MON	53	E3
HIGH ST	O	159	B1
HIGH ST	SC	169	B3
HIGH ST	SCR	53	E2
HIGHGRADE RD	MOD	7	E2
HIGHLAND AV	FRCO	57	D2
HIGHLAND AV	LA	181	C4
HIGHLAND AV	LA	184	C1
HIGHLAND AV	LACO	97	D3
HIGHLAND AV	LACO	Q	D4
HIGHLAND AV	LACO	S	A1
HIGHLAND AV	MB	189	A5
HIGHLAND AV	SBD	98	E1
HIGHLAND AV	SBD	99	C2
HIGHLAND AV	SDCO	V	C4
HIGHLAND AV	SDCO	111	D1
HIGHLAND AV	U	123	B3
HIGHLAND BLVD	RCO	99	D2
HIGHLAND DR	CLK	209	A5
HIGHLAND DR	LACO	R	A2
HIGHLAND DR	SNLO	172	A1
HIGHLAND RD	CC	M	C5
HIGHLAND RD	CC	46	B1
HIGHLAND WY	SCR	P	B5
HIGHLAND WY	SCR	54	B1
HIGHLND HOME RD	RCO	99	E3
HIGHLAND LK RD	ALP	42	B1
HIGHLAND SPG RD	LAK	31	D3
HIGHLND SPGS RD	RCO	99	E3
HIGHLAND VLY RD	SDCO	106	E4
HIGHLANDS LK RD	SHA	12	B4
HIGHLINE RD	IMP	109	C5
HIGHLINE RD	KER	79	B4
HIGHLINE RD	KER	79	C4
HIGH PRAIRIE RD	HUM	10	C5
HIGHRIDGE RD	LACO	S	B3
HIGH ROCK RD	LAS	21	E4
HIGH SCHOOL RD	SON	37	D2
HIGH VALLEY RD	KER	88	D1
HIGH VALLEY RD	LAK	31	E2
HIGH VALLEY RD	LAK	31	E3
HIGH VALLEY RD	LAK	32	A3
HY TO THE STARS	SDCO	107	A2
HIGUERA ST	SLO	76	A4
HIGUERA ST	SNLO	172	B3
HILDRETH LN	SJCO	40	B4
HILDRETH RD	MAD	57	D1
HILL	FRCO	58	B4
HILL AV	PAS	190	E2
HILL RD	COL	32	D2
HILL RD	CC	38	E5
HILL RD	KER	78	C4
HILL RD	KLAM	5	C2
HILL RD	MEN	23	B3
HILL RD	SMCO	N	C4
HILL RD	SCL	P	D5
HILL RD	SCL	54	D1
HILL RD	SIS	5	D3
HILL RD	YUB	33	E1
HILL RD E	MEN	23	A5
HILL ST	AVLN	105	B4
HILL ST	LA	185	D5
HILL ST	LA	186	A3
HILL ST	LACO	S	D2
HILL ST	ML	164	C4
HILL ST	SDCO	V	A3
HILL ST	SDCO	106	B3
HILL ST	SDCO	111	C1
HILLCREST AV	BEN	153	C4
HILLCREST AV	CC	39	C5
HILLCREST BLVD	LACO	R	D3
HILLCREST BLVD	MLBR	144	D5
HILLCREST BLVD	SMCO	N	C1
HILLCREST BLVD	SMCO	45	B3
HILLCREST RD	CC	M	C3
HILLCREST ST	KER	80	E1
HILLDALE AV	MCO	55	C1
HILLDALE AV	MCO	86	E1
HILLER RD	HUM	9	E4
HILLER ST	BLMT	145	C4
HILLGATE RD	COL	32	E3
HILLHURST AV	LA	182	C3
HILLMAN AV	BLMT	145	B4
HILLSBORO AV	LA	183	D3
HILLSDALE AV	SCL	P	B4
HILLSDALE BLVD	SMCO	N	C2
HILLSDALE BL E	FCTY	145	D2
HILLSDALE BL E	SM	145	B3
HILLSDALE BL W	SM	145	A4
HILLS FERRY RD	MCO	47	C4
HILLSIDE AV	RCO	98	E3
HILLSIDE BLVD	SMCO	L	B5
HILLSIDE BLVD	SMCO	N	B1
HILLSIDE BLVD	SMCO	45	B2
HILLSIDE DR	MPA	49	C3
HILLSIDE DR	SMCO	N	C1
HILLSIDE DR	SMCO	45	C3
HILLSIDE DR	SHA	18	D2
HILL SIDE STA	LAS	14	B3
HILLSIDE VIS RD	RCO	107	C1
HILLS VALLEY RD	FRCO	58	B4
HILLTOP	SHA	18	C2
HILLTOP DR	CC	L	C3
HILLTOP RD	SIS	5	A2
HILL VIEW TK TR	SBD	91	C2
HILMAR RD	STA	47	D4
HILT RD	SIS	4	A2
HILT HUNGRY RD	SIS	4	A2
HILTON PACK STA	MNO	51	A3
HILTONS RD	HUM	9	C2
HILTONS RD	HUM	10	A2
HIME RD	IMP	112	A3

STREET	CO.	PAGE	GRID
HI MOUNTAIN RD	SLO	76	C3
HINDS RD	STA	47	D1
HINKLEY RD	SBD	81	C5
HINTON AV	MCO	47	E4
HIRSCH RD	MPA	49	B4
HIRSCHDALE RD	NEV	27	E5
HITCHCOCK RD	MON	54	C4
HI YOU GULCH RD	SIS	3	D4
HOADLEY PKS RD	SHA	17	E1
HOAG RD	TEH	24	D2
HOAGLAND RD	HUM	16	D5
HOAGLIN RD	TRI	16	D5
HOAGLIN SCH RD	TRI	16	E5
HOBART AV	FRCO	56	B2
HOBART MILLS RD	NEV	27	D5
HOBBS RD	IMP	109	A2
HOBBS RD	SUT	33	C3
HOBO GULCH RD	TRI	11	B5
HOBSON AV	MON	65	B2
HOBSON WY	RCO	103	C5
HOFFMAN BLVD	R	155	A4
HOFFMAN LN	CC	39	C5
HOFFMAN RD	SBD	80	E3
HOFFMAN RD	SBD	81	A3
HOFFMAN RD	YUB	33	D3
HOFFMAN ST	AMA	40	E2
HFMN PLUMAS RD	YUB	33	D3
HOGAN	FRCO	58	A4
HOGAN LN	SJCO	40	B4
HOGAN DAM RD	CAL	40	E4
HOGAN DAM RD	CAL	40	E4
HOGBACK RD	INY	60	A4
HOG CANYON RD	KER	79	D3
HOG CANYON RD	SLO	76	B1
HOG CANYON EXT	SLO	66	B5
HOGIN RD	STA	47	C4
HOG LAKE TK TR	RCO	100	B5
HOGSBACK RD	TEH	18	D5
HOGSBACK RD	TEH	19	B4
HOKE RD	SUT	33	C2
HOLBROOK RD	MCO	48	D5
HOLCOMB CK RD	SBD	91	E5
HOLCOMB VLY RD	SBD	91	E5
HOLCOMBS RD	SIE	27	D4
HOLDEN	SJCO	40	C5
HOLDNER RD	SOL	39	B2
HOLDRIDGE DR	TUL	68	E3
HOLDRIDGE RD	IMP	112	C3
HOLE AV	RCO	99	A3
HOLENBECK	SJCO	40	C5
HOLIDAY AV	KER	89	C1
HOLIDAY RD	DN	2	B3
HOLLAND	YOL	39	D2
HOLLAND AV	BUT	25	B3
HOLLAND RD	RCO	99	C4
HOLLAND RD	SOL	39	C3
HOLLND TRACT RD	CC	39	D5
HOLLENBECK AV	LACO	U	A3
HOLLENBECK AV	SVL	149	D2
HOLLISTER AV	SB	87	B4
HOLLISTER ST	SDCO	V	C5
HOLLISTER ST	SDCO	111	D2
HOLLOW LN	SHA	18	C2
HOLLOW RD	CC	39	A5
HOLLOWAY RD	COL	32	E1
HOLLOWAY RD	KER	77	C1
HOLLOW LOG RD	PLA	34	E2
HOLLY AV	LACO	R	C3
HOLLY RD	SBD	91	A3
HOLLY RD	TRI	17	A3
HOLLY ST	SMCO	N	D2
HOLLYWOOD BLVD	LA	181	A4
HOLLYWOOD BLVD	LA	182	A4
HOLLYWOOD BLVD	LACO	97	D2
HOLLYWOOD BLVD	LACO	Q	D3
HOLLYWOOD FRWY	LA	181	B2
HOLLYWOOD FRWY	LA	185	D1
HOLLYWOOD FRWY	LA	186	A2
HOLLYWOOD FRWY	LACO	97	D1
HOLLYWOOD FRWY	LACO	Q	D3
HOLLYWOOD LN	SBD	101	D1
HOLLYWOOD WY	BUR	179	B3
HOLLYWOOD WY	LA	179	B3
HOLLYWOOD WY	LACO	97	D1
HOLLYWOOD WY	LACO	Q	D2
HOLMAN HWY	MONT	167	C5
HOLMAN HWY	MON	53	D4
HOLMAN HWY	MON	168	C1
HOLMES AV	KER	78	B5
HOLMES LN	SOL	39	A2
HOLMES RD	SBD	84	C4
HOLMES RD	TEH	24	E1
HOLMES ST	ALA	P	C1
HOLMES ST	ALA	46	C2
HOLMS FLAT RD	HUM	16	B3
HOLOHAN RD	SCR	54	C2
HOLSTEAD RD	SBD	81	C5
HOLT	SJCO	39	E5
HOLT AV	LACO	U	A2
HOLT BLVD	MTCL	203	B5
HOLT BLVD	ONT	203	B5
HOLT BLVD	ONT	204	A5
HOLT BLVD	POM	203	B5
HOLT BLVD	SBD	U	C2
HOLT BLVD	SBD	98	D2
HOLT RD	IMP	109	C5
HOLT RD	KER	79	E5
HOLT RD	KER	80	A5
HOLTON RD	IMP	109	B5
HOLTVLE DUMP RD	IMP	109	C5
HOLTZWL	MPA	48	E2
HOLTZWL	MPA	49	A2
HOLWORTHY DR	TUL	68	D2
HOLZHAUSER LN	SIS	11	D1

STREET	CO.	PAGE	GRID
HOME AV	SD	216	D3
HOME AV	SDCO	V	C3
HOME AV	SDCO	111	D1
HOMEDALE RD	KLAM	5	C1
HOMES RD	SBD	91	E4
HOMESTEAD AV	SAL	171	B4
HOMESTEAD RD	MON	54	C4
HOMESTEAD RD	SLO	76	B2
HOMESTEAD RD	SCL	P	A3
HOMESTEAD RD	SCL	45	E4
HOMESTEAD RD	SCLR	150	C3
HOMESTEAD RD	SCLR	151	A3
HOMESTEAD RD	SVL	150	C3
HOMEWOOD CYN RD	INY	71	B4
HONDA RD	SB	86	B3
HONEY BEE RD	SHA	18	B3
HONEY RUN RD	BUT	25	C3
HONEY SPGS RD	SDCO	112	B1
HONEY WAGON RD	IMP	108	E2
HONOLULU AV	IMP	108	C2
HONOLULU AV	LACO	Q	E2
HONOLULU RD	KER	78	A4
HOOD FRANKLN RD	SAC	39	E2
HOOKER CREEK RD	HUM	16	C5
HOOKER CREEK RD	TEH	18	C4
HOOKTON RD	HUM	15	D1
HOOPER RD	SUT	33	C2
HOOPER RD	YUB	33	D2
HOOVER RD	MCO	56	C1
HOOVER ST	LA	185	C3
HOOVER ST	LACO	Q	E4
HOOVER FLAT RD	LAS	14	C5
HOPE AV	KLAM	5	C1
HOPE ST	LA	185	E4
HOPKINS ST	ALA	L	C4
HOPLAND ST	SBD	91	B3
HOPPER RD	STA	47	E2
HOPYARD RD	ALA	M	B5
HOPYARD RD	ALA	46	B2
HORIZON RD	SBD	91	B3
HORIZON ST	SBD	91	C4
HORN LN	SIS	11	D1
HORN RD	LAS	8	C5
HORNBROOK RD	SIS	4	B3
HORNITOS RD	MPA	48	D3
HORR RD	SHA	13	D3
HORSE CANYON RD	KER	80	B1
HORSE CREEK RD	SIS	3	C3
HORSE LAKE RD	LAS	21	C1
HORSE LINTO RD	HUM	10	D4
HORSE RDG LKOUT	TRI	17	A4
HORSESHOE RD	STA	47	E1
HORSESHOE RD	STA	48	A1
HORSESHOE BR RD	PLA	34	B4
HORSESHOE HL RD	MAR	37	E5
HORSESHOE MDWS	INY	60	A4
HORTON CREEK RD	INY	51	C4
HOSFIELD DR	TUL	68	B2
HOSKING RD	KER	78	D3
HOSLER AV	BUT	25	A3
HOSPITAL LN	RED	122	C5
HOSTETTER RD	SCL	P	B3
HOTCHKISS RD	TRI	22	E1
HOT CK RANCH RD	MNO	50	E2
HOT CK RANCH RD	MNO	51	A2
HOTLUM	SIS	12	C1
HOT SPRINGS RD	ALP	36	B5
HOT SPRINGS RD	RCO	108	D1
HOT SPRINGS RD	TUL	68	E4
HOT SPRINGS RD	TUL	69	A4
HOUGHTON AV	TEH	24	D2
HOUGHTON RD	KER	78	C4
HOUSE RD	IMP	108	E5
HOUSE RD	LAS	14	C3
HOUSTON AV	KIN	67	D1
HOUSTON AV	TUL	68	B1
HOUT RD	AMA	40	D2
HOVLEY RD	IMP	109	A4
HOWARD	SJCO	47	A1
HOWARD AV	FRCO	57	A5
HOWARD AV	FRCO	57	A3
HOWARD AV	MCO	47	E4
HOWARD AV	MCO	48	A4
HOWARD AV	SD	214	A5
HOWARD RD	MCO	47	E4
HOWARD RD	RCO	107	B1
HOWARD RD	STA	47	B3
HOWARD RD	TUL	68	B4
HOWARD ST	MEN	23	A3
HOWARD CREEK RD	SIE	27	A3
HOWARD MTHWS RD	SJCO	40	A5
HOWRDS GLCH FTG	MOD	14	C1
HOWE RD	CC	L	E3
HOWE CREEK RD	HUM	15	E3
HOWELL AV	KER	80	C1
HOWELL AV	SIS	11	D1
HOWELL RD	IMP	109	A2
HOWELL MTN RD	NAPA	29	C2
HOWELL MTN RD	NAPA	38	B1
HOWELLS RD	PLU	26	B1
HOWLAND HILL RD	DN	1	D4
HOWSLEY RD	SUT	33	D4
HOY RD	SIS	12	C1
HOY RD	TEH	18	D5
HOYER RD	STA	47	C4
HUASNA RD	SLO	76	C4
HUASNA TOWNSITE	SLO	76	D4
HUB CT	CAL	41	A5
HUBBARD	PLA	34	B3
HUBBARD RD	LACO	89	E4
HUBBARD ST	LACO	89	C5
HUBBARD ST	LACO	Q	C1
HUDSON AV	FRCO	56	B2
HUDSON RD	CAL	41	A5
HUDSON RD	MON	65	A1

STREET	CO.	PAGE	GRID
HUDSON ST	SMCO	N	D2
HUDSON RD	SIS	4	A3
HUDSON RD	SUT	33	E3
HUDSON ST	SHA	13	C5
HUERHUERO L PNZ	SLO	76	C2
HUEY RD	SLO	76	A1
HUFF RD	IMP	108	E5
HUFF RD	SBD	91	E3
HUFF ST	RCO	107	C1
HUFFAKER RD	SUT	33	E3
HUFFMEISTER RD	COL	32	C2
HUFFORD RD	HUM	9	E2
HUFFORD RD	HUM	10	A2
HUGHES AV	CUL	183	C5
HUGHES AV	FRCO	57	C4
HUGHES AV	FRCO	67	C1
HUGHES AV	LA	183	C5
HUGHES LN	KER	78	D3
HUGHES RD	GV	127	C2
HUGHES RD	NEV	127	C2
HUGHES RD	SUT	33	C2
HULEN RD	MCO	47	C5
HULEN RD	MCO	55	C1
HULL AV	MCO	48	B4
HULL RD	GLE	24	A3
HULL CREEK RD	TRI	23	A1
HULL MTN RD	LAK	23	D5
HULL VALLEY RD	MEN	23	A2
HULTBERG RD	MCO	47	D4
HULTBERG RD	STA	47	D3
HUMBOLDT AV	FRCO	56	E3
HUMBOLDT AV	FRCO	57	A3
HUMBOLDT RD	BUT	19	D5
HUMBOLDT RD	BUT	25	B3
HUMBOLDT RD	C	124	E4
HUMBOLDT RD	DN	1	E4
HUMBOLDT RD	PLU	19	E5
HUMBOLDT RD	PLU	20	A5
HUMBLDT HILL RD	HUM	15	E1
HUMBUG RD	PLU	19	E5
HUMBUG RD	PLU	20	A5
HUMBUG CREEK RD	SIS	4	A4
HUMBUG HUMBOLDT	PLU	20	B4
HUME AV	KIN	67	E1
HUME RD	FRCO	58	E3
HUMPHREY CIR	PLU	20	D5
HUMPHREY RD	SUT	33	C2
HUN RD	SBD	84	C4
HUNEWILL RCH RD	MNO	43	B3
HUNGRY CK MTRWY	PLU	20	E5
HUNGRY CK LO RD	SIS	4	A2
HUNGRY VLY RD	VEN	88	D2
HUNT RD	CAL	40	E4
HUNT RD	CAL	41	A4
HUNT RD	IMP	112	B3
HUNT RD	LAS	14	C3
HUNT RD	MCO	47	C5
HUNTER	MON	54	C4
HUNTER BLVD	RCO	103	D4
HUNTER ST	CAL	41	A5
HUNTER CREEK RD	DN	1	E5
HUNTER CREEK RD	DN	2	A5
HUNTER MTN RD	INY	61	A4
HUNTERS VLY RD	MPA	48	E2
HUNTINGTON AV	SBR	144	C3
HUNTINGTON DR	LACO	97	E2
HUNTINGTON DR	LACO	R	B3
HUNTINGTON RD	MAD	57	C2
HUNTINGTON RD	STA	47	B2
HUTCHINS ST	SJCO	40	A4
HUTCHINSON RD	SJCO	47	B2
HUTCHINSON RD	SUT	33	C3
HUNTLEY MINE RD	MNO	50	E2
HUNTSMAN AV	FRCO	56	E4
HUNTSMAN AV	FRCO	57	A4
HUNTSMAN AV	FRCO	58	A4
HUPP COUTOLENC	BUT	25	D2
HURDS GULCH RD	SIS	3	D5
HURLES CIR	BUT	25	E4
HURLETON RD	BUT	25	E4
HURLTN SWDS FLT	BUT	25	E4
HURLEY FLATS RD	RCO	100	B3
HURRICANE RD	SLO	77	D4
HUSMAN RD	MCO	47	C5
HUSMAN RD	MCO	55	C1
HUSTED RD	COL	32	E2
HUSTON RD	IMP	109	B5
HUTCHINS	MCO	56	B1
HUTSELL RD	MEN	30	E3
HYAMPOM RD	TRI	17	A2
HYDE RD	IMP	111	E3
HYDE ST	FRCO	57	B5
HYDRIL RD	KIN	67	A3
HYPERION AV	LA	182	D4
I			
I AV	SBD	91	C4
I ST	BEN	153	A4
I ST	EUR	121	D1
I ST	MDO	162	B3
IBEX SPRING RD	SBD	72	D5
ICE HOUSE RD	ED	35	C3
ICE HOUSE RD	ED	35	C4
ICELAND RD	NEV	27	E5
IDAHO AV	KIN	67	D2
IDAHO RD	STA	47	D3
IDAHO ST	SDCO	V	C3
IDAHO ST	SDCO	111	D1
IDAHO-MARYLAND	NEV	34	C1
IDAHO-MARYLD RD	GV	127	D3
IDAHO-MARYLD RD	NEV	127	D3
IDALEONA DR	RCO	99	B3
IDLEWOOD LN	HUM	9	E3

STREET	CO.	PAGE	GRID
IDLEWOOD LN	HUM	10	A3
IGNACIO BLVD	MAR	L	A2
IKE CROW RD	STA	47	C4
ILLINOIS AV	STA	47	C2
ILLINOIS AV	TEH	24	E2
ILLINOIS VLY RD	DN	2	D2
IMLER RD	IMP	108	E4
IMOLA AV	NAPA	L	D1
IMOLA AV	NAP	133	C5
IMOLA AV W	NAP	133	B5
IMPERIAL AV	EC	217	B4
IMPERIAL AV	IMP	109	A5
IMPERIAL AV	SD	216	A4
IMPERIAL AV	SDCO	V	C3
IMPERIAL AV	SDCO	111	D1
IMPERIAL HWY	IMP	111	B3
IMPERIAL HWY	LA	189	B2
IMPERIAL HWY	LACO	97	D3
IMPERIAL HWY	LACO	98	B3
IMPERIAL HWY	LACO	Q	C5
IMPERIAL HWY	LACO	R	E5
IMPERIAL HWY	LACO	S	A1
IMPERIAL HWY	ORA	R	E5
IMPERIAL HWY	ORA	T	C1
IMPERIAL ST	KER	77	E2
IMPERIAL ST	KER	78	B2
IMPERIAL DAM RD	IMP	110	E5
IMPERL GABLS RD	IMP	110	B3
INCLINE RD	MPA	49	B2
INCLINE RD	MPA	63	A5
INDEPENDENCE RD	CAL	41	B2
INDPNDCE CEM RD	CAL	41	B2
INDEPNDNC LK RD	SIE	27	C5
INDEPNDNCIA MAT	BAJA	112	B4
INDIA ST	SD	215	C1
INDIAN AV	PMSP	206	B4
INDIAN AV	RCO	100	C3
INDIAN RD	LAS	21	A4
INDIANA AV	MCO	56	B1
INDIANA AV	STA	47	E2
INDIANA ST	LACO	R	B4
INDIANA RCH RD	YUB	26	A5
INDIANA SCH RD	YUB	26	A5
INDIAN CYN RD	KER	70	C5
INDIAN CYN RD	KER	80	C1
INDIAN CEM RD	ALP	36	B4
INDIAN COVE CIR	SBD	101	B2
INDIAN CV E RD	SBD	101	B2
INDIAN CV W RD	SBD	101	B2
INDIAN CV MT RD	SBD	101	B2
INDIAN CREEK RD	ALP	36	C5
INDIAN CREEK RD	KER	79	D3
INDIAN CREEK RD	MNO	51	D2
INDIAN CREEK RD	PLU	20	E5
INDIAN CREEK RD	RCO	100	A4
INDIAN CREEK RD	SIS	2	D2
INDIAN CREEK RD	SIS	3	D4
INDIAN CREEK RD	TRI	17	D2
INDIAN DIGGINS	ED	41	B1
INDIAN FLAT RD	NEV	34	C1
INDIAN GUIDE	FRCO	58	B3
INDIAN GULCH RD	MPA	48	E3
INDIAN GULCH RD	MPA	49	A4
INDIAN GLCH EXT	MPA	48	D4
INDIAN HILL BL	CLA	203	A3
INDIAN HILL BL	LACO	98	D2
INDIAN HILL BL	POM	203	B3
INDIAN HILL RD	RCO	100	C5
INDIAN HILL RD	SIE	26	C5
INDIAN HILL RD	STA	48	C2
INDIANOLA AV	FRCO	57	E4
INDIANOLA CTOFF	HUM	9	E5
INDIANOLA CTOFF	HUM	10	A5
INDIANOLA RESRV	HUM	15	D2
INDIAN OLE RD	LAS	20	C4
INDIAN PAINT DR	RCO	100	C5
INDIAN PASS RD	IMP	110	B4
INDIAN PEAK RD	MPA	49	B3
INDIAN POINT RD	KER	79	B4
INDIAN RANCH RD	INY	71	C2
INDIAN RES RD	AMA	40	D3
INDIAN ROCK RD	IMP	112	D5
INDIANS RD	MON	64	D2
INDIAN SCHL RD	LPAZ	104	A2
INDIAN SRVCE RD	TUL	69	A3
INDIAN SPGS RD	ALP	36	D5
INDIAN SPGS RD	NEV	34	B2
INDIAN SPGS RD	SBD	81	D4
INDIAN TOM LAKE	SIS	5	B2
INDIAN VLY RD	MAR	38	A4
INDIAN VLY RD	MON	66	A5
INDIAN VLY RD	SIE	26	C4
INDIAN VLY RD	SLO	66	A5
INDIAN VLY RD	TRI	17	A2
INDIAN WELLS ST	KER	80	D1
INDIO AV	SBDO	100	E1
INDUSTRIAL BLVD	MOH	96	B4
INDUSTRIAL PKWY	ALA	N	E1
INDUSTRIAL PKWY	ALA	P	A1
INDUSTRIAL PKWY	ALA	45	E2
INDSTRL FARM RD	KER	78	C2
INGHRAM RD	TEH	24	D2
INGLEWOOD AV	LACO	S	B1
INGLEWOOD BLVD	LA	188	A2
INGOMAR GRADE	MCO	55	D1
INGOMAR RD	MCO	47	D5
INGOMAR RD	MCO	55	D1
INGRAHAM ST	SD	212	B1
INGRAHAM ST	SDCO	V	A3
INGRAM LN	SUT	33	B1
INGRAM CREEK RD	STA	47	A3
INK GRADE	NAPA	32	B5
INK GRADE	NAPA	38	B1
INLAND DR	SJCO	40	A5

INDEXES

257
INLAND FRWY
STREET INDEX
KEYSTONE RD

STREET	CO.	PAGE	GRID
INLAND FRWY	SD	214	A3
INLAND FRWY	SD	216	C1
INLAND FRWY	SDCO	V	D4
INLAND FRWY	SDCO	106	C5
INLAND FRWY	SDCO	111	D2
INLAND CTR DR	SBDO	207	B4
INSKIP RD	TEH	19	A4
INTAKE BLVD	RCO	103	D5
INTERLAKE RD	SLO	65	D5
INTERNATIONL AV	FRCO	57	D2
INTERNATIONL AV	IMP	109	B3
INVESTOR AV	RCO	102	C4
INWOOD RD	SHA	19	A3
INYO N	INY	51	D3
INYO ST	DN	1	D4
INYOKERN RD	KER	80	D1
IONA AV	KIN	67	D2
IONE RD	SAC	40	C2
IONE BUENA VIS	AMA	40	D3
IONE MICHIGN BR	AMA	40	C2
IOWA AV	RCO	99	B2
IOWA AV	STA	47	C3
IOWA CITY RD	YUB	33	D1
IOWA HILL	PLA	34	D2
IRIS AV	RCO	99	B3
IRIS CT	KER	79	C1
IRIS DR	SAL	171	C2
IRIS LN	SDCO	106	D3
IRIS RD	LAS	13	E3
IRIS RD	LAS	14	A3
IRIS WY	CAL	41	B2
IRIS CANYON RD	MONT	167	E5
IRIS CANYON RD	MONT	168	E1
IRISH HILL RD	AMA	40	D2
IRISH TOWN PNE-			
-GRV WIELAND RD	AMA	41	A2
IRMULCO RD	MEN	22	E5
IRONAGE RD	SBD	101	E1
IRONE AV	KER	89	C1
IRON MTN RD	SBD	91	C1
IRON MTN RD	SHA	18	B1
IRON MTN PUMPNG	SBD	102	E1
IRONWOOD AV	RCO	99	C2
IRONWOOD CT	KER	79	B4
IRVINE AV	CM	199	C4
IRVINE AV	NB	199	C4
IRVINE AV	ORA	199	E1
IRVINE BLVD	ORA	98	C4
IRVINE BLVD	ORA	T	E3
IRVINE RD	IMP	109	C4
IRVINE CENTR DR	ORA	98	C4
IRVINE CENTR DR	ORA	T	E3
IRVINE LODGE RD	MEN	22	E4
IRWIN RD	SBD	81	E5
IRWIN RD	SBD	82	A5
IRWIN RD	SBD	208	B1
IRWIN RD	TEH	24	C2
IRWINDALE AV	LACO	R	E3
ISABELLA BLVD	KER	80	B4
ISABELA-WLKR PS	KER	79	D1
ISABELA-WLKR PS	KER	80	B1
ISHI PISHI RD	HUM	10	D2
ISLAND RD	SHA	13	D3
ISLAND RD	SIS	3	D5
ISLAND RD	SIS	11	D1
ISLAND BAR HILL	BUT	25	E4
ISLAND MTN RD	HUM	22	D1
ISLAND MTN RD	TRI	22	D1
ISLAND PARK RD	FRCO	58	B2
ISLETON RD	SAC	M	E1
ISPEN AV	MCO	48	E5
ITALIAN BAR RD	FRCO	50	A5
ITALIAN BAR RD	TUO	41	C4
IVANHOE RD	SBD	91	E4
IVANPAH RD	SBD	84	C3
IVANPAH CIMA RD	SBD	84	B3
IVERSON LN	LAS	14	B3
IVERSON RD	MEN	30	D4
IVERSON RD	MON	54	E5
IVERSON ST	SAL	171	B4
IVESGROVE DR	LACO	89	D3
IVORY MILL RD	GLE	24	A4
IVY AV	MCO	56	C1
J			
J ST	DVS	136	D2
J ST	MDO	162	B3
J ST	MER	170	C5
J ST	SCTO	137	E3
J ST	SDCO	V	C4
J ST	SDCO	111	D2
JACALITOS CK RD	FRCO	66	D3
JACARANDA DR	KER	79	B4
JACK AV	KER	78	B2
JACKASS FLTS RD	NEV	26	C5
JACKASS FLTS RD	NEV	34	C1
JACKASS GRADE	SBT	55	E4
JACKASS GRADE	SBT	56	A4
JACKASS HILL RD	TUO	41	C5
JACK CREEK RD	SLO	75	E2
JACK CREEK RD	SLO	76	A2
JACKLIN RD	SCL	P	B2
JACKLIN RD	SCL	46	B4
JACK PINE AV	KER	79	E5
JACK RABBIT TR	RCO	99	D3
JACK RANCH RD	KER	69	B5
JACK RANCH RD	KER	80	D1
JACKS RD	MON	54	E5
JACK SHAW RD	HUM	16	B2
JACK SLOUGH RD	YUB	33	D2
JACKSNIPE RD	SOL	38	E3
JACKSON	PLA	33	E4
JACKSON AV	KER	77	E1

STREET	CO.	PAGE	GRID
JACKSON AV	KER	78	B1
JACKSON AV	KIN	67	D2
JACKSON AV	SJCO	47	D1
JACKSON DR	SDCO	V	D2
JACKSON DR	SDCO	106	D5
JACKSON RD	IMP	109	B4
JACKSON RD	SAC	40	A1
JACKSON RD	SBD	91	D3
JACKSON RD	STA	47	C2
JACKSON ST	ALA	L	E5
JACKSON ST	ALA	M	A5
JACKSON ST	ALA	N	E1
JACKSON ST	ALA	P	A1
JACKSON ST	ALA	45	E2
JACKSON ST	RCO	99	A3
JACKSON ST	RCO	101	A4
JACKSON ST	SF	143	D3
JACKSON ST	TEH	18	D5
JACKSON ST W	ALA	N	E1
JACKSON ST W	H	146	D4
JACKSON GATE RD	AMA	40	E2
JACKSON MDWS RD	SIE	27	C4
JACKSON RCH RD	HUM	9	E5
JACKSON SLGH RD	SAC	M	D2
JACKSON VLY RD	AMA	40	D3
JACKSONVILLE RD	TUO	41	C5
JACK TONE RD	SJCO	40	B4
JACOBS	FRCO	58	B4
JACOBS RD	SJCO	40	A5
JACOBS WY	RCO	99	B4
JACOBY CREEK RD	HUM	10	A5
JACQUELINE	SIS	4	C2
JADE AV	SIS	4	C4
JAHANT	SJCO	40	A3
JAHANT RD	SJCO	40	B3
JAIL RD	AVLN	105	B5
JAKE RD	RCO	100	A5
JALAMA RD	SB	86	B4
JAMACHA BLVD	SDCO	V	D3
JAMACHA RD	SDCO	V	E3
JAMACHA RD	SDCO	111	D1
JAMAICA BLVD	MOH	96	B4
JAMBOREE BLVD	IRV	198	E4
JAMBOREE BLVD	IRV	200	C1
JAMBOREE BLVD	ORA	T	D4
JAMBOREE RD	IRV	198	E4
JAMBOREE RD	NB	200	A4
JAMBOREE RD	ORA	98	C5
JAMES RD	FRCO	56	E4
JAMES RD	IMP	109	B5
JAMES RD	KER	78	D2
JAMES DONLON BL	CC	M	C3
JAMES LICK FRWY	SF	142	E5
JAMES LICK FRWY	SFCO	45	C2
JAMES LICK SKWY	SF	142	D4
JAMES LICK SKWY	SF	143	D5
JAMESON AV	FRCO	57	B5
JAMESON AV	FRCO	57	B4
JAMESON RD	COL	32	E1
JAMESON RD	KER	79	D4
JAMISON CK RD	SCR	N	D5
JAMISON CK RD	SCR	53	D1
JANE RD	SBD	92	D4
JANES RD	HUM	10	A5
JANESVLLE GRADE	LAS	21	B4
JANICE AV	KER	79	E1
JANICE AV	KER	80	A1
JANICE RD	SIS	4	C2
JANICE ST	KER	80	A4
JANOPAUL AV	STA	162	C5
JANSS RD	VEN	96	D1
JAPATUL LN	SDCO	107	B5
JAPATUL LN	SDCO	112	B1
JAPATUL RD	SBD	91	C4
JAPATUL RD	SBD	91	D3
JAPATUL RD	SDCO	107	B5
JAPATUL RD	SDCO	112	B1
JAPATUL VLY RD	SDCO	107	C5
JAPATUL VLY RD	SDCO	112	C1
JAQUIMA DR	CAL	41	A4
JARDINE RD	SLO	76	B1
JARED LN	SB	86	E2
J ARTHR YNGR FY	SMCO	45	D3
J ARTHR YNGR FY	FCTY	145	D1
J ARTHR YNGR FY	SM	145	D1
JARVIS AV	ALA	N	E2
JARVIS AV	ALA	P	A2
JARVIS AV	ALA	45	E3
JARVIS RD	ALP	36	C4
JASMINE RD	SBD	92	B3
JASPER LN	YUB	33	E2
JASPER RD	IMP	112	B4
JASPER RD	TUO	48	B1
JASPER SEARS BR	MCO	55	C1
JASPER SEARS RD	MCO	55	C1
JAVA AV	KIN	67	C2
JAVA DR	SVL	148	E2
JAVIS AV	KER	80	C1
JAVIS AV	KER	80	E1
JAWBONE CYN RD	KER	79	E2
JAWBONE CYN RD	KER	80	B3
JAY DEE LN	RCO	100	C5
JAYMAR RD	HUM	16	B3
JAYNE AV	FRCO	66	D3
JAYNE AV	FRCO	67	A2
JEAN BLANC RD	INY	51	D3
JEANESE	TUO	41	C5
JEAN NICHOLS RD	RCO	99	D5
JEFF ST	KER	80	C1
JEFFERSON AV	FRCO	56	E4
JEFFERSON AV	FRCO	57	C4
JEFFERSON AV	FRCO	58	A4
JEFFERSON AV	RCO	99	C5
JEFFERSON AV	SM	N	D2

STREET	CO.	PAGE	GRID
JEFFERSON BLVD	CUL	183	D5
JEFFERSON BLVD	CUL	188	C1
JEFFERSON BLVD	LA	183	D5
JEFFERSON BLVD	LA	185	A5
JEFFERSON BLVD	LACO	97	D2
JEFFERSON BLVD	LACO	Q	D4
JEFFERSON BLVD	LACO	187	D4
JEFFERSON BLVD	LACO	188	A4
JEFFERSON BLVD	YOL	39	D2
JEFFERSON ST	MONT	167	D4
JEFFERSON ST	NAP	133	C4
JEFFERSON ST	ORA	T	D1
JEFFERSON ST	RCO	101	A4
JEFFERSON ST	SDCO	106	B3
JEFFERSON ST	SF	143	A2
JEFFERSON ST N	NAP	133	B1
JEFFERY RD	IMP	111	E3
JEFFREY RD	ORA	98	C4
JEFFREY RD	ORA	T	E4
JEFFREY RCH RD	MNO	51	D2
JELLYS FERRY RD	TEH	18	D4
JENEVEIN AV	SBR	144	B3
JENKINS RD	KER	78	C3
JENKS LAKE RD	SBD	100	A1
JENNINGS RD	STA	47	C3
JENNY LIND RD	CAL	40	D4
JENSEN AV	COL	32	E3
JENSEN AV	FRCO	56	C4
JENSEN AV	FRCO	57	A3
JENSEN RD	SLO	75	E1
JERROLD AV	FRCO	56	B2
JERRY COLLINS AV	MCO	48	B5
JERSEY	MCO	55	E2
JERSEY AV	KIN	67	C2
JERSEYDALE RD	MPA	49	C3
JERSEY ISLAND	CC	39	C4
JERSEY ISLND RD	CC	M	D3
JERUSALEM GRADE	LAK	32	B4
JESS VALLEY RD	MOD	8	B3
JESUS MARIA RD	CAL	41	A3
JETTY RD S	HUM	15	D1
JEWELL AV	PAC	167	A1
JEWELL RD	TEH	18	C4
JEWELL VLY RD	SDCO	111	A4
JEWETT RD	HUM	16	D5
JEWETT RD	SUT	33	C3
JEWETTA AV	KER	78	C3
J HELT RD	HUM	15	D2
JIM DAY RD	SHA	13	E4
JIM HARVEY RD	SHA	18	C2
JIMMY DURNTE BL	SDCO	106	C4
JIM NEGRA RD	MCO	55	C2
JOAQUIN RD	ML	164	D2
JOAQUIN RDG LKT	FRCO	66	C2
JOEGER	PLA	34	C3
JOE SMITH RD	INY	51	D4
JOHANSEN RD	STA	47	D2
JOHN ST	RCO	100	E3
JOHN ST	SAL	171	C4
JOHN DALY BLVD	SMCO	L	B5
JOHN DALY BLVD	SMCO	45	B2
J F KENNEDY DR	RCO	99	C3
J F KENNEDY DR	SF	141	B4
JOHN FOX RD	STA	47	E2
JOHN GIBSON BL	LA	191	A2
JOHN LADD CHROM	SIS	3	B3
JOHN MUIR PKWY	CC	L	D3
JOHN MUIR PKWY	CC	38	D5
JOHNNY MDW RD	MNO	43	E5
JOHNNY MDW RD	MNO	50	E1
JOHNNY MDW RD	MNO	51	A1
JOHNS DR	TUL	68	D3
JOHNS RD	KER	79	C3
JOHN SCHOOL RD	COL	33	A3
JOHN SCHOOL RD	YOL	33	A3
JOHN SMITH RD	SBT	55	A3
JOHNSON AV	MCO	47	D4
JOHNSON AV	SDCO	V	E2
JOHNSON AV	SDCO	106	E5
JOHNSON AV	SNLO	172	C3
JOHNSON AV	SLO	76	B3
JOHNSON CT	KER	79	C4
JOHNSON DR	TUL	58	B4
JOHNSON RD	HUM	10	B3
JOHNSON RD	HUM	15	E2
JOHNSON RD	KER	78	C3
JOHNSON RD	LAS	21	B3
JOHNSON RD	LACO	89	D3
JOHNSON RD	LACO	89	D4
JOHNSON RD	MCO	55	E1
JOHNSON RD	SBD	90	E3
JOHNSON RD	SBD	90	E4
JOHNSON RD	SBD	91	C3
JOHNSON RD	SJCO	40	C4
JOHNSON RD	TEH	18	B5
JOHNSON RD	TEH	18	D4
JOHNSON RD N	MCO	55	D1
JOHNSON ST	RCO	101	B5
JOHNSON ST	RCO	108	B1
JOHNSON ST	SBD	91	E3
JOHNSON ST	SB	87	D1
JOHNSON CYN RD	INY	72	A3
JOHNSON CYN RD	MON	54	E5
JOHNSON CYN RD	MON	55	A5
JOHNSON RCH RD	PLU	20	D5
JOHNSON SCH RD	LAS	21	B3
JOHNSTON AV	KER	80	D1
JOHNSTON AV	RCO	99	E4
JOHNSVILLE RD	SIE	26	D3
JOHNSVLL MCCREA	PLU	26	E3
JOHN WEST RD	MAD	49	D4
JOINES RD	YUB	33	E1
JOINT HWY 14	LAS	20	E3
JOINT HWY 14	LAS	21	A3

STREET	CO.	PAGE	GRID
JOINT RD	TEH	18	B5
JOJOBA RD	RCO	107	A1
JOJOBA RD E	RCO	107	A1
JOJOBA ST	RCO	102	C4
JOLON RD	MON	65	B3
JOLON PLEYTO	MON	65	B4
JONATA PARK RD	SB	86	D3
JONATHAN ST	SBD	91	B3
JONES AV	COL	32	E3
JONES LN	MOD	8	B1
JONES RD	LAS	8	B5
JONES RD	MCO	48	B4
JONES RD	SJCO	47	D1
JONES ST	FRCO	57	B5
JONES ST	SF	143	B2
JONES ST	SMA	173	D3
JONES BAR RD	NEV	34	C1
JONES BRADWAY	SBD	92	A3
JONES VALLEY RD	SIE	27	E4
JORDAN RD	HUM	16	A3
JORDAN RD	MCO	47	E4
JORDAN RD	MCO	48	A4
JORDAN CREEK RD	MPA	48	E1
JORDAN CREEK RD	MPA	49	A1
JORDON HILL RD	BUT	25	D2
JORGENSEN RD	MCO	47	C5
JORGENSEN RD	STA	47	C4
JOSE RD	SCR	P	B5
JOSE BASIN RD	FRCO	50	A5
JOSE BASIN RD	MAD	58	A1
JOSEPH PL	SIS	4	C2
JOSEPH CREEK RD	MOD	7	C5
JOSHUA BLVD	KER	80	C5
JOSHUA DR	SBD	100	D2
JOSHUA LN	SBD	100	E2
JOSHUA RD	SBD	91	C3
JOSHUA RD	SBD	91	D4
JOSHUA WY	KER	79	D5
JOSHUA TREE RD	SBD	92	C5
JOY RD	SON	37	C2
JOY ST	KER	70	A5
J T CROW RD	STA	47	C4
JUAN ST	SD	213	A5
JUAN ST	SDCO	V	B3
JUAN DIEGO-			
-FLATS RD	RCO	100	A5
JUBILEE PASS RD	INY	72	C4
JUDSON ST	SBD	99	C2
JULIAN AV	KER	89	D1
JULIAN AV	SDCO	107	A5
JULIAN RD	SDCO	107	A4
JULIAN ST	SCL	P	C3
JULIAN ST	SCL	46	B4
JULIAN ST	SJ	152	A4
JULIE ST	KER	79	C3
JUMAR CT	RCO	107	B1
JUMPER AV	KER	78	A2
JUNCAL RD	SB	87	D4
JUNE ST	SBD	99	B1
JUNE LK BCH RD	MNO	50	C1
JUNIPER AV	MCO	48	B4
JUNIPER LN	SIS	4	C5
JUNIPER RD	LAS	14	B3
JUNIPER RD	RCO	99	B3
JUNIPER ST	SDCO	106	C2
JUNIPER FLTS RD	RCO	99	D4
JUNIPER FLTS RD	RCO	101	A2
JUNIPER HILL RD	LACO	90	B4
JUNIPR KNOLL RD	SIS	5	A3
JUNIPER LAKE RD	LAS	20	A3
JUNIPERO ST	CAR	168	C4
JUNIPERO SRA BL	SCL	N	D3
JUNIPERO SRA BL	SCL	45	D4
JUNIPERO SRA FY	CPTO	149	C4
JUNIPERO SRA FY	CPTO	150	A4
JUNIPERO SRA FY	MLBR	144	A5
JUNIPERO SRA FY	SJ	150	A4
JUNIPERO SRA FY	SMCO	45	C3
JUNIPERO SRA FY	SCL	149	C4
JUNIPER STA RD	MOD	7	B5
JUNKANS RD	SHA	18	A3
JURS RD	CAL	41	B2
JURUPA AV	RCO	99	A2
JURUPA AV	SBD	99	A2
JURUPA RD	RCO	99	A2
JUSTICE CT	KER	79	D2
JUSTICE RD	TRI	16	E5
JUTLAND DR	SD	211	C4
J W BARR	SIS	12	C2
K			
K ST	BEN	153	A4
K ST	MDO	162	B3
KADOTA AV	MCO	48	D5
KAGEL CANYON RD	LACO	Q	D1
KAISER	SJCO	40	B5
KAISER RD	IMP	109	C3
KAISER RD	RCO	102	C4
KAISER RD	STA	47	D3
KALIN RD	IMP	109	A4
KAMM AV	FRCO	56	E5
KAMM AV	FRCO	57	C5
KAMM AV	TUL	57	D5
KAMM RD	IMP	109	C5
KANDRA RD	SIS	5	D2
KANE RD	HUM	9	E3
KANE RD	HUM	10	A3
KANE RD	SBD	91	E2
KANSAS AV	KIN	67	D2
KANSAS AV	MDO	162	A3
KANSAS AV	STA	47	C2
KANSAS AV	TEH	18	E5
KAPAPA RD	SBD	80	E1

STREET	CO.	PAGE	GRID
KAPRANOS RD	LAK	23	C5
KARCHNER RD	PLA	34	A3
KAREN AV	RCO	100	C3
KARLO RD	LAS	21	C2
KARNAK RD	SUT	33	C4
KASSON RD	SJCO	47	A2
KATELLA AV	ANA	193	C4
KATELLA AV	ANA	194	B4
KATELLA AV	OR	194	B4
KATELLA AV	ORA	98	B3
KATELLA AV	ORA	T	D2
KATHERINE RD	VEN	97	A1
KAUFENBERG RD	LAS	14	A4
KAUFFMAN AV	TEH	18	E5
KAUFMAN RD	STA	47	E2
KAUT RD	TRI	10	E5
KAVANAUGH RD	IMP	112	C3
KEARNEY AV	FRCO	57	A3
KEARNEY BLVD	FRE	165	B4
KEARNY ST	SF	143	C2
KEARNY VILLA RD	SD	213	E1
KEARNY VILLA RD	SD	214	A1
KEARNY VILLA RD	SDCO	V	C2
KEARNY VILLA RD	SDCO	106	D5
KEATON RD	MCO	47	D4
KECKS RD	KER	77	A1
KEEFER RD	BUT	25	A2
KEEGAN RD	COL	32	C2
KEELE RD	RCO	110	C1
KEIM BLVD	RCO	110	C1
KELBAKER RD	SBD	83	C3
KELBAKER RD	SBD	84	A5
KELBAKER RD	SBD	93	E2
KELBAKER RD	SBD	94	A1
KELLEMS LN	SIS	3	D5
KELLEMS LN	SIS	11	D1
KELLER RD	RCO	99	C5
KELLEY RD	SBD	101	D1
KELLOG RD	SUT	33	B2
KELLOGG DR	ORA	98	C3
KELLOGG DR	ORA	T	E1
KELLOGG RD	DN	1	D3
KELLOGG SRRA BL	RCO	100	C3
KELLY	SJCO	47	D1
KELLY RD	HUM	16	C2
KELLY RD	NAPA	L	D1
KELLY RD	NAPA	38	D3
KELLY RD	TEH	24	A2
KELLY RD	YUB	26	B5
KELLY GULCH RD	SIS	11	B2
KELSEY CREEK RD	SIS	3	B5
KELSEY CREEK RD	LAK	31	D3
KELSO AV	KER	79	E1
KELSO RD	ALA	M	E4
KELSO RD	ALA	46	D1
KELSO RD	KER	79	E1
KELSO RD	SBD	83	C4
KELSO AMBOY RD	SBD	93	E1
KELSO AMBOY RD	SBD	94	A1
KELSO CIMA RD	SBD	83	E5
KELSO CIMA RD	SBD	84	A4
KELSO CK VLY RD	KER	79	E1
KELSO VALLEY RD	KER	79	E2
KELSO VALLEY RD	KER	80	A2
KEMP CT	HUM	16	B3
KEMPER RD	KER	80	A5
KEMPER RD	STA	47	D2
KEMPTON RD	SUT	33	D3
KENDALL AV	KER	80	D1
KENDALL DR	SBD	99	B1
KENDLE RD	IMP	109	C4
KENMAR LN	KER	79	A4
KENMAR RD	HUM	15	E2
KENNEBRAW LN	HUM	16	C4
KENNEDY AV	BUT	25	A3
KENNEDY RD	STA	48	A1
KENNEDY RD	TRI	17	B1
KENNEDY MEADOW	TUL	70	A3
KENNEDY MEM DR	SHA	18	B2
KENNEFICK RD	SJCO	40	B4
KENNETH AV	SAC	34	B5
KENNETH RD	LACO	Q	D2
KENNETT RD	SHA	18	C1
KENNEY AV	TEH	18	C4
KENNY AV	MCO	48	B4
KENNY CAMP RD	TRI	11	D5
KENO WORDEN RD	KLAM	5	A1
KENSINGTON WY	S	160	B2
KENT AV	KIN	67	B2
KENT AV	KIN	67	C2
KENT AV	MAR	139	B5
KENT AV	SUT	33	C1
KENTUCKY AV	YOL	33	B5
KENTUCKY ST	FRFD	135	B3
KENWOOD	SDCO	111	E1
KENWOOD DR	SDCO	V	D3
KEOUGH HOT SPGS	INY	51	D5
KERN RD	SBD	101	D1
KERN ST	SAL	171	D4
KERN CANYON RD	KER	79	A2
KERN RIV CYN RD	KER	79	B2
KERTO RD	KER	78	A5
KERSHAW RD	IMP	109	B4
KESTER AV	LACO	Q	C3
KESWICK DAM RD	SHA	18	B2
KETTLEMAN LN	SJCO	40	A4
KETTNER BLVD	SD	215	D4
KETTNER BLVD	SDCO	V	B3
KEYES RD	MCO	48	B3
KEYES RD	STA	47	D3
KEYES RD	STA	48	A3
KEYES ST	SJ	152	D5
KEYS RD	SUT	33	D4
KEYSTONE RD	IMP	109	A5

INDEXES

258
KEYSVILLE RD — STREET INDEX — LEPRECHAUN LN

STREET	CO.	PAGE	GRID
KEYSVILLE RD	KER	79	C1
KEZAR DR	SF	141	D4
KIBBE RD	YUB	33	D1
KICKAPOO TR	SBD	100	D2
KIDDER AV	FRFD	135	C3
KIDDER CREEK RD	SIS	3	C5
KIDDER CK RD S	SIS	3	D5
KIDDER CK RD S	SIS	11	D1
KID LAKES	PLA	35	C1
KIDWELL RD	SOL	39	B1
KIEFER BLVD	SAC	39	E1
KIEFER BLVD	SAC	40	B1
KIEFER RD	IMP	112	C4
KIELY BLVD	SJ	150	E5
KIELY BLVD	SCLR	150	D3
KIERNAN AV	STA	47	B2
KIETZKE LN	RENO	130	E3
KIFER RD	SCLR	150	D1
KIFER RD	SVL	150	A1
KILAGA SPGS RD	PLA	34	B3
KILAGA SPG RD N	PLA	34	B3
KILBURN AV	NAP	133	A4
KILBURN RD	STA	47	C4
KILE RD	SJCO	39	E3
KILER CANYON RD	SLO	75	E1
KILER CANYON RD	SLO	76	A1
KILGORE RD	SUT	33	A2
KILKARE RD	ALA	46	B2
KILLGORE HLS RD	SIS	4	A4
KILROY	STA	47	D3
KILROY RD	MCO	47	D4
KIMBALL AV	SBD	98	D2
KIMBALL LN	YUB	33	D2
KIMBALL RD	TEH	18	D5
KIMBERLINA RD	KER	78	B1
KIMBERLY CT	KER	79	C5
KIMBERLY DR	KER	79	C5
KIMBERLY RD	SHA	18	D3
KIMTU CT	HUM	16	B5
KINCAID RD	SCL	P	D3
KINCAID RD	SCL	46	C4
KINE AV	RCO	99	C3
KINEVAN RD	SB	87	B4
KING AV	KIN	67	C2
KING RD	COL	32	C2
KING RD	IMP	112	C3
KING RD	KER	67	C5
KING RD	PLA	34	B4
KING RD	SJ	152	D1
KING RD	SCL	P	C3
KING RD	SCL	46	B4
KING RD	SCL	152	D1
KING RD	SOL	39	C2
KING RD	TEH	18	C5
KING RD	TRI	12	A4
KING ST	BKD	166	E4
KING CITY RD	SBT	65	C1
KINGDON	SJCO	40	A4
KING RANCH RD	BUT	25	E5
KING RIDGE RD	SON	37	A1
KINGS AV	FRCO	66	D2
KINGS RD	SBD	90	E4
KINGS RD	TUO	48	E1
KINGS RD	TUO	49	A1
KINGSBURY RD	TRI	17	B2
KINGS CANYON RD	FRCO	58	A3
KINGS HILL RD	PLA	34	D2
KINGSLEY ST	MTCL	203	A4
KINGS MTN RD	SMCO	N	D2
KINGS MTN RD	SMCO	45	C4
KINGS PEAK RD	HUM	16	A5
KINGSTON RD	SBD	83	E2
KINGS VALLEY RD	DN	1	E3
KINNEY RD	MEN	30	C3
KIOWA BLVD	MOH	96	B4
KIOWA RD	RCO	102	C3
KIOWA RD	SBD	91	C4
KIP ST	KER	80	C1
KIRBY RD	MCO	48	C4
KIRBY ST	CAL	40	D4
KIRK RD	SCL	P	B4
KIRKER PASS RD	CC	M	B3
KIRKVILLE RD	SUT	33	C3
KIRSCHENMANN RD	SB	87	D1
KIT CARSON RD	AMA	35	E5
KIT CARSON CPGD	ALP	36	B4
KLAMATH BCH RD	DN	1	E5
KLAMATH BCH RD	DN	9	E1
KLAMATH BCH RD	DN	10	A1
KLAMATH MILL RD	DN	2	A5
KLAMATH MILL RD	DN	10	A1
KLAMATHON RD	SIS	4	B3
KLAMATH RIV RD	SIS	3	D3
KLASSETTE ST	KER	80	A4
KLAU MINE RD	SLO	75	D1
KLIPSTEIN ST	KER	78	A5
KLIPSTEIN CY RD	KER	78	A5
KLOKE RD	IMP	112	B4
KLONDIKE RD	SBD	93	C3
KLONDKE MINE RD	TRI	17	A3
KNEELAND RD	HUM	16	B1
KNIEBES RD	MCO	47	D5
KNIGHTON RD	SHA	18	C3
KNIGHTS RD	SUT	33	C3
KNIGHTSEN AV	CC	M	D3
KNIGHTSEN AV	CC	39	C5
KNOB HILL RD	MEN	31	B2
KNOB PK LKOT RD	SHA	17	D3
KNOTT AV	ORA	98	D3
KNOTT AV	ORA	T	B2
KNOW	PLA	33	E5
KNOWLES RD	MAD	49	B5
KNOWLES RD	MCO	56	C1
KNOX RD	STA	47	E1

STREET	CO.	PAGE	GRID
KNOXVL DVLHD RD	NAPA	32	C4
KOALA RD	SBD	91	A3
KOCH RD	KER	78	B2
KOENIGSTEIN RD	VEN	88	C4
KOESTER RD	KER	79	D3
KONOCTI RD	LAK	31	D3
KOPTA RD	TEH	24	E2
KOSTER RD	SJCO	47	A2
KOSTER ST	EUR	121	B1
KOWOLOWSKI RD	MOD	6	A2
KRAEMER BLVD	ORA	T	D1
KRAFFT RD	MCO	48	D4
KRAFT RD	KER	78	E5
KRAMAR RD	IMP	111	E3
KRAMER BLVD	ORA	98	C3
KRAMER RD	LAS	14	B3
KRAMER RD	SBD	91	A1
KRATZMEYER RD	KER	78	C2
KREHE RD	SUT	33	C1
KROSENS RD	YUB	25	E5
KRUSE RD	COL	32	D1
KT RD	SBT	54	E3
KT RD	SBT	55	A3
KUBLER RD	IMP	111	E4
KUCK RD	SIS	4	B4
KUENZLI ST	RENO	130	D2
KUMBERG RD	IMP	112	C4
KUNA AV	SBD	92	E5
KURT RD	KER	77	E1
KUTZ RD	IMP	108	E5
KYLE AV	KER	70	A5
KYTE AV	KER	78	C2
L			
L ST	CC	M	C3
L ST	DVS	136	D3
L ST	DN	1	D4
L ST	MDO	162	B3
L ST	SCTO	137	B3
L ST	SDCO	V	C4
L ST	SDCO	111	D2
LA BARR MDWS RD	NEV	34	C2
LABP & L RD	SBD	91	A4
LA BREA AV	LA	181	C4
LA BREA AV	LA	184	C3
LA BREA AV	LACO	97	D2
LA BREA AV	LACO	Q	D5
LA BREA CK RD	SB	77	A5
LA BRISA DR	SBD	100	E1
LA BRISA DR	SBD	100	D1
LA BRUCHERIE RD	IMP	112	A3
LA CADENA DR	CLTN	207	A4
LA CADENA DR	SBD	90	E3
LA CADENA DR	SBD	99	B2
LACEY BLVD	KIN	67	C1
LA CIENEGA BLVD	BH	183	E2
LA CIENEGA BLVD	CUL	183	E5
LA CIENEGA BLVD	ING	188	E4
LA CIENEGA BLVD	ING	189	E2
LA CIENEGA BLVD	LA	183	E4
LA CIENEGA BLVD	LACO	97	D2
LA CIENEGA BLVD	LACO	Q	D4
LA CIENEGA BLVD	LACO	183	E2
LA CIENEGA BLVD	LACO	188	E1
LA CIENEGA BLVD	LACO	189	E2
LAC JAC	FRCO	58	A4
LACK RD	IMP	109	A4
LA COLINA	TUL	68	E3
LA COLINA LN	RCO	107	C1
LA CONTENTA RD	SBD	100	E2
LA COSTA AV	SDCO	106	C3
LA CRESCENTA AV	LACO	R	A2
LA CRESTA DR	SDCO	107	A5
LA CUARTA ST	LACO	R	D5
LADD RD	STA	47	C2
LADDER RIDGE RD	LAK	31	D2
LADINO AV	MCO	48	B4
LA ENTRADA AV	LACO	R	D5
LAFAYETTE RD	SIE	26	D5
LAFAYETTE ST	SCLR	151	B1
LAFAYETTE ST	S	160	D5
LA GLORIA RD	SBT	55	B5
LAGOMARSINO AV	MON	65	B2
LAGOON DR	KER	78	A2
LA GRANADA	SDCO	106	C4
LA GRANDE RD	COL	32	C2
LA GRANGE RD	MCO	48	C2
LA GRANGE RD	STA	48	C2
LA GRANGE RD	TUO	48	C1
LA GRANGE DM RD	STA	48	C2
LAGUE RD	YUB	26	A5
LAGUNA AV	FRCO	67	B1
LAGUNA FRWY	ORA	98	D4
LAGUNA FRWY	ORA	T	E4
LAGUNA RD	SON	37	D2
LAGUNA RD	VEN	96	C1
LAGUNA CYN RD	LAG	201	B2
LAGUNA CYN RD	ORA	98	D5
LAGUNA CYN RD	ORA	T	E5
LAGUNA CREEK TR	SOL	38	E3
LAGUNA MTN RD	SDCO	107	D5
LAGUNA SECA DR	SBD	91	D4
LAGUNA SECA RD	MCO	55	D3
LA HABRA BLVD	ORA	R	E5
LA HABRA BLVD	ORA	T	B1
LA HONDA RD	SMCO	N	C3
LA HONDA RD	SMCO	45	C4
LAIRD RD	PLA	34	B4
LAIRD RD	STA	47	C3
LAIRO RED ROCK	SIS	5	B3
LA JOLLA AV	SDCO	106	C5
LA JOLLA BLVD	SDCO	V	A2
LA JOLLA BLVD	SDCO	106	C5

STREET	CO.	PAGE	GRID
LA JOLLA AMAGO	SDCO	107	A2
LA JOLLA S DR N	SD	211	B2
LA JOLLA S RD S	SD	211	A4
LA JOLLA SHR DR	SD	211	A2
LA JOLLA VLG RD	SDCO	V	A2
LAKE AV	FRCO	56	E3
LAKE AV	FRCO	57	A3
LAKE AV	KER	79	C2
LAKE AV	LACO	98	A1
LAKE AV	LACO	R	B3
LAKE AV	PAS	190	D4
LAKE AV	SCR	54	C2
LAKE BLVD	SHA	18	C2
LAKE DR	SBD	91	C5
LAKE RD	FRCO	50	B5
LAKE RD	KER	80	C3
LAKE RD	MCO	48	C4
LAKE RD	STA	47	E2
LAKE RD	STA	48	A2
LAKE RD N	INY	51	B5
LAKE RD S	INY	51	C5
LAKE RD S	KER	78	B4
LAKE RD S	KER	78	C4
LAKE ST	MAD	57	A2
LAKE ST	RCO	99	B4
LK ALMANOR W DR	PLU	20	B4
LK ALMANR RD E	PLU	20	C4
LK ALPINE RD E	ALP	42	A1
LK ALPINE RD W	ALP	42	A2
LAKE ANNIE RD	MOD	7	D3
LK BRITTON LOOP	SHA	13	D4
LK BRITTON RAMP	SHA	13	D4
LAKE CALIF DR	TEH	18	D3
LAKE CANYON RD	LACO	89	B3
LAKE CANYON RD	LACO	89	C3
LAKE CITY RD	NEV	26	C5
LK CITY DUMP RD	MOD	7	D5
LAKE CREST RD	LAS	21	B4
LAKE DAVIS RD	PLU	27	B2
LAKE EARL DR	DN	1	D4
LAKE FOREST DR	ORA	98	D4
LAKE FRANCES RD	YUB	26	B5
LAKE HERMAN RD	SOL	L	E2
LAKE HERMAN RD	SOL	38	D4
LAKE HERMAN RD	SOL	153	C1
LK JENNINGS PK	SDCO	107	A5
LAKELAND RD	LACO	R	C5
LAKELAND RD	LACO	T	A1
LAKE LEAVITT RD	LAS	21	B3
LAKE MARY RD	ML	164	A4
LAKE MARY RD	MNO	50	D2
LAKE MATHEWS DR	RCO	99	B3
LAKE MCCUMBER	SHA	19	B2
LAKE MEAD DR	CLK	74	E3
LAKE MORENA DR	SDCO	112	D1
LAKE MURRAY BL	SDCO	V	D3
LAKE MURRAY BL	SDCO	106	D5
LAKEPORT BLVD	LAK	31	D3
LAKE POWAY RD	SDCO	106	E4
LAKERIDGE RD	SHA	19	A3
LAKE SHORE AV	O	158	B3
LAKESHORE BLVD	LAK	31	D3
LAKESHORE DR	KLAM	5	B1
LAKESHORE DR	LAK	32	A3
LAKESHORE DR	SHA	12	C5
LAKE SHORE DR	SIS	4	C5
LAKESHORE RD	MOD	7	B4
LAKESIDE DR	O	158	A3
LAKE SIDE LN	SIS	4	C2
LAKE STATION RD	KER	78	B4
LAKE TAHOE BLVD	SLT	129	A4
LAKEVIEW	KIN	67	C2
LAKEVIEW	PLA	34	A3
LAKEVIEW AV	ORA	T	E2
LAKEVIEW AV	RCO	99	D3
LAKEVIEW DR	AMA	40	D3
LAKEVIEW DR	LAK	31	D2
LAKE VIEW DR	LAS	21	B4
LAKE VIEW DR	SLO	75	D1
LAKEVIEW RD	MPA	49	B3
LAKEVIEW RD	SCR	54	C2
LAKEVIEW RD	SDCO	107	A5
LAKE VIEW RD	SIS	4	C3
LAKEVIEW RD	SON	38	B3
LAKEVIEW CEM RD	SIS	5	A3
LAKEVILLE HWY	SON	L	A1
LAKEVILLE RD	SON	L	B2
LK WILDWOOD DR	NEV	34	B1
LAKEWOOD BLVD	LACO	98	A3
LAKEWOOD BLVD	LACO	S	E2
LAKEWOOD DR	MEN	23	A5
LAKIN DAM RD	SIS	13	A2
LA LOMA AV	B	156	B2
LA LOMA AV	MDO	162	C3
LA LOMA AV	VEN	88	C5
LA LOMA RD	LACO	R	B3
LA LOMA RD	PAS	190	A5
LAMB BLVD	CLK	74	E2
LAMB CANYON RD	RCO	99	E3
LAMBERT LN	LAS	21	C4
LAMBERT RD	LACO	R	D5
LAMBERT RD	ORA	U	A4
LAMBERT RD	ORA	T	C1
LAMBERT RD	SAC	39	E3
LAMBERT BRDG RD	SON	31	D5
LAMBIE RD	SOL	39	B3
LAMBUTH RD	STA	47	D1
LAMERT LN	GLE	24	D5
LA MESA RD	SBD	90	E4
LA MIRADA AV	LACO	R	D5
LA MIRADA AV	LACO	T	B1
LA MIRADA BLVD	LACO	98	B3
LAMMERS RD	SJCO	46	E2
LAMPLEY RD	STA	48	A2

STREET	CO.	PAGE	GRID
LAMPSON AV	GGR	195	A1
LAMPSON AV	ORA	T	B2
LANCASTER BLVD	KER	90	B1
LANCASTER BLVD	LACO	90	A2
LANCASTER RD	LACO	88	E2
LANCASTER RD	LACO	89	A2
LANCASTER RD	STA	47	E1
LANCASTER RD	STA	48	A1
LANCHA PLANA-			
-BUENA VISTA RD	AMA	40	D3
LANDACRE RD	TRI	17	B2
LANDAU BLVD	RCO	100	D3
LANDECENA DR	TRI	17	D1
LANDER AV	MCO	47	D5
LANDER AV	STA	47	E3
LANDERGEN RD	HUM	15	E4
LANDES RD	TEH	18	C4
LANDESS RD	SCL	46	B4
LANDIS GULCH	TRI	17	C3
LANDRAM AV	MCO	48	B4
LANES RD	FRCO	57	C2
LANES VALLEY RD	TEH	19	A3
LANFAIR RD	SBD	84	D3
LANFAIR RD	SBD	94	E1
LANGDON RD	MCO	55	D2
LANGLL VLY RD E	KLAM	5	E1
LANGLL VLY RD E	KLAM	6	A1
LANGLL VLY RD W	KLAM	5	E1
LANGLL VLY RD W	KLAM	6	A1
LANGWORTH RD	STA	47	D2
LANINI RD	MON	54	E5
LANINI RD	MON	55	A5
LANKERSHIM BLVD	LA	179	A5
LANKERSHIM BLVD	LACO	97	D1
LANKERSHIM BLVD	LACO	Q	D2
LANNAGAN RD	TRI	11	B5
LANNAGAN RD	TRI	17	B1
LANPHERE RD	HUM	9	E5
LANSING AV	KIN	67	C2
LA PALMA AV	ANA	193	D1
LA PALMA AV	ANA	194	A1
LA PALMA AV	KER	80	A5
LA PALMA AV	ORA	98	A3
LA PALMA AV	ORA	T	B2
LA PALOMA	AVLN	105	A4
LA PALOMA DR	TUL	68	E3
LA PALOMA RD	MCO	48	C4
LA PANZA AV	SB	87	E2
LA PAZ RD	ORA	98	D5
LA PORTE RD	BUT	25	D5
LA PORTE RD	BUT	26	B4
LA PORTE RD	YUB	26	A5
LA POSTA RD	SDCO	112	D1
LA PUENTE RD	LACO	U	A3
LARCHMONT BLVD	LA	184	E1
LARGO GRANDE	RCO	107	B1
LARGO VISTA RD	LACO	90	D4
LARKELLEN AV	LACO	R	E4
LARKIN RD	BUT	25	C4
LARKIN RD	SUT	33	C1
LARKIN VALLEY	SCR	54	B2
LARKMEAD LN	NAPA	29	B2
LARKSPUR DR	MLBR	144	B5
LARREA AV	SBD	101	B1
LARRY FLAT	MOD	7	D3
LARSEN RD	IMP	109	A5
LARSON LN	MNO	42	E1
LARSON RD	RCO	107	C1
LA RUE RD	YOL	136	B3
LA SALLE CANYON	SB	86	B3
LAS AMIGAS RD	NAPA	38	C3
LAS ANIMAS RD	SCL	46	C5
LAS FLORES AV	KER	80	C1
LA SIERRA AV	RCO	99	A3
LAS LOMAS AV	AVLN	105	A5
LAS PALMAS AV	STA	47	C3
LAS PASOS	VEN	96	C1
LASPINA DR	TUL	68	B2
LAS PLUMAS AV	BUT	25	D4
LS PULGAS CY RD	SDCO	106	A2
LAS ROCAS	RCO	100	D4
LASSELLE ST	RCO	99	C3
LASSEN AV	BUT	25	B3
LASSEN AV	FRCO	67	A1
LASSEN AV	FRCO	57	A3
LASSEN LN	SIS	12	C2
LASSEN RD	TEH	25	A2
LASSEN ST	LAS	8	B4
LASSEN ST	NAP	133	A1
LASSEN TRAIL	TEH	19	D4
LASSEN CREEK RD	MOD	7	C4
LASSEN PARK HWY	SHA	19	D2
LASSICS LKOT RD	TRI	16	E4
LAST CHANCE CYN	KER	80	C2
LAST CHANCE MNE	NEV	26	E5
LAST CHANCE MNE	NEV	35	A1
LAS TUNAS DR	LACO	R	C3
LAS VARAS RD	SB	87	A4
LAS VEGAS BLVD	CLK	74	D3
LAS VEGAS BL S	CLK	209	C4
LAS VEGAS BL S	CLK	210	B5
LAS VEGAS BL S	LV	209	C4
LAS VIRGENES RD	LACO	97	A1
LATHAM RD	SUT	33	B3
LATHROP RD	MAN	161	A1
LATHROP RD	SJCO	47	A1
LATHROP RD	SJCO	161	D1
LATIGO CYN RD	LACO	97	A2
LA TIJERA BLVD	LA	188	C5
LA TIJERA BLVD	LACO	Q	D5
LATKA LN	TEH	19	B4
LATROBE RD	AMA	40	D1
LATROBE RD	ED	40	C1
LATROBE RD	SAC	40	B1

STREET	CO.	PAGE	GRID
LA TUNA CYN RD	LACO	97	D1
LA TUNA CYN RD	LACO	Q	D2
LAUFFER RD	HUM	22	D1
LAUGHLIN RD	STA	47	E2
LAURA DR	LAS	27	E1
LAUREL AV	KIN	67	B2
LAUREL AV	MLBR	144	C5
LAUREL AV	SUT	33	D3
LAUREL DR E	MON	171	E2
LAUREL DR E	SAL	171	E2
LAUREL DR W	SAL	171	A2
LAUREL DR W	MON	171	A2
LAUREL LN	YUB	33	D1
LAUREL ST	NAP	133	A4
LAUREL ST	SD	215	D2
LAUREL ST	SDCO	V	C3
LAUREL ST	SC	169	C3
LAUREL WY	TEH	18	C4
LAUREL CYN BLVD	LACO	97	D1
LAUREL CYN BLVD	LACO	Q	C1
LAUREL DELL RD	LAK	31	C2
LAURELES GRADE	MON	54	C5
LAUREL GLEN RD	SCR	P	B5
LAUREL GLEN RD	SCR	54	A1
LAUREL GROVE AV	MAR	139	B4
LAUREL GROVE AV	MAR	L	A3
LAUREL GROVE AV	ROSS	139	A4
LAURELLEN RD	YUB	33	D2
LAURENT ST	SC	169	B3
LAURJOE RD	SBD	91	E3
LAUSTEN RD	COL	32	D1
LAUX RD	COL	33	A1
LAVA BED RD	BUT	25	B3
LAVA BDS NAT MN	MOD	6	A4
LAVA BDS MED LK	SIS	5	C5
LAVAL RD	KER	78	E5
LAVER CROSSING	LAS	21	E5
LAVERNE AV	MAR	140	A3
LA VETA AV	OR	196	B1
LAVEZZOLA RD	SIE	26	D4
LAVIC RD	SBD	92	E2
LA VISTA AV	VEN	88	C5
LAWNCREST RD	SHA	18	C2
LAWRENCE	AMA	41	A1
LAWRENCE EXPWY	SCL	P	A3
LAWRENCE EXPWY	SCLR	150	C4
LAWRENCE EXPWY	SJ	150	C4
LAWRENCE EXPWY	SVL	150	C4
LAWRENCE RD	AMA	40	E1
LAWSON LN	HUM	15	E2
LAXAQUE RD	MOD	8	D1
LAYTNVL DOS RIO	MEN	22	E3
LAZARO CARDENAS	BAJA	112	B4
LAZARUS LN	RCO	100	A5
L B CROW RD	STA	47	C4
LEACH RD	YUB	33	D3
LEAR AV	SBD	101	B1
LEARY RD	SAC	M	D1
LEARY RD	SAC	39	D3
LEASTALK AV	SBD	84	C3
LEATHER RD	IMP	110	D5
LEAVENWORTH ST	SF	143	B2
LEAVESLEY RD	SCL	P	E5
LEAVESLEY RD	SCL	54	D1
LEAVITT RD	LAS	21	B3
LEE RD	MCO	48	A3
LEE RD	PLU	26	D1
LEE RD	SHA	13	E4
LEE RD	SUT	33	D4
LEEDS	MCO	48	C4
LEEGE AV	SB	86	B3
LEEK RD	STA	47	D2
LEE SCHOOL RD	SAC	40	B2
LEESVILLE RD	COL	32	C2
LEESVL-LODGA RD	COL	32	B1
LEFF RD	RCO	107	B1
LEFFINGWELL RD	LACO	R	C5
LEFFINGWELL RD	LACO	T	B1
LEGION AV	MCO	47	E4
LEGION AV	MCO	48	A4
LEGION PARK DR	MDO	162	E5
LE GRAND RD	MCO	48	D5
LEGRAY RD	KER	78	E5
LEIGHTON, H RD	SHA	18	C2
LEILA LN	SBD	101	E1
LEIMERT BLVD	LACO	Q	D4
LEININGER RD	TEH	25	A1
LEISER RD	SUT	33	C4
LEISURE TOWN RD	SOL	39	A2
LELITER RD	KER	70	C5
LEMON AV	SDCO	V	D3
LEMON AV	SDCO	111	E1
LEMON AV	SJCO	47	D1
LEMON AV	STA	47	B3
LEMON RD	SBD	91	C4
LEMON ST	ORA	T	C1
LEMON ST	VAL	134	D5
LEMON CANYON RD	SIE	27	C4
LEMOS RD	SIS	4	A2
LENAHAN RD	COL	32	D1
LENARD RD	LAS	14	C3
LENINGER RD	BUT	25	A2
LENTELL RD	HUM	15	E1
LENWOOD RD	SBD	91	D1
LEO RD	RCO	107	A1
LEON AV	MCO	56	B2
LEON RD	RCO	99	D4
LEONA AV	LACO	89	D3
LEONARD AV	FRCO	57	D4
LEONARD AV	KER	78	A2
LEONARD RD	MPA	49	C3
LEONI RD	ED	41	B1
LEOTA ST	MCO	55	D1
LEPRECHAUN LN	RCO	107	B1

INDEXES

COPYRIGHT, © 1989 BY Thomas Bros Maps

STREET	CO.	PAGE	GRID
LERDO HWY	KER	77	D2
LERDO HWY	KER	78	A2
LEROY AV	SJCO	47	B1
LESSING ST	SBD	91	A3
LETTS VALLEY RD	COL	31	E1
LEVEE RD	FRCO	56	E4
LEVEE RD	IMP	112	D5
LEVEE RD	YOL	39	C2
LEVERONI RD	SON	L	B1
LEVERONI RD	SON	38	B3
LEVERONI RD	SON	132	B5
LEVIATHAN LKOUT	ALP	36	D5
LEVIATHAN RD	ALP	36	D5
LEWELLING BLVD	ALA	146	B1
LEWELLING BL E	ALA	L	E5
LEWIS RD	MON	54	C2
LEWIS RD	SHA	13	E4
LEWIS RD	SOL	39	B3
LEWIS RD	STA	47	C4
LEWIS RD	VEN	96	C1
LEWIS RD	YUB	33	E3
LEWIS CREEK RD	MON	65	D2
LEWIS RIDGE RD	BUT	26	B4
LEWISTON AV	FRCO	67	C1
LEWISTON RD	SHA	18	A1
LEWISTON RD	TRI	17	D1
LEWISTON TURNPK	TRI	17	E1
LEXINGTON AV	MCO	56	A2
LEXINGTON AV	SDCO	106	E5
LEXINGTON ST	SCLR	151	B3
LEXINGTN HLL RD	PLU	26	C3
LIBERAL AV	TEH	24	D2
LIBERTY AV	MCO	48	A4
LIBERTY RD	SJCO	40	B3
LIBERTY RD W	BUT	25	B5
LIBERTY ISLD RD	SOL	M	D1
LIBERTY ISLD RD	SOL	39	C3
LIBRAMIENTO SUR	BAJA	111	D3
LIBRAMNT ORIENT	BAJA	111	D2
LICHEN WY	RCO	107	B1
LICHENS RD	SIS	4	B4
LIEBERT RD	IMP	111	E3
LIGGET AV	COL	32	E3
LIGHTHILL RD	SIS	3	D5
LIGHTHOUSE AV	MONT	167	D2
LIGHTHOUSE AV	MON	53	E2
LIGHTHOUSE AV	PAC	167	B2
LIGHTHOUSE RD	HUM	15	D4
LIGHTHOUSE RD	MEN	30	C3
LILI VALLEY WY	CAL	41	C2
LILLEY MTN DR	MAD	49	C5
LILY GAP RD	CAL	41	C2
LIM RD	LAS	14	C3
LIME CREEK RD	CAL	40	E3
LIMEDYKE LKOUT	TRI	16	E2
LIMEKILN RD	MON	54	D5
LIME KILN RD	NEV	34	C2
LIMEKILN RD	SBT	54	E4
LIMEKILN RD	SBT	55	A4
LIME KILN RD	TUO	41	C5
LIME SADDLE RD	BUT	25	C3
LIMONITE AV	RCO	99	A2
LINCOLN	LACO	97	C2
LINCOLN	MCO	48	B5
LINCOLN AV	ANA	193	B2
LINCOLN AV	ANA	194	B2
LINCOLN AV	FRCO	56	D4
LINCOLN AV	FRCO	57	A4
LINCOLN AV	FRCO	58	A4
LINCOLN AV	KIN	67	C2
LINCOLN AV	LACO	R	B2
LINCOLN AV	LACO	190	B1
LINCOLN AV	OR	194	E2
LINCOLN AV	ORA	98	B3
LINCOLN AV	ORA	T	B2
LINCOLN AV	PAS	190	B1
LINCOLN AV	RCO	U	E5
LINCOLN AV	RCO	98	E3
LINCOLN AV	SAL	171	C4
LINCOLN AV	SD	214	A5
LINCOLN AV	SDCO	106	D3
LINCOLN AV	SR	139	D3
LINCOLN AV	SA	196	C3
LINCOLN AV	SCL	P	B3
LINCOLN AV	SCL	46	B4
LINCOLN AV	YUB	33	E1
LINCOLN AV W	NAP	133	A3
LINCOLN BLVD	BUT	25	D5
LINCOLN BLVD	LA	187	A1
LINCOLN BLVD	LA	189	A1
LINCOLN BLVD	LACO	Q	B4
LINCOLN BLVD	LACO	187	D3
LINCOLN BLVD	MCO	47	E4
LINCOLN BLVD	MCO	48	A4
LINCOLN BLVD	SF	141	B2
LINCOLN BLVD	SMON	187	A1
LINCOLN RD	SBD	91	E4
LINCOLN RD	SUT	33	C2
LINCOLN RD	SUT	125	A5
LINCOLN RD	YUBA	125	A5
LINCOLN ST	NAPA	29	A1
LINCOLN ST	RCO	101	B5
LINCOLN ST	SC	169	D3
LINCOLN ST	S	160	D5
LINCOLN ST N	KER	77	E4
LINCOLN ST N	KER	78	A4
LINCOLN WY	AUB	126	D2
LINCOLN WY	SFCO	L	B5
LINCOLN WY	SF	141	C4
LINCOLN WY	SFCO	45	B1
LINCOLN WY E	AUB	126	D2
LINCOLN WY E	PLA	126	D2
LINDA DR	SIS	4	B2
LINDA VISTA AV	LACO	98	A1

STREET	CO.	PAGE	GRID
LINDA VISTA AV	LACO	R	B3
LINDA VISTA AV	NAP	133	A2
LINDA VISTA AV	PAS	190	A3
LINDA VISTA AV	TUL	68	D3
LINDA VISTA DR	SB	87	A3
LINDA VISTA RD	SBD	91	D1
LINDA VISTA RD	SD	213	B4
LINDA VISTA RD	SDCO	V	B3
LINDA VISTA RD	SDCO	111	C1
LINDBERGH BLVD	KER	80	B4
LINDBLOOM RD	MCO	55	D3
LINDEN AV	MCO	56	A1
LINDEN AV	SBD	99	B2
LINDEN AV	SSF	144	B1
LINDENBERGER RD	RCO	99	D4
LINDERO CYN RD	LACO	96	E1
LINDLEY AV	LA	178	E4
LINDLEY AV	LACO	97	C1
LINDLEY RD	HUM	15	E4
LINDSAY RD	IMP	109	A3
LINDSAY RD	KER	78	C4
LINDSEY AV	GLE	24	E3
LINE RD	YOL	39	D2
LINEA DEL CIELO	SDCO	106	C4
LINGARD RD	MCO	48	C5
LINN RD	SJCO	40	C4
LINNE RD	SJCO	46	E2
LINNE RD	SLO	76	B1
LINSON AV	SBD	91	A3
LINWOOD AV	STA	47	C3
LINWOOD RD	MCO	47	E3
LINWOOD RD	MCO	48	A3
LISBON ST	MCO	48	A5
LISBON ST	SDCO	V	D3
LISCOMB HILL RD	HUM	10	A5
LIST AV	TUL	68	C1
LITT RD	STA	47	D2
LITTLE AV	BUT	33	C1
LITTLE RD	LPAZ	104	A2
LITTLE BEAR RD	RCO	102	C4
LITL BLACK ROCK	TRI	17	C4
LTL BRWNS CK RD	TRI	11	D5
LTL BRWNS CK RD	TRI	17	D1
LITTLE GIANT ML	TEH	19	B4
LITTL GRASS VLY	PLU	26	C3
LITTL HONKR BAY	SOL	39	B3
LITTLE JOHN	SJCO	40	C5
LITTLE JOHN RD	CAL	41	A5
LITTLE LAKE RD	INY	70	C4
LITTLE LAKE RD	MEN	30	C1
LITL MORONGO DR	SBD	100	D1
LITL PANOCHE RD	FRCO	55	D4
LITL PANOCHE RD	SBT	55	D4
LITTLE RIVER	MEN	30	B1
LTL SLATE CK RD	SHA	12	B4
LTL SYCAMOR CYN	LACO	96	D2
LTL TUJUNGA RD	LACO	89	D5
LITTLE VLY RD	LAS	14	A4
LITTLE VLY RD	MEN	22	C4
LITTLE VLY DUMP	LAS	14	B5
LITL VIRGNIA LK	MNO	43	B4
LITTLE WALKR RD	MNO	42	E3
LITTLE WALKR RD	MNO	43	A3
LIVELY RD	BUT	25	B5
LIVE OAK	FRCO	58	B3
LIVE OAK AV	LACO	98	B1
LIVE OAK AV	SBD	99	A2
LIVE OAK AV	SCL	P	D5
LIVE OAK AV	SCL	54	C1
LIVEOAK DR	BUT	25	B3
LIVE OAK DR	SBD	99	D1
LIVE OAK RD	ORA	98	E4
LIVE OAK RD	SBT	55	B4
LIVE OAK RD	SJCO	40	A4
LIVEOAK RD	SLO	76	A1
LIVE OAK RD	TEH	18	C5
LIVE OAK CYN RD	SBD	99	D2
LIVERMORE RD	NAPA	32	A5
LIVNGSTN CRESSY	MCO	47	E4
LIVNGSTN CRESSY	MCO	48	A4
LIVORNA RD	CC	M	A4
LLAGAS RD	SCL	P	D5
LLAGAS RD	SCL	54	C1
LLANO RD	SON	37	E2
LLOYD LN	SHA	18	C3
LOBATA RD	YUB	33	E1
LOCAN AV	FRCO	57	D3
LOCH LOMOND RD	LAK	31	E4
LOCKHART RD	SBD	81	B4
LOCKWOOD RD	STA	47	D3
LOCKWOOD CEM RD	MON	65	C4
LOCKWD JOLON RD	MON	65	C4
LOCKWD SAN ARDO	MON	65	C4
LOCKWD SN LUCAS	MON	65	C3
LOCKWOOD VLY RD	VEN	88	C2
LOCO BILL RD	KER	79	D3
LOCUST AV	RCO	99	C2
LOCUST AV	SBD	81	A5
LOCUST AV	SBD	91	E4
LOCUST AV	STA	47	C3
LOCUST RD	SHA	18	D3
LOCUST TREE RD	SJCO	40	B4
LODGE RD	FRCO	58	A1
LODI LN	NAPA	29	B2
LODI RD	COL	33	A3
LOFGREN RD	BUT	25	B4
LOGAN AV	SD	216	E5
LOGAN LN	MEN	23	B2
LOG CABIN MINE	MNO	43	C5
LOGGING CAMP RD	MNO	50	E1
LOG HOUSE RD	SIS	4	E2
LOKERN RD	KER	77	D3
LOKOYA RD	NAPA	38	B2
LOLETA AV	TEH	24	D2

STREET	CO.	PAGE	GRID
LOLETA RD	HUM	15	D2
LOMA AV	MCO	56	B1
LOMA ALTA DR	LACO	98	A1
LOMA ALTA DR	LACO	R	B2
LOMA ALTA DR	STB	174	B4
LOMA PRIETA AV	SCR	P	B5
LOMA PRIETA RD	SCR	54	A1
LOMA RICA DR	NEV	34	C1
LOMA RICA RD	YUB	33	D1
LOMAS CONTADAS	CC	45	D1
LOMAS CANTADAS	CC	156	E2
LOMAS SANTA FE	SDCO	106	C4
LOMA VERDE RD	RCO	102	C4
LOMA VISTA DR	NAPA	38	C2
LOMBARD ST	SFCO	L	B4
LOMBARD ST	SF	142	A2
LOMBARD ST	SF	143	A3
LOMBARD ST	SFCO	45	B1
LOMBARDY AV	MCO	47	E3
LOMBARDY AV	MCO	48	A3
LOMITA	VEN	88	A4
LOMITA AV	MLBR	144	B4
LOMITA BLVD	LACO	97	D3
LOMITA BLVD	LACO	S	B2
LOMITAS DR	TUL	58	D5
LOMITAS DR	TUL	68	D1
LOMPOC-CASML RD	SB	86	B2
LONDALE RD	STA	47	D1
LONE BUTTE RD	KER	80	A5
LONE COMPANY RD	MNO	42	E1
LONE HILL AV	LACO	U	B2
LONE MTN RD	JOS	2	C2
LONE OAK AV	STA	47	E2
LONE PINE LN	SON	38	A1
LONE PINE CYN	SBD	90	E5
LONE PN NRRW GG	INY	60	B4
LONE STAR MN RD	MNO	51	C2
LONE STAR RD	COL	32	E2
LONE STAR RD	MNO	51	C2
LONE STAR RD	PLA	34	B3
LONE STAR RD	SBD	91	C2
LONE TREE	SJCO	47	C1
LONE TREE RD	BUT	25	D5
LONE TREE RD	MCO	48	B5
LONE TREE RD	SBT	55	A2
LONE TREE RD	SHA	18	D3
LONE TREE WY	CC	M	C3
LONE TREE WY	CC	39	B5
LONG BARN	TUO	41	E4
LONG BEACH BLVD	LB	192	E3
LONG BEACH BLVD	LACO	97	E3
LONG BEACH BLVD	LACO	S	D1
LONG BEACH BL N	LACO	S	D1
LONG BEACH FRWY	LB	192	C2
LONG BEACH FRWY	LACO	97	E3
LONG CANYON RD	SB	86	D1
LONG CANYON RD	RCO	100	D3
LONGCOR RD	TEH	18	C3
LONGDEN AV	LACO	R	C3
LONG FELLOW AV	BUT	25	B3
LONG GULCH RD	SIS	4	A4
LONG HAY FLAT	SHA	19	B3
LONG HOLLOW DR	MAD	49	C5
LONG HOLLOW DR	TEH	24	C2
LONGHORN DR	LAS	8	B4
LONGHORN LN	KER	79	B4
LONG PRAIRIE RD	SIS	5	A5
LONG RAVINE RD	NEV	34	B2
LONG RIDGE RD	TRI	16	E5
LONG VALLEY RD	ALP	36	C4
LONG VALLEY RD	LAK	32	A3
LONG VALLEY RD	SIE	27	E3
LONG VALLEY RD	PLU	20	C5
LONGVIEW AV	MCO	47	E4
LONGVIEW AV	MCO	48	A4
LONGVIEW RD	LACO	90	C3
LONOAK RD	MON	65	C2
LOOKOUT RD	CAL	41	C2
LOOKOUT ADIN RD	LAS	14	B3
LKOUT-HACKMR RD	MOD	6	B5
LKOUT-HACKMR RD	MOD	14	B1
LKOUT INDIAN RD	MOD	14	B3
LOOKOUT MTN RD	SLO	76	C3
LOONEY RD	MCO	48	B3
LOOP BLVD N	KER	80	B4
LOOP BLVD S	KER	80	B4
LOOP RD	HUM	16	A2
LOOP RD	RCO	101	B2
LOOP RD	SHA	19	C2
LOPES RD	SOL	38	E4
LOPEZ DR	SLO	76	B4
LOPEZ CANYON RD	LACO	Q	C1
LOPEZ CANYON RD	SLO	76	C4
LOQUAT AV	STA	47	B3
LORAINE AV	LACO	U	A1
LORENSON	PLA	34	B3
LORENTZ RD	AMA	40	D1
LORENZEN RD	SJCO	47	A2
LORETZ RD	CLO	32	D1
LORRAINE RD	SBD	92	E5
LORT DR	TUL	68	C1
LOS ALAMITOS BL	ORA	T	A2
LOS ALAMOS RD	RCO	99	C5
LOS ALTOS DR	LACO	R	D4
LOS ANGELES AV	VEN	89	A5
LOS ANGELES ST	KER	78	A2
LOS ANGELES ST	LA	185	E5
LS ANGLS AQDUCT	KER	80	B2
LS BURROS ARRYO	SLO	76	B4
LOS BURROS RD	MON	64	E4
LOS BURROS RD	MON	65	A4
LOS CERRITOS RD	MCO	48	B3
LOS CERRITOS RD	STA	48	B2
LOS COCHES RD	MON	65	A1

STREET	CO.	PAGE	GRID
LOS COCHES RD	SDCO	V	E2
LOS COCHES RD	SDCO	107	A5
LS COYOTES DIAG	LACO	S	E2
LS COYOTES DIAG	LACO	T	A2
LOS FELIZ BLVD	GLEN	182	E2
LOS FELIZ BLVD	LA	182	B3
LOS FELIZ BLVD	LACO	97	D1
LOS FELIZ BLVD	LACO	Q	E3
LOS FLORES RD	SBD	91	B5
LOS GATOS BLVD	SCL	P	B4
LOS GATOS BLVD	SCL	46	A5
LOS GATOS RD	FRCO	66	C2
LOS LOBOS RD	MON	65	D4
LOS NIETOS RD	LACO	98	A2
LOS NIETOS RD	LACO	R	C5
LOS OLIVOS ST	STB	174	A3
LOS OSOS VLY RD	SLO	75	E3
LOS OSOS VLY RD	SLO	76	A3
LOS PADRES RD	SBD	91	C3
LOS PALOS DR	SAL	171	D5
LOS PINOS DR	RCO	100	D5
LOS PRADOS	SM	145	C3
LS RANCHITOS RD	SR	139	B1
LOS ROBLES RD	LACO	98	A1
LOS ROBLES AV	LACO	R	B3
LOS ROBLES AV	PAS	190	C2
LOST RD	RCO	99	C4
LOST CREEK RD	TEH	19	E4
LOST CK DAM RD	YUB	26	B4
LOST HILLS AV	FRCO	66	D3
LOST HILLS RD	KER	77	D2
LOST LAKE RD	ALP	36	A5
LOST LAKE RD	FRCO	57	D2
LOST SECTION S	INY	72	C3
LOST SECTION RD	INY	72	C3
LOS VERJELES RD	BUT	25	E5
LOS VERJELES RD	YUB	25	E5
LOTT RD	BUT	25	B3
LOTUS RD	ED	34	D5
LOUIE RD	SIS	4	C5
LOUIS AV	BUT	25	D5
LOUISE AV	MAN	161	A2
LOUISE AV	SJCO	47	C1
LOUISIANA ST	SUIS	135	C4
LOUISIANA ST	VAL	134	C4
LOUMAS LN	KER	79	C4
LOUPE AV	SCL	P	C3
LOUPE AV	SCL	46	B4
LOVE CREEK RD	CAL	41	C3
LOVEKIN BLVD	RCO	103	D5
LOVELAND RD	IMP	109	A4
LOVELOCK RD	BUT	25	D2
LOVENESS RD	MOD	14	B1
LOW RD	IMP	111	E3
LOWDEN RD	RED	122	E3
LOWDEN RD	SHA	122	E3
LOW DIVIDE RD	DN	1	E3
LOW DIVIDE RD	DN	2	A3
LOWE RD	IMP	110	B3
LOWELL ST	SDCO	V	A3
LOWELL HILL RD	NEV	34	D1
LOWER RD	AVLN	105	B5
LOWER TER	AVLN	105	B5
LOWER AZUSA RD	LACO	98	B2
LOWER AZUSA RD	LACO	R	D3
LOWR CHILES VLY	NAPA	29	E2
LOWR CHILES VLY	NAPA	38	C1
LOWER COLFAX RD	NEV	34	C2
LOWER DORRAY RD	CAL	41	A2
LOWR ENTRPRS RD	BUT	25	E4
LOWER FIRE RD	SIS	4	D5
LOWER FORBESTWN	BUT	26	A4
LOWER GAS PT RD	SHA	18	B3
LOWR GLACIER RD	INY	51	E5
LOWER HONCUT RD	BUT	25	D5
LOWER JONES	SJCO	39	D5
LOWER KLAMTH HY	KLAM	5	B1
LOWER KUCK RD	SIS	4	C3
LOWER LAKE RD	DN	1	D3
LOWER LAKE RD	LAK	31	E3
LOWER LAKE RD	LAK	32	A3
LWR LITL SHASTA	SIS	4	B4
LOWER MAD RIVER	TRI	16	E3
LOWER RATLSNAKE	TRI	17	A3
LOWER SACRAMNTO	SJCO	40	A4
LOWER SPGS RD	SHA	18	B2
LOWER WSIDE RD	TRI	16	E4
LOWR WYANDTT RD	BUT	25	D5
LOWERY RD	HUM	15	D3
LOWERY RD	TEH	18	B5
LOWERY CEM RD	TEH	24	A1
LOWES CANYON RD	SLO	66	B5
LOW GAP RD	MEN	30	D1
LOW GAP RD	MEN	31	A2
LOW GAP RD	MEN	123	A2
LOW GAP RD	U	123	A2
LOYALTON RD	SIE	27	D3
LOYALTON RD	SIE	27	C3
LOZANO RD	MPA	48	D2
LOZANOS RD	PLA	34	B4
LUBKEN RD	INY	60	B4
LUCAS	SJCO	40	A4
LUCAS VALLEY RD	MAR	L	A3
LUCAS VALLEY RD	MAR	38	A4
LUCE GRISWLD RD	TEH	18	B4
LUCERNE VLY CTF	SBD	91	D2
LUCILLE	FRCO	66	D3
LUCILLE LN	RCO	107	C1
LUCINDA RD	SBD	81	C5
LUCKEHE RD	SUT	33	C1
LUCKY HILL RD	SIE	26	C3
LUCY BROWN RD	SLO	76	D1
LUDLOW RD	SBD	93	A2
LUDY BLVD	RCO	110	C1

STREET	CO.	PAGE	GRID
LUIS AV	MCO	55	C1
LUISENO RD	RCO	107	B1
LUKENS LN	RCO	99	C3
LULU MINE RD	TUO	41	C5
LULU MINE RD	TUO	48	C1
LUMGREY RD	SIS	3	E3
LUMPKIN RD	BUT	25	E4
LUMPKIN RD	BUT	26	B4
LUMPKIN-			
-LA PORTE RD	BUT	26	A4
LUMPKIN RDG RD	BUT	26	B3
LUNA RD	IMP	109	B3
LUNDY AV	SCL	P	B3
LUNDY LAKE RD	MNO	43	B4
LUNING AV	TEH	24	D1
LUNT RD	BUT	25	D3
LUPE RD	AMA	41	A2
LUPIN AV	MCO	48	B4
LUPINE	FRCO	58	B3
LUPINE LN	RCO	100	C5
LURLINE AV	COL	32	D2
LUTHER RD	PLA	34	C3
LUTHER RD	TEH	18	D5
LUTHER E GIBSON	SOL	38	E4
LUTHER GIBSN FY	BEN	153	D4
LUTIE AV	KER	80	A4
LUX AV	MCO	56	B1
LYERLY RD	IMP	109	B3
LYNCH RD	NAPA	38	D3
LYNCH CANYON DR	SLO	65	D5
LYNCH MDWS RD	BUT	25	D2
LYNN RD	VEN	96	D1
LYON AV	FRCO	56	C2
LYON AV	RCO	99	E3
LYON RD	STA	47	E2
LYON RD	STA	48	A2
LYONS AV	LACO	89	B4
LYONS AV	SLT	129	A3
LYONS RD	IMP	111	E4
LYONS RD	IMP	112	A4
LYONS ST	SNRA	163	C3
LYTLE AV	KER	68	B5
LYTLE CREEK RD	SBD	90	E5
LYTLE CREEK RD	SBD	99	A1
LYTTON ST	SDCO	V	A3
LYTTON SPG RD	SON	31	D5

M

STREET	CO.	PAGE	GRID
M ST	EUR	121	D1
M ST	FRE	165	D3
M ST	MCO	48	C4
M ST	MER	170	C5
M 1	TUL	69	A5
M 3	TUL	69	B5
M 8	LACO	90	C3
M 9	TUL	69	B5
M 10	TUL	69	B5
M 15	TUL	69	A4
M 33	TUL	68	E4
M 52	TUL	69	A4
M 56	TUL	69	B4
M 99	TUL	69	C4
M 107	TUL	69	C3
M 109	TUL	68	E4
M 109	TUL	69	A4
M 112	TUL	69	A4
M 117	TUL	68	D3
M 120	TUL	68	E3
M 176	TUL	68	E3
M 220	TUL	69	A2
M 231	TUL	69	A2
M 240	TUL	68	E2
M 276	TUL	69	A1
M 296	TUL	68	D1
M 348	TUL	68	E1
M 357	TUL	58	E5
M 357	TUL	59	A4
M 375	TUL	59	B5
M 453	TUL	58	D4
M 461	TUL	58	D4
M 465	TUL	58	D4
M 468	TUL	58	D4
M 469	TUL	58	D4
MABURY RD	SJ	152	D1
MABURY ST	SA	196	D3
MAC RD	RCO	107	C1
MACARTHUR BLVD	ALA	L	D5
MACARTHUR BLVD	ALA	45	D1
MACARTHUR BLVD	CM	197	B3
MACARTHUR BLVD	IRV	198	C3
MACARTHUR BLVD	IRV	200	B5
MACARTHUR BLVD	NB	198	C3
MACARTHUR BLVD	NB	200	B5
MACARTHUR BLVD	O	157	E1
MACARTHUR BLVD	O	158	B2
MACARTHUR BLVD	ORA	98	C4
MACARTHUR BLVD	ORA	T	C3
MACARTHUR BLVD	ORA	198	C3
MACARTHUR BLVD	SA	197	D3
MACARTHUR BLVD	SA	198	A3
MACARTHUR FRWY	ALA	45	D1
MACARTHUR FRWY	O	157	D1
MACARTHUR FRWY	O	158	B2
MACDOEL DIST RD	SIS	4	E4
MACDOEL DIST RD	SIS	5	A3
MACDONALD AV	CC	L	C3
MACDONALD AV	R	155	B3
MACDONALD LN	SIS	4	C5
MACE BLVD	YOL	39	C1
MACHADO LN	SIS	4	C5
MACHADO ST	RCO	99	B4
MACKERT RD	SUT	33	C4
MACKS GULCH RD	SIS	4	A5

260
MACKS GULCH RD
STREET INDEX
MEADOW GLEN RD

STREET	CO.	PAGE	GRID
MACKS GULCH RD	SIS	12	A1
MACKVILLE RD	SJCO	40	C3
MACLAY AV	LACO	89	D5
MACLAY AV	LACO	Q	C1
MACY ST	LA	186	C3
MACY ST	LACO	97	E2
MACY ST	LACO	R	A4
MADDALENA RD	PLU	27	C2
MADDEN AV	SUT	33	C2
MADDOCK RD	SUT	33	C4
MADEIRA AV N	MON	171	D3
MADEIRA AV N	SAL	171	D3
MADERA AV	FRCO	57	A4
MADERA AV	KER	78	B2
MADERA AV	KER	78	C2
MADERA AV	MAD	57	A2
MADERA RD	MCO	55	D1
MADERA RD	SBD	90	E3
MADERA ST	SDCO	V	D3
MADERA ST	SDCO	111	D1
MADISON AV	KIN	67	C2
MADISON AV	SAC	34	A5
MADISON AV	SAC	34	B5
MADISON AV	SBR	144	A4
MADISON AV	SD	214	A4
MADISON ST	KER	166	E5
MADISON ST	RCO	99	B2
MADISON ST	RCO	101	A4
MADISON ST	S	160	D3
MADONNA RD	SLO	76	A4
MADONNA RD	SNLO	172	A5
MADRE BLVD	LACO	98	A1
MAD RIVER RD	HUM	9	E5
MAD RIVER ROCK	TRI	16	E3
MADRONA ST	NAPA	29	B3
MADRONE RD	SON	38	B3
MADSEN	FRCO	57	E2
MADSEN AV	FRCO	57	E5
MAGEE CANYON RD	MNO	44	A5
MAGEE CANYON RD	MNO	51	B1
MAGEE HILLS RD	RCO	99	E5
MAGIC MTN PKWY	LACO	89	B4
MAGNOLIA	MAR	38	B5
MAGNOLIA	SJCO	47	D1
MAGNOLIA AV	FRCO	57	C5
MAGNOLIA AV	GLE	24	D3
MAGNOLIA AV	KER	78	A2
MAGNOLIA AV	LB	192	D3
MAGNOLIA AV	MAR	L	A3
MAGNOLIA AV	MCO	47	E4
MAGNOLIA AV	MCO	48	A4
MAGNOLIA AV	ONT	203	E5
MAGNOLIA AV	ORA	98	B4
MAGNOLIA AV	ORA	T	C2
MAGNOLIA AV	RCO	99	A3
MAGNOLIA AV	RIV	205	A4
MAGNOLIA AV	SDCO	V	E2
MAGNOLIA AV	SDCO	106	E5
MAGNOLIA AV	SDCO	107	A4
MAGNOLIA AV	MLBR	144	C4
MAGNOLIA AV	STA	47	B3
MAGNOLIA BLVD	BUR	179	B4
MAGNOLIA BLVD	LA	179	B4
MAGNOLIA BLVD	LACO	Q	C3
MAGNOLIA RD	YUB	33	D1
MAGNUS ORCHD RD	SIE	26	D5
MAGONIGAL RD	NEV	27	B5
MAHER RD	MON	54	C3
MAHOGANY WY	LAS	20	E2
MAHOGANY FLAT	INY	71	C2
MAHOGANY PK RD	SIS	5	B3
MAHON AV	SJCO	47	D1
MAHONEY RD	SLO	75	E1
MAHONEY RD	SB	86	B1
MAIDEN LN	AVLN	105	A4
MAIDU DR	AUB	126	C5
MAIL RD	SB	86	D3
MAIL RT	LAS	8	C5
MAIN AV E	SCL	P	D5
MAIN AV E	SCL	54	C1
MAIN RD N	KLAM	5	E2
MAIN RD S	MOD	7	A3
MAIN ST	A	157	C4
MAIN ST	AMA	40	D2
MAIN ST	BARS	208	A2
MAIN ST	CC	L	E4
MAIN ST	CC	M	A3
MAIN ST	CC	M	A4
MAIN ST	EC	217	B2
MAIN ST	ELS	189	A3
MAIN ST	GV	127	C3
MAIN ST	HUM	15	E3
MAIN ST	IMP	109	A5
MAIN ST	IMP	109	B2
MAIN ST	INY	51	D4
MAIN ST	IRV	198	B3
MAIN ST	KER	78	E3
MAIN ST	LAK	31	D3
MAIN ST	LAS	8	B4
MAIN ST	LAS	21	B4
MAIN ST	LV	209	C3
MAIN ST	LA	185	E5
MAIN ST	LA	186	A3
MAIN ST	LACO	88	E4
MAIN ST	LACO	Q	C5
MAIN ST	LACO	Q	E5
MAIN ST	LACO	R	B3
MAIN ST	LACO	S	A1
MAIN ST	LACO	S	C2
MAIN ST	MAN	161	C4
MAIN ST	MEN	30	C4
MAIN ST	MOD	14	B3
MAIN ST	NAP	133	C2
MAIN ST	NAPA	38	A1

STREET	CO.	PAGE	GRID
MAIN ST	ORA	98	B4
MAIN ST	ORA	T	D3
MAIN ST	PLCV	138	D3
MAIN ST	RCO	U	E5
MAIN ST	RCO	98	E3
MAIN ST	RCO	99	B4
MAIN ST	RCO	99	E4
MAIN ST	RCO	205	C2
MAIN ST	SAL	171	C4
MAIN ST	SBD	91	B4
MAIN ST	SBD	91	D1
MAIN ST	SBD	93	B2
MAIN ST	SCL	P	B3
MAIN ST	SD	216	B5
MAIN ST	SDCO	V	C5
MAIN ST	SDCO	V	E3
MAIN ST	SDCO	106	C2
MAIN ST	SDCO	107	A4
MAIN ST	SDCO	111	D2
MAIN ST	SF	143	E4
MAIN ST	SJCO	40	B5
MAIN ST	SLO	75	C2
MAIN ST	SLO	76	A2
MAIN ST	SA	196	B4
MAIN ST	SA	198	B3
MAIN ST	SB	76	C5
MAIN ST	SB	86	B1
MAIN ST	STB	173	A3
MAIN ST	SMA	173	A3
MAIN ST	SHA	18	C1
MAIN ST	SIE	26	D4
MAIN ST	SIS	3	D5
MAIN ST	SON	37	C2
MAIN ST	STA	47	E3
MAIN ST	S	160	E4
MAIN ST	SUIS	135	C4
MAIN ST	TEH	18	D3
MAIN ST	TUL	68	B1
MAIN ST	TUL	68	D3
MAIN ST	VENT	175	A2
MAIN ST	YUBA	125	D5
MAIN ST E	STA	47	E3
MAIN ST N	AMA	40	E2
MAIN ST N	LA	186	C2
MAIN ST N	LACO	R	A4
MAIN ST N	MON	54	C4
MAIN ST N	SAL	171	C2
MAIN ST S	SAL	171	B5
MAIN ST W	GV	127	A3
MAIN ST W	SB	76	B5
MAIN ST W	SB	86	A1
MAIN ST W	STA	47	D3
MAIN DRAIN RD	KER	77	D2
MAINE AV	LACO	R	E3
MAINE ST	SOL	38	C4
MAINE ST	VAL	134	C4
MAIN EAST WEST	MOD	5	E3
MAIN PRAIRIE RD	SOL	39	B3
MAJESTC OAK CIR	SHA	18	C3
MAJESTIC VW DR	SHA	18	C3
MALAGA AV	FRCO	56	E4
MALAGA AV	FRCO	57	C4
MALAGA RD	KER	78	E3
MALIBU CYN RD	LACO	97	A2
MALIN HWY	MOD	5	E2
MALLARD RD	MCO	55	E2
MALLARD RD	YOL	39	D2
MALLOTT RD	SUT	33	C2
MALTON AV	TEH	24	D2
MALUM RIDGE RD	MAD	49	E4
MALVERN AV	ORA	T	C1
MAMELUKE HLL RD	ED	34	E3
MAMMTH POOL RD	MAD	49	E5
MAMMTH POOL RD	MAD	50	A5
MAMMTH SCNC LP	MNO	50	D2
MAMMOTH TVRN RD	ML	164	D2
MANCHESTER AV	ANA	193	A2
MANCHESTER AV	ING	188	D5
MANCHESTER AV	LA	187	D5
MANCHESTER AV	LA	188	A5
MANCHESTER AV	LACO	97	D2
MANCHESTER AV	LACO	Q	E5
MANCHESTER AV	SDCO	106	C4
MANDEVLL CYN RD	LACO	97	C2
MANDRAPA RD	IMP	111	E4
MANGALAR RD	RCO	100	C5
MANGO ST	SBD	80	E5
MANGROVE AV	BUT	124	B2
MANGROVE AV	C	124	C3
MANHATTAN AV	LACO	97	D3
MANHATTAN AV	LACO	S	A1
MANHATTAN BLVD	LACO	97	D3
MANHATTAN BLVD	LACO	S	B1
MANIER DR	TUL	69	A3
MANILLA AV	AVLN	105	B5
MANKAS CORNR RD	SOL	L	E1
MANKAS CORNR RD	SOL	M	A1
MANKAS CORNR RD	SOL	38	E3
MANLY RD	KER	89	D1
MANN RD	ALA	M	C5
MANNEL AV	KER	78	B2
MANNER MTN TR	NEV	34	C1
MANNING AV	FRCO	56	B4
MANNING AV	FRCO	57	E4
MANNING RD	ALA	46	C2
MANOR RD	COL	32	C2
MANOR ST	KER	78	D2
MANTECA AV	KIN	67	C2
MANTECA RD	SJCO	47	B2
MANTON RD	TEH	18	E4
MANTON RD	TEH	19	A3
MANTON SCH RD	TEH	19	B3
MANUAL DOMINGOS	SB	86	C3
MANZANA DR	RCO	100	D3

STREET	CO.	PAGE	GRID
MANZANITA AV	BUT	25	B3
MANZANITA AV	BUT	124	C2
MANZANITA AV	RCO	99	C2
MANZANITA RD	ML	164	D2
MANZANITA RD	RCO	100	B5
MANZANITA RD	TRI	16	D1
MANZANITA LK RD	MAD	49	E5
MANZANITA LKOUT	MOD	14	D2
MANZNR REWRD RD	INY	60	A3
MAPES RD	LAS	21	C3
MAPES RD	RCO	99	C4
MAPLE AV	FRCO	57	C2
MAPLE AV	FRCO	67	C1
MAPLE AV	SBD	91	B4
MAPLE AV	STR	131	D4
MAPLE LN	NAPA	29	B2
MAPLE LN	SBD	100	A1
MAPLE ST	RCO	98	E3
MAPLE ST	SAL	171	C4
MAPLE ST	SDCO	107	A4
MAPLE CREEK RD	HUM	10	B5
MAPLE HILLS RD	HUM	16	B5
MARCH LN	S	160	A1
MARCIEL DR	MAD	57	B2
MARCONI AV	SAC	40	A1
MARCO POLO AV	RCO	100	A5
MARCUM RD	SUT	33	D4
MARCUSE RD	SUT	33	D3
MAR DE CORTEZ	AVLN	105	A4
MARE ISLAND BL	VAL	134	B4
MARE ISL CAUSWY	VAL	134	B3
MARENGO AV	LACO	R	B3
MARENGO RD	COL	32	D2
MARENGO ST	LA	186	E2
MARGUERITE AV	TEH	24	D2
MARGUERITE PKWY	ORA	98	D5
MARGUERITE RD	MCO	48	E5
MARGUERITE MN RD	AUB	126	C2
MARICOPA HWY	KER	78	B5
MARIE AV	KER	89	E1
MARIE DR	PLU	20	D5
MARIN AV	FRCO	56	D4
MARIN ST	VAL	134	C4
MARINA AV	ALA	P	C1
MARINA AV	ALA	46	C2
MARINA BLVD	ALA	L	D5
MARINA BLVD	ALA	45	D2
MARINA BLVD	SF	142	A1
MARINA BLVD	SUIS	135	C4
MARINA DR	IMP	108	C2
MARINA DR	MEN	31	B1
MARINA EXPWY	LACO	187	D3
MARINA FRWY	CUL	188	A3
MARINA FRWY	LA	188	A3
MARINA FRWY	LACO	97	C2
MARINA VISTA	M	154	B2
MARIPOSA ST	VAL	134	E3
MARINE AV	COL	32	E3
MARINE AV	MB	189	C5
MARINE AV	RB	189	C5
MARINE PKWY	RC	145	E4
MARINERS ISL BL	SM	145	C2
MARINETTE	TUL	68	B1
MARINE WORLD PY	SMCO	N	D2
MARINE WORLD PY	SMCO	45	D3
MARINO LN	KER	79	E2
MARIPOSA AV	BUT	25	B3
MARIPOSA AV	C	124	D2
MARIPOSA AV	RCO	99	B3
MARIPOSA AV	TUL	68	B1
MARIPOSA RD	SJCO	40	B5
MARIPOSA RD	SJCO	47	C1
MARIPOSA RD	STA	47	D2
MARIPOSA ST	SFCO	142	E4
MARIPOSA WY	MCO	48	C5
MARIPOSA DUMP	MPA	49	B3
MARITIME ST	O	157	B2
MARKET AV	CC	L	C3
MARKET ST	COL	33	A2
MARKET ST	O	157	E2
MARKET ST	RIV	205	B3
MARKET ST	RCO	99	B2
MARKET ST	SD	215	E4
MARKET ST	SD	216	A4
MARTN L KING WY	SDCO	V	C3
MARKET ST	SFCO	L	B5
MARKET ST	SF	142	B4
MARKET ST	SF	143	D4
MARKET ST	SFCO	45	B2
MARKET ST	SJ	152	B3
MARKET ST	SCLR	151	B3
MARKET ST	S	160	E5
MARKET ST	YUBA	125	D1
MARKET ST W	MON	171	B3
MARKET ST W	SAL	171	B3
MARKHAM ST	RCO	99	D3
MARK HOPKINS AV	SUT	33	D3
MARKLEEVLLE LKT	ALP	36	C5
MARKS	FRCO	57	D5
MARKS AV	FRCO	57	C4
MARKS RD	SBD	101	D1
MARK SPGS W RD	SON	37	E1
MARKWEST STA RD	SON	37	D1
MARLAY AV	SBD	99	A2
MAR MONTE AV	SCR	54	B2
MARNI CT	KER	79	C4
MAROA AV	FRE	165	C1
MAROA AV	FRCO	57	C3
MARQUARDT AV	LACO	T	B1
MARR RD	LAS	8	D5
MARSH RD	SCL	46	B3
MARSH RD	SMCO	N	D2
MARSH ST	SNLO	172	B3
MARSH ST	SLO	76	A3

STREET	CO.	PAGE	GRID
MARSHALL RD	ED	34	D4
MARSHALL RD	MCO	55	C1
MARSHALL RD	STA	47	C4
MARSHALL ST	RCO	99	C4
MARSHAL-PETALMA	MAR	37	D4
MARSHALL RCH RD	TRI	17	C2
MARSH CREEK RD	CC	M	B3
MARSH CREEK RD	CC	M	D4
MARSH CREEK RD	CC	39	B5
MARSH CREEK RD	CC	46	B1
MARSHES FLAT RD	TUO	48	D1
MARSHVIEW RD	SOL	38	D4
MART AV	STA	47	E2
MARTIN AV	FRE	165	C5
MARTIN AV	KER	78	B2
MARTIN LN	AMA	40	D3
MARTIN RD	FRCO	56	D4
MARTIN RD	IMP	109	A4
MARTIN RD	MON	64	D1
MARTIN RD	YUB	25	E5
MARTIN ST	LAK	31	D3
MARTIN ST	MONT	167	D4
MARTIN ST	MON	53	E3
MARTIN ST	RCO	99	B3
MARTINEZ RD	MON	65	C4
MARTINEZ CYN RD	LACO	89	A4
MARTINGALE LN	CAL	41	A4
MRTN LTHR KG BL	LA	184	C5
MRTN LTHR KG BL	LACO	Q	D4
MARTIS PEAK RD	PLA	35	E1
MARTY RD	SUT	33	A2
MARVIN RANCH RD	SIE	26	C4
MAR VISTA	SDCO	106	C3
MAR VISTA DR	MONT	168	D1
MAR VISTA DR	MONT	167	D4
MAR VISTA DR	MON	53	E3
MARX RD NO 1	SHA	18	A3
MARX RD NO 2	SHA	18	A3
MARYLAND ST	VAL	134	B5
MARYSVILLE BLVD	SAC	33	E5
MARYSVILLE RD	YUB	26	A5
MARYSVILLE RD	YUB	33	E1
MASON ST	SF	143	B2
MASON ST	STB	174	E3
MASON DIXON RD	SBD	100	E1
MASONIC AV	SFCO	L	B5
MASONIC AV	SF	142	A3
MASONIC RD	MNO	43	C2
MASSACHUSTTS AV	SDCO	V	D3
MASSACHUSTTS AV	SDCO	111	D1
MASSACK RD	PLU	26	D2
MASSEY RD	MPA	49	C3
MAST AV	KER	78	B1
MASTEN AV	SCL	P	E5
MASTEN RD	TEH	18	B5
MASTERS AV	FRCO	56	D4
MASTERSONS RD	SIS	11	E2
MATHER ST	O	158	B1
MATHER FIELD RD	SAC	40	A1
MATHESON RD	SHA	18	B2
MATHEWS RD	LAS	14	B4
MATHEWS RD	SJCO	40	A5
MATHEWS RD	SJCO	47	A1
MATHEWS RD	SIS	5	A2
MATHILDA AV	SCL	P	A3
MATHILDA AV	SCL	45	E4
MATHILDA AV	SVL	148	D5
MATILIJA RD	VEN	88	A4
MATLOCK LP	TEH	18	C4
MATTERHORN DR	KER	79	C5
MATTHEWS LN	YUB	33	D1
MATTOLE RD	HUM	15	C3
MATTOLE RD	HUM	16	E4
MAUI RD	SBD	92	C1
MAURICO AV	RCO	99	C4
MAWSON RD	SUT	33	A2
MAXSON RD	FRCO	58	B2
MAXWELL LN	SOL	39	C2
MAXWELL RD	AMA	40	C2
MAXWELL CYN RD	NAPA	38	C1
MAXWLL SITES RD	COL	32	C1
MAY	CC	38	C5
MAYARADA	SBD	101	E1
MAYARO LODGE RD	BUT	25	E2
MAYBECK	SJCO	40	A5
MAYBERT RD	NEV	26	E5
MAYER AV	KER	78	B2
MAYER RD	YUB	33	D2
MAYFIELD RD	RCO	102	A4
MAYHEW AV	TEH	24	D2
MAYNARD RD	SHA	18	D2
MAY SCHOOL RD	ALA	M	C5
MAY SCHOOL RD	ALA	46	C2
MAYS CANYON RD	SON	37	C2
MAYTEN RD	SIS	4	C5
MAZE BL	MDO	162	A3
MAZE BLVD	STA	47	C2
MAZOURKA CANYON	INY	60	A3
MCADAMS CK RD	SIS	3	D5
MCADAMS INDN CK	SIS	3	D4
MCARTHUR RD	SHA	13	C3
MCARTHUR RD	SUT	33	B2
MCAULIFFE RD	SHA	18	A3
MCAUSLAND RD	COL	24	E5
MCBEAN PKWY	LACO	89	B4
MCCABE RD	IMP	112	A3
MCCABE RD	MCO	47	B5
MCCABE RD	MCO	55	B1
MCCAHILL LN	HUM	15	E2
MCCAIN BLVD	COR	215	B5
MCCAIN VLY RD	SDCO	111	A4
MCCALL AV	FRCO	57	D3
MCCALL BLVD	RCO	99	C4
MCCANN RD	HUM	16	B4

STREET	CO.	PAGE	GRID
MCCART RD	KER	68	A5
MCCARTHY RES RD	CAL	41	B2
MCCARTY RD	RCO	U	D4
MCCARTY RD	RCO	98	E3
MCCARTY RD	SBD	98	E3
MCCARTY RD	TEH	24	B2
MCCATER RD	MCO	48	E5
MCCAY	MPA	48	E3
MCCLAIN LN	RCO	107	B1
MCCLATCHY RD	SUT	33	B2
MCCLELLAN RD	CPTO	149	B5
MCCLELLAN RD	LAS	14	C3
MCCLELLAND LN	LAS	21	C3
MCCLELLN MTN RD	HUM	16	C3
MCCLINTOCK RD	STA	47	C4
MCCLOSKEY RD	SBT	54	E3
MCCLOSKEY RD	SBT	55	A3
MCCLOSKEY RD	SOL	39	C3
MCCLOUD AV	SIS	12	C2
MCCLOUD DUMP RD	SIS	12	E2
MCCLURE AV	TEH	24	D1
MCCLURE RD	STA	47	D2
MCCLURE SUB RD	MEN	31	B2
MCCOMBS RD	KER	77	E1
MCCOMBS RD	KER	78	B1
MCCONAHUE GL RD	SIS	11	E1
MCCONNELL RD	IMP	109	B5
MCCORMACK RD	SOL	39	B3
MCCOURTNEY RD	NEV	34	B2
MCCOURTNEY RD	NEV	127	A5
MCCOURTNEY RD	PLA	34	A3
MCCOY AV	KER	77	E1
MCCOY RD	LAS	20	C3
MCCOY RD	MON	54	E5
MCCOY RD	MON	55	A5
MCCOY RD	TEH	18	C4
MCCRACKEN RD	STA	47	B3
MCCREERY RCH RD	SBT	55	C3
MCCRORY RD	SOL	39	A3
MCCULLACH RD	MCO	47	D4
MCCULLOCK BLVD	MOH	96	B4
MCCULLY RD	MOD	7	D5
MCCUNE RD	SOL	39	A2
MCDANIEL RD	IMP	112	D5
MCDERMOTT RD	COL	32	D1
MCDERMOTT RD	RCO	99	E4
MCDOEL DIST	SIS	4	E4
MCDOEL DORRS RD	SIS	5	A3
MCDONALD	SJCO	39	D5
MCDONALD AV	STA	47	C2
MCDONALD RD	IMP	109	A3
MCDOWELL BLVD	SON	L	A1
MCEWEN RD	CC	L	D3
MCEWEN RD	CC	38	D4
MCEWEN RD	STA	47	E2
MCFADDEN	MON	54	C4
MCFADDEN AV	SA	195	A5
MCFADDEN AV	SA	196	C5
MCFARLND-WDY RD	KER	78	C1
MCGARY RD	SOL	38	D4
MCGEE AV	STA	47	D2
MCGEE CREEK RD	MNO	51	A3
MCGOWAN	YUB	33	D2
MCGRATH RD	SUT	33	B2
MCHENRY AV	MDO	162	C3
MCHENRY AV	SJCO	47	C2
MCHENRY RD	MCO	48	C5
MCINTIRE RD	SJCO	40	C3
MCINTOSH RD	HUM	10	D4
MCKEAN RD	SCL	P	C4
MCKEAN RD	SCL	46	C5
MCKEE RD	MCO	48	C4
MCKEE RD	SJ	152	E2
MCKEE RD	SCL	P	C3
MCKEE RD	SCL	46	B4
MCKEE ST	MCO	48	D5
MCKEEN RD	SIS	11	D2
MCKELL RD	LAK	32	A5
MCKENZIE AV	FRE	165	D3
MCKENZIE RD	SAC	40	A3
MCKERNIE ST	RCO	99	E4
MCKIBBEN RD	KER	78	A1
MCKIM RD	IMP	109	B5
MCKINLEY AV	FRE	165	B2
MCKINLEY AV	FRCO	57	A3
MCKINLEY AV	SJCO	47	A1
MCKINLEY ST	RCO	99	A3
MCKINLEYVLLE AV	HUM	9	E4
MCKINNEY CK RD	SIS	3	D4
MCKNNEY RUBICN-			
-SPRING RD	PLA	35	D2
MCLAIN RD	YUB	26	B4
MCLAUGHLIN AV	LA	187	E1
MCLAUGHLIN AV	SCL	P	C3
MCMASTER RD	MCO	48	C5
MCMILLAN CYN RD	SLO	76	C1
MCMULLIN	SJCO	47	A2
MCMULLIN GRADE	FRCO	57	A4
MCMURRY MDWS RD	INY	59	D1
MCNAMARA RD	MCO	48	C5
MCNEILL LN	SOL	39	B1
MCNELLA LN	PLU	27	C3
MCNERNEY RD	IMP	109	A3
MCRAE RD	BUT	25	B4
MCRAE RD	TUO	41	C5
MCSWAIN RD	MER	170	A3
MCSWAIN RD	MCO	170	A3
MEACHAM RD	KER	78	B3
MEAD RD	IMP	109	B4
MEADE AV	SD	214	B5
MEADOW DR	AMA	41	B2
MEADOW DR	MCO	48	A4
MEADOW RD	TRI	17	D1
MEADOW GLEN RD	CAL	41	C2

INDEXES

COPYRIGHT, © 1989 BY Thomas Bros Maps

STREET	CO.	PAGE	GRID
MEADOW LAKE RD	NEV	26	E5
MEADOW LAKE RD	NEV	27	B4
MEADOW LAKE RD	SIE	27	B5
MEADOW RIDGE RD	MAD	49	D5
MEADOWS DR	VAL	134	A1
MEADOWS RD	IMP	112	B4
MEADOWSWEET DR	CRTM	140	C1
MEADOW VLY RD	YUB	26	A5
MEADOW VIEW DR	SHA	18	C3
MEADOWVIEW RD	SAC	39	E2
MEADOW VISTA RD	PLA	34	C3
MEALEY RD	IMP	108	E5
MEAMBER CK RD	SIS	3	C4
MEARS RIDGE RD	SHA	12	C3
MECCA DALE RD	RCO	101	E3
MECHAM RD	SON	37	E3
MEDFORD AV	KIN	67	C2
MEDFORD RD	FRCO	57	E1
MEDICINE LK HWY	MOD	5	E5
MEDICINE LK HWY	SIS	5	D5
MEDICINE LK RD	SIS	5	C5
MEDICINE LK RD	SIS	13	B2
MEDLIN RD	STA	47	C4
MEEKLAND AV	ALA	L	E5
MEEKLAND AV	ALA	M	A5
MEEKLAND AV	ALA	N	E1
MEEKLAND AV	ALA	P	A1
MEEKS RD	SBD	92	D5
MEHRING RD	IMP	110	D5
MEHRTEN DR	TUL	68	D1
MEIER RD	STA	47	E2
MEIER RD	STA	48	A2
MEIGS RD	STB	174	A5
MEIKLE RD	STA	47	E2
MEIKLE RD	STA	48	A2
MEISS RD	SAC	40	B2
MEISS LAKE-			
-SAMS NECK RD	SIS	4	E3
MEISS LAKE-			
-SAMS NECK RD	SIS	5	A3
MELCHER RD	KER	78	B1
MELLA DR	AMA	41	A2
MELLO AV	SJCO	47	C1
MELLOR RD	STA	48	A2
MELODY CT	HUM	10	A5
MELOLANO RD	IMP	109	B5
MELON ST	RCO	102	C4
MELONES CT	TUO	41	B5
MELROSE AV	LA	181	B5
MELROSE AV	LA	182	C5
MELROSE AV	LACO	Q	AV
MELROSE AV	LACO	183	D1
MELROSE DR	SDCO	106	C3
MEMORY LN	SA	195	E2
MEMORY LN	SA	196	A2
MENALTO AV	MP	147	C1
MENDENHALL RD	TEH	18	C5
MENDIBOURE RD	LAS	8	B4
MENDIBURN	KER	79	D5
MENDIBURN RD	KER	80	B4
MENDOCINO AV	FRCO	57	E2
MENDOCINO AV	STR	131	C1
MENDOCINO PASS	MEN	23	B2
MENIFEE RD	RCO	99	C4
MENLO AV	RCO	99	E4
MERCED AV	FRCO	66	D3
MERCED AV	KER	78	A2
MERCED AV	LACO	R	E4
MERCED AV	MCO	47	E4
MERCEDES AV	MCO	48	B4
MERCED FALLS RD	MPA	48	D3
MERCED FALLS RD	TUO	48	D2
MERIDIAN AV	SCL	151	E5
MERIDIAN BLVD	ML	164	C3
MERIDIAN RD	BUT	25	A3
MERIDIAN RD	SBD	91	E2
MERIDIAN RD	SCL	P	B3
MERIDIAN RD	SCL	46	B5
MERIDIAN RD	SOL	39	B3
MERIDIAN RD	SUT	33	A2
MERIDIAN ST	SJ	151	E5
MERLE AV	STA	47	D2
MERRIAM RD	STA	47	E3
MERRIAM RD	YUB	26	B5
MERRILL AV	FRCO	56	B2
MERRILL AV	SBD	98	D2
MERRILL RD	TEH	24	E2
MERRILL RD S	KLAM	5	C2
MERRILL ST	SBD	99	A2
MERRILL FLAT RD	LAS	20	D2
MERRILLVILLE RD	LAS	20	E2
MERRIMAC CTO RD	BUT	25	E3
MERRITT	LAK	31	D3
MERRITT DR	TUL	57	E5
MERRITT DR	TUL	58	A5
MERRITT LN	PLA	34	A3
MERVEL AV	MCO	55	E2
MESA DR	RCO	103	C5
MESA DR	RCO	110	C1
MESA DR	SBD	100	E1
MESA DR	SDCO	106	B3
MESA RD	MAR	37	E5
MESA RD	SBD	92	E5
MESA TK TR W	SDCO	107	C5
MESA COLLEGE DR	SD	213	D1
MESA COLLEGE DR	SDCO	V	B2
MESA GRANDE RD	SDCO	107	B3
MESQUITE RD	INY	61	B2
MESQUITE CYN RD	KER	80	C2
MESQUITE SPG RD	SBD	101	B1
MESQUITE VLY RD	INY	73	C3
MESSICK	SJCO	40	C4
MESSICK RD	SUT	33	D3
MESSILLA VLY RD	BUT	25	D3
MESSING RD	CAL	40	D4
MESTMAKER ST	KER	68	D5
METCALF RD	NEV	34	B2
METCALFE RD	SCL	P	D4
METCALFE RD	SCL	46	C5
METROPOLE AV	AVLN	105	B5
METROPOLITAN RD	HUM	15	E2
METTER RD	SUT	33	C1
METTLER AV	KER	68	B5
METTLER AV	KER	78	B2
METTLER RD	SJCO	40	A4
METTLER RD	STA	47	D1
METZ RD	MON	65	B1
METZGER RD	SHA	13	D3
MEXICAN LAKE RD	SBT	66	B1
MEYER RD	LACO	R	D5
MEYER RD	LACO	T	B1
MEYERS LN	SUT	33	B1
MEYERS GRADE RD	SON	37	B1
MICA RD	RCO	107	C1
MICHAEL RD	MCO	48	B5
MICHEL RD	CAL	41	B3
MICHELSON DR	IRV	198	C4
MICHELTORENA ST	STB	174	B3
MICHIGAN BAR RD	SAC	40	C2
MICHILLINDA BL	LACO	R	C2
MICHOACAN AVD	BAJA	112	B4
MICKE GROVE RD	SJCO	40	B4
MIDDLE AV	SCL	P	E5
MIDDLE AV	SCL	54	D1
MIDDLE RD	BLMT	145	C4
MIDDLE RD	MAR	37	D3
MIDDLE RD	SJCO	46	E1
MIDDLE TER	AVLN	105	B5
MIDDLE BAR RD	AMA	40	E3
MIDDLE BAR RD	AMA	41	A3
MIDDLE CREEK RD	SHA	18	B2
MIDDLE CREEK RD	SIS	3	C3
MIDDLE CK RCH	SIS	3	C3
MIDDLEFIELD RD	MP	147	A1
MIDDLEFIELD RD	PA	147	E3
MIDDLEFIELD RD	SCL	N	E2
MIDDLEFLD RD E	MVW	148	B4
MIDDLE FORK RD	MON	66	B4
MDDL FK GASQUET	DN	2	A3
MID FK HUMBG RD	SIS	3	E4
MIDDLE HARBR RD	O	157	C3
MIDDL HONCUT RD	BUT	25	D5
MIDDLE RIDGE RD	MEN	30	B2
MIDDLETON DR	DN	1	D3
MIDDLETON RD	SUT	33	B2
MIDDLETON RD	TRI	11	E3
MIDDLETOWN RD	PLCV	138	B2
MIDDLETWN PK DR	SHA	18	B2
MDL TWO ROCK RD	SON	37	E3
MDL TWO ROCK RD	SON	38	A3
MIDLAND AV	SDCO	106	D4
MIDLAND RD	RCO	103	B2
MIDLAND TR	KER	80	C2
MIDOIL RD	KER	77	E4
MIDWAY	BUT	25	B4
MIDWAY DR	SD	213	A5
MIDWAY DR	SDCO	V	A3
MIDWAY RD	ALA	M	E5
MIDWAY RD	KER	77	E4
MIDWAY RD	SBD	101	D1
MIDWAY RD	SOL	39	B2
MIDWAY WELLS	INY	61	D3
MIKISHA BLVD	SBD	92	D5
MILAN RD	KER	77	E2
MILE END	MON	64	E1
MILE END	MON	65	A1
MILES RD	MCO	48	C5
MILFORD RD	SBDO	81	A1
MILFORD CEM RD	LAS	21	C5
MILFORD GRADE	LAS	21	C5
MILGEO RD	SJCO	47	C2
MIL-GOR RD	SBD	101	E1
MILHAM AV	KIN	67	B3
MILITAR	BAJA	112	B4
MILITARY E	BEN	153	C4
MILITARY W	BEN	153	B4
MILITARY W	SOL	38	D4
MILITARY RD	SIS	13	A2
MILITARY PASS	SIS	12	D1
MILITARY PASS	SIS	13	A2
MILL AV	KER	78	B1
MILL RD	BUT	26	B4
MILL RD	MNO	52	C3
MILL RD	SLO	76	B1
MILL RD	TEH	19	C4
MILL RD	YUB	26	B4
MILL ST	GV	127	B4
MILL ST	NEV	34	C1
MILL ST	RENO	130	C3
MILL ST	SBD	99	C2
MILL ST	SBDO	207	C3
MILL ST	U	123	C3
MILLARD CYN RD	RCO	100	B2
MILLBRAE AV	MLBR	144	D5
MILLBRAE AV	SMCO	N	C1
MILLBRAE AV	SMCO	45	B3
MILLBROOK AV	FRCO	57	C2
MILL CANYON RD	MNO	42	E2
MILL CREEK RD	HUM	10	C3
MILL CREEK RD	MEN	31	B2
MILL CREEK RD	SBD	99	E1
MILL CREEK RD	SIS	3	D5
MILL CREEK RD	SIS	3	E4
MILL CREEK RD	SON	31	C5
MILL CREEK RD	SON	37	D1
MILL CK PWR HS	MNO	43	B4
MILLER	MAR	45	B1
MILLER AV	CPTO	150	A5
MILLER AV	FRCO	56	B2
MILLER AV	MAR	L	B4
MILLER AV	MV	140	A3
MILLER AV	VAL	134	E4
MILLER RD	COL	33	A3
MILLER RD	IMP	112	C3
MILLER RD	MCO	48	D4
MILLER RD	TRI	23	A1
MILLER RD	YOL	39	C2
MILLER ST	SMA	173	C3
MILLER RANCH RD	SIE	26	D4
MILLERTON RD	FRCO	57	D2
MILLERTON RD	MAD	57	D1
MILLIKEN AV	SBD	U	E3
MILLIKEN AV	SBD	98	E2
MIL POTRERO HWY	KER	88	B1
MILLS AV	CLA	203	A4
MILLS AV	LACO	R	D5
MILLS AV	MTCL	203	A4
MILLS RD	MCO	47	C5
MILLS RD	SOL	39	C2
MILLS RD	SUT	33	B2
MILLS ORCHDS RD	COL	32	C1
MILLS PARK RD	SIE	27	A3
MILLUX AV	FRCO	56	B2
MILLUX RD	KER	78	C4
MILLVL PLAIN RD	SHA	18	D3
MILLWOOD DR	TUL	58	C5
MILLWOOD RD	FRCO	58	C3
MILNES RD	STA	47	D2
MILPAS DR	SBD	91	D4
MILPAS ST	STB	174	D3
MILPITAS RD	MON	64	E3
MILPITAS RD	MON	65	B3
MILPITAS WSH RD	IMP	110	B2
MILSAP BAR RD	BUT	25	E3
MILSAP BAR RD	BUT	26	A3
MILSTEAD RD	MEN	22	D1
MILTON RD	CAL	40	E5
MILTON RD	NAPA	L	C1
MILTON RD	NAPA	38	C3
MILTON RD	SJCO	40	C5
MILTON RD	STA	40	E5
MINA RD	MEN	23	A1
MINE RD	VEN	89	A5
MINER RD	CC	L	D4
MINER RD	CC	45	D1
MINER ST	S	160	E4
MINERAL RD	IMP	108	E1
MINERAL RD	SHA	19	C3
MINERAL KING AV	TUL	68	A1
MINERAL KING RD	TUL	59	B5
MINERAL SCHOOL	SHA	19	A1
MINERET RD	ML	164	C2
MINERS CREEK RD	SIS	11	D2
MINES RD	ALA	P	D1
MINES RD	ALA	46	D3
MINES RD	SCL	46	D3
MING AV	KER	78	C3
MINI DR	VAL	134	C1
MINNEOLA RD	SBD	92	B1
MINNESOTA ST	SDCO	106	C2
MINNEWAWA AV	FRCO	57	D2
MINNEWAWA AV	FRCO	57	D5
MINNIEAR RD	STA	47	B3
MINNIETTA RD	INY	71	B2
MINT RD	MCO	56	B1
MINTURN RD	MCO	48	D5
MIRABEL RD	SON	37	D2
MIRAMAR RD	SDCO	V	B1
MIRAMAR RD	SDCO	106	D5
MIRAMAR WY	SDCO	V	B2
MIRAMAR WY	SDCO	106	D5
MIRA MESA BLVD	SDCO	V	B1
MIRA MESA BLVD	SDCO	106	C5
MIRANDA AV	CC	M	A4
MIRASOL AV	KER	77	E3
MIRASOL AV	KER	78	A3
MISSION AV	MCO	48	C5
MISSION AV	SD	214	A5
MISSION AV	SDCO	106	B3
MISSION AV	SR	139	C3
MISSION BLVD	ALA	45	E2
MISSION BLVD	ALA	146	C1
MISSION BLVD	H	146	D2
MISSION BLVD	MTCL	203	A5
MISSION BLVD	ONT	203	D5
MISSION BLVD	ONT	204	B5
MISSION BLVD	POM	203	A5
MISSION BLVD	RCO	99	A2
MISSION BLVD	SBD	U	D2
MISSION BLVD	SBD	98	D2
MISSION BLVD	SBD	203	A5
MISSION BLVD	SD	212	A1
MISSION BLVD	SDCO	V	A2
MISSION BLVD	SDCO	106	C5
MISSION DR	LACO	R	B3
MISSION FRWY	SDCO	V	A3
MISSION RD	LA	186	D2
MISSION RD	LACO	98	A2
MISSION RD	LACO	R	B3
MISSION RD	MON	65	B3
MISSION RD	SDCO	106	C2
MISSION RD	SMCO	L	B5
MISSION RD	SMCO	N	B1
MISSION RD	SMCO	45	B2
MISSION ST	SFCO	L	B5
MISSION ST	SF	142	C5
MISSION ST	SF	143	C5
MISSION ST	STB	174	A3
MISSION ST	SC	169	A4
MISSION TR	RCO	99	B5
MISSION BAY DR	SD	212	D1
MISSN BAY DR W	SD	212	B4
MISSION CTR RD	SD	213	E3
MISSION CK RD	RCO	100	C2
MISSION GRGE RD	SDCO	V	C2
MISSION GRGE RD	SDCO	106	E5
MISSION LKS BL	RCO	100	C2
MISSN OLIVE RD	BUT	25	E5
MISSION RDGE RD	STB	174	D2
MISSION VLY FWY	SD	213	C5
MISSION VLY FWY	SD	214	B4
MISSION VLGE DR	SD	214	C1
MISSION VLGE DR	SDCO	V	C2
MISSION VLGE DR	SDCO	106	D5
MISSOURI AV	STA	47	E2
MISTLETOE DR	VEN	88	C4
MITCHELL RD	HUM	10	C3
MITCHELL RD	HUM	15	E1
MITCHELL RD	LAS	8	A5
MITCHELL RD	LAS	14	E5
MITCHELL RD	STA	47	D4
MITCHLLS CMP RD	IMP	110	C2
MIX CANYON RD	SOL	38	E2
MOANING CAVE RD	CAL	41	B4
MOBLEY	SJCO	40	C5
MOBLEY	SJCO	47	C1
MOCAL RD	KER	77	E4
MOCAL RD	KER	78	D4
MOCKINGBIRD CYN	RCO	99	B3
MODJESKA CYN RD	ORA	98	E4
MODOC AV	FRCO	57	A3
MODOC COUNTY RD	MOD	5	D3
MOFFAT BLVD	MAN	161	C4
MOFFAT BLVD	SJCO	161	C4
MOFFAT RANCH RD	INY	60	A4
MOFFATT RD	MCO	47	D5
MOFFETT BLVD	MVW	148	A4
MOFFETT BLVD	SCL	N	E3
MOFFETT BLVD	SCL	P	A3
MOFFETT DR	TUL	68	D1
MOFFETT RD	STA	47	D3
MOFFETT CK RD E	SIS	3	E5
MOFFETT CK RD W	SIS	3	E5
MOHAVE RD	LPAZ	103	E3
MOHAVE ROSE DR	LACO	89	D3
MOHAVE VLY HWY	MOH	85	D5
MOHLER RD	SJCO	47	B2
MOJAVE AV	KER	89	C1
MOJAVE DR	SBD	91	B3
MOJAVE RD	SBD	91	B4
MOJAVE RD	SBD	101	C1
MOJAVE-RANDSBRG	KER	80	C4
MOJVE TRPICO RD	KER	79	E5
MOJVE TRPICO RD	KER	80	A5
MOJVE TRPICO RD	KER	89	E1
MOKELUMNE HILL-			
-CMP SECO TP RD	CAL	41	C3
MOLERA RD	MON	54	B3
MOLINO AV	MV	140	A3
MOLLER AV	TEH	24	E2
MONARCH MINE RD	SIE	26	E4
MONARCH MINE RD	SIE	27	A4
MONO DR E	MONO	43	C4
MONO WY	TUO	163	D4
MONROE	MCO	55	D1
MONROE AV	FRCO	57	B3
MONROE AV	FRCO	57	B5
MONROE AV	TEH	18	D5
MONROE ST	RCO	101	A4
MONROE ST	SCLR	150	C1
MONSON	FRCO	58	B4
MONTGUE AGER RD	SIS	4	B4
MONTAGUE EXPWY	SCL	P	B3
MONTAGUE GRNADA	SIS	4	B4
MONTANA AV	LA	180	A3
MONTANA AV	LACO	97	C2
MONTANA AV	SHA	18	C2
MONTANA ST	PAS	190	A1
MONTARA RD	SBD	91	E1
MONTE RD	IMP	109	A4
MONTEBELLO BLVD	LACO	R	C4
MONTE BELLO RD	SCL	N	E3
MONTE BELLO RD	SCL	45	D4
MONTE BLOYD RD	MEN	30	D2
MONTECITO RD	SDCO	107	A4
MONTECITO RD	SLO	75	E2
MONTECITO ST	STB	174	D3
MONTE DIABLO AV	S	160	A4
MONTEREY AV	FRCO	56	D4
MONTEREY AV	FRCO	66	D2
MONTEREY AV	MDO	162	D4
MONTEREY AV	RCO	100	E4
MONTEREY BLVD	SFCO	L	B5
MONTEREY BLVD	SFCO	45	B2
MONTEREY HWY	SCL	P	D4
MONTEREY HWY	SCL	54	D1
MONTEREY RD	LACO	R	B3
MONTEREY RD	SLO	76	A1
MONTEREY RD	SLO	76	A2
MONTEREY RD	SCL	46	B4
MONTEREY ST	SAL	171	C4
MONTEREY ST	SNLO	172	C3
MONTEREY PSS RD	LACO	R	B3
MONTE VERDE AV	CAR	168	B3
MONTE VISTA AV	MCO	48	A3
MONTE VISTA AV	SBD	U	C2
MONTE VISTA AV	SBD	80	E1
MONTE VISTA AV	SBD	98	D1
MONTE VISTA AV	STA	47	C3
MONTE VISTA AV	STA	48	A3
MONTE VISTA DR	SDCO	106	C3
MONTE VISTA RD	SHA	18	B3
MONTEZUMA RD	SDCO	V	C3
MONTEZUMA RD	SDCO	111	D1
MONTEZUMA HL RD	SOL	39	B4
MONTFORD AV	MV	140	A3
MONTGOMERY AV	BUT	25	A3
MONTGOMERY DR	STR	131	D3
MONTGOMERY RD	IMP	109	B3
MONTGOMERY RD	TRI	11	B5
MONTGOMERY ST	SF	143	C2
MONTGOMERY ST	MCO	48	C3
MONTGOMRY CK RD	TRI	11	D5
MONTGMRY RCH RD	SHA	18	B2
MONTICELLO RD	NAPA	133	E1
MONTPELIER RD	STA	47	E3
MONTPELIER RD	STA	48	A3
MONUMENT BLVD	CC	M	A3
MONUMENT RD	HUM	15	E3
MOODY RD	MEN	22	B2
MOODY ST	ORA	T	B2
MOON BEND RD	COL	32	A2
MOON BEND RD	COL	33	A2
MOONEY BLVD	TUL	68	B2
MOONEY RD	LAS	20	C2
MOONEY RD	LAS	20	C3
MOONEY FLAT RD	NEV	34	A1
MOONRIDGE RD	SBD	100	A1
MOONSHINE RD	YUB	26	B5
MOONWIND ST	KER	80	D1
MOORE RD	LAS	21	E4
MOORE RD	PLA	33	E4
MOORE RD	PLA	34	A4
MOORE RD	SUT	33	B2
MOOREHEAD RD	STA	47	C5
MOORES FLAT RD	NEV	26	D5
MOORPARK FRWY	VEN	88	E5
MOORPARK RD	VEN	96	D1
MOORPARK ST	LACO	Q	C3
MOORVILL RDG RD	BUT	26	B4
MOOSE CAMP RD	SHA	13	B5
MORADA LN	SJCO	40	B4
MORAGA AV	ALA	L	D4
MORAGA AV	ALA	45	D1
MORAGA AV	MCO	55	D1
MORAGA AV	O	158	E1
MORAGA AV	P	158	D1
MORAGA AV	SD	211	E5
MORAGA RD	CC	L	E4
MORAGA RD	CC	45	E1
MORAGA WY	CC	L	E4
MORAN AV	MCO	48	A4
MORAN RD	CAL	41	C3
MORAN RD	STA	47	C4
MORAN RD	TEH	24	D1
MORCOURT AV	KER	80	C1
MOREHEAD RD	DN	1	D3
MOREHEAD RD	SUT	33	B2
MORELLO AV	CC	L	E3
MORELLO AV	CC	154	E3
MORELLO AV	M	154	E4
MORENA BLVD	SD	211	C4
MORENA BLVD	SD	212	E1
MORENA BLVD	SD	213	A4
MORENA BLVD	SDCO	V	A2
MORENA BLVD	SDCO	111	C1
MORENA BLVD W	SD	213	A4
MORENA RES DR	SDCO	112	D1
MORENO AV	SDCO	V	E1
MORENO AV	SDCO	106	E5
MORENO RD	STB	174	C2
MORENO ST	MTCL	203	C3
MORENO BEACH DR	RCO	99	C2
MORGAN RD	CAL	41	B5
MORGAN RD	HUM	15	D2
MORGAN RD	LAS	21	C1
MORGAN RD	SBD	101	D1
MORGAN RD	STA	47	D3
MORGAN WY	LPAZ	104	A5
MORGAN CYN RD	FRCO	57	E2
MORGAN TERRITRY	CC	39	B5
MORGAN TERRITRY	CC	46	B1
MORGAN VLY RD	LAK	32	B4
MORLEY AV	MCO	48	D5
MORMON ST	LA	191	C3
MORMN EMGRNT TR	ED	35	C5
MORNING DR	KER	78	E3
MORNING STAR RD	ALP	36	C5
MORNING STR CTO	SBD	84	B3
MORNING STAR MN	SBD	84	B3
MORONGO DR	RCO	100	A3
MORONGO RD	SBD	101	B1
MORONI RD	SUT	33	B2
MORRETTI CYN RD	SLO	76	B4
MORRILL RD	STA	47	D2
MORRIS AV W	MDO	162	A2
MORRIS RD	COL	33	A2
MORRIS RD	KER	78	A3
MORRIS RD	STA	47	C4
MORRIS MINE RD	MNO	51	C2
MORRISON RD	STA	48	A1
MORRISN BRYN RD	TEH	24	B2
MORRISON CYN RD	ALA	P	B1
MORRISON CYN RD	ALA	46	A1
MORRIS RANCH RD	RCO	100	C5
MORRO RD	KER	91	C3
MORSE RD	SJCO	40	B4
MORSE RD	YOL	39	D3
MORTON AV	TUL	68	D3
MORTON BL S	MDO	162	C4
MOSAIC CANYON	INY	61	D4
MOSELEY RD	DN	1	D3
MOSHER	MPA	49	A3
MOSQUITO RD	ED	34	E4
MOSQUITO RDG RD	PLA	34	E3
MOSS OLD MLL RD	TRI	10	E5
MOTHER DR	ED	34	D5
MOTHER LODE TR	MAD	49	C4
MOTOR AV	LA	183	B3
MOTOR AV	LACO	Q	C4

INDEXES

STREET	CO.	PAGE	GRID
MOTT AIRPORT RD	SIS	12	D2
MOULTAN LOOP	TEH	19	A3
MOULTON PKWY	ORA	98	C4
MOUND SPGS RD	SBD	100	C1
MT ACADIA BLVD	SD	213	B2
MT ADA RD	AVLN	105	B5
MOUNTAIN AV	LACO	R	D2
MOUNTAIN AV	RCO	100	A4
MOUNTAIN AV	SBD	U	D2
MOUNTAIN AV	SBD	98	D1
MOUNTAIN AV	UPL	203	E2
MOUNTAIN BLVD	O	156	E5
MOUNTAIN DR	STB	174	B2
MOUNTAIN RD	SBD	90	D4
MOUNTAIN RD S	VEN	88	C5
MOUNTAIN ST	LACO	Q	E2
MTN CLIMBER WY	KER	79	C5
MTN HOME CK RD	SBD	99	E1
MTN HOME RCH RD	SON	38	A1
MTN HOUSE RD	ALA	M	E4
MTN HOUSE RD	ALA	46	D1
MTN HOUSE RD	MEN	31	C4
MTN HOUSE RD	SIE	26	D4
MTN LEMON RD S	VEN	88	C5
MTN MEADOW RD	SHA	19	C2
MTN QUAIL LN	MOD	7	B5
MOUNTAIN RCH RD	CAL	41	B3
MTN SCHOOL RD	SHA	13	B5
MTN SPRINGS RD	SBD	94	E1
MTN SPRINGS RD	SLO	76	A1
MOUNTAIN VW AV	FRCO	56	C5
MOUNTAIN VW AV	FRCO	57	D5
MOUNTAIN VW AV	SBD	99	C2
MOUNTAIN VW AV	RCO	99	E2
MOUNTAIN VW RD	HUM	16	B1
MOUNTAIN VW RD	KER	78	E3
MOUNTAIN VW RD	KER	79	A3
MOUNTAIN VW RD	MEN	30	E3
MOUNTAIN VW RD	RCO	100	D3
MOUNTAIN VW RD	SBD	92	B1
MOUNTAIN VW RD	SBD	91	C1
MOUNTAIN VW RD	STB	174	A4
MOUNTAIN VW RD	SCR	P	B5
MOUNTAIN VW RD	SCR	54	A1
MOUNTAIN VW RD	SHA	13	C5
MOUNTAIN VW RD	STA	47	D3
MOUNTAIN VW ST	BARS	208	A2
MTN VW-ALVSO RD	MVW	148	A5
MTN VW-ALVSO RD	SCL	P	B3
MTN VIEW RCH RD	SON	31	C5
MT AUKUM RD	ED	40	E1
MT AUKUM RD	ED	41	A1
MT BALDY LKOUT	SIS	2	D3
MT BULLION CTFF	MPA	49	A3
MT DIABLO SC BL	CC	M	B4
MT EATON RD	TUO	41	D5
MT EDEN RD	SCL	N	E4
MT EDEN RD	SCL	P	A4
MT EDEN RD	SCL	45	E5
MT EMMA RD	LACO	90	A4
MT GAINES	MPA	48	E3
MT GLEASON AV	LACO	Q	E2
MT HAMILTON RD	SCL	P	C3
MT HAMILTON RD	SCL	46	C4
MT HERMON RD	SCR	P	A5
MT HERMON RD	SCR	53	E1
MT HOUGH CRYSTL	PLU	26	D1
MT HOLLYWOOD DR	LA	182	A2
MT HOUSE RD	YUB	26	C5
MT MADONNA RD	SCL	54	C2
MT OLIVE RD	NEV	34	C2
MT OPHIR RD	MPA	49	A3
MT PIERCE LKOUT	HUM	15	E3
MT PINOS RD	KER	88	D2
MT PINOS RD	VEN	88	A1
MT PINOS RD	VEN	88	C2
MT REBA RD	ALP	42	A1
MT SHASTA DR	SIS	12	E2
MT VEEDER RD	NAPA	29	C4
MT VEEDER RD	NAPA	38	B2
MT VERNON AV	CLTN	207	B4
MT VERNON AV	KER	78	D3
MT VERNON AV	RCO	99	B2
MT VERNON AV	SBD	91	D1
MT VERNON AV	SBD	99	B2
MT VERNON AV	SBDO	207	B2
MT VERNON RD	PLA	34	B3
MT WHITNEY	FRCO	57	C5
MT WHITNEY AV	FRCO	66	D1
MT WHITNEY ST	KER	70	C5
MT WILSON	LACO	98	A1
MT WILSON RD	LACO	R	C1
MT ZION RD	AMA	41	A2
MOVIE RD	INY	60	A4
MOWRY AV	ALA	P	A2
MOWRY AV	ALA	46	A3
M T FREITAS PKY	SR	139	A1
MUCK VALLEY RD	LAS	14	B4
MUDD RD	IMP	109	A5
MUD LAKE RD	ALP	36	C4
MUD LAKE RD	MOD	6	A5
MUD LAKE RD	MOD	14	A1
MUELLER	SJCO	40	A5
MUELLER	SJCO	47	A1
MUIR AV	BUT	25	A3
MUIR MILL RD	MEN	22	E5
MUIR MILL RD	MEN	23	A5
MUIR MILL RD	MEN	30	E1
MUIR MILL RD	MEN	31	A1
MUIR WOODS RD	MAR	L	A4
MUIR WOODS RD	MAR	45	A1
MULBERRY AV	MCO	48	B4
MULBERRY AV	RCO	99	A2
MULBERRY DR	LACO	R	D5

STREET	CO.	PAGE	GRID
MULBERRY ST	C	124	D5
MULE BRIDGE RD	SIS	11	C2
MULE CANYON RD	SBD	92	A1
MULE CREEK RD	TRI	11	D5
MULE DEER LN	MOD	7	B5
MULE TOWN RD	SHA	18	B2
MULHOLLAND DR	LA	177	A5
MULHOLLAND DR	LA	181	A2
MULHOLLAND DR	LACO	97	C1
MULHOLLAND DR	LACO	Q	C3
MULHOLLAND HWY	LACO	97	A1
MULLER LN	DGL	36	B3
MULLER RD	KER	78	E3
MULLER RD	KER	79	A3
MULLOY RD	SIS	4	C3
MUMMA RD	COL	33	A3
MUMY RD	INY	51	C4
MUNCY RD	STA	47	C3
MUNJAR RD	BUT	25	A2
MUNRAS AV	MONT	167	D5
MUNRAS AV	MON	53	E4
MUNSEY RD	KER	80	C3
MUNRAS AV	MONT	168	D1
MUNZER RD	KER	78	B3
MURCHISON DR	MLBR	144	D5
MURIEL DR	BARS	208	C2
MURPHY AV	SCL	P	B3
MURPHY LN	SCL	P	E5
MURPHY LN	SCL	54	D1
MURPHY LN	SHA	19	A1
MURPHY RD	IMP	112	A3
MURPHY RD	MON	54	C2
MURPHY RD	NEV	26	C5
MURPHY RD	SBT	55	B3
MURPHY RD	SCR	54	C2
MURPHY RD	SJCO	47	C1
MURPHY RD	STA	47	C2
MURPHY RD	TUO	41	C5
MURPHYS GRD RD	CAL	41	B4
MURRAY RD	HUM	9	E4
MURRAY RD	HUM	10	A4
MURRAY RD	SJCO	40	C5
MURRAY RD	SUT	33	C3
MURRAY CK RD E	CAL	41	B3
MURRAY CK RD W	CAL	41	A3
MURRAY RIDGE RD	SD	214	A2
MURRIETA HT SPG	RCO	99	C5
MURRIETTA RD	RCO	99	C3
MUSCAT AV	FRCO	57	B4
MUSCAT AV	FRCO	57	D4
MUSCOTT ST	SBDO	207	A2
MUSTANG RD	RCO	100	A5
MUSTANG SPGS RD	SLO	76	A1
MUTAU FLAT RD	VEN	88	C2
MYER AV	TUL	68	C2
MYERS LN	COL	32	E2
MYERS RD	COL	32	D2
MYERS RD	SIS	4	E3
MYERS RD	SIS	5	A3
MYERS ST	BUT	25	D4
MYFORD RD	ORA	T	E3
MYKLE OAKS RD	MPA	49	A3
MYRA AV	LA	182	C5
MYRTLE AV	DN	1	E5
MYRTLE AV	EUR	121	E1
MYRTLE AV	HUM	9	E5
MYRTLE AV	HUM	15	E1
MYRTLE AV	LACO	R	D2
MYRTLEWOOD DR	MAD	57	C2

N

STREET	CO.	PAGE	GRID
NABORLY RD	SBD	101	D1
NACIMNTO-FER RD	MON	64	E3
NACIMNTO-FER RD	MON	65	A3
NACIMIENTO LAKE	MON	65	E4
NACMIENTO LK DR	SLO	75	E1
NACMIENTO LK DR	SLO	76	A1
NACIONAL ST	SAL	171	A3
NADEAU RD	INY	71	B1
NADER RD	PLA	34	A3
NAGEL CANYON RD	KER	79	D3
NAGLEE AV	SJ	151	D4
NANTES AV	MCO	55	E1
NAPA AV	FRCO	56	E5
NAPA RD	SBD	92	E5
NAPA RD	SON	38	B3
NAPA RD	SON	L	B1
NAPA RD	SON	132	D5
NAPA ST	SON	L	B1
NAPA ST E	SNMA	132	E4
NAPA ST E	SON	38	B3
NAPA ST W	SNMA	132	C4
NARANJO BLVD	TUL	58	D5
NARANJO BLVD	TUL	68	D1
NARBONNE AV	LACO	S	B2
NARRAGANSETT AV	SDCO	V	A3
NARRAGANSETT AV	SDCO	111	C1
NASHUA RD	MON	54	C3
NASON RD	MON	64	C1
NASON ST	RCO	99	C3
NATIONAL AV	SD	216	A4
NATIONAL AV	SDCO	V	C4
NATIONAL AV	SDCO	111	D1
NATIONAL BLVD	CUL	183	D5
NATIONAL BLVD	LA	180	E5
NATIONAL BLVD	LA	183	C4
NATIONAL BLVD	LACO	Q	C4
NATL TRAILS HWY	SBD	91	B2
NATL TRAILS HWY	SBD	92	A1
NATL TRAILS HWY	SBD	93	A2
NATL TRAILS HWY	SBD	94	A3
NATIVIDAD RD	MON	54	D4
NATOMAS RD	SUT	33	D4

STREET	CO.	PAGE	GRID
NATURAL BRDG RD	INY	72	B1
NAUMAN RD	VEN	96	B1
NAUTILUS ST	SD	211	A4
NAVAJO DR	SAL	171	C1
NAVAJO RD	RCO	99	C4
NAVAJO RD	SBD	91	C3
NAVAJO RD	SDCO	V	D2
NAVAJO RD	SDCO	111	D1
NAVARO ST	SDCO	V	A3
NAVARRO RDG RD	MEN	30	C2
NAVELENCIA AV	FRCO	58	A4
NAVY DR	SJCO	40	A5
NEAL SPRING RD	SLO	76	B1
NEBO ST	SBD	92	A1
NEBRASKA AV	FRCO	57	B4
NEBRASKA AV	FRCO	57	C4
NEBRASKA AV	TUL	58	A4
NEBRASKA ST	VAL	134	C3
NECKLE RD	IMP	112	A3
NECTAR RD	RCO	107	B1
NEEDHAM RD	STA	47	B3
NEEDHAM ST	MDO	162	A3
NEEDLE PEAK RD	SLT	129	D4
NEELEY	SJCO	40	A4
NEENACH RD	LACO	89	E2
NEES AV	FRCO	56	C3
NEES AV	FRCO	57	C3
NEGRO CREEK DR	TUL	58	C4
NEGRO HOLE RD	SIS	5	C4
NEIGHBORS BLVD	RCO	103	D5
NEIGHBORS BLVD	RCO	110	D1
NEILSON RD	CAL	40	E3
NELANDER	MCO	47	E4
NELSON	SJCO	47	C1
NELSON AV	BUT	25	C4
NELSON DR	TUL	69	B2
NELSON RD	BUT	25	B4
NELSON RD	TRI	17	C2
NELSON BAR RD	BUT	25	D3
NELSON CREEK RD	SHA	13	B4
NELSON PIT RD	IMP	112	C3
NELSON RES RD	LAS	8	B3
NELSONS CROSSNG	BUT	26	A3
NELSN SHPPEE RD	BUT	25	B4
NEROLY RD	CC	39	C5
NEROLY RD	CC	M	C3
NESTLE AV	LA	178	D5
NETHERLANDS RD	YOL	39	D2
NETHERTON RD	MCO	47	C5
NEUGERBAUER	SJCO	39	E5
NEUMARKEL RD	KER	79	A3
NEURALIA RD	KER	80	B4
NEVA AV	TEH	24	D2
NEVADA AV	KIN	67	B2
NEVADA AV	KIN	67	C2
NEVADA ST	AUB	126	B3
NEVADA ST	NEVC	128	C2
NEVADA ST	NEV	128	D2
NEVADA CITY HWY	GV	127	D2
NEVADA CITY HWY	NEV	127	D2
NEVADA CITY HWY	NEV	128	A5
NEVIS AV	KER	78	C1
NEW AV	LACO	R	C4
NEW AV	SCL	P	E5
NEW AV	SCL	54	D1
NEWARK BLVD	ALA	P	A2
NEWARK BLVD	ALA	45	E3
NEWBERRY RD	SBD	92	C1
NEW BIG OAK FLT	MPA	49	C1
NEW BIG OAK FLT	MPA	63	B4
NEWCASTLE	PLA	34	B4
NEWCASTLE RD	SJCO	40	B5
NEW CEMETERY RD	LAS	14	B3
NEW CHESTR DUMP	PLU	20	B4
NW CHG QRTZ MTN	AMA	40	E2
NEWCOMB AV	FRCO	56	C4
NEWCOMB ST	TUL	68	D3
NEW DOCK ST	LA	191	C2
NEW DOCK ST	LACO	S	C3
NEWHALL AV	LACO	89	B4
NEWHALL RD	MCO	48	B5
NEWHALL RD	SUT	33	B2
NEWHALL ST	SJ	151	D3
NEW HOPE RD	SAC	39	E3
NEW HOPE RD	SAC	40	A3
NEWHOPE ST	FTNV	197	B2
NEWHOPE ST	GGR	195	A3
NEWHOPE ST	ORA	T	C3
NEWHOPE ST	SA	195	A3
NEW IDRIA RD	SBT	55	E5
NEW IDRIA RD	SBT	56	A4
NEWLAND ST	ORA	T	B3
NEWMARK AV	FRCO	57	E4
NEW PLEYTO RD	MON	65	D4
NEW PEORIA FLAT	TUO	41	B5
NEWPORT AV	GLE	24	D3
NEWPORT AV	ORA	98	C4
NEWPORT AV	ORA	T	E2
NEWPORT BLVD	CM	199	C2
NEWPORT BLVD	NB	199	A4
NEWPORT BLVD	ORA	98	C4
NEWPORT BLVD	ORA	T	E2
NEWPORT FRWY	CM	197	E5
NEWPORT FRWY	CM	198	B3
NEWPORT FRWY	OR	194	E3
NEWPORT FRWY	OR	196	E3
NEWPORT FRWY	ORA	98	C4
NEWPORT FRWY	ORA	T	C4
NEWPORT FRWY	ORA	196	E3
NEWPORT FRWY	SA	196	E4
NEWPORT FRWY	TUS	196	E4
NEWPORT RD	MCO	48	A3
NEWPORT RD	RCO	99	C4
NEWPORT RD	RCO	99	D4

STREET	CO.	PAGE	GRID
NEWRIVER RD	TRI	11	A4
NEW ROME RD	NEV	34	C1
NEWSOM RD	MCO	47	C5
NEWSOM RD	MCO	55	C1
NEWTON AV	KIN	67	C3
NEWTOWN RD	ED	34	E5
NEWVILLE RD	GLE	24	B3
NEWVILLE RD	TEH	24	A2
NEW YORK DR	LACO	R	B2
NEW YORK DR	LACO	R	B2
NEW YRK FLAT RD	YUB	26	A4
NEW YRK HOUS RD	YUB	26	A5
NEW YORK MTN RD	SBD	84	C4
NEW YORK RCH RD	AMA	40	E2
NEW YORK RCH RD	AMA	41	A2
NICASIO VLY RD	MAR	37	E4
NICE LUCERNE	LAK	31	D2
NICHOLAS RD	MAD	57	E2
NICHOLLS RD	NEV	34	B2
NICHOLS RD	IMP	112	A3
NICHOLS RD	RCO	99	B4
NICHOLS CYN RD	LA	181	A3
NICHOLS MILL RD	SIE	27	B4
NICKEL RD	MCO	48	A5
NICOLAS RD	RCO	99	D5
NICOLAUS	PLA	33	E4
NICOLAUS AV	SUT	33	D3
NIDER RD	IMP	109	B3
NIDERER RD	SLO	75	E1
NIDERER RD	SLO	76	A1
NIELSON	SJCO	40	C5
NIELSON AV	FRE	165	A3
NIELSEN AV	FRCO	57	A3
NIELSEN RD	CAL	41	A3
NIESTRATH RD	SON	37	B1
NILAND AV	IMP	109	B3
NILAND MRINA RD	IMP	109	A2
NILE AV	SJCO	47	B1
NILE RD	SJCO	47	B1
NILES AV	KIN	67	D3
NILES ST	BKD	166	C2
NILES ST	KER	78	E3
NILES CANYON RD	ALA	P	B1
NILES CANYON RD	ALA	46	A3
NILL AV	KER	78	C1
NIMITZ BLVD	SD	212	C5
NIMITZ BLVD	SDCO	V	A3
NIMITZ BLVD	SDCO	111	C1
NIMITZ FRWY	ALA	45	D2
NIMITZ FRWY	ALA	146	C2
NIMITZ FRWY	H	146	C4
NIMITZ FRWY	O	157	D1
NIMITZ FRWY	O	158	B4
NIMITZ FRWY	O	159	C1
NIMITZ FRWY	SJ	152	A1
NINE RD	CAL	41	C4
NINE MILE CYN	INY	70	B4
NINTH ST	C	124	C5
NIPOMO ST	SNLO	172	B3
NIPTON RD	SBD	84	C2
NIPTON DESRT RD	SBD	84	C2
NIPTON MOORE RD	SBD	84	C2
NISQUALLY RD	SBD	91	B4
NISSEN RD	HUM	15	D2
NM 1	TUL	68	E5
NM 14	TUL	68	E4
NM 18	TUL	69	C4
NM 23	TUL	69	B4
NM 24	TUL	69	B4
NM 45	TUL	69	C4
NM 50	TUL	69	B4
NM 88	TUL	69	C4
NM 93	TUL	69	C4
NM 112	TUL	69	C3
NM 117	TUL	70	A3
NM 121	TUL	69	B3
NM 127	TUL	69	B3
NM 133	TUL	70	A3
NM 163	TUL	69	B3
NM 175	TUL	69	B3
NM 231	TUL	69	B2
NM 232	TUL	69	A2
NM 276	TUL	69	A1
NOBLE RD	YUB	33	D2
NOFFSINGER RD	IMP	109	B3
NOLAN RD	IMP	109	B4
NOLINA CIR	RCO	100	D4
NO NINE	MPA	48	E3
NONPAREIL AV	COL	32	E3
NOPEL AV	BUT	25	C2
NORD AV	BUT	124	A4
NORD AV	KER	78	C3
NORD HWY	BUT	25	A3
NORDAHL RD	IMP	110	D5
NORD GIANELLA	BUT	25	A3
NORDOFF ST	LACO	97	C1
NORFOLK ST	SM	145	A1
NORHAM PL	SBD	101	A1
NORIEGA RD	KER	78	C3
NORIEGA ST	SF	141	C5
NORMA ST S	KER	80	E1
NORMAL ST	SD	214	A5
NORMAL ST	SDCO	V	B3
NORMAL ST	SDCO	111	D1
NORMAN	SUT	33	B2
NORMAN AV	KER	80	B5
NORMAN RD	COL	24	E5
NORMANDIE AV	LA	182	B5
NORMANDIE AV	LA	185	B5
NORMANDIE AV	LACO	Q	E5
NORMANDIE AV	LACO	S	C2
NORMAN HILLS RD	RCO	107	C1
NORRBOM RD	SON	38	B3
NORRBOM RD	SON	132	D3

STREET	CO.	PAGE	GRID
NORRIS RD	KER	78	C2
NORRIS CYN RD	CC	M	A5
NORRIS CYN RD	CC	46	A2
NORRISH RD	IMP	109	C5
NORTH AV	FRCO	56	C4
NORTH AV	FRCO	57	B4
NORTH AV	KIN	57	D5
NORTH AV	MCO	47	E3
NORTH AV	MCO	48	A3
NORTH AV	ORA	T	C2
NORTH AV	SDCO	106	D3
NORTH AV	STA	47	C2
NORTH HWY	INY	61	E4
NORTH HWY	INY	62	A5
NORTH HWY	INY	72	B1
NORTH RD	STA	47	B2
NORTH ST	MAN	161	C3
NORTH ARM	PLU	20	D5
N BNK CHETKO RD	CUR	1	D2
NORTH BUSCH RD	MEN	23	B5
NORTH BUSCH RD	MEN	31	B1
NORTHCREST DR	DN	1	D4
NORTHRLY BR GRN	SLO	75	D2
NORTH FORK RD	HUM	15	D4
NORTH FORK RD	MAD	49	D5
NORTH FORK RD	SBT	66	A2
NORTH FORK RD	TUO	41	E4
N FK MAD RIV RD	TRI	17	B5
NORTHGATE BLVD	SAC	33	E5
NORTH GATE RD	CC	M	B4
NORTH GATE RD	CC	39	A5
NORTH GATE RD	SOL	39	A3
NORTH LIVERMORE	ALA	46	C2
NORTH RIDGE RD	SBD	100	C2
NORTHRUP RD	MCO	47	D4
NORTHRUP RD	MOD	8	A1
NORTHRUP RD	MOD	14	E1
NORTH SHORE	PLA	35	E1
NORTH SHORE DR	SBD	92	A5
NORTH SHORE RD	SIS	12	C2
NORTHSIDE DR	MPA	63	B2
NORTH SIDE RD	SBD	91	E3
NORTH STAR TR	SBD	100	C2
NORTH VALLEY RD	PLU	20	D5
NORTHWOODS BLVD	NEV	27	D5
NORTHWOODS BLVD	NEV	35	D1
NORTON RD	KER	80	B3
NORTON RD	SBT	55	E4
NORTON RD	SOL	39	C3
NORTONVILLE	CC	39	B5
NORVEL RD	LAS	20	C3
NORWALK BLVD	LACO	98	A3
NORWALK BLVD	LACO	R	C5
NORWALK BLVD	LACO	T	A1
NORWGIAN RCH RD	TRI	11	E4
NORWOOD AV	SR	139	A4
NOTRE DAME AV	BLMT	145	B5
NOVATO BLVD	MAR	L	A2
NOVATO BLVD	MAR	38	A4
NOYES VALLEY RD	SIS	11	E2
NTU RD	SB	86	B1
NUESTRO RD	SUT	33	C2
NUEVO RD	RCO	99	C3
NUNES LN	SHA	19	C2
NUNNIEMAKER RD	HUM	16	C4
NURSE SLOUGH LN	SOL	39	A3
NYON RD	SBD	100	B1

O

STREET	CO.	PAGE	GRID
O ST	FRE	165	D3
OAHU RD	SBD	92	C1
OAK AV	DVS	136	C3
OAK AV	LAKE	7	B1
OAK AV	MCO	48	B4
OAK AV	SUT	33	D3
OAK AV	TRI	17	B2
OAK DR	SDCO	112	D1
OAK RD	MPA	49	B3
OAK ST	BKD	166	A4
OAK ST	MCO	47	E4
OAK ST	MCO	48	A4
OAK ST	SF	141	E4
OAK ST	SF	142	A4
OAK ST	SHA	18	B3
OAK ST	S	160	B4
OAK ST	U	123	C2
OAK WY	BUT	25	A3
OAK CREEK RD	KER	79	D5
OAK CREEK RD N	INY	59	E3
OAK CREEK RD S	INY	59	E3
OAKDALE RD	MCO	48	A3
OAKDALE RD	MCO	48	B3
OAKDALE RD	STA	47	D2
OAKDALE CYN RD	LACO	89	A2
OAKDL WTRFRD HY	STA	47	E2
OAK FLAT RD	SLO	75	E1
OAK FLAT RD	SLO	76	A1
OAK FLAT RD	STA	47	B4
OAK GLENN AV	SCL	P	D5
OAK GLEN AV	SCL	54	C1
OAK GLEN RD	RCO	100	A5
OAK GLEN RD	SBD	99	E2
OAK GROVE	CC	38	E5
OAK GROVE	MPA	49	B4
OAK GROVE RD	CC	M	A3
OAK GRV SCHOOL	MPA	49	B4
OAK HILL RD	ED	34	E5
OAK HILL RD	SBD	91	A4
OAK KNOLL AV	LACO	R	B3
OAK KNOLL AV	NAPA	29	E5
OAK KNOLL AV	NAPA	38	C2
OAK KNL RNG STA	SIS	3	D3
OAKLAND AV	FRCO	67	A1

263
OAKLAND AV
STREET INDEX
PAINTER AV

STREET	CO.	PAGE	GRID
OAKLAND AV	O	158	B2
OAKLAND AV	P	158	C1
OAKLAND RD	SJ	152	B1
OAKLAND CP RD	PLU	26	D1
OAKLEA RD	STA	47	B3
OAKLEY LN	YUB	33	E3
OAK MEADOW RD	NEV	34	B2
OAKMONT TR	SHA	18	C1
OAKMORE ST	TUL	68	B2
OAK PARK BLVD	CC	L	E3
OAK PARK BLVD	CC	M	A3
OAK RANCH RD	SIE	26	D4
OAK RIDGE RD	SCL	P	D2
OAK RIDGE RD	TRI	17	A2
OAK RUN RD	SHA	18	D2
OAK RUN RD	SHA	19	A1
OAK RUN TO FERN	SHA	19	A1
OAK SPG RNCH RD	SBD	90	E4
OAK SPRINGS RD	SBD	91	D4
OAKS AV	ONT	203	D5
OAKS RANCHO RD	KER	79	B4
OAK TREE RD	NEV	26	B5
OAK VALLEY DR	SIS	4	A4
OAK VALLEY RD	YUB	26	C4
OAK VIEW CT	KER	79	B4
OAKVILLE CROSS	NAPA	29	D3
OAKVLLE CRSS RD	NAPA	38	C2
OAKVILLE GRADE	NAPA	29	C4
OAKVILLE GRADE	NAPA	38	B2
OAKWAY	BUT	25	D2
OAKWOOD	SJCO	40	C5
OAKWOOD	SJCO	47	C1
OASIS RD	MON	65	C3
OASIS RD	INY	52	C3
OASIS RD	RCO	102	C4
OASIS RD	SBD	90	D4
OASIS RD	SHA	18	C2
OAT GAP RD	MEN	23	C5
OAT HILL RD	LAK	32	B5
OAT HILL RD N	NAPA	32	B5
OATMAN RD	MOH	85	D5
OATMN TOPOCK HY	MOH	95	E1
OBANION RD	SUT	33	C3
OBERLIN RD	SIS	4	A4
OBRIEN RD	JOS	2	C2
OBSIDAN DOME RD	MNO	50	D1
O'BYRNES FERRY	TUO	41	B5
OCCIDENTAL RD	SON	37	D2
OCEAN AV	CAR	53	D5
OCEAN AV	CAR	168	B3
OCEAN AV	SFCO	L	B5
OCEAN AV	SFCO	45	B2
OCEAN AV	SB	86	B3
OCEAN BLVD	LB	191	E2
OCEAN BLVD	LB	192	B3
OCEAN BLVD	LACO	98	A4
OCEAN BLVD	LACO	S	D2
OCEAN DR	DN	1	D3
OCEAN DR	HUM	9	E4
OCEAN DR	MEN	22	C4
OCEAN BEACH FWY	SD	212	C5
OCEAN PARK BLVD	LA	180	C5
OCEAN PARK BLVD	LACO	Q	C4
OCEAN PARK BLVD	SMON	180	C5
OCEAN PARK BLVD	SMON	187	A1
OCEAN PARK RD	SB	86	A2
OCEANSIDE BLVD	SDCO	106	B3
OCEAN VIEW AV	INY	51	B3
OCEAN VIEW BLVD	LACO	R	A2
OCEAN VIEW BLVD	PAC	167	A1
OCEAN VIEW BLVD	SD	216	B4
OCEAN VIEW BLVD	SDCO	V	C4
OCEAN VIEW BLVD	SDCO	111	D1
OCEANVIEW DR	CUR	1	D2
OCEAN VIEW DR	DN	1	D3
OCONNOR WY	SLO	76	A3
OCOTILLO WY	SBD	91	C4
ODD FELLW PK RD	HUM	16	A3
ODOM LN	MEN	22	C5
O'FARRELL ST	SF	143	A5
OFFAL RD	MNO	42	E1
OFFIELD LOOKOUT	SIS	10	E1
OFFUTT RD	KER	78	B1
OGBURN CEM RD	SHA	19	A2
OGIER RD	IMP	112	C3
OGILBY RD	IMP	110	B4
OGULIN CANYON	LAK	32	A3
O'HARA AV	CC	M	D3
O'HARA AV	CC	39	C5
OHIO AV	FRCO	56	C3
OHIO AV	LA	180	B4
OHM RD	COL	32	E2
OHM RD	TEH	18	D5
OIL CANYON RD	FRCO	66	D2
OIL CITY RD	FRCO	66	D2
OILER CT	KER	79	C3
OILFIELDS RD	KER	78	D2
OIL PLANT RD	MNO	43	C5
OIL WELL RD	HUM	15	E2
OJAI DR	SHA	18	C3
OJAI FRWY	VEN	88	A5
OJAI FRWY	VENT	175	A2
OJAI FRWY	VEN	175	A2
OJAI ST	VEN	88	B4
O'KEEFE ST	MP	147	B1
O'KEEFE ST E	SMCO	147	C1
OKEEFFE RD	SIS	5	D2
OKLAHOMA AV	TEH	18	D5
OKLAHOMA SCH RD	SIS	5	B3
OLANCHA DRWN RD	INY	70	E1
OLD HWY	COL	32	D1
OLD HWY	LAS	21	D5
OLD HWY	MPA	49	A4
OLD HWY	PLU	26	D1

STREET	CO.	PAGE	GRID
OLD AIRLINE HWY	SBT	55	B4
OLD ALLRED RD	MPA	49	B3
OLD ALTURAS HWY	MOD	5	E2
OLD ALTURAS HWY	MOD	6	A2
OLD ALTURAS RD	SHA	18	D2
OLD ARCATA RD	HUM	9	E5
OLD ARCATA RD	HUM	10	A5
OLD AUBURN RD	SAC	34	A5
OLD BANNING-			
-IDYLLWILD RD	RCO	100	A3
OLD BAYSHRE HWY	SJ	152	A1
OLD BREA CYN RD	LACO	U	A3
OLD CAMP TWO RD	SIS	13	C2
OLD CASTLE RD	SDCO	106	D2
OLD CEMETERY RD	LAS	14	B3
OLD CHAMPS FLAT	LAS	20	D1
OLD CHISHOLM DR	SBD	101	B1
OLD COAST HWY	SB	86	D3
OLD COPPER CITY	SBD	81	D3
OLD CORNING RD	TEH	24	D2
OLD COULTRVLLE-			
-YOSEMITE RD	MPA	49	C1
OLD COULTRVLLE-			
-YOSEMITE RD	MPA	63	A4
OLD CUTOFF RD	LAS	21	B4
OLD DAVIS RD	SOL	39	C1
OLD DON PDRO RD	TUO	48	C1
OLD DRYTOWN-			
-PLYMOUTH RDYMT	AMA	40	D2
OLD EEL RIV RD	LAK	23	C5
OLD EEL ROCK	HUM	16	C4
OLD EL MIRAGE	SBD	90	D3
OLD ELSINORE RD	RCO	99	C3
OLDENBERG RD	SBD	91	D3
OLD FRIANT RD	FRCO	57	C2
OLD GASQUET TLL	DN	2	B3
OLD GULCH RD	CAL	41	B4
OLD HRLD PLM RD	LACO	90	A3
OLD HAUN RD	PLU	20	C4
OLD HERNANDZ RD	SBT	55	C5
OLD HWY RD	LAS	14	A4
OLD HWY RD	PLU	26	C1
OLD HWY RT 29	LAS	21	C5
OLD HWY S FORK	DN	2	A3
OLD HIGHWAY 99	SIS	12	B1
OLD HWY 138	LACO	89	D2
OLD HONEY RUN	BUT	25	C3
OLD KANE SPG RD	SDCO	108	A3
OLD KNOX RD	YUB	26	B4
OLD LAMBERT RD	AMA	40	C2
OLD LANDMARK DR	SBD	91	D1
OLD LEESVL GRAD	COL	32	C2
OLD LOMA RD	BUT	25	C1
OLD LONG VLY RD	LAK	32	A3
OLD MAIL RT	LAS	8	C5
OLD MAMMOTH RD	ML	164	A5
OLD MAMMOTH RD	MNO	50	D2
OLD MATTOLE RD	HUM	15	D4
OLD MIDLAND RD	KLAM	5	B1
OLD MILL RD	DN	1	D4
OLD MINE RD	SBD	101	A1
OLD MINE TR	RCO	100	B5
OLD MIRAMAR RD	SDCO	V	B2
OLD MIRAMAR RD	SDCO	106	C5
OLD MORGN HL RD	TRI	17	B2
OLD MORRO RD	SLO	76	A2
OLD NATL TR HWY	SBD	94	D2
OLD OAK FLAT RD	MPA	49	C1
OLD PARKER RD	SBD	103	E2
OLD PIEDMONT RD	SCL	46	B4
OLD PLYMTH SAC-			
-VIA FIN RCH RD	AMA	40	D2
OLD PONY EXPRSS	ALP	36	B4
OLD RAILROAD GR	SHA	12	B4
OLD RANCH RD	KER	79	C5
OLD REDWOOD HWY	SON	37	D1
OLD RENO RD	NEV	27	D5
OLD RIDGE RD	LACO	89	A2
OLD RIVER RD	KER	78	C3
OLD RIVER RD	KER	78	C4
OLD RIV SCHL RD	LACO	R	B5
OLD SN FRANCSCO	SVL	150	A1
OLD SCHOOL RD	SHA	13	D3
OLD SCH HOUS RD	TRI	22	E1
OLD SEIAD HWY	SIS	3	B3
OLD SEIAD CK RD	SIS	3	B3
OLD SHASTA RIV	SIS	4	A3
OLD SHERWIN GRD	INY	51	B3
OLD SHERWOOD RD	MEN	22	E4
OLD SKYLINE	KIN	67	A3
OLD SONOMA RD	NAP	133	B4
OLD SONOMA RD	NAPA	L	C1
OLD SONOMA RD	NAPA	38	C3
OLD SONOMA RD	NAPA	133	A5
OLD SPANISH TR	INY	72	E4
OLD SPANISH TR	INY	73	B4
OLD STAGE RD	MEN	30	D4
OLD STAGE RD	MON	54	D3
OLD STAGE RD	SIS	12	C2
OLD STAGE RD N	SIS	12	C1
OLD STAGEROAD	MEN	30	D4
OLD STATE HWY	HUM	9	E2
OLD STATE HWY	HUM	10	A2
OLD STATE HWY	INY	72	E3
OLD STATE HWY	INY	73	A3
OLD STATE HWY	KIN	67	B4
OLD STATE HWY	LAK	31	C2
OLD STATE HWY	MNO	43	C5
OLD STATE HWY	MNO	50	D2
OLD STATE HWY	SIS	4	E3
OLD STATE HWY	SIS	5	A4
OLD STEWRTS PT-			
-SKAGGS SPGS RD	SON	31	B5
OLD STOCKTON RD	AMA	40	D3

STREET	CO.	PAGE	GRID
OLD STOCKTON-			
-IONE HWY	AMA	40	D2
OLD STRWBRRY RD	TUO	41	E3
OLD STRWBRRY RD	TUO	42	A3
OLD SUTTER CK-			
-AMADOR CITY HY	AMA	40	E2
OLD STTR HLL RD	AMA	40	E2
OLD TELEGRPH RD	VEN	88	E4
OLD TELEGRPH RD	VEN	89	A4
OLD THREE CK RD	HUM	10	C5
OLD TIM BELL RD	STA	47	E2
OLD TOLL	MPA	49	A3
OLD TOLL RD	INY	71	A1
OLD TOLL RD	LAS	14	A3
OLD TOLL RD	MEN	31	C3
OLD TOLL RD	YUB	26	B5
OLD TOPANGA CYN	LACO	97	B2
OLD TRUCKEE RD	SIE	27	C4
OLD WESTSIDE RD	SIS	4	B5
OLD WILBUR RD	COL	32	C2
OLD WITR SPG RD	LAK	31	C2
OLD WOMAN SPGS	SBD	100	D1
OLD WOMN SPG RD	SBD	92	A4
OLD YERMO CTOFF	SBD	91	E1
OLD YOSEMITE RD	MPA	49	A1
OLD 44 DR	SHA	18	C2
OLEANDER	SJCO	47	B2
OLEANDER AV	BKD	166	C4
OLEANDER AV	RCO	99	B3
OLEMA ST	SBD	80	E1
OLINDA RD	SHA	18	C3
OLIVAS LN	SOL	39	A2
OLIVE AV	BUR	179	C5
OLIVE AV	COR	215	B5
OLIVE AV	FRE	165	B2
OLIVE AV	FRCO	57	A3
OLIVE AV	FRCO	57	C3
OLIVE AV	GLE	24	D3
OLIVE AV	MAR	L	A2
OLIVE AV	MCO	48	A4
OLIVE AV	MCO	48	C4
OLIVE AV	RCO	99	B5
OLIVE AV	RCO	99	D4
OLIVE AV	SDCO	106	C3
OLIVE AV	SJCO	47	B2
OLIVE AV	STA	47	B3
OLIVE AV	STA	47	E1
OLIVE AV	STA	48	A1
OLIVE AV	TEH	24	D1
OLIVE AV	TUL	68	D3
OLIVE AV W	MER	170	B2
OLIVE DR	KER	78	D2
OLIVE DR E	DVS	136	D3
OLIVE HWY	BUT	25	D4
OLIVE LN	GLE	24	A4
OLIVE RD	TEH	24	D2
OLIVE RD	VEN	88	B5
OLIVE ST	AVLN	105	A4
OLIVE ST	LA	185	E4
OLIVE ST	LACO	R	C3
OLIVE ST	MAR	38	B4
OLIVE ST	RCO	99	B4
OLIVE ST	SDCO	107	A4
OLIVE ST	SHA	18	B3
OLIVEHURST	YUB	33	D2
OLIVE LAKE BLVD	RCO	103	D5
OLIVENHAIN RD	SDCO	106	C4
OLIVE ORCHRD RD	CAL	40	D4
OLIVER RD	SBT	55	D4
OLIVERA DR	TUL	58	C5
OLIVE SCHOOL LN	SOL	39	A2
OLIVET RD	SON	37	D2
OLIVEWOOD AV	TEH	24	D2
OLNEY PARK DR	SHA	18	B2
OLSEN RD	MCO	48	B3
OLSEN RD	VEN	88	D5
OLSEN CREEK RD	TRI	16	E2
OLSON RD	LAS	8	B4
OLYMPIC	LAK	32	A3
OLYMPIC BLVD	BH	183	B2
OLYMPIC BLVD	LA	183	B2
OLYMPIC BLVD	LA	184	B2
OLYMPIC BLVD	LA	185	B3
OLYMPIC BLVD	LA	186	B4
OLYMPIC BLVD	LA	180	C4
OLYMPIC BLVD	LACO	97	D2
OLYMPIC BLVD	LACO	Q	D4
OLYMPIC BLVD	SMON	180	A5
OLYMPIC RD	MAD	57	B1
OLYMPIC RD	SBD	100	E1
OMAHA AV	KIN	67	B3
OMAHA AV	KIN	67	E3
OMEGA RD	NEV	26	E5
OMO RANCH RD	ED	40	E1
OMO RANCH RD	ED	41	B1
ONEAL RD	BUT	25	C4
ONEAL RD	MAD	57	D1
ONE HOLE SPG RD	SBD	92	C5
ONION VALLEY RD	ED	35	B4
ONION VALLEY RD	INY	59	E3
ONSTOTT RD	SUT	33	C2
ONTARIO AV	RCO	99	E5
ONTARIO AV	RCO	98	E3
ONYX AV	SIS	4	C5
OPAL RD	MCO	48	D4
OPAL WY	SHA	18	C1
OPAL FERRY RD	KER	88	D1
OPAL MTN RD	SBD	81	C4
OPENSHAW RD	BUT	25	C4
OPEN SHAW RD	PLU	20	D5
OPHIR RD	BUT	25	D5
OPHIR RD	INY	71	A2
ORANGE AV	BUT	25	E5
ORANGE AV	EC	217	D3

STREET	CO.	PAGE	GRID
ORANGE AV	FRCO	57	C4
ORANGE AV	FRCO	57	D4
ORANGE AV	KIN	67	A3
ORANGE AV	KIN	67	D3
ORANGE AV	LACO	Q	E2
ORANGE AV	LACO	R	D4
ORANGE AV	LACO	S	D2
ORANGE AV	ORA	T	B2
ORANGE AV	RCO	99	C3
ORANGE AV	SD	214	C5
ORANGE AV	SDCO	V	B4
ORANGE AV	SDCO	V	D5
ORANGE AV	SDCO	111	C1
ORANGE AV	SDCO	111	D2
ORANGE AV	SJCO	47	D1
ORANGE AV	SON	132	A4
ORANGE AV	STA	47	C3
ORANGE AV W	SSF	144	A1
ORANGE FRWY	ANA	194	A4
ORANGE FRWY	OR	196	A1
ORANGE FRWY	ORA	98	C3
ORANGE FRWY	ORA	194	A4
ORANGE FRWY	ORA	T	D1
ORANGE RD	SDCO	107	A3
ORANGE ST	KER	78	B2
ORANGE ST	RCO	99	B2
ORANGE ST	SBD	99	C2
ORANGE BLOSM RD	STA	48	A1
ORANGEBURG AV E	MDO	162	D1
ORANGEBURG AV W	MDO	162	B1
ORANGE GROVE AV	LACO	98	C2
ORANGE GROVE AV	LACO	R	C3
ORANGE GROVE AV	LACO	U	B2
ORANGE GROVE BL	LACO	R	B3
ORANGE GROVE BL	PAS	190	C3
ORANGE-OLIVE RD	OR	194	C3
ORANGE-OLIVE RD	ORA	98	C3
ORANGE-OLIVE RD	ORA	T	D2
ORANGE PARK BL	ORA	T	E2
ORANGE SHOW RD	CLTN	207	C5
ORANGE SHOW RD	SBDO	207	C5
ORANGETHORPE AV	ORA	98	B3
ORANGETHORPE AV	ORA	98	C3
ORANGETHORPE AV	ORA	T	B1
ORANGEWOOD AV	ORA	T	B2
ORANGEWOOD RD	TEH	24	D1
ORCHARD AV	H	146	E4
ORCHARD AV	SLO	76	C5
ORCHARD AV	TEH	24	D2
ORCHARD DR	FRCO	58	D4
ORCHARD DR	MCO	48	C5
ORCHARD RD	IMP	112	C3
ORCHARD RD	MCO	47	C5
ORCHARD RD	SJCO	40	B4
ORCHARD RD	STA	47	B2
ORCHARD ST	RCO	99	E2
ORCHARD WY	MCO	56	C1
ORCHARD PARK AV	MCO	48	B4
ORCHARD SPGS RD	NEV	34	D2
ORCUTT RD	SLO	76	B4
ORCUTT RD	SLO	172	D5
ORCUTT RD	SNLO	172	D5
ORCUTT RD	VEN	88	C4
ORCUTT-GAREY RD	SB	86	C1
ORD ST	SB	86	B2
ORD FERRY RD	BUT	25	A4
ORD MOUNTAIN RD	SBD	91	E2
ORD RANCH RD	BUT	25	C5
ORDWAY RD	SIS	12	C1
OREGON AV	SCL	N	E2
OREGON DR	MDO	162	D4
OREGON CREEK RD	SIE	26	D4
OREGON GULCH RD	BUT	25	D4
OREGON HILL RD	YUB	26	B5
OREGON MTN RD	DN	2	C3
OREGON-PAGE MLL	PA	147	D3
OREGON-PAGE MLL	SCL	45	E4
ORESTIMBA RD	STA	47	C4
ORINDA DR	SM	145	C4
ORLEANS AV	FRCO	55	E3
ORMONDE RD	SLO	76	B4
ORMSBY AV	FRCO	56	C2
ORNBAUN RD	MEN	30	E3
ORO FINO RD	SIS	3	D5
OROVILLE BANGOR	BUT	25	D4
OROVLL CHICO HY	BUT	25	B3
OROVLL DAM BL E	BUT	25	D4
OROVLLE GRIDLEY	BUT	25	C5
OROVLE QUNCY HY	BUT	25	D4
OROVLE QUNCY HY	BUT	25	E3
OROVLE QUNCY HY	BUT	26	A3
ORR RD	SAC	40	A3
ORR & DAY RD	LACO	R	C5
ORR & DAY RD	LACO	T	A1
ORR CREEK LN	PLA	34	B3
ORRIS RD	RCO	102	A4
ORRLAND AV	TUL	68	B3
ORR MTN LOOKOUT	SIS	5	A4
ORR SPRINGS RD	MEN	30	E1
ORR SPRINGS RD	MEN	31	A1
ORSI RD	STA	47	E1
ORTEGA HWY	ORA	98	E5
ORTEGA HWY	SCL	202	E1
ORTIGALITA RD	MCO	55	D2
OSAGE RD	SOL	39	B2
OSBORN RD	SIS	5	D2
OSBORN RD	TEH	24	B2
OSBORNE AV	RCO	102	C4
OSBORNE RD	SBD	91	D2
OSBORNE ST	LACO	97	C1
OSBORNE ST	LACO	Q	C2
OSBORNE PARK RD	IMP	109	D4
OSDICK RD	SBD	80	E3
OSGOOD RD	ALA	P	B2

STREET	CO.	PAGE	GRID
OSO PKWY	ORA	98	D5
OSO FLACO LK RD	SLO	76	B5
OSOS ST	SNLO	172	C3
OSPITAL RD	CAL	40	D4
OSTROM RD	YUB	33	E2
OSWALD RD	SUT	33	B2
OSWELL ST	KER	78	D3
OTAY LAKES RD	SDCO	V	D4
OTAY LAKES RD	SDCO	111	E2
OTAY MESA RD	SDCO	V	D5
OTAY MESA RD	SDCO	111	E2
OTAY VALLEY RD	SDCO	V	D5
OTAY VALLEY RD	SDCO	111	E2
OTIS DR	A	159	A2
OTIS ST	LACO	R	A5
OTOE RD	SBD	91	C3
OUR HOUS DAM RD	SIE	26	C5
OUTINGDALE	ED	40	E1
OUTINGDALE	ED	41	A1
OUTLAW MINE RD	RCO	102	A2
OUTPOST DR	LA	181	C3
OVERLAND AV	CUL	188	C1
OVERLAND AV	LA	183	B5
OVERLAND AV	LACO	Q	C4
OVERLAND AV	MCO	55	D1
OVERLAND DR	SHA	18	C3
OWENS	SJCO	47	D1
OWENS AV	CLK	74	E2
OWENS RD	INY	51	D4
OWENS RD	SIS	5	A2
OWENS GORGE RD	MNO	51	B2
OWENS RIVER RD	MNO	50	E1
OWENS RV RCH RD	MNO	50	E1
OWENYO LONE PNE	INY	60	B4
OWL HOLE SPG RD	SBD	82	B1
OXALIS AV	FRCO	56	B2
OXBOW PL	SB	86	E3
OXFORD AV	FRCO	56	A2
OXFORD RD	SOL	39	D3
OXFORD ST	B	156	A2
OXNARD BLVD	OXN	176	C1
P			
P ST	BKD	166	D5
P ST	FRE	165	E3
P ST	KER	166	D5
P ST	SCTO	137	A3
P ST	SBD	91	D1
PACHECO BLVD	CC	L	E3
PACHECO BLVD	CC	38	E5
PACHECO BLVD	CC	154	C2
PACHECO BLVD	M	154	C2
PACHECO RD	KER	78	D3
PACHECO PASS HY	SCL	54	E2
PACHECO PASS RD	SCL	54	D2
PACIFIC AV	DN	1	D4
PACIFIC AV	LB	192	D3
PACIFIC AV	LA	187	A2
PACIFIC AV	LA	191	A4
PACIFIC AV	LACO	97	D4
PACIFIC AV	LACO	S	C3
PACIFIC AV	LACO	S	D2
PACIFIC AV	PAC	167	C2
PACIFIC AV	SC	169	D3
PACIFIC AV	S	160	B1
PACIFIC AV	SUT	33	D3
PACIFIC AV	SUT	33	D4
PACIFIC AV	TUL	68	B2
PACIFIC BLVD	LACO	97	E2
PACIFIC BLVD	LACO	R	A4
PACIFIC BLVD	SM	145	B4
PACIFIC HWY	SD	213	A5
PACIFIC HWY	SD	215	C2
PACIFIC ST	MONT	167	E4
PACIFIC ST	SBD	99	C1
PACIFIC BCH DR	SD	212	A2
PACIFIC BCH DR	SDCO	V	A3
PACIFIC CST HWY	LB	192	D1
PACIFIC CST HWY	LA	192	D1
PACIFIC CST HWY	LACO	97	B2
PACIFIC CST HWY	LACO	S	B1
PACIFIC CST HWY	LACO	T	A3
PACIFIC CST HWY	ORA	T	A3
PACIFIC CST HWY	VEN	96	C2
PACIFC GRV-CRML	MONT	167	B4
PACIFC GRV-CRML	MON	53	D3
PACIFC GRV-CRML	MON	167	B4
PACIFC GRV-CRML	PAC	167	B4
PACIFIC HTS RD	BUT	25	C5
PACIFIC LUMBER	HUM	16	A1
PACIFIC MINE RD	SIE	26	C3
PACIFIC VIEW DR	MEN	30	C3
PACIFIC VIEW RD	VEN	96	C2
PACKER RD	COL	32	E1
PACKER LAKE RD	SIE	26	E3
PACKER LAKE RD	SIE	27	A3
PAC MINE RD	SIE	26	D3
PADUA AV	CLA	203	C1
PADUA AV	LACO	98	D1
PADUA AV	UPL	203	C1
PAGE AV	FRCO	67	B1
PAGE RD	STA	47	B2
PAGE MILL RD	PA	147	C5
PAGE MILL RD	SCL	N	E3
PAGE MILL RD	SCL	45	D4
PA HA LN	INY	51	D4
PAIGE AV	TUL	68	B2
PAIGE BAR RD	SHA	18	B2
PAINE RD	AMA	40	D2
PAINT RD	CAL	41	B4
PAINTED CAVE	SB	87	C4
PAINTED GORG RD	IMP	111	C3
PAINTER AV	LACO	98	B2

INDEXES

STREET	CO.	PAGE	GRID
PAINTER AV	LACO	R	D4
PAJARO ST	SAL	171	C4
PALA RD	DN	1	D3
PALA RD	RCO	106	D1
PALA TEMECLA RD	SDCO	106	D1
PALAZZO RD	MCO	47	E5
PALAZZO RD	MCO	48	A5
PALAZZO RD	MCO	55	E1
PALERMO RD	BUT	25	D5
PALRMO HONCT HY	BUT	25	D5
PALISADE AV	SBD	91	E3
PALISADES AV	RED	122	E1
PALISADES DR	LACO	97	C2
PALLETT CK RD	LACO	90	C4
PALM AV	AUB	126	C3
PALM AV	COR	215	C5
PALM AV	FRE	165	C2
PALM AV	FRCO	57	C3
PALM AV	KER	78	B1
PALM AV	KER	78	C3
PALM AV	LACO	R	C5
PALM AV	MCO	48	A4
PALM AV	RCO	99	B2
PALM AV	RCO	99	E4
PALM AV	SBD	99	B1
PALM AV	SDCO	V	C5
PALM AV	SDCO	V	D3
PALM AV	SDCO	111	D2
PALM AV	SDCO	111	E1
PALM AV	SCL	P	D4
PALM AV	SCL	54	C1
PALM AV	SHA	18	B3
PALM DR	RIV	206	E1
PALM DR	RCO	100	D3
PALM DR	SDCO	106	C4
PALM DR	SCL	N	E2
PALM ST	BKD	166	B4
PALM CANYON DR	PMSP	206	B5
PALM CANYON DR	RCO	100	D4
PALM CANYON DR	SDCO	107	E2
PALM CYN DR E	PMSP	206	C5
PALM CYN DR N	PMSP	206	A1
PALMDALE BLVD	LACO	90	B3
PALMDALE RD	SBD	90	E4
PALMDALE RD	SBD	91	A3
PALMER AV	FRCO	66	C2
PALMER RD	SB	86	C2
PALMER CREEK RD	HUM	15	E2
PALMETTO AV	BUT	124	C3
PALMETTO AV	C	124	C3
PALMETTO AV	ONT	203	E5
PALMETTO AV	ONT	204	A5
PALMETTO ST	SBD	80	E5
PALMETTO ST	SBD	81	A5
PALMETTO WY	LAS	20	D2
PALMS TO PINES	RCO	100	E4
PALO COLORDO RD	MON	64	B1
PALOMA RD	CAL	40	E3
PALOMAR AV	SDCO	V	C5
PALOMAR AV	SDCO	111	D2
PALOMAR ST	RCO	99	C5
PALOMAR APRT RD	SDCO	106	B3
PALOMAR DIV TK	RCO	106	D1
PALOMARES RD	ALA	M	A5
PALOMARES RD	ALA	P	A1
PALOMARES RD	ALA	46	A2
PALOMAS AV	KER	77	E3
PALOMAS AV	KER	78	A3
PALOMINO RD	SDCO	106	C2
PALOMINO WY	HUM	22	C1
PALO PRIETA CHO	SLO	76	D1
PALOS VERDES BL	LACO	S	B2
PALOS VRDS DR E	LACO	97	D4
PALOS VRDS DR E	LACO	S	B3
PALOS VRDS DR N	LACO	97	D3
PALOS VRDS DR N	LACO	S	B2
PALOS VRDS DR S	LACO	S	A3
PALOS VRDS DR S	LACO	97	D4
PALOS VRDS DR W	LACO	97	D4
PALOS VRDS DR W	LACO	S	B2
PALO VERDE AV	LACO	S	E2
PALO VERDE BLVD	MOH	96	B4
PALO VERDE RD	IMP	110	C1
PALO VERDE RD	SBD	100	C2
PALO VERDE ST	MTCL	203	C3
PAMELA ST	KER	79	C2
PAMO RD	SDCO	107	A3
PAMPA RD	KER	79	A3
PANAMA LN	KER	78	B3
PANAMA LN	KER	79	A3
PANAMA RD	KER	78	D3
PANAMA RD	KER	79	A3
PANAMINT VLY RD	INY	71	B1
PANCHO RD	RCO	107	A1
PANCHORICO RD	MON	65	E3
PANGBORN LN	INY	60	B4
PANOCHE RD	FRCO	56	D3
PANOCHE RD	SBT	55	B4
PANOCHE RD	SBT	56	A4
PANORAMA DR	KER	78	E2
PANORAMA PT RD	SHA	18	D3
PANORAMIC HWY	MAR	38	A5
PANORAMIC HWY	MAR	L	A4
PANORAMIC HWY	MAR	45	A1
PANTHER CK RD	TEH	19	C3
PANTHER GAP RD	HUM	16	A4
PAPPAS RD	KER	80	C3
PARADISE AV	MDO	162	A4
PARADISE AV	STA	47	C3
PARADISE DR	CRTM	140	D1
PARADISE DR	MAR	L	B3
PARADISE DR	MAR	45	B1
PARADISE DR	RCO	100	C5
PARADISE RD	CLK	74	D2
PARADISE RD	CLK	209	C4
PARADISE RD	CLK	210	E3
PARADISE RD	COL	24	E5
PARADISE RD	LV	209	C4
PARADISE RD	SJCO	46	E1
PARADISE RD	SJCO	47	A1
PARADISE RD	SB	87	B3
PARADISE RD	STA	47	C2
PARADISE SPG RD	SBD	81	E4
PARADISE SPG RD	SBD	82	B5
PARADISE VLY RD	SDCO	V	D4
PARADISE VLY RD	SDCO	111	D1
PARAISO SPGS RD	MON	64	E1
PARAISO SPGS RD	MON	65	A1
PARAMOUNT BLVD	LACO	98	A3
PARAMOUNT BLVD	LACO	R	C4
PARAMOUNT BLVD	LACO	S	E1
PARDEE DAM RD	CAL	40	D3
PARDOES	AMA	41	D1
PARIS AV	KIN	67	D3
PARIS VALLEY RD	MON	65	D3
PARK AV	BUT	25	B3
PARK AV	C	124	C5
PARK AV	LAG	201	C2
PARK AV	O	157	D1
PARK AV	SJ	151	D3
PARK AV	SJ	152	B4
PARK AV	SCLR	151	C3
PARK AV	TRI	17	D2
PARK AV W	NAP	133	A3
PARK BLVD	ALA	L	D4
PARK BLVD	ALA	45	D1
PARK BLVD	CC	L	C3
PARK BLVD	O	158	D3
PARK BLVD	SD	214	A5
PARK BLVD	SD	215	E3
PARK BLVD	SD	216	A1
PARK BLVD	SDCO	V	B3
PARK BLVD N	SA	196	B2
PARK DR S	CC	156	D1
PARK RD	BEN	153	D4
PARK RD	IMP	109	B4
PARK RD	SBT	55	A3
PARK RD E	COL	24	B5
PARK ST	ALA	L	D5
PARK ST	HUM	9	E5
PARK ST	S	160	B4
PARK ST	TUL	68	B3
PARK WY	LAK	31	D2
PARK CREEK RD	ED	35	B4
PARKER AV	CC	L	D3
PARKER RD	SBD	101	E1
PARKER RD	STA	47	D2
PARKER CREEK RD	MOD	7	B2
PARKER CREEK RD	MOD	8	B1
PARKER CK RD W	MOD	8	B1
PARKER DAM RD	SBD	104	B1
PARKER LAKE RD	MNO	43	C5
PARKER LAKE RD	MNO	50	C1
PARKER-POSTN RD	LPAZ	103	E4
PARKFIELD GRADE	FRCO	66	C3
PARKFLD CEM RD	MON	66	C4
PARKFLD-COALNGA	FRCO	66	C4
PARK HILL RD	SLO	76	B3
PARKMAN RD	IMP	110	D5
PARK MARINA DR	RED	122	D1
PARK MOABI	SBD	95	E2
PARKMONT DR	LACO	89	D3
PK PRESIDIO BL	SF	141	C3
PARKS RD	SUT	33	C3
PARKSIDE DR	RCO	101	D5
PARKSIDE DR N	CC	M	B3
PARKVIEW LN	KER	79	C5
PARKVILLE RD	SHA	18	D3
PARKWAY DR	DN	1	D4
PARKWAY DR	TEH	18	D4
PARLIER AV	FRCO	56	E4
PARLIER AV	FRCO	57	D4
PARLIER AV	FRCO	58	B4
PARNASSUS BLVD	SF	141	D5
PARR	CC	38	C5
PARROTTS FERRY	TUO	41	C4
PARSONS RD	FRCO	66	C2
PASADENA AV	LA	186	D1
PASADENA FRWY	LA	186	B2
PASADENA FRWY	LACO	97	E2
PASADENA FRWY	LACO	R	A3
PASCOE RD	KER	69	B5
PASEO AV	SUT	33	C1
PASEO DEL MAR	LACO	97	D4
PASEO DEL MAR	LACO	S	B3
PASKENTA RD	TEH	18	D5
PASKENTA RD	TEH	24	C1
PASKENTA CEM RD	TEH	24	B2
PASO ST	KER	78	A5
PASO NOGAL	CC	38	E5
PASO ROBLES BL	SLO	76	A1
PASO ROBLES HWY	KER	77	A1
PASQUALE RD	NEV	34	C1
PASS RD	SUT	33	A2
PASSONS BLVD	LACO	R	C5
PASSONS BLVD	LACO	R	C5
PAST TIME LN	RCO	100	A5
PATHFINDER RD	LACO	U	B3
PATRICIA AV	SIS	4	C2
PATRICIA LN	CAL	41	C3
PATRICIA LN	MNO	42	E1
PATRICIA LN	MNO	43	A1
PATRICK RD	LPAZ	104	A2
PATRICK WY	SBD	100	E1
PATRICKS CK RD	DN	2	B3
PATRICKS PT	HUM	9	E3
PATTERSON AV	SB	87	B4
PATTERSON LN	MOD	8	D1
PATTERSON RD	HUM	10	D4
PATTERSON RD	KER	89	B1
PATTERSON RD	STA	47	D2
PATTERSON RD	VEN	96	B1
PATTERSON CK RD	SIS	3	C5
PATTERSON CK RD	SIS	11	D1
PATTRSN MILL RD	MOD	8	E3
PATTERSON PS RD	ALA	M	D5
PATTERSON PS RD	ALA	46	C2
PATTERSON PS RD	SJCO	46	D2
PATTERSN RCH RD	TRI	17	A1
PATTERSN SAWMLL	LAS	8	D3
PATTISON RD	CAL	40	D3
PATTON	MCO	55	E1
PATTON MILLS RD	TEH	24	A2
PATTYMOCUS-			
PATWIN RD	SBD	90	E3
PAUBA RD	RCO	106	D1
PAUI RD	RCO	107	B1
PAULARINO AV	CM	197	E4
PAULINE AV	STA	47	C2
PAUL NEGRA RD	MCO	55	E3
PAXTON RD	SBDO	100	E1
PAXTON ST	LACO	Q	C1
PAYEN RD	SAC	40	C1
PAYMASTER MN RD	SBD	83	C4
PAYNE AV	CC	39	C5
PAYNE RD	IMP	108	E5
PAYNE RD	SUT	33	B2
PAYNE WY	KER	79	D3
PAYNES CK LOOP	TEH	19	A4
PAYNES CREEK RD	TEH	19	A4
PAYNES CREEK RD	TEH	18	D4
PEABODY RD	SOL	M	B1
PEABODY RD	SOL	39	A3
PEACEFUL GLEN	SOL	39	A2
PEACH AV	FRCO	57	D2
PEACH AV	FRCO	57	D5
PEACH AV	GLE	24	E4
PEACH AV	MCO	47	E4
PEACH AV	MCO	48	A4
PEACH TREE RD	MON	65	E2
PEACH TREE RD	MON	66	A2
PEACHY CYN RD	SLO	75	E1
PEACHY CYN RD	SLO	76	A1
PEAK RD	TRI	16	E5
PEAR AV	GLE	25	A4
PEAR AV	STA	47	C4
PEARBLOSSOM HWY	LACO	90	A4
PEARL RD	SJCO	40	B3
PEARL ST	SDCO	V	A2
PEARL ST	SDCO	106	C5
PEAR MAIN ST	SBD	91	B3
PEARSON RD	BUT	25	C3
PEARSON RD	INY	70	C5
PEASE RD	SUT	33	C2
PEAVINE RDG RD	ED	35	B4
PEBBLE BEACH DR	DN	1	D4
PEBBLY BEACH RD	AVLN	105	B5
PECHO VALLEY RD	SLO	75	E3
PECK RD	LACO	98	B1
PECK RD	LACO	R	D4
PEDERSON	FRCO	58	A3
PEDLEY RD	RCO	99	A2
PEDRICK RD	SOL	39	B2
PEDRICK RD	SOL	39	B1
PEDRO RANCH RD	MNO	51	C1
PEDROS RD	STA	47	D3
PEGASUS DR	KER	78	D2
PEGASUS ST	KER	79	B4
PELGER RD	SUT	33	B3
PELICAN RD	STA	47	B2
PELLERIN RD	STA	47	E2
PELLET RD	IMP	108	E4
PELLISER RD	KER	79	B4
PELTIER RD	SJCO	39	E3
PELTIER RD	SJCO	40	A3
PENCIL RD	MOD	7	B5
PENDLETON RD	SBD	92	A1
PENDOLA RD	YUB	26	B4
PENDOLA EXT	YUB	26	C4
PENDOLA GARDEN	MPA	49	A3
PENFIELD AV	LA	178	A4
PENINSULA AV	SMCO	N	C1
PENINSULA DR	HUM	15	E5
PENINSULA DR	PLU	20	B4
PENMAN SPGS RD	SLO	76	B1
PENNINGTON RD	BUT	25	B5
PENNINGTON RD	SUT	33	B1
PENNSYLVANIA AV	FRFD	135	B3
PENNSYLVANIA AV	LACO	Q	E2
PENNSYLVANIA AV	RIV	205	E3
PENNSYLVANIA AV	RCO	99	E3
PENNSYLVANIA AV	SOL	L	E1
PENNSYLVANIA AV	SOL	M	A1
PENNSYLVANIA AV	SOL	135	B4
PENNSYLV GCH RD	CAL	41	C4
PENON LOOKOUT	MPA	48	D1
PENOYAR GRAS LK	SIS	4	E5
PENOYAR TENNANT	SIS	5	A5
PENROSE ST	LACO	Q	D2
PENTLAND RD	KER	78	B5
PENTZ RD	BUT	25	C3
PENTZ MAGALIA	BUT	25	D3
PEORIA RD	YUB	34	A1
PEPPER AV	SBD	99	B2
PEPPER DR	KER	78	E3
PEPPER RD	SON	37	E3
PEPPER RD	SON	38	A3
PEPPER ST	MCO	47	E4
PEPPER ST	MCO	48	A4
PEPPER ST	SBD	80	E5
PEPPER ST	SBD	81	A5
PERALTA BLVD	ALA	P	A1
PERALTA BLVD	ALA	46	A3
PERALTA ST	ALA	L	C4
PERALTA ST	O	157	C2
PERCH ST	KER	79	C4
PERCY AV	YUBA	125	D3
PERCY RD	KER	79	D1
PEREZ RD	IMP	112	D5
PERI RD	MON	65	D4
PERIMETER RD	NEV	34	B2
PERINI RD	LAK	32	A4
PERKINS AV	KER	78	B1
PERKINS RD	CLO	33	A3
PERKINS RD	SB	87	C1
PERKINS ST	U	123	B3
PERRAL RD	KER	77	D2
PERRIN AV	FRCO	57	D2
PERRIN RD	SJCO	47	B2
PERRIS BLVD	RCO	99	C3
PERRY RD	COL	32	D1
PERRY RD	RCO	99	B4
PERRY CREEK RD	ED	41	A1
PERSHING AV	S	160	A1
PERSHING AV	SJCO	40	A5
PERSHING DR	LA	187	D5
PERSHING DR	LACO	Q	C5
PERSHING DR	SD	216	A3
PERSHING DR	SDCO	V	C3
PESCADERO RD	SMCO	N	C4
PESCADERO CK RD	SMCO	45	C5
PETALUMA AV	SON	132	B4
PETALUMA HLL RD	STR	131	D4
PETALUMA HLL RD	SON	38	A2
PETALUMA HLL RD	SON	131	D4
PETE MILLER RD	STA	47	C5
PETERSBOURGH S	CAL	40	E3
PETERSBURG RD	SIS	11	B3
PETERSON DR	NAPA	29	B2
PETERSON LN	LAK	31	D3
PETERSON RD	COL	32	C1
PETERSON RD	FRCO	58	B1
PETERSON RD	IMP	109	B3
PETERSON RD	KER	68	C5
PETERSON RD	KER	77	E1
PETERSON RD	KER	78	B1
PETERSON RD	LPAZ	104	A3
PETERSON RD	LACO	89	D4
PETERSON RDG RD	YUB	26	B5
PETRIFIED FORST	NAPA	38	A1
PETRIFIED FORST	SON	38	A1
PETRO RD	INY	72	C2
PETROGLYPH RD	MNO	51	D3
PETRLEUM CLB RD	KER	78	A4
PETTINGER RD	CAL	40	D4
PETTYJOHN RD	TEH	17	E5
PEW RD	SBD	85	C5
PEZZI RD	SJCO	40	B4
PFE RD	PLA	33	E5
PFITZER RD	MCO	47	D5
PHEASANT CT	KER	79	B4
PHEASANT DR	MOD	7	B5
PHEASANT LN	SIS	4	B4
PHELAN RD	HUM	15	D1
PHELAN RD	SBD	91	A4
PHELPS AV	FRCO	66	D2
PHILADELPHIA ST	LACO	98	E2
PHILADELPHIA ST	SBD	U	C3
PHILADELPHIA ST	SBD	98	E2
PHILBRIC RD	SB	86	C1
PHILBROOK RD	BUT	25	D1
PHILDOW RD	LAS	20	E3
PHILIP	PLA	33	E4
PHILIPS RD	MCO	55	E1
PHILLIPE LN	SIS	4	A4
PHILLIPS	LAK	32	A3
PHILLIPS BLVD	SBD	U	C3
PHILLIPS DR	SBD	82	A5
PHILLIPS RD	KER	78	C1
PHILLIPS RD	KER	78	D4
PHILLIPS RD	KER	80	B4
PHILLIPS RD	SHA	19	A1
PHILLIPS RD	SOL	39	B1
PHILLIPSVLLE RD	HUM	16	C4
PHILO GRNWD RD	MEN	30	C2
PHOENIX LAKE RD	TUO	41	D5
PHYLLIS RD	TEH	17	C4
PICACHO RD	IMP	110	D5
PICADOR BLVD	SDCO	V	D5
PICADOR BLVD	SDCO	111	D2
PICARD RD	SIS	4	E2
PICARD RD	SIS	5	A2
PICRD SAMS NECK	SIS	4	E2
PICARDY DR	S	160	B4
PICAYUNE RD	MAD	49	D5
PICKENS RD	LAS	21	D5
PICKERING AV	LACO	R	C5
PICKETT RD	IMP	109	B4
PICO BLVD	LA	180	D4
PICO BLVD	LA	183	B3
PICO BLVD	LA	184	C3
PICO BLVD	LA	185	A3
PICO BLVD	LACO	Q	C4
PICO BLVD	SMON	180	B5
PICO BLVD	SMON	187	A1
PICO CANYON RD	LACO	89	B4
PIEDMONT AV	B	156	B3
PIEDMONT AV	O	158	B1
PIEDMONT RD	SCL	P	C3
PIEDRA RD	FRCO	58	A3
PIEDRA AZUL	MCO	55	D3
PIEDRAS DR	RCO	99	B3
PIER AV	LACO	S	B1
PIERCE LN	SOL	38	E4
PIERCE RD	SCL	P	A4
PIERCE RD	SCL	45	E5
PIERCE RD	SUT	33	C3
PIERCE ST	BKD	166	A2
PIERCE ST	RCO	99	A3
PIERCE ST	RCO	101	B4
PIERCE CK MTWY	PLU	20	E4
PIERCE POINT RD	MAR	37	D4
PIERI RD	KER	78	B4
PIERLE RD	IMP	108	E5
PIERSON BLVD	RCO	100	C2
PIGEON PASS RD	RCO	99	C2
PIGEON POINT RD	HUM	15	E1
PIGEON SPG RD	KER	79	C5
PIKE RD	STA	47	D3
PIKE CITY RD	SIE	26	C5
PIKE CITY RD	YUB	26	C5
PILAR RD	SIS	4	D5
PILE ST	SDCO	107	A4
PILGRIM CK RD	SIS	12	E2
PILITAS HUERHRO	SLO	76	C2
PILOT SPRING RD	MNO	43	D5
PILOT SPRING RD	MNO	50	E1
PIMLICO DR	RCO	100	C5
PINAL ST	SB	86	D1
PINE AV	BUT	25	B3
PINE AV	LB	192	D3
PINE AV	MEN	31	C1
PINE AV	PAC	167	C2
PINE AV	SBD	U	D4
PINE AV	SBD	98	D2
PINE AV	TRI	17	B2
PINE DR	HUM	16	B4
PINE DR	LAS	20	E2
PINE DR	MPA	48	E1
PINE ST	C	124	C4
PINE ST	CC	L	E3
PINE ST	MONT	167	D2
PINE ST	MON	53	E2
PINE ST	NAP	133	B4
PINE ST	RED	122	B1
PINE ST	RCO	100	C4
PINE ST	SDCO	107	A4
PINE ST	SF	142	A3
PINE ST	SF	143	C4
PINE ST	SHA	18	C3
PINE ST	U	123	C2
PINE CANYON RD	MON	65	B3
PINE CANYON RD	SB	76	E5
PINE COVE TR	KER	79	D2
PINE CREEK BLVD	MOD	8	B1
PINE CREEK RD	INY	51	B4
PINE CREEK RD	HUM	10	C3
PINE CREEK RD	SIS	2	E3
PINE FLAT	SON	31	E5
PINE FLAT RD	SBD	91	E5
PINE FLAT RD	SCR	N	E5
PINE FLAT RD	SCR	53	D1
PINE GROVE	VEN	88	C4
PINE GROVE RD	KLAM	5	C1
PINE GRV TABEAU	AMA	41	A2
PINE GRV VOLCNO	AMA	41	A2
PINE GULCH RD	AMA	40	E2
PINE HILLS RD	SDCO	107	C4
PINE HOLLOW RD	CC	M	B3
PINEHURST RD	CC	45	D1
PINE MTN DR	TUO	48	E1
PINE MTN RD	KER	78	E1
PINE MTN RD	KER	79	A1
PINE MTN RD	MEN	31	D4
PINE NUT RD	MNO	42	E1
PINE RIDGE	FRCO	58	C3
PINE RIDGE RD	HUM	10	C3
PINE RIDGE RD	MEN	31	A2
PNES TO PLMS HY	RCO	100	B4
PINE TREE CY RD	KER	80	A4
PINE VALLEY RD	MON	65	D3
PINEVISTA CIR	RCO	100	A3
PINEWOOD LN	FRCO	58	B1
PINEY CK LOOP	MON	64	D2
PINKSTON CYN RD	BUT	25	D3
PINNACLE RD	SBD	81	A1
PINOLE VLY RD	CC	L	D3
PINOLI RIDGE RD	NEV	26	E4
PINOLI RIDGE RD	NEV	27	A4
PINON CANYON RD	KER	79	C4
PINON VILLGE RD	TUL	70	A3
PINTO DR	CAL	41	B4
PINTO RD	RCO	101	E4
PINTO BASIN RD	RCO	101	D4
PINTO MTN RD	SBD	101	C1
PIONEER AV	STA	47	D1
PIONEER BLVD	LACO	98	A3
PIONEER BLVD	LACO	T	A1
PIONEER DR	KER	78	E3
PIONEER RD	DN	2	B3
PIONEER RD	MCO	55	D1
PIONEER RD	STA	47	D3
PIONEER TR	SLT	129	C4
PIONEER CK RD	AMA	41	B2
PIONEERTOWN RD	SBD	100	D1
PIONEER TR RD	ED	36	A4
PIPE CREEK RD	RCO	100	C5
PIPE LINE AV	SBD	U	C3
PIPE LINE AV	SBD	98	D2
PIPER RD	CC	M	D3
PIPES RD	SBD	100	C1
PIPES CANYON RD	SBD	100	D1
PIPI RD	ED	41	C1
PIRCEN RD	LAS	14	B3
PIRU CANYON RD	LACO	89	A4
PIRU CANYON RD	VEN	88	E4
PISGAH CRATR RD	SBD	92	E2
PISTACHIO RD	KER	77	B1
PIT RD	MNO	51	A2
PIT #1 PWRHS RD	SHA	13	D4

STREET	CO.	PAGE	GRID
PITTMAN HILL RD	FRCO	58	A2
PITT RIV CYN RD	LAS	14	A4
PITT SCHOOL RD	SOL	39	B2
PITTVILLE RD	LAS	20	A1
PITTVILLE RD	SHA	13	E4
PITTVILLE BENCH	LAS	14	A4
PITTZER RD	IMP	112	B3
PIUMA RD	LACO	97	A2
PIUTE MTN RD	KER	79	D2
PIUTE PINES RD	KER	79	D3
PLACENTIA AV	CM	199	A3
PLACENTIA AV	NB	199	A3
PLACENTIA AV	ORA	T	C4
PLACER AV	FRCO	56	E4
PLACER CT	KER	79	D2
PLACER RD	SHA	18	B3
PLACER RD	SUT	33	E3
PLACER ST	RED	122	A2
PLACER ST	SHA	18	B2
PLACER ST	TRI	17	D1
PLACER HILLS RD	PLA	34	C3
PLACERITA CYN	LACO	89	C5
PLACERVILLE DR	PLCV	138	A3
PLACERVILLE RD	SAC	34	B5
PLAINS RD	CC	39	C5
PLAINSBURG RD	MCO	48	D5
PLANO ST	TUL	68	D3
PLANTATION ST	RCO	102	C4
PLANT FIVE RD	INY	51	C4
PLANZ RD	KER	78	D3
PLASKETT RDG RD	MON	64	E4
PLATEAU CIR	SHA	18	B2
PLATEAU PINE RD	SHA	19	B3
PLATFORM RD	MAR	37	E4
PLATINA RD	SHA	18	A3
PLATINA RD	SHA	17	D3
PLATINA SCH RD	SHA	17	D4
PLAYA AZUL	AVLN	105	B4
PLAZA ST	SDCO	106	C4
PLEASANT	CC	38	E5
PLEASANT AV	SON	37	E1
PLEASANT RD	SLO	66	B5
PLEASANT GROVE	PLA	33	D4
PLEASANT GROVE	SUT	33	E4
PLEASANT GRV LN	BUT	25	E5
PLEASANT HILL	SON	37	D2
PLEASANT HLL RD	CC	L	E4
PLEASANT HLL RD	CC	M	A3
PLEASNT HL RD E	M	154	C4
PLEASANT OAK DR	TUL	68	E3
PLEASNTN SNL RD	ALA	P	B1
PLEASNTN SNL RD	ALA	46	B2
PLEASANT PT RD	HUM	15	E2
PLEASNTS VLY RD	SOL	38	E2
PLEASNTS VLY RD	SOL	39	A2
PLEASANT VLY AV	O	156	B5
PLEASANT VLY RD	ALP	36	B5
PLEASANT VLY RD	ED	34	E5
PLEASANT VLY RD	NEV	34	B1
PLEASANT VLY RD	STA	47	D1
PLEASANT VLY RD	VEN	96	B1
PLEASNT VLY DAM	INY	51	C3
PLESANTE RD	MON	54	C3
PLEYTO CEM RD	MON	65	C4
PLINCO MINE RD	PLU	21	C5
PLUMAS AV	FRCO	57	A3
PLUMAS ST	RENO	130	B4
PLUMAS ARBGA RD	YUB	33	D3
PLUMB LN E	RENO	130	D5
PLUMB LN W	RENO	130	C5
PLUMBAGO RD	SIE	26	D5
PLUM CREEK RD	TEH	19	A4
PLUMMER LKOT RD	TRI	17	B3
PLUM VALLEY RD	MOD	7	C4
PLUNKETT RD	HUM	10	A5
PLYMIRE RD	TEH	18	C5
PLYMOUTH AV	KIN	67	A3
PLYMOUTH RD	SBD	80	E5
PLYMTH SHNDOAH	AMA	40	B1
POCK LN	SJCO	40	B5
POCKET RD	SAC	39	D2
POE RD	IMP	108	E3
POE POWERHOUSE	BUT	25	E3
POINSETTIA LN	SDCO	106	B3
PT LAKEVIEW RD	LAK	32	A3
POINT LOMA AV	SDCO	V	A3
POINT LOMA AV	SDCO	111	C1
POINT LOMA BL W	SDCO	V	A3
POINT LOMA BL W	SD	212	B5
PT OF TIMBER RD	CC	39	D5
PT PLEASANT RD	SAC	39	E3
POINT RANCH RD	MNO	43	B3
PT REYES RD	MAR	37	E4
PT REYES PETLMA	MAR	37	E4
POINT SAL RD	SB	86	A1
PT SAN PEDRO RD	MAR	L	B3
POKER BAR RD	TRI	17	D1
POKER FLAT RD	SIE	26	D3
POLE LINE RD	LAS	20	A1
POLE LINE RD	MCO	55	E2
POLELINE RD	SBD	93	A5
POLE LINE RD	SHA	13	E5
POLETA RD	INY	51	D4
POLETA LAWS RD	INY	51	D4
POLHEMUS RD	SMCO	N	C2
POLI ST	VENT	175	E2
POLK AV	FRCO	57	B3
POLK AV	FRCO	67	B1
POLK AV	FRCO	57	B5
POLK ST	LACO	Q	C1
POLK ST	RCO	101	B5
POLLACK FLAT	SIS	5	A5
POLSON RD	NAPA	38	D3
POMEGRANATE AV	STA	47	C3

STREET	CO.	PAGE	GRID
POMELO AV	STA	47	C3
POMERADO RD	SDCO	V	C1
POMERADO RD	SDCO	106	D5
POMEROY AV	SCLR	150	C3
POMEROY LS BERS	SLO	76	C5
POMONA AV	COR	215	C5
POMONA AV	CM	199	B3
POMONA AV	TEH	24	D1
POMONA BLVD	LACO	R	B4
POMONA FRWY	LACO	98	A2
POMONA FRWY	LACO	R	E4
POMONA ST	CC	38	D4
POMPONIO CK RD	SMCO	N	C3
POND RD	KER	68	A5
PONDER WY	SHA	18	B3
PONDEROSA BLVD	LAS	21	B4
PONDEROSA RD	CAL	41	C4
PONDEROSA WY	AMA	41	B3
PONDEROSA WY	BUT	25	C2
PONDEROSA WY	BUT	25	D3
PONDEROSA WY	BUT	26	A4
PONDEROSA WY	CAL	41	B3
PONDEROSA WY	MPA	49	B3
PONDEROSA WY	PLA	34	D3
PONDEROSA WY	SHA	19	B2
PONDEROSA WY	TEH	19	B3
PONDOSA WY	SIS	13	C3
PONY RD	SBD	92	C4
PONY WY	CAL	41	A4
PONY EXPRESS TR	ED	35	A4
POOLE AV	KER	80	C1
POOLE LN	SIE	27	D3
POOLE RD	HUM	15	D2
POOLE RD	MCO	48	D5
POOL STATION RD	CAL	41	A3
POONKINNEY RD	MEN	23	A3
POOP OUT HL RD	SBD	100	A1
POOR BOY CK RD	ALP	36	C5
POORE RD	IMP	109	C4
POPE ST	NAPA	29	C2
POPE CANYON RD	NAPA	38	C1
POPE VALLEY RD	NAPA	29	C1
POPE VALLEY RD	NAPA	32	B5
POPE VALLEY RD	NAPA	38	B1
POPLAR AV	KER	78	B3
POPLAR AV	MLBR	144	D5
POPLAR AV	SMCO	N	C1
POPPET FLAT RD	RCO	100	A3
POPPY BLVD	KER	80	B4
PORTAL RD W	MNO	43	C5
PORT CHICAGO HY	CC	M	A3
PORTER	FRCO	58	A4
PORTER AV	RCO	99	C3
PORTER RD	SOL	39	B2
PORTER CREEK RD	SON	37	E1
PORTER CREEK RD	SON	38	A1
PORTERVILLE HWY	KER	68	D5
PORTERVILLE HWY	KER	78	D1
PORTERVILLE WY	KER	78	C1
PORT KENYON RD	HUM	15	D2
PORTOLA AV	ALA	M	C5
PORTOLA AV	RCO	100	E4
PORTOLA BLVD	ALA	46	C2
PORTOLA DR	SFCO	L	B5
PORTOLA DR	SFCO	45	B2
PORTOLA RD	SLO	76	A2
PORTOLA RD	SMCO	N	D3
PORTOLA RD	SMCO	45	D4
PORTOLA STAT PK	SMCO	45	D5
PORTOLA S PK RD	SMCO	N	D4
PORTOLA MCLEARS	PLU	27	B3
PORTUGUESE BEND	SUT	33	C4
PORTUGUESE CYN	MON	66	B4
PORT WINE RIDGE	PLU	26	C3
PORT WINE RIDGE	SIE	26	C4
PORTY ST	KER	78	D4
POSO AV	KER	77	E1
POSO AV	KER	78	A1
POSO FLAT RD	KER	79	A1
POST AV	TEH	24	E2
POST RD	RCO	99	B4
POST ST	SF	142	B3
POST ST	SF	143	A4
POST MTN RD	TRI	17	B3
POTRERO AV	SF	142	D4
POTRERO RD E	VEN	96	D1
POTRERO RD W	VEN	96	C1
POTRERO ST	SFCO	L	C5
POTRERO GRDE BL	LACO	R	C4
POTTER RD	MON	54	D4
POTTEROFF RD	CAL	41	B3
POUND RD	IMP	109	A3
POUNDSTONE RD	COL	33	B3
POURROY RD	RCO	99	D5
POVERTY RD	SAC	M	D1
POVERTY RD	SAC	39	D3
POVERTY HILL RD	SIE	26	C4
POWAY RD	SDCO	V	C1
POWAY RD	SDCO	106	D4
POWDER HILL RD	SIS	5	C5
POWDER HILL RD	SIS	13	C1
POWELL AV	SON	37	D1
POWELL RD	SBD	92	D5
POWELL RD	SUT	33	B1
POWELL RD	VEN	88	E4
POWELLTOWN RD	BUT	25	D2
POWER RD	TRI	17	C1
POWER HOUSE RD	FRCO	57	E1
POWER HOUSE RD	MEN	23	B5
POWERHOUSE RD	TRI	11	E5
POWERHOUSE RD S	TEH	19	B3
POWER HSE HL RD	BUT	25	C5
POWER INN RD	SAC	40	A1
POWER LINE RD	MNO	52	C3

STREET	CO.	PAGE	GRID
POWER LINE RD	RCO	106	E1
POWER LINE RD	SAC	33	D5
POWER LINE RD	SBD	83	A3
POWER LINE RD	SBD	91	C3
POWER LINE RD	SHA	18	B2
POWER LINE RD	SUT	33	D4
POWERS AV	MAN	161	D3
POZOS RD	RCO	99	C3
PRADO RD	SNLO	172	A5
PRAHSER RD	SJCO	40	C5
PRAIRE WY	MEN	22	C5
PRAIRE WY	MEN	30	B1
PRAIRIE AV	LACO	S	B1
PRAIRIE AV	SBD	91	C1
PRAIRIE DR	LAS	8	A5
PRAIRIE CK RD	TRI	17	A1
PRAIRIE FLOWER	STA	47	D4
PRAIRIE FLWR RD	STA	47	D3
PRATT RD	TUL	68	B1
PRATT RANCH RD	MEN	31	C3
PRATVLL BTT RES	PLU	20	B5
PREFUMO CYN RD	SLO	75	E4
PREFUMO CYN RD	SLO	76	A4
PRELL RD	SB	86	C1
PRESCOTT AV	MONT	167	C3
PRESCOTT AV	MON	53	D3
PRESCOTT AV	PAC	167	C3
PRESCOTT RD	SJCO	47	B1
PRESIDIO AV	SF	142	A2
PRESIDIO BLVD	SFCO	L	B5
PRESIDIO BLVD	SFCO	45	B1
PRESSLEY RD	SON	38	A2
PRESTON	MPA	49	A5
PRESTON RD	BUT	25	C4
PRESTON RD	IMP	111	E4
PRESTON RD	MCO	47	C4
PREVITALI RD	AMA	41	A2
PRICE CREEK RD	HUM	15	E3
PRICE CK CAMPBL	TRI	17	B1
PRICE CK SCH RD	HUM	15	E2
PRICE CANYON RD	SLO	76	B4
PRIEST COLTRVLL	MPA	48	D1
PRIEST COLTRVLL	TUO	48	E1
PRIEST VLY RD	MON	66	A2
PRIM RD	IMP	109	B5
PRIMROSE MN RD	SIE	26	E4
PRINCE AV	FRCO	56	A2
PRINCE RD	MCO	47	C4
PRINCESS PAT MN	SBD	90	E2
PRINCETON	FRCO	58	A3
PRINCETON RD	MCO	48	B3
PROGRESS RD	SUT	33	B2
PROSPECT AV	KER	78	A1
PROSPECT AV	ORA	T	E2
PROSPECT AV	SDCO	V	E2
PROSPECT BLVD	PAS	190	A3
PROSPECT RD	SCL	45	E4
PROSPECT RD	SCL	P	A3
PROSPECT ST	SDCO	V	A2
PROSPECT ST	SDCO	106	C5
PROSPERITY AV	TUL	68	A2
PROSSER DAM RD	NEV	27	D5
PROUTY RD	SJCO	40	B3
PROVIDENCE RCH	SBD	84	B4
PRUNE AV	STA	47	C3
PRUNERIDGE AV	CPTO	150	A4
PRUNERIDGE AV	SJ	151	A4
PRUNERIDGE AV	SCLR	150	C4
PRUNERIDGE AV	SCL	151	A4
PUDDING CK RD	MEN	22	C5
PRUSSIAN HLL RD	CAL	41	B3
PUEBLO AV	KIN	67	C3
PUEBLO AV	NAP	133	B2
PUENTE AV	LACO	98	B2
PUENTE AV	LACO	R	D4
PULGA RD	BUT	25	D2
PULLMAN RD	IMP	111	E4
PUMICE MINE RD	MNO	50	D1
PUMICE MINE RD	MNO	51	C1
PUMICE MILL RD	MNO	51	D3
PUMP RD	MCO	55	E2
PUMP RD	STA	47	C4
PUMPHOUSE RD	COL	32	D2
PUMPHOUSE RD	SIS	4	B5
PUMPHOUSE RD	YOL	39	D2
PUNKIN CTR RD	LAS	14	B4
PURDON RD	NEV	26	C5
PURDY AV	KER	80	A5
PURISIMA RD	SB	86	B3
PURISIMA CK RD	SMCO	45	C4
PURITAN MINE RD	LACO	89	E4
PUTAH LN	LAK	32	A4
PUTAH CREEK RD	SOL	39	A1
PUTNAM RD	COL	25	A5
PUTNAM WY	COL	32	E3
PYLE RD	CAL	41	B5
PYLE RD	LAK	31	D2
PYRAMID HILLS	KIN	67	A5
PYRITE RD	RCO	99	A2

Q

STREET	CO.	PAGE	GRID
QUAIL AV	KIN	67	B3
QUAIL DR	RCO	100	B5
QUAIL HILL RD	HUM	16	A2
QUAIL ST	KER	80	C1
QUAIL WY	RCO	100	A5
QUAIL HILL RD	CAL	41	A5
QUAIL HOLLOW RD	SCR	N	E5
QUAIL SPGS RD	SBD	101	A1
QUAIL SPGS SPUR	SBD	101	A2
QUAKER ST	HUM	9	E5
QUAKR HL CRS RD	NEV	34	D1
QUALITY RD	KER	68	C5
QUARRY RD	HUM	9	E4
QUARRY RD	MAD	49	B5
QUARRY RD	PA	147	A3
QUARRY RD	SDCO	V	D4
QUARRY RD	SDCO	111	E1
QUARRY RD S	HUM	10	A5
QUARTZ AV	SIS	4	C4
QUARTZ ST	BUT	25	D2
QUARTZ ST	SBD	84	C3
QUARTZ ST	TUO	41	C5
QUARTZ HILL RD	SHA	18	C2
QUARTZ MT LKOUT	SIS	3	D5
QUARTZ MTN RD	MAD	49	D5
QUARTZ VLY DR	SIS	3	C5
QUARTZ VLY RD	SIS	3	C5
QUARTZ VLY RD E	SIS	3	C5
QUATAL CYN RD	KER	87	E2
QUATAL CYN RD	SB	87	E2
QUATAL CYN RD	VEN	88	A1
QUEBEC AV	KIN	67	E3
QUEBEC AV	KIN	67	A3
QUEEN OF SHEBA	INY	72	A3
QUEENS AV	YUBA	125	A1
QUEENS WY	LB	192	D4
QUESTHAVEN RD	SDCO	106	C3
QUICK RD	IMP	112	C5
QUIEN SABE RD	SBT	55	B3
QUIEN SABE RCH	SBT	55	B3
QUIMBY RD	SCL	P	C3
QUIMBY RD	SCL	46	C4
QUINCY RD	SIE	26	D3
QUINCY RD	STA	47	E3
QUINCY JCT RD	PLU	26	D1
QUINCY LA PORTE	PLU	26	D2
QUINCY LA PORTE	PLU	26	C4
QUINLEY AV	MCO	48	B5
QUINN RD	HUM	15	D1
QUINN RD	KER	68	D5
QUISENBERRY RD	STA	47	C3
QUITO RD	SCL	P	A4
QUITO RD	SCL	46	A5

R

STREET	CO.	PAGE	GRID
R ST	FRE	165	E3
R ST	MER	170	B4
RABBIT BRUSH LN	SIS	4	B4
RABBIT RANCH RD	MNO	51	C2
RABBIT SPGS RD	SBD	91	E4
RABBIT SPGS RD	SBD	92	A4
RABER ST	KER	80	A5
RACE ST	SJ	151	E4
RACE ST	SCL	P	B3
RACE TRACK RD	SAC	M	E1
RACE TRACK RD	SAC	39	D3
RACE TRACK RD	TUO	163	A3
RACETRACK VLY	INY	61	A2
RACINE AV	KIN	67	E3
RACQUET CLUB DR	SR	139	B3
RADIO LN	RED	122	C5
RADIO STATN RD	SOL	39	B2
RAGAN MEADWS RD	TRI	17	A3
RAG DUMP RD	BUT	25	D2
RAGLIN RIDGE RD	TEH	23	E1
RAGLIN RIDGE RD	TEH	24	A1
RAGSDALE RD	RCO	102	B4
RAHILLY RD	MCO	48	B5
RAIL CANYON RD	COL	24	B5
RAIL CANYON RD	GLE	24	B5
RAIL CREEK RD	SIS	12	A2
RAILROAD AV	CC	M	B3
RAILROAD AV	DN	1	D4
RAILROAD AV	HUM	16	D4
RAILROAD AV	RED	122	B3
RAILROAD AV	SMA	173	B2
RAILROAD AV	SOL	135	E3
RAILROAD AV	SUT	33	C2
RAILROAD AV	VAL	134	A4
RAILROAD ST	SBD	84	C3
RAILROAD CYN RD	RCO	99	C4
RAILRD FLAT RD	CAL	41	B3
RAINBOW	FRCO	57	E3
RAINBOW BASN RD	SBD	81	D5
RAINBOW CYN RD	SBD	93	B4
RAINBOW GLEN RD	SDCO	106	C1
RAINBOW LAKE RD	SHA	18	A3
RAINES RD	STA	47	B3
RAIN TREE LN	BUT	25	A2
RAJNUS RD	KLAM	5	E2
RALPH RD	IMP	109	A5
RALSTON AV	BLMT	145	C5
RALSTON AV	SMCO	N	C3
RALSTON AV	SMCO	45	C3
RAMAL RD	SON	38	C3
RAMBLA PACIFICO	LACO	97	B2
RAMELI GREIG RD	PLU	27	D2
RAMIREZ RD	YUB	33	D1
RAMON RD	PMSP	206	C4
RAMON RD	RCO	100	B3
RAMONA AV	LACO	U	B2
RAMONA AV	MTCL	203	B5
RAMONA AV	SBD	U	C3
RAMONA AV	SBDO	203	B5
RAMONA AV	SBD	91	C3
RAMONA AV	SBD	98	D2
RAMONA BLVD	LACO	R	D3
RAMONA BLVD	RCO	99	E3
RAMONA DR	SNLO	172	A2
RAMONA EXPWY	RCO	99	C3
RAMONA EXPWY	RCO	99	D3
RAMONA FRWY	SDCO	V	D3
RAMONA FRWY	SDCO	106	E5
RAMOS RD	MCO	55	D1
RAMP RD	MNO	43	B3
RAMSEY RD	RCO	107	B1
RAMSEY RD	SOL	38	E3
RAMSEY MINE RD	LPAZ	104	D4
RAMS HILL DR	SDCO	107	E3
RAMSHORN RD	TRI	12	A3
RAMS HORN GRADE	AMA	41	A2
RAMSHN MUMBO CK	TRI	12	B3
RANCH RD	HUM	15	E2
RANCH RD	MCO	48	C5
RANCH RD	MNO	52	C3
RANCH RD	SBD	92	E5
RANCHERIA RD	KER	69	C5
RANCHERIA RD	KER	78	E2
RANCHERIA RD	KER	79	A2
RANCHERIA RD	MEN	30	C3
RANCHERIA CK RD	SIS	4	A3
RANCHERIAS RD	SBD	91	C3
RANCHERIA-SAWML	KER	79	B1
RANCHERO	SBD	91	B4
RANCHITA CYN RD	MON	66	C5
RANCHITA CYN RD	SLO	66	B5
RANCHITO RD	MPA	48	D2
RANCHITOS RD	MAR	L	A3
RANCHLAND DR	SHA	18	B2
RANCH LAND RD	SDCO	106	E4
RANCHO AV	SBD	99	B2
RANCHO DR	KER	78	E4
RANCHO DR	KER	79	A4
RANCHO DR	SBD	91	A3
RANCHO RD	KER	78	E5
RANCHO RD	KER	79	A5
RANCHO RD	LV	209	A2
RANCHO RD	SB	76	C5
RANCHO RD	SB	86	B1
RANCHO RD	SHA	18	C2
RNCHO ALISAL RD	SB	86	E3
RCHO BAUTSTA RD	RCO	100	B5
RO BERNARDO RD	SDCO	106	D4
RANCHO CALIF RD	RCO	99	D5
RANCHO CALIF RD	RCO	106	C1
RANCHO CANADA	SDCO	107	A5
RNCHO CONEJO BL	VEN	96	D1
RO SANTA FE RD	SDCO	106	C3
RANCHO VIEJO RD	SJC	202	E1
RANDALL AV	SBD	99	A2
RANDALL RD	KER	77	E4
RANDOLPH RD	MCO	47	E4
RANDOLPH RD	SAC	40	A2
RANDSBURG RD	SBD	81	C2
RANDSBRG CUTOFF	KER	80	A4
RANDSBRG CUTOFF	SBD	80	E3
RANDSBG INYOKRN	KER	80	D1
RANDSBG WASH RD	SBD	80	E1
RANDSBG WASH RD	SBD	81	A1
RANGE RD	MCO	48	B5
RANGER STA RD	INY	51	B3
RANGER STA RD	INY	60	A4
RANGER STA RD	TRI	17	B1
RANNELS BLVD	RCO	103	C5
RANNELS BLVD	RCO	110	C1
RASOR RD	SBD	83	A4
RATTLESNAKE RD	NEV	34	C2
RATTLESNAKE RD	TRI	17	B3
RATTLSNK BTT RD	MOD	14	E1
RATTLSNK CYN RD	SBD	92	C5
RATTLSNAK CK RD	SIS	3	D5
RAWHIDE RD	TUO	41	C5
RAWSON RD	TEH	18	D5
RAY	SJCO	40	A3
RAY	SJCO	40	A4
RAY RD	SB	86	B1
RAYHOUSE RD	YOL	32	C4
RAYMOND AV	ORA	T	C1
RAYMOND RD	ALA	M	D5
RAYMOND RD	ALA	46	C2
RAYMOND RD	MAD	49	C5
RAYMOND RD	MAD	57	B1
RAYNOR RANCH	MCO	48	E5
READING RD	TEH	18	D5
REAL RD	BKD	166	A4
REAL RD	KER	166	A5
REALTY RD	SJCO	40	B4
REATA RD	INY	51	D4
RECALDE RD	SBT	55	E4
RECHE RD	SBD	92	D5
RECHE RD	SDCO	106	C2
RECHE CANYON RD	RCO	99	C2
RECLAMATION RD	LAK	31	D2
RECLAMATION RD	SUT	33	C3
RECTOR RD	NEV	34	C1
RED BANK RD	TEH	18	B5
RED BANK RD	TEH	24	C1
RED BOX RD	LACO	R	C2
RED CAP RD	HUM	10	D2
RED CLOUD MN RD	RCO	102	B4
REDDING AV	KIN	67	D3
REDDING CYN RD	INY	51	E4
REDDING CK RD	TRI	17	D2
REDDINGTON AV	COL	32	E3
RED DOG RD	NEV	34	D1
RED GRADE RD	TRI	17	D1
RED HEAD CYN RD	MON	65	D3
RED HILL AV	CM	198	A4
RED HILL AV	IRV	198	D3
RED HILL AV	ORA	T	D3
RED HILL BLVD	ORA	98	C4
REDHILL RD	CAL	41	B4
RED HILL RD	IMP	109	A3
RED HILL RD	INY	51	C4
RED HILL RD	TRI	17	C1
REDHILL RD	TUO	48	C1
REDINGER LK RD	MAD	49	E5
REDINGER LK RD	MAD	50	A5
REDLANDS BLVD	RCO	99	C2

INDEXES

266
REDLANDS BLVD
STREET INDEX
ROCKY CT

STREET	CO.	PAGE	GRID
REDLANDS BLVD	SBDO	207	D5
REDLANDS BLVD	SBD	99	C2
REDLANDS FRWY	RCO	99	D2
REDLANDS FRWY	SBD	99	D2
REDLANDS ST	SBD	99	D2
REDMEYER RD	MEN	31	B2
REDMOND RD	HUM	9	E5
RED MOUNTAIN RD	KER	80	E3
RED MOUNTAIN RD	MCO	55	B1
RED MOUNTAIN RD	RCO	100	A5
RED MOUNTAIN RD	SBD	80	E3
RED MOUNTAIN RD	SHA	13	C3
RED MOUNTAIN RD	TRI	17	B4
RED MTN LKOUT	GLE	24	A3
RED MTN MTWY	TRI	17	B4
RED MTN TK TR	RCO	106	C1
RED OAK CYN RD	SIE	26	E3
REDONDO AV	LACO	98	A4
REDONDO AV	LACO	S	E2
REDONDO BLVD	LA	184	B4
REDONDO BCH BL	LACO	S	B1
REDPARK RD	HUM	9	A1
RED ROCK RD	LAS	8	D4
RED ROCK RD	LAS	27	E2
RED ROCK RD	SIS	5	A3
REDROCK-INYOKRN	KER	80	C1
REDROCK-INYOKRN	KER	80	C2
REDROCK-RANDSBG	KER	80	B3
RED ROVER MN RD	LACO	89	E4
RED SHANK LN	RCO	100	A5
REDSTONE AV	KER	79	C3
RED TOP RD	SOL	38	D3
RED TOP MTN RD	MAD	57	C1
RED VISTA RD	ALP	36	A5
REDWING RD	SBD	91	D3
REDWOOD BLVD	KER	80	B4
REDWOOD DR	HUM	16	C5
REDWOOD DR	TUL	69	B2
REDWOOD HWY	CRTM	140	C2
REDWOOD HWY	DN	1	E3
REDWOOD HWY	DN	2	A5
REDWOOD HWY	DN	9	E3
REDWOOD HWY	HUM	15	E3
REDWOOD HWY	HUM	16	A3
REDWOOD HWY	HUM	16	B4
REDWOOD HWY	MAR	L	A2
REDWOOD HWY	MAR	38	A4
REDWOOD HWY	MAR	140	C2
REDWOOD HWY	MEN	22	D2
REDWOOD HWY	SR	139	D2
REDWOOD HWY	STR	131	C2
REDWOOD HWY	SON	31	C4
REDWOOD HWY	SON	37	E2
REDWOOD HWY	SON	38	A3
REDWOOD RD	ALA	L	E4
REDWOOD RD	ALA	47	E1
REDWOOD RD	NAPA	29	D5
REDWOOD RD	NAPA	38	C2
REDWOOD RD	STA	47	D3
REDWOOD ST	SOL	L	D2
REDWOOD ST	VAL	134	B3
REDWD HOUSE RD	HUM	16	B3
REDWOOD RTRT RD	SCL	P	D5
REDWOOD RTRT RD	SCL	54	C1
REED	FRCO	58	A4
REED AV	KER	80	A5
REED AV	SVL	150	B1
REED LN	SCL	P	A3
REED RD	KER	68	C5
REED RD	SUT	33	C2
REEDER RD	KLAM	5	C1
REED MTN RD	HUM	22	C1
REED ORCHARD RD	TEH	25	A1
REEDS CREEK RD	TEH	18	B5
REEDS TURNPIKE	CAL	41	A5
REED VALLEY RD	RCO	100	A5
REESE AV	COL	33	A1
REESE RD	BUT	25	A2
REEVES RD	VEN	88	B4
REEVES CYN RD	MEN	31	A1
REFUGIO RD	SB	86	E3
REGENTS RD	SD	211	D2
REGENTS RD	SDCO	V	A2
REGENTS RD	SDCO	106	C5
REGLI LN	HUM	15	E2
REICHART RCH RD	MNO	51	C1
REID AV	TUL	68	D3
REID RD	KER	79	E2
REID RD	KER	80	A2
REILLY RD	MCO	48	C5
REINA RD	KER	78	C2
REINO RD	VEN	96	D1
REIS AV	VAL	134	E5
RELIEF HILL RD	NEV	26	D5
RELIEZ RD	CC	38	E5
RELIZ CANYON RD	MON	65	A2
RELIEZ VLY RD	CC	L	E3
REMANN AV	SHA	19	E1
REMBACH WY	KER	79	C1
RENFRO RD	KER	78	C3
RENGSTORFF RD	SCL	N	E2
RENGSTORFF RD	SCL	P	A2
RENO AV	TEH	24	D1
RENWICK AV	SB	86	B3
REQUA RD	DN	1	E5
REQUA RD	DN	2	A5
RESEDA BLVD	LA	178	D3
RESEDA BLVD	LACO	97	C1
RESERVATION RD	COL	32	E1
RESERVATION RD	MON	54	B4
RESERVATION RD	TUL	68	E3
RESERVE RD	KER	77	D3
RESERVOIR RD	BUT	25	D5
RESERVOIR RD	ED	34	D3

STREET	CO.	PAGE	GRID
RESERVOIR RD	SOL	38	D4
RESERVOIR RD	STA	48	A2
RESERVOIR ST	LACO	98	D2
RETRAC WY	NEV	34	B2
RETSON RD	BUT	25	D2
REVIS RD	MAD	49	C5
REWARD RD	KER	77	D3
REYES ADOBE RD	LACO	96	E1
REYNARD WY	SD	215	D2
REYNOLDS AV	MCO	56	B2
REYNOLDS HWY	MEN	23	A5
REYNOLDS RD	SHA	13	E4
REYNLDS FRRY RD	TUO	41	B5
RHEEM BLVD	CC	L	E4
RHELM	CC	38	C5
RHONDA RD	SHA	18	C3
RIALTO AV	SBD	99	B1
RIALTO AV	SBDO	207	C2
RIATA RD	LAK	32	A4
RIATA WY	CAL	41	A4
RICE AV	SBD	101	A1
RICE AV	VEN	96	B1
RICE RD	FRCO	57	C2
RICE RD	MCO	48	B5
RICE RD	STA	47	E2
RICE RD	VEN	88	A4
RICE CANYON RD	LAS	21	B3
RICE CANYON RD	LAS	21	B3
RICE CREEK RD	LAK	23	D5
RICE CREEK RD	LAK	31	D1
RICES CROSNG RD	NEV	34	B1
RICES CROSNG RD	YUB	26	A5
RICES TEX HL RD	YUB	26	A5
RICETON HWY	BUT	25	C5
RICH LN	RCO	106	E1
RICH RD	KER	68	C5
RICHARD RD	SIS	4	D5
RICHARD ST	KER	70	A5
RICHARDS AV	BUT	33	C1
RICHARDS BLVD	DVS	136	D3
RICHARDSON AV	SF	142	A1
RICHARDSON RD	SBD	91	A3
RICHARDSON RD	SIS	4	E3
RICHARDSON RD	SIS	5	A2
RICHARDSON SPGS	BUT	25	B2
RICH BAR RD	PLU	26	B1
RICHEY RD	CLO	33	A3
RICHFIELD RD	TEH	24	D1
RICH GULCH RD	PLU	26	B1
RICHLAND RD	SUT	125	B5
RICHMOND RD	LAS	21	A3
RICHMOND ST	SD	215	E1
RICHVALE HWY	BUT	25	B4
RIDER ST	RCO	99	B3
RIDGE DR	SHA	18	B2
RIDGE RD	AMA	40	E2
RIDGE RD	CAL	41	B2
RIDGE RD	NEV	34	C1
RIDGE RD	NEV	127	A2
RIDGE RD	NEV	128	A4
RIDGE RD	SIE	26	C5
RIDGE RD	SIS	3	E4
RIDGE RD	TEH	18	C5
RIDGECREST BLVD	KER	80	D1
RIDGE ROUTE RD	ED	34	E4
RIDGEWAY DR	ED	35	B4
RIDGEWAY HWY	MEN	23	B5
RIDGEWOOD	MEN	23	A5
RIDGEWOOD DR	HUM	15	E1
RIDGEWOOD RD	SHA	18	C2
RIEBLI RD	SON	37	E1
RIEBLI RD	SON	38	A1
RIEFF RD	LAK	32	B4
RIEGO RD	SUT	33	D5
RIGGIN AV	TUL	68	A1
RIGGINS RD	SUT	33	C4
RIGGS RD	LAK	31	D3
RIGGS RD	SBD	83	B2
RIKER ST	SAL	171	B5
RILEY RD	BUT	25	B5
RILEY RD	SB	86	E3
RILEY RD	SAC	40	A2
RIM O T WRLD HY	SBD	91	C5
RIM O T WRLD HY	SBD	99	D1
RIMPAU BLVD	LA	184	C3
RIMROCK RD	BARS	208	D4
RIM ROCK RD	RCO	107	C1
RIMROCK RD	SBD	91	D1
RIMROCK RD	SBD	100	C1
RIM ROCK CANYON	RCO	107	C1
RINCON AV	SDCO	106	D3
RINCON AV	SON	38	A2
RINCON RD	SBD	91	C4
RINCNADA LS PIL	SLO	76	C3
RINGWOOD AV	SMCO	N	D2
RIO RD	CAR	168	C4
RIO RD	MON	168	C4
RIO BLANCO	SJCO	40	A4
RIO BONITO RD E	BUT	25	C5
RIO BONITO RD W	BUT	25	C5
RIO DEL SOL RD	RCO	100	E3
RIOLINDA AV	FRCO	57	B4
RIO LINDA BLVD	SAC	33	E5
RIO OSO RD	SUT	33	D3
RIORDON RD	COL	32	D1
RIOSA RD	PLA	33	E3
RIOSA RD	PLA	34	A3
RIO VISTA AV	FRCO	58	A4
RIO VISTA AV W	TEH	18	D4
RIO VISTA RD	SUIS	135	C4
RIO VISTA ST	ORA	T	D2
RIPONE RD	STA	47	C2
RIPPON RD N	SJCO	47	C1
RIPPON RD W	SJCO	47	B2

STREET	CO.	PAGE	GRID
RISING HILL RD	SIS	4	C5
RITCHEY ST	SA	198	E1
RITTER RD	SHA	13	D3
RITTS MILL RD	SHA	19	B2
RIVER AV	BUT	33	C1
RIVER BLVD	KER	78	D3
RIVER RD	BUT	25	A3
RIVER RD	COL	33	A1
RIVER RD	HUM	15	D3
RIVER RD	HUM	16	D5
RIVER RD	MAD	49	C5
RIVER RD	MAD	57	B1
RIVER RD	MCO	47	D4
RIVER RD	MON	54	D4
RIVER RD	RCO	U	E4
RIVER RD	RCO	98	E3
RIVER RD	RCO	99	C4
RIVER RD	SAC	M	D1
RIVER RD	SBD	85	C5
RIVER RD	SBD	95	D1
RIVER RD	SJCO	47	C1
RIVER RD	SLO	66	A5
RIVER RD	SLO	76	A1
RIVER RD	SLO	76	C3
RIVER RD	SON	37	D2
RIVER RD	STA	47	B3
RIVER RD	STA	47	D1
RIVER RD	TEH	24	D1
RIVER RD S	YOL	39	D2
RIVER ST	SC	169	C1
RIVER ST	SCR	169	C1
RIVER ST	SON	31	C4
RIVER BENCH RD	LAS	20	E3
RIVERBEND AV	FRCO	57	E3
RIVERCREST DR	HUM	16	B5
RIVEREDGE RD	SDCO	106	C1
RIVERFORD RD	SDCO	V	E2
RIVERFORD RD	SDCO	106	E5
RIVER GRADE RD	LACO	R	D3
RIV JCT FRMS RD	SJCO	47	B2
RIVER RANCH RD	SHA	18	C3
RIVER ROCK RD	TRI	17	D1
RIVERSIDE	WSH	130	B3
RIVERSIDE AV	MCO	47	D4
RIVERSIDE AV	RCO	103	C5
RIVERSIDE AV	SBD	99	B1
RIVERSIDE AV	SHA	18	C3
RIVERSIDE AV	TEH	18	D5
RIVERSIDE BLVD	SCTO	137	B4
RIVERSIDE BLVD	SAC	39	D1
RIVERSIDE DR	LA	179	B5
RIVERSIDE DR	LA	182	D3
RIVERSIDE DR	LACO	Q	E3
RIVERSIDE DR	LACO	Q	C3
RIVERSIDE DR	RED	122	A1
RIVERSIDE DR	RCO	99	B4
RIVERSIDE DR	SBD	U	C3
RIVERSIDE DR	SBD	98	D2
RIVERSIDE DR	SDCO	V	E2
RIVERSIDE DR	SDCO	106	E5
RIVERSIDE DR	SHA	18	C2
RIVERSIDE DR	SON	132	B3
RIVERSIDE DR	STA	47	D2
RIVERSIDE FRWY	ANA	194	C1
RIVERSIDE FRWY	ORA	98	C3
RIVERSIDE FRWY	ORA	T	E1
RIVERSIDE FRWY	RCO	99	A3
RIVERSIDE RD	HUM	10	A5
RIVERSIDE RD	INY	51	D4
RIVERSIDE RD	SBD	92	C1
RIVERSIDE ST	KER	78	A2
RIVERSIDE PK RD	HUM	16	A3
RIVER SPRINGS	MNO	44	B5
RIVERVIEW DR	SHA	12	C5
RIVER VIEW RD	SBD	91	C1
RIVERVIEW RD	TRI	17	B2
RIVER WAY DR	TUL	68	B1
RIVIERA	RED	122	A5
RIVIERA DR	SD	212	B2
RIVIERA DR	SDCO	V	A3
RIVIERA DR	SHA	18	C2
RIVIERA RD	SUT	33	C1
ROAD 1	LAS	20	B1
ROAD 1	MAD	56	B1
ROAD 4	LAS	20	B1
ROAD 4	MAD	56	C1
ROAD 5	MAD	56	C1
ROAD 5 1/2	MAD	56	C2
ROAD 6	MAD	56	C1
ROAD 7	MAD	56	C1
ROAD 8	MAD	56	C1
ROAD 8 1/2	MAD	56	C3
ROAD 9	LAS	20	B1
ROAD 9	MAD	56	C1
ROAD 10	MAD	56	D1
ROAD 10 1/2	MAD	56	D2
ROAD 11	MAD	56	D1
ROAD 12	MAD	56	D1
ROAD 12	TUL	57	E5
ROAD 13	MAD	56	D1
ROAD 14	MAD	56	D1
ROAD 14 1/2	MAD	56	D1
ROAD 15	MAD	56	D1
ROAD 15 1/2	MAD	56	D1
ROAD 16	MAD	56	D2
ROAD 16	TUL	57	E5
ROAD 16 1/2	MAD	56	D2
ROAD 17	MAD	56	D2
ROAD 18	MAD	56	E1
ROAD 18 1/2	MAD	56	E1
ROAD 19	MAD	56	E1
ROAD 19 1/2	MAD	56	E2
ROAD 20	MAD	56	E2
ROAD 20 1/2	MAD	56	E2

STREET	CO.	PAGE	GRID
ROAD 21	MAD	56	E2
ROAD 21 1/2	MAD	56	E2
ROAD 22	MAD	48	E5
ROAD 22 1/2	MAD	48	E5
ROAD 23	MAD	48	E5
ROAD 23 1/2	MAD	56	E1
ROAD 24	MAD	56	E1
ROAD 24	TUL	57	E5
ROAD 24	TUL	67	E2
ROAD 24 1/2	MAD	56	E2
ROAD 24 1/2	MAD	57	A2
ROAD 25	LAS	20	B1
ROAD 25	MAD	57	A2
ROAD 26	MAD	57	A2
ROAD 26 1/2	MAD	57	A2
ROAD 27	MAD	57	A1
ROAD 28	MAD	57	A2
ROAD 28	TUL	57	E5
ROAD 28	TUL	67	E2
ROAD 28 1/2	MAD	57	A2
ROAD 29	MAD	49	B5
ROAD 29 1/2	MAD	57	B2
ROAD 30	MAD	57	B2
ROAD 30 1/2	MAD	57	B2
ROAD 31	MAD	57	B3
ROAD 31 1/2	MAD	57	B2
ROAD 32	MAD	57	B2
ROAD 32	TUL	57	E5
ROAD 33	MAD	57	B2
ROAD 33 1/2	MAD	57	B2
ROAD 34	MAD	57	B3
ROAD 34	TUL	67	E4
ROAD 34	TUL	68	A4
ROAD 34 1/2	MAD	57	B2
ROAD 35	MAD	57	B2
ROAD 36	MAD	57	B2
ROAD 36	TUL	57	E5
ROAD 37	MAD	57	B2
ROAD 37 1/2	MAD	57	C2
ROAD 38	MAD	57	C2
ROAD 38	TUL	67	E4
ROAD 39	MAD	57	C2
ROAD 39 1/2	MAD	57	C2
ROAD 40	MAD	57	C2
ROAD 40	TUL	57	E5
ROAD 40 1/2	MAD	57	C2
ROAD 42	TUL	57	E4
ROAD 44	TUL	57	E5
ROAD 46	TUL	68	A4
ROAD 48	TUL	57	E4
ROAD 48	TUL	68	A1
ROAD 50	TUL	68	A4
ROAD 52	TUL	58	A4
ROAD 52	TUL	68	A1
ROAD 56	TUL	58	A5
ROAD 56	TUL	68	A1
ROAD 60	TUL	58	A5
ROAD 60	TUL	68	A1
ROAD 64	TUL	58	A4
ROAD 64	TUL	68	A1
ROAD 68	TUL	58	A5
ROAD 68	TUL	68	A1
ROAD 72	TUL	58	A4
ROAD 74	TUL	58	A5
ROAD 76	TUL	58	A5
ROAD 76	TUL	68	A1
ROAD 78	TUL	58	A4
ROAD 80	TUL	58	A5
ROAD 80	TUL	68	A2
ROAD 84	TUL	58	A5
ROAD 84	TUL	68	A1
ROAD 88	TUL	58	A5
ROAD 88	TUL	68	A3
ROAD 92	TUL	68	A2
ROAD 96	TUL	58	A4
ROAD 100	TUL	58	B5
ROAD 100	TUL	68	B1
ROAD 104	TUL	58	B5
ROAD 108	TUL	68	B1
ROAD 109	TUL	58	B4
ROAD 110	MEN	31	B3
ROAD 112	TUL	58	B5
ROAD 114	TUL	58	B4
ROAD 116	TUL	58	B5
ROAD 120	TUL	58	B5
ROAD 124	TUL	58	B4
ROAD 124	TUL	68	B2
ROAD 128	TUL	58	B4
ROAD 128	TUL	68	B3
ROAD 132	TUL	58	B4
ROAD 132	TUL	68	B1
ROAD 136	TUL	58	B4
ROAD 136	TUL	68	B3
ROAD 138	TUL	68	B1
ROAD 140	TUL	58	B4
ROAD 140	TUL	68	B1
ROAD 143	TUL	58	B4
ROAD 144	TUL	58	B5
ROAD 148	TUL	58	B5
ROAD 148	TUL	68	B1
ROAD 152	TUL	58	B4
ROAD 152	TUL	68	B1
ROAD 156	TUL	58	B5
ROAD 156	TUL	68	B1
ROAD 158	TUL	68	B1
ROAD 164	TUL	68	C1
ROAD 166	TUL	68	C1
ROAD 168	TUL	68	C1
ROAD 172	TUL	68	C2
ROAD 176	TUL	68	C3
ROAD 180	TUL	58	C5
ROAD 180	TUL	68	C1
ROAD 182	TUL	58	C5
ROAD 182	TUL	68	C1

STREET	CO.	PAGE	GRID
ROAD 184	TUL	58	C5
ROAD 188	TUL	68	C3
ROAD 190	TUL	68	C1
ROAD 192	TUL	68	C1
ROAD 194	TUL	58	C5
ROAD 196	TUL	58	C5
ROAD 196	TUL	68	C1
ROAD 197	TUL	58	C5
ROAD 200	TUL	58	C5
ROAD 200	TUL	68	C1
ROAD 202	TUL	68	C3
ROAD 204	MAD	57	C2
ROAD 204	TUL	58	C5
ROAD 205	MAD	57	C2
ROAD 206	TUL	58	C5
ROAD 208	TUL	58	C5
ROAD 208	TUL	68	C1
ROAD 209	MAD	57	C1
ROAD 210	TUL	68	C1
ROAD 212	TUL	58	C5
ROAD 212	TUL	68	C1
ROAD 216	MAD	57	D1
ROAD 216	TUL	68	C2
ROAD 220	TUL	58	D5
ROAD 220	TUL	68	D1
ROAD 222	TUL	68	D1
ROAD 224	TUL	68	D4
ROAD 228	TUL	68	D1
ROAD 232	TUL	68	D2
ROAD 235	MAD	50	A5
ROAD 236	TUL	68	D1
ROAD 240	TUL	68	D4
ROAD 244	TUL	68	D1
ROAD 248	TUL	68	D1
ROAD 252	TUL	68	D2
ROAD 256	TUL	68	D3
ROAD 260	TUL	68	D2
ROAD 264	TUL	68	D3
ROAD 266	TUL	68	D4
ROAD 268	TUL	68	D3
ROAD 272	TUL	68	D4
ROAD 276	TUL	68	D2
ROAD 296	TUL	68	E3
ROAD 320	TUL	68	E3
ROAD 406	MAD	57	C1
ROAD 434	MAD	49	D4
ROAD 601	MAD	49	D4
ROAD 602	MAD	57	B1
ROAD 612	MAD	49	C5
ROAD 810	MAD	49	C4
ROAD 812	MAD	49	C4
ROAN RD	CAL	41	B4
ROBB RD	RCO	99	B4
ROBBEN RD	SOL	39	B3
ROBBEN RD	SOL	39	B2
ROBBINS RD	SUT	33	B3
ROBBINS RNCH RD	NEV	26	D5
ROBBY RD	KER	79	B4
ROBERTA AV	LAKE	7	C1
ROBRTNO RIGHETI	SLO	76	B4
ROBERTS LN	KER	78	D2
ROBERTS RD	SJCO	40	A5
ROBERTS RD	SJCO	47	A1
ROBERTS RD	SON	38	A3
ROBERTS FRRY RD	STA	48	B2
ROBERTSON BLVD	BH	183	D2
ROBERTSON BLVD	CUL	183	D5
ROBERTSON BLVD	LA	183	D4
ROBERTSON BLVD	LACO	Q	D4
ROBERTSON BLVD	LACO	183	D2
ROBERTSON BLVD	MAD	56	D1
ROBERTS RES RD	MOD	14	B3
ROBIN AV	MCO	47	E4
ROBIN AV	MCO	48	A4
ROBINSON	SJCO	47	C1
ROBINSON RD	IMP	109	A5
ROBINSON RD	MCO	48	C3
ROBINSON RD	SOL	39	B3
ROBINSON CYN RD	MON	54	B5
ROBINSON CK RD	MEN	31	A2
ROBINSN MILL RD	BUT	25	E5
ROBNSN RCHRIA W	LAK	31	D2
ROBLAR AV	SB	86	E3
ROBLAR RD	SON	37	D3
ROBLEY POINT RD	BUT	25	D2
ROBS RD	MOD	8	B3
ROCA LN	SBD	90	E2
ROCK CANYON RD	LAS	14	A3
ROCK CANYON RD	RCO	107	C1
ROCK CREEK DR	BUT	25	B2
ROCK CREEK RD	CAL	40	E4
ROCK CREEK RD	CAL	41	A4
ROCK CREEK RD	ED	34	E4
ROCK CREEK RD	INY	51	A3
ROCK CREEK RD	MNO	51	A3
ROCK CREEK RD	NEV	34	C1
ROCK CREEK RD	SHA	18	B2
ROCK CREEK RD	SHA	19	B3
ROCK CK GRBG PT	MNO	51	B3
ROCKERFELLER RD	BUT	25	E3
ROCKHAVEN	SBD	101	A2
ROCKING CHR RD	SBD	101	A2
ROE RD	BUT	25	C3
ROCKLIN	PLA	34	B4
ROCK PILE RD	KER	79	A4
ROCKPILE RD	SON	31	B4
ROCKRIDGE RD	RCO	100	A5
ROCK RIVER RD	STA	48	B1
ROCK RIVER RD	TUO	48	B1
ROCK SPRINGS RD	SBD	91	C4
ROCKVILLE RD	SOL	L	E1
ROCKVILLE RD	SOL	38	D3
ROCKWOOD RD	IMP	112	A4
ROCKY CT	KER	79	D5

INDEXES

267

ROCKY LN

STREET INDEX

SANTA INEZ AV

STREET	CO.	PAGE	GRID
ROCKY LN	KER	79	D3
ROCKY RD	RCO	99	B5
ROCKY BAR RD	ED	41	A1
ROCKY BLUFF RD	RCO	99	B4
ROCKY CANYON RD	SLO	76	B2
ROCKYDALE RD	JOS	2	C1
ROCKY PT CMPGRD	PLU	20	B5
RODDEN RD	STA	47	E1
RODEO AV	TEH	24	D1
RODEO BLVD	LACO	Q	D4
RODEO RD	LA	184	A5
RODEO RD	SBD	91	C2
RODEO GULCH RD	SCR	54	A2
RODUNER RD	MCO	48	B5
ROEDING RD	STA	47	D3
ROEN RD	STA	48	A2
ROGERS RD	KER	80	B3
ROGERS RD	STA	47	B3
ROGERS CREEK RD	SIS	10	E1
ROHNERVILLE RD	HUM	15	E2
ROLAND DR	SIS	4	C5
ROLINDA AV	FRCO	57	B5
ROLLING HLLS RD	LACO	S	B2
ROLLINS RD	MLBR	144	E5
ROLLINS LAKE RD	PLA	34	D2
ROMEL ST	CAL	41	A4
ROMERO	MCO	55	C1
ROMERO RD	MCO	47	C5
ROMERO CYN RD	SB	87	D4
ROMERS DAIRY RD	MEN	31	B2
ROMIE LN E	SAL	171	C5
RONNIE AV	KER	79	B5
ROOP RD	SCL	P	E5
ROOP RD	SCL	54	D1
ROOSEVELT RD	MCO	48	C5
ROOST AV	KER	79	B4
ROOT AV	KER	78	B1
ROOT RD	RCO	99	E5
ROOT RD	STA	47	D2
ROSA RD	MCO	47	D4
ROSAMOND BLVD	KER	89	D1
ROSAMOND BLVD	KER	90	B1
ROSAMND HLLS RD	RCO	107	C1
ROSAMUND BLVD	KER	80	C5
ROSARITA DR	SAL	171	D2
ROSCOE BLVD	LACO	97	C1
ROSCOE RD	HUM	15	E4
ROSCOE RD	STA	47	E2
ROSE AV	FRCO	56	E4
ROSE AV	FRCO	57	C4
ROSE AV	LA	187	A2
ROSE AV	MCO	47	E4
ROSE AV	MCO	48	B4
ROSE AV	VEN	88	B5
ROSE AV	VEN	96	B1
ROSE DR	ORA	T	D1
ROSE RD	KER	79	E2
ROSE RD	KER	80	A2
ROSE RD	SIS	5	D2
ROSE RD	TRI	17	B1
ROSE RD	YOL	39	D2
ROSE ST	SDCO	106	D3
ROSEBURG AV	MDO	162	A1
ROSECRANS	LACO	97	D3
ROSECRANS AV	ELS	189	B5
ROSECRANS AV	MB	189	B5
ROSECRANS AV	ORA	98	B3
ROSECRANS AV	ORA	T	C1
ROSECRANS BLVD	SDCO	111	C1
ROSECRANS ST	SDCO	V	A3
ROSE GARDEN RD	MCO	47	C5
ROSEDALE HWY	KER	78	C3
ROSE HILLS RD	LACO	R	D4
ROSE LAWN AV	MCO	47	E3
ROSELAWN AV	MDO	162	A5
ROSE LAWN AV	STA	47	E3
ROSELLE AV	STA	47	D2
ROSE MARIE LN	S	160	A1
ROSEMARY RD	SB	86	C1
ROSEMEAD BLVD	LACO	98	A2
ROSEMEAD BLVD	LACO	R	C5
ROSE MINE RD	SBD	92	B5
ROSEMORE AV	STA	47	C2
ROSER RD	TEH	24	C2
ROSES RD	LACO	R	C3
ROSE VALLEY RD	VEN	88	B3
ROSEWOOD AV	VEN	96	C1
ROSEWOOD BLVD	KER	80	B5
ROSITA ST	LA	178	B5
ROSS AV	EC	217	A4
ROSS RD	IMP	111	E3
ROSS RD	IMP	112	D5
ROSSI ST	SAL	171	C3
ROSSMORE AV	LA	184	D2
ROSSMORE AV	LACO	Q	D4
ROSY RIDGE RD	RCO	107	B1
ROUGH&READY RD	NEV	34	B1
ROULTS RD	MNO	51	B3
ROUND HOUSE RD	MAD	49	D4
ROUND MTN LKOUT	SIS	13	D1
ROUND MTN RD	KER	78	D2
ROUND MTN RD	MNO	51	B2
ROUND ROBIN DR	RCO	100	B4
ROUND VALLEY RD	SBD	100	B1
ROUND VALLEY RD	TEH	23	D2
ROUND VLY RD N	INY	51	B4
ROUND VLY RD S	INY	51	C4
RND VLY TUNGSTN	INY	51	C4
ROUNDY RD	TRI	11	D5
ROUNDY RD	TRI	17	D1
ROUSE AV	STA	162	A5
ROUSE RD	RCO	99	C4
RT OLYMPC TORCH	LAS	20	D2
ROUTE 4 FRWY	CC	154	D3
ROUTE 4 FRWY	M	154	D3
ROUTE 47 FRWY	LB	191	E2
ROUTE 47 FRWY	LB	192	A2
ROUTE 47 FRWY	LA	191	E2
ROUTE 47 FRWY	LA	192	A2
ROUTE 47 FRWY	LACO	97	E4
ROUTE 47 FRWY	LACO	S	D2
ROUTE 52 FRWY	SD	211	E3
ROUTE 94 FRWY	SD	216	C3
ROUTE 101 FRWY	STB	173	D5
ROUTE 101 FRWY	SB	86	D4
ROUTE 101 FRWY	SB	87	D4
ROUTE 101 FRWY	SMA	173	C1
ROWDY CREEK RD	DN	1	E3
ROWENA AV	LA	182	D3
ROWLEE RD	KER	77	E2
ROWLEE RD	KER	78	A2
ROWLES RD	TEH	24	E2
ROXBURY DR	SIS	3	C4
ROXBURY RD	MCO	56	B1
ROXFORD ST	LACO	89	C5
ROXFORD ST	LACO	Q	B1
ROYAL AV	VEN	88	E5
ROYAL AV	VEN	89	A5
ROYAL OAKS DR	LACO	R	D3
ROY JONES RD	SIS	4	B3
ROYO RNCHERO DR	SUT	33	C2
RUBIDOUX BLVD	RCO	99	B2
RUBLE RD	STA	47	C3
RUCKER AV	SCL	P	E5
RUCKER AV	SCL	54	D1
RUDD RD	KER	78	C3
RUDDICK	MEN	31	B2
RUDGEAR RD	CC	M	A4
RUDNICK RD	KER	80	C4
RUDOLPH DR	KER	79	C4
RUDOLPH RD	INY	51	D3
RUEGGER RD	IMP	109	A3
RUFF LN	GLE	24	E5
RUFFIN RD	SDCO	V	C2
RUFFIN RD	SDCO	106	D5
RUGGED TRAIL RD	RCO	107	C1
RUMBLE RD	STA	47	C2
RUNGE RD	SOL	39	C2
RUSH ST	RCO	107	C1
RUSH CREEK DR	TRI	11	D5
RUSH CREEK RD	MNO	43	C5
RUSH CREEK RD	TRI	17	D1
RUSH CK SHORTCT	TRI	17	D1
RUSH CK CAMP RD	TRI	11	D5
RUSHING HILL LKT	TUO	48	B1
RUSS LN	HUM	15	D2
RUSSEL AV	KER	79	A4
RUSSELL AV	FRCO	56	A3
RUSSELL BLVD	DVS	136	B3
RUSSELL BLVD	YOL	38	E1
RUSSELL BLVD	YOL	39	A1
RUSSELL RD	CAL	41	A3
RUSSELL RD	SAC	39	D3
RUSSELL RD	STA	47	B2
RUSSELL RD	TEH	18	C3
RUTH AV	BLMT	145	C4
RUTH DUMP RD	TRI	17	A4
RUTHERFORD	NAPA	29	D3
RUTHERFORD RD	IMP	109	A4
RUTH HILL RD	FRCO	58	C3
RUTH HILL RD	FRCO	58	B3
RUTH ZENIA RD	TRI	16	E4
RYAN AV	KER	80	A4
RYAN RD	LAS	21	B3
RYAN RD	SLO	76	C2
RYAN CREEK RD	MEN	23	A5
RYE CANYON RD	LACO	89	B4
RYE GRASS SWALE	MOD	8	A1
RYE GRASS SWALE	MOD	14	E1
RYER RD E	SOL	39	D3
RYER ISLAND RD	SOL	M	D1
S			
S ST	EUR	121	E2
SABINANA RD	YUB	33	E1
SABODAN ST	KER	78	D5
SACHREITER RD	COL	33	A2
SACRAMENTO AV	BUT	25	A3
SACRAMENTO AV	C	124	A4
SACRAMENTO AV	FRCO	56	D4
SACRAMENTO AV	SUT	33	D3
SACRAMENTO BLVD	SCTO	137	E5
SACRAMENTO DR	SHA	18	C2
SACRAMNTO FWY N	SCTO	137	D1
SACRAMENTO ST	AUB	126	C4
SACRAMENTO ST	PLA	34	D1
SACRAMENTO ST	PLCV	138	C3
SACRAMENTO ST	VAL	134	B2
SACRMNTO VLY RD	SUT	33	C3
SACRMNTO VLY BL	SUT	33	C4
SADDLE CT	KER	79	C5
SADDLEBACK RD	SIE	26	D4
SADDLEHORN RD	SBD	84	C3
SADDLE PEAK RD	LACO	97	B2
SADDLE TRAIL RD	SHA	18	B3
SADDLE VIEW CT	SHA	13	E4
SAGE AV	SBD	100	D1
SAGE RD	HUM	15	D2
SAGE RD	RCO	99	E4
SAGEBRUSH LN	SIS	4	E3
SAGE CANYON RD	KER	80	B1
SAGE FLATS DR	INY	70	B2
SAGE HEN RD	MNO	51	A2
SAGE HEN RD	NEV	27	D5
SAGE HN MDWS RD	MNO	43	E5
SAGE HN MDWS RD	MNO	50	E1
SAGE HN MDWS RD	MNO	51	A1
SAGEHORN RD	MOD	7	D3
SAGELAND CT	KER	79	B4
SAGE VALLEY RD	LAS	21	D5
SAGINAW AV	FRCO	57	E4
SAHARA AV	LV	209	A4
SAHARA AV E	CLK	74	D2
SAHARA AV W	CLK	74	C2
ST CATHERINE WY	AVLN	105	B4
ST FRANCIS AV	STA	47	C2
ST GEORGE ST	LA	182	D3
ST HELENA HWY	NAPA	29	D4
ST HELENA RD	SON	38	A1
ST JAMES ST	SJ	152	C3
ST JOHN RD	TRI	16	E2
ST JOHN LOOP RD	TRI	16	E2
ST LOUIS AV	KER	80	A4
ST LOUIS RD	HUM	9	E5
ST LOUIS RD	HUM	10	A5
ST LOUIS RD	PLU	26	C3
ST MARYS AV	TEH	18	D5
ST MARYS RD	CC	L	E4
ST MARYS RD	CC	M	A4
ST MARYS RD	CC	45	E1
SALE LN	TEH	18	D5
SALEM AV	KIN	67	E3
SALEM RD	SOL	39	B3
SALINAS RD	MON	54	C2
SALINAS ST	STB	174	E3
SALINE VLY ALT	INY	70	E1
SALINE VLY RD	INY	60	C3
SALINE VLY RD	INY	60	D5
SALMON CREEK RD	HUM	16	B4
SALMON FALLS RD	ED	34	C5
SALMON LAKE RD	SIE	26	E3
SALMON LAKE RD	SIE	27	A3
SALMON RIVER RD	SIS	10	E2
SALMON RIVER RD	SIS	11	A2
SALT RD N	SHA	12	C4
SALT CREEK RD	MCO	55	D2
SALT CREEK RD	SHA	12	D5
SALTDALE RD	KER	80	C3
SALTON DR	IMP	108	C2
SALTON RD	SBD	80	E5
SALTON RD	SBD	81	A5
SALTON BAY DR	IMP	108	C2
SALTON VIEW RD	RCO	101	B3
SALT POOL RD	INY	72	A1
SALT SPG VLY RD	CAL	40	E4
SALT SPG VLY RD	CAL	41	A4
SALTUS RD	SBD	93	E3
SALTUS RD	SBD	94	A3
SALVADORI RD	SIS	4	B5
SAM ALLEY RIDGE	LAK	31	D2
SAMEL DR	SBD	100	D2
SAMPLE RD	FRCO	57	E2
SAMPSON ST	SD	216	B5
SAMSON AV	TEH	18	D5
SAMSON AV	TEH	24	D2
SAN ANDREAS RD	SCR	54	B2
SAN ANDREAS RD	SBD	100	E2
SAN ANDREAS ST	STB	174	A3
SN ANTONE CP RD	CAL	41	B4
SAN ANTONIO AV	CAR	53	D5
SAN ANTONIO AV	ONT	204	A3
SAN ANTONIO AV	SBD	98	D1
SAN ANTONIO AV	UPL	204	A3
SN ANTONIO AV N	CAR	168	B4
SAN ANTONIO DR	LACO	S	D2
SAN ANTONIO DR	LACO	T	A1
SAN ANTONIO RD	MON	65	D5
SAN ANTONIO RD	SB	86	B2
SAN ANTONIO RD	SCL	N	E3
SAN ANTONIO RD	SCL	P	A3
SAN ANTONIO RD	SCL	P	E3
SAN ANTONIO RD	SCL	45	E4
SAN ANTONIO ST	SJ	152	E3
SAN ANTONIO VLY	SCL	46	D4
SAN BENACIO RD	MON	54	C4
SAN BENITO AV	FRCO	56	D4
SAN BENITO AV	TEH	18	D5
SN BERNARDNO AV	FRCO	56	C3
SN BERNARDNO AV	SBD	98	D2
SN BERNARDNO FY	CLA	203	A3
SN BERNARDNO FY	LA	186	D3
SN BERNARDNO FY	LACO	98	B2
SN BERNARDNO FY	LACO	R	D4
SN BERNARDNO FY	MTCL	203	A3
SN BERNARDNO FY	ONT	203	A3
SN BERNARDNO FY	ONT	204	B3
SN BERNARDNO FY	SBD	98	E2
SN BERNARDNO FY	UPL	204	B3
SN BERNARDNO RD	LACO	U	A2
SN BERNARDNO RD	SBD	80	E1
SN BERNARDNO RD	UPL	204	C2
SN BERNARDNO ST	MTCL	203	B3
SN BERNARDNO ST	POM	203	C3
SN BERNARDNO ST	SBD	U	D2
SN BERNARDNO CK	SLO	75	E3
SN BERNARDNO CK	SLO	76	A3
SANBORN RD	SUT	33	C2
SANBORN RD S	SAL	171	E5
SAN BRUNO AV	SBR	144	B3
SAN BRUNO AV	SMCO	45	B2
SAN CARLOS AV	SMCO	N	D2
SAN CARLOS AV	SMCO	45	D3
SAN CARLOS RD	MCO	55	D2
SAN CARLOS ST	CAR	168	B4
SAN CARLOS ST	SJ	151	D5
SAN CARLOS ST	SJ	152	C4
SAN CARLOS ST	SCL	151	D5
SANCHES RD	MCO	47	C4
SANCHEZ RD	MON	54	E5
SAND CANYON AV	ORA	98	C4
SAND CANYON AV	ORA	T	E4
SAND CANYON RD	INY	51	C4
SAND CANYON RD	KER	70	C5
SAND CANYON RD	KER	79	D4
SAND CANYON RD	LACO	89	C4
SAND CANYON RD	SBD	99	D2
SAND CREEK RD	COL	32	D3
SAND CREEK RD	FRCO	58	B4
SAND CREEK RD	TUL	58	B4
SAND CREST DR	IMP	108	C2
SANDERS RD	STA	47	C3
SANDERS RD	SUT	33	C2
SANDERSON AV	RCO	99	E4
SAND FLAT RD	SIS	12	D2
SAND FLAT CTOFF	MNO	50	E1
SAND HILL RD	SMCO	N	D3
SAND HILL RD	SMCO	45	D4
SANDIA CREEK DR	SDCO	106	C1
SAN DIEGO AV	FRCO	56	C4
SAN DIEGO AV	SD	213	B5
SAN DIEGO FRWY	CUL	188	A1
SAN DIEGO FRWY	HAW	189	E3
SAN DIEGO FRWY	ING	188	D4
SAN DIEGO FRWY	IRV	198	E5
SAN DIEGO FRWY	LA	180	C2
SAN DIEGO FRWY	LA	188	D4
SAN DIEGO FRWY	LACO	97	C2
SAN DIEGO FRWY	LACO	180	C2
SAN DIEGO FRWY	LACO	189	E3
SAN DIEGO FRWY	LACO	S	B1
SAN DIEGO FRWY	ORA	98	D4
SAN DIEGO FRWY	ORA	197	A3
SAN DIEGO FRWY	ORA	198	A4
SAN DIEGO FRWY	ORA	202	C4
SAN DIEGO FRWY	ORA	T	B3
SAN DIEGO FRWY	SD	211	D1
SAN DIEGO FRWY	SD	212	E3
SAN DIEGO FRWY	SD	215	D3
SAN DIEGO FRWY	SD	216	A3
SAN DIEGO FRWY	SDCO	V	A2
SAN DIEGO FRWY	SDCO	106	B3
SAN DIEGO FRWY	SDCO	111	D2
SAN DIEGO FRWY	SJC	202	C4
SAN DIEGO ST	KER	78	B2
SN DIEGO MSN RD	SD	214	D2
SAN DIMAS AV	LACO	U	B2
SN DIMAS CYN RD	LACO	U	B1
SANDMOUND BLVD	CC	39	D5
SAN DOMINGO RD	CAL	41	B4
SAND RIDGE RD	ED	34	E5
SAND RIDGE RD	ED	40	E1
SANDRINI RD	KER	78	D4
SANDROCK RD	SD	214	B1
SANDROCK RD	SDCO	V	B3
SANDROCK RD	SDCO	106	D5
SAND SLOUGH RD	MCO	47	E5
SAND SLOUGH RD	MCO	48	A5
SANDY AV	KER	80	C1
SANDY DR	RCO	107	C1
SANDY RD	MON	66	B4
SANDY ST	KER	80	C1
SANDY HILLS RD	RCO	107	C1
SANDY MUSH RD	MCO	48	B5
SANDY PRAIRIE	HUM	15	E2
SAN FELIPE RD	SBT	54	E2
SAN FELIPE RD	SBT	55	A2
SAN FELIPE RD	SDCO	107	C2
SAN FELIPE RD	SCL	P	C3
SAN FELIPE RD	SCL	46	C4
SAN FERNANDO BL	BUR	179	C1
SAN FERNANDO BL	LA	179	C1
SAN FERNANDO RD	BUR	179	E2
SAN FERNANDO RD	GLEN	182	D1
SAN FERNANDO RD	LA	186	D1
SAN FERNANDO RD	LACO	89	B5
SAN FERNANDO RD	LACO	89	C5
SAN FERNANDO RD	LACO	97	E1
SAN FERNANDO RD	LACO	Q	C1
SANFORD RD	SON	37	D2
SANFORD RCH RD	MEN	31	B2
SN FRANCSQT CYN	LACO	89	B4
SAN GABRIEL BL	LACO	98	A2
SAN GABRIEL BL	LACO	R	C3
SAN GABRIEL FWY	LACO	98	A3
SAN GABRIEL FWY	LACO	S	E1
SAN GABRIEL RD	LACO	R	E3
SAN GABRIEL CYN	LACO	98	C1
SN GABRL CYN RD	LACO	R	E3
SN GABRL RV FWY	LACO	T	A1
SN GABRL RIV PY	LACO	R	C4
SAN GORGONIO AV	RCO	100	A3
SN GUILLERMO RD	VEN	88	B2
SANHEDRIN RD	GLE	24	A4
SAN IGNACIO RD	RCO	99	E5
SANITARIUM RD	NAPA	29	C2
SAN JACINTO RD	RCO	99	C4
SAN JACINTO ST	SBD	100	C2
SAN JACINTO RDG	RCO	100	A4
SAN JOAQUIN AV	FRCO	66	D3
SAN JOAQUIN AV	LAK	32	A3
SAN JOAQUIN RD	ORA	T	E3
SAN JOAQUIN ST	S	160	D3
SN JQUIN HLS RD	NB	200	A4
SAN JOSE BLVD	MAR	38	A4
SAN JOSE RD	CLO	32	E2
SN JOSE AVNALES	SLO	76	D3
SN JOSE L PANZA	SLO	76	C3
SN JOSE-STA MAR	SLO	76	B3
SN JS ST MAR LK	SLO	76	C3
SN JS ST MAR MT	SLO	76	D3
SAN JUAN AV	SAC	34	A5
SAN JUAN HWY	SBT	54	D2
SAN JUAN RD	MCO	56	B1
SAN JUAN RD	MON	54	C2
SAN JUAN CYN RD	SBT	54	D3
SAN JUSTO RD	SBT	54	D3
SANKEY RD	SUT	33	D4
SAN LUCAS RD	MON	65	C3
SAN LUIS BAY DR	SLO	76	A4
SAN LUISITO CK	SLO	75	E3
SAN LUISITO CK	SLO	76	A3
SAN MARCOS RD	SLO	76	A1
SAN MARCOS RD	SB	87	B4
SN MARCOS PS RD	SB	87	B3
SAN MARIN DR	MAR	L	A2
SAN MARTIN AV	SCL	P	E5
SAN MARTIN AV	SCL	54	D1
SN MARTNZ CHQT	LACO	89	A4
SN MARTNZ GD CN	LACO	89	A4
SAN MATEO AV	FRCO	56	D5
SAN MATEO AV	SBR	144	B1
SAN MATEO AV	SSF	144	B1
SAN MATEO RD	SDCO	105	E1
SAN MATEO ST	SBD	99	C2
SAN MIGUEL	CC	45	E1
SAN MIGUEL AV	SAL	171	C5
SAN MIGUEL DR	CC	M	A4
SAN MIGUEL DR	NB	200	C5
SN MGUEL CYN RD	MON	54	C3
SN MIGUELITO RD	SB	86	B3
SAN PABLO AV	ALA	L	D4
SAN PABLO AV	ALA	45	D1
SAN PABLO AV	CC	L	C3
SAN PABLO AV	CC	38	C5
SAN PABLO AV	ELC	155	E4
SAN PABLO AV	O	157	E2
SAN PABLO AV	R	155	D2
SAN PABLO AV	SP	155	B1
SN PABLO DAM RD	CC	L	D3
SN PABLO DAM RD	CC	38	C5
SN PABLO DAM RD	SP	155	C1
SAN PASQUAL RD	SDCO	106	D3
SAN PASQUAL RD	SB	86	B3
SAN PASQUAL VLY	SDCO	106	E3
SAN PEDRO AV	SBD	84	C3
SAN PEDRO RD N	MAR	L	B3
SAN PEDRO RD N	MAR	38	B5
SAN PEDRO RD N	MAR	139	C2
SAN PEDRO RD N	SR	139	C2
SAN PEDRO ST	LA	185	E5
SAN PEDRO ST	LA	186	A4
SAN PEDRO ST	LACO	S	C1
SAN RAFAEL AV	PAS	190	A4
SAN RAFAEL DR	RCO	100	C3
SN RAMON VLY BL	CC	M	B5
SN RAMON VLY BL	CC	46	A2
SANS BAKER RD	FRCO	58	C3
SN SIMEON CK RD	SLO	75	C1
SANTA ANA AV	CM	199	C3
SANTA ANA AV	NB	199	C3
SANTA ANA AV	ORA	T	C4
SANTA ANA AV	ORA	199	E1
SANTA ANA AV	SBD	99	A2
SANTA ANA BLVD	SA	196	A4
SANTA ANA FRWY	ANA	193	D4
SANTA ANA FRWY	LA	186	D3
SANTA ANA FRWY	LACO	98	A2
SANTA ANA FRWY	LACO	T	B1
SANTA ANA FRWY	ORA	98	A2
SANTA ANA FRWY	ORA	T	B1
SANTA ANA FRWY	SA	196	B2
SANTA ANA RD	VEN	88	A5
SANTA ANA ST	ANA	193	B2
STA ANA CYN RD	ORA	98	C3
STA ANA CYN RD	ORA	T	E2
STA ANA VLY RD	SBT	55	A3
SANTA ANITA AV	LACO	98	B2
SANTA ANITA AV	LACO	R	C4
SANTA ANITA AV	LACO	R	D2
SANTA ANITA RD	SBT	55	B3
STA BARBARA ST	SDCO	111	C1
STA BARBARA ST	STB	174	B2
STA BARBARA ST	SDCO	V	A3
STA BARB CYN RD	SB	87	D1
SANTA CLARA	A	159	A1
SANTA CLARA AV	O	158	B2
SANTA CLARA AV	SA	195	E2
SANTA CLARA AV	SA	196	A2
SANTA CLARA AV	VEN	88	B5
SANTA CLARA ST	SJ	152	C3
SANTA CLARA ST	SCL	P	C3
SANTA CLARA ST	SCL	46	B4
SANTA CLARA ST	VAL	134	B4
SANTA CLARA WY	SM	145	C3
SANTA CRUZ AV	SCL	P	A4
STA CRZ GUN CLB	MCO	55	E2
STA CRZ GUN CLB	MCO	56	A2
SANTA FE	MCO	48	C4
SANTA FE AV	KIN	67	E3
SANTA FE AV	LB	192	B2
SANTA FE AV	LA	186	C5
SANTA FE AV	LACO	R	A4
SANTA FE AV	LACO	S	D2
SANTA FE AV	MCO	48	D5
SANTA FE AV	SBD	81	B5
SANTA FE AV	SDCO	106	C2
SANTA FE AV	SJCO	47	D1
SANTA FE AV	STA	47	D2
SANTA FE BLVD	MAD	57	B2
SANTA FE DR	MCO	48	A3
SANTA FE DR	SDCO	106	C4
SANTA FE GRADE	FRCO	56	C3
SANTA FE GRADE	MCO	47	D4
SANTA FE RD	SBD	92	B4
SANTA FE ST	SBD	92	A1
SANTA FE WY	KER	78	B2
STA FE FIRE RD	SBD	91	A5
STA FE SPGS RD	LACO	R	C5
SANTA INEZ AV	SMCO	45	C3

INDEXES

STREET	CO.	PAGE	GRID
SANTA ISABEL	CM	199	D1
SANTA LUCIA	SBR	144	B4
SANTA LUCIA AV	CAR	168	B4
SANTA LUCIA AV	MCO	55	D1
SANTA LUCIA RD	SLO	76	A2
SANTA MARIA WY	SB	86	C1
STA MAR MESA RD	SB	86	C1
SANTA MONICA BL	BH	183	A2
SANTA MONICA BL	LA	180	C3
SANTA MONICA BL	LA	181	C5
SANTA MONICA BL	LA	182	A5
SANTA MONICA BL	LA	183	A2
SANTA MONICA BL	LACO	97	D2
SANTA MONICA BL	LACO	181	C5
SANTA MONICA BL	LACO	183	A2
SANTA MONICA BL	SMON	180	C3
SANTA MONICA FY	LA	184	A4
SANTA MONICA FY	LA	185	A4
SANTA MONICA FY	LA	186	A4
SANTA MONICA FY	LACO	97	C2
SANTA MONICA FY	LACO	Q	C4
SANTA MONICA FY	SMON	180	B5
SANTA PAULA FWY	VEN	88	B5
SANTA PAULA ST	VEN	88	C5
STA RITA GRADE	MCO	56	B1
SANTA RITA RD	ALA	M	B5
SANTA RITA RD	ALA	46	B2
STA RITA OLD CK	SLO	75	E2
SANTA ROSA AV	SON	37	E2
SANTA ROSA AV	STR	131	D4
SANTA ROSA RD	INY	60	D5
SANTA ROSA RD	RCO	99	B4
SANTA ROSA RD	SBD	91	D4
SANTA ROSA RD	SB	86	C3
SANTA ROSA RD	VEN	88	D5
SANTA ROSA ST	SNLO	172	C2
STA ROSA CK RD	SLO	75	C2
STA ROSA MTN TK	RCO	100	D5
SANTA TERESA BL	SCL	P	C4
SANTA TERESA BL	SCL	46	B5
SANTA TERESA BL	SCL	54	D2
SANTA YSABEL RD	SLO	75	E3
SANTIAGO BLVD	OR	194	E2
SANTIAGO BLVD	ORA	98	C3
SANTIAGO BLVD	ORA	T	E2
SANTIAGO CYN RD	ORA	98	D3
SANTIAGO CYN RD	ORA	T	E2
SN TIMTEO CY RD	RCO	99	D2
SN TIMTEO CY RD	SBD	99	D2
SAN TOMAS EXPWY	SJ	150	E5
SAN TOMAS EXPWY	SCL	P	B3
SAN TOMAS EXPWY	SCLR	150	E2
SAN TOMAS EXPWY	SCLR	151	A1
SAN TOMAS EXPWY	SCL	46	A5
SANTOS AV	SJCO	47	C1
SANTOS RD	SB	86	D3
SANTOS ST	SB	86	B1
SAN VICENTE BL	LA	180	A3
SAN VICENTE BL	LA	183	E2
SAN VICENTE BL	LA	184	B3
SAN VICENTE BL	LACO	97	C2
SAN VICENTE BL	LACO	Q	D4
SAN VICENTE RD	MON	55	A5
SAN VICENTE RD	MON	65	A1
SAN VICENTE RD	SDCO	107	A4
SAN VINCENTE AV	SAL	171	B4
SAPAQUE RD	MON	65	C5
SARATOGA AV	KER	80	E1
SARATOGA AV	SJ	150	E5
SARATOGA AV	SCL	P	A4
SARATOGA AV	SCLR	150	E5
SARATOGA AV	SCLR	151	A4
SARATOGA AV	SCL	45	E5
SARATGA-LS G RD	SCL	P	A4
SARTGA-LS GATOS	SCL	45	E5
SARATOGA SPGS	LAK	31	C2
SARATOGA SPG RD	SBD	72	D5
SARATOGA SPG RD	SBD	82	D1
SARATOGA-SVL RD	SCL	P	A4
SARATOGA-SVL RD	SCL	45	E5
SARATOGA-SVL RD	SVL	149	D2
SARBO RD	MCO	55	D1
SARDINE LAKE RD	SIE	27	A4
SARGENT RD	SJCO	40	A4
SARGENTS RD	MON	65	E4
SARGENTS RD	MON	66	A4
SARIDA AV	KER	79	C4
SARINA RD	DN	1	D3
SARON FRUIT COL	TEH	18	D4
SASIA RD	KER	79	B4
SATICOY AV	VEN	88	B5
SATICOY ST	LA	177	A1
SATICOY ST	LA	178	C1
SAUGUS VNTRA RD	LACO	89	A4
SAVANA	MCO	48	D5
SAVIERS RD	OXN	176	C5
SAWMILL	INY	51	C4
SAW MILL RD	ALP	36	B5
SAWMILL RD	BUT	25	C3
SAWMILL RD	KER	69	C5
SAWMILL RD	KER	79	C1
SAWMILL RD	MNO	50	E2
SAW MILL CREEK	SBT	66	B1
SAWMILL CRSSOVR	MNO	51	B1
SAWMILL CUTOFF	MNO	50	D2
SAWMILL FLAT RD	TUO	41	C4
SAWMILL MDWS RD	MNO	51	B1
SAWTELLE AV	SUT	33	C3
SAWTELLE BLVD	CUL	188	A1
SAWTELLE BLVD	LA	180	C3
SAWTELLE BLVD	LA	188	B2
SAWTOOTH PEAK	KER	80	C1
SAWYER AV	STA	47	D1
SAWYERS BAR RD	SIS	11	C1

STREET	CO.	PAGE	GRID
SAYLOR RD	STA	47	E3
SAYRE ST	LACO	Q	C1
SCALA LN	SIS	4	B4
SCALES RD	YUB	26	C4
SCANDIA RD	SOL	M	B1
SCANDIA RD	SOL	39	A3
SCARFACE RD	SIS	3	E5
SCARFACE RD	SIS	4	A5
SCARLT BUGLE RD	RCO	100	C5
SCARONI AV	KER	78	B2
SCENIC DR	STA	47	D2
SCENIC DR	MDO	162	D2
SCENIC DR	STA	162	D2
SCENIC RD	CAR	168	B4
SCHAAD RD	COL	32	D2
SCHADD RD	CAL	41	C2
SCHAEFER AV	SBD	98	E2
SCHAEFFER RD	SB	87	D1
SCHAFER AV	TEH	18	E5
SCHAGLE RD	SUT	33	C3
SCHALLOCK RD	KER	78	C5
SCHARTZ RD	IMP	109	B4
SCHATZ RD	KER	79	C4
SCHEAFER	MPA	49	B3
SCHEIBER RD	SUT	33	D3
SCHELL RD	IMP	112	C3
SCHILLING	MPA	48	E2
SCHILLING AV	FRCO	67	B1
SCHLAG RD	SUT	33	C2
SCHLEISMAN RD	RCO	98	E2
SCHMIDT DR	RCO	107	A1
SCHMIDT RD	MCO	47	C5
SCHOBER LN	INY	51	D4
SCHOOL RD	IMP	112	D5
SCHOOL RD	MNO	50	E2
SCHOOL RD	MNO	51	A2
SCHOOL ST	HUM	15	E2
SCHOOL ST	MEN	30	C3
SCHOOL ST	U	123	C2
SCHOOLER RD	SBD	101	D1
SCHOOL HOUSE RD	LAS	8	C5
SCHOOL HOUSE RD	MPA	49	A4
SCHLHOUSE HL RD	SIS	4	D3
SCHOTT RD	BUT	25	C3
SCHOTT RD	LAS	14	B3
SCHROEDER AV	SUT	33	C1
SCHROEDER MINE	SIS	3	E4
SCHUETTE RD	LAK	31	C2
SCHULMEYER RD	SIS	4	A4
SCHULTE RD	SJCO	46	E2
SCHULTZ RD	KER	80	D5
SCHUSTER RD	KER	68	B5
SCIARONE RD	ED	35	B5
SCOFIELD AV	KER	78	A1
SCOTT AV	LACO	R	D5
SCOTT BLVD	SCL	P	B3
SCOTT BLVD	SCLR	151	A2
SCOTT RD	CAL	41	C3
SCOTT RD	LAS	27	E2
SCOTT RD	MPA	49	C3
SCOTT RD	RC0	99	C4
SCOTT RD	SAC	40	C1
SCOTT RD	SIS	5	D2
SCOTT BAR RD	SIS	3	D4
SCOTT CREEK RD	ALA	P	B2
SCOTT CREEK RD	ALA	46	B3
SCOTT DAM RD	LAK	23	C5
SCOTT FORBES RD	YUB	34	A1
SCOTT LUMBER RD	SHA	19	C1
SCOTT MTN RD	SIS	11	E2
SCOTT RIVER RD	SIS	3	B4
SCOTTS CREEK RD	LAK	31	C3
SCOTTS FLAT RD	NEV	34	D1
SCOTTS VLY RD	LAK	31	C2
SCOTT VALLEY DR	SCR	P	A5
SCOTTS VLY RD	SCR	54	A1
SCOTT VALLEY RD	SIS	3	D5
SCOTT VALLEY RD	SIS	11	D1
SCOTT VLY AIRPT	SIS	3	D5
SCOUT RD	BUT	19	D5
SCOUT ST	SHA	18	B3
SCOVELL AV	RCO	99	E4
SCRANTON AV	TUL	68	D3
SEAL BEACH BLVD	ORA	98	A4
SEAL BEACH BLVD	ORA	T	A3
SEARLES STA RD	KER	80	E2
SEARLES STA RD	SBD	80	E2
SEARLES STA CTO	SBD	80	E2
SEARS RD	LAS	21	B4
SEARS RD	SOL	L	D2
SEARS POINT RD	SOL	38	C4
SEARS POINT RD	SOL	134	B2
SEARS POINT RD	SON	L	B2
SEARS POINT RD	VAL	134	B2
SEASIDE AV	LA	191	D3
SEASIDE BLVD	LACO	S	C3
SEATTLE AV	KIN	67	D3
SEA VIEW DR	IMP	108	C2
SEAVIEW RD	SON	37	A1
SEAVW QUARRY RD	SON	37	B1
SEAWARD AV	VENT	175	D3
SEBASTIAN RD	KER	78	E5
SEBASTIAN RD	KER	79	A5
SEBASTOPOL AV	STR	131	C4
SEBASTOPOL FRWY	STR	131	B4
SEBASTOPOL FRWY	SON	131	B4
SEBASTOPOL RD	SON	131	B4
SECO ST	PAS	190	A3
SECOND ST	C	124	B5
SECRETARIAT RD	KER	79	B4
SECRET SPGS RD	SIS	4	E3
SECTION OLD RED	PLU	19	E3
SEE CANYON RD	SLO	75	E4
SEE CANYON RD	SLO	76	A4

STREET	CO.	PAGE	GRID
SEE VEE LN	INY	51	D4
SEIAD CREEK	SIS	3	B3
SEIAD OAKS RD	SIS	3	B3
SEIDNER	SJCO	47	D1
SEIGLER CYN RD	LAK	32	A4
SEIGLER SPGS RD	LAK	31	E4
SELLERS AV	CC	M	D4
SELLERS AV	CC	39	C5
SELMADOLPH ST	SBD	91	E3
SELVA RD	ORA	202	A4
SEMINARY AV	ALA	L	D5
SEMINARY AV	ALA	45	D1
SEMINARY AV	O	159	E1
SEMINARY DR	MAR	140	C4
SEMINARY DR	MV	140	C4
SENATOR WASH RD	IMP	110	E5
SENECA RD	PLU	20	B5
SENECA RD	SBD	91	B4
SENECA RD	SBD	91	E3
SENILIS AV	SBD	100	C2
SENTER RD	SJ	152	E5
SENTER RD	SCL	P	C3
SENTER RD	SCL	46	B4
SEPULVEDA BLVD	CUL	188	A1
SEPULVEDA BLVD	ELS	189	C3
SEPULVEDA BLVD	LA	180	D3
SEPULVEDA BLVD	LA	183	A5
SEPULVEDA BLVD	LA	188	C4
SEPULVEDA BLVD	LA	189	C3
SEPULVEDA BLVD	LACO	97	C1
SEPULVEDA BLVD	LACO	Q	C2
SEPULVEDA BLVD	LACO	S	B2
SEPULVEDA BLVD	LACO	180	B2
SEPULVEDA BLVD	MB	189	C3
SEQUOIA BLVD	KER	80	B4
SEQUOIA RD	FRCO	58	D3
SEQUOIA RD	HUM	16	C4
SERENADE DR	SBD	80	E1
SERENE DR	SHA	18	B2
SERENO DR	VAL	134	C2
SERFAS CLUB DR	RCO	U	D5
SERFAS CLUB DR	RCO	98	E3
SERPA LN	SIS	3	D5
SERPA LN	SOL	39	B2
SERRAMONTE BLVD	SMCO	L	B5
SERRAMONTE BLVD	SMCO	N	B1
SERRANO RD	VEN	96	C2
SERVICE RD	SIE	26	C4
SERVICE RD	STA	47	C3
SESPE ST	VEN	88	D5
SESPE RIVER RD	VEN	88	B3
SEVEN HILLS RD	ALA	L	E5
SEVEN HILLS RD	ALA	M	A5
SEVEN MILE LN	BUT	25	A4
SEVEN MI SLOUGH	HUM	15	D2
SEVEN OAK RD	SBD	100	A1
SEVERE RD	IMP	109	A3
SEWARD DR	HUM	16	C4
SEXTON	SJCO	47	C1
SEYMOUR RD	SUT	33	B4
SEYMOUR CK RD	VEN	88	C2
SHABELL LN	INY	59	E3
SHACKELFORD RD	STA	47	B2
SHADOW CYN RD	SLO	75	E2
SHADOW MTN RD	SBD	83	D2
SHADOW MTN RD	SBD	90	E2
SHADOW MTN RD	SBD	91	A2
SHADOW MTN RD	SBD	101	D1
SHADY LN	SR	139	A4
SHADY DELL RD	SIS	5	A3
SHAFFER RD	MCO	48	B3
SHAFFER ST	OR	194	D3
SHAFTER AV	KER	78	B2
SHAFTER RD	KER	78	C4
SHAIN AV	FRCO	56	B2
SHAKELEY LN	AMA	40	D2
SHAKE RIDGE RD	AMA	40	E2
SHAKE RIDGE RD	AMA	41	A2
SHALE RD	KER	77	E4
SHAMROCK RD	SIS	4	A4
SHANDON CEM RD	SLO	76	D1
SHANDON-SN JUAN	SLO	76	D1
SHANK RD	IMP	109	B4
SHANNON DR	SBD	101	D1
SHANNONDALE RD	LACO	89	E4
SHANNON VLY RD	LACO	89	E4
SHARON RD	MCO	55	E2
SHARON RD	YOL	136	A1
SHARPE RD	SON	38	A1
SHARP PARK RD	SMCO	N	B1
SHARP PARK RD	SMCO	45	B2
SHASTA AV	FRCO	56	E3
SHASTA AV	FRCO	57	A3
SHASTA BLVD	TEH	18	E5
SHASTA BLVD	TEH	24	E1
SHASTA ST	VAL	134	D4
SHASTA WY	C	124	B4
SHASTA WY	KLAM	5	C1
SHASTA CO RD	MOD	13	E3
SHA DAM ACCS RD	SHA	18	B1
SHA SPG MCCLOUD	SIS	12	D2
SHASTA VIEW DR	MOD	14	E1
SHASTA VIEW DR	SHA	18	C2
SHASTA VISTA DR	SIS	4	C5
SHATTUCK AV	B	156	A2
SHATTUCK AV	O	156	A4
SHAVES AV	SBD	91	C1
SHAW AV	FRCO	57	C3
SHAWMUT RD	TUO	41	C5
SHAWMUT RD	TUO	48	C1
SHAW PIT RD	MOD	14	B2
SHAWS FLAT RD	SNRA	163	A2
SHAWS FLAT RD	TUO	163	A2
SHAWS FLAT RD	TUO	41	C5

STREET	CO.	PAGE	GRID
SHAWS FT JMSTWN	TUO	41	C5
SHAY CREEK RD	ALP	36	B5
SHEE CAMP RD	MNO	51	B2
SHEEP CREEK RD	SBD	90	E4
SHEEP CK SPG RD	SBD	82	E1
SHEEP CK TK TR	SBD	90	E5
SHEEP MTN RD	SIS	5	A3
SHEEP RANCH RD	CAL	41	B3
SHEEPY CREEK RD	SIS	5	B2
SHEEPY ISLND RD	SIS	5	B2
SHEFFIELD RD	SUT	33	C3
SHEKELL	VEN	88	D5
SHELBY ST	KER	78	B5
SHELDON RD	SAC	39	E2
SHELDON ST	LACO	Q	C2
SHELL AV	CC	L	E3
SHELL AV	MCO	56	A1
SHELL BLVD	CC	38	E5
SHELL BLVD	FCTY	145	D2
SHELL RD	FRCO	66	D2
SHELL RD	TUO	41	C5
SHELL CANYON RD	IMP	111	C3
SHELLCO RD	KER	67	C5
SHELL GULCH RD	SIS	11	D1
SHELL NO 2	YUB	33	D1
SHELLEY	SJCO	40	D4
SHELLEY RD	SIS	4	B4
SHELTER COVE RD	HUM	22	A1
SHELTER ISLD DR	SDCO	V	A3
SHELTON RD	SBD	101	D1
SHELTON RD	SJCO	40	C4
SHELTN BUTTE RD	HUM	10	D2
SHENANDOAH SCHL	AMA	40	E1
SHEPHERD AV	FRCO	57	C2
SHEPHERD RD	MOD	14	B3
SHEPPARD RD	VEN	88	C5
SHERIDAN	FRCO	58	A4
SHERIDAN RD	ALA	P	B2
SHERIDAN RD	ALA	46	B3
SHERIDAN RD	SLO	76	B5
SHERMAN RD	SBD	100	C2
SHERMAN WY	LA	177	B1
SHERMAN WY	LA	178	C1
SHERMAN WY	LACO	97	C1
SHERMAN ISLD RD	SAC	M	C2
SHERWIN CK RD	MNO	50	E2
SHERWOOD AV	KER	77	E1
SHERWOOD AV	KER	78	B1
SHERWOOD BLVD	TEH	24	E1
SHERWOOD DR	SAL	171	C3
SHERWOOD RD	MEN	22	E4
SHERWD RNCHERIA	MEN	22	E4
SHETLAND CT	CAL	41	B5
SHIELDS AV	FRCO	56	A3
SHIELDS AV	FRCO	57	A3
SHIELDS RD	SHA	17	C3
SHIELLS RD	STA	47	C4
SHILOH RD	SOL	39	B4
SHILOH RD	SON	37	E1
SHIMMINS RDG RD	MEN	22	E4
SHIMMINS RDG RD	MEN	23	A4
SHINGLE RD S	ED	40	C1
SHINGLETWN DUMP	SHA	19	B3
SHINGLETOWN RDG	SHA	19	A3
SHINN RANCH RD	LAS	21	D2
SHIPPEE RD	BUT	25	C4
SHIPPEE RD	MCO	48	B5
SHIRK RD	TUL	68	A1
SHIRLAND	PLA	34	C4
SHIRLEY RD	CAL	41	A5
SHIRLEY MDWS RD	KER	79	C1
SHIRT TAIL CYN	PLA	34	D2
SHIVELY RD	HUM	16	A3
SHOEMAKE AV	STA	47	B2
SHOEMAKER AV	LACO	T	B1
SHOEMAKER RD	HUM	10	C4
SHOEMAKER RD	SIS	4	E4
SHOP RD	MNO	42	E1
SHOP ST	INY	70	B2
SHORE RD	SBT	54	E2
SHORELINE DR	LB	192	D3
SHORELINE DR	STB	174	C5
SHORELINE HWY	MAR	L	A4
SHORELINE HWY	MAR	37	D4
SHORELINE HWY	MEN	22	C3
SHORELINE HWY	MEN	30	C4
SHORELINE HWY	MAR	140	B4
SHORT AV	KER	91	C3
SHORT RD	KER	78	A5
SHORT CREEK RD	MEN	23	B2
SHORTYS WELL RD	INY	72	A2
SHOSHONE VLY RD	SBD	93	B5
SHOSHONI LOOP	SHA	13	E4
SHOUP AV	LA	177	B3
SHOUP RD	SHA	18	A3
SHOWER PASS RD	HUM	16	B2
SHRODE LN	LAS	21	C4
SHULTZ RD	MCO	56	C1
SHUMWAY RCH RD	RCO	100	D5
SHUTE MTN RD	BUT	25	E3
SHUTT ST	DN	1	D3
SHY ST	MCO	47	C5
SHY ST	MCO	55	C1
SICARD FLAT RD	YUB	34	A1
SIDDING RD	KER	78	B3
SIDEWINDER RD	IMP	110	C5
SIDEWINDER RD	RCO	102	C3
SIDEWINDER RD	SBD	91	D2
SIDNEY GULCH RD	TRI	17	D1
SIEGLER SPGS RD	LAK	32	A4
SIERRA AV	FRCO	57	C3
SIERRA AV	NAP	133	A1
SIERRA AV	SBD	99	A2
SIERRA DR	MPA	48	E1

STREET	CO.	PAGE	GRID
SIERRA DR	MDO	162	B4
SIERRA HWY	KER	80	A5
SIERRA HWY	KER	90	A1
SIERRA HWY	LACO	89	C4
SIERRA PKWY	CAL	41	D3
SIERRA RD	LAS	20	E3
SIERRA RD	SCL	P	C3
SIERRA RD	SCL	46	B4
SIERRA RD	STA	47	E1
SIERRA ST	RENO	130	B2
SIERRA WY	KER	69	D5
SIERRA WY	KER	79	D1
SIERRA WY	SBDO	207	D3
SIERRA WY	SBD	99	C1
SIERRA WY	TUL	58	A5
SIERRA CTR DR	SHA	13	E4
SRA COLLEGE BL	PLA	34	B5
SIERRA DEL SOL	RCO	100	E3
SIERRA MADRE AV	LACO	98	C1
SIERRA MADRE AV	LACO	U	A1
SIERRA MADRE BL	LACO	R	C3
SIERRA MADRE BL	LACO	R	C2
SIERRA VISTA AV	TEH	24	D1
SIERRA VISTA ST	KER	80	C1
SIERRA VLY RD	PLU	27	C3
SIEVERS RD	SOL	39	B2
SIGNAL RD	IMP	111	E4
SIGNAL BUTTE RD	LAS	20	E1
SIGNAL RIDGE RD	MEN	30	D3
SIKES RD	SOL	39	C2
SILAXO AV	FRCO	56	C2
SILLS RD	COL	32	D3
SILSBEE RD	IMP	112	A3
SILURIAN LK RD	SBD	83	B2
SILVA RD	MPA	49	B3
SILVA RD	SIS	4	C3
SILVERA CT	BUT	25	C3
SILVERADO TR	NAP	133	E4
SILVERADO TR	NAPA	29	A1
SILVERADO TR	NAPA	38	C2
SILVER BAR RD	MPA	49	B4
SILVER BRDG RD	SHA	18	D2
SILVER CYN RD	INY	51	E4
SILVRADO CYN RD	ORA	98	E4
SILVER CREEK RD	MOH	85	D4
SILVER CREEK RD	SCL	P	C4
SILVER CREEK RD	SCL	46	B4
SILVER CK CMPGD	ALP	42	C1
SILVER HILL RD	ALP	36	C5
SILVER KING RD	SHA	18	B2
SILVER LAKE BL	LA	182	E4
SILVER LAKE BL	LA	185	D1
SILVER LAKE BL	LACO	Q	E4
SILVER LAKE RD	LAS	20	B3
SILVER BAR RD	MPA	49	B4
SILVER PUFF DR	KER	89	E3
SILVER QUEEN RD	KER	79	E5
SILVER QUEEN RD	KER	80	A5
SILVR RAPIDS RD	CAL	40	D4
SILVR STRAND RD	SDCO	V	B4
SILVR STRAND BL	SDCO	111	D2
SILVERTHORN RD	SHA	18	D1
SLVR TIP CPGRD	ALP	42	A2
SILVER VLY RD	SBD	92	B1
SILVEYVILLE RD	SOL	39	B2
SIMAS ST	SB	86	B1
SIMI VALLEY- -SN FERN VLY FY	LA	89	B5
SIMI VALLEY- -SN FERN VLY FY	VEN	88	E5
SIMMERHORN RD	SAC	40	A3
SIMMLER RD	SLO	77	A2
SIMMLR BITTRWTR	SLO	76	E1
SIMMLR BITTRWTR	SLO	77	A1
SIMMLR SN DIEGO	SLO	77	B3
SIMMLR SN DIEGO	SLO	77	C4
SIMMLER SODA LK	SLO	77	C3
SIMMONS RD	LAK	23	C5
SIMMONS RD	SHA	18	B2
SIMMONS RD	STA	47	C3
SIMPSON LN	MEN	22	C5
SIMPSON LN	YUB	33	D2
SIMPSON RD	IMP	109	B3
SIMPSON RD	RCO	99	D4
SIMPSON RD	TEH	24	C1
SIMPSN DATNI RD	YUB	33	D2
SIMS RD	TUO	41	C5
SIMS RD	TUO	48	C1
SIMS CREEK RD	TRI	17	C3
SIMS LOOKOUT RD	SHA	12	C4
SINCLAIR FRWY	ALA	46	B3
SINCLAIR FRWY	SJ	151	D5
SINCLAIR FRWY	SCL	46	B3
SINCLAIR FRWY	SCL	151	D5
SINCLAIR RD	IMP	109	A3
SINEX AV	PAC	167	B2
SINGLE SPRINGS	SIS	4	E5
SINGLETON RD	RCO	99	D2
SINGLE TREE	SBD	100	E2
SINGLETREE DR	CAL	41	A5
SINGLEY RD	HUM	15	E2
SINNARD AV	SUT	33	C1
SINTON RD	SB	86	B1
SIR F DRAKE BL	MAR	37	E4
SIR F DRAKE BL	MAR	38	A5
SIR F DRAKE BL	MAR	L	A3
SIR F DRAKE BL	ROSS	139	A4
SIR F DRAKE BL	SANS	139	A4
SISK RD	STA	47	C2
SISKIYOU AV	FRCO	57	A3
SISKIYOU AV	FRCO	67	A2
SITES-LODOGA RD	COL	24	B5
SITES-LODOGA RD	COL	32	B1
SIX MILE RD	CAL	41	B4

STREET INDEX

STREET	CO.	PAGE	GRID
SKAGGS ISLND RD	SOL	38	C4
SKAGGS SPGS RD	SON	31	C5
SKIDOO RD	INY	71	D1
SKI HILL RD	MOD	7	C5
SKI RUN BLVD	SLT	129	C3
SKITTONE RD	STA	47	D2
SKULL FLAT RD	CAL	41	B2
SKUNK RANCH RD	CAL	41	C4
SKYLINE BLVD	ALA	L	D4
SKYLINE BLVD	ALA	45	D1
SKYLINE BLVD	KIN	67	A3
SKYLINE BLVD	SMCO	N	B1
SKYLINE BLVD	SMCO	N	C2
SKYLINE BLVD	SMCO	45	C3
SKYLINE BLVD	SCL	N	E4
SKYLINE DR	KER	79	B4
SKYLINE DR	MONT	167	C4
SKYLINE DR	MON	53	D3
SKYLINE DR	SBD	100	E1
SKYLINE DR	SDCO	V	D4
SKYLINE DR	SDCO	111	D1
SKYLINE MTWY	PLU	20	D4
SKYLINE RD	KER	77	E3
SKYLINE RD	KIN	67	A3
SKYLINE RD	SON	31	A5
SKY LINE DR	VAL	134	E3
SKYLINE FRST DR	MONT	167	C5
SKYLINE FRST DR	MONT	168	C1
SKYLINE FRST DR	MON	53	D4
SKYLINE RCH RD	SBD	100	D1
SKY RANCH RD	MON	54	C5
SKY VALLEY RD	RCO	100	E3
SKY VALLEY RD	SOL	38	D4
SKY VIEW DR	IMP	108	C2
SKYVIEW RD	MAD	57	C2
SKYWAY	BUT	25	C2
SKYWAY DR	SB	86	B1
SKYWAY RD	BUT	19	D5
SKYWAY RD	BUT	25	D1
SLACKS CYN RD	MON	66	B3
SLASH X RCH RD	SBD	91	C2
SLATE RD	YUB	26	A4
SLATE CREEK RD	SHA	12	B4
SLATE CREEK RD	TRI	11	D5
SLATE GULCH	MPA	48	E3
SLATE MTN RD	TRI	12	A4
SLATE MTN LO RD	SHA	12	B4
SLATER AV	ORA	T	B3
SLATER RD	HUM	16	B2
SLATE RANGE	INY	71	B2
SLATER BUTTE LO	SIS	2	E3
SLAUGHTERHOUSE	MPA	49	B3
SLAUSON AV	CUL	188	D3
SLAUSON AV	LACO	97	D2
SLAUSON AV	LACO	Q	E4
SLAUSON AV	LACO	R	C5
SLAUSON AV	LACO	188	D3
SLAYTON RD	IMP	109	C5
SLIGER MINE RD	ED	34	D3
SLOAT BLVD	SFCO	L	B5
SLOAT BLVD	SFCO	45	B2
SLOAT RD	PLU	26	E2
SLOUGH RD	SIS	4	B5
SLOUGH RD	SIS	12	B1
SLOUGHHOUSE RD	SAC	40	B2
SLOVER AV	SBD	99	A2
SLUG GULCH RD	ED	41	A1
SLUSSER RD	SON	37	D2
SLY PARK RD	ED	35	A5
SMALLEY RD	FRCO	57	E1
SMARTS RANCH RD	SBD	92	B5
SMARTVILLE RD	YUB	34	A1
SMITH	YUB	33	E1
SMITH AV	FRCO	57	E4
SMITH AV	KER	78	B1
SMITH AV	KER	70	A5
SMITH GRADE	SCR	53	D1
SMITH RD	MON	65	C5
SMITH RD	SBD	80	E1
SMITH MTN RD	MON	66	B3
SMITH PK LKOUT	TUO	48	E1
SMITH PK LKOUT	TUO	49	A1
SMITHNECK RD	SIE	27	D4
SMITHSON RD	SBD	91	B2
SMITH STA RD	MPA	48	E1
SMITH STA RD	MPA	49	A1
SMITH STA RD	TUO	48	E1
SMITH STA RD	TUO	49	A1
SMOKE CK RCH RD	LAS	21	D3
SMOKE TREE RD	SBD	90	E4
SNAVELY RD	DN	1	E3
SNEATH LN	SMCO	N	B1
SNEATH LN	SMCO	45	B2
SNEATH LN	SBR	144	A2
SNELL ST	SNRA	163	B3
SNELLING HWY	MER	170	A3
SNELLING RD	MCO	48	C3
SNELL VALLEY RD	NAPA	32	B5
SNOW RD	KER	77	E2
SNOW RD	KER	78	C2
SNOW ST	KER	79	E1
SNOW ST	KER	80	A1
SNOW CAMP RD	HUM	10	B5
SNOWDN HOVEY GL	SIS	4	C4
SNOWS RD	ED	35	A5
SNOWSHOE SPGS	ALP	36	B4
SNOW TENT RD	NEV	26	D5
SNYDER RD	IMP	109	C5
SNYDER RD	MCO	47	D5
SOAP CREEK RD	SIS	3	E5
SOBOBA RD	RCO	99	E3
SOBOBA ST	RCO	100	A4
SOBRANTE AV	CC	L	D3
SOBRANTE AV	CC	38	C5
SODA BAY RD	LAK	31	D3
SODA CANYON RD	NAPA	38	C2
SODA CREEK RD	SHA	12	C3
SODA LAKE RD	KER	78	A5
SODA LAKE RD	KER	87	E1
SODA LAKE CK RD	SLO	77	B3
SODA LK SN DIEG	SLO	77	B3
SODA LK SN DIEG	SLO	77	D4
SODA ROCK LN W	SON	31	D5
SODA SPRINGS RD	BUT	19	D5
SODA SPRINGS RD	SON	30	E5
SOETH RD	GLE	24	B5
SOLANO AV	ALA	L	D4
SOLANO AV	NAP	133	A2
SOLANO AV	VAL	134	C5
SOLANO WY	CC	M	A3
SOLDIER MTN DR	SHA	13	D3
SOLDIER MTN RD	SHA	13	D3
SOLEDAD DR	MONT	167	D4
SOLEDAD DR	MONT	168	D1
SOLEDAD DR	MON	53	E4
SOLEDAD FRWY	SDCO	V	B2
SOLEDAD FRWY	SDCO	106	C5
SOLEDAD CYN RD	LACO	89	E4
SOLEDAD MTN RD	SD	211	B4
SOLOMAN RD	SB	86	B1
SOMAVIA RD	MON	54	D4
SOMEO ST	SB	86	B1
SOMERSVILLE RD	CC	M	B3
SOMERSVILLE RD	CC	39	B5
SONOMA AV	FRCO	56	D4
SONOMA AV	FRCO	66	D1
SONOMA AV	STR	131	E3
SONOMA BLVD	NAPA	L	D2
SONOMA BLVD	VAL	134	C4
SONOMA HWY	SNMA	132	C3
SONOMA MTN RD	SON	38	A2
SONORA	SJCO	40	D5
SONORA	STA	41	A5
SONORA RD	STA	40	D5
SONORA RD	STA	47	D1
SONORA RD	STA	48	A1
SONORA ELEM SCH	TUO	163	D4
SOPHIE ST	RCO	99	C4
SOQUEL AV	SC	169	D3
SOQUEL DR	SCR	54	A2
SOQUEL-SAN JOSE	SCR	54	A2
SORENSON RD	HUM	16	B3
SORENSON RD	RCO	107	B1
SORREL WY	CAL	41	A4
SORRENTO VLY RD	SDCO	106	C4
SORRENTO VLY RD	SDCO	V	A1
SOSCOL AV	NAP	133	D3
SOSCOL RD	NAPA	38	C3
SOTO ST	LA	186	D5
SOTO ST	LACO	R	A4
SOULE LN	SIS	4	C4
SOULSBYVILLE RD	TUO	41	D5
SOUTH AV	FRCO	56	E4
SOUTH AV	FRCO	57	B4
SOUTH AV	MCO	47	E4
SOUTH AV	MCO	48	A4
SOUTH AV	TEH	24	E2
SOUTH DR	SF	141	B4
SOUTH RD	MNO	51	C1
SOUTH RD	BLMT	145	C5
SOUTH ST	ANA	193	B3
SOUTH ST	ANA	194	A2
SOUTH ST	GLE	24	D3
SOUTH ST	LACO	98	A3
SOUTH ST	LACO	S	D1
SOUTH ST	LACO	T	A1
SOUTH ST	ORA	T	C2
SOUTH ST	RED	122	B2
SOUTH ST	SBD	90	E4
SOUTH ST	SNLO	172	B4
SOUTH ST	SHA	18	C3
SOUTHAM RD	COL	24	E5
SOUTHAMPTON RD	BEN	153	A3
SOUTH BANK RD	DN	1	E3
S BNK CHETKO RD	CUR	1	D2
SOUTH BAY FRWY	SDCO	V	D4
SOUTH BAY FRWY	SDCO	111	D1
SOUTHBAY FRWY	SVL	148	C4
SOUTHERN AV	SIS	12	E2
S EMBARCADRO FY	SF	142	E4
S EMBARCADRO FY	SFCO	45	C2
SOUTH FORK DR	TUL	58	E5
SOUTH FORK DR	TUL	68	E1
SOUTH FORK DR	TUL	69	A1
SOUTH FORK RD	DN	1	E4
SOUTH FORK RD	DN	2	A4
SOUTH FORK RD	SHA	18	B3
SOUTH FORK RD	SIS	2	E3
SOUTH FORK RD	TRI	10	D5
SOUTH FORK RD	TRI	16	E2
SOUTH FORK RD	TUO	41	D4
S FK LOOKOUT RD	SHA	18	B2
S FK MAD RIV RD	TRI	17	B5
S FORK MTN RD	LAS	8	B3
S FORK MTN RD	TRI	16	E3
S FK SALMON RIV	SIS	11	B2
SOUTH GRADE RD	SDCO	107	A2
SOUTH GRADE RD	SDCO	107	B5
SOUTHSIDE DR	MPA	63	B2
SOUTHSIDE RD	SBT	54	E3
SOUTHSIDE RD	SBT	55	A3
SOUTH VLY FRWY	SCL	54	C1
SW EXPWY	SCL	P	B3
SOUTHWORTH RD	CAL	40	D4
SOUZA RD	TRI	17	A4
SOWLES RD	SJCO	40	B3
SPA RD	IMP	108	E1
SPACER DR	TUL	68	B2
SPALDING RD	LAS	20	D1
SPANGLE GOLD RD	MAD	49	C5
SPANGLER RD	KER	68	C5
SPANISH DAGGER	RCO	100	C5
SPANISH DRY DGN	ED	34	D3
SPANISH RCH RD	PLU	26	B1
SPANSH RCH BUTE	PLU	25	E2
SPANSH RCH BUTE	PLU	26	A2
SPANISH VALLEY	NAPA	32	C5
SPARKS RD	MCO	47	C5
SPARKS RANCH RD	SOL	39	B1
SPEAR AV	HUM	10	A5
SPECIMAN SPG RD	MAD	49	B4
SPENCE RD	MON	54	D4
SPENCER LN	SON	32	A5
SPENCER LN	SON	38	A1
SPENCER RD	COL	24	E5
SPENCER RD	STA	47	A2
SPENCEVILLE RD	NEV	34	B2
SPENCEVILLE RD	YUB	33	E3
SPERRY AV	STA	47	B3
SPERRY RD	STA	47	E3
SPGNOLI MINE RD	AMA	41	A2
SPILLWAY RD	MNO	51	B2
SPINELLI RD	MAD	49	C5
SPINK RD	CAL	41	B2
SPLICER RD	COL	33	A3
SPOONER RD	LAS	8	A4
SPOONER RD	LAS	14	E4
SPORTS ARENA BL	SD	212	D5
SPORTS ARENA BL	SD	213	A5
SPRECKELS BLVD	MON	54	C4
SPRING RD	VAL	134	C4
SPRING ST	LACO	S	E2
SPRING ST	NAPA	29	C3
SPRING ST	U	123	B3
SPRING ST N	LA	186	B2
SPRING TR	LAK	31	D2
SPRING BRNCH RD	TEH	18	D3
SPRING BRNCH RD	TEH	19	A3
SPRINGBROOK RD	CC	L	E4
SPRINGBROOK RD	CC	M	A4
SPRING CREEK RD	SHA	13	D3
SPRINGDALE ST	ORA	T	B3
SPRINGER RD	SCL	N	E3
SPRINGFIELD AV	FRCO	56	E4
SPRINGFIELD AV	FRCO	57	B4
SPRING GAP RD	TUO	41	E3
SPRING GAP RD	TUO	42	A3
SPRING GARDEN	PLA	34	D3
SPRING GULCH RD	LAS	14	B4
SPRING GULCH RD	SHA	18	C3
SPRING HILL RD	LAS	14	E4
SPRING HILL RD	SON	37	E3
SPRING HILL RD	SON	38	A3
SPRING LAKE RD	KLAM	5	B1
SPRING MDWS RD	SIS	12	E3
SPRING MTN RD	NAPA	29	A2
SPRING MTN RD	NAPA	38	B1
SPRINGS RD	SOL	L	D2
SPRINGS RD	SOL	38	D4
SPRING VLY LTRL	COL	32	D2
SPRING VLY RD	COL	32	C2
SPRING VLY RD	MEN	31	B1
SPRING VLY RD	YUB	33	E1
SPRINGVILLE AV	TUL	68	D3
SPRINGVLLE MILO	TUL	69	A2
SPROUL CREEK RD	HUM	22	B1
SPRUCE AV	SSF	144	B1
SPRUCE RD	TUL	68	C2
SPRUCE RD EXT	LAK	32	A4
SPRUCE ST	B	156	A1
SPRUCE CAMP RD	MCO	55	E2
SPRUCE GROVE RD	LAK	32	B4
SPUNKY CYN RD	LACO	89	C3
SPUR ST	CAL	41	A4
SPYROCK RD	MEN	22	D2
SQUAW BUSH RD	SBD	92	B4
SQUAW FLAT RD	VEN	88	D3
SQUAW GULCH RD	SIS	11	D2
SQUAW VALLEY RD	SIS	12	D2
SQUAW VLY LP RD	SIS	12	D3
SQUIRREL CK RD	PLU	26	D2
STABLER LN	YUBA	125	A1
STADIUM WY	LACO	Q	E3
STADIUM WY	SD	214	B4
STADIUM WY	SDCO	V	B3
STADIUM WY	SDCO	111	D1
STAFFORD RD	HUM	16	A3
STAG RD	AVLN	105	B4
STAGE RD	BUT	25	C2
STAGE RD	LAS	8	D5
STAGE RD	LACO	T	B1
STAGE RD	SMCO	N	C4
STAGE RD	SMCO	45	C5
STAGE COACH LN	SDCO	106	C2
STAGECOACH RD	HUM	9	E4
STAGECOACH RD	SB	87	B3
STAGECOACH CYN	NAPA	32	C5
STAGE GULCH RD	SON	L	A1
STAGHORN RD	RCO	107	C1
STAHL RD	IMP	109	B4
STALLARD RD	IMP	110	C2
STALLION WY	CAL	41	B4
STAMPEDE DAM RD	SIE	27	E5
STAMPFLI LN RD	PLU	20	D5
STANDARD RD	TUO	41	D5
STANDARD MNE RD	PLU	20	C5
STANDIFORD AV	STA	47	C2
STANDISH PIT RD	LAS	21	B3
STANDLEY ST	U	123	B3
STANISLAUS AV	FRCO	66	D1
STANISLAUS RD W	STA	47	B3
STANLEY	SJCO	40	C5
STANLEY AV	VEN	88	A5
STANLEY BLVD	ALA	M	C5
STANLEY BLVD	ALA	P	C1
STANLEY BLVD	ALA	46	B2
STANLEY RD	CAL	41	B2
STANLEY RD	IMP	109	B3
STANLEY RD	RCO	100	A5
STANWOOD DR	STB	174	E2
STANYAN ST	SF	141	E3
STAPP RD	HUM	16	C2
STAR AV	STA	47	E2
STARBRIGHT MINE	SBD	82	A4
STARDUST RD	CLK	210	B1
STAR HILL RD	SMCO	N	C3
STARK	SJCO	40	A5
STARK	SJCO	47	A1
STARK RD	STA	47	B3
STARKEY RD	SLO	76	C1
STARLING ST	LACO	90	C2
STARLITE DR	INY	51	C4
STARLITE DR	INY	51	C4
STARR RD	IMP	109	C5
STATE LN	SBD	100	B1
STATE ST	LACO	R	A5
STATE ST	MTCL	203	B5
STATE ST	ONT	203	B5
STATE ST	POM	203	B5
STATE ST	RCO	99	E4
STATE ST	SB	87	C4
STATE ST	SD	215	D4
STATE ST	SDCO	V	B4
STATE ST	STB	174	B3
STATE ST N	MEN	31	B2
STATE ST N	U	123	C2
STATE ST S	MEN	123	D3
STATE ST S	U	123	D3
STATE COLLGE BL	ORA	98	C3
STATE COLLGE BL	ORA	T	D2
STATE COL BL N	ANA	193	E5
STATE COL BL N	OR	193	E5
STATE COL PKWY	SBD	99	B1
STATE FRSTRY RD	SON	31	A5
STATE LINE RD	MOD	5	E2
STATE LINE RD	MNO	52	C3
STATE LINE RD	INY	72	D1
STATE LINE RD	SIS	5	B2
STATEN ISLND RD	SJCO	39	D4
STATE RANCH RD	SUT	33	C5
STATION RD	KER	78	A3
STAVERVILLE RD	SIE	27	D3
STEARNS RD	STA	47	E2
STEARNS ST	LACO	S	E2
STEARNS ST	VEN	89	A5
STEEG RD	SBD	101	D1
STEEL BRIDGE RD	TRI	17	D1
STEELE LN	MEN	22	E3
STEELE LN W	STR	131	B2
STEELE CYN RD	NAPA	38	D2
STEELHEAD CIR	TRI	17	D1
STEELHEAD RD	HUM	16	D5
STEEL SWAMP RD	MOD	6	C3
STEFFAN ST	VAL	134	E5
STEIDLMAYER RD	CLU	33	A2
STEINEGUL	SJCO	47	D1
STEINER RD	AMA	40	E1
STEINER RD	SUT	33	B3
STEINER FLAT RD	TRI	17	C1
STELLAR RD	SBD	92	A4
STELLING RD N	CPTO	149	D5
STELLING RD S	CPTO	149	D5
STENT CUTOFF	TUO	41	C5
STEPHENSON BLVD	RCO	110	C1
STEPHENS RIDGE	BUT	25	E3
STERCHI LN	SIS	4	C4
STERLING AV	SBD	99	C2
STERLING RD	INY	70	C4
STERLING LAKE	NEV	27	B5
STETSON AV	RCO	99	E4
STEVEN ST	KER	78	B5
STEVENS RD	IMP	111	E3
STEVENS CK BLVD	CPTO	149	C5
STEVENS CK BLVD	CPTO	150	A5
STEVENS CK BLVD	SCL	P	B3
STEVENS CK BLVD	SCLR	150	A5
STEVENS CK BLVD	SCL	46	A4
STEVENS CK FRWY	MVW	148	A4
STEVENS CK RD	SCL	N	E3
STEVENS CK RD	SCL	P	A3
STEVENS CK RD	SCL	45	E5
STEVENSON BLVD	ALA	P	A2
STEVENSN BDG RD	SOL	39	B1
STEVENS MINE RD	SBD	80	E2
STEVENS MINE RD	SBD	81	A2
STEVENS PASS RD	SIS	5	A5
STEVENS PASS RD	SIS	13	B1
STEWART	MOD	14	D1
STEWART AV	BUT	124	A5
STEWART LN	INY	51	E5
STEWART LN	SOL	39	C4
STEWART RD	HUM	16	C4
STEWART RD	INY	51	D4
STEWART RD	SJCO	47	A1
STEWART RD	TEH	18	C5
STEWART ST	SB	86	C1
STEWARTS POINT- -SKAGGS SPGS RD	SON	30	E5
STEWARTS POINT- -SKAGGS SPGS RD	SON	31	A5
STEWART RCH RD	HUM	16	D4
STEWART SPGS RD	SIS	12	B1
STICE RD	TEH	18	D4
STIERLIN RD	SCL	N	E2
STIERLIN RD	SCL	P	A2
STILLWELL AV	MONT	167	D3
STILLWELL AV	MON	53	E3
STILSON CYN RD	BUT	25	B3
STIMPSON RD	BUT	25	D5
STIMPSON RD	BUT	33	D1
STINE RD	BKD	166	A5
STINE RD	KER	78	D3
STINGY LN	SHA	18	C3
STOCKDALE HWY	KER	78	A3
STOCKDALE RD	SLO	76	A1
STOCKER ST	LACO	Q	D4
STOCKTON AV	MCO	48	B4
STOCKTON AV	SJ	151	E3
STOCKTON BLVD	SCTO	137	E4
STOCKTON BLVD	SAC	39	E1
STOCKTON RD	VEN	88	D5
STOCKTON ST	SF	143	C2
STOCKTON ST	SNRA	163	A5
STOCKWLL MNE RD	INY	71	B4
STODDARD RD	STA	47	C2
STODDARD RD	STA	47	E2
STODDARD MTN RD	SBD	91	C2
STODDARD WELLS	SBD	91	D2
STOEKEL RD	SHA	18	B3
STONE AV	STA	47	C2
STONE RD	LAS	20	E1
STONE RD	MCO	55	D1
STONEBORO RD	MEN	30	C3
STONE CANYON RD	MON	66	B3
STONE COAL RD	MOD	14	B2
STONEHEDGE DR	YUB	25	E5
STONEHILL DR	ORA	202	B3
STONE HOUSE RD	SAC	40	C1
STONEHURST AV	LACO	Q	D2
STONERIDGE DR	ALA	46	A2
STONE VALLEY RD	CC	M	A4
STONE VALLEY RD	CC	46	A1
STONEWLL CYN RD	MON	65	A1
STONEY CREEK RD	LAS	21	D2
STONY CREEK RD	AMA	40	D3
STONYFD-LDGA RD	COL	24	B5
STONY POINT RD	STR	131	A3
STONY POINT RD	SON	38	A3
STONY POINT RD	SON	37	E2
STONY POINT RD	SON	37	E3
STONY POINT RD	SON	131	A4
STOREY	FRCO	56	C2
STORRIE RD	PLU	25	E2
STORY RD	SJ	152	E4
STORY RD	SCL	P	C3
STORY RD	SCL	46	B4
STORY RD	STA	47	E3
STOVALL RD	COL	32	D2
STOVEPIPE WELLS	INY	61	D4
STOVER RD	HUM	10	B4
STOW	SJCO	40	C5
STOW	SJCO	47	C1
STOWELL RD	STB	173	B4
STOWELL RD	SB	86	B1
STOWELL RD	SMA	173	B4
STRADLEY AV	KER	68	B5
STRAND, THE	LAS	20	E1
STRATTON LN	SOL	39	B4
STRAWBERRY DR	MAR	140	D3
STRAWBERRY LN	SHA	18	C3
STRAWBERRY RD	MON	54	C3
STREETER AV	RCO	99	B2
ST OF GL LNTERN	ORA	202	A4
STREET 200	MAD	57	D1
STREET 225	MAD	50	A5
STREET 600	MAD	49	B1
STREET 600	MAD	49	C4
STREET 603	MAD	57	B1
STREIBY RD	IMP	109	B4
STRINGTOWN RD	BUT	25	E4
STRIPLIN RD	SUT	33	D4
STROUD AV	FRCO	57	C5
STRUCKMAN RD	CAL	41	B3
STUBBLEFIELD RD	KER	78	A5
STUBBLEFIELD RD	KER	87	E1
STUBBY SPRGS TR	RCO	101	A2
STUDEBAKER RD	LACO	98	A3
STUDEBAKER RD	LACO	S	E1
STUDEBAKER RD	LACO	S	E2
STUDEBAKER RD	LACO	T	A1
STUHR RD	STA	47	C4
STUKEY ST	DN	1	D3
STUMPFIELD MTN	MPA	49	C3
STUMPTOWN RD	HUM	9	E4
STUNT RD	LACO	97	B2
STURGIS RD	VEN	96	B1
STURM RD	HUM	16	C3
SUBACO RD	SUT	33	B3
SUBSTATION RD	MNO	50	E2
SUCCESS DR	TUL	68	D3
SUCCESS VLY DR	TUL	68	E3
SUCKER RUN RD	BUT	26	A4
SUCKOW RD	KER	80	D5
SUDDEN RD	SB	86	B3
SUE AV	KER	89	C1
SUE ST	KER	81	B5
SUEY RD	SMA	173	E3
SUEY CREEK RD	SLO	76	D5
SUGAR CREEK RD	SIS	11	D2
SUGARLOAF RD	FRCO	58	A1
SUGAR LOAF RD	INY	51	D5
SUGRLF LKSHR RD	SHA	12	B5
SUGRLOAF LKT RD	SHA	12	B5
SUGARLOAF TK TR	SBD	99	E1
SUGAR PINE	PLA	34	E2
SUGAR PINE PL	BUT	25	C2
SUGAR PINE RD	TUO	41	E4
SUGAR PINE SPG	LAS	14	A3
SUISUN VLY RD	SOL	L	E1

SUISUN VLY RD

STREET INDEX

270

TRAILS END LN

STREET	CO.	PAGE	GRID
SUISUN VLY RD	SOL	38	E3
SULFUR RD	INY	52	D5
SULKEY CT	CAL	41	A5
SULLENGER RD	SUT	33	B2
SULLIVAN RD	KER	78	A2
SULLIVAN RD	MPA	49	B3
SULLIVAN RD	STA	47	C5
SULLIVAN ST	ORA	T	C3
SULLIVAN ST	SA	195	D5
SULPHUR BANK DR	LAK	32	A3
SULPHUR MTN RD	VEN	88	B4
SULPHR MTN RD E	VEN	88	B4
SULPHUR SPGS RD	MON	65	B3
SULTANA DR	MCO	48	A4
SULTZE AV	KER	78	B5
SUMMERHILL DR	TUO	42	A3
SUMMER HOMES RD	ML	164	C2
SUMMERS LN	KLAM	5	C1
SUMMERS RD	LAS	21	E5
SUMMERSET RD	SBD	91	C1
SUMMIT AV	GLE	24	D3
SUMMIT AV	SBD	99	A1
SUMMIT RD	BUT	25	D5
SUMMIT RD	KER	79	C4
SUMMIT RD	SCL	P	C5
SUMMIT RD	SCR	P	A5
SUMMIT RD	SCR	54	B1
SUMMIT CREEK RD	TRI	17	C2
SUMMIT LAKE DR	NAPA	38	B1
SUMMIT LEVEL RD	CAL	41	C3
SUMMITROSE ST	LACO	Q	E1
SUMMIT TRUCK TR	SBD	91	B5
SUMMY	SUT	33	B2
SUMNER AV	AVLN	105	B5
SUMNER AV	FRCO	56	E4
SUMNER AV	FRCO	58	B4
SUMNER AV	RCO	98	E2
SUMNER ST	BKD	166	E3
SUNBURST AV	SBD	100	E1
SUNEVER RD	SBD	101	A1
SUNFAIR RD	SBD	101	A1
SUNFLOWER AV	CM	197	D3
SUNFLOWER AV	CM	198	A3
SUNFLOWER AV	LACO	U	A2
SUNFLOWR SPG RD	SBD	94	D2
SUNFLR SPGS SPR	SBD	94	E3
SUNKIST ST	ANA	194	A2
SUNKIST ST	ORA	T	D2
SUNKIST TR	LPAZ	104	C4
SUNLAND BLVD	LACO	97	D1
SUNLAND BLVD	LACO	Q	D2
SUNLAND DR	INY	51	D4
SUNNY LN	AVLN	105	B5
SUNNY ACRES AV	MCO	47	E3
SUNNY ACRES AV	MCO	48	A3
SUNNYBRAE BLVD	SM	145	A2
SUNNY BRAE LN	HUM	10	A5
SUNNY HILL RD	SHA	18	A3
SUNNYSIDE AV	FRCO	57	D3
SUNNYSIDE AV	FRCO	57	D4
SUNNYSIDE AV	MAD	57	A1
SUNNYSIDE AV	MV	140	A2
SUNNYSIDE RD	LAS	21	B4
SUNNYSLOPE	FRCO	58	B2
SUNNYSLOPE RD	SBD	90	E4
SUNNYVALE AV	CPTO	149	D1
SUNNYVALE AV	SVL	148	E5
SUNNY VISTA RD	SBD	100	E1
SUNOL BLVD	ALA	P	B1
SUNRISE	SBD	101	B1
SUNRISE BLVD	SAC	34	A5
SUNRISE BLVD	SJCO	40	B2
SUNRISE HWY	SDCO	107	D4
SUNRISE HWY	SDCO	107	D5
SUNRISE WY	PMSP	206	C5
SUNRISE WY	RCO	100	D3
SUNRISE SPGS RD	SBD	93	A5
SUNSET	SAC	34	B5
SUNSET AV	FRFD	135	D3
SUNSET AV	KER	79	E5
SUNSET AV	LACO	R	D4
SUNSET AV	MAD	57	A2
SUNSET AV	MCO	55	D1
SUNSET AV	RCO	99	E3
SUNSET AV	SOL	135	D3
SUNSET BLVD	BH	183	A1
SUNSET BLVD	KER	79	A4
SUNSET BLVD	LA	181	B4
SUNSET BLVD	LA	182	A4
SUNSET BLVD	LA	185	D1
SUNSET BLVD	LA	186	A1
SUNSET BLVD	LACO	97	C2
SUNSET BLVD	LACO	Q	D2
SUNSET BLVD	SD	213	B5
SUNSET BLVD	SDCO	V	B3
SUNSET BLVD	SFCO	L	B5
SUNSET BLVD	SF	141	A5
SUNSET BLVD	SFCO	45	B2
SUNSET BLVD	LA	180	C1
SUNSET BLVD W	PLA	33	E4
SUNSET BLVD W	PLA	34	A4
SUNSET DR	IMP	108	C2
SUNSET DR	INY	60	B4
SUNSET DR	MCO	47	E4
SUNSET DR	MCO	48	A4
SUNSET DR	MONT	53	C2
SUNSET DR	PAC	167	B2
SUNSET DR	SDCO	106	C3
SUNSET PKWY	MAR	38	A4
SUNSET RD	CC	M	D3
SUNSET RD	CC	39	C5
SUNSET RD	CLK	74	D3
SUNSET RD	GLE	24	D3
SUNSET RD	SBD	100	E1

STREET	CO.	PAGE	GRID
SUNSET ST	FRCO	66	D2
SUNSET CYN DR	LACO	Q	D2
SUNSET CLIFFS BL	SD	212	B5
SUNSET CLIFFS BL	SDCO	V	A3
SUNSET CLIFFS BL	SDCO	111	C1
SUNSET CRSNG RD	LACO	U	B3
SUNSET LAKE RD	ALP	42	B1
SUNSHINE MNE RD	KER	80	E3
SUPERIOR AV	CM	199	A3
SUPERIOR AV	NB	199	A3
SUPERIOR RD	KER	78	B3
SURPRISE CYN RD	INY	71	C3
SURPRISE SPG RD	SBD	100	E1
SURPRISE VLY RD	LAS	8	E3
SURPRISE VLY RD	MOD	7	E3
SURPRISE VLY RD	MOD	8	E3
SUSAN HILLS DR	LAS	20	E3
SUSANVILLE RD	LAS	14	B3
SUSQUEHANNA RD	SIS	4	D3
SUTLIFF RD	SJCO	47	D1
SUTTENFIELD RD	SJCO	40	B3
SUTTER AV	FRCO	56	E4
SUTTER AV	FRCO	66	E3
SUTTER AV	MDO	162	A5
SUTTER LN	AMA	40	D2
SUTTER RD	HUM	9	E4
SUTTER RD	HUM	10	A4
SUTTER RD	YOL	39	D3
SUTTER ST	AMA	40	E2
SUTTER ST	SF	142	B3
SUTTER ST	SF	143	C4
SUTTER CK IONE-			
-BACK CUTOFF RD	AMA	40	D2
SUTTR CK VOLCNO	AMA	40	E2
SUTTR CK VOLCNO	AMA	41	A2
SUTTER ISLND RD	SAC	M	D1
SUTTER ISLND RD	SAC	39	D3
SUTTERVILLE RD	SAC	39	D1
SWAN RD	MCO	48	B4
SWAN RD	SOL	39	C2
SWAN MTN RD	PLU	20	B3
SWANSEA RD	LPAZ	104	D3
SWANSON AV	FRCO	57	B5
SWANSON AV	FRCO	57	C5
SWANSON RD	STA	47	E3
SWANTON RD	SCR	N	D5
SWANTON RD	SCR	53	D1
SWARTHOT CYN RD	SBD	91	A5
SWASEY DR	SHA	18	B2
SWEDE CREEK RD	SHA	18	D2
SWEDE CREEK RD	TRI	11	A5
SWEDES FLAT RD	BUT	25	E5
SWEENEY RD	ED	35	B5
SWEENEY RD	SB	86	C3
SWEENEY RD	SOL	39	A2
SWEENEY PASS RD	SDCO	108	A5
SWEENY RD	MCO	55	C2
SWEET RD	IMP	109	A5
SWEETEN LN	SBD	91	D1
SWEETLAND RD	NEV	26	B5
SWEETSER RD	KER	89	E1
SWEETWATER RD	SDCO	V	C4
SWEETWATER RD	SDCO	111	E1
SWEETWATER RD	SDCO	111	D2
SWEETWTR SPGS BL	SDCO	V	E3
SWEETWTR SPG RD	SON	37	D1
SWEITZER LN	SBD	92	D5
SWENSEN RD	MCO	47	D4
SWETZER RD	SUT	33	E3
SWIFT AV	MCO	56	A2
SWIFT RD	SBD	80	E5
SWIFT ST	SC	169	A4
SWIFT CREEK	TRI	11	E4
SWIGART RD	SIS	4	B4
SWISS RANCH RD	CAL	41	B3
SX RD	MOD	14	E1
SYCAMORE AV	FRCO	57	A4
SYCAMORE AV	SDCO	106	C3
SYCAMORE DR	LACO	88	E5
SYCAMORE LN	DVS	136	B3
SYCAMORE RD	ALA	P	B1
SYCAMORE RD	KER	78	E4
SYCAMORE RD	KER	79	A4
SYCAMORE RD	SDCO	V	C5
SYCAMORE RD	SDCO	111	D2
SYCAMORE RD	VEN	88	D4
SYCAMORE ST	ANA	193	B2
SYCAMORE ST	MCO	47	E3
SYCAMORE ST	MCO	48	A3
SYCAMORE CYN RD	SB	87	C4
SYCAMORE CYN RD	STB	174	E3
SYCAMORE CUTOFF	CLU	33	A2
SYCAMRE FLAT RD	MON	65	A2
SYCAMORE SL RD	COL	33	A2
SYCAMORE VLY RD	CC	M	B4
SYCAMORE VLY RD	CC	46	A1
SYDNOR AV	KER	80	D1
SYKES RD	INY	70	B3
SYLVAN AV	STA	47	D2
SYLVESTER RD	MCO	55	D1
SYMMES RD	INY	59	E3

T

STREET	CO.	PAGE	GRID
T ST	BKD	166	D4
T ST	STA	47	C4
TABL MTN OVRCRS	BUT	25	C4
TABLE BLUFF RD	HUM	15	D1
TABLE MTN BL	BUT	25	C4
TABLE MTN RD	FRCO	57	D2
TABLE MTN RD	RCO	100	C5
TABLE MTN TK TR	RCO	107	C1
TABLEROCK RD	SIS	4	C4
TABOOSE CK RD	INY	59	E1

STREET	CO.	PAGE	GRID
TABOR AV	FRFD	135	B2
TABOR AV	SOL	39	A3
TABOR AV E	FRFD	135	C2
TAECKER RD	IMP	109	B4
TAFT AV	OR	194	C3
TAFT AV	ORA	98	C3
TAFT AV	ORA	T	D2
TAFT HWY	KER	78	C3
TAFT ST	TEH	24	E1
TAGE RD	SBD	101	D1
TAGLIO RD	MCO	47	D5
TAHOE ST	MCO	48	B4
TAHQTZ-MCCLM WY	PMSP	206	A4
TALBERT AV	FTNV	197	A3
TALBERT AV	ORA	98	B4
TALBERT AV	ORA	T	B3
TALBERT LN	SOL	39	B4
TALBOT ST	SDCO	V	A3
TALC CITY RD	INY	70	D1
TALMAGE RD	U	123	D4
TAMALPAIS AV	MAR	38	B5
TAMALPAIS DR	CRTM	140	B1
TAMARACK AV	SDCO	106	B3
TAMARACK RD	SHA	13	C5
TAMARACK RD	SHA	19	C1
TAMARACK RD	TEH	19	C4
TAMARACK LK RD	TRI	12	B3
TAMARACK PK RD	SHA	13	C5
TAMPA AV	LA	178	B3
TAMPA AV	LACO	97	B1
TANABE RD	YUB	33	D1
TANATEA ST	RCO	107	C1
TANK FARM RD	KER	78	A4
TANK FARM RD	SLO	76	B4
TANNERY GLCH RD	TRI	11	D5
TAPADERO ST	CAL	41	A4
TAPIA LN	SBD	90	E2
TAPLIN RD	NAPA	29	C3
TAPO RD	VEN	89	A5
TAPO CANYON RD	VEN	89	A5
TARA AV	KER	69	B5
TAR CANYON RD	KIN	66	E4
TARKE RD	SUT	33	B2
TARPON DR	SIS	4	B3
TASSAJARA RD	MON	64	D2
TATE CREEK RD	SIS	13	A2
TAVERN RD	SDCO	107	B5
TAVERNETTI RD	MON	54	E5
TAVERNETTI RD	MON	55	A5
TAVERNOR RD	SAC	40	B2
TAYLOR AV	KER	78	B1
TAYLOR BLVD	CC	L	E3
TAYLOR BLVD	CC	M	A3
TAYLOR BLVD	CC	38	E5
TAYLOR BLVD	MLBR	144	C5
TAYLOR LN	SIS	5	B4
TAYLOR RD	CC	39	C4
TAYLOR RD	STA	47	C3
TAYLOR ST	SF	143	B2
TAYLOR ST	SJ	152	B2
TAYLORSVL TRANS	PLU	20	D5
TEAFORD SDLE RD	MAD	49	E4
TEAGUE AV	FRCO	57	D2
TEAGUE AV	MON	65	B2
TEAL DR	MOD	7	A5
TEALE RD	KER	78	D4
TEALE RD	KER	79	A4
TEAPOT	TUL	68	C3
TECHNR RBSN RD	SIS	5	A4
TECOLOTE RD	SDCO	V	B3
TECOLOTE RD	SDCO	111	C1
TECOPA HOT SPGS	INY	73	A4
TED ELDER RD	SHA	13	D3
TED KIPF RD	IMP	109	C3
TED KIPF RD	IMP	110	A4
TEDOC RD	TEH	17	D4
TEFFT ST	SLO	76	C5
TEGAN RD	SAC	39	E2
TEGNER RD	MCO	47	D4
TEHACHAPI BLVD	KER	79	D4
TEHACHP-WLW SPG	KER	79	D5
TEHAMA AV	KIN	67	A4
TEHAMA AV	TEH	24	D1
TEHAMA ST	GLE	24	D4
TEHAMA & VNA RD	TEH	24	E1
TEJON RD	LACO	90	C4
TELEGRAPH AV	B	156	B3
TELEGRAPH AV	O	156	B3
TELEGRAPH AV	S	160	A2
TELEGRAPH RD	CAL	40	E5
TELEGRAPH RD	CAL	41	A5
TELEGRAPH RD	LACO	89	A4
TELEGRAPH RD	LACO	98	A2
TELEGRAPH RD	LACO	R	B4
TELEGRAPH RD	MPA	49	B3
TELEGRAPH RD	VEN	88	E4
TELEGRPH CYN RD	SDCO	V	D5
TELEGRPH CYN RD	SDCO	111	D2
TELEGRAPH CK RD	HUM	22	A1
TELEGRAPH MN RD	SBD	83	D3
TELEPHONE RD	SB	86	C1
TELEPHONE RD	VEN	88	B5
TELESCOPE PK RD	RD	10	C4
TELL BLVD	DN	1	D3
TEMESCAL CYN RD	RCO	99	A3
TEMPERANCE AV	FRCO	57	D2
TEMPERANCE AV	FRCO	57	D5
TEMPLE AV	LACO	R	D4
TEMPLE AV	LACO	S	E2
TEMPLE ST	LA	185	C1
TEMPLE ST	LA	186	B2
TEMPLE CITY BL	LACO	R	C3
TEMPLE CREEK	SJCO	40	C5
TEMPLE CREEK	SJCO	47	C1

STREET	CO.	PAGE	GRID
TEMPLE HILLS DR	LAG	201	D2
TEMPLETON RD	SLO	76	A2
TENAJA RD	RCO	99	B5
TENAJA TRUCK TR	RCO	99	B5
TENMILE RD	MEN	30	D4
TENMILE CUTF RD	MEN	30	D4
TENNANT AV	SCL	P	E5
TENNANT AV	SCL	54	D1
TENNANT RD	SIS	4	E5
TENNANT RD	SIS	5	A5
TENNANT LAVA BD	MOD	5	E4
TENNANT LAVA BD	SIS	5	B5
TENNANT MT HRBN	SIS	5	A4
TENNESSEE ST	SBD	99	C2
TENNESSEE ST	VAL	134	C4
TENNESSEE ST E	FRFD	135	C3
TENNYSON RD	ALA	N	E1
TENNYSON RD	ALA	P	A1
TENNYSON RD	ALA	45	E2
TEPUSQUET RD	SB	86	D1
TEQUEPIS CYN RD	SB	87	A3
TERCEIRA RD	MCO	55	E2
TERMINAL RD	AVLN	105	B5
TERMINOUS RD	SAC	39	D4
TERMO GRASSHPPR	LAS	8	A5
TERMO GRASSHPPR	LAS	14	E5
TERRA BELLA ST	LACO	Q	C2
TERRACE	FRCO	58	A3
TERRACE RD	RCO	100	D4
TERRY MILL RD	SHA	13	A5
TERWER RIFFL RD	DN	10	A1
TERWILLIGER RD	RCO	107	C1
TESLA RD	ALA	M	D5
TESLA RD	ALA	P	D1
TESLA RD	ALA	46	C2
TESORO RD	SBD	90	E3
TEST STATION	MNO	43	C5
TEXAS AV	KER	79	E5
TEXAS AV	KER	80	A5
TEXAS RD	STA	47	C2
TEXAS ST	FRFD	135	A3
TEXAS ST	SD	216	B1
TEXAS ST	SDCO	V	B3
TEXAS ST	SDCO	111	D1
TEXAS ST N	SOL	M	A1
TEXAS ST N	SOL	38	E3
TEXAS ST N	FRFD	135	C3
TEXAS HILL	MPA	48	E2
TEXAS HILL RD	YUB	26	A5
TEXAS SPGS RD	SHA	18	B2
THATCHER RD	SHA	19	C2
THATCHER MLL RD	SHA	19	C2
THATCHER RDG RD	BUT	25	D1
THE BRADSHAW TR	RCO	102	A5
THEDA ST	RCO	99	C4
THE INDIAN RD	MOD	8	B3
THEODORE ST	RCO	99	D3
THEODORIC RD	SBD	84	C4
THING RD	SDCO	112	C2
THIRD ST	C	124	B5
THISSELL RD	SOL	39	B2
THOMAS	SON	31	E5
THOMAS	SON	37	E1
THOMAS RD	HUM	16	B5
THOMAS RD	KER	90	C1
THOMAS RD	MCO	55	C2
THOMAS RD	SBT	55	A4
THOMAS RD	SHA	18	B3
THOMAS RD	SHA	19	A1
THOMAS ST	KER	80	A4
THOME RD	YUB	33	D1
THOMES AV	TEH	24	D1
THOMPSON AV	FRCO	57	D3
THOMPSON AV	FRCO	57	D5
THOMPSON BLVD	VENT	175	B2
THOMPSON RD	IMP	109	A5
THOMPSON RD	LAS	14	B4
THOMPSON RD	MNO	43	B4
THOMPSON RD	SBD	81	C5
THOMPSON RD	SLO	76	C5
THOMPSON RD	SUT	33	C3
THOMPSON CYN AV	KER	79	C2
THOMPSON CYN RD	MON	65	B2
THOMSEN RD	SOL	39	C2
THORNBERRY RD	MAD	49	D4
THORNBURG ST	SMA	173	B3
THORNE AV	FRE	165	B4
THORNTON AV	ALA	P	A1
THORNTON AV	ALA	45	E3
THORNTON AV	ALA	46	A3
THORNTON RD	MCO	48	B4
THORNTON RD	SJCO	40	A4
THOUSND OAKS BL	LACO	96	E1
THOUSND OAKS BL	VEN	96	D1
THOUSND PLMS RD	RCO	100	E3
THOUSAND SPGS	SHA	13	D3
THREE CHOP RD	MEN	22	D5
THREE FLAGS HWY	KER	80	D1
THREE PINES CYN	KER	80	B1
THREE SLASHS RD	IMP	110	C2
THRIFT RD	MCO	48	C5
THRUSH DR	SIS	4	B3
THUNDER	SDCO	106	B3
THUNDERBIRD BL	KER	80	C4
THUNDERBIRD RD	SBD	91	C3
THUNDER CYN RD	SLO	75	D2
TIBURON BLVD	MAR	L	B4
TIBURON BLVD	MAR	140	E3
TICE VALLEY BL	CC	L	E4
TICE VALLEY BL	CC	M	A4
TICE VALLEY BL	CC	45	E1
TICINO ST	SB	86	B1
TIEDEMAN RD	STA	47	B2
TIERNEY RD	HUM	16	B3

STREET	CO.	PAGE	GRID
TIERRA BUENA RD	SUT	33	C2
TIERRA DEL SOL	SDCO	112	E2
TIERRA RJADA RD	VEN	88	E5
TIERRA SANTA BL	SDCO	V	C2
TIERRA SANTA BL	SDCO	106	D5
TIFFANY RCH RD	SLO	76	B4
TIGER CREEK RD	SIS	11	D2
TILTON AV	SCL	P	D4
TILTON DR	LACO	89	E3
TIM BELL RD	STA	48	A2
TIMBER COVE RD	SON	37	A1
TIMBER CRATER	SHA	13	D3
TIMBUCTOO RD	YUB	34	A1
TIMM RD	SOL	39	A2
TIMMONS AV	KER	68	B5
TIMMONS RD	SIS	4	B5
TIM MULLEN RD	HUM	16	B1
TIMS RD	SB	86	E2
TIN BARN RD	SON	31	A5
TIN BARN RD	SON	37	A1
TINDALL RCH RD	MEN	31	B2
TINNEMAHA RD	INY	59	E1
TIOGA PASS RD	MPA	42	E5
TIOGA PASS RD	MPA	43	A5
TIOGA PASS RD	MPA	50	A1
TIOGA PASS RD	MPA	63	D3
TIOGA PASS RD	MNO	43	A5
TIOGA PASS RD	TUO	42	E5
TIOGA PASS RD	TUO	50	A1
TIOGA PASS RD	TUO	63	A4
TIONESTA RD	MOD	5	E5
TIONESTA RD	MOD	6	A4
TIONESTA RD	SIS	5	D5
TIPPECANOE ST	SBD	99	C2
TIPTOP RD	MPA	49	C3
TISDALE	SUT	33	B3
TITLOW HILL RD	HUM	10	C5
TITSWORTH RD	IMP	109	C4
TIZON RD	RCO	107	B1
TOBACCO	SJCO	40	C5
TOBIN DR	VAL	134	B1
TODAYANA WY	PLA	34	D2
TODCO RD	KER	69	B5
TODD RD	SON	37	E2
TODD EYMANN RD	FRCO	58	D3
TODD VALLEY	PLA	34	D3
TOEWS AV	MCO	48	D4
TOFT DR	RCO	99	A4
TOKAY COLONY RD	SJCO	40	C4
TOLAND LN	SOL	39	C4
TOLAND RD	VEN	88	C4
TOLAND PARK RD	VEN	88	C4
TOLL GATE WY	BUT	25	C2
TOLL HOUSE RD	FRCO	57	D2
TOLL HOUSE RD	FRCO	58	A2
TOMALES RD	SON	37	E3
TOMALES PETALMA	MAR	37	D3
TOM GREEN MN RD	SHA	18	A1
TOMKI RD	MEN	23	B5
TOMPKNS HILL RD	HUM	15	E2
TOM SHAW RD	HUM	16	B2
TOM WELLS RD	LPAZ	104	A5
TONNER CYN RD	ORA	U	A4
TONZI RD	AMA	40	D2
TOOBY DR	FRFD	135	A3
TOOME CAMP	TEH	24	A2
TOOMES RD	STA	47	C2
TOPA LN	VEN	88	C4
TOPANGA CYN BL	LA	177	B3
TOPANGA CYN BL	LACO	97	B1
TOPAZ LN	MNO	42	E1
TOPAZ RD	SBD	91	B3
TOPEKA DR	LA	178	C4
TOPO RD	MON	65	B1
TOPO VALLEY RD	SBT	65	C1
TOPOCK DAVIS DM	MOH	95	E1
TOPPEN DORFF LN	HUM	15	D2
TORO CANYON RD	SB	87	D4
TORO CREEK RD	SLO	75	E2
TORO CREEK RD	SLO	76	A2
TORRANCE BLVD	LACO	97	D3
TORRANCE BLVD	LACO	S	B2
TORREY PINES RD	SD	211	B2
TORREY PINES RD	SDCO	V	A2
TORREY PINES RD	SDCO	106	C5
TORREY RD N	VEN	88	E4
TORREY RD S	VEN	88	E4
TOTH RD	HUM	22	A1
TOTTEN RD	SHA	13	E4
TOVEY AV	LACO	90	A3
TOWER RD	MCO	48	C4
TOWER RD	SLO	76	B1
TOWER LINE RD	KER	79	A4
TOWNE AV	LACO	U	C2
TOWNSEND RD	IMP	109	C5
TOWNSEND RD	SIS	4	C4
TOWNSEND ST	SBD	91	D1
TOWNSHIP AV	VEN	88	E5
TOWNSHIP AV	VEN	89	A5
TOWNSHIP RD	KLAM	5	B2
TOWNSHIP RD	YUB	34	A1
TOWNSHIP RD N	SUT	33	C2
TOWNSHIP RD S	SUT	33	C3
TOZER ST	MAD	57	A2
TRABUCO RD	ORA	98	D4
TRABUCO RD	ORA	T	E3
TRACTOR AV	FRCO	66	D2
TRACY AV	KER	78	A2
TRACY BLVD	SBD	100	D1
TRACY BLVD	SJCO	39	E5
TRACY BLVD	SJCO	46	E1
TRAGEDY SPGS RD	AMA	35	E5
TRAIL CANYON RD	INY	72	A1
TRAILS END LN	RCO	107	C1

INDEXES

STREET	CO.	PAGE	GRID
TRAILS END RD	SIS	4	C5
TRAILS END CAMP	SBD	96	B5
TRAMPA CYN RD	MON	64	C1
TRAMWAY RD	TEH	19	C4
TRANCAS ST	NAP	133	C2
TRANCAS ST	NAPA	133	D2
TRASK AV	GGR	195	B2
TRASK AV	ORA	T	B3
TRAUTWEIN RD	RCO	99	B3
TRAVIS BL	FRFD	135	B3
TRAVIS BLVD	SOL	L	E1
TRAVIS BLVD	SOL	M	A1
TRAYNHAM RD	COL	33	A3
TREAT BLVD	CC	M	A3
TREAT BLVD	CC	38	E5
TREAT BLVD	CC	39	A5
TREDWAY	SJCO	40	A4
TREFOIL LN	SHA	18	D3
TREMONT RD	SOL	39	C1
TREMONT ST	AVLN	105	B5
TRENTHAM RD	IMP	109	B5
TRES CERITOS AV	RCO	99	D4
TRESTLE GLEN	MAR	45	B1
TRESTLE GLEN RD	O	158	C3
TRETHEWAY RD	SJCO	40	B4
TRIANGLE RD	MPA	49	B3
TRIANGLE RCH RD	MOD	6	D4
TRIANGLE RCH RD	STA	47	D2
TRIMBLE RD	SCL	P	B3
TRIMMER SPGS RD	FRCO	58	A3
TRIMMER SPGS RD	INY	58	C2
TRINDADE RD	MCO	48	B4
TRNIDAD SCNC DR	HUM	9	E4
TRINITY	TEH	18	D5
TRINITY AV	FRCO	56	E3
TRINITY AV	FRCO	57	A4
TRINITY RD	SON	38	B2
TRINITY ST	FRE	165	C4
TRINITY ALPS RD	TRI	11	D5
TRINITY DAM BL	TRI	11	D5
TRINITY DAM BL	TRI	17	E1
TRINITY MTN RD	SHA	12	A5
TRINITY PINE DR	TRI	17	B3
TRIPP FLATS RD	RIV	100	B5
TRIUNFO CYN RD	LACO	96	E1
TRONA RD	SBD	80	E2
TRONA RD	SBD	81	A1
TRONA AIRPRT RD	INY	71	B4
TRONA WLDRSE RD	INY	71	B4
TROPICANA AV	CLK	74	D3
TROPICANA AV	CLK	210	C4
TROWER	MPA	49	A3
TROWER AV	NAP	133	A1
TROY RD	SBD	92	C2
TRUCKEE AV	TEH	24	D1
TRUCKE ARPRT RD	NEV	27	D5
TRUCKE-TAHO ARP	NEV	35	E1
TRUESDALE RD	SLO	76	D1
TRUEX RD	BUT	25	D3
TRUMAN RD	KER	89	D1
TRUMAN MDWS RD	MNO	44	C5
TRUMBULL RD	LAS	21	D2
TRUXTUN AV	BKD	166	B3
TRUXTUN AV	KER	78	D3
TSCHIRKY RD	SIS	5	D2
TUBBS RD	SOL	39	A2
TUCACOTA HLS RD	RCO	99	E5
TUCKER RD	KER	79	C4
TUCKER RD	LAS	21	D5
TUCKER CYN RD	SLO	76	D1
TUCSON AV	KIN	67	D4
TUDOR RD	SUT	33	C3
TUGG WY	CAL	41	A5
TUJUNGA AV	LACO	Q	D3
TUJUNGA CYN BL	LACO	Q	E1
TULARE AV	KER	77	E2
TULARE AV	FRCO	57	C3
TULARE AV	TUL	68	B1
TULARE ST	FRE	165	D4
TULAROSA RD	SB	86	C3
TULE LN	CC	39	C5
TULE LN	GLE	24	E4
TULE RD	COL	33	A3
TULE RD	YOL	39	D2
TULE CYN TK TR	RCO	107	C1
TULE CREEK RD	TRI	17	B2
TULEDAD RD	LAS	8	D5
TULE PEAK RD	RCO	107	B1
TULE SPRING RD	INY	72	A2
TULE SPGS TK TR	SDCO	107	B4
TULIP AV	STA	47	C4
TULLOCH RD	MCO	48	B1
TULLOCH RD	TUO	41	B5
TULLY RD	MDO	162	A2
TULLY RD	SJCO	40	C4
TULLY RD	SCL	P	C3
TULLY RD	SCL	46	B4
TULLY RD	STA	47	C2
TULLY CREEK RD	HUM	10	C3
TUMBLEWEED RD	LACO	90	C4
TUNA CANYON RD	LACO	97	B2
TUNGSTEN RD	MNO	51	D3
TUNGSTEN CTY RD	INY	51	C4
TUNITAS CK RD	SMCO	N	C3
TUNITAS CK RD	SMCO	45	C4
TUNNEL RD	B	156	C4
TUOLUMNE AV	FRCO	56	D4
TUOLUMNE BLVD	MDO	162	A4
TUOLUMNE DR	MLBR	144	B5
TUOLUMNE RD	STA	47	C3
TUOLUMNE ST	SOL	L	D2
TUOLUMNE ST	VAL	134	D2
TUPMAN RD	KER	78	B3
TURK ST	SF	142	A3
TURK ST	SF	143	B5
TURKEY AV	BUT	25	D5
TURKEY FLAT RD	MON	66	D4
TURKEY HILL RD	KLAM	5	E2
TURLOCK AV	SCL	P	E5
TURLOCK AV	SCL	54	D1
TURLOCK RD	MCO	48	B3
TURNBULL CYN RD	LACO	98	B2
TURNBULL CYN RD	LACO	R	D4
TURNELL RD	TEH	18	C4
TURNER AV	BUT	33	C1
TURNER AV	MCO	47	D4
TURNER AV	SBD	U	E2
TURNER AV	SBD	98	E2
TURNER DR	TUL	68	B2
TURNER RD	AMA	40	E2
TURNER RD	MCO	47	D4
TURNER RD	SJCO	39	E4
TURNER RD	SJCO	40	A4
TURNER RD	STA	47	D3
TURNER ISLND RD	MCO	56	A1
TURQUOISE ST	SD	211	A5
TURQUOISE ST	SDCO	V	A2
TURQUOISE ST	SDCO	106	C5
TURRI RD	SLO	75	E3
TURRI RD	SLO	76	A3
TURTLE MTN RD	SBD	95	C4
TURTLE VLY RD	SBD	91	C2
TUSCAN SPGS RD	TEH	18	D4
TUSSING RCH RD	SBD	91	C4
TUSTIN AV	CM	199	C3
TUSTIN AV	NB	199	C3
TUSTIN AV	OR	194	E3
TUSTIN AV	OR	196	E2
TUSTIN AV	ORA	98	C4
TUSTIN AV	ORA	196	E4
TUSTIN AV	ORA	199	C3
TUSTIN AV	SA	196	E4
TUSTIN AV	ORA	T	D2
TU SU LN	INY	51	D4
TUTTLECREEK RD	INY	60	A4
TUTTLETOWN RD	TUO	41	C5
TUXEDO AV N	S	160	C3
TUXFORD ST	LACO	Q	D2
TWEEDY BLVD	LACO	R	A5
TWENTIETH ST	C	124	E5
TWENTY-EIGHT MI	STA	47	E1
TWNTY MULE TEAM	INY	72	A1
TWNTY MULE TEAM	KER	80	C4
TWNTYNINE PALMS	SBD	100	E1
TWNTYNINE PALMS	SBD	101	D1
TWENTY-SIX MILE	STA	47	D1
TWIN RD S	MNO	43	A3
TWIN CITIES RD	SAC	39	E3
TWIN CITIES RD	SAC	40	A3
TWIN LAKES RD	MNO	43	B3
TWIN LAKES RD	TRI	12	B3
TWIN LKS CMPST	ALP	35	E5
TWIN OAKES RD	KER	79	D3
TWIN OAKS VLY	SDCO	106	C3
TWIN PEAKS RD	SDCO	106	D4
TWIN PINES RD	RCO	100	A3
TWIN VALLEY RD	LAK	31	E2
TWIN VIEW BLVD	SHA	18	C2
TWISSELMAN RD	KER	67	B5
TWIST RD	TUO	41	C5
TWIST RD	TUO	48	C1
TWITCHLL ISL RD	SAC	M	D2
TWITCHLL ISL RD	SAC	39	C4
TWO MILE RD	COL	32	D1
TWO MILE RD	SBD	101	B1
TYLER AV	LACO	R	C4
TYLER RD	AMA	40	E1
TYLER RD	TEH	18	D5
TYLER ST	MONT	167	E3
TYLER ST	RCO	99	A3
TYLER ST	RCO	101	B4
TYLER ST	SAL	171	B2
TYLER ST	SDCO	V	D3
TYLER ST	SDCO	111	D1
TYLER FOOT CRSG	NEV	26	B5
TYLER GULCH RD	SIS	3	D4
TYLER ISLAND RD	SAC	M	E2
TYLER ISLAND RD	SAC	39	D4
U			
U ST	FRE	165	E3
UBEHEBE RD	INY	60	E4
UGO ST	MCO	48	A4
UKIAH RD	MEN	31	B2
UKIAH BOONVILLE	MEN	30	E3
UKIAH BOONVILLE	MEN	31	A3
UKONOM LKOUT RD	SIS	2	E5
ULLREY AV	SJCO	47	C1
ULRIC ST	SD	213	D3
ULRIC ST	SDCO	V	B3
ULRIC ST	SDCO	111	C1
UNDERPASS RD	MEN	22	E4
UNDERSTOCK DR	BUT	25	C2
UNDERWOOD LN	INY	51	D4
UNDERWOOD RD	MON	54	C5
UNDERWD MTN RD	TRI	16	E1
UNDINE RD	SJCO	46	E1
UNION AV	BKD	166	E3
UNION AV	KER	166	E5
UNION AV	FRFD	135	C4
UNION AV	SB	86	C1
UNION AV	SCL	P	B4
UNION AV	SCL	46	B5
UNION AV	SOL	38	E3
UNION RD	KER	78	B4
UNION RD	MAN	161	A3
UNION RD	SBT	54	E3
UNION RD	SJCO	47	B1
UNION RD	SLO	76	B1
UNION ST	EUR	121	C2
UNION ST	HUM	15	E1
UNION CITY BLVD	ALA	N	E1
UNION CITY BLVD	ALA	P	A1
UNION CITY BLVD	ALA	45	E3
UNION HILL RD	TRI	17	D2
UNION RIDGE RD	ED	34	E5
UNION SCHOOL RD	SHA	18	C1
UNION SUGAR AV	SB	86	B3
UNITED ST	KER	80	A5
UNIVERSITY AV	ALA	L	D4
UNIVERSITY AV	KER	78	E2
UNIVERSITY AV	PA	147	B2
UNIVERSITY AV	RIV	205	B2
UNIVERSITY AV	RCO	99	B2
UNIVERSITY AV	SAL	171	A4
UNIVERSITY AV	SD	214	D5
UNIVERSITY AV	SD	215	D1
UNIVERSITY AV	SD	216	D1
UNIVERSITY AV	SDCO	V	B3
UNIVERSITY AV	SDCO	111	D1
UNIVERSITY AV	SMCO	N	E2
UNIVERSITY DR	IRV	200	C2
UNIVERSITY DR	ORA	98	C4
UNIVERSITY DR	ORA	T	D4
UPAS ST	SD	216	A1
UPHAM RD	BUT	25	E5
UPHILL RD	SBD	101	A1
UPJOHN RD W	KER	80	D1
UPLAND RD	VEN	88	C5
UPPER TER	AVLN	105	B5
UPPER BEAR RIV	HUM	15	D3
UPPR COUGR FIRE	SIS	4	D5
UPPR COUGR FIRE	SIS	12	D1
UPPER DIVISN CK	INY	59	E2
UPPER DORRAY RD	CAL	41	A2
UPPER FALL RD	SIS	13	A2
UPPER LK CTY RD	MOD	7	D5
UPR MAD RIV RD	TRI	17	A4
UPPER PALRMO RD	BUT	25	D5
UPPER SHOTGN RD	SHA	12	C4
UPPER S FORK RD	TRI	16	E2
UPPR SUMMRS MDW	MNO	43	B3
UPPER TOBY RCH	HUM	16	C5
UPPER WILLOW CK	SIS	4	C3
UPTON RD	AMA	40	E1
USAL RD	MEN	22	B2
USFS CAMP RD	TRI	17	A1
USONA RD	MPA	49	C4
USTICK RD	STA	47	C3
UTAH AV	SSF	144	C1
UTAH DR	INY	70	E1
UTAH ST	FRFD	135	B3
UTAH TR	SBD	101	C1
UTAH MINE RD	BUT	25	D2
UTICA AV	KIN	67	D4
UTICA PWRHSE RD	CAL	41	C4
UVAS RD	SCL	54	C1
UXMAL	BAJA	112	B4
V			
V ST	MER	170	A4
VADNEY AV	TEH	24	E2
VAIL	SJCO	39	E3
VAIL RD	IMP	109	A3
VAIRA RANCH RD	AMA	40	D2
VALDOR RD	TRI	17	C1
VALENCIA AV	LACO	89	B4
VALENCIA AV	ORA	98	C3
VALENCIA AV	ORA	T	D1
VALENCIA BLVD	TUL	58	C5
VALENCIA BLVD	TUL	68	C1
VALENCIA RD	SCR	54	B2
VALENSIN RD	SAC	40	A3
VALENTINE AV	FRCO	57	C4
VALENTINE AV	FRCO	67	C1
VALERIA AV	FRCO	56	B2
VALERIO ST	STB	174	B3
VALK RD	STA	47	E2
VALLECITO ST	SHA	18	C1
VALLECITOS RD	ALA	P	C1
VALLECITOS RD	ALA	46	B2
VALLE VISTA AV	VAL	134	C3
VALLE VISTA RD	SBD	101	B1
VALLEY AV	ALA	M	B5
VALLEY AV	ALA	P	B1
VALLEY AV	ALA	46	B2
VALLEY BLVD	LACO	97	E2
VALLEY BLVD	LACO	98	B2
VALLEY BLVD	LACO	R	C3
VALLEY BLVD	SBD	99	A2
VALLEY PKWY	SDCO	106	D3
VALLEY RD	ED	34	C5
VALLEY RD	KER	80	C3
VALLEY RD	MEN	23	A5
VALLEY RD	PLA	34	A3
VALLEY RD	SAC	34	C5
VALLEY RD E	SB	87	D4
VALLEY RD W	MOD	8	B3
VALLEY CTR RD	SBD	92	B1
VALLEY CTR RD	SDCO	106	E3
VALLEY CIR BL	LACO	97	B1
VALLEY CTOFF RD	LAS	14	B3
VALLEY FORD RD	SON	37	D3
VLY FRD/FRNKLN- -MARSH RD	MAR	37	D3
VLY FRD/FRNKLN- -SCHOOL RD	MAR	37	D3
VALLEY HOME RD	STA	47	D1
VALLEY SAGE RD	LACO	89	D4
VALLEY VIEW DR	CAL	41	C3
VALLEY VIEW DR	SBD	102	C1
VALLEY VIEW RD	JKSN	3	E1
VALLEY VIEW RD	SBD	91	C1
VALLEY VIEW ST	ORA	98	B3
VALLEY VIEW ST	ORA	T	B2
VALLEY VW LKOUT	TEH	24	A2
VALLEY VISTA BL	LA	178	E5
VALLEY WELLS RD	INY	71	B4
VALLEY WELLS RD	SBD	81	C5
VALLEY WEST RD	KER	78	A4
VALLOMBROSA AV	BUT	25	B3
VALLOMBROSA AV	BUT	124	D4
VALLOMBROSA AV	C	124	D4
VALOS RD	KER	78	E5
VALPARAISO AV	SMCO	N	D2
VALPARAISO AV	SCL	45	D4
VALPICO RD	SJCO	46	E2
VALPREDO AV	KER	78	D5
VAL VERDE	PLA	34	B4
VALYERMO	LACO	90	C4
VAN ALDEN AV	LA	178	C4
VAN ALLEN	SJCO	40	C5
VAN ALLEN	SJCO	47	C1
VAN ARSDALE RD	MEN	23	B5
VAN BRMMR LKOUT	SIS	5	B4
VAN BUREN BLVD	RCO	99	A2
VAN BUREN ST	MONT	167	E4
VAN BUREN ST	RCO	101	A4
VANCE AV	HUM	15	D5
VAN CLIFF	MCO	47	E5
VANDEGRIFT BLVD	SDCO	106	B2
VANDEGRIFT RD	SDCO	106	B2
VANDEN RD	SOL	39	A3
VANDENBERG RD	SB	86	B2
VANDER LINDN RD	IMP	112	C3
VANDER POEL RD	IMP	112	A3
VANDER VEER RD	RCO	101	C5
VAN DOLLEN RD	SLO	66	B5
VAN DUSEN CYN	SBD	92	A5
VAN DUZEN RD	TRI	16	E4
VAN DUZEN RD E	TRI	16	E3
VAN GORDN CK RD	SLO	75	C1
VAN LOON CUTOFF	MNO	51	D2
VAN NESS AV	FRE	165	D3
VAN NESS AV	FRCO	57	C3
VAN NESS AV	LACO	Q	D5
VAN NESS AV	SF	143	A4
VAN NESS AV	SFCO	L	B4
VAN NESS AV	SFCO	45	C1
VAN NESS AV S	SF	142	C4
VAN NESS RD	TRI	12	A5
VAN NUYS BLVD	LACO	89	C5
VAN NUYS BLVD	LACO	97	C1
VAN NUYS BLVD	LACO	Q	C1
VANOWEN ST	BUR	179	B2
VANOWEN ST	LA	177	A2
VANOWEN ST	LA	178	B2
VANOWEN ST	LA	179	B2
VAN SICKLE RD	SOL	39	A4
VARGAS RD	ALA	P	B1
VARGAS RD	ALA	46	B3
VARNER RD	RCO	100	D3
VARNI RD	SCR	54	B2
VASCO RD	ALA	M	D5
VASCO RD	ALA	46	C2
VASCO RD	CC	M	D4
VASCO RD	CC	46	C1
VASQUEZ CYN RD	LACO	89	C4
VASQUEZ CK RD	SBT	55	D4
VASSAR AV	MCO	48	C5
VASSAR ST	RENO	130	C4
VAUGHN AV	MCO	48	B4
VAUGHN RD	RCO	108	E1
VAUGHN RD	SOL	39	B2
VAWTER RD	COL	32	E3
VAWTER RANCH RD	RCO	99	E5
VEDDER RD	SHA	13	C5
VEE BEE ST	RCO	100	E3
VENCILL RD	IMP	112	C3
VENDEL RD	IMP	108	E4
VENICE BLVD	LA	183	C5
VENICE BLVD	LA	184	C3
VENICE BLVD	LA	185	C3
VENICE BLVD	LA	187	C2
VENICE BLVD	LA	188	A1
VENICE BLVD	LACO	97	C2
VENICE BLVD	LACO	Q	C4
VENTURA AV	FRCO	57	D3
VENTURA AV	MAD	56	D1
VENTURA AV	VEN	88	A5
VENTURA AV	VENT	175	B2
VENTURA BLVD	LA	177	D4
VENTURA BLVD	LA	178	A4
VENTURA BLVD	LACO	97	C1
VENTURA FRWY	BUR	179	C5
VENTURA FRWY	LA	177	C4
VENTURA FRWY	LA	178	B4
VENTURA FRWY	LA	179	C5
VENTURA FRWY	LACO	97	A1
VENTURA FRWY	VENT	175	C2
VENTURA FRWY	VEN	88	A5
VENTURA FRWY	VEN	96	C1
VENTURA RD	MCO	48	B5
VENTURA RD	OXN	176	A4
VENTURA RD	VEN	96	B1
VENTURA ST	FRE	165	D5
VENTURA ST	VEN	88	D4
VENTURE VLY RD	SDCO	107	D3
VENZKE RD	SHA	18	D3
VERA AV	KER	80	D1
VERANO AV	SON	132	C3
VERBENA AV	C	124	E2
VERBENA AV	SBD	91	B3
VERBENA DR	RCO	100	D2
VERDE AV	MCO	47	D4
VERDEMNT RCH RD	SBD	99	B1
VERDE SCHOOL RD	IMP	112	C3
VERDI PEAK RD	SIE	27	E4
VERDUGO AV	BUR	179	B4
VERDUGO AV	LACO	Q	D3
VERDUGO BLVD	LACO	R	A2
VERDUGO LN	KER	78	C2
VERDUGO RD	LACO	R	A3
VERMICULITE MN	SBD	100	E2
VERMONT AV	ANA	193	C3
VERMONT AV	LA	182	B5
VERMONT AV	LA	185	C5
VERMONT AV	LACO	97	D3
VERMONT AV	LACO	S	C2
VERMONT CYN RD	LA	182	B2
VERNON AV	LACO	97	D2
VERNON AV	LACO	Q	E4
VERNON AV	LACO	U	A1
VERNON RD	SUT	33	D4
VERSAILLES AV	A	159	A2
VESTA ST	SDCO	111	D1
VESTA ST	SDCO	V	C4
VESTAL RD	TEH	18	A4
VETERAN AV	LACO	Q	C5
VETERANS HALL	TRI	10	E5
VIA CAPRI	SD	211	A3
VIA DE LA VALLE	SDCO	106	C4
VIA DEL REY	MONT	167	D4
VIA DEL REY	MON	53	E3
VIADUCT BLVD	SBDO	207	B2
VIA GAYUBA	MONT	167	D4
VIA PARAISO	MONT	167	D4
VIA RANCHO PKWY	SDCO	106	D4
VIA SECO ST	SBD	92	A3
VIA VERDE	LACO	U	A2
VICHY SPGS RD	MEN	31	B2
VICKREY LN	SOL	38	E2
VICTOR AV	SHA	18	C2
VICTOR RD	SJCO	40	B4
VICTOR ST	KER	80	D1
VICTORIA AV	RCO	99	A3
VICTORIA AV	RIV	205	C4
VICTORIA CT	KER	79	C4
VICTORIA DR	SDCO	107	B5
VICTORIA DR	SHA	18	B2
VICTORIA ST	LACO	97	E3
VICTORIA ST	LACO	S	C1
VICTORIA ST	ORA	T	C4
VICTORIA ST	SM	199	A2
VICTORIA ST	STB	174	B4
VICTORY AV	STA	47	D1
VICTORY BLVD	BUR	179	B2
VICTORY BLVD	LA	177	C2
VICTORY BLVD	LA	178	B3
VICTORY BLVD	LA	179	B2
VICTORY BLVD	LACO	97	D1
VICTORY BLVD	LACO	Q	C2
VICTORY HWY	CC	M	C3
VICTORY HWY	CC	39	C5
VICTORY HWY	SAC	M	D1
VICTORY PL	BUR	179	D2
VICTORY PL	LACO	Q	D2
VICTORY RD	SJCO	47	D1
VIEJAS GRADE	SDCO	107	B5
VIERRA RD	YUB	26	A5
VIEUDELOU AV	AVLN	104	B4
VIEW DR	TUL	58	B4
VIEW LAND RD	LAS	21	D3
VILAS RD	BUT	25	C2
VILLA AV	EC	217	C1
VILLA AV	SR	139	D3
VILLA RD	IMP	109	B5
VILLA ST	SAL	171	B3
VILLA CREEK RD	SLO	75	D2
VILLAGE DR	AMA	40	D3
VILLAGE RD	SDCO	106	C5
VLLA L JOLLA DR	SD	211	C1
VLLA MANUCHA RD	STA	47	C4
VILLA PARK RD	ORA	T	E2
VINA RD	TEH	24	E2
VINCENT AV	LACO	R	E3
VINCENT RD	MCO	47	E3
VINCENT RD	MCO	48	A3
VINCENT RD	STA	47	E3
VINCENT RD	STA	48	A3
VINE AV	MCO	48	B4
VINE AV	SJCO	47	D1
VINE ST	LA	181	D5
VINE ST	LACO	Q	D3
VINE ST	SDCO	V	E2
VINE ST	SDCO	107	A5
VINE ST	SJ	152	B4
VINE WY	KER	79	C1
VINE HILL RD	SCR	P	B5
VINE HILL RD	SCR	54	A1
VINELAND AV	FRCO	57	A4
VINELAND AV	LACO	97	D1
VINELAND AV	LACO	Q	D2
VINELAND RD	KER	78	E4
VINEWOOD AV	MCO	47	E4
VINEWOOD AV	MCO	48	A4
VINEYARD AV	ALA	M	C5
VINEYARD AV	ALA	P	C1
VINEYARD AV	ALA	46	B2
VINEYARD AV	OXN	176	D1
VINEYARD AV	SBD	98	E2
VINEYARD AV	SBD	U	E3
VINEYARD AV	VEN	176	D1
VINEYARD DR	SLO	75	E1
VINEYARD DR	SLO	76	A1
VINEYARD RD	PLA	34	A5
VINEYARD RD	SJCO	40	A2
VINEYARD RD	STA	47	B3

272
VINEYARD RD
STREET INDEX
WILDWOOD RD

STREET	CO.	PAGE	GRID
VINEYARD RD	YUB	34	A2
VINEYARD WY	MCO	56	B1
VINEYARD CYN RD	MON	66	B4
VINNUM RD	HUM	16	B4
VINTON GULCH RD	BUT	25	D3
VINTON LOYALTON	PLU	27	D3
VIOLA AV	TEH	24	D2
VIOLA MINERAL	TEH	19	C3
VIRGIL AV	LACO	Q	E4
VIRGINIA	SBD	92	D5
VIRGINIA AV	KIN	67	E4
VIRGINIA AV	MDO	162	B2
VIRGINIA RD	LACO	R	B3
VIRGINIA RD	STA	47	E2
VIRGINIA RD	STA	48	A2
VIRGINIA RD	YUB	33	E1
VIRGINIA ST	RCO	99	D3
VIRGINIA ST N	RENO	130	B2
VIRGINIA ST S	RENO	130	B3
VIRGINIA LK RD	MNO	43	B4
VIRGINIATOWN RD	PLA	34	B3
VISALIA RD	FRCO	58	D4
VISALIA RD	TUL	68	C1
VISTA AV	MCO	48	D5
VISTA AV	RCO	98	E1
VISTA AV	SBD	98	D1
VISTA LN	LAS	21	B4
VISTA RD	SBD	91	B2
VISTA WY	SDCO	106	B3
VISTA CHINO	PMSP	206	A2
VISTA CHINO	RCO	100	D3
VISTA DEL MAR	LACO	97	C2
VISTA DL MAR BL	ELS	189	A4
VISTA DL MAR BL	LACO	Q	C5
VISTA DEL VALLE	LA	182	B1
VISTA DE ORO	RCO	100	E3
VISTA ENCINA AV	MDO	162	D3
VISTA GRANDE DR	KER	79	D1
VISTA MINE RD	IMP	110	A4
VIVIAN RD	STA	47	C3
VLASNIK RD	KER	77	E2
VOGEL RD	IMP	111	E3
VOGEL RD	KER	79	D5
VOLCANO CIR	BUT	25	B3
VOLCANO PIONEER	AMA	41	A2
VOLCANOVILLE RD	ED	34	E3
VOLLEY RD	PLA	34	C3
VOLTA RD	MCO	55	D1
VOLTAIRE ST	SDCO	V	A3
VOLTAIRE ST	SDCO	111	C1
VON GLAHN	SJCO	47	C1
VOORHESS RD	MCO	48	D5
VORDEN RD	SAC	M	D1
VORDEN RD	SAC	39	D3
VOTAW RD	AMA	40	E1
VULCAN MINE RD	SBD	84	A5
VULCAN MINE RD	SBD	94	A1
W			
WAALEW RD	SBD	91	C3
W A BARR RD	SIS	12	C2
WABASH AV	SBD	99	D2
WABASH BLVD	SD	214	C5
WABASH BLVD	SD	216	C5
WABASH BLVD	SDCO	111	D1
WABASH BLVD	SDCO	V	C5
WACHTEL WY	SAC	34	B5
WACKERMAN RD	TEH	24	C2
WADDELL ST	TUL	68	C2
WADDINGTON RD	HUM	15	E2
WADE AV	MCO	48	E5
WADLEIGH RD	COL	32	D1
WAGNER	SJCO	47	C1
WAGNER AV	ANA	194	A3
WAGNER AV	COL	32	E3
WAGON RD	BUT	25	C2
WAGON WHEEL	SBD	101	A1
WAGSTAFF RD	BUT	25	C3
WAHL RD	IMP	112	A3
WAINWRIGHT RD	MCO	47	D4
WAKEFIELD	FRCO	58	A4
WALCH AV	TEH	24	E2
WALDO RD	YUB	34	A2
WALERGA	PLA	33	E5
WALGROVE AV	LA	187	C1
WALKER DR	SHA	13	D4
WALKER PL	MNO	51	C1
WALKER RD	DN	1	E3
WALKER RD	IMP	108	E3
WALKER RD	LAS	14	C3
WALKER RD	MEN	23	A5
WALKER RD	MEN	31	A1
WALKER RD	NAPA	32	B5
WALKER RD	SBD	92	C5
WALKER RD	SIS	3	C3
WALKER RD	SON	37	E3
WALKER ST	GLE	24	D3
WALKER ST	ORA	T	B2
WALKER WY	IMP	110	B5
WALKER BASIN RD	KER	79	C3
WALKER CREEK RD	INY	70	B2
WALKER CREEK RD	SIS	3	B3
WALKR LANDNG RD	SAC	M	D1
WALKR LANDNG RD	SAC	39	D3
WALKER MINE RD	PLU	26	E1
WALKER MINE RD	SHA	18	B1
WALKER PLAINS	BUT	25	E2
WALKUP RD	COL	32	B1
WALL RD	SJCO	40	C4
WALLACE AV	VAL	134	D4
WALLACE RD	KER	78	C1
WALLACE RD	SON	37	E2
WALLACE RD	SON	38	A2

STREET	CO.	PAGE	GRID
WALLACE CK RD	SON	37	D1
WALLEN RD	TEH	18	D4
WALLER ST	SF	141	E4
WALLER ST	SF	142	A4
WALLIS RD	STA	48	A3
WALLY HILL RD	CAL	41	B4
WALMORT RD	SAC	40	A2
WALNUT AV	CC	M	A3
WALNUT AV	CC	38	E5
WALNUT AV	FRE	165	C5
WALNUT AV	FRCO	57	C4
WALNUT AV	LACO	Q	E2
WALNUT AV	MCO	48	A4
WALNUT AV	ORA	T	E3
WALNUT AV	STA	47	C3
WALNUT AV	STA	47	D1
WALNUT AV	TUL	68	B1
WALNUT AV	U	123	B3
WALNUT AV	YUB	33	D2
WALNUT BLVD	CC	M	A4
WALNUT BLVD	CC	M	D4
WALNUT BLVD	CC	39	C5
WALNUT BLVD	CC	46	C1
WALNUT DR	COL	32	D2
WALNUT DR	HUM	15	E1
WALNUT DR	NAPA	29	D4
WALNUT DR	SJCO	40	C4
WALNUT LN	GLE	25	A4
WALNUT RD	TEH	24	D2
WALNUT ST	ANA	193	B4
WALNUT ST	C	124	A5
WALNUT ST	ORA	T	C1
WALNUT ST	PAS	190	B3
WALNUT ST	TEH	18	C5
WALNUT ST	VAL	134	C1
WALNUT GROVE AV	LACO	R	C4
WALNUT GROVE RD	SJCO	39	E3
WALSER RD	KER	79	C2
WALTERS RD	LAS	14	C3
WALTERS RD	SOL	39	A3
WALTERS CAMP RD	IMP	110	C2
WALTERS MINE RD	BUT	26	B3
WALTHERS RD	SOL	M	A1
WALTON AV	SUT	33	C2
WALTON AV	SUT	125	A5
WALTZ RD	PLA	33	E3
WAMBLE RD	STA	47	E1
WAMBLE RD	STA	48	A1
WANGENHEIM RD	STA	47	C4
WARD AV	STA	47	B4
WARD RD	HUM	10	B5
WARD RD	LACO	89	E4
WARD RD	MCO	55	E1
WARD CREEK RD	PLU	26	E1
WARD LAKE RD	LAS	21	B3
WARDLOW RD	LACO	98	A3
WARDLOW RD	LACO	S	E2
WARDLOW RD	LACO	T	A2
WARDROBE AV	MCO	48	B4
WARDS FERRY RD	TUO	41	D5
WARDS FERRY RD	TUO	48	D1
WARE RD	COL	32	E2
WARE RD	IMP	112	B4
WARING RD	SDCO	V	C3
WARING RD	SDCO	111	D1
WARING RD	STA	47	E3
WARM SPRINGS BL	ALA	P	B2
WARM SPGS BLVD	ALA	46	B3
WARM SPRINGS RD	INY	51	D4
WARM SPRINGS RD	SON	38	B2
WARNER AV	FTNV	197	D2
WARNER AV	ORA	98	B4
WARNER AV	ORA	T	C3
WARNER AV	ORA	T	E3
WARNER AV	SA	197	D2
WARNER AV	SA	198	A1
WARNER AV	TUS	198	D2
WARNER RD S	LAS	8	C3
WARNER RD W	MOD	8	C1
WARNER ST	C	124	A3
WARNERVILLE RD	STA	47	E2
WARNERVILLE RD	STA	48	A2
WARREGARD RD	CAL	41	B3
WARREN AV	RCO	99	D4
WARREN AV	TEH	18	C4
WARREN FRWY	ALA	45	D1
WARREN FRWY	O	156	E5
WARREN RD	CAL	40	D4
WARREN RD	RCO	99	D5
WARREN RD	RCO	99	D4
WARREN VISTA AV	SBD	100	E1
WASCO WY	KER	78	A3
WASCO POND RD	KER	68	B5
WASHBURN WY	KLAM	5	B1
WASHINGTON AV	RCO	99	C5
WASHINGTON AV	SBD	99	B2
WASHINGTON AV	SDCO	V	E3
WASHINGTON AV	SDCO	106	E5
WASHINGTON AV	SA	195	D3
WASHINGTON AV	SA	196	A3
WASHINGTON BLVD	ALA	P	B2
WASHINGTON BLVD	CUL	183	D5
WASHINGTON BLVD	CUL	187	C3
WASHINGTON BLVD	CUL	188	A2
WASHINGTON BLVD	DN	1	D4
WASHINGTON BLVD	LA	183	D5
WASHINGTON BLVD	LA	184	D4
WASHINGTON BLVD	LA	185	B4
WASHINGTON BLVD	LA	186	C5
WASHINGTON BLVD	LA	187	A3
WASHINGTON BLVD	LACO	97	E2
WASHINGTON BLVD	LACO	98	A2
WASHINGTON BLVD	LACO	R	B2
WASHINGTON BLVD	LACO	R	C4

STREET	CO.	PAGE	GRID
WASHINGTON BLVD	MCO	47	E4
WASHINGTON BLVD	MCO	48	A4
WASHINGTON BLVD	PAS	190	A2
WASHINGTON PL	CUL	188	A2
WASHINGTON PL	LA	188	A2
WASHINGTON PL	SD	213	C5
WASHINGTON RD	MCO	56	B1
WASHINGTON RD	NEV	26	D5
WASHINGTON RD	SBD	92	A3
WASHINGTON RD	STA	47	D3
WASHINGTON ST	SB	87	C1
WASHINGTON ST	FRCO	66	D3
WASHINGTON ST	LA	187	B3
WASHINGTON ST	MONT	167	E4
WASHINGTON ST	RCO	99	B3
WASHINGTON ST	RCO	100	E4
WASHINGTON ST	RIV	99	D5
WASHINGTON ST	SD	213	D5
WASHINGTON ST	SD	215	C1
WASHINGTON ST	SDCO	V	B3
WASHINGTON ST	SDCO	111	C1
WASHINGTON ST	SCLR	151	C3
WASHINGTON ST	SNRA	163	B2
WASHINGTON ST	S	160	C5
WASHINGTON ST	TUO	163	B2
WASHINGTON ST E	SON	L	A1
WASHINGTON ST E	SON	38	A3
WASHOE	FRCO	56	C4
WASHOE AV	FRCO	56	C3
WASIOJA RD	SB	77	C5
WASIOJA RD	SB	87	B1
WATER LN	SMCO	N	C4
WATER ST	AMA	40	E2
WATER ST	SC	169	D2
WATER ST	SCR	54	A2
WATER CANYON RD	KER	80	B3
WATER CANYON RD	KER	79	C5
WATERFRONT RD	CC	L	E3
WATERFRONT RD	CC	M	A3
WATERFRONT RD	CC	154	E1
WATERLOO LN	DGL	36	C3
WATERLOO RD	SJCO	40	B5
WATERMAN AV	SBD	99	C2
WATERMAN AV	SBD	207	E3
WATERMAN AV	SBDO	207	E3
WATERMAN BLVD	FRFD	135	A2
WATERMAN RD	AMA	40	D2
WATERMAN RD	SAC	40	A2
WATERS RD	VEN	88	D5
WATERS END RD	SLO	76	C4
WATERTOWN RD	CAL	40	E3
WATER TROUGH RD	SON	37	D2
WATKINS DR	RCO	99	B2
WATKINS RD	TEH	24	D2
WATKINS TR	KER	79	C5
WATKINSON RD	SJCO	40	B3
WATMAUGH RD	SON	L	B1
WATSON RD	MEN	31	B2
WATSONVILLE RD	SCL	P	D5
WATSONVILLE RD	SCL	54	C1
WATT AV	SAC	34	A5
WATT AV	SAC	40	A1
WATT LN	BUT	25	C5
WATTENBURG RD	MEN	23	A3
WATTRSN TROUGHS	MNO	51	B2
WATTS AV	SUT	33	D3
WATTS DR	KER	79	C3
WATTS VALLEY RD	FRCO	57	E3
WATTS VALLEY RD	FRCO	58	A3
WAUCOBA SALINE	INY	60	C2
WAUKEENA RD	YOL	39	D2
WAVERLY	SBD	91	D1
WAVERLY	SJCO	40	D5
WAY RD	MCO	55	E1
WAYBUR RD	SUT	33	C3
WEAVER CREEK E	TRI	17	D1
WEAVER CT	KER	79	D3
WEAVER RD	IMP	109	A4
WEAVER HILLS DR	RCO	107	A1
WEAVERVLL SCOTT	TRI	12	A2
WEAVERVLL SCOTT	TRI	11	D5
WEAVERVLL SCOTT	TRI	11	E3
WEBB RD	IMP	109	C5
WEBB RD	SHA	18	D3
WEBB RD	SUT	33	C4
WEBER AV	FRE	165	A2
WEBER AV	S	160	C5
WEBER RD	SOL	39	B2
WEBSTER AV	RCO	99	C3
WEBSTER RD	SBD	91	E1
WEBSTER ST	A	157	E5
WEBSTER ST	ALA	45	D1
WEBSTER ST	FRFD	135	B4
WEBSTER ST	O	158	A3
WEDEL AV	KER	77	E1
WEED RD	IMP	112	A4
WEEDPATCH HWY	KER	78	E3
WEEDS POINT RD	YUB	26	C4
WEEKS RD	SCL	P	C5
WEEMASOUL RD	TEH	18	A5
WEGIS RD	KER	78	C3
WEIMAR CROSS RD	PLA	34	C3
WEINERT RD	IMP	109	A5
WEIR AV	MCO	47	E4
WEIR CANYON RD	ORA	U	C5
WEIR CANYON RD	ORA	98	D3
WEISS RD	SUT	33	B2
WEISER RD	KER	77	C1
WEITCHER RD	MOD	14	E1
WELCH CT	CAL	41	B5
WELCOME AV	KER	80	D1
WELDON	FRCO	58	A3
WELLBARN AV	FRCO	57	E1
WELLOCK RD	TRI	17	D1

STREET	CO.	PAGE	GRID
WELLS AV	RENO	130	C3
WELLS AV N	RENO	130	C2
WELLS DR	LA	178	C4
WELLS LN	SJCO	40	B4
WELLS RD	COL	32	D1
WELLS RD	MAD	49	C5
WELLS RD	RCO	103	D4
WELLS RD	VEN	88	B5
WELLSFORD RD	STA	47	D2
WELLSONA RD	SLO	76	A1
WELTY RD	STA	47	A3
WENDEL RD	LAS	21	D3
WENGLER HILL RD	SHA	19	A2
WENTE ST	ALA	P	C1
WENTE ST	ALA	46	C2
WENTWORTH ST	LACO	89	D5
WENTWORTH ST	LACO	Q	D1
WENTWTH SPGS RD	ED	34	E3
WENTWTH SPGS RD	ED	35	B3
WERICK RD	RCO	99	A3
WESCOTT RD	COL	33	A2
WEST AV	FRE	165	A1
WEST AV	FRCO	57	C4
WEST AV	FRCO	67	C1
WEST AV	RCO	110	C1
WEST DR	RCO	100	D2
WEST LN	S	160	E1
WEST LN	SJCO	40	A4
WEST LN	MCO	48	B4
WEST LN	SJCO	160	E1
WEST RD	COL	33	A3
WEST RD	LACO	R	D5
WEST RD	MEN	31	B1
WEST RD	STA	47	C4
WEST ST	ANA	193	B4
WEST ST	EUR	121	E1
WEST ST	O	157	E2
WEST ST	ORA	T	C2
WEST ST	TUL	68	A2
WESTBOROUGH	SMCO	N	B1
WESTBROOK LN	DN	1	E3
WESTCLIFF DR	NB	199	C4
WEST COAST RD	HUM	16	C5
W END OREGN MTN	TRI	17	C1
WESTERN AV	KER	78	A2
WESTERN AV	LA	182	A4
WESTERN AV	LA	185	A5
WESTERN AV	LACO	97	D3
WESTERN AV	LACO	Q	D5
WESTERN AV	LACO	Q	E2
WESTERN AV	LACO	S	C3
WESTERN AV	ORA	T	B2
WESTERN CYN RD	LA	182	A3
WESTERN HILL RD	RCO	100	B5
WESTERN MINE	LAK	32	A5
WESTRN MINERALS	KER	78	A5
WESTFALL	MPA	49	C3
WESTFALL W	MPA	49	A4
WESTGATE AV	HUM	9	E3
WESTGATE DR	HUM	15	E1
WESTGATE DR	NAPA	38	D2
WESTHAVEN DR	HUM	9	E4
WESTLAKE BLVD	VEN	96	E1
WEST LAWN AV	FRCO	57	B4
WEST LAWN AV	FRCO	57	B5
WESTMINSTER AV	GGR	195	B3
WESTMINSTER AV	ORA	98	A4
WESTMINSTER AV	ORA	T	A3
WESTMINSTER AV	SA	195	B3
WESTMORELAND RD	IMP	108	E5
WESTON RD	TEH	24	B2
WESTOVER DR	TEH	18	D5
WESTOVER DR	TEH	24	D1
WEST PORTAL RD	MNO	50	D1
WESTRIDGE RD	TRI	17	B3
WESTSIDE BLVD	MCO	47	E4
WESTSIDE BLVD	MCO	48	A4
WESTSIDE FRWY	FRCO	56	B4
WESTSIDE FRWY	FRCO	66	E2
WEST SIDE FRWY	KER	77	D1
WEST SIDE FRWY	KER	78	D4
WESTSIDE FRWY	KIN	67	B4
WESTSIDE FRWY	MCO	55	D1
WESTSIDE FRWY	STA	47	B3
WEST SIDE HWY	INY	72	A1
WEST SIDE HWY	KER	67	B5
WEST SIDE HWY	KER	78	A4
WESTSIDE RD	IMP	111	E3
WEST SIDE RD	JOS	2	C1
WEST SIDE RD	LAS	8	A5
WESTSIDE RD	MOD	7	B3
WESTSIDE RD	MOD	8	A2
WESTSIDE RD	SHA	18	B1
WESTSIDE RD	SIE	27	B3
WESTSIDE RD	SON	37	D1
WSIDE POTTR VLY	MEN	31	B1
WESTWOOD BLVD	LA	183	A4
WESTWOOD BLVD	LACO	Q	C4
WESTWOOD ST	TUL	68	D3
WET MEADOW RD	MNO	50	E1
WETMORE RD	ALA	P	C1
WETMORE RD	ALA	46	C2
WEYER RD	STA	47	E2
WEYMOUTH BLUFF	HUM	15	E2
WHEALAN RD	MCO	48	D5
WHEATLAND RD	SUT	33	E3
WHEDBEE DR	SOL	38	E3
WHEELER RD	IMP	108	E5
WHEELER RD	SBD	91	C2
WHEELER CYN RD	VEN	88	B5
WHEELER NURSERY	SHA	12	E5
WHEELER RIDGE RD	KER	78	E5
WHEEL GULCH RD	TRI	17	B1
WHEELOCK RD	BUT	25	C3

STREET	CO.	PAGE	GRID
WHIPPLE AV	SMCO	N	D2
WHIPPLE RD	ALA	P	A1
WHISKEY CK RD	COL	32	E3
WHISKEY CK RD	SHA	18	B2
WHSKEY SLIDE RD	CAL	41	B3
WHISLER RD	KER	78	B1
WHITAKER BLF RD	MAR	37	D3
WHITE AV	LACO	U	C2
WHITE DR	BUT	25	B4
WHITE LN	KER	78	D3
WHITE LN	NAPA	29	C3
WHITE LN	SJCO	40	B5
WHITE RD	COL	33	A3
WHITE RD	MCO	47	D3
WHITE RD	MON	66	C4
WHITE RD	SBD	91	A4
WHITE RD	SCL	P	C3
WHITE RD	SCL	46	B4
WHITE COTTGE RD	NAPA	29	C2
WHITE COTTGE RD	NAPA	38	B1
WHITE CRANE RD	MCO	47	E4
WHITE CRANE RD	MCO	48	A4
WHITEHORSE RD	MOD	13	E2
WHITEHORSE RD	MOD	14	A2
WHITEHURST RD	SCL	54	C2
WHITE MTN RD	INY	51	E4
WHITE MTN RD	INY	60	D4
WHITE OAK DR	SHA	18	C3
WHITE PINE LN	SB	86	E2
WHITE PINE LN	SB	87	A2
WHITEPINE ST	SIS	4	B3
WHITE RIVER RD	KER	69	A5
WHITE ROCK RD	ED	40	C1
WHITE ROCK RD	MPA	49	A4
WHITE ROCK RD	MPA	48	E5
WHITE ROCK RD	MCO	48	E5
WHITE ROCK RD	SAC	40	A1
WHITE ROCK RD	SHA	17	C3
WHTE ROCK LK RD	NEV	27	B5
WHITES BRDGE AV	FRCO	56	D3
WHITES BRDGE AV	FRCO	57	C3
WHITES GULCH RD	SIS	11	C2
WHITES MILL RD	KER	69	B5
WHITES MILL RD	KER	79	B1
WHITEWTR CYN RD	RCO	100	C2
WHITE WOLF RD	TUO	42	D5
WHITE WOLF RD	TUO	63	C3
WHITLEY AV	KIN	67	D3
WHITLOCK RD	IMP	109	C5
WHITLOCK RD	MPA	49	A3
WHITLOCK RD E	MPA	49	B3
WHITLOW RD	HUM	16	C4
WHITMORE AV	STA	47	D2
WHITMORE RD	SHA	18	E5
WHITMORE RD	SHA	19	A2
WHITMRE TUBS RD	MNO	50	E2
WHITMRE TUBS RD	MNO	51	A2
WHITNEY AV	VAL	134	D1
WHITNY PORTL RD	INY	60	A4
WHITSETT AV	LACO	Q	C3
WHITTIER AV	RCO	99	E4
WHITTIER BLVD	LA	186	D4
WHITTIER BLVD	LACO	98	A2
WHITTIER BLVD	LACO	R	B4
WHITTIER BLVD	LACO	R	D5
WHITTIER BLVD	ORA	R	D5
WHITTLE AV E	AVLN	105	B5
WHITTLE RD	CAL	41	B4
WHITWELL WY	RCO	107	C1
WHITWORTH RD	MCO	47	C5
WHITWORTH RD	MCO	55	C1
WIASMUL RD	RCO	107	B1
WIBLE RD	KER	166	B5
WIBLE RD	KER	78	D4
WICKENDEN WAY	MOD	8	A1
WICKMAN RD	BUT	25	B5
WICKS ST	SB	86	C1
WIDGEON RD	YOL	39	D3
WIDOW SPGS DR	SIS	12	E2
WIDOW VALLEY RD	MOD	13	E3
WIDOW VALLEY RD	MOD	14	A3
WIGHT WY	LAK	31	D3
WILBUR	CC	39	B5
WILBUR AV	LA	178	C3
WILBUR RD	BUT	25	C4
WILBUR SPRGS RD	COL	32	B3
WILCOX RD	SHA	19	D1
WILCOX RD	TEH	18	D4
WILCOX RANCH RD	TUO	41	C5
WILD RD	SBD	91	B2
WILDASS RD	SBT	66	B1
WILDCAT RD	MCO	55	C2
WILDCAT RD	SHA	18	E3
WILDCAT RD	SHA	19	A3
WILDCAT RD	TEH	19	A3
WILD CAT TR	RCO	100	A5
WILDCAT CK RD	SIS	11	D2
WILDCAT CYN RD	CC	L	D4
WILDCAT CYN RD	CC	45	D1
WILDCAT CYN RD	SDCO	107	A5
WILD DUCK RD	MCO	55	E2
WILDER RD	HUM	16	A2
WILDER RD	TEH	18	D5
WILDRNSS LDGE RD	MEN	22	D3
WILDER RIDGE RD	HUM	16	A4
WILDHORSE RD	SBD	92	B1
WILDHORSE CY RD	MON	65	C2
WILDMAN RD	KER	78	E4
WILD PLUM RD	SIE	27	A4
WILDROSE RD	INY	61	C5
WILD WASH RD	SBD	91	C2
WILDWOOD AV	SLT	129	D3
WILDWOOD RD	COL	32	E3
WILDWOOD RD	KER	78	A2

INDEXES

COPYRIGHT, © 1989 BY Thomas Bros Maps

STREET	CO.	PAGE	GRID
WILDWOOD RD	SJCO	47	C1
WILDWOOD RD	TRI	17	C2
WILDWOOD CYN RD	SBD	99	E2
WILEY WELLS RD	RCO	103	B5
WILFRED CYN RD	MNO	51	B2
WILHOLT RD	SJCO	40	A5
WILKIE AV	SUT	33	D3
WILKINS AV	STA	47	D1
WILKINS RD	IMP	109	B2
WILKINS RD	IMP	112	D5
WILKINSON RD	IMP	109	A3
WILLARD RD	TEH	18	C5
WILLARD CK RD	LAS	20	E3
WILLIAM RD	BUT	25	C3
WILLIAM ST	SJ	152	C4
WILLIAMS	SJCO	47	C1
WILLIAMS AV	MCO	47	D4
WILLIAMS RD	IMP	109	B4
WILLIAMS RD	KER	79	C2
WILLIAMS RD	KER	80	D4
WILLIAMS RD	LAS	8	B4
WILLIAMS RD	MON	54	D4
WILLIAMS RD	SHA	13	E4
WILLIAMS CK RD	HUM	15	D2
WILLIAMSON RD	KER	79	D4
WILLIAMSON RD	RCO	107	A1
WILLIAMSON RD	TUO	41	B5
WILLIAM TELL TR	KER	79	C5
WILLIAMS VLY RD	PLU	20	C5
WILLIAMS WLL RD	SBD	81	E5
WILLIS RD	MCO	56	B1
WILLISTON RD	SUT	33	C1
WILLMOTT RD	MCO	55	D1
WILLMS RD	STA	48	A1
WILLOUGHBY RD	IMP	112	A4
WILLOW AV	CRTM	140	B1
WILLOW AV	FRCO	57	D2
WILLOW AV	GLE	24	E5
WILLOW AV	KER	89	C1
WILLOW DR	KER	78	A2
WILLOW DR	MAD	57	B1
WILLOW RD	MP	147	A2
WILLOW RD	SBD	91	C4
WILLOW RD	SDCO	107	A5
WILLOW RD	SLO	76	B5
WILLOW RD	SMCO	N	E2
WILLOW RD	SMCO	45	D3
WILLOW ST	LACO	97	E3
WILLOW ST	LACO	S	D2
WILLOW ST	SJ	152	C5
WILLOW WY	LAS	20	E2
WILLOW CREEK RD	AMA	40	D2
WILLOW CREEK RD	INY	52	D4
WILLOW CREEK RD	SBT	55	C5
WILLOW CREEK RD	SLO	75	E1
WILLOW CREEK RD	SLO	76	B1
WILLOW CREEK RD	SIS	4	C3
WILLOW CREEK RD	YUB	26	B5
WLLW CK RED RCK	SIS	5	B3
WILLOW GLEN DR	SDCO	111	E1
WILLOW GLEN RD	YUB	26	A5
WILLOW PASS RD	CC	M	A3
WILLOW PASS RD	CC	M	B3
WILLOW PASS RD	CC	39	A5
WILLOW POINT RD	YOL	39	D2
WILLOW RCH RD S	MOD	7	C3
WILLOWS RD	SDCO	107	B5
WILLOW SPGS EXT	SIS	13	A2
WILLOW SPGS RD	KER	79	D5
WILLOW SPGS RD	KER	89	D1
WILLOW SPGS RD	KER	90	A1
WILLOW SPGS RD	LAS	14	A5
WILLOW SPGS RD	LACO	89	C3
WILLOW SPGS RD	SCL	P	D5
WILLOW SPGS RD	SCL	54	C1
WILLOW VLY RD	NEV	34	C1
WILL S GREEN RD	COL	32	E2
WILMINGTON AV	LACO	97	E3
WILMINGTON AV	LACO	S	D2
WILMINGTON BLVD	LA	191	B1
WILMINGTON BLVD	LACO	S	C2
WILSHIRE AV	SBD	101	C1
WILSHIRE BLVD	BH	183	B2
WILSHIRE BLVD	LA	180	D2
WILSHIRE BLVD	LA	183	B2
WILSHIRE BLVD	LA	185	A2
WILSHIRE BLVD	LACO	97	D2
WILSHIRE BLVD	LACO	Q	D4
WILSHIRE BLVD	LACO	180	D2
WILSHIRE BLVD	SMON	180	A4
WILSHIRE RD	SBD	92	A4
WILSON AV	COL	32	E3
WILSON AV	MAR	38	A4
WILSON AV	VAL	134	A3
WILSON DR	LA	181	A2
WILSON DR	TUL	68	E3
WILSON RD	IMP	112	D5
WILSON RD	KER	78	D3
WILSON RD	MCO	55	D1
WILSON RD	SUT	33	D3
WILSON ST	KER	79	C3
WILSON ST	RIV	100	A3
WILSON ST	TEH	24	E1
WILSON WY	PLA	34	B3
WILSON WY	SJCO	40	B5
WILSON BEND RD	COL	33	B3
WILSON CREEK RD	DN	1	E5
WILSON HILL RD	MAR	37	E4
WILSON HILL RD	SHA	19	A3
WILSON LAKE RD	TEH	19	D4
WILSON LANDING	BUT	25	A2
WILSON RANCH RD	SBD	90	E4
WILSON SPGS RD	LAS	14	A5
WILSON VLY RD	RCO	107	A1

STREET	CO.	PAGE	GRID
WILTON PL	LA	181	E5
WILTON PL	LA	182	A5
WILTON PL	LA	184	E3
WILTON PL	LA	185	A3
WILTON RD	SAC	40	A2
WIMER RD	SJCO	40	D4
WINCHESTER BLVD	SCL	P	B3
WINCHESTER BLVD	SCL	46	A5
WINCHESTER RD	RCO	99	D4
WINCHUCK RD	CUR	1	D2
WINDING WY	SR	139	B4
WINDING WY	SHA	18	D2
WINDING WY	SIS	12	E2
WINDLASS DR	RCO	101	C5
WINDSONG WY	RCO	107	B1
WINDSOR AV	LACO	R	B2
WINDSOR RD	SON	37	D1
WINDSOR RIV RD	SON	37	D1
WINE CREEK RD	SON	31	D5
WINE CREEK RD	SON	37	D1
WINEMAN RD	SLO	76	C5
WINEVILLE AV	SBD	99	A2
WINGATE RD	INY	71	C3
WINGFIELD RD	LAS	21	A3
WING LEVEE RD	SJCO	46	E1
WINNETKA AV	LA	178	A3
WINNETKA AV	LACO	97	B1
WINSHIP RD	SOL	39	C2
WINSHIP RD	YUBA	125	D4
WINSLOW RD	IMP	109	A2
WINSOME WY	SHA	18	B2
WINTER GRDNS BL	SDCO	V	E2
WINTER GRDNS BL	SDCO	106	E5
WINTERGREEN RD	SBD	90	E4
WINTERS RD	SBD	100	E1
WINTERS RD	SOL	39	A1
WINTRS GULCH RD	SIS	4	A5
WINTON AV W	ALA	45	E2
WINTON AV W	H	146	C4
WINTON AV W	ALA	L	E5
WINTON AV W	ALA	N	E1
WINTON RD	CAL	41	B2
WINTON WY	MCO	48	B4
WINTOON WY	SIS	12	E2
WIRT RD	IMP	109	B3
WISCONSIN AV	COL	32	E3
WISCONSIN AV	TEH	24	E2
WISE RD	PLA	33	E3
WISE RD	PLA	34	A3
WISHON AV	FRE	165	C2
WISHON DR	TUL	69	B2
WISTOS LN	LAS	21	B3
WITHERS AV	CC	L	E3
WITHERS AV	CC	38	E5
WITHROW RD	SHA	19	A2
WITTER SPG E RD	LAK	31	C2
WIXOM RD	IMP	111	E3
WOHLFORD RD	SDCO	106	E3
WOLF RD	NEV	34	C2
WOLF CREEK RD	ALP	36	C5
WOLF CREEK RD	NEV	34	C2
WOLFE RD	CPTO	150	A4
WOLFE RD	SCL	P	A3
WOLFE RD	SCL	45	E4
WOLFE RD	SCL	46	A4
WOLFE RD	SVL	150	A3
WOLFE RD	VEN	96	C1
WOLFE GRADE	MAR	L	B3
WOLFE GRADE	MAR	139	C5
WOLFSEN	MCO	47	E5
WOLFSEN	MCO	55	E1
WOLFSKILL	SOL	39	A1
WONDER AV	KER	80	A4
WONDERLAND BLVD	SHA	18	C1
WONDERLAND DR	RCO	100	A3
WONDER STUMP RD	DN	1	E3
WONDERVIEW RD	RCO	100	A3
WOO RD	MCO	55	E2
WOOD RD	RCO	99	B3
WOOD RD	SUT	33	B2
WOOD RD	VEN	96	C1
WOOD ST	GLE	24	D4
WOODBINE RD	RCO	100	C5
WOODBRIDGE RD	SJCO	39	E4
WOODBRIDGE RD	SJCO	40	B4
WOODBURY RD	LACO	R	B2
WOODBURY RD	PAS	190	A1
WOOD CANYON RD	INY	71	D1
WOODCUTTERS WY	SHA	19	B3
WOODEN VLY RD	NAPA	38	D2
WOODFORD-TEH RD	KER	79	C4
WOODHILL DR	SHA	13	A5
WOODHOUSE MINE	CAL	41	B2
WOODLAND AV	MCO	48	C4
WOODLAND AV	SR	139	E5
WOODLAND AV	STA	47	C2
WOODLAND AV	TEH	24	D1
WOODLAND DR	MPA	49	C3
WOODLAND WY	SHA	19	B3
WOODLF TUNNL RD	BUT	26	B4
WOODLEY RD	SDCO	106	C4
WOOLEY RD E	VEN	96	B1
WOODMAN AV	LACO	97	C1
WOODMAN AV	LACO	Q	C2
WOOD RANCH RD	LAS	21	B2
WOODRIDGE RD	SHA	19	B3
WOODROW AV	SC	169	C5
WOODRUFF AV	LACO	S	E2
WOODRUFF AV	LACO	T	A2
WOODRUFF LN	YUB	33	D1
WOODSBRO RD	SJCO	40	A5
WOODSIDE AV	SDCO	V	E2
WOODSIDE AV	SDCO	106	E5
WOODSIDE RD	SMCO	45	D3

STREET	CO.	PAGE	GRID
WOODSIDE RD	SMCO	N	D2
WOODS LAKE RD	ALP	36	A5
WOODSON AV	TEH	24	D2
WOODSON RD	SJCO	40	A3
WOOD VALLEY RD	SDCO	106	E3
WOODVIEW LN	MPA	49	B4
WOODWARD AV	SJCO	47	A1
WOODY RD	KER	78	D1
WOODY ST	KER	78	E1
WOODY-GRANIT RD	KER	68	E5
WOODY-GRANIT RD	KER	69	A5
WOODY-GRANIT RD	KER	78	E1
WOODY-GRANIT RD	KER	79	A1
WOOKEY RD	BUT	25	A2
WOOLEY RD	OXN	176	A4
WOOLLOMES AV	KER	68	A5
WOOLNER AV	FRFD	135	A4
WORDEN AV	MCO	48	C5
WORDEN RD	CAL	41	B3
WORK RD	KER	90	B1
WORKMAN ST	LACO	Q	C1
WORKMAN MILL RD	LACO	98	A2
WORKMAN MILL RD	LACO	R	C4
WORMWOOD RD	IMP	111	E4
WORSLEY RD	RCO	100	C2
WORTH AV	TUL	68	D3
WORTH RD	SUT	33	D4
WORTHINGTON RD	IMP	108	E5
WORTHINGTON RD	MCO	47	C5
WORTHINGTON ST	KER	79	E1
WRAGG CANYON RD	NAPA	38	D2
WRAN RD	LAS	21	C4
WREN RD	STA	47	E2
WRIGHT AV	SVL	149	B3
WRIGHT AV	TUL	68	B3
WRIGHT RD	IMP	109	C5
WRIGHT RD	SIS	5	D3
WRIGHTS LAKE RD	ED	35	D4
WRIGLEY RD	HUM	15	E1
WRIGLEY TER RD	AVLN	105	B5
WUNPOST RD	MCO	65	E4
WYANDOTTE AV	BUT	25	D4
WYNDTT MNRS RCH	BUT	25	D4
WYE RD	INY	51	D4
WYER RD	COL	32	E3
WYLIE DR	MDO	162	E1
WYLIE ST	SB	87	D1
WYMAN CREEK RD	INY	52	A3
WYNCOOP RD	SUT	33	B2
WYNDAM LN	RED	122	C4
WYNDHAVEN DR	TEH	18	D4
WYO AV	GLE	24	E3
WYSE RD	LACO	89	D4
X			
XIMENO AV	LACO	S	E3
Y			
YAJOME ST	NAP	133	C2
YANKEE HILL RD	TUO	41	C4
YAQUI GULCH RD	MPA	49	B3
YAQUI PASS RD	SDCO	107	E3
YARD RD	TEH	18	D4
YELLOW BUTTE RD	SIS	4	D5
YELLW JACKET RD	MNO	51	C1
YELLW JACKET RD	TEH	19	C4
YERBA BLVD	KER	80	B4
YERBA BUENA RD	VEN	96	D2
YERMO RD	SBD	82	C5
YERMO RD	SBD	92	A1
YERMO CUTOFF	SBD	81	E5
YERMO CUTOFF	SBD	82	A5
YGNACIO VLY RD	CC	M	A3
YGNACIO VLY RD	CC	45	E1
YGNACIO VLY RD	CC	39	A5
YMCA RD	FRCO	58	D3
YOAKIM BRDG RD	SON	31	C5
YOCUM RD	IMP	109	B3
YOKE ST	SHA	18	C3
YOLANDA AV	KER	89	C2
YOLANO RD	SOL	39	C2
YOLO AV	FRCO	56	E4
YOLO ST	STA	47	C4
YOLO CO LINE RD	COL	32	E3
YOLO CO LINE RD	COL	33	A3
YORBA LN	SBD	90	E3
YORBA LINDA BL	ORA	98	C3
YORBA LINDA BL	ORA	T	D1
YORK AV	KIN	67	A5
YORK BLVD	LACO	97	E1
YORK BLVD	LACO	R	A3
YORK RD	IMP	110	D5
YORK RD	SIS	4	C3
YORK ST	NAP	133	C3
YOSEMITE AV	MAN	161	A4
YOSEMITE AV	MCO	48	C4
YOSEMITE AV	SJCO	47	B1
YOSEMITE BLVD	MDO	162	E3
YOSEMITE BLVD	STA	47	D2
YOSEMITE BLVD	STA	48	B2
YOSEMITE RD	TUO	41	D5
YOSEMTE OAKS RD	MPA	49	B3
YSMTE SPGS PKWY	MAD	49	C5
YOU BET RD	NEV	34	D2
YOUD RD	MCO	48	B3
YOUNG AV	COL	32	E3
YOUNG RD	COL	24	E5
YOUNG RD	IMP	109	B3
YOUNG RD	STA	47	C3
YOUNG ST	RCO	99	E4
YOUNG LOVE AV	SC	169	B4
YOUNGS HILL RD	YUB	26	C4

STREET	CO.	PAGE	GRID
YOUNGSTOWN RD	MCO	47	E4
YOUNT ST	NAPA	29	D4
YOUNTVLL CRS RD	NAPA	29	D4
YOUNTVLL CRS RD	NAPA	38	C2
YOWELL RD	MOD	14	B3
YREKA AGER RD	SIS	4	B4
YREKA MONO	SIS	4	A4
YREKA WALKER RD	SIS	3	D3
YREKA WALKER RD	SIS	4	A4
YTURRIARTE RD	SBT	55	D4
YUBA AV	FRCO	56	E3
YUBA NEVADA RD	YUB	26	B5
YUBA PASS RD	SIE	27	B4
YUCAIPA BLVD	SBD	99	D2
YUCCA RD	RCO	107	C1
YUCCA RD	SBD	90	E3
YUCCA TR	SBD	100	E1
YUCCA LOMA RD	SBD	91	C4
YUCCA MESA RD	SBD	100	E1
Z			
ZABALA RD	MON	54	D4
ZABRISKIE PT RD	INY	72	A1
ZACA STATION RD	SB	86	E2
ZACHARIAS RD	STA	47	B3
ZACHARY AV	KER	78	C1
ZANES RD	HUM	15	E1
ZAPPONE RD	IMP	110	A4
ZAYANTE RD	SCR	54	A1
ZAYANTE RD E	SCR	P	A5
ZEDIKER AV	FRCO	57	E3
ZEDIKER AV	FRCO	57	E4
ZEERING RD	STA	47	C3
ZEIGLER PT RD	HUM	10	D5
ZELDA LN	SBD	101	E1
ZENIA RD	MEN	23	A2
ZENIA BLUFF RD	HUM	16	D5
ZENIA LK MTN RD	TRI	17	A5
ZENIA LK MTN RD	TRI	23	A1
ZENO RD	LAK	31	D2
ZERKER RD	KER	78	C2
ZERMATT DR	KER	79	C5
ZINC HILL RD	INY	70	E1
ZINC MINE RD	SBD	84	A3
ZINFANDEL DR	SAC	40	A1
ZINFANDEL LN	NAPA	29	C3
ZINK RD	BUT	25	E3
ZITZMAN RD	SIS	3	C5
ZLABEK RD	SIS	5	D2
ZOGG MINE RD	SHA	18	B2
ZOO DR	LACO	Q	E3
ZULU QUEN MN RD	RCO	102	A2
ZUMWALT	SJCO	47	C1
ZUMWALT AV	TUL	68	A2
ZUMWALT RD	COL	32	D2
ZZYZX RD	SBD	83	B4
NUMERIC STREETS			
1ST AV	BARS	208	B1
1ST AV	BUT	25	B3
1ST AV	GLE	24	E3
1ST AV	IMP	112	D5
1ST AV	LPAZ	104	B2
1ST AV	LACO	R	D5
1ST AV	LACO	T	B1
1ST AV	MCO	47	E4
1ST AV	PLU	20	A4
1ST AV	SBD	208	C1
1ST AV	SD	215	D4
1ST AV	SDCO	V	B3
1ST AV	SDCO	V	C4
1ST AV	SDCO	111	D2
1ST ST	ALA	M	C5
1ST ST	ALA	46	C2
1ST ST	BEN	153	B4
1ST ST	DN	1	D3
1ST ST	DVS	136	D3
1ST ST	FRCO	57	C3
1ST ST	LA	186	A2
1ST ST	LACO	Q	E4
1ST ST	NAPA	L	C1
1ST ST	NAP	133	C4
1ST ST	ORA	98	B4
1ST ST	ORA	T	D3
1ST ST	RCO	U	E4
1ST ST	RCO	98	E3
1ST ST	SF	143	D4
1ST ST	SCL	P	B3
1ST ST	SJ	151	E1
1ST ST	SJ	152	B3
1ST ST	SA	195	A4
1ST ST	SA	196	A4
1ST ST	SCL	46	A4
1ST ST	SCL	54	D2
1ST ST	SHA	18	C3
1 1/2 AV	KIN	68	A1
2ND AV	COL	33	B3
2ND AV	GLE	24	E3
2ND AV	KIN	68	A1
2ND AV	LPAZ	104	B1
2ND AV	MCO	47	D4
2ND AV	RCO	103	D4
2ND AV S	MCO	48	A4
2ND ST	FRFD	135	A3
2ND ST	KER	68	B5
2ND ST	LA	186	A2
2ND ST	LACO	S	E3
2ND ST	MER	170	A5
2ND ST	SDCO	V	E3
2ND ST	SDCO	106	B3
2ND ST	SDCO	106	E5
2ND ST	SR	139	C4

STREET	CO.	PAGE	GRID
2ND ST E	BEN	153	C4
2ND ST E	RENO	130	B3
2ND ST E	SOL	38	D4
2ND ST W	RENO	130	A3
2 1/2 AV	KIN	67	E2
3RD AV	FCTY	145	C1
3RD AV	GLE	24	E3
3RD AV	LPAZ	104	B1
3RD AV	MCO	47	D4
3RD AV	NAPA	38	D3
3RD AV	RCO	103	D4
3RD AV	SBD	99	B1
3RD AV	SDCO	V	C4
3RD AV	SDCO	111	D2
3RD AV	SMCO	N	C1
3RD AV	SMCO	45	C3
3RD AV	TEH	18	E5
3RD AV	TEH	24	E1
3RD ST	BH	183	C1
3RD ST	CC	38	C5
3RD ST	COR	215	B5
3RD ST	DVS	136	D3
3RD ST	EUR	121	C1
3RD ST	LB	192	D3
3RD ST	LA	183	C1
3RD ST	LA	184	B1
3RD ST	LA	185	A1
3RD ST	LA	186	A3
3RD ST	LACO	Q	D4
3RD ST	NAP	133	C4
3RD ST	RIV	205	C2
3RD ST	SBDO	207	D2
3RD ST	SBD	99	C1
3RD ST	SFCO	L	C5
3RD ST	SF	143	D4
3RD ST	SR	139	C4
3RD ST	SHA	18	C3
3RD ST	TEH	24	D2
3RD ST	YOL	137	A2
4TH AV	CAR	168	C3
4TH AV	GLE	24	E3
4TH AV	KIN	67	E1
4TH AV	MCO	47	D4
4TH AV	MON	168	C3
4TH AV	RCO	103	D4
4TH AV	SD	215	D3
4TH AV	SDCO	V	C4
4TH AV	SDCO	111	D2
4TH ST	ALA	L	D4
4TH ST	BKD	166	C4
4TH ST	COR	215	C5
4TH ST	EC	217	D4
4TH ST	EUR	121	C1
4TH ST	KER	166	C4
4TH ST	LA	186	A3
4TH ST	MAR	L	A3
4TH ST	MAR	38	B5
4TH ST	MOD	8	B1
4TH ST	ONT	203	D3
4TH ST	ONT	204	B3
4TH ST	RCO	99	C4
4TH ST	SBD	99	D2
4TH ST	SDCO	V	C4
4TH ST	SDCO	111	C1
4TH ST	SJ	152	B2
4TH ST	SR	139	B3
4TH ST	SA	196	B4
4TH ST	SCL	54	E3
4TH ST	SHA	18	D3
4TH ST	STR	131	D3
4TH ST E	RENO	130	B2
4TH ST W	RENO	130	A2
5TH AV	CAR	168	B3
5TH AV	GLE	24	E3
5TH AV	GLE	24	E3
5TH AV	KIN	67	E1
5TH AV	LPAZ	104	A2
5TH AV	LACO	R	D3
5TH AV	SBD	92	D5
5TH AV	SBD	99	D2
5TH AV	SDCO	106	D3
5TH AV	SR	139	B3
5TH AV E	SIS	4	B4
5TH ST	DVS	136	C3
5TH ST	EUR	121	C1
5TH ST	HUM	9	E5
5TH ST	LA	186	A3
5TH ST	RCO	99	A3
5TH ST	SCTO	137	A3
5TH ST	SBD	99	C1
5TH ST	SBD	207	C2
5TH ST	SBDO	207	C2
5TH ST	SF	143	C5
5TH ST	SA	195	C4
5TH ST	SOL	L	D2
5TH ST	TEH	24	E1
5TH ST	VAL	134	D5
5TH ST	VEN	96	B1
5TH ST E	BEN	153	C5
5TH ST E	OXN	176	D4
5TH ST E	VEN	176	D4
5TH ST W	LACO	90	A2
5 1/2 AV	KIN	67	E2
6TH AV	CAR	168	B3
6TH AV	GLE	24	E3
6TH AV	KIN	67	E1
6TH AV	MCO	47	E4
6TH AV	RCO	103	D4
6TH AV	SD	215	E3
6TH AV	SDCO	V	B3
6TH ST	GLE	24	D3
6TH ST	LB	192	D3
6TH ST	LA	184	C2
6TH ST	LA	185	C2

STREET	CO.	PAGE	GRID
6TH ST	LA	186	A3
6TH ST	ONT	203	D3
6TH ST	RCO	99	A3
6TH ST	YUB	33	E2
6 1/2 AV	KIN	67	E2
7TH	CC	38	C5
7TH AV	CAR	168	B3
7TH AV	KIN	67	E1
7TH AV	LPAZ	104	A2
7TH AV	LACO	R	D4
7TH AV	SF	141	D4
7TH AV	SFCO	L	B5
7TH AV	SFCO	45	B2
7TH AV	SCR	54	A2
7TH AV	YUB	33	D2
7TH ST	EUR	121	C1
7TH ST	IMP	109	A4
7TH ST	KER	78	B1
7TH ST	LB	192	D3
7TH ST	LA	185	C2
7TH ST	LA	186	A3
7TH ST	LACO	97	C2
7TH ST	LACO	98	A4
7TH ST	LACO	S	E2
7TH ST	O	157	C3
7TH ST	O	158	A4
7TH ST	RIV	205	B2
7TH ST	RCO	99	B2
7TH ST	RCO	99	E4
7TH ST	SBD	91	B4
7TH ST	SBD	99	B2
7TH ST	SBD	99	D2
7TH ST	SJ	152	B3
7TH ST	SLO	75	E3
7TH ST	STA	47	E3
7TH ST	UPL	203	E3
7TH ST N	MDO	162	B3
7TH ST S	MDO	162	C4
7TH ST S	STA	162	C4
7TH ST W	BEN	153	B4
7TH STANDARD RD	KER	77	C2
7 1/2 AV	KIN	57	E5
8TH AV	CAR	53	D5
8TH AV	CAR	168	B3
8TH AV	KIN	67	D1
8TH AV	RCO	103	D4
8TH AV	SD	215	E3
8TH ST	ALA	L	C4
8TH ST	BKD	166	C4
8TH ST	BUT	25	C5
8TH ST	EC	217	C3
8TH ST	IMP	112	A3
8TH ST	LA	185	A2
8TH ST	LA	186	A3
8TH ST	O	157	C3
8TH ST	RCO	99	E3
8TH ST	SBD	U	E2
8TH ST	SBD	98	E2
8TH ST	SDCO	V	C4
8TH ST	SDCO	106	B3
8TH ST	SDCO	111	D1
8TH ST	SJCO	40	B5
8TH ST	SON	L	B1
8TH ST	UPL	203	E2
8TH ST E	DVS	136	C3
8TH ST W	DVS	136	B3
8 1/2 AV	KIN	57	D5
9TH AV	KER	68	C5
9TH AV	KIN	67	D1
9TH AV	LPAZ	104	A2
9TH AV	SD	215	E4
9TH AV	SDCO	106	D3
9TH ST	GGR	195	A2
9TH ST	LB	192	C2
9TH ST	LA	185	A3
9TH ST	LA	186	A4
9TH ST	LA	191	A4
9TH ST	LACO	S	C3
9TH ST	MDO	162	B3
9TH ST	SBD	203	E2
9TH ST	SBDO	207	C1
9TH ST	SF	143	B5
9TH ST	UPL	203	E2
9TH ST	UPL	204	B2
9TH ST S	MDO	162	C4
9TH ST S	STA	162	C4
9 1/2 AV	KIN	67	D1
10 MI HOUSE TR	BUT	25	C2
10TH	CC	38	C5
10TH AV	KIN	67	D1
10TH AV	RCO	103	D5
10TH ST	LB	192	D2
10TH ST	RCO	99	D3
10TH ST	SF	142	D4
10TH ST	SJ	152	B2
10TH ST	UPL	203	E2
10TH ST	YUB	33	D2
10TH ST E	LACO	90	A3
10TH ST W	BEN	153	A3
10TH ST W	CC	M	C3
10TH ST W	LACO	89	E3
10 1/2 AV	KIN	67	D2
11TH AV	KIN	67	D1
11TH AV	LPAZ	104	A2
11TH AV	RCO	103	D5
11TH AV	SBD	91	E1
11TH AV	SD	215	E4
11TH AV	SDCO	V	B3
11TH ST	LAK	31	D3
11TH ST	MDO	162	B3
11TH ST	SBD	91	B4
11TH ST	SJCO	47	A2
12TH AV	KIN	67	D1
12TH AV	LPAZ	104	A2

STREET	CO.	PAGE	GRID
12TH AV	SD	215	E4
12TH AV	SDCO	V	B3
12TH ST	BUT	25	C4
12TH ST	HUM	15	E2
12TH ST	MOD	8	A1
12TH ST	O	157	C2
12TH ST	SCTO	137	C3
12TH ST	YUB	33	D2
12TH ST E	O	159	C1
12TH ST N	SCTO	137	C2
12 3/4 AV	KIN	67	D1
13TH AV	ALA	L	D4
13TH AV	ALA	45	D1
13TH AV	CAR	168	B4
13TH AV	KIN	67	D1
13TH AV	LPAZ	104	A2
13TH AV	O	158	C4
13TH ST	CC	38	C5
13TH ST	SJ	152	B2
13 1/4 AV	KIN	67	D1
14 MILE HOUSE	BUT	25	C2
14TH AV	KIN	67	D1
14TH AV	LPAZ	104	A2
14TH AV	O	158	C4
14TH AV	RCO	100	D3
14TH AV	RCO	103	D5
14TH ST E	ALA	L	E5
14TH ST E	ALA	L	E5
14TH ST E	CC	M	C3
14TH AV E	O	158	D5
14TH ST	ALA	146	B1
14TH ST	CC	39	B5
14TH ST	EUR	121	B2
14TH ST	MDO	162	B3
14TH ST	O	157	C2
14TH ST	RIV	99	E2
14TH ST	RIV	205	C3
14TH ST	RCO	99	B2
14TH ST	SBD	99	D2
14TH ST E	ALA	45	E2
14TH ST E	DVS	136	C2
14TH ST E	O	159	D1
14TH ST W	DVS	136	C2
14 1/2 AV	KIN	67	D2
15TH AV	KIN	67	D1
15TH AV	RCO	103	C5
15TH AV	SDCO	106	D3
15TH ST	KER	80	A5
15TH ST	MDO	162	B3
15TH ST	SCTO	137	B4
15 1/2 AV	KIN	67	C1
16TH AV	KIN	67	C1
16TH AV	RCO	100	D3
16TH AV	RCO	103	D5
16TH ST	MER	170	B3
16TH ST	SCTO	137	C4
16TH ST	SBD	98	D1
16TH ST	SBD	99	D2
16TH ST	SD	215	E4
16TH ST	SD	216	A4
16TH ST	SDCO	V	B3
16TH ST	YUMA	112	C5
17 MILE DR	MON	53	B3
17 MILE DR	MON	167	A3
17 MILE DR	PAC	167	B2
17TH AV	KIN	67	C1
17TH AV	SCR	54	A2
17TH ST	CM	199	B3
17TH ST	MDO	162	C3
17TH ST	ORA	98	C4
17TH ST	ORA	T	B4
17TH ST	ORA	T	C4
17TH ST	ORA	T	D3
17TH ST	SF	141	E5
17TH ST	SF	142	A5
17TH ST	SJ	152	C2
17TH ST	SA	195	D3
17TH ST	SA	196	A3
18TH AV	KIN	67	C1
18TH AV	RCO	100	D3
18TH AV	RCO	103	D5
18TH ST	BKD	166	B3
18TH ST	LAK	32	A3
18TH ST	SDCO	V	C4
18TH ST	SDCO	111	D2
18 3/4 AV	KIN	67	C1
19TH AV	KIN	67	C3
19TH AV	SFCO	L	B5
19TH AV	SFCO	45	B2
19TH ST	BKD	166	B3
19TH ST	CM	199	A2
19TH ST	KER	80	A5
19TH ST	ORA	T	C4
19TH ST	SBD	98	D1
20TH AV	KIN	67	C1
20TH AV	RCO	100	D3
20TH AV	RCO	103	C5
20TH ST	KER	80	B5
20TH ST	KIN	80	A5
20TH ST E	LACO	90	A3
20TH ST W	KER	89	E1
20 1/2 AV	KIN	67	C2
21ST AV	KIN	67	C3
21ST ST	BKD	166	B3
21ST ST	MER	170	D3
21ST ST	SCTO	137	C4
21ST ST	SJ	152	C2
21 1/2 AV	KIN	67	C1
22ND AV	KIN	67	C1
22ND AV	RCO	100	E3
22ND AV	RCO	103	C5
22ND ST	RCO	100	A3
22ND ST	YUB	33	D2
22 1/2 AV	KIN	67	C1

STREET	CO.	PAGE	GRID
23RD AV	KIN	67	C1
23RD AV	O	158	C4
23RD ST	BKD	166	C3
23RD ST	CC	L	C3
23RD ST	CC	38	C5
23RD ST	R	155	B3
23RD ST	SP	155	B3
23RD ST	SMON	187	B1
23 1/2 AV	KIN	67	B1
24TH AV	KIN	67	B1
24TH AV	RCO	100	E3
24TH AV	RCO	103	C5
24TH ST	BKD	166	C2
24TH ST	KER	78	D3
24TH ST	SAC	39	E1
24TH ST	SBD	98	D1
24TH ST	SDCO	V	C4
24TH ST	SDCO	111	D2
24TH ST	SJ	152	D2
24TH ST	YUMA	112	C5
24 1/2 AV	KIN	67	B1
25TH AV	KIN	67	B1
25TH AV	KIN	67	B4
25TH AV	RCO	103	C5
25TH AV	SF	141	B3
25TH AV	SM	145	A3
25TH ST	LACO	S	C3
25TH ST	SD	216	A4
25TH ST	SDCO	V	B3
25TH ST E	LACO	90	A3
25TH ST W	KER	89	E1
26TH AV	RCO	101	A3
26TH AV	RCO	103	C5
26TH ST	SD	216	B5
26 1/4 AV	KIN	67	B1
27TH AV	KIN	67	B1
27TH ST	SDCO	V	C5
27TH ST	SDCO	111	D2
28TH AV	KIN	67	B2
28TH AV	RCO	101	A3
28TH AV	RCO	110	D1
28TH AV	SM	145	A3
28TH ST	SD	216	B4
28TH ST	SDCO	V	C3
28TH ST	SDCO	111	D1
29TH AV	ALA	L	D4
29TH ST	SCTO	137	D4
30TH AV	KIN	67	B3
30TH AV	RCO	100	D3
30TH AV	RCO	110	C1
30TH ST	BKD	166	D2
30TH ST	KER	80	B5
30TH ST	SD	214	B5
30TH ST	SD	216	B4
30TH ST	SDCO	V	C4
30TH ST	SDCO	111	D1
30TH ST	SDCO	111	D2
30TH ST E	LACO	90	A3
30TH ST W	KER	89	E1
30TH ST W	LACO	89	E2
31ST AV	SM	145	A4
32ND AV	RCO	101	A3
32ND AV	RCO	110	C1
32ND ST	KER	80	B5
32ND ST	LAK	32	A3
32ND ST	SD	216	C4
32ND ST	SDCO	111	D1
32ND ST	YUMA	112	C5
34TH AV	RCO	100	D3
34TH AV	RCO	110	C1
34TH ST	BKD	166	C2
35TH AV	ALA	L	D4
35TH AV	O	158	E5
35TH AV	RCO	110	C1
36TH AV	KIN	67	A4
36TH AV	RCO	100	D4
36TH AV	RCO	110	D1
36TH ST	LAK	32	A3
37TH ST	KER	80	B5
38TH AV	RCO	101	A4
38TH AV	RCO	110	D1
38TH ST	SD	216	D5
39TH AV	SM	145	C3
40TH AV	RCO	101	A4
40TH AV	SF	141	A3
40TH AV	SM	145	B4
40TH ST	SBD	99	B1
40TH ST	SD	214	D5
40TH ST	SDCO	V	C4
40TH ST E	LACO	90	A3
40TH ST W	KER	89	E1
40TH ST W	LACO	89	E2
41ST AV	SCR	54	A2
41ST ST	LACO	Q	E4
42ND AV	RCO	101	A4
42ND AV	SM	145	B4
43RD ST	SD	214	E5
43RD ST	SD	216	E1
44TH AV	RCO	100	E4
47TH AV	RCO	101	A4
47TH AV	SAC	39	E1
47TH ST E	LACO	90	A3
48TH AV	RCO	101	A4
50TH AV	RCO	101	A4
50TH ST E	LACO	90	A3
50TH ST W	KER	89	E1
50TH ST W	LACO	89	E2
51ST ST	LACO	Q	E4
52ND AV	RCO	101	A4
54TH AV	RCO	101	A4
54TH ST	RCO	99	A2
54TH ST	SDCO	V	C3
54TH ST	SDCO	111	D1
55TH ST E	LACO	90	B3

STREET	CO.	PAGE	GRID
57TH ST E	LACO	90	B3
58TH AV	RCO	101	A5
60TH AV	RCO	101	A5
60TH ST	SDCO	V	C4
60TH ST E	LACO	90	B2
60TH ST W	KER	89	E2
60TH ST W	LACO	89	E2
62ND AV	RCO	101	B5
64TH AV	RCO	101	B5
65TH EXPWY	SAC	39	E1
65TH ST E	LACO	90	B2
65TH ST W	LACO	89	E2
66TH AV	RCO	101	B5
67TH ST	RCO	101	A5
68TH AV	RCO	101	B5
68TH AV	TEH	18	E5
70TH AV	RCO	101	B5
70TH ST	SDCO	V	D3
70TH ST	SDCO	111	D1
70TH ST E	LACO	90	B3
70TH ST W	LACO	89	E2
72ND AV	RCO	101	B5
73RD AV	ALA	L	D5
74TH AV	RCO	101	B5
76TH AV	RCO	101	B5
76TH ST E	LACO	90	B3
78TH AV	RCO	108	B1
80TH AV	RCO	107	C1
80TH AV	RCO	108	B1
80TH ST E	LACO	90	B3
80TH ST W	KER	89	D2
80TH ST W	LACO	89	D3
81ST AV	RCO	108	B1
82ND AV	RCO	108	B1
84TH AV	RCO	108	B1
85TH ST W	LACO	89	D3
87TH ST E	LACO	90	B4
87TH ST W	LACO	89	D3
90TH ST E	LACO	90	B3
90TH ST W	KER	89	D2
90TH ST W	LACO	89	D3
92ND ST	LACO	Q	E5
92ND ST W	LACO	89	D3
95TH ST W	LACO	89	D3
96TH ST E	LACO	90	B4
97TH ST W	LACO	89	D3
98TH AV	ALA	L	E5
98TH AV	ALA	45	D2
98TH AV	O	159	D4
98TH ST W	LACO	89	D3
99-97 CUTOFF	SIS	4	B4
100TH ST E	LACO	90	B2
100TH ST W	KER	89	D2
103RD ST	LACO	Q	E5
105TH ST E	LACO	90	B3
106TH ST E	LACO	90	B4
110TH ST E	LACO	90	B3
110TH ST W	KER	79	D5
110TH ST W	LACO	89	D2
115TH ST W	KER	79	D5
120TH ST E	LACO	90	B2
120TH ST W	LACO	89	D2
121ST ST E	LACO	90	B4
130TH ST E	LACO	90	C2
130TH ST W	LACO	89	D2
131ST ST E	LACO	90	C4
135TH ST	LACO	S	C1
137TH ST E	LACO	90	C2
140TH ST E	LACO	90	C2
140TH ST W	KER	89	D1
145TH ST	KER	89	D1
145TH ST E	LACO	90	C3
146TH ST	KER	89	D1
147TH ST	KER	89	C1
149TH ST	KER	89	C1
150TH ST E	LACO	90	C3
152ND ST W	KER	89	C1
155TH ST	KER	89	C1
157TH ST W	KER	89	C1
160TH ST W	LACO	89	C2
164TH ST	LACO	S	B1
165TH ST E	LACO	90	C3
170TH ST E	LACO	90	C3
170TH ST W	KER	89	C2
170TH ST W	LACO	89	C2
175TH ST E	LACO	90	C3
176TH ST	KER	89	C1
177TH ST	KER	89	C1
180TH ST E	LACO	90	C3
180TH ST W	LACO	89	C2
182ND ST	LACO	S	C1
185TH ST E	LACO	90	C3
185TH ST W	KER	89	C2
190TH ST	LACO	97	D3
190TH ST	LACO	S	B1
190TH ST E	LACO	90	C2
190TH ST W	LACO	89	C2
195TH ST	LACO	S	E1
195TH ST	LACO	T	A1
195TH ST E	LACO	90	C2
195TH ST W	KER	89	C2
200TH ST E	LACO	90	D2
200TH ST E	LACO	90	C3
204TH ST E	LACO	90	D4
210TH ST	KER	89	C1
210TH ST E	LACO	90	D3
215TH ST W	KER	89	C2
220TH ST	LACO	S	C2
220TH ST E	LACO	90	D3
223RD ST	LACO	S	C2
223RD ST E	LACO	90	D4
225TH ST E	LACO	90	D2
228TH ST	LACO	S	C2
230TH ST E	LACO	90	D3

STREET	CO.	PAGE	GRID
230TH ST W	KER	89	B2
233RD ST E	LACO	90	D4
235TH ST W	KER	89	B2
235TH ST W	LACO	89	B2
240TH ST E	LACO	90	D3
295TH ST W	KER	89	B2
300TH ST W	KER	89	B2
8001	MAD	50	A5
8003	MAD	50	A4
8004	MAD	50	A4
8005	MAD	50	A4
8006	MAD	50	A4
8007	MAD	50	A4
8008	MAD	50	A5
8009	MAD	50	A4
8009	MAD	50	A5
8013	MAD	50	B4
8014	MAD	50	B4
8015	MAD	50	B4
8016	MAD	50	A4
8020	MAD	50	A4
8021	MAD	49	E4
8023	MAD	50	B3
8024	MAD	50	A3
8026	MAD	50	B3
8027	MAD	50	B3
8029	MAD	50	A4
8041	MAD	49	E4
8042	MAD	49	D3
8046	MAD	49	D3
8063	MAD	57	C1
8066	MAD	57	D1
8067	MAD	57	E1
8080	MAD	57	D1
8081	MAD	49	D5
8082	MAD	49	D5
8083	MAD	49	D5
8086	MAD	49	C5
8087	MAD	57	C1
8089	MAD	49	D4

HIGHWAY INDEX

FEDERAL

ROUTE NO.	CO. ABBR.	PAGE	GRID
6	ESM	44	E4
6	MIN	44	D5
6	MNO	51	C1
50	CRSN	36	B2
50	DGL	36	B2
50	ED	35	B4
50	ED	36	A3
50	LYON	36	D1
50	SAC	40	A1
60	LPAZ	104	D4
93	CLK	74	E2
93	MOH	85	E1
95	CLK	74	D2
95	LPAZ	103	E5
95	MIN	44	A1
95	NYE	62	B2
95	RCO	103	E2
95	SBD	85	B4
95	SBD	95	B1
95	SBD	103	D1
95	YUMA	112	E5
97	KLAM	5	B1
97	SIS	4	D5
97	SIS	5	A3
97	SIS	12	C1
101	CUR	1	C1
101	DN	10	A1
101	HUM	9	E3
101	HUM	10	A2
101	HUM	15	D2
101	HUM	16	B4
101	HUM	22	C1
101	LACO	97	B1
101	LACO	Q	D3
101	MAR	38	B5
101	MAR	45	B1
101	MAR	L	B2
101	MEN	22	C2
101	MEN	31	A1
101	MON	54	C3
101	MON	55	A5
101	MON	65	B2
101	SB	86	C1
101	SB	87	A4
101	SBT	54	D3
101	SCL	46	A4
101	SFCO	45	B1
101	SFCO	L	B4
101	SLO	76	A1
101	SMCO	45	C2
101	SMCO	L	C5
101	SMCO	N	C1
101	SCL	54	D1
101	SCL	P	C3
101	SON	32	D5
101	SON	37	E1
101	SON	33	A3
101	VEN	88	A5
101	VEN	96	D1
197	DN	1	E3
199	DN	1	E3
199	DN	2	C3
395	CRSN	36	C2
395	DGL	36	C3
395	INY	51	C3
395	INY	59	E1
395	INY	60	A3
395	INY	70	B1
395	KER	70	C5
395	KER	80	D1
395	LAKE	7	C1
395	LAS	8	B3
395	LAS	21	B3
395	LAS	27	E1
395	MOD	7	C3
395	MOD	8	B2
395	MNO	42	E2
395	MNO	43	A2
395	MNO	50	D1
395	SBD	80	E3
395	SBD	91	A2
395	WSH	28	A3

INTERSTATE

ROUTE NO.	CO. ABBR.	PAGE	GRID
5	COL	32	D1
5	COL	33	A3
5	FRCO	55	E3
5	FRCO	56	B4
5	FRCO	66	D1
5	GLE	24	D3
5	JKSN	4	A1
5	KER	77	E2
5	KER	78	B3
5	KER	88	D1
5	KIN	67	C4
5	LACO	88	E2
5	LACO	89	A3
5	LACO	97	E1
5	LACO	98	B3
5	LACO	Q	D2
5	LACO	R	C5
5	MCO	47	C5
5	MCO	55	E2
5	ORA	98	B3
5	ORA	105	E1
5	ORA	T	E3
5	ORA	U	A5
5	SAC	39	E2
5	SDCO	106	A2
5	SDCO	111	D2
5	SDCO	V	A2
5	SJCO	39	E4
5	SJCO	40	A4
5	SJCO	47	A2
5	SHA	12	C3
5	SHA	18	C2
5	SIS	4	B3
5	SIS	12	D2
5	STA	47	A3
5	TEH	18	D4
5	TEH	24	D1
5	YOL	33	A4
8	IMP	111	B4
8	SDCO	107	A5
8	SDCO	111	C1
8	SDCO	112	D1
8	SDCO	V	B3
8	YUMA	112	D5
10	LPAZ	103	E5
10	LACO	97	D2
10	LACO	98	A2
10	LACO	Q	D4
10	LACO	U	B2
10	RCO	99	E3
10	RCO	100	A3
10	RCO	101	A4
10	RCO	102	D4
10	RCO	103	B5
10	SBD	99	A1
10	SBD	U	E2
15	CLK	74	E1
15	RCO	99	B4
15	SBD	82	C5
15	SBD	83	D3
15	SBD	84	A2
15	SBD	91	D2
15	SBD	92	B1
15	SDCO	106	D3
15	SDCO	V	C1
15	SBD	99	A1
40	SBD	92	A1
40	SBD	93	D2
40	SBD	94	D2
40	SBD	95	C1
80	ALA	L	C4
80	CC	38	C5
80	CC	L	C3
80	NEV	27	C6
80	NEV	35	D1
80	PLA	34	D2
80	PLA	35	A1
80	SAC	33	E5
80	SAC	34	A5
80	SAC	39	E1
80	SFCO	45	C1
80	SFCO	L	C4
80	SOL	38	E3
80	SOL	39	A2
80	WSH	28	A4
80	YOL	39	D1
105	LACO	Q	D5
105	LACO	S	B1
110	LACO	97	D3
110	LACO	Q	E5
110	LACO	S	C1
205	SJCO	46	D2
210	LACO	89	E5
210	LACO	97	E1
210	LACO	98	B1
210	LACO	Q	C1
210	LACO	R	A2
210	LACO	U	A2
215	SBD	99	B1
238	ALA	45	E2
238	ALA	L	E5
280	SCL	45	E4
280	SCL	N	E3
280	SCL	P	A3
280	SFCO	45	B2
280	SFCO	L	C5
280	SMCO	45	B2
280	SMCO	N	C2
380	SMCO	45	C2
380	SMCO	N	C1
405	LACO	97	C1
405	LACO	Q	B3
405	LACO	S	C2
405	ORA	98	B4
405	ORA	T	A2
480	SFCO	45	C1
505	SOL	39	A2
505	YOL	33	A4
505	YOL	39	A1
580	ALA	45	A1
580	ALA	46	A2
580	ALA	L	D4
580	ALA	M	A5
580	CC	L	C3
580	MAR	38	B5
580	SJCO	46	D2
605	LACO	98	B2
605	LACO	R	D4
605	LACO	S	E2
605	LACO	T	A2
680	ALA	46	B2
680	ALA	P	B1
680	CC	38	E5
680	CC	46	A1
680	CC	L	E4
680	CC	M	A3
680	SCL	46	B4
680	SCL	P	B2
680	SOL	38	E4
680	SOL	L	E2
780	SOL	38	D4
780	SOL	L	E2
805	SDCO	106	C5
805	SDCO	111	D2
805	SDCO	V	B1
880	ALA	P	B2
980	ALA	45	D1
980	ALA	L	D4

STATE

ROUTE NO.	CO. ABBR.	PAGE	GRID
1	HUM	15	D3
1	LACO	96	D2
1	LACO	97	B2
1	LACO	Q	C4
1	LACO	S	B2
1	MAR	37	E4
1	MAR	45	A1
1	MAR	L	B4
1	MEN	22	C2
1	MEN	30	C3
1	MON	54	B3
1	MON	64	B2
1	MON	65	A4
1	ORA	98	C5
1	ORA	105	D1
1	ORA	T	B3
1	SFCO	45	B1
1	SFCO	L	B4
1	SLO	65	A5
1	SLO	75	B1
1	SLO	76	A4
1	SMCO	45	B2
1	SMCO	L	B5
1	SMCO	N	B1
1	SB	86	B2
1	SCR	53	C1
1	SCR	54	B2
1	SCR	N	D5
1	SON	30	D5
1	SON	37	B1
1	VEN	96	C1
2	LACO	90	C4
2	LACO	97	E1
2	LACO	Q	C4
2	LACO	R	A1
2	SBD	90	E5
3	SIS	3	D5
3	SIS	4	A4
3	SIS	11	D1
3	SIS	12	A2
3	TRI	11	E4
3	TRI	12	A3
3	TRI	17	B2
4	ALP	36	C5
4	ALP	42	B1
4	CAL	41	D2
4	CC	38	D5
4	CC	39	C5
4	CC	L	E3
4	CC	M	B3
4	SJCO	39	E5
4	SJCO	40	B5
4	STA	40	E5
9	SCL	45	E5
9	SCL	N	E4
9	SCL	P	A4
9	SCR	53	D1
9	SCR	N	E4
9	SCR	P	A5
12	CAL	40	D4
12	CAL	41	A3
12	NAPA	38	C3
12	NAPA	L	C1
12	SAC	39	C4
12	SAC	M	E2
12	SJCO	39	E4
12	SJCO	40	A1
12	SOL	38	E3
12	SOL	39	A3
12	SOL	M	B1
12	SON	37	E2
12	SON	38	A2
13	ALA	45	D1
13	ALA	L	D4
14	KER	80	C1
14	KER	89	E1
14	LACO	89	E2
15	SDCO	V	C3
16	COL	32	C3
16	SAC	39	E1
16	SAC	40	A1
16	YOL	32	D4
17	SCR	54	A1
17	SCR	P	B5
18	LACO	90	D4
18	SBD	91	A4
18	SBD	92	A4
18	SBD	99	C1
19	LACO	98	A3
19	LACO	R	C3
19	LACO	S	E1
20	COL	32	E2
20	COL	33	A2
20	LAK	31	E3
20	LAK	32	A3
20	MEN	22	D5
20	MEN	31	C2
20	NEV	34	C1
20	SUT	33	C2
20	YUB	33	E1
22	ORA	98	B4
22	ORA	T	A3
23	LACO	96	E2
23	VEN	88	D5
23	VEN	96	E1
24	ALA	L	D4
24	CC	38	E5
24	CC	45	E1
24	CC	L	E4
24	CC	M	A3
25	MON	65	D2
25	SBT	55	A3
25	SBT	65	D1
26	CAL	41	B2
26	SJCO	40	D4
27	LACO	97	B1
27	LACO	Q	A2
28	CRSN	36	B2
28	PLA	35	E1
28	WSH	36	A1
29	LAK	31	D2
29	LAK	32	A4
29	NAPA	38	B1
29	NAPA	L	D1
29	SOL	38	D4
30	LACO	98	D1
30	LACO	U	C2
30	SBD	98	E1
30	SBD	99	B1
30	SBD	U	E1
31	RCO	98	E2
31	RCO	U	E4
32	BUT	25	A3
32	GLE	24	D3
32	TEH	19	E4
33	FRCO	56	B2
33	FRCO	66	D2
33	KER	67	B5
33	KER	77	B1
33	KER	78	A5
33	KIN	67	A4
33	MCO	47	C5
33	MCO	55	C1
33	SJCO	47	A2
33	SLO	87	E1
33	SB	87	E1
33	STA	47	B3
33	VEN	88	A2
34	VEN	88	C5
34	VEN	96	C1
35	LACO	T	A1
35	SFCO	45	B2
35	SFCO	L	B5
35	SMCO	45	C3
35	SMCO	L	B5
35	SMCO	N	B1
35	SCL	46	A5
36	HUM	15	E2
36	HUM	16	C3
36	LAS	20	E3
36	LAS	21	A3
36	PLU	20	A4
36	SHA	17	E4
36	TEH	17	E4
36	TEH	18	C4
36	TEH	19	C4
36	TRI	16	E3
36	TRI	17	A3
37	MAR	L	B2
37	SOL	38	D4
37	SOL	L	C2
37	SON	38	C4
38	SBD	91	E5
38	SBD	92	A5
38	SBD	99	E1
38	SBD	100	B1
39	KLAM	5	C1
39	LACO	98	C1
39	LACO	R	E3
39	LACO	U	A2
39	ORA	98	B4
39	ORA	R	D5
39	ORA	T	C1
41	FRCO	57	C3
41	KIN	67	C2
41	MAD	49	D4
41	MAD	57	C2
41	MPA	63	C5
41	SLO	66	D5
41	SLO	76	A2
42	LACO	97	E2
42	LACO	Q	C5
42	LACO	R	B5
43	FRCO	57	D5
43	KER	68	B5
43	KER	78	B2
43	KIN	67	E2
43	TUL	68	A3
44	LAS	20	A2
44	SHA	18	C2
44	SHA	19	C2
45	COL	32	E1
45	COL	33	A2
45	GLE	24	E3
45	YOL	33	C4
46	JOS	2	D1
46	KER	77	A1
46	KER	78	B1
46	SLO	66	D5
46	SLO	75	E2
46	SLO	76	B1
47	LACO	191	C3
48	LACO	89	A2
49	AMA	40	D1
49	CAL	41	A3
49	ED	34	D4
49	MAD	49	D4
49	MPA	48	E2
49	MPA	49	A3
49	NEV	34	C1
49	PLA	34	C3
49	PLU	27	D3
49	SIE	26	C4
49	SIE	27	C4
49	TUO	41	C5
49	TUO	48	D1
49	YUBA	26	C4
50	ED	34	C5
50	SAC	39	E1
50	SAC	40	A1
52	SDCO	106	C5
52	SDCO	V	B2
53	LAK	32	A3
54	SDCO	111	E1
54	SDCO	V	D4
55	ORA	98	C4
55	ORA	T	D3
56	SDCO	106	D4
57	LACO	98	C2
57	LACO	U	B3
57	ORA	98	C3
57	ORA	T	D1
58	KER	77	E3
58	KER	78	B3
58	KER	80	A4
58	SBD	91	C1
58	SLO	76	B3
58	SLO	77	A3
59	MCO	48	C4
60	LACO	98	B2
60	LACO	R	D4
60	RCO	99	B2
60	SBD	98	D2
60	SBD	U	E3
61	ALA	45	D2
61	ALA	L	D5
62	RCO	100	C2
62	RCO	102	E2
62	SBD	101	A1
62	SBD	102	A2
62	SBD	103	B2
63	FRCO	58	B4
63	TUL	58	B5
63	TUL	68	B2
65	KER	68	D6
65	KER	78	D2
65	PLA	34	A3
65	TUL	68	C2
65	YUB	33	D3
66	JKSN	4	A1
66	KLAM	4	D1
66	SBD	98	E1
66	SBD	99	B1
66	SBD	U	D2
67	SDCO	106	E4
67	SDCO	107	A4
67	SDCO	V	E2
68	MOH	85	D4
68	MON	54	B4
70	BUT	25	D3
70	KLAM	5	D1
70	LAS	27	E2
70	PLU	26	A1
70	SUT	33	D4
70	YUB	33	D1
71	LACO	98	D2
71	LACO	U	C3
71	RCO	98	D2
71	SBD	98	D2
71	SBD	U	C3
72	LPAZ	104	B2
72	LACO	97	E2
72	LACO	98	A2
72	LACO	R	B4
73	ORA	98	C4
73	ORA	T	D4
74	ORA	98	E5
74	ORA	99	A5
74	RCO	99	C4
74	RCO	100	A4
75	SDCO	111	C1
75	SDCO	V	B4
76	SDCO	106	D2
76	SDCO	107	B2
77	ALA	L	D5
77	ALA	45	D1
77	ALA	159	C1
78	IMP	108	C3
78	IMP	109	A4
78	IMP	110	C2
78	RCO	103	D5
78	RCO	110	C1
78	SDCO	106	C3
78	SDCO	107	C3
78	SDCO	108	A3
79	RCO	99	E3
79	RCO	106	D1
79	SDCO	107	B1
80	SFCO	L	C5
82	SCL	46	A4
82	SCL	P	A3
82	SMCO	45	C2
82	SMCO	N	B1
83	SBD	98	D2
83	SBD	U	D3
84	ALA	45	E3
84	ALA	46	B3
84	ALA	M	C5
84	SMCO	45	D4
84	SMCO	N	D3
84	YOL	39	D1
85	SCL	45	E4
85	SCL	P	A3
86	IMP	108	C2
86	IMP	109	A4
86	RCO	101	B4
86	RCO	108	B1
87	SCL	46	B4
87	SCL	P	B3
88	ALP	36	C4
88	AMA	35	D5
88	AMA	41	A2
88	DGL	36	C3
88	SJCO	40	C3
89	ALP	36	B4
89	ED	35	E3
89	ED	36	A4
89	MNO	36	D5
89	NEV	27	D5
89	PLA	35	D1
89	PLU	20	A4
89	PLU	26	C1
89	SHA	13	C3
89	SHA	19	E1
89	SIE	27	C4
89	SIS	12	E2
89	SIS	13	B3
89	TEH	19	D3
90	LACO	Q	D4
90	ORA	98	C3
90	ORA	T	E1
91	LACO	97	E3
91	LACO	S	C1
91	ORA	98	C3
91	ORA	T	C2
91	RCO	99	A3
91	RCO	U	D5
92	ALA	45	D3
92	ALA	N	E1
92	SMCO	45	D3
92	SMCO	N	C2
94	SDCO	111	E1
94	SDCO	112	D2

HIGHWAY INDEX

ROUTE NO.	CO. ABBR.	PAGE	GRID
94	SDCO	V	D3
95	LPAZ	104	B2
95	MOH	85	D5
95	MOH	95	D1
95	MOH	96	B3
96	HUM	10	C3
96	SIS	2	E4
96	SIS	3	C3
96	SIS	10	E1
98	IMP	111	C3
98	IMP	112	C4
99	BUT	25	B3
99	FRCO	57	B3
99	JKSN	3	E1
99	KER	68	B5
99	KER	78	C2
99	MAD	56	D1
99	MAD	57	B2
99	MCO	48	B4
99	MCO	56	D1
99	SAC	39	E2
99	SAC	40	A2
99	SJCO	40	B4
99	SJCO	47	B1
99	STA	47	D3
99	SUT	33	C3
99	TEH	18	D5
99	TUL	57	E5
100	CRSN	36	C2
103	LACO	97	E4
103	LACO	S	D2
104	SAC	40	C2
107	LACO	97	D3
107	LACO	S	B2
108	MNO	42	E2
108	STA	47	D2
108	TUO	41	D4
108	TUO	42	B2
110	LACO	97	E2
110	LACO	R	B3
111	IMP	108	D1
111	IMP	109	B3
111	IMP	112	B3
111	RCO	100	C3
111	RCO	101	A4
111	RCO	108	D1
112	ALA	45	D2
112	ALA	L	E5
113	SOL	39	B2
113	SOL	M	C1
113	SUT	33	C3
113	YOL	33	C5
114	SMCO	N	D2
115	IMP	109	B3
115	IMP	112	C3
116	SON	37	D2
116	SON	38	A3
116	SON	L	A1
117	SDCO	111	E2
117	SDCO	V	D5
118	LACO	89	B5
118	LACO	Q	C1
118	VEN	88	C5
118	VEN	89	A5
119	KER	78	B3
120	MNO	43	C5
120	MNO	51	B1
120	SJCO	47	B1
120	STA	48	A1
120	TUO	41	C5
120	TUO	48	C1
120	TUO	49	B1
121	NAPA	38	D2
121	NAPA	L	C1
121	SON	38	B3
121	SON	L	B1
123	ALA	L	D4
124	AMA	40	D2
125	SDCO	106	E4
125	SDCO	V	D2
126	LACO	89	A4
126	VEN	88	D4
126	VEN	89	A4
127	INY	72	D2
127	SBD	72	E5
127	SBD	83	B2
128	MEN	30	C2

ROUTE NO.	CO. ABBR.	PAGE	GRID
128	MEN	31	B4
128	NAPA	38	B2
128	SON	31	D5
128	SON	38	A1
128	YOL	39	A1
129	SCR	54	D2
130	SCL	46	C4
130	SCL	P	C3
131	MAR	38	B5
131	MAR	45	B1
131	MAR	L	B4
132	MPA	48	D2
132	SJCO	47	A2
132	STA	47	B2
132	STA	48	B2
133	ORA	98	D5
133	ORA	T	E4
134	LACO	97	D1
134	LACO	Q	E3
134	LACO	R	A3
135	SB	86	C1
136	INY	60	B4
137	TUL	68	B2
138	LACO	88	E2
138	LACO	89	A2
138	LACO	90	A3
138	SBD	91	A5
139	LAS	14	C3
139	LAS	20	E1
139	LAS	21	A3
139	MOD	5	E3
139	MOD	6	A4
139	MOD	14	D1
139	SIS	5	E3
140	KLAM	5	C1
140	LAKE	7	A1
140	MCO	47	D4
140	MCO	48	A4
140	MPA	48	E4
140	MPA	49	C2
142	ORA	T	E1
142	ORA	U	B4
142	SBD	98	D2
144	SB	87	C4
145	FRCO	57	A4
145	FRCO	66	E1
145	MAD	57	B2
146	CLK	74	E3
146	MON	55	B5
146	SBT	55	C5
147	PLU	20	C4
149	BUT	25	C4
150	SB	87	E4
150	VEN	88	B4
151	SHA	18	C1
152	MAD	56	C1
152	MCO	55	E1
152	MCO	56	B1
152	SCL	54	D2
152	SCR	54	C2
154	SB	87	A3
155	KER	68	B5
155	KER	69	B5
155	KER	79	C1
156	CLK	72	E1
156	CLK	74	A1
156	MON	54	C3
156	SBT	54	E2
156	SBT	55	A2
157	CLK	73	E2
157	CLK	74	A2
158	CLK	73	E1
158	CLK	74	A1
160	CLK	73	E3
160	CLK	74	B3
160	NYE	73	C2
160	SAC	39	E1
160	SAC	M	D2
161	CLK	74	C5
161	SIS	5	B2
162	BUT	25	B5
162	GLE	24	B4
162	GLE	25	B5
162	MEN	22	E4
162	MEN	23	A3
163	CLK	85	C4
163	SDCO	106	D5

ROUTE NO.	CO. ABBR.	PAGE	GRID
163	SDCO	V	B3
164	CLK	84	E2
164	LACO	98	A1
165	MCO	47	E5
165	MCO	55	E2
166	KER	77	A4
166	KER	78	B5
166	SB	86	B1
166	SLO	76	D5
167	MNO	43	E4
168	FRCO	50	B5
168	FRCO	57	E2
168	FRCO	58	A1
168	INY	51	E5
168	INY	52	C3
168	MNO	52	C3
169	DN	1	E5
169	DN	2	A5
169	DN	10	A1
169	HUM	10	C3
170	LACO	97	D1
170	LACO	Q	C2
172	TEH	19	D4
173	SBD	91	C5
174	NEV	34	D2
175	LAK	31	E3
175	LAK	32	A5
175	MEN	31	C3
176	SB	86	C1
177	RCO	102	D2
178	INY	72	D3
178	INY	73	A3
178	KERN	69	E5
178	KER	70	A5
178	KER	78	E2
178	KER	79	A2
178	KER	80	B1
178	SBD	81	A1
180	FRCO	56	E3
180	FRCO	57	C3
180	FRCO	58	B3
180	FRCO	59	A3
182	MNO	43	C2
183	MON	54	C3
184	KER	78	E3
185	ALA	45	D1
185	ALA	L	D5
188	SDCO	112	C2
189	SBD	91	C5
190	INY	61	D4
190	INY	70	C1
190	INY	72	C1
190	TUL	68	B3
190	TUL	69	A3
191	BUT	25	C3
192	SB	87	C4
193	ED	34	E4
193	PLA	34	B3
195	RCO	101	B5
198	FRCO	66	E2
198	KIN	67	C2
198	MON	65	D2
198	MON	66	A2
198	TUL	58	E5
198	TUL	59	A5
198	TUL	68	B1
200	HUM	9	E5
200	HUM	10	A5
201	TUL	58	B5
202	KER	79	C4
203	MNO	50	D2
204	KER	78	D3
206	DGL	36	B3
206	SBD	99	B1
207	DGL	36	B3
208	DGL	36	E4
208	MEN	22	B2
209	SDCO	111	C1
209	SDCO	V	A4
213	LACO	S	C3
213	LACO	97	D3
215	RCO	99	C3
216	TUL	68	C1
217	SB	87	B4
218	MON	54	B4
219	STA	47	C2
220	SOL	39	D3

ROUTE NO.	CO. ABBR.	PAGE	GRID
221	NAPA	L	D1
221	NAPA	38	D3
223	KER	78	D4
223	KER	79	A4
224	SB	87	E4
225	SB	87	C4
227	SLO	76	B4
229	SLO	76	B2
232	VEN	88	B5
233	MAD	56	D1
236	SCR	53	D1
236	SCR	N	D4
237	SCL	46	B4
237	SCL	P	A3
238	ALA	46	A2
238	ALA	P	A1
243	RCO	100	A3
245	TUL	58	C4
245	TUL	68	C1
246	SB	86	C3
247	SBD	91	E2
247	SBD	92	B4
247	SBD	100	D1
249	FRCO	58	D4
250	ORA	98	C3
253	MEN	31	A3
254	HUM	16	B4
255	HUM	9	E5
255	HUM	10	A5
259	SBD	99	B1
262	ALA	46	A3
262	ALA	P	B2
263	SIS	4	A4
264	ESM	52	A1
265	ESM	52	E1
266	ESM	52	E3
266	MNO	52	C3
267	ESM	61	C1
267	PLA	35	E1
267	PLA	36	A1
269	FRCO	67	A1
270	MNO	43	B3
271	MEN	22	C1
273	SHA	18	C2
274	SDCO	106	C5
274	SDCO	V	B2
281	LAK	31	E3
282	SDCO	111	C1
282	SDCO	V	B4
284	PLU	27	D2
299	HUM	10	B4
299	LAS	14	A3
299	MOD	7	C5
299	MOD	8	B1
299	MOD	14	D1
299	SHA	13	B5
299	SHA	18	B2
299	TRI	10	D5
299	TRI	16	E1
299	TRI	17	D1
330	SBD	99	C1
338	LYON	43	B1
341	LYON	36	D1
341	WSH	28	C5
359	MIN	44	B2
360	MIN	44	C3
371	RCO	100	B5
372	NYE	73	B2
373	NYE	62	D5
374	NYE	62	A3
380	SMCO	N	B1
428	WSH	36	C1
429	WSH	36	B1
430	WSH	28	B4
431	WSH	28	B5
431	WSH	36	B1
445	WSH	28	D1
446	WSH	28	E2
447	WSH	28	E2
480	SFCO	L	C4
512	CRSN	36	C2
513	CRSN	36	C2
604	CLK	74	E2
666	WSH	28	B4
710	LACO	97	E2
710	LACO	R	B5
710	LACO	S	D2

ROUTE NO.	CO. ABBR.	PAGE	GRID
880	ALA	45	E2
880	SCL	46	B4
COUNTY			
1	LPAZ	103	E3
1	LPAZ	104	A1
3	LPAZ	104	B2
10	LPAZ	104	A2
14	LPAZ	103	E2
14	LPAZ	104	A2
17	LPAZ	103	E2
17	LPAZ	104	A2
21	LPAZ	103	E3
21	LPAZ	104	A3
25	LPAZ	103	E3
29	LPAZ	103	E2
30	LPAZ	103	E3
30	LPAZ	104	A3
34	LPAZ	103	E3
38	LPAZ	103	E3
44	LPAZ	103	E3
44	LPAZ	104	A3
50	LPAZ	103	E4
56	LPAZ	103	E4
A 1	LAS	20	D2
A 2	LAS	14	C3
A 3	LAS	21	B4
A 5	TEH	18	C3
A 6	TEH	18	E4
A 6	TEH	19	B3
A 7	TEH	18	D5
A 8	TEH	18	D5
A 9	TEH	24	D2
A10	SIS	12	C2
A11	TEH	24	D1
A12	SIS	4	B5
A13	PLU	20	B4
A14	PLU	27	A3
A15	PLU	27	B2
A16	SHA	17	E3
A16	SHA	18	A3
A16	SHA	122	A2
A17	SHA	18	D3
A17	SHA	19	A3
A18	SHA	18	C2
A19	SHA	13	D3
A21	LAS	20	C2
A22	PLU	20	D5
A23	PLU	27	C2
A23	SIE	27	C3
A24	PLU	27	D3
A25	LAS	21	D5
A26	LAS	21	D5
A27	LAS	21	B3
B 2	BUT	25	D4
D 1	DN	1	E3
D 2	DN	1	D4
D 3	DN	1	D3
D 5	DN	1	D2
E 1	ALP	36	C5
E 4	YOL	32	E4
E 4	YOL	33	A4
E 6	YOL	39	B1
E 6	YOL	136	A2
E 7	SOL	39	B1
E 7	YOL	33	B5
E 8	YOL	33	C4
E 8	YOL	39	C1
E 8	YOL	136	E1
E 9	YOL	39	D2
E10	YOL	33	B4
E11	YOL	33	B4
E13	SAC	39	D3
E16	AMA	40	E1
E16	ED	35	B4
G 1	SBT	54	E3
G 2	SCL	46	A4
G 2	SCL	P	A3
G 2	SCLR	150	C2
G 3	PA	147	D2
G 3	SCL	45	D4
G 3	SCL	147	B6
G 3	SCL	N	E3
G 4	SCL	46	A4
G 4	SCL	P	B3
G 4	SCLR	150	E1
G 4	SCLR	151	A1

ROUTE NO.	CO. ABBR.	PAGE	GRID
G 5	PA	147	C6
G 5	SCL	45	E4
G 5	SCL	147	A5
G 5	SCL	149	A3
G 5	SCL	N	E3
G 6	MVW	148	C5
G 6	SCL	45	E4
G 6	SCL	46	A4
G 6	SCL	148	C5
G 6	SCLR	151	B1
G 6	SVL	148	C5
G 7	SCL	54	D2
G 8	SCL	46	B5
G 8	SCL	54	C1
G 8	SCL	P	B4
G 9	SCL	54	D2
G10	SCL	46	B5
G10	SCL	P	B4
G11	MON	54	C3
G12	MON	54	C3
G13	MON	65	C2
G13	SBT	65	C1
G14	MON	65	B3
G15	MON	65	B1
G16	MON	54	B5
G16	MON	64	C1
G16	MON	65	B1
G16	MON	168	E4
G17	MON	54	C4
G17	MON	65	A1
G18	MON	65	D4
G19	MON	65	E5
G20	MON	54	C5
J 1	FRCO	55	E3
J 1	FRCO	56	A3
J 1	SBT	55	B4
J 2	ALA	46	C2
J 2	ALA	M	D5
J 2	ALA	P	D1
J 2	SJCO	46	E1
J 3	S	160	E2
J 3	SJCO	47	B2
J 3	SJCO	160	E2
J 4	CC	46	D1
J 4	SJCO	46	E2
J 4	SJCO	47	A2
J 5	SJCO	40	B4
J 5	SJCO	47	C1
J 6	SJCO	40	C5
J 6	SJCO	47	D1
J 7	MCO	47	E3
J 7	MCO	48	A3
J 7	SJCO	40	B5
J 7	SJCO	47	C1
J 7	STA	47	D2
J 8	SCTO	137	D5
J 9	SJCO	47	C1
J 9	STA	47	D1
J 9	STA	48	A3
J11	SAC	39	D3
J11	SJCO	39	D3
J12	SJCO	40	C3
J13	SJCO	46	E1
J14	STA	40	E5
J14	STA	47	E1
J15	TUL	68	B2
J16	MPA	48	E3
J16	MCO	48	B3
J16	STA	47	D3
J17	MCO	48	A3
J17	STA	47	C3
J18	STA	47	C4
J19	FRCO	58	B4
J19	TUL	58	A5
J20	MPA	48	E2
J20	TUO	48	E1
J21	TUL	58	D5
J22	TUL	68	B4
J23	TUL	58	C5
J23	TUL	68	C2
J24	TUL	68	B4
J25	TUL	68	A1
J27	TUL	68	C2
J28	TUL	68	C2
J29	TUL	68	D2
J30	TUL	68	B1
J32	TUL	68	A1

ROUTE NO.	CO. ABBR.	PAGE	GRID
J34	TUL	68	A1
J38	TUL	57	E5
J38	TUL	58	B5
J40	TUL	58	A5
J41	TUL	70	B4
J42	TUL	68	E3
J42	TUL	69	A3
J44	TUL	68	C5
J59	MCO	48	C2
J59	TUO	48	C1
N 1	LACO	97	B2
N 2	LACO	89	A2
N 3	LACO	89	E5
N 3	LACO	90	A4
N 5	LACO	90	A2
N 6	LACO	90	C4
N 7	LACO	S	B3
N 8	LACO	98	C2
N 8	LACO	R	D5
N 8	LACO	U	A3
N 8	LACO	T	B1
N 9	LACO	96	E2
N 9	LACO	97	A2
R 2	RCO	102	B4
R 3	RCO	99	E5
R 3	RCO	100	A5
R 3	RCO	106	E1
R 3	RCO	107	A1
S 1	SDCO	107	D4
S 1	SDCO	112	D1
S 2	IMP	111	B3
S 2	SDCO	107	C3
S 2	SDCO	108	A4
S 2	SDCO	111	B3
S 3	SDCO	107	E3
S 4	SDCO	106	D4
S 4	SDCO	V	C1
S 5	SDCO	106	D4
S 6	SDCO	106	E2
S 6	SDCO	107	A2
S 7	SDCO	107	A2
S 8	SDCO	106	C4
S 9	SDCO	106	C4
S10	SDCO	106	C3
S11	SDCO	106	C3
S12	SDCO	106	D3
S13	SDCO	106	C1
S14	SDCO	106	C3
S15	SDCO	106	C2
S16	RCO	106	D1
S16	SDCO	106	D1
S17	SDCO	V	E3
S17	SDCO	111	E1
S17	SDCO	112	A1
S18	ORCO	98	D4
S19	ORCO	98	E4
S20	SB	86	B2
S21	SDCO	V	A1
S21	SDCO	106	C5
S22	IMP	108	C2
S22	SDCO	107	E2
S22	SDCO	108	B2
S24	IMP	112	D5
S24	IMP	110	D5
S26	IMP	109	A4
S27	IMP	109	A5
S28	IMP	109	A5
S28	IMP	112	C3
S29	IMP	108	E5
S29	IMP	111	E3
S30	IMP	109	A3
S30	IMP	112	A3
S31	IMP	109	B4
S31	IMP	112	B3
S32	IMP	109	C4
S32	IMP	112	C3
S33	IMP	109	C4
S33	IMP	112	C4
S34	IMP	110	B4
S80	IMP	108	C5
S80	IMP	109	A5
S80	IMP	111	D3
S80	IMP	112	A3

HIGHWAY NAME	HWY NO.	CO. ABBR.	PAGE	GRID
ANGELES CREST HWY	2	LACO	90	B5
ANGELES CREST HWY	2	SBD	90	E5
ANTELOPE VALLEY FWY	14	KER	89	E2
ANTELOPE VALLEY FWY	14	KER	90	A2
ANTELOPE VALLEY FWY	14	LACO	89	D4
ANTELOPE VALLEY FWY	14	LACO	90	A2
ARROYO PKWY	110	LACO	190	C5
ARTESIA FWY	91	LACO	97	E3
ARTESIA FWY	91	LACO	S	C1
ARTESIA FWY	91	ORA	98	A3
BAKERSFIELD-MCKITTRICK HWY	58	KER	78	A3
BARSTOW FWY	15	SBD	82	C5
BARSTOW FWY	15	SBD	83	D3
BARSTOW FWY	15	SBD	84	A2
BARSTOW FWY	15	SBD	91	B5
BARSTOW FWY	15	SBD	92	B1
BARSTOW FWY	215	SBD	99	B1
BAY HWY	1	SON	37	C3
BAYSHORE FWY	101	SCL	N	E3
BAYSHORE FWY	101	SCL	P	A3
BAYSHORE FWY	101	SCL	46	A4
BAYSHORE FWY	101	SCL	147	D1
BAYSHORE FWY	101	SCL	148	A3
BAYSHORE FWY	101	SCL	151	D1
BAYSHORE FWY	101	SCL	152	B1
BAYSHORE FWY	101	SMCO	L	C5
BAYSHORE FWY	101	SMCO	N	D2
BAYSHORE FWY	101	SMCO	45	D3
BAYSHORE FWY	101	SMCO	144	C1
BAYSHORE FWY	101	SMCO	145	D4
BOULDER HWY	93	CLK	74	E2
BOULDER HWY	95	CLK	74	E2
BURNS FWY	101	HUM	9	E5
BURNS FWY	101	HUM	10	A5
BURNS FWY	101	HUM	15	E1
CABRILLO FWY	163	SDCO	V	B3
CABRILLO FWY	163	SDCO	111	C1
CABRILLO FWY	163	SDCO	213	D3
CABRILLO FWY	163	SDCO	215	E2
CABRILLO HWY	1	MAR	53	D4
CABRILLO HWY	1	MON	54	B4
CABRILLO HWY	1	MON	64	B2
CABRILLO HWY	1	MON	65	A4
CABRILLO HWY	1	MON	168	C2
CABRILLO HWY	1	SB	86	B1
CABRILLO HWY	1	SCR	N	D5
CABRILLO HWY	1	SCR	53	C1
CABRILLO HWY	1	SCR	54	B2
CABRILLO HWY	1	SCR	169	A4
CABRILLO HWY	1	SLO	65	A5
CABRILLO HWY	1	SLO	75	B1
CABRILLO HWY	1	SLO	76	B5
CABRILLO HWY	1	SLO	172	B1
CABRILLO HWY	1	SMCO	L	B5
CABRILLO HWY	1	SMCO	N	B2
CABRILLO HWY	1	SMCO	45	B3
CALF CANYON HWY	58	SLO	76	C2
CENTRAL EXPWY	82	SCL	N	E3
CENTRAL FWY	101	SFCO	142	C5
CENTRAL SKYWAY	101	SFCO	142	C4
CENTRAL SKYWAY	101	SFCO	143	C5
CENTRAL VALLEY HWY	43	KER	78	B1
CENTURY FWY	105	LACO	Q	D5
COAST HWY	1	ORA	105	D1
COAST HWY	1	ORA	199	C4
COAST HWY	1	ORA	201	A2
COAST HWY	1	ORA	202	D5
COAST HWY	1	SON	30	D5
COAST HWY	1	SON	37	B2
COAST HWY E	1	ORA	200	A5
CORONA DEL MAR FWY	73	ORA	T	D4
CORONA DEL MAR FWY	73	ORA	98	C4
CORONA DEL MAR FWY	73	ORA	197	D4
CORONA DEL MAR FWY	73	ORA	198	A5
CORONA EXPWY	71	LACO	U	C3
CORONA EXPWY	71	LACO	98	D2
CORONA EXPWY	71	RCO	98	D2
CORONA EXPWY	71	SBD	U	C3

HIGHWAY NAME	HWY NO.	CO. ABBR.	PAGE	GRID
CORONA EXPWY	71	SBD	98	D2
CORONA FWY	15	RCO	99	B4
COSTA MESA FWY	55	ORA	T	C4
COSTA MESA FWY	55	ORA	98	C4
COSTA MESA FWY	55	ORA	194	E3
COSTA MESA FWY	55	ORA	196	E4
COSTA MESA FWY	55	ORA	198	D2
DEVORE FWY	15	SBD	99	A1
EASTSHORE FWY	80	ALA	L	D3
EASTSHORE FWY	80	CC	L	D3
EASTSHORE FWY	80	CC	38	C5
EASTSHORE FWY	80	CC	155	D3
EL CAMINO REAL	101	MON	54	D4
EL CAMINO REAL	101	MON	55	A5
EL CAMINO REAL	101	MON	65	B2
EL CAMINO REAL	101	MON	66	A5
EL CAMINO REAL	101	MON	171	D3
EL CAMINO REAL	101	SB	86	C1
EL CAMINO REAL	101	SB	87	A4
EL CAMINO REAL	101	SBT	54	D2
EL CAMINO REAL	101	SCL	54	D2
EL CAMINO REAL	82	SCL	147	B3
EL CAMINO REAL	82	SCL	149	E2
EL CAMINO REAL	82	SCL	150	B2
EL CAMINO REAL	82	SCL	151	A2
EL CAMINO REAL	101	SLO	66	A5
EL CAMINO REAL	101	SLO	76	A4
EL CAMINO REAL	101	SLO	172	B4
EL CAMINO REAL	82	SMCO	145	A3
EL DORADO FWY	50	SAC	40	A1
EL SEGUNDO FWY	105	LACO	Q	C5
ELVAS FWY	80	SAC	137	E2
EMBARCADERO SKYWAY	480	SFCO	45	C1
ESCONDIDO FWY	215	RCO	99	C4
ESCONDIDO FWY	15	SDCO	V	C1
ESCONDIDO FWY	15	SDCO	106	D2
ESCONDIDO FWY	15	SDCO	216	D3
EVAN HEWES HWY	8	IMP	111	B4
EVAN HEWES HWY	8	IMP	112	A5
EVAN HEWES HWY	8	IMP	112	D3
FAMOSO HWY	46	KER	78	A1
FOOTHILL FWY	210	LACO	Q	B1
FOOTHILL FWY	210	LACO	R	B2
FOOTHILL FWY	210	LACO	U	A2
FOOTHILL FWY	210	LACO	89	D5
FOOTHILL FWY	210	LACO	97	D1
FOOTHILL FWY	210	LACO	98	A1
FOOTHILL FWY	210	LACO	190	B2
GARDEN GROVE FWY	22	ORA	T	C3
GARDEN GROVE FWY	22	ORA	98	B4
GARDEN GROVE FWY	22	ORA	195	B2
GARDEN GROVE FWY	22	ORA	196	C1
GIBSON, LUTHER E FWY	680	SOL	L	E2
GIBSON, LUTHER E FWY	680	SOL	38	E4
GIBSON, LUTHER E FWY	680	SOL	153	E4
GLENDALE FWY	2	LACO	R	A3
GLENDALE FWY	2	LACO	97	E1
GOLD COUNTRY HWY	49	AMA	40	D1
GOLD COUNTRY HWY	49	CAL	41	A3
GOLD COUNTRY HWY	49	ED	34	C4
GOLD COUNTRY HWY	49	ED	40	A1
GOLD COUNTRY HWY	49	ED	138	B1
GOLD COUNTRY HWY	49	MPA	48	D1
GOLD COUNTRY HWY	49	MPA	49	A3
GOLD COUNTRY HWY	49	NEV	34	C1
GOLD COUNTRY HWY	49	NEV	127	B5
GOLD COUNTRY HWY	49	NEV	128	A2
GOLD COUNTRY HWY	49	PLA	34	C3
GOLD COUNTRY HWY	49	PLA	126	B1
GOLD COUNTRY HWY	49	PLU	27	D3
GOLD COUNTRY HWY	49	SIE	26	C4
GOLD COUNTRY HWY	49	SIE	27	C3
GOLD COUNTRY HWY	49	TUO	41	A3
GOLD COUNTRY HWY	49	TUO	48	D1
GOLD COUNTRY HWY	49	TUO	163	B1
GOLDEN CENTER FWY	20	NEV	127	E2
GOLDEN GATE FWY	101	MAR	L	B4
GOLDEN GATE FWY	101	SFCO	L	B4

HIGHWAY INDEX

HIGHWAY NAME	HWY NO.	CO. ABBR.	PAGE	GRID
GOLDEN GATE FWY	101	SFCO	45	B1
GOLDEN STATE FWY	5	LACO	Q	B1
GOLDEN STATE FWY	5	LACO	R	C5
GOLDEN STATE FWY	5	LACO	88	E2
GOLDEN STATE FWY	5	LACO	89	B4
GOLDEN STATE FWY	5	LACO	97	D1
GOLDEN STATE FWY	5	LACO	179	C1
GOLDEN STATE FWY	5	LACO	182	D2
GOLDEN STATE FWY	5	LACO	186	D3
GROVE SHAFTER FWY	980	ALA	L	D4
GROVE SHAFTER FWY	980	ALA	45	D1
GROVE SHAFTER FWY	24	ALA	156	A5
GROVE SHAFTER FWY	980	ALA	158	A2
GUADALUPE PKWY	87	SCL	151	D1
GUADALUPE PKWY	87	SCL	152	A3
HARBOR FWY	110	LACO	Q	E5
HARBOR FWY	110	LACO	S	C2
HARBOR FWY	110	LACO	97	D4
HARBOR FWY	110	LACO	185	D4
HARBOR FWY	110	LACO	191	A2
HOLLYWOOD FWY	170	LACO	Q	C2
HOLLYWOOD FWY	101	LACO	Q	D3
HOLLYWOOD FWY	101	LACO	97	D1
HOLLYWOOD FWY	170	LACO	97	D1
HOLLYWOOD FWY	101	LACO	181	C2
HOLLYWOOD FWY	101	LACO	182	A5
HOLLYWOOD FWY	101	LACO	185	D1
HOLLYWOOD FWY	101	LACO	186	A2
HOLMAN HWY	68	MON	168	C1
IDYLLWILD NATL FOREST HWY	74	RCO	100	A4
INLAND FWY	805	SDCO	V	A1
INLAND FWY	805	SDCO	106	C4
INLAND FWY	805	SDCO	111	D2
INLAND FWY	805	SDCO	214	B3
INLAND FWY	805	SDCO	216	C1
JAMES LICK FWY	80	SFCO	L	C4
JAMES LICK FWY	80	SFCO	45	C1
JAMES LICK FWY	101	SFCO	142	D5
JAMES LICK SKYWY	80	SFCO	142	D4
JAMES LICK SKYWY	101	SFCO	143	C5
JOHN T KNOX FWY	580	CC	L	C3
JOHN T KNOX FWY	580	CC	155	B4
JUNIPERO SERRA FWY	280	SCL	N	D2
JUNIPERO SERRA FWY	280	SCL	P	A3
JUNIPERO SERRA FWY	280	SCL	45	D3
JUNIPERO SERRA FWY	101	SCL	149	C4
JUNIPERO SERRA FWY	101	SCL	150	A4
JUNIPERO SERRA FWY	280	SMCO	N	B1
JUNIPERO SERRA FWY	280	SMCO	45	B2
JUNIPERO SERRA FWY	280	SMCO	144	A5
KNOX, JOHN T FWY	580	CC	L	C3
KNOX, JOHN T FWY	580	CC	155	B4
LAGUNA FWY	133	ORA	T	E4
LAGUNA FWY	133	ORA	98	D5
LAKEVILLE HWY	116	SON	L	A1
LICK, JAMES FWY	80	SFCO	L	C4
LICK, JAMES FWY	80	SFCO	45	C1
LICK, JAMES FWY	101	SFCO	142	D5
LICK, JAMES SKYWY	80	SFCO	142	D4
LICK, JAMES SKYWY	101	SFCO	143	C5
LONG BEACH FWY	710	LACO	R	B4
LONG BEACH FWY	710	LACO	S	D2
LONG BEACH FWY	710	LACO	97	E3
LONG BEACH FWY	710	LACO	192	C2
LOS BANOS HWY	59	MCO	170	C5
LUTHER E GIBSON FWY	680	SOL	L	E2
LUTHER E GIBSON FWY	680	SOL	38	E4
LUTHER E GIBSON FWY	680	SOL	153	E4
MACARTHUR FWY	580	ALA	L	D4
MACARTHUR FWY	580	ALA	45	D1
MACARTHUR FWY	580	ALA	158	B2
MARICOPA HWY	166	KER	78	B5
MARINA EXPWY	90	LACO	187	D3
MARINA FWY	90	LACO	Q	C4
MARINA FWY	90	LACO	97	C2
MARINA FWY	90	LACO	188	A3
MARINE WORLD PKWY	37	SOL	134	B2
MIDLAND TRAIL	14	KER	80	C2

HIGHWAY NAME	HWY NO.	CO. ABBR.	PAGE	GRID
MISSION VALLEY FWY	8	SDCO	V	B3
MISSION VALLEY FWY	8	SDCO	111	C1
MISSION VALLEY FWY	8	SDCO	213	E4
MOORPARK FWY	23	VEN	88	D5
MOORPARK FWY	23	VEN	96	E1
NEEDLES FWY	40	SBD	92	A1
NEEDLES FWY	40	SBD	93	D2
NEEDLES FWY	40	SBD	94	D2
NEEDLES FWY	40	SBD	95	C1
NIMITZ FWY	880	ALA	L	E5
NIMITZ FWY	880	ALA	P	B2
NIMITZ FWY	880	ALA	45	D2
NIMITZ FWY	880	ALA	46	A3
NIMITZ FWY	880	ALA	146	C4
NIMITZ FWY	880	ALA	157	D1
NIMITZ FWY	980	ALA	158	B4
NIMITZ FWY	880	ALA	159	C1
NORTH HWY	190	INY	72	B1
OCEAN BEACH FWY	8	SDCO	212	C5
OJAI FWY	33	VEN	88	A5
OJAI FWY	33	VEN	175	A2
ORANGE FWY	57	LACO	U	B3
ORANGE FWY	57	LACO	98	C3
ORANGE FWY	57	ORA	T	D1
ORANGE FWY	57	ORA	U	A4
ORANGE FWY	57	ORA	98	C3
ORANGE FWY	57	ORA	194	A4
ORTEGA HWY	74	ORA	98	E5
ORTEGA HWY	74	ORA	99	A5
ORTEGA HWY	74	ORA	202	E1
PACIFIC COAST HWY	1	LACO	Q	C4
PACIFIC COAST HWY	1	LACO	S	B1
PACIFIC COAST HWY	1	LACO	96	E2
PACIFIC COAST HWY	1	LACO	97	B2
PACIFIC COAST HWY	1	ORA	T	A3
PACIFIC COAST HWY	1	ORA	98	C5
PACIFIC COAST HWY	1	VEN	96	C2
PASADENA FWY	110	LACO	R	A3
PASADENA FWY	110	LACO	R	A3
PASADENA FWY	110	LACO	97	E2
PASADENA FWY	110	LACO	186	B2
PASO ROBLES HWY	46	KER	77	A1
PINES TO PALMS HWY	74	RCO	100	B4
POMONA FWY	60	LACO	R	E4
POMONA FWY	60	LACO	98	B2
POMONA FWY	60	SBD	U	D3
POMONA FWY	60	SBD	98	D2
PORTERVILLE HWY	65	KER	68	D5
PORTERVILLE HWY	65	KER	78	D1
PORTERVILLE HWY	65	TUL	68	C2
RAMONA FWY	125	SDCO	V	D2
REDLANDS FWY	10	RCO	99	D2
REDLANDS FWY	10	RCO	100	A3
REDLANDS FWY	10	SBD	99	D2
REDONDO BEACH FWY	91	KER	97	E3
REDONDO BEACH FWY	91	LACO	S	C1
REDWOOD HWY	101	DN	1	E3
REDWOOD HWY	199	DN	2	B3
REDWOOD HWY	101	DN	10	A3
REDWOOD HWY	101	HUM	9	E3
REDWOOD HWY	101	HUM	10	A2
REDWOOD HWY	101	HUM	15	E3
REDWOOD HWY	101	HUM	16	B4
REDWOOD HWY	101	HUM	22	C1
REDWOOD HWY	101	MAR	L	A2
REDWOOD HWY	101	MAR	38	A4
REDWOOD HWY	101	MAR	45	B1
REDWOOD HWY	101	MAR	139	D2
REDWOOD HWY	101	MAR	140	C2
REDWOOD HWY	101	MEN	22	C2
REDWOOD HWY	101	MEN	31	A1
REDWOOD HWY	101	SON	L	A2
REDWOOD HWY	101	SON	31	C4
REDWOOD HWY	101	SON	37	D1
REDWOOD HWY	101	SON	38	A3
REDWOOD HWY	101	SON	131	C2
RIVERSIDE FWY	91	ORA	T	D2
RIVERSIDE FWY	91	ORA	U	C5

HIGHWAY INDEX

HIGHWAY NAME	HWY NO.	CO. ABBR.	PAGE	GRID
RIVERSIDE FWY	91	ORA	98	C3
RIVERSIDE FWY	91	ORA	194	D1
RIVERSIDE FWY	91	RCO	U	C5
RIVERSIDE FWY	91	RCO	99	A3
RIVERSIDE FWY	91	RCO	205	C2
ROSEDALE HWY	58	KER	78	C3
ROUTE 4 FWY	4	CC	M	B3
ROUTE 4 FWY	4	CC	154	C3
ROUTE 8 FWY	8	SDCO	106	D5
ROUTE 8 FWY	8	SDCO	107	A5
ROUTE 8 FWY	8	SDCO	111	A4
ROUTE 8 FWY	8	SDCO	112	D1
ROUTE 17 FWY	17	SCL	46	A5
ROUTE 17 FWY	17	SCR	P	B4
ROUTE 17 FWY	17	SCR	54	A1
ROUTE 52 FWY	52	SDCO	211	E3
ROUTE 67 FWY	67	SDCO	106	E5
ROUTE 78 FWY	78	SDCO	106	C3
ROUTE 94 FWY	94	SDCO	V	D3
ROUTE 94 FWY	94	SDCO	216	D3
ROUTE 101 FWY	101	SB	86	D2
ROUTE 101 FWY	101	SB	173	C1
SAN BERNARDINO FWY	10	LACO	U	B2
SAN BERNARDINO FWY	10	LACO	98	B2
SAN BERNARDINO FWY	10	LACO	186	D3
SAN BERNARDINO FWY	10	SBD	U	D2
SAN BERNARDINO FWY	10	SBD	98	D2
SAN BERNARDINO FWY	10	SBD	99	A1
SAN BERNARDINO FWY	10	SBD	203	B3
SAN BERNARDINO FWY	10	SBD	204	D3
SAN DIEGO FWY	405	LACO	Q	B3
SAN DIEGO FWY	405	LACO	S	B2
SAN DIEGO FWY	405	LACO	97	C2
SAN DIEGO FWY	405	LACO	180	C2
SAN DIEGO FWY	405	LACO	188	D4
SAN DIEGO FWY	405	LACO	189	E5
SAN DIEGO FWY	405	ORA	T	B3
SAN DIEGO FWY	405	ORA	98	B4
SAN DIEGO FWY	5	ORA	98	D4
SAN DIEGO FWY	5	ORA	105	D1
SAN DIEGO FWY	405	ORA	197	D4
SAN DIEGO FWY	405	ORA	198	A4
SAN DIEGO FWY	5	ORA	202	D3
SAN DIEGO FWY	5	SDCO	V	A2
SAN DIEGO FWY	5	SDCO	106	A2
SAN DIEGO FWY	5	SDCO	111	D2
SAN DIEGO FWY	5	SDCO	211	C4
SAN DIEGO FWY	5	SDCO	212	E3
SAN DIEGO FWY	5	SDCO	215	E3
SAN DIEGO FWY	5	SDCO	216	B5
SAN GABRIEL RIVER FWY	605	LACO	R	D4
SAN GABRIEL RIVER FWY	605	LACO	S	E2
SAN GABRIEL RIVER FWY	605	LACO	T	A2
SAN GABRIEL RIVER FWY	605	LACO	98	A2
SAN VICENTE FWY	67	SDCO	106	E5
SANTA ANA FWY	5	LACO	98	A2
SANTA ANA FWY	5	LACO	186	D3
SANTA ANA FWY	5	ORA	T	B1
SANTA ANA FWY	5	ORA	U	A5
SANTA ANA FWY	5	ORA	98	A2
SANTA ANA FWY	5	ORA	193	D4
SANTA ANA FWY	5	ORA	196	B2
SANTA MONICA FWY	10	LACO	Q	C4
SANTA MONICA FWY	10	LACO	97	D2
SANTA MONICA FWY	10	LACO	180	B5
SANTA MONICA FWY	10	LACO	183	B4
SANTA MONICA FWY	10	LACO	184	D4
SANTA MONICA FWY	10	LACO	185	D4
SANTA MONICA FWY	10	LACO	186	A5
SANTA PAULA FWY	126	VEN	88	B5
SEBASTOPOL FWY	12	SON	131	B4
SHORELINE HWY	1	MAR	L	B4
SHORELINE HWY	1	MAR	37	D4
SHORELINE HWY	1	MAR	45	A1
SHORELINE HWY	1	MAR	140	B4
SHORELINE HWY	1	MEN	22	C3
SHORELINE HWY	1	MEN	30	C4
SILVERADO TRAIL	121	NAPA	133	E4

HIGHWAY NAME	HWY NO.	CO. ABBR.	PAGE	GRID
SIMI VLY-SN FERNANDO VLY	118	LACO	Q	C1
SIMI VLY-SN FERNANDO VLY	118	LACO	89	B5
SIMI VLY-SN FERNANDO VLY	118	VEN	88	E5
SIMI VLY-SN FERNANDO VLY	118	VEN	89	B5
SINCLAIR FWY	680	ALA	P	B2
SINCLAIR FWY	680	ALA	46	B2
SINCLAIR FWY	680	CC	46	A1
SINCLAIR FWY	680	SCL	P	B2
SINCLAIR FWY	680	SCL	46	B4
SINCLAIR FWY	280	SCL	151	D5
SINCLAIR FWY	280	SCL	152	D4
SNELLING HWY	59	MCO	170	C5
SOLEDAD FWY	52	SDCO	V	B2
SOLEDAD FWY	52	SDCO	106	C5
SONOMA HWY	12	SON	132	C3
SOUTH BAY EXPWY	54	SDCO	V	D4
SOUTH BAY EXPWY	54	SDCO	111	D1
SOUTHBAY FWY	237	SCL	P	A3
SOUTHBAY FWY	237	SCL	46	A4
SOUTHBAY FWY	237	SCL	148	C4
SOUTHRN EMBARCADERO FY	280	SFCO	L	C5
SOUTHRN EMBARCADERO FY	280	SFCO	45	C2
SOUTHRN EMBARCADERO FY	280	SFCO	143	E5
SOUTH VALLEY FWY	101	SCL	54	C1
STEVENS CREEK FWY	85	SCL	N	E3
STEVENS CREEK FWY	85	SCL	P	A3
STEVENS CREEK FWY	85	SCL	45	E4
STEVENS CREEK FWY	85	SCL	148	A4
TAFT HWY	119	KER	78	C3
TERMINAL ISLAND FWY	103	LACO	192	A2
THREE FLAGS HWY	395	KER	80	D1
TWENTYNINE PALMS HWY	62	RCO	100	C2
TWENTYNINE PALMS HWY	62	RCO	102	C2
TWENTYNINE PALMS HWY	62	SBD	100	C2
TWENTYNINE PALMS HWY	62	SBD	101	C1
TWENTYNINE PALMS HWY	62	SBD	102	A2
VENTURA FWY	134	LACO	Q	E3
VENTURA FWY	134	LACO	R	A3
VENTURA FWY	101	LACO	97	B1
VENTURA FWY	134	LACO	97	B1
VENTURA FWY	101	LACO	177	C4
VENTURA FWY	101	LACO	178	B3
VENTURA FWY	101	LACO	179	D5
VENTURA FWY	101	VEN	87	E5
VENTURA FWY	101	VEN	88	A5
VENTURA FWY	101	VEN	96	D1
VENTURA FWY	101	VEN	175	C3
WARREN FWY	13	ALA	L	D4
WARREN FWY	13	ALA	45	D1
WARREN FWY	13	CC	156	E5
WESTSIDE FWY	5	FRCO	55	E3
WESTSIDE FWY	5	FRCO	56	B4
WESTSIDE FWY	5	FRCO	66	E2
WEST SIDE FWY	5	KER	77	D1
WEST SIDE FWY	5	KER	78	B3
WEST SIDE FWY	5	KER	88	D1
WESTSIDE FWY	5	KIN	67	C4
WESTSIDE FWY	5	MCO	47	C5
WESTSIDE FWY	5	MCO	55	D1
WESTSIDE FWY	5	SAC	39	E2
WESTSIDE FWY	5	SJCO	39	E4
WESTSIDE FWY	5	SJCO	40	A4
WESTSIDE FWY	5	SJCO	47	A2
WESTSIDE FWY	5	STA	47	B3
WESTSIDE FWY	5	YOL	33	A4
WEST SIDE HWY	33	KER	67	B5
WEST SIDE HWY	33	KER	77	C1
WEST SIDE HWY	33	KER	78	A4
YOUNGER FWY	92	ALA	N	D1
YOUNGER FWY	92	ALA	45	D2
YOUNGER FWY	92	SMCO	N	D1
YOUNGER FWY	92	SMCO	45	D2
YOUNGER FWY	92	SMCO	145	D1

✈ AIRPORTS

NAME & ADDRESS	PAGE	GRID
ALTURAS MUNICIPAL AIRPORT, 1 mi W of Alturas	8	A1
AMADOR COUNTY AIRPORT, near Amador	40	D2
ANTIOCH AIRPORT, Lone Tree Wy, Antioch	M	C3
ARCATA AIRPORT, off Hwy 101 at Airport Rd	10	A4
AUBURN AIRPORT, 4 mi N of Auburn	34	C3
BAKERSFIELD AIRPARK, Watts Dr & Union Av	78	D3
BARSTOW-DAGGETT, Nat'l Trails Hwy, Barstow	92	B1
BENTON AIRPORT, Gold St, Redding	122	A3
BISHOP AIRPORT, 2 mi E of Bishop	51	D4
BRACKETT FIELD, McKinley Av, La Verne	U	C2
BUCHANAN FIELD AIRPORT, John Glenn Dr, Concord	M	A3
BURBANK-GLENDALE-PASADENA, 2627 N Hollywood Wy	179	B1
CALAVERAS CO AIRPORT, Hwy 49 S of San Andreas	41	A4
CANNON INTERNATIONAL AIRPORT, 2 of Reno	28	C4
CARSON AIRPORT, Carson City, Nevada	36	C1
CATALINA AIR & SEA TERMINAL, Harbor Blvd	191	B3
CHICO MUNICIPAL AIRPORT, 5 mi NW of Chico	25	B2
CHINO AIRPORT, Hwy 83, Chino	U	D3
COLUSA COUNTY AIRPORT, 3 mi S of Colusa	33	A2
DELANO MUNICIPAL AIRPORT, Hwy 99, Delano	68	B5
DOUGLAS COUNTY AIRPORT, Minden, Nevada	36	C3
FANTASY HAVEN AIRPORT, 2 mi SE of Tehachapi	79	D4
FRESNO AIR TERMINAL, 5175 E Clinton Av	57	D3
FRESNO-CHANDLER DOWNTOWN AIRPORT, Amador & Thorne	165	B4
IMPERIAL COUNTY AIRPORT, Hwy 86 at Main, Imperial	109	A5
INYOKERN COUNTY AIRPORT, Hwy 395, Inyokern	80	D1
JOHN MCNAMARA FIELD, nr Crescent City	1	C4
JOHN WAYNE AIRPORT, MacArthur Blvd	198	B5
KERN VALLEY AIRPORT, Sierra Wy N of Lake Isabella	69	D5
LAKEVIEW MUNICIPAL AIRPORT, near jct of 140 & 395	7	B1
LAMPSON AIRPORT, SW of Clear Lake off Hwy 175	31	D3
LIVERMORE AIRPORT, Stanley Blvd, Livermore	M	C5
LONE PINE AIRPORT, 1 mile south of Lone Pine	60	B4
LONG BEACH MUNICIPAL, 4100 Donald Douglas Dr	S	E2
LOS ANGELES INTERNATIONAL, 1 World Wy	189	C2
MADERA AIRPORT, Hwy 99 & Av 17	57	A2
MARIPOSA YOSEMITE AIRPORT, near Mariposa	49	A3
McCARRAN INTERNATIONAL, 5 miles S of Las Vegas	210	C5
MEADOWS FIELD, Skyway & Airport Drs	78	D2
MENDOCINO COUNTY AIRPORT, Hwy 1 S of Little River	30	B1
MERCED MUNICIPAL AIRPORT, 2 mi SW of Merced	170	A5
MONTEREY PENINSULA AIRPORT, off Hwy 68	54	B1
NEEDLES MUNICIPAL, Airport Rd & Hwy 95, Needles	95	D2
NORTH LAS VEGAS AIR TERMINAL, 3.5 miles NW of L V	74	D2
OAKDALE AIRPORT, 8191 Laughlin Rd, Oakdale	47	E1
OAKLAND INTERNATIONAL, Doolittle & Airport Wy	159	B4
OCOTILLO WELLS AIRPORT, HWY 78, Ocotillo	108	B3
ONTARIO INTERNATIONAL AIRPORT, 2 mi E of Ontario	204	E5
OROVILLE AIRPORT, 3 mi SW of Oroville	25	C4
PALMDALE AIRPORT, Sierra Hwy	90	A3
PALM SPRINGS REGIONAL, 2 mi E of Palm Springs	206	E3
PEARCE AIRPORT, Hwy 53 S of Clearlake	32	A3
PLACERVILLE AIRPORT, S of Hwy 50 near Smithflat	34	E5
REDDING MUNICIPAL AIRPORT, 7 miles SE of Redding	18	C2
SACRAMENTO CO METRO ARPRT, 12 mi NW of Sacramento	33	D5
SACRAMENTO EXECUTIVE AIRPORT, 6151 Freeport Blvd	39	D1
SALINAS MUNICIPAL AIRPORT, off Hwy 101	54	D4
SAN DIEGO INTERNATIONAL AIRPORT, Lindbergh Field	215	B2
SAN FRANCISCO INTL, Airport Wy off Bayshore Fwy	144	D3
SAN JOSE INTERNATIONAL AIRPORT, 1661 Airport Bl	151	C1
SANTA BARBARA AIRPORT, James Fowler Rd	87	B4
SANTA MARIA PUBLIC AIRPORT, Skyway Dr, Sta Maria	86	B1
SANTA MONICA MUNICIPAL AIRPORT	187	C1
SHAFTER-KERN COUNTY AIRFIELD, Lerdo Hwy	78	B2
SISKIYOU COUNTY AIRPORT, Montague	4	C4
STOCKTON METRO AIRPORT, 5000 S Airport Wy	40	B5
SUSANVILLE AIRPORT, 5 mi SE of Susanville	21	B3
SUTTER COUNTY AIRPORT, off Samuel Dr	125	E4
TAFT-KERN AIRPORT, West Side Hwy, Taft	78	A4
TAHOE AIRPORT, Pioneer Trail Rd	36	A3
TEHACHAPI-KERN CO AIRPORT, Green & J Sts	79	D4
TRUCKEE AIRPORT, 4 miles E of Truckee	35	E1
TULELAKE MUNI AIRPORT, N of Hw 139 near Newell	5	E3
UKIAH AIRPORT, State St	123	D5
VENTURA COUNTY AIRPORT, Oxnard	176	A4
YUBA COUNTY AIRPORT, Olivehurst	33	D2
YUCCA VALLEY AIRPORT, Hwys 62 & 247, Yucca Valley	100	D1

⌂ AMUSEMENT PARKS

NAME & ADDRESS	PAGE	GRID
DISNEYLAND, Harbor Blvd, Anaheim	193	B4
Amusement park-7 theme sections, rides, shops.		
KNOTTS BERRY FARM, 8039 Beach Bl, Buena Park	T	B2
Ride 'Corkscrew' & 'Log Ride'; shops, rstrnts.		
MARINE WORLD AFRICA, 1000 Fairgrounds, Vallejo	134	E1
Land & sea animal shows; natural setting		
MARRIOTT'S GREAT AMERICA, 1 Great America Pkwy	P	B3
Family amusement park, American history theme.		
OASIS WATER PARK, 1500 Gene Autry Tr, Palm Spgs	100	D3
Wave pool, speed slide, hydro tubes, lagoon.		
RAGING WATERS, 111 Via Verde, San Dimas	U	B2
Pools, slides, picnic area.		
RAGING WATERS, off Capitol Expwy, San Jose	P	C3
Pools, slides, picnic area.		
SAN DIEGO WILD ANIMAL PARK, 5 mi W of Escondido	106	D3
Tour through preserve for endangered species.		
SEA WORLD, 1720 S Shores Rd, Mission Bay Park	212	C4
Marine life amusement pk, shows; Japanese Vlg.		
SIX FLAGS MAGIC MOUNTAIN, I-5 at Valencia Av	89	B4
Family amusement park; thrill rides and shops.		
SPLASHDOWN WATERSLIDE, 200 Dempsey, Milpitas	P	C2
Water flumes; picnic area.		
UNIVERSAL STUDIOS & AMPHITHEATER, Univ City Plaza	181	B1
Features tours of movie and TV sets; shows.		
WET 'N WILD, 2600 Las Vegas Blvd, Las Vegas	209	C4
Wave pool, flumes, water roller coaster.		
WILD RIVERS, Irvine Center Dr, Irvine	98	D4
Water slides and activities.		
WINDSOR WATERWORKS, 8225 Conde, Windsor	37	E1
Pool, flumes, picnic area.		

POINTS OF INTEREST INDEX

NAME & ADDRESS	PAGE	GRID	NAME & ADDRESS	PAGE	GRID
BEACHES			HUNTINGTON BEACH STATE PARK, Huntington Beach	T	B4
			Sandy beach, good surfing, picnicking.		
			ISLA VISTA COUNTY BEACH PARK, Camino Del Sur	87	B4
			Sandy beach, tidepools.		
ARROYO BURRO BEACH COUNTY PARK, 2981 Cliff Dr	87	C4	J D PHELAN BEACH, El Camino del Mar, Sn Francisco	141	A2
Swimming, picnicking, surf fishing.			Swimming cove protected from the wind.		
ASILOMAR STATE BEACH, Sunset Dr, Pacific Grove	167	A1	LAS TUNAS STATE BEACH, near Jct Hwy 1 & Hwy 27	Q	A4
Conference facilities in a beautiful setting.			Swimming in the surf, fishing, and picnicking.		
ATASCADERO STATE BEACH, Jct Hwy 1 and Hwy 41	75	D3	LEADBETTER BEACH, Shoreline Dr, Santa Barbara	174	C5
Swimming, fishing and camping.			Very wide, sandy beach; picnic facilities.		
AVILA STATE BEACH, Front St	76	A4	LEO CARRILLO STATE BEACH, S of Hwy 101	96	D2
Fishing, fire rings, swimming.			Good surfing, diving and swimming.		
BAKER BEACH, NW shore Presidio, San Francisco	141	B2	LEUCADIA STATE BEACH, Leucadia	106	B4
Fishing, hiking nearby, no swimming.			Scenic beach for fishing and swimming.		
BEAN HOLLOW STATE BEACH, S of Half Moon Bay	N	B4	LITTLE RIVER STATE BEACH, South of Trinidad	9	E4
Fishing and camping on the beach.			Beautiful beaches, delta, nature trails.		
BOLSA CHICA STATE BEACH, N of Huntington Beach	T	A3	MALIBU LAGOON STATE BEACH, near Malibu	97	B2
Sandy beach, body surfing, picnicking.			Site of famous surfrider beach, swimming.		
BOOMER BEACH, Coast Blvd, La Jolla	105	B2	MANCHESTER STATE BEACH, near Point Arena	30	B3
Scenic beach, swimming and fishing.			Beaches, sand dunes, Point Arena Lighthouse.		
CABRILLO BEACH, E of Pacific Av, San Pedro	S	C3	MANHATTAN STATE BEACH, Manhattan Beach	S	A1
Public boat ramp, surf fishing, barbeque pits.			Public fishing pier, swimming, surfing.		
CAPISTRANO BEACH, San Juan Capistrano	202	D5	MANRESA STATE BEACH, off San Andreas Rd	54	B2
Sandy beach, body surfing, picnicking.			Sandy beach, tide pools.		
CAPITOLA CITY BEACH, 30th Av, Capitola	54	A2	MARINA STATE BEACH, 10 mi N of Monterey	54	B4
Swimming and fishing.			Good fishing area.		
CARDIFF STATE BEACH, Cardiff	106	B4	MARINE STREET BEACH, La Jolla	105	A3
Fine beach for fishing or swimming.			Fishing, swimming and sunbathing.		
CARLSBAD STATE BEACH, 3 mi S of Carlsbad Bl	106	A3	MCGRATH STATE BEACH, S of Santa Clara River	96	A1
Fish, swim, surf, camp, store, concessions.			Hiking, camping, fishing.		
CARMEL RIVER STATE BEACH, Scenic Rd	168	B4	MONTARA STATE BEACH, N of Half Moon Bay	N	A2
Skin diving, fishing, bird watching sites.			Fishing beach.		
CARPINTERIA STATE BEACH, Linden Av	87	D4	MONTEREY STATE BEACH, Park Av	54	B4
Camping, picnicking. fishing pier, boat ramp.			Sandy beach, fishing, swimming in summer.		
CASA BEACH, Coast Blvd, La Jolla	105	A3	MOONLIGHT STATE BEACH, Encinitas	106	B4
Swimming and fishing.			Sandy beach for swimming and fishing.		
CASPER HEADLANDS STATE RESERVE, Hwy 1 near Casper	22	A5	MORRO STRAND STATE BEACH, end of Yerba Buena Rd	75	D2
Scenic environment with good fishing.			Sand dunes, streams; camping permitted.		
CASPER STATE BEACH, off Hwy 1 near Casper	22	B5	MOSS LANDING STATE BEACH, off Hwy 1	54	B3
Scenic area for picnicking and fishing.			Fishing and equestrian trails.		
CAYUCOS STATE BEACH, on Ocean Front Rd	75	D2	NATURAL BRIDGES STATE BEACH, W Cliff Dr	53	E2
Fishing pier, barbeque & picnic facilities.			Natural sandstone formation; picnics, fishing.		
CORAL BEACH, Hwy 1 W of Malibu Beach	97	A2	NEW BRIGHTON STATE BEACH, off Hwy 1	54	A2
Fishing, swimming and picnicking.			Sandy beach, tide pools.		
CORONA DEL MAR STATE BEACH, Corona Del Mar	T	D5	NEWPORT DUNES AQUATIC PARK, off Pacific Coast Hwy	199	D4
Sandy beach, tidepools, body surfng, picnckng.			Swimming and other aquatic recreation.		
DOCKWEILER STATE BEACH, Venice	187	A4	OCEANSIDE CITY BEACH, The Strand & Pacific	106	A3
Swimming, picnicking, fishing.			Popular resort; 4 mi beach, swim, skin dive.		
DOHENY STATE BEACH, Puerto & Del Obispo Sts	202	B4	PACIFICA STATE BEACH, Hwy 1, Pacifica	N	B1
Surfing, camping, fire rings & picnic areas.			Fishing, hiking, tidepools.		
EAST BEACH, E Cabrillo Blvd, Santa Barbara	174	E4	PELICAN STATE BEACH, 21 miles N of Crescent City	1	D2
BBQ & picnic facilities, volleyball courts.			Fishing; no swimming.		
EL CAPITAN STATE BEACH, Avenida del Capitan	87	A4	PESCADERO STATE BEACH, Hwy 1 S of Half Moon Bay	N	B4
Surfing, hiking, camping, boat rentals.			Good beach for fishing.		
EL DORADO BEACH, off Hwy 50, South Lake Tahoe	129	A3	PISMO STATE BEACH, off Hwy 101, Pismo Beach	76	B5
On the south shore of lovely Lake Tahoe.			Camping & hiking among sandy beaches & dunes.		
EMMA WOOD STATE BEACH, Hwy 101 & Hwy 33	88	A5	POINT DUME STATE BEACH, Hwy 1	96	E2
Camping, fishing and swimming.			Good beach for picnicking, hiking or fishing.		
GAZO CREEK ANGLING ACCESS, Gazo Creek Rd	N	C4	POINT REYES NATIONAL SEASHORE, near Olema	37	D5
Beach access for fishing.			Sandy beach, tide pools; picnic, camp, hike.		
GOLETA BEACH COUNTY PARK, 5990 Sandspit Rd	87	B4	POINT SAL STATE BEACH, Sal Point Rd	86	A1
Fishing pier, swimming, boat hoist.			Many varieties of marine life.		
GRAYWHALE COVE STATE BEACH, N of Half Moon Bay	N	A1	POMPONIO STATE BEACH, Hwy 1 S of Half Moon Bay	N	B3
Good beach for fishing.			Lovely beach for picnicking and fishing.		
HALF MOON BAY STATE BEACH, near Half Moon Bay	N	B2	PORT HUENEME BEACH, off Hueneme Rd	96	B1
Camp on bluffs above beaches, hike, picnic.			Fishing pier, playground, bike paths.		
HERMOSA BEACH, btwn Redondo & Manhattan Beaches	S	A1	REDONDO STATE BEACH, Redondo Beach	S	A2
Public fishing pier, swimming, surfing.			Adjacent to King Harbor Marina; swim, fish.		

NAME & ADDRESS	PAGE	GRID
REFUGIO STATE BEACH, Refugio Rd	86	E4
Tidepools; camping, fishing.		
ROBERT H MEYER MEM STATE BEACH, Hwy 1 W of Malibu	96	E2
Swimming, picnicking facilities, fishing.		
ROBERT W. CROWN MEMORIAL STATE BEACH, Alameda	L	D5
Day use only; youth programs offered.		
ROYAL PALMS STATE BEACH, Paseo dl Mar, Ls Angeles	S	C3
Good beach to swim, picnic, or fish.		
SALINAS RIVER STATE BEACH, Potrero Rd	54	B3
Wide sandy beach & dunes; clamming & fishing.		
SAN BUENAVENTURA STATE BEACH, Harbor Bl, Ventura	175	C3
Good swimming, beach equipment rentals.		
SAN CLEMENTE STATE BEACH, San Clemente	105	D1
Surfing, camping; BBQ & picnic facilities.		
SAN ELIJO STATE BEACH, Cardiff	106	B4
Good beach for camping, fishing and swimming.		
SAN GREGORIO STATE BCH, Hwy 1 S of Half Moon Bay	N	B3
Good fishing beach; picnicking.		
SAN ONOFRE STATE BEACH, San Onofre	105	E2
Surf fishing, clamming; surfing & camping.		
SAN SIMEON STATE BEACH, Hwy 1	75	B1
Camping, hiking; dunes to explore.		
SANTA CRUZ BEACH, Beach St	169	D4
Swimming, surfing, surf fishing.		
SANTA MONICA STATE BEACH, Palisades Beach Rd	Q	B4
Most popular beach in the Los Angeles area.		
SEACLIFF STATE BEACH, 5 mi S of Hwy 1	54	B2
Swimming; marine museum - open in summer.		
SILVER STRAND STATE BEACH, Hwy 75, S of Coronado	V	B4
Beautiful beach to swim, picnic, or fish.		
SONOMA COAST STATE BEACH, N of Bodega Bay	37	B2
Camp, hike, picnic; scenic beaches.		
SOUTH CARLSBAD STATE BEACH, S of Carlsbad	106	B3
Camping, fishing and swimming.		
STILLWATER COVE, Hwy 1 S of Walsh Landing	37	A1
Good swimming and fishing.		
SUNSET STATE BEACH, W of Watsonville	54	B2
Scenic bluffs; camp, fish, clam dig, picnic.		
THORNTON STATE BEACH, off Hwy 35 E of Daly City	L	B5
Good fishing; hiking trails.		
TOPANGA STATE BEACH, Topanga Canyon Blvd	Q	A4
Swimming in the surf, picnicking.		
TORREY PINES STATE BEACH, S of Del Mar	V	A1
Scenic beach for hiking, swimming, exploring.		
TRINIDAD STATE BEACH, off Hwy 101, Trinidad	9	E4
Beaches, bluffs, nature trails, picnicking.		
TWIN LAKES STATE BEACH, Santa Cruz	54	A2
Swimming, fire pits; day use only-no camping.		
VENTURA RIVER BEACH PARK, Hwy 101, Ventura	175	A2
Extends along E bank Ventura River to beach.		
WEST BEACH, Cabrillo Bl, Santa Barbara	174	D4
Sandy beach; restaurants & specialty shops.		
WESTPORT UNION LANDING STATE BEACH, N of Westport	22	B3
Fishing and camping.		
Wm. RANDOLPH HEARST STATE BEACH, Hwy 1, Sn Simeon	75	B1
Picnic facilities; boating, fishing, swimming.		
WILL ROGERS STATE BEACH, N of Santa Monica	Q	B4
Wide sandy beach; surfing, picnicking.		
WINDANSEA BEACH, foot of Palomar St	V	A2
Surfboarding & spectator beach; no swimming.		
WIPEOUT BEACH, Coast Blvd, La Jolla	105	A3
Sandy beach, swimming and fishing.		
ZMUDOWSKI STATE BEACH, 1 mi N of Moss Landing	54	B3
Fishing and horseback riding.		

CAMPGROUNDS

NAME & ADDRESS	PAGE	GRID
ANDREW MOLERA STATE PARK, W of Hwy 1, Big Sur	64	B2
Camping, hiking, sandy beaches and meadows.		
ANZA BORREGO DESERT STATE PARK, San Diego County	108	A4
Beautiful wildflowers in spring; camp & hike.		
ATASCADERO STATE BEACH, Jct of Hwy 1 & Hwy 41	75	D3
Camping and picnicking facilities.		
AUSTIN CREEK STATE RECREATION AREA, E of Ft Ross	37	C1
Primitive camping; picnicking area.		
BENBOW LAKE STATE REC AREA, 2 mi S of Garberville	22	B1
Camp, fish, horse trails, swim, & picnic.		
BIG BASIN REDWOODS STATE PARK, on Hwy 236	N	D4
Camping alongside the historic redwoods.		
BOLSA CHICA STATE BEACH, N of Huntington Beach	T	A3
Camping, body surfing, picnicking & swimming.		
BOTHE-NAPA VALLEY STATE PARK, on Hwy 29	38	A1
Camping, swimming, picnicking & hiking.		
BRANNAN ISLAND STATE REC AREA, S of Rio Vista	M	D2
Camping, fishing, swimming, boating; Vis Ctr.		
BUTANO STATE PARK, E of Hwy 1 at Gazos Creek Rd	N	C4
Camping and recreational facilities.		
CALAVERAS BIG TREES STATE PARK, E of Arnold	41	D3
Camping among the redwood groves.		
CARPINTERIA STATE BEACH, Linden Av	87	D4
Camping, picnicking, fishing pier, boat ramp.		
CASTLE CRAG STATE PARK, S of Dunsmuir	12	D3
Camping, fishing, hiking, swimming.		
CASTLE ROCK STATE PARK, near Jct Hwy 9 & Hwy 35	N	E4
Scenic park for camping, picnicking, & hiking.		
CASWELL MEMORIAL STATE PARK, Hwy 99 S of Manteca	47	B2
Camping, fishing, swimming, and hiking.		
CHINA CAMP STATE PARK, N of San Rafael	L	B3
Camping and recreation facilities.		
CLEAR LAKE STATE PARK, near Lakeport	31	D3
Camping, hiking, picnicking and boating.		
COLUSA-SACRAMENTO RIVER STATE REC AREA, Colusa	33	A1
Camping, fishing, boating and waterskiing.		
CUYAMACA RANCHO STATE PARK, on Hwy 79, Julian	107	C4
In old Indian territory; camp, hike; horses.		
DEL NORTE COAST REDWOODS ST PK, S of Crescnt City	1	E4
Camping, picnicking, hiking, fishing&exhibits.		
D. L. BLISS STATE PARK, N of Emerald Bay	35	E3
Camping, beach, trails, dense forest.		
EL CAPITAN STATE BEACH, Avenida del Capitan	87	A4
Surfing, hiking, camping & boat rentals.		
EMERALD BAY STATE PARK, Hwy 89 near Emerald Bay	35	E3
Scenic; camping, picnicking and swimming.		
EMMA WOOD STATE BEACH, Jct Hwy 101 & Hwy 33	88	A5
Camping, swimming and fishing.		
FOLSOM LAKE STATE REC AREA, 1 mile N of Folsom	34	B5
Camping, boating, fishing, waterskiing;horses.		
FOREST OF NISENE MARKS, 4 miles N of Aptos	P	B5
Camping, picnicking, hiking trails.		
FREMONT PEAK STATE PARK, S of San Juan Bautista	54	D3
Camping, hiking trails, picnicking.		
FURNACE CREEK CAMPGROUND, Furnace Creek Ranch	62	A5
Camping facilities in the heart of Death Vly.		
GAVIOTA STATE PARK, Gaviota Beach Rd	86	D4
Camping, fishing, boat launch, picnic areas.		
GEORGE HATFIELD STATE REC AREA, 28 mi W of Merced	47	D4
Camping, hiking, fishing, and picnicking.		
GRIZZLY CREEK REDWOODS STATE PARK, E of Fortuna	16	B3
Scenic; camp, fish, nature trails, creeks.		
GROVER HOT SPRINGS STATE PARK, W of Markleeville	36	B5
Camping; fishing and swimming in hot creeks.		

POINTS OF INTEREST INDEX

NAME & ADDRESS	PAGE	GRID
HENDY WOODS STATE PARK, near Philo on Hwy 128 Camp, picnic, fish, hike, swim.	30	D3
HENRY COE STATE PARK, 14 mi NE of Morgan Hill Picturesque camping and picnic grounds.	P	E4
HENRY COWELL REDWOODS STATE PARK, N of Santa Cruz Equestrian trails, camping, hiking, fishing.	N	E5
HIDDEN VIEW, 17 miles N of Madera Scenic area to camp, swim and fish.	49	B5
HOLLISTER HILLS VEHICULAR REC AREA, Cienega Rd Camping, motorcycling & 4-wheel drive trails.	54	E3
HUMBOLDT REDWOODS STATE PARK, Redwood Highway Tallest redwoods; camp, fish, hike, picnic.	16	A4
HUNGRY VALLEY STATE VEHICULAR REC AREA, Gorman Primitive camping; off-road vehicle use.	88	E2
INDIAN GRINDING ROCK STATE HIST PK, S of Volcano Restored Miwok Indian Vlg; camping facilities.	41	A2
J SMITH REDWOODS STATE PARK, NE of Crescent City Camping, picnicking, hiking, fishing&exhibits.	1	E4
LAKE ELSINORE STATE REC AREA, near I-5 & Hwy 74 Camping, swimming, fishing and boating.	99	B4
LAKE OROVILLE STATE REC AREA, NE of Oroville Camp, fish, boat, waterski, horseback ride.	25	D4
LAKE PERRIS STATE REC AREA, off Ramona Expwy Camping, bicycle trails, boat rentals.	99	C3
LEO CARRILLO STATE BEACH, S of Hwy 101 Good surfing, diving and swimming.	96	D2
LITTLE GRASS VALLEY RESERVOIR, W of Gibsonville Camping and recreational facilities.	26	C3
MacKERRICHER STATE PARK, N of Fort Bragg Rocky beaches, sand dunes, nature trails.	22	B5
MALAKOFF DIGGINS STATE HIST PK, NE of Nevada City Camping along colorful slopes.	26	D5
MANCHESTER STATE BEACH, near Point Arena Camping on sandy beaches among sand dunes.	30	B3
McARTHUR-BURNEY FALLS MEM STATE PK, NE of Burney Well developed park with camping and fishing.	13	C4
McCONNELL STATE RECREATION AREA, 5 mi SE of Delhi Camping, picnicking, fishing and swimming.	48	A3
MILLERTON LAKE REC AREA, 22 miles E of Madera Camping, boating, fishing & horseback riding.	57	D1
MONTANA DE ORO STATE PARK, Pecho Valley Rd Barbeque facilities; camping, riding & hiking.	75	E3
MORRO BAY STATE PARK, on Morro Bay Camping, fishing, clam digging, boating.	75	D3
MT SAN JACINTO STATE PARK, Hwy 111 near Palm Spgs Hiking, picnicking and limited camping.	100	B3
MOUNT TAMALPAIS STATE PARK, 6 mi N of Hwy 1 Camping, hiking, equestrian trails.	L	A3
NEW BRIGHTON STATE BEACH, off Hwy 1 Scenic camping; fishing and swimming.	54	A2
OAKWOOD LAKE RESORT, off I-5 S of Manteca Camping, watersports and shopping.	47	A1
OCOTILLO WELLS STATE VEHICULAR REC AREA, Hwy 78 Off-road 4-wheel drive vehicle trails.	108	B3
PALOMAR MOUNTAIN STATE PARK, Birch Hill Rd Beautiful area to camp or enjoy a picnic.	107	A2
PATRICKS POINT STATE PARK, N of Trinidad Camping, hiking, biking, picnicking.	9	D3
PAUL M. DIMMICK WAYSIDE CAMPGROUND, W of Navarro Primitive campgrounds; swim, fish, picnic.	30	C2
PFEIFFER BIG SUR STATE PARK, E of Hwy 1, Big Sur Hiking, camping, swimming and fishing.	64	B2
PICACHO STATE RECREATION AREA, W of Picacho Camping, fishing, hiking and sailing.	110	C4
PISMO DUNES STATE VEHICULAR REC AREA, Pismo Beach Off-road, 4-wheel drive trails; camp & picnic.	76	B5
PISMO STATE BEACH, off Hwy 101, Pismo Beach Camping & hiking along sandy beaches & dunes.	76	B5
PLUMAS EUREKA STATE PARK, Hwy A14 at Johnsville Camping, scenic creeks, trails, lakes & mtns.	26	E2
POINT MUGU STATE PARK, Hwy 1 Camp near the ocean; hiking, swimming&fishing.	96	C2
PORTOLA STATE PARK, W of Hwy 35 Camping, recreational facilities.	N	D4
PRAIRIE CREEK REDWOODS STATE PARK, N of Orick Camping, fishing, picnic areas, hiking.	10	A1
PROVIDENCE MTNS STATE REC AREA, Essex Rd Camping facilities in scenic surroundings.	94	B1
RED ROCK CANYON STATE PARK, Hwy 14 at Ricardo Camping, picnicking, hiking and exhibits.	80	B3
REFUGIO STATE BEACH, Refugio Rd Tidepools; camping and fishing.	86	E4
RICHARDSON GROVE STATE PARK, S of Garberville Scenic camping area; fish, swim, hike.	22	B1
RUSSIAN GULCH STATE PARK, S of Fort Bragg Camp, hike to waterfall, rocky headlands.	30	A1
SADDLEBACK BUTTE STATE PARK, E of Lancaster Camping, picnicking, and hiking trails.	90	C3
SALTON SEA STATE RECREATION AREA, off Hwy 111 Good area to camp, boat, waterski, or hike.	108	E2
SALT POINT STATE PARK, N of Fort Ross off Hwy 1 Camping, beaches, underwater preserve, trails.	37	A1
SAMUEL P. TAYLOR STATE PARK, off Hwy 1 near Olema Camping, fishing, winter sports, riding.	37	E4
SAN CLEMENTE STATE BEACH, San Clemente Surfing, camping; barbeque, picnic facilities.	105	D1
SAN ELIJO STATE BEACH, Cardiff Camping & picnicking on the beach; swimming.	106	B4
SAN LUIS RES STATE REC AREA, 16 mi W of Los Banos Lovely area to camp, waterski, fish & hike.	55	C1
SAN ONOFRE STATE BEACH, San Onofre Surf fishing, clamming, surfing and camping.	105	E2
SAN SIMEON STATE BEACH, Hwy 1, Morro Bay Camping and hiking; sand dunes to explore.	75	B1
SILVERWOOD LAKE STATE RECREATION AREA, Hwy 138 Camping, swimming, boating and fishing.	91	B5
SINKYONE WILDERNESS ST PK, Humboldt & Mendocno Co Tent camping, picnicking, hiking and fishing.	22	A1
SONOMA COAST STATE BEACH, N of Bodega Bay Camp, hike, picnic; scenic beaches.	37	B2
SOUTH CARLSBAD STATE BEACH, S of Carlsbad Scenic beach for camping, fishing or swimming.	106	B3
STANDISH HICKEY STATE REC AREA, 1 mi N of Leggett Camping, fishing, hiking trails, swimming.	22	C2
STOVEPIPE WELLS CAMPGROUND, Death Valley Natl Mon 200 campsites (RV & tents) in the valley.	61	C4
SUGARLOAF RIDGE STATE PARK, Adobe Canyon Rd Camping, fishing and riding.	38	A2
SUGAR PINE POINT STATE PARK, N of Meeks Bay Camping, swimming, fishing and hiking.	35	E2
SUNSET CAMPGROUND, Furnace Creek Ranch, Death Vly Campsites near the heart of Death Valley.	62	A5
SUNSET STATE BEACH, W of Watsonville Scenic beach to camp, fish, dig for clams.	54	B2
TAHOE STATE RECREATION AREA, N of Tahoe City Camp, swim, fish, boat, picnic.	35	E2
TEXAS SPRINGS CAMPGROUND, Furnace Creek Ranch RV and tent campsites in scenic Death Valley.	62	A5
TUOLUMNE MEADOWS, Tioga Pass Rd Camp, fish, backpack, mtn climb, horses.	43	A5
TURLOCK LAKE STATE REC AREA, SW of La Grande Waterski, fish, boat, hike and camp.	48	B2
WESTPORT UNION LANDING STATE BCH, N of Westport Camping and fishing.	22	B3
WOODSON BRIDGE STATE REC AREA, SE of Corning Camping, fishing, swimming, nature trail.	24	D2

NAME & ADDRESS	PAGE	GRID
COLLEGES & UNIVERSITIES		
CAL STATE COLLEGE, BAKERSFIELD, 9001 Stockdale Hy	78	C3
Small campus; good student-professor ratio.		
CALIF STATE POLYTECH UNIV, POMONA, 3801 W Temple	U	B2
Outstanding programs in architecture.		
CAL STATE POLYTECH UNIV, SAN LUIS OBISPO	172	B1
Noted for studies in agriculture & business.		
CAIFORNIA STATE UNIVERSITY, CHICO, W 1st St	124	B4
Offers a variety of quality academic programs.		
CALIF STATE UNIV, DOMINGUEZ HLLS, 1000 E Victoria	S	D1
Noted as a leader in innovative programs.		
CALIF STATE UNIV, FRESNO, Shaw & Cedar Av	57	C3
Noted for agriculture, business, engineering.		
CAL STATE UNIV, FULLERTON, 800 N State College Bl	T	D1
Good academic opportunities in many subjects.		
CALIF STATE UNIV, HAYWARD, 25800 Carlos Bee Bl	M	A5
Strong programs in sciences & liberal arts.		
CALIF STATE UNIV, LONG BEACH, 1250 Bellflower Bl	T	A2
One of largest universities in CSUC system.		
CALIF STATE UNIV, LOS ANGELES, 5151 State Coll Dr	R	B4
Wide spectrum of programs with an urban focus.		
CAL STATE UNIV, NORTHRIDGE, 18111 Nordhoff St	Q	B2
A broad range of educational opportunities.		
CALIF STATE UNIV, SACRAMENTO, 6000 J St	39	E1
Situated halfway between S F & the Sierras.		
CAL STATE UNIV, SAN BERNARDINO, 5000 University	99	B1
On a 3-3 system: 3 quarters, 3 classes.		
CAL STATE UNIV, STANISLAUS, 801 W Monte Vista Av	47	D3
Small, intimate campus in San Joaquin Valley.		
CAL TECH-CALIF INSTITUTE OF TECH, 1201 E Calif Bl	190	D4
Largest private technical college in Calif.		
CLAREMONT COLLEGES, College Av & Foothill Blvd	203	A1
Distinguished group of six schools & colleges.		
CLAREMONT GRADUATE SCHOOL, Claremont Colleges	203	A1
Studies in educatn, business, history, Englsh.		
CLAREMONT McKENNA COLLEGE, Claremont Colleges	203	B2
Studies in political science & economics.		
HARVEY MUDD COLLEGE, Claremont Colleges	203	A1
Studies in sciences, engineering, mathematics.		
HUMBOLDT STATE UNIV, Arcata	10	A5
Beautiful campus in a redwood forest.		
LOYOLA-MARYMOUNT UNIV, LA, Loyola Bl & W 80th St	188	A4
Fine academic Catholic university.		
PEPPERDINE UNIV, 24255 W Pacific Coast Hy, Malibu	97	A2
Private univ; noted for studies in business.		
PITZER COLLEGE, Scott Hall, Claremont Colleges	203	B1
Studies in liberal arts and humanities.		
POMONA COLLEGE, Sumner Hall, Claremont Colleges	203	B2
Studies in history, social & natural sciences.		
ST MARYS COLLEGE, St Marys Rd, Moraga	L	E4
Studies in liberal arts & economics.		
SAN DIEGO STATE UNIV, 5300 Campanile Dr	V	C3
Largest in the CSUC system.		
SAN FRANCISCO STATE UNIV, 1600 Holloway Av	L	A5
Many interdisciplinary programs.		
SAN JOSE STATE UNIVERSITY, 125 S 7th St	152	C4
Campus of 27,000 students in Santa Clara Vly.		
SCRIPPS COLLEGE, Balch Hall, Claremont Colleges	203	B1
Studies in social sci, literature, fine arts.		
SCRIPPS INST OF OCEANOGRAPHY, San Diego	211	A1
Branch of UCSD, oceanographic research.		
SCRIPPS INST SUBMERGED LAND AREA, San Diego	211	A1
Part of Scripps Institute of Oceanography.		
SONOMA STATE UNIV, 1801 E Cotati Av	38	A3
Offers programs in sciences and liberal arts.		

NAME & ADDRESS	PAGE	GRID
STANFORD UNIVERSITY, Junipero Serra Blvd	147	A3
Distinguished univ; beautifl church on campus.		
UNIV OF CALIF, BERKELEY, 2200 University Av	156	B2
Oldest & largest of the Univ Of Cal campuses.		
UNIV OF CALIF, DAVIS, Russell Bl & La Rue	136	B3
Studies in law, medicine, agricultre, science.		
UNIV OF CALIF, IRVINE, Campus Dr	200	D2
Good programs in sciences & medicine.		
UNIV OF CALIF, LOS ANGELES, 405 Hilgard Av	180	C1
Outstanding liberal arts & medical schools.		
UNIV OF CALIF, RIVERSIDE, 900 University Av	205	E3
Desert campus lies at base of foothills.		
UNIV OF CALIF, SAN DIEGO, La Jolla Village Dr	V	A2
Specializes in physicl & naturl sci, medicine.		
UNIV OF CALIF, SAN FRANCISCO, 3rd & Parnassus Avs	141	E5
Small campus, tours available.		
UNIV OF CALIF, SANTA BARBARA, Ward Memorial Bl	87	A4
Beautiful campus beside the ocean.		
UNIV OF CALIF, SANTA CRUZ, Hill St	169	A1
Overlooks bay, excellent marine research dept.		
UNIVERSITY OF NEVADA, LAS VEGAS, Flamingo Rd	210	E3
Noted for music & theater; concert hall.		
UNIVERSITY OF NEVADA, RENO, N Virginia & 9th Sts	130	B1
Beautiful site overlooking Truckee Meadows.		
UNIVERSITY OF THE PACIFIC, Stadium Dr, Stockton	160	B2
Noted for Liberal Arts & Sciences.		
UNIVERSITY OF SAN DIEGO, Alcala Park	213	B4
Fine academic programs, small campus.		
UNIVERSITY OF SAN FRANCISCO, 2130 Fulton St	141	E3
Fine academic programs on a small campus		
UNIVERSITY OF SANTA CLARA, The Alameda	151	C3
Mission Santa Clara is on this campus.		
UNIV OF SOUTHERN CALIF, 3551 University Av, L A	185	C5
Largest private university in California.		
GOLF COURSES		
ALMADEN GOLF & COUNTRY CLUB, San Jose	P	B4
Konica San Jose Classic, LPGA.		
BERMUDA DUNES COUNTRY CLUB, 42360 Adams St	101	A4
Bob Hope Desert Classic, PGA.		
CYPRESS POINT COUNTRY CLUB, 17 Mile Dr	53	A4
AT&T Pebble Beach National Pro-Am, PGA.		
DESERT INN & COUNTRY CLUB, Las Vegas	210	C1
Panasonic Las Vegas Invitational.		
ELDORADO COUNTRY CLUB, Indian Wells	100	E4
Bob Hope Chrysler Classic.		
FAIRBANKS RANCH COUNTRY CLUB, San Diego	106	C4
Kyocera Inamori Classic.		
INDIAN WELLS COUNTRY CLUB, 4600 Club Dr, Riversde	100	E4
Bob Hope Classic, PGA.		
LA COSTA COUNTRY CLUB, Carlsbad	106	C3
MONY Tournament of Champions, PGA.		
LA QUINTA COUNTRY CLUB, Eisenhower Dr & 50th Av	101	A4
Bob Hope Classic, PGA.		
MISSION HILLS COUNTRY CLUB, Rancho Mirage	100	D4
Nabisco Dinah Shore Invitational, LPGA.		
OAKMONT COUNTRY CLUB, Glendale	Q	E2
GNA Classic.		
PEBBLE BEACH GOLF LINKS, off 2nd Av	168	B3
AT&T Pebble Beach National Pro-Am, PGA.		
RIVIERA COUNTRY CLUB, Pacific Palisades	Q	B4
Los Angeles Open, PGA.		
SPYGLASS HILL G C, Spyglass Hill & Stevenson	53	B4
AT&T Pebble Beach National Pro-Am, PGA.		
TAMARISK C C, 70240 F Sinatra Dr, Rancho Mirage	100	D4
Bob Hope Desert Classic, PGA.		

POINTS OF INTEREST INDEX

NAME & ADDRESS	PAGE	GRID
TORREY PINES GOLF COURSE, La Jolla	V	A1
Shearson Lehman Bros-Andy Williams Open, PGA.		

HARBORS

NAME & ADDRESS	PAGE	GRID
ALAMEDA HARBOR, Embarcadero & 9th Av	158	B4
Major shipping center of northern California.		
BODEGA HARBOR, Hwy 1 at Bodega Bay	37	C3
Small but busy harbor; parks nr harbor & bay.		
INNER HARBOR, between Oakland & Alameda	157	D4
Busy commercial section of SF Bay.		
LONG BEACH HARBOR, Ocean Blvd	192	A5
Shares largest man-made harbr with Ls Angeles.		
LOS ANGELES HARBOR, Seaside Av	191	C5
Busy commercial port of state's largest city.		
PORT HUENEME HARBOR, end of Hueneme Rd	96	B1
Dominated by US Naval installation.		
PORT OF SACRAMENTO, off Lake Washington	39	D1
Furthest inland port of Sac deep-watr channel.		
PORT OF STOCKTON, off Hwy 5 in Stockton	160	A5
Busy inland agricultural seaport.		
RICHMOND INNER HARBOR, Richmond	155	B5
Commercial port in San Francisco Bay.		
SAN DIEGO BAY, W of I-5	V	C4
Busy deepwater port, home of USN 11th Fleet.		
SAN FRANCISCO HARBOR, Fisherman's Wharf	L	B4
Major commercial port; 1st in W Coast shippng.		
SANTA CRUZ HARBOR	169	E4
Small commercial harbor in Monterey Bay.		

HISTORICAL SITES

NAME & ADDRESS	PAGE	GRID
ALPINE COUNTY HIST COMPLEX, Hwy 89, Markleeville	36	C5
Historic museum and restored buildings.		
ANDERSON MARSH STATE HIST PARK, near Clear Lake	32	A3
Buildings from Anderson Ranch & Indian site.		
ANGELS HOTEL, Angels Camp	41	B4
Hotel in Twain's 'The Jumpng Frog of Calv Co'.		
ARROYO DE CANTUA, off Hwy 5	66	D1
Headqrtrs of notorious bandit Jquin Murieta.		
ASTRONOMICAL OBSERVATORY, off Shake Ridge Rd	41	A2
1st observ in Cal - discvrd Great Comet 1861.		
AVERY HOTEL, Moran Rd, Avery	41	C3
Wooden hotel built in 1853.		
BALE GRIST MILL ST HISTORIC PARK, on Hwy 29	38	B1
Restored mill was built in 1846.		
BANNING PARK, 401 E M St, Wilmington	S	C2
House built in 1850s by Gen Phineas Banning.		
BARNSDALL PARK, 4800 Hollywood Bl	182	B4
Site of Frank Lloyd Wright's Hollyhock House.		
BENICIA CAPITOL STATE HISTORIC PARK, H & 1st Sts	153	B4
Capitol of California in 1853.		
BIDWELL MANSION ST HIST PK, 525 Esplanade, Chico	124	B4
Restored Victorian home of Chico founder.		
BODIE STATE HISTORICAL PARK, Bodie, off Hwy 395	43	C3
Gold boom town, now a restored ghost town.		
BOK KAI TEMPLE (CHINESE JOSS HOUSE), Marysville	33	D2
Only temple in USA for worship of River God.		
BORAX MUSEUM, Furnace Creek Ranch, Death Valley	62	A5
Memorabilia from the old borax mine.		
BOWERS MANSION, Washoe Valley	36	B1
Granite home built 1864 wth rewards of mining.		
BRAND PARK, San Fernando Bl, Los Angeles	Q	D2
Picturesque atmosphere of early Cal missions.		
BRIDGEPORT COVERED BRIDGE, Bridgeport	34	B1
Longest single-span wood-covered bridge in US.		

NAME & ADDRESS	PAGE	GRID
BURBANK MEMORIAL GARDENS, Santa Rosa Av	131	D4
A living memorial dedicated to the naturalist.		
CALICO GHOST TOWN, 10.5 miles NE of Barstow	92	A1
Restored mining town - tour of mine & museum.		
CALIFORNIA STANDARD OIL WELL, McKittrick Field	77	E3
Discovery well started new oil field in 1899.		
CALIF STATE MINING & MINERAL EXHIBIT, Mariposa	49	B3
Displays of Calif gold, diamonds and fossils.		
CAMP CURTIS, 1 mi N of Arcata.	9	E5
Estab for the protection of white settlers.		
CAMP SALVATION, Calexico	112	B4
Refugee ctr for emigrants in search of gold.		
CAMRON STANFORD HOUSE, 14418 Lakeside Dr	158	A3
Built in 1876 it serves as the Oakland Museum.		
THE CASTLE, 70 S B St, Virginia City	36	D1
Built 1868 - restored; antique furnishings.		
CATALINA ISLAND MUSEUM, Casino Building	97	B4
Features displays on the island's history.		
CHARCOAL KILNS, near Wildrose, Death Vly Natl Mon	71	D2
Large old kilns used during the mining days.		
CHILDREN'S PARK, S Morton Bl, Modesto	162	D4
Childrens playground wth old train & airplane.		
CHINESE TEMPLE, E of Oroville	25	D4
A temple of worship for over 10,000 Chinese.		
COL THOMAS BAKER MEMORIAL, City Hall, Bakersfield	166	C3
Civic Center commemorates friend of travelers.		
COLUMBIA CITY HOTEL, Main St, Columbia	41	C4
Hotel built in 1856 which is still in use.		
COLUMBIA STATE HISTORIC PARK, N of Columbia	41	C4
Gold boom town in 1850s, now preserved.		
CONCANNON VINEYARD, S of Livermore	P	D1
Estab Livermore Vly as a select wine district.		
CONGREGATIONAL CHURCH, Jesus Maria Rd	41	A3
Built 1853 - oldest Congregtnl Church in Ca.		
COTTONWOOD CHARCOAL KILNS, N of Cartago	70	B1
Bit 1870s to char wood for mines at Owens Lk.		
DEATH VALLEY GATEWAY, mouth of Furnace Creek	72	B1
Natural entrance to Death Vly used by settlrs.		
DE LA GUERRA PLAZA, 15 E De La Guerra St	174	C4
Shopping arcade in historic adobes.		
DEL NORTE COUNTY HISTORICAL MUSEUM, Crescent City	1	D4
Largest museum in Northern California.		
DIEGO SEPULVEDA ADOBE, 1900 Adams Av, Costa Mesa	197	A5
Old ranch adobe now houses a museum.		
DRYTOWN, N of Amador	40	E2
1st town in Ama, in which gold was discvrd.		
D STEWART COUNTY STORE, in Ione	40	C2
The 1st brick bldg, built in Ione Vly, 1856.		
DUNSMUIR HOME & GARDENS, 2960 Peralta Oaks Ct	L	E5
Blt 1899, Greek revival mansion, 48 acre grdn.		
EL PRESIDIO DE SANTA BARBARA, 210 E Canon Perdido	174	C3
One of four presidios built in Calif, 1782.		
EL PUEBLO DE LOS ANGELES, Main & Arcadia Sts	186	B3
State historic pk with many historic landmrks.		
EMPIRE MINE STATE HIST PK, Colfax Rd	127	D4
Oldst quartz mine in operatn for over 100 yrs.		
ESTUDILLO HOME, S of San Leandro	L	E5
Home of the family which founded San Leandro.		
EUGENE O'NEILL NATIONAL HIS SITE, NW of Danville	M	A4
Rangr-guided tour of O'Neill's 1937 Tao House.		
FELTON COVERED BRIDGE, off Graham Hill Rd, Felton	P	A5
1 of 3 remaining coverd bridgs in Sta Cruz Co.		
FERNANDO PACHECO ADOBE, Concord	M	B3
Restored adobe house originally built in 1843.		
FORESTIERE UNDERGROUND GARDENS, Shaw Av, Fresno	57	B3
7 acres of grottos, vines and courts.		
FORT HUMBOLDT STATE HISTORIC PARK, Eureka	121	A3
Exhibits of logging & military life.		

NAME & ADDRESS	PAGE	GRID	NAME & ADDRESS	PAGE	GRID
FORT JANESVILLE, near Janesville	21	B4	LELAND STANFORD WINERY, off Hwy 680	P	B2
Fort built for protection from Indian attacks.			Founder of Stanfrd Uni, operated here in 1869.		
FORT MASON, Golden Gate National Recreation Area	143	A1	LIVERMORE MEMORIAL MONUMENT, Livermore	P	C1
Former army hdqurtrs houses mus; cultural ctr.			Remembrance of the 1st settler of Livermore.		
FORT POINT NATL HISTORIC PARK, Golden Gate Park	141	C1	L A CO MUSEUM OF NATURAL HIST, 900 Exposition Bl	185	C5
Built in 1861 to control access to SF Bay.			Exhibits include Indian artfcts, gems & mummy.		
FORT TEJON STATE HISTORIC PARK, Ft Tejon Rd	88	D1	LOS ENCINOS STATE HIST PK, 16756 Moorpark St	Q	B3
Former military center; summer programs.			This historic park features 1849 Osa Adobe.		
FRESNO FLATS HISTORIC PARK, Rd 427, Oakhurst	49	D4	LOS ROBLES ADOBE, 3 mi N of Lemoore	67	C1
Historic buildings and artifacts of Madera Co.			Restored adobe house, built in 1849.		
FT ROSS STATE HIST PARK, at Fort Ross	37	A1	LOTT HOME, 1735 Montgomery St, Oroville	25	C4
Restored American outpost; museum and beach.			Restored; furnished 1856 home of Judse C Lott.		
GASLAMP QUARTER, Downtown San Diego	215	E4	LOWER LAKE STONE JAIL, Lower Lake	32	A3
Victorian bldgs, shops, nightclubs, theaters.			Claimed to be smallest jail in US, built 1876.		
GIANT DESERT FIGURES, 18 miles north of Blythe	103	C3	LUMMIS HOME STATE HISTORIC MNT, 200 E Av 43, LA	R	B3
3 giant figures - 2 animals, 1 coiled serpent.			Built 1895 by Charles F Lummis.		
GOLD BUG MINE, off Bedford Rd, Placerville	138	E1	MALAKOFF DIGGINS STATE HIST PK, NE of Nevada City	26	D5
Exposed gold veins in old mine shaft; tours.			Colorful slopes exposed by hydraulic mining.		
GOLD COUNTRY, HIGHWAY 49, from Mariposa to Vinton	41	A3	MARIPOSA COUNTY COURTHOUSE, Mariposa	49	B3
300 mi drive through the historic Mother Lode.			Built 1854 after Mariposa became the Co seat.		
GRANVILLE P SWIFT ADOBE, N of Orland	24	D3	MARIPOSA COUNTY HIST CENTER, 12th St & Jessie St	49	B3
Rodeos were held annually at this site.			Early Gold Rush equip, stamp mill, buildngs.		
GRASS VALLEY MUSEUM, Chapel St, Grass Valley	127	B4	MARSHALL'S BLACKSMITH SHOP, Gold Trail Pk	34	E4
Built in 1855; artifacts from early Grass Vly.			Marshall was a smithy & qualified carpenter.		
HARMONY BORAX WORKS, Furnace Creek, Death Valley	62	A5	MARSHALL GOLD DISCOVERY STATE HIST PARK, Hwy 49	34	D4
Preserved processing plant nr borax discovery.			Marshall's discov in 1848 started 'Gold Rush'.		
HAROLD LLOYD ESTATE, 1740 Greenacres, Beverly Hls	Q	C3	MARY AARON MUSEUM, 704 D St, Marysville	33	D2
Once home to the silent screen actor.			Restored home - gold rush tools, pictures.		
HEARST SAN SIMEON STATE HIST MONUMENT, off Hwy 1	75	B1	MARY AUSTIN'S HOUSE, Independence	59	E3
Tours of fabulous estate of William R Hearst.			Wrote books depicting beauty of Owens Valley.		
HERITAGE HILL, Lake Forest Dr & Serrano, El Toro	98	D4	McKITTRICK BREA PIT, 1/2 mi W of McKittrick	77	E3
Restored historicl bldgs of central Orange Co.			Animals were trapped in ancient asphalt pit.		
HOTEL LEGER, Main St, Mokelumne Hill	41	A3	MENDOCINO PRESBYTERIAN CHURCH, Main St, Mendocino	30	C1
Victorian style hotel, garden pool & theatre.			Blt 1868 of redwood, 1 of oldest still in use.		
INDIAN GRINDING ROCK STATE HIST PK, S of Volcano	41	A2	METHODIST CHURCH, S of Ione	40	C3
Restored Miwok Indian village, museum.			Dedicatd 'Lone City Centenary Church' in 1866.		
IOOF HALL, Mokelumne Hill	41	A3	MONO COUNTY HISTORICAL MUSEUM, Bridgeport City Pk	43	B3
1st 3-story bldg in the interior of the state.			Restored ele sch, houses many histrcl artfcts.		
JACK LONDON STATE HISTORIC PARK, Broadway	38	B2	MONTEREY STATE HIST PARK, 210 Olivier St	167	E3
Museum is in House of Happy Walls.			Includes many buildings of historic interest.		
JACOBY BUILDING, 8th & H, Arcata	10	A5	MORMON STATION STATE HIST MON, N of Gardnerville	36	B3
Princpl supply store for Klmth-Trnty miners.			Museum has pioneer items & displays; old fort.		
J. J. JACKSON MUSEUM, Highway 299, Weaverville	17	D1	MORMON STOCKADE, Court St, San Bernardino	207	D2
Trinity Co. history; Indian & mining displays.			Site of 1851 stockade built for protection.		
JOHN MUIR NATIONAL HISTORIC SITE, 4204 Alhambra	154	B4	MORRO ROCK, off the coast of Morro Bay	75	D3
House built 1882; visitor's center & tours.			Important navigational landmark for 300+ yrs.		
JOSE E BORONDA ADOBE, 333 Boronda Rd, Salinas	171	A2	MOTHER COLONY HOUSE, 400 N West St, Anaheim	193	B2
Restored adobe, artifacts, historic photos.			First house built in Anaheim.		
KEANE WONDER MINE & MILL, off Daylight Pass Ctoff	61	E4	MT SHASTA MUSEUM, off Hwy 5 north of Dunsmuir	12	C2
Well-preserved historic remains of silvr mine.			Features the geology & history of gold mining.		
KENTUCKY MINE HISTORIC PARK, NE of Sierra City	27	A4	MURPHYS, 9 mi NE of Angels Camp	41	C4
Restored stamp mill & old gold mine buildngs.			Victorian houses, old jail, hotels, church.		
KERN CO MUSEUM & PIONEER VILLAGE, 3801 Chester	166	C2	MURPHY'S HOTEL, off Hwy 4 in Murphys	41	C4
Exhibits of pioneer and Indian history.			Early guests included Mark Twain & Gen Grant.		
KEYESVILLE, 4 miles W of Isabella	79	C1	MUSEUM OF NATURAL HIST, State Pk Rd, Sta Barbara	174	B2
Center of placer & quartz gold mining,1853-70.			Displays, films & lectures.		
KIT CARSON MARKER, Kit Carson	35	D5	NAPA COUNTY HISTORICAL MUSEUM, in Calistoga	38	A1
Replica of orig instriptn cut from Kit's tree.			County history of the late 1800s.		
LAKE COUNTY MUSEUM, 255 N Forbes St, Lakeport	31	D3	NAPA VALLEY RAILROAD DEPOT, Calistoga	38	B1
In old courthouse, Indian & pioneer displays.			Built 1868, is now the Southern Pacfic depot.		
LAKEPORT HISTORICAL MUSEUM, 175 3rd St, Lakeport	31	C3	NATIONAL HISTORIC SHIPS, Hyde St Pier, Aquatic Pk	143	B1
Displays of indian baskets & other artifacts.			Museum of 5 ships; includes the Balclutha.		
LA PURISIMA MSSN STATE HIST PK, 3 mi NE of Lompoc	86	C2	NATIONAL HOTEL, 2 Water St, Jackson	40	E2
Restored mission, exhibits. Open 9-4:30 daily.			Built in 1849, survived the 1862 fire.		
LARKIN HOUSE, Jefferson St & Calle Principal	167	E4	NEVADA STATE HIST MUS, 1650 N Virginia St, Reno	28	B4
Served as American Consulate 1843 to 1846.			Indian, pioneer, mineral, gambling exhibits.		
LAWS RAILROAD MUSEUM & HIST SITE, NE of Bishop	51	D3	OCTAGON HOUSE, 2645 Gough St, San Francisco	143	A2
Restored 1880's RR depot, locomotive, equip.			Eary San Francisco home built in 1861.		

NAME & ADDRESS	PAGE	GRID	NAME & ADDRESS	PAGE	GRID
ODD FELLOWS MEMORIAL, Kirkwood	36	A5	SAINT TERESA'S CHURCH, Bodega	37	C3
Here rests the Unknown Pioneer, 1849.			Built of redwood in 1859; still in use.		
OLD CUSTOM HOUSE, Fisherman's Wharf	167	E3	SAINT VINCENT'S SCHOOL, north of San Rafael	L	B3
Oldest government building in California.			Founded in 1855.		
OLDEST HOUSE NORTH OF SF BAY, N of Novato	L	A2	SALVIO PACHECO ADOBE, Concord	M	B3
Built 1776 by an Indian chief.			Two-story home was the 1st built in the vly.		
OLD FIREHOUSE No 1, 214 Main St, Nevada City	128	C2	SAN DIEGO PLAZA, Old Town, San Diego	213	A5
Indian baskets, pioneer and Donner Party itms.			Center of Mexican Pueblo, blt 1830s; restored.		
OLD FOLSOM POWERHOUSE, Folsom	34	B5	SAN FRANCISCO MARITIME NAT'L HIST PK, end Hyde Av	143	B1
Long distance generating plant built in 1890s.			Historic ships, guided & self-guided tours.		
OLD HOMESTEAD, Crockett	L	D3	SAN JUAN BAUTISTA STATE HIST PARK, 2nd St, SJB	54	D3
Built in 1867 - 1st American home in Crockett.			Incl mission, Plaza Hotel, & house built 1841.		
OLD SACRAMENTO STATE HISTORIC PARK, 2nd & I Sts	137	A2	SAN PASQUAL BATTLEFIELD STATE HIST PARK, Hwy 78	106	E3
Business district during Gold Rush; restored.			Battle site between Dragoons & Californios.		
OLD SPANISH LIGHTHOUSE, Point Loma	V	A4	SAN RAFAEL ADOBE, 1330 Dorothy Dr, Glendale	Q	E2
Lighthouse constructed 1854 - 1855.			Adobe and hacienda built in 1865.		
OLD STOVEPIPE WELL, off Hwy 190, Death Valley	61	D4	SANTA BARBARA HISTORICAL MUS, 136 E De La Guerra	174	C3
Site of underground well marked by stovepipe.			Exhibits of state & local history.		
OLD TOWN SAN DIEGO STATE HISTORIC PARK	213	A5	SANTA CRUZ CITY MUSEUM, 1305 E Cliff Dr	169	E3
Restored Spanish-style bldgs; museums, shops.			Natural history of Santa Cruz County.		
OLVERA STREET, 130 Paseo de la Plaza	186	B2	SANTA CRUZ COUNTY HIST MUS, Cooper & Front Sts	169	D3
Shopping & dining in birthplace of Ls Angeles.			Artifacts & history of early Santa Cruz Co.		
PEPPARD CABIN, off Hwy 70 in Quincy	26	C2	SANTA MARIA VALLEY HIST MUSEUM, 616 S Broadway	173	C3
Cabin built in 1888; made of hand hewn logs.			Pioneer Indian & Spanish historical exhibits.		
PERALTA HOME, W of Castro Valley	L	E5	SCOTT MUSEUM, off Hwy 3 in Trinity Center	11	E4
The first brick home built in Alameda County.			Features Indian artifacts and antiques.		
PETALUMA ADOBE ST HISTORIC PARK, Adobe Ranch Rd	L	A1	SKIDOO, off Skidoo Rd in Death Valley	61	D5
Relics displayed in 1836 adobe house.			Ruins of mining town that once flourished.		
PETER LASSEN GRAVE, 5 mi E of Susanville	21	A4	SNELLING COURTHOUSE, Snelling	48	C3
In memory of a pioneer killed by Indians.			1st courthouse in Merced County, built 1857.		
PETER L TRAVER BUILDING, off Hwy 4	41	C4	SONOMA HISTORIC PARK, W Spain St & 3rd St W	132	D3
Served as a generl store & Wells Fargo Office.			Home of General Vallejo built in 1850.		
PIGEON PT LIGHTHOUSE, Pigeon Pt Rd, San Mateo Co.	N	C4	STEVENSON HOUSE, 530 Houston St, Monterey	167	E4
Constructed in 1872 and still in use.			Living quarters of Robert Louis Stevenson.		
PIONEER YOSEMITE HISTORY CENTER, Wawona	49	C3	STONE HOUSE, 6 mi N of Middleton	32	A4
Historical buildings, covered bridge, cabins.			Oldest building in Lake County, 1st blt 1854.		
PIONEER SCHOOLHOUSE, 2 mi E of Quincy	26	C1	SUSPENSION BRIDGE, S of Chico	25	B3
1st schoolhouse in Plumas Co, built in 1857.			Bidwell Bar Bridge was the 1st in Calif, 1856.		
PLUMAS COUNTY MUSEUM, 500 Jackson Street, Quincy	26	C2	SUTTER'S FORT STATE HIST PARK, 28th & L Sts, Sact	137	D3
Artifacts of early Plumas County			Features relics of Gold Rush Era.		
PLYMOUTH TRADING POST, Plymouth	40	E2	TEMPLE OF KUAN TI, Albion St, Mendocino	30	B1
Office & commissary of the many small mines.			Chinese house of worship.		
POINT FERMIN HISTORIC LIGHTHOUSE, Paseo Del Mar	S	C3	TUMCO MINES, 4 mi NE of Ogilby	110	C5
Located in Angels Gate Park.			Largest stamp mill in US was located here.		
POINT SUR STATE HISTORIC PARK, Monterey County	64	A1	VALLECITO BELL MONUMENT, Vallecito	41	B4
Ranger-guided tours of lighthouse & Moro Rock.			Used to call the town together until 1939.		
PONY EXPRESS REMOUNT STATION, off Hwy 88	36	B4	VIRGINIA CITY, NE of Carson City, Nevada	36	D1
An important remount station in the 1860s.			Old mining town - churches, hotels, homes.		
PRESIDIO OF MONTEREY, Pacific St	167	E3	VOLCANO, 12 mi NE of Jackson	41	A2
Now House Defense Language Institute.			Gold rush bldgs - hotel, jail, brewery, PO.		
PRESIDIO OF SAN FRANCISCO, NW end Lombrd	141	C2	WATTS TOWER STATE HISTORIC PARK, 1765 E 107th St	R	A5
Active Army Post fr 1776; 1450 Acres, hikng.			Unusual tower studded with glass & shell.		
RAILTOWN 1897 STATE HISTORIC PARK, Jamestown	41	B5	WEAVERVILLE JOSS HOUSE STATE HIST PK, Weaverville	17	C1
26 acre park with trains on exhibit.			Chinese worship house built in 1874.		
RED BRICK GRAMMAR SCHOOL, Altaville	41	A4	WILL ROGERS STATE HISTORIC PARK, Sunset Blvd	Q	B4
Built 1848 - it is one of the oldest in Ca.			Will Rogers' home located in 186 acre park.		
RENEGADE CANYON NATURL HIST LNDMRK, nr China Lake	70	D5	WOODLAND OPERA HOUSE STATE HIST PARK, Woodland	33	C5
Remarkable prehistoric rockpile collection.			Built in 1895 to serve Sacramento Valley.		
RHYOLITE, off Hwy 374, Nevada	62	A2	YORBA-SLAUGHTER ADOBE, 5.5 miles south of Chino	U	D3
Once a booming silver town, now in ruins.			Early American architecture, built in 1850s.		
RICHARDSON ADOBE, 2.5 mi S of Soledad	65	B1	YUCAIPA ADOBE, Yucaipa	99	D2
Built 1843, later used as stage station & PO.			Oldest house in San Bernardino Co, built 1842.		
ROCKVILLE STONE CHAPEL, Rockville	L	D1			
Volunteer pioneers built chapel in 1856.					
ROOP'S FORT, Weatherlow St, Susanville	20	E3	**HOTELS**		
Built in 1854 - Emigrant trains stopped here.					
ST JAMES EPISCOPAL CHURCH, Sonora	163	C3	* Indicates information obtained from AAA.		
Oldest Episcopal Church in California.			*ADOBE INN-CARMEL, Dolores St & 8th Av	168	B3

COPYRIGHT. © 1989 BY Thomas Bros Maps

NAME & ADDRESS	PAGE	GRID
19 units; fireplaces, pool, sauna; restaurant.		
*AHWAHNEE HOTEL, E end of Yosemite Valley	63	D1
An elegant hotel built in the 1920's.		
*AIRPORTER INN, 18700 MacArthur Blvd	198	C5
Across from John Wayne Airport.		
*ALADDIN, 3667 Las Vegas Bl, Las Vegas	210	B2
Casino, restaurants, entertainment, shops.		
ALEXIS PARK RESORT, 375 E Harmon Av, Las Vegas	210	D3
500 rooms; pools, putting green, tennis.		
*AMERICANA CANTON HOTEL, S Palm Canyon	100	C4
460 rooms; golf, tennis, health spa, 3 pools.		
AMFAC HOTEL, 8601 Lincoln Blvd, Los Angeles	188	A5
750 rooms; pool, entertainment, diningroom.		
ANAHEIM HILTON & TOWERS, 777 N Convention Wy	193	C5
1600 units; restaurants, entertainment.		
*ANAHEIM MARRIOTT HOTEL, 700 W Convention Wy	193	C5
1043 units;pool,whirlpool, balconies & patios.		
ARROWHEAD HILTON, in Lake Arrowhead Village	91	C5
257 rooms; pool, whirlpool, boat dock.		
BAKERSFIELD HILTON INN, Rosedale Hwy, Bakersfield	166	A2
197 units; pool, whirlpool, disco.		
*BALLY'S, 3645 Las Vegas Blvd, Las Vegas	210	B2
Casino, restaurants, entertainment.		
*BALLYS HOTEL - RENO, 2500 E 2nd St, Reno	28	C4
Casino, restaurants, theatres, shows, shops.		
*BARBARY COAST HOTEL, 3595 Las Vegas Blvd S	210	B2
Casino, restaurant, entertainment.		
BARNEY'S, Hwy 50 in South Lake Tahoe	129	E1
Casino, shows and restaurant.		
*BEST WESTERN CAMERON PARK INN, on US Hwy 50	34	C5
61 rooms; pool. Restaurant adjacent.		
*BEST WESTERN CAVALIER INN, 3.5 mi S of Sn Simeon	75	C1
66 rooms; oceanfront, pool, restaurant.		
*BEST WESTERN DANISH INN LODGE, 1455 Mission Dr	86	E3
81 rooms; pool, garage, dining room.		
*BEST WESTERN FLAGWAVER, 937 North H St, Lompoc	86	B3
72 rooms; pool, coffeeshop opposite.		
*BEST WESTERN LAWRENCE WELK VILLAGE INN, Escndido	106	D3
132 rooms; pool, golf, tennis, entertainment.		
*BEST WESTERN PONDEROSA MOTOR INN, H St near 11th	137	C2
98 units; pool & sauna, 3 blocks from capitol.		
*BEST WESTERN ROYAL LAS VEGAS, 99 Convention Ctr	209	D5
237 units; pool, restaurant and casino.		
*BEST WESTERN ROYAL SCOT, 1680 Oceanside Blvd	106	B3
80 rooms; pool & sauna, movies, dining room.		
*BEST WESTERN STATION HOUSE INN, S Lake Tahoe	36	A3
100 rooms; near beach, casinos and skiing.		
BEST WESTERN BONANZA INN, 1001 Clark Av, Yuba Cty	125	C2
125 rooms; convention center, restaurant.		
*BEVERLY GARLAND HOTEL, 1780 Tribute, Sacramento	39	E1
210 rooms; pool & whirlpool, playground.		
BEVERLY HERITAGE, 3350 Av of the Arts, Costa Mesa	198	A3
238 rooms; near the Performing Arts Center.		
*BEVERLY HILLS HOTEL, 9641 Sunset Blvd	183	A1
Excellent accomodations on beautiful grounds.		
*BEVERLY HILTON HOTEL, 9876 Wilshire Blvd	183	A2
Large hotel offers exceptional facilities.		
*BEVERLY WILSHIRE HOTEL, 9500 Wilshire Blvd	183	C2
Long established with excellent accomodations.		
*BILTMORE HOTEL, 515 S Olive St, Los Angeles	186	A3
Lovely long established hotel of the 1920's.		
BINION'S HORSESHOE HOTEL, 128 Fremont	209	C2
Casino, pool, cafe.		
BOURBON STREET HOTEL, 120 E Flamingo St, Ls Vegas	210	B3
Casino, restaurant, shows.		
*BREAKERS MOTEL, Morro Bay Bl & Market, Morro Bay	75	E3
25 rooms; ocean view, pool, restaurant.		
BUENA PARK HOTEL, 7675 Crescent Av, Buena Park	T	B2

NAME & ADDRESS	PAGE	GRID
350 rooms, near Knott's Berry Farm.		
BURBANK AIRPORT HILTON, 2500 Hollywood Wy,Burbank	179	B2
277 rooms; pool, sauna, whirlpool.		
*CAESAR'S PALACE, 3570 Las Vegas Bl, Las Vegas	210	B2
Casino, restaurants, entertainment, shops.		
*CAESAR'S, 1 blk N of US 50, Stateline, Nevada	129	E1
Cafe, convention facilities, golf, hlth club.		
*CALIFORNIA CLUB, 1st & Ogden, Las Vegas	209	C2
325 units; dining room & coffee shop, casino.		
CARLTON OAKS LODGE & COUNTRY CLUB, Santee	V	D2
59 rooms; pool, sauna, tennis.		
*CARRIAGE HOUSE INN, Junipero Av nr 8th Av, Carml	168	C3
13 units; fireplaces, bay windows; early Amer.		
CENTRE PLAZA HOLIDAY INN, 2233 Ventura St, Fresno	165	E4
320 rooms, near the convention center.		
*CENTURY PLAZA HOTEL, 2025 Avenue of the Stars	183	A2
Near Shubert Theater & ABC Entertainment Ctr.		
*CIRCUS-CIRCUS, 2880 Las Vegas Blvd	209	B5
Casino, entertainment, game room, circus acts.		
*CIRCUS-CIRCUS, 500 N Sierra St, Reno	130	B2
Hotel, casino, restaurant, entertainment.		
*CLAREMONT RESORT, Ashby & Domingo Avs, Oakland	156	C3
Lovely hotel & tennis club with vw of S F Bay.		
CLARION HOTEL, 401 Millbrae Av, Millbrae	144	E5
223 rooms; dining room & coffee shop, pool.		
CLARION HOTEL, 700 16th St, Sacramento	137	C2
248 rooms, near State Capitol.		
*CLIFT HOUSE, 495 Geary St, San Francisco	143	C3
329 units; newly renovated rooms, restaurant.		
COLONIAL INN, 910 Prospect St, La Jolla	105	B2
75 rooms; swimming pool, dining room.		
CONCORD HILTON, 1970 Diamond Blvd, Concord	38	E5
340 rooms; pool & whirlpool, restaurant.		
*CONESTOGA INN, 1240 S Walnut St, Anaheim	193	B4
254 units; pool, whirlpool, restaurant.		
*COTO DE CAZA, 14 mi E of I-5 via El Toro Rd	98	E5
100 rooms; pools & saunas, fishing, tennis.		
*DEL WEBB'S HIGH SIERRA, 255 N Sierra St	129	E1
Casino, restaurant, entertainment, shops.		
*DESERT INN, 3145 Las Vegas Bl, Las Vegas	209	B5
Casino, restaurants, entertainment.		
*DISNEYLAND HOTEL, 1150 W Cerritos Av	193	B4
Served by Disneyland Monorail.		
DOUBLETREE HOTEL, 1000 The City Dr, Orange	195	E1
460 rooms; tennis, pool, whirlpool.		
DREAM INN, 175 West Cliff Dr, Santa Cruz	169	D4
163 rooms; entertainment, pool, whirlpool.		
*DUNES, 3650 Las Vegas Bl, Las Vegas	210	B2
Casino, restaurants, entertainment, shops.		
EL CORTEZ HOTEL, 600 E Fremont St, Las Vegas	209	E1
316 room with a convenient downtown location.		
*EL DORADO HOTEL, 4th & Virginia, Reno	130	B2
Casino, restaurant and entertainment.		
EL RANCHO HOTEL, on the Strip, Las Vegas	209	C5
Newly renovated; casino, shows & restaurant.		
EMBASSY SUITES, 211 E Huntington Dr, Arcadia	R	D3
194 suites, pool and sauna.		
EMBASSY SUITES, 7762 Beach Blvd, Buena Park	T	B2
203 rooms; whirlpool & pool, dining.		
EMBASSY SUITES, 1211 Garvey, Covina	98	C2
264 rooms; restaurant, attractive grounds.		
EMBASSY SUITES, 8425 Firestone Blvd, Downey	R	B5
220 rooms; sauna, whirlpool & swimming pool.		
EMBASSY SUITES, 1440 Imperial Av, El Segundo	189	C2
351 rooms; near Los Angeles Internatl Airport.		
EMBASSY SUITES, 4550 La Jolla Village Dr	V	B2
Near beaches, freeways and unique shopping.		
EMBASSY SUITES, 333 Madonna Rd, San Luis Obispo	172	B4

POINTS OF INTEREST INDEX

NAME & ADDRESS	PAGE	GRID
400 rooms; entertainment, diningroom, pool.		
IMPERIAL PALACE, 3535 Las Vegas Blvd, Las Vegas	210	B2
1500 rooms; pools, entertainment, casino.		
INLAND EMPIRE HILTON, Waterman Av, San Bernardino	207	D5
247 rooms; dining room, pool & whirlpool.		
INN AT THE PARK, 1855 S Harbor Blvd, Anaheim	193	C4
500 units; pool, restaurant & coffee shop.		
IRVINE HILTON, 17900 Jamboree Blvd, Irvine	198	E4
550 units; close to John Wayne Airport.		
*JADE TREE INN, Junipero St near 5th, Carmel	168	C3
55 units; ocean view, fireplace, pool, lanais.		
LA CASA DEL ZORRO, Borrego Springs	107	E2
Studios, suites and casitas.		
*LA COSTA HOTEL & SPA, Costa del Mar Rd, Carlsbad	106	C3
547 rooms & houses; golf, tennis, health spa.		
LA JOLLA MARRIOTT, 4240 La Jolla Village Dr	V	B2
360 rooms, pool, whirlpool, dining room.		
LANDMARK HOTEL, Paradise Rd, Las Vegas	209	D5
Lovely rooms; restaurant, showrooms & casino.		
*LA QUINTA HOTEL, Eisenhower Dr, La Quinta	100	E4
269 rooms; lovely grounds, pool, tennis, golf.		
LA SIESTA VILLAS, Hwy 111, Palm Springs	100	C3
18 luxurious villas; swimming pool.		
*LAS VEGAS HILTON, 3000 Paradise Rd	209	D5
Casino, restaurants, star entertainment.		
LE BARON HOTEL, 1350 N First St, San Jose	151	E1
327 rooms, pool, steamroom, entertainment.		
*L'ERMITAGE, 9291 Burton Wy, Beverly Hills	183	C1
Elegant suites in the European tradition.		
LOS ANGELES AIRPORT HILTON, Century Bl,Ls Angeles	189	D1
1281 rooms; pool, diningroom, entertainment.		
*LOS ANGELES HILTON HOTEL, Wilshire at Figueroa	185	E3
900 units; pool, shopping; public facilities.		
*MADONNA INN, US 101 at Madonna Rd, Sn Luis Obspo	172	B4
109 unusually decorated rooms; restaurnt,cafe.		
MARINA DEL REY MARRIOTT, Maxella Av,Marina dl Rey	187	D3
283 rooms; whirlpool & pool, dining room.		
*MARINA HOTEL, 3805 Las Vegas Blvd	210	B4
870 units; pool, 2 restaurants, casino.		
*MARINA INTERNATIONAL HOTEL, 4200 Admiralty Wy	187	C3
136 units; patios/balconies, pool; LAX trans.		
*MARINERS INN, 6180 Moonstone Beach Dr, Cambria	75	C2
26 rooms; whirlpool. Across from the beach.		
*MARK HOPKINS HOTEL, 1 Nob Hill, San Francisco	143	C3
Elegnt lndmrk htl, panoramic vw 'Top of Mark'.		
MARRIOTT FISHERMAN'S WHARF, 1250 Columbus Av, S F	143	B1
257 rooms, restaurant and lounge.		
MARRIOTT HOTEL, 18000 Von Karman, Irvine	198	D4
502 rooms; tennis, exercise room, pool.		
*MARRIOTT HOTEL, 5855 W Century Bl, Los Angeles	189	D1
Very large hotel, transport to airport.		
*MARRIOTT INN, 200 Marina Blvd, Berkeley	L	C4
376 rooms; indoor pool, sauna, restaurant.		
MARRIOTTS DESERT SPRINGS RESORT, Palm Desert	100	E3
900 rooms, pool, tennis, golf, restaurant.		
*MARRIOTT'S RANCHO LAS PALMAS RESORT, Bob Hope Dr	100	E4
456 rooms; pools, golf, tennis, bicycles.		
*MARRIOTT'S SANTA BARBARA BILTMORE, 1260 Channel	87	D4
229 rooms; overlooks ocean, pool, restaurant.		
*MAXIM, 160 E Flamingo, Las Vegas	210	B3
Casino, restaurant, entertainment, shops.		
MENDOCINO HOTEL, 45080 Main St, Mendocino	30	B1
Restored 1878 Victorian hotel.		
MERIDIEN HOTEL, 50 3rd St, San Francisco	143	D3
700 rooms, restaurant, lounge, downtown.		
MIRAMAR SHERATON, 101 Wilshire Bl, Santa Monica	Q	B4
300 rooms, near Santa Monica Beach.		
MONTECITO INN, 1295 Coast Vlg Rd, Montecito	87	D4

NAME & ADDRESS	PAGE	GRID
60 rooms & suites; restored historic inn.		
MONTEREY PLAZA, 400 Cannery Row, Monterey	167	E3
291 rooms, pool, restaurant and lounge.		
*MOONSTONE INN, 5860 Moonstone Beach Dr, Cambria	75	B2
9 rooms with an ocean view from each.		
MURPHY'S HOTEL, off Hwy 4 in Murphys	41	C4
Historical monument still in full operation.		
*NAPA VALLEY LODGE BEST WESTERN, Yountville	38	C2
55 rooms; lovely view, pool & whirlpool.		
NEWARK HILTON, 39900 Balentine, Newark	P	A2
318 rooms; pool, sauna, whirlpool, dining.		
NEW OTANI HOTEL, Los Angeles St, Los Angeles	186	B3
448 rooms; beautiful garden, pool & sauna.		
NEWPORT BCH MARRIOTT, Newport Ctr Dr, Newport Bch	200	A4
603 rooms; 2 pools, tennis, dining.		
NEWPORTER RESORT, 1107 Jamboree Rd, Newport Beach	199	E4
325 rooms, tennis, pool, golf, restaurant.		
OAKLAND AIRPORT HILTON, Hegenberger Rd, Oakland	159	D4
367 rooms; pool, restaurant, entertainment.		
ONTARIO AIRPORT HILTON, 700 'G' St, Ontario	U	E2
309 rooms; dining, whirlpool & swimming pool.		
PACIFICA HOTEL, 6161 Centinela Av, Culver City	188	C3
375 rooms; swimming pool, restaurant.		
*PACIFIC PLAZA, 501 Post St, San Francisco	143	C3
140 units; restaurant, pay valet garage.		
PALA MESA RESORT, Jct I-15 & Hwy 76, Fallbrook	106	C2
135 rooms; pool, whirlpool, golf, tennis.		
PALM SPRINGS HILTON RIVIERA, Palm Springs	206	B2
467 rooms; 2 pools, wading pool, tennis.		
*PALM SPRINGS SPA HOTEL, Indian Av N & Tahquitz-M	206	B3
230 units; pool, 2 hot minerl pools, steam rm.		
PASADENA HILTON, 150 Los Robles Av, Pasadena	190	C4
253 rooms; entertainment, dining room, pool.		
*PEPPER TREE INN, 3850 State St, Santa Barbara	87	C4
150 rooms; patios, 2 pools & sauna, restaurnt.		
*PICADILLY INN AIRPORT, 5115 E McKinley, Fresno	57	D3
185 rooms; pool, whirlpool, restaurant.		
*PICADILLY INN-SHAW, 2305 W Shaw Av, Fresno	57	C3
203 rooms; pool, airport trans, restaurant.		
PINE INN, Ocean Av, Carmel	168	B3
49 rooms; Victorian decor, beautiful view.		
PLEASANTON HILTON, Johnson Dr, Pleasanton	M	B5
298 rooms; racquetball, tennis, swimming pool.		
*QUAIL LODGE, 8205 Valley Greens Dr, Carmel Vly	54	B5
100 rooms; scenic grounds, golf, tennis.		
QUALITY INN, 616 Convention Wy, Anaheim	193	C5
281 rooms; pool, dining & entertainment.		
QUALITY ROYALE, 1433 Camino del Rio, San Diego	214	A4
265 rooms; pool, sauna, putting green.		
*QUEEN MARY, Pier J, Long Beach	192	E4
British liner now serves as hotel & restrnt.		
*RAMADA HOTEL, 6th & Lake St, Reno	130	B2
250 units; casino and restaurant.		
RAMADA INN, 1331 Katella Av, Anaheim	193	E4
240 rooms; pool, jacuzzi, restaurant & lounge.		
*RAMADA INN, 114 E Highway 246, Buellton	86	D3
98 rooms; pool, convention & conference facil.		
RAMADA RENAISSANCE HOTEL, 55 Cyril Magnin St, S F	143	C3
1015 rooms; downtown, restaurant and lounge.		
*RANCHO BERNARDO INN, 17550 Bernardo Oaks Dr	106	D4
236 rooms; 2 pools, golf, bicycling, tennis.		
RED LION INN, Camino del Rio Ct, Bakersfield	166	A2
262 units; pool, whirlpool.		
RED LION INN, 3050 Bristol, Costa Mesa	198	A4
Near the Orange County Performing Arts Center.		
*RED LION MOTOR INN, 1830 Hilltop Dr, Redding	18	C2
194 rooms; pool, putting green, dining room.		
*RED LION MOTOR INN, 2001 Point West Wy, Sacto	39	E1

NAME & ADDRESS	PAGE	GRID	NAME & ADDRESS	PAGE	GRID
448 rooms; pools, airport trans, dining room.			265 rooms; dining room, swimming pool.		
*RENO HILTON, 255 N Sierra	130	B3	SHERATON TOWNHOUSE, 2961 Wilshire Bl, Los Angeles	185	C2
Lovely hotel with pool, casino & restaurants.			300 rooms, pool, sauna, tennis, dining room.		
RESIDENCE INN, 1700 S Clementine, Anaheim	193	C4	SHERATON UNIVERSAL, off Lankershim,Universal City	181	A1
Near Disneyland, convention center & freeways.			475 rooms; entertainment, pool & sauna.		
RESIDENCE INN, 201 N State College Bl, Orange	196	A1	SHERATON VALLEY INN, 5101 California Av, Bakrsfld	78	C3
Near Anaheim Stadium and freeways.			200 rooms; pool and restaurant.		
*RIO BRAVO RESORT, 11200 Lake Ming Rd, Rio Bravo	78	E2	*SHORE CLIFF LODGE, 2555 Price St, Pismo Beach	76	B4
112 rooms; tennis, golf, pools, airstrip.			99 rooms; ocean view, heated pool, restaurant.		
RITZ CARLTON, 33533 Shoreline Dr, Dana Point	105	D1	*SILVERADO COUNTRY CLUB RESORT, 1600 Atlas Peak	38	D2
393 rooms; golf, tennis, pools, ocean view.			260 rooms; 8 pools, golf, tennis, bicycles.		
*RIVIERA, 2901 Las Vegas Bl, Las Vegas	209	C5	*SMUGGLERS INN, 3737 N Blackstone Av, Fresno	57	C3
Casino, restaurants, entertainment, shops.			210 rooms; beautiful landscape, pool, restrnt.		
SACRAMENTO HILTON, 2200 Harvard, Sacramento	39	A3	*STANFORD COURT, 905 California St, Nob Hill	143	C3
336 rooms, pool, restaurant and lounge.			Gracious 1900s decor in Old Stanford House.		
*SACRAMENTO INN, 1401 Arden Wy	39	E1	*STOCKTON HILTON, 2323 Grand Canal	40	A5
387 rooms; pools, putting green, dining room.			202 rooms; 3 pools, dining room & coffee shop.		
*SAHARA (DEL WEBB'S), 2535 Las Vegas Bl, Ls Vegas	209	C4	STOUFFER CONCOURSE, 5400 Century Bl, Los Angeles	189	E1
Casino, restaurants, entertainment, shops.			750 rooms; restaurant, swimming pool.		
*SAN DIEGO HILTON, 1775 E Mission Bay Dr	212	E3	SUNDANCE HOTEL, 301 E Fremont St, Las Vegas	209	C2
356 units; pool, beach, rental boats & bikes.			650 units; restaurant, buffet and casino.		
*SANDS, 3355 Las Vegas Bl, Las Vegas	210	B2	*SUNNYVALE HILTON INN, 1250 Lakeside Dr	P	A3
Casino, restaurants, star entertainment.			372 rooms; pool, restaurant, airport trans.		
*SANDS REGENT, Arlington & 3rd Sts, Reno	130	A2	*TAHOE SEASONS RESORT, Saddle & Keller, Lk Tahoe	129	E3
Casino, cafe, and shops.			160 units; tennis courts and restaurant.		
SAN DIEGO MARRIOTT, 333 W Harbor Dr	215	D4	THE CHATEAU, 4195 Solano Av, Napa	38	C2
1350 rooms, near several points of interest.			115 rooms; Country-French atmosphere, pool.		
SAN FRAN AIRPORT MARRIOTT, Bayshore Hy,Burlingame	N	C1	*THE INN AT RANCHO SANTA FE, Linea del Cielo	106	C4
689 rooms; dining, health club, pool.			80 rooms and cottages on tree-shaded grounds.		
*SAN LUIS BAY INN, Avila Beach	76	A4	THE LODGE AT PEBBLE BEACH, on the 17 Mile Drive	53	B5
76 rooms; ocean view, golf, swim, dining room.			159 units; pool, sauna, golf course.		
*SANTA CLARA MARRIOTT, Great America Parkway	P	B3	THE PARK HOTEL, 300 N Main St, Las Vegas	209	E1
764 rooms; near Great America Theme Park.			435 rooms, entertainment, casino.		
SHERATON-ANAHEIM, 1015 W Ball Rd, Anaheim	193	B3	*THE SHASTA INN, 2180 Hilltop Dr, Redding	18	C2
500 rooms; entertainment, dining, pool.			148 rooms; pool & whirlpool, restaurant.		
*SHERATON AT FISHERMAN'S WHARF, 2500 Mason St, SF	143	B1	*THE TREE HOUSE BEST WESTERN, off I-5, Mt Shasta	12	C2
525 units; pool, restaurant and coffee shop.			94 rooms; indoor pool, bicycles, dining room.		
SHERATON GRANDE, 333 S Figueroa St, Los Angeles	186	A3	*TICKLE PINK MOTOR INN, 155 Highland Dr, Carmel	54	A5
470 rooms, near Music Center & downtown.			35 rooms; beautiful view and lovely location.		
SHERATON HARBOR ISLAND E, 1380 Harbor Island Dr	215	B2	TORRANCE MARRIOTT, 3635 Fashion Wy, Torrance	S	B2
750 rooms, tennis courts, swimming pool.			487 rooms; 2 pools, sauna, whirlpool.		
SHERATON HARBOR ISLAND W, 1590 Harbor Island Dr	215	A2	TOWN & COUNTRY, Hotel Circle, San Diego	213	D4
350 rooms, near San Diego Internat'l Airport.			966 rooms; 4 pools, sauna & whirlpool.		
*SHERATON HOTEL, 45 John Glenn Dr, Concord	M	A3	*TROPICANA, 3801 Las Vegas Bl, Las Vegas	210	B4
331 rooms; conference center, entertainment.			Casino, cafe, entertainment, theater, shops.		
SHERATON HOTEL, Industry Hills Pkwy, Industry	R	E4	*UNION PLAZA HOTEL, 1 Main St, Las Vegas	209	C1
298 rooms; golf, tennis, 2 swimming pools.			Casino, restaurant, entertainment.		
SHERATON INN, 1177 Airport Blvd, Burlingame	N	D1	*UNIVERSITY HILTON, 3540 E Figueroa St, LA	185	C5
316 rooms; dining room & coffee shop; pools.			241 units; next to USC campus; pool.		
*SHERATON NEWPORT BEACH, 4545 MacArthur Blvd	198	B5	U S GRANT HOTEL, 326 Broadway, San Diego	215	D3
Beautiful facilities, entertainment.			283 rooms, 1900's decor, restaurant, lounge.		
SHERATON-PALACE HOTEL, 639 Market St, Sn Francsco	143	D3	*VACATION VILLAGE, Mission Bay Pk, San Diego	212	B3
592 rooms, lounge and restaurant, downtown.			449 bungalows, rooms & suites; 5 pools.		
*SHERATON PLAZA, 6101 W Century Blvd	189	C1	VEGAS WORLD HOTEL, 2000 Las Vegas Bl S, Las Vegas	209	C4
Beautiful facilities, easy access to LAX.			529 rooms, casino, entertainment.		
*SHERATON PLAZA, 400 E Tahquitz-McCallum Wy	206	B4	*VISCOUNT HOTEL, 700 Queenswy Dr, Long Beach	192	D4
258 units; pool, saunas, whirlpools, tennis.			Located on the waterfront next to Queen Mary.		
SHERATON PREMIERE, off Lankershim, Universal City	181	A1	VISCOUNT HOTEL, 9750 Airport Blvd, Los Angeles	189	D1
450 rooms; exercise room, pool & whirlpool.			575 rooms, near Los Angeles Intrnat'l Airport.		
SHERATON RIVERSIDE, 3400 Market, Riverside	205	B2	WAWONA HOTEL, S entrance to Yosemite Valley	49	D3
296 units; dining room and entertainment.			A grand mountain resort built in the 1800's.		
SHERATON ROUND BARN INN, 3555 Round Barn Bl	37	E2	*WEST BEACH MOTOR LODGE, Cabrillo Bl & Bath St	174	C4
252 rooms, pool, golf and tennis.			45 units; across from yacht harbor & beach.		
*SHERATON SANTA BARBARA HOTEL, 1111 E Cabrillo	87	D4	*THE WESTGATE, 2nd Av at C St, San Diego	215	D3
174 rooms; ocean view, pool, dining room.			223 units; elegant decor, restaurant.		
*SHERATON SUNNYVALE INN, 1100 N Mathilda Av	148	D4	*WESTIN BONAVENTURE, 6th & Flower, Los Angeles	186	A3
174 rooms; pool, restaurant, cocktail lounge.			Rooftop restaurnt & revolvng cocktl lounge.		
SHERATON SUNRISE, Point East Dr, Rancho Cordova	40	B1	*WESTIN ST FRANCIS, Union Square, San Francisco	143	C3

NAME & ADDRESS	PAGE	GRID
Fashionable shops, skyline view from elevator.		
*WESTIN SOUTH COAST PLAZA, 666 Anton Bl,Costa Msa	198	A3
400 units; pool, putting green, tennis.		
*WESTWOOD MARQUIS, 930 Hilgard Av, Westwood	180	D2
250 elegant suites; pool, sauna, whirlpool.		
WHITTIER HILTON, 7320 Greenleaf Av, Whittier	R	D5
206 rooms, whirlpool, pool, dining room.		

✝ MISSIONS

NAME & ADDRESS	PAGE	GRID
MSN BASILICA SAN DIEGO DE ALCALA, 10818 SD Msn Rd	214	E3
1769, 1st missn estblshd along El Camino Real.		
MISSION LA PURIMISA CONCEPCION, 15 mi W of US 101	86	B2
1787, 11th missn, rebuilt by original methods.		
MISSION NUESTRA SENORA DE LA SOLEDAD, off US 101	65	A1
1791, 13th missn, stood in ruins for 100 yrs.		
MISSION SAN ANTONIO DE PADUA, off U S 101	65	B3
1771, 3rd msn, one of largest restored missns.		
MISSION SAN ANTONIO DE PALA, off Hwy 76	106	E2
Built in 1816 to help the Sn Luis Rey Mission.		
MISSION SAN BUENAVENTURA, Main & Figueroa Sts	175	B2
1782, 9th missn, last founded by Father Serra.		
MISSION SAN CARLOS BORROMEO, Lasuen Dr, Carmel	168	B4
1770, 2nd missn, burial place of Father Serra.		
MSN SAN FERNANDO REY DE ESPANA, 15151 SF Msn Bl	Q	C1
1797, 17th msn, destroyed by '71 quake; rstrd.		
MISSION SAN FRANCISCO DE ASIS, Dolores & 16th Sts	142	C4
1776, 6th missn, chapel unchanged for 175 yrs.		
MISSION SAN FRANCISCO SOLANO, Spain & 1st Sts	132	D3
1823, 21st missn, northernmost & last of msns.		
MISSION SAN GABRIEL ARCANGEL, 1120 Old Mill Rd	R	C3
1771, 4th missn, at crossroads in early Calif.		
MISSION SAN JOSE, 43300 Mission Blvd	P	B2
1777, 14th missn, noted for outstanding music.		
MISSION SAN JUAN BAUTISTA, off US 101	54	D3
1797, 15th msn, near othr buildngs of msn era.		
MISSION SAN JUAN CAPISTRANO, off I-5 at Ortega	202	E1
1776, 7th mission, swallows return annually.		
MISSION SAN LUIS OBISPO, Chorro & Monterey Sts	172	C3
1772, 5th mission, 1st misn to use tile tools.		
MISSION SAN LUIS REY DE FRANCIA, on Hwy 76	106	B3
1798, 18th missn, most successful of all msns.		
MISSION SAN MIGUEL ARCANGEL, 801 Mission St	66	A5
1797, 16th missn, last msn secularized - 1834.		
MISSION SAN RAFAEL ARCANGEL, A St & 5th Av	139	D3
1817, 20th missn, founded to aid sick Indians.		
MISSION SANTA BARBARA, Laguna & Los Olivos Sts	174	B2
1786, 10th missn, famed as most beautiful msn.		
MISSION SANTA CLARA DE ASIS, Grant & Franklin St	151	B2
1777, 8th missn, bell dated 1798 still clangs.		
MISSION SANTA CRUZ, School & Emmet Sts	169	D2
1791, 12th msn, destroyed, replica built 1931.		
MISSION SANTA INES, 1760 Mission Dr	86	E3
1804, 19th mission, favorite mission of many.		
MISSION SANTA YSABEL, Hwy 79 near Julian	107	C3
Blt 1818, contains mus & Indian burial grnds.		

🌲 PARKS (STATE & FEDERAL) & NATIONAL FORESTS

NAME & ADDRESS	PAGE	GRID
ADM WILLIAM STANDLEY STATE REC AREA, Laytonville	22	C3
Beautiful scenery; no camping facilities.		
AHJUMAWI LAVA SPRINGS STATE PARK, Island Rd	13	E3
Accessible by boat only.		
ALAMEDA PARK, Micheltorea & Anacapa Sts	174	C3
Displays 280 species of plants and shrubs.		
AMERICAN RIVER PARKWAY, from Nimbus Dam	137	B1

NAME & ADDRESS	PAGE	GRID
23 mi long greenbelt along banks of Sacto Riv.		
ANCIENT BRISTLECONE PINE FOREST, White Mountn Rd	52	A3
4600 yr old pine forest, nature trails.		
ANDREW MOLERA STATE PARK, W of Hwy 1, Big Sur	64	B2
50 campsites, sandy beach, hiking, meadows.		
ANGELES NATIONAL FOREST, N of Los Angeles	Q	D1
In rugged mtns of LA, hiking & winter sports.		
ANGEL ISLAND STATE PARK, E San Francisco Bay	L	B4
Isl pk has hiking, bike rentl, picnc, day use.		
ANNADEL STATE PARK, Channel Dr	38	A2
Riding & hiking.		
ANTELOPE VALLEY CAL POPPY RESERVE, W of Lancaster	89	D2
Scenic area for picnicking.		
ANZA BORREGO DESERT STATE PARK, San Diego County	108	A4
Beautiful wildflowers in spring; camp, hike.		
ARMSTRONG REDWOODS STATE RESERVE, E of Fort Ross	37	C1
Giant redwoods, picnicking, hiking trails.		
AUBURN STATE REC AREA, 1 mile South of Auburn	34	D3
Camp; riding & hiking trails on American Rivr.		
AUSTIN CREEK STATE RECREATION AREA, E of Ft Ross	37	C1
Camp, horseback ride, meadows, vllys, forests.		
AZALEA STATE RESERVE, off Hwy 101, Arcata	10	A4
Beautiful azaleas bloom late May - early June.		
BENBOW LAKE STATE REC AREA, 2 mi S of Garberville	22	B1
Horse trails, fish, hike, swim, picnic.		
BENICIA STATE RECREATION AREA, W of Benicia	L	D2
Good fishing; picnicking facilities.		
BIG BASIN REDWOODS STATE PARK, on Hwy 236	N	D4
First state park to preserve redwoods.		
BOGGS MOUNTAIN STATE FOREST, N of Hwy 175	32	A4
Picnicking; hiking trails.		
BONELLI REGIONAL COUNTY PARK, Park Rd, San Dimas	U	B2
Picnicking facilities and hiking trails.		
BORDER FIELD STATE PARK, 15 mi S of San Diego	V	B5
Good area to picnic, fish, swim, or hike.		
BOTHE-NAPA VALLEY STATE PARK, on Hwy 29	38	A1
Hiking, picnic & camping areas, swimming pool.		
BRANNAN ISLAND, South of Rio Vista	M	D2
Boat, fish, camp, hike; visitors center.		
BROOKSIDE PARK, Rosemont Av, Pasadena	190	A3
Site of Rosebowl; swimming, hiking, golfing.		
BUCKSKIN MOUNTAIN STATE PARK, Hwy 95, Arizona	104	C1
Scenic area to hike and picnic.		
BURTON CREEK STATE PARK, E of Tahoe State Park	35	E1
Camping and picnicking.		
BUTANO STATE PARK, E of Hwy 1 at Gazos Creek Rd	N	C4
Camping, recreational facilities.		
CABRILLO NATIONAL MONUMENT, Point Loma, San Diego	V	A4
Visitors ctr with historic progrms & displays.		
CALAVERAS BIG TREES STATE PARK, E of Arnold	41	D3
2 giant Redwood groves - self-guided tours.		
CANDLESTICK POINT RECREATION AREA, US 101	L	C5
Scenic hiking trails; picnicking & fishing.		
CASTLE CRAG STATE PARK, S of Dunsmuir	12	D3
Pinnacles, crags, cliffs, green pines, rec.		
CASTLE ROCK STATE PARK, near Jct Hwy 9 and Hwy 35	N	E4
Nature & hiking trails; picnicking & camping.		
CASWELL MEMORIAL STATE PARK, Hwy 99 S of Manteca	47	B2
Camp, fish, swim, hike, picnic.		
CHABOT REGIONAL PARK, Lake Chabot	L	E5
5000 acre park; fish, picnic, moto-X, boat.		
CHANNEL ISLANDS NATIONAL PARK, off Santa Barbara	87	C5
Consists of 5 islands, 20 to 60 mi offshore.		
CHINA CAMP STATE PARK, N of San Rafael	L	B3
Recreational facilities and camping.		
CHINO HILLS STATE PARK, off Hwy 71, Orange Co	U	C4
Hiking trails, picnic areas.		
CLEAR LAKE STATE PARK, near Lakeport	31	D3

POINTS OF INTEREST INDEX

NAME & ADDRESS	PAGE	GRID	NAME & ADDRESS	PAGE	GRID
Beautiful streams, mountains, forests.			Scenic area for picnicking, hiking & camping.		
MT DIABLO STATE PARK, Diablo Rd	M	B4	SALTON SEA STATE RECREATION AREA, off Hwy 111	108	E2
Hiking trails, campsites on peak.			Camp, hike, picnic, boat, waterski.		
MT SAN JACINTO STATE PARK, Hwy 111 near Palm Spgs	100	B4	SALT POINT STATE PARK, N of Fort Ross off Hwy 1	37	A1
Hiking, picnicking, some camping.			Underwater presrve, beachs, tidepools, trails.		
MT TAMALPAIS STATE PARK, 6 mi N Hwy 1, Marin Co	L	A3	SAMUEL P TAYLOR STATE PARK, off Hwy 1	37	E4
Hiking, equestrian trails, camping.			Camping, fishing, riding, winter sports.		
MUIR WOODS NATL MONUMENT, Mt Tamalpais State Park	L	A4	SAN BERNARDINO NATIONAL FOREST, Hwy 18	U	D1
Named for naturalist John Muir; day hikes.			Camping, picnicking; year-round sports.		
NEVADA STATE PARK, N of Carson City, Nevada	36	C1	SAN BRUNO MOUNTAIN STATE PARK, S of Daly City	L	B5
Rec at Washoe Lake-camp, boat, nature trails.			Enjoy a picnic amid the beautiful scenery.		
NOJOQUI FALLS COUNTY PARK, S of Solvang	86	E3	SAN FRANCISCO BAY WILDLIFE REFUGE, south S F Bay	N	E2
Picnic facilities with a view of the falls.			Preservation of nature at its best.		
OCOTILLO WELLS STATE VEHICULAR REC AREA, Hwy 78	108	B3	SAN FRANCISCO FISH & GAME REFUGE, off Hwy 280	N	B1
Trails for off-road vehicle use; camping.			Lovely area for hiking and picnicking.		
OREGON CAVES NATIONAL MONUMENT, off Hwy 46	2	E2	SAN GABRIEL WILDERNESS AREA, off Hwy 2	R	E1
Spectacular formations of mineral deposits.			Preserve of natural & rugged mountain country.		
PALOMAR MOUNTAIN STATE PARK, Birch Hill Rd	107	A2	SAN ONOFRE STATE PARK, off I-5, San Onofre	105	E1
Sierra-like country, many camps, picnic sites.			Scenic area for hiking and picnicking.		
PARK MOABI, off I-40	95	D2	SANTA MONICA MTNS NAT'L REC AREA, Los Angeles Co	96	E2
Boat rentals & ramp, camping, fishing.			Nature trails to hike and ranger programs.		
PATRICKS POINT STATE PARK, N of Trinidad	9	D3	SEQUOIA NATIONAL PARK, Hwy 198	59	B5
Camping, hiking, biking, picnicking.			With Kings Canyon, museum, logging, rec area.		
PAUL M. DIMMICK WAYSIDE CAMPGROUND, W of Navarro	30	C2	SEQUOIA NATIONAL FOREST, Hwy 198	69	D2
Primitive campground with swimming & fishing.			Fishing, camping, boating, winter sports.		
PETRIFIED FOREST, on Petrified Forest Hwy	38	A1	SHADOW CLIFFS REGIONL RECREATION AREA, Pleasanton	P	C1
Ancient redwoods preserved in volcanic ash.			Swim, fish, boat, picnic, bike & waterslide.		
PFEIFFER BIG SUR STATE PARK, E of Hwy 1, Big Sur	64	B2	SHASTA NATIONAL FOREST, off I-5	13	D2
215+ dev sites - hiking, store, swim , fish.			Large lakes, steep mountains, rec facilities.		
PINNACLES NATIONAL MONUMENT, on Hwy 146	55	B5	SHASTA STATE HISTORIC PARK, 6 miles W of Redding	18	B2
Remnant of volcanic mtn; hike & explore caves.			Restored buildings were blt in Gold Rush days.		
PIO PICO STATE HIST PARK, Whittier Blvd, Whittier	R	D4	SIERRA NATIONAL FOREST, S of Yosemite Natl Park	49	C3
Second adobe home of last Mexican governor.			Grand sequoias; wtrsports at lakes, hunting.		
PISMO DUNES STATE VEHICULAR REC AREA, Pismo Beach	76	B5	SINKYONE WILDERNESS ST PK, Humboldt & Mendocno Co	22	A2
Sand dunes, off-road trails; swim, camp, fish.			Tent camping, picnicking, hiking & fishing.		
PLACERITA CYN STATE PARK, Hwy 14 N of Sn Fernando	89	C5	SISKIYOU NATIONAL FOREST, SW Oregon	1	E2
Scenic area for picnicking and hiking.			Rugged mtns, winding creeks, old mining towns.		
PLUMAS EUREKA STATE PARK, Hwy A14 at Johnsville	26	E2	SIX RIVERS NATIONAL FOREST, NW corner of CA	10	D3
Scenic creeks, mountains, lakes and trails.			Many rivers, good fishing, forest-coverd mtns.		
PLUMAS NATIONAL FOREST, south of Hwy 36	20	B5	SMITHE REDWOODS STATE RESERVE, E of Hwy 101	22	C2
Waterfall, lakes, grassy valleys, woodlands.			Trails to waterfall, Eel River, picnicking.		
POINT LOBOS STATE RESERVE, W of Hwy 1	54	A5	STANDISH HICKEY STATE REC AREA, 1 mi N of Leggett	22	C2
Spectacular view of coast; swim in China Cove.			Picnicking, hiking, biking, camping.		
POINT MUGU STATE PARK, Hwy 1	96	C2	STANISLAUS NATIONAL FOREST, SE of Hwy 4	41	D4
Scenic campsite; fish, swim, picnic, hike.			Deep, stream-cut canyons, meadows, evergreens.		
PORTOLA STATE PARK, W of Hwy 35	N	D4	SUGARLOAF RIDGE STATE PARK, Adobe Canyon Rd	38	B2
Camping, recreational facilities.			Fishing, riding & camping.		
PRAIRIE CREEK REDWOODS STATE PARK, N of Orick	10	A1	SUGAR PINE POINT STATE PARK, north of Meeks Bay	35	E2
Good camping, scenic trails thru lush forest.			Grove of sugar pines; camp, cross-country ski.		
PROVIDENCE MTNS STATE REC AREA, Essex Rd	94	B1	TAHOE NATIONAL FOREST, W of Lake Tahoe	26	E3
Scenic area for camping; exhibits.			Good fishing, camping, snow skiing, scenic.		
RANCHO SIERRA VISTA, Ventura County	96	C1	TAHOE STATE RECREATION AREA, N of Tahoe City	35	E2
Native American Cultural Center.			Good camping, boating, beach, nature trails.		
RED ROCK CANYON STATE PARK, Hwy 14 at Ricardo	80	B3	TECOLOTE CYN NATURAL PK, Linda Vista Rd, Sn Diego	213	B2
Picnicking, hiking trails, camping facilities.			Large natural park in the city of San Diego.		
REDWOOD NATIONAL PARK, Crescent City, Orick	2	A4	TOIYABE NATIONAL FOREST, E Sierra Nev into Nevada	73	D1
Giant redwoods, picturesque coast & rivers.			Camp, fish, hunt; forest, grass, sagebrush.		
RICHARDSON GROVE STATE PARK, south of Garberville	22	B1	TOMALES BAY STATE PARK, Tomales Bay	37	D4
Scenic, camp, fish, swim, hiking trails.			Hike to scenic beaches; rocky, wave-cut coves.		
ROBERT LOUIS STEVENSON STATE PK, off Hwy 29	32	A5	TOPANGA STATE PARK, Hwy 27, in Santa Monica Mtns	Q	A4
Scenic area for picnicking and hiking.			Picnicking, hiking, horseback riding.		
ROEDING PARK, north of Belmont Av	165	B2	TORREY PINES STATE RESERVE, S of Del Mar	V	A1
Picnic areas, boat rides, children's zoo.			Beautiful hiking area; nature trail, exhibits.		
ROGUE RIVER NATIONAL FOREST, South Central Oregon	3	C2	TRINITY NATIONAL FOREST, along Hwy 299	17	B3
Fishing & white-water rafting on Rogue River.			Good hunting and fishing; rivers & lakes.		
RUSSIAN GULCH STATE PARK, S of Fort Bragg	30	A1	TULE ELK RESERVE STATE PARK, Tupman Rd	78	B3
Rocky headlands, camping, hike to waterfall.			Several acres grazed by native valley elk.		
SADDLEBACK BUTTE STATE PARK, E of Lancaster	90	C3	TURLOCK STATE REC AREA, Hwy 132 East of Modesto	48	B2

POINTS OF INTEREST INDEX

NAME & ADDRESS	PAGE	GRID
Camp; hiking, swimming and fishing available.		
VAN DAMME STATE PARK, south of Fort Bragg	30	C1
Camp near beach, hiking trails, Pygmy Forest.		
W. IDE STATE HISTORIC PARK, 2 mi NE of Red Bluff	18	D4
Home of the California Pioneer. Picnic & swim.		
WILL ROGERS STATE HISTORIC PARK, Sunset Bl	Q	B4
Will Roger's home locatd within 186 acre park.		
WOODSON BRIDGE STATE REC AREA, SE of Corning	24	D2
Camping, fishing, swimming, nature trail.		
YOSEMITE NATIONAL PARK, off Hwy 120	49	D1
Beautiful wtrflls, lakes, cyns, streams, mtns.		

POINTS OF INTEREST

NAME & ADDRESS	PAGE	GRID
A B C STUDIOS, 2020 Avenue of the Stars	182	C4
Tour sets & watch filming of TV programs.		
ACADEMY OF SCIENCES, Golden Gate Park	141	D4
Renowned science museum incl Morrsn Planetarm.		
AEROSPACE HISTORY CENTER, Balboa Park, San Diego	215	E2
Aeronautical displays of the past and present.		
ALCATRAZ ISLAND, San Francisco Bay	L	B4
Former maximum security prison; 1/2 day tours.		
AMADOR COUNTY MUSEUM, 225 Church St, Jackson	40	E2
Working models of old gold mines.		
AMER CAROUSEL MUSEUM, 633 Beach St, San Francisco	143	B1
Carousel art from New York and Philadelphia.		
AMERICAN FOREST PRODUCTION MILL, North Fork	49	E5
Tours of the lumber mill are conducted daily.		
AMERICAN VICTORIAN MUSEUM, 325 Spring St	128	B2
Collection of Victorian artifacts.		
AMTRAK STATION, Kettner & D St, San Diego	215	C3
Train station with access to zoo & othr sites.		
ANAHEIM CONVENTION CENTER, Katella & Harbor	193	B5
Concerts, sports events, shows.		
ANAHEIM STADIUM, 2000 State College Bl, Anaheim	194	A5
Home of Angels baseball & Rams football teams.		
ANGEL'S CAMP MUSEUM, Main St, Angels Camp	41	B4
History museum; also known for Frog Jumping.		
ANO NUEVO STATE RESERVE, off Hwy 1, San Mateo Co.	N	C5
Reserve for seals, sea lions & elephant seals.		
ANTELOPE VALLEY INDIAN MUSEUM, 15701 E Avenue 'M'	90	C3
Exhibits of Indian artifacts.		
ANZA-BORREGO VISITOR CENTER, State Park Headqtrs	107	D2
Information and Ranger Station.		
ARCO PLAZA, 505 S Flower St, Los Angeles	186	A3
Subterranean shopping center.		
ARTIST'S DRIVE, Death Valley National Monument	72	A1
Rainbow-colored canyon of geological interest.		
ASIAN ART MUSEUM, near Japanese Tea Garden, GGP	141	C4
Outstanding Oriental collection; jade display.		
ATMOSPHERIUM & PLANETARIUM, University of Nevada	130	A1
Space & star programs shown on dome ceilings.		
AVENUE OF THE GIANTS, N of Garberville	16	C4
Scenic route thru groves of majestic redwoods.		
BADWATER, in Death Valley, south of Hwy 190	72	A1
Lowest pt in N America, 282' below sea level.		
BALBOA PARK, off Hwy 163 in San Diego	216	A2
Large central park; gardens, zoo, museums.		
BALBOA PAVILION, Balboa Bl, Newport Beach	199	D5
Beautiful landmark of Newport Bay; cruises.		
BATTERY POINT LIGHTHOUSE, Crescent City	1	D4
Tours & museum include history of lighthouse.		
BAY MEADOWS RACETRACK, S Delaware, San Mateo	145	B3
Thoroughbred, harness & quarter horse racing.		
BERKELEY AQUATIC PARK, Polk St, San Francisco	L	C4
Curved fishing pier creates cold swim lagoon.		
BERKELEY ROSE GARDENS, Euclid Av & Bayview	156	A1

NAME & ADDRESS	PAGE	GRID
1000's of different varieties of roses.		
BIDWELL PARK, E 4th St, Chico	124	D4
Swimming pool, picnic, golf, nature trails.		
BIRD ROCK, Bird Rock Av, La Jolla	105	B5
Birdwatching in a natural coastal setting.		
BOWERS MUSEUM, 2002 N Main St, Santa Ana	196	B3
Historical pioneer, Indian & Spanish displays.		
BRADBURY BUILDING, 304 Broadway, Los Angeles	186	B3
Distinguished 19th Century structure.		
BRIDALVEIL FALL, Yosemite National Park	63	A2
Beautifl waterfall drops 600' to Yosemite Vly.		
BROOKS HALL, under San Francisco Civic Center	143	B4
Subterranean hall built in 1958 for shows.		
BUFFALO PRESERVE, Golden Gate Park	141	A4
10 acres downtown SF used for bison preserve.		
BURBANK STUDIOS, 4000 Warner Blvd	179	C5
Offers tours of day's activity on the lot.		
CABLE CAR MUS, Washington & Mason, San Francisco	143	C2
World's first cable car&cable winding machine.		
CABOTS PUEBLO MUSEUM, 67624 Desert View	100	C3
Indian, Eskimo & early settler artifacts.		
CABRILLO MARINE MUSEUM, 3720 Stephen M White Dr	S	B3
Beautiful exhibits of fish, birds & whales.		
CALAVERAS COUNTY MUSEUM, 30 N Main, San Andreas	41	A3
In old courthouse; Indian arts, guns, gems.		
CALICO MTNS ARCHAEOLOGICAL PROJ, Hwy 15, Barstow	82	B5
Tours available Wednesday through Sunday.		
CALIFORNIA ALMOND GROWERS EXCHANGE, 216 O Street	137	C2
Offers tours and films daily.		
CALIFORNIA CAVERNS, Cave City Rd, San Andreas	41	B3
Tours of the caves available.		
CALIFORNIA LIVING MUSEUM, Hwy 178, Rio Bravo	78	E2
Informative contemporary museum.		
CALIF MUSEUM OF SCIENCE & INDUSTRY, 700 State Dr	185	C5
Fascinating do-it-yourself mus in Expositn Pk.		
CALIFORNIA OIL MUSEUM, 1003 Main St, Santa Paula	88	B5
History of discovery & drilling of oil in Cal.		
CALIFORNIA RAILROAD MUSEUM, E of I-5 on Front St	137	A2
Exhibits housed in restored railway station.		
CALIFORNIA RODEO GROUNDS, 1034 N Main St	171	C2
Parades & square dancing at rodeo.		
CALIFORNIA STATE ARCHIVES, 1020 O St	137	B3
Features historical documents of California.		
CALIFORNIA STATE CAPITOL MUSEUM, Sacramento	137	B3
Exhibits and tours offered daily from 9 to 5.		
CALIFORNIA WESTERN RAILROAD, Laurel St, Ft Bragg	22	B5
Train trips through picturesque redwoods.		
CAMPANILE, center of Univ of Berkeley campus	156	B2
Landmark chimes hourly from 12 bronze bells.		
CANDLESTICK PARK, Gilman Av east of Bayshore Fwy	L	C5
Home of San Francisco 49ers & Giants.		
CANNERY ROW, south of Pt Alones, Monterey	167	E2
Famous location of John Steinbeck's novels.		
CARIZZO GORGE RAILROAD TRESTLE, N of Jacumba	111	A4
Highest wooden trestle still in use.		
CARNEGIE STATE VEHICULAR REC AREA, W of Tracy	P	E1
Motorcycle trails and camping facilities.		
CARSON MANSION, 143 M St, Eureka	121	D1
Fabulous Victorian home; carved redwood walls.		
CASINO, St Catherine Wy, Catalina Island	97	B4
Features grand ballroom where big bands play.		
CASTLE AIR MUSEUM, Heritage Wy, Atwater	48	B4
Air Force museum; open daily.		
CATALINA ISLAND, 21 mi SW of Los Angeles	97	D5
Boats depart from Long Beach & LA Harbors.		
CEC SEABEE MUSEUM, Naval Battalion Center	96	A1
History of the Naval Construction Battalion.		
CEDAR GROVE, Kings Canyon National Park	59	B3

NAME & ADDRESS	PAGE	GRID
Base for trail trips by horseback or backpack.		
CENTER OF THE WORLD, Felicity, California	112	C5
Pyramid built at point determned world center.		
CHINATOWN, 900 N Broadway, Los Angeles	186	C2
Authentic Chinese shops and restaurants.		
CHINATOWN, between Stockton & Kearny Sts, SF	143	C2
Largest Chinese settlement in America.		
CHURCH BUILT FROM ONE TREE, Santa Rosa	131	D4
Built from a single redwood tree.		
CHURCH FINE ARTS BUILDING, University of Nevada	130	B1
Art exhibits & theater productions.		
CIVIC MEMORIAL AUDITORIUM, Center St, Stockton	160	D4
Various shows, conventions, exhibits&displays.		
CLARK BIRD REFUGE, E of Santa Barbara	87	C4
Wild birds in their natural habitat.		
CLARK MEMORIAL MUSEUM, 240 E St, Eureka	121	C1
Victorian furniture & clothing, antique guns.		
CLEAR LAKE WILDLIFE REFUGE, off Hwy 139	6	B3
Hunting of waterfowl, good photography.		
CLIFF HOUSE, 1090 Point Lobos Av	L	A4
Famous restaurant with magnificent view.		
COIT TOWER, top of Telegraph Hill	143	C2
Volunteer firefighter mem, good view of city.		
COLEMAN FISH STATION, 12 mi SE of Anderson	18	D3
Large salmon hatchery; spawning fall & winter.		
COLUSA NATL WILDLIFE REFUGE, on Hwy 20	32	E2
1000's of birds to view on self-guided tour.		
COMMUNITY MEMORIAL MUS, Butte House Rd, Yuba City	125	B2
Memorabilia of early Indians and Pioneers.		
COW MOUNTAIN REC AREA, near Cow Mountain	31	C2
Camp, boat, wtrski, hike, fish, swim, hunt.		
COW PALACE, Geneva Av & Santos St, Daly City	L	B5
Arena, exhibition center; sports events.		
CROCKER ART MUSEUM, 210 O Street, Sacramento	137	A3
Paintings, furniture, sculpture.		
CRYSTAL CATHEDRAL, Chapman Av, Garden Grove	195	D1
Features religious and secular concerts.		
DAFFODIL HILL, 3 mi N of Volcano	41	B2
Blossoms from late March through mid-April.		
DANTES VIEW, above Badwater, Death Vly Nat'l Mon	72	B2
Beautiful vw of Badwater & Death Vly from mtn.		
DEATH VALLEY JUNCTION, Hwy 190 & Hwy 127	72	D1
Home of Marta Beckets Amargosa Opera House.		
DELEVAN NATIONAL WILDLIFE REFUGE, SE of Delevan	32	E1
Nesting area for migrating waterfowl.		
DESCANSO GARDENS, 1418 Descanso Dr	R	A2
1000s of beautifl flowrs frm around the world.		
DESERT MINING MUSEUM, Butte St, Randsburg	80	D3
Large gem & mineral exhibits, mine guides.		
DEVIL'S GOLF COURSE, S of Hwy 190, Death Valley	72	A1
Unusual salt formations from ancient lakebed.		
DEVIL'S HOLE, DEATH VALLEY NATIONAL MONUMENT	72	E1
A deep water-filled cave, preserves pupfish.		
DE YOUNG MEMORIAL MUSEUM, Golden Gate Park	141	C4
Oldst municipl US art mus; hses wrld of art.		
DISNEY STUDIOS, Alameda Av at Buena Vista, Burbnk	179	D4
Creative team for Disney Productions.		
DODGER STADIUM, 1000 Elysian Park	186	B1
Home of the Los Angeles Dodgers		
EASTERN CALIFORNIA MUSEUM, Hwy 395, Independence	60	A3
Exhibits of local and natural history.		
EMBARCADERO, Embarcadero Center on the waterfront	143	D2
Centers on 4 towers; shops, hotels & restrnts.		
EMBARCADERO, Harbor Drive, San Diego	215	C2
Restored old ships, maritime mus, restaurants.		
EMPIRE COMPANY FIRE MUSEUM, Curry St, Carson City	36	B2
Old firefighting trucks, equipment & pictures.		
EQUESTRIAN CENTER, 34th Av & Kennedy Dr	141	B4

NAME & ADDRESS	PAGE	GRID
Horses for rent for use in Golden Gate Park.		
EUREKA VALLEY SAND DUNES, S Eureka Rd	60	D1
Home to a variety of rare plants & animals.		
EXPLORATORIUM & PALACE OF FINE ARTS,Goldn Gate Pk	142	A1
A fascinating 'hands on' science museum.		
EXPOSITION PARK, Exposition Bl	Q	E4
Includes memorial coliseum & sports arena.		
FARMER'S MARKET, 3rd St & Fairfax Av	184	A1
Acres of markets, restaurants & gift shops.		
FEATHER RIVER HATCHERY, Lake Oroville	25	E4
View millions of salmon & steelhead.		
FEATHER RIVER RAILROAD MUSEUM, Portola	27	B2
Over 50 trains; summer train rides.		
FERRY BUILDING EMBARCADERO, foot of Market St	143	E2
Bay trafic hist, world trade ctr, mineral mus.		
FISHERMAN'S WHARF, off Foam St, Monterey	167	E3
Art gallery, shopping & theater.		
FISHERMAN'S WHARF. ft of Taylor at Jefferson, S F	143	B1
Open air markets, restaurants, vw fshng fleet.		
FLEET SPACE THEATER & SCIENCE CENTER, Balboa Park	216	A2
Exquisite celestial displays and films.		
FLYING LADY MUS, 15060 Foothill Rd, Morgan Hill	P	E5
Features vintage airplanes and cars.		
FOREST LAWN MEMORIAL PARK, 1712 S Glendale Av	179	D5
Large collection of stained glass & statuary.		
THE FORUM, Manchester & Prairie Sts	Q	D5
Popular center for sports & entertainment.		
FRESNO CONVENTION CENTER, Tulare & M Sts	165	E4
Various shows, conventions, exhib & displays.		
FRESNO METROPOLITAN MUSEUM, Van Ness Av, Fresno	165	D3
Natural and historical exhibits.		
FRONTIER MUSEUM, Rancho California Rd, Temecula	99	C5
Collection of artifacts of early settlers.		
FROST AMPHITHEATER, Stanford University	147	A3
Outdoor theater which seats 9,500.		
FURNACE CREEK VISITOR CENTER, Death Valley	62	A5
Ranger talks, museum, information & gift shop.		
GAMBLE HOUSE, 4 Westmoreland Pl, Pasadena	190	B3
Great architectural work, originl furnishings.		
GENERAL GRANT GROVE, Redwd Mtn Kings Cyn Nat'l Pk	58	E4
Seasonal festivities, horse & foot trails.		
GEORGE G HOBERG VISTA POINT, 875 Lakeport Bl	31	D3
Picnic, old Indian prayer hill, wildflowers.		
GHIRARDELLI SQUARE, N Point, Beach & Larkin Sts	143	A1
Shops, outdoor cafes by old chocolate factory.		
GIANT FOREST, Sequoia National Forest	59	A4
One of largest & finest Sequoia groves.		
GLACIER POINT, S of Curry Village	63	D2
3200' abve the vly, vw vly & snow-covrd peaks.		
GOLDEN CANYON, S of Hwy 190, Death Valley	62	A5
Hike through dramatically colored, scenic cyn.		
GOLDEN GATE BRIDGE, on Hwy 101	141	C1
Famous bridge offers spectacular view.		
GOLD COUNTRY, HIGHWAY 49, Mariposa to Vinton	27	D3
Historic 300 mi drive through the Mother Lode.		
GOLDEN GATE PROMENADE, along SF Bay shoreline	141	D1
Walkway along marina green.		
GRAND CANYON OF THE TUOLUMNE, N of White Wolf	42	C5
Trails to deep-cut canyons, waterfalls, mdws.		
GRAND CENTRAL MARKET, Hill & 4th Sts	186	A3
Food bazaar specializing in foods of Mexico.		
GREAT PETALUMA MILL, 6 Petaluma Bl N	L	A1
Shops & restaurants in restored grain mill.		
GREAT VLY MUS NATURL HIST, 1100 Stoddard, Modesto	162	A3
Plants & animals indigenous to Central Valley.		
GREYSTONE MANSION, 501 N Doheny Rd, Beverly Hills	Q	C3
Historic mansion and surrounding park.		
GRIFFITH OBSERVATORY, 2800 Observatory Rd	182	B3

NAME & ADDRESS	PAGE	GRID
Mining, railroad & Indian artifacts displayed.		
MONO HOT SPRINGS, northeast of Lakeshore	50	D4
Hot and cold currents, beach, near campsites.		
MONTEREY BAY AQUARIUM, Cannery Row, Monterey	167	E2
Unique aquarium with 'hands on' exhibits.		
MORETON BAY FIG TREE, Chapala & Montecito	174	D4
Largest fig tree of its kind in the nation.		
MORMON TEMPLE, 10777 Santa Monica Bl	180	D3
One of the largest Mormon temples in the US.		
MORRISON PLANETARIUM, in Golden Gate Park	141	D4
Interesting celestial films and displays.		
MORRO BAY AQUARIUM, 595 Embarcadero	75	D3
More than 300 fish & marine animal displays.		
MORRO BAY NATURAL HISTORY MUS, Morro Bay State Pk	64	A4
Chumash Indians, wildlife & marine displays.		
MT SHASTA, off Hwy 5 N of Dunsmuir	12	D1
Mighty 14,162 ft mtn covered by 5 glaciers.		
MT SHASTA FISH HATCHERY, 1 mi W of Mt Shasta	12	C2
Trout produced to stock Northern Cal streams.		
MT WHITNEY, Whitney Portal Rd	59	E4
At 14,495' it is highest mtn in contiguous US.		
MOUNT WILSON OBSERVATORY, Mt Wilson Rd	R	C2
Famous for huge Hooker telescope & camera.		
MOVIELAND WAX MUSEUM, 7711 Beach Bl, Buena Park	T	B2
Wax displays of celebrities & movie scenes.		
MUD BATHS, in Calistoga	38	A1
Attracts visitors year around.		
MUSIC CONCOURSE, Golden Gate Park	141	D4
Free opn air concrts givn alng tree lined wlk.		
MUSEUM OF CONTEMPORARY ART, 250 S Grand, L A	186	A3
Permanent collection of international flavor.		
MUSEUM OF MINING, Johnsville	26	E3
Historical museum of mining in California.		
NATIONAL MARITIME MUSEUM, foot of Polk Street	143	A1
Displays nautical models, figureheads, photos.		
NATURAL BRIDGE, Death Valley National Monument	72	B1
Colorful hike to natural arch in Black Mtns.		
NBC STUDIOS, 3000 W Alameda Av, Burbank	179	D5
A look at behind-the-scenes TV production.		
NEVADA STATE CAPITOL, N Carson St, Carson City	36	B2
Built 1871, silver dome caps large stone bldg.		
NEVADA ST MUS, N Carson at Robinson, Carson City	36	B2
Mining, pioneer, R R objects & exhibits.		
NOB HILL, at Calif, Sacramento, Jones & Tyler Sts	143	C3
Symbolic of elegant living; cable car access.		
NORTON SIMON MUSEUM, 411 W Colorado Blvd	190	B4
Outstanding collection of art & sculpture.		
OAKDALE MUSEUM, 1st & F Sts, Oakdale	47	E2
Features local and natural history artifacts.		
OAKLAND-ALAMEDA COUNTY COLISEUM, Nimitz Fy, Av 66	159	D2
2 bldg sprts complex, indr arena, outdr stadm.		
OAKLAND MUSEUM, 1000 Oak St at 10th St	158	A3
Unusual environmtl mus follows Calif history.		
OAKWOOD LAKE RESORT, off I-5 S of Manteca	47	A1
Water theme park with camping facilities.		
OAKLAND WORLD TRADE CENTER, Embarcadero	157	E4
Busy trade center near Inner Harbor at SF Bay.		
OAKLAND ZOO, Knowland Dr & 98th Av	L	E5
Picinic area, amusmt pk, aerail trm, baby zoo.		
OIL MUSEUM, Hwy 33, Taft	78	A5
History of oil industry & processing methods.		
OLD EAGLE THEATER, J & Front Sts	137	B2
First theater in California, opened in 1849.		
OLD FAITHFUL GEYSER OF CALIFORNIA, on Tubbs Rd	38	A1
Eruptions occur every 50 minutes.		
OLD GOVERNOR'S MANSION, 16th & H Sts, Sacramento	137	C3
Victorian gothic mansion built in 1877; tours.		
OLD TIMERS MUSEUM, Highway 4, Murphys	41	C3

NAME & ADDRESS	PAGE	GRID
Built 1865; Indian display, historic items.		
OLD TOWN ART GUILD, G & 2nd Sts, Eureka	121	C1
Galleries, gift shops, art supplies.		
ONE LOG HOUSE, Phillipsville	16	C4
2000 year old log home hewn from 40 ton tree.		
ORANGE EMPIRE RAILWAY MUSEUM, Perris	99	B4
An extensive collection of early trains.		
PACIFIC SW RAILWAY MUSEUM, Highway 94, Campo	112	D2
Exhibits of the Pacific SW Railway.		
PAGE MUSEUM, 5801 Wilshire Blvd	184	B2
Exhibits of prehistoric animals from tar pits.		
PAINTED GORGE, off Hwy 195, N of Salton Sea	101	C5
Bluffs of colorfully layered rock.		
PALM SPRINGS AERIAL TRAMWAY, Tramway Dr	100	C3
Spectacular view of desert floor below.		
PALOMAR OBSERVATORY, Hwy 56, Mt Palomar	107	A2
Operated by Cal Tech; tours; 200" telescope.		
PAULEY PAVILION, U C L A Campus	180	C1
Features many sports events.		
PELTON WHEEL MINING MUSEUM, Allison Ranch Rd	127	B4
Pelton waterwheel, old mining tools.		
PIER 39, northern waterfront, San Francisco	143	C1
Recreates old SF street scene; shops, rstrnts.		
PIONEER MUSEUM & HAGGIN GALLERIES, Stockton	160	B4
Historical displays, paintings & art objects.		
PLACER COUNTY MUSEUM, 1273 High St, Auburn	126	C4
Displays of early mining equipment.		
PLACER COUNTY VISITORS INFORMATION CTR, Newcastle	34	B4
Historical & informational displays 24 hours.		
PLANES OF FAME MUSEUM, Chino Airport	U	D3
World War II memorabilia & plane collection.		
PT ARENA LIGHTHOUSE & MUS, off Hwy 101, Pt Arena	30	B3
Daily tours; maritime artifacts.		
POINT HUENEME, end of Hueneme Rd	96	B1
Marks entrance to Port Hueneme Harbor.		
POINT LOMA, 10 miles W on Catalina Bl	V	A4
Site Cabrillo Nat Monmt, lighthse, scenic vw.		
POINT PINOS LIGHTHOUSE, Monterey Harbor	167	A1
Oldest lighthouse still in use on West Coast.		
PONDEROSA RANCH, Tahoe Blvd, Incline Village	36	B1
Westrn town amusmnt pk, 'Bonanza' TV shw site.		
PORTS O'CALL VILLAGE, on Harbor Blvd, San Pedro	191	B4
Nautical shopping village with harbor tours.		
QUEEN MARY, Pier J, Long Beach	192	E4
Tours, restaurants & hotel on famous liner.		
RACETRACK, Death Valley National Monument	60	E3
Clay playa, rocks tilt during high winds.		
RAINBOW BASIN/OWL CANYON, 10 mi N of Barstow	81	D5
Natural landmark of color sediment layers.		
RAMONA BOWL & MUSEUM, 2 mi SE of Hemet	99	E4
Home of the annual Ramona Pageant.		
RANCHO SANTA ANA BOTANIC GARDENS, Foothill Blvd	203	A1
Exclusively native plants of California.		
REDDING CONV & VISITORS BUREAU, 777 Auditorium Dr	122	C1
Local information and event schedule.		
REDDING MUSEUM & ART CENTER, 1911 Rio, Redding	18	B2
Interesting Indian relics & art coll displayd.		
RICHMOND ART CENTER, Barrett Av, Richmond	155	B3
Displays of painting & other art objects.		
RIM OF THE WORLD HIGHWAY	99	E1
Scenic route leads to mountain resort areas.		
RIVERSIDE INTERNATIONAL RACEWAY, on Hwy 60	99	B3
Features many varieties of auto racing.		
ROARING CAMP/BIG TREES NARROW GAUGE RAILRD,Felton	P	A5
Restored 1880's steam locomotives featured.		
ROBERT RIPLEY MEMORIAL MUSEUM, in Juilliard Park	131	D4
Museum is in the Church of One Tree.		
ROSE BOWL, in Brookside Park	190	A3

NAME & ADDRESS	PAGE	GRID
Famous stadium of New Year's Football game.		
ROSICRUCIAN EGYPTIAN MUS & PLANETARIUM, San Jose	151	D4
Largest Egyptian collection on the West Coast.		
ROY ROGERS MUSEUM, I-15, Victorville	91	B3
Memorabilia of Roy Rogers and Dale Evans.		
SACRAMENTO HIST CTR, 101 'I' St, Old Sacramento	137	A2
17th century maps and gold nugget collections.		
SACRAMENTO NATIONAL WILDLIFE REFUGE, S of Willows	24	D5
Nesting area for migratory waterfowl.		
SACRAMENTO SCIENCE CTR & JR MUSEUM, 3615 Auburn	33	D5
Nature trails and animals to touch.		
SALTON SEA NATIONAL WILDLIFE REFUGE, E of Hwy 111	109	A3
Scenic view of nesting birds at Salton Sea.		
SAN BERNARDINO COUNTY MUSEUM, Redlands	99	C2
Artifacts and history of the early settlers.		
SAND DUNES, E of Stovepipe Wells, Death Valley	62	D4
Shifting sand creates scenic area for a walk.		
SAN DIEGO-LA JOLLA UNDERWATER PK, Torrey Pines Rd	V	A1
Protected marinie life area open to public vw.		
SAN DIEGO MUSEUM OF ART, Balboa Park, San Diego	216	A2
Contains American and European art.		
SAN DIEGO WILD ANIMAL PARK, 5 mi W Esconddo CA 78	106	D3
Tour through preserve for endangered species.		
SAN DIEGO ZOO, Balboa Park, San Diego	215	E1
One of the largest and lovliest in the world.		
SAN FRANCISCO ART INSTITUTE, 800 Chestnut, SF	143	B2
Three galleries; tours available.		
S.F. MUSEUM MODERN ART, Van Ness & McAllister	143	B4
20th century art, changing exhibits.		
SAN FRANCISCO-OAKLAND BAY BRIDGE, I-80	L	C4
Main link to East Bay.		
SAN FRANCISCO ZOO, Sloat Bl & 45th Av	L	B5
Rated among the top six zoos in the world.		
SAN LUIS OBISPO CO HIST MUSEUM, 696 Monterey	172	B3
Displays of early Californian & Indian relics.		
SAN ONOFRE VISITOR'S CENTER, off I-5	105	E1
Nuclear power generating plant with displays.		
SANTA ANITA PARK, 285 W Huntington Dr	R	D3
One of the nation's famous horseracing tracks.		
STA BARBARA BOTANICAL GARDEN, 1212 Mission Cyn Rd	174	B1
65 acres of native Calif trees, plants, cacti.		
SANTA BARBARA CO COURTHOUSE, downtown Sta Barbara	174	C3
One of the most beautiful buildings in West.		
SANTA BARBARA MUSEUM OF ART, State & Anapamu Sts	174	B3
Orientl & American art glasswares, sculptres.		
STA CRUZ BIG TREES & PACIFIC RR, 6 mi from S Cruz	53	E1
Historic RR from Roaring Camp to Santa Cruz.		
SANTA CRUZ BOARDWALK, near Municipal Pier	169	D4
Shopping, restaurants, outdoor shows, rides.		
SANTA CRUZ MUNICIPAL PIER, off West Cliff Dr	169	E5
Shops and arcades over the ocean.		
SAUSALITO FERRY TERMINAL, Anchor St	L	B4
Commuter service to San Francisco.		
SCOTIA LUMBER MILL, Main St, Scotia	16	A3
Tour mill, debarking, sawing, shipping logs.		
SCOTTY'S CASTLE, Death Valley National Monument	61	B1
Tour unique mansion built by Death Vly Scotty.		
SCRIPPS AQUARIUM MUSEUM, 8602 La Jolla Shores	211	A1
Sea exhibits & tidepools.		
SEAL ROCKS, Golden Gate National Recreation Area	L	A5
View of seal and bird habitats.		
SESPE WILDLIFE AREA, E of I-5 off Hwy 126	88	C4
Established to preserve near-extinct condors.		
SEVENTEEN MILE DRIVE, Monterey Peninsula	53	B2
Magnificent drive between Carmel & Monterey.		
SHASTA DAM & POWER PLANT, 15 miles NW of Redding	18	B1
2nd largest dam in US; exclnt vw of Mt Shasta.		
SHRINE DRIVE-THRU TREE, Myers Flat	16	B4

NAME & ADDRESS	PAGE	GRID
Drive through living tree; logging display.		
SIERRA BUTTES, N of Sierra City	27	A4
Giant rugged granite outcrops, scenic.		
SIERRA NEVADA MUSEUM OF ART, 549 Court St, Reno	130	A3
Collections of art from all over the world.		
SIERRA MONO MUSEUM, St 274 & St 225, North Fork	49	E5
Artifacts of Native Indian Tribes.		
SILVERADO MUSEUM, 1490 Library Ln	38	B1
Memorabilia of Robert Louis Stevenson.		
SILVER WINGS AVIATION MUS/PLANETARIUM, Mather AFB	40	A1
Facilities provide Space & Aviation exhibits.		
SISKIYOU COUNTY MUSEUM, 910 S Main St, Yreka	4	A4
Indn objects, displays of old & new indstry.		
SOLAR ONE, National Trails Hwy, Daggett	92	A1
Nation's first solar electric power plant.		
SOLVANG, Hwy 246	86	E3
Authentic Danish village.		
SOUTH COAST BOTANIC GARDENS, 26300 Crenshaw Bl	S	B2
Calif native plants & trees; man-made lake.		
SPACE SHUTTLE LAUNCH COMPLEX, Vandenberg AFB	86	A3
Closed to the public.		
SPORTS ARENA, Exposition Park, Los Angeles	185	C5
Sports events for college & profesnl athletes.		
SPRUCE GOOSE, Queens Wy, Long Beach Harbor	192	E4
Features Howard Hughes' airplane made of wood.		
STATE CAPITOL, Capitol Mall, Sacramento	137	B3
Daily guided tours through capitol building.		
STATE INDIAN MUSEUM, 2618 K St, Sacramento	137	D3
Features various California Indian cultures.		
STEARNS WHARF, lower State St	174	E4
The main pier extends beyond State Street.		
STEINBECK HOUSE, 132 Central Av, Salinas	171	B3
Birthplace of author; restaurant & gift shop.		
STEINHART AQUARIUM, Golden Gate Park	141	D4
In Acadmy of Sci; features circular fish tank.		
STRYBING ARBORETUM, South Dr, Golden Gate Park	141	C4
More than 5000 plant species displayed.		
TECOPA HOT SPRINGS, west of Hwy 127	72	E4
Old Indian healing pl, baths open to public.		
TELEGRAPH HILL, at Lombard & Kearny Sts	143	C2
Park, Coit Tower at top with view; tours.		
TELEVISION CITY - CBS, 7800 Beverly Blvd	184	A1
Actual site of many telecasts.		
TITUS CANYON, E of Hwy 374, Death Valley Natl Mon	62	D3
Colorful, exciting drive thru a narrow canyon.		
TOWE FORD MUSEUM, 2200 Front St, Sacramento	137	A3
Most complete collection of antique Fords.		
TREES OF MYSTERY, 16 miles S of Crescent City	1	E5
Unusual&handcarved redwood trees; Indian Mus.		
TRONA PINNACLES, S of Trona near Pinnacle	81	B1
Tall pinnacles formed by algae of a sea.		
TUCKER WILDLIFE SANCTUARY, 28322 Modjeska Canyon	98	D4
Features a variety of hummingbirds.		
TULARE COUNTY MUSEUM, 27000 S Mooney, Mooney Grve	68	B2
Restored buildings; Indian & Pioneer artifcts.		
TULE LAKE NATL WILDLIFE REFUGE, S of Tulelake	5	D3
Great stopping point for migrating waterfowl.		
TUOLUMNE COUNTY MUSEUM, 158 W Bradford, Sonora	163	B3
Located in the old jail; gold rush objects.		
TUOLUMNE COUNTY VISITORS BUREAU, 55 Stockton Rd	163	C3
Local information and event schedule.		
20TH CENTURY FOX STUDIO, Pico Blvd	183	B3
One of the oldest studios in Hollywood.		
UBEHEBE CRATER, Death Valley National Monument	61	A2
Crater created by volcanic steam explosion.		
UNDERSEA WORLD, Hwy 101 S of Crescent City	1	D4
View sea plants & animals, scuba diving show.		
UNION SQUARE, Geary, Powell, Post & Stockton Sts	143	C3

NAME & ADDRESS	PAGE	GRID
Fashionable shopping center; park, fountain.		
UNION STATION, 800 N Alameda St, Los Angeles	186	C2
One of the landmarks of Los Angeles.		
VICTORIAN TOUR HOUSE, 401 Pine St, Nevada City	128	C2
Privately owned restored home-tours by appt.		
VIKINGSHOLM, at Emerald Bay	35	E3
Large Scandanavian castle with furnishings.		
VISITOR CENTER YOSEMITE VILLAGE, Yosemite Lodge	63	C1
Displays, photos of Yosemite, films.		
WARM SPGS DAM & FISH HATCHERY, 11 mi NW Healdsbrg	31	C5
Visitor ctr & camping; dam created Lk Sonoma.		
WASSAMA ROUND HOUSE STATE HIST, 55 mi N of Fresno	49	C4
Picturesque picnic area.		
WAYFARER'S CHAPEL, 5755 Palos Verde Dr	S	B3
Striking glass church sits atop hill by sea.		
WESTERN RAILWAY MUSEUM, Highway 12 E of Fairfield	M	B1
Restored rail cars, rides, exhibits & museum.		
WHISKEYTOWN-SHASTA-TRINITY REC, NW of Redding	18	A1
Camp, backpack, picnic, boat, water sports.		
WHITNEY PORTAL, W from Lone Pine	59	E4
Starting point for Mt Whitney trail.		
WILLIAM S HART PARK, Newhall Av at Sn Fernando Rd	89	B5
Tour the silent screen actor's beautiful home.		
WINCHESTER MYSTERY HOUSE, Winchester Bl, San Jose	151	B5
Fascinating house and museum.		
WINNERS CIRCLE RCH, 59911 Lakeview Hy, Petaluma	L	B1
Miniature horses bred and trained; sales.		
WOODMINSTER AMPHITHEATER, S of Orinda	L	E4
Centerpiece of pk, sumr concerts, light opera.		
WRIGLEY MEMORIAL & BOTANICAL GARDN, Avalon Cyn Rd	97	A5
Beautiful cactus, flowers & trees at monument.		
YOSEMITE FALLS, Yosemite National Park	63	D1
Two beautiful waterfalls fall over 2,400 feet.		
YOSEMITE MTN SUGAR PINE RR, Hwy 41 N of Sugr Pine	49	D3
4 miles trip on a steam-powered railroad.		
YOSEMITE VALLEY, Mariposa County	63	A1
Picturesque, campng, domes, wtrflls, meadow.		
YREKA WESTERN RR, off I-5 & Central Eureka Exit	4	B4
'Blue Goose' shortline RR through Shasta Vly.		
YUMA TERRITORIAL PRISON ST HIST PK, off I-8, Yuma	112	D5
Blt 1876, operated until 1909; museum & tour.		
ZABRISKIE POINT, off Hwy 190 in Death Valley	62	B5
Overlooks Death Vly from badland of Black Mtn.		
ZALUD HOUSE MUSEUM, 393 N Hocket, Porterville	68	D3
1891 home with period furniture.		

⛵ RECREATION LAKES, RIVERS & MARINAS

NAME & ADDRESS	PAGE	GRID
ALPINE LAKE, 51 mi NE of Angels Camp	42	A1
100+ dev sites - boat, backpack, fish, swim.		
ANDERSON RESERVOIR, Hwy 101, S of San Jose	46	D5
Fishing and boating facilities.		
ANTELOPE LAKE, 45 miles NE of Quincy	21	A4
200+ dev sites - boat, waterski, fish, hike.		
AQUATIC PARK, foot of Polk St, San Francisco	143	A1
Curved fishing pier creates cold swim lagoon.		
BALBOA MARINA, 2751 W Pacific Coast Hwy	199	B4
One of the largest marinas on the west coast.		
BARNHILL MARINA, Inner Harbor, Alameda	157	E4
Pleasure boat marina in the Inner Harbor.		
BASS LAKE, E of Oakhurst	49	E4
220+ dev sites - boat, waterski, fish, hike.		
BENICIA MARINA, end of E 3rd St	153	B5
Pleasure boat marina south of Benicia Point.		
BERKELEY AQUATIC PARK, Foot of Bancroft Av	L	C4
Saltwatr lake, watr sports, model boat racing.		
BERKELEY MARINA, foot of University Av	L	C4

NAME & ADDRESS	PAGE	GRID
Base for poplr sport fshng fleet, fshng pier.		
BETHANY RES ST REC AREA, Christensen Rd, Alameda	M	E4
Day use only; boat, bicycle, picnic, and fish.		
BIG BEAR LAKE, off Hwy 18	91	E5
Resort area has many winter & summer sports.		
BIG BEND RESORT, Parker Dam Rd, S of Lake Havasu	96	C5
Waterskiing, boating and fishing.		
BIG SAGE RESERVOIR, NW of Alturas	7	A5
Boating, fishing, no camping facilities.		
BLACK BUTTE LAKE, 9 miles west of Orland	24	B3
90+ dev sites - boat, waterski, fish, hike.		
BLUE LAKE, 42 mi SE of Alturas	8	C3
40+ dev sites - boat, waterski, fish, hike.		
BLUE LAKES, Hwy 20 & Blue Lakes Rd	31	C2
RV & tent camping; boat, fish, swim and hike.		
BOCA RESERVOIR, NE of Truckee	27	E5
90+ dev sites - boat, waterski, fish, hike.		
BOWMAN LAKE, 40 mi NE of Nevada City	27	A5
Primitive sites-fish, backpack, swim, picnic.		
BRANNAN ISLAND STATE REC AREA, S of Rio Vista	M	D2
Water ski, fish; swim, picnic; visitor center.		
BRIDGEPORT RESERVOIR, just north of Bridgeport	43	B3
60+ dev sites - boat, fish, swim, backpack.		
BUCKS LAKE, southwest of Quincy	26	B2
70+ dev sites - boat, waterski, fish, hike.		
BUENA VIS AQUATIC REC AREA, 25 mi SW Bakersfield	78	B4
Fish, swim, camp, waterski or boat.		
BULLARDS BAR RESERVOIR, E of Camptonville	26	B5
90+ dev sites - boat, watrski, fish, picnic.		
BUTTE LAKE, Lassen Volcanic National Park	20	A2
90+ dev sites - sail, fish, swim, backpack.		
BUTT VALLEY RESERVOIR, off Prattville Butt Res Rd	20	B5
Sailing; recreational facilities.		
CAMANCHE RESERVOIR, W OF San Andreas	40	C3
1150+ dev sites - boat, fish, hike, swim.		
CAMP FAR WEST RESERVOIR, 29 mi NW of Auburn	34	A2
30+ dev sites - boat, waterski, fish, swim.		
CAPLES LAKE, near Kirkwood on Hwy 88	36	A5
30+ dev sites - boat, fish, hike, horses.		
CASTAIC LAKE STATE RECREATION AREA, N of Castaic	89	B4
Boating, picnicking and swimming.		
CATALINA YACHT HARBOR, Avalon Bay, Catalina Islnd	97	B4
Yacht moorings, glass bottom boat tours.		
CHANNEL ISLANDS HARBOR, Oxnard	96	A1
Small marina, Channel Islands Museum.		
CHERRY LAKE, 31 mi E of Tuolumne	42	B4
40+ dev sites - boat, waterski, fish, horses.		
CLEAR LAKE, near Lakeport	31	D2
140+ dev sites - boat, waterski, fish, hike.		
COLORADO RIVER, on the California-Arizona border	110	C3
Camp, hike along the river; boat, swim.		
COLUSA-SACRAMENTO RIVER STATE REC AREA, Colusa	33	A1
Undev camps, boat, fish, picnic, waterski.		
CONVICT LAKE, 37 miles north of Bishop	50	E2
90+ dev sites - boat, fish, backpack, horses.		
COYOTE RESERVOIR, N of Gilroy	P	E5
70+ dev sites - boat, waterski, fish, hike.		
CUYAMACA RESERVOIR, off Hwy 79 south of Julian	107	C4
Camping, fishing, duck hunting; no swimming.		
DANA POINT MARINA, S of Del Obispo St	202	B5
Shopping, restaurants, boating facilities.		
DESERT SHORES MARINA, Hwy 86, near Desert Shores	108	B1
Boating and fishing facilities.		
DON PEDRO RESERVOIR, W of Coulterville	48	C2
500+ dev sites - hseboat, watrski, fish, hike.		
DORRIS RESERVOIR, east of Alturas	8	B1
Good fishing & swimming; day use only.		
DOWNTOWN LONG BEACH MARINA, off Shoreline Dr	192	E4

POINTS OF INTEREST INDEX

NAME & ADDRESS	PAGE	GRID	NAME & ADDRESS	PAGE	GRID
Boating and fishing facilities.			20+ dev sites - boat, fish, mtn climb, hike.		
LITTLE GRASS VALLEY RESERVOIR, W of Gibsonville	26	C3	ST FRANCIS YACHT CLUB, off Marina Bl, Sn Francsco	142	A1
240+ dev sites - boat, waterski, fish, hike.			Long established yacht club in the Bay Area.		
LONG BEACH MARINA & MARINE STADIUM, Long Beach	S	D3	SALTON BAY MARINA, off Hwy 86 near Salton City	108	D2
One of the largest marinas on the west coast.			Fishing and boating facilities.		
LOON LAKE, NW of Emerald Bay	35	D3	SALTON SEA STATE RECREATION AREA, off Hwy 111	108	E2
50+ dev sites - boat, fish, hike, picnic.			Boat, waterski, hike, camp, fish, picnic.		
LOPEZ LAKE, 23 mi N of Santa Maria	76	C4	SALT SPRINGS RESERVOIR, 20.5 mi SE of Hams Sta	41	D1
300+ sites - boat, waterski, fish, picnic.			20+ dev sites - boat, fish, swim, hike.		
LOWER NEWPORT BAY, Newport Beach	199	C5	SAN FRANCISCO BAY	L	C5
Leads to vast estuary in Upper Newport Bay.			Boat tours of the bay, harbor and Alcatraz.		
LUNDY LAKE, 12 miles north of Lee Vining	43	B4	SAN LUIS RES STATE REC AREA, 16 mi W of Los Banos	55	C1
30+ dev sites - boat, fish, picnic, backpack.			70+ dev sites - boat, waterski, fish, hike.		
MAMMOTH POOL RESERVOIR, east of Bass Lake	50	B4	SANTA BARBARA YACHT HARBOR, W Cabrillo Bl	174	D4
60+ dev sites - boat, waterski, fish, hike.			Boat rentals, hoist & ramp, sport fishing.		
MANZANITA LAKE, Lassen Volcanic National Park	19	D2	SANTA MARGARITA LAKE, 19 mi from San Luis Obispo	76	C3
170+ dev sites - sail, fish, hike, horses.			80+ dev sites - boat, fish, swim, hike, picnc.		
MARINA DEL REY, Via Marina	187	C4	SAN VICENTE RESERVOIR, Moreno Av, off CA 67	V	E1
Berths more than 10,000 yachts.			S D City lake, day use; boat, fish, no swim.		
MARTINEZ LAKE, Fishers Landing Rd, Yuma Co.	110	E4	SCOTTS FLAT RESERVOIR, E of Nevada City	34	D1
Marina on the Colorado River; boat & fish.			180+ dev sites - boat, waterski, goldpn, fish.		
MARTINEZ YACHT HARBOR, Martinez	154	B1	SHAVER LAKE, south of Camp Sierra	58	B1
Small pleasure craft marina.			60+ dev sites - boat, waterski, fish, hike.		
MARTIS CREEK RESERVOIR, SE of Truckee	35	E1	SILVER LAKE, 50 mi NE of Jackson	35	E5
20+ dev sites - sail, fish, swim, hike.			90+ dev sites - boat, fish, horseback ride.		
MEDICINE LAKE, 48 miles NE of McCloud	5	D5	SILVERWOOD LAKE STATE RECREATION AREA, Hwy 138	91	B5
70+ dev sites - boat, waterski, fish, horses.			Swim, fish, camp, boating & water ski.		
MELONES RESERVOIR, end of Reynolds Ferry Rd	41	B5	SOUTH LAKE, 22 mi SW of Bishop	51	C5
Boat, fish, picnic, camp; RV parking area.			Dev sites - boat, fish, backpack, picnic.		
MILLERTON LAKE REC AREA, 22 miles East of Madera	57	D1	SOUTH LAKE TAHOE-EL DORADO STATE REC AREA, Hwy 50	129	A3
130+ dev sites - boat, waterski, fish, horses.			Boating, fishing, swimming, picnicking.		
MISSION BAY, Mission Bay Park, W of I-5	212	D2	STAMPEDE RESERVOIR, 15 mi N of Truckee	27	D4
Separate courses for diverse water sports.			250+ dev sites - boat, waterski, fish, hike.		
MONO LAKE TUFA STATE RESERVE, Hy 395 @ Lee Vining	43	D4	STATE UNDERSEA PARK, Hwy 1 & Temple Hills	201	B3
Interesting salt formatns surround saltwtr lk.			Good divng area, fish, shells, rock formtions.		
MONTEREY MARINA, Ocean View Blvd	167	E3	STONY GORGE RESERVOIR, 20 miles west of Willows	24	B4
Small craft harbor near Fisherman's Wharf.			140+ dev sites - boat, waterski, fish, swim.		
MORENA LAKE, Oak Dr & Buckman Spgs Rd, W of I-8	112	D1	STOW LAKE, Stow Lake Dr in Golden Gate Park	141	C4
Campsites, fishing, boating, hiking, horses.			Largest manmade lake in park, boating.		
NEEDLES MARINA, Hwy 40, Needles	95	D2	SUTHERLAND RESERVOIR, Sutherland Dam Dr, Hwy 78	107	B3
Waterski, boating and fishing.			Fish, boat, camp nrby Black Cyn, El Loro Rnch		
NORTH SHORE MARINA, Hwy 111, near Desert Beach	108	C1	TIOGA LAKE, 12 miles west of Lee Vining	43	B5
Boating and fishing facilities.			10+ dev sites - boat, fish, picnic, hike.		
NOYO HARBOR, south of Fort Bragg	22	B5	TOPAZ LAKE, east of Markleeville	36	E5
Small, scenic eastern-like fishing village.			200+ dev sites - boat, waterski, fish, swim.		
OCEANSIDE HARBOR, 1540 Harbor Dr N	106	A3	TRINITY LAKE, 44 mi NW of Redding	12	A4
Deep sea & sport fishing; pier fishng; sailng.			400+ dev sites - sail, wtrski, fish, horsbck ride.		
OTAY RESERVOIR, Wueste Rd, E Chula Vista	V	E4	TULLOCH RESERVOIR, SE of Copperopolis	41	B5
S D City lk, co campgrd; fish, boat, no swim.			60+ dev sites - boat, fish, swim, picnic.		
PARDEE RESERVOIR, 3.5 mi E of Buena Vista	40	D3	TWIN LAKES, 13 miles southwest of Bridgeport	43	A3
180+ dev sites & pool - boat, fish, bicycle.			180+ dev sites - boat, fish, backpack, horses.		
PICACHO STATE RECREATION AREA, W of Picacho	110	C4	UNION VALLEY RESERVOIR, 17 mi N of Riverton	35	C4
Fish, boat, camp, picnic or hike.			270+ dev sites - boat, fish, swim, hike.		
PINE FLAT RESERVOIR REC AREA, 20 mi N of Fresno	58	B2	VALLEJO MARINA, off Mare Island Causeway	134	A4
Dev camps - houseboat, waterski, fish, hike.			Recreational marina near Mare Islnd Naval Res.		
PROSSER CREEK RESERVOIR, N of Truckee	27	D5	VENTURA HARBOR, 1603 Anchors Way Dr	175	D5
Dev & undev sites - boat, fish, swim, picnic.			Includes 2 marinas, boat rentals, launch ramp.		
PYRAMID LAKE RECREATION AREA, off I-5	88	E3	VIRGINIA LAKES, 18.5 miles north of Lee Vining	43	B4
25+ dev sites-boat, waterski, fish, swim.			40+ dev sites - boat, fish, backpack, horses.		
RICHMOND MARINA BAY, 1340 Marina Wy S, Richmond	155	B5	WEST VALLEY RESERVOIR, 22 miles SE of Alturas	8	B3
Large boat marina on San Francisco Bay.			Camp, boat, waterski, fish, swim, hike, hunt.		
ROCK CREEK LAKE, SW of Toms Place	51	B3	WHISKEYTOWN LAKE, S of Hwy 299, W of Redding	18	A2
220+ dev sites - boat, fish, backpack, picnic.			150+ sites - sail, fish, waterski, hike, swim.		
ROLLINS RESERVOIR, N of Colfax	34	D2	WILD & SCENIC RIVER, Middle Fork Feather River	26	C2
240+ dev sites - boat, waterski, fish, hike.			Designated by Congress as a wild & scenic riv.		
RUTH LAKE, N of Ruth	16	E4	YOSEMITE LAKE & PARK, N of Merced off Lake Rd	48	C4
60+ dev sites - boat, waterski, fish, horses.			Boat, sail, waterski, fish, hike, picnic.		
SADDLEBAG LAKE, 12.5 miles north of Lee Vining	43	B5			

POINTS OF INTEREST INDEX

POINTS OF INTEREST INDEX

NAME & ADDRESS	PAGE	GRID
EL DORADO VINEYARDS, 3551 Carson Rd, Camino	35	A5
Wine tasting.		
EL PASO DE ROBLES, 3551 Carson Rd, Paso Robles	76	A1
Wine tasting room & sales; picnic area.		
EMILE GUGLIELMO, 1480 E Main Av, Morgan Hill	P	E5
Winery tours by appointment; tasting & sales.		
ESTATE WILLIAM BACCALA, 10400 S Hwy 101, Ukiah	31	B3
Tasting room & retail sales; picnic area.		
ESTRELLA RIVER WINERY, Hwy 46, Paso Robles	76	B1
Tours and tasting available.		
FERRARA WINERY, 1120 W 15th Av, Escondido	106	D3
Informal tours; wine tasting and sales.		
FETZER VINEYARDS, 1150 Bel Arbes Rd, Redwood Vly	31	B3
Tasting room; tours by appointment only.		
FIELD STONE WINERY, 10075 Hwy 128, Healdsburg	31	E5
Retail sales and tasting room; tours by appt.		
FIRESTONE WINERY, Hwy 176, Los Olivos	86	E2
Wine tasting, tours & sales.		
FITZPATRICK WINERY, 7740 Fairplay Rd, Somerset	41	A1
Tasting room; premium varietal wines.		
FOLIE A DEUX WINERY, 3070 St Helena Hy, St Helena	29	B2
Tasting, retail sales, picnic area.		
FOPPIANO, 12707 Old Redwood Hwy, Healdsburg	37	D1
Tasting room open daily; tours by appointment.		
FORTINO WINERY, 4525 Hecker Pass Hwy, Gilroy	54	C2
Wine tasting, retail sales & tours available.		
FRANCISCAN VINEYARDS, 1178 Galleron Rd, Rutherfrd	29	C3
Tasting and self-guided tours daily.		
FRANZIA BROS. WINERY, Hwy 120, Ripon	47	B1
Tasting room & retail sales; picnic area.		
FRASINETTI WINERY, 7395 Frasinetti Rd, Sacramento	40	A2
Winery and tasting room open Tuesday - Sunday.		
FREEMARK ABBEY WINERY, Hwy 29, St Helena	29	B2
Guided tours and retail sales daily.		
FRENCH VLY VINEYARDS, 36515 Briggs Rd, Murrieta	99	C5
Open daily for tours and tasting.		
FREY VINEYARDS, 14000 Tomki Rd, Redwood Valley	31	B1
Tasting, retail sales & picnic; tours by appt.		
FRITZ CELLARS, 24691 Dutcher Ck Rd, Cloverdale	31	C4
Tours & tasting by appointment; open daily.		
GAINEY VINEYARD, E Highway 246, Santa Ynez	86	E3
Winery tours and wine tasting daily.		
GALLEANO WINERY INC, 4231 Wineville Rd, Mira Loma	99	A2
Tours, wine tasting & sales; picnic area.		
GEYSER PEAK WINERY, 2281 Chianti Rd, Geyserville	31	C5
Wine tasting daily; tours by appointment.		
GIRARD WINERY, 7717 Silverado Tr, Oakville	29	D3
Tours & tasting by appointment; retail sales.		
GIUMARRA VINEYARDS, Edison Hwy, Edison	78	E3
Tasting room open Tuesday through Saturday.		
GLEN ELLEN WINERY, London Ranch Rd, Glen Ellen	38	B2
Tasting room, retail sales; no tours.		
GLORIA FERRER, 23555 Highway 121, Sonoma	L	B1
Tasting room open daily; groups by appointmnt.		
GOLD MINE WINERY, Parrotts Ferry Rd, Columbia	41	C4
Open daily for tasting & sales; picnic area.		
GRAND CRU, 1 Vintage Ln, Glen Ellen	38	B2
Open daily for tasting; tours by appointment.		
GREENSTONE WINERY, Hwy 88 & Jackson Vly Rd, Ione	40	C3
Tasting room open daily; tours by appointment.		
GREENWOOD RIDGE VINEYARDS, 5501 Hwy 128, Philo	30	E2
Winery is open daily; tours available.		
GRGICH HILLS CELLAR, Hwy 29 north of Rutherford	29	C3
Informal tours and sales daily.		
GUENOC WINERY, 21000 Butts Cyn Rd, Middletown	32	B6
Wine tasting, tours & retail sales; picnics.		
GUNDLACH-BUNDSCHU, 2000 Denmark St, Sonoma	L	B1
Open daily for tasting and tours.		

NAME & ADDRESS	PAGE	GRID
HACIENDA, 1000 Vineyard Ln, Sonoma	L	C1
Open daily for tasting; tours by appointment.		
HALLCREST VINEYARDS, 379 Felton Empire Rd	N	E5
Open daily for tasting and tours.		
HANDLEY CELLARS, 3151 Highway 128, Philo	30	D2
Winery and tasting room are open daily.		
HANNS KORNELL CHAMPAGNE CELLARS, Larkmead Ln	29	B2
Guided tours and tasting daily.		
HAYWOOD WINERY, 18701 Gehricke Rd, Sonoma	L	C1
Open daily for tasting & retail sales.		
HECKER PASS WINERY, 4605 Hecker Pass Hwy, Gilroy	54	C2
Wine tasting & retail sales; tours by appt.		
HEITZ CELLARS, 436 St Helena Hwy	29	C3
Tours by appointment only.		
HERITAGE CELLARS, 2310 S Railroad Av, Fresno	57	C3
Winery and tasting room are open daily.		
HIDDEN CELLARS WINERY, 1500 Cunningham Rd, Ukiah	31	B2
Winery and tasting room are open daily.		
HOP KILN WINERY, 6050 Westside Rd, Healdsburg	37	D2
Historic landmk; tasting & sales; picnic area.		
HUSCH VINEYARDS, 4900 Hwy 128, Philo	30	D2
Winery tours, tasting room open daily.		
INGLENOOK VINEYARD, 1991 St Helena Hwy S, Ruthrfd	29	C3
Wine tasting, museum & gift shop; tours.		
J CAREY VINEYARDS, 1711 Alamo Pintado Rd, Solvang	86	E3
Open for tours and tasting.		
JEKEL VINEYARD, 40155 Walnut Av, Greenfield	65	A1
Guided tours, sales & wine tasting; picnic.		
J FILIPPI VINTAGE CO, 13052 Jurupa Av, Fontana	98	E2
Winery and tasting room are open daily.		
J. LOHR, 1000 Lenzen, San Jose	151	E4
Tasting, sales & guided tours.		
JOHNSON'S ALEXANDER VLY, 8333 Hwy 128, Healdsburg	31	D5
Open daily for tours and tasting.		
JOSEPH MATHEWS WINERY, 1711 Main St, Napa	133	C3
Winery and tasting room are open daily.		
JOSEPH PHELPS VINEYARDS, 200 Taplin Rd, St Helena	29	D3
Guided tours by appointment; sales Mon-Sat.		
J ROCHIOLI VINEYARDS, 6192 Westside Rd, Healdsbrg	37	C1
Daily tasting and sales; picnic area.		
J W MORRIS WINERY, 101 Grant Av, Healdsburg	37	E1
Tasting room open Thur-Mon; groups by appt.		
KENDALL-JACKSON, 700 Matthews Rd, Lakeport	31	D3
Open daily for tasting and tours.		
KENWOOD, 9592 Sonoma Hwy, Kenwood	38	B2
Open daily for tasting; tours by appointment.		
KIRIGIN CELLARS, 11550 Watsonville Rd, Gilroy	P	D5
Tasting room open daily; tours by appointment.		
KONOCTI CELLARS, Hwy 29 at Thomas Dr, Kelseyville	31	D3
Tasting room, group tours by appointment.		
KORBELL CHAMPAGNE CELLARS, 13260 Old River Rd	37	C1
Champagne tasting room; tours.		
LAKE SONOMA WINERY, 9990 Dry Ck Rd, Geyserville	31	C5
Open daily for tours and tasting.		
LAMBERT BRIDGE, 4085 W Dry Creek, Healdsburg	31	C5
Daily tasting & sales; picnic area.		
LANDMARK VINEYARDS, 9150 Los Amigos Rd, Windsor	37	E1
Open Sat & Sun, or by appointment; tours.		
LAS MONTANAS WINERY, 8860 Highway 12, Kenwood	38	B2
Open for tasting and tours; closed Tuesdays.		
LEEWARD WINERY, 2784 Johnson Dr, Ventura	88	B5
Winery and tasting room are open daily.		
LIVE OAKS WINERY, 3875 Hecker Pass Hwy, Gilroy	54	D1
Tasting room open daily; groups by appointmnt.		
LIVERMORE VLY CELLARS, 1508 Wetmore Rd, Livermore	P	C1
Winery tours daily; wine tasting and sales.		
LOUIS M MARTINI, 254 St Helena Hwy	29	C3
Guided tours and wine tasting room open daily.		

NAME & ADDRESS	PAGE	GRID
SANTA YNEZ VALLEY, 365 N Refugio Rd, Santa Ynez	86	E3
Tours and tasting on Saturday; M-F by appoint.		
SANTINO WINERY, Steiner Rd, Plymouth	40	E1
Informal tours and tasting room.		
SATIETY, Highways 113 & 25A, Yolo	33	C5
Tasting room and winery are open daily.		
SAUSAL WINERY, 7370 Highway 128, Healdsburg	31	E5
Winery and tasting room are open daily.		
SCHARFFENBERGER CELLARS, 7000 Highway 128, Philo	30	D3
Winery & tasting room open daily except Wed.		
SEA RIDGE, 935 Highway 1, Bodega Bay	37	B1
Open daily for tasting.		
SEBASTIANI VINEYARDS & WINERY, 389 4th St E	132	E4
1st vineyard in Sonoma Vly; tours and tasting.		
SEQUOIA GROVE, 8338 St Helena Hwy, Napa	29	D3
Winery tours by appointment; tasting & sales.		
SHENANDOAH VINEYARDS, 12300 Steiner Rd, Plymouth	40	E1
Winery and tasting room are open daily.		
SHOWN & SONS VINEYARDS, 3514 St Helena, Rutherfrd	29	D3
Winery is open daily; appointments suggested.		
SIERRA WINERY, 1925 N Mooney Blvd, Tulare	68	B2
Tasting and sales daily; picnic area.		
SIMI WINERY, 16275 Healdsburg Av, Healdsburg	31	D5
Wine tasting, guided tours.		
SMITH & HOOK, 37700 Foothill Rd, Soledad	65	A1
Open for tours and tasting daily.		
SMOTHERS BROS WINES, 9575 Highway 12, Kenwood	38	B2
Open daily for tours and tasting.		
SODA ROCK, 8015 Hwy 128, Healdsburg	31	D5
Wine tasting; historic stone winery building.		
SOUVERAIN, Independence Ln & Hwy 101, Geyserville	31	D5
Open daily for tasting and tours; restaurant.		
SPRING MOUNTAIN VINEYARDS, 2805 Spring Mtn Rd	29	B3
Tours by appointment only.		
STAG'S LEAP WINE CELLARS, 5766 Silverado Tr, Napa	29	E4
Tasting room open daily; appt req for tours.		
STEPHEN ZELLERBACH, 14350 Chalk Hill Rd, Healdsbg	32	B5
Picnic, tasting, retail sales; tours by appt.		
STEPHEN ZELLERBACH VINEYARD, 4611 Thomas, Hldsbrg	37	E1
Tasting room open daily; appt req for groups.		
STERLING VINEYARDS, 1111 Dunaweal Ln, Calistoga	29	A2
Tasting & tours; aerial tramway to hlltp wnry.		
STEVENOT WINERY, San Domingo Rd near Murphys	41	B4
Tasting room and retail sales.		
STONEGATE WINERY, 1183 Dunaweal Ln, Calistoga	29	A2
Tours by appointment; retail sales most days.		
STUERMER WINERY, Highway 29, Lower Lake	32	A4
Tasting room open Thurs-Sun; groups req appts.		
SUMMER HILL VINEYDS, 3920 Hecker Pass Hwy, Gilroy	54	D2
Wine tasting & retail sales; picnic area.		
SUTTER HOME, 227 St Helena Hwy S, St Helena	29	C3
Tasting room and gift shop.		
SYCAMORE CREEK VINEYARDS, 12775 Uvas Rd	P	D5
Tours and tasting offered daily.		
THE WINERY AT ASTI, 26150 Asti Rd	31	C4
Open daily for tasting and tours.		
THOMAS VINEYARD, 8916 Foothill Blvd, Cucamonga	U	E2
Wine tasting & sales; picnic; historic landmk.		
THOMAS KRUSE WINERY, 4390 Hecker Pass Hwy, Gilroy	54	C2
Retail sales & wine tasting; picnic area.		
TRENTADUE, 19170 Redwood Hwy, Geyserville	31	D5
Open all week for tasting.		
VALLEY OF THE MOON, Madrone Rd, Glen Ellen	38	B2
Tasting room, retail sales; no tours.		
VEGA VINEYARDS, 9495 Santa Rosa Rd, Buellton	86	D3
Tours and tasting available.		
VENTANA VINEYARDS, Los Coches Rd W of Greenfield	65	B1
New Monterey district winery.		

NAME & ADDRESS	PAGE	GRID
VIANO VINEYARDS, 150 Morello Av, Martinez	154	E2
Tasting room open daily; appt req for groups.		
VICHON WINERY, 1595 Coombsville Rd, Napa	29	C4
Tours by appt; wine tasting & retail sales.		
VILLA MT EDEN, Oakville Cross Rd, Oakville	29	D3
Tours weekdays by appointment.		
VOSE VINEYARDS, 4035 Mt Veeder Rd, Napa	29	C4
Tasting room is open daily.		
V SATTUI WINERY, White Ln at Hwy 29 S, St Helena	29	C3
Tasting room, tours, gift shop; founded 1885.		
WEIBEL CHAMPAGNE, Stanford Av, Mission San Jose	P	B2
Champagne tasting room.		
WEIBEL VINEYARDS, 7051 N State St, Redwood Valley	31	B1
Tasting room and gift shop; no tours.		
WENTE BROS, 5555 Tesla Rd, Livermore	P	D1
4th generation winery; excellent tour/tasting.		
WENTE BROS SPARKLING WINE CELLARS, Livermore	P	D1
Hourly tours available; restaurant.		
WERMUTH WINERY, 3942 Silverado Tr, Calistoga	29	B2
Open daily for tasting and tours.		
WHALER VINEYARD, 6200 Eastside Rd, Ukiah	31	B2
Tasting room open daily; appointmnts suggestd.		
WHITEHALL LANE WINERY, St Helena Hwy S	29	C3
Retail sales.		
WHITE OAK VINEYARDS, 208 Haydon St, Healdsburg	37	E1
Open daily for wine tasting.		
WILLIAM WHEELER WINERY, 130 Plaza St, Healdsburg	37	E1
Open Thursday - Monday for tours and tasting.		
WINDSOR VINEYARDS, 11455 Old Redwood Hwy, Hldsbrg	37	D1
Tasting room is open daily.		
WINTERS WINERY, 15 Main St, Winters	39	A1
Wine tasting and retail sales daily.		
WOODEN VALLEY WINERY, 4756 Suisun Vly Rd, Suisun	L	E1
Tasting room and sales area are open Tues-Sun.		
YANKEE HILL WINERY, Yankee Hill Rd, Columbia	41	C4
Wine tasting; tours by appointment.		
YORK MOUNTAIN WINERY, Hwy 46, Templeton	75	E2
Tasting room; tours by appointment only.		
ZACA MESA WINERY, Foxen Cyn Rd, Los Olivos	86	E2
Tour provides a good overview of winemaking.		